The Oxford Encyclopedia of

ISLAM AND WOMEN

The Oxford Encyclopedia of Islam and Women

Natana J. DeLong-Bas
EDITOR IN CHIEF

VOLUME 2
Names and Naming–Ziyārah

OXFORD
UNIVERSITY PRESS

OXFORD
UNIVERSITY PRESS

Oxford University Press is a department of the University of Oxford.
It furthers the University's objective of excellence in research,
scholarship, and education by publishing worldwide.

Oxford New York
Auckland Cape Town Dar es Salaam Hong Kong Karachi
Kuala Lumpur Madrid Melbourne Mexico City Nairobi
New Delhi Shanghai Taipei Toronto

With offices in
Argentina Austria Brazil Chile Czech Republic France Greece
Guatemala Hungary Italy Japan Poland Portugal Singapore
South Korea Switzerland Thailand Turkey Ukraine Vietnam

Published by Oxford University Press, Inc.
198 Madison Avenue, New York, NY 10016
www.oup.com

Library of Congress Cataloging-in-Publication Data
The Oxford encyclopedia of Islam and women / Natana J. DeLong-Bas, editor in chief.
p. cm.
Includes bibliographical references and index.
ISBN 978-0-19-976446-4—ISBN 978-0-19-999803-6—ISBN 978-0-19-999804-3
1. Women in Islam—Encyclopedias. I. DeLong-Bas, Natana J.
BP173.4.O94 2013
297.082'03—dc23
2012050203

Printed in the United States of America
on acid-free paper

THE OXFORD ENCYCLOPEDIA

OF

ISLAM AND WOMEN

N

NAMES AND NAMING. "Choose for your children pleasant and beautiful names," the Prophet reportedly said. As a measure of how significant names could be, he changed one individual's name that he thought improper. Care about names has perhaps developed from the sensitivity and piety to God's ninety-nine beautiful names in the Qurʾān (17:110).

In general Muslims in the Islamic heartlands have followed naming practices established early in Islamic times: the only name "given" is the first name, because the Qurʾān instructed, "Call them after their true father's names" (33:5), thereby dictating that the second name will be the father's, while the third may well be the grandfather's. There has seldom been variation in this rule, whether for boys or girls, because Islamic inheritance laws depended on it and claims had to be validated according to it. Girls legally retained their patronymic even after marriage, rather than assuming their husbands' names (as is traditional in much of the West), which is sometimes challenging for Muslim immigrant women at passport controls.

The naming of a child need not occur until the moment of registration with the state, which may be delayed, especially if the actual birthdate is not considered auspicious or if important family members are absent. During this interim a male child may be called "Muḥammad" and a female "Fāṭimah," as recommended in certain prophetic traditions. Once the decision is made, elaborate celebrations are usually held. South Asian Ismāʿīlīs perform a ceremony called a *chanda*, sprinkling blessed water over the child at a special rite in the *jamāʿat-khānah*; the names, dates of birth, and professions of the parents are then registered.

Because of its importance for identity, the greatest variation has taken place in the first name (*ism*). Religious conviction has been a fundamental determinant: Sunnīs have preferred the names of Muḥammad and the first three rightly guided caliphs, while Shīʿah have opted for ʿAlī and other figures of historical importance. Favorite names for girls have been less clearly sectarian, with the possible exception of ʿĀʾishah, since the wives and daughters of the Prophet are universally appealing. Also broadly acceptable are combinations reflecting religious resonances—names attributed to God, prefixed with "slave of," as ʿAbd al-Raḥmān, or to religion, as Quṭb al-Dīn, "pole of religion." Among Arabs, if a family had previously lost boys, they might give a new son a girl's name to deflect the attention of evil powers. Such a name could follow him into adulthood. Ethnic or heroic popularity sometimes overcame religious influences, such as Timur among Turkish-speaking peoples; tribal influence may also play a role (as in the Sudan). Names can anticipate a characteristic, as "Fayṣal" (arbiter or peacemaker) or "Saʿīd" (happy), or hope, "Umm al-Saʿādah" (mother of happiness). Throughout Islam, where one name is religious, a local name or nickname, is customarily added, resulting in long given names.

Modernity has had dramatic impacts on naming, one is that long names are simplified or replaced. Traditional names in Turkey, for example, have been eroded in concert with secular reforms. Since the 1970s political identity markers, such as Lenin or Russia, or places (Misra, Mecca), have surfaced. Others favor a great performer, Umm Kulthūm, or a leader, Nāṣir.

The patronymic has also undergone some modification over time. The *kunyah* or honorific name originated among pre-Islamic Arabs and became a mark of special caliphal recognition. It could also reflect one's tribe, birthplace, or even legal school. If the honor was included in the father's name, it could become part of the child's legal name. Special linkage phrases amplified an underlying relationship, thus the prefixes "ibn" (son of) or "Abū" (father of) in Arabic or the suffixes "-zādeh" or "-oghlu", both also meaning "son of" in Persian and Turkish, respectively. Magnifiers, such as "Magdī "(my glory)," were added to a father's or grandfather's name. Officially one's name included the *kunyah* and became part of a perpetually retained ancestral name.

Where an individual's given and ancestral names are conventional and liable to be confused with others, an addition, called *laqab* in Arabic, serves as a special indicator. Indicators vary: to profession (al-Naqqāsh, "the painter"), to a concept (al-Mulk, "of the kingdom"), or to a physical characteristic (al-Aʿmā, "the blind"). Conventionally, the assignment of a place name (*nisbah*) did not occur unless an individual became famous and was associated with a location, for example, Dhū al-Nūn al-Miṣrī (Dhū al-Nūn "of Egypt").

Names marking special recognition have been popular. These include titles like *shaykh*, *aga*, or *beg*; descriptors like "Ḥajjī" or "Ḥājjah," denoting someone who has completed a pilgrimage; and respectful designators like *shāh* ("saint," when a prefix to a name). These may become part of the individual's official name.

Professionals in Muslim countries may shorten to the given and indicator names, although locals will recognize someone by the professional title and given name. Migrants to the West have had considerable trouble with these traditions. Early immigrants were often assigned "Western-sounding" names, for example, "Sid" for "Saʿīd". European language influences have affected name spellings in India, Pakistan, and Africa. Indigenous languages also affected the form of names adopted from Arabic; thus in Swahili, "Fāṭimah" became "Fatuma" and "Abū Bakr" became "Bakāri".

Among the Hui of China, only surnames reflect Muslim ancestry. Early in the expansion of Islam into China, "Muḥammad" was shortened to "Ma," or a Muslim derivative as "Bai," (from Turkish *bey*). Since Muslim law has not applied to Chinese Muslims, their first names did not need to carry the individual's prime identity. Names like "Fāṭimah" are maintained, however, in Sinicized form. While in Indonesia Muslim identity has depended less on naming practices, perhaps indicative that the presence or absence of Islamic law is a factor in maintaining naming traditions.

Nevertheless Muslim naming protocols continue to be important identity markers. Converts are given Muslim names befitting the person, sometimes reflecting the convert's own choice, sometimes reflecting the new believer's social position, while African American converts actively adopt Muslim names; one of the Black Muslim converts, Malcolm X, had six names before his death as el-Hajj Malik el-Shabazz.

BIBLIOGRAPHY

A helpful overview of Arab traditions carried on into Islam is Frederick Mathewson Denny, "Names and Naming," in *Encyclopedia of Religion*, edited by Mircea Eliade, vol. 10, pp. 300–307 (New York: Macmillan, 1987). Naming trends are covered in two important articles by Richard W. Bulliet, "Conversion to Islam and the Emergence of a Muslim Society in Iran," in *Conversion to Islam*, edited by Nehemia Levtzion, pp. 30–51 (New York: Holmes and Meier, 1979), on medieval Iran; and "First Names and Political Change in Modern Turkey," *International Journal of Middle East Studies* 9 (1978): 489–495. G. W. Murray, *Sons of Ishmael: A Study of the Egyptian Bedouin* (London: Routledge, 1935) is an older source with useful ethnographic materials. Finally Dale F. Eickelman, a foundational writer on modern Moroccan Islam, covers the topic in "Rites of Passage: Muslim Rites," in *Encyclopedia of Religion*, edited by Mircea Eliade, vol. 12, pp. 380–403 (New York: Macmillan, 1987), and *Moroccan Islam: Tradition and Society in a Pilgrimage Center* (Austin: University of Texas Press, 1976). More recent and popular publications include Ahmed Abdul Hakeem, *Treasury of Favorite Muslim Names* (Chicago: Pearl Publications, 1997), and Salahuddin Ahmed, *The Dictionary of Muslim Names* (New York: New York University Press, and London, Hurst and Co., 1999).

EARLE WAUGH

NANA ASMA'U. (1793–1864), West African Qādirīyah Ṣūfī scholar, poet, teacher. Nana Asma'u bint Shehu Usuman Dan Fodio was a quadrilingual (Arabic, Fulfude, Hausa, Tamchek), classically trained scholar whose father, Shehu Usuman Dan Fodio, led the Sokoto jihad of Islamic reform (1803–1830) in what is now known as northern Nigeria. Like her father before her, Asma'u was taught by her mother and grandmother. In the Fodio (Fulfulde, "learned") family, literacy and the pursuit of knowledge was central to an activist life. Asma'u studied the classical canon contained in her father's extensive library, wrote Arabic poems that were admired by scholars as far away as Morocco, taught classes to both young men and young women, and was the trusted advisor to her father, brother Bello, and husband Gidado, who were instrumental figures during the Sokoto jihad's period of itinerancy and warfare. In the aftermath of these wars, Asma'u saw a need to educate and re-socialize refugees, particularly women. To this end she organized women students into groups known as the 'Yan Taru (the Associates), led by women known as *Jaji* (Hausa, "leader," no plural). The Jajis and their 'Yan Taru members would study with Asma'u until they had memorized the poetry she wrote as mnemonic instructional devices. Although Asma'u wrote works in Arabic (for the widest circle of scholars far beyond her region) and Fulfulde (for her clan, whose first language was Fulfulde), the educational poems were written and delivered in the language used by the masses, usually Hausa. Once they had memorized and learned how to teach these works, 'Yan Taru groups would follow their Jaji in procession from Asma'u's home to rural communities, where they would stay for the time necessary to teach women in those places what was contained in the poetry. The poems focused on ethics, attire, behavior, and theology. One poem contained in just thirty verses all the 114 names of Qur'ānic chapters; this material was then "unpacked" in lessons teaching the message of each chapter. Another poem, called "Ṣūfī Women" was based on tenth- and twelfth-century classical works of the same name, but Asma'u's version also included the names of nineteenth-century Ṣūfī women who were her peers, thereby elevating their status to that of Ṣūfī women in history. Nana Asma'u's activism and development of the 'Yan Taru program established a model for Muslim women's scholarly activity that thrives in the twenty-first century.

Asma'u's collected works of sixty-four long poems were published in English translation in 1997. Since then, women of American Qādirīyah Muslims affiliated with the Sokoto Fodio community have begun to develop their own 'Yan Taru groups of activist Muslimahs, led by a Jaji in each community, and a national Jaji to oversee 'Yan Taru education throughout the United States. The curriculum followed by American 'Yan Taru members is rigorous, including lessons in Arabic literacy, Qur'ānic study, social behavior, jurisprudence, doctrine, history of Asma'u and other women scholars in Islam, and media training, many of which were written by Asma'u, Shehu Usuman Dan Fodio, and his son, Caliph Bello.

Bibliography

Boyd, Jean. *The Caliph's Sister.* London: Frank Cass, 1989.

Boyd, Jean, and Beverly Mack. *The Collected Works of Nana Asma'u bint Sheu Usman dan Fodio (1793–1864).* East Lansing: Michigan State University Press, 1997.

Mack, Beverly, and Jean Boyd. *One Woman's Jihad: Nana Asma'u, Scholar and Scribe.* Bloomington: Indiana University Press, 2004.

Beverly Mack

Nāṣif, Malak Ḥifnī. Malak Ḥifnī Nāṣif (1886–1918) was an Egyptian feminist and writer known as Bāḥithat al-Bādiyah (Searcher in the Desert). Daughter of a scholar and littérateur, Nāṣif entered the 'Abbās Primary School when the state opened a girls' section in 1895. Receiving her diploma in 1901, she began to teach while enrolled in the Teachers' Training Program at Sanīyah School, where she received her certificate in 1905. She left her teaching post two years later upon marriage to 'Abd al-Sattār al-Baṣṣāl, a Bedouin chief, and settled with him in Fayyûm oasis. Although obliged by the Ministry of Education as well as personal circumstances to stop teaching after marriage, Nāṣif continued to write, publishing under the name "Bāḥithat al-Bādiyah." She spoke in the women's lecture series begun in 1909 and held at the Egyptian University and in the offices of the liberal newspaper, *Al-jarīdah.* Her essays, newspaper articles, and speeches were collectively published in *Al-nisā'īyat* (Women's/"Feminist" Pieces), a pioneering feminist book.

A reformer in the Islamic modernist tradition focusing on gender, Nāṣif inveighed against men's abuses relating to divorce and polygamy. Appropriating a male Muslim nationalist forum, the Egyptian Congress meeting in Heliopolis in 1911, she sent a list of feminist demands, insisting specifically that women be allowed to participate in congregational worship in mosques, to study in all fields, and to enter all occupations and professions, and, more generally, that women be permitted to develop themselves (as enjoined by Islam upon all believers) and to contribute to the welfare of the *ummah* (the community and nation). She also called for reform of the Muslim Personal Status Code. Unswerving in her goals but cautious in her methods, Nāṣif did not advocate uncovering of the face (although she knew this form of veiling was not ordained by Islamic religion) until society was better prepared to accept this change. Following the Italian invasion of Libya in 1911, Nāṣif initiated a program in Cairo to train women as nurses. In 1914 she participated in founding the Women's Refinement Union (al-Ittiḥād al-Nisā'ī al-Tahdhībī) and the Ladies Literary Improvement Society (Jam'īyat al-Raqy al-Adabīyah li-al-Sayyidāt al-Miṣrīyat). When Nāṣif died in 1918 at the age of thirty-two, women and men alike paid her homage. In commemorating her life and work, future feminist leader Hudā Sha'rāwī publicly pledged to continue her struggle on behalf of women.

[*See also* Feminism *and* Sha'rāwī, Hudā.]

BIBLIOGRAPHY

Abu-Lughod, Lila. *Remaking Women*. Princeton, N.J., 1998.

Badran, Margot. *Feminists, Islam, and Nation: Gender and the Making of Modern Egypt*. Princeton, N.J., 1995.

Badran, Margot. "From Consciousness to Activism: Feminist Politics in Early Twentieth-Century Egypt." In *Problems of the Middle East in Historical Perspective*, edited by John P. Spagnolo, pp. 27–48. London, 1992.

Goldschmidt, Arthur, Amy T. Johnson, and Barak A. Salmoni, eds. *Re-Envisioning Egypt, 1919–1952*. Cairo, 2005.

Kurzman, Charles. *Modernist Islam, 1840–1940: A Sourcebook*. New York, 2002.

Nāṣif, Malak Ḥifnī. *āthār Bāḥithat al-Bādiyah Malak Ḥifnī Nāṣif, 1886–1918 (Works of Bāḥithat al-Bādiyah)*. Edited by Majd al-Dīn Ḥifnī Nāṣif. Cairo, 1962.

Ziyādah, Mayy. *Bāḥithat al-Bādiyah: Dirāsah Naqdīyah (Bāḥithat al-Bādiyah: A Critical Research)*. Beirut, 1983. Originally published in 1920.

MARGOT BADRAN

NGOs AND WOMEN. The term "NGO" or "nongovernmental organization" was introduced in 1945 by the United Nations Charter, which grants consultative status to certain civil society organizations. For many years, the term was primarily used in relation to international organizations working with the UN system or with topics related to the UN's own areas of competence and intervention, most often secular or Christian Western organizations.

Today, the term is more broadly used, covering regional, national, and local organizations, non-Western organizations, various religious organizations, as well as organizations that are not connected to the UN. There is no scholarly consensus on a definition of what constitutes an NGO, but the term has primarily been used in relation to organizations involved in topics such as development, humanitarian aid, human rights, environment, and culture.

NGOs are often moral actors. They are, as Berger (2003:17) formulates it, actors who have "challenged the 'Wrong' in favor of the 'Right' and sought to alter inequitable distributions of power and resources in favor of the disenfranchised." This does not, however, mean that they are moral in a certain way; nor does it mean that they are always successful in their moral endeavors.

In relation to Islam and women, three different kinds of NGOs are relevant to discuss: secular women's NGOs, Muslim NGOs, and Muslim women's NGOs.

Secular Women's NGOs. Secular women's NGOs address the situation of women both in Muslim majority countries and in countries where Muslims constitute a minority. They typically rely on a liberal, rights-based approach, which refers to the UN Convention on the Elimination of All Forms of Discrimination Against Women (CEDAW) and various frameworks for reproductive rights, such as the Beijing Platform for Action.

Examples of secular women's NGOs include international organizations such as Development Alternatives with Women for a New Era (or DAWN), national organizations such as the Pakistani Women's Action Forum, and some local associations, for instance those sponsored by the Bangladesh Rural Advancement Committee (or BRAC).

The efforts of these NGOs include calls for reforms of laws, for instance. Personal status codes, which discriminate against girls and women with regard to family matters, such as marriage, divorce, custody, or heritage. They also work to combat discriminatory patriarchal practices, for instance, with regard to housework, access to education, or professional opportunities. In addition, many seek to counter violent practices such as female genital mutilation and so-called honor killings.

Secular NGOs have drawn the ire of various Muslim organizations, who accuse their feminist approach of prioritizing the rights of the individual woman over those of her family and community. Their notion of gender has also been criticized for glossing over what many Muslims see as natural and important differences between men and women. Whereas the secular NGOs advocate for gender equality, their Muslim opponents advocate for relations of equity and complementarity between men and women. Even though some adherents of secular NGOs are in fact practicing Muslim women, these organizations have been criticized for representing a "foreign" and westernized approach, which claims "universality" but disrespects Muslim identity and traditions (Ezzat, 2001).

Muslim NGOs and Women. Since the 1960s, Muslim majority countries, as well as countries with strong Muslim minorities, have seen a sharp increase in the number of Muslim NGOs, that is, NGOs with an explicitly Muslim identity. In Africa, for instance, the number of local and national Muslim NGOs has increased sixfold between 1980 and 2000, meaning that more than 15 percent of all NGOs are Muslim (Salih, 2002).

The group of Muslim NGOs is far from homogeneous. It includes international NGOs, such as Islamic Relief Worldwide, national organizations, such as Indonesia's Muhammadiyah or Ghana's Islamic Council for Development and Humanitarian Services, as well as numerous local Muslim associations, driven by volunteers and mosque personnel. Some are related to political movements (for example, the Muslim Brotherhood or Jamāʿ at i-Islāmī); others are explicitly nonpolitical.

Few of these organizations work specifically with "women's rights," as understood in a secular NGO context. Instead, they engage more indirectly with women's issues, in particular through their health, educational, and financial services to the poor. The Jordanian Islamic Center Charity Society, for instance, offers educational programs specifically for girls, and the Kuwaiti International Islamic Charitable Organization directs its microfinance projects primarily at women.

Internally, the majority of Muslim NGOs include women as staff members or volunteers. For many women, these organizations are the only venues for legitimate participation in the public sphere, providing them with a space for empowerment that is acceptable to their surroundings. For others, however, the patriarchal structures and management style of many Muslim organizations is a constraint. Very few Muslim NGOs, for instance, would allow a female director, even among Western organizations such as Muslim Aid, based in Britain.

Muslim Women's NGOs. A large part of Muslim NGOs consists of women's organizations, which address issues of relevance to Muslim women from an explicitly Muslim perspective. Like other Muslim organizations, and perhaps even more so, these organizations provide women, especially from conservative environments, with possibilities for public participation, without having to compromise on Islamic practices of gender segregation, for example, and—just as importantly—without having to reproduce secular, liberal discourses on women's rights.

Muslim women's NGOs comprise a wide and dynamic field of organizations, including local pious study groups of the Cairene mosque movement; national organizations, such as Islah Charitable Society in Yemen; and international networks, such as the International Muslim Women's Union.

These organizations often engage in religious studies, cultural activities, and social welfare activism, including literacy programs, vocational training, and charity. Whereas secular women's NGOs have been criticized for imposing a "foreign" approach, they in turn criticize many

Muslim women's NGOs for perpetuating traditional gender roles, for instance, via their vocational training, which often focuses on traditional women's responsibilities such as childcare, cooking, or sewing.

Yet, since the 1990s, a new kind of Muslim women's NGO has emerged, inspired by the controversial trend of "Islamic feminism." While constituting a highly heterogeneous group, these organizations combine rights-based advocacy with a specifically Muslim approach, arguing that ignorance and patriarchal traditions prevent women from enjoying the rights bestowed on them by Islam. Examples include Junta Islamica Catalana from Barcelona, the Malaysian NGO Sisters in Islam, and the international Musawah.

Blurred Boundaries between Muslim and Secular NGOs. When it comes to women, Muslim and secular NGOs have traditionally been viewed (and defined themselves) in opposition to each other. However, boundaries between them are increasingly blurred as they learn from each other.

Muslim NGOs involved in women's issues increasingly adopt historically secular development discourses and rights-based approaches. Secular women's NGOs, on their side, are becoming more attentive to the potentially positive role of Islam in shaping the lives of Muslim women, reflecting a general awareness of religion among secular NGOs in recent years.

Accordingly, in many instances, it may make more sense to think of the relationship between these organizations not in terms of stark oppositions between "Muslim" and "secular," but rather as a continuum on which the organizations move up and down to different degrees and at different times emphasizing different interpretive approaches to Islam.

[*See also* Convention on the Elimination of All Forms of Discrimination against Women (CEDAW) *and* Musawah.]

BIBLIOGRAPHY

Abu-Lughod, Lila. *Remaking Women: Feminism and Modernity in the Middle East.* Princeton, N.J., and Oxford: Princeton University Press, 1998.

Ahmed, Leila. *Women and Gender in Islam.* New Haven, Conn., and London: Yale University Press, 1999.

Badran, Margot. *Feminism in Islam: Secular and Religious Convergences.* Oxford: Oneworld, 2009.

Balchin, Cassandra. "With Her Feet on the Ground: Women, Religion and Development in Muslim Communities." *Development* 46, no. 4 (2003): 39–49.

Basu, Amrita. "Globalization of the Local/Localization of the Global. Mapping Transnational Women's Movements." *Meridians: Feminism, Race, Transnationalisms* 1, no. 1 (2000): 68–84.

Berger, Julia. "Religious Non-governmental Organizations." *Voluntas: International Journal of Voluntary and Nonprofit Organizations* 14, no. 1 (2003): 15–39.

Clarke, Janine. *Islam, Charity and Activism: Middle Class Networks and Social Activism in Egypt, Jordan and Yemen.* Bloomington: Indiana University Press, 2004.

Daly, Sunny. "Young Women as Activists in Contemporary Egypt: Anxiety, Leadership, and the Next Generation." *Journal of Middle East Women's Studies* 6, no. 2 (2010): 59–85.

Deeb, Lara. *An Enchanted Modern: Gender and Public Piety in Shi'i Lebanon.* Princeton Studies in Muslim Politics, Princeton, N.J.: Princeton University Press, 2006.

Ezzat, Heba Raouf. "The Silent Ayesha: An Egyptian Narrative." In *Globalization, Gender, and Religion: The Politics of Women's Rights in Catholic and Muslim Contexts,* edited by Jane H. Bayes and Nayereh Esfahlani Tohidi, pp. 231–258. New York: Palgrave, 2001.

Ferree, Myra Max, and Carol McClurg Mueller. "Feminism and the Women's Movement: A Global Perspective." In *The Blackwell Companion to Social Movements,* edited by David A. Snow, Sarah A. Soule, and Hanspeter Kriesi, pp. 576–607. Oxford: Blackwell Publishing, 2004.

Haddad, Yvonne, Jane I. Smith, and Kathleen Moore. *Muslim Women in America. Gender, Islam and Society.* New York: Oxford University Press, 2006.

Hafez, Sherine. *An Islam of Her Own. Reconsidering Religion and Secularism in Women's Islamic Movements.* New York: New York University Press, 2011.
Jouili, Jeanette S. "Beyond Emancipation: Subjectivities and Ethics among Women in Europe's Islamic Revival Communities." *Feminist Review* 98 (2011): 47–64.
Juul Petersen, Marie. "Islamizing Aid: Transnational Muslim NGOs After 9.11." *Voluntas: International Journal of Voluntary and Non-Profit Organizations*, early online access March 2011.
Mahmood, Saba. *Politics of Piety. The Islamic Revival and the Feminist Subject.* Princeton, N.J., and Oxford: Princeton University Press, 2005.
Mir-Hosseini, Ziba. "Muslim Women's Quest for Equality: Between Islamic Law and Feminism." *Critical Inquiry* 32, no. 4 (2006): 629–645.
Moghadam, Valentine M. *Modernizing Women: Gender and Social Change in the Middle East.* Boulder, Colo. Lynne Rienner Publishers, 2003.
Morgan, Robin (ed.). *Sisterhood Is Global. The International Women's Movement Anthology.* New York: Feminist Press, City University of New York, 1996.
Pruzan-Jørgensen, Julie. "Islamic Women's Activism in the Arab World. Potentials and Challenges for External Actors", *DIIS Report*, 2012: 02, Copenhagen: Danish Institute for International Studies.
Salih, Mohammed. *Islamic NGOs in Africa: The Promise and Peril of Islamic Voluntarism*, Copenhagen: Centre of African Studies, University of Copenhagen, 2001.
Shehabuddin, Elora. *Reshaping the Holy: Development, Democracy, and Muslim Women in Bangladesh.* New York: Columbia University Press, 2008.
Zahedi, Ashraf. "Muslim American Women in the Post 11-September Era." *International Feminist Journal of Politics* 13, no. 2 (2011): 183–203.

Marie Juul Petersen and
Julie Pruzan-Jørgensen

Nigeria. Nigeria is a country of diverse cultures with rich religious traditions. Its inhabitants consist of different ethnic groups and tribes who speak different languages: Hausa, Igbo, Yoruba, and others. Since its amalgamation into one country in 1914, it remains the largest nation in Africa, with a population of more than 160 million, an estimated 50 percent of whom are Muslim, 40 percent Christian, and 10 percent indigenous religious practitioners. Although women have contributed to the advancement and progress of Nigeria, they have received little recognition for their contributions, particularly in economics and education. They sometimes suffer from abuses, often attributed to the andocentric nature of Nigerian society. Even though women have achieved some progress and enjoy participation in the new democratic government, they still lag behind in many areas of social and political life.

History of Nigeria. The major tribes in Nigeria are the Fulani, Hausa, Ibo, Tiv, and Yoruba. The groups were separated geographically and politically from one another before colonial rule but engaged in mutual trade relations. They practiced animist religions until Islam was introduced into the North in the eleventh century by North African Arab Muslims. Christianity came to Eastern Nigeria in the seventeenth century through the Portuguese. The Yoruba held on to their *Orisha* religion until they were introduced to Islam in the 1800s and later colonized by the British. The British established their colonial occupation of Nigeria in the early 1900s and united Nigeria under one government in 1914.

Although Islam came to Nigeria in the eleventh century (Hiskett, 1985, p. 59), it was not fully spread in Northern Nigeria until the early sixteenth century when Shaykh Muḥammad Abd al-Karim al-Maghili (d. 1505) of Algeria visited Northern Nigeria. Hunwick mentions that al-Maghili established Islamic schools, taught scholars, and wrote for the King of Kano, Rumfa, a treatise called *On Obligation of Princes*, a guidebook on how to govern Muslims in accordance with Islam. Islam was not truly adhered to or the religion of the state until the jihad of Usuman Dan Fodio, the Muslim reformer of West Africa (*mujaddid*) (d. 1817). He established an Islamic state in Northern Nigeria in the 1800s, resulting in a stable government. When

Lord Lugard, the British governor, conquered the North in 1903, he retained the Northern leaders in their positions. They were governed through "indirect rule," in which the British supervised them and made minor changes to the existing Islamic system (Crocker, 1936, p. 213).

Women's role in Dan Fodio's government appears to have been minimal. Dan Fodio educated the Hausa women and included them in his classes despite strong opposition from his contemporary scholars. There is no substantial record of women's full participation in the government, although his daughter, Nana Asma'u, was a recognized scholar and leader within the movement (Badran, 2011, pp. 31–32). Mack has analyzed how Nana Asma'u became a great scholar in the Fodiyo community and how her scholarship helped Hausa women learn the Qur'ān and ḥadīth. Her embrace of and practice of Sufism, and composition of religious poetry in native (*A'Ajami)* language assisted other women in affiliating with the Qadiriyah Ṣūfī Order in West Africa (Badran, 2011, pp. 23–23). When the British took over Northern Nigeria, they relegated women's role to homemakers and educated men and appointed them in strategic positions. The British replaced women who held positions, such as in administration and management of the market, by men. Under British rule, a few women received Western education and served as midwives, nurses, teachers, and clerks. However, Muslim women generally did not fare well in this regard because Muslim parents did not enroll their children in British schools owing to concerns about their potentially being converted to Christianity. Even after independence, Christian schools insisted that Muslim students should receive Christian religious instruction or withdraw from the schools (Clark and Linder, 1984, pp. 15–18). After the establishment of an additional twelve states in 1975 and the adoption of Universal Basic Education (UBE) and Universal Primary Education policy in Nigeria in 1976, the government ensured that boys and girls were admitted into schools and received both Islamic and Christian education. In the old Western Region (today's Oyo, Ogun, Lagos, and Oshun states), parents were fined through the Local Welfare Offices for not sending their children (male or female) to schools. Today, with encouragement from the government and awakening from women's organizations, such as Abeokuta Women Organization and the Federation of Muslim Women Association of Nigeria, female enrollment in school has increased.

Women's Education and Employment. The percentage of Nigerians, males and females, attending school today has grown. Girls' enrollment jumped from 43.6 percent enrollment in high school in 2006 to 49.9 percent in 2008 (*Gender Statistics Newsletter*, 2011, p. 11). Boys and girls often attend the same schools and are taught by both male and female teachers, although public interaction is less frequent between men and women in Northern Nigeria. At the college level, women still lag behind men because of early marriage, religious orientation, and parental constraints. Many Muslim parents, especially in the North, do not want their daughters to attend college, preferring them to get married to protect their modesty. They strongly believe that Islam requires women to have early marriage so as not to engage in any immoral relationship. In the job market, males win more jobs than females due to job discrimination and inadequate training of women, although today an increasing number of women travel to Europe and America for education and business and to the Middle East and West Africa, mainly for business.

Before the production of petroleum in Nigeria, 70 to 80 percent of Nigerians engaged in farming. Although both men and women tilled the soil and planted the crops, women were responsible for harvesting and selling them (Adekanye, Otitolaiye, and Opaluwa, 2009). Furthermore, nearly all food processing was done by women, especially in the North, despite the fact that many of them observed seclusion, working from home, and not appearing or selling in public (Zakaria, 2001). Today, women work mostly as educators in junior and high schools and as nurses (Boserup; Adekanye, 1985; and Banwo). Muslim women are engaged in business as entrepreneurs in most of the capital cities, including Lagos, Abuja, Ibadan, Kano, Onisha, Calabar, Jos, and Kaduna. Between 25 and 30 percent of registered businesses in Nigeria today are owned by women (Halkias et al. 2011). Despite women's activity in business and as entrepreneurs, they continue to face challenges, such as lack of access to capital, culture, and inadequate education whereby certain professions are exclusively reserved for men, for example, carpentry, bricklayers, and shoemaking. Some women's groups, such as the Federation of Muslim Women Association of Nigeria (FOMWAN) and the International Women Society of Nigeria (IWSN), are working to promote the welfare of poor women, in particular, by increasing their access to education, agriculture, and economic decision making. One important organization in this regard is Country Women Organization of Nigeria (CWON), which focuses on entrepreneurial education, training, and access to credit. (Supprakit)

Although men and women interact with one another at government institutions, such as colleges, universities, banks, and factories, and work together in agriculture and in the markets, in occupational jobs, such as fashion design, textile dyeing, carpentry, and others, women are often segregated from men. Only about 10 percent of women are professionals, such as lawyers, doctors, professors, engineers, senators, or mayors, even though they are qualified (*Gender Statistic Newsletter* 4, Nigeria Bureau of Statistics, 2011). Many Nigerian women are housewives. Even though they are proud of being mothers and educators, their private contributions are not formally recognized.

Women's Organizations. After independence, women established many organizations, such as the National Council of Women's Societies (NCWS), Women in Nigeria (WIN), Civil Liberty of Nigeria (CLN), and International Women's Society of Nigeria (IWSN), which is one of Nigeria's oldest women's organizations. These organizations seek to address the injustice and gender inequality Nigerian women often face, as well as human rights concerns, including polygamous marriage (which is practiced more by Muslims than by any other group in Nigeria) and female circumcision, which is occasionally enforced on them by their parents at times and by societal pressure occasionally as part of the culture. Many women's rights organizations are petitioning the government to put a legal system in place that will protect women from abuse and discrimination.

Three major Muslim women's organizations in Nigeria are Federation of the Muslim Women's Association of Nigeria (FOMWAN); Muslim Sisters Organization of Nigeria (MSON); and Women Living under Muslim Laws International Solidarity Network: Africa and Middle East, which has branches throughout Africa and the Middle East and fights for women's rights in all African countries. Based in Lagos, Women Living under Muslim Laws International Solidarity Network: Africa and Middle East offers solidarity and social and political support to women, regardless of their status as Muslim or non-Muslims. It also collects and disseminates information regarding women's rights in Africa and the Middle East and provides various training programs for its members. Along with other organizations, such as Women in Law and Development in Africa (WILDAF), it has worked to demonstrate against certain verdicts of Sharī`ah courts in Northern Nigeria, most famously in the cases of Safiyat Hussaini and Amina Lawal, both of whom were sentenced to death by stoning. Both were accused of committing adultery. These groups, with the support of other women's organizations in Nigeria and abroad, successfully lobbied the government for the freedom of both women.

FOMWAN was established by Muslim women in 1985, largely out of frustration that more secularly feminist-oriented organizations were not serving the interests of Muslim women who cherish both their religion and their relationships with their husbands, whom they view as life partners, rather than oppressors. It has branches in thirty-six states in Nigeria, more than five hundred affiliate groups, and consulate status with the United Nations. FOMWAN is a nonprofit and nongovernment organization that aims at promoting health, literacy, and economic empowerment for Muslim women, providing its members with social and educational services. It seeks to enhance positive social behavior for Muslim girls and improve the socioeconomic status of Nigerian women. It also collaborates with other women's organizations to empower women to be role models and have an impact on the religious and secular lives of Nigerian women. The Muslim Sisters Organization of Nigeria (MSON) is a women's wing of the Islamic Educational Trust of Nigeria, which was established in Minna in 1969 by Dr. Ahmed Lemu, Hajiya Aishah Lemu, and Alhaji Sani Ashafa Sulaiman. The MSON operates primarily in Niger, Kaduna, and Sokoto States. It promotes girls' and women's education, advocating the importance of Islamic and Western education and encouraging young mothers to enroll their children in schools. It also provides financial and spiritual support for its members.

Women Leaders in Nigeria. No woman has ever become head of state, prime minister, or governor in Nigeria. Particularly in Northern Nigeria, women seem to be removed from positions of political leadership, such as in Zamfara State where, from 1999 until 2009, there were no women among the members of the Zamfara House of Assembly or serving as the head of any local governments. Nevertheless, in other parts of the country, women have been more successful in gaining access to the corridors of power. Muslim women were elected as deputy governors in Lagos in 1999 (Alhaja Lateefat Okunnu) and Ogun States in 2003 (Alhaja Salimot Makanjuola Badru). Women also achieved important victories across the board in the 2007 elections: six were elected deputy governors, nine senators, twenty-seven national representatives, and fifty-two members of the various Houses of Assembly. Women have also served in ministerial positions, including minister of women's affairs, education, port-authority, health, and the central bank. Nevertheless, as of 2011, 92.5 percent of the members of the Nigerian Senate were males and only 7.5 percent were females (Nigeria Bureau of Statistics, 2011).

Prominent women leaders in Nigeria who have had an impact on politics, education, law, the economy, and women's rights include Farida Waziri, Abigail Olufunmilayo Rasome-Kuti, Lateefat Okunnu, Hauwa Ibrahim, and Ayesha Imam.

Farida Mzamber Waziri attained one of the highest positions in the Nigerian police. Born in 1946 in Gboko, Benue State, she received her law degree at the University of Lagos and joined the Nigerian Police Force in 1965. She gradually rose to the top position of Assistant Inspector General of Police and served at different strategic positions. In 2008, she was appointed chairperson of the Economic and Financial Crime Commission (EFCC), the most powerful anti-corruption agency in Nigeria. During her tenure, she worked to promote women's rights and to recruit women into the police force, encouraging women to challenge men in all leadership positions. She left office in November 2011.

Abigail Olufunmilayo Ransome-Kuti was an educator. Born in October 1900 in Abeokuta, she completed her college education in London. On her return to Nigeria, she became a teacher and later joined politics, where she fought for women's rights. She was the mother of the Fela Ransome-Kuti, the founder of Reggae music in Nigeria. She encouraged women's participation in politics and education and served as the treasurer for the political party of the National Council of Nigeria and Cameron (NCNC) in the 1950s. She founded the Egba Women's Union in 1946, which later became Abeokuta Women's Union. The Union promoted women's education and fought against social abuses and discrimination against women. She received the National Honor of the Order of the Federal Republic of Nigeria (OFR) in 1965. She died in April 1978.

Alhaja Lateefat Okunnu was born in Lagos in 1939. She earned her BA degree in Geography and then a post-graduate diploma (MA degree) in administration from the University of California. She started her career as an educator, teaching at colleges and serving as educational administrator at different levels in Lagos. She became the first female Deputy Governor of Lagos State in 1999. She also served at the national level as the Chairperson of the Caretaker Committee of the National Republican Convention, which led to the formation of Nigeria's popular democracy. Okunnu is one of the founding members of FOMWAN and the Muslim League for Accountability (MULAC), which fosters government transparency in keeping with Islamic principles. Okunnu has also formerly served as a member of the Nigerian Inter-Religious Council (NIREC) and the Nigeria Supreme Council for Islamic Affairs. She won the Federal National Award, Order of Federal Republic of Nigeria (OFR) in 2002 for her contributions to the development of Nigeria.

Hauwa Ibrahim was born in 1967 in Gombe. She received a law degree and started her private law practice in 1999, having previously worked in different judicial departments. Ibrahim came to fame through her participation in the defense of the rights of Safiya Hussaini and Amina Lawal, both of whom had been sentenced to death by stoning at the Sharīʿah courts in Northern Nigeria following accusations of adultery. Mrs. Ibrahim was a member of their defense team, which argued that Safiyatu and Amina Lawal had been denied their fundamental right to a fair hearing because the trial court had not explained to them their right to have lawyers. In addition, the defense team found many errors in the proceedings and judgments of the Upper Shariah Court that tried the cases. Eventually, both cases were dismissed on a technicality (Yawuri, 2007, pp. 129–139): not on the ground that Islamic law is wrong but that it is arbitrarily applied to women. Mrs. Ibrahim is an advocate for justice and defends women's rights, as well as the rights of men who have been harshly sentenced by literal applications of Sharīʿah. Her participation in winning freedom for both Safiyat and Amina brought her to international attention. Since that victory, she has been invited to Europe and America to lecture on Islamic law. She received the Sakharov Prize, given by the European parliament to honor exceptional individuals who combat intolerance, fanaticism, and oppression, in 2005. Ibrahim believes that the Sharīʿah should be understood properly and applied correctly without any discrimination, in order to serve human beings and promote justice.

Ayesha Imam is one of Nigeria's most distinguished scholars and leading feminists. An educator, researcher, human rights activist, and prolific author, she was educated in Nigeria and the United Kingdom and has taught at universities in Nigeria, Canada, the United Kingdom, and Senegal. Since the 1990s, she has been engaged in social research, writing proposals, project management and implementation, research methodologies, data analysis, and group conflict resolutions. She offers training workshops for many organizations in West Africa and the Middle East under the umbrella of the United Nations. Her greatest impact has been in promoting gender equality and preventing abuses against women and the poor. She founded the first feminist organization in Nigeria—Women in Nigeria (WIN). She has served as the director for the Council for the Development of Social Sciences in Africa (CODESRIA) in Senegal and the coordinator of the International Solidarity Network of women living under Muslim laws in West Africa and the Middle East (WLUML) (Badran, 2011, 195–196). In 2002, she received the John Humphrey Freedom Award for her contributions to human rights and promotion of gender equality.

Conclusion. Nigerian women, although often marginalized by patriarchal society, have played an important role in the global struggle for women's rights and gender equality. They initiated and participated in women's rights conferences in Nigeria, West Africa, the Middle East, the United Kingdom, Canada, the United States, and other countries. They attended the International Women Year Conference in Mexico in 1975, the Conference on Women Forum in Copenhagen in 1980 and in Nairobi in 1985, the World Conference on Women in Beijing in 1995, Beijing +5 and Beijing +10 in New York in 2000 and 2005, and the 9th Annual Conference of the African Leadership Forum in Accra, Ghana, in 1997. In all of these conferences, they have sought to remain informed and to help their own people elevate their status and eliminate discrimination against women. They hold the Nigerian government responsible for the implementation of the UN Convention on the Elimination of Discrimination Against Women (CEDAW) by fighting for gender equality, fair treatment, and good quality of life for all Nigerian women. Although Muslim women still lag behind in Northern Nigeria, there are concerted efforts by the government to enhance their education and improve their social status.

BIBLIOGRAPHY

Adekanye, T. O. "Innovation and Rural Women in Nigeria." In *Technology and Rural Women: Conceptual and Empirical Issues*, edited by I. Ahmed, I. London: Allen & Unwin, 1985.

Adekanye, T. O., J. O. Otitolaiye, and H. I. Opaluwa "Food and Agricultural Production in Nigeria: Some Empirical Considerations for Engendering Economic Policy for Africa." Paper presented at the IAFFE Conference on Feminist Economics, Boston, Mass., 26–28 June, 2009.

Badran, Margot, ed. *Gender and Islam in Africa: Rights, Sexuality, and Law.* Washington, D.C.: Woodrow Wilson Press, 2011.

Banwo, Adeyinka. "Women in the Traditional Economy." In *Understanding Yoruba Life and Culture*, edited by Nike S. Lawal, Matthew N. O. Sadiku, and P. Ade Dopamu. Trenton, N.J.: Africa World Press, 2004.

Clarke, Peter, and I. Linder. *Islam in Modern Nigeria: A Study of a Muslim Community in a Post-Independence State, 1960–1983.* Naubz: Craunwald: Munich, Chr. Kaiser Verlag, 1984.

Crocker, W. R. *Nigeria: A Critique of British Colonial Administration.* London: George Allen & Unwin, 1936.

Denzer, LaRay. "Nigerian Women's Empowerment: The Voice of Folayegbe Mosunmola Akintunde-Ighodalo, 1953 to the Present." http://www.yorku.ca/nhp/conferences/dartmouth/LaRay_Denzer. Program of African Studies, Northwestern University.

Federation of Muslim Women's Associations in Nigeria. http://www.fomwan.org/.

Halkias, S. D., C. Nwajiuba, N. Harkiolakis, and S. M. Caracatsanis. "Challenges Facing Women Entrepreneurs in Nigeria." *Management Research Review* 34, no. 2 (2011): 221–235.

Hiskett, M. *The Development of Islam in West Africa.* London and New York: Longman, 1984.

Hunwick, John O. *Shari'a in Songhay: The Replies of al-Maghili to the Questions of Askia al-Hajj Muhammad.* Edited and translated with an introduction and commentary. Oxford: Oxford University Press, 1985.

International Humanist and Ethical Union. http://www.iheu.org/node/1134; http://www.iheu.org/node/979; http://www.wildaf-ao.org/eng/articlephp3?id_article=46.
Juang, Richard M., and Noelle Anne Morrissette, eds. *Africa and the Americas: Culture, Politics, and History, A Multidisciplinary Encyclopedia*, pp. 822–825. Santa Barbara, Calif.: ABC-CLIO, 2008.
Mack, Beverly B. "Muslim Women's Knowledge Production in the Greater Maghreb: The Example of Nana Asma'u on Northern Nigeria." In *Gender and Islam in Africa: Rights, Sexuality, and Law*, edited by Margot Badran.Washington, D.C.: Woodrow Wilson Press, 2011.
Nigeria Bureau of Statistics (NBS). *Gender Statistics Newsletter* 2.4 (July–Dec. 2011).
Owhonda, John. *Nigeria: A Nation of Many People.* Parsippany, N.J: Dillion Press, 1998.
Saturday Tribune. "How Have the Women Fared?" http://www.tribune.com.ng/sat/index.php/women-affairs/1158-democracy-in-nigeria-how-have-the women-fared.html. 28 May 2010.
Supprakit, Sasiya. "Challenges and Obstacles Facing Women Entrepreneurs: The Case of Nigeria." *Journal of African Business* 10, no. 1 (2011): 105–121.
Yawuri, Aliyu Musa. "On Defending Safiyatu Hussaini and Amina Lawal." In *Shari'ah Implementation in Northern Nigeria 1999–2006*, edited by Philips Ostein, pp. 129–139. Ibadan, Nigeria: Spectrum Books, 2007.
Zakaria, Y. "Entrepreneurs at Home: Secluded Muslim Women and Hidden Economic Activities in Northern Nigeria." *Nordic Journal of African Studies* 10, no. 1 (2001): 107–123.
Zamfara State House of Assembly. http://zamfarastatehouseofassembly.org.

Yushau Sodiq

Noor al-Hussein. (b. 1951), Queen Dowager of Jordan, Queen Consort from 1978 to 1999, and human rights and women's rights activist.

Noor al-Hussein's paternal great-grandfather was one of the earliest Arab immigrants to the U.S., arriving in the early 1890s. Her father was Najeeb Halaby, a prominent businessman and aviation expert, who served as a State Department advisor, head of the Federal Aviation Administration, and CEO and chair of Pan Am. Born Lisa Najeeb Halaby, she earned a BA in Architecture and Urban Planning from Princeton University in 1974, as part of the Ivy League school's first coeducational freshman class. She later worked for Royal Jordanian Airlines, during which she met King Hussein bin Talal. They wed in 1978; upon marriage, she converted to Islam and changed her name to "Noor al-Hussein," a name chosen by her husband, which means "light of Hussein." They had four children: Princes Hamzah and Hashim, and Princesses Iman and Raiyah.

Queen Noor took up many causes during her tenure; she was mainly interested in cultural issues, women's advancement, and regional economic development. One of the numerous projects she supported was the National Handicraft Development Program, established by her foundation as a way to celebrate Jordanian culture and to empower women to generate income for themselves and their families. The queen became known for wearing traditional, handcrafted Jordanian dresses or robes as a way of highlighting and generating an interest in local and culturally relevant fashion. She also took up the cause of children in the country; in addition to supporting programs focused on education and women's and children's health, particularly childhood immunization and antipoverty programs, she helped establish the Children's Heritage and Science Museum and the Mobile Life and Science Museum in the 1980s.

She has been quite popular in the United States; like other American women who had gone on to marry royalty (such as Princess Grace of Monaco), she captured the imaginations of her native country. She was frequently compared to Princess Diana of Wales in terms of her involvement in human rights issues. After the death of Diana,

Queen Noor became the chief spokesperson to bring world attention to the effort to lobby against land mines.

Queen Noor serves as the chairperson of the Noor Al Hussein Foundation (NHF), a nonprofit non-governmental organization (NGO) she founded in 1985. The NHF supports, among other things, job creation, microfinancing opportunities, family health care, and women's economic and social advancement. She also chairs the King Hussein Foundation (KHF), which she established in 1999 after the king's death.

She serves on the boards of, or presides over, numerous organizations devoted to global conflict resolution, including United World Colleges, Global Zero, International Campaign to Ban Landmines, Refugees International, Seeds of Peace, Council of Women World Leaders, Women Waging Peace, the International Union for Conservation of Nature, and the International Commission on Missing Persons.

Noor al-Hussein has been honored with many awards, including the Healing the Planet Award from Physicians for Social Responsibility, the Global Environmental Citizen Award from Harvard Medical School's Center for Health and the Global Environment, the Inspiration Award from the Dag Hammarskjöld Fund for Journalists, and the Woman of Compassion Award from UNICEF.

BIBLIOGRAPHY

DeLong-Bas, Natana J. *Notable Muslims: Muslim Builders of World Civilization and Culture*. Oxford: OneWorld, 2006.

Noor Al Hussein Foundation. http//:www.nooralhusseinfoundation.org.

Queen Noor. *Hussein of Jordan*. Amman, Jordan: KHF Publishing, 2000.

Queen Noor. *Leap of Faith: Memoirs of an Unexpected Life*. New York: Miramax Books, 2003.

SUSAN MUADDI DARRAJ

NÜ AHONG. The contestations surrounding the application of the Chinese/Farsi title of *nü ahong* to Chinese female religious leaders reveal the volatile history of women's entry into Islamic leadership positions in China's vast Muslim diaspora. *Ahong* functions as a generic title, and can refer to both female and male religious practitioners in a position of authority. They commonly preside over the religious affairs of the mosque to which they are contracted. The title embraces a range of functions that vary according to the contracted duties of an individual *ahong*, the needs of a given *fang* (congregation of believers belonging to a particular mosque), and the individual qualities of learning and charismatic leadership an *ahong* brings to her position. Duties assigned include religious instruction and specialized training of future religious personnel, leading collective worship and giving sermons, presiding over rites and ceremonies, and sharing in the administrative and representational duties associated with the public standing of her mosque. In modern times, the title of *ahong* is increasingly interchangeable with the title of imam, suggestive of formal rank and contractual status with respect to a mosque or other Islamic institution. The enduring controversy over the use of the title by women, and over the authority invested in the person of a female *ahong*, is intimately linked to parochial and gendered understanding of women's value and place in the history of Islam's survival in China. In Muslim communities in which independent female religious institutions were either short-lived or never allowed to emerge in the first place, the title of *nü ahong* is commonly rejected as *huai bid'ah* (reprehensible innovation). Instead, women of learning and religious authority may be addressed as *jiaozhang* (a person teaching at an advanced level), *shiniang* or *shimu* (title of respect given to the female kin of a male teacher or *ahong*), *jiaoyuan* (teacher of Islam), or *hailifan* (student of Islam). This is not unlike the practice in Iran where the Farsi term *ākhūnd* (preacher) only applies to men who preach from the pulpit. In contrast, female religious leaders are called *khanom* and confine their teaching and counseling to guiding women on personal and family-related issues.

Authority of an *Ahong*. An individual *ahong* contributes to her female congregation's aspiration for recognition and standing in the community through the caliber of her learning, the integrity of her leadership, and the moral purity of her conduct. In her role as broker between a mosque organization and its female congregation, between her mosque and the adjacent men's mosque, between mosque and the Muslim community, between the local Muslim community and national as well as international political and religious actors, and, most importantly, in her role as mediator between God and the women for whose afterlife she is responsible, she can either establish a reputation from which all associated with the mosque benefit, or she can reduce it to a marginal and inconsequential position.

From "Symbolic Shelter" to *Dulixingde Nüsi* (Independent Women's Mosque). The historical origin of the *nü ahong* tradition in China can be traced back to the late sixteenth and early seventeenth centuries, when a Hui Muslim intellectual and religious elite confronted the imminent prospect of the demise of Islam and utter assimilation of the Hui population by engaging in innovative, influential, intellectual, and pedagogical projects. Women constituted both the primary targets of their strategy to popularize Islamic knowledge and their indispensable handmaidens as teachers of women in a strictly gender-segregated society. The combination of women's transformation of assigned segregated space into a rich source of collective identity and changes brought about by political and gender-related advances—especially during the early years of the twentieth century and again under Communist Party rule—contributed to a process of indigenization that culminated in women's own unique institutions.

The historical circumscription of female-led Islamic institutions combined with Confucian ethical-philosophical gender norms has left enduring traces in the gendered architecture of women's mosques, their material and religious culture, and, crucially, in the assigned *nei*-associated (pertaining to women's secluded realm) functions, status, and restricted mobility of women *ahong*. Reforms of women's religious education as part of the national campaign to strengthen the Chinese nation during the Republican era (1912–1949) combined with improved training of women *ahong* and greater exposure to growing attention to the "women's question" arguably had an impact on some of the more independent-minded *ahong*. Many features reflecting the early conception of women's places of education and prayer as an extension of the domestic home were altered to reveal an active quest by women for spiritual equality. In all these important reforms, the role of women *ahong* was decisive; some started to implement fixed regimes of instruction and prayer, prioritizing the improvement of female religious and overall education.

After years of brutal silencing of public expressions of faith, the early 1980s brought increased access by religious women to legal and sociopolitical resources to which all Chinese women have been entitled, resulting in a new phase of consolidation and expansion. Since then, Muslim women have acquired a basis on which to challenge the norms and teachings traditionally legitimizing their institutional subordination to men. For this reason, rather than resenting mandatory state registration (which came into force in 1994) as intrusive and restrictive, female *ahong* aspire to qualify for state registration, celebrating registration as a milestone in the history of women's spiritual progress, and as due official recognition and affirmation of their equal standing in all spheres of society. For a number of ambitious leaders of women's mosques, the raised living standard and higher incomes of recent years, noticeable even in Muslim communities in the poorer rural areas, are providing opportunities to turn their mosques into highly visible symbols of women's capacity for spiritual devotion.

The greatest change in current times has been the widening of a woman *ahong*'s sphere of activity both inside and beyond the mosque gates, adding to her authority on issues of increasing complexity at both the local and international levels. The obstacles faced by female *ahong*-led women's mosques are numerous and serious. They include being subjected to critical exposure in fundamentalist Muslim websites and scrutiny by the growing number of returned pilgrims, eager to enforce conformity with a more "authentic" Arab-Muslim gender paradigm in their communities, exacerbating the vulnerability of women's institutions.

Conclusion. In the twenty-first century, women *ahong* in a number of Hui Muslim communities in central China, presiding over officially registered women's mosques, claim equal status according to law with men's mosques. They are situated at the most *dulixingde* (independent) end of the spectrum of women's mosques to be found in central China. Offering a poignant contrast with the status of the more dependent women's mosques elsewhere where *nü ahong* have come to rely in all respects on the management and guidance of leaders from adjacent men's mosques, the more independent *nü ahong* represent what is most innovative and yet what is also entirely consistent with the spirit of generations of female leaders before them.

BIBLIOGRAPHY

Allès, Èlisabeth. *Musulmans de Chine: Une Anthropologie des Hui du Henan*. Paris: Éditions de l'École des Hautes Études en Sciences Sociales, 2000. A comprehensive ethnographic study of the most populous Muslim minority, among ten Muslim minorities, in central China.

Bano, Masooda, and Hilary Kalmbach, eds. *Women, Leadership and Mosques: Changes in Contemporary Islamic Authority*. Leiden, Netherlands: Brill, 2012. A wide-ranging edited volume that brings together current international scholarship on contexts and contestations relating to women in positions of religious leadership.

Jaschok, Maria, and Shui Jingjun. *The History of Women's Mosques in Chinese Islam: A Mosque of Their Own*. Richmond, U.K.: Curzon, 2000. The first comprehensive historical, ethnographic study of the origin, evolution, and current status of female-led madāris and mosques in China.

Jaschok, Maria, and Shui Jingjun. *Women, Religion and Space in China*. New York, Routledge, 2011. A historical and ethnographic study of the changing functions and significance of local Muslim, Daoist, and Catholic female-led institutions in a provincial city in central China.

MARIA JASCHOK

NŪR JAHĀN. Mihrunnisā', "Nūr Jahān," (1577–1645), last wife of the Mughal emperor Jahāngīr (r. 1605–1627) and empress of Mughal India (r. 1611–1627), was born in Kandahār. Her father, Mirza Ghiyas Beg, and her mother, Asmat Begam, were on their way from Persia to the court of Akbar (r. 1556–1605) in Agra when their daughter was born. Later known as Nūr Mahāl, "Light of the Palace," and Nūr Jahān, "Light of the World," Mihrunnisā' married a Turkish soldier, Sher Afgan, during the family's early years in India. Upon his death in 1607, she entered more fully into courtly life, learning the arts and letters of the Persian and Hindu cultures around her. In 1611, Mihrunnisā' met and married the emperor Jahāngīr, and she began an ascent to power and influence that quickly reached throughout the empire and abroad to Europe.

Almost immediately, Nūr Jahān began assuming the reins of governance. Jahāngīr was increasingly under the influence of wine and opium, and more inclined toward natural science and the arts, so the details of court were left to a family group: Nūr Jahān, her father (now Itimaduddaula), her brother, Āṣaf Khān, and her stepson, Khurram (later Shāh Jahān). Under this rubric, and more often on her own, Nūr Jahān put her seal on grants of land, minted coins in her name, processed petitions from nobles, collected duties on lands and on goods from merchants, engaged in her own trade across the Mughal Empire in India, and used new contacts with the English at court to set up trade in luxury goods. Her involvement in trade was an important achievement, for she and Jahāngīr's mother ran ships exporting indigo and textiles, and importing embroidery and paintings.

Nūr Jahān participated in her husband's religious explorations and herself engaged in charity work and donations of food to pilgrims and the poor. She became an expert marksperson, and was said to be the empire's best shot in killing tigers. Moreover, Nūr Jahān continued to exert considerable influence in the arts. Her imported embroidery patterns are seen on two Mughal mausoleums, those of Itimaduddaula and of Shāh Jahān's favorite wife and her niece, Mumtāz Maḥal (the Taj Mahal), and she is associated with unique rug, jewelry, and dress designs, and with styles of cooking. Miniature painting under Nūr Jahān increasingly focused on women and courtly life, and drew upon Hindu themes at court. Nūr Jahān also built caravanserai and gardens, and under her direction some of the most magnificent examples were established in northern India and Kashmir.

Although the family's rule was extensive and prosperous, it collapsed around 1620. Nūr Jahān had failed in betrothing her only child, Ladli, to Jahāngīr's eldest son, Khusrau; in early 1622, Khusrau was reported dead, probably murdered, while in Shāh Jahān's care; Nūr Jahān's father died in early 1622; and Shāh Jahān (in league with his now father-in-law Āṣaf Khān) went into slow rebellion against his father in late 1620, only to return to claim the throne in 1627–1628. This left Nūr Jahān at the helm, tending to Jahāngīr's illnesses in the last years and making trips to Kashmir for his health. A final revolt in 1626 by a trusted general, Mahābat Khān, put Nūr Jahān's military skills on display again as she fought attackers while on elephant back in the middle of a river. When Jahāngīr died in 1627, Nūr Jahān went into quiet widowhood with her daughter's family in Lahore, devoted now to charitable works. She herself died in 1647 and is interred there in a tomb of her own design.

[*See also* Mughal Empire.]

BIBLIOGRAPHY

Beach, Milo Cleveland. *The Grand Mogul: Imperial Paintings in India, 1600–1660*. Williamstown, Mass.: Sterling and Francine Clark Art Institute, 1978. An annotated assessment of paintings during the height of the Mughal period, with attention paid to those commissioned by Jahāngīr. Miniature paintings are an important source for the history of the time.

Findly, Ellison Banks. *Nur Jahan: Empress of Mughal India*. New York: Oxford University Press, 1993. A biography of Nūr Jahān taken from primary sources of the period.

Foster, William, ed. *The Embassy of Sir Thomas Roe to the Court of the Great Mogul, 1615–1619, As Narrated in His Journal and Correspondence*. 2 vols. London: Hakluyt Society, 1899. Memoirs of the first official English ambassador to the Mughal court, including his encounters with both Jahangir and Nūr Jahān.

Rogers, Alexander, trans., and Henry Beveridge, ed. *The Tuzuk-i-Jahangiri, or Memoirs of Jahangir*. 2 vols. 1909–1914. 2nd ed., Delhi: Munshiram Manoharlal, 1968. Personal memoirs of Jahāngīr, with details of his life with Nūr Jahān.

ELLISON BANKS FINDLY

O

OBAID, THORAYA. (b. 1945), a distinguished leader in the field of human development and women's rights.

Obaid served for a decade as under-secretary-general of the United Nations and executive director of the United Nations Fund for Population Activities (UNFPA). Prior to her appointment at UNFPA, Obaid served the United Nations in various capacities starting in 1975.

Born in Saudi Arabia, Obaid was the first Saudi national to lead a United Nations agency. She also made history in the 1960s as the first woman to be supported by a scholarship from the Kingdom of Saudi Arabia to study in the United States. In her 2002 commencement address at her alma mater, Mills College, a historic women's college in Oakland, California, Obaid championed her father's support and firm commitments to education for girls, a principle that he believed to be firmly rooted in the Islamic tradition. She also noted the influence of the American civil rights discourses of the 1960s and 1970s on her intellectual formation during her student years. Following her graduation from Mills College, Obaid went on to earn a doctorate in English literature, with a minor in cultural anthropology, from Wayne State University, Detroit, Michigan.

In her professional life, Obaid is widely recognized by her colleagues for her vision, humility, and dedication to many causes, from maternal and child health to the mobilization of indigenous youth. Under her tenure as its executive director, UNFPA focused extensively on the empowerment of women, especially in the area of reproductive health, bringing awareness to critical and culturally controversial issues, including early marriage, obstetric fistula, female genital cutting, family planning, and domestic violence. She is celebrated as well for her successful fundraising, which nearly doubled yearly contributions to the UNFPA and increased dramatically the number of countries providing contributions.

Drawing on both her professional and personal backgrounds, Obaid's leadership helped to introduce a culturally sensitive approach to development interventions within the United Nations systems. In particular, she advocated vigorously for practitioners in the field to give greater recognition of the role of religion in bringing about human rights and dignity, a contribution for which she has been recognized widely. Against a tide of secularist thought, she successfully embraced religious leaders as potential catalysts for social change and worked with religious institutions providing social services to poor populations. She is credited as well for her leadership in engaging men in efforts to promote women's welfare and human development; she has spoken at length about the interconnections between gender justice and universal values of human dignity.

Obaid is the recipient of numerous awards and recognitions for contributions toward advancing human rights and for her long and distinguished service to the United Nations, among them the Second Century Award for Excellence in Health Care from Columbia University in New York in 2003, the Louis B. Sohn Human Rights Award from UNA-NCA in Washington, D.C., in 2009, and the Millennium Development Goals Lifetime Achievement Award from the United Nations in 2010. She was also the first Muslim to be awarded the Union Medal from New York's Union Theological Seminary in 2011, the highest honor bestowed by that institution. In addition, in 2011, for her service to humanity, the government of Japan awarded Obaid the Grand Cordon of the Order of the Rising Sun, the highest honor bestowed by the emperor of Japan on a non-national. She has been recognized in Forbes' 2004 and 2010 ranking of the 50 Most Powerful Arab Women.

[*See also* Saudi Arabia; United Nations Population Fund; *and* Women's Rights.]

BIBLIOGRAPHY

DeLong-Bas, Natana J. *Notable Muslims: Profiles of Muslim Builders of the World Civilization and Culture*. Oxford: Oneworld, 2007. Includes a profile of Thoraya Obaid.

"Thoraya Ahmed Obaid." United Nations Fund for Population Activities. http://web.unfpa.org/ed/bio.htm. Includes a listing of Obaid's appointments, activities, and awards through 2008.

CELENE AYAT LIZZIO

OMAN. According to the 2010 Omani national census, the population of the Sultanate is around 3 million, and women account for half of this number. Many Omanis and non-Omanis consider the palace coup of July 1970 to be the date that best represents the modern history of the nation. In other words, the Sultanate of Muscat and Oman, as it was known until 1970, was one of the last nations on Earth to confront the difficult choice between the traditional economy of the interior and the emerging integration of Muscat into a modern economy, accepting the pressures of development and "modernization." The exploration of oil on a large scale in the late 1960s and early 1970s, the Dhofar military insurgence in the south of the country (1968–1976), and the reluctance of the previous sultan to modernize Oman, jointly contributed to the political change in 1970, which ended the rule of Sa'id bin Tymur (1932–1970) and brought his 29-year-old son, Qaboos, to power.

Sultan Qaboos's government initiated socioeconomic plans aimed at developing the infrastructure of the country from scratch. Women, akin to men, particularly those who returned to Oman after the 1970 palace coup, worked together in the development of the country. Prior to this time, women were prohibited from entering any of the three schools in Oman. Hence, the condition of Omani women has been thoroughly transformed since 1970, predominantly because of education opportunities for women. Whereas in the 1970s, no schools existed for girls, the most recent figures available from the Ministry of Education report an enrolment rate nearing 90 percent of all girls eligible for elementary school. The proportion of female students in education demonstrates an overall increase from 12.7 percent in 1971–1972 to 33 percent in 2005, reaching 49 percent in 2006–2007—a fourfold increase in thirty-eight years. In 2004, the sultan appointed four women to ministerial level. This step of political enhancement was internationally observed as an indication of the state's willingness to increase women's role in decision-making in Oman. In 2005, a woman was appointed as the ambassador to the United States, following the appointment of a woman a few years earlier to serve as the Omani ambassador to the Netherlands. More women have also been appointed to serve in the Majlis al-Dawla, or the State's Council, which is an appointed council with duties similar to the duties of the elected parliament, Majlis al-Shūrā, although members are appointed and not elected.

Yet the 1970 change in Oman was not a complete departure from the past. Oman is an Arab and Islamic society, and thus change for women's status has not come effortlessly. The Basic Status of the State (or the State's Constitution), promulgated in 1996, stipulates that Oman is an Arab and Islamic state. The second article plainly says that "the state's religion is Islam and Islamic Sharīʿa is the basis for legislation," and, despite the fact that the third chapter of the Law recognizes personal liberties, civil rights, and equality including gender equality, the Basic Status of the State (hereafter the Basic Law, as in Arabic al-Nizam al-Asasi) also contains extensive references to Sharīʿah, particularly in Articles 1, 2, 7, 12(2), 13 (4), and 38. Similarly, the Basic Law places emphasis on national heritage. Thus, Islam in Oman is not only the religion of the state, but in fact it shapes the identity of the nation and is the main source of value for the overall majority of Omanis.

In 1997, one year after the sultan proclaimed the Basic Law, he issued the first Law of Personal Status that governs family, women, and children's rights. This law is based on the Sharīʿah or, more precisely, early Islamic jurisprudence (*fiqh*). The law prohibits women from getting married without the consent of a male guardian. It also gives a husband the right to divorce his wife on a whim and it favors the male line to the female (*ʿAsaba*) in terms of inheritance. For instance, a son will inherit twice the amount of that inherited by his sister. The law also does not prevent the early marriage of a female child and does not protect a female who decides to marry by her own volition if her male guardian(s) reject(s) her selection of husband. Similarly, the criminal law treats women unequally. For instance, the law of "blood money," known in Arabic as *diyah*, considers the blood money of a woman to be half a man's. Also, the law treats a woman's testimony or *shahādah* as being half as valuable as a man's. It appears that the Criminal Law analogized the *diyah* and the *shahādah* with inheritance, in which a male (son) is granted a portion equal to two portions of that of the female. The latter is based on Qurʾān 4:11, which states, "Allah (thus) directs you as regards your children's (inheritance): to the male, a portion equal to that of two females." In 2010, the state's land law was amended and women were, for the first time, allowed to receive state land. Men, on the other hand, have been allowed to receive one or more lands since 1970. This division was legitimized by local patriarchal and Islamic tradition, which considers the man to be the breadwinner and not the woman. Although women in Oman were allowed to work outside of the home and earn salaries as early as 1970, society has—generally—maintained the idea that men are financially responsible for the household and house maintenance. In 2005, for instance, the female minister of Social Development (ousted from office in 2011) issued a decree obliging women to share the financial responsibility of the family; yet this was abolished in 2011 as an answer to the growing public demand to reverse this regulation. As can be seen, although the state has taken a number of political measures to enhance women's role in society, the family remains male-dominated. Owing to the changing economic and educational conditions of Omani women on one hand, and the patriarchal, social, and cultural nature of society on the other, two strong views have developed, occasionally resulting in a conflict between those who advocate social reform and those who oppose it.

The sultan appears to be the main advocate of reform in the country and hence the Omani State also appears to be committed to reform and, in particular, to the policy of "women's empowerment" and women's full participation in society. In one of his early speeches in the 1970s, the sultan called "upon Omani women everywhere, in the villages and the cities, urban and bedu (nomad) communities... to roll up their sleeves and contribute to the process of economic and social development." Also, following the failure of Omani women to enter the Majlis al-Shūrā (an elected "parliament") in 2007, the sultan first appointed 14 women out of a total of 83 members to the Majlis al-Dawla and, second, publicly stated, for the first time, that gender equality is important for the development of the country and that Islam and tradition should not prevent women's contribution to the nation's development. He went further, announcing that one day every year should be celebrated nationwide as "Omani women's day."

The State's mufti, Shaykh Ahmad bin Hamad al-Khalili, and many other Ibadi scholars denounce gender equality and women's participation on an equal footing with men in society, women's emancipation, and the competence of women to compete with men on an educational level. To them, women should be allowed to study and work only insofar as they are segregated from men. A number of Ibadi scholars interviewed in 2005 stated that women's physiological nature prevents them from being equal to men or having equal rights to study and work, particularly in a mixed male–female environment. Women, as the *mufti* stated in one of his famous lectures presented in the late 1980s, are naturally seductive and, thus, gender segregation should be applied in society, including educational and work places. These conservative views, however, are no different from those held by many Muslim scholars elsewhere. During the short-lived "Omani uprising" (January–May 2011), public demands for gender segregation, an increase in the role of Islamic education in society, and stronger integration of Sharīʿah, in the state's laws were advocated. Although the current Omani ruler belongs to the Ibadi *madhhab* (school of thought), Ibadi history has historically acknowledged a strong resentment toward the monarchy, and, despite the tactical relationship between the monarchy and the Ibadi religious authority in Oman, one can argue that the hidden suspicion between the two has not completely disappeared. Therefore, one considerable difference between Oman and many other Arab countries lies in the political history and contemporary political nature of the state: the two are very much interwoven, and it is in this context of the modern history of the country that "women and Islam" in Oman can be better understood.

Oman is home to al-Ibadiyah, or Ibadis, or, as sometimes referred to in English, *Ibadism*, which is a school of Islamic thought (*madhhab*) originating from the ancient Islamic faction of al-Khawarij, or the Kharijites, in the seventh century CE, when a group of Muslims broke away from al-Khawarij, during the first Muslim civil war. Ibadis take their name from the seventh century CE ʿAbdullah bin Ibad. Ibadi resources claim that the Ibadi School emerged in Basra in Iraq, in the first Islamic century, and thus their school is the first to be established in Islam, before the establishment of the Sunnī or the Shīʿī schools. An Ibadi group called the "carriers of knowledge" (*Hamalat al-ʿIlm*) traveled from Basra in the eighth century, carrying the Ibadi teachings to Oman, and eventually were able to establish a religious-tribal authority in Oman called the Imamate. This Imamate system of ruling continued, albeit with disruption, until the middle of the twentieth century when the father of Sultan Qaboos, Sultan Sa'id, supported by the British Royal Air Force (RAF), put an end to the Ibadi imamate in the late 1950s. Ibadi political tradition advocates a self-sufficient economic, social, and political organization based on Ibadi heritage, which is associated with tribalism. The ruler, according to this tradition, should be "elected" by the religious notables in society and can be any male (Ibadi) Muslim, as far as his personality, knowledge, and reputation are tied to Ibadi theology. Hence, this tradition is different from that of the monarchic system.

Again in 1962, resistance to the monarchy in Oman started to gain momentum, this time emanating from Dhofar, the southern region of Oman. By June 1965, the revolt against Sultan Sa'id had intensified and a number of tribally orientated Dhofaris joined the resistance in the mountains of Dhofar. The insurgency progressed from rebellious actions to a revolutionary armed struggle spreading all over the country, resulting in a real threat to the sultanate monarchical system. Eventually Sultan Sa'id was ousted from power and the Dhofari movement was militarily ended in 1976. The Dhofari movement was a result of the political failure of both the sultanate and imamate systems in Oman. The Dhofari movement was not only hostile toward the sultan, but it was also suspicious of, if not openly hostile to, the Imam. So the other contemporary history that affected the policy of the 1970 Omani state toward women, as mentioned earlier, was the leftist movement of the 1960s and early 1970s.

Sultan Qaboos's government, with strong British involvement, has developed what appears to be a counter-modern plan toward change in Oman espousing some of the ideas that have been expressed before by the policies of the Dhofari movement. For instance, the movement abolished the ongoing practice of slavery in the areas that it occupied in Dhofar. It also set up health centers and educational classes on politics and literacy. Two schools for 2,000 pupils were established, health centers were founded, and barefoot doctors trained. An interview, conducted by Halliday with a number of Omani women in Dhofar in early 1970, provides an indication of the movement's goals and highlights its rejection of the tribal-religious–based social system. An Omani woman associated with the movement stated that "we have suffered from four Sultans; we had the political Sultan: the Sultan of Muscat, the tribal Sultan: the Shaykh, the religious Sultan: the Imam, and the family Sultan: the father, brother and husband." Thus, from the middle of the twentieth century until late 1970, Oman suffered profound social and political instability and was scarred by the struggle against the al-Sa'id ruling family. It is in this context that one should evaluate the post-1970 Qaboos era toward women and Islam. There is, on one hand, the state's desire to keep politics in the hands of the sultan, who has proven to be an advocate for women's participation in society. On the other, however, there is the strong Ibadi tradition that considers women as the core of the family unit, so that any wide change to the status of women could eventually break down this long-time ongoing system. The Omani state therefore has taken a middle ground view toward Islam and local tradition on one hand and women's status on the other. Principally, it maintains the importance of the two, propagating the notion that there is no conflict between them. The Omani laws, regulations, and policies therefore attempt to go in this direction. Arguably, this method has enabled the post-1970 Omani state to maintain the status quo for more than forty years.

BIBLIOGRAPHY

Al-Azri, Khalid. *Social and Gender Inequality in Oman: The Power of Religious and Political Tradition in Oman*. London: Routledge, 2012.

Al-Abri, Fatma. *Life-Paths of Educated Omani Women*. Muscat: Ministry of Social Development, 2010.

Al-Kumi, Basma. "Al-Mara'a fi 'Uman: Wazira Taht Sultat al-Wali." http://www.rezgar.com/debat/show.art.asp?aid=59021.

Chatty, Dawn. "Women Working in Oman: Individual Choice and Cultural Constraints." *International Journal of Middle East Studies* 32, no. 2 (2000): 241–254.

Eickelman, Dale F. "From Theocracy to Monarchy: Authority and Legitimacy in Inner Oman, 1935–1970." *International Journal of Middle Eastern Studies* 17, no. 1 (1985): 3–24.

El-Haddad, Yahya. "Major Trends Affecting Families in the Gulf Countries." http://www.un.org/esa/socdev/family/Publications/mtelhaddad.pdf.

Halliday, Fred. *Arabia without Sultans*. Harmondsworth: Penguin, 1974.

Kelly, John Barret. "Sultanate and Imamate in Oman." London: Oxford University Press, 1959.

Limbert, E. Mandana. "Marriage, Status and the Politics of Nationality in Oman." In *The Gulf Family: Kinship Policies and Modernity*. London: Saqi, 2007.

Peterson, J. E. "The Emergence of Post-Traditional Oman." http://eprints.dur.ac.uk/archive/00000139/01/Peterson.pdf.

Peterson, J. E. *Oman in the Twentieth Century*. London: Croom Helm, 1978.

Savage, Elizabeth. "Survival through Alliance: The Establishment of the Ibadiyya." *British Society for Middle Eastern Studies* 17, no. 1 (1990): 5–15.

Uzi Rabi. "The Ibadhi Imamate of Muhammad bin Abdullah al-Khalili (1920–45): The Last Chapter of a Lost and Forgotten Legacy." *Middle Eastern Studies* 44, no. 2 (2008): 169–211.

Khalid al-Azri

One Million Signatures Campaign

[*This entry contains two subentries,*

Iran *and*

Morocco.]

Iran

The One Million Signatures Campaign in Iran, also known as the Change for Equality campaign, was established in Tehran on 12 June 2006 by fifty-four Iranian women's rights activists, including Shirin Ebadi, a lawyer and Nobel laureate, and the journalists Noushin Ahmadi Khorasani, Nargest Mohammadi, Parvin Ardalan, Zhila Bani Yaghoob, Fariba Davoodi Mohajer, and Bahareh Hedayat. Other prominent Iranians supported the campaign, whose goals were to educate Iranians about laws discriminatory to women and collect a million signatures in support of legal reforms. The campaign was formally announced 27 August 2006 at a seminar on The Impact of Laws on Women's Lives. The campaign has also involved legal battles for the rights to publicly demonstrate and circulate petitions.

The One Million Signatures Campaign spread to more than fifteen Iranian provinces and became known outside Iran through social and foreign media. It produced a booklet, available online, titled the "Effect of Laws on Women's Lives," which explained the desired reforms. These would equalize women's rights with men's with regard to marriage and divorce, end polygamy and temporary marriage (*sīgheh*), allow women to confer citizenship upon their children, and equalize the *dhiyyeh* (compensation, or "blood money" given upon murder or bodily injury) for a women with that provided for men. Reforms would also equalize inheritance, make eighteen the age at which women and men are criminally responsible, make women's testimony in court equal to that of men's, and oppose legal loopholes which exempt or reduce the punishment of murderers in honor killings. The activists also called for an end to executions by stoning for *zinah* (adultery or fornication), and opposed compulsory wearing of the hijab. The changes they sought were not anti-Islamic; rather, they critiqued incorrect interpretations of Islam in current laws. They did not politically oppose Iran's Islamic regime, but sought to influence the public and lawmakers. The activists were careful to include only signatures by Iranians among the million, although many outside Iran signed the petitions in support. Nevertheless campaigners were denied the right to meet in public places and they were harassed and defamed. Many were detained, interrogated, and imprisoned for their activities. Some had their passports taken away, and were prevented from leaving Iran as occurred when Parvin Ardalan attempted to travel to Sweden to receive the Olaf Palme Prize for her campaign role, or when California State University student Esha Momeni interviewed activists for a film and was detained and prevented from leaving Iran. Iranian newspapers and media were not permitted to cover the campaign.

The campaign took longer than the initially planned two years to collect signatures. Its success was seen with parliament's amendment of the inheritance law in 2008. Women were granted rights to *dhiyyeh* (blood money) equal to men's in accidents covered by insurance companies in 2008. Also parliament defeated a family protection bill supported by the Ahmadinejad government, which would have permitted men to marry additional wives without the consent of their first wife.

Bibliography

Alikarami, Leila. "One in One Million" *New Internationalist*. Issue 426, 2007. http://www.newint.org/features/special/2009/10/22/leila-alikarami/.

Casey, Maura J. "Challenging the Mullahs, One Signature at a Time." *New York Times*, February 7, 2007.

"One Million Signatures: The Battle for Gender Equality in Iran." *Tavana*. Exclusive Case Study. http://www.tavaana.org/viewcasestudy.jsp?pageId=2071502000341264606266439&lang=en&restrictids=nu_repeatitemid&restrictvalues=01011418707013018588104441/.

Tahmasebi, Sussan. "One Million Signatures Campaign: Answers to Your Most Frequently Asked Questions." *Change for Equality*, February 28, 2008. http://www.we-change.org/english/spip.php?article226/.

Tohidi, Nayereh. "Iran's Women's Rights Activists Are Being Smeared." *Women's eNews*, September 17, 2008.

Tohidi, Nayereh. "Iran's Women's Rights Movement and the One Million Signatures Campaign." *Payvand*, December 16, 2006.

Sherifa Zuhur

Morocco

The Union de l'Action Feminine (Women's Action Union) and other Moroccan women's groups began campaigning in 1990 to overhaul Morocco's personal status (family) code known as the *mudawanna*, which had been adopted in 1958. Some clerics and conservatives opposed any change to this area of law and considered the campaign to be targeting Islamic values. For two years meetings and seminars were convened. Reformers marched and demonstrated in cities like Rabat and Casablanca, and lobbied the government. In 1993 they launched the One Million Signatures campaign, intending to demonstrate popular support for the reform of the *mudawwana*, which severely restricted women's rights with regard to divorce, marriage, custody of children, and inheritance. The campaign was supported by the UAF founder Latifa Jbabdi, publisher of the feminist magazine *8 Mars*, and other feminists.

According to the *mudawanna* men could repudiate, or divorce, their wives easily, but women faced great difficulty obtaining a divorce. Women could not marry without the legal approval of a male guardian or a marital tutor, yet men could marry up to four wives without their initial or subsequent wives' assent. Married women must obey their husbands according to the law, even if their husbands' wishes were detrimental to their interests.

The campaign initially used the argument that the *mudawwana* was a man-made law and could therefore be altered by the government. However opponents held that the *mudawwana* derived from God's law, the Sharīʿah. The reformers eventually utilized religious arguments in favor of reform and took on the task of carefully explaining the reforms to Morocco's large illiterate population.

With over 1 million signatures from a population of about 25 million, the campaign was empowered to argue more effectively for the *mudawwana*'s reform. King Hassan II enacted a limited reform of the *mudawwana* in 1993. This reform meant that women could select the male guardian who was to represent them, but did not undo the concept of guardianship. Fathers could no longer compel their daughters to marry someone they did not want. The reformers were not satisfied with the limited amendments, but Moroccans were nevertheless able to see that the *mudawwana* was not, as enemies of reform had argued, a sacred inviolable text that could never be altered. The *mudawwana* was more thoroughly overhauled in 2004 under the new king, Mohammed VI (Hassan's son). This second reform made polygamy more difficult for men as a woman's consent was needed and the husband must appear before a judge. Women gained the right to specify in their marriage contracts that their husbands would not marry additional wives. Women no longer needed a guardian or marital tutor to act on their behalf once they had come of age. Men could no longer repudiate their wives outside of a court, and women could divorce more easily. Divorces were arranged in a civil divorce court rather than merely before a religious official. Other changes were also made in family law at that time.

The One Million Signatures campaign inspired a similar campaign in Iran. It also inspired a campaign to collect 1 million signatures in Morocco to demonstrate civil society's support for the Sahara autonomy plan put forth in 2010 and which was opposed by the Polisario, the political leadership of the Sahrawi refugees.

BIBLIOGRAPHY

Brand, Laurie A. *Women, the State and Political Liberalization: Middle Eastern and North African Experiences.* New York: Columbia University Press, 1998.

Charrad, Mounira M. *States and Women's Rights: The Making of Postcolonial Tunisia, Algeria, and Morocco.* Berkeley: University of California Press, 2001.

Freedom House. Morocco Country Report. "Women's Rights in the Middle East and North Africa." 2010. http://www.freedomhouse.org/report-types/women's-rights-middle-east-and-north-africa/.

"Moudawana: A Peaceful Reform for Moroccan Women." Available at Tavaana. Case Studies. http://www.tavaana.org/.

Sherifa Zuhur

Orientalism. "Orientalism" is a multifaceted term, broadly referring to encounters between the "Orient" (the East) and the West (Europe and the United States). In its oldest form, Orientalism simply referred to scholarship about the "Orient," which encompassed most of the "Old World" beyond Europe from the Near and Middle East, to North Africa, China, Japan, and South Asia. In modern usage, however, "Orientalism" has come to refer to a particular discourse.

In his landmark 1978 book, *Orientalism*, Edward Said redefined the word "Orientalism" to refer to the problematic Western discourse of knowledge of, and stereotypical representations of, the East (including the Far, Near, and Middle East), such as depictions in artistic works, photography, pop culture, media, nonfiction literature, poetry, and fiction, as well as scholarly work from lexicography to historical and cultural studies. Said's book revolutionized the field of Middle

Eastern studies by challenging the epistemological hegemony of "Oriental" cultural studies. Said borrowed Foucault's concept of knowledge and power, the ontological and epistemological authority manifesting political domination over an "Other" through discourse (the sum of assumptions that forms a collective common sense) to argue that Western scholarship on the Near and Middle East was tainted by racism, skewed by positions of privilege and airs of superiority, and driven by colonial and imperial political motivations. Said argued that this problematic relationship, and the manifestation of the "Other" (the conception of a fundamental and static distinction in another, which creates a polarity in the subject-object relationship) in the language of a broad variety of writers (poets, novelists, scholars, and nonfiction writers) addressing the Middle East from the eighteenth to the early twentieth centuries, can be particularly observed in nineteenth-century literary narratives, from the blatant bigotry in Rudyard Kipling's "The White Man's Burden" (1899), to the themes in Joseph Conrad's *Heart of Darkness* (1899), to the sexualized, exotic conceptions and portrayals of the Orient evident in the escapades of Sir Richard Burton, the novels of Gustave Flaubert, and the characterization of the Orient in the ethnographies of Edward Lane. Each of these characters portrayed their preoccupation with Orient as an exotic Other in various ways and from different approaches. Although Flaubert and Burton both wrote about their adventures with local prostitutes, Flaubert was a French novelist who wrote autobiographical/fiction and Burton was more like a mercenary/spy/scholar. Burton translated an uncensored (sexually explicit) *1001 Nights* from Arabic into English that was banned and circulated only among the members of an exclusive book club in the U.K. Burton dressed and spoke like a local in the lands he was visiting, he traveled to Mecca (while doing so was forbidden to non-Muslims) and developed a pseudoscientific theory about sexuality related to climate.

Said argued that Orientalism, as a discourse, develops through the accumulation of reinforced stereotypes that constitute a sum of perceptions, which Said calls "imagined geographies" of the Other. This process of Othering enables the colonizer to morally justify the subjugation of a target population through the deliberate misunderstanding of the "imagined" manufactured representation, thus giving license to exploit, subjugate, and "civilize" the Other. Furthermore, Orientalism is one-sided discourse, produced by Westerners for Western audiences. Orientalism is thus, in essence, a packaged political vehicle, a manufactured representation evident in art, literature, pop culture, and the media, as well as the framing of images. Since its initial publication, *Orientalism* has been controversial and highly influential, inspiring critical inquiry in all disciplines (anthropology, comparative literature, comparative religion, history, political science) relating to cultural studies, and inspiring a whole new field of postcolonialism.

Many scholars, including anthropologists and specialists in gender and women's studies, have taken issue with the role of gender and race in Orientalist discourse. While Said did not focus on gender construct in *Orientalism*, he made note of persistent misconceptions of and preoccupations with Middle Eastern sexuality by Orientalist travelers. Postcolonial critique and gender studies share a similar base in critical theory; both have been influenced by the same discursive critique of analyzing the role of images and narrative to establish and reinforce popular ideals of gender and race while adhering to social hierarchy, and both aim at challenging contemporary hegemony. Nevertheless, scholars and advocates of these disciplines have not always been aware of each other's problems or agendas. There is an abundance of scholarship based on the intersection of Orientalism, race, gender, and related topics, including women in Islam, the role of women in the proliferation of Orientalism (from nineteenth-century art history to contemporary politics) and the role of gender and Orientalism in human-rights discourse and foreign policy.

Orientalism has been influential not only as reference for critical scholarship, but as a point of contention. While Said provided a framework on which advocates might base further critique, *Orientalism* was also very controversial, not only for attacking the old guard of Western epistemological authority over the "Orient," but also because Said went so far as to say that all previous Western scholarship was tainted, providing endless material for other scholars to present the inevitable multitude of exceptions. Said's critics took issue with his blanket charge, arguing that he overlooked centuries of significant contributions innocent of political or ideological motives. Others have taken issue with Said's methodological paradox of avoiding objectification of the Other by reinforcing the differences he claimed he was trying to diminish, thereby reinforcing the polarized binary of East and West, and "us" and "them."

The major impact of the scholarly debates sparked by Said's book has been the negative connotation now surrounding "Orientalism," both as a term and as a means of depicting and framing the Middle East, whether from the perspective of culture, history, religion, or gender. Said, and scholars of cultural studies and postcolonialism, argue that Orientalism persists in Western media and foreign policy to this day. Said was critical of several contemporary scholars including Bernard Lewis, Samuel Huntington, and Fouad Ajami, accusing their scholarship of portraying the Middle East as culturally rigid and static, fundamentally different from the West, and in favor of hawkish foreign policy. Huntington' s sociopolitical concept of a "clash of civilizations" is a famous theory that has been described as the epitome of modern Orientalism.

Critics suspicious of Western foreign policy in the Middle East have described American exceptionalism and Eurocentricism as "Orientalist" ideologies. Scholars, suspicious of groups advocating regime change or military action for the purpose of rescuing women from oppressive social conditions, have argued that such policies have failed to change the plight of local women, and that women's realities are very different from the media's portrayal, which conforms to Orientalist stereotypes. Orientalism is also referenced in regard to its inverse manifestation, Occidentalism, and Middle Easterners' preconceived notions of the West and Westerners.

BIBLIOGRAPHY

Asad, Talal. "Review of *Orientalism*." *English Historical Review* 95 (1980): 648–649.

Buruma, Ian, and Avishai Margalit. *Occidentalism: The West in the Eyes of Its Enemies*. New York: Penguin Books, 2004.

Carrier, James G. *Occidentalism: Images of the West*. Oxford: Clarendon Press, 1995.

Dobie, Madeleine. *Foreign Bodies: Gender, Language, and Culture in French Orientalism*. Stanford, Calif.: Stanford University Press, 2001.

Foucault, Michel, and Paul Rabinow. *The Foucault Reader*. New York: Pantheon Books, 1984.

Huntington, Samuel P. *The Clash of Civilizations and the Remaking of World Order*. New York: Simon & Schuster, 1996.

Irwin, Robert. *Dangerous Knowledge: Orientalism and Its Discontents*. Woodstock, N.Y.: Overlook Press, 2006.

Lewis, Reina. *Gendering Orientalism: Race, Femininity, and Representation*. New York: Routledge, 1996.

Lewis, Reina, and Sara Mills. *Feminist Postcolonial Theory: A Reader*. New York: Routledge, 2003.

Macfie, A. L. *Orientalism: A Reader*. New York: New York University Press, 2000.

Mazumdar, Sucheta, Vasant Kaiwar, and Thierry Labica. *From Orientalism to Postcolonialism: Asia, Europe and the Lineages of Difference*. London: Routledge, 2009.

Naghibi, Nima. *Rethinking Global Sisterhood: Western Feminism and Iran*. Minneapolis: University of Minnesota Press, 2007.

Nayak, Meghana. "Orientalism and 'Saving' US State Identity after 9/11." *International Feminist Journal of Politics* 8 (2006): 42–61.

Nayak, Meghana V., and Christopher Malone. "American Orientalism and American Exceptionalism: A Critical Rethinking of US Hegemony." *International Studies Review*11 (2009): 253–276.

Richardson, Michael. "Enough Said: Reflections on Orientalism." *Anthropology Today* 6 (1990): 16–19.

Said, Edward W. *Orientalism*. New York: Vintage Books, 1979.

Skeet, Charlotte Helen. "Globalisation of Women's Rights Norms: The Right to Manifest Religion and 'Orientalism' in the Council of Europe." *Public Space: The Journal of Law and Social Justice* 4 (2009): 34–78.

Tavakoli-Targhi, Mohamad. *Refashioning Iran: Orientalism, Occidentalism, and Historiography*. New York: Palgrave, 2001.

Tibawi, Abdul Latif. *English-Speaking Orientalists: A Critique of their Approach to Islam and Arab Nationalism*. Geneva, Switzerland: Islamic Centre, 1965.

AARON ALBERT HALEY

OTTOMAN EMPIRE.

[*This entry contains two subentries,*

Overview *and*
Women's Socioeconomic Role]

OVERVIEW

As elsewhere, the quest to understand the role of women in the Ottoman Empire in the larger context of social history has led to a rewriting of Ottoman history. Such rewriting reveals the original contributions of non-Western societies to global projects of modernity and constitutes an alternative to man-centered nationalist history writing. However, despite the valuable contributions of scholars in disassociating the harem from eroticism and the Ottoman Empire from the harem, Orientalist tendencies that feed from ahistorical interpretations of Islamic histories continue to influence the contemporary perception of Ottoman history.

The Early and Classical Periods. The Ottoman Empire was founded at the end of the thirteenth century as an emirate that quickly grew toward Byzantine borders. Intermarriage and conversions guaranteed more physical expansion. Love between Muslim warriors and Byzantine women, or bilateral cultural expansion, became an asset for foundation in both myth and reality. Expansion continued with changing capital cities during the fourteenth century, and the Muslim dream of conquering İstanbul became a reality with Mehmed II the Conqueror (1432–1481) in 1453. Mehmed II also changed how Ottoman sultans procreated: He did not have any children with his Christian wives and relied on his concubines for procreation. This was a strategy that was to guarantee undivided power, and this is the story of how the imperial harem started to become synonymous with an Ottoman rule that lasted for over six centuries. Thus, concubinage as an ultimate form of reproduction and sexual politics was only invented by the Ottoman sultans in the fifteenth century.

In fact, dwelling on the history of how the sultans related to women and how they procreated is synonymous with dwelling on Ottoman history. However, this sexual dimension of politics is overemphasized in the Ottoman context with the key word "harem." Both the imperial harem and ordinary harems are discussed in reference to women's life in the Ottoman Empire here, but see the entry on HAREM for more in-depth treatment. Harem is a major issue concerning women in the Ottoman Empire as depictions of the harem were used for the eroticization and exoticization of Muslim women for centuries. These depictions are still an important obstacle to a complete understanding of how multifarious and changing the lives of women were in the empire. Leslie Peirce's *Imperial Harem* (1993) has unclouded the concept of harem to stand for a space of dignity and piousness, a sacred space for imperial women and the women who served and accompanied them, as well as those women who educated other women in the sixteenth century. Peirce's account is also one that describes women in the Ottoman Empire in the fifteenth and sixteenth centuries. She presents in detail the debated subject of the Rule of Women (*Kadınlar Saltanatı*) that started with the much-beloved concubine of Sultan Süleyman the Magnificent (1494/95–1566), Hürrem (1500/06–1558), in the middle of the sixteenth century and lasted for over a century.

A century after Mehmed II's institutionalization of imperial procreation with concubines, concubines who influenced rulers, either with love, by bearing children, or as the mothers of those children who would become sultans, evolved into a political asset and the "Rule of Women" lasted for a century. Acknowledging the power of women and observing that they derive this power from a politico-sexual strategy that instrumentalizes them as slaves might have been empowering; however, the problem with such a paradigm is that the debate on the rule of women indicates this rule started a downward path for the empire. The ruthlessness and ambition attributed to these influential women, the most famous of whom were Hürrem Sultan and Kösem Sultan (1590–1651), also take away from any suggestion of empowerment. Political acts that are regarded as normal for men become character flaws in women according to the Rule of Women paradigm, and character flaws degenerate Ottoman politics.

The very same period of the Rule of Women, when viewed from the angle of women's support of *ḥammām* and city culture, takes a different turn. The *ḥammām*, or the public bath, has a special place among historical spaces in the Ottoman Empire, shared with the Mediterranean region. The Roman bathing culture was made a part of Islamic culture by the Ottomans during this period. Like the mosque, the school/*medrese*, and the saintly tomb/*türbe*, the *ḥammām* became a part of mosque complexes. Women have used *ḥammāms* perhaps more frequently than other parts of these complexes. The complexes were commonly founded by women like Hürrem, who is most famous for being the patron of the Haseki *ḥammām* in Istanbul. Such endowments were acts of concern that powerful women initiated, out of which residential and commercial areas developed, drawing new populations to these locales. In other words, powerful women, by founding spaces that incorporated new districts in the city, facilitated new urban as well as political patterns. These patterns grew markedly in the sixteenth century, continuing into the seventeenth and marking the classical age of the Ottoman Empire.

It is not uncommon to evaluate everything that happened after the rule of Sultan Süleyman as stagnation and decline as the boundaries of the empire that almost included the Mediterranean from Algeria to Vienna in the sixteenth century started shrinking in the seventeenth century after a series of revolts that followed expansion. The classical periodization of the Ottoman Empire as such is not typical of current historiography. In line with İnalcık and Quataert's conceptualization (1995), it is now more common to roughly periodize the empire in terms of its beginnings up to the fifteenth century, the classical period up to the eighteenth century, and the age of reforms for the nineteenth century. In this conceptualization, women are not regarded as a reason for decline; instead, they are part of a story of modernization, a story experienced parallel to that of Europe.

Age of Reforms. As in Europe, a different class of women became the symbol of a new kind of ruling strategy by the eighteenth century: women who belonged to a newly forming moneyed class increased their outdoor activities to declare their newly acquired power and became more visible to the Ottoman state, so officials stepped in to regulate these activities in a direct manner. Their early attempts consisted of enforcing punitive measures on women's activities. Decrees that regulated women were issued repeatedly, and through such repetitions, it became obvious that most women resisted the regulations. The law, like the women who came into contact with the law through their actions and the groups they represented, became reflexive and fluid. As a result, the state modernized and unified the code on men's attire in 1829 and remained silent on women's dress, but eventually stopped regulating women's attire as well. This was an acknowledgment of different demands for power in the empire from a new class that consisted of people from different religions. However, whereas the Muslim members of this class could acquire more power through *iltizam*, or buying tax-farms from the state, Christians had to be content with the relative equality that the reforms of Tanzimat brought in 1836. In the meanwhile, they began to invest in nationalism.

The multiethnic makeup of the empire had long been leading to its shrinking, particularly where the Balkan and Greek populations declared and struggled for various forms of independence. As the more Christian-populated of the lands declared independence and some Muslim populations living there migrated to what remained of the empire, the general population of the Ottoman Empire became increasingly Muslim. Young Ottoman thought, symbolized most commonly by Mehmet Namık Kemal (1840–1888), reinvented a Muslim past in the golden age of Islam, simultaneously imagining a multiethnic form of Ottoman citizenship where each group lived peacefully side by side. Ideas such as democracy and equality that made this paradoxical but sound approach possible were to be found in the age of the Prophet and in the key words *meşveret* (consultation), *ijmāʿ* (consensus), and *ijtihād* (independent reasoning).

The non-Muslim groups that remained in the empire also adopted Ottomanism, and they, too, had long wanted their own modernization projects to reach fruition. From 1861 onward, female education was so advanced in the Greek communities of the Ottoman Empire that soon unemployment grew among the growing number of women teachers. Educated young women tended to marry later, sometimes remained single, and increased their bargaining power with education. Meanwhile, the existence of birth control practices and frequent postponement of marriage also influenced other urban communities in the empire in the nineteenth century and led to the prolongation of youth and education. The Hamidian state (1876–1909) was especially notable for its contribution to this prolongation via its development of girls' education and for its efforts toward modernization, even though such efforts always supported further centralization and state power. It initiated and continued programs of occupational and systematic education for women in Istanbul and other cities, an effort that built on the developments of girls' education that had started in 1850. This emerging interest in education is vital to conceptualizing the dynamics within the modernizing Ottoman state and its relation to the changing society, as well as a better understanding of women's role in this transformation.

Through its struggles for independence against not only the Ottoman Empire, but also France and Britain, Egypt had developed outstanding institutions of education, especially girls' education, and media. At the end of the nineteenth century, Egypt, together with Tunisia, Algeria, and Libya, were no longer parts of the Ottoman Empire.

Until then, Cairo and Istanbul had shared a flourishing feminist movement that combined the forces of education and media. Qāsim Amīn (1863–1908) was a lot like Namık Kemal in many ways, a proto-feminist man who saw himself as a savior of women. There are parallels between the lives of Egyptian feminists, such as Hoda Shaarawi (1879–1947), and feminists in Istanbul such as Fatma Âliye Hanım (1862–1936) and Halide Edip Adıvar (1884–1964). They all had a problematic relationship with local politicians and Western elites, remaining between the two. Due to this tension, their struggle for rights mostly concurred with centralization and nationalization and was scorned when it did not.

The long history of the feminist movement in Turkey was uncovered as recently as the 1990s (see Demirdirek, 1998; the original appeared in Turkish in 1993). This process represented the collaboration of academic and political feminisms. Related works show that, by 1908, these efforts were best revealed in the social currents aroused after the Constitutional Revolution. Now, women's feminist discourse—instead of men's discourse on women's emancipation—became an important part of the evolving media. It should be noted that just as a Turkish, Kurdish, and Armenian nationalist spirit developed alongside Balkan, Greek, and Arab forms of nationalism, the feminist priorities of the writers in corresponding journals coexisted with and were soon replaced by nationalist sentiments. Turkish feminists developed a nationalistic pro-military attitude supporting the armed struggle for the foundation of the Turkish republic.

The legacy of the Ottoman feminists can be understood better through the history of the media, demonstrating the transition from the impermanence of women in industry and social life to a position of relative stability. This stability was achieved by women mostly via a successful instrumentalization of the media during the post-1908 period. However, the more women were included in industry and social life, the more feminism was excluded from the dialogue. Biographies and autobiographies of women like Fatma Âliye and Halide Edip who achieved this stability at the turn of the century clearly demonstrate these processes of inclusion and exclusion. Fatma Âliye is a product of Young Ottoman thought that centered on the public sphere. She was educated by Ahmet Mithat, a prominent novelist and journalist of the Young Ottoman era. Âliye was the founder of one of the first and most influential philantropic organizations together with her sister Emine Semiye. Together, they contributed to the media, literature, civil society, and education and tried to establish a variety of practices and freedoms for women in Islam.

A generation younger, Halide Edip was also a journalist, novelist, activist, and educator. However, she was more of a nationalist, being one of the Young Turks who had transformed Young Ottoman thought into a more nationalistic and more state-based phase. Unlike most Young Turks, however, she critiqued her own nationalism, as well as the Young Turk Union and Progress Party (İttihat ve Terakki). These militarized Young Turks, just like Sultan Abdülhamid II, against whom they won and secured the second constitution of 1908, sought to increase the homogeneity of the empire rather than the heterogeneity emphasized by the Young Ottomans. The first half of the twentieth century was the end of an Ottomanist dream shared not only by the heavily Muslim population as a result of the nationalization of the Ottoman Empire, but also by other nations that emerged, and that strove to emerge. Edip continued to participate in and critique these processes together with her second husband, Adnan Adıvar, until the founding of the Turkish republic and beyond.

Zabel Yesayan, part of an Armenian feminist line, is another such woman who wrote both on nationalism and various tides of annihilation and displacement of Armenian populations from Anatolia, and on Armenian nationalism as well. A socialist, during Stalin's Great Purge, she was ironically accused of nationalism, a critique she withstood despite all reactions. Ottoman activists who acted out of feminist concerns contributed greatly to the history of the press in the late Ottoman Empire and the history of girls' education.

Women's memoirs in the early twentieth century can be fully comprehended only when evaluated together with discussions pertaining to the close relationship between nationalism and women's history. These memoirs solicit women as readers and as witnesses. Numerous examples of how their class origins influenced women's feminist and nationalist activities in different ways are also revealed. These movements influenced, and were influenced by, the intellectual formation and paradoxes of women on violence and on participating in nationalist politics. As a result, only by carefully considering primary sources, such as newspapers, journals, and memoirs, can the various tides of nationalism that immensely influenced the twentieth century be fully understood.

The most ruthless nationalist politics of population was a trademark of the Young Turk era (1908–1918), as well as a perceived atmosphere of freedom that drastically increased the space for mass media. The contemporary feminist texts that directly address women's participation in public activities in the Ottoman Empire mainly focus on the journals that women read, created, or contributed to during the late nineteenth and early twentieth centuries. It is just as important to acknowledge the insider critique of both mainstream and revolutionary activities voiced by these women.

By means of new studies that take their muse from a variety of voices and sources which Ottoman women mobilized, the mist is vanishing around the knowledge of both Ottoman women and the Ottoman Empire. As a result, it is now possible to view both as producers of goods, ideas, networks, resistance, and identities.

BIBLIOGRAPHY

Badran, Margot. *Feminists, Islam, and Nation: Gender and the Making of Modern Egypt*. Princeton, N.J.: Princeton University Press, 1995.

Demirdirek, Aynur. "In Pursuit of the Ottoman Women's Movement." In *Deconstructing Images of "The Turkish Woman,"* edited by Zehra F. Arat, pp. 65–82. New York: St. Martin's Press, 1998.

Faroqhi, Suraiya. *Subjects of the Sultan: Culture and Daily Life in the Ottoman Empire*. London: I. B. Tauris, 2000.

İnalcık, Halil, and Donald Quataert. *An Economic and Social History of the Ottoman Empire, 1300–1914*. Cambridge, U.K.: Cambridge University Press, 1995.

Peirce, Leslie. *The Imperial Harem: Women and Sovereignty in the Ottoman Empire*. New York and Oxford: Oxford University Press, 1993.

Quataert, Donald, ed. *Consumption Studies and the History of the Ottoman Empire 1550–1922*. Albany: State University of New York Press, 2000.

Tamboukou, Maria. "Tracing Heterotopias: Writing Women Educators in Greece." *Gender and Education* 16, no. 2 (2004): 189–207.

Tucker, Judith E. *In the House of the Law: Gender and Islamic Law in Ottoman Syria and Palestine*. Berkeley: University of California Press, 1998.

Zilfi, Madeline. *Women in the Ottoman Empire: Middle Eastern Women in the Early Modern Era*. Leiden, Netherlands: Brill, 1997.

Elif E. Akşit

Women's Socioeconomic Role

It is impossible to study the role of women in the economic life of the Ottoman Empire without dealing also with some social and even legal issues characterizing their situation. For example, women were entitled to part of the estates left after the death of members of their family, but they were only entitled to half of what men were entitled to. Women were also entitled to bride-price, paid upon marriage, and to deferred bride-price, paid upon dissolution of the marriage (either by death of the husband or by divorce). Thus some properties were supposed to come into the possession of women during their life, whether or not they had any business acumen or interest in conducting business. Moreover Islamic law also ruled that women were supposed to be in full and unlimited control of their properties even if they married, the husband alone being, at the same time, responsible for the necessary economic expenditures of the family. All these were laws inscribed in the law books and hence theoretical rights of women, although it is not clear whether this was also the situation in real life and furthermore does not reveal what other pursuits women actually had in the life of city and country in the place and era. The Ottoman Empire, a vast area that existed over a long period, has received little empirical research on the economic life of women. What is more troublesome methodologically is that there were considerable differences between various cities and areas, hard and fast generalizations being at present quite hazardous. This article uses one compact case study, the seventeenth-century western Anatolian city of Bursa, to indicate and detail divergences in other places.

It is quite evident that women in Bursa inherited property. A large number of women were specified as receiving shares of estates of deceased people, and a large number of documents in the *kadi* tribunal dealt with women demanding and receiving their shares in their inheritance, sometimes in the face of counter-demands posed by relatives of all sorts, including sons, a potentially sensitive issue.

However women got their property, in Bursa they were not at all quick to get rid of it, as some scholars in the past have claimed. On the contrary, they seem avidly interested in conducting business and making money. Thus women had a great many houses (in about a third of women's estates there were houses), and in many documents they were found selling and buying in what seems to be roughly the same proportion. Moreover women were in many cases owners of shops and even of workshops. It is not easy to discern if they actually worked in these institutions. In any event it is clear that women for the most part were assertive enough to uphold the right to deal freely with their property, independently of their husband. An illustration of this is the case of a woman who sued her husband for building an annex to the family home, which was her own property. She demanded that the court order the demolition of this addition, which was granted. This particular family was certainly not a patriarchal one. Not surprisingly, women were found doing business not only with complete strangers but also even with members of their family, buying and selling mulberry orchards and houses and receiving formal documents from the court. For many, verbal agreements were not sufficient.

Women in seventeenth-century Bursa were occupied in production of various goods, a topic almost totally missing from accounts of the lives of women in other places. One woman was found in the guild of candlemaking, but it seems that this was the only involvement of women with the guilds, a highly regulated and exclusionary organization. However a great many women worked in less monopolistic trades. One such was the putting-out system, where an entrepreneur producing fabrics, usually silk, would distribute raw materials to women processing the fabrics, then returning the materials to the producer for further distribution. Of three hundred silk spinning wheels (*mancinik*) in Bursa in 1678, about half belonged to women and were probably operated by women. Other women in Bursa produced various textiles on their own and in their houses, which they then marketed themselves in the streets and even in front of the established shops in the markets. This kind of marketing incensed the shop owners, but their recourse to the *kadi* made no difference, since it was proven to be an ancient custom.

Women were also seriously engaged with credit operations. This sometimes took substantial proportions, and it certainly involved risks, including face-to-face relations with unrelated males. But it was still less onerous than the production of leather or soap, or international trade that involved trips lasting several months. Possibly it was one line of business that women preferred. Many women gave loans to their husbands. A large number of estates postmortem of men in Bursa included sections on outstanding debts of the deceased, and more often than not these lists included debts to wives, besides the universally present deferred bride-price. The inclusion of these sums in recorded documents indicates that they were given with every intention of retrieving them back. One can also imagine that many more loans of this nature were given without documentation.

Women of course also gave large sums in loan to businessmen. Many of these loans smack of being business ventures. Such was maybe the loan of 3,600 akçe that one woman in Bursa gave to a baker, which included hidden interest of 600 akçe, an unusually exorbitant rate for the time, when the usual rate would be around 10 percent. This could not have been a friendly loan. Such may also have been the loan of 2,200 kuruş (an enormous sum, equal to a number of houses) extended by one Ai'se Hatun to one Haj Mustafa.

Women were also involved with the financing of silk-buying expeditions to Iran, where Bursa merchants joined (possibly organized) caravans going to Iran to purchase raw silk. Some women were involved with money lending to such an extent that it may be possible to call them semiprofessional, if not professional, money lenders. Several such women were owed, at the time of their death, large sums by several people, sometimes people not residents of Bursa. Clearly women constituted an important sector of the credit institution of seventeenth-century Bursa, a surprisingly developed and under-researched institution.

Many women were involved with agriculture, sometimes impressively so. Women were often registered as owners of orchards, but this may be looked at as a second-class agriculture, since the main crop in all traditional societies, and certainly in the Ottoman Empire, was cereals (mainly wheat), and hence the ownership of sown land and related properties was given a special status in Islam in general and the Ottoman Empire in particular. Thus sown land was considered state land that could be possessed rather than owned outright. As a corollary, sown land was subject to *kānūn* law, which stated, among other things, that if a man had male children, his wife and daughters were debarred from the inheritance of sown land. But it turned out that often people had, at their death, only wives and daughters, and in such cases daughters were liable to inherit. The outcome is that in many instances women in Bursa left in their estates agricultural farms (*çiftlik*) that included sown land, in addition to fruit gardens and mulberry orchards. In quite a number of incidences women who, at their death, had a husband and children left in their estates not only commercial quantities of wheat and barley but even wheat sown in the ground, indicating that they actually had sown land and an agricultural business which they had operated.

Bursa was apparently an exceptional place. Other places that have been the subject of studies have not yielded such rich texture of women's activity, although on the whole all extant studies have rejected the highly negative picture depicted of women's position in the past.

One useful study that allows comparison between Bursa and other places is the historian Ronald C. Jennings's study on Kayseri, a city in central Anatolia. Seventeenth-century Kayseri resembled Bursa in that women received property via inheritances and the delayed bride-price, property in which they traded with apparent enthusiasm. They also sued relatives without any hesitation when they thought their rights were violated. But Jennings also found that Kayseri women sold houses and other real estate properties much more often than they bought them, thus affirming a generalization claiming that women tended to turn real estate properties into cash as soon as possible. In addition Jennings did not find Kayseri women who were involved with production, investment, and agricultural properties. More or less the same picture appears from the cultural historian Yvonne J. Seng's study of women in Üsküdar in the first half of the sixteenth century. Suraiya Faroqhi, a leading authority on Ottoman history, found some women engaged in truly large-scale business, but the examples are too isolated to allow clear interpretation.

The material presented here, and especially that from Bursa, seems to stand in serious contradiction to a series of generalizations concerning Middle Eastern societies in the past. They may all be summarized by the concept of patriarchal society that is said to have dominated that society and dictated that women should be banned from the public sphere, including fighting for rights in the court and pursuing economic interests in the public arena. One feels that latter-day models of social organization have been projected backward on to periods concerning which little was actually known. But this model evidently does not fit these periods, and the important question is why and in what ways?

Part of the problem is that scholars did not realize in the past that demographic conditions in traditional Middle Eastern societies were such that mortality was extremely high (whether from plagues or from more mundane reasons), so that even if that society was patriarchal, it often had to shelve such cultural assumptions in the face of widowed women who had to take care of children with no supporting family behind them. Such women had to go into the world and assume every task their male family members would have undertaken—had they lived longer. And it is one small step from such a situation to one where, as a consequence, patriarchal feelings and assumptions, being unworkable for practical reasons, get weaker also in principle.

But there is also an even more important explanation. A 2007 study by the professor Hülya Canbakal on seventeenth-century ʿAyntāb, a city in south central Anatolia, throws an important sidelight on Bursa. ʿAyntāb was controlled by a patriarchal elite featuring several families of notables who played central roles in the city, from running all matters in the judiciary to playing key parts in all economic affairs in the town. Bursa had no trace of such a social elite, and not at all because it was run by the central government (which it was not to any particular extent). The reason was that Bursa sat astride important international routes of commerce and movement, and it was therefore a cosmopolitan city, based on an economy of production and international trade. It seems that such a society featured patriarchal tendencies to a much smaller extent than ʿAyntāb and probably many other towns in Anatolia. This could reasonably account for the much freer position of women in Bursa than in other places. Only future research will tell what other cities the model of Bursa represented.

[*See also* Borrowing and Credit, Women's: Contemporary and Historical Practice; Guilds; Ottoman Empire; *and* Property.]

BIBLIOGRAPHY

Canbakal, Hülya. *Society and Politics in an Ottoman Town: ʿAyntāb in the 17th Century*. Leiden and Boston: Brill, 2007.

Faroqhi, Suraiya. "Two Women of Substance." In *Stories of Ottoman Men and Women: Establishing Status, Establishing Control*, pp. 151–166. Istanbul: Eren, 2002.

Gerber, Haim. "Social and Economic Position of Women in an Ottoman City: Bursa, 1600–1700." *International Journal of Middle Eastern Studies* 12, no. 3 (November 1980): 231–244.

Jennings, Ronald C. "Women in Early 17th Century Ottoman Judicial Records: The Sharia Court of Anatolian Kayseri." *Journal of the Economic and Social History of the Orient* 18, no. 1 (January 1975): 53–114.

Seng, Yvonne J. "Standing at the Gates of Justice: Women in the Law Court of Early Sixteenth-Century Üsküdar, Istanbul." In *Contested States: Hegemony and Resistance*, edited by Mindie Lazarus-Black and Susan F. Hirsch, pp. 184–206. London: Routledge, 1994.

Haim Gerber

P

PAINTING. [*This article contains two subentries:*
Overview *and*
Women's Representation and Production.]

OVERVIEW

The theological aversion to figural imagery largely discourages the life like depictions of religious figures in the world of Islam. Religious texts, such as the Qurʾān, contain elaborately calligraphed pages in a variety of scripts and richly colored illumination with geometric ornamentation, but do not have any illustrations as visual aids for narrating stories, let alone images of living beings.

What we can call "Islamic" painting does, however, exist in the sense in which illustrations of the lives of the Prophet Muḥammad and other major religious figures are done in a respectful manner, often veiled. Muḥammad's heavenly journey (*miʿrāj*), for instance, formed the basis for a poetic and pictorial tradition in the Islamic world, and it is represented in diverse media from medieval to modern times. By contrast, it is difficult to trace the role of women in the development of pictorial conventions in the Islamic religious sphere. Two of the powerful female members of the family of the Prophet Muḥammad—his first wife Khadīja (d. c. 619) and their daughter Fātimah (d. 633)—are almost never pictured or worshipped as icons, in comparison with the female saints of Christendom who enjoyed their popularity in the visual culture of the Western world.

In secular contexts, the production of manuscripts served to establish a long tradition of book illustrations in the Islamic world before the introduction of European-style painting in modern times. Manuscripts of science, medicine, history, folktale, romance, epics, poetry, and animal fables were illustrated as storytelling images, and illustrated copies of such writings survive from the years since around 1000 CE These often contain the detailed depiction of humans and animals, accentuated by jewel like colors and motifs (thus widely appreciated as "miniatures" in the past), whereas single-page portraits also developed into a long-lasting pictorial tradition in the Islamic world. In the Persian cultural domain, Firdawsi's Shāhnāma ("Book of Kings") became the most commonly illustrated type of literature. Female images were also widely found in these illustrated manuscripts in the form of certain characters, as well as dancers and musicians.

Late Antique heritage was deeply rooted in the early periods of Islamic rulership in the East Mediterranean, and female figures often appeared in the pictorial decoration of secular buildings in the region. In some cases, they were represented as being undressed, for example, those found in the Umayyad bath house Qsayr ʿAmra in modern-day Jordan.

Little is known about individual painters of the Islamic world before modern times, and very few pieces of information on female Muslim painters, if they ever existed, are available. What is clear is that such anonymous painters, normally attributed to workshops or schools, were receptive of foreign pictorial traditions, and cultural contacts with non-Islamic lands, such as Byzantium and China, resulted in bringing a number of concepts for the figural arts to the Islamic sphere. This followed the introduction of European prints and oil paintings that exerted a decisive impact on the shaping of human imagery among Muslim painters at the courts of early-modern Muslim dynasties. Riza ʿAbbasi, one of the named Persian painters of the Ṣafavid period (1501–1732), extensively used women for his pictorial models. Royal palaces of the same dynasty were, for example, decorated with large-scale mural paintings that illustrated historical subjects and figures, including women.

Before the introduction of European-style painting, Muslim artists confined themselves to the experimental use of perspective and shading. In modern times, especially during the late nineteenth and early twentieth centuries, the painting style of the Islamic world dramatically changed, culminating in the rise of modernism in the region. Painting was no longer confined to manuscript painting, yet numerous pictorial forms began to flourish. Together with individual sociopolitical and economic factors, regional variations emerged in the painting style of the Islamic world, and it was increasingly difficult to treat it as a single cultural entity of Muslim visual culture.

It is widely considered that the classical-style, Ottoman pictorial tradition ended with the late eighteenth century, and the history of modern, "Turkish" painting began in the mid-nineteenth century. The works of Turkish painters, with a variety of training in sketching, draftsmanship, and engineering, were no longer the products of a court atelier system. They were graduates of the new engineering and military academies under governmental sponsorship, and the majority of them were sent to Europe to complete their education under famous artists of the time. Works of Osman Hamdi Bey (1842–1910), one of the pioneering modern Turkish painters, were executed under the inspiration of European Orientalist painters, who often used Muslim women as the mirror of the declining Orient; yet he painted daily lives, with the emphasis of realism, including women in the harem or on the street.

Qājār Persia (1779–1924) experienced the emergence of a distinctive painting style under the complex amalgamation of indigenous Persian pictorial concepts and newly acquired European visual concepts. Many pictorial arts of the time—not only life-size portraits done in oil but also lacquer book-bindings and pen boxes—depicted women of the court, for example, dancers, musicians, and servants, with attempts to apply Western pictorial techniques and to give scrupulous attention to the representations of costumes and jewelry.

Based on a long and rich tradition of painting in a variety of media in Hindu, Buddhist, and Islamic traditions, Muslim painters of South Asia equally became very familiar with European painting style in early modern times, particularly under Mughal rule. Pictorial elements and subject matters derived from European conventions served to make the painting style of Islamic South Asia even more eclectic than before.

With the introduction of fine-arts schools and the increasing accessibility of education to women beginning in the nineteenth century, women have become important members of the art community throughout the Islamic world. However, they faced the same barriers to success and recognition as their counterparts in the West throughout the nineteenth and twentieth centuries. This was due to more restricted access to major centers of art training and fewer chances to be included in gallery and museum collections than male artists of the same period had.

As dramatic changes affected the cultural climate of the Islamic world, the development of modern- to contemporary-style painting took a variety of paths. In Iran, many avant-garde artists left the country after the Iranian Revolution of 1979, but kept their profiles in Europe and the United States. In the Arab world, particularly North Africa and Lebanon, where there was significant cultural contact with France, Arab artists worked to develop the cultural institutions necessary to support an art community that encouraged women to pursue an artistic career. Another center of contemporary art of the Islamic world was set up in the Gulf region, in which artistic activities and cultural institutions emerged only in the past few decades. In many cases, female Muslim artists began to enjoy their freedom of artistic expression.

Although the impact of Western art remains predominant, Islamic forms of pictorial arts have also been explored by Muslim artists. Observing Islamic religious values, nonfigural representations of the faith, diverse cultures, and sociopolitical themes place an important position in the contemporary art scene in many Islamic countries. Several Muslim artists explored calligraphic arts in an innovative yet traditional form, whereas they seek for several means of nonfigural pictorial representations in the form of geometric patterns and abstraction.

BIBLIOGRAPHY

Ali, Wijidan. *Contemporary Art from the Islamic World.* London: Scorpion Publishing, 1989.

Ali, Wijdan. *Modern Islamic Art: Development and Continuity.* Gainesville: University of Florida Press, 1997.

Arnold, Thomas W. *Painting in Islam: A Study of the Place of Pictorial Art in Muslim Culture.* Oxford: Clarendon Press, 1928.

Baer, Eva. *The Human Figure in Islamic Art: Inheritances and Islamic Transformations.* Costa Mesa, Calif.: Mazda Publications, 2004.

Diba, Layla S., and Maryam Ekhtiar. *Royal Persian Painting: The Qajar Epoch, 1785–1925.* London: I. B. Tauris, 1998.

Gruber, Christiane J., and Frederick Colby, eds. *The Prophet's Ascension: Cross-Cultural Encounters with the Islamic Miʿrāj Tales.* Bloomington: Indiana University Press, 2010.

Porter, Venetia. *Word into Art: Artists of the Modern Middle East.* London: British Museum Press, 2006.

Shaw, Wendy M. K. *Ottoman Painting: Reflections of Western Art from the Ottoman Empire to the Turkish Republic.* London: I. B. Tauris, 2010.

Sims, Eleanor. *Peerless Images: Persian Painting and Its Sources.* New Haven, Conn.: Yale University Press, 2002.

Nancy Micklewright
Updated by Yuka Kadoi

Women's Representation and Production

Any discussion of the representation of women in painting or their role(s) in painterly production is complicated, because even though the female figure was an appropriate subject, women as painters, collectors, or patrons of art were fundamentally neglected until the feminist movement. Thereby, few critical studies of women as either subjects or producers of paintings predate the 1970s, and if such studies exist they are more descriptive than critical analyses. By contrast, late twentieth-century feminist scholars have examined the symbolism of female imagery in art to gain an understanding of women's roles both within artistic and religious traditions and within the wider culture. Such studies indicate that images reveal cultural perceptions of gender, power, and religion, and function as critical vehicles for cultural histories. Images are neither benign expressions nor neutral objects; rather, they are central to the socialization process as constructs of being male or female by visualizing attitudes of proper and inappropriate female behavior. Further, and especially critical to the study of women, many paintings were lost in wars, invasions, or religious iconoclasm, as well as through such natural disasters as earthquakes, tsunami, or fires, to the extent that the surviving works may be limited in scope or subject matter. For example, feminist scholars argue that fundamental Western patriarchal attitudes resulted in the destruction, if not total elimination, of any paintings in which female motifs of power and authority were central.

This generic problematic is complicated further by the complex disposition of the role of women in Islamic society and culture, whether historical or contemporary. Moreover, there is the precarious nature of painting itself in Islamic society and culture. Traditionally, Islamic painting is identified with book illustration and thereby heavily dependent on textual sources, as portraiture, history painting, and genre paintings are minor subcategories. In addition, the painter who may generally fulfill multiple tasks including witness, archivist, activist, and storyteller is in questionable, if not dangerous, standing in Islamic society. The continuing and unresolved debate over the acceptability of representational images that traditionally have been condemned as idolatrous by Islamic theologians has been complicated by the reality that the visual arts featuring people and animals have existed from earliest Islamic times to the present, especially during periods of royal patronage. The escalating tolerance of *taṣwīr* as a consequence of the modern media from film and television to the Internet as suppliers of figural, popular, and pervasive imagery, especially of women, was witnessed in the daily, if not hourly, media coverage of the Arab Spring.

Woman as Subject and as Painter. Although the Western definitions of culture and art are not universally valid, there is a recognition that the long-standing distinctions between women's art and men's art can be found throughout the Islamic world even unto the continuing classifications of folk and high art. Traditionally, women's art flourished within the domestic sphere, such as embroidery, tapestry, and song. The popular practices of women's art reveal the daily experience of human life in a multiplicity of settings. The iconography of women follows historical patterns matching their societal, political, and religious subordination as communicated through the symbolism of gestures, postures, attributes, and emblems of common female experiences, such as birth, puberty, marriage, reproduction, and death. Thereby, woman as the subject of painting should be depicted in the sanctioned stages of life: virgin, wife, mother, and widow; however, narrative or patronage requirements included the presentations of courtesans, dancers, acrobats, and servants.

These motifs were prominent in Persian and Ottoman miniatures. Small paintings on paper, miniatures were made either as book illustrations or for inclusion in albums—Persian *muraqqa* or Turkish *murrakka*. Despite social and religious constraints, the daughters of elite families often learned poetry, music, or art. The visual art form deemed most appropriate was, of course, calligraphy. According to tradition, a daughter of the Abbasid Caliph al-Mahdi painted golden calligraphy onto a glass. However, before the twentieth century, women as artists, patrons, critics, models, and muses found their greatest venue for artistic expression in Islamic Spain and the post-1876 Ottoman Empire.

The growing interest in women's position(s) in Islamic society, hastened as much by technology as by globalization and politics, has expanded the boundaries in the arts throughout the Middle East. Initially, art institutions such as the College of Fine Arts in Cairo (1908) were founded under colonialism. However, since the 1980 and 1990s there has been a rapid growth in the establishment of national museums of modern art, art academies, and private galleries. Many of these institutions have supported the training and the exhibitions of woman painters and curators who have moved beyond the artistic influences of either nineteenth-century Orientalist painters or the hegemony of modern art from the West. For example, in Jordan, Wijdan Ali worked on the establishment of the Royal Society of Fine Arts (1979), the National Gallery of Fine Arts (1980), and the faculty of Arts and Design at the University of Jordan (2001) and continues to curate exhibitions and author definitive scholarly catalogues.

From 9/11 to the "Arab Spring." Even before 9/11, there was the overarching question of the social and cultural role(s) for women in the Islamic world during a time of dramatic pressures toward modernization.

Islamic women artists, curators, critics, and collectors expanded the borders of Islamic painting beyond the incorporation of nationalism, denial of colonialism, and revival of folk motifs, especially for tourism. Affirmed within the categories of feminist art, their paintings (and exhibitions) are critiques of the political, economic, and ideological power of society and thereby subversive challenges to the premise of patriarchal culture and authority. Their concern for gender equality and cultural integrity melded with a call for the end of violence and commoditization of women to launch new styles and motifs as visual critiques of both the West and also national governments within Arab countries and throughout the Arab diaspora. Clearly the extremes of xenophobia and Islamophobia since 9/11 have layered the representations and perceptions of Islam and women with new political, religious, and social ramifications.

Highlighting the "new" place of Islamic women artists and curators is a series of international art exhibitions that evolved from Contemporary Art from the Islamic World (1989) beginning with the first traveling exhibition of contemporary Arab women's art titled Dialogue with the Present, The Work of 18 Arab Women Artists (1999). International exhibitions such as Breaking the Veils: Women Artists from the Islamic World (launched in Crete, 2002) supported the re-visioning of attitudes of and toward Islamic women painters. More recently, and in fortuitous coordination with the "Arab Spring," were two major exhibitions. Fluidity, Layering, Veiling: Perspectives from South Asian and Middle Eastern Women Artists (2011) displayed a diversity of generations, media, and religious perspectives of Islamic women artists from South Asia, Middle East, Europe, and the United States while the critically praised Dream and Reality (2011) introduced those "nearly forgotten women painters" from the Ottoman era.

BIBLIOGRAPHY

Resources on the topic of women and the arts are predominantly surveys or monographs on the history of women artists in Western culture; few specialized sources exist from the perspective of non-Western cultures.

Denny, Walter. "Women and Islamic Art." In *Women, Religion, and Social Change*, edited by Yvonne Yazbeck Haddad and Ellison Banks Findly, pp. 147–180. Albany: State University of New York Press, 1985.

Keelan, Siumee H., curator, and Fran Lloyd, ed. *Contemporary Arab Women's Art: Dialogues of the Present*. London: I. B. Tauris, 1999. See especially Tina Sherwell, "Bodies in Representation: Contemporary Arab Women's Art," pp. 58–69.

Sloman, Paul, ed. *Contemporary Art in the Middle East.* London: Black Dog Publishing, 2009.
Walther, Wiebke. *Women in Islam.* Rev. ed. Princeton, N.J.: Markus Wiener, 2009. English translation of *Die Frau im Islam*, first published in 1980. See especially "Women in Islamic Culture," pp. 143–154.

DIANE APOSTOLOS-CAPPADONA

PAKISTAN. Women in Pakistan have marked their presence in public spaces since the 1950s. Whether in circumscribed spaces for women or gender-mixed spaces, Pakistani women are increasingly participating in public debates and have become more visible in national discourses. The national public sphere in Pakistan is important in this regard because it serves as a theatrical "stage" for political performance, where women and men across ethnic, class, and ideological lines have orchestrated acts of protest and performed as agents of social change. This is a platform contested and shared by political parties, social movements, and grassroots organizations. Rhetorically skilled and activist women use the national public sphere as a political stage to promote their emergent causes in front of local as well as global audiences.

Particularly in urban sectors, women have demonstrated their demands for justice and condemned institutional violence against women through street mobilization, public assemblies (*jalsa*), print journalism, and TV media. Most effectively, using methods of collective mobilization, women in Pakistan have claimed a female voice in male-dominated discourses by seizing upon public places and spaces: the scene of the street as disseminated by the media. With this in view, both Islamic and secular women can be seen as proactive agents in the national public sphere, exposing the limits of the political and linking the spectacular and theatrical with their claims to authority as they critique corruption, nepotism, and inequality in society and in the state apparatus. Ideologically apart, Islamic women use religious tradition as a means to reach their political ends whereas secular women use UN-sanctioned human rights to voice a consistent criticism against ideas and practices of gender bias. Pakistani women have thus contested the national public sphere among themselves and with their male counterparts—they have used it successfully to create a national focus and attract global attention to their demands. While outspoken women have created public awareness around cultural, social, political, and legal subjects related to the status of women and/or their own identities in private and public, middle-class and working-class women have performed quotidian roles in a broad spectrum of social, cultural, and work spaces. Additionally, the urbanization schemes of the major cities of Karachi, Lahore, and Islamabad, along with the administrative reform in 1972, opened up positions for secretarial work in government services, in the nongovernmental organization sector, and in other such white-collar occupations.

The boom of media enterprise continues to add new avenues in broadcasting and journalism—modern jobs that Pakistani women compete for. There are female academics with prominent profiles, as well some outstanding women politicians (there is a quota for women in the National Assembly of Pakistan). Whether in sight, leading public exposés in political arenas, or out of sight, in novel workspaces, the actions of Pakistani women demonstrate how cultural conventions of exposure and discourses on domesticity, and thus ideals of womanhood, have taken new forms and continue to change with time. The perception of Pakistani women as only domestic daughters, sisters, and wives who act in the private sphere, circumscribed by *purdah* (seclusion) norms, is thus changing. In the early twenty-first century Pakistani women are actively engaged in the fields of philanthropy, politics, governance, religion, law, activism, human rights, education, sports, literature, music, arts, fashion, and, most popularly, in the media.

Since 1999, the year in which the army chief Pervez Musharraf (r. 1999–2008) seized power via a nonviolent coup, the media landscape in Pakistan has seen a dramatic change. Musharraf opened up the airways to a free and independent media when he issued countless TV licenses his predecessors had vehemently blocked. GEO broadcast was among the first TV channels. It moved its headquarters from Dubai to Lahore and competed for audiences with the state-governed channel, Pakistan Television Corporation (PTV), which had been broadcasting news and religious and social programs to the public since 1964. Following in its trail, more than forty-five private TV channels mushroomed alongside print newspapers in more than eleven languages. This explosion of broadcast media outlets and subsequently new media spaces, such as YouTube, heralded the emergence of a new mediatized public sphere where social, political, and human rights activists—men and women alike—articulated counter-discourses to state-sponsored rhetoric. In particular, urban-educated Pakistani youth have become proactive in social media, exploiting the opportunity to develop new modes of critical expression. Feminist critics, journalists, and writers have published their writings in the press and media—for example the journalist Razia Bhatti (1944–1996) was a critic who broke many taboos—making TV journalism and broadcasting a platform for engagement, criticism, and contestation. Often TV journalists take up the role of moral crusaders advocating for public ethics and attacking discrimination and corruption. They also employ the media to transmit local events to a global audience. Countless foundations, networks, and resources for Pakistani journalists have materialized as part of the rapid development in modern media communication, predominantly in the urban landscape—some exclusively directed at women, such as the Women Media Center (WMC). WMC, founded by the feminist journalist Fauzia Shaheen, is a nonprofit organization that works toward creating a professional and unbiased environment to empower and increase women's presence in the media via training and workshop participation. The key objective of the organization is to create visible and competent female newsmakers—both as sources and subjects of news.

Women parliamentarians working for state power and influence are prominent in mediatized discourses. There is a higher number of women in parliament than the constitutionally imparted quota; women across political parties possessed altogether 91 out of 342 seats in the National Assembly after the 2008 election—the highest representation of women in the country's history. In comparison, the 1988 elections elected only eight women to the National Assembly. Moreover, after 2008 five women have assumed positions at the federal level and as ministers of state. This indicates that the visibility of women in the polity and legislature has increased and is increasing, despite the apparent rise of Islamism in the country.

Not limited to state politics, women in diverse political and social public domains also manifest their interests, needs, resistance, and collective mobilizations against discrimination and hegemonic power. Indeed, the role of Pakistani women is shifting national politics as new aspects of participation and public representations are structured within and around women's agency. This has been true of the rising political engagement, visibility, and achievements of women from the upper classes, but is now increasingly so also for the middle classes, who associate the status of Pakistani women with that of progress and democracy, manifested in the supreme symbol of

Pakistan's first female prime minister, Benazir Bhutto (1953–2007), first elected in 1988.

Even prior to Benazir Bhutto, however, a series of women pioneered political discourses and were engaged in Pakistan's nation-building project. Women's role has been, and still is, enmeshed in Pakistani nationhood, idealized in cultural performances (as daughters, sisters, and mothers who preserve honor and respect, balancing domestic duties with public engagement) and cultural clothing (ideally with a light chiffon scarf on the head to demonstrate respect for tradition). Their public involvement necessitated symbols of modest conduct and dress codes immersed in new combinations of representation with respect to so-called traditional values and domestic awareness—whether in rural or urban areas. Tradition in this way is an essential part of facilitating changes and engaging in complex ways in political strategizing.

After the independence of Pakistan in 1947, women from the upper and upper-middle classes (often wives of political leaders) participated in the birth of national politics, legislation, and representation. In particular, the public face of Fatimah Jinnah (1893–1967), the sister of the nation's founding father, Mohammad Ali Jinnah (1876–1948), was seen to connote strength in support of a nation in the making. Fatimah Jinnah ran for presidency in the 1965 elections with support from the conservative religious movement Jamāʿat-i Islāmī, but her opponent, Ayub Khan (r. 1958–1969), defeated her. Nationally and internationally recognized Begum Rana Liaquat Ali Khan (1905–1990), the wife of Pakistan's first prime minister, Liaquat Ali Khan (1896–1951), held several state positions; among others, she was the first female ambassador to the Netherlands, Italy, and Tunisia from 1954 to 1963. Later, in 1973, she was appointed as the first female governor of Sindh Province. Begum Rana Liaquat Ali Khan also established the All Pakistan Women's Association (APWA) in 1949, whose members were mainly drawn from the minority elite. It was a serious and collective attempt to improve women's status in society and was state sponsored until 1977. APWA hosted welfare projects for low-income women in both rural and urban areas, predominantly in the fields of education, health, social rights, and law. This image and the welfare work of "do-good begums" were an essential aspect of the nation-building project in the early years. They articulated discourses of anticolonial nationalism and the integration of migrants (*muhājir*) coming from India. Thus, both Fatimah Jinnah and Begum Rana Liaquat Khan figured as symbols of motherhood: Madar-e-Millat (Mother of the Nation).

Another influential group, the Women's Action Forum (WAF), was formed in 1981. A secular feminist movement shaped within a liberal framework of religious tolerance and freedom, its founders were educated activists who contested a series of women's predicaments and Islamic laws that discriminated in favor of men, such as the *ḥudūd* punishments introduced by the general Zia ul-Haq (r. 1977–1988) in 1979. Using the national public sphere as an arena for political performance, WAF women took to the streets and demonstrated against legal injunctions oppressing women and denying their rights. The legislation of the Muslim Family Law Ordinance (1961), the Hudood Ordinance (1979), the Law of Evidence (1984), and the Law of *Qiṣāʿ* (retribution) and *Diyāt* (blood money) (1985) has been under immense criticism from Pakistani feminists and human rights activists. All four laws do not protect women's legal rights vis-à-vis men—on the contrary, they institutionalize the devaluation of women. In cases of testimony, inheritance, marriage, or guardianship of children, the legislation prevents women from exercising their fundamental rights on equal terms with men. For example, in cases of financial transactions, the testimony of two women equals that of one man, and in cases of rape the evidence of four righteous Muslim men is needed to prove that adultery has not taken place and that a sexual attack was in fact rape. In particular, the Hudood Ordinance, in which the distinction between rape and adultery is blurred, has been the subject of constant criticism. WAF also defended the right of sportswomen to participate in the Asian Games. During the military government of General Zia ul-Haq women were banned from spectator sports as a result of an androcentric religious lobby that considered women's participation in sports as obscene. However, since the mid-1990s, women have become increasingly visible in national and regional sports fields; in team-oriented performances; and as individual performers in cricket, football, tennis, squash, badminton, swimming, skiing, mountain climbing, cycling, and running, where women set new directions for emerging currents of change. Since the first women's cricket team was assembled in 1996 by Shaiza and Sharmeen Khan, young Pakistani women have been inspired and encouraged to ignore criticism from orthodox religious groups. However, limited funds for women's sports have made it extremely difficult for Pakistani women to qualify for international sports competition.

In contrast to the secular WAF, young Islamist women in the cross-gendered seminary-mosque movement Jamia Hafsa–Lal Masjid (Seminary Hafsa–Red Mosque) are a contemporary example of how female religious actors have contested and performed in the national public sphere. The movement first came into the limelight through national media in early 2007. Reportedly seven thousand adolescent girls, young women, female teachers, and students from Jamia Hafsa assembled in the courtyard of the Red Mosque on 28 January 2007 in Islamabad to protest against seven mosque demolitions in the capital. More broadly, the movement was agitating for Islamic revivalism and Islamic legalization in the social, political, and legal institutions of Pakistan. As an essential part of the scene, all students and teachers were dressed in black burqa uniforms (long female kaftan dresses that include head and face covers), while the adolescent girls, modestly dressed with pastel-colored scarves over their head, lined up in row after row behind their leaders. Local Pakistanis, regardless of religious conviction, were appalled by this urban female face of Islamism, not only because they perceived the burqa as an imported alien dress code by contrast to their own *shalwar kamiz* (trouser and tunic), but also because religion had taken a radical form in which women replicated androcentric Islamist discourses in the public sphere. The authorities ignored the powerful and intimidating public representation of women from Jamia Hafsa and their demands for a "system change" based on religious tenets. They responded with a military operation, however, as the movement sought to alter what its members perceived to be rampant social change in their immediate local community, overtly attacking "un-Islamic" activities and "un-Islamic" places in Islamabad. Young Islamist women took part in moral crusades in public spaces—and equally encouraged other religiously ethically minded Muslim men and women (*ghairat-mand*) to do the same—precipitating a vigilante movement of Sharīʿah enforcement (*Nifazat-e-sharīʿah*) in the country. In the discourses of Jamia Hafsa the notion of *ghairat* applies to "ethical shame" or "ethical consciousness" directed by religion. The idea of *ghairat*, generically meaning honor, jealousy, courage, modesty, and shame, is enacted in various cultural contexts, often in relation to women's modesty and sexuality. It is a complex concept that applies to both men and women. Motivated by *ghairat*, the movement violated the law as members occupied the national children's library of the city, kidnapped a local prostitute, and forced film and music shops to shut down, burning their DVDs and CDs alleged to contain "sinful" music, women's dancing and singing, or displays of immodest sexuality.

Regardless of background and ideology, and despite their visibility in the national public sphere, one has to keep in mind that women in Pakistan face disproportionate hurdles in achieving success. Access to power in Pakistan is structured around social background and family names. The distribution of welfare, education, power, and privilege as preconditions for social mobility is still highly unequal. While the deterioration in the status of the majority of rural and lower-class women continues, politically or financially endowed women have increasingly progressed in activities at the state and grassroots levels, in national and international arenas. In a complex and gender-organized society like Pakistan, however, women must still contend with prejudice and patriarchal perceptions, regardless of social background and social status. These construct cultural boundaries and maintain systematic modes of subordination that either marginalize women in subtle ways or in more overt and brutal ways. Furthermore, institutional discrimination toward women still persists and takes different forms both in rural and urban configurations: in the house, the society, or the state, women at some level encounter the face of a structurally entrenched androcracy. Pakistan remains in many respects a patriarchal feudal society, typified by traditions that authorize men to keep their families' daughters, sisters, and wives within either close kinship or domestic proximity. Such traditions provide a set of rules, perceptions, and behaviors to govern, inculcate, and reproduce sharply distinct gender roles in culturally structured ideologies and practices.

[*See also* Bhutto, Benazir; *and* Women's Action Forum.]

BIBLIOGRAPHY

Abu-Lughod, Lila. *Remaking Women: Feminism and Modernity in the Middle East*. Princeton, N.J.: Princeton University Press, 1998.

Asif, Iram Nisa. "Urban Islamism with a Gendered Perspective: The Case of Jamia Hafsa." Ph.D. diss., University of Copenhagen, forthcoming.

Eglar, Zekiye Suleyman. *A Punjabi Village in Pakistan*. New York: Columbia University Press, 1960.

Mumtaz, Khawar, and Farida Shaheed. *Women in Pakistan: Two Steps Forward, One Step Back?* London and Atlantic Highlands, N.J.: Zed Books, 1987.

"Pakistan's media scene/ Swat Valley: Al Jazeera Listening Post." http://blip.tv/al-jazeera-listening-post/pakistan-8217-s-media-scene-sawt-valley-2368628. (Accessed on 20 November 2011.)

Ring, Laura A. *Zenana: Everyday Peace in a Karachi Apartment Building*. Bloomington: Indiana University Press, 2006.

Talbot, Ian Arthur. *Pakistan: A Modern History*, 3d ed. London: Hurst & Co., 2009.

Weiss, Anita M. "Women's Position in Pakistan: Sociocultural Effects of Islamization." *Asian Survey* 25, no. 8 (August 1985): 863–880.

Werbner, Pnina. "Revisiting the UK Muslim Diasporic Public Sphere at a Time of Terror: From Local (Benign) Invisible Spaces to Seditious Conspiratorial Spaces and the 'Failure of Multiculturalism' Discourses." *South Asian Diaspora* 1, no. 1 (2009): 19–45.

"Women Media Center Pakistan": http://wmcpk.org/wp/.

"Women's Parliamentary Caucus": http://www.wpcp.org.pk/wpcp/Home.aspx.

IRAM NISA ASIF

PAKZAD, SURRAYA. (b. 1968), Afghan women's rights advocate. Pakzad was born in Herat, Afghanistan, to a family of sixteen children. She came of age during the Soviet invasion and occupation (1979–1989) of Afghanistan. Pakzad was married at the age of fourteen. In 1990, she graduated from Kabul University, having studied in the Faculty of Literature. She has six children and lives and works in Herat.

Having experienced firsthand the tragedies of war, Pakzad maintains an unwavering commitment to supporting Afghan women's rights in a country where nearly half of the population is female. Under the rule of the Taliban (1996–2001), women were subjected to an interpretation of Sharīʿah laws that sought to deny them equal rights and access to education. During this time, Pakzad helped to establish the Voice of Women Organization (VOW) in Kabul, where groups of girls were taught how to read. In 2002, VOW was officially registered as a nongovernmental organization, with a mission statement that it "advocates for women's rights, gender equality, legal & social protection, economic opportunities, political participation, freedom from violence." Supported by international donors, VOW provides vocational, legal, and educational services, including shelters for women, literacy programs, legal services, psychosocial support, job training, and raising awareness of gender-based violence.

Like other women in her country, Pakzad lives in a constant state of fear, given the rampant lawlessness and lack of security endemic to Afghanistan. There also continues to be staunch opposition to recognition of Afghan women as equal to their male counterparts; this was evident with the passage of the 2009 Shīʿī Personal Status Law. Like contemporary Afghan women's rights activists, including Massouda Jalal, Malalai Joya, and Fawzia Koofi, Pakzad is vigilant in uniting Afghan women in the twenty-first century, irrespective of the tribal, ethnic, or religious divisions that have plagued the country for decades. In describing Pakzad, Khalid Hosseini (2009) quoted her namesake, the twentieth-century Afghan Queen Soraya: "Do not think, however, that our nation needs only men to serve it. Women should also take their part, as women did in the early years of Islam."

While working to empower the women in her country, Pakzad is an outspoken critic of the inefficiency of aid distribution and the implementation of development projects throughout Afghanistan since 2001. Despite these realities, Pakzad is committed to changing the situation of women in her native country. She was quoted by Katie Glueck (2010) as saying: "Someone needs to be in the front line, to pave the road for a bright future for the next generation. If I shall die today, at least the next generation shall enjoy freedom. My life shall be at risk, but it is my pleasure to save the lives of the women of the future."

Pakzad has been recognized internationally for her work. In 2008, she received the National Medal (Malali Medal) from the Afghanistan President Hamid Karzai, and, from the U.S. Department of State, the Women of Courage Award. In 2009, she was named one of *Time* magazine's "People of the Year."

BIBLIOGRAPHY

Glueck, Katie. "Suraya Pakzad and the Long, Tough Fight for Afghan Women." *Politics Daily/Huffington Post*, 2010. http://www.politicsdaily.com/2010/03/11/suraya-pakzad-and-the-long-tough-fight-for-afghan-women/.

Hosseini, Khalid. "Heroes and Icons: Suraya Pakzad[21]." *Time* magazine, April 30, 2009. http://www.time.com/time/specials/packages/article/0,28804,1894410_1894289_1894277,00.html.

Voice of Women Organization. http://vwo.org.af/index.php?option=com_content&view=category&layout=blog&id=38&Itemid=63.

YALDA ASMATEY

PALACES. Traditionally, in Islamic lands, the palace functioned as both a political and a familial entity, serving as a site for diplomatic transactions and outward displays of splendor, as well as housing several generations of a ruling family. In many instances, from the Abbasid palaces in Sāmarrā (ninth century, Iraq) to the Alhambra in Granada (fourteenth century, Spain), palaces took the form of extensive complexes composed of several courtyards, buildings, and gardens, with secondary dwellings for servants and dependents. To what extent these palace layouts continued the older traditions of Mesopotamian, Persian, and Byzantine practices, and to what extent they were newly created to reflect the aspirations of Muslim dynasties is debatable, but it is clear that, within the social structure of Islam, the protection and privacy of women grew to be a principle concern. In palaces, this concern found spatial expression in the subdivision of the household into two main sections: the area where guests were received and the private area reserved in particular for women and children. This more restricted space is usually referred to as the *harem*, which derives from the Arabic root *h-r-m*, indicating sanctity and deference, as well as prohibition and inviolability. The concept of carving out a more private space for the life of the ruling family is by no means unique to Muslim polities; for example, the main residence of the czar at the Kremlin (fifteenth-century, Moscow) had no public rooms, and the upstairs living quarters of the imperial family were barred from courtiers.

In Islamic lands, domestic structures tend to have a lower survival rate than public monuments such as mosques and *madrasahs*, and the range of palatial architecture sites remains quite limited. Although archaeological discoveries from early Islamic times are plentiful—including a range of Umayyad villas, the Abbasid palace at Sāmarrā, and Lashkari Bazaar in Afghanistan and Afrasiyab (old Samarqand) in Central Asia—the exact locations of separate women's zones are difficult to pinpoint. Recent scholarship has demonstrated, however, that the dynamics of gender in ruling households were far more complicated than once imagined. The constant presence of male children and eunuchs transgressed divisions of gender. The half-naked stucco statues of richly attired female attendants from the Umayyad desert palace at Khirbat al-Mafjar (early eighth century) near Jericho represent the earliest surviving depictions of women in palatial architecture. The discovery of a ninth-century fresco of two dancing women each pouring wine into the other's cup from the excavations of the Jawsaq al-Khaqani palace in Sāmarrā also suggests a convivial atmosphere in the private quarters of palaces in early Islamic times.

In the early modern period, from which the best-studied examples of royal residences come, women developed several means to assert their imperial presence. The Topkapı Palace in Istanbul, home to the Ottoman ruling family for approximately four hundred years, stands as the best-preserved example of a harem space. Although the harem was by far the most restricted part of the palace, its location within the complex afforded some of the best views of the surrounding landscape. Additionally, in the late sixteenth and seventeenth centuries, the Valide Sultans (mothers of the rulers) increasingly gained political power, and renovations to the harem quarters allowed these figures to supervise imperial council meetings—and thus, official affairs of state—from a screened window. Such devices created an asymmetrical reality, whereby occupants of the harem could look out and enjoy the privilege of the royal gaze, but could not be viewed by the outside world. Royal Ottoman women also followed the tradition of female patronage within Islamic architecture. Such major commissions as the Yeni Valide Mosque (seventeenth century, Eminönü, Istanbul) allowed female patrons to establish their imperial presence within the urban landscape, extending their influence beyond the physical confines of the palace.

BIBLIOGRAPHY

Hambly, Gavin, ed. *Women in the Medieval Islamic World: Power, Patronage and Piety*. New York: St. Martin's Press, 1998.

Peirce, Leslie P. *The Imperial Harem: Women and Sovereignty in the Ottoman Empire.* New York: Oxford University Press, 1993.

Ruggles, D. Fairchild, ed. *Women, Patronage, and Self-Representation in Islamic Societies.* Albany: State University of New York Press, 2000.

EMILY NEUMEIER

PALESTINE. This entry covers the area that presently constitutes the State of Israel and the Occupied Palestinian territories of the West Bank and Gaza Strip, from the end of the Ottoman Empire (1917) until the establishment of the state of Israel (1948). During this time the area was under British rule, in accordance with the Sykes–Picot Agreement. After having defeated the Ottoman army, British forces set up a military administration of the area, which was replaced by a civil one in 1920. The League of Nations formalized British rule into a mandate in 1922. The British Mandate of Palestine (excluding the autonomous Transjordan) had direct control over legislative, judicial, and military matters, as well as foreign relations, and also supervised religious affairs. The Mandate was to be responsible for effectuating the Balfour Declaration by establishing a national home for the Jewish people, while at the same time ensuring that nothing was done that could prejudice the civil and religious rights of the non-Jewish communities in Palestine.

Zionist immigration had swelled the numbers of Jews in Palestine to 85,000, or 10 per cent of the total population by the beginning of World War I. Already then, Jewish land appropriation caused friction and disputes with the local population. An additional 100,000 Jewish immigrants arrived during the first decade of the British Mandate, and, between 1929 and 1939, more than one-quarter million Jewish immigrants came to Palestine, fleeing increased persecution in Europe. Throughout the Mandate period, Palestinian notable leaders voiced increasing criticism at the British at what they saw as unrestricted immigration and land purchase. Attempts on the part of the Mandate administration to establish joint Jewish-Arab self-governing institutions failed. The Zionist Commission was recognized as the representative for the Jewish community in Palestine, while the Supreme Muslim Council (SMC) was established by the Mandate to be in charge of Muslim community affairs. From 1920 on, the Palestinian Arab leadership, encompassing both Muslims and Christians, began calling for autonomy and for the rejection of the Balfour Declaration. Although united in its opposition to British rule and Zionist expansion, and with a common nationalist agenda, the leadership nevertheless suffered deep internal division. This division crystallized around the grand Jerusalem families of Husseini and Nashashibi; the former led the SMC, the latter included the mayor of Jerusalem. The rivalry deepened while the influence of Zionist institutions grew and became increasingly assertive.

Social Conditions for Women during the British Mandate. Even if Palestinian society was to remain predominantly rural throughout the period, towns such as Jerusalem, Jaffa, and Haifa experienced increased urbanization at the beginning of the twentieth century. In particular, the latter two towns became important port cities as international trade increased, and urban bourgeoisie and notable families gained in political influence at the expense of the rural elite. Rural village society was characterized by strong clan ties, communal farming practices, and customary law. Labor division was gendered, but women's participation in both domestic and agricultural work was crucial to family survival and valued as such. Poor urban women participated in the workforce, for example, as domestic servants and street vendors. Because of their obligations, both rural and poor urban women were freer to move about in their communities than was the case in particular for women of the middle and upper classes and tended to veil to a lesser degree. Common to women of all classes, however, was the fact that they were expected to be predominantly oriented toward their families, and that marriage and motherhood were seen as the essential milestones in their lives.

Promulgated in 1917, the Ottoman Law of Family Rights (OLFR) constituted the first official codification of Islamic family law in the modern era and was considered an instrument to improve women's status, in particular in the field of marriage and divorce rights. Whereas the OLFR was intended to be valid for non-Muslims as well as Muslims, the British Mandate administration repealed the sections applying to Christians and Jews, encouraging non-Muslim communities to apply family laws specific to their faiths. From the 1900s onward, an increasing number of upper- and middle-class girls received education, in particular at Christian missionary schools, and some embarked on a professional career as well. Melia Sakakini, who became a headmistress in Jaffa, is considered a pioneer. A few women went abroad to study, and the first Muslim woman to do so was Sa'ida Jarallah, who went to England in 1938. She was typical of women who achieved this—supported by her father, a judge at the Islamic Court, and by the fact that her family was highly respected. The British Mandate did not put women's education high on the agenda and differentiated between rural and urban girls in the sense that rural education focused almost entirely on practical issues, such as home economics and hygiene. What existed of institutions of higher education—training colleges for women—served to reinforce women's domestic role by teaching child and family care, handicrafts, and nutrition, but became more academic in the 1930s. The colleges mainly educated women to become teachers in the countryside and remained expensive establishments for the elite.

Women's education was clearly valued in the Palestinian community at the time, both because it contributed to women's respectability in itself and because it was linked to women's economic and social welfare. An educated woman was seen as cultured and refined and, therefore, valued as a marriage partner. Education was also seen as a safety net in the event of widow- or spinsterhood. An increasing number of work opportunities opened up, in the Mandate administration, public offices, and as nurses, doctors, and midwives, and all required a certain level of education. Courses in, for example, typing and first aid were offered, and women emerged in the public space in increasing numbers.

Women's Organization in the 1920s. It was among the educated women that the first initiatives toward women's organizations emerged in the first decades of the twentieth century. The earliest groups raised funds for and carried out charitable work, a necessary and welcome activity because poverty was widespread after World War I and institutions were not functioning after the collapse of the Ottoman Empire. Among the first organizations was the Orthodox Ladies Society of Jaffa, founded in 1910, and Jaffa's Arab Women's Union, which may have predated World War I. The British Mandate attempted to organize Palestinian and Jewish women in a Palestinian Women's Council under the auspices of prominent British women, but the initiative came to nothing. Although women sporadically joined in protests against Jewish immigration and British policies in the 1920s, the efforts were mostly disorganized. A group of twenty-nine Christian and Muslim women sent a letter to the British administration in 1920, protesting the Balfour Declaration. Later that year, violent protests calling for Palestinian independence and rejecting plans for a Jewish national home broke out in Jerusalem. The incident served to orient the leading members of the Arab community more directly toward Palestinian national objectives, which also inspired Palestinian women's activism. In 1921, women participated in violent protests in Jaffa, and later that year were involved in raising money for an Arab delegation to London, both of which demanded the abolition of the Balfour Declaration. Groups of women organized throughout the country, writing letters to the British administration, and women also participated in debates in the local press. Not all cases were national, though—women also engaged in press debates over veiling and women's rights and duties in society.

The riots of 1929 sparked the first publicly acknowledged political action of Palestinian women. In August of that year, long simmering conflicts between Muslims and Jews over access to the Wailing Wall erupted in Jerusalem and subsequently spread to other parts of Palestine. Jewish individuals and businesses were the main targets of the riots, which were violently put down by the British Mandate's police forces. One hundred and thirty-three Jews and 116 Arabs died in the riots, and 1,300 individuals were arrested, mostly Arabs. Three Arab men were executed. The riots and their aftermath increased the resentment of the Palestinian Arab population toward the Zionist settlers and toward the British Mandate, who were seen to have formed an alliance thwarting Palestinian national ambitions.

The Palestine Arab Women's Congress (AWC), which assembled in October 1929, attracted 200 women from all over the country. A delegation led by, most prominently, Matiel Mogannam visited the High Commissioner for Palestine and presented the AWC resolutions in support of the male national leadership, protesting the Balfour Declaration, Jewish immigration, collective punishment enforced as a response to the riots, mistreatment of Palestinian prisoners, brutality against demonstrators, and preferential treatment of Jews over Palestinians. Transported in a convoy of honking cars, they visited other foreign representatives throughout Jerusalem. The initiative was well planned and received widespread attention. The Congress elected an Arab Women's Executive Committee that became the executive leadership of the Arab Women's Association (AWA). The leadership was constituted mainly of urban, educated middle- and upper-class women, many of whom were related or married to members of the Arab Executive Committee. According to its bylaws, the AWA was sought to "elevate the standing of women" and to support "national institutions" (Fleischmann, 2000, p. 19). The AWA also aimed at inspiring women all over Palestine to organize, and branches were later established in the major towns.

The 1936–1939 Revolt and After. In the years leading up to the 1936–39 revolt, tensions between the Arab and Jewish communities became more radicalized, and both groups had established armed groups. Among them was the Black Hand organization led by Izz al-Din al-Qassam, who was widely supported, in particular by the increasingly marginalized peasants and the urban poor. A women's organization, Rifaqat al-Qassam (the comrades of al-Qassam, who are in this case exclusively women), was also established, although it is not known if they participated in militant activism. The revolt of 1936–1939 was sparked by the death of al-Qassam at the hands of the British in 1935 and by fears that increased Jewish immigration would lead to a Jewish takeover of Palestine. From April 1936, a general strike was declared to persuade the British to change their policies and stop Jewish immigration, disallow Jewish takeover of Arab land, and establish a national Palestinian government. The British Mandate administration attempted to crush the strike with brutally repressive means, including confiscation of property, preventive detentions, deportations, and even torture.

During this period, the activities of the women's organizations remained largely peaceful. The women of the AWA wrote protest articles in newspapers and also letters to the British Mandate leadership on behalf of imprisoned Palestinian activists, demanding reduced sentences, amnesties, and releases. The AWA also provided economic assistance to prisoners' families and to the prisoners themselves. After the revolt had begun, the number of prisoners multiplied, and the AWA also supported the wounded and their families, as well as families of martyrs. The women also actively protested the increasingly repressive British policies, in particular after martial law was declared in 1937. An increasing number of women joined demonstrations, often at the front, and, in particular, the Haifa and Jaffa AWA chapters were known for militancy. Sadhij Nassar, leader of the Haifa Women's Union, was among the first women to be arrested without trial for her political activism. It is particularly noteworthy that peasant women participated in the revolt. Bearing the brunt of the Jewish takeover of land, peasant women had violently opposed Zionist immigration since its inception. Most of their activities were spontaneous and disorganized, and little of it has been recorded. Peasant women helped rebels hide in the countryside, and smuggled food, arms, and messages to fighters. They were also effective in inciting their men to take up arms and join the fighting.

During the revolt, the AWA split into two factions along the lines of the rivalry between the leading Palestinian families that had taken opposite sides during the revolt. While the Husseini family supported the revolt, the Nashashibi family favored dialogue with the British. The rivalry went so far as to allege that the Nashashibis organized anti-revolt militias, joining the British and their allied Jewish armed groups. The Arab Women's Union (AWU) remained allies with the Husseini faction and tended to be a more political organization, whereas the Arab Women's Association that supported the Nashashibi side was more charity oriented. The revolt of 1936–1939 was brutally crushed by the British and that, combined with the internal rivalry, almost completely incapacitated the Palestinian national leadership and made it difficult to actively resist the partition plan and organize resistance in the period leading up to the 1948 war. The women's movement organized demonstrations and boycotts against Jewish products. When the war broke out, some women formed secret paramilitary cells and fought with the Arab Salvation Army.

BIBLIOGRAPHY

Esposito, J. L. with N. DeLong-Bas. *Women in Muslim Family Law*. Syracuse, N.Y.: Syracuse University Press, 2001.

Fleischmann, E. L. "The Emergence of the Palestinian Women's Movement 1929–39." *Journal of Palestine Studies* 29, no. 3 (2000): 16–32.

Fleischmann, E. L. *Jerusalem Women's Organizations during the British Mandate, 1920s–1930s*. Jerusalem: PASSIA, 1995.

Kimmerling, B., and J. S. Migdal. *Palestinians: The Making of a People*. New York: The Free Press, 1993.

Sayigh, R. "Introduction." In *Portraits of Palestinian Women*, by O. A. Najjar. Salt Lake City: University of Utah Press.

Segev, T. *One Palestine, Complete: Jews and Arabs under the British Mandate*. London: Abacus, 2001.

HILDE GRANÅS KJØSTVEDT

PAMPHLETS AND TRACTS. Although religious pamphlets and tracts are a worldwide phenomenon in Islam, this article concentrates on their presence in the Arab world. To walk the streets of any city in the Middle East or North Africa is to be confronted by a world of pamphlets and booklets. At the same time, the transnational nature of culture generally means that some of the same pamphlets resurface in Western cities with large Muslim and arabophone populations. In these Western cities one will also find pamphlets with Islamic content produced in French, English, and other European languages. Most pamphlets are religious in nature, for several reasons beyond the fact that the Islamist movement may be one of the most significant intellectual and cultural forces in the region. Other trends have come together with this movement, including the increased Arabization of previously Francophone-dominated areas like North Africa, and the economic upsurge brought about by the oil boom in the Gulf states.

Pamphlets are normally packaged and sold for mass consumption; hence their low prices. In certain heavily Islamized city neighborhoods, for example in Fez, pamphlets are produced in offset editions, bound with simple covers, and distributed free (except to the unsuspecting Westerner, who invariably pays for them). In Tunisia, however, religious pamphlets are unavailable, the regime having clamped down on the activities of the Islamists.

Religious pamphlets cover a varied range of topics and are addressed to both genders. Although they are more often written by men (the names of the leading shaykhs, al-Shaʿrāwī, Kishk, and al-ʿUthaymīn, figure prominently here), women can still have a strong presence in this textual world. Thus one of the most popular religious pamphlets to date was written by a woman, Niʿmat idqī; titled *al-Tabarruj* (Female Adornment), this booklet has seen several editions and is as easily obtained in Saudia Arabia as it is in Morocco. Peddlers on busy streetcorners hawk individual *suwar* of the Qurʿān. The more adventurous reader can delight in miniature booklets setting forth advice on proper behavior, legal injunctions (*fatāwā*; sing., *fatwā*), or even mini-manuals to help one interpret dreams. A woman is told how to win her husband in the 67-page *Kayfa taksibīna zawjak*.

The appeal of these pamphlets goes beyond their content. Many sport brightly colored covers rich in semiotic significance. Like the stained-glass windows of a Christian cathedral, the covers tell a visual story as powerful in its own way as the verbal story within. Series like *Silsilat al-marʾah al-Muslimah* (Series on the Muslim Woman) have their visual stamp on the cover, permitting potential readers to spot them readily. The more astute connoisseur of pamphlets learns in time to recognize the distinctive visual style of certain artists (e.g., al-Zuhayrī) whose names are now important in the cultural segment of the Islamist movement. Like their counterparts in the more secularized culture of the contemporary Middle East and North Africa, they are helping to shape a new popular culture, transmitted through pamphlets.

BIBLIOGRAPHY

Abrahamian, Ervand. *Radical Islam: The Iranian Mojahedin*. London: I. B. Tauris, 1989.

Douglas, Allen, and Fedwa Malti-Douglas. *Arab Comic Strips: Politics of an Emerging Mass Culture*. Bloomington, Ind., 1994. Discusses the visual world of Islamist artists.

Kepel, Gilles. *Les banlieues de l'Islam: Naissance d'une religion en France*. Paris, 1987. Includes analyses of some pamphlet literature in France.

Malti-Douglas, Fedwa. "An Anti-Travel Guide: Iconography in a Muslim Revivalist Tract." *Edebiyāt* 4, no. 2 (1993): 205–213. Study of the iconographic and textual dimensions of an Islamist pamphlet.

Malti-Douglas, Fedwa. *Medicines of the Soul: Female Bodies and Sacred Geographies in a Transnational Islam*. Berkeley: University of California Press, 2001.

FEDWA MALTI-DOUGLAS

PARĪ-KHĀN KHĀNUM I. (c. 1507–c. 1552), daughter of Shāh Ismāʿīl I of the Ṣafavid dynasty (b. 1487 CE, r. 1501–1524), and full sister of Ṭahmāsp Mīrzā, i.e., Shāh Ṭahmāsp I (b. 1514 CE,

r. 1524–1576). Her mother, Shāh Begī Begam (d. 1540 CE), known as "Tājlū" Khānum ("tāj" meaning "crown"), was the principal spouse of the Shah and a daughter of an important Turkman *amīr* of the Mawṣillū tribe, Maḥmād Beg b. Ḥamza Beg Bektāsh Mawṣillū, whose military and political support was essential to the Ṣafavid state, at the time still in the process of formation. In addition to Shāh Ṭahmāsp, Parī-Khān I was full sister to Bahrām Mīrzā (b. 1517 CE), and to Mahīn Bānu (b. 1519 CE), the youngest sister, who was later to become renowned as a counsellor of Shāh Ṭahmāsp, under the honorific name of Shāhzāda Sulṭanum. Among her full siblings, Parī-Khān Khānum I is the least known, probably because she might have left the royal court following her marriage, and her activities thereafter took place in the provinces.

As a representative of the Ṣafavid dynastic family, she played an instrumental role in the process of the consolidation of Ṣafavid power in the western regions of the state, especially the Shirvan, and the countries of origin and the governorships of her successive husbands. Parī-Khān Khānum I descended both from the Ṣafavids and from a Qizilbāsh tribe—blood ties that proved of great importance for her dynastic family in their fight for power. Although the historical sources are scarce and the information partly difficult to interpret (mostly because of the fact that there seems to have been some confusion about a "sister" and a "daughter" of Shāh Ismāʿīl present during the same period of time in the same area), it is clear that her first marriage was to Sulṭān-Khalīl b. Shaykh Shāh (r. 1524–1535), ruler of Shirvan. After his death in 1535, having left behind no children, Parī-Khān I proved to be an important political figure, as she actively worked toward strengthening the Ṣafavid grip on the Caucasian provinces of Shirvan and Gilan. In particular, she intervened in the struggle for power in Shirvan by supporting one of the candidates against most of the local military and court dignitaries—as a result of which she had to flee to the royal court around 1537.

It is possible, although far from certain, that in 1539 or 1540, Parī-Khān Khānum I became the wife of Darvīsh Muḥammad Khān (d. before 1551), ruler of Shakki. After he died, she wed the Ṣafavid *amīr*—and her own first cousin (his mother was Fāṭima-Sulṭān Begam, a sister of Shāh Ismāʿīl I)—ʿAbd Allāh Khān b. Qarā Khān Ostājalū (d. 1566 or 1567), one of the most influential dignitaries of the state and commander in chief of the army, who was appointed governor of Shirvan in 1551. In 1553–1554, two chronicles mention her participation—as well as that of her mother-in-law (and paternal aunt), Fāṭima-Sulṭān—in a military campaign alongside ʿAbd Allāh Khān. She led a mounted support detachment of three thousand camp guards, Qizilbāsh soldiers and servants, and some servant girls, or *kanīzān*, into battle.

Her marriage to ʿAbd Allāh Khān Ostājalū produced a son, variously named in the sources as Shāh-Qulī/ʿAlī Mīrzā (*mīrzā* being the title given to all Ṣafavid princes of the time, both in paternal and maternal lines), or Sulṭān-ʿAlī Khān Ostājalū, with whom Anthony Jenkinson (traveller and merchant, and a unique European eyewitness testimony of the Qazvin court) met at the royal court in Qazvin in 1562, and a daughter named Māh-Parvar Khānum. In general, Parī-Khān Khānum I and ʿAbd Allāh Khān's descendants played an important role in later Ṣafavid history and politics, especially their grandson Salmān Khān Ostājalu b. Shāh-Qulī Mīrzā, (d. 1623–24) a high dignitary of Safavid provincial and central administrations, and at the same time the great amir of the Qizilbāsh Qstājalu tribe.

BIBLIOGRAPHY

ʿAbdī Beg Shīrāzī Navīdī. *Takmilat al-akhbār*. Edited by ʿAbd al-Ḥusayn Navāʾī. Tehran, Iran: Nay, 1990. The author's patron was Parī-Khān Khānum II, daughter of Shāh Ṭahmāsp, who was a niece of Parī-Khān Khānum I and an important political figure of her times.

Aubin, Jean. "L'avènement des Safavides reconsidéré." *Moyen Orient et Océan Indien* 5 (1988): 1–130.

Ilchī, Khurshāh b. Qubād al-Ḥusaynī. *Tārīkh-i Ilchī-yi Niẓāmshāhī*. Ms British Library, Or. 203. The author travelled to the Ṣafavid court in 1545–1547.

Iskandar Beg Turkmān Munshī. *History of Shah ʿAbbas the Great*. 2 vols. Translated by R. M. Savory. Boulder, Colo.: Westview Press, 1978.

Jenkinson, Anthony. *Early Voyages and Travels to Russia and Persia*. London: Hakluyt Society, 1886.

Khuzānī Iṣfahānī, Fażlī b. Zaynal. *Afżal al-tavārīkh*. vol. 2. Ms British Library, Or. 4678. Second part of a chronicle of the early Ṣafavids, especially devoted to the reign of Shāh Ṭahmāsp.

Marʿashī, Mīr Tīmūr. *Tārīkh-i khāndān-i Marʿashī-yi Māzandarān*. Edited by Manūchihr Sutūda, Tehran, Iran: Iṭṭilāʿāt, 1985.

Membrè, Michele. *Mission to the Lord Sophy of Persia (1539–1542)*. Translated by A. H. Morton. London: University of London, 1993. Eyewitness account of the Ṣafavid state and court written by a Venetian merchant.

Qumī, Qāżī Aḥmad. *Khulāṣat al-tavārīkh*. 2 vols. Edited by Iḥsan Ishrāqī. Tehran, Iran: Dānishkada-i Tehrān, 1980 and 1984. One of the most important and detailed Ṣafavid chronicles, until the arrival to power of Shāh ʿAbbās I.

Rūmlū, Ḥasan Beg. *Aḥsan al-tavārīkh*. Edited by ʿAbd al-Ḥusayn Navāʾī. Tehran, Iran: Intishārāt-i Bābāk, 1978.

Sayyid Ḥasan Mudarresī Ṭabāṭabāʾī, ed. *Turbat-i Pākān*. vol. 1. Qum, Iran, 1977.

Szuppe, Maria. "'The Jewels of Wonder': Learned Ladies and Princess Politicians in the Provinces of Early Safavid Iran." In *Women in the Medieval Islamic World: Power, Patronage, and Piety*, edited by Gavin R. G. Hambly, pp. 325–347. New York: St. Martin's Press, 1998.

Szuppe, Maria. "La Participation des femmes de la famille royale à l'exercice du pouvoir en Iran safavide au XVIe siècle. Part 1." *Studia Iranica* 23.2 (1994): 211–258. Detailed study of the women of the Ṣafavid dynasty, and their participation in the public sphere.

Szuppe, Maria. "La Participation des femmes de la famille royale à l'exercice du pouvoir en Iran safavide au XVIe siècle. Part 2." *Studia Iranica* 24, no. 1 (1995): 61–122. Detailed study of the women of the Ṣafavid dynasty, and their participation in the public sphere.

Szuppe, Maria. "Status, Knowledge, and Politics: Women in Sixteenth-Century Safavid Iran." In *Women in Iran from the Rise of Islam to 1800*, edited by Guity Nashat and Lois Beck, pp. 140–169. Urbana: University of Illinois Press, 2003.

Walther, Wiebke. *Women in Islam: From Medieval to Modern Times*. 3d ed. Translated by Guity Nashat. Princeton, N.J.: Markus Wiener Publishing, 1993.

Maria Szuppe

People of the Book. "People of the book" (*ahl al-kitāb*) is the Qurʾānic designation for Jews, Christians, and occasionally other groups, such as Sabaeans and Zoroastrians, who, according to Islamic tradition, were entrusted with divinely revealed books prior to the Qurʾān. These books explicitly include al-Tawrāh (the Torah), al-Zabūr (the Psalms), and al-Injīl (the Gospel).

Islamic tradition and Qurʾānic interpretation are historically divided about the past and present status of al-Tawrāh, al-Zabūr, and al-Injīl. In one line of reasoning, Jews and Christians are accused of deceptively corrupting or altering these divinely revealed texts (2:75–79, 5:13). The original revealed books are thus construed as lost, though portions or selections are conceivably embedded or incorporated in canonical Hebrew and Christian scriptures.

Other Muslim interpreters, including Al-Ghazālī, Al-Rāzī, Al-Tabarī, Ibn Kathīr, Ibn Khaldūn, Sayyid Ahmad Khān, and Muhammad Abduh, appear to acclaim Jewish and Christian Scriptures not only as divinely revealed, but divinely preserved texts along with the Qurʾān. Any "corruption" is not in the biblical books themselves, but in erroneous interpretations or representations of them (2:62, 2:83–87, 2:89, 2:91, 2:97, 2:136, 2:140, 3:2–3:3, 3:50, 3:81, 3:84, 3:119, 4:47,

4:136, 4:163, 5:44–47, 5:66, 5:68–69, 6:91–92, 6:154, 10:37, 10:94, 16:43, 16:84, 17:55, 19:30, 21:7, 21:105, 29:46, 35:31, 40:78, 42:3, 42:13, 57:27, and 61:6).

The Qur'ān and Islamic tradition are of two minds about people of the book, sometimes treating them appreciatively and respectfully, at other times condemning them or calling for their subjugation. The Qur'ān denounces particular Jews who are prophet-killers and idolaters (2:91–96, 3:181, 5:70, cf. 4:157, 5:78, cf. 3:110), mischief-makers (5:64–68), and Sabbath-breakers, who are characterized as apes and swine (cf. 2:63–66, 5:59–60, 7:160–166, cf. 4:46–47). *Sūrah* 5:51 warns against having Jews and Christians as close friends or protectors, perhaps due to the history of early conflict with Medina's Jewish tribes. Jews are rebuked for claiming that "Ezra" is the son of God (a saying contrary to mainstream Judaism), and Christians are censured for worshipping Mary, as well as Jesus (5:116, 9:30). *Sūrah* 5:82 speaks harshly of Jews but favorably of Christians.

Sūrah 9:29 prescribes fighting, or forcing at least some people of the book to pay a religious penalty or poll tax (*jizyah*), so they "feel themselves subdued." These subjugated Jews and Christians were called dhimmī, or "protected" peoples, and, unlike pagans or idolaters, they were allowed some freedom of worship if they abided by fluctuating religious and legal restrictions.

More positive portrayals of people of the book emphasize their common monotheistic heritage as recipients of revelation (3:64, 29:46), and praise for people of the book who hasten to do good deeds, whom God consequently rewards in the hereafter (2:62, 3:114–115, 5:48, 5:69). The Qur'ānic Arabic *ahl* in *ahl al-kitāb*, moreover, connotes "family," so that "family of the book" might supplement "people of the book" to signify that Muslims, Jews, and Christians are individually and collectively the prophet Abraham's legitimate spiritual heirs. *Sūrah* 5:5 subsequently stipulates that Muslims and people of the book may eat each other's food, and that Muslim men may marry wives from among the people of the book.

Tradition indicates that the Muslim prophet Muḥammad wed several Jewish and Christian wives or concubines: Maria al-Qibtiyya (Christian), Rayhana Bint Zayd, and Safiyya bint Huyayy (both Jewish). Muslims customarily refer to the prophet's wives as "Mothers of the Believers." The Qur'ān also extols biblical figures like Mary, the virgin mother of Jesus, who is the only woman the Qur'ān names (3:42–45, 5:75, 19:16–33, 66:12). The Qur'ān further favorably alludes to Eve (2:35–36, 20:117), the Queen of Sheba (27:23–44), and possibly Hagar (2:158).

Controversies involving Muslims, women, and people of the book are numerous. One concern is Muslims invoking Islamic blasphemy laws against religious minorities and women. Another is perceived kidnapping, forced marriage, and conversion of non-Muslim women to Islam in Egypt, Pakistan, and India. This reported phenomenon is complicated by Egyptian Coptic Christian disapproval of divorce. If a Coptic Christian woman desires to divorce her Christian husband, converting to Islam is one way to expedite her divorce, and Muslims historically frown upon or forbid Muslim women from marrying or remaining married to non-Muslim men. Critics decry double standards in some contexts that prohibit Muslims from converting or "apostasizing," which at the same time urge Jews and Christians to embrace Islam. Compounding these are child custody laws and norms that favor Islam over other religions, and Muslims over non-Muslim parents.

Fortunately, conflict need not characterize interreligious relations. Christian Ethiopians sheltered early Muslim refugees. Fatimid Caliphs Al-ʿAziz and Al-Zahir supported Jewish and Christian communities, allowing them some leadership within the state. Al-Zahir took a Jewish wife who mothered Caliph Al-Mustansir.

The Canadian convert to Islam Ingrid Mattson envisions an "Axis of Good" connecting Muslims and other communities. Jewish Coalition for Disaster Relief assists Muslims in Sudan, Turkey, Indonesia, and Kosovo. The Pentecostal Assiout (renamed Thrasher) Orphanage and the Presbyterian Fowler Home served thousands of orphans and widows in Egypt. Contemporary Christians and Muslims cooperate to provide relief for the poor through the Christian nongovernmental organization World Vision. Corners for Creativity Cultural Center in Alexandria, Egypt, partners Christians with Muslim women and men in writing, visual arts, and fine arts classes. Dialogue through the Muslim-initiated *Dialogue Through the Muslim Interfaith Initiative: A Common Word* (3:64) and its derivatives incorporates women's voices. These are just a few examples of how Jews, Christians, and Muslims—whose populations combined embody more than half of the global population and more than half of the world's women—seek to love God, each other, and God's creation together.

BIBLIOGRAPHY

Menocal, Maria Rosa. *The Ornament of the World: How Muslims, Jews, and Christians Created a Culture of Tolerance in Medieval Spain.* Boston: Little, Brown, and Company, 2002. An idyllic glimpse at a comparably amicable multireligious milieu.

Moffett, Samuel Hugh. *A History of Christianity in Asia.* 2 vols. Maryknoll, N.Y.: Orbis Books, 2005. An erudite, highly readable history, especially of Christian-Muslim relations in Asia.

Smith, Jane Idleman. *Muslims, Christians and the Challenge of Interfaith Dialogue.* New York: Oxford University Press, 2007. An exploration of contemporary issues, particularly in America.

Ye'or, Bat. *Islam and Dhimmitude: Where Civilizations Collide.* Madison, N.J.: Farleigh-Dickinson University Press, 2001. A meticulously documented, sometimes polemical record of Jews and Christians under Muslim rule by an Egyptian-born Jewish woman.

BENJAMIN B. DEVAN

PERSIAN LITERATURE.

PERSIAN LITERATURE. In the earliest extant New Persian poetry from the tenth and eleventh centuries we encounter glimpses of a female beloved in both the courtly ode (*qaṣīdah*) and the newly emergent short lyric (*ghazal*). Even at this very early stage in the development of New Persian poetry, though, the preference in both the *qaṣīdah* and the *ghazal* is for a male beloved (typically a pubescent boy or youth) who acts as the wine server (*sāqī*) or slave attendant (*ghulām*) at the drinking bout (*majlis-i sharāb*). In such poetry, the prevailing amorous mood is male homoerotic. This said, a female presence is preserved in New Persian lyric poetry, albeit indirectly, via the feminization of the wine and its eroticization as a virginal, female object of desire (a trope most likely adopted from the early Arabic *khamrīyah*). The female element in Persian epic poetry, which emerged during the same period, is altogether different. In epic, the love relationships depicted are almost exclusively heteroerotic. Firdawsī's *Shāhnāmah* (*Book of Kings*, completed 1010) contains several strong female characters, and there are numerous Persian romances that showcase bold female heroines, such as Unṣurī's *Vāmiq u 'Adhrā'* (early eleventh century), Gurgānī's *Vīs u Rāmīn* (1055), and Niẓāmī's romance masterpieces, *Khusraw va Shīrīn* (1180) and *Laylī u Majnūn* (1192). In their positive and nuanced depictions of female protagonists, these poets relied on material of a chiefly pre-Islamic, rather than Islamic, origin, be that Persian, Greek, or Arab.

Woman as Poet in the Medieval Period. Up until the mid-twentieth century, the contribution of women to Persian literature was almost exclusively confined to poetry. Evidence for Persian women poets and their poetry in the early medieval period is fragmentary at best and is found in male-authored texts, primarily poetic anthologies (sing. *taẕkirah*) that also contain brief biographical sketches. This paucity of material reflects dominant socio-religious anxieties around the female voice, and around women engaging in reading, writing, and poetic performance. The male homosocial space of the *majlis* (the courtly or other elite gathering at which poetry would be recited or sung to musical accompaniment) was not considered an appropriate space for free Muslim women. This said, some poetry penned by women has survived from the medieval period, a fact which itself is testament to the impact a number of women poets must have had on the literary scene of their day, and evidence that some were able to carve out a niche for themselves in a male-dominated poetic tradition.

One of the earliest women to write in New Persian was an Arab-descent native of Balkh named Rābiʿah who is believed to have lived in the tenth century and to have been a contemporary of Rūdakī (d. 941), the "father" of New Persian verse. Rābiʿah wrote in both Arabic and Persian, and at least one *mulammaʿa* (mixed Arabic/Persian poem) is ascribed to her. She is believed to have composed Persian poetry of an amorous nature; indeed, disclosure of her love for the slave-boy Baktāsh is said to have led to her death at the hands of her own brother.

Another medieval woman poet of note, one who is frequently described in impious terms, is Mahsatī Ganjavī. Mahsatī is thought to have lived in the twelfth century and to have been a poet-singer at the court of the Seljuk ruler Sultan Sanjar (d. 1157). Most of the poems attributed to Mahsatī are in the quatrain or *rubāʿī* form, and bear an erotic tone. Mahsatī is a master of the *shahr-āshūb* (lit. "city-disturber"; a short poem in which the physical charms of young male apprentices of the marketplace are extolled). Unsurprisingly, there are ongoing debates as to the validity of the attribution of these poems to Mahsatī, although early sources do associate her name with the *rubāʿī* and the *shahr-āshūb* genre.

One woman poet of medieval Iran about whom we have more reliable biographical information, and who left to posterity the largest poetic output of any woman poet writing in Persian until the modern period, is Jahān-Malik Khātūn (d. after 1389). A princess of the Īnjūid dynasty, Jahān lived in Shiraz in the fourteenth century and was a contemporary of ʿUbayd-i Zākānī (d. 1371) and Ḥāfiẓ (d. 1389). Like Ḥāfiẓ, Jahān focused her poetic efforts on the *ghazal*, recording over 1,400 of her *ghazal*s in writing (Jahān also composed a smaller number of *qaṣīda*s and *rubāʿī*s). There is much overlap in terms of theme, meter, refrain, and content between Jahān's poetry and that of Ḥāfiẓ, and there is evidence that she moved in the same court literary circles as her more celebrated male counterparts. In the preface to her *dīvān*, Jahān speaks openly of her anxiety about composing poetry as a woman, and recording her poetry in writing. She justifies her art by mentioning earlier women poets (e.g., ʿĀʾishah Muqriya, and two other royal women, Qutlugh-shāh Khātūn and Pādshāh Khātūn, d. 1295) in an attempt to emphasize the notion of a "sisterhood" of female poets, and to argue that she is part of an established tradition of women poets writing in Persian. Jahān's *dīvān* was not printed until 1995 and she has yet to receive substantial attention from scholars.

The Early Modern Period: Ṣafavid Iran and Mughal India. Fakhrī Hiravī's *Javāhir al-ʿajāʾib* (Wondrous Jewels, 1556) is the earliest known all-female *tazkirah*. Compiled in Mughal India in the middle of the sixteenth century, this anthology contains whole poems or poetic fragments from more than twenty women poets. Some pre-Tīmurid poets are mentioned (including Mahsatī, Pādshāh Khātūn, and Jahān), but the majority of the poets featured are late Tīmurid contemporaries or near-contemporaries of the compiler. These women poets were active in a range of cities in eastern Iran and Central

Asia. Most of them wrote in Persian, and some in Chaghatai Turkish. Persian poetry thrived in India in the Mughal period (1526–1858), a period that witnessed the production of fine poetry by a number of talented women drawn from both the ruling elite (such as Nūr Jahān, Sālima-Sulṭān Bigum, and Zīb al-Nisāʾ), as well as from more humble strata of society (such as Bījā Shāhī). Women poets of Ṣafavid Iran (1501–1722) include Nihānī, who was active in the late seventeenth century.

Neoclassical Awakening in the Eighteenth and Nineteenth Centuries. The so-called Bāzgasht-i adabī or "Literary Return," a neoclassical poetic movement that rejected the ornate Ṣafavid-Mughal style and advocated the emulation of "classical"—that is, pre-Tīmurid—Persian poetry, began in Isfahan in the eighteenth century and came to fruition in Tehran at the court of Fatḥ-ʿAlī Shāh Qājār (r. 1797–1834). One of the pivotal figures in the Bāzgasht, Hātif Iṣfahānī, had a daughter, Rashḥah (lit. "sprinkling"), who was an accomplished poet. In the early nineteenth century, Rashḥah gained entry to court circles in Tehran and produced praise poetry for royal patrons, who included ẓiyāʾ al-Salṭana (1799–1873), Fatḥ ʿAlī Shāh's private secretary and his favorite daughter. ẓiyāʾ al-Salṭanah, herself a poet, commissioned her full brother, Maḥmūd Mīrzā, to compile a *tazkirah* of women poets. Maḥmūd Mīrzā's *Nuql-i Majlis* (Confection of the Assembly, completed 1825) is the earliest female-only *tazkirah* from the nineteenth century and the key source for the poetry of what was a not insignificant number of women poets who were active at the royal court and in other elite circles circa 1810–1825.

Women poets of the mid-nineteenth century include the Qājār princess Ḥusn-i Jahān Khānum and her co-wife, Mastūrah (who wrote in both Persian and Kurdish). The female poet of this period who has had the most lasting impact on Persian literary history is Ṭāhirah Qurrat al-ʿAyn (b. 1814 or 1817). Ṭāhirah was a revolutionary Bābī preacher from Qazvin who expressed her reformist socio-religious vision through her poetry. Her most captivating poems are those in which she expresses her devotion to Sayyid ʿAlī Muḥammad Shīrāzī, the Bāb, through the medium of love poetry. Ṭāhirah, whose most transgressive act was her public unveiling in 1848, was executed for her religious convictions in Tehran in 1852.

The last truly neoclassical woman poet of the nineteenth century was a granddaughter of Fatḥ-ʿAlī Shāh, Gawhar, better known by her epithet, Shamsat al-Shuʿarāʾ ("Sun of Poets"). Shamsat al-Shuʿarāʾ was patronized by her cousin, Malik-Jahān Khānum ("Mahd-i ʿUlyā"; d. 1873), the powerful mother of Nāṣir al-Dīn Shāh (r. 1848–1896). Gawhar's *dīvān* (containing more than six thousand lines of poetry) was the first of any woman poet to be printed in Iran (in Isfahan in 1902).

The Twentieth Century: Poetry. The tradition of neoclassical Qājār women poets was continued at the start of the twentieth century by Faṣl-i Bahār Khānum (1878–1940), known best by her pen name, Jannat ("Paradise"). Jannat was one of a handful of women poets in the first decades of the twentieth century to be taken seriously by their male peers. The most radical woman poet of this period was Shams Kasmāʾī (1883–1961), who was born in Yazd and who, as a young woman, lived in Russian Turkistan for almost a decade. After returning to Iran in 1918, Kasmāʾī became an active member of a group of reformist poets and social progressives in Tabriz and, in 1920, she published a poem titled "Parvarish-i tabīʿat" ("Nurturing Nature"), which in all likelihood was the first modernist Persian poem ever to have been published. Other women poets of the era include the Bahāʾī social activist Ṭāyirah ("Bird," 1872–1911), who produced conservative neoclassical *ghazals*, but who also published advocacy pieces in the socially progressive newspapers of Tehran in which she opposed polygamy and promoted modern education for girls. Another woman who managed to penetrate the male-dominated journalistic world was Fakhr-i ʿUẓmā Arghūn ("Fakhrī," 1899–1966) who not only served as editor of a successful journal, but also wrote unabashedly patriotic poetry.

The establishment of independent women's societies (sing. *anjuman*) grew exponentially in the period following the Constitutional Revolution of 1906–1911. One young woman who fought valiantly to set up her own *anjuman* and establish a women's periodical was Zand-dukht Shīrāzī (1909–1952). Zand-dukht, in both her editorial pieces and her poems, called for the greater involvement of women in the public sphere, in particular in the workforce. Like many women of her generation, Zand-dukht admired Reza Shah (r. 1925–1941) and his aggressive modernization program, which included the forced unveiling act (Kashf-i ḥijāb) of 1936. Not all women poets of the period, though, were so eager to promote a public persona. ʿĀlam-tāj Qāʾim-maqāmī ("Zhālah," 1883–1946) was intensely private. In her poetry, which was only published after her death, we find perhaps the most nuanced, lyrical, and overwhelmingly bitter plea of any Iranian woman from the first half of the twentieth century. Zhālah decried forced marriage, the veil, and women's confinement to the domestic space, which she repeatedly depicted in her verses as a prison.

By far the most popular woman poet of the first half of the twentieth century was Parvin Eʿtesami (1907–1941). Eʿtesami, who received an excellent education and whose father was a major literary figure and translator in his day, speaks with a chaste, often conservative voice in her poetry. Although her poetry conforms to classical conventions, the content is modern in the sense that it is concerned with the stark inequalities and injustices in her society, in particular the suffering of the urban and rural poor. Although perhaps not as concerned with women's rights as some of her contemporaries, Parvin Eʿtesami's vision is one that advocates social equality for all, whether male or female. Although she lacked a strident gendered voice, there are strong feminine elements in her poetry, in particular in her penchant for setting the narratives in her poems within the private, domestic space.

Iran's most celebrated living poet is Simin Behbahani (b. 1927; eldest daughter of Fakhr-i ʿUẓmā Arghūn mentioned above). Behbahani's poetry shares many similarities with that of Eʿtesami in form (Behbahani writes almost exclusively in *ghazal*). Like Eʿtesami before her, Behbahani tackles painful issues around social inequality and inhumanity in contemporary Iran. Through her masterful reconfiguration of the millennium-old *ghazal*, Behbahani has succeeded in writing poems that marry neoclassical form with sociopolitical critique. Bolder than many of her female predecessors, Behbahani has made daring choices in her poetry, most notably in those poems that center on such marginalized and disenfranchised female figures as gypsies, dancing girls, and prostitutes. The communicative power of Behbahani's poetry and her ability to voice the concerns of the Iranian everywoman resonate with many up to today.

The woman poet of the modern era who has had the most lasting impact on the trajectory of Persian poetry, and who has played the most significant role in bringing women poets into the mainstream as equal colleagues alongside their male peers, is Forugh Farrokhzad (1935–1967). Although she began writing in a style sympathetic to the classical canon, Farrokhzad rapidly, first in terms of content, and then in terms of form, diction, and imagery, aligned herself with modernist Persian poetry or *shiʿr-i naw*.

Farrokhzad is the most outspoken female poet of modern Iran and the most translated. She is best remembered by some for breaking social expectations in Iran in the 1950s and 1960s, and for certain aspects of her personal life, but it is in her poetry that Farrokhzad displayed the greatest degree of audacity. Although she began her career as a poet intimately concerned with the tribulations of young Iranian women from middle-class backgrounds such as herself, by the end of her short life she surpassed the feminine and wrote poetry of a broader, comprehensively human nature.

The deeply felt influence of Farrokhzad's poetry is evident in the writing of many of the most talented contemporary Iranian women poets. One such poet is Granaz Moussavi (born in Iran but now living in Australia), in whose poetry we see echoes of Farrokhzad's demand for the fundamental right to a voice in Iranian society and the ongoing struggle against outmoded socio-religious codes that persist in stifling women's expression in Iran.

The Twentieth Century: Prose. By far the most celebrated woman novelist and short story writer of pre-revolutionary Iran, Simin Daneshvar (1921–2012), best demonstrated her female-centered narrative style in her novel *Savūshūn* (1969). In this post-colonial, anti-British novel—hailed as the first best seller of artistic merit in the history of the Iranian novel—Daneshvar raises the private, female sphere to the same level as the male, public sphere.

Other significant women prose writers of the 1960s and 1970s include Mahshid Amirshahi (*Sār-i Bībī Khānum*, Bībī Khānum's Starling, 1968). By locating women protagonists firmly at the center of their fiction, Daneshvar, Amirshahi, and their contemporaries tackled gender issues in fresh and provocative ways. They sought to explore the complex relationship between gender and power in a still largely patriarchal society by disrupting the dominant male-centered modes of fictional writing.

In the Wake of the Islamic Revolution (1978–1979). Following the example set by figures such as Simin Daneshvar, many younger women writers began to take center stage on the Iranian literary scene from the 1970s onward. Some have produced short stories and novels with a strident, often feminist tone (the best examples being the works of Moniru Ravanipur [*Kanīzū*, 1988; *Sang'hā-yi shayṭān*, Satan's Stones, 1990] and Shahrnush Parsipur [*Ṭūbā va ma'nā-yi shab*, Touba and the Meaning of Night, 1978; and *Zanān bidūn-i mardān*, Women without Men, 1990]), while others have produced works of a less overtly politicized tone. Among this second group can be counted Goli Taraghi, a writer who rose to fame in 1970 with *Man ham Chih Guvārā hastam* ("I Too Am Che Guevara"), and who now straddles Paris and Tehran and is as much part of the exilic literary scene as she is of the domestic one. Taraghi has grown in popularity since the revolution, and her short stories (in particular "Khāṭirah'hā-yi parākandah," Scattered Memories, 1992), which draw primarily on her middle-class 1950s Tehrani childhood, have proved extremely popular. Although not overtly political, the poignancy of Taraghi's longing for a lost Tehran cannot go unnoticed and could be understood as a critique of the contemporary status quo.

A younger writer, who in terms of her prose style could be regarded as following in the footsteps of Taraghi, is Zoya Pirzad, who has enjoyed remarkable success, in particular with her novel *Chirāgh'hā-rā man khāmūsh mī-kunam* (I Will Turn Off the Lights, 2001), which is centered on the lives of an Armenian extended family in 1960s Abadan. This is the first mainstream Iranian novel in which almost all the main characters come from one of Iran's religious minority communities. Like Taraghi, Pirzad's prose is tinged with nostalgia for pre-revolutionary Iran, and it is similarly lacking in overtly political or social comment. This is of course in part because of Iran's strict censorship laws.

Another best-selling novel of recent years is *Bāmdād-i khumār* (Morning of Intoxication, 1996) by Fattaneh Hajj Sayyid Javadi. Although it is inferior to *Chirāgh'hā-rā man khāmush mī-kunam* in literary terms, *Bāmdād-i khumār*'s popularity and instant success is noteworthy. This novel is similarly nostalgic, but is set in early-twentieth-century Iran and focuses on the lives of the members of a wealthy, aristocratic (Muslim) extended family.

Women Writers of the Iranian Diaspora. Just as women writers have been increasing in both number and popularity within Iran, so, simultaneously, expatriate women writing primarily in English and French have come to dominate the Iranian literary scene abroad. Although a few novels written by Iranian women writers of the diaspora have enjoyed some success (such as Bahiyyih Nakhjavani's *The Saddlebag*, 2000), it is in the genre of autobiography or memoir that they have excelled. An early example in English is Shusha Guppy's *The Blindfold Horse* (1988), which, although focused on personal life experiences (in particular childhood), manages to touch on broader aspects of twentieth-century Iranian history. More recent examples that deal more specifically with the 1978–1979 revolution, the Iran–Iraq War (1980–1988), and the early years of the Islamic Republic are Roya Hakakian's *Journey from the Land of No: A Girlhood Caught in Revolutionary Iran* (2004) and Marjane Satrapi's immensely successful *Persepolis* (2000–2003), a memoir in graphic-novel form written in French and subsequently translated into numerous languages. (In 2007, Satrapi's graphic novel was turned into an animated film of the same name, directed by the author and Vincent Paronnaud. The film won the Jury Prize at the 2007 Cannes Film Festival.) Some writing by women writers of the Iranian diaspora has provoked more controversy than others, most notably Azar Nafisi's *Reading Lolita in Tehran: A Memoir in Books* (2004). This autobiographical novel spawned heated debate among expatriate Iranian intellectuals and inspired the writing of a book-length response, Fatemeh Keshavarz's *Jasmine and Stars: Reading More than Lolita in Tehran* (2007). Nafisi subsequently published a more straightforward memoir, *Things I've Been Silent About* (2008), in which she in turn responds to the criticisms directed at her by certain elements within the expatriate Iranian community.

A number of diasporic Iranian women writers who consider themselves to belong to both their Iranian and their adopted cultures have tackled directly issues of identity and belonging in their autobiographies. This sort of memoir is most commonly found in the American context, and Azadeh Moaveni's *Lipstick Jihad* (2005) is an important example. Literature of the Iranian diaspora produced in English is of course not confined to prose genres. A number of women poets who have grown up largely (or exclusively) outside of Iran, and who often do not possess a fluent command of Persian, nevertheless proudly identify themselves as Iranian and draw upon classical and contemporary Persian literature through translation as sources of inspiration for their own brand of Iranian literary expression. The poetry of Mimi Khalvati is perhaps the best exemplar of this phenomenon.

Bibliography

Behbahani, Simin. *A Cup of Sin: Selected Poems*. Edited and translated by Farzaneh Milani and Kaveh Safa. Syracuse, N.Y.: Syracuse University Press, 1999.

Brookshaw, Dominic Parviz. "Odes of a Poet-princess: The *Ghazals* of Jahan-Malik Khatun." *Iran* 43 (2005): 173–195.

Brookshaw, Dominic Parviz, and Nasrin Rahimieh, eds. *Forugh Farrokhzad, Poet of Modern Iran: Iconic Woman and Feminine Pioneer of New Persian Poetry*. London and New York: I. B. Tauris, 2010.

Daneshvar, Simin. *A Persian Requiem*. Translated by Roxane Zand. London: Halban, 1991.

Eʿtesami, Parvin. *A Nightingale's Lament: Selections from the Poems and Fables of Parvin Eʿtesami (1907–1941)*. Translated by Heshmat Moayyad and Margaret Arent Madelung. Lexington, Ky.: Mazda Publishers, 1985.

Farrokhzad, Forugh. *Sin: Selected Poems of Forugh Farrokhzad*. Translated by Sholeh Wolpé. Fayetteville: University of Arkansas Press, 2007.

Guppy, Shusha. *The Blindfold Horse: Memories of a Persian Childhood*. London: Heinemann, 1988.

Hakakian, Roya. *Journey from the Land of No: A Girlhood Caught in Revolutionary Iran*. New York: Crown, 2004.

Keshavarz, Fatemeh. *Jasmine and Stars: Reading More than Lolita in Tehran*. Chapel Hill: University of North Carolina Press, 2007.

Khalvati, Mimi. *Child: New and Selected Poems 1991–2011*. Manchester, U.K.: Carcanet, 2011.

Milani, Farzaneh. *Veils and Words: The Emerging Voices of Iranian Women Writers*. Syracuse, N.Y.: Syracuse University Press, 1992.

Milani, Farzaneh. *Words, Not Swords: Iranian Women Writers and the Freedom of Movement*. Syracuse, N.Y.: Syracuse University Press, 2011.

Moaveni, Azadeh. *Lipstick Jihad: A Memoir of Growing Up Iranian in America and American in Iran*. New York: Public Affairs, 2005.

Nafisi, Azar. *Reading Lolita in Tehran: A Memoir in Books*. New York: Random House, 2004.

Nafisi, Azar. *Things I've Been Silent About: Memories*. New York: Random House, 2008.

Pirzad, Zoya. *Things We Left Unsaid*. Translated by Franklin Lewis. Oxford: Oneworld, 2012.

Ṭāhirah Qurrat al-ʿAyn. *Tahirih: A Portrait in Poetry*. Edited and translated by Amin Banani. Los Angeles: Kalimát Press, 2005.

Satrapi, Marjane. *Persepolis: The Story of a Childhood*. New York: Pantheon, 2003.

Satrapi, Marjane. *Persepolis 2: The Story of a Return*. New York: Pantheon, 2004.

Sharma, Sunil. "From ʿĀ'esha to Nūr Jahān: The Shaping of a Classical Persian Poetic Canon of Women." *Journal of Persianate Studies* 2 (2009): 148–164.

Taraghi, Goli. *A Mansion in the Sky and Other Short Stories*. Translated by Faridoun Farrokh. Austin: University of Texas Press, 2003.

Dominic Parviz Brookshaw

Pesantren. The word *Pesantren* refers to a type of boarding school in Indonesia offering training in Islamic subjects. Although it has been long held that *pesantren* emerged during the sixteenth century as Islam spread throughout the region, recent opinion has tended to identify the nineteenth century as the formative period for this institution, when the Dutch colonial regime opened up areas of east Java to commercial agriculture. *Pesantren* are private ventures founded and run by scholars called *kiais*, usually with the assistance of their families. Many schools do not survive the founder, but others continue over the course of several generations. Prestige is gained through contacts with other scholarly families and through students who establish new *pesantren* recognizing the original scholars as progenitors.

Students in earlier times remained at a *pesantren* until they believed they had learned enough and then returned to society. Committed students, often sons of scholars, moved among schools whose scholars had reputations for special knowledge. A good number then traveled to Mecca to complete their education. In the early twenty-first century, students usually stay at a particular school for a full education. *Pesantren* were once primarily a rural phenomenon. Scholars provided education, gave advice to villagers, and legitimized local ceremonies. Some scholars were regarded as "blessed" and were believed capable of providing cures and supernatural assistance, both during their lifetimes and after death at their tombs. Villagers supported schools with food and assistance; in some places, pious endowments were also given. Students often worked in the agricultural fields of the school since fees were seldom charged. Currently, some *pesantren* are located in urban areas, and many rely on fees charged to students.

A Traditional Education. Learning was traditionally based on the *kitāb kuning* ("yellow books") of prominent Muslim scholars, usually from the Shāfiʿī legal school. Study always included Arabic grammar (*naḥw*) and conjugation (*ṣarf*), Qurʾānic recitation (*qirāʾah*), Qurʾānic exegesis (*tafsīr*), theology (*tawḥīd*), jurisprudence (*fiqh*), ethics (*akhlāq*), logic (*manṭiq*), history (*tārīkh*), and mysticism (*taṣawwuf*). Instruction was given in Javanese and other local languages. The *weton* or *ḥalqah* system, in which students sat in a semicircle before a seated scholar, who called on them in turn for recitation, was the norm. After Indonesia won independence, the educational system underwent a rapid expansion, as the Dutch had provided education only to a tiny minority. Trained citizens were considered a necessity to the new nation and efforts to produce such citizens intensified during the development-oriented Suharto regime. Only students who followed a curriculum focusing on general subjects could obtain a state-recognized certificate enabling them to attend a university. Many Indonesians sought an education that would lead to a job in the civil service or the rapidly expanding private sector. In this context, a purely religious education constituted an obstacle to both societal and personal goals. *Pesantren* traditionally had not given any form of diploma to their graduates and they risked becoming less attractive to prospective students. Subsequently, many *pesantren* modified their curriculum to include training in nonreligious subjects. More conservative schools retaining a primarily religious curriculum, called *salafiyah pesantren*, are at a disadvantage, as their graduates are often unable to go on to further study in the state educational system, where they would be trained in skills that are marketable in wider society.

Although there is an outside perception that *pesantren* are a hotbed of radical ideas and perhaps even a breeding ground of terrorism, this is not the reality. Some perpetrators of the 2003 Bali bombing were associated with a *pesantren* located near Yogyakarta, but this is a rare case. Of the some fourteen thousand *pesantren* in Java, perhaps fifty have radical leanings and many of these were founded in opposition to the politically moderate norm prevailing in most *pesantren*.

Women and *Pesantren*. *Pesantren* rarely accepted female students until the 1950s, when male Islamic leaders concluded that young women could receive an education in a safe, disciplined environment. The experience was not originally intended to empower women, or encourage involvement in the social or political arena. To some extent, the curriculum taught to women *pesantren* students reflected the preconceptions of male religious educators. Although women were taught using the same traditional texts, it was assumed that they would not be able to cover as much material as men and that their training would primarily prepare them for the roles of wife and mother. Recently, female enrollment has grown dramatically and their time at *pesantren* is often regarded as preparation for a higher education in Islamic subjects. Some surveys show that close to 50 percent of current *pesantren* students are women. Although not all *pesantren* accept women, at some, the women outnumber the male students. Classes and dorms remain segregated.

In general, female *pesantren* students do not see any conflict between aspirations for a career or community service and expected domestic responsibilities. For example, some become involved in NGOs such as the Perhimpunan Pengembangan Pesantren dan Masyrakat (P3M, the Center for the Development of Pesantren and Society), an organization that applies *fiqh* to modern situations to make *pesantren* relevant to society's development. To this end, workshops tackle such issues as reproductive rights and domestic violence. Similarly, many individual graduates do outreach work in their communities, counseling women on their rights when confronted by spousal abuse. Many female students hope to go on to teach, either in the state schools or universities, or perhaps in a *pesantren*.

Although, in recent decades, women have made inroads in teaching at *pesantren*, most teachers are still male. A few women have established their own *pesantren* for female students, although these schools tend to rely on the sponsorship of husbands or fathers. At many *pesantren*, the wife or other female relatives of a *kiai* have overall responsibility for female students and take the title of *nyai*. Women teachers are generally only allowed to teach female students. If a *nyai* operates her own *pesantren*, she usually finds it financially difficult as she seldom has access to the endowments and donations typically available to her male colleagues. Female *pesantren* teachers must be deeply religious and highly motivated individuals in order to overcome the skepticism that tends to discourage female participation in the public sphere.

Interpreting Traditional Texts. As an institution, the *pesantren* is closely linked to Nahdlatul Ulama (NU), an important player in civil society and politics that is seen as the protector of traditionalist Islam in Indonesia. Although NU promotes a conservative outlook, it has proven tolerant of local practices, such as visiting gravesites of local holy men in order to receive their blessing and has been accommodating toward religious pluralism and political liberalism. The movement's main goal is training religious scholars, who are expected to make an impact in their communities. Since the 1970s, *pesantren* curriculum has been revised to achieve this goal. Many of the classical texts taught at *pesantren*, often written centuries ago in the Middle East, exhibit a marked patriarchal and, in some cases, misogynist perspective. The *Kitb Syarh 'Uqud Al-Lujain fi Bayan Huquq Al-Zaujain* (Notes on the Mutual Responsibility Concerning the Clarification of the Rights of Spouses [or *Kitb Syarh*]), written in the nineteenth century in Mecca and long influential in the world of NU *pesantren*, sees a female role of total subservience to men as sanctioned by Islam. The text informs women that they are to accept even abuse without complaint and that they are worth intrinsically less than men. Such views are still accepted uncritically and even promoted by some male NU members. However, by allowing female *pesantren* students to study and critique these texts, the NU has opened space for them to challenge the patriarchal order, while remaining faithful to the essence of community traditions.

A notable example of this process was the reinterpretation by the NU scholars of the P3M, both male and female, of the *Kitb Syarh*; they found that many of the ḥadīth (traditions) used to justify its positions were weak or even falsely reported. Also, it was acknowledged that institutions that had once been socially acceptable (such as slavery) and thus condoned by religion might later be condemned. Consequently, texts promoting female subservience also need reevaluation. In addition, classical texts have been examined to produce more progressive interpretation, still grounded in traditional values, on issues like contraception. Women working within the *pesantren* world have gained power and status from their firm knowledge of the classical Islamic tradition and in many cases have used this position to foster female empowerment within their sometimes conservative communities.

[*See also* Madrasah.]

BIBLIOGRAPHY

Dhofier, Zamarkhsyari. *The Pesantren Tradition: The Role of the Kiai in the Maintenance of Traditional Islam in Java*. Tempe: Monograph Series Press, Program for Southeast Asian Studies, Arizona State University, 1999.

Sciortino, Rosalia, Lies Marcoes Natsir, and Masdar F. Mas'udi. "Learning from Islam: Advocacy of Reproductive Rights in Indonesian Pesantren." *Reproductive Health Matters* 4, no. 8 (November 1996): 86–96.

Srimulyani, Eka. "Muslim Women and Education in Indonesia: The *pondok pesantren* Experience." *Asia Pacific Journal of Education* 27, no. 1 (March 2007): 85–99.
Van Doorn-Harder, Pieternella. *Women Shaping Islam: Reading the Qur'an in Indonesia*. Chicago: University of Illinois Press, 2006.

MICHAEL WOOD

PHILANTHROPY AND WOMEN, CONTEMPORARY AND HISTORICAL. Philanthropy, literally meaning "love of mankind" is commonly used as a synonym for charity. It refers to private initiatives for public good, focusing on the improvement of human wellbeing and welfare. It is manifested in a wide range of practices, including individual-to-individual giving for immediate assistance to institutional giving through endowments allocated for socially useful purposes. The form and content of philanthropy vary over time and space.

Almost every religion has a philanthropic component. Islam gives vital importance to philanthropy by presenting it as a form of worship, a tool for self-purification, and a source of social security. Three major forms of philanthropy in Islam are *zakāt* (charitable wealth tax), *ṣadaqah* (voluntary charity), and *waqf* (permanent endowment or Islamic charitable foundation). As stated in both the Qur'ān and ḥadīth, *zakāt* is one of the five pillars of the Islamic faith, which obliges Muslims to give a fixed portion of their wealth to the poor and needy. *Ṣadaqah*, as mentioned in the ḥadīth, is a voluntary act of giving alms for the cause of God. A common practice in Islamic civilization, although not stated in the Qur'ān, a *waqf* (Islamic charitable foundation) is the creation of charity organizations by individuals, families, or institutions. These organizations often have income-producing activities attached to them. *Awqāf* may endow mosques, hospital, clinics, schools, baths, and other institutions serving the public good. Historical and current philanthropic acts of Muslims mainly fall into one of these religiously based charity types.

Muslims prefer to give their charity secretly and directly to the person in need, mainly relatives and neighbors. According to Islamic texts, those deemed deserving of giving include invalids, elderly individuals, single women, and mothers with small children. Muslim men are supposed to provide the obligatory support of dependents, including orphans, widows, and divorced women.

Although the study of charity, philanthropy, and poverty has, in the last decades, become a growing field of Islamic social history, there has been a scarcity of studies addressing women's philanthropy.

Historical Muslim Women's Philanthropy. Historically, women are often considered as beneficiaries of philanthropy, despite the fact that they become involved in philanthropy as donors and volunteers/social entrepreneurs as well. According to Islamic law, Muslim women can be property owners because they are given a dower by husbands and shares of the estates of deceased kin and engage in trade activities. Thus, they have access to economic and social power, making their participation in philanthropic activities possible. Since the early days of Islam, Muslim women's traditional philanthropic activities have involved caring for the poor, widows, and orphans; assisting marriages monetarily; freeing slaves; endowing religious foundations; donating sums to the establishment of mosques, religious schools, fountains, and soup kitchens; and undertaking other forms of charity. Women also play substantial roles in service provision of philanthropic organizations.

The first well-known woman Muslim philanthropist is the first Muslim, Khadīja, the wife of Prophet Muḥammad. She was a wealthy businesswoman and trader who supported the Prophet not only morally but also financially in his efforts to deliver the message of Islam. She fed and clothed the poor, assisted her relatives financially, and helped those who had no means to marry. It was noted that she gave away all of her wealth in the name of charity.

Another prominent Muslim female philanthropic figure is Queen Zubayda, wife of the ninth-century Caliph Harun Al-Rashid of the ʿAbbasid dynasty. She built a water system in Mecca and created a path from Baghdad to Mecca, including building up walls that provided shelter for travelers, mosques, and hostels along the way to make it easier to travel to Hajj In the same century, Fatima al-Fihriyya emerged as a female philanthropist in Fez, Morocco. She used the inheritance from her business father to build Al-Qarawwiyyin Mosque in 859 CE, one of the largest mosques and the oldest academic degree granting university in Africa. The eleventh century saw Banafshaaʾ al-Rumiyya, who restored schools, bridges, and public housing for homeless women in Baghdad. She also had a school endowment.

Between the fifteenth and seventeenth centuries, Ottoman women, particularly women from the imperial family and upper class, became involved in philanthropic activities. They established endowments to build mosques and public fountains. For example, Hafsa Sultan, the mother of Sultan Suleyman (1494–1566), founded the mosque complex with its college, soup kitchen, and hospital in Manisa, a city located in Western Anatolia. Bezmi Alem Valide Sultan, the wife of Mahmut II (1789–1839), is also known for her extensive charities. She established a hospital, mosque, and school complex in Istanbul, capital of the Ottoman Empire. In general, wives and mothers of the imperial household took initiatives to establish endowments of great importance. Such initiatives of imperial women were considered a tangible expression of the ruler's benevolence toward the empire's subjects. It served to broadcast not only their personal piety and generosity, but that of the whole dynasty as well.

In the early twentieth century, Muslim women created organizations to carry on philanthropic activities in a more organized fashion. Some of these organizations became visible in the late Ottoman Empire. Two prominent organizations were *Osmanlı Kadınları Sefkat Cemiyet-i Hayriyyesi* and *Cemiyet-i Hayriyye-yi Nisvaniyye*. While the former were concerned with helping poor women and orphaned girls, the latter focused on improving women's educational facilities in Istanbul and Salonika. These organizations became necessary as both government and religious foundations had failed to provide basic services because of the ongoing World War I and had not been interested in providing services for women's education, such as women's schooling. Women became more visible as activists and innovators in organizations, giving support in the newly established Muslim nation-states such as Turkey and Egypt. In Turkey, the Children's Protection Society and the Turkish Red Crescent were established. One of the earlier organizations in Egypt is the New Woman Organization founded in 1919 by a group of upper-class women. It provided care services for poor women and children, organized workshops for girls in poor areas to produce carpets using modern equipment, and worked for advocating women's education.

Historically, the main feature of women's public charity was the usage of Muslim means. Women often aimed at helping less fortunate women such as orphans, paupers, prisoners, and prostitutes, in addition to female family members and retainers, in need. Charities targeting individuals and endowments transformed into women's philanthropic organizations by broadening the scope of their activities. Women asserted the prerogative of claiming and organizing the sector of public life for the welfare of the public and women.

Contemporary Muslim Women's Philanthropy. Muslim philanthropy has attracted growing public attention since September 11 because of the supposed link between charity and extremist violence as portrayed in the media. Thus, the number of studies addressing Islam and philanthropy has been on the rise. It has been observed that nongovernmental organizations (NGOs) have become important avenues for philanthropic acts of Muslims. NGOs are concerned with a wide range of philanthropy-related issues, including poverty alleviation, education, and care for women and children. However, NGOs in the Muslim world remain weak and diffuse compared to those in Western countries. Although women are among the primary supporters of the philanthropic sector in many Muslim countries, their contribution has been rarely studied in academic research.

The philanthropy sector is very attractive to Muslim women. There are many women-only organizations, along with mixed-gender organizations. It is important to identify some main features of philanthropic women's NGOs.

1. Although some organizations are autonomous, some of them have an auxiliary role to the government or donors. In some cases, women NGOs integrate themselves into a male-dominated religious body/movement, as occurred in the Muslim Brotherhood in Egypt and Refah Party in Turkey.
2. Most of the organizations are established by upper- and middle-class women. In addition to funds directly provided by wealthy women, women generate innovative fund-raising methods for providing income. But women's organizations are still undercapitalized, particularly in terms of endowment funds, compared to organizations run by men.
3. Although the older organizations did not have specialization of services, now there has been the tendency toward increasing specialization. Although some of them concentrate on meeting the daily needs and demands of poor women and families, others provide training to women to have access to different professions. Their services involve a mixture of philanthropy, social work, and advocacy.
4. Women's involvement in the philanthropic field is often tolerated in countries where women have limited access to the public sphere, as in oil-rich Muslim countries. For both Muslim men and women, philanthropic organizations are legitimate spaces for social interaction outside the walls of women's own homes because they fit into the desired image of a Muslim woman as responsible for her family and household.
5. Although it is difficult to measure the impact of involvement of philanthropic activities on women's empowerment, it is found that it brings women feelings of self-satisfaction, self-confidence, happiness, and meaning in life. It also provides opportunities to build networks and gain new skills, as well as to acquire social, cultural, and symbolic capital. For some women, philanthropy can also act as a channel for raising social status and a stepping-stone for a professional career. It can create opportunities for women who had limited access to the formal labor sector to work as service workers and to be involved in economic projects. Nora Derbal (2011) argues that women involved in philanthropic NGOs can build parallel power structures outside of the male-dominated areas, such as politics and business, as well as homes in the Saudi Arabian case. Creating new power structures may enable women to gain political power and advocate for obtaining legal rights and recognition.

Some contemporary examples of philanthropic activities conducted by Muslim women individually or organizationally include humanitarian efforts by Sheikha Al Mayassa Bint Hamad Bin Khalifa Al-Thani in Qatar, who has worked with Qatar's Red Crescent organization to raise money for clothing and school equipment for the children of Iraq in 2003. Since 2005, she has served as the chair of the Qatar Foundation's "Reach Out to Asia" initiative aiming to provide those in need with quality education. It operates in ten countries across Asia.

In Saudi Arabia, women are usually denied access to involvement in the activities of social welfare agencies funded by the government and male donors because of the strict gender segregation in public places. Nevertheless, Saudi women have pioneered the establishment of the civil society organizations (philanthropic societies) throughout the country since 1962. At present, of 872 civil society organizations in Saudia Arabia, 30 are women's philanthropic societies. These organizations help mainly poor families and Saudi women by providing services in caring of children, the elderly, people with special needs; services in adult education, training, and rehabilitation; and health care. Philanthropic organizations provide Saudi women free action space.

In Egypt, religion has been a primary factor in the birth and development of women's philanthropy since the nineteenth century. Egyptian women's voluntary organizations established schools and training centers to enable poor women to have access to certain professions (sewing, nursing, producing carpets). Women's philanthropic organizations have pursued a mix of social welfare activities and advocacy. Thus, there has been a close relationship between women's voluntary organizations and the Egyptian women's movement that were both greatly influenced by the Egyptian state.

In Turkey, one of the oldest and the biggest women's philanthropic foundations is the Philanthropist Foundation, which has been active since 1928. It established dormitories, schools, centers for blood donation, health centers, classes for disabled students, and a home for aged people. Since the 1990s, women's philanthropic organizations have directed their resources to creating social development projects in collaboration with international organizations, including the United Nations, European Union, and the Global Fund for Women. Priority issues include education, reproductive health, and violence against women. Family foundations are also influential in the philanthropic sector of Turkey. They establish schools, universities, sports facilities, libraries, dormitories, and orphanages. One of the most well known is the Sabanci Foundation led by Guler Sabancı, a successful businesswoman. Women's foundations also contribute to promoting and protecting the human rights of women and girls in Turkey.

Muslim women living in Western Europe and North America tend to concentrate on helping poor Muslims living in their home countries and Muslims in conflict regions, as well as those living in regions where natural disasters occur. Female Muslim philanthropists are engaged with the activities of relief, aid and charity organizations, as observed in the Islamic Relief and Asian Relief based in the United States. The aim is often to meet immediate needs and rebuild their lives, families, and communities. Muslim women also become involved in activities of aid-development organizations, as in the U.K.-based Muslim Aid and U.S.-based Muslim Women's Giving Circle, Muslim Women's Alliance, and the Muslim Women's Fund. These organizations contribute to the elimination of poverty by focusing on issues including education, skills training, provision of clean water, health care, and income generation projects.

Bibliography

Afif, Suad. "Voluntary Work in Civil Society: Saudi Women Volunteers as a Social Capital." Paper presented at the Ninth International Conference of the International Society for Third Sector Research, Kadir Has University, Istanbul, Turkey, July 7–10, 2010.

Ali Rida, Najla. "Field of Volunteering Services in Philanthropic Societies." Paper presented at the First Forum for Philanthropic Societies: Hopes and Expectations." Paper no. 23, Workshop for Social Services in Societies, King Khaled Foundation, Riyadh, Saudi Arabia, 2003.
Benthall, Jonathan, and Bellion-Jourdan Jerome. *Charitable Crescent: Politics of Aid in the Muslim World.* London: I. B. Tauris. 2009.
Bonner, Michael, Mine Ener, and Amy Singer. *Poverty and Charity in Middle Eastern Contexts.* New York: State University of New York Press, 2003.
Clark, Janine. *Islam, Charity, and Activism: Middle Class Networks and Social Welfare in Egypt, Jordan and Yemen.* Bloomington: Indiana University Press, 2004.
Derbal Nora. "Philanthropy in Jeddah, Saudi Arabia Lifestyle and Liberty in Name of Piety and Islam." In *The First Annual Conference on Arab Philanthropy and Civic Engagement. Selected Research, Amman, Jordan, April 16–17, 2011.* Cairo: The American University in Cairo Press.
Ibrahim, Barbara, and Sherif, Dina H. *From Charity to Social Change: Trends in Arab Philanthropy.* Cairo: The American University in Cairo Press, 2008.
Kandil, Amani. "Women and Philanthropy in Egypt," In *Women, Philanthropy, and Civil Society*, edited by Kathleen D. McCarthy, pp. 191–225. Bloomington: Indiana University Press, 2001.
Karakaya-Stump, Ayfer. "Debating Progress in a 'Serious Newspaper for Muslim Women': The Periodical *Kadın* of the Post-revolutionary Salonica, 1908–1909." *British Journal of Middle Eastern Studies* 30, no. 2 (2003): 155–181.
Konyalı, Ibrahim Hakki Konyalı. "Kanun î Sultan Süleyman'ın Annesi Hafsa Sultan'ın Vakfiyesi ve Manisa'daki Hayir Eserleri." *Vakıflar Dergisi* 8 (1969): 47–56.
Mosaic: Recognizing Extraordinary Muslim Women. http://mosaicofmuslimwomen.wordpress.com/2011/12/19/then-queen-zubaida-bint-jafar-al-mansour/.
Pierce, Leslie. 1993. *The Imperial Harem: Women and Sovereignty in the Ottoman Empire.* New York: Oxford University Press, 1993.
"Reachout Asia." http://www.reachouttoasia.org/en/aboutus.
Sabra, Adam Abdelhamid. *Poverty and Charity in Medieval Islam: Mamluk Egypt, 1250–1517.* Cambridge, U.K.: Cambridge University Press, 2006.
Singer, Amy. *Charity in Islamic Societies.* Cambridge, U.K.: Cambridge University Press, 2008.

Zeynep Şahin-Mencütek

Philippines. Philippine Muslim women are active participants in the local and global discourses and activities on the promotion and maintenance of women's rights. Individually or through various organizations, they have subverted traditional narratives on Philippine Muslim women, which present females primarily as wives, mothers, homemakers, and caregivers. In such narratives, although protected and esteemed, they are perceived as subordinate to males, who are portrayed as fathers, economic providers and heads of households, and participants and guardians of social, political, economic, and religious institutions. These narratives reflect the lived realities of Philippine Muslims, in which interpretations of Islam and customs restrict women's roles in society.

There have been Muslim women who held formal positions of leadership or exercised power informally through family networks. Site Cabil, also known as Sultana Nur al Azam, governed as sultana for several years in Sulu in the 1800s. Inok, the wife of Datu Piang (1846–1933), who took over her husband's role in the anticolonial struggle, was appointed by the American colonial government as municipal president in Buluan, Cotabato, from 1909 to 1913. Tarhata Kiram (1904–1979) and Dayang Dayang Hadji Piandao (1884–1946), though they did not hold formal positions of power in the Sulu sultanate, continued to exert their influence in the predominantly male political circles in Sulu until they died.

The first recorded Muslim women's group in the Philippines was organized by Tarhata Kiram in Sulu during the American period (1898–1946). This organization became part of the National

Federation of Women's Clubs, which was involved in projects like lobbying for women's inclusion in provincial and municipal boards of education and the campaign for suffrage, a thirty-year effort culminating in a constitutional amendment granting women the right to vote.

After World War II, an increasing number of Muslim women pursued university education and professional careers. In politics, Tarhata Alonto Lucman was elected governor of Lanao del Sur in 1971, and Santanina Rasul became the first Muslim woman senator in 1987, after serving in various capacities in the local government of Sulu. Her Magbassa Kita Foundation, which initially focused on adult literacy programs, has now expanded to include skill-training programs, microfinancing, and peace advocacy. In 2001 two Muslim women were elected to the House of Representatives, Soraya Jaafar of Tawi Tawi and Faysah Maniri Racman-Pimping Dumarpa of the first district of Lanao del Sur. Others have been elected to provincial and local levels of government.

Muslim women have also increased their participation in the field of education. Muslim women educators include Bai Matabay Namli Plang, who founded the Mindanao Institute of Technology (now the University of Southern Mindanao); Emily Marahomsar, the former president of Mindanao State University; Carmen Abubakar, the former dean of the Institute of Islamic Studies at the University of the Philippines; and Luningning Mizuareh-Umar, the former president of Basilan State College and commissioner of the Commission on Higher Education of the Philippines.

Political and economic developments in the Philippines in the late 1960s and the declaration of martial law in 1972 opened up other areas of women's involvement in the public sphere. One of the reasons for the declaration of martial law by President Ferdinand Marcos was the rebellion launched by the Moro National Liberation Front (MNLF) in the southern Philippines in 1969. Although the leadership of the front consisted of male Moros (ethnic Muslims in the southern Philippines), the membership included women, whose range of activities included intelligence, propaganda, support for the fighters, and, for some, actual involvement in armed conflict. When the MNLF and the Philippine government negotiated for a solution to the conflict, women were not involved in the formal process, but the Women's Committee fulfilled critical tasks behind the scenes.

The war generated other issues, such as internal displacement of peoples, disruption of education, increased poverty, and peace and security. These problems motivated MNLF women like Eleanora Roida Tan, Tarhata Maglangit, and Hadja Bainon Caron, who were members of the MNLF Women's Committee, to start nongovernment organizations that include programs for livelihood-skill training, education, and empowerment of women.

In the 1970s women's issues gained global attention when the United Nations launched initiatives on women's rights and the protection of women against discrimination. The United Nation's gender agenda includes topics like human trafficking, prostitution, and labor migration, but it is on the issues of the feminization of poverty and gender rights that Muslim activists and groups tend to focus. In response to these issues, Muslim women activists and groups have created their own feminism, which affirms the different contexts and experiences of these issues for Philippine Muslim women. In 1975 Zorayda Tamano organized the Philippine Muslim Women Association to foster unity and empower Muslim women representing various tribes in the southern Philippines. It is affiliated with such national women's organizations as the National Council of Women of the Philippines. Yasmin Busran Lao, founder of the Al Mujadilah Development Foundation (inspired by chapter 58 of the Qurʾān), and Raissa Jajurie of the Nisa ul-Haqq fi Bangsamoro (Women for Justice in the Bangsa Moro), organized seminars to raise awareness, and promote the provisions, of the Convention on the Elimination of all Forms of Discrimination against Women (CEDAW), adopted by the United Nations in 1979 and enforced in the Philippines since 1981. As Muslims have historically experienced discrimination in the country, knowing the CEDAW provisions is particularly important, although the task is complicated by perceptions of incongruity among some CEDAW provisions, interpretations of the Qurʾān, and local customs. Most Philippine Muslim women do not know their rights under the Code of Muslim Personal Laws, which was promulgated in the country in 1976, so Al Mujadilah is engaged in popularizing the code and examining which provisions need to be changed to ensure gender equity. Also working for women's rights, as well as promoting democracy, is Amina Rasul, who established the Philippine Center for Islam and Democracy.

Interpreting the Qurʾān is the domain of male religious leaders, but there is now an organization of women religious scholars, Aleemat, headed by Khadija Mutilan, who graduated from Al-Azhar University. She and Albaya Barodin are members of the National Ulama Conference of the Philippines, which was organized under the auspices of the Philippine Center for Islam and Democracy in 2009.

Although Philippine Muslim women leaders are involved in transnational organizing and they participate in international women's conferences on women's issues, it is the Muslim women masses who form the strength of the Philippine Muslim women's movement, as they participate locally in the programs and activities, and contribute to the definition of what it means to be a Philippine Muslim woman in the twenty-first century.

[*See also* Convention on the Elimination of All Forms of Discrimination against Women (CEDAW); Rasul-Bernardo, Amina; *and* Southeast Asia and the Pacific.]

BIBLIOGRAPHY

Angeles, Vivienne SM. "Philippine Muslim Women: Tradition and Change." In *Islam, Gender, and Social Change*, edited by Yvonne Haddad and John Esposito, pp. 209–234. New York: Oxford University Press, 1998.

Bragado, Erlinda, ed. *Filipinas in Dialogue: Muslim-Christian Women's Response to Contemporary Challenges*. Manila: Dela Salle University Press, 1995.

Code of Muslim Personal Laws of the Philippines. Manila: Ministry of Muslim Affairs, 1981.

Lacar, Luis Q. "Philippine Muslim Women: Their Emerging Role in a Rapidly Changing Society." In *Mindanao: Land of Unfulfilled Promise*, edited by Mark Turner and Lulu Turner, pp. 109–125. Quezon City: New Day Publishers, 1992.

VIVIENNE SM. ANGELES

PLURALISM. A pluralistic approach to religious diversity is central to the Qurʾānic message (28:46 and 4:163–164). Muslim scholars of diverse orientations have advocated a pluralism that affirms principles of freedom, difference, and co-existence, based on interpretations of Qurʾānic teachings regarding the equality of all people. Their starting point is the Qurʾān's statement that God deliberately created humanity to consist of different nations, ethnicities, tribes, and languages (30:22 and 48:13). This assertion is bolstered by 2:251, which states that God created difference in order to foster competition between nations and to guarantee progress. Qurʾānic passages regarding the plurality of civilizations, systems, and laws (5:48 and 5:69) are interpreted as encouraging people to understand one another better and co-exist, rather than engage in conflict. Moderate Islamists also assert that God created the Muslim community as a "middle community" (*ummah wasaṭ*) as a reflection of His favor for moderation and desire to avoid extremes, so that seeking the negation or eradication of the religious Other is not permitted. Discussions of pluralism have branched out into debates about not only the possibility of normal relations between Islamic and non-Islamic states, but also the toleration of political and religious differences within an Islamic state, the creation of opportunities for religious minorities, and assurance of gender equality and public roles for women within an Islamic state.

For example, the Egyptian scholar Fathi Osman has pointed to the Qur'ānic title of "Children of Adam" (17:70) given to all people as a sign that God confers honor and dignity on all of humanity. This must be assured through guarantees of freedom of faith, opinion, and expression for all people (2:256 and 2:282). He also asserts that 30:22 and 49:13 recognize ethnic and racial pluralism, which he interprets as a call for cooperation among different races, ethnicities, and social ranks. Because "every human being has his or her spiritual compass and has been granted dignity by God" (7:172–173), he contends that scripture supports the development of universal relations and global pluralism, including not only Jews and Christians, but also Hindus, Buddhists, Taoists, and people of other faiths (Osman, 1996, p. 65). This is a task to be carried out without gender distinction.

Similarly, the Indonesian scholar Nurcholish Madjid (1996, 2003) argued that salvation is available to all who submit to the will of God, including the "people of the book" who share a common tie to both monotheism and divine revelation, regardless of gender. 2:62 simply states that "those who believe—the Jews, the Christians, and the Sabaeans—whosoever believe in God and the Last Day and do good works, they shall have their reward from their Lord and shall have nothing to fear, nor shall they come to grief." According to this verse, salvation depends on "faithfulness to God and the Day of Judgment and the carrying out of good deeds," not on "factors of descent." This verse is not specific to men. Madjid taught that, because Islam recognizes that true faith can exist in forms other than Islam, the critical issue of faith is whether a person is sincere in his or her faith and engages in righteous conduct, not whether he or she believes in the prophecy of Muḥammad.

Some scholars have focused on the social justice dimension of pluralism to address gender justice. The South African scholar and anti-apartheid activist Farid Esack (1997) has focused on the divine command to Muslims to be just, honest, and charitable, and to fight oppression of the poor and powerless, as highlighting God's concern for cooperation based on social ethics and social justice, rather than on differences in beliefs. Esack has defined religious pluralism as the creation of an environment in which everyone is safe and free to be human and to serve God. He calls for a consistent application of morality that asserts the right of every human being to experience justice and be free from oppression, tyranny, and conflict. Esack's vision of religious and social pluralism embraces all marginalized groups. More than a matter of tolerating or co-existing with the Other, this vision calls for valuing and being enriched by the Other without establishing boundaries, whether legal or ritual. The goal is to free people from injustice and servitude to other human beings so that they are free to worship God. Esack assigns a special role to Muslim intellectuals in this struggle, encouraging them to set aside arguments about how to sight the moon or slaughter a cow correctly in favor of working on important issues, such as fighting tribalism, gender discrimination, and racism within the Muslim community. This vision of pluralism is more than functional or utilitarian; it embraces the theological legitimacy of other faiths based on the Qur'ānic proclamation of the single brotherhood of all people.

American scholar Abdulaziz Sachedina (2007) believes that the essential message of the Qur'ān is the unity of humanity as evidenced by the common origins of all human beings and their right to God's mercy and forgiveness. Qur'ān 2:213 states that humanity is a single community that God has the power to unite, making religious pluralism a necessary corollary to the diversity that characterizes human existence on earth. Thus, he concludes, although differences between religious traditions and the specifics of worship exist, greater attention should be given to the common human experiences of God, including judgment on Judgment Day, the requirement to be moral citizens, and the need to acknowledge God as the Creator of all of humanity. According to Sachedina's construct, the desired outcome of religious pluralism is the creation of an ethical public order that requires human beings to live and work together for justice and peace for the entire world. Broad human acceptance of this order would be possible because every person possesses *fiṭrah*, or a primordial nature that allows each person to deal with others in fairness and equity. Sachedina believes that this moral ability should lead to the development of a global ethic of pluralism that embraces understanding and active engagement with the religious Other. Nowhere does he suggest that this process should be exclusive to men.

Muslim women's engagement in debates about pluralism has been limited to date, although many women are active in interfaith dialogue, particularly with Christians and Jews, with special attention given to building relationships between people of different faith traditions.

BIBLIOGRAPHY

Esack, Farid. *Qur'an, Liberation & Pluralism: An Islamic Perspective of Interreligious Solidarity Against Oppression*. Oxford: Oneworld, 1997.

Esposito, John L. *The Future of Islam*. New York and Oxford: Oxford University Press, 2010.

Madjid, Nurcholish. "In Search of Islamic Roots for Modern Pluralism: The Indonesian Experience." In *Toward a New Paradigm: Recent Developments in Indonesian Islamic Thought*, edited by Mark R. Woodward, pp. 89–116. Tempe: Arizona State University, Program for Southeast Asian Studies, 1996.

Madjid, Nurcholish. "Islamic Faith and the Problem of Pluralism: Relations Among the Believers." In *The True Face of Islam: Essays on Islam and Modernity in Indonesia*, by Nurcholish Madjid. Ciputat: Voice Center Indonesia, 2003.

Osman, Mohamed Fathi. *The Children of Adam: An Islamic Perspective on Pluralism*. Washington, D.C.: Center for Muslim-Christian Understanding, Georgetown University, 1996.

Sachedina, Abdulaziz. *The Islamic Roots of Democratic Pluralism*. New York and Oxford: Oxford University Press, 2007.

Smith, Jane I. *Muslims, Christians, and the Challenge of Interfaith Dialogue*. New York and Oxford: Oxford University Press, 2007.

JOHN L. ESPOSITO

POLITICAL ACTIVISM, WOMEN'S.

[*This entry contains two subentries:*

Historical Discourse *and*
Contemporary Discourse.]

HISTORICAL DISCOURSE

Muslim women's political activism spans the globe and encompasses numerous individual and collective efforts. For centuries, Muslim women have interpreted scriptures and *aḥādīth* in ways that they found to be the most representative of men's and women's roles as discussed by the Prophet and in the Qur'ān. For example, in 1909, Malak Hifni Nasif, an Egyptian, published *al-Nisa'iyyat* (Feminist Pieces), a book of essays on women's rights in relation to Islam.

Beginning in the late 1800s and early 1900s, like their counterparts elsewhere around the globe, Muslim women began rallying for political enfranchisement. Ottoman women's efforts for enfranchisement began in the late 1800s, and Turkish women were enfranchised in the early 1930s. Syrian women became enfranchised in 1949, Egyptian women in 1957, Kuwaiti women in 2006, and Saudi women are set to become enfranchised in 2015.

Much of Muslim women's political activism has focused on trying to change personal status laws. For example, in Egypt, the debate concerning reforms to personal status law centered on *khulʿ*, a type of divorce that, since reforms in 2000, can be initiated by a woman but does not require consent from the husband. Reforms to laws governing *khulʿ* accompanied a new form of marriage contract that allowed women to make stipulations regarding their dowries, rights, and grounds for divorce. Changes to Morocco's personal status law in 2004 were the result of a lengthy, calculated effort by many women's groups to attract the king's support. The changes incorporated language that states that men and women are equal before the law and that women are human beings rather than dependents. Furthermore, guardianship rights were set, forcible marriage was outlawed, the minimum age for marriage was increased to eighteen, polygyny was highly restricted, divorce was made a right for both men and women, and property was recognized to be that of both spouses.

Iran's personal status laws were first codified in the early 1930s under Reza Shah Pavlavi as part of his modernization reforms. Reza Shah adopted European codes in most areas of law, but family law was left almost entirely unaltered. Mohammad Reza Shah initiated rights in the 1960s that gave men and women equal access to divorce and child custody rights; such initiatives were supported by women's rights activists and journals. After the 1979 revolution, Ayatollah Khomeini almost instantaneously instigated a return to Sharīʿah (Islamic) law. Women gradually organized and lobbied for changes to the law in the 1980s and 1990s. Under President Khatami, the Parliament initiated thirty-three bills to address gender-based discrimination. However, the Guardian Council used its veto power or substantially rewrote each of the bills. Mahmoud Ahmadinejad's election and rule has only served to radicalize women's desire for change in Iranian law and society.

The other large focus of women's activism has been efforts to secure access to education. Many scholars of Islam have adamantly argued that Islam guarantees equal access to religious, theoretical, and technical education for men and women. Such scholars and activists argue that it is governments who have unjustly prohibited women from attending school and justified the prohibition based on incorrect interpretations of Islam. Despite this, United Nations Development Program statistics regarding adult populations demonstrate that, in most Arab states and Muslim majority countries, women are systematically excluded from education or parts of the education process and that women are illiterate at significantly higher rates than men. The reasons given for excluding women from the educational process are many, but two predominant ones are that women are the bearers of culture and family, and, if they are educated, they will cease to want to be mothers, thus signifying the end of culture and kinship, and the idea that education for a woman is not ideal, because a girl who is educated will be difficult to marry off. Nevertheless, attitudes are starting to change in some places, notably the Arab Gulf countries, as educated girls, particularly those who are employed, are considered more desirable marriage partners. Furthermore, many Arab and Muslim cultures are apprehensive about the genders mixing, and the education of girls thus requires coeducational classrooms, costly extra schools, and, generally, mothers appearing in public more often in order to take their female children to school and back. In some countries, including Afghanistan, Yemen, Iraq, and Turkey, families' (particularly those in rural areas) concerns include a lack of female teachers and poverty, as poor families will typically choose to send sons to school in order for them to acquire the skills necessary to find employment, while keeping their daughters at home to tend to the house, grow crops, and produce handicrafts.

Muslim women around the world have worked to overturn laws and cultural norms that prevent them from obtaining an education. In the late 1800s and early 1900s, elite Ottoman women lobbied the government to allow them to attend university classes, a right that was acknowledged in the 1910s. Beginning in the 1920s and 1930s, modern Turkey and Iran both mandated young girls attend school. In Saudi Arabia, where education is typically gender segregated, girls have staged protests over the unequal facilities, resources, and treatment of girls and boys. Owing to the Taliban's interpretation of Islam, Afghani girls were banned from attending schools for several years in the 1990s, despite women in 1970s Afghanistan having attended school regularly. Organizations such as the United Nations build schools for girls and try to keep them operational, despite attacks aimed at school-attending girls and their families. Women justify their desire for education based on several interlocking tenets, including that Islam guarantees men and women have equal access to education, that educated women make better mothers, that education helps women to better serve God, and that education allows women to earn money to help support their families.

Women across Muslim countries have coordinated and compared their political activism through the help of nongovernmental organizations (NGOs). Two of the most prominent of these organizations are Women Living Under Muslim Laws, founded in 1984, and the International Muslim Women's Union, founded in 1996. Muslim women have also joined global causes outside the feminist agenda. Muslim women can be found in NGOs working for humanitarian, environmental, interfaith, and peace causes. With rising educational levels, professional Muslim women can also be found in different executive positions in international organizations.

Bibliography

Al-Atraqchi, Leila. *The Women's Movement and the Mobilization for Legal Change in Egypt: A Century of Personal Status Law Reform*. Unpublished Ph.D. dissertation, Concordia University, 2003.

Mir-Hosseini, Ziba. "How the Door of *Ijtihad* Was Opened and Closed: A Comparative Analysis of Recent Family Law Reforms in Iran and Morocco." *Washington and Lee Legal Review* 64 (2007): 1499–1511.

Women Living Under Muslim Laws. http://www.wluml.org.

Zvan-Elliott, Katja. "Reforming the Moroccan Personal Status Code: A Revolution for Whom?" *Mediterranean Politics* 14, no. 2 (July 2009): 213–227.

Sarah Fischer

Contemporary Discourse

Though stereotypes about the passivity or victimization of Muslim women persist, a growing body of scholarship also documents the political activism of Muslim women, their contributions to various political movements, and the gendered impacts of political processes. The turbulence and dramatic changes of the twentieth and early twenty-first centuries have affected the Muslim world in different ways, but Muslim women have hardly been passive onlookers. Instead, they have actively taken part in movements (revolution, national liberation, democratization) for social and political change, and they have formed and led their own movements and organizations.

Patterns of women's political activism vary across the Muslim world, affected by the nature of the state, social class, ethnicity, and ideology. Grievances and demands are also context-shaped, but some common patterns may be identified. One is that at least since the United Nations World Decade for Women (1976–1985), Muslim women have been inspired by the global women's rights agenda, launching campaigns to improve their legal status and social positions and to ensure that their governments implement the agreements that they have signed (such as the 1979 Convention on the Elimination of All Forms of Discrimination against Women and the 1995 Beijing Declaration and Platform for Women). Another is that the spread of fundamentalist movements and political Islam has affected women across the Muslim world, generating polemics about the hijab and Muslim family law. A third observable pattern is that women are major contributors to, and participants in, civil society and democracy movements, as they see a democratic polity as both a desirable alternative to authoritarianism and a pathway to their own equality and rights. This essay thus focuses on women's political activism, and their demands for participation, rights, and equality, in connection with (a) nationalist and revolutionary movements, (b) fundamentalism and political Islam, and (c) civil society, feminism, and democratization.

Women in Nationalist and Revolutionary Movements. Studies show that nationalist movements and revolutions may be imbued with concepts of inclusion and equality, of modernity and progress, in which case they are often compatible with women's advancement, rights, and participation. Or they may be infused with cultural defensiveness and nostalgia for a bygone era or invented golden age, in which case they may place on women the burden of reproducing cultural values and traditions through prescribed dress and comportment.

Early-twentieth-century nationalist movements tended to equate women's seclusion and illiteracy with national backwardness or stagnation. Progress and national integration were advanced via social and educational reforms, the promotion of a national language, and the establishment of a modern nation-state (Moaddel, 2005). Muslim women (as well as non-Muslims) responded enthusiastically to the reform agendas of nationalist, constitutionalist, and revolutionary movements in Egypt, Iran, and Turkey, as well as in the Soviet republics (Jayawardena, 1986; Afary, 1996; Fleischmann, 1999), where women's rights leaders were advocates of nationalist causes, as well as of women's advancement. For example, in October 1938 in Cairo, Huda Sharawi and the Egyptian Feminist Union sponsored the Eastern Women's Conference for the Defense of Palestine (Weber, 2008). The great anticolonial, nationalist, and Third World movements of the mid-twentieth century likewise saw active participation by women, in Algeria, Egypt, Indonesia, Morocco, Tunisia, and elsewhere.

Yet feminist scholars have noted tensions between the goals of women's rights and those of national liberation. At the first and second Eastern Women's Congresses (1930 in Damascus, 1932 in Tehran), the hostility of conservative male leaders to feminist demands for political rights and for equality within the family, for instance, forced women leaders to retreat to the more acceptable minimalist demand for access to education. While nationalist leader Kemal Atatürk granted Turkish women the right to vote in 1930, women did not receive the vote in Egypt, Iran, or Syria until much later. Modernization affected many institutions and laws in Muslim-majority countries, but family law remained patriarchal almost everywhere. In law and tradition alike, men were designated the guardians of women, with authority over them. Notions of male domination seeped into nationalist movements, especially as the movements took on a more religious character in the latter part of the twentieth century. The evolution of the Palestinian nationalist movement is a case in point.

Initially, the Palestinian nationalist movement allowed women politically to participate in what became the most secular and democratic movement in the Arab world. In the 1970s Palestinian women's political activity and participation in resistance groups expanded, be it in Lebanon, the West Bank or Gaza, in universities or refugee camps. During the first Intifada, Palestinian women organized themselves into impressive independent political groups and economic cooperatives. Internationally, the best-known Palestinian women have been the guerrilla fighter Leila Khaled and the diplomat and English professor Hanan Ashrawi—two contrasting examples of roles available to Palestinian women in their movement. The nationalist movement also produced notable writers with feminist consciousness. Samira Azzam and Fadwa Tuqan, for example, combined a critique of patriarchal structures and a fervent nationalism to produce compelling work.

At the same time, the Palestinian movement exalted women as mothers and as mothers of martyrs. During the latter part of the 1980s, another trend emerged among the Palestinians, especially in the impoverished Gaza Strip: Islamist vigilantes insisting that women cover themselves when appearing in public. The frustrations of daily life, the indignities of occupation, and the inability of the secular and democratic project to materialize may explain this shift. What began in the early 1990s as a sophisticated women's movement that sought feminist interventions in the areas of constitution writing and social policy experienced setbacks toward the end of the decade as the West Bank and Gaza faced Islamization and continued Israeli occupation (Gerner, 2006).

Algerian women have been involved twice in conflicts that have profoundly affected them: the war of liberation in the 1950s and early 1960s, and the civil conflict between Islamists and the state in the 1990s. While their earlier participation was conducted within a nationalist framework, the later struggle was framed as feminist, modernist, and antifundamentalist (Cherifati-Merabtine, 1995; Moghadam, 2011). In the Islamist terror campaign that followed the military's decision to prevent the Front Islamique du Salut from taking power after the 1991 elections, numerous women and girls were raped or killed and a number of women activists assassinated. Nonetheless, Algerian women formed many new women's organizations and developed critiques of both state autocracy and political Islam. Throughout the decade, they championed modernity and individual rights while also holding on to the socialist legacy of equality of citizens.

Iranian women were active participants in the 1978–1979 Iranian revolution against the shah's rule, although in sheer numbers, men dominated the street protests. Many women sided with communist organizations; others with liberal groups or Muslim organizations. It is safe to say that even the Muslim women who initially supported the agenda of Ayatollah Khomeini did not expect the harsh laws, political repression, and systematic discrimination against women that characterized Islamization in the 1980s. Here political Islam overtook and eventually eliminated the liberal nationalism and revolutionary Marxism of the anti-shah coalition.

Fundamentalism, Political Islam, and Women's Activism. The rise of Islamic fundamentalism and political Islam has significantly affected women throughout the Muslim world, and women themselves have been divided for and against these movements. Whether seeking state power through force or influencing public policies to take part in governance nonviolently, Islamist movements have been preoccupied with cultural identity and authenticity, and this has had implications for women's autonomy and range of choices. Women's crucial role in the socialization of the next generation makes them symbols of cultural values and traditions, and thus they are expected to behave and dress in prescribed ways. Some Muslim women regard this role as an exalted one and gladly assume it, becoming active participants, though rarely ideologues, in Islamist movements. Other women find it an onerous burden, and they resent restrictions on their individuality, mobility, and personal freedoms. Such nonconformist women may rebel in various ways: they may discreetly pursue alternative lifestyles, they may leave the country and settle elsewhere, and/or they may join or form feminist organizations.

The spread of the hijab since the 1980s has been tackled by feminist scholars in different ways. Some, such as Fadwa El Guindi and Arlene MacLeod, emphasize the personal choice and enhanced opportunities for mobility that veiling represents, especially for women of the lower middle class and conservative families. Others, pointing out that veiling is compulsory in some countries (notably Saudi Arabia and Iran) and required by strong social pressure on women elsewhere, have stressed its link to fundamentalism and religious identity among women (see contributions by Margot Badran, Nayereh Tohidi, Binnaz Toprak, Ayesha Imam, and Sondra Hale, among others, in Moghadam, 1994). What is more, such social pressures may take the form of harassment and intimidation by self-styled enforcers of correct religious behavior and public morality, as has occurred in Sudan, Iran, Algeria, Afghanistan, and even within immigrant communities in Europe. In sum, veiling may be regarded as an identity marker of piety, of tradition, or of a distinct cultural or religious group, or it can be seen as a sign of affiliation with political Islam.

Islamization in Iran following the 1979 revolution saw the strengthening or introduction of Muslim family law across the Muslim world, latterly in Malaysia. Holdouts were Afghanistan and the Muslim-majority republics of the Soviet Union, but that changed in the 1990s with the collapse of the communist bloc. There are, of course, women in the Muslim world who embrace Islamic laws, and many of them are related to male Islamists. Indeed, Rachel Rinaldo (2010) shows how Islamic piety can be a resource for Muslim women's political mobilization in Indonesia. But many women object to the second-class citizenship of women and bias in favor of men within certain interpretations of Islamic law; the harsh penalties for adultery, which women suffer more than men; and the absence of women from political decision making. An early response was the formation of an international solidarity network called Women Living under Muslim Laws (WLUML), which since 1984 has drawn attention to discriminatory family laws and harsh criminal codes; extended solidarity and support to women victims; and promoted legal reform, gender equality, and pluralist politics. In the twenty-first century, Muslim women's groups from Africa and Asia have worked with the Women's Learning Partnership for Rights, Development, and Peace (WLP) to promote women's human rights. Another response has taken the form of "Islamic feminism," which is an intellectual, theological, and activist project of Muslim women to recoup what they believe to be the essentially egalitarian and emancipatory Qurʾānic message from the patriarchal misinterpretations of the medieval era as well as from the extremist positions of contemporary movements (Mirza, 2006). In Malaysia, the group Sisters in Islam draws on theology and feminist discourses alike to criticize compulsory veiling, polygamy, and women's subordination. Although its focus is domestic, it works with WLUML and WLP to advance the human rights of all women in the Muslim world.

Civil Society, Feminism, and Democratization. In the 1990s, studies began to document the expansion of associational life in Muslim-majority countries. This incipient civil society was seen as the result of the aspirations of the growing middle and professional classes, and as a response to global trends. In particular, the UN global women's rights agenda was a factor in the emergence of all manner of women's organizations. Preparations for the Fourth World Conference on Women (Beijing, September 1995) and the post-Beijing follow-up helped generate legitimacy and support for the types of women's organizations that were proliferating: professional associations, women-in-development NGOs, research centers and women's studies institutes, women-led publishing houses, and women's rights or feminist organizations. ("Feminism" here refers to a discourse that critiques women's subordination, calls for women's participation and rights, and seeks the necessary legal, policy, and cultural changes for gender equality.) Where political pluralism existed, women's auxiliaries of the major political parties and trade unions also could be found, along with more traditional charitable organizations led by women and official or state-supported women's organizations. Even in a poor Muslim majority country, such as Mali, women-led credit associations and advocacy groups, such as l'Association Juristes Maliennes and l'Observatoire des Droits de la Femme et de l'Enfant, were formed (Wing, 2002).

The emergence of the newer associations reflected the changing sociopolitical dynamics of women's activism, with its discourse of women's participation, human rights, civil society, modernity, citizenship, and democratization. Advocacy became more pointed, with a focus on the need to reform discriminatory family laws and bring them in line with constitutional guarantees of equality, as well as with global standards and trends (e.g., the UN Women's Convention); to criminalize domestic violence and other forms of violence against women, including "honor crimes," and prohibit sexual harassment; to grant women equal nationality rights so that their children may acquire citizenship through the mother and not just the father; and to create mechanisms for greater access by women to employment and political decision making.

Strategies to achieve goals included coalition building with other civil-society organizations, appeals to transnational advocacy networks, the study and reinterpretation of Islamic texts, and consensus building to gain elite allies or mobilize grassroots support. Such strategies were used for the removal of the Sharīʿah sentence against a Nigerian woman accused of adultery in the late 1990s; for the right of Egyptian women to a *khulʿ* divorce, which was won in 2000; for family-law reform in Morocco, which was won in 2003–2004 after a decade-long campaign; for the establishment of counseling centers and hotlines (*centres d'écoutes*) for women victims of domestic violence and sexual harassment, which are in place in North Africa; for an end to discriminatory family laws and reform of the criminal code to remove stoning in Iran, a campaign launched in 2006 but repressed by the government.

The strategies deployed by activists to advance women's participation and rights are rarely confrontational and as such differ markedly from the tactics and strategies of many Islamist movements. Since women's groups tend to have limited leverage and relatively few resources, and since many governments in the Muslim world are authoritarian, consensus building is a reasonable strategic choice, as well as a democratic practice. In fact, many women's groups call themselves "democratic," as well as "feminist," and their practices appear to contribute to the making of democratic society.

The political scientist Yesim Arat (1994) points out that in the 1980s, at a time when Turkey's civil society was under tight military control, the new feminist movement helped to usher in democratization through campaigns and demands for women's rights, participation, and autonomy. In her study of the Palestinian women's movement, Andrea Barron (2002) explains that in the 1990s, the three top priorities for women's rights advocates were changing the personal status laws, fighting domestic violence, and increasing women's political participation. The movement was identified as an agent for democracy "because of the *substance* of its goals—obtaining equal rights for half of Palestinian society—and because of the *process* it is using to accomplish its objectives." In particular, Barron cites four "democratic practices" of the movement: (1) establishing an autonomous social movement with strong ties to political society, (2) expanding political participation and knowledge about the laws and customs that affect women, (3) campaigning for equal protection of the laws, and (4) cultivating a democratic political culture that supports pragmatic decision making and respects political differences (Barron, 2002, pp. 80–81). Even after the second intifada emerged, the women's movement was still regarded as an important national agent of democratization, although it subsequently faced many obstacles.

Yet another example comes from Morocco. When Abdelrahman Yousefi was appointed prime minister in 1998 and formed a progressive cabinet, women's groups allied themselves to the government in the interest of promoting both women's rights and a democratic polity (Sadiqi and Ennaji, 2006; Skalli, 2007; Moghadam and Gheytanchi, 2010). Subsequently, Moroccan feminist organizations endorsed the truth and reconciliation commissions that were put in place to assess the repressive years prior to 1998. A number of key Moroccan women leaders previously associated with left-wing political groups (notably Latifa Jbabdi of l'Union d'Action Feminine) gave testimony about physical and sexual abuse (Slyomovics, 2005). More recently, women's rights groups have helped form a coalition known as the Springtime of Dignity, which includes physician groups, in a new campaign for penal code reform spearheaded by the Association Démocratique des Femmes Marocaines (WLP, 2011). Such activities and strategies demonstrate the democratic and democratizing nature of women's rights groups.

At the same time, women's groups are wary of a democratic transition that could bring to power political forces inimical to the rights of women (and minorities). The historical record shows that women can pay a high price when a democratic process that is institutionally weak, or not founded on principles of equality and the rights of all citizens, or not protected by strong institutions, allows a political party advocating patriarchal norms to come to power and immediately institute laws relegating women to second-class citizenship and instituting controls over their bodies and mobility. This was the Algerian feminist nightmare, which is why so many educated Algerian women opposed the Islamist Front Islamique du Salut after its expansion in 1989.

Even before Egypt's mass protests of 2011, calls were issued for political reform and democracy by the secular Kefaya (Enough) movement, as well as by the Muslim Brotherhood. The latter demanded "the freedom of forming political parties" and "independence of the judiciary system," which are laudable goals, but also "conformity to Islamic Sharia Law," which is not conducive to gender equality or the equality of Muslim and non-Muslim citizens in all domains (Brown, Hamzawy, and Ottaway, 2006). After the resignation of President Hosni Mubarak, Egyptian women were excluded from the constitution-writing process, and groups such as the Egyptian Center for Women's Rights complained regularly, questioning whether Egypt can effect a democratic transition if half the population is excluded from shaping the political process. In Tunisia, where mass protests led to the departure of President Ben Ali, some women were incorporated into the new political process, but many Tunisian feminists, noting that men continue to dominate the emerging institutions, remain skeptical of the agenda of the Islamic parties. Time will tell if the democracy movements in Egypt and Tunisia will result in equality of all citizens—women and men, Muslim and non-Muslim—or if some version of the status quo ante is achieved. What is clear, however, is the democratizing and modernizing nature of women's rights activism.

[*See also* Algeria; Convention on the Elimination of All Forms of Discrimination against Women (CEDAW); Egypt; Iran; Tunisia; Veiling; *and* West Bank and Gaza.]

BIBLIOGRAPHY

Afary, Janet. *The Iranian Constitutional Revolution 1906–1911: Grassroots Democracy, Social Democracy, and the Origins of Feminism*. New York: Columbia University Press, 1996.

Arat, Yesim. "Toward a Democratic Society: The Women's Movement in Turkey in the 1980s." *International Women's Studies Forum* 17 (1994): 241–248.

Barron, Andrea. "The Palestinian Women's Movement: Agent of Democracy in a Future State?" *Middle East Critique* 11, no. 1 (2002): 71–90.

Brown, Nathan, Amr Hamzawy, and Marina Ottaway. "Islamist Movements and the Democratic Process in the Arab World: Exploring Gray Zones." Paper no. 67 (March 2006). Carnegie Endowment for International Peace, Washington, D.C. http://www.carnegieendowment.org/files/cp_67_grayzones_final.pdf.

Cherifati-Merabtine, Doria. "Algerian Women at a Crossroads: National Liberation, Islamization, and Women." In *Gender and National Identity: Women and Politics in Muslim Societies*, edited by Valentine M. Moghadam, pp. 40–62. London: Zed Books, 1995.

Fleischmann, Ellen. "The Other 'Awakening': The Emergence of Women's Movements in the Modern Middle East, 1900–1940." In *Social History of Women and Gender in the Modern Middle East*, edited by Margaret Meriwether and Judith Tucker. Boulder, Colo.: Westview Press, 1999.

Gerner, Deborah. "Mobilizing Women for Nationalist Agendas: Palestinian Women, Civil Society, and the State-Building Process." In *From Patriarchy to Empowerment: Women's Participation, Movements, and Rights in the Middle East, North Africa, and South Asia*, edited by Valentine M. Moghadam, pp. 17–39. Syracuse, N.Y.: Syracuse University Press, 2006.

Jayawardena, Kumari. *Feminism and Nationalism in the Third World*. London: Zed Books, 1986.

Mirza, Qudsia, ed. *Islamic Feminism and the Law*. London: Routledge, 2006.

Moaddel, Mansoor. *Islamic Modernism, Nationalism, and Fundamentalism: Episode and Discourse*. Chicago: University of Chicago Press, 2005.

Moghadam, Valentine M. "Algerian Women in Movement: Three Waves of Feminist Activism." In *Confronting Global Gender Justice: Women's Lives, Human Rights*, edited by Debra Bergoffen, Paula Ruth Gilbert, Tamara Harvey, and Connie L. McNeely, pp. 180–199. London: Routledge, 2011.

Moghadam, Valentine M., ed. *Identity Politics and Women: Cultural Reassertions and Feminisms in International Perspective*. Boulder, Colo.: Westview Press, 1994.

Moghadam, Valentine M., and Elham Gheytanchi. "Political Opportunities and Strategic Choices: Comparing Feminist Campaigns in Morocco and Iran." *Mobilization: An International Quarterly of Social Movement Research* 15, no. 3 (September 2010): 267–288.

Rinaldo, Rachel. "The Islamic Revival and Women's Political Subjectivity in Indonesia." *Women's Studies International Forum* 33 (2010): 422–431.

Sadiqi, Fatima, and Moha Ennaji. "The Feminization of Public Space: Women's Activism, the Family Law, and Social Change in Morocco." *Journal of Middle East Women's Studies* 2, no. 2 (Spring 2006): 86–114.

Skalli, Loubna Hanna. "Women, Communications, and Democratization in Morocco." In Valentine M. Moghadam, ed., *Empowering Women: Participation, Rights, and Women's Movements in the Middle East, North Africa, and South Asia*. Syracuse, N.Y.: Syracuse University Press, 2007.

Slyomovics, Susan. *The Performance of Human Rights in Morocco*. Philadelphia: University of Pennsylvania Press, 2005.

Weber, Charlotte. "Between Nationalism and Feminism: The Eastern Women's Congresses of 1930 and 1932." *Journal of Middle East Women's Studies* 4, no. 1 (Winter 2008): 83–106.

Wing, Susannah D. "Women Activists in Mali." In *Women's Activism and Globalization: Linking Local Struggles and Transnational Politics*, edited by Nancy Naples and Manisha Desai, pp. 172–185. London: Routledge, 2002.

WLP [Women's Learning Partnership for Rights, Development, and Peace]. "Springtime of Dignity: Coalition for a Penal Code That Protects Women from Discrimination and Violence." http://www.learningpartnership.org/lib/morocco-springtime-dignity-coalition.

VALENTINE M. MOGHADAM

POLITICS AND POLITY (THEORETICAL OVERVIEW). *Politics and Polity* was chosen to reflect the importance not only of political developments and their impact on women, but also the importance of women's participation in a variety of political processes, demonstrating that women are not simply the subjects of political entities, but also play an active role in guiding and shaping them. Articles contained therein give attention to the forms of various political systems, showing where women are present and have voices, as well as discussing how women living under various political systems formulate their understanding of their rights and responsibilities and how they seek to engage them, either within the existing system or by working to change it. Women's participation in the political arena has occurred both directly, for example, by voting, and indirectly, such as via influence over a male political figure. Participation has further come from within the system, such as by election or appointment to office, as well as from outside it, either in cases in which women have been shut out of the system, such as in the Guardian Council in Iran where only men may serve, or in circumstances in which it is believed that the system is beyond repair and needs a complete overhaul, as in the cases of the Arab Spring in Libya, Egypt, and Tunisia, for example.

Although the entries themselves are fairly standard, such as articles on individual countries, the content deliberately focuses on women's participation, contributions, and challenges, both historically and in the contemporary period. In cases where women have accessed the circles of political power, this is mentioned. In cases where they have not, the reasons for that are examined. Each country article contains at least a broad historical overview to emphasize the reality that women have always lived in and contributed to the economies, cultures, political systems, and societies of these countries, whether directly or indirectly. Restoring these voices to history is part of the goal of this Encyclopedia in general.

Particularly prominent women, such as rulers, major philanthropists, and those who have broken the proverbial glass ceilings in various professions, have received their own separate entries that nevertheless tie them to broader issues and trends. For example, female rulers of past major dynasties, such as Abish Khatun, Radiyya bint Iltutmish, Khayr al-Nisa' Begum, Khanum Pari-Khan I, Qutlugh Terken Khatun, Soghaghtani Beki, and Baghdad Khatun, among others, receive the same kind of coverage male rulers often receive in historical volumes, highlighting their achievements and major life events. In some cases, multiple female figures are portrayed in discussions of dynasties, rather than individually, such as in the cases of the Sulayhid, Mamluk, Fatimid, Qajar, Timurid, and Rasulid Dynasties; the Mughal, Safavid, and Ottoman Empires; the Sokoto Caliphate; and the Delhi Sultanate. This fulfills not only the function of restoring these women to history, but also of demonstrating through their examples that women have, indeed, served in ruling capacities in the past in Muslim-majority countries and dynasties, often with success. All of this sets the stage for contemporary political figures, such as Nadia Yassine, Benazir Bhutto, Sheikha Hasina Wazed, and Khaleda Zia, placing them within the framework of continuity with historical example, rather than as contemporary aberrations. Finally, although some have downplayed the importance of "royal consorts," such as Hurrem Sultan, Nur Jahan, and Shajarat al-Durr, inclusion of their biographies serves as a reminder that "soft" forms of power, such as influence over a powerful man, have long been ways for women to insert their voices into political projects and even to take over the position of ruler.

Women warriors, both past and present, are included to show the role that women have played in battles, defending both Islam and nation—a theme of particular importance in the unfolding of the Arab Spring, where women played prominent roles as leaders, organizers, and publicists, as well as participants, in overthrowing old regimes and demanding a voice at the table in the creation of new states and constitutions. Giving consideration to past examples of women's participation in the struggle for liberation only to be set aside in the construction of the new polities that followed underscores the importance of including their voices in the construction of new polities today.

Contemporary figures are also included to draw attention to the variety of fields in which women are taking on public roles and the impact this has not only for matters of their own personal visibility, but also for the impact this is expected to have in opening doors for other women. Thus, Rola Dashti, for example, is not celebrated simply for her personal success in being elected to parliament in Kuwait, but also to demonstrate the increasingly public and political roles that women in the Gulf are taking on with the express purpose of ensuring that women's voices are included in national decision making, rather than simply within the home.

At no time has this project been more important, as debates about the "appropriate" status and role of women, with respect to the state, the community, and the family, are intimately tied to visions of new polities. It is hoped that the information contained in this Encyclopedia will encourage serious consideration of the importance of including women's voices in the discussion and decision-making processes, rather than making decisions about and for them.

NATANA J. DELONG-BAS

POLYGYNY. Polygyny, the practice of having more than one wife at the same time, may seem outdated in the modern era. However, when sūrah 4:3 ("... Marry women of your choice, two, three, or four; but if ye fear that ye shall not be able to deal justly [with them], then [marry] only one...") was revealed to the Prophet Muḥammad, it produced nothing short of a revolution in the way it improved conditions for women. Life in the seventh-century tribal culture of the Arabian Peninsula had been patriarchal and misogynistic. Women were not considered fully independent human beings and had no right to own or inherit property. Men were permitted to take an unlimited number of wives, and concubinage, enslavement of women and girls, and incestuous marriages were prevalent. Sexual abuse and the killing of baby girls were widely practiced, and upon marriage, women were required to surrender all financial protection from their natal family.

Immediately preceding the revelation of sūrah 4:3, a large number of Muslim men had been killed in the Battle of Uhud in 625 CE, leaving behind a great number of widows and orphans without personal or legal status, or any means of financial support. The Qur'ān's admonition thus had a double impact: it restricted previously unchecked polygyny and at the same time ensured that large numbers of vulnerable war widows and orphans would be cared for. Sūrah 4:3 was part of a sequence of revelations that provided greater protection for women, including the right to receive their own dower and the right to enter into marriage contracts as equal partners instead of subjects of those contracts. In this way, the Qurʿān shifted focus from the tribe as the most important social unit to the family as the foundation of society.

Because of patrilineal social structures that provided status and inheritance rights through male family members, as well as the importance placed on clearly establishing the paternity of children, women were not given a similar right to marry more than one husband (polyandry). If a woman took a second husband, that marriage was void, and any children fathered by the second husband were considered illegitimate and therefore excluded from inheritance.

The Qurʿān does not allow a man to take more than one wife in all circumstances. The language of sūrah 4:3 makes clear that more than one wife may not be taken if any inequity would result. This limitation is consistent with other verses counseling against multiple marriages, including sūrah 4:129, which warns that "Ye are never able to be fair and just as between women, even if it is your ardent desire," and sūrah 33:4, which states, "Allāh has not made for any man two hearts in his one body," taken to mean that it is impossible to love equally more than one woman at a time.

In Sunnī Islam, women may generally stipulate in their marriage contracts that their husbands may take no other wives. If the stipulation is violated, a wife has the right to obtain a divorce. The right to enter into stipulations in the marriage contract is more limited in the Shīʿī branch of Islam.

The Shīʿī branch recognizes an additional form of multiple marriage, called *nikāḥ al-mutʿah*, or temporary marriage. According to Shīʿī believers, sūrah 4:24 of the Qurʿān authorizes *mutʿah*, which consists of a contractual relationship between a man and a woman for a fixed period of time, after which it automatically expires and the man and woman have no further relationship with each other. Sunnī believers, however, consider *mutʿah* to be forbidden.

Beginning in the second half of the twentieth century, national laws limiting or restricting polygyny were enacted in approximately half the fifty-seven countries comprising the Organization of the Islamic Conference. In 1956, Tunisia became the first country to outlaw polygyny altogether on the basis that it was humanly impossible for a man to give equal treatment to more than one wife. Since then, a number of countries, including Algeria, Indonesia, Egypt, Senegal, Bangladesh, Gambia, Jordan, Libya, and Malaysia, have enacted legislation limiting the practice of polygyny in some way, most commonly by requiring that the first wife be notified if a husband intends to take another wife and permitting divorce if all wives are not treated equally. In 2004 the Family Code of Morocco was enacted, stating that polygyny is not permitted unless a judge verifies a husband's ability to guarantee equality among wives and children and finds that there is an objective and exceptional motive that justifies taking another wife. A woman has the right to a divorce if any harm results from her husband taking another wife.

Some scholars believe that legislative changes to traditional interpretations of Islamic law relating to polygyny are justified by Islam's overarching objectives, which emphasize justice, equality, and tolerance, while others believe that new interpretations are permitted by the use of *ijtihād*.

In some African countries in which Islamic law is influential, polygyny has been outlawed by national legislation. However, it is often still practiced since the demands of agricultural economies require multiple wives and children to provide essential labor.

The new constitutions of some states, including Afghanistan and Iraq, provide that Islam is the official religion and a fundamental source of legislation, and that no law contradicting Islam may be established. Thus, an increase in polygyny may be seen in the future despite a decline in recent years resulting from organized action on the part of local women's groups and national legislation restricting the right of a man to take more than one wife.

BIBLIOGRAPHY

Arshad, Amna. "Ijtihad as a Tool for Islamic Legal Reform: Advancing Women's Rights in Morocco." *Kansas Journal of Law and Public Policy* 16 (2006): 129–156.

Barlas, Asma. *Believing Women in Islam: Unreading Patriarchal Interpretations of the Qur'an*. Austin: University of Texas Press, 2002.

Esposito, John L. *Women in Muslim Family Law*. 2d ed. Syracuse, N.Y.: Syracuse University Press, 2001.

Jansen, Yakare-Oule. "Muslim Brides and the Ghost of the Shari'a: Have the Recent Law Reforms in Egypt, Tunisia and Morocco Improved Women's Position in Marriage and Divorce, and Can Religious Moderates Bring Reform and Make it Stick?" *Northwestern University Journal of International Human Rights* 5 (2007): 181–212.

Mashhour, Amira. "Islamic Law and Gender Equality—Could There Be a Common Ground? A Study of Divorce and Polygamy in Sharia Law and Contemporary Legislation in Tunisia and Egypt." *Human Rights Quarterly* 27 (2005): 562–596.

Sonn, Tamara. "Islam." In *Ethics of Family Life*, edited by Jacob Neusner. Belmont, Calif.: Wadsworth/Thomson Learning Press, 2001.

CHRISTIE S. WARREN

POPULAR RELIGION.

[*This entry contains five subentries:*

Europe and the Americas
Middle East and North Africa
South Asia
Southeast Asia *and*
Sub-Saharan Africa.]

EUROPE AND THE AMERICAS

In highlighting historic and contemporary geographies associated with Islam and Muslims, Europe and the Americas are predictable candidates for neglect since Islam arose in the Arabian Peninsula and grew rapidly across North African and South Asian population centers. Yet Muslim presence spans hundreds of years in the Americas and exceeds a thousand years in Europe. Muslims entered the Iberian Peninsula or al-Andalus, now Spain and Portugal, after 700 CE. Turks, Tatars, and other Muslims conquered portions of the Mediterranean, Byzantine Empire, and surrounding areas, capturing Constantinople in 1453 and besieging Vienna, Austria, in 1683. Muslim numbers in Western Europe multiplied in the 1900s, so that, by 2010, of total populations, an estimated 9 percent of France, 5 percent of Germany, and greater than 6 percent of the Netherlands were Muslim.

The first recorded Muslims in the Americas arrived among North and West African slaves and were, on rare occasions, European colonists. In the 1800s and 1900s, Muslims from Africa, Asia, and Europe immigrated or traveled to the United States and Latin America as temporary workers or indentured servants. African-Brazilian Muslims briefly organized a Muslim state in 1830. The heterodox Nation of Islam movement materialized in Detroit during the 1930s. By 2010 several million Muslims lived in North America and composed about 2 percent of Argentina, 7 percent of Guyana, almost 16 percent of Suriname, and over 6 percent of Trinidad and Tobago in Latin America and the Caribbean, where they brought what might be termed informal or popular religious practices with them.

At least three overlapping themes emerge surveying women, Islam, and popular religion in

Europe and the Americas beyond formal religious rites and clerical elites. One is portrayals of Muslim women; another is non-Muslim women's perceptions of Islam and Muslims; and the last is Muslim women embodying "popular religion" in politics, conversation, work, media, and the arts.

European and American popular portrayals of Muslim women range from mysterious exotics to sufferers of Muslim misogyny and non-Muslim stereotypes, to models of virtue and creativity. Eugene Delacroix (1798–1863) and Gustave Flaubert (1821–1880) rendered Muslim women residents in lavish, lascivious imperial harems. Films such as *Sex in the City* 2 (2010) visualize Muslim women shrouding their hair and sexuality beneath burqas or other enveloping garb. Presumably, Muslim women huddle shyly from men in Jackie Chan's comedy *The Accidental Spy* (2001). Ayaan Hirsi Ali and the assassinated Dutch filmmaker Theo Van Gogh's *Submission, Part I* (2004) depict Muslim women tattooed with Qur'ānic quotations praying amid their anger and heartache. *Not without My Daughter* (1991), *The Stoning of Soraya M* (2008), and the 9 August 2010, cover of *Time* magazine picture women victims of Muslim men.

More lightheartedly, the reality TV series *All American Muslim* (2011) and the Canadian drama *Little Mosque on the Prairie* (2007–2012) try to dispel stereotypes by focusing on Muslims' daily lives. Legendary Persian Princess Scheherazade in *One Thousand and One (Arabian) Nights* is a daring empowering classical figure who spins narrative intrigue to win her life and love from a would-be executioner. "Nadia," a recurring character in the popular television serial *Lost* (2004–2010), is brave, compassionate, and persevering. The 1960s Nation of Islam *Muhammad Speaks* comic strips sketched Muslim women modestly dressed and self-assured. The Marvel Comics superhero "Sooraya Qadir/Dust" joined *X-Men* in 2002.

European and American non-Muslim women's perceptions and interactions with Islam and Muslims vary comparably. Maria Martin (1807) and Eliza Bradley (1823) alleged reports on women captives of Mediterranean Muslim Corsairs. Susannah Rowson's more congenial play *Slaves in Algiers* (1794) featured a former Algerian slaver turned abolitionist. Christian missionary women in the 1900s sought to convert and serve Muslims through education, hospitals, and orphanages. Helen Barrett Montgomery (1910) and Ruth Frances Woodsmall (1936) lamented what they believed was Islamic misogyny and fatalism, proposing Christianity as the cure for both. The Pentecostal Assiout (renamed Lillian Thrasher) Orphanage and Presbyterian John and Esther Fowler Home helped thousands of orphans and widows in Egypt. The American schoolmistress Mary Mills Patrick (1850–1940) sought to aid Turkey's transition to a secular state. The Italian Catholic Annalena Tonelli (1943–2002) assisted Muslim orphans, the disabled, refugees, and tuberculosis patients in Kenya and Somalia, prompting support from the World Health Organization, UNICEF, and Catholic charities.

European and American women criticizing Islam and insisting their critique speaks for repressed Muslim women are the *New York Times* best-selling author and Lebanese-American Birgitte Gabriel, Syrian-American Wafa Sultan, British journalist Melanie Phillips, and Italian Oriana Fallaci in *La Rabbia e l'Orgoglio* (The rage and the pride, 2002) and *La forza della ragione* (The force of reason, 2004). The African-American minister, Elreta Dodds, shares contextual concerns in *The Trouble with Farrakhan and the Nation of Islam* (1997), as does Egyptian-American Nonie Darwish in founding the organization Arabs for Israel and directing the civil rights group Former Muslims United. Pamela Gellar is perhaps most polarizing as a leading activist for the international human rights organization Stop Islamization of Nations.

British pundit Karen Armstrong replied to Islam's critics by praising and defending Islam in *Islam: A Short History* (2000) and her two biographies of the Muslim prophet Muḥammad (1992, 2007). Cuban-born Maria Rosa Menocal contributed *The Ornament of the World: How Muslims, Jews, and Christians Created a Culture of Tolerance in Medieval Spain* (2002), and with Jerrilynn Dodds and Abigail Krasner, *The Arts of Intimacy: Christians, Jews, and Muslims in the Making of Castilian Culture* (2009). Evangelical Christians building relationships and writing favorably about Muslim women are Miriam Adeney, Iranian-American Shirin Taber in *Muslims Next Door: Uncovering Myths and Creating Friendships* (2004), Dayna Curry and Heather Mercer in *Prisoners of Hope: The Story of Our Captivity and Freedom in Afghanistan* (2002), and Yale University's Melissa Yarrington who has co-edited *A Common Word: Muslims and Christians Loving God and Neighbor* (2010).

Muslim women themselves contribute significantly to popular religion in Europe and the Americas. Venetian Fatima Hatun née Beatrice Michiel converted to Islam and functioned as a viceroy of sorts for Venice and Constantinople in the 1500s. Tansu Penbe Ciller was Turkey's first female prime minister (1993–1996), and Kosovo elected Atifete Jahjaga in 2011. U.S. President Barack Obama appointed Dalia Mogahed to advise the White House Office of Faith Based Partnerships. The Dutch-Somali member of parliament (2003–2006) and former Muslim Ayaan Hirsi Ali published *New York Times* best sellers in 2007 and 2010, and wrote *Newsweek* magazine's 24 September 2012 cover article. Ugandan-Canadian Irshad Manji's *The Trouble with Islam Today: A Muslim's Call for Reform in Her Faith* (2003) likewise became a *New York Times* best seller. Through subsequent opportunities, these women and others like them continue to operate as unofficial spokespersons for Muslims, former Muslims, and Islam in public discourse.

Additionally noteworthy early-twenty-first century Muslim women authors and academics include Indian-American lawyer Sumbul Ali-Karamali, Iranian-American Qur'ān translator Laleh Bakhtiar, the Egyptian-American Harvard professor Leila Ahmed, and Ṣūfī phenomenologist Anna Marie-Schimmel. African-American Amina Wadud, Indian-American Asra Nomani, and Pakistani-Canadian Raheel Raza bridge academic and popular priorities by campaigning for women leading mosque prayers. Brazilian Maria Moreira calls for increasing Latin American consciousness of Islam. Saleemah Abdul-Ghafur edited *Living Islam Out Loud: American Muslim Women Speak Out* (2005), interweaving Muslim women's poetry and prose exploring cultural identity, spirituality, and sexuality.

In interreligious pursuits, Asma Afsaruddin, Riffat Hassan, Rabia Terri Harris, and S. Ayse Kadayifci-Orellana dialogue with Evangelical Christians (2009). Ranya Idilby enjoys repartee with Jewish and Episcopalian friends in *The Faith Club* (2007). Lejla Demiri, Maleiha Malik, and Mona Siddiqui contribute to Building Bridges Seminars in Sarajevo, Bosnia-Herzegovina, and elsewhere. The Canadian convert to Islam Ingrid Mattson was the Islamic Society of North America's (ISNA) first female president and has been on the faculty at Connecticut's historically Christian Hartford Seminary, which pioneered the training of Muslim women and men in the United States as university and military chaplains. Muslim women also participate in forums online, including Altmuslimah, Beliefnet, Huffington Post, Middle East Experience, Parliament of World Religions affiliate State of Formation, Patheos, and Religion Dispatches.

Marrying Muslim men is one reason European and American women give for converting to Islam. Converts such as the former American Queen Noor of Jordan have garnered much attention. Karin van Nieuwkerk (2006) cites further motives, including Muslim family and community values; a sense of spirituality, morality, and rationality; and disillusionment with non-Muslim religions. These reasons parallel Muslim women's explanations for converting to Christianity, along with Bible reading, visions of Jesus, and the personal assurance of life after death.

European and American Muslim women congruently excel in sports; fashion; and the culinary, visual, and fine arts. Laila Ali, the daughter of Muhammad Ali, captured multiple boxing titles, finishing with a 24–0 record in 2007. Lebanese-American Muslim Rima Fakih won the 2010 Miss USA pageant. The Council on American Islamic Relations (CAIR) has held women's fashion extravaganzas. *Azizah Magazine* similarly displays trendy attire. Kristen Ghodsee introduces her readers to "Silvi," a Bulgarian Muslim "Avon Lady." Katie Brown of Sapelo Island on the Georgia coast remembers her grandmother Margret making "saraka" cakes for her community and chanting *dhikr*. British-born Soraya Syed Sanders has taught and exhibited calligraphy in London. Bosnian Alma Suljevic clears minefields and sells the soil she collects to art galleries. British Bangladeshi Afshan Azad played "Padma Patil" in the blockbuster *Harry Potter* movies. Mara Brock Akil has produced and written for television shows, such as *The Jamie Foxx Show* and *Girlfriends*, and the motion picture *Sparkle* (2012). Iranian-American Shohreh Aghdashloo has appeared in multiple films and television, enacting the role of "Elizabeth," a Jew, in *The Nativity Story* (2006) and of "Dr. Kavita Rao" in *X-Men: The Last Stand*. She also received an Academy Award nomination for her portrayal of "Nadi" in *House of Sand and Fog* (2003).

The above examples representing Muslim women in Europe and the Americas demonstrate innovative vitality belying assumptions that Muslim women must universally or overwhelmingly conform their religious practices, styles of dress, and personal expressions to prescriptions or presumptions of conventional Muslim authorities, cultural pressures, or non-Muslim expectations. Yet Muslim women may still choose to adopt or appreciate particular religious traditions and their precedents. Muslim women in Europe and America actively converse and collaborate with Christians, Jews, and others who mutually enrich and influence each other. Some women convert to or away from Islam to other religions such as Christianity, or confess atheism, as Ayaan Hirsi Ali does at the time of this writing. Muslim women are role models in scholarship, sports, and the arts who publicly and privately exemplify their religious identities to others. Their words and achievements inform and reshape popular perceptions and portrayals of women and Islam, concurrently patterning possibilities for Muslim and other women to blossom as boxers, actresses, poets, even prime ministers. Future dynamics involving women, Islam, and popular religion in Europe and the Americas may prove even more fascinating.

BIBLIOGRAPHY

Abu-Nimer, Mohammed, and David Augsburger, eds. *Peace-Building by, between, and beyond Evangelical Christians and Muslims*. Lanham, Md.: Rowman & Littlefield, 2009.

Adeney, Miriam. *Daughters of Islam: Building Bridges with Muslim Women*. Downers Grove, Ill.: InterVarsity, 2002.

Ali, Ayaan Hirsi. *Infidel*. New York: Free Press, 2007.

Ali, Ayaan Hirsi. *Nomad: From Islam to America: A Personal Journey through the Clash of Civilizations*. New York: Free Press, 2010.

Dursteler, Eric R. *Renegade Women: Gender, Identity, and Boundaries in the Early Modern Mediterranean*. Baltimore: Johns Hopkins University Press, 2011.

Ghanea Bassiri, Kambiz. *A History of Islam in America: From the New World to the New World Order*. New York: Cambridge University Press, 2010.

Ghodsee, Kristen Rogdeh. *Muslim Lives in Eastern Europe: Gender, Ethnicity, and the Transformation of*

Islam in Postsocialist Bulgaria. Princeton Studies in Muslim Politics. Princeton, N.J.: Princeton University Press, 2010.

Gomez, Michael A. *Black Crescent: The Experience and Legacy of African Muslims in the Americas*. Cambridge, U.K.: Cambridge University Press, 2005.

Haddad, Yvonne Yazbeck, Jane I. Smith, and Kathleen M. Moore. *Muslim Women in America: The Challenge of Islamic Identity Today*. New York: Oxford University Press, 2006.

Idilby, Ranya, Suzanne Oliver, and Priscilla Warner. *The Faith Club: A Muslim, a Christian, a Jew—Three Women Search for Understanding*. New York: Simon & Schuster, 2007.

Kidd, Thomas S. *American Christians and Islam: Evangelical Culture and Muslims from the Colonial Period to the Age of Terrorism*. Princeton, N.J.: Princeton University Press, 2009.

Nieuwkerk, Karin van. *Women Embracing Islam: Gender and Conversion in the West*. Austin: University of Texas Press, 2006.

Zebiri, Kate. *Muslims and Christians Face to Face*. Oxford: Oneworld, 1997.

Benjamin B. DeVan

Middle East and North Africa

"Popular" Islam—the term used for the variations in belief and practice in Islam as they are locally understood and observed throughout the Muslim world—is also public Islam. Traditionally educated religious scholars (*ʿulamāʾ*) and self-appointed contemporary Islamist spokespersons sometimes dismiss as non-Islamic or "incorrect" local practices that they believe conflict with their idea of Islamic principles, even though the people who maintain such traditions usually consider their practices authentic. These practices include special respect for people who claim to be descendants of the Prophet Muḥammad, the veneration of saints or "pious ones" (*al-ṣāliḥūn*), possession cults (*zār*), participation in religious brotherhoods (*ṭarīqahs*), and commemoration of the Prophet's birth (*mawlid al-nabī*; Turkish, *mevlûd*) in which women play dominant roles.

The "Pious Ones" or Saints. In Arabic, a *ṣāliḥ* is a person, living or dead, who serves as an intermediary in securing God's blessings (*barakah*) for clients and supporters. The term does not imply that God has intermediaries, a notion at odds with Qurʾānic doctrine, although implicit in local beliefs. Shrines associated with these saints are the focus of local pilgrimages and annual festivals. Some offerings are annual obligations that ensure that the social groups involved "remain connected" with the saint to secure his blessings. Annual festivals for major saintly figures attract tens of thousands of clients. At the same time, public collective recitations of poetry in praise of the Prophet Muḥammad are popular events that reinforce community ties and bring blessings to the reciters and their audiences.

In addition to offering collective sacrifices to "remain connected," individuals give gifts or sacrifices for specific requests. For instance, it is common for women to go to certain shrines to ask for a saint's help in becoming pregnant. A woman may tear a strip of cloth from her dress and attach it to the door of a shrine as a reminder to the pious one. If the request is granted, she and her spouse give the promised payment. For a North African who implicitly accepts such beliefs, the main issue is not the existence of pious ones—that is taken for granted—but whether particular pious ones will exercise their powers on one's behalf.

Use of the term "pious one" instead of "marabout" or "saint" evokes the multifaceted nature of the concept in North African thought. Shrines dot the landscape throughout North Africa, and the significance of pious ones is formally acknowledged in a variety of ways. In North Africa, it is common for people going on the pilgrimage to Mecca first to visit local shrines or sanctuaries and to do so again on their return. Such ritual activities suggest that believers have an integrated vision of local religious practices and more universally accepted rituals such as the pilgrimage to Mecca. The Arabic word for pilgrimage (*ḥajj*) is not used to describe such local visits; the pilgrimage to Mecca is conceptually a separate phenomenon.

Religious Orders and Rituals in the Modern World. Religious brotherhoods (*ṭarīqahs*) and lodges (*zāwiyah*; Persian, *khānqāh*; Turkish, *tekke*), associated with mysticism, also figure in popular religious practices throughout the Muslim-majority world. Popular religious expression often reflects social differentiation. In North Africa, for instance, the Tijānīyah order—and today the Būshīshīyah in Morocco—had numerous government officials among its adherents, as did the Bektāshīyah order in Turkey. Other orders were associated with particular crafts or trades. Some were considered highly respectable; others less so. Less emphasized until recent years has been the vital role that women have played in sustaining the mystic tradition, an integral element of Islamic religious expression, throughout the Muslim world. In recent times, some orders are enjoying a revival as religious traditions become "re-imagined" and integrated into modern life.

Sometimes popular religious practices have been dismissed as little more than an affective complement to the formal side of Islamic practice and involving women more than men. Such characterizations can be highly misleading. For example, *zār* cults are prevalent throughout Egypt, Sudan, and East Africa. Because women often play a major role in these practices, some observers have speculated that they compensate for their often subordinate social status. More recent studies suggest, however, that the elaborate array of spirits called up by participants in *zār* cults, in which both men and women participate, offers a conceptual backdrop against which villagers and others can imagine alternative social and religious realities, much like the veneration of saints, the "invisible friends" of early Latin Christianity.

Women also predominate in the ceremonies that mark the birth of the Prophet Muḥammad, the *mevlûd* in Turkey, while men predominate in activities that take place in mosques. Rather than seeing the *mevlûd* as primarily a women's activity, it is best to see it as complementary to mosque activities and an integral element of the way Islam is understood locally and practiced by both women and men acting as households.

Popular elaboration of ritual also distinguishes communities within the Muslim world. The ritual cycle of mourning for the betrayal of the Prophet's grandson Ḥusayn (d. 680) provides Shīʿī Muslims with a sense of self-renewal and victory over death and strengthens a sense of sectarian identity. On *ʿāshūrāʾ*, the tenth of the month of Muḥarram, funerary processions in Shīʿī communities throughout Iran, Afghanistan, southern Iraq, Pakistan, and Lebanon reenact the last episodes of Ḥusayn's life and his burial. Central to these occasions is a mourning play (*taʿzīyah*) about his martyrdom, its many versions varying according to local circumstances. The intensity of such public performances, especially when they accompany other religious events, provides Shīʿī leaders with a means of mobilizing public opinion.

Popular religious expression involves both explicit discussion and debate, and an implicit reimagination of belief and practice, which together contribute to a continuing reconfiguration of religious thought throughout the world of Islam. Thus, the theologian Ibn Taymīyah (d. 1328) condemned celebration of the Prophet's birth as a harmful innovation (*bidʿah*). Many other theologians, however, tolerate it as an acceptable innovation (*bidʿah ḥasanah*) because it promotes reverence for the Prophet. In other regions, including villages in the Chitral region of Pakistan's North-West Frontier Province, austere and rigid Wahhābī-inspired representations of Islam clash with a lively tradition of Ṣūfī-inspired poetry and music recitals that balance the formality of public ritual.

Islam's "New" Intellectuals. A major development in the popular understanding of Islam is associated with the rise of mass education and the new media. Traditionally educated religious scholars (*'ulamā'*) now compete for public space alongside media-wise preachers and others who capture a public audience and suggest to a wide public how to live Islamic lives in the modern world. The proliferation of new communications media has also opened public space for women. Not all Muslims regard the authoritative voice of an established man of learning as a prerequisite to legitimate religious knowledge. Increasingly, the carriers of religious knowledge are those who claim a strong Islamic commitment, as is the case with many educated urban youths. Freed from traditional patterns of learning and scholarship, which have often been compromised by state control, religious knowledge is increasingly interpreted in a directly political fashion. Photocopied tracts, Web blogs, and the clandestine dissemination of sermons on cassettes and CDs have begun to complement the male-oriented mosque as the vehicle for disseminating visions of Islam that challenge those sanctioned by the state. Likewise, the religious interpretation of dreams and visions cuts across all social classes, gender, and educational levels throughout the region and in places as diverse as Pakistan, Egypt, and Morocco can have profound personal and political significance.

The overall trend is toward open competition for who speaks for Islam to thinkers and activists from wider backgrounds than male-dominated religious schools. Potential audiences for religious thought and activism are increasingly younger and educated, familiar with competing secular ideologies and open to the idea of women and men sharing public space. The key terms in persuasive public appeals for social justice, often derived from Qur'ānic verses and religious slogans, are more evocative for their intended audiences than are the language and arguments of secular appeals alone. Sometimes these invocations of religious themes are only tangentially based on Islamic tradition as it is more universally understood. Such competing voices, however, have profoundly altered the competition over who speaks for Islam throughout the Muslim-majority world and how they do so.

BIBLIOGRAPHY

Afsaruddin, Asma, ed. *Hermeneutics and Honor: Negotiating Female Public Space*. Cambridge, Mass.: Harvard University Press, 1999. Excellent survey of how women past and present have contributed publicly to defining the moral order.

Boddy, Janice. *Wombs and Alien Spirits: Women, Men, and the Zār Cult in Northern Sudan*. Madison: University of Wisconsin Press, 1989. Rich, evocative account of possession cults and how they relate to both Islam and ideas of gender and person.

Çinar, Alev. *Modernity, Islam, and Secularism in Turkey: Bodies, Places, and Time*. Minneapolis: University of Minnesota Press, 2005. Fascinating account of changing notions of the moral authority of women in Turkish public space.

Deeb, Lara. *An Enchanted Modern: Gender and Public Piety in Shi'i Lebanon*. Princeton, N.J.: Princeton University Press, 2006.

Eickelman, Dale F. *The Middle East and Central Asia: An Anthropological Approach*. 4th ed. Upper Saddle River, N.J.: Prentice Hall, 2002. Chapter 10 provides an extensive account of religious practices throughout the region.

Eickelman, Dale F. *Moroccan Islam: Tradition and Society in a Pilgrimage Center*. Austin: University of Texas Press, 1976. Thorough account of saints in a Moroccan context and the ambiguous tension between their veneration and other interpretations of Islam.

Mahmood, Saba. *Politics of Piety: The Islamic Revival and the Feminist Subject*. Princeton, N.J.: Princeton University Press, 2005.

Mittelmaier, Amira. *Dreams That Matter: Egyptian Landscapes of the Imagination*. Berkeley: University of California Press, 2011.

Salvatore, Armando, and Dale F. Eickelman, eds. *Public Islam and the Common Good*. Leiden, Netherlands, and Boston: E. J. Brill, 2004. Discusses the role that Islam plays in politics and society throughout the Middle East, Turkey, and South Asia.

Schielke, Samuli. "On Snacks and Saints: When Discourses of Order and Rationality Enter the Egyptian Mawlid." *Archives de Sciences Sociales des Religions* 135 (2006): 117–140.

Smith, Margaret. *Rābiʿa the Mystic and Her Fellow-Saints in Islām*. Cambridge, U.K.: Cambridge University Press, 1928 (reprinted 2010). Remains the classic account of the role of female mystics in the Muslim tradition.

Tapper, Nancy, and Richard Tapper. "The Birth of the Prophet: Ritual and Gender in Turkish Islam." *Man* 22, no. 1 (March 1987): 69–92. One of the best accounts of the complementarity of men's and women's religious practices for the entire region.

Waugh, Earle H. *Memory, Music, and Religion: Morocco's Mystical Chanters*. Columbia: University of South Carolina Press, 2005.

Dale F. Eickelman

South Asia

Muslim women's experience in the religious landscape of South Asia is diverse. Since the introduction of Islam to the subcontinent in the early eighth century CE, women have been involved in myriad ways with the propagation and practice of various interpretations of Islam. From the shrines of religious saints to marking the cycle of the religious calendar, the ambit of women's religious experiences and rituals covers many areas of social life. In the last century, in particular, popular forms of women's Islam have been the focus of religious revival and reform movements.

The first Muslim women in South Asia were largely high status, typically local wives of Arab traders or soldiers. The Arab elite in the region did not undertake a program of mass conversion, and records indicate that men and women affiliated with Islam in its initial presence in the area sought to be or already were at the top of local hierarchies. As Muslim presence in the region continued over centuries, more popular engagements with Islam would dramatically expand the number of those considering themselves Muslim.

Women's religious practices were an important factor in the wider adoption of Islam in the subcontinent. As Muslim rulers altered the built environment and developed an Indo-Muslim culture, groups of women worked, as men did, as artisans and craftspeople involved in creating religious artifacts and structures. As Muslim rulers moved nomadic populations in the northwest and northeast of South Asia toward systems of settled agriculture, the peasant populations that emerged were more closely acquainted with Islamic cosmologies and narratives. A particularly important set of locales where larger swathes of women engaged with Islam were saintly shrines.

As tomb-sites and successor institutions to Ṣūfīs (Muslim mystics) sprang up across the region, women from preexisting religious communities increasingly associated with these *dargahs* (shrines). A number of syncretic and heterodox practices developed at shrines, although themes and perspectives from the Qurʾān and the life of the Prophet were salient in these observances. Practices included learning religious creeds and stories through rhyme and verse. Every year, an *ʿurs* (commemoration of a saint's death) would gather large numbers of devotees. In the cycle of women's shrine visitation and returning home, Islamic parables and lessons spread to their surrounding communities. Thus, women's popular practice was a major vehicle for the gradual conversion of entire villages and family networks. As is the case today, in most shrines women sat together in a separate section from men across a screen or on another side of the saints' tombs.

Women continue to visit shrines for a whole host of concerns. Instances of spirit possession are remedied through exorcisms. Aside from seeking a saint's intercession through prayer, some women affiliated with shrines also served as healers, treating various illnesses and infertility. Examples abound of women's close association with shrines across South Asia. One is the Yusufayn shrine in Hyderabad, India, where Muslim women join with one another and groups of non-Muslim women to offer prayers. Another is the shrine of Sakhi Sarwar in Pakistan's Punjab province: a centuries-old tradition is practiced whereby women bring toy cradles to the shrine and pray for the ability to conceive children.

Women have been traditionally prohibited from attending congregational prayers in the mosque by religious scholars, including on ʿĪd (the festival marking the end of Ramaḍān and the *ḥajj*). In practice, the ban was not absolute. Because women generally observe the five daily prayers at home, South Asian Muslim women have crafted spaces for religious devotion and observance in and around the home. During major religious rites and festivals, for example, marriage and funerals, women often assumed community-oriented roles centered on building solidarity with other women, food preparation, and gender-segregated religious rituals.

There are several occasions in the religious calendar where women's practices are an important part of community building. *Milad*s (commemorations of the Prophet's birth) have long been socially recognized as primarily a women's ritual. During these occasions, hymns are recited, some having been transmitted orally over generations and others representing new arrangements composed by the reciters. Talks are also given concerning the circumstances and signs of the Prophet's birth. *Ifṭārs* (fast-breaking meals during Ramaḍān) and the commemoration of the death of the Prophet's grandson Ḥusayn during Muḥarram, the first month of the Islamic calendar, are marked by the preparation of particular foods and various genres of oral recitation. Often, roles in life cycle rituals and commemorations will be specific to a woman's life stage. Factors such as whether a woman has passed puberty or is married impact her authority in religious spaces and the amount of responsibility she is given for conducting ceremonies and rites.

A class-based separation in the normative conception of Muslim women took place after the Indian Mutiny of 1857. British colonial authorities took direct control of much of the region and created a personal law based on their understanding of Islam, mixing British legal principles and the input of particular religious scholars. The *shurafāʾ*, Muslim elites in northern India, began to elaborate on the idea of purdah (women's seclusion) as an important part of solidifying and strengthening the Muslim community in the face of increasing politicization of religious identity. At the same time, popular heterodox religious practices were discounted as the result of being uneducated or naive in their religious tradition. In an important sense, the reform of many practices associated with women's religious life was an organizing principle of Islamic revivalism during the early twentieth century. The legislative arrangements undertaken by both the British and Muslim elite reform projects afforded low value to the lived experiences of many Muslim women. They had worked alongside men in manual and agricultural labor, and their shared religious observances with other faith communities were the basis for long-standing cooperation and peace among Muslims, Hindus, and others. Likewise, the legalistic understanding behind reform movements directly before the end of the colonial era served to undermine long-standing forms of public piety among women.

Nevertheless, in contemporary popular Islam, women often hold strong continuities with their forebears in terms of ritual practice and devotion.

Pīrs, religious saints and their descendants, continue to serve as a resource for divine intercession on matters from family strife to medical concerns. Rituals and objects are used as protection against *naẓar* (the "evil-eye"), a frequent social concern. Muslim women are also engaged in various grassroots movements throughout the region, among which are efforts to educate women about their rights under Islamic marriage contracts, improve health and education for girls, and create employment opportunities for girls. For example, women deploying religious themes have been at the forefront of agitation for political autonomy in Kashmir. Not only elite Muslim women, but also poorer women gather in study circles for *dār*s or religious education.

Over the last few decades, there has been a rise of *fatwā*s or legal opinions of male scholars concerning women's practice at the local level, which in turn has diminished certain popular practices and forms of women's community building. In spite of the effects of urbanization and the impact of religious fundamentalism, Muslim women in South Asia continue to imbue their day-to-day lives and communities with religious devotion and meaning-making.

Bibliography

Abbas, Shemeem B. *The Female Voice in Sufi Ritual: Devotional Practices of Pakistan and India*. Austin: University of Texas Press, 2003.

Aftab, Tahera. *Inscribing South Asian Muslim Women: An Annotated Bibliography and Research Guide*. Boston: Brill, 2008.

Metcalf, Barbara. *Islam in South Asia in Practice*. Princeton, N.J.: Princeton University Press, 2009.

Abbas Jaffer

Southeast Asia

The majority of the world's Muslim population lives in island Southeast Asia in what is known as the "Muslim Archipelago." The modern nation-states of Indonesia, Malaysia, and Brunei Darussalam have Muslim-majority populations totaling more than 210 million. Muslims constitute a minority in Singapore, the Philippines, and the Buddhist-dominant cultures of Thailand, Myanmar, Cambodia, Laos, and Vietnam in mainland Southeast Asia. There are similarities between the Muslim cultures in the world's largest Muslim-majority nation-state of Indonesia and the Muslim Malay cultures in Malaysia, Brunei Darussalam, Singapore, southern Thailand, and the southern Philippines.

Muslims in Southeast Asia are predominantly Sunnī, following the Shāfiʿī school of Islamic law, and are part of the wider Muslim community known as Ahl al-Sunnat wa-al-Jamāʿat (the people of the Sunnah and the community). What this means in practice, however, may vary from place to place and from group to group. This is because, in Southeast Asia, there is a diversity of ethnic groups that practice Islam in local ways, integrating and co-existing with indigenous customs and pre-Islamic ways of life. These kinds of Islamic practices contrast with those of Salafis who seek to purify their understanding of Islam from cultural elements. Women in such Salafi groups also deserve attention in this review of women and popular religion, given the increasing popularity of Salafi movements in Southeast Asia.

Muslim communities had developed in Southeast Asia in the thirteenth century as a result of increasing maritime trade at the time. Islam arrived in Southeast Asia in its Ṣūfī form, emphasizing mystical practice and saint veneration. Ṣūfism has been more prominent in Indonesia than in other Muslim-majority cultures since the fourteenth century, where it characterized Islamic practice. Ṣūfī orders (Malay, *tarekat*; Arabic, *ṭarīqah*) are found not only in Indonesia but also in southern Thailand, southern Philippines, Singapore, Brunei Darussalam, and Malaysia.

Urbanization processes and globalizing forces have facilitated the reinvention of popular Ṣūfism among the educated middle classes in urban areas, signaling a move from the traditional association of Ṣūfism with Islamic boarding schools in rural areas.

Ṣūfī cultural practices contrast with the modernist, reformist, or Salafī movements that characterize what have been termed "scripturalist" and "literalist" versions of Islam. The latter subscribe to Arab-derived gender ideologies that differ from Southeast Asia's emphasis on bilateral gender relations as "separate but complementary," affording women significantly high levels of social mobility and autonomy in daily life. Before Islam's arrival in island Southeast Asia, Hindu-Buddhist and indigenous "animist" religious practices were the prevalent form of religiosity for approximately eight centuries. The introduction of Islam as Ṣūfī practice integrated well with the existing Hindu-Buddhist and indigenous cultures—an example is the replacement of ancestor worship with the Ṣūfī practice of saint veneration at graves. Scholars have described this amalgamation as syncretic, giving rise to culturally rich diverse forms of Islamic practice. There are thus varieties of religious practice in island Southeast Asia that are historically rooted in pre-Islamic Hindu-Buddhist and indigenous worldviews and practices. These practices integrate with an Islamic worldview to form popular modes of religiosity in daily life.

Popular Islam. Popular religion refers to the ways in which ordinary people interpret, understand, and practice religion, in this case Islam, as it integrates with local cultural beliefs and practices. This means that, although Islam is identifiable as a coherent set of beliefs and practices, it is also expressed and practiced in culturally specific ways across the ethnic and linguistic diversity of Southeast Asia's island world. Literature has tended to identify women's practices with culture rather than Islam, and as a result, there is a lack of literature that deals with popular religion as Islamic.

For ordinary Muslim women, popular Islam consists of various practices determined by one's preferred interpretation of Islam. Class, ethnicity, educational background, and status also exert an influence on and shape the kinds of popular religious practices women perform. More generally, popular practices include attending weekly sermons at the local mosque or the mosque of a preferred organization or group (of which there are many to choose from), or joining a Qurʾānic study group. Other popular Islamic practices include prayers for the dead and prayer meals, recitations asking God to bless the Prophet and his family, and celebrating the birth of the Prophet Muḥammad.

The popularity of celebrity male and female Muslim preachers on television or attending their sermons in person shows that women actively seek Islamic knowledge and instruction. Muslim women may choose to be active in an Islamic organization, to be part of an established Ṣūfī order, or to attend the lectures or sermons of a charismatic Muslim figure in a new religious or spiritual movement. Muslim women who de-emphasize culture in their religiosity generally do not participate in Ṣūfī orders, local rituals, or cultural practices. Instead, they typically practice their preferred interpretation of Islam as part of organizations or reformist movements popularly described as Salafī. Salafī (and Wahhābī) women often face challenges in their communities in part because of the proselytizing practices of their husbands or families that focus on deculturalizing Islam. Therefore, Salafī women are rarely involved in rituals or important aspects of communal religiosity, but rather take on significant roles within their exclusive Salafī community.

Popular Village Religion. Popular religion differs for women living in urban and rural areas.

The emphasis on communal living in rural areas means that local custom (Malay, *adat*) is socially valued, and therefore, Muslim women who live in village areas of Southeast Asia play important roles in the everyday life of popular religion in several domains of social life. This includes, but is not limited to, communal rituals such as feasts, preparation of offerings, healing and communicating with unseen worlds, potent ancestors, and deceased Muslim saints. Malays (and non-Malay groups) practice popular expressions of "village Islam" through life-crisis rituals and popular feasts (Malay, *kenduri*) known by various local terms in Indonesia (*slametan, syukuran, kenduren/kenduri, tahlilan, roahan*), Malaysia (*kenduri*), Brunei Darussalam (*majelis doa slamet/doa kesyukuran*), Singapore (*kenduri*), southern Thailand (*kenduri*), and the southern Philippines (*kanduli*). The ritual feasts vary from place to place, but are usually performed for major life crises (birth, circumcision, marriage, pregnancy, death), as well as for celebratory events including personal achievements, recovery from illness, performing the *ḥajj*, death anniversaries (varying from 3, 7, 9, 40, and 100 days and one and two years after death, and sometimes 1,000 days), and so on. The rituals are also performed within Islamic organizations, *madrasahs* (*pondok/pesantren*), Ṣūfī orders; at saints' tombs; and in city neighborhoods.

The anthropologist Clifford Geertz's classic account of Javanese religion (1976) revealed the central place these ritual feasts occupy in Javanese Islamic religiosity. They are communal-based and serve important functions in village life by keeping the religious aspects of daily life alive. Feminist scholars such as Bianca J. Smith (2008) and Norma Sullivan (1994) have challenged Geertz's male-biased rendition of the rituals, which focuses on the rituals' formality involving male community members who pray and feast together under the guidance of the village Muslim leader. Androcentric readings of these popular rituals have failed to acknowledge the role of Muslim women's religiosity in the maintenance of popular religion in village life. At these rituals, women are responsible for the preparation of food and offerings. In Indonesia, female religious specialists are often required for the female ritual aspect called *rewang* (cooking ritual food for the feast and preparing offerings).

In the Malay Archipelago, women midwife specialists (*dukun bayi/bidan*) are required for Islamicized rituals surrounding pregnancy, birth, and its aftermath. Ordinary Muslim women consult these ritual specialists on food taboos, herbal medicines, and massage during pregnancy and postpartum (especially during the first forty or so days after birth that a woman must spend indoors), as well as for ritual cleansing and burial (or floating in a river or ocean) of the spiritually important placenta. Use of magic spells (*jampi*) and spiritual power (*ilmu*) for healing by Muslim or indigenous healers (*dukun/bomoh/orang pandai/orang pintar*), who use a combination of local magic and Qurʾānic verses, is still popularly practiced by Muslim women in Southeast Asia. Female specialists also offer sex/love magic and beauty-enhancing practices for brides and magical amulets for protection against evil.

Women may become religious specialists with a range of expertise that draws on local and Islamic knowledge. Scholars have argued that the patriarchal public sphere of Islam has reinforced women's identification with local practices that have been categorized as "un-Islamic" or "traditional" (indigenous or Hindu-Buddhist). Research has shown, however, that Muslim women also can and do become specialists of Islam in their own right in *madrasahs*, Islamic boarding schools (*pondok pesantren*), and Ṣūfī orders, often acquiring status and expertise that is recognized by the wider Muslim community. In Indonesia, scholars have documented a number of cases where Muslim women have become legitimate heads of *madrasahs*, Islamic boarding schools, and Ṣūfī orders. Muslim women regularly visit living male or female Muslim leaders or Ṣūfī masters to request help, advice, blessings, or healing as part of their Muslim lifestyles.

Popular Ṣūfism. Popular Ṣūfī practices have been integrated into wider cultural practices that include periodic and calendrical pilgrimages (*ziyārah*) to the tombs of Ṣūfī saints, heroes, kings, and spiritually powerful Muslim leaders for any number of reasons, including for worldly and otherworldly pursuits. Infertile women or those desiring pregnancy believe that performing such pilgrimages leads to a blessed pregnancy. In some parts of the Muslim Archipelago, women and their families take newborn babies to Muslim saints' graves for blessing, or to request general health, success, or recovery from an illness. The tombs of historical female figures are also popular among women seeking pregnancy, love, or other forms of worldly assistance. For Ṣūfī women (and men) ascetics, the acquisition of supernatural power is sought through meditation at Muslim saints' graves. Women constitute a significant percentage of participants in the varieties of Ṣūfī orders in Muslim Southeast Asia; in some cases, they acquire leadership roles through kinship-based inheritance or achieve spiritual potency.

Bibliography

Frisk, Sylva. *Submitting to God: Women and Islam in Urban Malaysia*. Denmark: NIAS Press, 2009.

Geertz, Clifford. *The Religion of Java*. Chicago: University of Chicago Press, 1976. This was the first influential ethnography to detail the role of the communal ritual feast (*slametan*) in Java, Indonesia. Despite Geertz's identification of the ritual as characteristic of village animism, the scholarly consensus is that ritual feasts share an Islamic identity across the Muslim world, and are especially similar to the Malay Muslim *kenduri* and South Indian Muslim *kanduri*.

Peletz, Michael. *Reason and Passion: Representations of Gender in a Malay Society*. Berkeley and London: University of California Press, 1996.

Smith, Bianca J. "Kejawen Islam as Gendered Praxis in Javanese Village Religiosity." In *Indonesian Islam in a New Era: How Women Negotiate Their Muslim Identities*, edited by Susan Blackburn, Bianca J. Smith, and Siti Syamsiyatun, pp. 97–118. Melbourne: Monash University Press, 2008.

Smith, Bianca J., and Mark Woodward, eds. *Gender and Power in Indonesian Islam: Leaders, Feminists, Sufis and Pesantren Selves*. London and New York: Routledge, forthcoming.

Sullivan, Norma. *Masters and Managers: A Study of Gender Relations in Urban Java*. St. Leonards, NSW: Allen & Unwin, 1994. Following a Geertzian approach to the Javanese *slametan* communal feast, Sullivan also overlooked the Islamic-ness of the ritual feast in her significant inquiry into the female aspect of the ritual. See Bianca J. Smith (2008) for a feminist critique of Geertz and an ethnographic account of Muslim women's contribution to ritual feasts as Islamic practice in Java.

Watson-Andaya, Barbara. *The Flaming Womb: Repositioning Women in Early Modern Southeast Asia*. Honolulu: University of Hawai'i Press, 2006.

Bianca J. Smith

Sub-Saharan Africa

For the past thousand years, Islam, in the form of the practice of Muslims and outward expressions of Muslim consciousness, icons, and social organization, has widely contributed to cultural appropriations and adaptations across the African continent. During the nineteenth century, and to an even greater extent under colonial domination in the twentieth century, the velocity of Islamization picked up. During the twentieth century, the population of Muslims has increased exponentially from an estimated 11 million in 1900 to 234 million in 2010. Previously, many of the regions of sub-Sahara had had little or no direct contact with the Islamic world, but, with the advent of Christian missionary activity, Islam became a counterweight to European-inflected monotheism. Toward the end of the twentieth century, independent Africa was visited by yet another wave of Muslim influence in the form of nongovernmental organizations mainly from the Arabian Peninsula, which further differentiated Islamic practice in the heartlands from local praxis.

One result of this long history is that popular expressions of piety in Islamized Africa exhibit rich diversity, both within individual societies and in developments across time, and cultural expressions of Islam extend into political arenas well beyond simple acts of conversion and opposition. The steady rise of the population coupled with the large geographical expanse of sub-Saharan Africa means that to refer to popular religion in broad brush strokes is almost impossible. This is because popular religion is exactly about a localized phenomenon that cannot be generalized easily over nations and cultures. Examples of popular religion in sub-Saharan Muslim societies may, however, be grouped into three categories that broadly elucidate the phenomenon: culturally specific social behavior and religious ideas that include appropriations of Islamic motifs; the permeation of symbols of literacy (e.g., the Qurʾān), into everyday life; and ritual practice.

Islam and Local Culture. Islamization in sub-Saharan Africa has been by no means systematic; it has affected some individuals and communities and left others untouched. Frequently, it is Islamic dress that most effectively distinguishes converts from non-Muslims living around them. That dress is generally a variation on the *jallābīyah* and cap (*kaffīyeh*)—both sometimes bearing elaborate embroidery that may be an indicator of economic class—and ornament in the form of talismans in leather amulet pouches tied to the arm or hung around the neck, *tasbīḥ* (prayer beads), and, for the traveler, a rolled prayer mat and a kettle of water carried for ablutions. To be so equipped is to be identified as a Muslim in sub-Sudanic African societies where specific local customs relating to diet, marriage, divorce, or inheritance may conflict with Islamic law or where the full weight of orthopraxy may not be felt.

The decorative arts of local cultures across Muslim Africa, such as their music and poetry, reveal great local genius in the appropriation of Islamic symbols. Islamic symbols and elements of Muslim material culture have also entered African arts in such forms as elaborately woven prayer mats, amulet-case designs in metal or leather, jewelry, and ornament in mask designs. Analogous to these representations in the arts are Islamic motifs in music and verse. Distinctive Islamic dress and Islamic motifs in the arts of many sub-Saharan African societies are the result of centuries of contact with Muslim lands.

Qurʾān and Popular Piety. The most pervasive example of Qurʾānic transcendence in popular usage throughout sub-Saharan Africa is the talisman or amulet industry, the products of which adorn babies, children, and adults as well as protect many a home and car. Talismans are mainly utilized for their preventative or palliative powers, which underlines an important therapeutic attraction of Islam among peoples on the fringe of the Muslim world. The use of "washings" (typically inked or chalked verses from the Qurʾān, washed into a vial to be periodically drunk or dabbed on the body) to cure or at least mitigate a variety of ills has long been part of the repertoire of holy men and seers throughout Muslim Africa. In the same fashion, talismans hung at a prescribed spot or worn on the body can serve a range of purposes: protection in armed conflict or everyday affairs, for individuals or whole communities; security for safe travel, avoidance of slander, or assurance of success or influence; advantage to cause and then protect pregnancies, cure disease, or promote intelligence; and punishment in the form of proactive measures against enemies. A common adornment for masks used in communal cleansing ceremonies well beyond the pale of Muslim communities are talismans with appropriate prayers or Qurʾānic messages to aid the process.

Washings and talismans are at the juncture of medicine (*ṭibb*) and esoteric sciences (*bāṭinīyah*) in Islamic learning, and these specifically Islamic cures compete with other therapeutic remedies readily available in most African societies. It is to specialists in social problems that politicians and businessmen apply for formulas for success, and there are few heads of state, Muslim or Christian, who are not reputed to retain a personal *mallam* (religious leader) or marabout (Ṣūfī mystic).

The Ṣūfī brotherhoods have long been the vanguard of Islamization in sub-Saharan Africa, and with them have arisen popular attachments to individual *shaykh*s, analogous to the special relation between *shaykh* and student in many other parts of the Muslim world. Pilgrimage to the tombs of saints may have therapeutic effects, most frequently for women to safeguard pregnancies. The desire for prayers of intervention on behalf of individuals has spawned a minor prayer industry for *shaykh*s. This mediating role, most frequently played by Ṣūfī leaders, has led to the veneration of both dead saints and living *shaykh*s. The Ṣūfī *shaykh* as a conduit between the supernatural and the common folk has long been an important fixture in the moral economy of Muslim communities. Whether he is a writer of simple talismans or an accomplished jurist, a *shaykh*'s authority rests largely on his near-monopoly over the scripture, but his *barakah* (blessing) may also be sought for its own sake.

The title "al-Shaykh," like the pilgrim's title "al-Ḥājjī," connotes local recognition of the religious, objects of veneration among their followers and subjects of snickers among their critics. Inexpensive cassette tapes of sermons and readings by both pan-Islamic notables and local preachers have become available on national markets in sub-Saharan Africa, providing an electronic form of mediation and translation of the Word in local settings that now competes with the scripture in the economy of popular piety. With the increased activity of Muslim nongovernmental organizations and the return home from local students subsidized to study in the Hejaz at the end of the twentieth century, there has come a new level of competition for the minds of the faithful between the *shaykh*s and "modernist" practice.

Ritual Practice. Piety in most sub-Saharan African Islamic communities, as elsewhere in the Islamic world, is most publicly displayed at prayer and most effectively demonstrated on festival days. These are the occasions for new outfits for children, new gowns for adult members of the household, lavish displays of food for dependents, and generous dispensing of cash gifts—all widely accepted as indices of religiosity. Although the relative importance of individual festival days varies from region to region, the end of Ramaḍān generally competes in importance as a principal festival. Celebration of the Prophet's birth, the *mawlid*, is a minor holiday in parts of sub-Saharan Africa, although it has been appropriated by the Ṣūfī brotherhoods in many countries for an annual display of piety before saints' tombs. Large followings of some local saints have spawned individual festivals. The centrality of the visitation of saints' tombs varies across Africa's Muslim populations.

Elements of life-cycle rituals in Muslim societies are popularly understood to be linked to Islamic prescriptions. In sub-Saharan Africa, these focus on naming ceremonies (which frequently involve an imam or local *shaykh* and elaborate displays of hospitality), the acts of circumcision and clitoridectomy, the formalities and types of marriage (dowers, the degrees of proximity permitted in Islamic law, the number of wives, etc.)

and divorce, and burial rites. In each Islamized society, compromise is negotiated among local custom, scripturally sanctioned practice, and orthopraxy in neighboring Muslim communities and lands. It is generally with respect to Islamic laws of inheritance and, in particular, land that local custom has proven most intractable.

Since the mid-twentieth century, as a result of increased communication between the Muslim heartlands and sub-Saharan Africa and also as a result of increasing numbers of African pilgrims traveling to the Hejaz, there has been a gradual but perceptible homogenization within national Muslim cultures. This is most noticeable in ritual life, where the political influence of religious leaders has been recognized by national authorities and ritual reinforcement of that influence has been encouraged (a contrast with the official wariness toward that same influence during colonial times). As a result, national Islamic political cultures have emerged in many countries.

[*See also* Astronomy and Astrology; Dress; Sufism and Women, *subentries on* Historical Overview *and* Contemporary Thought and Practice; *and* Ziyārah.]

BIBLIOGRAPHY

Bravmann, René A. *African Islam.* Washington, D.C.: Smithsonian Institution Press, 1983. Elegantly illustrated exhibition catalogue with extended essays on the material culture of Muslim societies in sub-Saharan Africa.

Le Grip, A. "LeMahdisme en Afrique noire." *L'Afrique et l'Asie* 18 (1952): 3–16. Remains one of the best brief surveys of Mahdism in Sudanic Africa during the nineteenth and twentieth centuries.

Lewis, I. M., ed. *Islam in Tropical Africa.* 2d ed. London: International African Institute, 1980. Decades after its first appearance, this study remains one of the most succinct and comprehensive surveys of orthopraxy and popular piety in sub-Saharan African communities; includes an updated introduction.

Nimtz, August H., Jr. *Islam and Politics in East Africa.* Minneapolis: University of Minnesota Press, 1980. Surveys Ṣūfī brotherhoods in East Africa (with particular reference to Tanzania) and their gradual involvement in national politics.

Owusu-Ansah, David. *Islamic Talismanic Tradition in Nineteenth-Century Asante.* Lewiston, N.Y.: Edwin Mellen Press, 1991. Detailed study of a set of over five hundred folios of instructions on the manufacture of talismans recovered from a non-Muslim state on the Gold Coast in the early nineteenth century.

Pewton Forum on Religion and Public Life. "Tolerance and Tension: Islam and Christianity in Sub-Saharan Africa." 2010. http://www.pewforum.org/uploaded-Files/Topics/Belief_and_Practices/sub-saharan-africa-full-report.pdf.

Roberts, Allen F., and Mary Nooter Roberts, with Gassia Armenian and Ousmane Guye. *Saint in the City: Sūfī Arts of Urban Senegal.* Los Angeles: UCLA Fowler Museum of Cultural History, 2003, distributed by University of Washington Press. This richly illustrated (274 color photos) museum catalogue narrates the development and diffusion of mainly *murīd* expressions of visual arts.

Saul, Mahir. "Islam and West African Anthropology." *Africa Today* 53 (2006): 2–33. Surveys the ways anthropologists have ignored the syncretism in West African societies that reflects the long-standing influence of Islam.

Tom, Abdullahi Osman el-. "Drinking the Koran: The Meaning of Koranic Verses in Berti Erasure." In *Popular Islam South of the Sahara,* edited by J. D. Y. Peel and Charles C. Stewart, pp. 414–431. Manchester, U.K.: Manchester University Press, 1985. This collection also includes six contributions that address aspects of popular Islam in Sudan, Nigeria, and Senegal.

Charles C. Stewart
Updated by Zahraa McDonald

Pottery. *See* Ceramics, Women's Representation in

Pregnancy and Childbirth.

Islam from the beginning encouraged its followers to marry in order to establish a loving relationship between spouses and procreate: "His proofs are that He created for you spouses from among yourselves, in order to have tranquility and contentment with each other, and He placed in your hearts love and care towards your spouses. In this, there are sufficient proofs for people who think" (Qur'ān' 24:32).

The Qur'ān'ic understanding of pregnancy and childbearing challenged the *Jāhilīyah* (pre-Islamic) tradition of oppressive and violent treatment of girls and women within the family and society. For instance, according to the fourth chapter of the Qur'ān', "Women" (*an-Nisa*), woman's womb is the source of human relationships, and reciprocity and mutuality. A Muslim doctor, Ibn Qayyim, was the first to introduce similarities between the Qur'ānic and Galenic (referring to Galen, who was born in 131 CE in what is today Turkey) view of the development of the embryo. Islam's view of procreation is similar to the Galenic view on the contribution of both the male and the female and different from the Aristotelian doctrine that presents the view,

> that the male gives the active principle while the female is passive and only provides the place for the activity of the male semen. This doctrine, of course, flows directly from the Aristotelian doctrine (which he applies universally to explain all phenomena) of form and matter, the active and the passive factor, "the matter," is not something negative, however, but also has a positive "tendency to become" something, while the active factor, "the form," fashions matter into that something. Although Aristotle believed that the woman contributed only the menstrual blood that fashioned the body of the child and that its souls came from the male, according to the Islamic doctrine the contribution of both spouses produce the entire organism of the child; in a deeper sense, of course, the entire process is the creation of God. (Rahman, 1979, pp. 111–112)

It should be mentioned, however, that medieval Muslim scholars, such as Ibn Qayyim and Avicenna, used the works of Galen or other Greek philosophers and doctors to understand and interpret the Qur'ānic verses about pregnancy and childbearing. The ḥadīth literature, for instance, has been used to supplement the understanding of Qur'ān'ic verses. In this article, the Qur'ān'ic verses, ḥadīth literature, and the works of traditional and contemporary Muslim scholars are used to describe briefly and analyze the Islamic theology of pregnancy and childbearing.

Importance of Motherhood and Childbearing in Islam. The gender dynamic in many Qur'ān'ic references is more explicit in the verses that describe both God's attributes as well as references to pregnancy, childbearing, and birth and display the importance of motherhood and childbearing in the Qur'ān'. For instance, the word used for womb in the Qur'ān' is *rahim*, which derives from the same root of "mercy" as *raḥma*, *raheem*, and *rahman*, which are among God's most important attributes or "names." The Qur'ān' also describes a womb as a firm, secure, and fixed place for an embryo: "Thereafter We made him as a Nutfah in a *qaraar makeyn* [a fixed place]" (23:13). According to one *qudsī ḥadīth* (this kind of ḥadīth refers to the sayings of the prophet Muḥammad, but signifies that the meaning of the ḥadīth is from God; the other popular kind of ḥadīth is the exemplary sayings and actions of the Prophet Muḥammad), God said, "I am God and I am the All-merciful. I created the womb and I gave it a name derived from my own name. Hence if someone cuts off the womb, I will cut him off, but if someone joins the womb, I will join him to Me." These examples in the Qur'ān' are grammatically feminine in order to show the gender dynamic, like many other names of God that represent forgiveness and mercy.

Many Qur'ān'ic verses and aḥādīth extol the merits of marriage, procreation, and fecundity.

> Man, We did create from a quintessence (of clay); Then We placed him as (a drop of) sperm in a place of rest firmly fixed; Then We made the sperm into a clot of congealed blood; then of that clot We made a (foetus) lump; then We made out of that lump bones and clothed the bones with flesh; then We developed out of it another creature: so blessed be God, the Best to create! (Qur'ān' 23:12–14; see also 22:5)

Also, Muḥammad is reported to have said, "Marry the affectionate and the fecund so that the number of my people exceeds that of others."

The emphasis on childbearing in the Qur'ān' and the ḥadīth literature has created a culture that gave importance to procreation and made childbearing a spiritual experience. For instance, Khalaf and Callister reported the experience of one woman:

> During childbirth the woman is in the hands of God. Every night during my pregnancy I read from the Holy Qur'an to the child. When I was in labor I was reading a special paragraph from the Holy Qur'an about protection. The nurses were crying when they heard what I was reading. I felt like a miracle might happen—that there was something holy around me, protecting me, something beyond the ordinary, a feeling, a spirit about being part of God's creation of a child. (p. 383)

However, childbearing also became one of the most significant responsibilities of women in many Muslim societies, and barren women became stigmatized and criticized for not being able to conceive and bear a child to their husbands. This is one of the main reasons for divorce or polygamy in some Muslim families. Moreover, the majority of Muslim women believe that God alone is the creator; therefore, only God can influence the outcomes of their pregnancy and birth. Many Muslim women, especially those who live in developing countries, use Qur'ān'ic verses and prayer (*du'a*) from the ḥadīth as charms and talismans to conceive a child or visit the tombs of Ṣūfī masters (Muslim saints) to ask God for help to ensure pregnancy and positive birth outcomes. They may also use a special amulet consisting of Qur'ān' verses written with musk water or ink, and sew it to the mother's clothing or use it as bracelet with a strong belief that the amulet protects the unborn baby from the unseen creatures, disease, and the evil eye. An example of such prayer is the prayer of the Prophet Zakariah in his old age for his barren wife. "O my Lord! Grant me from You, a good offspring. You are indeed the All-Hearer of invocation" (Qur'ān 3:38).

A Basic Knowledge of Pregnancy in Islam. Basim Musallam mentions a ḥadīth that narrates that Muhammad was once asked: "From what is the child created?" He replied: "It is created from both the semen of the man and the semen of the woman. The man's semen is thick and forms the bones and tendons, while the woman's is fine and forms the flesh and blood" (46:39). The other version of the ḥadīth by Ibn Qayyim al-Jawziyyah states that, once A'isha and Umm Salama asked him, "Should a woman wash [her clothes] after nocturnal emission [*idha ihtalamat*]?" The Prophet said that she should if there is a trace of the fluid. They asked again: "Do women have nocturnal emissions?" The Prophet said: "How else do their children resemble them?" In another version of the same ḥadīth, it is said: "When her semen dominates the man's semen, the child [will] look like her brothers and when the man's semen dominates her semen, the child [*boy*] will look like his brothers."

The Qur'ān and the ḥadīth offer Muslims basic knowledge of pregnancy and childbearing. For instance, according to Islam, pregnancy is developed in three trimester periods. The first three stages of forty days, or the first trimester of embryonic development, comprise the drop stage (*nutfa*), the leech-like clot or substance stage (*'alaqa*), and the tissue stage (*mudgha*). The other two stages of prenatal development mentioned in the Qur'ān are the stages of *'aadam* (bones) and the dressing of the bones with muscle. In a famous ḥadīth found in the collection of al-Bukhari,

> Each one of you in creation amasses in his mother's womb [in the form of a drop (*nutfa*) for forty days; then he becomes a blood clot (*'alaqa*) for the same period; then he becomes a lump of flesh (*mudgha*) for the same period; then the angel is sent with a mandate [to write down} four things [for the child]: his sustenance, his term of life, his deeds, and whether he will be miserable (*shaqi*) or happy (*sa'id*).]

Many Muslim scholars agree that ensoulment occurs after 120 days of gestation. Some scholars report that ensoulment takes place on the fortieth, forty-second, or forty-fifth night. Ensoulment means the progressive development of the embryo and its viability that grants moral and legal rights and inherent dignity to the embryo (Sachedina, 2009). Therefore, in Islam, life is a precious gift from God, but humans are responsible for how they use this gift. Humans are responsible for preserving their life and the lives of others. However, the latter argument complicates the picture of terminating pregnancy and leads to the possibility of either the legitimate and illegitimate termination of pregnancy in Muslim societies—a point that has divided society into two groups: the proponents and opponents of abortion. Hence, the Qur'ān is clear in its message that "a mother should not be made to suffer because of her child" (2:233), implying that not only preserving life, but also the quality of life is important. Taking this perspective into account, many Islamic authorities issued rules (*fatāwā*) allowing women access to abort unwanted pregnancies. A similar *fatwā* was issued for Bosnian women raped by the Serbian army and Azerbaijani women raped by the Armenian soldiers, allowing them to abort these unwanted pregnancies. This was based on a similar *fatwā*, which was issued in Algeria, when Algerian women were raped by French soldiers. Later on, Muhammad Saeed Tantawi, the Grand Sheikh of Al Azhar, approved a draft of laws allowing women to abort a pregnancy that is the result of a rape.

Moreover, the Qur'ān draws attention to the burden, *dhat haml*, of pregnancy and the special care legally due to pregnant women: "and every pregnant woman (*dhat haml*) will drop her burden" (22:2); "And for those who have a burden (pregnant) their term is when they bring forth their burden. . . . If they have a burden (pregnant) then spend on them until they bring forth their burden." (65:4,6).

***Nasab*, the Proper Lineage of the Child.** In many societies, the proper lineage of the child to his or her family is important to ensure the healthy and virtuous upbringing of the child. According to Islamic legal understandings, pregnancy is the fertilization and development of one or more embryos or fetuses in a woman's uterus, which cannot be replaced by something else for the gestation of a child. This is one of the reasons that the traditional and contemporary Islamic sources consider the mother's womb and, therefore, motherhood, sacred. Furthermore, Islam gives importance to the preservation of proper lineage (*nasab*), which relates the child to the father or mother via blood relationships and demands a proper registration of pregnancy and birth in order for the child to be related to his or her biological parents; this is one of the main purposes of the sacred law of Islam, the Sharī'ah. Another Qur'ānic verse advises the divorced woman to wait for three monthly periods after her divorce in order to make sure that she is not pregnant before marrying another man (2:228) in order to ensure knowledge of parentage.

Nevertheless, from an Islamic perspective, the child's rights over his or her parents begin before the mother's pregnancy. It means that both spouses are responsible for the physical, psychological, and spiritual formation of the child and women are the visible and most important participants in the procreation process.

Conclusion. The traditional Islamic theology of pregnancy and childbearing is God-centered and aims not only to create an awareness of God and the importance of mutual love between husband and wife, as well as the new life, but also human frailty, finitude, and death, and individual and social responsibility before the pregnant woman gives birth and after the child is born. However, it has also created a culture that makes Muslim women responsible for childbearing, as well as one in which Muslim women frequently use the Qurʾān and prayers (*duʿa*) as charms and talismans to conceive a child and give birth to a healthy baby. As Muslim women seek new roles and voices within Muslim societies, they are adapting traditional Islamic sources and creating new understanding in order to bring an Islamic dimension to the universal physical, spiritual, and psychological experience of women.

BIBLIOGRAPHY

Hassan, R. "An Islamic Perspective." In *Women, Religion, and Sexuality: Studies on the Impact of religious teachings on women*, edited by Jeanne Becher, pp. 92–128. Philadelphia: Trinity Press International, 1990.

Isgandarova, Nazila. "Islamic Spiritual Care in a Health Care Setting." In *Spirituality and Health: Multidisciplinary Explorations*, edited by A. Meier, T. O'Connor, and P. VanKatwyk. Waterloo, Ontario: WLU Press, 2005.

Khalaf, I., and L. C. Callister "Cultural Meanings of Childbirth: Muslim Women Living in Jordan." *Journal of Holistic Nursing* 15, no. 4 (1997): 373–388.

Musallam, B. F. *Sex and Society in Islam: Birth Control before the Nineteenth Century*. Cambridge, U.K.: Cambridge University Press, 1983.

Rahman, F. *Islam*. Chicago: University of Chicago Press, 1979.

Sachedina, A. *Islamic Biomedical Ethics: Principles and Application*. New York: Oxford University Press, 2009.

NAZILA ISGANDAROVA

PRINT JOURNALISM.

Journalism is a cultural practice embedded in its broader political, economic, and sociocultural realities. As a cultural practice, it reflects as well as contributes to shaping the values and norms of the society where journalism is produced and consumed. Print journalism in Muslim countries is no exception, especially when analyzed in its relation to Muslim women and gender issues. This relationship has been complex, evolving, and rife with tensions and contradictions spanning at least a century. This article highlights major trends characterizing the relationship between print journalism and Muslim women, focusing on both journalistic content *about* Muslim women and journalistic content produced *by* Muslim women. The overview of women's different stages of journalistic experiences helps identify those trends that remained constant, despite changes in the larger context of journalism, and those that evolved over time.

Women's Discovery and Development of Journalistic Agency. The late nineteenth century marked women's entrance into a long trajectory in journalism as readers, writers, editors, and subjects of journalistic content. The surrounding context of colonialism, struggles for national liberation, and nation-building impacted the nature and development of women's place in print journalism. Before the 1950s, women's investment in the journalistic field was characterized by at least three important and interrelated processes: the affirmation of the right to exist, confirmation of women's writing competence, and the search for a unique identity in print journalism. The post-independence phase has been characterized more by women's struggles over representational power and equality in the profession.

Muslim women's early experiments in journalism appealed to the nationalist fervor to justify their right to exist along with men's voices. Hence, when the first generation of Lebanese,

Syrian, and Egyptian women became involved in print culture as administrators, editors, and/or writers in national journals, their mission was defined in terms of educating women to better serve the nation's future generation of male leaders. In India and Pakistan, although there were very few Muslim women in print journalism prior to independence, those who started writing were also encouraged by the nationalist ethos.

Because education was the rallying call of most nationalists, women invested their journalistic talents in the mission of raising women's consciousness, denouncing harmful cultural practices, and defining women's roles and responsibilities in advancing their nation's progress. The right to exist was also defended in terms of women's right to self-expression and freedom from the forces that restrict women's contribution to national development. Those who questioned the status quo were a minority of privileged urban middle- and upper-class women who took advantage of their social status and capital to launch women's careers in print journalism and print culture in general. By the 1920s, nearly twenty-five Syrian journals were owned by women and nearly the same number of journals and periodicals were launched in Cairo. This explains why Muslim women's entrance to journalism is referred to as an "awakening." Their writing and publishing reflected and contributed to the larger *nahḍah* (intellectual awakening) that was taking place across the Muslim world.

Muslim women's participation in the *nahḍah* entailed defending their right to exist as a public presence that is capable and *competent*. As journalists, readers, and writers, the pioneers faced cultural, psychological, and patriarchal barriers that had inhibited their writing. Some women decided to go anonymous in their early journalistic experiences, such as the Moroccan Malika El Fassi. Others opted for the subversive act of unveiling their name and identity, such as Herawati Diah, who pioneered the role of Indonesian women in journalism. In all cases, women's early struggles with themselves and their societies were part of the identity construction and affirmation of an autonomous writing and thinking subject proud to reveal other skills than those prescribed by traditional societies.

Defending women's voice to exist also meant a search for their unique identity that is anchored in the Muslim context and its realities. Much of the journalistic effort of the early women was preoccupied with its relation to, *but* independence from, women's writings in Western and European contexts. The search for an indigenous voice was a self-conscious endeavor to silence critics accusing Muslim women of emulating colonial practices and betraying their Muslim nation. Preoccupation with "authenticity" and "indigeneity" has remained a thorny issue as local and global cultures intersect more intensely.

Despite the considerable achievements since the *nahḍah,* women's experiences with journalism entered a phase of crisis and "stagnation" in the second decade of the twentieth century. In the immediate post-independence years, women's voices not only were marginalized, but also were mostly expected to regain their silent domesticity. This should come as no surprise since the process of nation-building has often meant setbacks in women's emancipation as Kumari Jayawardena reminded us in her seminal work on feminism and nationalism (1986). Thus, what characterized the 1960s and 1970s were trends in journalism that trivialized Muslim women's capabilities and competences and undermined their role in the development of their countries. This was done by a thriving commercial press that gradually started confining women to consuming home–beauty–fashion images. This trend is another constant feature of journalism, even as the lives of many Muslim women have been changing under the combined effects of education, urbanization, modernization, and Islamist revival.

What this means is that the culture of journalism has not kept pace with the direction of change in women's lives in Muslim countries. Although a greater number of women are accessing education, contributing to public and private sectors of the economy, and as many are seeking greater public roles as political actors, writers, lawyers, and teachers, their representational images in print journalism have stubbornly clung to outmoded models of feminine passivity and submissiveness. This disjuncture between the changing reality of women and the unchanging culture of journalism is the feature of print journalism that is a cause of serious concern and contestation by women.

The Cost of Professionalization. In fact, two simultaneous but contradictory processes have defined Muslim women and print journalism since the 1980s: the increasing professionalization of women in journalism *and* the increasing violence (real and symbolic) against Muslim women in general, and those in the profession in particular.

As Muslim women's movements started gathering momentum in many Muslim countries since the 1990s, rights activists turned to print journalism as a strategic space for both challenging entrenched patriarchal practices and for producing alternative knowledge about women. Thus, the generation of women who institutionalized women's struggles since the 1990s used the communicative power of journalism to reach out to the elite male readers, policy makers, and religious power wielders in their countries. Their calls for women's rights were made on the pages of the feminist press including the *Thamania Mars* (March 8)—one of the early feminist periodicals published by the Moroccan Union of Feminist Action, the Egyptian *Noun* under the leadership of Nawāl al-Saʿdāwī, or the Iranian *Zanan* founded by Shahla Sherkat.

In terms of professionalization, more women are receiving their journalistic training from schools and centers. Many are more confident, competent, and aggressive in reporting on often silenced subjects such domestic violence, rape, female genital mutilation, or sexual harassment. This has often meant "elbowing their way" into a hostile journalistic culture, as the Jordanian Mahassen Al Imam and Rana Husseini expressed it. Husseini, for instance, uncovered the cultural and legal institutions that in/directly sanction "honor crimes" in Jordanian society. Her speaking out about this violence triggered a public debate that built sufficient momentum for activists to call for legal reforms. Other professionals used journalism to engage in broader issues of justice and freedom. The Egyptian women's rights activist Iqbal Baraka, the editor of *Hawaa*, started out as a war correspondent in the Sinai and wrote a highly charged political weekly column for *Al Ahram* when fewer women were permitted or expected to report on politics. The Iranian Shahla Lahiji, who started writing for newspapers at age fifteen, opted for a career in publishing and became the first woman publisher when she founded Roshangaran Publishing in 1983. As a writer, feminist activist, and director of the publishing house, she gave visibility to more than two hundred works by women or dealing with women's issues.

The cost for being a daring woman journalist in a Muslim country is often very high. The jailing, harassing, and killing of female journalists are among the risks they face in addition to their discrimination on the job. Women journalists are often targeted by conservative groups, religious and political, that perceive their voices as a threat or deviance. The torture and killing of women journalists during the Algerian civil war is a clear example of this: "we shall fight with the sword those who fight us with the pen" said the Armed Islamic Group to justify their killing of female journalists. The recent incident of arrest, interrogation, and beating of Mona El Tahawi in Egypt's

Tahrir Square is a reminder that the more vocal and visible women are, the higher their risk of gender-based violence.

Although the number of women journalists is on the increase, they remain considerably underrepresented in management and decision-making positions. The socioeconomic and political structures within which media professionals function are based on entrenched power differentials that disadvantage women irrespective of their degree of competence or areas of expertise. A recent survey of women journalists in North Africa documents the frustrations of generations of journalists who see their careers reaching the same dead-end no matter what the qualifications they bring to the job. Similar observations have been made about women journalists in Saudi Arabia. Being a vocal Muslim female media professional has always been, and remains, an act of heroism.

The symbolic violence perpetrated by print journalists against Muslim women is no less vexing. In 2006, the Center of Arab Women for Training and Research (CAWTAR) and the United Nations Development Fund for Women released the "Arab Women Development Report: Arab Women and the Media" that surveyed twenty-three studies on media images of women between 1995 and 2005. The report revealed that 79 percent of the images of women were negative, focusing on women as sex objects, materialistic, manipulative, opportunistic, and inexperienced. The Global Media Monitoring Project (GMMP), the largest international monitoring mechanism on gender fairness in reporting, further confirmed this. In its 2010 report, it noted that although news media in all regions have made progress in outputting stories that challenge stereotypes, the Middle East registered no progress. The report adds that Latin America has the highest percentage of stories that challenge stereotypes (13 percent) and the Middle East has the highest percentage (81 percent) of those that reinforce stereotypes. It also notes that, in all regions, stories by female reporters challenge stereotypes between 1.2 and 7 times more than those by male reporters—in the Middle East "the output of female reporters challenges stereotypes 7 times more than that by male reporters" (GMMP 2010, 18).

A New Era of Women and Journalism? Although Muslim women have consistently been marginalized by and within the print culture, their subordinate position should not prevent us from seeing important ways in which women's rights activists are combating the trend from within and without. Important initiatives and strategies emerged most visibly since the turn of the new millennium. These include the creation of research centers that monitor the media and produce evidence-based knowledge to trace the continuity of symbolic violence against Muslim women. This is the role, for instance, of the Tunis-based CAWTAR. Other centers, such as the Jordanian Arab Women Media Center, are more focused on training women journalists and empowering them to promote the culture of human rights and democracy. The research and reports published by these centers form the basis for calling for reforms and building transnational support networks for advancing women's rights under Muslim law.

In addition to research institutes, an increasing number of conferences and fora bring together women professionals to share their expertise, build coalitions, and establish a common ground for defending their rights. In 2002, the General Women's Union in the United Arab Emirates convened more than one thousand women to the Arab Women's Media Forum to discuss ways to improve both the media's portrayal of their gender and women's participation in journalism. Among the achievements of the forum is the adoption of the Abu Dhabi Declaration, a document that calls on media organizations to remove discrimination against women in the media industry.

In terms of international networks and coalitions, Muslim women are receiving training opportunities from international organizations that support gender equality. The Institute of War and Peace, based in the United Kingdom, The Netherlands, and Washington, D.C., has tailored its Women's Reporting & Dialogue Programme to the needs of Muslim women. The program offers them training with the aim of forming a regional network of journalists whose reporting will serve as a source of information on gender issues in their countries. Other programs target Muslim men journalists with gender awareness programs in an effort to build the values of gender fairness in the profession.

The aforementioned initiatives, and many others, seek to prepare a younger generation of Muslim journalists to transform the entrenched patriarchal culture and practices of print journalism.

BIBLIOGRAPHY

Akeel, Maha Mustafa. *Al-Mar'ah al-Sa'udiyyah fi al-ilam: Dirasah hawla al-tajarib wa-al-dawr wa-al-ta'thir.* Beirut, Lebanon: Arab Scientific Publishers, 2010.

Baron, Beth. *The Women's Awakening in Egypt: Culture, Society, and the Press.* New Haven, Conn.: Yale University Press, 1994.

CAWTAR-UNIFEM. 2006. Arab Women Development Report: Arab Women and the Media. http://www.cawtar.org.

GMMP. Who Makes the News? Preliminary Report. World Association for Christian Communication. 2010. http://www.whomakesthenews.org/images/stories/website/gmmp_reports/2010/gmmp_2010_preliminary.pdf.

Jayawardena, Kumari. *Feminism and Nationalism in the Third World.* London: Zed Books, 1986.

Kalla, Jurj. *Tarikh al-Sihafa al-niswiyah: nashatuha wa-tatawwuruha, 1892–1932.* Beirut, Lebanon: Dar al-Jil, 1996.

Minault, Gail. "Les revues féminines en langue urdu au début du XX e siècle." *Women Living Under Muslim Laws* 9 (1991): 9–10.

Naji, J. E. *Profession: Journalisme Maghrebin au féminin.* Rabat, Morocco: UNESCO, 2006.

Sakr, N. *Women and Media in MENA: Power through Self-Expression.* London: I. B. Tauris, 2004.

Skalli, L. H. "Constructing Female Leadership in the Middle East: The Gender of Politics in Moroccan Media." *Gender and Society* 25.4 (2011): 473–495.

Skalli, L. H. *Through A Local Prism: Gender, Globalization and Identity in Moroccan Women's Magazines.* Lanham, Md.: Roman & Littlefield, 2006.

LOUBNA H. SKALLI

PROPERTY. Ownership is mentioned in the Qurʾān many times: the Creator is the owner of everything; and He made subject to human beings the earth, sun, moon, sea, and rivers. (14:32–34, 16:12–14, 31:20, and 45:13). The human race, or Adam's children, is assigned to be a vicegerent that is required to act in accordance with the rules set forth by the Real Owner. Sharīʿah considers property rights as God-given and God-regulated.

Nature of Ownership. Ownership is defined in Sharīʿah as "an exclusivity over an object vesting the owner, alone, with a legal authority of its use, enjoyment and disposal" (ʿAbbādī, 1974, p. 150). The object of property can be material, abstract, intellectual, and financial. Property carries a moral connotation. As Islamic morality condemns alcohol and other intoxicants, these are not recognized to be property of Muslims.

Private ownership rights are established in numerous verses in the Qurʾān and by the practice of the Prophet in Medina. Accordingly, ownership rights apply to all people with no discrimination on the basis of color, gender, religion, or ethnicity. Some Arabs had a tradition of dividing the estate among male heirs only and they were worried that the Qurʾānic verses gave women the right to own real estate. In reply, 4:7 asserted women's right to inheritance: "From what is left by parents and those nearest related, there is a share for men and a share for women, whether the property be small or large, a determinate share." Thus, Islam may be one of earliest legal systems in the world that granted full ownership rights to women. This is reflected in all Arab civil laws since the time of the Majallah (civil law of the Ottoman Empire issued in the middle of the nineteenth century). However, actual—and in violation of law—practices in several rural areas in the Arab countries use various means of persuasion and pressure to deprive women heirs of their right to inherit land and buildings on the pretense of family pride and legacy.

The Islamic definition of ownership implies that it is a right or set of rights granted by God, the Ultimate Lawmaker. Most Sharīʿah scholars therefore assert that neither the society nor its lawmaking body have any power to alter these basic God-given rights, including property rights. Second, private property is protected by Sharīʿah and its basic sources, the Qurʾān and the sunnah of the Prophet Muḥammad. Third, property rights entitle the owner to full authority to use, invest, and dispose of an owned object. "Owners are absolute masters of their properties" is a statement one finds in all major jurists' writings. This implies a wide range of economic freedom. Fourth, property rights are free of prejudice on the basis of gender, religion, color, or ethnicity.

Property may be private or public. Some writers add a third category, *waqf* (charitable endowment) property. While private property is owned by persons, public property is owned collectively by the whole society. It covers things that belong to the society such as parks, rivers, forests, and mineral resources. The government administers public property on behalf of people and in their best interests.

Public land can be divided into three types: (1) community lands, such as roads and village pasture areas. Community land cannot be sold or disposed of by the government, nor can it be acquired or owned by private persons. In some African countries, community land still exists and is often associated with a tribal social system. It is called *arāshī* land in Algeria and Tunisia. Tribal traditions determine the distribution of community lands among families for cultivation. (2) **Free** land covers all lands not used in economic production. This land is called *mawāt* (dead). Individuals have the right of *iḥyāʾ* (revivification) of *mawāt* land by putting it into economic use. This is a sufficient cause for earning private ownership of the land. The government can regulate the exercise of this right, but it cannot eliminate it. (3) State public property. This category covers all other public properties, with respect to which the only Sharīʿah restriction on the behavior of the government is the criterion of serving the best interests of the people.

Acquisition of Private Property. Sharīʿah recognizes six ways of acquiring property rights:

1. Acquisition of unowned mobile things, such as filling a pitcher from a river, hunting, and collecting firewood.
2. Revivification of *mawāt* land. Land revivification means making it productive in agriculture, industry, or any other economic use.
3. Increment of an already owned property with or without labor involved. This includes fruits of owned trees and offspring of owned livestock.
4. Contractual relationships including exchange contracts, such as sale and hiring, and contributory contracts, such as gifts and last wills.
5. Tort liabilities that create a right of compensation.
6. Inheritance, for which details of heirs and their shares are mostly given in the Qurʾān. Noticeably, the first three ways create new property rights, and the last three transfer an existing property from one person to another.

On the other hand, there are three means of acquisition not recognized in Sharīʿah: (1) noncontractual grabbing of property including theft, swindling, looting, coercive and fraudulent practices; (2) acquisition of *mawāt* land without its revivification; and (3) exchange relationships that are either invalid or prohibited. Invalid relationships include contracts lacking basic requirements, such as the consent of parties. Prohibited exchanges include interest on loans, since the Qurʾān mentions that a lender is only entitled to get the principal back and considers any increment oppressive (2:279); income from gambling (5:90–91); bribery and similar exercises; prostitution, etc. Things acquired by prohibited means remain the property of their original owner and should be returned to her or him or to the rightful heirs.

Restrictions on Property. Sharīʿah prescribes four kinds of restrictions on property. (1) While using one's own property for enjoyment and ornamentation is permissible (7:31–32), the Qurʾān forbids wastefulness, "for God loveth not the wasters" (7:31), and considers spendthrifts as "brothers of Satan" (17:27). Wasters and spendthrifts can be pronounced incapable of using their own property and subject to legal guardianship. (2) Use of one's property is constrained by others' rights. Extracting benefit and enjoyment of one's property must not be at the expense of the rights of others or of society as a whole. Examples of such restricted actions are raising one's building to reduce the ventilation and sunshine of a neighbor's property (individual harm) and monopolistic practices (societal harm). (3) Distribution of one's property after death is set by the Qurʾānic inheritance system. Since the true owner is God, private ownership rights hold as long as the owner lives. Upon death, they go back to the true owner. The Islamic inheritance law is founded on this principle. Shares are assigned to different heirs by God in the Qurʾān. The owner has no right to change these shares under any circumstances. Heirs are lineage- and marriage-based. (4) The fourth type of restriction is the right of God on private property, *zakāh*. *Zakāh* is a religious obligation on every Muslim who owns property. It ranks as the third pillar of Islam. Its rate is 2.5 percent of wealth and savings and should be distributed to the poor and needy.

BIBLIOGRAPHY

ʿAbbādī, ʿAbd al-Salām. *Al-milkīyah fī al-sharīʿah al-Islāmīyah.* Amman, Jordan: Maktabat al-Aqṣá, 1974.

Abū Zahrah, Muḥammad. *Al-milkīyah wa-nazḥarīyat al-ʿaqd fī al-sharīʿah al-Islāmīyah.* Cairo, Egypt: Dar al Fikr al Arabi, 1976.

Chapra, Mohammed Umer. *Towards a Just Monetary System: A Discussion of Money, Banking, and Monetary Policy in the Light of Islamic Teachings.* Leicester, U.K.: Islamic Foundation, 1985.

Gulaid, Mohamoud Awaleh. *Land Ownership in Islam: A Survey.* Jiddah, Saudi Arabia: Islamic Research and Training Institute, 1991.

Sait, Siraj, and Hilary Lim. *Land, Law and Islam: Property and Human Rights in the Muslim World.* London: Zed Books, 2006.

Tripp, Charles. *Islam and the Moral Economy: The Challenge of Capitalism.* Cambridge, U.K., and New York: Cambridge University Press, 2006.

MONZER KAHF

PROPHETHOOD. *Nubuwwah* and *risālah* are the Arabic terms that denote prophethood in the Islamic religious vocabulary. The derivative words *nabī* (pl. *anbiyā*) and *rasūl* (pl. *rusul*) are both used in the Qurʾān to mean "prophet." Distinguishing between *nubuwwah* and *risālah*, Muslim scholars have generally regarded the former as the quality of receiving divine revelation and the latter as the mission of some prophets who were also given a religious law (Sharīʿah) recorded in scripture. In this sense, a *nabī* follows and applies the Sharīʿah of the previous *rasūl*. However, such distinction is not explicit in the Qurʾān. The

Qur'ān emphasizes the humanness of the prophets (14:11; 17:93; 18:110; 41:6), although they are able to receive divine messages (4:163–165; 10:2; 12:109; 21:25). The divine revelation makes them the bearers of good news (*mubashshir*) and warners (*mundhir*) (2:213; 4:165; 6:48). The prophets are not responsible for the people's rejection of their message; their task is only to preach, warn, and remind (3:20; 5:99; 11:12; 16:35; 88:21). They will be accepted on Judgment Day as witnesses (*shahīd* and *shāhid*) for or against the people to whom they were sent (4:41; 16:84, 89; 28:75; 33:45; 48:8).

According to the Qur'ān, God has sent his messengers to every human community throughout history (16:36; 17:15; 35:24), although the Qur'ān names only a number of them, most of whom are the biblical patriarchs and prophets. The universal message of all the prophets was monotheism, the belief in "one God" (16:36; 21:25; 43:45). Besides this universal message, the prophets were also given local messages that concerned the special situation of their own people.

According to the Qur'ān, prophethood is not something that can be attained through personal effort; only God can designate a prophet (6:124: 43:31–32). The Qur'ān also emphasizes that the prophetic office was eternally closed with Muḥammad, "the Seal of the Prophets" (*khātam al-nabiyyīn*), namely, the last prophet (33:40).

Classical Islamic scholars adopted the doctrine of the impeccability (*'iṣmah*) of the prophets. They also put emphasis on miracles (*mu'jizah*) as the external evidence of prophethood. The Qur'ān attributes many supernatural occurrences to the miraculous intervention of the prophets. In the case of Prophet Muḥammad, the Qur'ān presents itself as his miracle, which no human is able to imitate (2:23–24).

A disagreement about the nature of prophethood occurred between medieval Islamic philosophers and theologians. The philosophers considered the functions of *nubuwwah*, such as receiving divine revelation (*waḥy*), to be within natural human abilities and regarded the law (Sharī'ah) as an expression of the higher philosophical truth simplified through symbolism for the common people. The theologians, who insisted on the role of divine grace in prophethood, rejected these ideas.

Another controversy among Muslim scholars concerned whether or not a woman could be a prophetess. The majority of them did not approve of the idea that prophethood was available to women. However, Ibn Ḥazm (d. 1064), the great Andalusian thinker, argued for the possibility of a female prophetess drawing on the Qur'ānic verses that express divine communication with women either by means of angelic appearance, as in the case of Mary (3:42–47; 19:17–21) or Sarah, Abraham's wife (11:71–73; 51:29), or by divine revelation, as in the example of Moses's mother (28:7). He also considers Pharaoh's wife, Āsiya, who took Moses under her protection, a prophetess because of prophetic traditions that praise her. But what Ibn Ḥazm means here is *nubuwwah*, not *risālah*, for the Qur'ān restricts the latter only to men (12:109; 16:43; 21:7). Al-Ash'arī (d. 935/6), one of the founders of the orthodox theology, is also said to have considered four women the recipients of *nubuwwah*. Another scholar who insists especially upon the prophethood of Mary is al-Qurṭubī (d. 1273), the renowned Andalusian exegete.

BIBLIOGRAPHY

Ash'arī, Abū al-Ḥasan 'Alī b. Ismā'īl. *Mujarrad maqālāt al-shaykh Abī al-Ḥasan al-Ash'arī* (The Unadulterated Statements of the Master Abū Ḥasan al-Ash'arī). Edited by, Daniel Gimaret (Beirut, Lebanon: Dār al-Mashriq, 1987). In this work, al-Ash'arī's thoughts were compiled by Ibn Fūrak (Abū Bakr Muḥammad ibn al-Ḥasan) (d. 1015/6).

Ibn Ḥazm, 'Alī b. Aḥmad. *al-Faṣl fī al-milal wa-al-ahwā' wa-al-niḥal* (The Judgment about Religions,

Heresies, and Sects). 5 vols. (Jiddah, Saudi Arabia: Sharikat Maktabāt ʿUkāẓ, 1982). Very important treatise on religions and Islamic sects.

Kerr, David A. "Prophethood". In *The Oxford Encyclopedia of the Islamic World*. 6 vols. Edited by John L. Esposito. New York: Oxford University Press, 2009.

Qurṭubī, Muḥammad b. Aḥmad. *al-Jāmiʿ li-aḥkām al-Qurʾān: tafsīr al-Qurṭubī* (The Compendium of Legal Provisions of the Qur'an: al-Qurṭubī's Commentary). 20 vols. Beirut. Lebanon: Dār al-Kitāb al-ʿArabī, 1997. Voluminous Qurʾānic commentary that focuses on jurisprudential aspect of the verses.

Rahman, Fazlur. *Prophecy in Islam: Philosophy and Orthodoxy*. London: Allen & Unwin, 1958. Useful work on classical Islamic debates about the nature of prophethood.

Rahman, Fazlur. *Major Themes of the Qur'an*. Minneapolis, Minn.: Bibliotheca Islamica, 1994. It contains an insightful chapter on prophethood and revelation according to the Qurʾān.

DAVID A. KERR
Updated by HALIM CALIS

PROPHETS. Narratives about prophets (*anbiyāʾ*) and messengers (*rusul*) are found throughout the Qurʾān and Muslim literary genres. The Qurʾān mentions by name, in addition to Muḥammad, twenty-four prophets and alludes to others, among the most significant of whom are Moses, Abraham, and Jesus. Jesus is referred to mainly in connection with stories of the nativity and of his mother, the Virgin Mary (3:35–48; 19:16–34). Some Qurʾānic verses seem to suggest that women such as Mary and the mother of Moses had prophetic experiences (3:42, 28:7), and in a similar vein Sarah (cf. 11:71), Abraham's wife, and Āsiyah, Pharaoh's wife, for her true intuition (28:10, 66:11), are also mentioned. Other prophets to whom the Qurʾān devotes notable space are Adam (e.g., 2:30–38, 7:11–25); Noah (7:59–64, 11:25–49); Lot (11:77–83); Joseph (12:3–101); David (21:78–80, 38:17–26); and Solomon (27:15–44).

The distinctive style of the Qurʾān shaped the stories about the prophets; the Qurʾānic passages reflect a dramatic construction whose aim is to underline the prophets' relation to God Almighty, while simultaneously dealing with questions relevant to Muḥammad's mission when he was in Mecca and Medina. Further, these stories reflect a format that focuses on the important religious themes, values, and messages of their stories, rather than historically linear narratives and chronological details. The important role of prophets and messengers in the Qurʾān paved the way for the enrichment of the traditions and literature that spread in the generations following Muḥammad's death. Later exegetical discussion asserted that women cannot be prophets, although Mary and Āsiyah are mentioned by some prophetic sayings as examples of perfection. Traditions and legends regarding all the prophets and mentioning Mary, Āsiyah, Sarah, Moses's sister Miriam, and Noah's and Lot's wives recur in every literary genre, but they are especially prominent in four important genres: Qurʾānic exegesis; collections of the sayings of Muḥammad (ḥadīth); historiography; and the stories of the prophets (*qiṣaṣ al-anbiyāʾ*).

The first works of *qiṣaṣ al-anbiyāʾ* have been lost or only partially preserved. The earliest partially preserved collections are those of Isḥāq ibn Bishr (d. 821) and ʿUmārah ibn Wathīmah al-Fārisī (d. 902). The works of al-Thaʿlabī (d. 1035) and al-Kisāʾī (twelfth century) constitute the major examples of the genre and are the most renowned works dealing with the topic. These works and later examples of *qiṣaṣ al-anbiyāʾ* conventionally display a fixed structure describing the story of the world from its creation to the story of Jesus and the apostles. Chapters dedicated to the various prophets and including the women connected to their lives collect traditions from a range of sources and attribute these to figures and authors of previous generations, along with Qurʾānic quotations. The attitude of the contemporary Muslim world toward these figures and the related literature varies. For some Muslims, the rich traditions and medieval literature about prophets and messengers have constituted a problem. The accusation, which originated with Ibn Taymīyah and Ibn Kathīr in the fourteenth century, that biblical and extraneous material on this topic was introduced into Muslim literature gained currency in the early part of the twentieth century. In the early twenty-first century the accusation that a work is full of *isrāʾīlīyāt* (i.e., narratives of Jewish origin) is an easy way to dismiss traditions included in medieval works.

BIBLIOGRAPHY

Brinner, William M., trans. *ʿArāʾis al-majālis fī qiṣaṣ al-anbiyāʾ* ("Lives of the Prophets" as Recounted by Abū Isḥāq Aḥmad ibn Muḥammad ibn Ibrāhīm al-Thaʿlabī). Leiden, Netherlands: E. J. Brill, 2002.

Clarke, L. G. "Prophecy and Women Prophets." In *Encyclopedia of Women & Islamic Cultures*, Vol. 5, edited by Joseph Suad, pp. 315–354. Leiden, Netherlands, and Boston: E. J. Brill, 2007.

Knappert, Jan. *Islamic Legends: Histories of the Heroes, Saints, and Prophets of Islam*. 2 vols. Leiden, Netherlands: E. J. Brill, 1985.

Schwarzbaum, Haim. *Biblical and Extra-Biblical Legends in Islamic Folk-Literature*. Walldorf-Hessen, Germany: Verlag für Orientkunde Vorndran, 1982.

Speyer, H. *Die biblischen Erzählungen im Qoran* (The Biblical Stories in the Qurʾān). Hildesheim, Germany: G. Olms, 1961. The first edition was published in 1931 (Gräfenhainichen, Germany: C. Schulze).

Stowasser, B. F. *Women in the Qurʾān, Traditions, and Interpretation*. New York and Oxford: Oxford University Press, 1994.

Ṭabarī, al-. *The History of al-Ṭabarī*. vols 1–4. SUNY Series in Near Eastern Studies. Albany: State University of New York Press, 1985–.

Thackston, W. M., Jr., trans. *The Tales of the Prophets of al-Kisaʾi*. Boston: Twayne, 1978.

Tottoli, Roberto. *Biblical Prophets in the Qurʾan and Muslim Literature*. Richmond, U.K.: Curzon, 2002.

Tottoli, Roberto, ed. *The Stories of the Prophets by Ibn Muṭarrif al-Ṭarafī*. Berlin: Klaus Schwarz, 2003.

Wheeler, Brannon M. *Prophets in the Quran: An Introduction to the Quran and Muslim Exegesis*. London and New York: Continuum, 2002.

ROBERTO TOTTOLI

PROSTITUTION. Scattered sources and a virtual absence of historical writing on the subject of prostitution in the Arabo-Islamic world have led some historians to rightly characterize it as a "history consigned to collective forgetfulness." From the scholarship to date, the overall picture is one in which prostitutes were often tolerated in Islamic societies and in some contexts required to pay taxes like other professions. Prostitutes were a tax farm in the Fatimid, Ottoman, and Safavid empires, as well as Andalusian Spain where prostitutes were called "*kharajiyyat*" after the tax they paid to the Muslim authorities.

Although tolerance predominated, there is some evidence that Muslim empires targeted prostitutes in an attempt to relegate sex work to certain parts of the city, or, at other times, crack down on the sex trade at the behest of disapproving clerics. The sixteenth-century Safavid Shah Abbas I attempted to ban prostitutes from holy sites, as did the eighteenth-century Damascus governor Asʿad pasha al-ʿAzm. Yet, Damascene barber and chronicler Ahmad al-Budayri writes that when pressured to control the bold, defiant acts of local prostitutes in public, the governor was reluctant to abolish prostitution altogether out of fear of losing his popularity with the troops. Succumbing to pressure in 1749, Asʿad pasha banned prostitutes from the city, yet the ban was ineffective overall and short lived. Like the Damascus governor, the nineteenth-century Khedive Muḥammad ʿAli exiled prostitutes and dancers to Upper Egypt in 1834 under the pretext of protecting the army from a menace to societal morals, military discipline, and public health. Large urban areas such as Cairo, Tunis, Istanbul,

Aleppo, Damascus, and Isfahan lay along prominent centers of commerce and imperial administration that attracted foreign merchants, government officials, and troops who served as patrons to local prostitutes. There is evidence that Damascene prostitutes forged strong links with troops and Ottoman officials to the extent they were invited to festivities, including the wedding of the Ottoman treasurer's daughter. Such associations between troops and prostitutes were frequent enough that accusing a woman of associating with soldiers was considered a slanderous accusation of unlawful intercourse. Links with powerful patrons could assist prostitutes in evading punishment, whereas prostitutes lacking connections to powerful men were more vulnerable to prosecution.

In Aleppo, virtually all defendants brought to court on prostitution charges were Muslim women, some of whom have been identified as non-local. There is some evidence of male prostitution in public coffeehouses and private homes; however, such references are restricted to a handful of documents. Prostitutes brought to Aleppo's Sharīʿah court were convicted of conducting business in private homes that spanned the city, rather than in central brothels or designated districts. Conversely, prostitution in eighteenth-century Istanbul appears to have been conducted in brothels in the red-light district of Galata, an old Genoese colony with a conspicuous non-Muslim community. In colonial Tunis, prostitution predominated in the Sidi ʿAbdallah Guèche district, an area that continues to be associated with moral vice. As with Galata, Tunis's red light district was settled by new immigrants beginning around 1830, among them were female sex workers seeking patronage from French officers stationed abroad.

Prostitution occupies an unusual place in Islamic law, making it sometimes difficult to discern prostitution cases from accusations of illicit sexual intercourse (*zinah*) and other criminal charges. In theory, prostitution constitutes a *zinah* crime; however, in practice the courts rarely referred to cases of prostitution in such terms and instead couched accusations in euphemism. From the few studies published thus far, it appears prostitution was treated distinctly from *zinah* crimes and most frequently punished with banishment from the city or city quarter rather than with the required penalties for *zinah* found in the Sharīʿah. However, judges often ruled in prostitution cases without proper evidence or trial; judges would receive hearsay evidence to rule against alleged prostitutes rather than follow the strict criteria of evidence required in the Sharīʿah. Historians have unearthed examples of the slippery legal framing of illicit sex. Julia Clancy-Smith suspects that prostitution charges in colonial Tunisia were campaigns of revenge against individuals who violated appropriate communal boundaries between Muslims and non-Muslims, while Leslie Peirce argues that charges of illicit sexual conduct in sixteenth-century Aintab may have shrouded accusations of heresy.

Ottoman law left the interpretation of the law and protection of public interest to the judge's discretion. Although prostitutes were subjected to the power of the courts and the venom of their neighbors who facilitated these cases, there is some evidence that they were also viewed by some jurists as victims of circumstance. Prominent eleventh-century Hanafi jurist al-Marghinani discouraged the use of banishment as a punishment for female adulterers because removing women from their "means of subsistence" might lead them to prostitution, "the ugliest form of *zinah*." Furthermore, punishment for prostitution varied mostly because judges applied discretionary punishment (*taʿzir*) that left it to judges to determine the outcome of cases.

Scholarship produced thus far indicates that punishment for prostitution varied according to context. In Ottoman Bursa, women were punished by beating the soles of their feet. In nineteenth-century Tunis, convicted women were stripped naked, paraded publicly, then drowned in the sea or a lake, while in other places, such as Aleppo, the punishment appears to have been noncorporal and nonlethal expulsion from the city quarter. Ottoman court cases studied thus far indicate that judges may have been reluctant to apply the stricter punishment of the death penalty in prostitution cases since jurists argued that prostitution was not the same as willing *zinah* because women were forced into prostitution either by circumstance or by procurers. Those who procured prostitution were given some of the harshest penalties in Ottoman imperial law, including discretionary punishment and parading him or her publicly, fining, or flogging. The sixteenth-century *kannunname* of Sultan Suleyman called for the branding of a procurer and *siyasetnames* called for female procurers to have their noses cut off. Although there is little evidence in Sharīʿah court records that these punishments were implemented, the code nevertheless sent a strong message that procuring prostitution warranted a harsh penalty.

Muḥammad Ali's modernization initiative in nineteenth-century Egypt, in emulation of Europe, included attempts to ban prostitution, as well as other vice-ridden institutions such as taverns, in areas where troops were housed in order to halt the spread of syphilis and protect overall public health. In the colonial period, specific zones of prostitution were established across several colonies in North Africa and the Middle East. Some of these zones and *maisons de tolerance* were enacted along with policies and regulations that sought to control public health threats, such as venereal disease, by subjecting prostitutes to periodic examinations. These laws, originating in Europe, resulted in the predominance of an occidental-style prostitution, or what historian Christelle Taraud has called "the public harem," in some parts of North Africa.

BIBLIOGRAPHY

Bouhdiba, Abdelwahab. *Sexuality in Islam*. Translated by Alan Sheridan. London: Routledge & Kegan Paul, 1985.

Clancy-Smith, Julia. *Mediterraneans: North Africa and Europe in an Age of Migration, c. 1800–1900*. Berkeley: University of California Press, 2011.

Fahmy, Khaled. "Prostitution in Egypt in the Nineteenth Century." In *Outside-In: On the Margins of the Modern Middle East* edited by Eugene Rogan, pp. 77–103. New York: I. B. Tauris 2002.

Peirce, Leslie. *Morality Tales: Law and Gender in the Ottoman Court of Aintab*. Berkeley: The University of California Press, 2003.

Rafeq, Abdul-Karim. Public Morality in the 18th Century Ottoman Damascus. *Revue du monde musulman et de la Méditerranée* 55–56 (1990): 180–196.

Semerdjian, Elyse. "'Because He Is So Tender and Pretty': Sexual Deviance and Heresy in Eighteenth-Century Aleppo." *Social Identities: Journal for the Study of Race, Nation, and Culture* 18, no. 2. (March 2012): 179–199.

Semerdjian, Elyse. *"Off the Straight Path": Illicit Sex, Law, and Community in Ottoman Aleppo*. Syracuse, N.Y.: Syracuse University Press, 2008.

Taraud, Christelle. *Prostitution Coloniale: Algerie, Tunisie, Moroc (1830–1962)*. Paris: Payot & Rivages, 2003.

Zarinebaf, Fariba. *Crime & Punishment in Istanbul, 1700–1800*. Berkeley: University of California Press, 2011.

ELYSE SEMERDJIAN

PURIFICATION. According to the ḥadīth, "Purity is half of faith," underlining the importance of purity and purification in the Islamic tradition. The fundamental notion of purity is also reflected in the Islamic concept of *fiṭrah* (human nature), which, according to the ḥadīth, involves circumcision, removing hair from under the armpits and pubic area, paring the nails, proper cleanliness, and perfuming oneself. Each of these acts has direct relevance to notions of purity and purification in Islam.

For both men and women, a state of purity is a precondition for worship (*ʾubūdīyah*) because every act of worship is an encounter with God. The purification ritual is intended to prepare the believer in both body and mind. In fact, the purification ritual in Islam is one of numerous means by which sins and infractions are forgiven. Therefore, acts related to worship, such as touching the Qurʾān, fulfilling the obligatory prayer (*ṣalāḥ*), and circumambulating the Kaʿbah (*ṭawāf*), must be performed in a state of purity.

Physical purification rituals culminate in spiritual purity in acts of worship. Both the discipline of the ritual acts and their aesthetic dimensions contribute to the deepening of the purification process at the nonmaterial, spiritual level. Purification norms and rituals also function at the interpersonal level. For example, sexual relations between husband and wife are conditional upon a certain degree of ritual purity and both husband and wife are expected to purify themselves after such relations.

The Islamic legal tradition (Sharīʿah) has set out rules and regulations for the successful fulfillment of purification rituals. A distinction is made between real impurity (*ḥaqīqī*) and conceptual impurity (*ḥukmī*). Real impurities include feces, urine, blood, semen, and alcohol—material impurities that defile objects or persons. In these cases, purity is attained by simply removing the defiling object by washing, rubbing, drying, or exposure to the sun. By contrast, conceptual impurities are states or conditions in which humans find themselves; they may or may not involve actual defilement by real impurities. Conceptual impurity arises through elimination, touching a corpse, disbelief, menstruation, and postnatal bleeding. In such cases, purity can only be attained by special ritual acts after the defiling impurity, if any, has been removed.

The idea of removing impurities implies that purity is the natural human state. A person remains in a constant state of purity as long as this state is not nullified by any real or conceptual impurity. According to classical Arabic lexicons, moreover, "purity" (*ṭahūr*) is defined as the opposite of "menstruation." In Islamic tradition, maintaining purity reflects an ancient avoidance of menstrual bleeding; hence, a vast number of traditional rules of purity deal with the purity of women. The culture of purification has, however, expanded beyond this original idea. This association between purity in general and menstrual purity in particular may be understood in the sense that purity is an original state broken by temporary periods of impurity.

There are two major purification rituals in the Sharīʿah—the bath (*ghusl*) and the ablution (*wuḍūʾ*)—and one minor ritual for exceptional circumstances. The *ghusl* is a major ritual that becomes necessary under the following conditions: conversion to Islam, sexual relations, ejaculation, and for women, the end of the menstrual period or postnatal bleeding. According to the Shīʿah, the *ghusl* is also obligatory after having washed a corpse, while Sunnīs vary in their opinion, with many believing that it is only recommended. In addition, both Sunnīs and Shīʿah recommend *ghusl* for numerous other occasions like Fridays, the days of the two Muslim festivals (ʿĪd), the pilgrimage, and entering Mecca. Like other acts of worship in Islam, the *ghusl* must be preceded by an intention to purify oneself. This is then followed by a general washing of every part of the body.

There are other forms of defilement that reduce the conceptual purity of a person only to a limited degree, such as elimination, flatulence, or irregular bleeding in a woman. In such a case, *ghusl* would not be obligatory; only the minor form of purification, *wudūʾ*, would be necessary to restore purity.

The essentials of *wuḍūʾ* are: washing the face, washing both arms up to the elbows, wiping part of the head, and washing both feet (Qurʾān 5:6). In exceptional circumstances, a person may be unable to maintain the condition of purity for a sufficient time to fulfill the obligation of prayers or other necessary rituals. Such a person is called *maʿdhūr* ("excused") and may fulfill the duties of worship as long as the *wuḍūʾ* is performed on every occasion. A woman who bleeds irregularly is said to be in a state of *istiḥāḍah* and would also be considered excused.

The Sharīʿah has also made provision for conditions when a person is ill and cannot use water, or when water is not available in the immediate vicinity. In such cases, the ritual of *tayammun* (dry ablution) may be substituted for either the *ghusl* or the *wuḍūʾ*, using clean dust or sand in the place of water.

Both men and women are expected to maintain the basic minimum of ritual purity with *ghusl*. Whenever any of the conditions that necessitate a *ghusl* exists, it is to be performed immediately. The *ghusl* is a precondition for all forms of worship in Islam. For example, entry to a mosque is not permitted to a person without the *ghusl* level of purity. Thus, according to many Sunnī schools, women who are menstruating and therefore require *ghusl* may not even pass through a mosque, although this clearly remains a matter of personal conscience on the part of the woman. Some Shīʿah restrict this prohibition only to the great mosques in Mecca and Medina. Similarly, menstruation and postnatal bleeding preclude women from fasting during Ramaḍān. There is a difference of opinion on whether menstruating women may recite the Qurʾān without touching it. The state of *ghusl* is thus the first key to worship in Islam; it opens the door to an encounter with God.

Modern technological developments, such as advances in plumbing and sanitation, have resulted in certain traditional texts, such as those dealing at length with clean pools and wells, becoming obsolete for most Muslims living in towns and cities. For the most part, however, modern Islamic practice follows the standards established by traditional manuals. Islamic purification practice in the early twenty-first century is poised between traditional requirements and modern possibilities.

BIBLIOGRAPHY

Ashraf, Sayyed Ali. "Inner Meaning of the Islamic Rites." In *Islamic Spirituality: Foundations*, edited by Seyyed Hossein Nasr, pp. 111–130. New York: Crossroad, 1987.

Denny, Frederick Mathewson. *An Introduction to Islam* 4th ed. New York and London: Collier Macmillan, 2011. Contains a detailed section on the various purification rituals in Islam.

Katz, Marion Holmes. *Body of Text: The Emergence of the Sunni Law of Ritual Purity*. Albany: State University of New York, 2002.

Khomeini, Ruhollah. *The Practical Laws of Islam*. 2d ed. Tehran: Islamic Propagation Organization, 1985. Abridged version of *Risālah-yi Tawẓiḥ al-masāʾil*. Khomeini's juridical opinions on essential Islamic rules.

Lazarus-Yafeh, Hava. "Some Differences between Judaism and Islam as Two Religions of Law." *Religion* 14 (April 1984): 175–191. Good account of the general differences between classic Islamic and Judaic rules.

Maghen, Zeʿev. *Virtues of the Flesh: Passion and Purity in Early Islamic Jurisprudence*. Leiden, Netherlands: E. J. Brill, 2005.

Sābiq, al-Sayyid. *Fiqh us-Sunnah: Purification and Prayer*. Translated by Muhammad Saʿeed Dabas and Jamal al-Din M. Zarabozo. Indianapolis, Ind.: American Trust, 1405/1985. Partial translation of a very popular Arabic compendium of Islamic Sharīʿah from a revivalist perspective.

al-Sharif, Mohammed Mahdi, trans. *Al-Ghazali's Ihya Ulum ad Din: New English Complete Translation*. Beirut: Dar al-Kutub al-Ilmiyah, 2008. Description of the inner and mystical experience of purity by one of the greatest scholars in Islamic history.

ABDULKADER I. TAYOB
Updated by NATANA J. DELONG-BAS

Q

QĀḌĪ. Throughout most of Islamic history, judicial authority over Muslims has rested with the *qāḍī*, or judge, who referred to the Sharīʿah law. Caliph Hārūn al-Rashīd (d. 809 CE) was the first to recognize the *qāḍī* of Baghdad as the *qāḍī al-quḍāt* or "judge of judges." Such recognition of a presumed jurisdictional hierarchy also implied systematic appointments of *qāḍīs* throughout the caliphal realm. In time, appointments were made by local dynasts who sometimes rejected the *qāḍī* of Baghdad's legitimacy. Regional differentiation was accompanied by gradual recognition of four "orthodox" schools of Islamic law. Although each recognized the legitimacy of the others, authorities might grant precedence to the *qāḍī* of a locally "preferred" school. Potential problems surfaced in Syria and Egypt when the Fāṭimids recognized four chief judges, two representing Fatimid Shīʿī heterodoxy. When the Ayyūbids assumed control, they eliminated the Shīʿī judges and removed the Mālikī judge as well, giving to a Shāfiʿī Qadi al Qudat the responsibility of appointing all *qāḍīs*.

Generally speaking, a *qāḍī*'s position as a "simple" judge did not invite individual contribution to the growing corpus of Islamic *fiqh*. Some exceptions occurred, however, as in the case of Qāḍī ʿIyād (d. 1149), a North African Mālikī judge who composed a major work (Al-shifāʾah bi taʿrīf huqūq al-muṣṭafa [Recognition of the Rights of the Chosen One], usually referred to as Al-shifāʿah), that became a highly popular legal "manual" of morals for Muslims.

During the early modern period, trends toward providing essentially secular definitions of key areas of law began to affect the traditional jurisdiction of the *qāḍī*. The historic experience of the Ottoman Empire and its successor states in the Middle East provide something of a prototype. Beginning in the 1830s, Ottoman Tanzimat decrees gradually reduced the *qāḍīs*' jurisdiction over areas of law susceptible to secular codification. Conservative Tanzimat Council reformers tried to develop a somewhat eclectic model of Islamic provisions as a general civil code (the Mecelle) to be applied in a partially secularized court system. Such changes led to a need for totally different professional qualifications than those possessed by the *qāḍīs*. This was the case in Egypt, where a system of *majālis maḥallīyah* (local councils) heard many cases deemed inappropriate for judgment in the *qāḍī*'s court. Originally, such *majālis* included *ʿulamāʾ* to consult on overlapping areas of law. Until drastic secular reforms were imposed by the First Turkish

Republic and adopted in other formerly Ottoman areas in the interwar period, personal status cases—including a wide range of issues involving women's legal status—remained under the *qāḍīs'* jurisdiction well into the twentieth century. In Egypt, the post of *qāḍī al-quḍāt* in Cairo also continued until 1947. Eight years later the early Nasser regime moved to abolish all remnants of the *maḥkamah* jurisdiction.

While a wide spectrum of measures have been adopted by various Islamic countries to redefine and redirect judicial authority traditionally vested in the *qāḍī*, debates over personal status law, particularly laws affecting the rights of women, continue. Questions of not only appropriate jurisdiction, but also the social and cultural objectives of family law, are inextricably linked to women's interests in Sharīʿahtic provisions for, for example, rights of individual testimony, inheritance, and marriage and divorce law (including child custody and polygamy).

Nothing in Islamic law specifically proscribes a woman's right to appear before the *qāḍī*, either to represent her own interests or to serve in some auxiliary status, such as agent (*amīn*) for another woman. Cultural tradition, however, seems to have mitigated against such in-court appearances by women of higher social status. Such litigants were most often represented by a legally recognized delegate, or *wakīl*.

Although cases of women being appointed as *maḥkamah* judges appear to have been rare, there are different legal points of view on the question. Whereas the Shāfiʿī school's early opposition to such appointments appeared in Abū al-Ḥasan al-Māwardī's (tenth century CE) work, followers of Abū Hanifa traditionally recognized the right of women *qāḍīs* to settle cases in which women have the right of testimony.

Contemporary circumstances vary from region to region. Whereas two women were appointed as *qāḍīs* in Malaysia in 2010, steps to do the same in Kenya in 2011 led to open debate as to whether such measures fit in with efforts to reform the overall justice system.

BIBLIOGRAPHY

Agmon, Iris. *Family and Court: Legal Culture and Modernity in Late Ottoman Palestine*. Syracuse, N.Y.: Syracuse University Press, 2006.

Shaham, Ron. "Judicial Divorce at the Wife's Initiative: The Sharīʿah Courts of Egypt, 1920–1955." *Islamic Law and Society* 1, no. 2 (1994): 217–257.

Shehada, N. Y. "Uncodified Justice: Women Negotiating Family Law and Customary Practice in Palestine." *Development* 47 (2004): 103–110.

Sonbol, Amira. "Women in Sharīʿah Courts: A Historical and Methodological Discussion." *Fordham International Law Journal* 27 (2003): 225–253.

Tillier, Mathieu. "Women before the Qadi under the Abbasids." *Islamic Law and Society* 16 (2009): 280–301.

BYRON CANNON

QĀJĀR DYNASTY. The Qājār dynasty ruled Iran from 1796 until 1925. During most of this time, Iran suffered a political, economic, and social decline. In general it can be said that the condition of women for much of the Qājār era continued the practices of Ṣafavid Iran.

Women were on the lower rungs of the social ladder in every part of Qājār society, only just above servants and slaves. Their social function was limited to being wives and mothers. As Lady Sheil (1865, p. 86), who lived in Tehran from 1849 to 1854, remarked, "In Persia, a woman is nobody." For the women of wealthy families, there was complete seclusion and a life of tedium occasionally interrupted by a women-only gathering for a religious ritual, a *sufrah* (votive offering of a meal), a *rawẓah-khānī* (recital of a story about the sufferings of the Shiite Imams), or an outing to a local shrine. The epitome of this was Fatḥ ʿAlī

Shāh (1772–1834) who had 157 wives who could be named (and possibly more than a thousand in all). Despite this, one of his daughters, ẓiyā' al-Salṭanah, was her father's secretary and treasurer as well as an accomplished calligrapher. She managed to avoid marriage during her father's lifetime, but when he died was forced to marry on pain of death by her half-brother Muḥammad Shah. Lower-class women helped to support their families by working as seamstresses, spinners, maids, and midwives, while also participating in women's religious rituals. Outside the home, women wore the chador, an all-enveloping black piece of cloth. The education of women was opposed by the clerical class and almost all women were illiterate. Consequently superstitions and thaumaturgy formed a large part of women's lives (Donaldson, 1938).

The most powerful woman in the first half of the Qājār era was Malik Jahān Khānum Mahd-i Ulyā (d. 1873), the mother of Nāṣir al-Dīn Shāh. A determined woman and politically astute, she competed against powerful prime ministers such as Ḥājjī Mīrzā Āqāsī, who dominated her husband Muḥammad Shāh (r. 1834–1848), and Mīrzā Taqī Khān the Amīr Kabīr, the equally dominant first prime minister of her son Nāṣir al-Dīn Shāh (r. 1848–1896), eventually overcoming both. Subsequently, from 1851, she dominated the political scene for a decade, the next prime minister, Mīrzā Āqā Khān Nūrī being initially her ally.

While Mahd-i Ulyā acquired power in the way traditional for women in the Islamic world, through manipulating their husbands and sons, her contemporary, Qurrat al-ʿAyn Ṭāhirah (1817–1852), marks the emergence of Iranian women into the modern world. She was the educated daughter of an eminent Qazvīn clerical family, but chose to follow what had become regarded as a heterodox movement, the Shaykhī school. Then in 1844, she went even further and became a Bābī, a religious movement that was to break away from Islam altogether. Of particular note is the fact that the Bāb (1819–1850), the founder of the movement, signaled a new social equality for women by designating her as one of the Letters of the Living (Ḥurūf-i Ḥayy), the highest rank in the religion's hierarchy. She is also famous for having appeared publicly unveiled at a conference of Bābīs at Badasht, near Shahrud, in 1848. Her path led her to divorce and loss of her children and eventually to her being killed in 1852. Succeeding generations of Iranian women, as well as the Bahāʾī community that emerged from the Bābī movement, have taken her as an icon and role model, while traditionalists stigmatize her as a promiscuous heretic.

After Ṭāhirah, the historical record goes quiet for several decades. During this time a few writers, such as the secular Mīrzā Fatḥ ʿAlī Akhūndzādah (1812–1878) and the Azalī Bābī/secular Mīrzā Āqā Khan Kirmānī (1853–1896), advocated women's rights (albeit only as a minor theme in their writings) and the Bahāʾīs continued to work for them behind closed doors, but there was little outward signs of advancement. Then in 1891/2, women emerged marching in the streets in the protests against the Tobacco Regime, and again in 1905–1911 in support of the Constitutional Revolution. There also developed a debate in the reformist press about the position of women. Despite the important role they played in the Constitutional Revolution, women were denied the vote in the constitution that was promulgated. However, this revolution marks the beginning of many further advances, such as the establishment of girls' schools, the formation of women's societies, and the emergence of women writers advocating women's rights. Among the prominent women of this period were Bībī Khānum Astarābādī (1858–1921), who founded a girls' school and wrote a refutation of an attack on women; Tāj al-Salṭanah (1884–1936), a Qājār princess who supported constitutionalism and feminism; and Ṭāyirah Khānum (1872–1911), a Bahā'ī who wrote articles advocating feminist issues in the press, was possibly the first Iranian woman to wear clothes made in a Western style, and strove to advance the social role of women in the Bahā'ī community.

It is no coincidence that almost all of these powerful and assertive women were described by their contemporary detractors as being promiscuous and a danger to religion. This was inevitable from the traditional viewpoint that saw women in a stereotyped domestic role and thus could only see any deviation from that as resulting from irreligion and lasciviousness. There was a great fear of women who stepped into the public arena as citizens and a rancorous public debate, epitomized by the dual meanings in Persian of the word *zan*—which means both wife (and a traditionalist protection/possession paradigm in relation to a husband) and woman (and a modern partnership/parity relation to men) (Najmabadi, 2005, 207–231).

Marriage. Marriage was a sexual contract for procreation and men often looked for friendship and companionship elsewhere. Polygyny was practiced mainly by the richer classes. Although in theory in Shiite law, divorce was more difficult and women had greater rights over property and inheritance than in Sunni law, the extent to which a women could exert these rights varied greatly—most women could not exert them unless they themselves came from a wealthy and influential family that was prepared to defend these rights.

Temporary Marriage (*mutʿah, sīgheh*). This provision in Shiite law allowed men to contract with a woman to be married for a fixed term and for a fixed monetary consideration. It was frequently practiced between women of low social class and men of high social class and was also very prevalent at sites of pilgrimage, such as Mashhad and Qom, where large numbers of male pilgrims could be expected to be without their wives.

Minorities. The religious minorities in Qājār Iran lived in their own quarters in each city and their women were largely confined to those quarters. This may have been partly out of fear, since stories circulated of the abduction of such women and a forced conversion followed by forced marriage (how common such episodes were is not possible to determine). In general, Zoroastrian, Jewish, and Christian women had more freedoms and rights within their communities than did Muslim women. Owing to the establishment of schools by their co-religionists from abroad, women of these religious minorities were among the best educated in Qājār Iran. The Bahā'īs were different, however, in that, except in a few places, they did not have a separate quarter and lived among Muslims, who were often unaware of their religious affiliation. They also were early promoters of girls' schools and of advancing the social role of women.

Tribes and Rural Areas. Women had some advantages in some tribal societies in that they mixed freely with men, often did not veil, and polygyny was less prevalent. But this was offset by the fact that women often had no property or inheritance rights and were frequently subject to pre-pubertal arranged marriage. In some rural areas, especially Māzandarān and Gīlān, women mixed freely with men and worked alongside them in the fields unveiled, while other rural communities were as socially strict as urban ones.

Bibliography

Afary, Janet. *The Iranian Constitutional Revolution, 1906–1911: Grassroots Democracy, Social Democracy, and the Origins of Feminism*. New York: Columbia University Press, 1996. Chapter 7 is a good account of women's contributions to the Constitutional Revolution of 1906–1911.

Amanat, Abbas. *Pivot of the Universe: Nasir al-Din Shah Qajar and the Iranian Monarchy, 1831–1896*. Berkeley: University of California Press, 1997. A biography of Nāṣir al-Dīn Shah with a good analysis of the impact of his mother, Mahd-i Ulyā.

Brookshaw, Dominic Parviz. "Żiā'-al-Salṭana." *Encyclopaedia Iranica*, online edition, published 15 August 2006. http://www.iranicaonline.org/articles/zia-al-saltana. On Dhiyā' al-Salṭanah.

Donaldson, Bess Allen. *The Wild Rue: A Study of Muhammadan Magic and Folklore in Iran*. London: Luzac, 1938. Contains acute observations of women's lives in the late Qājār period, especially superstitions and thaumaturgy.

Haeri, Shahla. *Law of Desire: Temporary Marriage in Shīʿi Iran*. London: I. B. Tauris, 1989. Addresses issues related to *mutʿah* marriage.

Javadi, Hasan, and Willem Floor. *The Education of Women and The Vices of Men: Two Qajar Tracts*. Syracuse, N.Y.: Syracuse University Press, 2010. The translation of a tract attacking women by an anonymous author, together with Astarābādī's spirited reply.

Karbalā'ī, Ḥasan. *Qarārdād-i Rizhī 1890 M. yā Tārīkh-i Inḥiṣār-i Dukhāniyat*. 2d printing. Tehran: Intishārāt-i Mubārizān, 1982. Includes an account of women's protest against the Tobacco Regime.

Milani, Farzaneh. *Veils and Words: The Emerging Voices of Iranian Women Writers*. London: I. B. Tauris, 1992. Chapter 4 is a good analysis of the life and impact of Ṭāhirah Qurrat al-ʿAyn.

Momen, Moojan. "The Role of Women in the Iranian Bahā'ī Community during the Qajar Period." In *Religion and Society in Qajar Iran*, edited by Robert M. Gleave, pp. 346–369. London: RoutledgeCurzon, 2005.

Najmabadi, Afsaneh. "Ṭāyirah." *Nīmih-yi Dīgar* 2/3 (Winter 1997): 146–195. A detailed account of Ṭāyirah Khānum.

Najmabadi, Afsaneh. *Women with Mustaches and Men without Beards: Gender and Sexual Anxieties of Iranian Modernity*. Berkeley: University of California Press, 2005. The first thorough analysis of the role of gender and sexuality in the shaping of the culture and politics of modern Iran.

Paidar, Parvin. *Women and the Political Process in Twentieth-century Iran*. Cambridge, U.K.: Cambridge University Press, 1995. Includes a good survey of the late Qājār period, although containing some inaccuracies.

Rāvandī, Murtidhā. *Tārīkh-i Ijtimāʾī-yi Īrān*. 10 vols. 3d ed. Tehran: Amīr Kabīr, 1978. The author uses a wide variety of sources to create a social history of Iran. See especially 3:280–283 (tribal women), 713–729 (women in Qājār Iran).

Sheil, Mary Leonora. *Glimpses of Life and Manners in Persia*. London: John Murray, 1856. As wife of the British minister in Tehran, Lady Sheil, an acute observer, had access to the women's quarters of some of the leading Iranian families.

Tāj al-Salṭanah. *Crowning Anguish: Memoirs of a Persian Princess from the Harem to Modernity, 1884–1914*. Edited by Abbas Amanat; translated by Anna Vanzan and Amin Neshati. Costa Mesa: Mage Publishers, 1996.

MOOJAN MOMEN

QATAR. Qatar is a small Persian Gulf state bordering Saudi Arabia, with a population just under 2,000,000. It received independence from Britain in 1971. Today, Qatar is one of the wealthiest countries in the world, though it was once among the poorest. Historically, it existed at the intersection of two economies: the desert and the sea. The settled population engaged in fishing, long-distance trade, and pearl diving. Women did not sail, but they engaged in commercial activity and, during the summer pearling season, when nearly the entire adult male population left for several months, their responsibilities for family and property grew.

While a settled population hugged the coast, a Bedouin population migrated annually into Qatar's interior from the Arabian Peninsula when summer rainfall made grass available for livestock. In the Bedouin camps, women engaged in household chores, raised livestock, wove rugs, and sold products. Although work was gendered (men hunted and maintained equipment related to camp movement), men and women could and did do all types of work.

Both settled and Bedouin societies were organized along kinship lines. Marriages were typically within the same tribe or larger kinship group. Because each coastal settlement or desert camp typically comprised a single tribe or clan, women moved about relatively freely. When entering mixed society, women covered their face with a mask called a *batula* and their head and body with a cloak called an *abaya*. Today most Qatari women wear an *abaya* and cover their heads with a *shayla*. A few cover their faces with a *niqab*.

Qatar underwent rapid, dramatic change in the mid-twentieth century. The pearling industry collapsed in the 1930s with the invention of Japanese cultured pearls. Shortly thereafter, oil was discovered. In 1935, the *amīr* granted a concession to the Qatar Petroleum Company, which found oil in commercial quantities in 1940 and began exporting oil in the 1950s.

In 2013, Qatar was one of the wealthiest countries in the world, owing to the development of oil and natural gas, with a per capita GDP of $102,700. Wealth transformed society, most notably by prompting an influx of foreign workers who now constitute the majority of the population. Because these workers are predominantly men, women constitute a much smaller percentage of the total population, only about a quarter, than in most countries. A smaller number of non-national women work largely in domestic labor. Many face abuse, but are reluctant to pursue legal remedies owing to fear of deportation.

Life is materially far better for women than it was even a few decades ago. Life expectancy has grown from sixty years in 1960 to eighty years for women (compared to seventy-six for men). Women also have access to state-supported education, public sector jobs, and a variety of social services. The family has also changed as women marry later (today the mean age at first marriage for women is twenty-four) and have fewer children. There has been some movement away from extended families toward nuclear families. Nonetheless, most marriages take place within a kinship framework and the elder men remain society's primary decision-makers.

Access to education has improved dramatically. The first girls' school opened in 1956 (the first boys' school in 1952). Previously, settled girls had access to Qur'ānic education and basic literacy but Bedouin education was informal. With the rise of the oil economy, state expenditures on education rose exponentially. Female enrollment in K–12 education is virtually equal to male (49 percent). Qatar's educational system is segregated by gender. At the university level, women's participation exceeds men's: 75 percent of university students are women. It is not uncommon in Qatar to find families in which all the adult women have college degrees (and some graduate degrees) but few of the men do.

Qatari women's labor force participation rate (34.5 percent) is lower than men's (65.5 percent), but this figure increases with higher education levels and is rising. Employed women are significantly more educated than their male counterparts. Women are more likely than men to work in the public sector, especially in health care and education, although several government initiatives now encourage female participation in the private sector. Maternity leaves are generous. Although reproductive rights are not typically discussed publicly, married women have access to birth control, and abortion is legal in the first trimester with a physician's, and husband's consent.

Article 35 of Qatar's 2004 constitution bans discrimination on the basis of sex. The 2006 Family Law gives women additional protections. Women now are granted custody of boys younger than fourteen and girls younger than sixteen (previously custody went to fathers when boys turned seven and girls reached puberty). Before 2006, personal status law (family and probate) was interpreted by Sharīʿah court judges who exercised tremendous judicial discretion. Many initiatives aimed at improving women's rights have been introduced by the *amīr*'s wife, Shaikha Mouza bint Nasser al-Misnad, who heads the Supreme Council for Family Affairs.

The *amīr* granted women suffrage in 1999. Since then, women have voted for and run in Municipal Council elections (thus far Qatar's only elected office). In 2003, a woman won a seat on the Council. A small number of women have also been appointed to public office and have served as minister of health, minister of education, and president of Qatar University, although it is important to note the role of close kinship ties in determining selection.

Women's rights are shaped more by social and religious norms than by law. Qataris are predominantly Sunnī and practice a mild form of Wahhābīyah, one less restrictive than that found in neighboring Saudi Arabia. Extended family dominates women's lives and is reinforced by the social norm of endogenous marriages (about a third of Qataris marry first cousins). A woman's consent is legally required for marriage, but her guardian carries out the legal contract, giving him effective veto power. Polygyny remains legal, albeit rare. Women do not have equal inheritance rights, nor may they divorce without cause as can men. Qatari women married to non-nationals cannot pass on citizenship automatically as can their husbands. Qatari women (but not foreign women) are required to obtain permission from their guardian to get a driver's license. Gender mixing used to be avoided in schools, workplaces, restaurants, and other public settings, yet it is increasingly more tolerated within a frame of social norms.

BIBLIOGRAPHY

Abu Saud, Abeer. *Qatari Women: Past and Present.* London: Longman, 1984.

Breslin, Julia, and Toby Jones. "Qatar." In *Women's Rights in the Middle East and North Africa: Progress amid Resistance*, edited by Sanja Kelly and Julia Breslin. New York: Freedom House and Lanham, Md.: Rowman & Littlefield, 2010.

Ferdinand, Klaus. *Bedouins of Qatar.* New York: Thames and Hudson, 1993.

Fromherz, Allen J. *Qatar: A Modern History.* Washington, D.C.: Georgetown University Press, 2012.

JILL CRYSTAL

QUR᾿ĀN. [*This entry contains five subentries,*

Historical Female Reciters
Portrayals of Women
Contemporary Female Reciters
Women's Exegesis, *and*
Women's Status.]

HISTORICAL FEMALE RECITERS

Female reciters played vital roles in the Muslim community during the revelation of the Qur᾿ān and in the centuries that followed. Women learned and practiced recitation as an expression of personal piety and a way of passing the Qur᾿ān on to future generations. Women gained respect and renown for both their recitation skills and the moral excellence that recitation conveyed. Female reciters often taught recitation and religious subjects to other Muslims, and they also gained opportunities for leadership. Even when women pursued other professions, their skills, knowledge, and reputation as reciters were often critical to their development and success.

Historical Survey. The ḥadīth (reported sayings of the Prophet) provide strong documentation of the roles of early female reciters. Through recitation, women were involved in early efforts to collect the verses of the Qur᾿ān. Several women, including the Prophet's wives ʿĀ᾿ishah and Ḥafṣa, dictated and corrected verses as scribes assembled them into written form. Ḥafṣa (d. 665), the daughter of the caliph ʿUmar, was a devout reciter dedicated to prayer, fasting, and meditation. She regularly memorized verses of the Qurʾān when they were revealed and focused on their meaning and interpretation. Another early reciter was Sayyida Nafīsah (762–824), a descendant of the Prophet's grandson al-Ḥasan. In her youth she became a *ḥāfiza* (one who has memorized the Qurʾān) and later established herself as a highly respected scholar in Egypt. Her biographer Mūnāwī (d. 1621) reported that when she dug a grave in anticipation of her death and welcomed union with God, she recited the entire Qurʾān six thousand times from within it.

Female reciters also served and emerged from early Muslim courts. The *qayna* (pl., *qiyān*), or singing slave girl, was responsible for providing a variety of forms of entertainment in the courts of the Umayyads, ʿAbbāsids, Fāṭimids, and Mamlūks. The *qiyān* had been important pre-Islamic musical entertainers, and following the revelation, they were also trained in Qurʾānic recitation. In the Umayyad era, the slave girl Hawā was known as a talented reciter and poet. One of the best-known *qiyān* was the Medinese Sallāma al-Qass (d. after 740?), who served Yazīd ibn ʿAbd al-Malik (r. 720–724) and his son Walīd (r. 743–744). Sallāma was known for her abilities as a reciter of the Qurʾān, singer, *ʿūd* (lute) player, andcomposer.

During subsequent centuries, many female reciters excelled in multiple readings (*qirāʾat*) of the Qurʾān. Numerous readings had developed during the first three centuries following the revelation. In the ninth century, scholars strove to standardize these recitation practices and recognized seven to ten prominent readings. Seven major readings were mastered by Fayiz al-Qurṭubī's daughter (d. 1055) of Cordoba, Umm al-ʿIzz bint Muḥammad ibn ʿAlī al-ʿAbdarī al-Dānī (d. 1214), the Moroccan reciter and *ḥāfiza* Khadījah bint Hārūn ibn ʿAbdullah al-Maghribiyya al-Dukkāliyya (1243–1296), and Bayram bint Aḥmad ibn Muḥammad al-Dayrūṭiyya (fifteenth century), a reciter who taught pious women and men in Jerusalem.

Women's skills as reciters and teachers of recitation were also cultivated in the courts of Mughal India. The daughters of Mughal emperors often received instruction in recitation from a very early age. In the court of the Mughal emperor Shāh Jahān, one important reciter and teacher of recitation was Sati-un-Nisa (1616–1646). This highly educated Persian woman held numerous administrative posts and taught Shāh Jahān's daughter Jahānārā (1614–1681). Jahānārā in turn became a skilled reciter, mystic, writer, poet, and patron of literary and religious projects. Jahānārā's brother, the Mughal emperor Awrangzīb, also ensured that his daughters had sound knowledge of the Qurʾān, including recitation. When one of them, the princess Zebunissa (1638–1702), became a *ḥāfiza* at the age of seven, Awrangzīb celebrated her accomplishment by holding a feast for the army in Delhi, closing public offices for two days, and donating money to the poor. Zebunissa became a scholar and was asked to resolve religious conflicts at court. She also began to write a commentary on the Qurʾān.

Leadership Roles. Female reciters often took on leadership roles as ascetics, religious leaders, and teachers. Many Ṣūfī women gained renown as reciters. In the seventh century, Shaʿwāna of al-Ubulla preached and recited the Qurʾān for ascetics and worshippers and was known for her melodious voice. Ḥafṣa bint Sīrīn (d. 719?) mastered the art of recitation by age twelve. She became an ascetic, reciting half of the Qurʾān each night and remaining in her private place of worship for thirty years. When Muslims asked her brother Muḥammad how to recite properly, he directed them to her as the expert. The Tunisian Ṣūfī ʿĀʾishah bint ʿImrān bint Sulaymān al-Manūbī (d. 1481) was a *ḥāfiza* who performed a complete recitation 1,520 times and devoted herself to charity in her community.

Historically, women used their skills as reciters when leading Muslims in prayer and other religious rituals. The Prophet's wife ʿĀ᾿ishah, for example, served as a prayer leader for women. Umm Waraqa, a reciter and *ḥāfiza*, was directed by the Prophet to lead her family in prayer. Ghazāla al-Harūriyya (d. 696) recited two lengthy chapters of the Qur᾿ān when leading male fighters in prayer in Kufa. In early twentieth-century China, female imams led other women in prayer and recitation in women's mosques.

Women reciters have long played important roles as teachers. Among the early generations of Muslims, women like Umm Jamīlah al-Saʿdīyah taught recitation to newcomers to the faith. Fāṭimah bint ʿAbd al-Raḥman ibn Muḥammad al-Qurṭubī (d. 1221) of Cordoba taught scholars the Warsh reading of the Qur᾿ān. Ḥukāymah bint Maḥmūd (b. 1299) was a Qur᾿ān reciter in the Hijaz who had a general *ijāzah* (certificate) for the transmission of recitation and taught many scholars. Khadījah bint al-Qayyim al-Baghdādiyya (d. 1300) was a reciter and preacher from Baghdad who taught *tajwīd* (proper recitation) to many other Muslims. Lalla Fatma N'Soumer (1830–1863) was an Algerian *ḥāfiza* who directed her father's Qur᾿ān school after his death and then led the Algerian resistance against the French. Ruqayyah bint Muḥammad (d. 1924) was the daughter of a *shaykh*, a *ḥāfiza*, and the first woman teacher in Illīgh, Morocco. Fāṭimah bint Muḥammad ibn Muḥammad (d. 1931) was a Ṣūfī and *ḥāfiza* who founded and taught at a girls' *madrasah*.

Preparation for Related Careers. For many women, the early acquisition of recitation skills provided a pathway to further religious studies. Amat al-Wāḥid bint al-Ḥusayn (d. 987), the daughter of a Baghdad judge, was a *ḥāfiza* who memorized multiple readings of the Qur᾿ān and later became an expert on *fiqh* (Islamic jurisprudence). Some reciters became scholars of ḥadīth and calligraphers. ʿĀ᾿ishah bint Ibrāhīm ibn al-Ṣiddīq (1262–1340) was both an excellent reciter and a scholar of ḥadīth. Umm Hani Maryam (1376–1466) memorized the Qur᾿ān as a child and then pursued other subjects including theology, law, history, and grammar. Subsequently, she studied ḥadīth with leading scholars in Cairo and Mecca and then trained later scholars in Egypt. In addition to being a *ḥāfiza*, she was known for her skill in calligraphy and poetry and her diligent observance of her religious obligations, performing the pilgrimage thirteen times. Calligraphers who had memorized the Qur᾿ān were thought to be especially trustworthy in their craft. Fāṭimah bint ʿAlī ibn Mūsā (d. 1071), who became a *ḥāfiza* at age nine, and Salmā bint Muḥammad ibn Muḥammad (d. 1428), who had memorized ten readings of the Qur᾿ān, were among the important female calligraphers. Zulaykhah Khātimī al-Saʿdī, a Turkish reciter and *ḥāfiza*, completed a highly embellished, gilded copy of the Qur᾿ān in 1859 that has been described as one of the most beautiful in existence.

Female reciters also achieved success in other vocal arts. One of the best known and most successful female reciters of the twentieth century was the Egyptian singer Umm Kulthūm (1904–1975). As the daughter of a poor imam of a village mosque, Umm Kulthūm learned to recite as a child by attending her local religious school. She learned to sing by imitating her father and studying with other singers of religious songs. Her style of singing was firmly rooted in principles of Qur᾿ānic recitation, including precise pronunciation, nasality, breath control, careful manipulation of durations, and concern for the meaning of the text. In addition to shaping her singing style, recitation remained a regular part of her life. She recited the Qur᾿ān when traveling and before the curtain rose on her concert stage. She recited throughout

Ramaḍān in the evenings and on other religious holidays. She recorded a short portion of recitation in one of her films (*Sallāma*, 1945) and planned to record additional recitation later in life, but was reportedly blocked by religious authorities. Nevertheless, she became an important influence on and role model for other female reciters, including several from Malaysia who visited her in Egypt and sought her advice in the 1960s.

Women have been active reciters since the time of the revelation. Still, our current understanding of their accomplishments is limited. Much relevant information is concentrated in key sources of historiography and prosopography documenting the lives of the Companions, ascetics, and religious scholars up to the seventeenth century. Other relevant information is limited to brief references to reciters in works focusing on other subjects. More research is needed to understand their achievements and their contributions to their communities and long-standing religious traditions.

[*See also* ʿĀʾishah; Calligraphy and Epigraphy; Ḥadīth, *subentry on* Transmission; Qurʾānic Recitation Schools for Girls; Tajwīd; Umm Kulthūm; *and* Umm Waraqa.]

BIBLIOGRAPHY

Bewley, Aisha. *Muslim Women: A Biographical Dictionary*. London: Ta-Ha, 2004. Short descriptions of important women from the seventh through the nineteenth centuries.

Danielson, Virginia. *The Voice of Egypt: Umm Kulthūm, Arabic Song, and Egyptian Society in the Twentieth Century*. Chicago: University of Chicago Press, 1997. Particularly thorough in its documentation of Umm Kulthūm's career up to 1964.

Mukherjee, Soma. *Royal Mughal Ladies and Their Contributions*. New Delhi: Gyan Books, 2001.

Srivastava, Gouri. *The Legend Makers: Some Eminent Muslim Women of India*. New Delhi: Concept Publishing, 2003.

al-Sulamī, Abū ʿAbd al-Raḥmān. *Early Sufi Women: Dhikr an-Niswa al-Mutaʿabbidāt al-Ṣūfiyyāt*. Edited and translated by Rkia Elaroui Cornell. Louisville, Ky.: Fons Vitae, 1999.

Sultanova, Razia. *From Shamanism to Sufism: Women, Islam, and Culture in Central Asia*. London: I. B. Tauris, 2011.

Laura Lohman

Portrayals of Women

Women appear in the Qurʾān in a variety of ways. They are sometimes directly and at other times indirectly addressed in injunctions, instructions, exhortations, threats, and promises. In the Qurʾānic stories, women appear as both heroines and villains. The Qurʾān is the *axis mundi* of Islam; its significance as the word of God for believing Muslims cannot be understated. The language of the Qurʾān is at times ambiguous and, like all sacred texts, contains symbolic and allegorical elements. To draw absolute legal and ethical statements from such a text is an arduous, if not impossible, task. The absoluteness of God has often been translated into the absoluteness of the word of God, the Qurʾān. It must be noted that there is a distinction between the oral revelation and the *mushaf*, the written book, a text that is a product of a set of decisions made by Muslim authorities. The relation between the two has been debated within Islamic thought from early in its history. This distinction is important, because the Qurʾān is no longer an oral discourse, but is a written text that needs to be interpreted. To understand the limitations of any given interpretation, it is important to note that our human understanding of the Qurʾān evolves in time and place, and is filtered through our limited cognitive universe, and hence no interpretation can be absolute. Interpreters have often offered general statements about women. Islamic jurisprudence has prescribed a gendered order that appears to be monolithic. Yet today in the early twenty-first century, many Muslims believe that Islam proclaims the equality of men and women. Some have come to the awareness that in the course of history, men have been the primary mediators between religious truth and women, and that this has had an indelible impact on the image of woman in Islam.

Women in the Text. Chapter 4 of the Qur'ān is titled *An-nisa'* (Women), but mention of women is not limited to this chapter alone. While in the Qur'ān the term *nisa* is repeated twice as many times as the term *rijal* (men), only one woman is mentioned by name: Maryam (Mary, mother of Jesus). Her name is the title of chapter 19 and is mentioned over thirty times in the book. The Qur'ān holds Maryam in the highest regard. It is written that she was "chosen by God above all other women" (3:42), and that "no man could have been like this woman" (3:36). The complete story of Maryam can be found sporadically in seven chapters of the Qur'ān: 3, 4, 5, 19, 21, 23, 66. These stories include not only the annunciation of Jesus's birth, but also the conception of Maryam herself and the divine favors granted to her. However, the Qur'ān does not directly refer to Maryam as a *nabī* (prophet). Thus there is disagreement among scholars as to whether or not Maryam could be considered a prophet. It is not difficult to ascertain that Maryam's experience is fundamental to constituting and projecting prophetic authority for John and Jesus, as well as for her guardian, Zachariah. The scandal of a woman becoming pregnant outside of marriage is explained in the Qur'ān by appealing to prophecy as superseding the traditional patriarchal expectations about women and their bodies. In fact, in the Qur'ān, the figures of Maryam and Issa (Jesus) manifest themselves collectively as a single prophetic figure.

The Qur'ān makes reference to other exceptional women—the wife of Pharaoh and adoptive mother of Moses (Asiya), the wives of the Prophet, the wife of Adam (Eve), and the Queen of Sheba—but does not mention them by their proper names. The various representations of women in the Qur'ānic stories serve as a clear indication that the Qur'ānic view of women is not a monolithic one. The stories of the Qur'ān mention prophets such as Abraham, Isaac, Ishmael, Moses, Zachariah, Jesus, and John, introducing them as exceptional men. It also refers to Maryam as an exceptional figure (3:36). And sets the wife of Pharaoh up as an example to those who believe (66:11). She convinced Pharaoh not to kill Moses and adopted him as her son. She distanced herself from Pharaoh and his oppressive rule (28:9), thus becoming one of the four noblest women of the world. The Queen of Sheba is mentioned as having a mighty throne (27:23) and as joining Solomon in submission to God (27:44). Several verses throughout the Qur'ān are direct exhortations addressed to believing men and women. Some aim at organizing relations between men and women. They include laws about marriage and divorce, sexuality, and adultery.

The Best Story of the Qur'ān. The story of Yusuf (Joseph) in chapter 12 is that of a prophet who had to overcome many adversities. However, it is the story of Yusuf and Zulaykha (wife of Potiphar, according to tradition) that has received the most attention, both in commentaries of the Qur'ān and in folklore and poetry. The story has been an inspiration for numerous works of mystical and love poetry in various Muslim languages. It is in these works that *kayd* (guile) has often been presented as a quintessential female trait. This chapter refers to the guile of women several times in the story (12:34, 12:50, 12:28). Zulaykha is consumed with love for Yusuf and is the living manifestation of *nafs lawwama*, the blaming soul (75:2). However, after long years of suffering, she is eventually united with her beloved as the *nafs mutma'inna*, the soul at peace (89:27).

Created Equal, Treated Unequally. The Qur'ān does not give details of separate creation of woman and man. It speaks instead of the creation of all humanity from one soul (*nafs*), the creation of one soul from another, and the creation of humanity from the two (4:1). From this verse, it cannot be ascertained whether the first created being was a man or a woman. The word *nafs* is feminine, and the mate created from it is masculine. Of the five references to the creation story in the Qur'ān, the woman is mentioned only in three of them, each time where the emphasis of the narrative is disobedience. Yet it is Adam that Iblis (Satan) whispers to in order to tempt him to eat from the forbidden tree (20:120). In chapter 7, both man and woman are deceived by Iblis and are banished from the Garden.

One of the most difficult verses of the Qur'ān (in terms of principles of gender relations) is the one that states that men are *qawwamun* (maintainers/protectors of women) because God has given one more than the other. This verse also describes righteous women as those who are devoutly obedient. If the husband fears disloyalty (*nushuz*) on the part of his wife, the husband is told first to advise her, second to refuse to share a bed with her, and lastly to beat her lightly (4:34), although this translation of *nushuz* is contested in the modern period. Translators of the Qur'ān translated *nushuz* as "disloyalty" in this verse with reference to the actions of the wife. The same term, with reference to the actions of the husband, is translated as "cruelty" or "desertion" (4:128). The reason for this difference in translation can be found in the remedy suggested for a husband's *nushuz*. While the previous verse suggests that fear of *nushuz* on the part of the woman calls for the man to take the three measures above, in the case of the husband's *nushuz*, the verse simply suggests that there will be no blame on husband and wife if they reach an amicable agreement (4:128).

In particular issues, such as the rules of inheritance and requirements of witnesses, women are clearly not on a par with men in the Qur'ān. While it is suggested that men receive half or one-fourth in inheritance from the departed spouse, women receive only one-fourth or one-eighth in inheritance from the departed husband (4:12). The rule of thumb is that the male shall receive the equivalent of two females' shares (4:176). For contracts, the Qur'ān calls for two male witnesses, or one male witness and two female witnesses (2:282). In marriage, men are given conditional permission to marry up to four wives (4:3). In divorce, men have the upper hand and have few restrictions (other than the general condition of releasing women in kindness) as to the reasons for divorce, because men have precedence over women (2:227–228, 2:236).

These instances indicate unequal status for men and women in the realm of social and economic roles, as well as in gender relations. On other issues, the Qur'ān addresses both *muslimin* (Muslim men) and *muslimat* (Muslim women), *mu'minin* (faithful men) and *mu'minat* (faithful women), and gives them both tidings of God's forgiveness and great reward (33:35).

Morally Subordinate or Autonomous? A simple reading of the Qur'ān that does not challenge its commonly accepted translations may reveal a high level of autonomy for men and a certain level of subordination for women. Even a perfunctory reading of the verses reveals that this autonomy is directly related to financial maintenance in exchange for exclusive sexual relations of the wife with the husband (4:34). On the issue of moral and religious responsibility, however, the Qur'ān is clear about the autonomy of women as well as that of men. While several verses may seem to maintain that women are subordinate to their spouses on matters of faith (36:55–56, 37:22, 43:70), in all these verses the term *azwaj* refers not to marital partners but to partners in action, those similar to them in action. Several verses of the Qur'ān affirm the moral autonomy of every single individual regardless of gender. The promise of the Qur'ān is that no righteous act will be lost, regardless of the gender of the person who acts (4:124, 3:195, 40:40, 33:35). Where spouses are mentioned, the promise of paradise is conditioned on righteousness and is not automatic (13:23, 37:22–23). Further examples from the Qur'ān's narratives support the view that women are morally autonomous. In the stories of the wives of Noah and Lot, not only is there no indication that they will enter paradise simply because they were married to righteous men; rather, they are asked to enter the fire (66:10). While the wives of Lot and Noah are examples for those who disbelieve, the wife of Pharaoh is an example to those who believe. She believed and acknowledged the truth of the message of the prophet Moses, and her husband's disbelief did not diminish or alter her faith (33:35).

Clearly, the narratives and stories of the Qur'ān do not attempt to depict a monolithic view of women. There are examples of righteous women, not-so-righteous women, and women who aspire to do wrong. The Qur'ān promises that each will receive her due reward in paradise if she acts autonomously in matters of faith. According to Muslim commentaries, Maryam did not abide by the rules of segregation as set by the historical context of her time. She resided in the temple at a time when women were not allowed to enter its confines. Asiya, the wife of Pharaoh, not only did not abide by the status quo; she supported Moses, who turned out to be her husband's most formidable enemy. Both women are depicted as exemplary for all times.

If women have autonomy in matters of faith and are religiously and morally responsible, if they will be judged according to their actions, how can they be commanded to be subordinate in matters of relationships and transactions? The approach that distinguishes between *'ibadat* (matters of worship) and *mu'amalat* (transactions) proves to be perceptive. Transactions are conditioned upon the vicissitudes of time and place. If Islamic jurisprudence's use of the Qur'ān in establishing a guideline for gender relations is to have a timeless application, it needs to consider the historical context and the time and place. It is always important to remember that no ruling of jurisprudence can be confirmed as truth or rejected as false with absolute certainty. Islamic jurisprudence is at its best a collective human understanding of Divine words and is not to be considered Divine.

[*See also* Mary.]

BIBLIOGRAPHY

Abu Zayd, *Naqd al-khitab al-dini*. Cairo: 1992.

Arkoun, Mohammed. *Rethinking Islam: Common Questions, Uncommon Answers*. Translated by Robert D. Lee. Oxford: Westview Press, 1994.

Barlas, Asma. *"Believing Women" in Islam: Unreading Patriarchal Interpretations of the Qur'an*. Austin: University of Texas Press, 2002.

Davary, Bahar. *Women and the Qur'an: A Study in Islamic Hermeneutics*. Lewiston, N.Y.: Edwin Mellen Press, 2009.

Lybarger, Loren D. "Gender and Prophetic Authority in the Qur'ānic Story of Maryam: A Literary Approach." *Journal of Religion* 80, no. 2 (April 2000): 240–270.

McAuliffe, Jane D. "Chosen of All Women: Mary and Fatima in Quranic Exegesis." *Islamochristiana* 7 (1981): 19–28.

Stowasser, Barbara F. *Women in the Qur'an, Traditions, and Interpretation*. New York: Oxford University Press, 1994.

Thurlkill, Mary F. *Chosen among Women: Mary and Fatima in Medieval Christianity and Shi'ite Islam*. Notre Dame, Ind.: University of Notre Dame Press, 2007.

Wadud, Amina. *Qur'an and Woman: Rereading the Sacred Text from a Woman's Perspective*. New York: Oxford University Press, 1999.

BAHAR DAVARY

Contemporary Female Reciters

Continuing centuries-old practices, women recite the Qur᾽ān in many situations and for many reasons in contemporary Muslim societies. Women perform recitation as part of daily, annual, and life-cycle rituals. Through recitation, women cultivate piety, gain various forms of literacy, and enjoy enhanced social standing in their communities. Female reciters provide important services in their communities, engage in processes of self-development, and contribute to religious revitalization on a national scale.

Daily and Annual Rituals. Women perform Qur᾽ānic recitation in daily prayer rituals. The recitation of the opening chapter and other portions of the Qur᾽ān is part of required daily prayer and constitutes a primary mode of piety. In addition to private prayer, women recite when leading congregations in prayer, amid conflicting legal opinions of such leadership. In Canada, for example, women have led female and mixed-gender congregations in prayer in mosques, homes, and other community venues. While China's female imams do not necessarily lead congregations in prayer, recitation remains an important part of their duties, which include teaching other women how to pray and recite the Qur᾽ān, visiting the sick, washing the bodies of deceased women, and providing women with spiritual assistance. Recitation abilities are normally required for women to become religious leaders in other communities. Moroccan women hoping to be certified as *mourchidate* (female spiritual guides) must have memorized half of the Qur᾽ān and meet stringent educational requirements before they can apply for training. They continue to study Qur᾽ānic recitation during their year-long training.

Women also recite the Qur᾽ān in Shīʿī women's prayer meetings. These are daily rituals in places like Tehran, where one hundred or more women spend several hours reciting the Qur᾽ān and discussing the meaning of the verses. Under the reciter's leadership, women cultivate piety, self-esteem, and social worth. Women place objects, such as medicine, in front of the leader when she recites so her breath can transmit blessings to them. In Iran, these meetings (*jaleseh*) are often dedicated to important figures for Shīʿah, such as the Prophet's daughter Fāṭima and his grandson Imām Ḥusayn.

Women recite the Qur᾽ān in annual religious rituals. In Indonesia, women recite the entire Qur᾽ān during Ramaḍān in an evening prayer cycle (*tarāwīḥ*). In the Hejaz, women, often of Malaysian or Egyptian heritage, recite the Qur᾽ān in women's celebrations of the Prophet's birthday. In Iran, Pakistan, and Lebanon, Shīʿah women recite the Qur᾽ān in mourning ceremonies held during Muḥarram and Ṣafar to commemorate the killing and imprisonment of Imām Ḥusayn and his family members at Karbala in 680 CE. Recitation of the opening chapter of the Qur᾽ān induces an atmosphere of spiritual contemplation before women recite prayers and poetry to inspire hope for redemption and intercession.

Women reciters also lead rituals in various Ṣūfī orders. These include the Moroccan Qādirīyah-Boutchichīyah Ṣūfī order and the Süleymanlı organization, a branch of the Naqshbandīyah Ṣūfī order that stresses Qur᾽ānic recitation and has a strong presence in Turkey and Western Europe. In such orders, women may direct the recitation and chanting in women's ecstatic rituals (*zikr*) and give lessons on ḥadīth (reported speech of the Prophet), recitation, and prayer.

Life-Cycle, Healing, and Blessing Rituals. Female reciters also lead life-cycle rituals, such as mourning ceremonies. In Yemen, a female reciter leads the visitation ceremony on a loved one's death and other women of the community respond to her recitations with interjections praising the Prophet Muḥammad. In Bosnia, the *tevhid* mourning ritual is performed five times after a loved one has died, beginning on the burial day. When women gather independently of men at the home of the deceased, a female reciter leads the ceremony. She leads prayers as the main reciter and directs other women to recite, following a hierarchy of age and skill. In addition to paying respects to the deceased, the *tevhid* allows women to praise God, reaffirm their membership in the Muslim community, earn *sevap* (religious merit), and display religious knowledge, including their ability to recite. On rare occasions, women may recite in a small mixed-gender *tevhid* held in the deceased's home.

Female reciters also conduct healing ceremonies. Bosnian faith healers (*bulas*) are middle-aged women who heal others through Qur'ānic recitation, prayer, and divination. Qur'ānic recitation forms part of two of the *bulas*' healing practices. The first is "praying of *istiḥāra*," a traditional form of healing and divination in which Islamic prayers and Qur'ānic recitation are performed as the *bula* prays for a dream and interprets it. The second healing practice is "casting horror," in which a lump of lead is heated, thrown into water, and interpreted to diagnose and relieve the problems of the patient, usually a woman who has lost a loved one or is otherwise distraught. Qur'ānic recitation is performed along with the casting of lead to identify the problem and address the woman's anxiety.

Women participate in group recitation (*khatm* or *khatam al-Qur'ān*) to acknowledge or call for good fortune. During a *khatm*, many individual reciters simultaneously recite different parts of the Qur'ān so that the entire text is recited within one hour. In Oman, a *khatm* may be performed when a loved one is recovering from illness, a woman is pregnant, or a family wants continued good health for its members. The *khatm* is normally conducted in the morning with provisions of coffee, fruit, and incense. Women attend and participate by reciting chapters from the Qur'ān. Their seating arrangement reinforces their social status and holding a *khatm* in one's home enhances a family's social prestige. In Bosnia, male reciters normally perform this complete recitation, but female reciters may do so when men are unwilling or unable to. The ritual brings *sevap* for those who recite, those who sponsor the recitation, and those for whom the recitation is performed. In Indonesia, this complete reading is normally performed by women who have memorized the entire Qur'ān in addition to fully mastering the rules of recitation.

Developing and Demonstrating Skills. In addition to helping preserve the revelation within their community, female reciters also gain a broad range of skills including pronunciation, reading, and comprehension of classical Arabic. Aspiring to learn to recite the Qur'ān also provides an incentive to become literate in a broader sense. Female reciters' skills are honed and evaluated through a variety of educational methods, including private and public instruction from the preparatory to university levels. After receiving instruction early in life, women may go on to teach recitation or join adult study groups focusing on recitation. For example, Bangladeshi women often join study groups where they emphasize the meaning of the Qur'ān and enjoy a sense of female community. In Indonesia, women's study groups discuss the rules of recitation, the melodic modes used in recitation, and their effect.

Where the melodically elaborate *mujawwad* style of recitation has been influential, female reciters' skills may include several forms of performance and improvisation using melodic modes. In Indonesia, female reciters have gained fluency in two separate modal systems, the Meccan modes and the Egyptian modes (*maqāmāt*), as a growing culture of recitation competitions made the latter normative. These reciters make extensive use of their chest voice and develop a range of about two octaves. Such melodic and vocal fluency enables reciters to perform genres of music, including the Arabic-language genres *tawshīḥ* (hymn) and *qaṣīdah* (ode). As a result, female reciters may become valued members of the community for their ability to perform in multiple art forms used in various rituals and celebrations.

Women also increasingly participate in recitation competitions. They have recited in Southeast Asian national competitions since the mid-twentieth century, and female divisions have been established more recently in other national and regional competitions, such as those in Toronto and Sharjah in the United Arab Emirates. Female reciters compete for honors and monetary prizes and may serve as judges. Competitions encourage women to gain fluency in recitation, recognize their achievements, and help them establish careers as teachers, professional reciters, and businesswomen. Recitation competitions also promote deeper and distinctly national forms of Islamic piety. International competitions attract female participants from Africa, Eastern Europe, and Asia, and female reciters from Indonesia, Malaysia, Thailand, the Philippines, and Pakistan have placed highly.

The best known contemporary female reciter is Hajja Maria ʿUlfah, who became the female champion in the 1980 Indonesian national recitation competition and the international competition in Kuala Lumpur. She subsequently served as recitation teacher, coach, judge, and lecturer in Indonesia, in addition to touring and lecturing internationally as a master reciter. She co-founded an Islamic boarding school with her husband and has served as an administrator at the Indonesian Institute for Qurʾānic Studies since 1988.

Although few female reciters have achieved this level of renown, they play important roles as teachers, healers, and spiritual leaders in Muslim communities around the world. They are respected and valued in these communities, and they merit greater scholarly attention.

Bibliography

Bringa, Tone. *Being Muslim the Bosnian Way: Identity and Community in a Central Bosnian Village*. Princeton, N.J.: Princeton University Press, 1995. An ethnographic study of women's roles in defining this Muslim community, highlighting the contributions of female reciters.

Gade, Anna M. *Perfection Makes Practice: Learning, Emotion, and the Recited Qurʾān in Indonesia*. Honolulu: University of Hawai'i Press, 2004.

Nelson, Kristina. *The Art of Reciting the Qurʾan*. Austin: University of Texas Press, 1985. Seminal study of Egyptian recitation practices, focusing on male reciters.

Rasmussen, Anne K. *Women, the Recited Qurʾan, and Islamic Music in Indonesia*. Berkeley: University of California Press, 2010.

Sultanova, Razia. *From Shamanism to Sufism: Women, Islam, and Culture in Central Asia*. London: I. B. Tauris, 2011.

Torab, Azam. "Piety as Gendered Agency: A Study of Jalaseh Ritual Discourse in an Urban Neighbourhood in Iran." *Journal of the Royal Anthropological Institute* 2, no. 2 (June 1996): 235–252. In-depth ethnographic exploration of women's prayer meetings in Tehran.

Van Doorn-Harder, Nelly. *Women Shaping Islam: Indonesian Women Reading the Qurʾan*. Champaign-Urbana and Chicago: University of Illinois, 2006.

Laura Lohman

Women's Exegesis

Women have been interpreting the Qurʾān since its revelation. Although women's access to formal scholarship and active participation in *tafsīr* sciences has been limited historically, there are nevertheless notable exceptions. Women from *ʿulamāʾ* families or Ṣūfī *shaykhah*s, as far back as the *tafsīr* tradition itself, produced partial or complete commentaries on the Qurʾān, or held classes for other women where they would provide live exegesis on the Qurʾān. Their perspectives on the Qurʾān were similar to those of the larger exegetical traditions that they followed; these included schools of thought such as *al-tafsīr bi al-ma'thūr* and *al-tafsīr bi al-riwāyah* (interpretation by community tradition and ḥadīth transmission), *al-tafsīr bi al-ra'y* (interpretation based on reasoning), and various strands of Ṣūfī *tafsīr*.

The Basis of Women's *Tafsīr*. The best-known women's *tafsīrs* are from the contemporary period, which by and large did not grow out of a historical tradition of women's participation in *tafsīr*. Rather, most contemporary women's *tafsīr* developed from the late nineteenth- and early twentieth-century Islamic modernist movements that responded to traditionalism in *tafsīr* studies, even though women have participated in traditionalist *tafsīr* sciences at Islamic learning centers such as the women's sections of al-Azhar University and Qom Seminary.

The modernists' *tafsīrs* of the Qur'ān were premised on the idea that scientific developments and modern notions of equality, progress, nationalism, and rights are compatible with Islam in its earliest form. They felt that, over the course of centuries, generations of Muslims after the Prophet Muḥammad lost sight of the spirit of Islam that accommodated these ideas. Sayyid Aḥmad Khān (1817–1898), Muḥammad ʿAbduh (1849–1905), and Fazlur Rahman (1919–1988) in particular inspired the *tafsīr* methodologies and hermeneutics of contemporary women exegetes. Three elements of their approaches in particular are the starting point of contemporary women's *tafsīr*. First is the use of reason in interpreting Qur'ān verses in order to adapt the text for modern applications and avoid literalism and superstition. The second is insistence on understanding the Qur'ān with respect to its historical context (*siyāq*). The third element, having to do with the interpreters, is that the text is available to all to interpret, but difficulties in understanding the Qur'ān are due to human limitations.

Parallel to social movements in Muslim countries throughout the twentieth century, female scholars, along with male allies, turned to *tafsīr* to connect gender and social equality to the foundational text of Islam. Building upon modernists' impetus to resist traditionalism in *tafsīr*, women began from the late 1980s onward to challenge male-centered *tafsīr*, as well as exclusive male authority to interpret the Qur'ān. Several terms have been used to describe the genre of women's *tafsīr* that emerged, including feminist *tafsīr*, pro-feminist *tafsīr*, and pro-women's *tafsīr*. Although decidedly non-feminist exegesis by women exists, the female exegetes who adopted modernist *tafsīr* foundations advocated for reading male–female equality and studied gender in the text, regardless of whether or not they adopted the often problematic term "feminist" to describe their scholarship.

Aysha Hidayatullah argues that Qur'ānic studies on gender topics is now dominated by a cohesive subfield of Muslim feminist theology that is inspired simultaneously by gender egalitarianism that feminist scholars find in the Qur'ān, feminist sensibilities of modernity, and occasional conversation with Christian and Jewish feminist theology. Juliane Hammer has pointed out that, since traditional education in *tafsīr* sciences in the *madrasah* or *ḥawẓah* has been largely closed off to women, many female Qur'ān scholars who are personally committed to bringing about change in Qur'ānic interpretation are carving out a new space for exercising their agency to interpret the Qur'ān by occupying academic positions.

In addition to critiquing traditional interpretive methodologies and developing Muslim feminist hermeneutics, feminist *tafsīr* has focused on issues that fall under three major categories: creation and ontology of the human being and conceptualizations of gender; female characters in the Qur'ān such as Adam's wife, Maryam the mother of Jesus, the Queen of Sheba, and references to the Prophet's wives; and legalistic verses about women or gendered themes such as marriage, polygyny, divorce, procedures of inheritance and testimony, and veiling.

Women *Tafsīr* Scholars. Riffat Hassan was among the first scholars to approach the Qur'ān from a feminist perspective. She argues for gender equality in the Qur'ān through a rereading of the creation story. Recognizing that, for centuries, Muslims have internalized woman's inferiority to man because of the belief that woman was created from the rib of man, and is therefore understood to be crooked, stubborn, and instrumental for man, Hassan argues that the Qur'ānic account of creation is entirely gender-egalitarian. She identifies verse 4:1 as the Islamic or Qur'ānic account of creation, in which the human being is made from a single soul (*nafsin wahidatin*). Additionally, she points out that the term *adam* is used mostly as a generic name for humans (rather than the specific person of Adam), meaning that man is not the primary creation. She argues that this is evidence that the spouse of Adam was not created for Adam, but rather as an equal human being. She further points out that, in the Qur'ānic account, both Adam and his wife are led astray by Satan. Azizah al-Hibri also relies on the creation story and the fact that Iblīs (the deviant angel who is considered to be Satan) refused God's command because he thought he was superior to human beings in order to argue that patriarchy is inspired by a satanic complex of superiority.

In the Western academy, the most influential work on gender in the Qur'ān has been Amina Wadud's *Qur'ān and Woman: Rereading the Sacred Text from a Woman's Perspective*. Wadud criticizes interpretive methodologies of medieval exegetes who read the Qur'ān in atomistic fashion. She argues that their reading of verses in isolation from one another with an emphasis on grammar constructions led their medieval, patriarchal gender sensibilities to affect the understanding of verses on gender relations, rendering women inferior in exegesis and interpretation of the Qur'ān for centuries. She proposes, instead, a hermeneutic that first examines verses in relation to one another, both linguistically and in terms of content, then examines the historical context of revelation that would shed light on the potential meanings of verses, and finally proposes to read verses in relation to the worldview, or weltanschaaung, of the Qur'ān.

Wadud applies this methodology to a variety of verses, such as those about men's alleged superiority in creation, in the world and hereafter, those about men's *qiwama* over women (generally translated as "men as maintainers of women"), their *darajah* (rank) over women (which she argues is a gender-neutral rank of one person above others for whom they have responsibility), veiling, divorce, and more. For each, she applies her methodology and interprets absolute gender equality in Qur'ānic verses with regard to gender relations in the *dunyā* (temporal world) and in the *ākhirah* (next life).

Wadud draws on Fazlur Rahman's trajectory argument regarding slavery, which states that, although the Qur'ān is not meant to be an abolitionist text, its regulation of slavery and repeated commands to free slaves functions as a moral trajectory prescribed by the text in which slavery is not considered ethical or acceptable. Likewise she argues that, given the novelty of the Qur'ān and the Prophet Muḥammad's religion, the Qur'ān functioned as a regulation of prior gender practices of Arabia that were unjust, with a view to the moral trajectory of complete equality in social relations. Wadud argues that human beings are created in the "tawḥīdic paradigm," in which there can be no hierarchy among human beings without violation of *tawḥīd* or the unity of God because only God can "lord" over others and every human being is directly a subject of God.

Drawing on the methodologies of Fazlur Rahman and Farid Esack in her work, *"Believing Women" in Islam: Unreading Patriarchal Interpretations of the Qur'ān*, Asma Barlas also advocates for changes to interpretive models of the Qur'ān.

Rather than focusing her study on interpretations of specific verses as Wadud does, Barlas is concerned with the history and context of the Qur᾽ān and unreading patriarchy as a methodology. She argues that understandings of the Qur᾽ān took a turn for sexist interpretation during the generations following the Prophet's death during the Umayyad dynasty's rule, continuing through ʿAbbāsid rule, as a matter of convenience of adhering to hierarchical models. Leila Ahmed likewise argues that the egalitarianism of the Qur᾽ān was corrupted by male-centered interpretation of the scriptural text in Muslim history; male jurists created a legalistic and gender-biased Islam for men to follow and prescribe, while women were left with an Islam of pietism and rituals. Barlas proposes methods that uncover these layers of patriarchy by reading the Qur᾽ān in a contemporary context. Further, she argues that it is not necessary to be a specialist in the Arabic language to approach the Qur᾽ān. The Qur᾽ān is meant to be an accessible and universal text. This is in contrast to Nimat Hafez Barazangi's approach to the Qur᾽ān, in which she advocates for greater education of women in Qur᾽ānic Arabic so that they may approach the text without intermediaries. However, both advocate for democratization of the text.

Finally, some scholars suggest that pro-women's *tafsīr* is not limited to the work of academicians. Saʿdīyah Shaikh argues that lay women carry out *tafsīr* in praxis, through first interpreting, then acting on their understanding of the Qur᾽ān's message. She found that women who turned to the Qur᾽ān in situations of domestic violence created a *tafsīr* or interpretation of the Qur᾽ān by the conscientious action they took in resisting abuse.

[*See also* Ahmed, Leila; Barazangi, Nimat Hafez; Barlas, Asma; Esack, Farid; Feminism; Gender Equality; Islam and Women, *subentry on* Contemporary Debates; Religious Authority of Women; Wadud, Amina; *and* Women and Islam, *subentry on* Role and Status of Women.]

BIBLIOGRAPHY

Ahmed, Leila. *Women and Gender in Islam: Historical Roots of a Modern Debate.* New Haven, Conn.: Yale University Press, 1992.

Ali, Kecia. "Timeless Texts and Modern Morals: Challenges in Islamic Sexual Ethics." In *New Directions in Islamic Thought: Exploring Reform and Muslim Tradition*, edited by Kari Vogt, Lena Larsen, and Christian Moe, pp. 89–99. New York: I. B. Tauris, 2009.

Anwar, Ghazala. "Muslim Feminist Discourses." In *Feminist Theology in Different Contexts*, edited by Elisabeth Schüssler Fiorenza and M. Shawn Copeland, pp. 55–61. Concilium 1996/1. Maryknoll, N.Y.: Orbis, 1996.

Badran, Margot. *Feminism in Islam: Secular and Religious Convergences.* Oxford: Oneworld Press, 2009.

Barazangi, Nimat Hafez. *Woman's Identity and the Qur᾽ān: A New Reading.* Gainesville: University Press of Florida, 2004.

Barlas, Asma. *"Believing Women" in Islam: Unreading Patriarchal Interpretations of the Qur᾽ān.* Austin: University of Texas Press, 2002.

Hammer, Juliane. "Identity, Authority, and Activism: American Muslim Women Approach the Qur᾽ān." *The Muslim World* 98 (2008): 443–464.

Hassan, Riffat. "An Islamic Perspective." In *Women, Religion, and Sexuality: Studies on the Impact of Religious Teachings on Women*, edited by Jeanne Becher, pp. 93–128. Philadelphia: Trinity Press International, 1990.

Roald, Anne Sofie. "Feminist Reinterpretation of Islamic Sources: Muslim Feminist Theology in the Light of the Christian Tradition of Feminist Thought." In *Women and Islamization: Contemporary Dimensions of Discourse on Gender Relations*, edited by Karin Ask and Marit Tjomsland, pp. 17–44. New York: Berg, 1998.

Shaikh, Saʿdīyah. "A *Tafsīr* of Praxis: Gender, Marital Violence, and Resistance in a South African Muslim Community." In *Violence against Women in Contemporary World Religions: Roots and Cures*, edited by Saʿdīyah Shaikh and Dan Maguire, pp. 66–89. Cleveland, Ohio: Pilgrim Press, 2007.

Stowasser, Barbara Freyer. "Gender Issues and Contemporary Qur'ān Interpretation." In *Islam, Gender, and Social Change*, edited by Yvonne Yazbeck Haddad and John L. Esposito, pp. 30–44. New York: Oxford University Press, 1998.

Wadud, Amina. *Inside the Gender Jihad: Women's Reform in Islam*. Oxford: Oneworld Press, 2006.

Wadud, Amina. *Qur'ān and Woman: Rereading the Sacred Text from a Woman's Perspective*. New York: Oxford University Press, 1999.

ZAHRA AYUBI

WOMEN'S STATUS

Given the extensive body of references to the role of women in Islam appearing in religious texts beginning with Qur'ānic scripture and extending to the corpus of Sharīʿah law, care has been taken here to confine references to the text of the Qur'ān itself. This may beg the question of making distinctions between the content of Qur'ānic verses referring to women, which are relatively limited in scope, and wider discussion of issues of gender raised by traditional legal scholars (*fuqahā'*) as well as contemporary commentators. With respect to *fiqh*, it should be noted that, although precepts drawn from the Sharīʿah cannot contradict specific provisions in the text of the Qur'ān, they can and do draw from a diverse body of legal sources based on the collected sayings and practices of the Prophet, commonly referred to as the *sunnah*, and other recognized components of *uṣūl al fiqh*.

Examination of the content of Qur'ānic verses dealing with issues of gender suggests a dichotomy of foci, one abstract in nature, the second quite specific, thus frequently taken to represent Qur'ānic laws. Specific verses make passing references to historically identifiable women, either within the chronological narrative associated with Muḥammad's prophetic mission or as symbolic figures drawn from pre-Islamic models. More abstract verses address broad issues related to gender, such as exhortations calling for modesty on the part of women, legal guidelines for marriage and divorce, polygyny and adultery, and rights of inheritance.

The Qur'ān offers several symbolic images of women that relate in one way or another to the religious mission of the Prophet. References such as those in Qur'ānic 53 to the three daughters—al-Lat, al-Uzza, and Manat—of the pre-Islamic (thus polytheistic) god appear in translation as "mere names," possessing no claims for recognition by the true God. In a different context, specifically 19, the Qur'ān provides (as part of Islam's recognition of preceding prophetic monotheistic missions) a version of the divine conception and the throes of delivery experienced by Mary. This is followed by an account of Mary's presentation of the infant Jesus to those who would greet him as a prophet. Believers are exhorted to show deference to the woman who bore him.

Accounts of a number of women who were contemporaries of Muḥammad—particularly his wives—are woven into the Qur'ānic revelation in ways that demonstrate adherence to a specific verse. Qur'ān 33:50, for example, defines appropriate marriage ties open to the Prophet. One possibly significant exception that does not fit into such standard narrative contexts is that of Zaynab, Muḥammad's daughter-in-law who divorced his adopted son in order to marry Muḥammad himself. This act became the subject of a specific revelation (33:37), which was needed in order to clarify an action that appeared to contradict Qur'ānic rules prohibiting marriages within certain family boundaries (see the discussion of Qur'ānic 4).

Although stated in very general terms, the Qur'ān upholds the principle of equality between men and women, beginning, symbolically, with their creation from the same source (Qur'ān 96). Equal status as believers is vouchsafed for both men and women as they embody the same religious values of devotion, truthfulness, patience, humbleness, and chastity, as well as the *ʿibādāt*, including fasting and almsgiving (33).

Numerous references enjoin the two genders to live righteous lives in harmony with each other. A prime example appears in Qurʾān 9, which cites the pleasure God derives from the closeness of their friendship—again tied to mutual observance of Islam's precepts.

Although reliable sources are limited, scholars often suggest that the status of women in Arabia before Islam was extremely precarious, and that the Qurʾān held a promise of improvements relating to personal security and dignity. In various places within the Revelation, one finds condemnations of former pagan practices, especially female infanticide. Such suggestions further imply the unacceptability, for example, of former conditions of polygamy (which are, in essence, redefined in the Qurʾān), but lack guidelines that could clarify how marriages were contracted and dissolved prior to the Islamic Revelation. Such lacunae are largely resolved by very specific terms laid down in the Qurʾān. Indeed, the most often cited areas in the Qurʾān in which women's relative position and status vis-à-vis men, and where rights and obligations are specifically defined, involve conditions of marriage and divorce.

Many verses from Qurʾān 34 clearly exhort believers to see to it that their women marry under the proper conditions. Marriage is assumed to be the fulfillment of God's will, not only for purposes of procreation but also to assure the security of women. Qurʾān 4 sets certain legal boundaries for marriage, forbidding nuptials with already married women (excepting one's own slave women who may already be married). The same chapter explicitly prohibits incestuous marriage with direct female relations and extends such prohibition to the mothers of one's wives, foster-mothers or foster-sisters, and stepdaughters (if marriage has been consummated with the biological mother; if not, marriage is permitted).

Several references in the Qurʾān sanction marriage with more than one wife, depending on one's material means. Concerning polygyny (apparently practiced widely and without legally defined constraints before the advent of Islam), a very specific Qurʾānic injunction appears in 4:3, which recognizes the legality of four wives on the condition of treating all equally, including in matters of dowry. Yet, men are assumed to have certain obligations toward their wives. Qurʾān 4 stipulates that, in cases where mistreatment or unequal treatment by the husband occurs (in the latter case of one or another wife in a polygynous marriage), an aggrieved wife is justified in expecting (as does God) the man to reform his behavior.

Such references notwithstanding, the Qurʾān is usually understood to affirm, specifically in 4:34, a higher status for men over women—mainly because of men's responsibility to provide for women's livelihood. Such a role may involve chastisement in cases where a woman's deference falls short of expected propriety, although what form this is to take is a matter of intense debate in scholarly and religious circles.

The most specific injunctions concerning women—bearing the nature of specific laws—appear in verses treating divorce, as well as those dealing with sexual transgressions, particularly cases of adultery. Qurʾān 65 is devoted entirely to divorce. Qurʾān 2 also contains many specific references, including one that allows a woman to remarry a man who has divorced her three times, but prevents a fourth marriage until she consummates a union with another man from whom she has been divorced.

In all divorce cases, it is essential to determine whether the wife may be pregnant. When there is evidence of regular menstruation and an extended commitment to abstention, divorce proceedings can go forward. Failure to maintain abstinence is taken (again, in Qurʾān 65 and 2) as a sign of reconciliation. If, however, a woman gives birth to a child conceived by a man who has divorced her, the former husband must provide for the mother and infant (or for a wet nurse) until the child is weaned. Another imposition of responsibilities on a husband seeking divorce can occur if there has been no consummation of the marriage; in such cases, the man must provide some material compensation and return all or part of the dowry. In all instances, it is recommended that two witnesses, one male and one female, be called to attest to the honorability of the divorce proceedings.

Adultery by either men or women is condemned and is subject to at least two forms of punishment. Qur'ān 24, which also contains a strong denunciation of prostitution, refers (as does 65) directly to adultery, prescribing a punishment of one hundred lashes for both the male and female offender. Although there is historical evidence that accused adulteresses could be condemned to death by stoning, no Qur'ānic reference specifies this extreme punishment.

Several sections of the Qur'ān call on both women and men to practice modesty in appearance and behavior. Some practices that have become characteristic of Muslim women throughout the world—wearing of various forms of head coverings and veils, for example—are implicit, but not necessarily explicit in the Qur'ān. What is certain is that the Qur'ān contains many injunctions calling on women especially to observe high standards of modesty. Qur'ān 24 exhorts women to avert direct eye contact and, in their clothing and adornment, to guard against any immodest exposure in the presence of males who are not direct family members. This can even include rapid movements of arms or legs—movements that can cause sounds revealing jewelry under outer garments. Qur'ān 33 echoes a similar theme, making it a woman's duty (specifically referring here to the Prophet's wives) to avoid arousing men's desires by using soft feminine tones when she speaks.

Comparison of such Qur'ānic injuctions with equally strict provisions in the earlier (but secularly based) sixth-century CE Frankish *Lex salica* suggests that the latter leveled warnings against what might become improper tendencies and intentions on the part of men rather than women.

Finally, one other body of Qur'ānic references lends itself to categorization as legally binding: matters of inheritance. Qur'ān 4 establishes specific rules for inheritance, guaranteeing that both men and women should inherit, but making distinctions between shares granted to males and females, involving smaller proportional amounts to female descendants. In cases of two heirs of different genders, the woman is to receive half the amount given to the man. If there are several female heirs, two-thirds of the inheritance is to be divided among their total number. Other provisions in the same chapter define conditions of inheritance when a son or daughter predeceases their parents or siblings. Here again, if both parents remain, a smaller proportion (than that of a father or brother) is allotted to the mother and sister of a childless male or female descendant.

Although all such Qur'ānic references may appear quite distant and isolated in time and space, by logic and necessity they bear close relation to issues of concern to Muslim women in the contemporary world. It is generally assumed that—with regard to issues affecting women's status or any other subject—if a specific citation appears in the Qur'ān, little room exists for debate. Sharī'ah-based interpretations, on the other hand, offer the potential of incorporating—through *uṣūl al fiqh*—broader conclusions depending on differing contexts. Such interpretations can and have been referenced by legislators in various Islamic countries endeavoring to make modern laws respecting the spirit of Qur'ānic revelation, while at the same time adapting legislation to reflect contemporary modes of life.

Most issues affecting women's legal status in modern times fall under the purview of personal status law, although they may also involve matters of civil law (e.g., property rights and contracts). A prime example among a number of prototypic twentieth-century measures to integrate Qur'ānic principles as bases of secular codes was the work of the jurist ʿAbd al-Razzāq al-Sanhūrī, the "father" of Egypt's 1949 Civil Code. Al-Sanhūrī and most of his generation chose, however, to put personal status questions involving women's status aside, mainly because these involved very close reference to religiously sanctioned laws. Even after 1979, when President Anwar el-Sadat decreed "progressive" changes in family laws affecting women, opposition reasserted itself, causing Egypt's High Constitutional Court in 1985 to reverse the changes. The gradual introduction of amendments after 2000 has allowed Egypt and other Islamic countries (important comparisons go back to the 1950s in Tunisia and are ongoing in twenty-first-century Malaysia) to reopen debates over the extent to which Qur'ānic revelation and Sharīʿah-based interpretation of the same can or should be integrated into legislative reform movements focused on women's legal status. Feminist interpreters of the Qur'ān are challenging some of the legal inequalities that have developed over the centuries as the result of specific masculinist interpretations of scripture and developing alternative, gender-egalitarian readings of it.

In such cases, the goal seems to be to address issues that many modernist interpreters consider excessively archaic, such as Qur'ānic provisions in 58 for recognizing the validity of a husband's simple verbal declaration of his intention to divorce. Other focal points are those in which the Qur'ān applies unequal "measures" to men and women. The most apparent may be inheritance, in which Qur'ānic laws as traditionally applied tend to depart from widely recognized areas of secular legislation, frequently sparking conflicting claims of jurisdictional precedence.

BIBLIOGRAPHY

Al Hāshimi, ʿAbdel-Munʿim. *Les femmes dans le récit coranique.* Beirut: Dar Ibn Hazm, 2005.

Barazangi, Nimat Hafez. *Women's Identity and the Qur'an: A New Reading.* Gainesville: University Press of Florida, 2004.

Barlas, Asma. *"Believing Women" in Islam: Unreading Patriarchal Interpretations of the Qur'an.* Austin: University of Texas Press, 2004.

Ismatu ad-Din Karkar. *Al mar'atu min khilâl al 'ayâti al-qur'âniyah.*Tunis: Société Tunisinne de Diffusion, 1979.

Mallat, Chibli, and Jane Frances Connors. *Islamic Family Law.* Leiden, Netherlands: E. J. Brill, 1990.

Stowasser, Barbara Freyer. *Women in the Qur'an, Traditions and Interpretation.* New York: Oxford University Press, 1996.

Wadud, Amina. *Qur'an and Woman: Re-reading the Sacred Text from a Woman's Perspective.* New York: Oxford University Press, 1999.

BYRON CANNON

QUR'ĀNIC RECITATION SCHOOLS FOR GIRLS.

Girls gain knowledge of proper recitation and learn to embody the Qur'ān through the vocal act of recitation in schools around the world. Often, the study of Qur'ānic recitation is introduced at an early age and memorization of the Qur'ān through recitation is a prerequisite for other studies. In addition to offering instruction in recitation as an essential mode of piety, these schools provide girls with basic literacy skills, social skills, and discipline, as well as opportunities for employment and leadership roles.

Private and Public Schooling. Girls have learned Qur'ānic recitation for centuries through both private instruction and public schooling. Private tutors have often taught daughters of religious leaders and the wealthy, such as upper-class

Ottoman girls and daughters in the royal families of Mughal India. In nineteenth-century Russia, the daughters of religious leaders (*mullahs*) received private instruction in the recitation and meaning of the Qur'ān and often became *abystais* (female religious leaders). Private instruction continues today, as Bangladeshis, for example, hire a teacher of recitation (*moulobi*) when their children reach age six to eight.

Public schools have provided instruction in recitation to a broader range of girls. Such schools, when supported by private donations or religious foundations, have offered free or less expensive education. Ottoman mosque schools taught girls and boys recitation, prayers, writing, and arithmetic. While girls often did not continue their studies as long as boys, in nineteenth-century Russia, similar numbers of boys and girls studied in Qur'ān schools through levels covering recitation, reading, and writing. More recently, girls have gained greater access to such schools. For example, in the Moroccan *kuttāb*, girls aged three to six receive instruction in Qur'ānic recitation and memorization. Girls and boys may be seated in separate halves of one classroom. The *kuttāb* also teaches socialization and keeps children off the streets—meaningful benefits for lower-income families who send their children to these schools for free. These schools now employ female teachers, who are perceived as gentler and better suited to teaching young children than traditional male teachers. As most of these female teachers have a public school education, including study at the *kuttāb*, their employment illustrates how girls can gain future income and respect through such early education.

Girls have also studied Qur'ānic recitation up to the university level. From the fifteenth century, Sudanese girls attended religious seminaries (*khalwah/khalāwī*), where they learned recitation, memorized the Qur'ān, and studied Islamic law, sometimes becoming female preachers and jurists. In Northern Nigeria, schools such as the Salamatu Institute for Arabic and Islamic Studies in Kaduna, founded in 1987, provide girls with instruction in recitation and other subjects at the junior secondary level. Islamic boarding schools (*pondok pesantren*) have been maintained in Indonesia since the sixteenth century and serve both boys and girls. Ranging from twenty students to thousands of students, these boarding schools provide instruction in recitation and other religious subjects from the preparatory to university levels.

Segregated Instruction. Girls commonly study recitation with other female students in communities where there is concern that a female reciter may be spiritually distracting to male listeners. Some institutions provide separate instruction for male and female students. In the University of Jordan's Faculty of Islamic Law, male and female students take courses on recitation separately, while studying other religious subjects together. Separate training for girls is also provided within the Süleymanlı organization, a branch of the Naqshbandīyah Ṣūfī order that emphasizes Qur'ānic recitation and has a strong following among Turkish Muslims in Europe. Like boys, girls learn recitation in Süleymanlı mosques and become initiates. For some, this first step leads to advanced studies to attain the position of *hoca hanum* (female preacher).

Separate institutions have also been established for female students. In China, Qur'ānic schools for girls were established starting in the late seventeenth century in Shanxi and Shandong Provinces and ultimately developed into women's mosques. In the 1980s girls' schools were established in South Africa, and in 1977 the Institut Ilmu al-Qur'an, a women's college, was founded in Jakarta. At this college, female students study the rules and melodic aspects of recitation, Arabic, and Islamic law, in addition to regular university courses.

One of the largest networks of girls' schools is the al-Huda International Institute of Islamic Education for Women. Begun in 1994 in Islamabad, al-Huda provides religious instruction across urban Pakistan and the diaspora as a supplement to secular schooling. In courses ranging from short summer programs to eighteen-month diploma programs, girls study the Qur'ān, with emphasis on recitation, listening, translation, and comprehension. Al-Huda focuses not on memorizing the entire Qur'ān, but rather on using recitation as part of character development. Girls are encouraged to gain a well-rounded education, engage in self-reflection, and participate in both public life and spiritual development. Graduates go on to teach at and found new branches, and they often lead informal study groups in women's homes.

Some segregated study leads to a certificate (*ijāzah*). Young female reciters may travel across the world to gain certificates indicating that they have mastered a particular tradition of recitation from an unbroken chain of reciters going back to the Prophet and ultimately to Gabriel and God. Focusing on the recitation, memorization, and comprehension of verses, young reciters are guided by female teachers who prepare them to pass a final examination administered by a *shaykh* who can confer a certificate. Once certified in that recitation tradition, the young reciter is expected to never reject any student who wants to study with her.

In these varied institutions, numerous teaching methods are used. Instruction typically begins with the shortest chapters. Students may learn by rote and by ear, reciting individually and in groups. Some schools, such as al-Huda, have created specialized teaching materials. In Indonesia, distinct pedagogies have developed, allowing parents to choose between a slow method of instruction aimed at deep understanding and more modern, rapid instruction. Despite these differences, recitation schools provide girls with a path to piety and literacy, ensure that they can preserve the community's knowledge of the Qur'ān, and allow them to gain religious authority and respect as adults.

BIBLIOGRAPHY

Boyle, Helen Nolan. *Quranic Schools: Agents of Preservation and Change*. New York: Routledge, 2004. Examines contemporary schools in Morocco, Yemen, and Nigeria.

Mattson, Ingrid. *The Story of the Qur'an: Its History and Place in Muslim Life*. Oxford: Blackwell, 2008. Includes a detailed account of how a young woman earns a certificate in recitation in Syria.

Mushtaq, Faiza. "New Claimants to Religious Authority: A Movement for Women's Islamic Education, Moral Reform and Innovative Traditionalism." PhD diss., Northwestern University, Evanston Ill., 2010. Extensive discussion of al-Huda International Institute of Islamic Education for Women.

Rasmussen, Anne K. *Women, the Recited Qur'an, and Islamic Music in Indonesia*. Berkeley: University of California Press, 2010. Several sections address instruction in recitation.

Laura Lohman

Qur'ānic Schools for Girls. In Sunnī Muslim communities, the commonly used term for a school is *madrasah* (pl. *madāris*). Female students either memorize the Qur'ān to become *hafizah* (masc. *hafiz*), someone who has memorized the complete Qur'ān, or they may also undertake more scholarly study to become *ʿalimahs* (masc. *ʿalim*) or scholars. In Shīʿī communities, the term for a religious school is *ḥawẓah*(pl. *ḥawẓāt*) *ʿilmīyah* or "enclaves of knowledge," and female students may study to become *mubālaghah* (masc. *mubālagh*). Other terms such as *maktab*, *dār al-ʿulūm*, or *jāmiʿah* may also be used. Subjects pursued in such schools can include Qur'ān studies, covering exegesis and commentary (*tafsīr*), along with other disciplines such as ḥadīth studies (sayings of the Prophet), *sīrah* (life history of Muḥammad), *fiqh* (jurisprudence), and *manṭiq* (logic).

The Era of the Prophet. During the lifetime of the Prophet, the ḥadīth indicate that men and women shared the same space, usually in the mosque, to learn the Qur'ān. However, the first indication of what may be understood as a Qur'ānic school specifically for females, albeit perhaps for women and not just girls, can be traced back to a ḥadīth stating, "Some women requested the Prophet to fix a day for them as the men were taking all his time. On that he promised them one day for religious lessons and commandments" (*Ṣaḥīḥ Bukhārī*, Vol. 1, Book 3, No. 101). Aisha Bewley (1999), a Muslim scholar and translator of the Qur'ān, also notes that the Prophet Muḥammad, after asking the women of the Anṣār to gather in one house, sent his companion 'Umar ibn al-Khaṭṭāb to teach women the basis of Islam.

These Qur'ān schools illustrate that education was a priority in early Muslim communities, not just for men, but also for women, and that facilities existed—some more organized as in the two instances mentioned above, and others less formal, such as when women approached the Prophet or his wives for scholarly advice. Indeed, 'Ā'ishah, the wife of the Prophet, praised the women of Anṣār when she said, "Modesty (or shyness) did not prevent them from becoming learned in the *Dīn*" (*Ṣaḥīḥ Muslim*, Book 3, No. 649). Women from this era were also involved in the memorization and transmission of Qur'ānic verse and ḥadīth. Some sources note that Zaynab bint 'Alī, Muḥammad's granddaughter, held regular meetings in Medina for this specific purpose.

History. As early Muslim communities grew, there was an increased need for educational facilities. Usually, centers of learning, as in the Prophet's time, were attached to mosques. It is not clear whether there were separate facilities for males and females, and it seems that usually males and females continued to share the same space. Furthermore, a number of references can be found in biographical sources about individual Muslim women who pursued both Qur'ānic and ḥadīth studies under their fathers and other scholars, and who became scholars and teachers themselves. However, there is little mention of specific schools for women or, indeed, for men.

In 859 CE, partly due to the efforts of Fāṭimah bint Muḥammad al-Fihri (d. 880), a center of learning was established at the Qarawīyīn Mosque in Fez, Morocco, which became what is recognized as the first formal school of Islamic studies, including the study of the Qur'ān (now the modern-day University of al-Karaouine), and where there were special facilities for women to listen to scholars. Bewley further mentions the al-Andalus Mosque, also in Fez, set up by Fāṭimah's sister Maryam, which became a branch of the Qarawīyīn Mosque and also a center of learning. Here, both male and female students were taught by a female teacher, Āliyya bint al-Ṭayyib (c. tenth century), and specific times were allocated for students to attend classes—after the *'aṣr* (evening) prayers for women and before the *dhuhr* (afternoon) prayers for men (Bewley, 1999).

Around this time, more organized facilities for teaching and learning Islamic sciences began to evolve and terms such as *madrasah* began to be used more frequently. In the late 'Abbāsid period, Niẓām al-Mulk (1018–1092), a Seljuk vizier, founded a number of schools that later came to be known as Madrasah Niẓāmiyyah. During the Fāṭimid and Mamlūk periods, schools flourished under royal patronage. However, there are considerable lacunae in recorded history around this period and, although a number of female scholars and ḥadīth transmitters can be traced back to this time, it is difficult to re-create an accurate picture of the facilities that existed for girls to study the Qur'ān.

Qur'ān schools for girls continued to develop in various formats, often under the patronage of female scholars and or female members of various royal families. For example, in fourteenth-century Cairo, Fāṭimah bint al-ʿAbbas al-Baghdadiyya, a Ṣūfī scholar and poet, established an all-female institute, the Ribat al-Baghdadiyya, which also offered women social support. In the fifteenth century, Umm ʿAbdullah taught mixed classes of more than fifty students in Damascus, and, in Cairo, Fāṭimah bint Muḥammad similarly taught men and women. Ghalayana, a Moroccan scholar who lived in the seventeenth century, is reported to have included many women and girls among her students. In China, also around the seventeenth century, schools were built for the Islamic education of Muslim women. The practice of *nu ahong*, or female spiritual leaders, continues to be widespread in Chinese Muslim communities.

Another women's education movement, Yan Taru ("those who congregate together" or "sisterhood") was established by the scholar and daughter of the founder of the Sokoto Caliphate (in Nigeria), Nana Asma'u, in the eighteenth century and still exists in the early twenty-first century. Asma'u trained older, more mature women to become teachers or *jajis* who taught the Qur'ān and Islamic studies to their local communities, sometimes through the medium of poetry.

Such examples indicate the historical continuity, geographical spread, and richness of Qur'ānic schools and wider educational developments for girls and women in the Islamic world that continued in various forms through the nineteenth and twentieth centuries. For example, Nawab Sultan Jahan Begam (1838–1901) introduced many educational reforms in her state of Bhopal (modern-day India); and, more recently, Farhat Hashimi's organization for women, Al-Huda International (established in 1994), has enabled women to set up study circles in their local communities aimed at studying the Qur'ān and Islam.

Contemporary Qur'ānic Schools for Girls. Modern Qur'ānic schools for girls exist all over the world in Muslim-majority communities and also in minority communities, such as in India and in the West. These schools follow a variety of pedagogic and curricula models (for example, the Darse Nizami that originated in the Indian Subcontinent). In most cases, girls, as do boys, start their Qur'ānic studies at an early age (four to five years). These classes, depending on sociocultural contexts, may be held in a school that includes both Islamic and "secular" curricula, or a supplementary school affiliated with a mosque or in institutions that only teach Islamic studies. At a young age, students are taught to read Arabic and memorize selected chapters of the Qur'ān. For example, the *pesantren* Islamic boarding schools in Indonesia offer young men and women the opportunity to undertake rigorous religious studies. Some may also focus, though, on vocational training and certain aspects of secular education.

Depending on the type of school and also the resources that students have access to, their career and further education opportunities may be limited or enhanced. Some *madāris*—in partnership with local universities—now offer women the opportunity to achieve a degree-level education.

Issues and Controversies. Some scholars have argued that modern Qur'ān schools for girls indoctrinate them in a worldview that is limiting and non-emancipated, encouraging them to lead secluded and domestic lives and that the curriculum taught to girls is less prestigious than what is offered to boys. There are also reports about the radicalization of girls and women (and young men), for example, in the female *madrasah* Jamia Hafza affiliated with the Red Mosque in Islamabad, Pakistan. However, in many rural and impoverished areas, these schools are the only source of literacy for Muslim girls, offering them routes out of their poverty by opening up teaching careers or leading to better marriage prospects. There is also more recent scholarship and activism that position these schools as agents of change that equip girls with knowledge of their rights and roles as outlined in the Qur'ān and that give them the tools to challenge patriarchy in Muslim communities. For example the PBS documentary *The Light in Her Eyes* shot in Syria before the 2012–2013 uprisings describes a school for girls run by a conservative teacher and its impacts on the lives of its students.

BIBLIOGRAPHY

Bano, M., and H. Kalmbach, eds. *Women, Leadership and Mosques: Changes in Contemporary Islamic Authority*. Leiden, Netherlands: E. J. Brill, 2012.

Bewley, A. *Islam: The Empowering of Women*. London: Ta-Ha, 1999.

Bewley, A. *Muslim Women—A Biographical Dictionary*. London: Ta-Ha, 2004.

Lambert-Hurley, S. *Muslim Women, Reform and Princely Patronage: Nawab Sultan Jahan Begam of Bhopal*. London: Routledge, 2007.

Meltzer, J., and L. Nix, dir. *The Light in Her Eyes*. PBS documentary, 2012. http://www.pbs.org/pov/thelightinhereyes/.

Mukadam, M., A. Scott-Baumann, A. Chowdhury, and S. Contractor. *Muslim Faith Leader Training: An Independent Review*. London: Department of Communities and Local Government, October 2010. http://www.communities.gov.uk/documents/communities/pdf/1734121.pdf.

Nadwi, M. *Al-Muḥaddithāt: The Women Scholars in Islam*. Oxford: Interface, 2007.

Reiser, E. "Between Expectations and Ideals: Hui Women Finding a Place in the Public Sphere through Islamic Education." Islam in China, 2011. http://islaminchina.info/between-expectations-and-ideals-hui-women-finding-a-place-in-the-public-sphere-through-islamic-education/.

SARIYA CHERUVALLIL-CONTRACTOR

QUTLUGH TERKĀN KHĀTŪN. (r. 1257–1283), powerful and influential ruler of the Persian province of Kerman for twenty-six years during the Ilkhanid period of Mongol Ascendancy.

> She was a queen whose character was righteous, whose mystery was pure, whose outer garments were modesty, whose insignia was chastity, . . . whose days were resolute. She was the jeweled knot and springtime of the kings of the Qarā Khitā'ī of Kirman. (Munshi, *Simt al-'ula*, p. 37)

The remarkable career of Qutlugh Terkān Khātūn began in the slave markets of Turkistan and came to a peaceful close in the sumptuous Ilkhanid courts of Tabrīz, the capital of the mighty Mongol kings of Iran. Born into a noble family of the Qara Khitai, a Turco-Mongol people originally from Northern China, Halal Khātūn (Lady Halal) fell victim to the wars being played out by rival statelets and warlords in Turkistan for domination over the eastern lands of the Islamic empire. The Qara Khitai, though their monarchs were usually infidels, ruled Islamic eastern Turkistan from their capital of Kashgar with the support of their Muslim subjects and the recognition of the Caliph in Baghdad.

Jealous of their growing power and influence, the mediaeval Islamic world's most powerful ruler, the Khwarazmshah 'Alā' al-Dīn bin Tekish, who had ambitions far beyond Central Asia, launched repeated attacks on his neighbors, including the Qara Khitai, and it was after one such attack that the future queen of Kerman found herself a slave in the markets of Bokhara. Fortunately her wit, beauty, and dispassionate, iron will served her well and her new master, the aged Hajji Salih of Isfahan, reputedly fell in love with her and she was accepted into his family. The Muslim accounts of these early years written from within her own *dīwān* (court) treat this delicate subject of female modesty and chastity with extreme sensitivity avoiding any suggestion of impropriety or hint at any compromising situation that might tarnish their Muslim queen's reputation. Therefore the various owners who took possession of the very self-assured "moon-faced beauty" apparently all treated her as a daughter rather than a concubine. As she changed hands—bartered as a commodity, or part of the spoils of war—the list of owners stretched to include a prince, chief judges, and an atabeg.

Her last owner, the wily Qutlugh Sultan Baraq Hājib of Kerman (r. 1222–1235), who acquired her as part of a peace settlement with the Atabeg of Yazd, is said to have adopted her as his daughter, though Waṣṣāf claims that the two produced a daughter, Maryam Khātūn. The court histories make no reference to this and claim that on his deathbed Baraq Ḥājib gave Quṭb al-Dīn, his nephew and heir to his throne, his "daughter's" hand in marriage though it is more realistic to assume that following steppe practice after his death, Baraq Ḥājib's male heirs inherited the deceased's wives and concubines. What is certain is that Quṭb al-Dīn, the heir to the throne of Kerman took Terkān Khātūn as his chief wife and that shortly after, his position as sultan and ruler of Kerman was endorsed with a *yarligh* (edict) from the Great Khan, Möngke (d. 1259) in Qaraqorum. Then—his position secured, his relations close with the Great Khan's brother and first Ilkhan (Mongol Emperor of Persia) of Iran, Hülegü Khan (d. 1265)—Quṭb al-Dīn, the new Qutlugh Sultan of Kerman, quite unexpectedly dropped dead, leaving an infant son and a grieving wife, Terkān Khātūn. However, the redoubtable Terkān Khātūn wasted no time in grief and she immediately travelled to Hülegü's new capital in Maragha, about 150 kilometers south of Tabrīz and ensured that she be appointed regent for her son Hajjāj. She had already been recognized as the real power behind the throne while her husband still lived, so her bid for full recognition of her authority was endorsed by not only the notables of Kerman but crucially by the *ʿulemā* as well. Hülegü Khan issued a *yarligh* awarding her the title of Qutlugh Sultan along with political and military control of the province and dispatched a *shahna/basqaq* to enforce his decision and support her throne. She cemented her position through marriage ties, betrothing her son Hajjāj to the daughter of Arghun Aqa, the former military governor of Iran and a leading Mongol official, and her daughter Pādeshāh Khātūn to Hülegü Khan's son and successor, Abaqa Khan. Though her court historians reported her anguish at contravening Islamic strictures in marrying her Muslim daughter to an infidel, political expediency prevailed and the capable Pādeshāh Khātūn entrenched herself securely at the heart of her husband's court, even marrying his son Geikhatu Khan (r. 1291–1295) on his death in 1282.

Terkān Khātūn oversaw a period of stability, prosperity, and security often described as Kerman's "Golden Age." She enjoyed the support of not only her political masters in Tabrīz and by extension in Khanbaliq (Beijing) but also of the notables and elite at home in Kerman. She had the backing of the merchants and traders who benefited from her royal connections and the links she was able to establish with people and places throughout the Mongol Empire as well as the endorsement of the conservative *ʿulemā*, who were prepared to serve under a female sovereign because their interests were well served through her considerable influence in the pagan royal courts and her sound judgments reflected well on them. Even the Tabrīz-appointed *basqaq* seemed to work for her interests rather than for his political masters in Azerbaijan.

Her daughter and successor, Pādeshāh Khātūn, was able to express in Persian verse a dilemma at the heart of her court, which her mother was able to resolve to her advantage. They were Turco-Mongols assimilated into sedentary Persian culture, three generations out from the steppe. Qutlugh Terkān was able to successfully identify with her Mongol masters in Tabrīz and at the same time play the Persian Muslim queen at home, accepted by her Persian subjects and trusted by her Mongol masters. Pādeshāh Khātūn's verse captures her own crisis of identity as she yearns for the freedom of the steppe while living the life of a Persian princess.

> Although I am the child of a mighty Sultan
> And the fruit of the garden that is the heart of the Turks,
> I laugh at fate and prosperity,
> But I cry at this endless exile
> (Munshī, p.70; *Tārīkh-i-Shāhī*, intro., p. 61; Shabānkāra'ī, p. 201. Lane, *Early Mongol Rule*, p. 110)

Women in the steppe culture of the Turco-Mongols enjoyed a far higher status than their sisters south of the Oxus and often exercised considerable political clout. Under Ilkhanid rule the women from those of Iran's ruling houses with some claim to Turkic ethnicity were able to assume unprecedented authority and were appointed to positions of real power. Qutlugh Terkān Khātūn was able to take full advantage of this turn of fate and her ascendancy signalled the beginning of a unique period in Iranian history when women relished the recognition of their unfettered abilities.

[*See also* Ābish Khātūn bint Saʿd II *and* Baghdād Khātūn.]

BIBLIOGRAPHY

Anon, (ed) Mohammad Ibrāuīm Bāstānī Pārīzī, *Tārīkh-i-Shāhī*, Inteshārāt-i-Baniyād Farhang Iran. Tehran, 1976.

Howorth, Henry Hoyle. *History of the Mongols: The Mongols of Persia*. Lightning Source UK: Milton Keynes, 2011.

Lambton, A. K. S. *Continuity and Change in Medieval Persia. Aspects of Administrative, Economic, Social History in 11th–14th Century Persia*. London: I. B. Tauris, 1988.

Lane, George. *Early Mongol Rule in Thirteenth-Century Iran*. London: RoutledgeCurzon, 2003.

Lane, George. *Daily Life in the Mongol Empire*. Westport, Conn.: Greenwood Press, 2006.

Munshī, Nasīr al-Dīn, 'Abbās, ed. *Simt al-ʿulā: Tārīkh-i-Qarakhitā'īān-i-Kirmān*, Inteshārāt Esatīr, Tehran, 1983.

Wassāf, Shihab al-Dīn 'Abdallah Sharaf Shīrāzī, M. M. Isfahānī, *Tārīkh-i-Wassāf*, Tehran, 1959.

GEORGE LANE

R

RĀBIʿAH AL-ʿADAWĪYAH. Ṣūfī mystic (713/17–801), Rābiʿah of Basra was a freedwoman from the tribe of Qays ibn ʿAdi; hence, her surname al-ʿAdawīyah. Born to a family of modest means in Basra, Rābiʿah (meaning "the fourth") was so called because she had three older sisters. Her life was struck by tragedy at a very young age, when she lost both her father and mother and was sold into slavery. Moved by her piety and prayerfulness, her master is said to have taken pity on her and eventually manumitted her. Rābiʿah is then reported to have wandered off into the desert, in pursuit of solitary contemplation of the divine. Upon her return from the desert, she acquired a simple room where she dedicated herself solely to the worship of God. According to the thirteenth-century mystic Fāriḍ al-Dīn ʿAṭṭār (d. c. 1221) who composed a hagiography of her life, Rābiʿah was inclined to fast all day and pray through the night. Many wondrous deeds and miracles are attributed to her. Her emphasis on the selfless love of God is exemplified in the well-known tradition, "If I worship You for fear of Hell, then burn me in Hell, and if I worship You in hope of Paradise, then exclude me from therein, but if I worship You for Your own sake, then do not withhold from me Your eternal beauty."

Unlike most mystics in Islam, Rābiʿah never married and is said to have refused many offers of marriage. Many of her friends and confidants were, however, prominent male scholars, such as Sufyān al-Thawrī (d. 778) and al-Hasan al-Baṣrī (d. 728), who are reported to have freely visited her and sought her advice on many matters.

Rābiʿah was almost ninety when she died in 801; she is buried in Basra. All her life she had been in preparation for her final meeting with the divine Beloved. Her shroud is said to have been always placed before her in her customary place of worship in order to serve as a reminder of the reality of the next world and of the ultimate union with the Beloved. According to ʿAṭṭār, she offered posthumous testimony to two visitors to her grave, asserting that she, in fact, had "attained that which I saw."

Some later non-Ṣūfī biographers developed ambivalent views of Rābiʿah and her overall contribution to scholarship. Thus, the historian Muḥammad ibn Aḥmad al-Dhahabī (d. 1348) praised her abstemiousness and God-fearing character (*al-zahida al-khashiʿa*), but tended to be dismissive of miracles attributed to her. Earlier non-Ṣūfī authors, such as the famous belle-lettrist al-Jāḥiẓ (d. 869), who was a younger near-contemporary of Rābiʿah, were more favorably disposed toward her. Ṣūfī biographers, like Abū Ṭālib al-Makkī (d. 996), however, held her in practically universal high esteem and praised her single-minded devotion to God and abstemiousness. They also tended to assign to her a much higher spiritual status than her distinguished male contemporaries or near-contemporaries. Through her exceptional piety and learning, Rābiʿah appears to have transgressed the usual social boundaries progressively erected for women, demonstrating through her life (even when viewed under the layers of legend) that a general respect for piety and learning, regardless of gender, remained a predictable constant of societies influenced by the Islamic Weltanschauung.

BIBLIOGRAPHY

ʿAṭṭār, Fāriḍ al-Dīn. *Muslim Saints and Mystics: Episodes from the Tadhkirat al-Auliya'* (Memorial of the saints). Translated by A. J. Arberry. Persian Heritage series. Boston: Routledge & Kegan Paul, 1979.

ʿAṭṭār, Fāriḍ al-Dīn. *Tadhkirat al-Awliya'* (Notes on the intimates of God). Edited by R. A. Nicholson. London: Luzc, 1905.

Makkī, Abū Ṭālib al-. *Qut al-qulub* (Nourishment of the hearts). Cairo: al-Maṭba'a al-miṣrîya, 1351[1932].

Smith, Margaret. *Rabiʿa the Mystic and Her Fellow-Saints in Islam*. Cambridge, U.K., and New York: Cambridge University Press, 1984. Originally published in 1928.

ASMA AFSARUDDIN

RADIYYA BINT ILTUTMISH. (d. 1240), sultan of Delhi (1236–1240). The eldest daughter of Sultan Shams al-Dīn Iltutmish by his chief wife, she was at one point groomed for the succession, according to the contemporary historian Jūzjānī, who quotes a remark by her father that none of his sons was worthy of the throne. This story was conceivably a later fabrication aimed at disparaging Iltutmish's dynasty, whose removal (1266) may already have been anticipated at the time Jūzjānī wrote (1260). Whatever the case, when Iltutmish died in 1236, he was instead succeeded by a son, Rukn al-Dīn Fīrūz Shāh. But Fīrūz Shāh's brief reign witnessed a number of revolts. The prominence of his mother, Shāh Terken, who had one of his half-brothers killed, was resented; and her attempt to arrest Radiyya provoked an uprising in the capital in the princess's favor, spearheaded by a significant element among her father's Turkish household slave (*ghulām, banda*) officers. Both the sultan and his mother were put to death, and Radiyya was enthroned in his place.

As a ruler, Radiyya displayed considerable energy and initiative, winning over or dispersing the other rebel amirs who had defied her brother. It soon became clear, however, that she had no intention of being a cipher. Jūzjānī tells us that she donned male attire and appeared in public mounted on an elephant. But her real offense was to reduce the power of the Turkish slave amirs who had enthroned her. When her deputy in command of the army (*nā'ib-i lashgar*), the Turk Qutlugh Khān, died in 1237, she replaced him, not with a Turk, but with an immigrant *malik* from Ghūr; she further aroused the Turks' resentment by promoting Jamāl al-Dīn Yāqūt, a slave officer of African (*Ḥabashī*) origin. In April 1240 she was lured out of Delhi on a campaign against the Turkish slave commander Altunapa, who had rebelled at Tabarhindh. On the march the Turks and their allies mutinied, put Yāqūt to death, and deposed Radiyya. She was incarcerated at Tabarhindh under Altunapa's supervision, and her brother Muʿizz al-Dīn Bahrām Shāh was proclaimed sultan, with Altunapa's confederate Aytegin as his viceroy (*nā'ib*). When Bahrām Shāh in turn grew restless, however, and had Aytegin murdered, Altunapa reacted by marrying Radiyya and making a bid to restore her as sultan. Defeated near Kaithal by Bahrām Shāh's forces, they were abandoned by their supporters and killed by local Hindus while in flight on 13 November 1240.

Radiyya's enthronement may possibly be connected with the fact that a number of her known *ghulām* supporters originated among the Central Asian (though in origin East Asian) people of the Qara-Khitan, over whom female sovereigns had ruled at times during the 12th century. Yet she also clearly enjoyed considerable popularity among the Muslim populace of the capital, and her memory seems to have been long revered; the Moroccan traveler Ibn Baṭṭūṭa, who visited the sultanate in the late 1330s, reports that her tomb near Delhi had become a focus of pilgrimage.

BIBLIOGRAPHY

Habibullah, A. B. M. "Sultānah Rāziah." *Indian Historical Quarterly* 16 (1940): 750–772.

Jackson, Peter. *The Delhi Sultanate: A Political and Military History*. Cambridge, U.K.: Cambridge University Press, 1999. See pp. 46–47, 66–67.

Jackson, Peter. "Sultān Radiyya bint Iltutmish." In *Women in the Medieval Islamic World: Power, Patronage, and Piety*, edited by Gavin R. G. Hambly, pp. 181–197. New York: St. Martin's Press, 1998.

PETER JACKSON

RAḤMĀN, ʿĀʾISHAH ʿABD AL-. ʿĀʾishah ʿAbd al-Raḥmān (1913–1998), was an Egyptian writer and professor of Arabic language and literature and Qurʾānic studies. Under the pseudonym Bint al-Shāṭiʾ, ʿAbd al-Raḥmān was the author of more than sixty books on Arabic literature, Qurʾānic interpretation, the lives of women of the early Muslim community (especially members of the Prophet's family), contemporary social issues, and fiction.

Raised in the Delta port city of Dumyat (Damietta), ʿAbd al-Raḥmān studied the Qurʾān and classical Arabic literature under the guidance of her father, an al-Azhar-educated teacher at a mosque-based religious institute. Although he educated her in the traditional style at home, mosque, and Qurʾānic school (*kuttāb*), he objected to her attendance at public schools. With the assistance of her mother and maternal great-grandfather, she managed to get a secular education despite her father's objections. ʿAbd al-Raḥmān began her literary career by writing poems and essays for a women's magazine called *Al-Nahḍah*, and became a literary critic for the semiofficial newspaper *Al-Ahrām* in 1936. That same year she entered the Faculty of Letters at Fuʾād I University (later Cairo University), assuming the pen name Bint al-Shāṭiʾ ("Daughter of the Shore") in order to conceal her identity from her father. Her first articles for *Al-Ahrām* focused on conditions in the Egyptian countryside, but she is best known for her later works on religious and literary topics. She received her doctorate in 1950 with a thesis on the poet Abū al-ʿAlāʾ al-Maʿarrī (d. 1058). In 1951, she became professor of Arabic language and literature at ʿAyn Shams University in Cairo. Throughout the 1960s she participated in international literary conferences, served on several government-sponsored committees on literature and education, and was a visiting professor at the Islamic University in Omdurman (Sudan), the University of Khartoum, and the University of Algiers. After retiring from her position at ʿAyn Shams University, she became professor of higher Qurʾānic studies at al-Qarawīyīn University in Fez, Morocco. Her regular articles for *Al-Ahrām*, her biographies of the women of the Prophet's household, and especially her exegesis of the Qurʾān brought her recognition and distinction in Egypt and throughout the Arab world.

ʿAbd al-Raḥmān's pursuit of public education offered her little challenge after her early education at the hands of her father, until she met Professor Amīn al-Khūlī when she was a student at Fuʿād I University. He introduced her to the literary analysis of the Qurʿān that later became her trademark. In her autobiography ʿAlā al-jisr (On the Bridge), she described her entire life as a path to this encounter with Amīn al-Khūlī, whom she married in 1945. Her work is seen as the best exemplification of his method, and she was much more prolific than her teacher, who died in 1966.

ʿAbd al-Raḥmān's two-volume Rhetorical Exegesis of the Noble Qurʿān makes a plea for removing the Qurʿān from the exclusive domain of traditional exegesis and placing it within literary studies. However, whereas some earlier exegetes allowed for a multiplicity of interpretations of any single Qurʿānic verse, seeing in this multiplicity a demonstration of the richness of the Qurʿān, ʿAbd al-Raḥmān argues that every word of the Qurʿān allows for only a single interpretation, which should be elicited from the context of the Qurʿān as a whole. She rejects extraneous sources, particularly information derived from the Bible or Jewish sources (Isrāʾīliyāt), the inclusion of which in traditional Qurʿānic exegesis she sees as part of a continuing Jewish conspiracy to subvert Islam and dominate the world. She also argues that no word is a true synonym for any other in the Qurʿān, so no word can replace another. Whereas some scholars believe certain phrases in the Qurʿān were inserted to provide the text with its characteristic rhythm and assonance, ʿAbd al-Raḥmān insists that every word of the Qurʿān is there solely for the meaning it gives.

ʿAbd al-Raḥmān was both deeply religious and very conservative, despite her active public life. On the subject of women's liberation, she affirmed the principle of male guardianship over women but firmly rejected male responsibility for the behavior of women. She insisted that a proper understanding of women's liberation does not abandon traditional Islamic values. She was consistently supported and honored by successive Egyptian regimes until her death in 1998.

Bibliography

Primary Sources

Al-Tafsīr al-bayānī lil-Qurʾān al-Karīm (The Rhetorical Exegesis of the Noble Qurʿān). 2 vols. Cairo, 1962–1969. Her most important work, reprinted in a number of editions.

Al-Sayyidah Zaynab, baṭalat Karbalāʾ (Sayyida Zaynab, Heroine of Karbalāʾ). Cairo, n.d. (1965?). Life of the granddaughter of the Prophet, who is credited with heroism at the battle of Karbala, in which her brother Husayn and other male relatives were killed.

ʿAlā al-jisr: Usṭūrat al-zamān (On the Bridge: A Legend of Time). Cairo, 1966. Autobiographical work that centers on the author's education, culminating in her encounter with Amīn al-Khūlī. Written in the year of his death, her entire life is seen as a path leading to this meeting, as a result of which she is "born again."

Al-Qurʾān wa-al-tafsīr al-ʿaṣrī (The Qurʿān and Modernist Exegesis). Cairo, 1970. Written against a book on "modernist" or "scientific" exegesis by the physician and television personality Muṣṭafā Maḥmūd.

Al-Isrāʾīlīyāt fī al-ghazw al-fikrī (The Israelite Tales in the Intellectual Conquest). Cairo, 1975.

Banāt al-nabī (Daughters of the Prophet). Cairo, 1963.

The Wives of Prophet Muhammad. Piscataway, N.J.: Gorgias Press, LLC, 2007.

Umm al-nabī (Mother of the Prophet). Cairo, n.d. (1961?).

Secondary Sources

Badran, Margot. *Feminists, Islam, and Nation: Gender and the Making of Modern Egypt*. Princeton, N.J.: Princeton University Press, 1995. Provides the broad Egyptian context for understanding Bint al-Shāṭiʾ's work and contributions.

Boullata, Issa J. "Modern Qurʿan Exegesis: A Study of Bint al-Shāṭiʾ's Method." *Muslim World* 64 (1974): 103–113. Positive evaluation of Bint al-Shāṭiʿ ontribution to Qurʿānic exegesis.

Hoffman-Ladd, Valerie J. "Polemics on the Modesty and Segregation of Women." *International Journal of*

Middle East Studies 19 (1987): 23–50. Analyzes Bint al-Shāṭi'’s stance on women's social roles.

Jansen, J. J. G. *The Interpretation of the Koran in Modern Egypt*. Leiden: E. J. Brill, 1974. Chapter 4, on "philological exegesis," deals primarily with Bint al-Shāṭi'’s exegesis, which he believes to be the best example of contemporary exegesis focusing on language analysis.

Kooij, C. "Bint al-Shāṭi': A Suitable Case for Biography?" In *The Challenge of the Middle East*, edited by Ibrahim A. A. El-Sheikh, et al., pp. 67–72. Amsterdam: Institute for Modern Near East Studies—University of Amsterdam, 1982. Critical description of Bint al-Shāṭi', which includes impressions gained from personal interviews with her, as well as interviews in Arabic literature. The author depicts her as both charming and domineering, and stresses Bint al-Shāṭi'’s self-centeredness, claiming that her autobiography, *'Alā al-jisr*, romanticizes and distorts reality.

Stowasser, Barbara Freyer. *Women in the Qur'an, Traditions, and Interpretation*. New York: Oxford University Press, 1994.

VALERIE J. HOFFMAN

RAHNAVARD, ZAHRA. (b. 1945)., Iranian artist and political activist. Zahra Rahnavard was born in the western Iranian city of Boroujerd. Raised in a religious Shī'ī family, she defines her life as a constant struggle between modern and traditional values. She received her undergraduate degree in sculpture from Tehran University and in 1995 earned her PhD in political science from Islamic Azad University.

According to Rahnavard, three women were influential in shaping her accomplishments in life: her "exceptional" grandmother who taught Persian and French literature; her poet mother; and her aunt who was well versed in the Qur'ān and Islamic tradition. She met Mir Hossein Mousavi at an exhibition of her work in 1969 and married him in September of that year. With Rahnavard an accomplished artist, several important exhibitions have showcased her artistic oeuvre over the years. One of her sculptures depicting motherly love, *Narcissus of Lovers*, has been on public display in the center of Mother Square in Tehran since 1994.

Rahnavard was a student and devotee of Ali Shari'ati, one of Iran's greatest intellectuals. Inspired by Shari'ati, she became actively involved in overthrowing the Pahlavi monarchy. After Shari'ati's arrest in 1976, she left for the United States, but returned to Iran shortly before the Iranian Revolution. Rahnavard and her husband became instrumental in developing many of the new Islamic Republic's political, cultural, and economic programs. According to Janet Afary (2001), Rahnavard's story is that of a generation of Islamist women who took official positions after the 1979 Islamic Revolution, only to become advocates of women's rights during the 1990s.

Rahnavard began her research on Qur'ānic topics in 1971. Her love of the Qur'ān led to more than forty years of research, earning her the nickname *Khadem-ol-Qur'ān* (the servant of the Qur'ān). Her numerous publications on art, literature, poetry, religion, and politics have been translated into Turkish, Arabic, Urdu, and English. Many of her writings center on issues that pertain to women's rights and status in Islam, including "The Rise of Muslim Woman" and "The Colonial Motives for the Unveiling of Women," both of which have circulated widely among educated youth in Iran.

Long active on the Iranian political scene, Rahnavard participated in the struggle to oust the Shah in the late 1970s. She became a senior advisor on cultural affairs to Iran's reformist president Mohammed Khatami during his second administration from 1997 to 2005. She was the first Iranian woman appointed as a chancellor of a university since the Iranian Revolution and headed Tehran's Al-Zahra University from 1998 to 2006. Rahnavard's outspoken criticism of President Mahmoud Ahmadinejad's policies resulted in her removal from the post at Al-Zahra. Even her impeccable revolutionary credentials did not withstand Ahmadinejad's reactionary pronouncement.

In 2009 Rahnavard was chosen as the third most influential global thinker by *Foreign Policy* magazine. She was an active participant in her husband Mir-Hossein Mousavi's 2009 presidential campaign. Under house arrest as of 2013, she is one of the leaders of Iran's opposition Green Movement. Throughout her life and in her work, Zahra Rahnavard has advocated for greater freedom and equality for women. She condemns the inequality of men and women in laws pertaining to divorce and citizenship. She has called for Iran to join the United Nations Convention on the Elimination of All Forms of Discrimination Against Women (CEDAW), stating publicly that equality of the sexes is a goal for which she would be willing to sacrifice her life.

BIBLIOGRAPHY

Afary, Janet. "Portraits of Two Islamist Women: Escape from Freedom or from Tradition?" *Middle East Critique* 10, no. 19 (2001): 47–77.

Cole, Juan Ricardo, and Nikki R. Keddie. *Shi'ism and Social Protest*. New Haven, Conn.: Yale University Press, 1986.

"Interview with Zahra Rahnavard, the Director of the Council." *Zan-i Rouz* 1221 (Tir 3, 1368) (24 June 1989): 8–9.

Ebadi, Shirin. "Zahra Rahnavard." *Time International (Atlantic Edition)* 175n no. 18 (2010).

Rahnavard, Z. (1990). *The Message of Hijab*. London: Al-Hoda Publishers.

Rahnavard, Z. *Toloueh Zaneh Mosalman*. Tehran: Mahboubeh publication, 1979. Analysis of the evolution of Muslim women.

Rahnavard, Zahrā. *Zindagīnāmah Va Khadamāt-I ʿilmī Va Farhangī-I Duktur Zahrā Rahnavard*. Tihrān: Anjuman-i Āṣār va Mafākhir-i Farhangī, 2004. Biography, and Academic Contributions of Zahra Rahnavard.

SAMANEH OLADI GHADIKOLAEI

RAMADAN, TARIQ.

RAMADAN, TARIQ. (b. 1962) is a Swiss theologian and academic who advocates a reinterpretation of Islamic texts. Tariq Said Ramadan calls on believers to establish a new Islam by engaging local Western societies. His emphasis on religion as an antidote to contemporary secular life in the West, along with his unabashed defense of certain controversial issues, drew the ire of American officials, who barred him from teaching in the United States in 2004. Four years later, *Foreign Policy* placed him eighth on a list of the world's top 100 contemporary intellectuals.

Ramadan was born in Geneva, Switzerland, on August 26, 1962, to Saʿīd Ramaḍān, a member of the Muslim Brotherhood who was expelled from Egypt by Gamal Abdel Nasser, and Wafa Al-Bana, the eldest daughter of Ḥasan al-Bannā His maternal grandfather founded the Brotherhood in 1928 and was assassinated in Cairo on February 12, 1949 Ramadan is married to a French convert to Islam. They have four children. His brother Hani is the Imam of the Geneva Mosque.

Tariq studied philosophy, literature, and social sciences at the University of Geneva and earned a master's degree in French literature and a doctorate in Arabic and Islamic studies at Al-Azhar University in Egypt, although his dissertation was on Nietzsche ("Nietzsche as a Historian of Philosophy"). He held two lectureships in religion and philosophy at the University of Fribourg and the Collège de Saussure, both in Switzerland. In October 2005 he accepted a visiting fellowship at St. Antony's College at the University of Oxford in Britain, and since 2005 has been a senior research fellow at the Lokahi Foundation. While in Britain, he was invited by the Tony Blair government to join a task force examining the role of Muslims in European societies. This work was a follow-up to his Mouvement des Musulmans Suisses, which engaged in various interfaith seminars. Officials at the European Union sought his advice on religious issues and appointed him to a commission dealing with Islam and secularism.

In February 2004 Ramadan accepted a tenured position as the Luce Professor of Religion at the Joan B. Kroc Institute for International Peace Studies at the University of Notre Dame in South Bend, Indiana. Before his scheduled arrival, the United States Department of State revoked his visa in late July 2004, citing the "ideological exclusion provision" of the Patriot Act as its grounds. The department later argued that Ramadan had provided support to a terrorist organization. Between December 1998 and July 2002, Ramadan had given donations totaling $940 to two Palestinian charity organizations designated as terrorist fund-raising groups for their alleged links to Ḥamās. On July 17, 2009, a federal appeals court reversed the government's decision, and on January 20, 2010, after more than five years of waiting, Secretary of State Hillary Clinton lifted the ban that prohibited Ramadan from entering the United States. On April 8, 2010, Ramadan spoke as part of a panel discussion at the Great Hall of Cooper Union in New York City, his first public appearance in the United States after the ban was lifted.

Ramadan believes in a reinterpretation of the Qur'ān to understand Islamic philosophy better. He emphasizes the difference between religion and culture, which he believes are too often confused. Most important, he rejects the separation of people into *dār al-islām* and *dār al-harb* (the Islamic and non-Islamic realms), because, he asserts, these classifications are suspect according to scripture. Instead, he proposes that Western Muslims live in *dār al-shahādah* (the realm of witness), where they can practice fundamental principles of faith and take responsibility for themselves and their actions.

In his 2009 book on the Prophet, which was intended as a rereading of his life stressing both spiritual and contemporary-daily-life lessons that can be drawn from Muḥammad's life as an exemplary paradigm, Ramadan argued that the Prophet treated women as women, not just as mothers, sisters, or daughters. According to this reading, women must be treated as equals to men before God and given the same universal rights and responsibilities in society, even when local norms and traditions restrict freedoms. Ramadan posited that the Prophet respected women, and while wearing the veil (*niqāb*) was recommended for the women in his immediate family, he did not impose such a rule on everyone throughout the ages. On the contrary, Ramadan affirms that according to several ḥadīths, Muḥammad set an example on dealing with women, including welcoming them in the mosque to pray and practice their religion. Muḥammad believed that women could and ought to study scripture to become better Muslims and stood by ʿĀʾishah bint Abū Bakr, his beloved spouse, who was also a scholar, when controversies arose within the ultraconservative Quraysh tribe. In one of the more colorful testimonies that Ramadan frequently quotes, when the Prophet welcomed his daughters Zaynab, Ruqayyah, Umm Kulthūm, and Fātimah Zahrāʾ, he invariably stood up, kissed them in front of people, and spoke with them at length. This was, Ramadan posits, a solid illustration of the respect that Muḥammad accorded to women in general and his daughters in particular, hoping that Arabian tribal values dismissive of women would change. Ramadan believes that the Prophet wanted Muslim women to be involved at all levels of life—social, political, and scholarly—even if this interpretation is not universally shared. Critics of Ramadan's writings pointed to various inconsistencies regarding physical violence against women, sexuality, contraception, and abortion, all of which he addressed in frank ways, but which were all reinterpreted through the Prophet's prism for tolerance and respect. Ramadan comprehensively rejects violence against women and believes that women can be good believers if they follow scripture and the Prophet's ḥadīths.

Because Ramadan has spoken on controversial subjects, including critical evaluations of Israeli treatment of Palestinians, and has opposed the U.S. military campaign in Iraq, many of his more conciliatory views were overlooked. For example, Ramadan condemned suicide bombings and violence as a tactic and declared that terrorism was never justifiable. He cautioned Muslims not to overreact to Pope Benedict's controversial September 12, 2006, speech on Islam at the University of Regensburg in Germany, when the Catholic Pontiff quoted the obscure Byzantine emperor Manuel II Paleologus, who infamously claimed, "Show me just what Muhammad brought that was new and there you will find things only evil and inhuman, such as his command to spread by the sword the faith he preached." While the Pope intended to discuss the relationship between faith and reason, his comments were deemed offensive. Ramadan urged caution, though critics frequently charged him with saying different things to different audiences. Many suspect that he speaks to radical Islamists or young Muslims in one way and to Western media or academics in another. Such criticisms notwithstanding and regardless of how convoluted some of his presentations may appear to outsiders, there is consistency in Ramadan's discourse—much like that of Ḥasan al-Bannā in Egypt. Since 2005 Ramadan has taught theology at the University of Oxford and simultaneously held a guest professorship for identity and citizenship at Erasmus University in Rotterdam. In August 2009 the City of Rotterdam and Erasmus University dismissed him from his positions as "integration adviser" and professor, declaring that his involvement with the Iranian television program *Islam and Life* was "irreconcilable" with his duties in Rotterdam. Ramadan described this move as Islamophobic and politically charged. In September 2009 Ramadan was appointed to the newly created Chair in Contemporary Islamic Studies at Oxford University, named after the ruler of Qatar, His Highness Shaykh Hamad bin Khalifah Al Thani.

BIBLIOGRAPHY

Landau, Paul. *Le sabre et le coran: Tariq Ramadan et les Frères Musulmans à la conquête de l'Europe.* Monaco: Rocher, 2005. Argues that Ramadan relies on the "word" to conquer Europe.

Ramadan, Tariq. *Faut-il faire taire Tariq Ramadan?* Paris: Archipel, 2005. A highly readable conversation with Ramadan on controversial subjects.

Ramadan, Tariq. *In the Footsteps of the Prophet: Lessons from the Life of Muhammad.* New York: Oxford University Press, 2009.

Ramadan, Tariq. *Islam, the West, and the Challenge of Modernity.* London: Islamic Foundation, 2009.

Ramadan, Tariq. *The Quest for Meaning: Developing a Philosophy of Pluralism.* London: Penguin Global, 2010.

Ramadan, Tariq. *Radical Reform: Islamic Ethics and Liberation.* New York: Oxford University Press, 2008.

Ramadan, Tariq. *Western Muslims and the Future of Islam.* New York: Oxford University Press, 2005.

Ramadan, Tariq. *What I Believe.* New York: Oxford University Press, 2009.

JOSEPH A. KÉCHICHIAN

RAPE AS WAR TOOL. Rape is frequently used as a weapon in times of social as well as armed conflict, such as war, in order to humiliate opponents and break their morale. In Arab societies, the codes of honor—related to virginity and to crimes meant to, symbolically, douse the family's or tribe's honor or pride in blood—are connected to rape, which is associated with death. Men prove their masculinity through sexual acts of violence against women of other clans, symbolically inflicting death through the "death" of the clan's honor, as embodied in its women, thereby reinforcing the system of the clan by making women vulnerable and in need of men's protection, as well as limiting women to the role of symbolizing the group's honor. Rapes can end in death or suicide, as only death can recover the clan's or tribe' s honor.

The sexual act itself, in many men's imagination and practice, can be associated with rape; it is an aspect of the system of power through which they prove their masculinity and domination. Metaphorically, and from an anthropological approach, the city is often conceived as a woman to be raped, because she is like a prostitute who incarnates all the decadent moral values of industrial and modern life. But rape is not enough: it has to reach its limits via total destruction. The devastation has to spread to other cities/women in the world, leading to annihilation and oblivion. Rape/destruction can be considered as a form of masculine cruelty, sadism, and violence that surfaces in times of disorder. Rape can also be used metaphorically to convey the suppression or defeat of one ethnic or national group by another; the victors "rape" the male victims, who are utterly frustrated and depressed because they are rendered powerless.

Rites surrounding virginity, purity, and chastity, and the notion of women as the exclusive property of men, lead to violence and crimes and are at the foundation of a society built on divisions and exclusion. In such a system, women are dominated, taken for granted, raped, led to suicide, or killed by men who are themselves manipulated by political power. Ancient traditions that adopted such perspectives continually resurface in culture, even when rooted in contradicting origins, ranging from paganism to pre-Islamic religious traditions. It is a vicious cycle of power struggles in which women are the ultimate victims. Sexual relations conceived in a system of power struggles and a structure of submission/domination result in the abuse of women, from denying their rights to raping their bodies. Rape is also associated with the trauma of unwanted pregnancies and abortions.

Rape during wartime is often a way for men to prove their masculinity through control and domination, not only of seized land, but also of fertile women who have an analogical relation to the earth. Many cases have been reported of rape in Iraq during the American invasion, causing shock in the U.S., and necessitating investigation and legal punishment of some soldiers. Hence, the phenomenon be documented in societies in many Muslim countries, as well as in the contemporary Western context and imagination. Spreading fear is one of the primary targets of the use of rape as a war tool, leaving scars not only on bodies but also on the collective memory of groups and nations.

Only different visions, new actions, and altered relationships based on trust, recognition, and acceptance of the other can help heal the wounds of rape and war. Many women's organizations have addressed this issue of rape in war and how to support women who have had to face such violence in their lives. They try to help women find a meaningful place for themselves in society after suffering such terrible trauma.

BIBLIOGRAPHY

Connell, Bob. "Masculinity, Violence and War." In *War/Masculinity*, edited by Paul Patton and Ross Poole. Sydney, Australia: Intervention, 1985.

cooke, miriam. *War's Other Voices: Women Writers on the Lebanese Civil War*. New York: Cambridge University Press, 1988.

Corm, Georges. *Géopolitique du conflit libanais: Étude historique et sociologique*. Paris: La Découverte, 1986.

Crittenden, Amy. "Nations Are Like Children," *The Nation*, February 4, 1991.

Enloe, Cynthia E. *Does Khaki Become You?: The Militarisation of Women's Lives*. London: Pluto Press, 1983.

Farrar, Adam. "War, Machining Male Desire." In *War/Masculinity*, edited by Paul Patton and Ross Poole. Sydney, Australia: Intervention, 1985.

Lapierre, Dominique. "Femmes: Une oppression millénaire." *Alternatives non-violentes: Femmes et violences 40* (Spring 1981): 12–26.

Makarem, May. "Avec la non-violence Laure Moghaïzel, l' autre visage du Liban," *L' Orient-Le Jour* (Beirut), March 16, 1988.

Reardon, Betty. *Sexism and the War System*. New York: Teachers College Press, 1985.

Wafa, Stephan. "Women and War in Lebanon." *Al-Raïda* 30 (1984).

Evelyne Accad

Rasul-Bernardo, Amina.

(b. 1954), Filipino educator, women's rights and peace activist, and journalist.

Born on 5 April 1954 in Jolo, Sulu, the Philippines, Amina Tillah Rasul-Bernardo is the daughter of Abraham Rasul and his wife Santanina Tillah. Her father served as a judge and was then appointed Ambassador to Saudi Arabia. Her mother was the first Filipina Muslim senator in the Philippines, serving from 1987 until 1995. The family also descended from the hereditary chief ministers of the Sultanate of Sulu.

Rasul-Bernardo was educated at Notre Dame High School in Jolo, Sulu, and then earned a BA in Economics from the University of the Philippines. She earned a master's degree in Public Administration from the Harvard Kennedy School of Government and an MBA from the Asian Institute of Management at Makati City, Philippines. She is married to Ramon Bernardo, a former Under-Secretary of Finance in the Philippines.

Rasul-Bernardo initially became known for her expertise in business and finance. She has served as director of the Philippine National Oil Corporation and the Development Bank of the Philippines, and she was the founding director of the Local Government Guarantee Corporation. As a recognized expert on the Muslim insurgency on Mindanao Island, she has worked on practical initiatives aimed at community reconciliation, including literacy and poverty alleviation in this area. She has also worked extensively with youth as a presidential advisor on youth affairs and chairman and CEO of the National Youth Commission from 1994 to 1998. She has also written a manual on Islamic peace education.

Rasul became an environmentalist, being a founder of the Bantay Dagat ("Sea Patrol" or "Watch the Seas") Movement, which has been involved in protecting the seas and the management of coastal resources, particularly by working to prevent illegal fishing techniques and overfishing, to reduce pollution, and to preserve coral reefs and mangrove swamps. She has held a variety of academic appointments, such as with the U.S. Institute of Peace, the Asian Institute of Management Policy Center, and the National Defense College of the Philippines.

Rasul-Bernardo has also served as the director of the Philippine Council on Islam and Democracy and director of the Board of Trustees for Promotion for Peace and Prosperity in the Philippines. She is a founding member of Women in International Security–Philippines and Muslim Women Peace Advocates–Sulu. In 2007, she received the Muslim Democrat of the Year Award from the Center for the Study of Islam and Democracy in Washington, D.C.

Bibliography

Angeles, Vivienne S. M. "Philippine Muslim Women: Tradition and Change." In *Islam, Gender, and Social Change*, edited by Yvonne Yazbeck Haddad and John L. Esposito, pp. 209–234. Oxford: Oxford University Press, 1988.

Rabasa, Ángel. *Building Moderate Muslim Networks*. Santa Monica, Calif.: Rand Corporation, 2007.

Rasul, Amina. *The Road to Peace and Reconciliation: Muslim Perspectives on the Mindanao Conflict.* Makati City, Philippines: Asian Institute of Management, 2003.

JUSTIN J. CORFIELD *and* NATANA J. DELONG-BAS

RASŪLID DYNASTY. The Sunnī Rasūlid dynasty (1229–1454 CE) is considered to mark the zenith of Islamic civilization in medieval Yemen. In its heyday, the Rasūlid Empire stretched across the coastal plain of the Red Sea (Tihama) and included the southern highlands of Yemen, up to the city of Sanaa in the north.

The dynasty's founder, Nūr al-Dīn ʿUmar bin ʿAlī (r. 1229–1250 CE), was a trusted fief-holder under the Ayyūbids when they ruled Yemen. Nūr al-Dīn demonstrated outward allegiance to the Ayyūbid sultans until 1235, when the ʿAbbāsid caliph al-Mustanṣir officially authorized him as ruler, marking the beginning of an independent Rasūlid state.

Rasūlid women played an integral part in politics throughout the two centuries of Rasūlid rule. The example of al-Dar al-Shamsi, the daughter of al-Manṣūr ʿUmar, the first Rasūlid sultan, illustrates the extent of women's involvement in politics during the Rasūlid era. Al-Dar al-Shamsi's political acumen was so well respected that she was called Bilqis al-Sughra (the younger Queen of Sheba). When her father died, a fight over succession erupted as her brother al-Muẓaffar Yusuf's right to the throne was challenged by his half-brother, al-Mufaḍḍal Quṭb al-Dīn, and his cousin, Fakhr al-Dīn Abū Bakr ibn Hasan. Her brother's rivals attacked the city of Zabīd while al-Dar al-Shamsi was there. With the help of Taj al-Dīn Badr, she barricaded the city, bribed many possible supporters of her brother's rivals, and kept the rival factions at bay. Her political clout and intelligence ensured her brother's political success in the region.

Al-Muẓaffar Yusuf reigned for forty-five years, dexterously ruling over his territories from the capital of Taʾizz. *Madrasahs* and mosques proliferated during this period and peace and stability were the norm. Many of these religious institutions were patronized by Rasūlid women. The trading port of Aden was incredibly active during this time. Commerce and trade thrived and a wide variety of goods made their way across East Africa, Egypt, the Mediterranean, India, and as far east as China. Historians have postulated that Rasūlid women with political connections engaged in trading during this era.

Al-Muẓaffar died in 1295 CE and was succeeded by his son al-Ashraf ʿUmar. Al-Dar al-Shamsi continued to be politically active during the reign of her nephew al-Ashraf ʿUmar. Even after her death, she had an impact on Rasūlid politics. Al-Dar al-Shamsi bequeathed her property to her nephew al-Muʾayyad Dawud. The value of this property, though unknown, is thought to have been so substantial that it led the sultan al-Ashraf ʿUmar to fear that his sibling, al-Muʾayyad Dawud, would use his inheritance to fund a rebellion against him. A long line of his descendants followed the reign of al-Ashraf ʿUmar, many of whom were skilled rulers, although none surpassed Al-Muẓaffar in his competency. Over the decades, the Rasūlid dynasty suffered from the transgressions of rebellious tribes and slave revolts as well as the near-constant scuffle over Sanaa with the Zaydī imams. After the death of ʿAmal al-Dīn al-Shaʿbi in 1283 CE, contentions over Sanaa exacerbated and the Zaydīs all but won the city.

During these decades, Rasūlid women continued to remain politically active and important. Rasūlid rulers correctly identified that alliances with Rasūlid women were often vital to ensuring political stability and to safeguarding male rulers. Marriage alliances were especially important in consolidating power and in preventing dangerous rifts that often plagued the reign of Rasūlid sultans. In addition to coveting the widows of previous rulers and daughters of political elites, Rasūlid sultans were also eager to marry daughters of prominent Ṣūfī *shaykh*s and other religious elites. A good example of this is the life of Jihat Ṣalāḥ (d. 1364), the daughter of Shaykh Ismāʿīl ibn ʿAbd Allāh al-Halabi. The life history of Jihat Ṣalāḥ also illustrates the political influence that elite Rasūlid women wielded in their own right. Jihat Ṣalāḥ was the wife of Sultan al-Muʾayyad Dawud and mother to the sultan al-Mujāhid ʿAlī (r. 1322–1363 CE). Her political skill was vital to the preservation of the men in her life. In 1323, when a serious revolt attempted to topple her son, she rescued him from prison. Two decades later, in 1353, her son was captured by the Mamlūks and imprisoned in Cairo. As this series of events unfolded, Jihat Ṣalāḥ immediately returned to Yemen and acted as her son's regent. She also secured her son's release by pressuring Indian merchants in Aden to lend her 400,000 dinars for al-Mujāhid's ransom. Rasūlid women of this era also played a critical role in bringing together different factions to support the heir to the throne. For example, upon the death of Sultan al-Afdal ʿAbbās in 1376, his wife Jihat Tayy immediately summoned state officials, tribal chiefs, and army generals to pledge allegiance to her son al-Ashraf Ismāʿīl.

While alliances with elite Rasūlid women and female participation in politics continued to be important and often led to political stability, the Rasūlid dynasty was plagued by a host of problems that eventually led to its demise. A quick succession of sultans followed al-Nāṣir Aḥmad (r. 1400–1424), none of whom managed to hold the dynasty together. Slave revolts increased and there was an outbreak of plague in the land. Constant fighting occurred among the Rasūlid *amīrs*. In 1454 CE the Rasūlid dynasty came to its official end as Aden fell to the Ṭāhirids and Rasūlid control over Tihama and southern Yemen was also lost.

At the height of the Rasūlid Empire, many religious institutions were built by Rasūlid elites, both men and women. Although few records exist detailing the estates of Rasūlid women, judging from the religious monuments that they financed, it would be safe to say that they had considerable finances at their disposal. Historians have identified forty-two religious monuments patronized by nineteen Rasūlid women, including *madrasahs*, mosques, public fountains, and a *khānqāh*. These monuments were located in the Zabīd region, Taʾizz, Jiblah, and the surrounding areas. Most of these monuments were named after their female patrons, while some were intentionally commissioned by these women in the name of a family member. Most of these monuments have not survived over the centuries. In Zabīd, only two monuments that had female patrons have survived: the *madrasah* al-Fatiniyah, commissioned by Jihat Fatin (d. 1366/1367) and the *madrasah* al-Farhaniyah built by Jihat Farhan (d. 1432/1433).

Like Rasūlid sultans, elite Rasūlid women were politically powerful, financially independent, and economically active. The political, financial, and artistic achievements of the Rasūlid dynasty would have been significantly fewer without the active participation of Rasūlid women in all these realms.

BIBLIOGRAPHY

Khazraji, ʿAli ibn al-Hasan al-. *The Pearl-Strings: A History of the Rasulid Dynasty of Yemen by ʿAli Ibn al-Hasan*. Translated by James W. Redhouse. Leiden. Netherlands: E. J. Brill. See especially pp. 1906–1918.

Sadek, Noha. "In the Queen of Sheba's Footsteps: Women Patrons in Rasulid Yemen." *Asian Art* 6, no. 2 (1993): 14–27.

Sadek, Noha. "Patronage and Architecture in Rasulid Yemen, 626–858 A.H./1229–1454 A.D." PhD diss., University of Toronto, Toronto, 1990.

Sadek, Noha. "Rasulid Women: Power and Patronage." *Proceedings of the Twenty-Second Seminar for Arabian Studies* 19 (1989): 121–136.

Shamrookh, Nayef Abdullah. "The Commerce and Trade of the Rasulids in the Yemen, 630–858/1231–1454." PhD diss., University of Manchester, Manchester, U.K., 1996.

Smith, G. Rex, ed. *The Ayyubids and Early Rasulids in the Yemen, 567–694, 1173–1295*. London: Luzac for the Trustees of the E. J. W. Gibb Memorial, 1978.

MASHAL SAIF

RAWẒAH KHVĀNĪ. One of the foremost characteristics of Shīʿī Muslims is the veneration they express for the family of the Prophet and his martyred grandson, Imam Ḥusayn. These expressions take various forms, the most common of which are public mourning ceremonies such as the *rawẓah khvānī* (narrative accounts of the martyrdom of Imam Ḥusayn), *taʿzīyah* (passion plays), and *dastah* (processions). The *rawẓah khvānī* is the remembrance, through recitations and chanting, of the suffering and death of Imam Ḥusayn and other Shīʿī martyrs at the battle of Karbala on the tenth of Muḥarram (ʿĀshūrāʾ) in 680 CE, while fighting against the forces of Yazīd, whom the Shīʿī consider an illegitimate, oppressive usurper of the caliphate.

Origin and Definition of the *Rawẓah Khvānī*. These recitations are performed at various types of religious gatherings held weekly throughout the year, especially on the anniversaries of the death dates of the Imams and other saintly figures such as Fāṭimah, the daughter of the Prophet and wife of ʿAlī, the first Imam. The rituals of lamentation reach their pinnacle of significance during the months of Muḥarram and Ṣafar when gatherings are held in mosques, *ḥusaynīyahs*, *zaynabīyahs*, in the courtyards of the bazaar, and in private homes to express grief over a death seen not only as a tragic event in itself but as an act of self-sacrifice on behalf of justice and truth.

The name *rawẓah khvānī* is derived from the title of the book *Rawḍāt al-shuhadāʾ* (Garden of Martyrs), the most comprehensive Shīʿī martyrology of its time (1502 CE), although its author, Ḥusayn Vāʿiẓ Kāshifī, was a Sunnī Muslim. This work and similar later books, such as Jawharī's *Ṭūfān al-bukā* (Tempest of Tears) or the *Asrār al-shahādāh* (Mysteries of Martyrdom) by Ṭabāṭabāʾī are part of a literary genre known as *maqtal*, a development of a broader genre of poetic eulogies (*manāqib*) and elegies (*marāthī*). These and still more recent works form the basis of the material used by the reciters (*rawẓah khvān*) in preparing their narrations.

The *rawẓah*, as it is popularly known in Iran, varies in length from about two hours to sessions lasting through the night. The usual format begins with the reading of verses of the Qurʾān followed by a sermon given by a preacher (*vāeʿiz*) who offers comments and advice on moral, religious, and social issues and/or the recitation of religious poetry by a panegyrist (*maddāḥ*) who eulogizes the family of the Prophet and the Imams. The eulogy leads into the *rawẓah khvānī* proper, at the conclusion of which is the chanting of dirges (*nawḥah*). Narrators are paid for their services and informally ranked on the basis of their rhetorical skills and the degree to which they can evoke intense emotional responses from their audiences. The *rawẓah khvān* achieves this by recounting explicit details of the agony and torment suffered by Imam Ḥusayn and his followers, all the while emphasizing their human compassion, kindness, and love for their families. This elicits profuse weeping, cries of lamentation, and commonly ecstatically induced rhythmic chest beating.

Many of the *rawẓah* are sponsored as expressions of thankfulness to God for the fulfillment of a vow and to ensure further blessings, as sponsoring or participating in such an event accrues religious merit (*savāb*). Weeping for Imam Ḥusayn, in particular, is believed to ensure his intercession on the Day of Judgment. Tears shed for the Imam are also believed to have curative powers and some individuals collect tears in small bottles that are used to cure various afflictions, a practice criticized by many as one of the traditional folk beliefs that needs to be reformed.

Women also sponsor and participate in gatherings where a *rawẓah* is performed, often by a professional woman narrator. These gatherings, although organized ostensibly for religious purposes, are also important occasions that allow women to get together outside their homes and socialize with others. There is an element of entertainment (*tafrīḥ*), social status, and community support in these rituals (for men as well as for women). The most popular such occasion for women is known as a *sufrah* (a ritual votive meal held to express gratitude for the fulfillment of a vow), especially that dedicated to ʿAbbās (also known by his epithet Abū al-Fazl), who was also martyred at Karbala. The *rawẓah* associated with this event focuses in detail on ʿAbbās's sufferings on the battlefield; participants weep and strike their chests or thighs in sympathy with his tribulations. In return for their empathic compassion, it is believed that ʿAbbās will act as an intercessor and mediator in the granting of wishes or responses to prayers.

Rawẓah Khvānī and Social Change. With greater literacy and religious understanding many of the practices and ideas associated with the *rawẓah* are being reevaluated by the lay public and pious Shīʿīs, who criticize them as un-Islamic and "ignorant" customs that are religious anachronisms incompatible with a modern nation-state. Such attitudes are also an aspect of a reformist Islam that seeks to purify the faith of folk beliefs and practices. Many such criticisms are directed at the reciters themselves who, generally, are poorly educated and limited in their formal knowledge of Islam and often have rather "mythical" understandings of the events at Karbala. Younger, pious Muslims tend to avoid "traditional" *rawẓah khvānī* with its emphasis on intense emotional outbursts and chest-beating rituals and seek those gatherings with a greater stress on the sermon and its meaning, where lessons can be learned in a less emotional setting.

All rituals, however, are polysemic and have many broader social, economic, or political implications. Despite criticism of such practices by the majority of the *ʿulamāʿ*, the *rawẓah* has served them well over the centuries with its ability to evoke and maintain intense emotional passions often used to arouse mass opposition to tyrannical governments, repression, and injustice. Abū Muslim, who led the movement to overthrow the Umayyad dynasty in the eighth century CE, encouraged his followers by recounting the injustices suffered by Ḥusayn and the family of the Prophet. In the period preceding the Iranian Revolution of 1979, religious gatherings (*hayʿat-i maẕhabī* for men; *jaleseh* for women) were organized daily within the quarters of the city by neighborhood groups and associations or by the guilds within the bazaar. Although they were intended to fulfill various religious goals, they almost always ended in a *rawẓah khvānī*, the not-so-latent message of which was opposition to the government. Ḥusayn's sister Zaynab, who was taken to Damascus after the battle of Karbala in chains as a prisoner along with other surviving members of Ḥusayn's group, became an important role model of one who speaks up against tyranny, injustice, and oppression. In fact, the ubiquity of *rawẓah khvānī* gatherings and their symbolic focus on the defiant roles of Ḥusayn and Zaynab was instrumental in arousing the populace against the shah, and ultimately leading to his downfall and the establishment of the Islamic Republic of Iran.

The message of the Islamic Revolution in Iran resonated throughout the world and more specifically in Lebanon, where several Israeli invasions have left hundreds of thousands of people homeless and poor. One consequence of this was the rise of the Shīʿī Ḥizbullāh political party, whose militant resistance movement fought to oust the Israeli occupiers while the party offered social assistance to those in need. Many fighters died in these encounters and they were seen as martyrs. Among the Lebanese Shīʿī it is considered an honor to be the mother, wife, or sister of a martyr, emulating the sacrifices of the women of the *ahl al-bayt*. Women use the role model of Zaynab in particular as an outspoken, strong, and compassionate activist to push the boundaries of what is acceptable and expected for pious Lebanese Shīʿī women. They play an increasingly active role by engaging in public community service activities (see Deeb for an extensive discussion of these ideas).

The *rawẓah* is thus a vitally important religious ritual embodying the very ethos of Shiism with its focus on tragedy, oppression, suffering, intercession, and final redemption—themes that also lend themselves to multiple meanings. But as the Lebanese and Iranian examples show, there is less emphasis on passive mourning and victimization in women's ritual gatherings in particular and a move toward a more active engagement to bring about social, political, and religious change. Shīʿī women are pushing against the social and cultural boundaries of society by adopting traditional imagery and using it to their religious and social advantage.

Comparable gatherings of lamentation and activist reformulations are found in most Shīʿī communities throughout the Muslim world. They have different names and differing sociopolitical functions depending on the local language and context. In Lebanon, for example, the word *majālis ʿāza* (mourning ceremonies) is used and *qāriʿ* (reciter) for the narrator of the Karbala drama. In Iraq, women's *rawẓah* assemblies are referred to as *qarāyā* or *dhikrā*; among the Shīʿīs of India, Pakistan, and the Indo-Muslim diaspora it is known as *majālis ʿāza* or simply *majlis*; *zākir* (male) and *zākirah* (female) are terms that refer to the reciters of the mourning rituals.

[*See also* Martyrdom.]

BIBLIOGRAPHY

Aghaie, Kamran Scot. *The Martyrs of Karbala: Shīʿī Symbols and Rituals in Modern Iran*. Austin: University of Texas Press, 2004.

Aghaie, Kamran Scot, ed. *The Women of Karbala: Ritual Performance and Symbolic Discourses in Modern Shīʿī Islam*. Austin: University of Texas Press, 2005.

Ayoub, Mahmoud M. *Redemptive Suffering in Islam: A Study of the Devotional Aspects of ʿĀshūrāʾ in Twelver Shiism*. The Hague: de Gruyter, 1978. Important study of the theological and folk beliefs associated with Imam Ḥusayn's martyrdom.

Chelkowski, Peter. "Popular Shīʿī Mourning Rituals." *Al-Serāt* 12, no. 1 (1986): 209–226. Excellent article by one of the leading authorities on popular Shīʿī ritual practices, especially the *taʿziyah*.

Deeb, Lara. *An Enchanted Modern: Gender and Public Piety in Shīʿī Lebanon*. Princeton, N.J. and Oxford: Princeton University Press, 2006. Perhaps the finest ethnographic study of a Shīʿī community in Lebanon, with a focus on public and private piety in the context of a changing society and its effect on women's lives.

Hegland, Mary Elaine. "Flagellation and Fundamentalism: (Trans)Forming Meaning, Identity, and Gender through Pakistani Women's Rituals of Mourning." *American Ethnologist* 25, no. 2 (1998): 240–266.

Hyder, Syed Akbar. *Reliving Karbala: Martyrdom in South Asian Memory*. Oxford: Oxford University Press, 2006.

Mahdjoub, Mohammad-Djaʿfar. "The Evolution of Popular Eulogy of the Imams among the Shia." In *Authority and Political Culture in Shiism*, edited by Said Amir Arjomand, pp. 54–79. Albany, N.Y.: State University of New York Press, 1988.

Thaiss, Gustav. "Religious Symbolism and Social Change: The Drama of Hussein." In *Scholars, Saints, and Sufis*, edited by Nikki R. Keddie, pp. 349–366.

Berkeley: University of California Press, 1972. Study of the organization of religious gatherings, especially those of the guilds, in modern Tehran, and their role in facilitating the Iranian Revolution of 1979.

Torab, Azam. *Performing Islam: Gender and Ritual in Iran*. Leiden, The Netherlands: E. J. Brill, 2007. A major anthropological study of Shīʿī ritual practices in Iran.

GUSTAV THAISS

REAL ESTATE. The advent of Islam in the seventh century granted women the indisputable right to inherit and own property. Scholarship on women's property rights in the Muslim world has focused predominantly on urban women, addressing access to property through dower, buying and selling, paid labor, inheritance, and *waqf*. Sharīʿah court records, particularly from the thirteenth century onward, provide insight into women's access to property, including transfer, management, and/or disposal. Women (whether Muslim, Christian, or Jewish) were actively engaged in buying and selling property, both commercial and residential. Owning property did not necessarily require significant financial resources as an individual could own a portion or share of a particular property. Historically, men in the Muslim world tended to diversify their investments, while women preferred investing their resources in real estate. This is probably due to the fact that women received a smaller portion of an inheritance than men, rendering their overall holdings more limited. Real estate ownership was most popular among middle-class women, while wealthy women also invested in various trade/commercial undertakings. Legal evidence indicates that women were adept at using the legal system to defend their property rights. Finally, depending on their social class and the nature of the property, women have used real estate to strengthen nonconjugal and/or conjugal ties.

Women and *Waqf*. Women's involvement in founding, managing, transmitting, and benefiting from *waqf* properties (religious endowments) is well documented in Ottoman history. Scholars have used court records to document women's property rights throughout the empire, particularly in and around urban centers such as Tripoli, Nablus, Bursa, Kayseri, Damascus, and Aleppo. Through the *waqf ahlī* (family endowment), a family could transfer an entire estate (rather than just the one-third maximum permitted for gifts under Islamic inheritance laws) and could designate any family member(s) or line of descent as the beneficiary(ies). The founder also had the right to designate whomever he or she wanted as the *waqf* manager. Thus, families bypassed the rigidities of Islamic law and afforded women access to various kinds of property. Women's access to *waqf* as beneficiaries, however, often depended on the importance accorded to the conjugal family unit in property transmission. Evidence largely indicates that women gained more access to family resources through *waqf* than they did through inheritance.

The most common forms of endowed real estate included urban real estate (houses, shops, warehouses) and land on the outskirts of towns and cities, including orchards, olive groves, vegetable gardens, and vineyards. The latter lands were considered *mulk* or private property (unlike arable lands, which were mostly state-owned) that could be sold, endowed, bought, or leased. Women mostly owned urban real estate or small lands around urban centers.

Although most arable lands in the Ottoman Empire belonged to the state and/or provincial notables (particularly after the eighteenth century), there are documented cases of women having property rights over arable lands. Women in Ottoman Bursa and Egypt had usufruct rights on arable lands and often treated them as their own, buying, selling, and mortgaging them.

Upper-class women also gained access to agricultural lands via *waqf* endowments, as beneficiaries, founders, or managers.

Real Estate and Familial Bonds. Property rights have had an impact on women's overall economic status and position within the family unit. Based on evidence from fifteenth-century Muslim Spain, Shatzmiller (2007) maintains that property rights for women helped mitigate the negative impact of patriarchal practices. Acquiring most of their property through inheritance, women (as wives, sisters, daughters, or mothers) played a key role in transmitting family property. Thus, family members consciously sought to protect women's inheritance rights in order to ensure economic stability. In fifteenth-century Granada, women's property was typically under the control of a guardian (*walī*, which could be a woman according to Maliki law, the dominant law school in Muslim Spain) for a prolonged period, that is, beyond majority or puberty. This often worked to the benefit of women because it allowed them time to mature as wives and economic players, while preventing husbands from taking advantage of women's property rights. Once a woman gained full control over her property, she gained significant economic bargaining power in her marriage, such as trading her property rights for her husband's renunciation of his right to divorce or engage in polygyny. In this context, it was in the husband's interest to cooperate/collaborate with his wife, even against other family members.

Through the modern period, women in the Muslim world have used or given up property to strengthen various social and familial relationships. Women in early-twentieth-century Jaffa and Haifa, for example, used *waqf*s to ensure that real estate remained in the hands of their children and/or natal extended families, thus strengthening non-conjugal family ties. These same women also used the courts to handle property transactions and disputes. Upper-class urban women in early-twentieth-century Jabal Nablus and the West Bank, on the other hand, often invested their dower in their husband's property or house (a trend also noticeable among rural women after the 1950s)—believing this would help secure their futures. This reflected their status as dependent, nonproductive individuals. While women's access to inheritance does vary based on urban versus rural backgrounds (with urban women enjoying more protection given the greater adherence to scriptural Islam in the cities and the nature of the property involved), claims to property are also shaped by other factors, including a woman's relationship to her non-conjugal kin and her marital status. Women in Jabal Nablus, for example, often left their inheritance shares to their brothers to strengthen their non-conjugal familial bonds and ensure that their brothers cared for them in the long term. Widows could bolster their social standing by giving up inheritance rights to their sons. Thus, the ways in which women have used real estate, rather than the ownership of real estate itself, provides more insight into gendered power relations; renouncing property ownership is not necessarily an indication of women's subordination.

In her study of modern Morocco, Vanessa Maher (1974) argues that access to real estate does not always translate into greater economic and/or social freedom for women. Comparing the status of townswomen and village women in the Middle Atlas, Maher asserts that, despite access to marketable capital, townswomen are less likely to seek divorce when facing marital pressures because marriage serves to build economic alliances. In such cases, the dower (which is treated by a woman's family as her inheritance) comes under the husband's management during marriage, although it remains for the woman upon divorce. Given their more secluded and subordinate status as wives, women are less likely to seek divorce. This secluded status also means that their family ties are weaker. Among townspeople, divorce could result in the disruption of the property-owning networks to which both husband and wife belong. Village women (*ksar*), on the other hand, tend to inherit landed property, which is rarely sold and ensures that a woman remains vested in her home community. These women usually maintain strong non-conjugal ties after they get married, thus weakening the position of the husband vis-à-vis his wife and ensuring that women are less dependent, particularly in the early years of marriage. For the *ksar*, therefore, divorce does not result in capital withdrawal for men or loss in social standing for women; many families welcome these women back home.

Assessment. Historical evidence indicates that women actively used Islamic courts to carry out various property transactions and protect their property rights. *Waqf* provided an important institution through which women gained access to and/or control over real estate. Although Islam supports women's property-owning rights (albeit unequal to those of men), not all women accumulated enough property to gain significant financial independence from their male kin. Furthermore, while access to property does not necessarily translate into power for all women, relinquishing property rights does not necessarily result in women's subjugation by their male kin either. Research indicates that women's access to real estate and their social and economic manipulation of property varied depending on several factors, including context (i.e., rural vs. urban), class background, marital status, and position within the conjugal and non-conjugal family units. Ultimately, real estate provided an important means through which women negotiated their status within the family unit and the broader community.

BIBLIOGRAPHY

Agmon, Iris. "Women, Class, and Gender: Muslim Jaffa and Haifa at the Turn of the 20th Century." *International Journal of Middle East Studies* 30, no. 4 (1998): 477–500. Illustrates how women used the courts to protect their property rights and how they endowed *waqf* properties to secure their children's futures or strengthen natal family ties.

Ahmed, Leila. *Women and Gender in Islam: Historical Roots of a Modern Debate*. New Haven, Conn., and London: Yale University Press, 1992. Provides a historical overview of women and gender in Islam, from the ancient world through the modern period.

Doumani, Beshara. "Endowing Family: Waqf, Property Devolution, and Gender in Greater Syria." *Comparative Studies in Society and History* 40, no. 1 (1988): 3–41. Using *waqf* endowments in the Islamic court records of nineteenth-century Tripoli and Nablus, Doumani explores how the transmission of property shaped family structures and the status of women, with the latter enjoying greater access to property when the conjugal family unit was given preference.

Fay, Mary Ann. "Women and Waqf: Toward a Reconsideration of Women's Place in the Mamluk Household." *International Journal of Middle East Studies* 29, no. 1 (1997): 33–51. Explores the economic power of the Mamlūk female elite as evidenced in their buying and selling of property, founding of *waqfs*, and/or administration of property. Women's property ownership contributed toward maintaining and reproducing the household.

Gerber, Haim. "Social and Economic Position of Women in an Ottoman City, Bursa, 1600–1700." *International Journal of Middle East Studies* 12 (1980): 231–44. Through the use of Islamic court records, the author addresses the overall economic role of women, with emphasis on how women inherited property, used the courts to handle various property disputes, and were involved in the buying, selling, and leasing of real estate.

Maher, Vanessa. "Divorce and Property in the Middle Atlas of Morocco." *Man*, n.s. 9, no. 1 (1974): 103–122. Examines the relationship between the type of property owned, women's social group status, and the frequency of divorce in modern-day Morocco.

Meriwether, Margaret L. "Woman and Waqf Revisited: The Case of Aleppo, 1770–1840." In *Women in the Ottoman Empire: Middle Eastern Women in the Early*

Modern Era, edited by Madeline C. Zilfi, pp. 128–52. Leiden, Netherlands: Brill, 1997. Provides evidence that women acted as founders, beneficiaries, and overseers of *waqf* properties, which allowed them greater access to family resources and a more pronounced public role. The Islamic courts often upheld women's right as beneficiaries and administrators.

Moors, Annelies. *Women, Property and Islam: Palestinian Experiences 1920–1990*. Cambridge, U.K.: Cambridge University Press, 1995. Provides an anthropological study of how the practice of property exchange or transfer as it affects women often diverges from Islamic law, with women's claims to property rights depending on their social status, class background, and how they gain access to property.

Shatzmiller, Maya. *Her Day in Court: Women's Property Rights in Fifteenth-Century Granada*. Cambridge, Mass. Islamic Legal Studies Program, Harvard Law School, 2007. Part 1 of the book deals most explicitly with the exchange, sale, and/or transfer of real estate to women and how such transactions impacted their status within the family unit.

Tucker, Judith. *Women in Nineteenth Century Egypt*. Cambridge, U.K.: Cambridge University Press, 1985. Chapter 1 provides insight into the peasant family's relationship to the land, particularly in the context of nineteenth-century transformations.

SABRINA JOSEPH

REFUGEES. Refugees are involuntary migrants who have fled their usual place of residence for fear of persecution, have crossed a border, and are no longer protected by their government. According to the 1951 Refugee Convention, a refugee under international law is someone who, "owing to a well-founded fear of being persecuted for reasons of race, religion, nationality, membership of a particular social group or political opinion, is outside the country of his nationality, and is unable to, or owing to such fear, is unwilling to avail himself of the protection of that country." The Convention does not specifically list gender or sex as grounds for persecution, which has led some human rights activists to raise concerns about the legal and social invisibility of gender-based violence in international refugee law, and about the inherent assumption that refugees and asylum seekers will be treated equally regardless of gender. However, others have argued that the Convention's five existing grounds are adequately broad, but that the interpretation of refugee law needs to be expanded to account for gender-specific forms of harm, gender-related persecution, and women's relationships with state institutions.

The United Nations High Commissioner for Refugees (UNCHR), created in 1951 to alleviate the crisis of uprooted people after World War II, estimates that in the first half of 2011 there were 10.5 million refugees who fell under its mandate worldwide, roughly half of whom were women. Furthermore, the number of internally displaced peoples (IDPs), forced migrants who have not crossed international borders, was approximately 27.5 million in 2011. In addition, the United Nations Relief and Works Agency for Palestine Refugees (UNRWA), established in 1949, assists an additional 5 million registered Palestinian refugees in the Middle East. A great number of refugees and other forced migrants originate from and are hosted by Muslim states; in fact, in 2011, at least half of individuals "of concern" to UNHCR lived in Muslim-majority countries.

Concepts of Migration and Asylum in Islam. Formal concepts of migration and asylum in Islam primarily draw from the migration of Muḥammad and his followers from Mecca to Medina (*al-hijrah*) in 622, which marks the beginning of the Islamic calendar, and from the Qurʾān and ḥadīth literature. Doctrines of *hijrah* (to migrate, to break ties with someone) in Islam also develop and expand *Jāhilīyah* notions of protection and hospitality, and Jewish and Christian concepts of sanctuary. Written after the *hijrah*, the Constitution of Medina secured the integration of Meccan refugees (*al-muhājirūn*) into the host community of Medina (called al-Anṣār, the helpers) by guaranteeing them rights agreed upon by both groups. The Constitution also provided a legal framework for protecting non-Muslims in Islamic states.

The Qur'ān contains multiple references to *hijrah* and elaborates on the duties of Muslims when it comes to seeking asylum from religious persecution and protecting refugees, even when the latter are not Muslims. Qur'ānic verse 9:6 states, "If any one of the idolaters should seek your protection [Prophet], grant it to him so that he may hear the word of God, then take him to a place safe for him, for they are people with no knowledge [of it]." As Muddathir ʿAbd al-Rahim (2008) notes, the term that indicates safe conduct in this passage, *ma'man*, is derived from *amān* (safety), which as an institution mandates that refugees, asylum seekers, and other travelers be respected and not forced to return to where they may be harmed. In modern refugee law, this concept of non-extradition is also a central tenet, and is referred to as *non-refoulement*. However, under *amān*, the ability to grant asylum was not restricted to state institutions.

In Qur'ānic verse 4:97, Muslims themselves, with the exception of women, children, and those too weak to travel, are exhorted to emigrate rather than live under oppression. Historically, the extent to which migration is a duty in Islam and the specific conditions of oppression that would require it have been disputed. As Khaled Abou El Fadl (1994) has explained, the obligation to emigrate has been an important matter of debate since the twelfth century, when large groups of Muslims came under non-Muslim powers at a magnitude not previously experienced in Islamic history. Some Ṣūfīs responded to this dilemma by reinterpreting the duty to undertake *hijrah* as a spiritual withdrawal from worldly tyranny and desires, rather than a literal one.

Refugees in Islamic History. In addition to the 622 *hijrah*, there have been other important mass migrations in the history of Islam. Between 613 and 615, a group of Muslims traveled to Abyssinia, seeking refuge from Meccan persecution. This journey was completed in two stages. Muslim women participated in both migrations to Abyssinia, as they would also in the *hijrah* to Medina.

Beginning in the eleventh century, Muslims from al-Andalus left the territories newly conquered by Christian armies, usually settling in the Kingdom of Granada. However, not long after Granada fell under Christian rule in 1492, Muslims were obligated to choose between conversion to Christianity or expulsion. Most chose conversion due to the difficulties and dangers of leaving the peninsula for safer grounds. Nevertheless, by 1614 all Moriscos (Muslims who had converted to Christianity) had been expelled. It is estimated that around 300,000 Moriscos were forced to leave Spain. Most of these refugees initially established themselves in North Africa, which also received a significant number of Jewish refugees from Spain. In fact, when Jews were expelled from Spain in 1492, most of them sought asylum throughout the Islamic world.

The weakening of the Ottoman Empire, which had traditionally offered asylum and support to large numbers of Muslim and Jewish refugees, also caused massive population shifts in southeastern Europe, North Africa, and Asia. This phenomenon intensified with the emergence of Russia as a major military power in the eighteenth century, and of nationalist movements within the empire itself. As the Ottoman Empire receded, Muslims living in the periphery were pushed toward the interior. Hundreds of thousands more became refugees during the Russian conquest of the Caucasus, and in the aftermath of the Crimean War (1853–1856), the Russo-Turkish War (1877–1878), and the Balkan Wars (1912–1913). In addition, Muslims who suddenly found

themselves as minorities in non-Muslim states were expelled or persuaded to leave.

European colonial expansion in the nineteenth century also drove many Muslims to leave their homelands as refugees. As national borders became fixed in the nineteenth and twentieth centuries, refugees fleeing conflict found asylum increasingly difficult to find, despite religious and ethical imperatives to protect migrants and travelers. For instance, shortly after World War I, Muslims in British India migrated, mostly to Afghanistan, fueled by support for the Pan-Islamic *khilāfat* movement. Like the Ottoman Muslim refugees, this group of Indian Muslims was referred to as *muhājirūn*, echoing the history of migration in early Islam. However, despite the religious discourse surrounding the movement, the migrants did not receive the support from their host society that they were expecting. Many of them did not survive the harsh conditions of the journey. Survivors were refused asylum after arrival or turned back at the border. A second, much larger number of refugees (over 13 million) resulted from the partition of British India in 1947, and the massive population exchanges between the newly established Pakistan and India that followed it.

Between 1946 and 1948, about 750,000 Palestinians were displaced from their homes with the establishment of the state of Israel and became refugees. The 1967 war caused yet another mass displacement. Palestinian refugees have also been forced to flee during other conflicts, most notably from Lebanon during the civil war (1975–1990) and from Kuwait during the Gulf War in 1991. Some have been displaced several times. As Janet Lippman Abu-Lughod (1995) has pointed out, the case of Palestinian refugees is unique due to their country's disappearance, its subsequent transformation, and the state of Israel's lack of recognition of their right of return, which has meant that the only direction in which Palestinians can migrate is out.

In recent years, major refugee and IDP crises have occurred in the Muslim world not only as a result of colonialism, war, and conflict, but also because of famines and natural disasters, as has been the case in Somalia, Pakistan, and Mali, among others. The Bosnian war left around 2 million refugees when it ended in 1995. The forced migration of Afghans, which began with the 1979 Soviet invasion, has continued with the U.S.-led invasion following September 2001. It is estimated that 6 million Afghans have been displaced in the last 30 years. In addition, the 1991 Gulf War and the 2003 U.S. invasion of Iraq have made Iraqi refugees one of the largest refugee populations in the world, with around 1.8 million living outside Iraq and 1.7 million IDPs unable to return home. Protracted refugee and IDP situations exist also in Algeria, Bangladesh, Iran, and Sudan.

Asylum and Refugee Law and Muslim Refugee Women. Countries that have signed the 1951 Convention and/or the 1967 Protocol, which expanded the definition of a refugee by removing geographical and temporal limitations, build domestic refugee law on the language of these documents. However, how the terms defined by the Convention and the Protocol are understood varies significantly. Applicants seeking asylum must prove that they have been persecuted or that they have well-founded fears that they may face serious harm. Their claims must satisfy the international legal definition of what constitutes a refugee in addition to its interpretation by the legal authorities from the host country.

Given the absence of gender as a recognized basis for persecution in the Convention, asylum petitions must incorporate the experiences of female applicants into the existing legal grounds. Depending on domestic interpretations of international refugee law, however, some countries approve asylum requests only if the perpetrators are state actors, actors affiliated officially or unofficially with the state, or actors who are tolerated by the state. These interpretations discriminate against the many female asylum-petitioners who seek protection from non-state agents, or whom the state has repeatedly failed to protect. Furthermore, most interpretations of refugee law have understood persecution in terms of men's experiences in the public sphere, thus dismissing the political implications of what are usually considered private acts of harm toward women and alternative forms of political participation or resistance that may cause women to be targeted for violence.

In order to address these issues, gender asylum law has sought to synchronize human rights norms with international refugee law. It recognizes that women are more likely to face certain forms of harm, such as rape, sexual and family violence, and human trafficking, and that therefore they may constitute a "particular social group" in the Convention grounds. In other instances, they may be targeted for persecution because they are women. Some legal advocates, however, have expressed concern over the increasing representation of Muslim women's asylum cases as gender-based persecution, where women are members of a particular social group and Islam (as a general category) is the persecuting agent. They fear that this is an Orientalist depiction of Islam and a misrepresentation of Muslim women's actual claims to persecution, which are usually embedded in complex economic, social, political, and religious structures. Violence against women is also widespread, which leads to questions regarding the unidirectional movement of the refugee system, in which Western countries usually determine asylum cases originating from the Global South.

Other legal and structural barriers affect Muslim refugee women. The UNRWA, for example, only recognizes the descendants of Palestinian refugee men as refugees. This excludes the children of women who are not born from a Palestinian man and the women themselves from services. In refugee camps worldwide, unequal access to food, water, education, and health care affect refugee women and girls, who are also especially vulnerable to sexual violence, even after displacement. In some cases, sexual violence is perpetuated by the same people who are entrusted with protecting refugees and IDPs.

After September 2001, Muslim communities in non-Muslim countries have faced violent attacks, harassment, and discriminatory policies, which have affected some Muslim refugee women specifically. They have also been subjected to increased police surveillance because of anti-terrorism provisions, which have led to more restrictive immigration measures that affect refugees and their families. In certain countries, secular laws have conflicted with Muslim refugee women's religious practices, especially with regard to wearing the *hijab* or *niqāb* in public settings.

BIBLIOGRAPHY

Abdel Haleem, Muhammad A. S. *The Qur'an: A New Translation*. New York: Oxford University Press, 2005.

Abou El Fadl, Khaled. "Islamic Law and Muslim Minorities: The Juristic Discourse on Muslim Minorities from the Second/Eighth to the Eleventh/Seventeenth Centuries." *Islamic Law and Society* 1, no. 2 (1994): 141–187. Contains a significant discussion on the position of various Muslim jurists on the obligation to emigrate.

"Afghan Refugees." In *Costs of War*. Providence, R.I.: Eisenhower Study Group, Brown University, Watson Institute of International Studies. http://costsofwar.org/article/afghan-refugees. An extensive, interdisciplinary analysis of the wars in Afghanistan and Iraq ten years after their onset. Includes a paper by Nora Niland, "The Great Deception: Only Democratic Delusions for Afghans."

Akram, Susan Musarrat. "Orientalism Revisited in Asylum and Refugee Claims." *International Journal of Refugee Law* 12, no. 1 (2000): 7–40. Useful critique of Orientalist portrayals of Islam in refugee rights advocacy, with an emphasis on Muslim women's asylum claims. The author argues that stereotyping Islam may adversely affect refugee and asylum claims, as well as silence refugee voices.

Cesari, Jocelyn. "'Islamophobia' in the West: A Comparison between Europe and America." In *Islamophobia: The Challenge of Pluralism in the 21st Century*, edited by John Esposito and Ibrahim Kalin, pp. 21–43. New York and Oxford: Oxford University Press, 2011. Examines structural forms of discrimination against Muslims in Europe and the United States.

Cohen, Robin, ed. *The Cambridge Survey of World Migration.* Cambridge, U.K.: Cambridge University Press, 1995. See especially Janet Lippman Abu-Lughod, "The Displacement of the Palestinians," pp. 410–413, and Astri Suhrke, "Refugees and Asylum in the Muslim World," pp. 456–460. Broad collection of essays on world migration and its political and economic contexts, beginning in the sixteenth century.

Elmadmad, Khadija. "An Arab Convention on Forced Migration: Desirability and Possibilities." *International Journal of Refugee Law* 3, no. 3 (1991): 461–481. Argues that because the 1951 Convention was written without the participation of Muslim-majority countries, it lacks the important perspective of those countries where refugee and IDP situations are most acute. She proceeds to outline a set of recommendations on how Islamic principles on asylum may help improve the current refugee situation.

Gender Related Asylum Claims in Europe: Comparative Analysis of Law, Policies and Practice Focusing on Women in Nine EU Member States. London: Asylum Aid, 2012. http://www.unhcr.org/refworld/docid/4fc74d342.html.

Guterres, António. "OIC Ministerial Conference on Refugees in the Muslim World." Opening remarks, United Nations High Commissioner for Refugees, May 11, 2012, Ashgabat, Turkmenistan. http://www.unhcr.org/4fb270979.html.

Haque, C. Emdad. "Dilemma of 'Nationhood' and Religion: A Survey and Critique of Studies on Population Displacement Resulting from the Partition of the Indian Subcontinent." *Journal of Refugee Studies* 8, no. 2 (1995): 185–209. Overview and analysis of population studies dealing with the displacement caused by the partition of British India in 1947.

Masud, Muhammad Khalid. "The Obligation to Migrate: The Doctrine of *Hijra* in Islamic Law." In *Muslim Travellers: Pilgrimage, Migration and the Religious Imagination*, edited by Dale F. Eickelman and James Piscatori, pp. 29–49. Berkeley: University of California Press, 1990.

Musalo, Karen. "A Short History of Gender Asylum in the United States." *Refugee Survey Quarterly* 29, no. 2 (2010): 46–63. Description and analysis of U.S. policies regarding extending protection to refugees for gender-related claims, with a historical overview of UNCHR guidelines.

Muzaffar, Saeher A. F. "Practicable Ideals? A Proposal for Revitalizing the Rights of Forced Migrants in Islam." *Journal of Refugee Studies* 14, no. 3 (2001): 250–275. Explores Islamic doctrines regarding refugees and asylum and assesses the current state of refugee assistance in the Muslim world.

"Refugees and Health." In *Costs of War*. Providence, R.I.: Eisenhower Study Group, Brown University, Watson Institute of International Studies. http://costsofwar.org/article/refugees-and-health. Includes a paper by Omar Dewachi, "Insecurity, Displacement and Public Health Impacts of the American Invasion of Iraq."

Sexual and Gender-Based Violence Against Refugees, Returnees and Internally Displaced Persons: Guidelines for Prevention and Response. UN High Commissioner for Refugees, May 2003. http://www.unhcr.org/refworld/docid/3edcd0661.html. UNCHR guidelines to respond to and prevent sexual and gender-based violence in the organization's operations around the world.

Türk, Volker, ed. *Special Issue: Asylum and Islam. Refugee Survey Quarterly* 27, no. 2 (2008). See especially Muddathir ʿAbd al-Rahim, "Asylum: A Moral and Legal Right in Islam," pp. 15–23; Sharifah Nazneen Agha, "The Ethics of Asylum in Early Muslim Society," pp. 30–40; and Khadija Elmadmad, "Asylum in Islam and in Modern Refugee Law," pp. 51–56. Contains extensive information about the development of asylum policies in Islam and Muslim countries, with comparisons to contemporary refugee policies.

MANUELA CEBALLOS

RELICS. The remains of holy persons may serve as a focus for devotional practices in Islam. These relics include physical remains—of the prophet Muḥammad, saints, and martyrs—and of objects associated with them. Many people believe that contact with such relics transfers powers of healing or blessing (*barakah*). Purported relics of the Prophet—for example, hair, teeth, and clothing—can be found throughout the Muslim world.

The veneration of relics is most commonly expressed in pilgrimage (*ziyārah*) to tombs. The model for this is the pilgrimage to the Prophet's tomb in Medina (*ʿumrah*), an act recommended by all schools of thought in Islam. Among Shīʿī Muslims, *ziyārah* also comprises pilgrimage to the tombs of the imams. The most common form of tomb visitation in the Muslim world is *ziyārah* to the tombs of purported Ṣūfī saints, both male and female. Many believe that the saints continue to exist in a spiritual state at their tombs (*dargāhs*). From these *dargāhs*, they may intercede with God on behalf of their devotees, and so tombs are often seen as sites of miracles. People go to tombs for many reasons: to fulfill vows, to gain blessings for themselves or their families, to seek cures for illness or relief from misfortune, to obey a command by a living *shaykh* or a spiritual command received in a dream, or simply to show love and devotion to the person buried within.

Such devotion reflects a long tradition of personal allegiance in Islam. From its onset, Islam challenged people to give allegiance to both the word of God revealed in the Qurʿān, but also to God's messenger. That allegiance also extended to those considered the legitimate successors to the Prophet. For the Shīʿīs, this means the imams and the male and female members of the Prophet's family in general. Pilgrimage to their tombs thus becomes an act of devotion and love toward persons loved by God and the Prophet. Both Sunnīs and Shīʿīs alike visit Ṣūfī tombs.

Pilgrimage to tombs has long been a target of criticism by Islamic reformers. Some reformers particularly condemn women' pilgrimages to Ṣūfī tombs. Scholars such as Ibn Taymīyah (d. 1328) have objected to it as a form of *shirk*, or the association of others with God, the most heinous sin in Islam. Numerous Muslim reform movements have continued this criticism since then. In the nineteenth century, Saudi Wahhābīs attempted unsuccessfully to stop visitation of even the tomb of Muḥammad. In Egypt, the Muslim Brotherhood is critical of festivals (*mawlids*) at Ṣūfī tombs. In South Asia, the reformist Deobandīs have counseled against this practice as well. Some Muslim reformers have objected to visiting tombs on the grounds that it is contrary to Islam and an impediment to progress.

Western scholars such as Ignácz Goldziher have shared this negative perspective about pilgrimage to tombs. However, most Muslims who visit tombs do not see their devotions as non-Islamic. Indeed, there are numerous Muslim organizations, and even religious scholars (*ʿulamāʾ*), that explicitly defend pilgrimage to tombs on the basis of the Qurʿān and ḥadīth.

[*See also* Sainthood; Sufism and Women; *and* Ziyārah.]

BIBLIOGRAPHY

Aydın, Hilmi. *The Sacred Trusts: Pavilion of the Sacred Relics, Topkapı Palace Museum, Istanbul.* Somerset, N.J.: The Light, 2004. Provides an inventory as well as historical context of the relics of the Prophet contained in the Topkapı Palace Museum.

Goldziher, Ignác. *Muslim Studies.* Vol. 1. Albany: State University of New York Press, 1971. Goldziher's discussion of relics and tombs in the Muslim world, titled "The Veneration of Saints in Islam," is typical of the critical Western accounts.

Hoffman, Valerie. *Sufism, Mystics, and Saints in Modern Egypt.* Columbia: University of South Carolina Press, 1995. Discusses the significance of relics and pilgrimage to Ṣūfī tombs in light of the continued importance of Ṣūfīs (both male and female) in Egyptian social life.

Kugle, Scott. *Sufis and Saints' Bodies: Mysticism, Corporeality and Sacred Power in Islam.* Chapel Hill: University of North Carolina Press, 2007. Provides insight into the connections between corporeality, pilgrimage, and the role of saints in South Asia and North Africa.

Metcalf, Barbara D. *Islamic Revival in British India: Deoband, 1860–1900*. Princeton, N.J.: Princeton University Press, 1982. Provides an interesting discussion of a reformist group critical of pilgrimage to tombs and the veneration of deceased Ṣūfīs.

Nasr, Seyyed Hossein. *The Heart of Islam: Enduring Values for Humanity*. New York: HarperCollins, 2004. Discusses pilgrimage to tombs within the broader context of pilgrimage in Islam.

Pemberton, Kelly. *Women Mystics and Sufi Shrines in India*. Columbia: University of South Carolina Press, 2010. Discusses the importance of relics and pilgrimage to tombs from a gender-focused perspective.

Troll, Christian W. *Muslim Shrines in India*. Delhi: Oxford University Press, 1989. Contains excellent discussions of pilgrimage to tombs and its critics in the South Asian context.

Wheeler, Brannon. *Mecca and Eden: Ritual, Relics, and Territory in Islam*. Rev. ed. Chicago: University of Chicago Press, 2006. Discusses the significance of relics and their associated rituals in Islam in light of pre-Islamic Prophetic lore.

Vernon James Schubel
Updated by Kelly Pemberton

Religion: Theory, Practice, and Interpretation (Theoretical Overview). The importance of religion as a global presence is undeniable. In the world of Islam, religion manifests itself in multiple ways and is woven into the daily warp and weft of human lives and into the daily rhythms of society. In this section, we have sought to do justice to religion through the three dimensions of theory, practice, and interpretation. The intertwining of these three dimensions lends greater vividness and thickness to our approach to religion, as we seek to gauge the myriad ways in which it influences the lives of people and of societies. It is not a one-way street however—people and societies also leave their broad imprint on religious beliefs and practices as they struggle to make their way in the world and to live faithful lives, sometimes in the face of great challenges. Discourses on religion need to be contextualized—temporally, spatially, and politically, above all. While it is useful and necessary to understand religion in the abstract, we also must complementarily understand it as a lived phenomenon, which is dynamic, often malleable, and irreducible to a monolith.

We now proceed to discuss each of these three dimensions of religion and focus on how they have served as broad guiding principles undergirding our treatment of this critical subject.

Theory. Religion, particularly as codified in sacred texts, is a powerful moving force at both the individual and communal levels. Religion frequently encodes the vertical relation between humans and a supreme being in elaborate doctrine and ritual practices, which often constitute its fundamental core. For the horizontal relation between humans, religion often prescribes ethical practices and codes of conduct that, ideally speaking, adherents are expected to implement in their lives. Knowledge of the theoretical basis of religion and its animating tenets is a *sine qua non*, therefore, for the study of religious traditions and communities.

We have accordingly included an introduction to the five pillars of Islam, which represent the tradition's bedrock core, adherence to which creates a singular commonality among Muslims everywhere. Worship is a central feature of the Islamic tradition, which calls for private and public adoration of the Divine Being; the article *Ibadah* elucidates this central feature. In addition to the daily prayers, the congregational prayer on Friday is an important faith-based activity that brings millions of Muslims together every week, as described in one of the entries. The fifth pillar of Islam is pilgrimage (*hajj*) to Mecca during the prescribed month of

Dhu'l-hijja at least once in one's lifetime if financial and physical conditions permit. Many Muslims are able to perform more easily the *umrah*—"the minor pilgrimage"—as described in one of the entries. Other essays deal with the centrality of the Qur'ān as liturgical text and women's engagement with it through formal oral recitation. After the Qur'ān, the Hadith literature, which contain the sayings of the Prophet Muhammad, is next in importance; one important essay discusses its transmission, study, and interpretation. Discussions of the concept of prophecy and prophethood, of afterlife in Islam, and inter faith relations further enrich this section.

Practice. Beliefs and doctrine do not manifest themselves in a historical vacuum. Although it is rightly suggested that a shared core of beliefs and ethical worldview produce remarkable uniformity among Muslim-majority societies, to a certain extent, the sheer cultural and ethnic diversity of these societies in their aggregate also create a rich mosaic of distinctive, regionally accented faith-based customs and practices. While learned men and women engage in the deep study of texts and explicate religious tenets and legal principles, rank-and-file practitioners live their faith more in the ordinary interstices of life. The emotive power of religion is often harnessed by them in creative ways to negotiate the daily challenges of earning a livelihood, raising a family, mourning the loss of a loved one, and all of life's vicissitudes. We also focus on how religious observances and rituals are negotiated by the faithful in ways that are contextually meaningful for them, and how gender often impacts their performance.

This section therefore includes discussions about women's religious celebrations, about prayer ablutions, relics, visitation of shrines, and other aspects of popular religion in South and Southeast Asia, the Middle East and North Africa, Sub-Saharan Africa, Europe, and the Americas. It seeks to answer questions about how women use space in the mosque not only to worship, but also to carve out a religious space for themselves in which they assert their right to be present in the house of God.

It is people, after all, who imbue religious doctrines and rituals with meaning and normativity. It is important, therefore, for us to ask, for example: Who exercises authority, where, why, and how? Thus, we include essays on the religious authority of women and on female reciters of the Qur'ān in the pre-modern and modern periods. We also discuss women's status in the Qur'ān and its implications for contemporary Muslim women.

It is also pertinent to ask: Who serves as role models for contemporary Muslims? Why are they regarded as worthy of emulation? Who exerts influence on the young people of today and why? Many of the answers are provided in the entries on a host of historical and contemporary figures—from Muḥammad the Prophet, ʿA'isha, his beloved learned wife, and other women in the seventh century to Amr Khaled and Mustafa Cerić in the twenty-first.

Interpretation. Religious authority in the Islamic milieu is epistemic—that is, based on knowledge especially of scripture and other ancillary texts of Arabic grammar and law, among other disciplines. A mere passive knowledge of these texts and sciences is not enough; a learned scholar must also authoritatively interpret these texts after having acquired the necessary tools to do so. Thus we focus on Qur'ānic schools where girls learn not only to recite the Qur'ān professionally, but also to engage with it as a living text. We discuss specifically women's exegesis of the Qur'ān—one of the most prominent names in the field in the modern period is that of Bint al-Shāṭiʾ, the pseudonym of ʿĀ'ishah ʿAbd al-Shāṭiʾ Raḥmān. Women's activist groups like Sisters in Islam and Musawah established by the Malaysian feminist Zainah Anwar engage in woman-friendly, egalitarian interpretations of the Qurʾān as discussed in three of our entries. The names of women exegetes have begun to proliferate in the recent period, and we have attempted to give them ample coverage and foreground their seminal contributions to the field of Qurʾānic studies.

Women have often lurked in the shadows of official historical narratives of the growth of religious traditions. Here we shine the spotlight on them and illuminate their seminal contributions to the shaping of one such global tradition.

[*See also* ʿIbādah; Khaled, Amr; Musawah; Rahman, ʿĀʾishah ʿAbd al-; Sisters in Islam, *and* ʿUmrah.]

Asma Afsaruddin

Religious Authority of Women.

Women hold positions of religious authority in many contemporary Muslim communities despite historical male dominance of formal religious leadership and the institutions and spaces associated with it. Although their authority is often limited by long-standing, often gendered, practices, their activities are significant because they have ended the near-monopoly of men over public religious leadership and increased female participation in lessons and prayer. This article refers to "female Islamic leadership" to specify the role of female authority in an explicitly religious context.

Although historical examples of female Islamic leadership exist, its expansion in the twentieth century needs to be seen alongside more recent changes in society and the place of women within it. Muslim women occupy leadership roles in a wide range of contexts, from the mosques and *madrasah*s of conservative piety movements, to official religious institutions, to movements trying to transform gender relations completely in Islam.

Authority in Islam is less centralized than in many religions, as is demonstrated by the proliferation of individuals claiming to speak for Islam in the twentieth century. The lack of a single, centrally regulated path to leadership increases the importance of peers and audiences in judging who is a legitimate leader. This less centralized structure provides women with opportunities and challenges. On the one hand, it lowers barriers to entry, making it possible for women—even those without significant religious education—to establish, or rise within, new religious organizations. On the other, it increases the role played by audience expectations, which are often shaped by long-standing sociocultural norms that place additional restrictions on women. What people expect to see in a religious authority is influenced by past examples, and what they expect to hear is influenced by past interpretations, making it difficult for women to advocate change explicitly without losing legitimacy.

Female Islamic Leadership in History. Prominent historical examples of female Islamic leadership are of several varieties. Women are featured in biographical dictionaries of Islamic scholars before the sixteenth century, often as Companions of the Prophet and ḥadīth transmitters, but occasionally as instructors or scholars. There are also many examples of female Ṣūfī leaders, as women could inherit the *barakah* of a Ṣūfī saint even in periods and places where women were excluded from the centers of Islamic scholarship in which would-be religious leaders mastered and demonstrated their knowledge. Many contemporary female Islamic leaders are aware of (and cite) these historical examples. It is important, however, to place the significant expansion of female authority within Islam in the context of twentieth-century social and cultural changes.

Women in Twentieth-Century Piety Movements. Mass movements spreading particular forms of Islamic practice are a major vehicle for female Islamic leadership worldwide, starting in the early twentieth century as social changes increased the public presence and education of women, and especially since the 1970s, with the spread of revivalist movements furthering specific forms of Islamic piety across the Middle East, South and Southeast Asia, Europe, and North America. Female leaders help the movements attract and engage female members.

These leaders often have some formal religious education, possibly provided within the movements themselves, but a significant part of their authority rests on building a reputation within the movement as a committed volunteer, knowledgeable instructor, and pious person. Many of these women are active in spaces that have long been central to religious practice, such as mosques or *madrasahs*, while others utilize alternative spaces such as public or semi-public spaces outside of mosques (rented premises, universities, other community facilities), private homes, or virtual spaces (television, Internet).

These leaders tend to spread conservative social and religious practices. Further female education and involvement within conservative contexts, where restrictive sociocultural practices are often justified through reference to religion regardless of the degree of support given to them in Islamic texts, nevertheless can enable women to have more influence over their daily lives through explicit reference to Islam.

Positions for Women in Official Islam. Female leaders have also been invited by states or male leaders to exercise religious leadership within official circles, though often with status lower than their male colleagues. For instance, state-run programs in Morocco and Turkey certify women to work as state employees preaching, teaching, and, in Turkey, even issuing *fatwās*. Hui women in China capitalized upon past invitations to leadership, as well as the gender-equality policies of the communist state, to establish women-only mosques. Women are serving as deputy muftis focusing on women's issues in India and Syria, and as judges (*qāḍīyahs*) in Palestine and Indonesia, the latter being the only setting where *qāḍīyahs* are equal to their male colleagues.

Opportunities for women to pursue formal religious education also expanded significantly in the second half of the twentieth century, for instance with a women's section of al-Azhar in Cairo and numerous female *madrasahs* in Qom. However, this expansion in education has not led to a rise of similar magnitude in the number of women recognized as top religious scholars, perhaps because the emphasis of many of these schools is on proselytization and outreach. The women who have emerged as prominent scholars in the twentieth century include Suʿad Saleh and Abla al-Kahlawy of Egypt, Noṣrat Amīn and Zohreh Ṣefātī of Iran, and Hajjah Maria Ulfah of Indonesia.

Religious Authority and Women Seeking Gender Justice. A final group of female Islamic leaders aim to change gendered hierarchies radically within Islam. Women such as North America's Amina Wadud, Asma Barlas, and Kecia Ali, and Germany's Rabeya Mueller, and organizations such as Malaysia's Sisters in Islam, combine reinterpretation of the Qurʾān with action, such as leading mixed-gender communal prayer. In North America, women have sought positions on the communal boards that run mosques, and equal distribution of mosque space. In Europe, these groups and thinkers are influential among women trying to figure out how to be Muslim while living in Europe. These female leaders make up a highly visible and inspirational vanguard arguing for major change within Islam. At the same time, this emphasis on change limits their audience and authority to groups and individuals sympathetic to this change.

Women who exercise Islamic religious authority are a heterogeneous group pursuing diverse goals. At the same time, the fact that so many women have successfully established themselves as people who can legitimately speak on behalf of Islam is a significant development that increases the influence and voice of women in a wide range of communities.

[*See also* Amīn, Noṣrat; Barlas, Asma; Education and Women, *subentry on* Women's Religious Education; Gender Construction; Gender Equality; Islam and Women; Islamic Biographical Collections, Women in; Kahlawy, Abla al-; Mujtahida; Qurʾān, *subentry on* Women's Exegesis; Saleh, Suʿad; Ṣefātī, Zohreh; Sisters in Islam; Ulfah, Hajjah Maria; Wadud, Amina; *and* Women and Islam.]

BIBLIOGRAPHY

Bano, Masooda, and Hilary Kalmbach, eds. *Women, Leadership, and Mosques: Changes in Contemporary Islamic Authority*. Leiden: E. J. Brill, 2012. A 22-chapter volume discussing female Islamic authority in the Middle East, Asia, Africa, Europe, and North America.

Jaschok, Maria, and Jingjun Shui. *The History of Women's Mosques in Chinese Islam: A Mosque of Their Own*. Richmond: Curzon, 2000.

Kalmbach, Hilary. "Social and Religious Change in Damascus: One Case of Female Islamic Authority." *British Journal of Middle Eastern Studies* 35, no. 1 (2008): 35–57.

Kuenkler, Mirjam. "Of *ʿĀlimahs*, *Wāʿiẓahs*, and *Mujtahidas*: Forgotten Histories and New State Initiatives." *Journal of the Royal Asiatic Society* (forthcoming).

Mahmood, Saba. *Politics of Piety: The Islamic Revival and the Feminist Subject*. Princeton, N.J.: Princeton University Press, 2005.

van Doorn-Harder, Pieternella. *Women Shaping Islam: Indonesian Women Reading the Qurʾān*. Urbana: University of Illinois Press, 2006.

Hilary Kalmbach

Religious Biography and Hagiography. Religious biography assumed a large importance in Islamic civilization from the earliest period when various biographical genres enumerated the virtues of the Prophet's associates, established priority in joining the Muslim community, and traced tribal genealogies and affiliations. Muslim women were part of this biographical process from the beginning due to their presence and participation in the Muslim community as authorities, scholars, leaders, and, in some cases, warriors for the faith.

However, female authorship of biographical works is unknown in the early centuries and hardly evidenced in pre-modern times. The relationship between early biography and the hadith collections was particularly important in verifying the reliability (taʿdīl) of hadith transmitters, among whom were many women. Some early women of the Prophet's family, in particular Fāṭimah and ʿĀʾisha (Spellberg, Elsadda), who came to represent political or interpretive positions within early Islam, generated extensive subsequent biographical reflections and representations.

The presence of women in early biographical compendia is significant, and the *Kitāb al-Ṭabaqāt al-Kabīr* of Ibn Saʿd (d. 845) contains some 4,250 biographical notices of men and women of the first Islamic generations, dedicating one of its nine volumes to females of the early Muslim community. However, recent scholarship qualitatively demonstrates declining numbers of women being cited in these biographical collections over the centuries (Roded, Nadwi).

Coupled with the wide dispersal of biographical information across Islamic writings, there exist a significant number of what might be termed specifically biographical "genres," such as Ṭabaqāt, malfūẓāt, manāqib, tadhkirah, and sīrah (siyar). Additional sources such as poetry and *waqf* documents can provide glimpses, however fleeting, into the lives of pre-modern Muslim women.

Classical biographical collections are a rich source for gender research although they lack the context found in some other sources. They also represent male perspectives on female biography—perspectives that often make female activities marginal or invisible.

Increasing numbers of women cited in hagiographies memorializing the golden age of Sufism indicate the significant role of women in the formative stage of religious movements. These alternative, idealized images may overemphasize the ascetic dimension of these women's lives and make them conform to male norms of piety, as in the famous characterization of Attar regarding Rabia of Basra (d. c. 801) that "she was a man on the path of God."

Scholarly and popular interest in recovering women's history has led to a scouring of pre-modern biographical sources to find out how Sufi and scholarly women were depicted, and the extent to which their contributions have been preserved (Cornell).

Individual biographies (*tarjamah*) and autobiographies were less common in the early periods of Islamic history, although a small number may be found, including the notable "Deliverance from Error" of Abū Ḥāmid al-Ghazālī. Hakim al-Tirmidhi's brief autobiographical notice, for example, describes the dreams and spiritual achievements of his wife.

The male-composed works of al-Subki (d. 1370) and al-Sakhawi (d. 1497) display the recognition of female contributors to Islamic scholarship (Lutfi), while poetic works by pre-modern Muslim women may in rare cases serve biographical functions (Homerin).

Developments. Many of the traditional genres of religious biography persist in religious contexts and in more traditional segments of Muslim societies. In the modern period, however, a number of new developments have occurred. Among these are the uses of religious biography for personal edification, reinforcing symbols of national or regional identity, and inspiring or legitimating political action. The increased sense of the modern individual as agent, whether influencing surrounding events, as in the life accounts of leaders and heroes, or in choosing to "convert" from one persuasion or affiliation to another, has also become more prominent in life accounts.

Modernity also brings greater attention to female biography and autobiography with its increasing numbers of female writers and activists. This, coupled with growing Muslim and non-Muslim interest in the role of women in past epochs, results in a new level of production of scholarly, religious, and popular female biographical and autobiographical writings.

For example, the biographical genre was strategically employed by the influential Iranian intellectual, ʿAlī Shariʿati (d. 1978), who composed inspiring biographies of early Islamic figures including the female Shīʿī heroines, Fāṭimah and Zaynab. These biographies, which combined the use of traditional Islamic sources with a more "Western" existential focus, were written so as to explicitly link the events and challenges of the past to contemporary problems.

Bint al-Shāṭīʾ (ʿĀʾishah ʿAbd al-Shāṭiʾ Raḥmān) (d. 1998), a female Egyptian religious writer, specialized in the biographies of early Muslim heroines. While many conservative male Muslim scholars present early Muslim women in ways that honor their contributions to Islamic history while continuing to reinforce traditional patterns of female behavior, in contrast, the Moroccan feminist historian Fatima Mernissi takes a revisionist look at the lives of a number of prominent early Muslim women demonstrating their independence and defiance of patriarchal cultural norms.

Scholarly efforts to recover the experiences of those further from the light of history have increasingly mined court and *waqf* records to piece together details of females' social and personal lives. Works by academic scholars of female biography demonstrate the shift in contemporary Egypt from nationalist themes in female biography (Booth) to a focus on female piety and even abandonment of secular lifestyles in favor of pious "Islamic" ones (Malti-Douglas).

The importance of the genre is evidenced by the fact that more women of Islamist persuasion have begun to participate in the biographical and autobiographical tradition. Zaynab al-Ghazālī (d. 2005), an Egyptian female activist in the Muslim Brotherhood, offered her prison memories in Hayātī (*My Life*) in the form of a heroic narrative with certain hagiographic undertones. The "voice from prison" genre is a classical form in Islamic poetry, and post-imprisonment narratives have also emerged from secular representatives, such as Egyptian feminist Nawāl al-Saʿdāwī. Maryam Jameela, an American convert from Judaism who affiliated herself with the Pakistani Jamaʿat-i Islami movement in the 1950s, found her collected letters transformed into a novelistic biography by the writer Deborah Baker in *The Convert: A Tale of Exile and Extremism* (2011).

In fact, the return to or embracing of Islam versus abandoning the tradition are competing themes represented in modern female autobiographies that increasingly follow the genre of "conversion" narratives, including the controversial "escape-from-Islam" narratives "Infidel" (Hirsi Ali) and "What's Wrong with Islam" (Irshad Manji).

Furthermore, a number of works by contemporary Muslim feminist scholars are either implicitly or explicitly autobiographical including Leila Ahmed's *A Border Passage*, Mernissi's *Dreams of Trespass*, and Amina Wadud's *Inside the Gender Jihad*.

In response to perceived misunderstandings of Islam, collected autobiographical testimonials of female Muslims living in diaspora contexts have been produced to demonstrate the shared humanity, diversity, and independence of Muslim women, for example, *Love insha Allah: The Secret Love Lives of American Muslim Women* (Mattu and Maznavi) and *Living Islam Out Loud: American Muslim Women Speak* (Abdul-Ghafur). A further autobiographical genre are the Ṣūfī convert narratives of Western Muslim women such as *Journey through 10,000 Veils* (Faye), *The Butterfly Mosque* (Wilson), or *The Sky Is Not the Limit* (Armstrong).

As the forces of Westernization have increasingly penetrated many Muslim societies, the canons of modern literature have tended to favor the novel, short story, and poetry written in free verse over classical biographical forms. With a decline in popular Sufism, the audience for collective memorials and devotional biographies has also decreased. Religious biography has adapted to these new circumstances. On the one hand, historians are studying classical biographical materials to recover and assess the roles and lives of Muslim women of the past, while contemporary Muslim women increasingly produce biographies and autobiographies of their own that engage religious issues in varying degrees.

[*See also* ʿĀʾisha bint Saʾd bint b. Abi Waqqas; Fāṭimah; Islamic Biographical Collections, Women in; Saʿdāwī, Nawāl al-; *and* Sainthood.]

Bibliography

Ahmed, Leila. *A Border Passage: From Cairo to America—A Woman's Journey*. New York, 1999.

ʿAṭṭār, Farīd al-Dīn. *Muslim Saints and Mystics*. Translated by A. J. Arberry. London, 1966.

Booth, Marilyn. *May Her Likes Be Multiplied: Biography and Gender Politics in Egypt*. Berkeley, Calif., 2001.

Elsadda, Hoda. "Discourses on Women's Biographies and Cultural Identity: Twentieth-Century Representations of the Life of ʿĀʾisha Bint Abi Bakr." *Feminist Studies* 27, no. 1 (Spring 2001): 37–64.

Fay, Mary Ann, ed. *Auto/biography and the Construction of Identity and Community in the Middle East*. New York, 2002.

Hatem, Mervat. ʿĀʾisha Abdel Rahman: An Unlikely Heroine." *Journal of Middle East Women's Studies* 7, no. 2 (Spring 2011): 1–26.

Hermansen, Marcia K. "Interdisciplinary Approaches to Islamic Biographical Materials." *Religion* 18, no. 4 (1988): 163–182.

Hoffman, Valerie. "An Islamic Activist: Zaynab al-Ghazālī." In *Women and the Family in the Middle East*, edited by Elizabeth Fernea, pp. 233–254. Austin, Tex., 1985.

Homerin, Th. Emil, trans. *Emanations of Grace: Mystical Poems of A'ishah Al-Ba'uniyah*. Lousiville, Ken., 2011.

Lutfi, Hoda. "Al-Sakhāwī"s *Kitāb Al-Nisā'* as a Source for the Social and Economic History of Muslim Women during the Fifteenth Century AD." *Muslim World* 71, no. 2 (1981): 104–124.

Malti-Douglas, Fedwa. *Medicines of the Soul: Female Bodies and Sacred Geographies in a Transnational Islam*. Berkeley, Calif., 2001.

Mernissi, Fatima. *Dreams of Trespass: Tales of a Harem Girlhood*. Reading, Mass. MA, 1994.

Mojaddedi, J. A. *The Biographical Tradition in Sufism: The Ṭabaqāt Genre from al-Sulamī to Jāmī*. Richmond, U.K., 2001.

Nadwi, Mohammad Akram. *Al-Muhaddithat: The Women Scholars in Islam*. Oxford: 2007.

Spellberg, Denise A. *Politics, Gender, and the Islamic Past: The Legacy of 'Ā'isha Bint Abi Bakr*. New York, 1996.

Roded, Ruth. *Women in Islamic Biographical Collections: From Ibn Sa'd to Who's Who*. Boulder, Colo., 1994.

Wadud, Amina. *Inside the Gender Jihad*. Oxford, 2006.

Marcia K. Hermansen

REVELATION. The term *waḥy*, from the Arabic verb *waḥa*, "to put in the mind," is sometimes understood as "inspiration." The Qur'ān uses this term not only for divine inspiration to humans but also for spiritual communication between other created beings. Revelation, however, refers specifically to the *waḥy* that is divine inspiration given to select humans, known as prophets, for the purpose of guidance. Beginning with the first human and prophet, Adam, this process of revelation has continued throughout human history until the message of the revelation was finally preserved intact in the form of the Qur'ān as delivered to the Prophet Muḥammad, which Muslims consider to be the last of the revelations sent to humanity.

Muslims accept not only the Qur'ān but also the Torah, the Psalms of Dā'ūd (David), the Gospels of Jesus, and other works as links in the chain of divine revelation. They believe that each contains the same basic message; however, the cultural, historical, and linguistic terms of particular revelations correspond to the time and place in which each was revealed. It is the ultimate principles within the revelation that transcend time and place to provide a message of universal significance to humankind.

Understanding revelation requires careful consideration of both the particulars of context and the universals of the message for humankind. Since revelation is given to guide human affairs, then intellectual understanding and practical implementation through a reliable example are also necessary. Thus, the prophets are both messengers and models. However, how they serve as models for Muslims has largely depended on how their examples have been interpreted in a given historical context.

Throughout history, debates have raged over how Muslims ought to evaluate the relative value of knowledge received from divine revelation and knowledge arrived at through independent reasoning. According to some philosophers, human reason can be sufficient to guide affairs and therefore, on occasion, equals guidance from revelation, especially since the two often coincide. If the Qur'ān is the revelation of God's will, however, it must be unchallengeable and without equal. Scholars belonging to more orthodox camps of Islamic thought—although by no means denying the reasonableness of revelation—oppose the idea that all things can be known by human reason alone. Humanity requires revelation for clear information about such areas as the unseen—the hidden mysteries of existence that inform us of the relationship between the absolute and the manifest.

Muslim thinkers such as Fazlur Rahman and Amina Wadud have expressed the need for interpretation of the Qur'ānic revelation free from narrow literalism and the verse-by-verse, atomistic methods of earlier exegetes. This has led to a new hermeneutics that addresses the universal relevancy of the revelation in a world of rapid and radical change. Such hermeneutics agree with the traditional opinion that revelation is a special body of knowledge linking the divine creator to humans who possess free will and an independent capacity for reasoning. Scholars have also debated how the act of transmission of revelation by prophets, along with the role of prophecy as intermediary between the divine and humanity, has shaped revelation in languages intelligible to human beings, and its message as contingent on the historical context of revelation. This idea carries great implications for pro-women interpretations of the Qur'ānic text.

No amount of literal and philological analysis can reveal information about the inner dimension of divine–human exchange. Since such information—which cannot be known through empirical means or through logical, sense-based reasoning—is nevertheless considered vital to correct guidance, humanity cannot come to know the ultimate truths except through divine revelation. Thus, revelation is considered a unique and necessary area of knowledge.

In traditional Muslim thought, prophethood is defined by the ability to receive *waḥy* and since all of the prophets have been men, only men are able receive *waḥy*. However, with an increase in women's perspectives in the genre of Qur'ān commentary, scholars have problematized the notion of receiving *waḥy* as an exclusively male experience by pointing to Maryam, the mother of Isa (Jesus), as a recipient of divine communication in the Qur'ān.

[*See also* Prophethood.]

BIBLIOGRAPHY

Arberry, A. J. *Reason and Revelation in Islam*. London: Allen & Unwin, 1971.

Chittick, William C., ed. *The Essential Seyyed Hossein Nasr*. Bloomington, Ind.: World Wisdom, 2007.

Kakar, Palwasha Lena. "Is She a Prophet? Maryam: Mother of Jesus." *Azizah* 3, no. 1 (2003): 14.

Qadir, C. A. *Philosophy and Science in the Islamic World*. London and New York: Croom Helm, 1988.

Soroush, Abulkarim. *The Expansion of Prophetic Experience: Essays on Historicity, Contingency, and Plurality in Religion*. Leiden, Netherlands: E. J. Brill, 2009.

Wadud, Amina. *Qur'an and Woman: Rereading the Sacred Text from a Woman's Perspective*. New York: Oxford University Press, 1999.

Ward, Keith. *Religion and Revelation: A Theology of Revelation in the World's Religions*. Oxford and New York: Oxford University Press, 1994.

AMINA WADUD
Updated by ZAHRA M. S. AYUBI

RITES. Rites within Islamic communities specifically concerning women are often related to what Western academics call "rites of passage": birth, puberty, marriage, death, and burial. These suggest that rites will have both a religious and cultural component. Furthermore, some women's voices within Islamic environments regard these life-course activities as only a small part of the ritual world they inhabit, and although such rites of passage may be explicitly expressed in the Qur'ān, they do not constitute all the complex ways in which Muslim women act ritually. Consequently, the emphasis here will first be the traditional conception of women's rites of passage, followed by some reference to the rich tapestry of ritual available to women throughout the Muslim world.

Some reference should also be made to the features of culture and agency. Qur'ānic sensitivity to the cultural matrix into which Islam came generated the notion of *jāhilīya*, a term that distinguished what was genuinely Islamic from its embedded (presumably pagan) environment. Yet, it was not a wholesale rejection. Crucial elements of Muslim ritual activity, such as pilgrimage and prayer, were clearly carry-overs from earlier days, so there was no set formula on what would be accepted or rejected. The early history of Islam indicates a prolonged process of negotiation and dialogue with its receiving cultures, often mediated by the fledgling growth of Sharī'ah (Islamic law). Agency, too, was an important issue. What Muslim women were expected to do, how they should conduct themselves, whether they were to act as they had as pagan Meccans, whether they were to perform the rituals of Islam in the same way as men, and whether they could carve out a distinct role for women believers in the ongoing development of the Islamic milieu were all complicated issues. Lines of demarcation between Islam and its cultural environment are still subject to debate; if the early borders were porous, then they have remained porous to the present. Students of Islamic society should be aware of this dynamic relationship within the tradition and its cultural situation, as these issues have direct relevance in any survey of women's rites.

The first rite of passage was and is essential for the ongoing identity of Islamic life: birth. God's Word and the Prophet's values were quite clear: if boys are favored, girls are equally part of God's purpose, for the expansion of society has been sanctioned by God (Qur'ān 4:1; 16:72). The practice of "exposing" girls to the elements (essentially constituting female infanticide) was forbidden (81:8; 6:151), and the importance of equality of the sexes became a key ingredient in Islamic self-awareness. Both Sunnī and Twelver Shī'ah mothers-to-be may undertake visitations to holy shrines or make offerings to revered saints as ways of guaranteeing the birth of a son, but, for both, regardless of the outcome, the birth of a healthy daughter also requires a gift to the saint afterward. Iranian (Shī'ah) mothers may plead for help from two Qur'ānic prophets, Elias and Khezr (i.e., Elijah and Khidr), for an easy delivery. Women in rural areas within Islamic countries are still regarded as responsible for providing the children in a marriage, and failure to do so may lead to divorce or a second marriage for their husbands.

However, at the birth of a girl, the same duties should apply: in Sunnī circles, the first duty of the new father is to whisper the *adhān* (call to prayer) in the right ear of the child; in some Shī'ah communities, the local mullah is called to whisper the *adhān* in the right ear and the *iqāmah* (second call to prayer) in the left. This is done because it is believed that the first words a Muslim child hears should be related to worshipping God. In the first few days or weeks following birth, the girl's head is shaved and the weight of the hair in gold or silver donated to charity. Her birth is welcomed by a large celebration called an *'aqīqah* (from the Arabic word *aqqa*, "to sacrifice an animal"), during which time the parents sacrifice a domestic animal (frequently a sheep) and invite the entire community to the feast. Usually, this takes place on an auspicious seventh, fourteenth, or twenty-first day. A naming ceremony also occurs, with considerable variety of procedures on determining the official name of the child. There is precedent in the Qur'ān for the mother to choose the name of her children (3:36), but normally naming is a joint procedure. For both Sunnīs and Shī'īs, it is usually regarded as the father's responsibility to reveal the name at the public celebration, thereby officially acknowledging the baby as his child. A differentiation may take place at this time that reflects the dominance of male heirs: a mother of a boy will be named as "mother of" (e.g., Umm 'Alī); a mother of a girl will not be similarly recognized. Some of these rituals are rooted in times and places predating Islam.

Other rites are less universal. One is the rite of circumcision. Where boys are required to undergo the rite as a sanctioned health and identity ritual, many regard the female equivalent as entirely noncanonical; still, for a few Muslim authorities, it is "praiseworthy." The extent of the female rite varies greatly within Muslim cultural milieu, but continues within some Arab and African contexts, both Sunnī and Shīʿah, although it is critiqued harshly by Muslim feminists.

A limited practice is the rubbing of a baby's gums with a bit of date or its juice and pronouncing prayers in preparation for mother's milk. This rite is called *taḥnīk* and is regarded as having been instituted by the Prophet on the authority of Abū Musa. Breastfeeding is still regarded as normative within Islamic societies because it is sanctioned by the Qurʾān (where children are to be suckled for two whole years, 2:233). Islamic law has also recognized the rights of a wet nurse as a legal foster mother, and it provides "milk siblings" with equivalent status to regular siblings.

Protection for the baby is an important part of a mother's responsibility. Iranian women are usually sheltered from outside visitors for forty days afterward; their first bath after delivery comes after a week of convalescence, and may be an event of joyful gathering with female relatives and close friends. For the first few weeks, both boys and girls may be dressed in long white gowns, with amulets protecting them from the evil eye and other negative forces. After a little time, however, girls' ears will be pierced and gifts of gold jewelry and earrings will be sent by close relatives of the family. Dressy clothes and formal attire will be given by relatives soon after the baby is out of danger from an early death. They also take great care to never allow the child to be out of their sight for the first forty days. These rites are obviously related to fears about evil spirits deriving from an earlier time, or are traceable to Zoroastrian tradition.

The second rite of passage relates to a girl's coming-of-age. Puberty is defined as the time when reproduction can take place. It is recognized as critical by the Qurʾān: "And when the children among you attain the age of puberty, then let them also ask for permission (to enter)" (24:59).

Non-Islamic and pagan cultures designate puberty as a special transition time and prescribe impressive rituals for girls. In most Islamic societies, behavioral codes rest on actions deemed to be Islamic, but whose relationship to the Qurʾān or *sunnah* of the Prophet might only be tangential. For example, a female undergoes processes of transition from the relative freedom of a "nongendered" child to that of a responsible adult participant in a Muslim home. The canonicity of these processes might be strongly debated within Islamic households, depending on class, educational status, conservative viewpoints, socioreligious milieu of the family, and community norms. These behavioral codes might entail such restrictions as seclusion in the home or restrictive protocols of dress in public (i.e., the burqa), limitations on visitation with nonfamily males, and required permission from fathers or husbands for some public activity, such as visits to medical clinics.

Great variations attend these codes across the world of Islam. Regardless, puberty is an important marker for Muslim women and, while it has no universal rite attached to it, puberty does signal a moment when agency shifts toward the young woman. Religiously, the transition may include such things as the beginning of full participation in prayers and Ramaḍān; culturally, proper deferential characteristics for young women (e.g., shyness, Qurʾān 28:25); and socially, preparation for distinctive women's experience (menstruation, pregnancy, labor, breastfeeding). One finds great diversity in modern debates concerning this period in a young woman's life, both within the

Islamic world and without. In Western contexts, a full discussion of the applicability of Middle Eastern concepts such as so-called honor killings has erupted, with the implication that these are sanctioned by Islam. Muslims usually point to the complex roots of this concept, that is, its significance only in some societies, its relationship to kin-based tribal cultures, and its dependency on a strong patriarchal system. Most Muslims prefer to argue that the religious content relates to whether the traditional role of remaining dutiful to parental advice will be upheld in a daughter's life choices (17:23).

At the same time, puberty provides transitions to new statuses and achievements. To name only a few: young Muslim women begin accumulating accessories for a prospective home, since the model of Muslim life is creating a family. Whereas beforehand she may have had little interest in food and its preparation, she now faces the responsibilities of learning to provide healthy sustenance for a husband and children. She may also become aware of the role she will soon assume as Islamic educator of her young children. In addition, the transition to adulthood brings with it certain defined legal rights and responsibilities, such as her rights according to Sharīʾah, her position as custodian of her own name in marriage, or her legal right to dower, and the family rites involved in carrying out these processes. In effect, there are a plethora of customs, rites, and cultural rituals associated with this transition that will need to be acquired, encountered, and embedded in the young Muslim woman's consciousness. Hence, in Islamic communities, puberty entails a series of lifestyle and behavioral shifts that mark the movement toward responsible adulthood. Collectively, they constitute a significant rite of passage from childhood to adulthood for a female. From this point forward, she has available to her all the formal and informal rituals of Islam.

Of critical importance are rites related to the five pillars. The first is the rite of ablution. These are known as *wuḍūʾ*, that is to say ritual washing, which also apply to men. The major washing, called *ghusl,* is mandatory after sexual relations, menstruation, childbirth, or contact with blood or the dead. The fast during Ramaḍān applies to women, but only when they are not menstruating; they are expected to make up the time later. There is resistance to the idea of a menstruating woman entering a mosque, and in Medina, she is forbidden from the Prophet's mosque. Handling the Qurʾān is also restricted during the menstrual cycle. Islam's emphasis on cleanliness spawned the famous *ḥammāms* (public baths), where times were set aside for women to bathe, becoming part of the public life of medieval society. The Prophet's *sunnah* also stressed the importance of women's cleanliness and dress, emphasizing the importance of women paying special attention to beauty. These elements informed the development of Islamic cultures, and have impacted fashion and codes of adornment. Evidence of their significance can be seen in the tastes and family rites of the modern Muslim woman.

Marriage constitutes a third rite of passage. Many current debates focus on rites related to marriage and divorce. The key issue is the woman's agency. The validity of marriage is attested to in both the Qurʾān and the ḥadīth. Marriage as a mutually supportive activity for both sexes is mandated, and its role in securing and growing the Muslim community is central. However, unlike in Christianity, it is not considered a sacred covenant. Rather, marriage is a civil contract between two people or, more traditionally, between two families. It is the culminating event of a significant process of negotiation and exchange. Central to the negotiation is the amount and kind of the *mahr* (dower). The dower is the Islamic means of guaranteeing the validity of the marriage offer, and reflects both the status of the families and their mutual interests in uniting in this way. The amount of the dower is a matter of serious negotiation between the respective families, and once decided upon, it becomes a personal asset of the bride and she retains it throughout the marriage. She need never forfeit it unless she seeks a divorce. The dower is thus distinguished from the custom in other cultures, which require a dowry to be paid to the father. A contract is drawn up that is mutually acceptable to both parties, and this is critical for the marriage ceremony. That contractual ceremony, called *nikāḥ*, takes place after agreement has been reached and is the formal act of acceptance; traditionally, the rite involves the groom appearing at the bride's house, during which time he orally proposes marriage to his bride, and she must publicly accept the proposal. The contract is then signed in the presence of two witnesses. A celebration follows, attended by well-wishers and relatives.

There are certain Islamic restrictions imposed on marriage negotiations. Muslim women are legally allowed only to marry Muslim men, while Muslim men may marry any woman from the "people of the book." Hence, Muslim women must require conversion of potential spouses not already within Islam, which then entail rites of conversion by the intended groom. Contemporary young Muslim women believe this inequitable, especially when they live in Western countries without a history of Muslim communities. In traditional Muslim environments, there are great differences of opinion surrounding what constitutes a permissible age for marriage, with legal limits defined between 9 and 15. It is therefore possible for someone still legally regarded as a child in some Western jurisdictions to marry in certain Muslim countries. All Muslim legal schools require puberty to have taken place before marriage.

Women's agency in marriage is often challenged by critics, but the fact is that Khadījah, the Prophet's first wife, proposed to him, apparently because of her higher social status. The Prophet was clear on women's agency in marriage: in the language of the *sunnah*, "A matron should not be given in marriage except after consulting her, and a virgin should not be given in marriage without taking her permission" (*Ṣaḥīḥ al-Bukhārī*). Thus, although writing the contract might fall to the male members of the family, it was not their place to dictate the persons named in the contract. On several occasions, the Prophet acted on a woman's wishes concerning marriage, even to the point of dissolving a marriage because of a wife's complaints about her husband's looks. According to Ibn ʿAbbās, the Prophet said: "A woman previously married has more right to her person than her guardian. And a virgin also should be consulted, and her silence implies her consent." Historically, then, women required the involvement of guardians/fathers in the legal matters related to marriage, but the women themselves provided approval of the legal document. And it is evident that widows and divorcees could act on their own behalf in legal matters and exercise their own personal freedom to choose what they wished to do. An examination of particular cases within the Sharī'ah also demonstrate that women's views held greater sway in the workings of the court than popular perceptions afford. For example, widows and divorcees could dispose of assets without a guardian's approval. In that case, these women had greater personal agency than those who were married. They could also undertake activities dedicated to the betterment of the community, such as setting up *waqf*s for religious or charitable purposes with their assets.

Studies have shown that, among some strata of Muslim societies, widows and divorcees experienced discrimination; those that were poor had little hope of remarrying. Islamic law provided one kind of outlet—the legal provision of several wives. Throughout Islamic history, divorced and widowed women from leading families and the upper classes had much greater potential for remarriage, a feature that still remains the norm in some societies. In Western countries, however, where different cultural norms shape marriage and where the application of Islamic law is blunted or refuted, issues are far more complex. Women's choices might be governed by identity concerns, and by a more intimate Muslim community whose restrictions have to be taken into consideration.

There are also some differences between Sunnī and Shīʿī law with regard to types of marriage. Shīʿah law recognizes *mutʿah,* or temporary marriage, contracts, by which a union may be undertaken for a specific period of time, at the end of which, a sum of money will be paid to the wife and both parties go their separate ways. While not permitting *mutʿah,* Sunnī law does recognize so-called lesser-contract marriages. These are designated as *ʿurf* (customary), *sirr* (secret), or *misyar* (itinerant) marriages. Lesser-contract marriages do not carry the same inheritance or maintenance rights, but children are regarded as legitimate.

Traditional marriage laws have collided with change in the Muslim world and, consequently, on the rites women practice. In countries where marriage must be delayed for financial or educational purposes, *ʿurf* is a favored option, but it has disadvantages for women. The "marriage," while performed by a Muslim cleric, is not recorded by the state, so technically no claims can be made when it ends. Children are not supported according to the long standing principles of Islamic law. Rites associated with marriage are likewise absent—such favorites as having one's hands and feet painted with patterns of henna, parties with girlfriends, the choices of gown and wedding day planning, and the arrival of the groom's entourage at the bridal home with the husband-to-be escorting his bride to the place of marriage—all these joyful occasions are forfeited by the *ʿurf* system. The fact is that the role of such marriages remains controversial, but they are increasingly common in the Muslim world. It is important to note that the same legal restrictions apply in the West against such temporary marriages.

Other issues also are involved: ethnicity plays an unofficial role in who will be considered a likely mate. In the past in Muslim countries, it was permissible for Muslim men to marry several wives, depending on the legal situation of their home cultures. As a result of reforms made since the early twentieth century, many jurisdictions removed that possibility, or seriously restricted it. Western countries do not allow such unions. However, polygamy was sanctioned by the Qurʾān and the Prophet, and the conservative movement throughout the Muslim world has once again brought the practice to the fore. Most modern Muslim states require the man to negotiate the potential to marry a second wife in the marriage contract, and authorities can grant a woman a divorce on judicial grounds if such a right has not been included in the contract. In China, however, Uighur culture still supports polygamy, a feature that is reflected in the Uighur language with expressions like *palančinig čoṇ xotuni* (the big wife). As a consequence, marriage in the West, where such contracts do not have the same force of law, can present several challenges to women who offer the contract as evidence of breach of agreement. On the other hand, there is also evidence of the severe repression of married women in places like Afghanistan, where, under the 2009 Shiite Personal Status Law, a man can withhold food and water if his wife does not cooperate with his sexual demands. Finally, same-sex marriages are forbidden in all legal schools of Islam and in all modern Islamic countries.

A marriage in a woman's life may indeed end with divorce, and various rites attend the process. There is significant difference in Islamic law over the kinds and validity of divorces, depending on social reforms within Muslim countries. It is in Islamic divorce that a woman's agency is most challenged. Because marriage is a civil contract, it requires only a civil action to rescind it. Couples need not live together if they clearly cannot do so peaceably and with mutual benefit. In traditional law, the power to divorce rests primarily with males. The Sharīʾah does not require men to state why they wish to divorce their wives, even though divorce without a reason is regarded as *makrūh* (morally reprehensible). The most familiar rite of divorce is the so-called *ṭalāq* formula ("I hereby divorce you!"), repeated by the man three times over a period of three menstrual cycles, which formally ends the relationship. A divorced woman must have the remaining amount of the dower paid to her, and she cannot remarry for a period of time designated as *ʿiddah* (probation) or three months and thirteen days after the divorce is finalized. During this time, her ex-husband must continue to cover her expenses. There are very few equivalent divorce options open to women, although in some Islamic jurisdictions a wife can petition the court for a divorce called *khulʿ* or an annulment (*faskh*). In some modern Islamic countries, women's rights have been expanded.

In the case of *ʿurf*-type marriages, several high-profile cases in Egypt have uncovered the loss of rights for women and children in such liaisons, causing women's organizations to campaign for a state law to step in to protect women and children in these cases; the government responded with new divorce laws, but it has not necessarily alleviated the problems. In Saudi Arabia, where the divorce rate has now reached 60 percent, a new phenomenon has evolved—that of forced divorce. This arises when the family is not satisfied with the terms of the contract, or one of the persons in the marriage is deemed unsuitable. A forced divorce may take place regardless of the happiness of the couple or whether they have children.

There is considerable social opprobrium toward divorced women in many Muslim countries—in some jurisdictions, spinsters have more status than divorcees. Most agree that, in Muslim society, someone is to be "blamed" for the failure of a marriage and, unfortunately, that blame usually falls on the woman. The Saudi psychologist Madiha al-Ajroush argues that Arab women are more disadvantaged by a divorce than men because women are fearful of losing their children if their former mates challenge their choice of new partner in court, and they often have to settle for a new husband of a lower social status. Most cannot return to their family home, and the social supports they might receive are few. Many therefore remain in unhappy marriages because there are few palatable options as a divorcee. Furthermore, significant differences exist in the application of divorce law across the Muslim world.

What is evident is that the rites which women have practiced (and which continue to be the norm) have arisen within traditional cultural patterns, and modernity has intercepted and changed the effectiveness of these practices. To give but one example: the contemporary businesswoman. In today's world, especially in North America and Europe, the business luncheon is the environment for important and sometimes critical decisions—it is a "rite" of business. Women and men freely engage in negotiations there. Yet, under traditional Muslim norms, the appearance in public of such a woman without her husband or a close family member would be forbidden and perhaps even the cause for divorce. Muslim businesswomen normally try to avoid such situations, but often cannot. In such a case, the business rite operates above that of Muslim cultural rites. Modernity thus brings its own kind of complexity to a woman's life.

The fourth rite of passage is death. The end of human life, whether male or female, is in the hands of God. Consequently, even in the most retractable of conditions, it is not up to a man or woman to limit his or her existence. Indeed, in situations of prolonged suffering, as now takes place in hospitals and institutions, an individual cannot take any action that would end his or her life before God wills it. This includes the withholding of sustenance and hydration. Therefore, a Muslim—be it man or woman—has virtually no agency over his or her life's end, and often leaves all issues relating to withholding of medical services to a spouse or oldest son. There is also some continuing belief in the benefits of suffering when facing death. The classic case is that of Rābiʿah al-ʿAdawīyah, the famous saint. When a friend counselled her to pray to God to relieve her suffering, she replied: "O Sufyan! Do you not know who has willed my suffering? Is it not God? Why do you ask me to pray for what contradicts his will?" In Islam, human society must step back and acknowledge the primacy of God in life, and death must be faced as a matter that is quite beyond one's control. Steadfastness when facing death is thus a measure of abiding Islamic faith.

The fifth rite of passage is that associated with mourning. Unless there are valid reasons for an autopsy, the body must remain inviolate from the moment of death until it is prepared for burial. That preparation is undertaken by close female relatives if the deceased is female, and they provide a ritual bath (*ghusl*) to the deceased and wrap her in a plain white shroud (*kafan*). She will be carried on the shoulders of male relatives to her final resting place. Elaborate wailing is frowned upon, and the body is carried to a mosque for a prayer before burial. This prayer, called *ṣalāt al-janāzah*, is the responsibility of the male members of the household and the community. Following this, the bier is carried to the cemetery, where she is buried facing Mecca. Following an offering of perfume, the body will be covered with boards and family members take turns throwing sand on the open grave. It is then filled and the family returns home.

What then comes into play are expressions of grief. This is the occasion when both family and religious rites mediate the potentially high emotional reactions. In Islamic communities, grief is lessened by the recognition that, once death has taken someone, that person belongs to God. Consequently, the family will support an event of remembrance and reflections for their departed. They may host a day of Qurʾān recitation to which members of the community will come to pay their respects. Visitation of women members of the community is handled by the deceased's daughters or female relatives. Families demonstrate their sense of loss by contributing to the poor as a gesture of their appreciation for her life. Among some Muslim cultures, for example, in Mecca, a specific meal is cooked to mark the end of condolences on the third day. A dish of rice and hummus, said to have been the favorite of the Prophet, is made by the family's women and served to all those who can attend. Responsibility for such rites lies entirely with women. Remembrance ceremonies may also be held after forty days and annually for a period of time. These rites are integrated into mourning procedures in Muslim countries and are obviously truncated among migrants to the West. Nevertheless, the deceased may continue to influence the family and community through a designation of *waqf* (religious estate) for the building of mosques or schools to benefit the poor or some other worthwhile group of people. In these cases, the Muslim woman still retains agency over such things as her *mahr* and gifts that have been given to her throughout her life, as well as any funds she has managed to accumulate on her own. Another rite sometimes practiced in Iran and other Muslim cultures is the cemetery visitation. In homes that have lost loved ones, women are often those who maintain fresh memories, and the visitation may include a picnic at the gravesite and the telling of stories and anecdotes about the deceased. Not only does this provide a way to conduct a family rite outside the home, but it also allows women who might tend to cloister themselves after the death of a key person to visit outside the home—an important event for them. It follows that the role of women in this remembrance activity is crucial.

This survey of rites in women's lives now shifts to a different terrain. While in the previous paragraphs, the material has been directly related to what might be termed "standard" ritual activity, this is only a small part of the way that rites relate to a Muslim woman. Furthermore, it might appear that women have little leeway in carrying out these activities, whereas in local situations, variations and local customs modify intentionality. Still, it is necessary to point to ways in which different conceptions of rites apply in situations other than birth, puberty, marriage, death, and burial.

Women's cultural rites with Islamic content are diverse and wide-ranging. For example, apart from the rather shop worn notion that Muslim women are confined to the house is a more convincing truth: many Muslim women believe their role as mother and head of the family establishment is a God-given responsibility. This entails constructing home rites that reflect an "Islamic" home. As such, they not only train their daughters on the etiquette of a fine Muslim home, but also lead them in spiritual development. It is also often the mother's role to train both sons and daughters about distinctive Muslim cultic practices, to inculcate proper norms, and to provide rudimentary understandings of Islam. It follows that mothers establish procedures to do this that are rich and multifaceted, even though such activity may not be recognized publicly. Thus, it is not unusual in visiting a Muslim home to find a mother engaged in the nightly ritual of listening to her children recite the Qur'ān. The fact is that Muslim women are the custodians of hospitality. Furthermore, since a mother's position in the family rests with their eldest son, they command a significant part of the nonpublic face of the family, entailing such activities as choosing marriage partners for children, approving how family assets are spent, and making decisions that will impact on the family's well-being.

There are family traditions (a favorite meal or a favored beverage) around the occasions for making these decisions, with the central focus on mothers. The delicate and sometimes onerous role they play in mediating various possibilities among family members speaks to a career of negotiating moral and religious truth in the midst of a busy family life. These are often "dressed" as family rites to provide them with authority. To this is added the significant skills they pass on in the preparation of correct culinary and Islamically sanctioned foods, particularly to daughters. Teaching their children the cultural dimensions of eating is not a simple task like providing a quick lesson: it involves developing and sustaining family rites that are experienced and appropriated almost by osmosis by the children. It is mothers who prepare the household for all the major events of the Muslim calendar: the cleaning and care of the family for special events, the special foods at Ramaḍān, hospitality to visiting relatives at other times of the year, provision of special dishes during birth celebrations, special rites for family events such as birthdays. All these elements have customs and rituals that are sometimes subtle and often require consummate abilities to carry out, and most of them are based on long protocols within the Islamic community reaching back to the Prophet's life and the Qur'ān.

Furthermore, most Sunnī communities have been blessed with women whose vision of their significance is not limited to the rites of passage or roles in the home. They see their role as a "mother of the community," by which they understand that Islamic society requires models of piety. One example of this was the writer Qūt al-Qulūb of Cairo, who wrote in French in the twentieth century and who movingly portrayed her early life in the Demirdash order. These women therefore take on teaching roles, often directed at young women, as a way to invigorate Islam and assure its proper maintenance. They are available for counseling, lead young women in deeper perceptions of prayer and meditation, and fundamentally hold that a life lived in conscious dedication to Islam's great spiritual values can transform a community. There are women like this all over the Muslim world, mostly unsung, who nevertheless provide guidance to young Muslim girls and women—women like Siddiqah Sherif el-Din of Jeddah who, in the early twentieth century, formed a Qur'ān school for girls, as well as academic schools for women. Although the academic schools are those most lauded today, it is the spiritual community that serves Islam. There are no guidelines for the rites that these women espouse; there is little national or international recognition of them. Still, it is important to point to them as crucial preservers of Islamic traditions, for they utilize notable rites such as Qur'ān recitation, but add to it spiritual activities that deepen and enhance religious meaning. Within their societies, their role is seen as a special blessing from God, with clearly significant ritual content, but they remain mostly unrecorded and unheralded.

There are others who have taken what might be termed a more pronounced political stance and developed ways for women to express their concerns through acts that will speak of Islamic values. The most evident of these in the early twenty-first century is the Al-Huda movement in Pakistan's notorious North-West Frontier Province. One group, called Bibiane, destroys the simple binary of public-private; in this culture, women play a key role in expressing both intra- and inter-familial relationships in ceremonies that bridge the family environment with the public culture. However, many other types of rites could be cited; one example would be the heroic activities of Meena Kashwar Kamal who founded the Revolutionary Association for Women of Afghanistan (RAWA) in 1977 and stood firm for the equality of men and women based on Islam and the Qur'ān in the face of fierce conservative opposition. Using such rites as silent vigils and prayerful demeanor in public places, RAWA encourages women to take a stand for the Qur'ān's values of equality.

In other contexts, such as Ṣūfī environments, such pious women are critical for tending to the moral and spiritual welfare of young devotees, particularly young women. Rābiʿah al-ʿAdawīyah is well known for her role in the early days of Sufism, and women were perceived to have more time for spiritual enterprises and could dedicate their lives to that purpose once their families were grown. While men obviously dominated the official structure of Ṣūfī orders, women formed lay divisions that stressed prayer and meditation and provided a substrate of piety expressed throughout most Islamic societies. The Bektashi tradition integrated women with men in ceremonial life. Sometimes these women themselves become the head or *shaykha* of the order. In these cases, they exemplify a spiritual role in the community that rises above any gendered view of their person. They themselves preserve and enhance the *barakah* (spiritual presence) held to reside in the lineage of the order. Women's roles in Sufism are complicated and reflect local growth and evolution, but do include participation in *dhikr*, carrying out the role of chanter, providing counseling and support for members in times of crises, and education. Since Sufism has placed less stress on law and doctrine, and more emphasis on personal experience and individual piety, it has opened many possibilities to women to address spiritual needs not captured in regular Islamic rituals.

In Shīʿah communities, some women become the heart and soul of *muḥarram* rites. This is because many of them have considerable skills as storytellers, and it is culturally acceptable for them to express emotions publicly. This may be noted particularly in the Twelver rituals associated with the martyrdom of Ḥusayn at Karbala. These are rituals of meditation and celebration of the life and meaning of the early martyrs of Shiism. The telling of the stories of their suffering becomes a crucial element in the remembrance rites of these events and their continuous impact on the Shīʿah community. It is the women who articulate these stories in the ceremonies of *taʿzīyah* (mourning or compassion) in large community meetings attended by women. In the public space, men march in procession and ritually beat their breasts or use chains to strike their backs to a rhythmic chant. These women reciters are talented performers, and their skills at retelling the history of these early events makes the hearers live again the agony of deception and woe that gave birth to their alternative vision of Islamic belief. They draw on the fact that it was women who were eyewitnesses to the original martyrdom and who could then relay the message to believers. In effect, it was women who guaranteed that a crucial part of Islamic history was preserved and remembered, and their importance is highlighted in Shīʿah Islam.

Finally, there are rites throughout the Islamic world that provide an outlet for women exclusively; examples of this are the *zār* in Egypt or the Gnawa *derdeba* in Morocco. Both of these rites feature women in trance, and both are critiqued as extra-canonical by the orthodox. Both are regarded as healing rites directed specifically at women. In the *zār*, rituals of trance are carried out for women who require some type of healing. These feature *dhikr*-type rites, led by women, with music inducing the candidate into a trance in which she makes contact with a spiritual force that provides healing. The Gnawa, a people of exclusively African origin in Morocco, have developed a distinctive type of Ṣūfī ceremony designed for the transference of spiritual power and the exorcism of evil. In this ceremony, a candidate responds to the music by dancing in trance, and during the rite, she encounters spiritual forces while under the trance. A long popular history also exists of women associated with rites of exorcism, black magic, and rites associated with the evil eye.

These are but a few of the ways that one can conceive of the roles of rites in Muslim women's lives; they speak to a complex life lived under the umbrella that is Islam. It points to porous boundaries and many variations within Islamic ritual sensitivity and its related embodiment of proper Islamic moral rectitude.

Bibliography

Abbas, Shemeem Burney. *The Female Voice in Sufi Ritual: Devotional Practices of Pakistan and India*. Oxford and New York: Oxford University Press, 2003.

Abbas, Shemeem Burney. "Sakineh[PB1]: The Narrator of Kerbala: An Ethnographic Description of Women's *Majles* Ritual in Pakistan." In *The Women of Kerbala: Ritual Performance and Symbolic Discourse in Modern Shiʿi Islam*, edited by Kamran Scot Aghaie. Austin: University of Texas Press, 2005.

Ahmad, Amineh. "Women's Agency in Muslim Society." In *The Sage Handbook of Islamic Studies*, edited by Akbar S. Ahmed and Tamara Sonn, pp. 213–239. London: SAGE, 2010.

Badran, Margot. *Feminism in Islam: Secular and Religious Convergences*. Oxford and New York: Oxford University Press, 2009.

Caprioni, Elena, and Eva Sajoo. "Gender and Identity." In *A Companion to Muslim Cultures*, edited by Amyn B. Sajoo, pp. 77–102. London: I.B. Tauris, 2012.

Dogan, Recep. "Is Honor Killing a 'Muslim Phenomenon'? Textual Interpretation and Cultural Representations." *Journal of Muslim Minority Affairs* 31, no.r 3 (September 2011): 423–440.

Esposito, John, and Yvonne Yazbeck Haddad. *Muslims on the Americanization Path?* Oxford and New York: Oxford University Press, 2000.

Ghadially, Rehana. "Gender and Moharram Rituals in an Isma'ili sect of South Asian Muslims." In *The Women of Karbala: Ritual Performance and Symbolic Discourses in Modern Shi'i Islam*, edited by Kamran Scot Aghaie, pp. 183–198. Austin: University of Texas Press, 2005.

Griffith, Ruth Marie, and Barbara Dianne Savage. *Women and Religion in the African Diaspora: Knowledge, Power, and Performance.* Baltimore, Md.: Johns Hopkins University Press, 2006.

Hoffman-Ladd, Valerie J. "Women and Islam: Women's Religious Observances." In *The Oxford Encyclopedia of the Modern Islamic World*, Vol. 4, edited by John L. Esposito, pp. 327–331. Oxford and New York: Oxford University Press, 1995.

Islamic Beliefs, Practices, and Cultures. Tarrytown, N.Y.: Marshall Cavendish, 2010.

Mageed, Dina Abdel. "Divorce a Labyrinth for Arab Wives." http://worldmuslimcongress.blobspot.ca/2007/03/divorce-arab-wives.html.

Rahman, Fazlur. *Health and Medicine in the Islamic Tradition: Change and Identity.* New York: Kazi, 1987.

Sengers, Gerda. *Women and Demons: Cultic Healing in Islamic Egypt.* Leiden, Netherlands: E. J. Brill, 2002.

Smith, Antar Ibn Stanford. *Muslim Names and Birth Rites.* Jackson, Mich.: Qur'anic Civilization Association, 1985.

Smith, Jane I., and Yvonne Yazbeck Haddad. *The Islamic Understanding of Death and Resurrection.* Oxford and New York: Oxford University Press, 2006.

Sultanova, Razia. *From Shamanism to Sufism: Women, Islam and Culture in Central Asia.* London: I. B. Tauris, 2011.

Waugh, Earle H. *Memory, Music and Religion: Morocco's Mystical Chanters.* Columbia: University of South Carolina Press, 2005.

Waugh, Earle H. *Visionaries of Silence: The Reformist Sufi Order of the Khalwatiya al-Demirdashiya of Cairo.* Cairo: American University in Cairo Press, 2008.

Waugh, Earle H., and Frank Reynolds, eds. *Religious Encounters with Death.* University Park: Pennsylvania State University Press, 1977.

EARLE WAUGH

ROSTAMANI, AMINA AL-. Influential business leader in the Middle East. Amina al-Rostamani is the CEO of TECOM Business Parks, the umbrella organization for nine of Dubai's free zones. Listed among Arabian Business.com's 100 most powerful Arab women in the Arab world, al-Rostamani rose from rank 80 to 69 in 2010 and then to 9 in 2011. A total of fifteen Emirati women were included in the list for 2011.

Al-Rostamani joined TECOM in 2001 as a project engineer for Samacom, the satellite communication services provider of the Dubai Holding Group. Then, as director of broadcasting for Dubai Media City, she developed the design and oversaw the implementation of satellite TV broadcasting and video-encoding facilities for broadcasters in Dubai Media City. In 2005 al-Rostamani was appointed executive director of media for TECOM Investments under the directive of Sheikh Muḥammad Rāshid bin Saʿīd Āl- Maktūm, crown prince/? of Dubai.

As CEO of TECOM Business Parks, al-Rostamani oversees Dubai Internet City, Dubai Media City, Dubai Knowledge Village, Dubai Studio City, Dubai Knowledge Village, International Media Production Zone, DuBiotech, Dubai Outsource Zone, Dubai International Academic City, and Enpark. A board member of the Dubai International Film Festival (DIFF), al-Rostamani is working to make Dubai a global hub for the movie industry. As of 2006, Dubai Media City includes more than 120 publishing houses. Dubai Studio City boasts fourteen sound stages, a 3.5 million square foot back lot for outdoor shooting, commercial offices, pre-built studios, a business center, and post-production studios. As of 2008, Studio City had become a virtual souk for industry professionals from around the world, a place to convene and trade. Al-Rostamani is also a board member of the UAE National Media

Council, which regulates the media sector in the United Arab Emirates (UAE).

Beyond developing and diversifying the economy, creating jobs, and enhancing prospects for tourism, al-Rostamani has a drive to develop and empower a specific aspect of a knowledge economy. Her vision is to bring together cultures, a subject she had addressed in several presentations at film festivals where she promoted the idea of "building cultures, meeting minds." She also strives to develop new young talent in the filmmaking industry.

Al-Rostamani's entrepreneurial accomplishments are significant to the region as women have only recently risen to such large-scale leadership positions. She is a resounding example for aspiring young women, especially in the business world. Her vision of women's participation in the development of the economy and other fields also guides her support. In 2005 she inaugurated the Dubai Ladies Club exhibition that featured the work of five Emirati women who produced art from traditional and contemporary materials. She has played a significant role in establishing the Dubai International Film Festival and strives to showcase the works of talented Emirati filmmakers. She has further demonstrated to others how a woman can lead a major corporation through a time of economic crisis with a belief in herself and relying on qualities usually not demonstrated by her male counterparts.

In addition, al-Rostamani has attained several notable academic achievements, receiving a BS, MS, and DSc degree in electrical engineering from George Washington University, Washington, D.C. She is an acknowledged authority on wireless technologies and parts of her PhD dissertation have been published in leading engineering journals, such as the *IEEE Transactions on Communications* and the *IEEE Journal in Selected Areas in Communications.*

BIBLIOGRAPHY

"100 Most Powerful Arab Women 2011. No. 9: Dr Amina Al Rostamani." http://arabianbusiness.com/100-moset-powerful-arab-women-2011-384182.html.

"Dr. Amina Al Rustamani Appointed Executive Director of Dubai Media City." *Middle East Print Communication Magazine*, July 23, 2005. http://www.meprinter.com/EN/News/Show.asp?Id=236.

"DSC Launches Online Film Souk." February 25, 2008. http://www.tradearabia.com/news/MEDIA_139254.html.

al-Rustamani, Amina, Branimir Vojcic, and Andrej Stefanov. "Greedy Detection." *Journal of VLSI Signal Processing Systems* 30, no. 1–3 (February 2002): 179–195.

WANDA KRAUSE

ROXELANA, HÜRREM. (c. 1505–1558), legendary wife of the sixteenth-century Ottoman emperor Sulaymān I, the Magnificent (r. 1520–1566). Roxelana was born in western Ukraine, then a part of Poland, and originally named Aleksandra Lisowska. She was captured by Tatar raiders and brought as a concubine to the Ottoman harem in 1520, where she was converted to Islam and was given the name Hürrem, which represented her lively and joyful nature. Soon she became the Sultan's favorite concubine, *haseki*, bearing him four sons and a daughter and outshining his former one, Mahidevran, the mother of his firstborn son, Muṣṭafā. This marked a breach in the imperial harem code, as concubines were not allowed the opportunity to bear more than one son, and concubines who already had a son were required to accompany him to provincial posts in due time. The purpose of sending the son to a provincial post was to allow him to gain practical administrative experience while preventing the mother from having too much influence over the father (the reigning sultan) by trying to sway him in favor of one son over another. Hürrem was exempted from these rules.

These concessions granted to Hürrem by the sultan, as well as his decision to accept monogamy and take Hürrem as his wedded wife, for the first time in Ottoman royal history, generated rumors about Hürrem being a schemer and a sorceress who, with all her intrigues and witchcraft, would eventually bring about the decline of the Ottoman Empire. These rumors have successively filled the records of the Western ambassadors to the Ottoman lands of the time, the pages of history books, and finally of history novels and plays from the East and the West alike, which often portray Hürrem as an insatiably power-greedy woman who held a tight grip on her husband, manipulated his political decisions, and defied the norms of the imperial court. Speculations of this sort focus primarily on the growing tension and competition between Hürrem and some of the most beloved and respected figures in the sultan's life, such as his mother, Hafsa Hatun, his former *haseki* Mahidevran, his first son, Muṣṭafā, and his successful grand vizier Ibrāhīm Pasha who was his best friend and loyal companion at times of war and peace. The unexpected murder of Ibrāhīm Pasha in 1536 and the execution of *şehzade* Muṣṭafā in 1553, at the order of the sultan, upon his suspicion of conspiracy, are often attributed to the intrigues of Hürrem and her intricate network of informants and allies, including her son-in-law Rüstem Pasha who held the position of grand vizier from 1544 to 1553 and then from 1555 to 1561. Hürrem is said to have reached her goal of becoming *valide sultan*, the mother of a sultan, when her son Selim ascended the Ottoman throne after Sulaymān's death in 1566 and ruled as Selim II until his death in 1574.

Considering that life in the harem was inaccessible to the outside world and the portrayal of Hürrem in the diplomatic, historical, and fictional texts since her time must be largely based on imagination rather than facts, today's scholars and writers explore why Hürrem figured in the works of traditional writers and scholars the way she did, namely as a woman with immense but disruptive power, one who paved the way for the so-called Sultanate of Women such as Safiye Sultan (1550–1605) or Kösem Sultan (c. 1589–1651), which they often associate with the decline of the empire. Although these women did not rule directly, their influence over the ruling sultans was such that the title "sultan" was associated with their names. Contemporary literature and scholarship focus on how even such traditional approaches, either consciously or inadvertently, point to the repressive aspects of the imperial order, especially as manifested in the codes of the harem, which prevented men and women from actualizing their potential as individuals—including the sultans, let alone the women in the harem. Reading between the lines, Hürrem emerges as a woman who had insight into her husband's dilemmas—his determination to expand Ottoman territories and resources on one hand, and his love of nature, arts, and poetry on the other—and who stimulated both his desires as an emperor and as a man with emotions who would rather have a kindred soul as a spouse than merely a subject. The glory of Sulaymān's reign, during which the empire reached its greatest heights, finds its counterpart in the glory of Hürrem Sultan, who still inspires writers as well as scholars of history, literature, and culture.

BIBLIOGRAPHY

İnalcık, Halil, and Cemal Kafadar, eds. *Süleymân the Second and His Time*. Istanbul: Isis Press, 1993.

Peirce, Leslie P. *The Imperial Harem: Women and Sovereignty in the Ottoman Empire*. New York: Oxford University Press, 1993.

Yermolenko, Galina, ed. *Roxolana in European Literature and Culture*. Burlington, Vt.: Ashgate Press, 2010.

ÖZLEM ÖĞÜT YAZICIOĞLU

S

Saʿdāwī, Nawāl al-. Nawāl al-Saʿdāwī (b. 1931) is a leading feminist of the Arab world. Al-Saʿdāwī evokes more passion and controversy than any other Arab writer, male or female, inside or outside of the Middle East. At various times, she has been subject to governmental harassment and arrest, or, conversely, the recipient of special protective measures. Her diverse career as a writer, feminist activist, and physician has brought her international fame as well as political adversity in her native country of Egypt.

Born in 1931 in the village of Kafr Ṭaḥlah in the Egyptian Delta, al-Saʿdāwī studied medicine in Cairo. As a physician she has practiced in the areas of public health, thoracic medicine, and psychiatry. In 1982, she founded the Arab Women's Solidarity Association (AWSA), with its official organ, Nūn, devoted to women's issues and feminist politics. She was appointed Egypt's minister of health in 1958, but was dismissed from that post in 1972 because of her frank writings on the sexuality of Arab women. In 1981, when the regime of President Anwar el-Sadat imprisoned numerous intellectuals of different political persuasions, al-Saʿdāwī found herself sharing prison accommodations with both leftists and Islamists. Her name has appeared on a death list drawn up by Islamic opposition groups. The assassination of the secularist Faraj Fawdah in 1992 sent shock waves through the Egyptian secular intellectual community and prompted government protection of intellectuals, al-Saʿdāwī among them. That same year, she lost a court case contesting the governmental closing of AWSA and the diversion of its funds to the Association of the Women of Islam. Nūn had been shut down a few months earlier, thus censoring an important source of feminist theory and criticism.

These political setbacks have not kept al-Saʿdāwī from indulging in her favorite activity: writing. The life of the pen has always had a greater attraction for the feminist physician than the life of the scalpel. Her extensive literary corpus covers a wide range of prose genres: novels, short stories, drama, travel and prison memoirs, and programmatic works. She wrote her first novel, *Mudhakkirāt ṭiflah ismuhā Suʿad* (Memoirs of a Girl Called Suʿād), at the age of thirteen. Her most recent novel, *Al-ḥubb fī zaman al-nafṭ* (Love in the Time of Oil, 1993), like all her writings, reflects her deep commitment to exposing gender inequality and the hardships endured by Arab women. Al-Saʿdāwī tackles difficult subjects with a frankness few Arab writers display, forcefully illuminating sexuality, gender roles, and male/female relations in Arab society in a straightforward, accessible prose. Much in her fiction revolves around the body, and powerful physical images permeate her writings.

Al-Saʿdāwī has gained an international readership and is perhaps the most visible of modern Arabic writers. *The Hidden Face of Eve* is a classic in the West. Her popularity in the West has meant that many of her works have been translated into several European languages, and her novels have received a number of international awards. Consequently, she has been accused by some of writing for a Western audience. But anyone familiar with al-Saʿdāwī's writings recognizes that they only make sense within an Arab-Islamic cultural context. Her plots, her linguistic games, her literary allusions, her religious-legal intertextual references are all part of what makes Nawāl al-Saʿdāwī a powerful Arab- and Arabic-writer.

[*See also* Feminism.]

BIBLIOGRAPHY

cooke, miriam. *Women Claim Islam: Creating Islamic Feminism through Literature*. London: Routledge, 2000.

Malti-Douglas, Fedwa. *Men, Women, and God(s): Nawal El Sadawi Writes Arab Feminism*. Berkeley, 1995. In-depth analysis of al-Saʿdāwī's literary writings.

Malti-Douglas, Fedwa. *Woman's Body, Woman's Word: Gender and Discourse in Arabo-Islamic Writing*. Princeton, 1991. Discusses al-Saʿdāwī's fiction and sets it in the broader context of corporality and Arabo-Islamic prose, classical and modern.

Saadawi, Nawal El. *A Daughter of Isis: The Autobiography of Nawal El Saadawi*. London: Zed Books, 1999.

Saadawi, Nawal El. *The Hidden Face of Eve: Women in the Arab World*. Translated by Sherif Hetata. London: Zed Press, 1980. Classic work on the status of women and Arab feminism; originally published in Arabic as *Al-Wajh al-ʿĀrī lil-Marʾah al-ʿArabīyah*.

Saadawi, Nawal El. *The Nawal El Saadawi Reader*. London: Zed Books, 1997.

Saadawi, Nawal El, and Sherif Hetata. *Walking through Fire: A Life of Nawal El Saadawi*. London: Zed Books, 2002.

Ṭarābīshī, Jurj. *Woman against Her Sex: A Critique of Nawal el-Saadawi*. Translated from the Arabic by Basil Hatim and Elisabeth Orsini. London, 1988. Translation of a psychoanalytic work very critical of al-Saʿdāwī's positions. Al-Saʿdāwī appended a response to the English translation.

FEDWA MALTI-DOUGLAS

ṢAFAVID DYNASTY. The Ṣafavid dynasty ruled Iran from 1501, the year Shāh Ismāʿīl I declared Tabrīz his capital and Twelver Shiism the religion of his realm, until 1722 CE, when a small band of invading Afghan tribesmen captured its capital, Isfahan. In these two centuries, the Ṣafavids evolved from a tribal band of warriors imbued with a mystical interpretation of Islam and guided by Turco-Mongol principles to a bureaucratic fiscal state following Iranian nonmigratory patterns and professing an increasingly exclusionary form of Twelver Shiism. Almost all the sources available for the period, both indigenous and foreign, are written by men, look at Iranian society from an urban-based male perspective, and thus pay almost no attention to women, who were much less visible in public life than men. The result is that we know little about the life and activities of upper-class women, less about ordinary women, and almost nothing about women in the rural parts of the country.

Court Women. The available sources suggest that court women played a role of importance from the beginning of Ṣafavid rule. Foreign observers claim that the women in the entourage of Shāh Ismāʿīl were highly visible and even took part in combat, causing modern scholars to argue that women were rather free and unencumbered during the early period. In keeping with the evolution of the Ṣafavids from a semi-nomadic tribal disposition along Turco-Mongol lines to a more restrictive urban-centered polity, the public role of women did narrow over time—with the clerically instigated restrictions imposed on women at the accession of Shāh Sultan Ḥusayn in 1694, prohibiting them from going out in public without male supervision, as the signal moment. There are good reasons to doubt that women literally participated in armed combat. European visitors who saw unveiled women on horseback accompanying the shah and called them royal women may have been confused, not recognizing the difference between court women who were secluded starting at an early age, and the prostitutes and dancing girls who invariably were part of the entourage of the shah and other dignitaries.

As elsewhere, elite women were central to sexual politics, solidifying alliances through marriage arrangements. Before they attained political power, the Ṣafavids themselves had married into the house of Uzun Ḥasan, the ruler of the dynasty they would overthrow. Mahdi ʿUlyā (Khayr al-Nisāʾ Begam), the wife of the dynasty's fourth ruler, Muḥammad Khudābanda, came from the ruling family of Māzandarān, thus strengthening the ties between the court and this region. Ṣafavid women were also given in marriage to local rulers as a reward for submitting to Ṣafavid rule, as was the case with the daughter of Amira Dubaj, the ruler of Gilan. Over time, marriage to members of the regional dynasty of Georgia became common, to the point where, in the seventeenth century, most royal wives and concubines were of Georgian (and Circassian) background. So as to strengthen ties with the religious classes, the shah and the elite also increasingly married into them.

In keeping with the Islamic custom whereby married women retain possession of the property they bring to a marriage, elite women also are known to have endowed property for religious purposes, focusing on the feeding of the poor, pilgrims, and students, especially in the late seventeenth century. A large portion of the Ṣafavid ancestral shrine of Ardabīl was thus endowed by women. Females are known, too, to have endowed villages, caravanserais, and bridges.

Examples of high-ranking women wielding considerable political power may be found throughout the period. Court women were taught to read and write, and some are known to have cultivated an interest in the arts, including calligraphy and poetry. Some also exchanged letters with their husbands, fathers, and sons, as well as with court women in the Ottoman Empire.

The most prominent woman of rank in the sixteenth century is Parī Khān Khānum (1548–1578). This favorite daughter of Shāh Ṭahmāsp (r. 1524–1576), born of a Circassian mother, managed to take control of the court after her father's death, plotting to help her brother Ismāʿīl Mīrzā assume the throne, while trying to have her other brother, Ḥamza Mīrzā, killed. Once Ismāʿīl mounted the throne as Ismāʿīl II (r. 1576–1578), he sought to neutralize her influence. She survived him, nevertheless, and continued to serve as de facto ruler until 1578, when she was assassinated at the behest of Mahdi ʿUlyā, the wife of the new shah, Muḥammad Khudābanda (r. 1578–1587).

Taking advantage of the partial blindness of her husband, the ambitious Mahdi ʿUlyā next took the reins of power and soon entered into conflict with the powerful Qizilbash, the Turcoman tribesmen who formed the backbone of Ṣafavid military power and who resented her pro-Tajik (ethnic Iranian) policy. Following accusations of sexual indecency, they called for her execution, which occurred by strangulation in 1578.

Important changes took place under Shāh ʿAbbās (1587–1629), the dynasty's most powerful ruler. The most important of these, a shift away from succession on the basis of collective legitimacy toward a more fixed patrilineage, restricted direct female access to power. Yet another development, the practice of immuring the heir-to be in the palace, which was instituted by Shāh ʿAbbās I, increased the importance of the harem as the center of power. The two developments combined to lessen the influence of daughters and sisters and to increase the role of aunts and great aunts and especially of queen-mothers as powerbrokers. The power of the latter was enhanced by the fact that she served as the patron of the Armenian suburb of New Jolfa. The first representative of the shah's new order was Zaynab Begam, a daughter of Shāh Ṭahmāsp and an aunt of Shāh ʿAbbās, whose advice the latter is said to have valued above anyone else's. Another example is Anna Khānum, the mother of Shāh ʿAbbās II (r. 1642–1666), who wielded power as a member of a ruling troika for the first years of her underage son's reign. The women and eunuchs of the harem are said to have formed a pacifist camp and, as such, they became in part responsible for the peace of Zuhāb of 1639, which terminated almost a century and a half of warfare with the Ottomans.

Increasingly the locus of power, the royal harem grew to enormous proportions, reportedly housing up to one thousand women under the last two shahs, Sulaymān (1666–1694), and even more under Sultan Ḥusayn (1694–1722). The former was persuaded by his mother, Nekahat Khānum, to give up the profligacy that nearly bankrupted the court in the early days of his rule. Maryam Begum, the great-aunt of the latter, wielded such extraordinary power at the court that she virtually controlled her feeble great-nephew until her death at an advanced age in 1720. It was she who quelled a court revolt against the shah in 1717, and it was at her behest that, after much dithering, the shah eventually mounted a campaign against Baluchi and Afghan invaders. Upon her death, she left the enormous sum of 200,000 tumans in cash, aside from vast amounts of jewelry, gold, silver, and landed property. Both women are known to have financed pious endowments.

Ordinary Women. The sources yield little information about ordinary women. The glimpses we get of rural and, especially, tribal women suggest that they were typically not veiled and that they were very active in the labor force, participating in agricultural activities and buying and selling in the market. It appears that urban females were veiled, in the early period as much as in the waning days of Ṣafavid rule, with Muslim women wearing a full cover whereas Armenian women covered their faces only up to their noses with the so-called *yagmaq*. Zoroastrian women, too, were not as heavily veiled as Muslim women.

Urban centers were also home to a large number of prostitutes, their ranks swollen by the ease of divorce and the destitution it brought for many women. Isfahan alone in the seventeenth century is said to have counted some twelve thousand. "High-class" courtesans rode horses, with their faces unveiled, and are said to have led lives of opulence. Much more numerous were the bedraggled women who were offered at prostitution markets in urban centers. Rather than leading a furtive existence, they were licensed and taxed.

[*See also* Iran.]

BIBLIOGRAPHY

Aubin, Jean. "L'avènement des Safavides reconsidéré." *Moyen Orient et Océan Indien* 5 (1988): 1–130.

Babaie, Sussan, et al. *Slaves of the Shah: New Elites of Safavid Iran*. London and New York: I.B. Tauris, 2004.

Babayan, Kathryn. "The "Aqa'id al-Nisa': A Glimpse at Safavid Women in Local Isfahani Culture." In *Women in the Medieval Islamic World*, edited by Gavin R. G. Hambly, pp. 349–382. New York: Palgrave, 1998.

Babayan, Kathryn. *Mystics, Monarchs, and Messiahs: Cultural Landscapes of Early Modern Iran*. Cambridge, Mass.: Harvard University Press, 2003.

Birjandifar, Nazak. "Royal Women and Politics in Safavid Iran." MA thesis, McGill University, Montreal, 2006.

Diba, Layla S. "Lifting the Veil of Depiction: The Representation of Women in Persian Painting." In *Women in Iran: From the Rise of Islam to 1800*, edited by Guity Nashat and Lois Beck, pp. 206–236. Urbana and Chicago: University of Illinois Press, 2003.

Ferrier, Ronald. "Women in Safavid Iran: The Evidence of European Travelers." In *Women in the Medieval Islamic World*, edited by Gavin R. G. Hambly, pp. 383–406. New York: Palgrave, 1998.

Golsorkhi, Shohreh. "Pari Khan Khanum: A Masterful Safavid Princess." *Iranian Studies* 28 (1995): 143–156.

Matthee, Rudi. "Courtesans, Prostitutes and Dancing Girls: Women Entertainers in Safavid Iran." In *Iran and Beyond: Essays in Middle Eastern History in Honor of Nikki R. Keddie*, edited by Rudi Matthee and Beth Baron, pp. 121–150. Costa Mesa, Calif.: Mazda, 2000.

Matthee, Rudi. "From the Battlefield to the Harem: Did Women's Seclusion Increase from Early to Late Safavid Iran?" In *New Perspectives on Safavid Iran: Empire and Society*, edited by Colin P. Mitchell, pp. 97–120. New York: Routledge, 2011.

Matthee, Rudi. *Persia in Crisis: Safavid Decline and the Fall of Isfahan*. London: I.B. Tauris, 2012.

Rizvi, Kishwar. "Gendered Patronage: Women and Benevolence during the Early Safavid Empire." In *Women, Patronage, and Self-Representation in Islamic Societies*, edited by D. F. Ruggles, pp. 123–153. Albany: State University of New York Press, 2000.

Szuppe, Maria. "The 'Jewels of Wonder': Learned Ladies and Princess Politics in the Provinces of Early Safavid Iran." In *Women in the Medieval Islamic World*, edited by Gavin R. G. Hambly, pp. 325–348. New York: Palgrave, 1998.

Szuppe, Maria. "La participation des femmes de la famille royale à l'exercice du pouvoir en Iran safavide au XVIe siècle." *Studia Iranica* 23 (1994): 211–258; 24 (1995): 61–122.

Szuppe, Maria. "Status, Knowledge, and Politics: Women in Sixteenth-Century Safavid Iran." In *Women in Iran: From the Rise of Islam to 1800*, edited by Guity Nashat and Lois Beck, pp. 140–169. Urbana and Chicago: University of Illinois Press, 2003.

Zarinebaf-Shahr, Fariba. "Economic Activities of Safavid Women in the Shrine-City of Ardabil." *Iranian Studies* 31 (1998): 247–261.

BIANCAMARIA SCARCIA AMORETTI
Updated by RUDOLPH MATTHEE

SAINTHOOD. Sainthood in Islam could be compared to the station of *insān al-kāmil* (the perfect human being) or of *walī* (the friend of God). Piety, mercy, purity, gnosis, and self-restraint are among the characteristics denoting a *walī*. Ṣūfī literature mainly deals with the *walī*'s acts and teachings, so that the terms "saint" and "Ṣūfī mystic" are often used interchangeably. Nevertheless, a saint is not always a Ṣūfī mystic, such as in the case of the personalities from the early history of Islam, like the Prophet's mother Āmīnah and his daughter Fatima, or other leading religious personalities in Islamic history. Moreover, the definition of the saint and his or her status is complex and controversial because, in Sunnī Islam, it is established informally by local and popular recognition.

Scholars agree in reporting the openness of Ṣūfī intellectual and mystical traditions toward women's access to the state of sainthood. Several Ṣūfī masters stressed that "any woman who engages in the Path of Divine Love is not to be deemed female" but rather to be judged only by her humanity (Nurbakhsh, 1980, p. 12). Regarding the gender to be attributed to a *walī*, the famous Ṣūfī master Fāriḍ al-Dīn ʿAṭṭār reported a *ḥadīth* according to which the Prophet claimed: "Do not look at a person's outward appearance but rather consider his good actions and his goodwill." Fāriḍ al-Dīn ʿAṭṭār (1976) pointed out that all women who practice mercy and worship are accredited to the Court of the Highest Lord, so that, as men of the elite, we cannot address them as women. This statement was made in reference to Rābiʿah al-ʿAdawīyah, a former slave who became one of the most popular saints in Islam. Introducing into Ṣūfism the idea of absolute Love for God, Rābiʿah al-ʿAdawīyah, who lived apart in the seclusion of holiness and extreme poverty, became the model of mercy and love of God. Other examples of female mystics are reported especially during the early history of Islam when Ṣūfī movements were characterized by ascetic life through practices such as fasting, seclusion, prolonged prayers, and vigils. Some of these individuals gained the title of "fool" (*majnuna*), because of their "foolish" love for God, a common theme in Ṣūfī literature; others were believed to perform miracles (*karāmāt*), gaining respect and veneration among believers. Among these Ṣūfī personalities, there were some who became famous not only for their sainthood, but also for their knowledge of religious sciences, becoming teachers and religious leaders.

Scattolin (1993) pointed out some general characteristics belonging to female Ṣūfī saints recorded in historical sources. First of all, several examples show an extreme asceticism that garnered them high respect within their community and a degree of freedom far beyond the restrictions of Islamic law pertaining to women. Second, several chose celibacy, gaining more freedom and autonomy. Even when these female saints married, it is recorded that they avoided sexual relations. They also denied their female nature through biological signs such as amenorrhea. By arresting their menstrual cycle, they overcame the source of ritual impurity for women. The last characteristic is that of mystical love, which is the real goal of the Ṣūfī spiritual way. According to other authors, like Amber (2009) and Coulon (1988), women could be recognized as saints and impose their leadership within Ṣūfī brotherhoods, thanks to their *barakah* (blessing), knowledge, purity, and the image of the ideal woman.

Even if the mystical way is open to every human being without distinction of gender, class, or race, fewer female saints and Ṣūfī women are recorded in historical sources compared to their male counterparts and they are not included in the genealogies of the main Ṣūfī brotherhoods.

Popular in the early history of Islam, later emerging personalities were less known until recent times. From the Maghreb and sub-Saharan Africa to Asia, several female leading personalities or saints are reported to have gained a high position only in the nineteenth and twentieth centuries in Islamic societies. Their roles appear particularly relevant within Ṣūfī sects where we can find many examples of female saints. Like their masculine counterparts, their role is strongly entwined with the concepts of wealth, power, and knowledge. Within nineteenth-century Islamic renewal, they assumed a leadership role within Ṣūfī orders in Africa and beyond, often as a result of particular circumstances, such as internal conflicts within the *ṭarīqah* of male elites or the absence of male family members to manage the Ṣūfī center. When they were alive, all saints were believed to have *barakah* (blessings) and to perform miracles (*karāmāt*). Women leaders at Ṣūfī centers are described either as active female Muslim leaders or as agents integrating non-Islamic elements within their Ṣūfī centers.

When saints' charisma gains regional popularity, their teachings are often transmitted through mystical poems, songs, dances, and music—that is to say, through a wide and heterogeneous variety of religious practices. Around these charismatic personalities and their holy shrines, some communities and solidarity networks were often established, such as charities and informal institutions.

Practices. Some scholars prefer to underscore the difference between a Muslim saint and a Ṣūfī, especially when the issue of the cult of saints is addressed. As Reeves (1995) pointed out, even if the Muslim cult of saints and Ṣūfī brotherhoods are two historically related topics, in some cases the cult of the saint could involve a broader part of the population than the Ṣūfī sects. Moreover, while Muslim saints have often been initiated into one or more Ṣūfī brotherhoods, their followers could eventually belong to anyone of them.

A popular practice in Muslim societies is pious visitation of living or dead saints, the so-called *ziyārah*. Despite theological critics who target this practice, people often make *ziyārah* to visit Ṣūfī *shaykhs* and leading Muslim personalities because they are believed to have *barakah*, a beneficent force of divine origin that may lead to prosperity and wealth. Through *ziyārah*, believers hope to receive blessings, as well as relief, instructions, or answers to their requests. The saint's residence, or his or her shrine after death, could become the center of a regional cult where gatherings and religious practices are performed. Attendance at these gatherings is considered to have therapeutic value in resolving personal troubles. Several scholars have discussed whether *ziyārah* practices were especially attractive to women. Certain holy places or saints became the focus of women's piety where they could perform parallel and often sexually segregated practices, "which alternately earned them praise or condemnation from legalists" (Cuffel, 2005, p. 401). Cuffel also pointed out how the widespread criticism in medieval sources of women holding interfaith celebrations at holy shrines was a discourse designed to "denigrate these practices and discourage women and men from participating in them" (p. 401). Other academic researchers questioned the tendency of some scholarly and theological critics to claim the "unorthodoxy" of women's practices at shrines. This is the case of ecstatic dances and possession rituals, such as *zār-ḥaḍrah* sessions in North East Africa, which are the target of legalists' critics. Coulon (1988) pointed out that women have the capability to participate in Islamic practices, manipulating and adapting them according to their needs. In participating within Ṣūfī groups and cultic religious practices, women could gain more freedom and agency. Some practices performed at holy shrines and sanctuaries involve exclusively feminine communities while crossing their religious affiliations. Women's devotion to certain holy shrines was the result of their connection with childcare and birth. In fact, some sanctuaries are devoted to solving fertility and sexual problems in several Islamic societies and beyond. Mernissi (1977) pointed out how, in the Maghreb, the visit to a sanctuary is among the rare situations in which women are not in a subordinate position. Within the sanctuaries, women can create an exclusively female collective endeavor, a "therapeutic network of communication among them" (p. 104). Such a gathering stimulates their "energies against their discontent and allows them to bathe in an intrinsically female community of soothers, supporters, and advisors." According to Mernissi, the sanctuary should be viewed as "an informal women's association" (p. 105). As observation of these women's communities affiliated with several cults of saints in the Maghreb and North East Africa shows that religious gatherings at holy shrines or the residences of living saints may be sexually mixed and not necessarily based on gender.

Still, we may take notice of living saints who attract believers, as well as troubled or sick people, during the *ziyārah*. When a saint dies, his or her shrines are considered blessed places where pilgrims perform *ḥaḍrah* sessions and chant *dhikr*, seeking the saint's *barakāt* (blessings).

BIBLIOGRAPHY

ʿAṭṭār, Fāriḍ al-Dīn. *Le mémorial des saints*. Paris: Seuil, 1976.

Bruzzi, Silvia, and Meron Zeleke. "Women Religious Leaders: A Comparative Study on Sufi Shrines in Eritrea and Ethiopia." *Northeast African Studies* 12, no. 2 (2012).

Clancy-Smith, Julia. "The House of Zainab: Female Authority and Saintly Succession in Colonial Algeria." In *Women in Middle Eastern History*, edited by Nikki R. Keddie and Beth Baron, pp. 254–274. New Haven, Conn., and London: Yale University Press, 1992.

Coulon, Christian. "Women, Islam and Baraka." In *Charisma and Brotherhood in African Islam*, edited by Donal B. Cruise O'Brien and Christine Coulon, pp. 113–133. Oxford: Clarendon, 1988.

Cuffel, Alexandra. "From Practice to Polemic: Shared Saints and Festivals as 'Women's Religion' in the Medieval Mediterranean." *Bulletin of the School of Oriental and African Studies* 68, no. 3 (2005): 401–419.

Gemmeke, Amber B. "Marabout Women in Dakar: Creating Authority in Islamic Knowledge." *Africa* 79, no. 1 (2009): 128–147.

Gürsoy-Naskali, Emine. "Women Mystics in Islam." In *Women in Islamic Societies*, edited by Bo Utas, pp. 238–243. London: Curzon, 1983.

Mernissi, Fatima. "Women, Saints, and Sanctuaries." *Signs* 3, no. 1 (1977): 101–112. Journal available in book form as *Women and National Development: The Complexities of Change* from University of Chicago Press.

Nurbakhsh, Javad. *Sufi Women.* 2nd Rev. ed. London New York: Khaniqahi-Nimatullahi, 1990.

Reeves, E. "Power, Resistance, and the Cult of Muslim Saints in a Northern Egyptian Town." *American Ethnologist* 22, vol. 2 (1995): 306–323.

Scattolin, Giuseppe. "Women in Islamic Mysticism." *Encounter* 198 (October 1993): 3–26.

Schimmel, Annemarie. *My Soul Is a Woman: The Feminine in Islam.* New York: Continuum, 2003.

Smith, Margareth. *Rabi'a the Mystic and Her Fellow-Saints in Islam.* Cambridge, UK, and New York: Cambridge University Press, 1984. Originally published in 1928.

SILVIA BRUZZI

SALAFI GROUPS. In "Women in Islamist Movements: Toward an Islamist Model of Women's Activism," Omayma Abdellatif and Marina Ottaway (2007) make the crucial but often forgotten point that female activists are of great importance in the Islamic political and social realm because they represent almost 50 percent of the population across the Middle East. As such, Muslim women represent, and will continue to represent, an already potent resource—particularly as participants in the continually changing sphere of twenty-first-century Islamic social dynamics, including in the realm of Salafism.

Salafism, in the strictest sense of the word, advocates a return to the first generation of Muslims (the Salaf, or pious leaders) and a period of history that was considered to be the pristine time of Islam characterized by an uncorrupted religious community. Islam is thought to have entered decline after the period of the Rightly Guided Caliphs due to the un-Islamic innovations that were introduced, particularly through Islam's historical encounter with the West. Those who seek a return to the first generation of Islam are known as Salafis, and they are said to desire a purge of these un-Islamic influences. Wiktorowicz (2001) explains this as reliance only on those who learned Islam directly from the Prophet or from those who knew him, which the Salafis believe grants them a pure understanding of religion.

While Wiktorowicz notes that the contemporary Salafi movement represents the most recent resurgence of puritanical reformism, Haykel (2009) and Bakr (2012) believe that this modern Salafist landscape is rife with diversity and competing political ideologies, resulting from three major categories of Salafism: Salafi jihadis, who call for the use of violence as a means to establish the Caliphate; activists, who call for nonviolent political activism; and quietists (aka scholastic or traditional Salafis, or independent Salafis), who espouse a traditional outlook where all forms of political organization and action, including violence, are forbidden, as they may promote civil strife among Muslims, and promote disobedience to Muslim rulers. As a result, there is not one modern Salafism but many, and as Wiktorowicz notes, divisions exist among them all.

These Salafisms also have competing social ideologies, particularly regarding women. The strictness or liberalness of gender roles within the construct of these Salafi social ideologies actively reflects the nature and dichotomy of the various Salafi groups. Given the association of Salafism with Wahhābīyah and Islamism as radical male-dominated versions of Islam, it seems perhaps counterintuitive that women would become Salafis. Yet, all of the various Salafisms hold fast to the traditional outlook of women as following the Qurʾān and *sunnah*, and looking to the Salaf as paradigmatic Muslims. Outward signs of piety—including conservative dress, and education of their children in Islam, among other things—characterize a general Salafi woman's role. This belief that true Islam is embodied in a strict literal interpretation and implementation of Islamic law and theological tenets, with the Qurʾān and *sunnah* as the only valid legal and religious interpretations of Islam, is reflective of the quietist stream of Salafism. Clearly, women have found a comfortable space to exist here, with the Salafi Sisters being an example. But they have also found a comfortable space to exist within Salafi activist expressions, represented thus far by the al-Nour political party in Egypt. Al-Nour has clearly expanded upon the Quietist definition and role of Salafi women. Though they espouse the traditional (Quietist) Salafi outlook, they have allowed a woman, Insaf Khalil, to run for office as a member of the Egyptian Parliament in the Independent Member District category for the coastal city of Ismailia. Al-Nour allowed her to show her face on a campaign poster, whereas previously they had placed only flowers there. Though she eventually lost the race to a male al-Nour candidate, her popularity tripled as a politician, as did that of the party in the region in late 2011.

Women's roles have also evolved within Salafism to include a niche in Salafi-jihadi groups. In the North Caucasus region of Dagestan, as of September 2012, Salafi groups have claimed over 100 suicide-bombing deaths. The bombers themselves wanted Dagestan to become an Islamic republic with Sharīʿah law, a typical Salafi-jihadi tenet; but, atypically, the bombers were women. These women, like the men of the Salafi groups in the region, believe that violence is permissible when striving for an Islamic republic. These women also believe that, if men are not willing to engage in violent jihad, not only are they not worthy of marriage, but also women themselves must pick up the slack, so to speak, and train to become suicide bombers and fighters.

Still another variant of Salafism reveals that just as many women embrace toleration, rather than don suicide vests. Salafyo Costa is an Egyptian Salafi group that works to dispel negative stereotypes regarding Salafis, simultaneously working alongside other groups of varying ideologies to promote diversity and striving to improve Egypt's social concerns. Their name is a play on the anti-Western stereotype of continually a Salafi who would never drink coffee at the popular European coffee chain Costa, and is also intended to remind themselves that Salafis do not have a monopoly on Islam.

As Esposito and Haddad (1998), among other modern scholars, note, the Qurʾān (51:49) sees men and women as equals in the eyes of God. God's preference is for faith, not gender. But, as illustrated by the examples above, there are many interpretations of the role of women in Islam, and particularly within the Salafi tradition. There are, therefore, clearly many Salafisms, each constructing its gender roles differently and each defining appropriate roles for women differently, depending on each group's interpretation of what it means to be a Salafi. Modern social, economic, and cultural realities have undeniably affected what constitutes the interpretation of the paradigmatic Salafi woman for some Salafis. The fact that women are even an active part of some Salafi groups indicates that the tradition is evolving, and will ensure that gender constructs and women's roles will be continually redefined along the spectrum of Salafis, from Quietists to jihadis, for some time to come.

BIBLIOGRAPHY

Abdel-Latif, Omayma, and Marina Ottaway. "Women in Islamist Movements: Toward an Islamist Model of Women's Activism." Carnegie Endowment for International Peace, July 2007. http://carnegieendowment.org/files/cmec2_women_in_islam_final1.pdf.

Bakr, Ali. "Egypt's Salafist's: A Closer Look." http://english.ahram.org.eg/NewsContentP/18/55636/Books/Egypts-Salafists-A-closer-look.aspx, 15 October 2012.

Esposito, John. *What Everyone Needs to Know About Islam*. New York: Oxford University Press, 2011.

Esposito, John, and Yvonne Haddad. *Islam, Gender and Social Change*. New York: Oxford University Press, 1998.

Haykel, Bernard. "On the Nature of Salafi Thought and Action." In *Global Salafism: Islam's New Religious Movement*, edited by Roel Meijer, pp. 33–57, New York: Columbia University Press, 2009.

Nemtsova, Anna. "Female Terrorists of Dagestan." Pulitzer Center on Crisis Reporting, September 6, 2012. http://pulitzercenter.org/reporting/russia-dagestan-terrorist-attack-religion-salafi-islam-female-menaces.

Al-Rashed, Abdul Rahman. "Who Are the Salafists, the Liberals, the Muslim Brotherhood?" *Asharq Alawsat*, December 17, 2011 http://www.asharq-e.com/news.asp?section=2&id=27738.

Wiktorowicz, Quintan. *The Management of Islamic Activism: Salafi's, the Muslim Brotherhood, and State Power in Jordan*. Albany: State University of New York Press, 2001.

CHRIS LAROSSA

SALEH, SUʿAD. (Suʿād Ibrāhīm Ṣāliḥ) (b. 1946) is professor of comparative Islamic jurisprudence (*al-fiqh al-muqāran*), former dean of Islamic studies at al-Azhar University, and a well-known preacher whose media appearances answering women's religious questions earned her the epithet of *muftiyat al-nisāʾ* (women's female jurisconsult). Born in Cairo to a religious instructor at one of al-Azhar's intermediate institutes, Saleh is the second of nine children, all encouraged by their Azharite father to pursue higher education. As one of a few female experts in Islamic law throughout Egypt and the Arab world, Saleh belongs to the first generation of students to graduate from al-Azhar since it opened a faculty for women in 1962. In 1967, she obtained the Higher License in Islamic Studies (*al-ijāza al-ʿulyā*) with honors. Soon after, in 1968, she began teaching at al-Azhar University. In 1973, she was awarded a master's degree with distinction for a thesis that questioned men's unconditional right to divorce. In 1975, Saleh was the first Women's Faculty graduate to be awarded a doctorate in comparative jurisprudence at al-Azhar.

Saleh became professor in comparative jurisprudence at al-Azhar in 1987, the first female dean of Islamic Studies at the Women's Faculty (1996–1998), and rapporteur of al-Azhar's standing academic promotions committee (1990s). She has also taught in Saudi Arabia (1981–1984, and 1999) and the United Arab Emirates (1997) (Ismāʿīl 2002: pp. 8–9). During those years, Saleh published several thematic studies in comparative jurisprudence, focusing on women, ritual law, family, and economics.

Saleh has become particularly associated with the call for appointing women as *muftīs* (jurisconsults authorized to give legal opinions [*fatwā*]). Historically, very few women jurists are known to have issued *fatwās* in an official capacity (Roded, 1993, pp. 84); generally, the popular Muslim perception is that *fatwās* are dispensed by men. In the late 1990s, Saleh contributed to opening and publicizing the debate when she submitted a request to the-then Grand Muftī of Egypt, Shaykh Naṣr Farīd Wāṣil, to allocate space in Dār al-Iftāʾ al-Miṣriyya (the official body for issuing *fatwās* in Egypt) for well-qualified female jurists to answer women's questions (Khalīl, 2002). Saleh maintained that there is unanimity in the Islamic scholarly tradition that maleness is not a condition for issuing valid *fatwās*. Nevertheless, her request was not granted, and her second attempt in 2003 with Wāṣil's successor, Shaykh Aḥmad al-Ṭayyib, also failed (Khalīl, 2003). Following the advice of the Grand Imām of al-Azhar, Shaykh Muḥammad Sayyid Ṭanṭāwī (d. 2010), she applied for council membership on the prestigious Majma' al-buḥūth al-islāmiyya bi'l-Azhar (the Higher Institute of Islamic Research at al-Azhar), a competitor of Dār al-Iftā'. Saleh, however, received only one favorable vote from the all-male members of the council. In her writings, public presentations, and media contributions, Saleh continues her advocacy for appointing women *muftīs* (f. *muftiya*). She has deliberately focused her efforts on shifting social attitudes through her embodied practice of this role in the media. She has gained considerable public prominence through her regular engagement with Arab satellite television channels, including her own *fatwā*-oriented program *Fiqh al-mar'a* (Women's Jurisprudence, broadcast since 2011 on the Egyptian satellite channel al-Ḥayāt 2). Informed by her lifelong research into gender aspects of Islamic law, Saleh's *fatwā* activism aims to achieve gender justice within an Islamic framework. One of her daring *fatwās* in this respect permits women to become heads of state on the basis that they are only barred from the office of caliphate, which no longer exists. Another significant *fatwā* permits the medical restoration of virginity to unmarried young women to protect their right to live without social stigma. Her most contentious to date is her 2006 *fatwā* against the *niqāb* (face-veiling). She declared that not only is the practice not obligatory, but that it is a pre-Islamic custom with no religious merit, further expressing her revulsion at the misuse of *niqāb* in identity fraud crimes. Her position provoked a furor of formal complaints, media hostilities, and even death threats from radical *salafī* preachers.

In addition to her religious and intellectual activities, Saleh joined al-Wafd, a secular political party in the opposition, in 2010. Since 2011, she has openly supported the 25 January Egyptian Revolution.

Bibliography

Badran, Margot. "Interview on Islamic Feminism." *Women Living Under Muslim Law*, 29 May 2005. http://www.wluml.org/fr/node/2204.

Bano, Masooda, and Hilary Kalmbach, eds. *Women, Leadership & Mosques: Changes in Contemporary Islamic Authority*. Leiden: Brill, 2012.

Ismā'īl, Bakr. *Al-Ustādha al-duktūra Su'ād Ibrāhīm Ṣāliḥ, ḥayātuhā wa-fikruhā* (Professor Su'ād Ibrāhīm Ṣāliḥ: Her life and works. Cairo: Maktab Alba Press, 2002. A short biography of Su'ad Saleh, including key works and excerpts.

Khalīl, Muḥammad. "'Ulamā' al-dīn yakhtalifūn ḥawl 'amal al-mar'a bi'l-iftā." *Al-Sharq al-awsaṭ*, 9 December 2002. http://www.aawsat.com/details.asp?article=140443&issueno=8777.

Khalīl, Muḥammad. "Ustādha fī jāmi'at al-Azhar tuṭālib muftī misr bi-ta'yīn muftiya li'l-nisā' wa-tattahim Shaykh al-Azhar bil-taharrub min maṭālibihā." *Al-Sharq al-awsaṭ*, 2 March 2003. http://www.aawsat.com/details.asp?article=155703&issueno=8860.

Kovach, Gretel, and Carla Power. "Changing the Rule of Law: Souad Salah is Challenging the Islamic Establishment." *Newsweek Magazine*, 30 December 2002.

Nkrumah, Gamal. "Profile: Souad Saleh: Time to tear down the divides." *Al-Ahrām Weekly*, no. 766, 27 Oct.–2 Nov., 2005.

Otterman, Sharon. "Fatwas and Feminism: Women, Religious Authority, and Islamic TV." *Transnational Broadcasting Studies*, no. 16, June–Dec. 2006. http://www.tbsjournal.com/Otterman.html.

Roded, Ruth. *Women in Islamic Biographical Collections: From Ibn Sa'd to Who's Who*. Boulder, Colo.: Lynne Rienner Publishers, 1993.

Sheikholesami, Hosna. *Film Review: Veiled Voices, Journal of Middle Eastern Women's Studies* 7, no. 2 (2011): 123–125.

Primary Works

Aḍwā' 'ala niẓām al-usra fi'l-islām (Illuminations on the family system in Islam), Jiddah: Maktabat tihāma, 1982.

Aḥkām al-waṣiyya wa'l-mirāth fi'l-sharī'a al-islāmiyya (Judgments pertaining to will and inheritance in Islamic law), al-Qāhira: Dār al-ḍiyā', 1991.

Aḥkām 'ibādāt al-mar'a fi'l-sharī'a al-islāmiyya: Dirāsa fiqhiyya muqārana (Judgments pertaining to women's ritual worship in Islamic Law: A comparative jurisprudential study), 3d ed., al-Qāhira: Dār al-ḍiyā', 1993.

Aḥkām taṣarrufāt al-safīh fi'l-sharī'a al-islāmiyya (Judgments pertaining to imbeciles in Islamic Law), Jiddah: Maktabat tihāma, 1984.

Aḥkām taṣarrufāt al-ṣaghīr fi'l-sharī'a al-islāmiyya (Judgments pertaining to children in Islamic Law), Jiddah: Maktabat tihāma, 1985.

'Alāqat al-abā' bi'l-abnā' fi'l-sharī'a al-islāmiyya: Dirāsa fiqhiyya muqārana (The parent-child relationship in Islamic Law: A comparative jurisprudential study),3d ed., al-Qāhira: Dār al-ta'āwun, 1998.

Al-Ḥajr 'ala al-ṣaghīr wa'l-safīh fi'l-sharī'a al-islāmiyya (Placing the child and the imbecile under interdiction in Islamic law), PhD Thesis, al-Qāhira: Jāmi'at al-Azhar, 1975.

Mabādi' al-niẓām al-iqtiṣādī fi'l-islām wa-ba'ḍ taṭbiqātuh (Principles of the economic system in Islam and some of its applications), al-Riyāḍ, KSA: 'Ālam al-kutub, 1997.

Al-Ṭalāq bayn al-iṭlāq wa'l-taqyīd (Divorce, a restricted or an absolute [male right]?), al-Qāhira: Dār al-ta'āwun, 1998.

Qaḍāyā al-mar'a al-mu'āṣira: ru'ya shar'iyya wa-naẓra wāqi'iyya (Women's Contemporary Issues: An Islamic legal perspective and a contextual viewpoint), al-Qāhira: Maktabat al-turāth al-islāmī, 2003.

Ru'ya wa-mawqif (A Vision and a Stance), *Silsilat al-nukhbah wa'l-muqaddasāt*, no. 6, n.d.

Documentary Films

Al- 'Arabiyyah Channel. *Wujūh Islāmiyya: Ma' al- duktūra Su'ād Ibrāhīm Ṣāliḥ*. Broadcast on 30 August 2009. http://www.alarabiya.net/programs/2009/08/ 30/83377.html. A biographical documentary in Arabic.

Maher, Brigid. *Veiled Voices: Syria, Egypt, Lebanon.* United States: Typecast Films, 2009. Documentary film in English featuring Su'ad Saleh.

Thomas, Anthony. *Inside the Qur'an*. London, U.K.: Juniper Communications Limited, 2008. Documentary film in English featuring Su'ad Saleh.

SHURUQ NAGUIB

SAUDI ARABIA. Women in Saudi Arabia have long made headlines in the international media. Any reading of Saudi women's status will end up going back to as early as the beginning of Islam, looking for explanations and sometimes justifications. Thus, it is important from the outset to investigate the context that created, affected, and shaped the case of the 'Saudi woman' and how she interacted with and responded to it, both internally and externally. The "Saudi woman's" case needs to be contextualized within the debates about modernity, Islamic conservatism/revivalism, and the response to narrow interpretations of Islam in the Muslim world and in Saudi Arabia. Saudi women's issues are not ancient ones, nor are they inherent to Islam; most of them are a reflection of the inability to deal with modernity when it hits this sacred part of society, that is, women.

Historical Factors. Saudi Arabia's history has been shaped by three major factors in recent decades: geographic location, Islam, and oil. Perhaps this is a simplification, but it gives, at least, a structure to how one can understand the major players in Saudi Arabia's current history. What formed the history of the state shaped also the past and present of Saudi women.

Saudi Arabia is situated on the Arabian Peninsula, which is flanked on the east by the Arabo-Persian Gulf and by the Red Sea on the west, guaranteeing its economic access to Asia from one side and Africa from the other. This was reflected in Arabia's rich historical relationships with India, Persia, Mesopotamia, the Levant, Egypt, Abyssinia, and Europe. Arabia was in the middle of the major ancient world civilizations and routes. It participated, transferred, and contributed to it prior to and after the advent of Islam in Makkah in 610 CE.

Alliance. Saudi Arabia is a modern nation state that emerged in 1932 but claims a longer history that dates back to 1744, when Muḥammad ibn Saud, one of central Arabia's leaders, from Diriyah (north of Riyadh, Saudi Arabia's capital today), decided to ally with a religious activist who critiqued the practices of his fellow men and women in Najd (central Arabia) in particular and who advocated for a puritanical reformation in Islam based on the early sources of religion, the Qurʾān and *sunnah*. This background is important for understanding the modern history of Saudi Arabia, which became indebted to this alliance throughout its political, economic, educational, and social decisions. Women were always an important component in the power equation of state and society in Saudi Arabia.

Oil. In 1933, Saudi Arabia signed a concession treaty with Standard Oil of California. In 1938, it began producing oil and, in 1939, the first shipment of oil left the Gulf to the United States. In 1973, Saudi Arabia led the famous oil embargo on the states that were supporting the Israelis in the 1973 Arab–Israeli War. In 1974, oil prices boomed. Since then, oil has become a major factor in the relationship between power and modernity.

Women and Modernity. Women's status in Saudi Arabia was formed in part by its sacred spatial location as the cradle of Islam. The government, therefore, carries a sacred responsibility for protecting the holy sites, leading some to claim that Saudi Arabia is the only true representative of Islam, following a strict adherence to the Qurʾān, *sunnah*, and Ḥanbalī school of Islamic law.

At the same time, Saudi Arabia was faced with accepting the challenge of modernity that was not limited to modern technology, but also included ideas, concepts, philosophies, and ideologies that touched on society, education, health, the economy, women, and even religion. Modernity meant also the adoption of the modern nation-state's components of institutions, administrative and bureaucratic systems, legal bodies, organized defense, etc. Where women fit within this modernity has long represented a challenge.

Muslims, in general, tend to think of "modernity" in two ways: (1) as modernization, which is associated with science, technology, and material progress, and (2) as Westernization, which is associated with promiscuity and all kinds of social problems. Although "modernization" is considered highly desirable, "Westernization" is considered equally undesirable. Because an emancipated Muslim woman is seen by many Muslims as a symbol not of "modernization" but of "Westernization," some conservative Muslims have also gone to the extreme of considering such "Westernization" as disguised "modernization."

Saudi Arabia therefore faced the additional challenge of conforming every modern innovation with religious guidance, often resulting in conflict between the religious establishment and the state on one side, and society on the other. As the state succeeded from early stages in gaining the grounds against fanatical tribes through the famous battle of Sbela in 1929, the battle to win over society continued unresolved. In 1961, the state managed to pass a law introducing public schools for girls. However, this was done under the condition of keeping girls' education under the control of a committee of religious scholars chaired by the Grand Mufti, separate from the ministry that runs boys' education. This was done to follow the objective of keeping the schools' curriculum in the private sphere to train girls to be good mothers and obedient wives. This situation continued until 2003, when, following a fire at a girls' school in which many students died because they were prevented from leaving the building unveiled, the education ministry was merged with the High Presidency for the Education of Girls.

Saudi women's twenty-first century story has been much affected by the religious discourse that dominated forty years of governing girls' education, curriculum, self-image, role, and position in society, indoctrinating women's inferiority to men and their only purpose of existence as a man's appendix, as N. Barazangi (2004, p. 54–58) puts it. Also impacting women's status were strict interpretations of various Qur'ān verses limiting women's movement, interaction, work, and education, justified as protecting women and society from gender mixing and social decay.

State Regulation of Women's Lives. To achieve this, Saudi Arabia adopted strict regulations that affected education, economic and political participation, public appearance, and legal status. Women were limited to traditional disciplines in education and were averted from some others, such as engineering and archaeology. Other regulations limited their work opportunities within strict boundaries in compliance with the state's guidelines that prevent gender mixing in the workplace. Publicly, women were barred from any political post and were prevented from being in control of their own movement by prohibiting them from driving cars or traveling without the consent of their guardians, even if these were their own sons. Also although the Basic Law gives women a legal capacity equal to that of men, it has mostly exceptional clauses that lead to undermining women's equity or freedom (for details see Al-Jarbou' and al-Muḥaysin, 2010, pp. 51–59). Despite all of the aforementioned, women's response was unexpected. They overwhelmed the education system and shortly came to outnumber male students in schools and universities, even though some disciplines remain denied to them. Some progress in opening new disciplines, such as law, engineering, (interior architecture, not pure engineering), and computer and information technology, has occurred in recent years.

The paradox is that, prior to modernization in the 1950s, women in Saudi Arabia were active in all turns of daily life inside and outside the home, more so in the rural areas than the urbanized cities, bearing in mind that class and racial relations determine some classes for certain professions and exclude some from others. Some jobs were known to be traditional and date back to time unknown. Women worked as farmers, weavers, nurses, wet nurses, midwives, sellers, healers, herders, painters, business women, and more. They were also teachers, poets, and, in some instances, even warriors. Although this is not an exhaustive account, the list gradually decreased as we move into modern times and urbanization. In other words, women lost much of their initiative and economic participation in these traditional jobs to modern jobs of teaching in schools and healing in hospitals. After the seizure of the Grand Mosque by armed militants in 1979, the hand of the religious establishment was strengthened in the public arena. Constraints were subsequently imposed on women, pulling them away from the public sphere. The resulting limitations on education, work, and movement were reflected in women's economic participation confining them to jobs that conform to rules of segregation. This has resulted in turning Saudi women into the least economically productive persons in the world, with only 10.5 percent economic participation, not by their own choice, but by state and religious establishment unconscious design.

The Advent of Reform. Under internal and international pressure after the second Gulf War (1990–1991), some reforms started to take shape in the form of the promulgation of the Basic Law, the formation of the Shūrā Council, the declaration of a Succession Law, and the Provinces law. However, none of this was meant to ameliorate women's status. It was not until the new millennium and the 11 September 2001 terrorist attack on the United States involving fifteen Saudi men, followed on

13 May 2003 by the shocking attack inside Riyadh, the Saudi capital, that the issue of women's status was raised to the "A" list of debate and reform.

Although none of the relevant organizations were civil society institutions, the debate front that was established through many platforms, such as the King Abdulaziz Center for National Dialogue, resulted in identifying female activism in the country that could belong to roughly three categories:

1. The traditional position that considers "feminism" and "emancipation" to be bad words and actions. This trend follows the official line that denies anything wrong with women's status. The belief that any change in women's status should be led by the state only or the traditional educational institutions.
2. The "enlightened" position that began in the 1930s with pioneering male activists who called for women's right to education, such as Muḥammad Hassan Awwad in 1926, Muḥammad Said Khoja in 1932, Ahmad al-Sibaei in 1935, all from Makkah; ʿAbdullah al-Qasseemi in Qasseem in 1946; Abdel-Kareem al-Juhaiman in 1955 in Dhahran; and Abdallah Abdeljabbar in Makkah/Jeddah (al-Qashʿami). Following this voice were women who were educated early in the twentieth century and studied abroad or in private girls schools or private home schooling. Many of them came back with a new vision of women's rights and individually held positions outside the country in international organizations or universities, such as Dr. Thoraya Obaid, UN Under Secretary and Executive Director for the United Nations Population Fund (UNPDF) between 2000 and 2011, or Dr. Thoraya al Turki, anthropology professor at the American University of Cairo. Other women made a collective move that reached its peak on November 6, 1990, when forty-seven women took to their cars and drove in Riyadh, challenging the ban on driving. The movement marked the beginning of Saudi women's public activism and signaled the embarkment of Saudi feminism. The debate that took place in society after this incident was as remarkable as it was vicious. Those women were sacked from their jobs, banned from traveling, defamed on the podiums of mosques, and, nationally, a *fatwā* was issued to prohibit women from driving cars. In spite of that, the demonstration succeeded in attracting attention to the status of Saudi women, both nationally and internationally. Since then, many active nonofficial women's groups have emerged to form pressure groups for reform, such as the Sunday Women's Group (1994–) in Riyadh. More groups were set up after 9/11, such as the Family Safety Program, a civil society initiative that was adopted by King ʿAbdullah and became a national program in 2005 to counter domestic violence against women and children. These campaigns and groups also include the national Saudi Women Writers Group (2006–), the Society for Defending Saudi Women's Rights (2007–) in Dammam, The Divorce Initiative (2008) in Khobar, the national Business Women Demand the Abolition of a Legal Guardian to Start a Business *Wakil* (2009) campaign, the national No to Minor Marriage campaign, the Women 2 Drive (2011) campaign, and so on.
3. The third voice is the revival Islamist that follows, on the one hand, a radical line that believes in women's rights through *Sharīʿah*, and, on the other, believes in women's right to reinterpret their position in Islam, challenging the religious establishment, which could be coined as Islamic feminism.

Despite the absence of unions and civil society platforms, which makes it hard on women to organize fully and be of real effect, they were able to break the silence, voice their demands, and sometimes even mobilize beyond the restricted lines to a relatively large extent. In addition to the preceding examples, women used writing, forming pressure groups, campaigning through journalism, new social media, cyber media, writing petitions, and networking.

This activism came to fruition on September 25, 2011, when King ʿAbdullah granted women their full political rights in the only two quasi-democratic institutions, the Shūrā Council and the Municipal Councils. They are to be part of these bodies similar to men, as appointees for the Shūrā Council and as appointees, voters, and candidates for the Municipal Councils in the 2013 and 2015 elections. This development was owed in part to the vital transformation in the Arab world wrought by the Arab Spring that began in December 2010. On January 13, 2013, thirty women were appointed to the Shūrā Council, increasing their number to twenty percent of the Council's membership, the minimum percentage required from now on, which is the result of women's demands. To the surprise of many, there was limited segregation and women shared the hall with men without barriers.

In the face of the limited opportunities given to Saudi women in private and public life, there are very significant examples of women who made it to the top in many areas of specializations. Pioneering women were able to lead their fields after continuing their education abroad, while others were able to break through by challenging the system internally through a constant struggle, or merely with social and economic class support that enabled them to excel as well. Another sort of support that is essential in the Saudi context is familial support, mainly by the male members of a woman's family.

Today, there are many reference books dedicated to collecting biographies of Saudi women achievers, including *Asbar, Mu'jam al-nisaa' al-sa'udiyyat* (Dictionary of Saudi Women, 1997), *Mu'jam asbar li al-'atibbaa' wa al-tabibat al-mu'asereen*(Asbar Dictionary of Saudi male and female medical doctors), and *Mu'jam nisaa' min al-mamlakah al-'arabiyyah al-Sa'udiyyah* (Dictionary of Women from Saudi Arabia, 2006). Some of these books are inspired by pride in Saudi women's achievements and some by public relations program. Regardless, the achievement of any Saudi woman should be counted as double or triple in size or weight compared to that of her male counterpart to account for the immense gender gap.

BIBLIOGRAPHY

Abu Zaid, B. *Ḥirāsat al-faḍīlah* (Guarding the Virtue). 6th ed. Riyadh, Saudi Arabia: Dār al-ʿĀṣimah, 2000.

Al-Bakr, Fawziyah. *al-Mar'ah al-su'udiyyahwa al-ta'leem* (Saudi woman and education). 2d ed. Cairo, Egypt: Al-'ilmiyyah, 1997.

Al-Bakr, Fawziah. "Report on Saudi Women." [http://www.aicongress.org/about/AIC_Annual%20Report_2009-1.pdf]. *American Islamic Congress Annual Report*, 2009.

Al-Fassi, Hatoon. "Saudi Women: Modernity and Change.", In *Industrialization in the Gulf: A Socioeconomic Revolution*, edited by Jean-Francois Seznec and Mimi Kirk, pp. 157–170. London: Routledge, 2010a.

Al-Fassi, Hatoon. "al-Khitab al-nisawi al-su'udi ma bayn al-hawiyyahwa al-khuṣuṣiyyah al-thaqafiyyah" (The Saudi feminist discourse between identity and the cultural particularism), pp. 213–226. *Multaqa khitabuna al-thaqafi* (The Cultural Discourse Conference). Makkah, Saudi Arabia: Maṭbu'atnādi Makkah al-thaqafi al-'adabi, 2010b.

Al-Fassi, Hatoon. "hal hunaa nusawiyyah su'udiyyah?" Beirut: Markaz Dirasat al-Wihda al-ʿArabiyyah and al-Bahithat al-Lubnaniyyat, 2012.

Hassan, Riffat. "Feminist Theology: The Challenges for Muslim Women." *Journal for Critical Studies of the Middle East* 9 (1996): 53–65.

Al-Jarbou', Ayyub bin Maoṣour, and Khalid bin ʿAbdelmuḥsin al-Muḥaysin. *al-Markaz al-qāanūnīlilmar'ahfī al-mamlakah al-'arabiyyah al-su'udiyyah* (The legal position of women in Saudi Arabia). Riyadh, Saudi Arabia: 2010.

MacFarquhar, Neil. "Saudi Monarch Grants Women Right to Vote." *New York Times*, 25/9/2011. http://www.nytimes.com/2011/09/26/world/middleeast/women-to-vote-in-saudi-arabia-king-says.html?_r=1&pagewanted=all.

Al-Qashʿami, Muhammadʿ Abd al-Razzaq. "Bidāyātta'līm al-mar'ahfīal-mamlakahal-'arabiyyahal-suʿudiyyah" (The beginning of women's education in Saudi Arabia), pp. 1–135. Introduction by Hatoon al-Fassi, the book of *al-Majallah al-ʾArabiyyah* 170. Riyadh, Saudi Arabia, 2011.

Al-Rasheed, Madawi. *A History of Saudi Arabia* 2d ed. Cambridge, U.K.: Cambridge University Press, 2010. A comprehensive account of the history of Saudi Arabia.

Al-Turki, Thoraya, Abu Bakr Bāqādir, and Amal Ṭanṭāwi. *Jiddah, Umm al-raḫawa al-shiddah. Taḫawulāt al-ḫayah al-ʾusariyyahbaynfatratayn* (Jiddah, town of welfare and hardship, the familial transformation between two periods). Cairo, Egypt: Dar al-Shuruq, 2006.

Hatoon Al-Fassi

Scholarly Approaches and Theoretical Constructs (Theoretical Overview). It would be difficult to imagine constructing a volume of this type without giving consideration to the core scholarly issues and approaches used in analyzing questions and conducting research related to women and gender in Islam. The goal of addressing *Scholarly Approaches and Theoretical Constructs* as its own theme was to bring attention to the ways in which "women," "gender," and "women's rights," particularly as related to "Islam," are conceived and defined, as well as to analyze the broader meaning of the conceptualization process, particularly its impact on contemporary events. The articles within this theme give attention to how gender roles have been defined in different Islamic contexts and time periods and according to what criteria, how and why women's status has changed over time and space, and definitions of what feminism and women's rights are, and whether and how they are applied and reinterpreted in different Islamic contexts. It has also been important to resist oversimplification of these topics by asserting a monolithic identity to "women," "gender," "women's rights," and even "Muslim women" by recalling the variety of historical, geographical, and cultural experiences contained within each category.

Feminism has been split into three separate articles, so as to focus on the major components of and developments in each. The article on Sources examines the awakening of awareness of "women's issues," looking at the relationship between modernization and development of the nation and women's status and roles, with particular focus on the rise of women's organizations and writings about the status of women in Egypt and Turkey in the late nineteenth century, as well as the impetus for a more "Islamic" version of feminism that emerged in the 1970s. The article addressing Concepts and Debates addresses questions related to "women's rights"—who has defined them since the nineteenth century, in particular, what this phrase means and to whom, and how to move the quest for achieving these rights forward. Finally, given the developments of the past few decades, the nature of Islamic feminism deserved an article of its own, as Islamists and Muslim women have struggled to decide not only how best to define these rights, but also how to structure the quest for these rights within the context of their faith, including questions related to who has the right to define what rights are and how to remain authentic to faith and scripture while seeking fulfillment of these rights. These debates are particularly critical today as new governments and state structures are being formed in response to the Arab Spring and questions about authenticity and legitimacy, often defined by the status and role of women as the culture bearers, are resurfacing.

Similarly, gender construction was broken out into three different time periods—early Islam, historical, and contemporary—as a means of looking for both continuity and change. Understanding how gender is considered and constructed allows for recognition of the human role at play, even where divine texts are under consideration. Gender studies as specific scholarly endeavors were given their own articles, examining both the history and development of the field and the methodologies used. In addition, articles examining women and gender themes in Sunnī, Shīʿī , and Ṣūfī thought, practice, and devotional literature have also been included, both to show where women are represented and have represented themselves in source materials, as well as to investigate where and how women have inserted themselves *as women* into religious conversation and practice, often with their own special rituals and customs.

Major scholarly debates, such as Hagarism, Orientalism, and the impact of patriarchy on interpretations and understandings of gender roles, perceptions of women, and women's activities, particularly within the family and with respect to access to public space, have also received attention. Because many of the major debates about women and their status in "Islam" began in earnest in the eighteenth century and continue through the present, articles addressing their role and status in "Islam," as well as the eighteenth century through the early twentieth century, and contemporary debates are addressed in separate articles.

Perhaps most prevalent among stereotypes of Muslim women is the direct correlation, at least in Western minds, between veiling and oppression, repression and suppression of women and their rights, creating a facile equation in which the religion of Islam is blamed for the perceived problem. Consequently, it was important to give attention to veiling as a historical phenomenon, as well as the contemporary resurgence of veiling, specifically looking at symbolism and meaning—not simply as assigned from the outside, but, more importantly, from the perspective of the *muḥajjabah* (veiled woman) herself, where the veil often serves as a symbol of agency, self-determination, and even liberation.

Finally, the question of women's agency is covered in articles analyzing social reform by geographic region, as well as political activism, allowing for discovery of the interplay among culture, politics, and religion as reforms take on different approaches in different contexts, while also offering insight into what might be considered transnational issues that Muslim women seek to address.

NATANA J. DELONG-BAS

SCIENCE, MEDICINE, AND EDUCATION (THEORETICAL OVERVIEW).

Like religion, science, medicine, and education have historically produced orthodoxies about the nature of women, and, therefore, what sorts of activities women were meant to perform in society. Strikingly, the lens through which these paradigms have focused their normative ideas about women has been on their reproductive capacity, not on their ability to use their bodies and brains in the interest of society. Rather than treat these institutional structures as separate or disconnected sources, we created *Science, Medicine, and Education* to reveal the vibrant interplay and overlap between those official systems of knowledge production and practices that have often worked through Islam to authorize women's roles, on the one hand, and women's initiatives within and responses to those very scripts, on the other. Our interest, however, was not to portray women as one-dimensional or reactionary actors to knowledge and practices sanctioned by science, medicine, or education. Nor did we intend to present these as monolithic systems that either derived exclusively from Islam or exercised a singular and identical effect on all Muslim women. Rather, we sought to showcase the dynamic engagement and, in some cases, contentious exchange between knowledge-producing institutions—both religious and secular—that circumscribed the terms of woman's nature, and, thus, their social functions, and female bodily and intellectual expressions. As such, *Science, Medicine, and Education* reiterates the emphasis of *Self and Body* by similarly focusing on the "creative ways in which women have negotiated their identities in a constant, often tense, dialectic" with, in this case, mutually reinforcing patriarchal institutions such as science, medicine, and education.

Entries on fertility, family planning, pregnancy, mothering, birthing, childrearing, and health care, for example, demonstrate what official discourses expected from women's societal roles. Through their orthodoxical views, medicine and education, especially, were each able to generate effective cultural norms that ultimately circumscribed women's experiences as women, especially in matters concerning sexuality, family planning, pregnancy, mothering, and childrearing. These cultural norms expected women to fulfill an ideal that did not always consider the views, activities, and visions that women had in relation to their own bodies. It is in these instances that we see a great deal of disparity between women's practice and official discourse. Particularly poignant demonstrations of this point are the articles "Fertility and Infertility Treatments," "Women in the Medical Profession: Historical," "Childrearing Practices," and "Women and Education: Contemporary Discourse."

Despite the regulatory, even exclusionary, impulses of science, medicine, and education, the articles brilliantly portray the varied and multifaceted articulations of female agency. Indeed, we see a myriad of vibrant female expression as it relates to reproductive and intellectual activity. In fact, although these formal systems have constrained women's agency in noteworthy, even debilitating, ways, they have also and paradoxically created significant opportunities for women to define, shape, and authorize their own meanings, and, by extension, their roles in society. An illustrative example of this is women and education. We learn that, despite the eventual erosion of women's educational rights, especially after Muḥammad's death, we still see dazzling moments of historical agency, when women excelled as judges, hadith narrators, ascetic devotees, medical scholars, and physicians. Their successes can partly be explained by, among other contextual variables, the high value Islam's scriptural sources placed on education as a universal right of all Muslims and how women in different Muslim societies have capitalized on this right.

More striking are those instances when women deviated from the expectations of the official scripts. An important example here is women's use of contraceptives. Despite there being two conflicting forces that have each determined the legal use and availability of contraception (e.g., Islam's pronatalist policy versus the state's national family planning programs), it was women who ultimately chose to use or not use contraception and which methods. Interestingly, women often utilized a variety of contraceptive methods other than those sanctioned by Muslim jurists. And their choices have had real and far-reaching implications for national and global population growth rates in Muslim countries, especially today. Similar examples can be found in the articles on medicine, as women historically pursued forms of medical practice, such as midwifery, that science and medicine had sanctioned, but also, at different points, discouraged and made illegal.

Whatever the relationship between women's practices and the official discourse, the articles here collectively agree that women's agency mattered. Women's roles, practices, and choices mattered when navigating the bodily world of reproduction or the intellectual world of ideas. Whether as wives who sought fertility treatments or postponed pregnancy, as mothers who gave birth to or raised children, as midwives and healers or as physicians with a state license, as poor women who faced no health care or life-threatening health challenges, their agency mattered to them, and to their societies that were invariably impacted. Therefore, the authors here echo the findings found throughout the encyclopedia: women's bodies were more than just acted upon; they became the prime locus for women's own agency.

We hope that readers will take away from this theme a more complex and nuanced understanding of women's activity involving their bodies and brains, and how reproduction in particular has historically been a central construct around which official scripts, such as science, medicine, and education, have organized to ultimately shape, regulate, and control women's corporeal and intellectual expression. Whether women fulfilled or defied the gender norms sanctioned by these institutions, what is clear is women's ongoing, dynamic interplay, and the brilliant snapshots of female expression and, by extension, societal notions of intimacy, that are produced.

Hibba Abugideiri

Seclusion. In Muslim society, the religiously sanctioned cultural practice of female seclusion is intended to shield female bodies from the penetrating male gaze. The norm of female seclusion complements sartorial norms, sanctioned by Islam, that regulate female dress, such as the headscarf. In tandem, regulations governing seclusion and dress function to indicate a female's sexual availability and, in the view of religious scholars, prevent social discord (*fitnah*).

Often, female seclusion has traditionally signaled social and economic prestige as well. The Qurʾānic prescription that men should speak to women from behind a curtain originally applied to the Prophet's wives only: "And when you ask them for something, ask from behind a veil; that is purer for your hearts and for theirs" (33:53). Lower- and working-class, rather than upper-class, women held jobs that often involved interaction with men. Even the headscarf originally signaled class status; slave women were prohibited from veiling their hair. Eventually, however, the norms governing seclusion spread to non-elites. It became a cultural norm throughout different regions of Muslim civilization—the Middle East, North Africa, and South Asia—to control and restrict female sexuality in public life.

Several Arabic and Persian terms signal the importance of seclusion, separation, and privacy to the organization of female space in Muslim society. Although, today, the Arabic word "hijab" generally denotes the headscarf worn by Muslim women, it originally referred to a veil or curtain that physically separates female from male space, as in the Qurʾānic verse mentioned earlier ("ask from behind a veil [hijab].") "Purdah" is a Persian word that also means "curtain," but it denotes the cultural institution of female seclusion; today, the term is especially applied in South Asia.

The harem, popularized in the Western imagination by the famous collection of stories, *The One Thousand and One Nights*, literally means "sacrosanct" and "inviolable," but denotes female members of the household or the physical space that they inhabit. Beginning in the Umayyad period (late seventh century), elite Muslim males, including the caliph, adopted the institution of the harem. The harem had been a Near Eastern cultural practice for thousands of years prior to the advent of Islam.

A few additional observations help place female seclusion in its proper social and cultural context. First, notwithstanding the fantasies of European Orientalists, the ideal of female seclusion did not always manifest itself in Muslim society. Despite the frustrations of many Muslim religious scholars, women in fourteenth-century Cairo could still be found roaming the cemeteries, markets, mosques, and festivals alongside men. Second, female Muslim space has varied across time and place. Local politics and culture, not just Islam, have shaped gendered space; female space thus has shifted along with the shifting interplay of religion, culture, and politics. It is therefore possible to understand why female seclusion is not exclusively "Islamic." The South Asian practice of purdah, for example, is not restricted to Muslims, but shared across other religious communities as well. In Muslim society, public life was not traditionally the exclusive preserve of men, nor was private life the exclusive preserve of women; the boundary separating public from private was porous. Premodern Muslim women did have a limited role in public life—at the markets, through scholarship, and even in politics. More recently, modern Muslim feminists in various majority-Muslim countries have struggled to normalize female participation in mixed gendered settings such as schools, cafes, and offices.

Another very different type of seclusion is denoted by the Arabic term, *khalwah*, which refers to spiritual and social seclusion as experienced by Muslim mystics, or Ṣūfīs. Many Ṣūfīs were women, like the famous Iraqi female mystic, Rāb'ia al-'Adawiyya (d. 801), who chose not to marry in order to devote her entire life to worshipping God. In contrast to the types of seclusion mentioned above, this mystical lifestyle choice of self-imposed seclusion appears to affirm female agency and freedom from male patriarchy.

BIBLIOGRAPHY

Afsaruddin, Asma, Anan Ameri, et al., eds. *Hermeneutics and Honor: Negotiating Female "Public" Space in Islamic/Ate Societies*: Cambridge, Mass.: Harvard University Press, 1999.

Ahmed, Leila. *Women and Gender in Islam: Historical Roots of a Modern Debate*. New Haven, Conn.: Yale University Press, 1992.

'Attār, Farīd al-Dīn. *Muslim Saints and Mystics*. Translated by A. J. Arberry. London: Routledge, 1983.

Lutfi, Huda. "Manners and Customs of Fourteenth-Century Cairene Women: Female Anarchy Versus Male Shar'i Order in Muslim Prescriptive Treatises." In *Women in Middle Eastern History*, edited by Nikki R. Keddie and Beth Baron, pp. 99–121. New Haven, Conn.: Yale University Press, 1991.

Stowasser, Barbara Freyer. "The Ḥijāb: How a Curtain Became an Institution and a Cultural Symbol." In *Humanism, Culture, and Language in the Near East*, edited by Asma Afsaruddin and A.H. Mathias Zahniser, pp. 87–104. Winona Lake, Inc.: Eisenbrauns, 1997. pp. 87–104.

YOUSHAA PATEL

ṢEFĀTĪ, ZOHREH. (b. 1948), Iran's most influential *mujtahida*, Zohreh Ṣefātī (whose full surname is Ṣefātī-Dezfūlī) remains the most prominent female religious authority of the Islamic Republic. She is a long-time member of the Women's Socio-Cultural Council (shūrā-ye farhangī ejtemā-ye zanān), where she heads the committee on *fiqh* and law. She was married to Ayatollah Moḥammad Ḥasan Aḥmadī Faqīh (d. 2010), with whom she had four daughters and two sons.

Ṣefātī grew up in Abadan and moved to Qom in the 1970s to seek religious training at a time when a number of *ḥawẓa* opened women's sections. After the establishment of Jāmi'at al-Zahrā' in Qom in 1985, the Islamic Republic's largest women's theological seminary, Ṣefātī became an instructor there, teaching inter alia the highest level of learning, the *dars-e khārej*, which leads to permission to engage in *ejtehād* (reasoning based on the Sharī'ah).

Ṣefātī received her first *revāya* in 1996 from Ayatollah Āqā Aslī 'Alī Yāri Gharavī Tabrīzī and from Ayatollah Mohammad Fāzel Lankarānī (1931–2007). She claims that after having read her book *Pazhūhishī-ye feqhī pīrāmūn-e senn-e taklīf* (A jurisprudential inquiry on the age of maturity, 1997), Ayatollah Loṭf-Allāh Ṣāfī Golpāyegānī (b. 1918) first granted her certification in *ejtehād*. Following Ṣāfī's *ejāzeh* (authorization), Ṣefātī received another certification in *ejeihād* from Ayatollah Moḥammad Ḥasan Aḥmadī Faqīh (d. 2010), who would become her husband. According to Ṣefātī, she herself has granted *ejāzehs* of *revāya* to more than forty male scholars.

Apart from her book on maturity, Ṣefātī has also published on the virtues of pilgrimage in *Ziyārat dar partaw-e velāyat* (Pilgrimage under the radiance of guardianship) and on women's *feqh* (jurisprudence) in *Naw-āwarihā-ye feqhī dar ahkām-e bānūwān* (Jurisprudential innovations in women's sentences).

Ṣefātī was consulted in the early 2000s by Iran's Expediency Council on the age of marriage. While the reformist-oriented parliament sought to raise the marriage age to eighteen and sixteen for boys and girls, respectively, the Guardian Council had rejected the bill as "un-Islamic." When issuing the final version of the bill, the mediating Expediency Council formulated a compromise with reference to a distinction Ṣefātī had made between the age of *taklīf*—when one is required to oblige by religious instructions such as *ḥejāb* (Ar. *hijab*)—and the age of marriage. When the bill became law in 2002, Ṣefātī's line of argumentation was followed in that the law stipulated the marriage age at thirteen for girls and fifteen for boys—higher than the age of *taklīf* (nine for girls), but lower than what the parliament had demanded.

In 2006 rumors suggested that women's groups were planning to nominate Ṣefātī for the Assembly of Experts, an 86-member *mojtahed* council that elects the supreme leader of Iran and holds the mandate to supervise his actions. Ṣefātī commented that she did not intend to run for the council, but that theoretically women were eligible for any office in the Islamic Republic, including those of the president, the clerical councils, and even the supreme leader.

Contrary to the majority opinion among Shīʿī jurists, Ṣefātī believes that a female *mojtahed* may be emulated by both men and women and that female religious authorities can attain the status of *marjaʿ* (source of emulation). She argues that prerequisites are purely meritocratic and that Islam does not discriminate on the basis of gender. She laments that few women ayatollahs exist in Iran in the early twenty-first century, and suggests that this is not due to their a priori exclusion from the system of clerical authority, but the fact that few women are sufficiently ambitious and industrious to embark on the challenging path required for the attainment of religious authority.

BIBLIOGRAPHY

Primary Works

Nawāwarihā-ye feqhī dar ahkām-e bānūwān (Jurisprudential innovations in women's sentences).

Pazhūhishī-ye feqhī pīrāmūn-e senn-e taklīf. Tehran: Nashr-e Moṭahhar, 1997/98.

"Senn-e Bolūgh-e Sharʿī-ye Dokhtarān" (The legal age of maturity for girls). In *Bolūgh-e Dokhtarān*, edited by Mehdī Mehrīzī, pp. 379–390. Qom, Iran: Daftar-e Tablīghāt-e Islāmī-ye Ḥawzah-ye ʿElmīyah-ye Qom (Islamic Propagation Office of the Religious Seminaries), 1997.

Ziyārat dar partaw-e velāyat: Sharḥī bar ziyārat-e ʿĀshūrā. Qom, Iran: Mujtamaʿ-i ʿUlūm-e Dīnī-e Ḥaḍrat-e Valī-e ʿAṣr, 1997.

Secondary Work

Künkler, Mirjam, and Roja Fazaeli. "The Life of Two Mujtahidahs: Female Religious Authority in 20th century Iran." In *Women, Leadership and Mosques: Changes in Contemporary Islamic Authority*, edited by Masooda Bano and Hilary Kalmbach, pp. 127–160. Leiden, Netherlands: Brill, 2012.

MIRJAM KÜNKLER

SELF AND BODY (THEORETICAL OVERVIEW). Women are often defined by their physicality and therefore it is not surprising that an encyclopedia on women's issues in general should include a section on self and body. By consciously choosing this particular subtext instead of other possibilities, we wish to highlight the individuality and specificity of women's bodies and their agency in constructing the self above and beyond cultural abstractions. Assigning these topics to a broader, more generic culture and society designation, for example, would have elided these specificities and masked the different creative ways in which women have negotiated their identities in a constant, often tense, dialectic with the larger (usually patriarchal) society.

Although topics such as beauty and aesthetics and cosmetics may seem rather traditional, the fact remains that women through time have often expressed themselves through bodily adornment and made their mark in society through their affinity for that which is considered beautiful and aesthetically pleasing. Cosmetics often had medicinal properties in addition to their beautifying purpose; therefore, their benefits could be conceived of in non-gendered terms as well. There was another important social and cultural dimension that is worthy of note—the preparation and application of cosmetics in a social setting often fostered female companionship and provided an outlet for expressing feminine solidarity. Among the venues where women's solidarity came to the fore were *ḥammāms*—bathhouses in the Islamic world reserved for women. The *ḥammāms* spawned almost-ritualized practices connected with cleaning and beautifying the body, reinforcing the idea of membership in a special club or a selective guild catering only to women. *Ḥammāms* could also serve as an important venue for political networking and intrigues, especially those that were frequented by women of noble birth—sometimes on a par with bathhouses and other places frequented by men.

The harem—the subject of many Western lurid fantasies and prurient voyeurism—was a gender-segregated domestic space distinctive of pre-modern Muslim societies. If we do not subscribe to the usual private–public dichotomy applied to post-industrial Western societies with its overt political implications, then it is possible for us to appreciate how an all-female domain, such as the harem, could be empowering for women, in which they could feel free to be themselves without male intrusion and supervision. In particularly elite households, women could wield disproportionate social and political influence, as has been cogently demonstrated in relation to the Ottoman imperial harem. But, seclusion as one of the outcomes of the harem system could have repressive consequences and stultify the expression of the feminine self. Studies on the harem and the socially instituted practice of seclusion point to the historical development of such traditional features of Islamicate societies and situate them in broader sociopolitical contexts.

A very important component of this discussion is sexuality and sexual expression, which constitute the human self and body to a considerable degree. Traditional pre-modern patriarchal societies defined and regulated women's sexuality on their behalf often through complex cultural notions of honor and virtue. Such notions gained considerable traction when legitimized through religious rhetoric, in the articulation of which women themselves rarely played a role. Practices that pre-date the rise of Islam and were deeply embedded in cultural rituals continued to be observed in Muslim-majority societies, even when understood to be in violation of Islamic precepts and values and/or not intrinsic to the Islamic worldview. Some of these practices became emotively associated in many cases in the postcolonial Islamic world with "cultural authenticity" that had to be preserved against encroaching Westernization.

Hijab is one of these variegated practices that has acquired great emotional and political resonance in Muslim-majority societies (in addition to Europe and North America as well). Although its specifically Islamic origins are contested, it has become in many ways the most easily identifiable marker of Muslim identity for women. Women choosing to wear hijab (primarily understood to mean headscarves with loose clothing that covers the whole body except for the face, hands, and feet) often express a multitude of reasons for doing so, not least of which is that it is an outward marker of religious piety and signifies their adherence to Islamic ideals of modesty and feminine dignity. That same marker of feminine Muslim identity however has called forth derision directed at vulnerable women, particularly in Europe recently, where specific forms of the hijab have been banned in an attempt in many cases to reverse what is perceived as the "threat" of Islamization and to "liberate" women, usually without their consent. In Turkey, a Muslim-majority society, the headscarfed woman until very recently was considered a pariah in official circles because of the supposed affront she posed to the statist policy of secularism.

Other contested cultural practices that have become associated with Islam include female genital cutting and honor killings. While arguments justifying these practices are crafted by some in a religious vocabulary, a historical and ethnographic study of such practices reveals that they have to do primarily with specific regional and tribal practices, ethnicity, and levels of education. At a popular level, however, and often in Western media depictions of these practices, they are regarded as symptomatic of what is assumed to be a fundamental disregard for women's rights in Islamicate societies.

This brings us to the final point of this essay—that women's bodies often become co-opted as the site of culture wars against their will and frequently used as pawns in political-cultural skirmishes. This is as true of debates over abortion in the United States as it is of debates over the hijab, for example, in non-Muslim and Muslim-majority societies. Women's own voices and preferences frequently become elided in these debates, because it is not their agency or lack thereof that usually concerns the larger society but rather the fraught symbolism of the practice in question and the political fallout from these debates. Throughout history, women's selves and bodies have often been "constructed" by others (men) and "packaged" to conform to cultural expectations of beauty and feminine propriety. Depending on their circumstances, women have sometimes been complicit in these ventures but they have also sometimes challenged their representation by others and undermined systems that relegated them to the sidelines.

Asma Afsaruddin

Sexual Education. Perspectives on what constitutes sexual education, and where, how, when, and to whom it should be offered, are wide-ranging and differ across Muslim societies. The contestations on these fronts make apparent not only the diversity of views on this topic, but also the varied ideological commitments and investments that inform them.

Broadly defined, sexual education is concerned with the scientific understanding of reproduction, but it additionally refers to a field of knowledge that entails a discussion of cultural and religious values and sex differences. In Western contexts, sexual education has been aimed primarily at promoting responsible sexual behaviors in teenagers. This has often meant educating youth about the risks of unprotected sexual intercourse and the ways in which they can protect themselves, raising awareness about sexually transmitted diseases, and maintaining healthy sexual relationships. Within this framework, schools are positioned as the ideal institutions responsible for disseminating information about sexual health.

Muslim engagement with, and responses to, sexual education can be located on a continuum, influenced by understandings of whether or not the curricula and educational approaches align with Muslim cultural and religious values. This multiplicity of views is exhibited by contestations over the role of schools in the production and transmission of knowledge about sexual health.

Scholars such as Fida Sanjakdar, Mark Halstead, and Muhammad Zain al-Dein, among others, have examined the different perspectives on and engagement of Muslims with school-based sexual education programs in Australia, Great Britain, and Canada, respectively. As their research highlights, some Muslims in the West argue that including sexual education in school curricula is a form of institutionalized consent for premarital sex, and imparting this information in co-educational settings incites early sexual practices in teenagers. Sexual desire in and of itself is not considered unhealthy; it is the expression of that desire outside the context of marriage that is understood as unethical, impulsive, and risky. It is, therefore, proposed that parents, and not schools, should be responsible for educating youth in single-sex settings. The underlying commitment is to protect the image of children as asexual and innocent. Other Muslims note that liberal values about sexualities and sexual relations, assumed to be incompatible with the Quʾrān and *ḥadīth*, are promoted in the garb of school-based sexual education. The perception is that sexual education programs which fail to privilege heterosexuality and abstinence in social relations are a threat to the heteronormative gender and sexual order. Accordingly, some Islamic centers, in Canada, for example, have taken the responsibility of educating young people about sexuality, sexual relations, and sexual health. In other instances, private and independent schools have emerged that design and implement sexual education curricula inspired by Muslim traditions and sexual ethics. An example is the curriculum prepared by Amira Al-Sarraf, head of the New Horizon School, an independent school in the United States that seeks to ground its teaching in Islam.

Nevertheless, other Muslims advocate an approach to sexual education that affirms their view of sexual desires as a positive aspect of human experience, presents scientific knowledge about sexual health, and places the onus of making responsible decisions within sexual relationships on the individuals. Although this approach seeks to employ the language of science and religion to promote a progressive agenda, it, too, assumes youth to be impulsive, which legitimizes supervision, policing, and surveillance by adults in and through sexual education programs.

Since sexuality and gender are intricately connected, school-based sexual education programs in the West also become a site where debates about appropriate gender roles, the symbolic connection between family honor and female sexual purity, division of labor within the institution of marriage, etc. are played out, which has implications for both women and men. At the core of these contestations then lies the project of organizing sexualities, and controlling sexual and gender behaviors.

BIBLIOGRAPHY

DeLong-Bas, Natana J. *Notable Muslims: Muslim Builders of World Civilization and Culture*. Oxford: Oneworld, 2006.

Halstead, Mark. "Muslims and Sex Education." *Journal of Moral Education* 26, no. 3 (1997): 317–330.

Rasmussen, Mary Lou. "Secularism, Religion and 'Progressive' Sex Education." *Sexualities: Studies in Culture and Society* 13, no. 6 (2010): 699–712.

Sanjakdar, Fida. *Living West Facing East: The (De)Construction of Muslim Youth Sexual Identities*. New York: Peter Lang, 2011.

Zain al-Dien, Muhammad. "Perceptions of Sex Education among Muslim Adolescents in Canada." *Journal of Muslim Minority Affairs*, 30, no. 3 (2010): 391–407.

SHENILA S. KHOJA-MOOLJI

SEXUALITY. Muslim women's sexuality is typically debated, in academic literature, either with respect to family honor and shame or in a lesbian context. Women are seldom given the opportunity to speak or write trivially about their bodies, sexuality, and physical pleasures in candid and banal ways. It has been only recently that some exceptions to this discursive tradition began to emerge, especially in the field of *fine* literature and other creative artistic writings, for example, the writings of Ahlam Moustaghanimi and Joumana Haddad.

In the mid-1970s, academic literature began to take interest in "Muslim sexuality" in general, with a clear emphasis on Muslim women's sexuality. Abdelwahab Bouhdiba showed how women in Muslim societies practiced their sexuality with relative freedom in the "Golden Age" of Islam. In a similar way, Fatima Mernissi explained, based on her experience in a bourgeois household in the city of Fez, how Moroccan women try frequently to transgress the sexualized boundaries and challenge the gender segregation and control over women and their sexualities imposed by tradition and some false *aḥādīth*. Both authors call for a return to the *origins* of Islam to look for some essence of "Islamic feminism," as Mernissi called it, while Bouhdiba termed the same period the age of "sublimed sexuality." Both approaches tend to a certain *essentialism*.

Islamic canonical texts, in general, promote licensed sex within marriage and recognize that the purpose of sex is not restricted to procreation, as conjugal pleasure is also taken into account. There is almost no Islamic canonical text that deals with female sexual pleasure as a value in and of itself outside the framework of marriage or independently from the tutorship of a man, whether father, husband, elder brother, or other male guardian. Polygyny in the *sunnah* and zawaj al-mutʿa (literally, marriage of pleasure) in the Shīʿī tradition are the only licit conjugal institutions that allow some "sexual mobility" in which men have more opportunity than women to have sex without being committed to procreation. To allow sex without the restraint of procreation, contraception has been always tolerated in Islam, both in its more primitive forms, such as coitus interruptus, (*ʿazl*) and its scientific medical forms, for example, birth control pills, male and female condoms, vaginal ring, the cap or diaphragm, and other methods, including abortion.

For men as for women, *zinah* (sexual activity outside of marriage, whether fornication or adultery) is categorically forbidden and severely punished, at least *de jure*. Lesbianism is not regarded as *zinah*, as it is outside the equation of licit/illicit. There is a flagrant similitude between the canonical Islamic sources and popular discourse concerning the silence that enveloped the subject of sexuality. In practice, as with homosexuals, hermaphrodites (*Khuntha*), and effeminate men, lesbians are tacitly tolerated on society's margins.

A woman's virginity is a major consideration for marriage, and early marriage is encouraged to avoid *zinah* and illicit relationships. Teenage girls are not encouraged to engage in romantic relationships because of the risk that it would lead them to sexual and/or romantic relations that could cause them to lose their virginity. Regardless, the practices of everyday life in a given Muslim society are far from the puritan regulations prescribed by Sharīʿah texts, the burden of tradition, and the authority of men. In the 1990s, several academic monographs, aware of the dissymmetry between the religious statutes and Muslim women's sexuality as it was practiced in everyday life, tried to bridge this gap. In addition, Judith Tucker's study, *Women in Nineteenth-Century Egypt*, showed the darker aspects of the modernization process and how the introduction of new technologies in Egypt exposed women to slavery (including sexual exploitation), rather than liberating them from it.

Sexuality, Gender, and Islamic Feminism. Women's status and their sexuality in Muslim societies are determined by several factors: (1) how space, time, labor, and capital are divided and gendered; (2) the factuality of biology that men are physically *stronger* than women; (3) the banality of the practices of everyday life; and, only then, (4) what God and other Islamic texts say. The last factor becomes significant when women have recourse to justice, religious authority, or the state in general, as arbiter in issues related to Personal Status or Family Law, including divorce, child custody, adultery, rape, conjugal betrayal, marital rape, and other domestic conflicts.

Women in Muslim societies face many difficulties in speaking out about their sexual practices outside private feminine space. Usually, symbolism and metaphors replace straightforward language, which is qualified as shameful. The sexual linguistic limits concerning sexuality may be illustrated in the North African tradition, which survived until the mid-twentieth century: A woman who had been forced into sodomy by her husband would go to a *qāḍī*, take off her shoes, and put one shoe on the other on the floor, displayed before the court, the jury, and the audience, providing a symbolic gesture to replace the "rude" and "choking" words that a woman could not pronounce in public.

The language of sexuality in Arab-Muslim societies is more masculine than feminine, rendering sexuality as gendered as the language itself. There are some words, expressions, sentences, and phrases that are specific to men and others that can be pronounced only by women. Usually, when the sexual semantic field is evoked and sexuality is spoken about in proper terms, it is to designate subjects other than sexuality itself. Anthropologists and ethnologists who have tried to focus on sexual practices in Arab-Muslim societies find it very difficult to have people (especially women) speak in a direct way about their sexual practices, including favorite positions, oral sex, masturbation, orgasm, and other aspects. The same difficulty is confronted by women ethnologists working on women's sexuality, even when these ethnologists are originally from the same societies under study, such as in the case of the contributors of *L'Année du Maghreb*, 2010, which was devoted entirely to sexual practices in cotemporary North African societies. The conclusions and deductions that the scholars reached in this study were achieved in indirect ways, either by observations or interpretations of some acts, words, and behaviors. This does not mean that the language is lacking words, terms, and adjectives to describe sexual acts and practices, but that what is needed in Arab-Muslim societies is something to enable men and women to speak of their sexual practices in medical terms or in a clinical way.

The "genderfication" of the sexual semantic field in Arab-Muslim societies is accompanied by another gendered division of space and time that is also dictated by societal "logic." Thus, the indoors are reserved for women, outdoors for men, housework for women, outside work for men, public space for men, private space for women; nighttime is not for women, and both daytime and nighttime are for men. These divisions are always challenged, contested, and transgressed by the conditions of the societal milieu (urban/rural, agrarian/industrial), ecological factors (nomadic/sedentary/transhumance), the necessities of modern life, and the will of women to emancipate their "Self."

The 1990s and the first decade of the twenty-first century witnessed the emergence of several feminist activist voices, from outside as well as from within Muslim societies, which asked for parity between men and women, equality between sexes, and political recognition of "deviant" identities that stem from "illicit" sexual relations, for example, male and female homosexuality. Thus, several studies have tried to understand the impact of these movements on their societies, while others turned directly to study societal phenomena that were regarded as deviant and taboo. The trend took advantage of the fact that the 1990s were the heyday of the American academic and ideological movements of feminism, gender studies, gay and lesbian studies, subaltern studies, and postcolonial theory. Many of these methodologies and theories were imported into the field of Middle Eastern Studies, granting the researchers and scholars, foreign and locals who ventured into the field, a sophisticated analytic arsenal. The latter was/is an efficient method to argue for liberating bodies and freeing identities that were born from all kinds of "deviant" or "illicit" sexual relationships.

The 1990s feminist wave also opened up venues for sensitive topics and subjects that were and still are considered as taboo (e.g., homosexuality, masturbation, oral sex, eroticism, pornography, sadomasochism, virginity, women's sexual desire), not only in academic literature, but also in the popular press, mass culture, yellow press, digital communications technologies, and social networks. Thus, several daily newspapers in countries such as Morocco, Egypt, and Lebanon, added supplements of "sexual education" where youngsters could ask questions about their sexualities and have them answered by professional sexologists and psychotherapists, a trend that witnessed a large popularity, not only among youth, but also among their parents who felt the need, like their children, to understand their sexuality. This sociopsychological situation reached its apogee with the emergence in 2008 in Beirut, Lebanon, of the first erotic magazine *Jasad*. *Jasad* was founded by a young intellectual Lebanese woman, Joumana Haddad. The articles, which bear the real names of the authors—no pseudonyms are allowed—are in Arabic because sex and sexuality are typically debated in today's Arab-Muslim societies in foreign languages, namely English and French.

In this vein, on the level of academic discourse, several interesting studies on women's sexuality—not necessarily on lesbianism, shame and honor, or prostitution—have been published. The aim behind them is to understand women's sexuality and the place, in private and public space, of women's bodies in contemporary modern Arab-Muslim societies. One of these studies was *Sexuality in the Arab World*. Based on a conference held at the American University of Beirut, some chapters of the book attempt to address the subject with an anthropological approach, for example, how women live, practice, and talk about their sexual practices in everyday life.

BIBLIOGRAPHY

Abu-Lughod, Lila, ed. *Remaking Women: Feminism and Modernity in the Middle East*. Princeton, N.J.: Princeton University Press, 1998.

Abu-Lughod, Lila. *Veiled Sentiments: Honor and Poetry in a Bedouin Society*. Berkeley: University of California Press, 1986.

Ahmed, Leila. *Women and Gender in Islam: Historical Roots of a Modern Debate*. New Haven, Conn.: Yale University Press, 1992.

L'Année du Maghreb. "Dossier: Sexe et sexualités au Maghreb." *Essais d'Ethnographies Contemporaines*." 6 (2010).

Badran, Margot. *Feminists, Islam, and Nation: Gender and the Making of Modern Egypt*. Princeton, N.J.: Princeton University Press, 1995.

Baron, Beth. "Women, Honour and the State: Evidence From Egypt." *Middle Eastern Studies* 42, no. 1 (2006): 1–20.

Beaumont, Valérie, Corinne Cauvin Verner, and François Pouillon. "Sexualité au Maghreb." *L'Annee de Maghren* 6 (2010): 3–14.

Bouhdiba, Abdelwahab. *Sexuality in Islam*. Translated by Alain Sheridan. London: Saqi Books, [1975] 1998.

Charrad, Mounira M. *States and Women's Rights: The Making of Postcolonial Tunisia, Algeria, and Morocco*. Berkeley: California University Press, 2001.

Haddad, Joumana. *I Killed Scheherazade: Confessions of an Angry Arab Woman*. London: Saqi Books, 2011.

Jasad Magazine. http://www.jasadmag.com/.

Khalaf, Samir, and John Gagnon. *Sexuality in the Arab World*. London: Saqi Books, 2006.

Mernissi, Fatima. *Beyond the Veil: Male-Female Dynamics in Modern Muslim Society*. Cambridge, Mass.: Shenkman, 1975.

Mernissi, Fatima. *Sex, Idéologie, Islam*. Casablanca: Edition Tierce, Le Fennec, 1984–1985.

Mosteghanemi, Ahlam. *Memory in the Flesh*. Cairo: American University in Cairo Press, 2003.

Mussalem, Basim F. *Sex and Society in Islam: Birth Control before the Nineteenth Century*. Cambridge, U.K.: Cambridge University Press, 1983.

Naamane-Gessous, Soumaya. *Au-delà de toute pudeur: La sexualité feminine au Maroc*. Casablanca: Edition Eddif, 1991.

Najmabadi, Afsaneh, ed. *Women's Autobiographies in Contemporary Iran*. Cambridge, Mass.: Harvard University Press, 1990.

Omnia, El Shakry. "Barren Land and Fecund Bodies: The Emergence of Population Discourse in Interwar Egypt." *International Journal of Middle East Studies* 37 (2005): 360–361.

Paidar, Parvin. *Women and Political Process in Twentieth-Century Iran*. Cambridge, U.K.: Cambridge University Press, 1995.

Saad Khalaf, Roseanne. "Breaking the Silence: What AUB Students Really Think about Sex." In *Sexuality in the Arab World*, edited by Samir Khalaf and John Gagnon, p. 187. London: Saqi Books: 2006.

Tucker, Judith E. *Women in Nineteenth-Century Egypt*, pp. 164–193. Cambridge, U.K.: Cambridge University Press, 1995.

SAMIR BEN-LAYASHI

SHAFĪQ, DURRĪYAH. Durrīyah Shafīq (1908–1976), also known as Doria Shafik, was an Egyptian scholar, teacher, journalist, and feminist activist. The writings and activism of Durrīyah Shafīq followed in the secular, democratic tradition of the Egyptian feminists Hudā Shaʿrāwī and Amīnah al-Saʿīd. Shafīq was educated in Western schools, first in a kindergarten run by Italian nuns and then at a French mission school. She was an admirer of Shaʿrāwī from youth, and it was with Shaʿrāwī's assistance that Shafīq was able to attend the Sorbonne, where she received a doctorate in 1940.

Upon returning to Egypt Shafīq taught at Alexandria College for Girls and at the Sannia School; she then worked for the Ministry of Education as a French-language inspector before beginning her career as a journalist and political activist. In 1945 she founded the magazine *Majallat bint al-Nīl* (Daughter of the Nile Magazine), which included a segment devoted to promoting political rights for women called "Bint al-Nīl al-siyāsīyah" (Political Daughter of the Nile).

In 1948 Shafīq founded the Ittiḥād Bint al-Nīl (Daughter of the Nile Union), a middle-class feminist association with branches in several provincial cities, dedicated to encouraging female literacy and full political rights for women. In a bid to gain international recognition for Egyptian feminism, Shafīq affiliated the Union with the International Council of Women under the name of the National Council for Egyptian Women.

In 1951 a thousand members of Shafīq's Union disrupted the Egyptian parliament in a demonstration calling for the vote and other political rights for women. The demonstration sparked a reaction on the part of religious conservatives, and the Union of Muslim Associations in Egypt, which included the Muslim Brotherhood, demanded that the king abolish all women's organizations that called for participation in politics, that women be encouraged to stay at home, and that the use of the veil be enforced. Shafīq responded with a "White Paper on the Rights of Egyptian Women" (Al-kitāb al-abyad li-ḥuqūq al-marʿah al-Miṣrīyah), in which she argued in the reformist tradition of Muslim feminists that Islam speaks for the equality of women and requires neither the veil nor domesticity.

The following year political opposition groups conducted a series of strikes against foreign interests in a bid to undermine the British occupation, and the paramilitary arm of Shafīq's Union joined in the strike by picketing Barclay's Bank. After the Free Officers came to power in 1952, Shafīq continued to agitate for political rights for women. She founded a short-lived Daughter of the Nile political party, which was disbanded with all other political parties in 1953 by the revolutionary government. In 1954, when the constitutional assembly formed by President Gamal Abdel Nasser to adopt or reject a proposed new constitution included no women, Shafīq carried out a much-publicized hunger strike to demand political rights for women, in which she was joined by members of the Bint al-Nīl Union in Cairo and Alexandria. Having sought and gained international recognition for her strike, Shafīq was rewarded when the governor of Cairo agreed to put in writing that the constitution would guarantee full political rights for women. The 1956 constitution did in fact grant women the right to vote, but only to those who formally applied for it, while for men the right to vote was automatic. Consequently, Shafīq filed a legal protest.

The following year marked Shafīq's political undoing. She announced to Nasser and the press that she was going on a hunger strike to protest Nasser's dictatorship, as well as the lingering Israeli occupation of the Sinai in the wake of the Suez invasion, which should have ended with the UN-ordered withdrawal. Shafīq's colleagues at the Bint al-Nīl Union not only failed to support her but asked her to resign, and, along with other women's associations, they denounced her as a traitor. She was placed under house arrest, and the Bint al-Nīl Union and magazine were closed down. In the following years Shafīq experienced repeated emotional breakdowns and eventually committed suicide in 1976.

Shafīq, like her predecessor Hudā Shaʿrāwī, had anticipated erroneously that women's participation in the struggle for national liberation would engender popular support for feminist causes. Shafīq miscalculated on two counts—first on the strength of Islamic conservative reaction, and second on the charisma of Nasser, who in spite of his repression of democracy enjoyed great popularity for having initiated the final evacuation of the British from Egypt.

In addition to her political writings, Shafīq wrote *Al-marʿah al-Miṣrīyah min al-farāʿinah ilā al-yawm* (Egyptian Women from the Pharaohs until Today), and, with Ibrāhīm ʿAbduh, *Taṭawwur al-nahḍah al-Miṣrīyah*, 1798–1951 (Development of the Women's Renaissance in Egypt), as well as several books of poetry and prose published in France.

[*See also* Feminism; *and* Shaʿrāwī, Hudā.]

BIBLIOGRAPHY

Ahmed, Leila. *Women and Gender in Islam: Historical Roots of a Modern Debate*. New Haven, 1992. Excellent discussion of the development of nineteenth- to twentieth-century feminism in the Middle East.

Badran, Margot, and miriam cooke, eds. *Opening the Gates: A Century of Arab Feminist Writing*. Bloomington, Ind., 1990. Includes a sample of Shafīq's political writing, "White Paper on the Rights of Egyptian Women" (pp. 352–356).

Nelson, Cynthia. *Doria Shafik, Egyptian Feminist: A Woman Apart*. Gainesville, Fla., 1996.

Nelson, Cynthia. "Doria Shafik's French Writing: Hybridity in a Feminist Key." *Alif: Journal of Comparative Politics* 20 (2000): 109–139.

Sullivan, Earl L. *Women in Egyptian Public Life*. Syracuse, N.Y., 1986.

ELEANOR ABDELLA DOUMATO

SHAJAR AL-DURR. (d. 1257), briefly Sultan of Egypt (1250). Originally a slave (usually described as Turkish, but possibly Armenian), Shajar became the favorite concubine of the Ayyūbid Sultan al-Ṣāliḥ Ayyūb and bore him a son, Khalīl (in 1240). Even after the child's early death, she was accordingly known as *Wālidat* (or *Umm*) *Khalīl* (Khalīl's mother). Following Ayyūb's own death near al-Manṣūra in November 1249, at the height of the invasion of Egypt by the ill-fated Seventh Crusade, she was one of a group of three, including the commander in chief Fakhr al-Dīn Ibn al-Shaykh, who concealed Ayyūb's death and issued decrees in his name, while secretly summoning his son al-Muʿaẓẓam Tūrān Shāh from Ḥiṣn Kayfā in Mesopotamia to assume the throne.

One source claims that Shajar herself was adept at forging Ayyūb's signature.

When Tūrān Shāh arrived, however, his arbitrary conduct rapidly alienated many of his father's faithful, in particular the corps of Mamlūk guards, the Baḥrīya. He allegedly ordered Shajar al-Durr to surrender the jewelry that Ayyūb had given to her, and she appealed to the Baḥrīya for assistance. On 2 May 1250, less than four weeks after triumphing over the Crusaders, Tūrān Shāh was cut down by Baḥrī Mamlūks, and Shajar al-Durr was proclaimed sultan, with the Mamlūk officer ʿIzz al-Dīn Aybak al-Turkumānī as her commander in chief (*atābak al-ʿasākir*).

Shajar al-Durr's Mamlūk backers saw her as providing legitimacy and continuity with Ayyūb's reign. Yet her rule was never acknowledged in his Syrian territories. The enthronement of a woman as sovereign (as opposed to regent) was virtually unprecedented in the Islamic Near East, and the circumstances of Shajar al-Durr's accession guaranteed hostility from Ayyūb's kin in Syria. In July 1250 the Ayyūbid Sultan of Aleppo, al-Nāṣir Yūsuf, was welcomed into Damascus as its ruler and prepared to invade Egypt. When this news reached Cairo, the Baḥrīya and their supporters recognized the need for a male ruler.

They deposed Shajar al-Durr and proclaimed Aybak as sultan on 30 July, only to dethrone him five days later, when the seizure of Kerak and al-Ṣubayba by other Ayyūbid princes made clear the need to restore the Ayyūbid line in Cairo. An infant grandson of al-Ṣāliḥ Ayyūb was made sultan, though Aybak served a second time as *atābak*. Once al-Nāṣir Yūsuf's attempt to conquer Egypt had been thwarted in 1251, however, and the threat from Syria had receded, Aybak removed the boy from the throne and again became sultan. At an uncertain date, he married Shajar al-Durr.

In the wake of her deposition, Shajar al-Durr nonetheless retained considerable authority, continuing to sign decrees as late as 1255. But in time Aybak, already emboldened by his success in moving against the more prominent among his fellow Baḥrīs, seemingly grew restless and contracted to marry a princess from Mosul (al-Mawṣil) in a bid to counter her influence. Shajar al-Durr reacted by arranging his murder on 10 April 1257, but she was killed in retaliation by Aybak's own Mamlūks in Cairo on 28 April. She was clearly a woman of strong character and is described by the Christian author Bar Hebraeus as possessing rare beauty. A significant body of folklore about her later evolved, most notably in the apocryphal details found in the fourteenth/fifteenth-century *Romance of Baybars*. In the modern period, she has served as an inspiration to feminist writers.

BIBLIOGRAPHY

The only full study is Götz Schregle, *Die Sultanin von Ägypten; Šağarat al-Durr in der arabischen Geschichtsschreibung und Literatur* (Wiesbaden, Germany: Harrassowitz, 1961); see also David J. Duncan, "Scholarly Views of Shajarat al-Durr: A Need for Consensus," *Arab Studies Quarterly* 22 (2000): 51–69; L. Ammann, "Shadjar al-Durr," *Encyclopaedia of Islam*, 2d ed., edited by C.E. Bosworth, Vol. 9, p. 176 (Leiden, Netherlands: Brill, 1997); and for further literature, Peter Thorau, *The Lion of Egypt: Sultan Baybars I and the Near East in the Thirteenth Century*, translated by P. M. Holt (Harlow, U.K.: Longman, 1992), chapters 5–6.

PETER JACKSON

SHAME. The concept of shame (Ar., *ḥashm*; Pers., *sharm*) is an aspect of social status often paired with honor as opposites of moral evaluation. This is at once too narrow and too broad. Notions of shame draw in religious injunctions to modesty, temperance, and body covering that symbolically limit interaction with others. Local, tribal, and class-bound notions are commonly merged with understandings of Islamic concepts, which are used to justify and rationalize specific social constraints, particularly on women and sexuality. The same words gloss a range of experiences from misery to embarrassment, and from bashful to coy behaviors. Rather than being the contrary of honor, shame might be understood better as one of its companions in ensembles of ideas about social status and self-presentation.

The exteriority that makes seclusion, veiling, and segregation of women available to analysis has tended to skew understandings of shame toward an emphasis on extramarital sexual relations. More nuanced accounts of honor as performance have shown the equation to be too narrow; shame gives meaning to such behavior rather than taking meaning from it. The problematic identity attributed to women inheres in their ambiguous status in patrilineally denominated relationships of descent and kinship. Strong concerns with virginity and chastity mark their symbiotic and symbolic relationship to paternity.

Additional grounds for shame are as diverse as experiences of it. Where land and control of productive resources are important, as in tribal and peasant societies, a person who must exchange labor for livelihood is in a position of social shame as a dependent and should act modestly. Such generic shame is relative; in commercial settings, artisans may have less social honor than traders but more than common laborers. More specific shame arises with bad dealings and social failures, which may be caused by another person or self-inflicted. Shame can thus be an aspect of status, performances, and attitudes.

Indigenous understandings of shame are grounded in notions of persons and behaviors as balances of *ʿaql* and *nafs*—or cognitive and affective capacities—that inform a comprehensive social metaphysics. This metaphysics highlights control and self-possession, with shame marking their absence, lapse, or compromise in a problematic moral universe. Shame is involuntary and emotional, but also figures in the responses of shyness and modesty.

Shame can powerfully motivate efforts to overcome or wipe it out. It is the negative motive of *jihad*, the struggle to subordinate one's own life and the social environment to the dictates of religion. Shame is also the harborage of revenge, which wipes out a shame and at the same time affirms it. Much ritual politeness of Muslim society is a matter of avoiding shame, shaming, or calling attention to the shame of another, lest these consequences be invoked. Shame unrestrained or unmitigated can lead to violence equally without restraint. Recognition of this power underwrites tendencies to avoid degrading another.

[*See also* Honor; Modesty; *and* Seclusion.]

BIBLIOGRAPHY

Anderson, Jon W. "Social Structures and the Veil: Comportment and the Composition of Interaction in Afghanistan." *Anthropos* 77 (1982): 397–420.

Delaney, Carol. "Seeds of Honor, Fields of Shame." In *Honor and Shame and the Unity of the Mediterranean*, edited by David D. Gilmore, pp. 35–48. Washington, D.C., 1987.

Wikan, Unni. "Shame and Honor: A Contestable Pair." *Man* 19 (1984): 635–652.

JON W. ANDERSON

SHAʿRĀWĪ, HUDĀ. Hudā Shaʿrāwī (1879–1947),was an Egyptian feminist leader. Born in Minyā in Upper Egypt to Sulṭān Pāshā, a wealthy landowner and provincial administrator, and Iqbāl Hānim, a young woman of Circassian origin, Nūr al-Hudā Sulṭān (known after her marriage as Hudā Shaʿrāwī) was raised in Cairo. Following her father's death when she was four, Hūdā was raised in a household headed by both her mother and a co-wife. Tutored at home, Hudā became proficient in French (the language of the elite) but, despite efforts to acquire fluency in Arabic, was permitted only enough instruction to memorize the Qurʿān. Through comparisons with her younger brother, Hudā became acutely aware of gender difference, the privileging of males, and the restrictions placed upon females. At thirteen, she reluctantly acquiesced to marriage with her paternal cousin, ʿAlī Shaʿrāwī, her legal guardian and the executor of her father's estate. At fourteen she began a seven-year separation from her husband. During this time (the 1890s), she attended a women's salon, where through discussions with other members, Hudā became aware that veiling the face and female confinement in the home were not Islamic requirements, as women had been led to believe. (Such critical examination of customary practice vis-à-vis religious prescription was part of the Islamic modernist movement initiated by Shaykh Muḥammad ʿAbduh in the nineteenth century.) In 1900 Shaʿrāwī resumed married life. She gave birth to a daughter, Bathna, in 1903 and a son, Muḥammad, in 1905. In 1909 Shaʿrāwī helped found the secular women's philanthropy, the Mabarrat Muḥammad ʿAlī, bringing together Muslim and Christian women to operate a medical dispensary for poor women and children. That same year she helped organize the first "public" lectures for and by women, held at the new Egyptian University and in the offices of the liberal newspaper, *Al-jarīdah*. In 1914 she participated in forming the Women's Refinement Union (al-Ittiḥād al-Nisāʾī al-Tahdībī) and the Ladies Literary Improvement Society (Jamʿīyat al-Raqy al-Adabīyah li-al-Sayyidāt al-Misrīyāt). Shaʿrāwī was active in the movement for national independence from 1919 to 1922. An organizer of the first women's demonstration in 1919, she became the president of the Women's Central Committee (Lajnat al-Wafd al-Markazīyah li-al-Sayyidāt) of the (male) nationalist Wafd party. Shaʿrāwī led militant nationalist women in broadening the popular base of the party, organizing boycotts of British goods and services, and assuming central leadership roles when nationalist men were exiled.

In 1923, the year after independence, Shaʿarāwī spearheaded the creation of the Egyptian Feminist Union (al-Ittiḥād al-Nisāʾī al-Miṣrī; EFU) and, as president, led the first organized feminist movement in Egypt (and in the Arab world). That same year, while returning from the Rome Conference of the International Woman Suffrage Alliance (which she attended as an EFU delegate), she removed her face veil in public in an act of political protest. Shaʿrāwī generously donated her personal wealth to the work of the Egyptian Feminist Union, while also supporting other organizations and individuals. She opened the House of Cooperative Reform (Dār al-Taʿāwun al-Iṣlāḥī), a medical dispensary for poor women and children and a center for crafts training for girls, in 1924 under the aegis of the EFU, and the following year founded *L'Egyptienne*, a monthly journal serving the feminist movement. Several years later, in 1937, she established the Arabic bimonthly *Al-miṣrīyah* (The Egyptian Woman).

The feminist movement of which Shaʿrāwī was a leader brought together Muslim and Christian women of the upper and middle classes who identified themselves as Egyptians. Although a secular movement, its agenda was articulated within the framework of modernist Islam. The feminist movement supported women's right to all levels of education and forms of work, called for full political rights for women, advocated reform of the Personal Status Code, pressured the government to provide basic health and social services to poor women, and demanded an end to state-licensed prostitution. Along with these woman-centered reforms, Shaʿrāwī stressed the nationalist goals of the feminist movement, calling for Egyptian sovereignty, including an end to British military occupation and the termination of the capitulations, which extended privileges and immunities to foreigners. In 1937 she created three dispensaries, a girls' school, and a boys' school in villages in the province of Minyā, and later a short-lived branch of the Egyptian Feminist Union in the city of Minyā. As a nationalist feminist, Shaʿrāwī was active in the international women's movement, serving on the executive board of the International Woman Suffrage Alliance (later called the International Alliance of Women for Suffrage and Equal Citizenship) from 1926 until her death. In 1938 she hosted the Women's Conference for the Defense of Palestine. Shaʿrāwī played a key role in consolidating Pan-Arab feminism, which grew out of Arab women's collective national activism on behalf of Palestine, organizing the Arab Feminist Conference in Cairo in 1944. She was elected president of the Arab Feminist Union (al-Ittiḥād al-Nisāʿī al-ʿArabī), created in 1945. Shortly before her death in 1947, the Egyptian state awarded Shaʿrāwī its highest decoration.

[*See also* Feminism.]

BIBLIOGRAPHY

Primary Works

"Asas al-Nahḍah al-Nisāʿīyah wa-Taṭawwuratihā fiMiṣr" (The Foundation of the Feminist Renaissance and Its Evolution in Egypt). *Majallat al-Shuʿūn al-Ijtimāʿīyah* (Cairo) (August 1941): 16–24. Broad overview.

"Discours de Mme. Charaoui Pacha, Presidente de l'Union Feministe Egyptienne." *L'Egyptienne* (December 1933): 10–14. Speech given at a ceremony honoring the first women to graduate from university in Egypt, dealing with the evolution of Egyptian women with a focus on education.

Harem Years: The Memoirs of an Egyptian Feminist. Translated, edited, and introduced by Margot Badran. London, 1986. English translation of the Mudhakkirāt.

Mudhakkirāt Hudā Shaʿrāwī, rāʿidat al-marʿah al-ʿarabīyah al-ḥadīthah (The Memoirs of Hudā Shaʿrāwī, Pioneer of the Modern Arab Woman). Introduction by Amīnah al-Saʿīd. Cairo, 1981.

Secondary Sources

Badran, Margot. "From Consciousness to Activism: Feminist Politics in Early Twentieth-Century Egypt." In *Problems of the Middle East in Historical Perspective*, edited by John P. Spagnolo, pp. 27–48. London, 1992.

Badran, Margot. "Dual Liberation: Feminism and Nationalism in Egypt from the 1870s–1925." *Feminist Issues* 8, no. 1 (Spring 1988): 15–34.

Badran, Margot. *Feminists, Islam, and Nation: Gender and the Making of Modern Egypt*. Princeton, 1995.

Golley, Nawar al-Hassan. *Reading Arab Women's Autobiographies: Shahrazad Tells Her Story*. Austin, Texas, 2003.

Kahf, Mohja. "Packaging 'Huda': Shaʿrawi's Memoirs in the United States Reception Environment." In *Going Global: The Transnational Reception of Third World Women Writers*, edited by Amal Amireh and Lisa Suhair Majaj, pp. 148–172. New York, 2000.

Subkī, Āmāl al-. *Al-ḥarakāh al-nisāʿīyah fiMiṣr mā bayna althawratayn 1919 wa 1952*. Cairo, 1986.

MARGOT BADRAN

SHARĪʾAH, FIQH, PHILOSOPHY, AND REASON (THEORETICAL OVERVIEW).

Debates about Sharīʾah, what it is, who should interpret it, and the relative role it should play in the lives of Muslims have been at center stage in discussions throughout Islamic history about how Islam is to be lived and interpreted. For the purposes of this encyclopedia, we elected to address "Sharīʾah, Fiqh, Philosophy, and Reason" separately from "Religion: Theory, Practice, and Interpretation" both to highlight the important role of Islamic law and its multiple definitions and applications among Muslims and to draw attention to the important role played by human beings in that interpretive process.

Major debates have been occurring over the past few decades about relative levels of authority between Sharīʾah and fiqh. Sharīʾah, as divinely revealed law, is intended to hold the highest level of authority, while fiqh, as human interpretation, should be considered less authoritative. Nevertheless, the current reality is that, in some societies, this distinction is not being made because of the perceived need to adhere to "tradition," whether scripturally based or not. The main battleground has to do with *ijtihad* (independent reasoning)—who has the right to engage it, when, where, and to what degree? Since the publication of Wael Hallaq's pivotal work questioning whether the gate to *ijtihad* was ever truly closed, the question of *ijtihad* and its appropriateness in the contemporary era, when societies face new challenges not only because of advancements in science, medicine, and technology, but also due to new realities of transnationalism, globalization, and mass migration, has resulted in heated debates. Muslim women today are increasingly demanding their right to participate in the conversation on the basis of their merit as scholars (such as Leila Ahmed and Azizah al-Hibri), judges (Tahany el Gebaly), muftis (Su'ad Saleh and Abla el Kahlawy), and even ayatollahs (Noṣrat Amīn and Zohreh Ṣefātī).

Debates and even conflicts have also erupted over Sharī'ah and where and when it should be applied, with some countries and states passing legislation either banning Sharī'ah from the legal system or banning the right of individuals to adhere to certain aspects of it. Of greatest concern internationally has been the question of *ḥudūd*, those punishments specified in the Qur'ān for certain crimes, as punishments have been upheld by or added into various legal systems, without necessarily adhering to the parameters for witnesses and evidence. One prominent case that has reverberated internationally occurred in Nigeria with respect to women found to be pregnant outside of marriage and thus accused of illicit sexual activity (*zinah*), which is punishable by death by stoning in some interpretations. Muslim women legal scholars, and activists employed a variety of legal arguments against stoning, including highlighting that this punishment is not specified in the Qur'ān, that there are strict regulations concerning witnesses for *zinah*, and, most successfully, turning to classical interpretations of Islamic law that forbid the use of pregnancy as evidence of illicit sexual activity. Similarly, Muslim women activists have worked to address cases of women being charged with *zinah* because they are unable to prove that they were raped, such as in Pakistan, a reality that pressures women to remain silent about sexual assaults rather than face the death penalty. These cases are important because they highlight women's agency and use of Sharī'ah, fiqh, reason, and historical example to create new spaces for the insertion of women's voices into these traditionally male domains, producing outcomes that both insist upon strict adherence to the guidelines for witnessing and evidence, while giving attention to the broad values that the Sharī'ah is supposed to protect and uphold. With the events of the Arab Spring and the rise of Islamist-oriented governments in countries such as Tunisia and Egypt, questions about the role of Sharī'ah in the new state, how it is to be applied, and who is to interpret it are likely to remain battlegrounds for the foreseeable future.

Questions related to family law, particularly marriage, divorce, inheritance, and child custody, also remain central concerns for women, particularly as marriage and divorce patterns are changing as demographics, educational levels, and women's employment are also undergoing significant transformations. Marriage and divorce particularly highlight differences between legal theory and actual practice, as seen both historically and in the contemporary era with the development of new kinds of marriage, such as *misyar* and *misfar*, which seem to meet the legal parameters for making sexual relations licit without providing any of the financial support and security, particularly maintenance (*nafaqah*), that a standard marriage (*nikah*) would provide. Similarly, women are demanding increasing agency in decision-making within the marriage, greater access to divorce, and stronger rights with respect to child custody as women in many Muslim-majority countries are entering the paid workforce and contributing to household finances as a matter of necessity. Reconfiguration of the logistics of the household is argued by some as justification for legal reconfiguration of the power structure within the household and greater autonomy for women.

Finally, this theme gives attention to the question of international standards of human rights, social justice, and women's rights, not only in terms of where they are perceived to fall short in the Muslim world, but also challenging the right of the West to define the terms and standards and questioning whether exemptions should be allowed for non-Western countries with alternative definitions of what constitutes "human rights" or "women's rights." At heart is the concern that "international standards" simply represent another form of neo-colonialism, albeit in global disguise.

In all of these topics, women are not only the subjects and objects of debate, as has been the case historically, but also emerge as participants in, as well as drivers of, both the topics and methods of analysis.

NATANA J. DELONG-BAS

SHAYKH, HANAN AL-. (b. 1945), Lebanese author. Born in Beirut, Hanan al-Shaykh grew up in a strict Shīʿa family, although her father supported her right to an education. She attended the Almillah Primary School for Muslim girls and then the Ahliyyah School for Girls, proceeding to the American Girls' College in Cairo, Egypt. Upon graduating in 1966, she returned to Lebanon to start work on the newspaper *Al-Nahar*. In 1975 she was forced to leave Beirut with the outbreak of the Lebanese Civil War. She moved initially to Saudi Arabia and later to London.

The author of a number of books, short stories, and plays, al-Shaykh has written about the influences on her own life and the controls her father and brother imposed in her youth. She was also deeply marked by her mother's desertion of the family when Hanan was very young. Much of al-Shaykh's work challenges the notions of obedience, modesty, and submissiveness by which she was raised, as well as portraying certain aspects of so-called honor killings. She believes in the importance of writing about issues that she sees as key, including controversial topics such as same-sex love and prostitution, seeking to bring issues that were previously hidden from society into public view.

As in the work of many other novelists, there are aspects of al-Shakyh's writings that derive from her own life experiences, yet she allows her fictional characters to take a different path, such as in *The Story of Zahra* (1980), in which the central female character evinces strength because of her ability to establish her own boundaries, rather than live in an environment dictated by men. *Beirut Blues* (1996) provides a thoughtful account of the Lebanese civil war through a number of letters from a woman who decided to remain in Beirut rather than flee, as al-Shakyh had done.

It was not long before some conservative countries in the Middle East either banned al-Shakyh's works, or made them hard to access. This was particularly true of *The Story of Zahra*, which discussed formerly taboo subjects, including abortion, divorce, and sexual promiscuity. Her later *Women of Sand and Myrrh* (1992) proved even more controversial for its coverage of a lesbian relationship.

The attempts to censor the writings of Hanan al-Shakyh in parts of the Middle East have not affected her book sales in North America and

Europe, where an avid readership remains. Al-Shaykh's works have been translated into English, French, Dutch, German, Danish, Italian, Korean, Spanish, and Polish.

BIBLIOGRAPHY

DeLong-Bas, Natana J. *Notable Muslims: Muslim Builders of World Civilization and Culture*. Oxford: Oneworld, 2006.

Sakkut, Hamdi. *The Arabic Novel: Bibliography and Critical Introduction, 1865–1995*. 6 vols. Cairo: American University in Cairo Press, 2000.

Shaykh, Hanan al-. *The Locust and the Bird: My Mother's Story*. London: Bloomsbury, 2009.

Shaykh, Hanan al-. *Only in London*. New York: Pantheon Books, 2001.

Shaykh, Hanan al-. *Women of Sand and Myrrh*. New York: Doubleday, 1992.

JUSTIN CORFIELD *and* NATANA J. DELONG-BAS

SHĪʿĪ ISLAM AND WOMEN.

[*This entry contains two subentries,*

Historical Overview *and*
Contemporary Thought and Practice.]

HISTORICAL OVERVIEW

The position of women in Shīʿī history has been, in theory, greatly enhanced by the prominent place accorded to the Prophet's daughter Fātimah, both in Shīʿī history and in the Shīʿī interpretation of the Qurʾān. There are, however, some negative factors for women in Shīʿism, such as the practice of temporary marriage (*mutaʿah*), which is accepted by Twelver Shīʿīs but not by Ismāʿīlī Shīʿīs. The actual status of women in Shīʿī societies has, in fact, been determined more by local cultures than by any theoretical considerations. We are still a long way from fully understanding this, as women remained invisible in most of the available historical sources. The evidence available so far, however, indicates that Shīʿī women had no more rights and were no freer than their Sunni counterparts in most of the Islamic world for most periods of history. Women who lived on the outer margins of the Islamic world were relatively freer than those living in the Islamic heartlands.

The Holy Family and Early Shīʿī Women of Bahrain and Iran. For Shīʿīs, Fātimah holds a special place both as the only child of the Prophet Muḥammad to grow to adulthood and to have descendants, thus becoming the progenitor of the line of Shīʿī Imāms. While Sunnīs interpreted Qurʾān 33:32–33 as honoring Muḥammad's wives, Shīʿīs considered these verses to refer to Fātimah and her daughters and female descendants. Furthermore, in the Akhbārī interpretation of the Qurʾān, she is the niche in the Light Verse of the Qurʾān (24:35), and the lamp in that verse symbolizes her sons, Ḥasan and Ḥusayn. She is also the brilliant light (*kawākibun durrīyun*) in that verse. In Twelver collections of Traditions, she is placed alongside the Prophet Muḥammad and the twelve Imāms as the Fourteen Immaculate Ones (*chāhārdah maʿsūmīn*), the lights that were the first things to separate from God. These, in the fully developed philosophy of *ḥikmat-i ilāhī* (the School of Isfahan), replace the Primal Will or Primal Intellect as the first emanations from God and the cause of the whole of the rest of creation. Consequently she is deemed capable of interceding for believers (Shīʿīs) on the Day of Judgment. Historically, Fāṭimah's insistence on her right to her inheritance from her father (the oasis of Fadak) had an effect on women's legal rights of inheritance. Also important in Shīʿī history are Khadījah (the first wife of Muḥammad, the mother of Fāṭimah, and the first woman believer, who supported Muḥammad in the difficult early years of his prophethood), and Zaynab (the daughter of Fāṭimah and ʿAlī, who championed the cause of the family of ʿAlī after its defeat and massacre at Karbalā).

These three women—Fāṭimah, Khadījah, and Zaynab—have provided role models for Shīʿī women, both domestically as good daughters, wives, and mothers, and also publicly for social engagement and occupying high positions in society. Also from this period is Shahrbānū, the daughter of the last Sasanian monarch Yazdigird. Her marriage to the third Imam, Ḥusayn, served the cause of Iranian nationalism well, but is likely just a pious fiction (Amir-Moezzi, 2011, pp. 45–100). Historically, for the first 300 years of Shīʿī history, the only Shīʿī women mentioned in the histories were descendants of the Prophet Muḥammad, such as the sister of the eighth Imam Fāṭimah Maʿṣūmah (d. 816 CE), whose shrine is the center of the religious complex at Qum, and occasionally the womenfolk of prominent Shīʿī families.

While the central orthodoxy of Islam became increasingly patriarchal in the years following the death of Muḥammad, groups situated on the margins of Islamic society, both religiously and geographically, often allowed women more of a social role. The Qarmaṭī Ismāʿīlī Shīʿīs of Bahrayn and al-Aḥsā (tenth century), are reported, for example, to have allowed women to go unveiled and to mix freely with men (Ahmed, 1992, pp. 98–99), although this may have been an attempt by the enemies of the Qarmaṭīs to blacken their name by attributing sexual license to them (Cortese and Calderini, 2006, pp. 26–27). Occasionally in the tenth to twelfth centuries, we read of exceptional Shīʿī women rising to positions of power, such as Sayyidah Khātūn (also known as Shīrīn, d. A.D. 419/1028 CE), a Bavand princess married to Fakhr al-Dawlah who held the reins of power in western Iran under the Buyid dynasty for some thirty years. Women are said to have had an important place in society in Daylām (now the province of Gīlān in Iran), whence the Buyids came (Busse, 1975, pp. 252–253, 306–308). It is from the Buyid period that we have the earliest evidence for the existence of ritual mourning for the martyred Imam Ḥusayn and for women's participation in this rite (Aghaie, 2005, p. 5).

Ismāʿīlī Shīʿīs in North Africa and Yemen. The Ismāʿīlī Shīʿī Fatimid dynasty, which ruled in North Africa from 909, in Egypt and Syria from 969, and in Arabia from 1037, until the final fall of the dynasty in 1171, depended for its legitimacy on descent through a woman, Fāṭimah, the daughter of the Prophet, and for this reason called itself Fatimid. Women seem to have played a prominent role in the early phase of the Ismāʿīlī mission (*daʿwah*) in North Africa, probably due to the greater social role of women in the Berber tribes of North Africa. The women of that area continued to appear prominently in the annals of the Zirid dynasty that ruled there, at first on behalf of the Fatimids and later independently (Cortese and Calderini, 2006, pp. 28–29, 58–60, 92–93).

During Fatimid times, the mothers of caliphs often played an important role in ensuring the succession of their sons, which enabled them to become powerful figures at court: Karīmah ensured the succession of her son al-Manṣur in 946 CE And Rasad ensured the succession of her son al-Mustanṣir in 1036 CE, then only seven years old, and she played an important role in state affairs until 1073 CE At other times, it was the aunt of the caliph who ensured the succession and wielded power afterwards: Sitt al-Mulk (970–1023 CE) was influential during the reign of her brother al-Ḥakīm and, after his disappearance in 1021 CE, ensured the succession of al-Ẓāhir and ruled as regent until her death. Aunts of the caliphs also attained positions of power in the reigns of the last three Fatimid caliphs, who all were children when they acceded to the caliphate. As distinct from many other dynasties, which would use marriages of the royal women to create alliances and reward allies, the Fatimids appear to have kept many of the women of the royal household unmarried. Nevertheless, these women, as well as the womenfolk of high government officials, possessed great wealth in their own right, some of it given to them by their menfolk and some of it earned through trade and other activities. With this wealth, they built and endowed mosques and other public buildings. It appears that under the Fatimids, ordinary women were relatively free to go out into the streets, go to the market or the public baths, and mix freely with men. Toward the end of their dynasty, however, the Fatimids seem to have become more disposed to controlling the activities of their women subjects. The caliph al-Ḥakīm, in particular, instituted a number of decrees against women, ordering that they not go out at night, that they not wear jewelry in public, and eventually even that they not go to public baths and cemeteries (Cortese and Calderini, 2006, pp. 114–127, 163–176, 191–199).

In Yemen, where women appear to have held a more prominent place in society (indeed, it has been suggested that Yemen had a matrilineal society in pre-Islamic times), two Ismāʿīlī Shīʿī queens together ruled for almost a century. The first was Asmā, who, from 1037 CE, ruled at first jointly with her husband, ʿAli, the founder of the Ṣulayḥī dynasty and, after his death in 1067 CE, continued to play an important role until her death in 1074 CE The second was her daughter-in-law Arwā (al-Sayyidah al-Ḥurra), who, from 1074 CE until her own death in 1137 CE, held both spiritual and temporal authority in Yemen on behalf of the Fatimid caliph, initially in the name of her paralyzed first husband al-Mukarram and then in the name of her son al-Mukarram junior and, after his death, in the name of her second husband Sabā (Mernissi, 1993, pp. 146–158; Cortese and Calderini, 2006, pp. 127–140). During this period, the lands under the rule of these two women prospered. Interestingly, today's Ṭayyibī Ismāʿīlīs (the Dawoodi and Sulaymani Bohras of India and Yemen) trace the spiritual authority of their leaders back to the appointment of the first of them by Arwā.

The Ṣafavids in Iran. It was the Ṣafavid dynasty (1501–1722) that established Twelver Shiʿism as the main religion of the people of Iran. Sources for women during this period are, however, scant and more research is needed. The Ṣafavids, in contrast to the Fatimids, used royal women to create alliances with surrounding dynasties through marriage, especially in the early years of the dynasty. In later years, as a result of a change in priorities, royal women tended to be married to prominent religious leaders. The women of the Ṣafavid courts of the sixteenth century were well educated, independently wealthy, patrons of the arts and letters, and often involved in political, administrative, and sometimes even military decisions. Shah Ismāʿīl's wife, Tājlū Khānum (d. 1540), was a counselor to her husband and the power behind the throne during the early years of the reign of her son Ṭahmāsp I. Parī Khān Khānum (1548–1578) played a prominent political role during the reign of her father, Shah Ṭahmāsp I, and after his death in 1576 held the reins of power as de facto ruler for varying periods of time (1577–1578). Khayr al-Nisā Bigum (d. 1579) was involved in all important decisions from the start of the reign of her husband, Shah Muḥammad Khudābandah, in 1578, and ruled Iran for some seventeen months during her husband's illness in 1578–1579, during which time she led the Ṣafavid army to war against the Ottomans. She came from Māzandarān in north Iran, and there seems to have been a tradition of women taking an active role in social affairs in that province and the neighboring province of Gīlān (Szuppe in Hambly, 1998, pp. 329–335; Babayan in Hambly, 1998, pp. 352–356).

In seventeenth-century Ṣafavid Iran, however, as Twelver Shiʿi Islam became more legalistic and rigid in its interpretations, both the women of the royal court and women in society generally became much more confined in their social freedom, participation in social and political affairs, and ability to control their own lives. Nevertheless, the accession of Shāh Sulṭān Ḥusayn in 1694 was largely secured by his great aunt Maryam Bigum, who exercised great influence. It is in the Ṣafavid period that there was the full development of the Shīʿī practice of *Rawẓah-khānī* (the emotive recounting of the story of the martyrdom of the Shīʿī Imams, especially Imam Ḥusayn), and performance of *taʿziyah* (a passion play of the story of the Imams and their martyrdoms). These practices became important for the development of women's religious life in all parts of the Shīʿī world.

India. The largest and most well-established Shīʿī community in India was in Awadh (Oudh, now part of Uttar Pradesh) and its capital Lakhnau (Lucknow). The nawabs of Awadh were Shīʿīs and founded a state in 1722 that was independent of the Mughal Empire from 1819. The women of the court of the nawabs played an important role in social and political affairs, as well as being great patrons of the arts and religious commemorations. In the late eighteenth century, Bahū Begam and Ṣadr al-Nisā Begam, the wife and mother of the Shujāʿ al-Dawlah (r. 1754–1776), had extensive staffs of some tens of thousands of people and were so wealthy that they could subsidize the state treasury when it needed to pay a large sum to the British. They patronized the arts, literature, dance, music, and architecture, as well as sponsoring religious ritual performances. Fakhr al-Nisā Begam (d. 1893), the daughter of Muḥammad ʿAlī Shāh, built the imposing Imambara of Mughal Saheba. The court women often led court factions usually focused on one or another possible successor to the current nawab. There were also courtesans, some of whom gained sufficient wealth and property to be independent. Indeed, the women in Lakhnau became so influential that British and Muslim observers in the nineteenth century condemned the rulers of Awadh as effeminate and dominated by their women—a circumstance that the British used to justify taking control of the area in 1856 (Fisher in Hambly, 1998, pp. 489–520).

In this marginal area of the Shīʿī world, women were relatively freer and more able to make decisions about their own lives, both at the level of the court and in the middle classes. This freedom allowed them, for example, sometimes to adopt a few Hindu practices and beliefs. They were, however, devout Muslims and particularly devoted to the Shīʿī rituals of mourning. There are occasional reports here, as in Lebanon, of families with only daughters switching from Sunnī to Shīʿī Islam to take advantage of the Shīʿī laws of inheritance, which are more generous to women (Cole, 2005, pp. 138–160).

Qājār Iran. The Qājār dynasty ruled Iran from 1794 to 1925. Women in Qājār Iran inherited the restrictive interpretations of Islamic law in relation to women formulated by the clerics of the late Ṣafavid period, such as Muḥammad Bāqir Majlisī. Some of the women of the wealthier classes spent most of their time doing nothing at all or, at most, cooking and preparing sweetmeats. When the American missionary S. G. Wilson (*Persian Life and Customs*, 1895, p. 259) asked some of them how they spend their time, they replied, "We do nothing but sleep, eat, and wonder what we will have for the next meal." Despite this, some women did influence their husbands and sons, and through them had an effect on society. Mahd-i Ulyā (d. 1873), for example, was able to exert great influence on state affairs during the reign of her husband, Muḥammad Shāh, and the early years of the reign of her son Nāṣir al-Dīn Shāh, except when Amīr Kabīr was prime minister.

Although women wore various types of outdoor clothes in Ṣafavid times, by the late Qājār period, this variety had been reduced to the *chādur*, a uniform black piece of cloth covering the whole body. During the Qājār period, typical religious activities for women included attending *Rawẓah-khānī* and *taʿziyah*, which were sometimes female-only; visiting the shrines of descendants of the Imāms; offering *naẕr*, votive offerings of food to the poor; and holding *sufras*, votive offerings of a meal usually in the name of a female member of the house of the Prophet. Crying during the commemorations of the martyrdoms of the Imāms had both a ritual and a cathartic aspect to it. Religious gatherings were one of the main ways in which women would meet and obtain advice and support from one another (Mahdavi, 1994).

In general, it was not thought necessary or even advisable to educate women. Nevertheless, some women of the upper classes did manage to obtain an education, and in a few clerical families, there seems to have been a tradition of educating the women. Examples of this include the Majlisī family of Isfahan from the Ṣafavid period and the Baraghānī family of Qazvīn from the Qajar period. From the latter family came Qurrat al-ʿAyn Ṭāhirah (1817–1852), who rebelled against the norms imposed upon her gender, left her husband, and proceeded to Karbalā to pursue her studies. Defying her family, she later joined the Bābī movement, was appointed by the Bāb to be one of his eighteen leading disciples, and famously appeared unveiled at a conference of the Bābīs, thereby announcing the abrogation of the Islamic sharīʿah, and was eventually executed for her beliefs (Milani, 1992, pp. 77–99).

Another woman who strove to break the restrictions imposed upon her gender, but this time under the influence of Western ideas, was Tāj al-Salṭanah (1883–1936). A further indication of the influence of the West upon women was the fact that women took part in the street demonstrations against the Tobacco Régie (monopoly) in 1893 and in favor of the Constitution in 1905–1911, even going so far as to mob the shah's carriage and create a human chain to prevent attacks on the male demonstrators. Despite this active involvement, they were not granted the vote in the Constitution. Yet after the Constitutional Revolution, an increasing number of girls' schools were founded.

Assessment. In conclusion, although there have been periods when Shīʿī women have played a significant social role, this has been as a result of local cultural factors rather than owing to Shīʿī Islam itself. In general, Shīʿī Islam has not been any more advantageous to women than Sunni Islam, despite some theoretical advantages. One caveat pertaining to this entry is that there is a great dearth of reliable information about women throughout the whole of Shīʿī history. For some important areas of the Shīʿī world (such as Iraq and Lebanon), there is insufficient material to assess the history of Shīʿī women. Hence, this survey has perforce been mainly about those women who rose to prominence rather than about women in general. Yet even some prominent women may have remained hidden because of bias against women. The general view in the Islamic world has been that women are not fit to govern or to play any leading role in society, and thus those who do succeed in doing so, despite this bias, are often subject to a collective amnesia or denigration of their efforts. A great deal more scholarship is needed to uncover their stories and the stories of the lives of ordinary women who remain invisible in the accounts of classical Islamic historians.

[*See also* Gender Themes, *subentry on* Shīʿite Devotional Literature.]

BIBLIOGRAPHY

Aghaie, Kamran Scott, ed. *The Women of Karbala: Ritual Performance and Symbolic Discourses in*

Modern Shiʿi Islam. Austin: University of Texas Press, 2005. Although primarily about women's experience of the Karbala rituals in the present, the first two chapters (by Negar Mottahedeh and Kamran Scott Aghaie) deal with the Qājār period.

Ahmed, Leila. *Women and Gender in Islam*. New Haven, Conn.: Yale University Press, 1992. A key foundational work on women and Islam but concentrates mainly on Sunni Islam.

Amir-Moezzi, Mohammad Ali. *The Spirituality of Shiʿi Islam*. London: I. B. Tauris, 2011. Although this book is not primarily on history or women, there is much about Fāṭimah and Shahrbānū in the book.

Busse, Heribert. "Iran under the Buyids." In *The Cambridge History of Iran*, vol. 4: *The Period from the Arab Invasion to the Saljuqs*, edited by R. N. Frye, pp. 250–304. Cambridge, U.K.: Cambridge University Press, 1975.

Cole, Juan. *Sacred Space and Holy War: The Politics, Culture, and History of Shiʿite Islam*. London: I. B. Tauris, 2005. Chapter 8 of this book is on women and concentrates exclusively on Shiʿi women of Awadh. Unlike most other studies of Shiʿi women, the author manages to create a picture of life among women of the middle and lower strata of society.

Cortese, Delia, and Simonetta Calderini. *Women and the Fatimids in the World of Islam*. Edinburgh: Edinburgh University Press, 2006. Thanks to the researches of these two authors, the premodern period for which we perhaps have the best information about Shiʿi women is during the Ismāʿīlī Shiʿi Fatimid dynasty in Egypt.

Donaldson, Bess Allen. *The Wild Rue*. London: Luzac, 1938. Contains acute observation of the lives of women in Iran during the late Qājār period.

Hambly, Gavin. *Women in the Medieval Islamic World: Power, Patronage, and Piety*. New York: St. Martin's Press, 1998. A collection of articles that ranges across both Shiʿi and Sunni societies. It is particularly good for Ṣafavid Iran. This article refers to the chapters by Maria Szuppe ("The 'Jewels of Wonder': Learned Ladies and Princess Politicians in the Provinces of Early Ṣafavid Iran," pp. 325–348), Kathryn Babayan ("The ʿAqa'id an-Nisa': A Glimpse at Ṣafavid Women in Local Isfahani Culture," pp. 349–381), and Michael Fisher ("Women and the Feminine in the Court and High Culture of Awadh 1722–1856," pp. 489–520).

Mahdavi, Shireen. "Women, Ideas, and Customs in Qajar Iran." In *Persian Studies in North America: Studies in Honor of Mohammad Ali Jazayery*, edited by Mehdi Marashi, pp. 373–393. Bethesda, Md.: Iranbooks, 1994. Good coverage of the Qājār period, although now a little dated.

Mernissi, Fatima. *The Forgotten Queens of Islam*. Minneapolis: University of Minnesota Press, 1993. Useful chapters on the Ismāʿīlī Queens of Yemen and Sitt al-Mulk of Egypt.

Milani, Farzaneh. *Veils and Words: The Emerging Voices of Iranian Women Writers*. London: I. B. Tauris, 1992. Describes the emergence of women writers in Iran as they struggled to come out from behind the veil, both the physical and cultural one. Chapter 4, pp. 77–99, deals with Qurrat al-ʿAyn Ṭāhirih.

Momen, Moojan. *An Introduction to Shiʿi Islam: The History and Doctrines of Twelver Shiʿism*. New Haven, Conn.: Yale University Press, 1985.

Najmabadi, Afsaneh. *Women with Mustaches and Men without Beards*. Berkeley: University of California Press, 2005. Gender roles and the figuration of women in Qājār, Iran.

Moojan Momen

Contemporary Thought and Practice

Modern Shiism offers fascinating examples of how gender-coded symbols and rituals can be used for social, cultural, religious, and political purposes. Women as symbols have always been central to Shiism, in particular, the women in the family of the Prophet Muḥammad, such as his daughter, Fāṭimah, and his granddaughter, Zaynab bint ʿAlī. However, the gendered dimensions of Shīʿī Islam have until recently been understudied. One of the pioneers of scholarship on this topic is Elizabeth Warnock Fernea, beginning with her 1969 book based on her stay in Iraq, titled *Guests of the Sheikh*. More systematic, book-length studies on women and Shīʿī Islam did not emerge until between 2004 and 2006, beginning with Kamran Scot Aghaie's 2004 monograph, titled *The Martyrs of Karbala: Shiʿi Symbols and Rituals in Modern Iran*, and 2005 multi-authored volume, titled *The Women of Karbala: Ritual Performances and Symbolic*

Discourses of Modern Shiʿi Islam. This was followed the next year by three more books in quick succession. Azam Torab's *Performing Islam: Gender and Ritual in Iran*, Lara Deeb's *An Enchanted Modern: Gender and Public Piety in Shiʿi Lebanon*, and Roxanne Varzi's *Warring Souls: Youth, Media, and Martyrdom in Post-Revolutionary Iran*. Since then, there has been Mary Thurlkill's 2007 publication of *Chosen Among Women: Mary and Fatima in Medieval Christianity and Shiʿite Islam*, Elizabeth Bucar's 2011 publication of *Creative Conformity: The Feminist Politics of U.S. Catholic and Iranian Shiʿi Women*, and Ingvild Flaskerud's 2012 publication of *Visualizing Belief and Piety in Iranian Shiʿism*. All of these texts are either focused specifically on questions of gender and Shīʿī Islam, or they contain significant treatments of the gender dynamics of ritual participation and symbolic representations of sacred themes. It should also be mentioned that, since the 1990s or earlier, there have been several important article-length studies focusing on women or gendered aspects of Shīʿī Islam, most notably by Mary Elaine Hegland, who has authored several important articles in which she explores the participation of women in South Asia, Iran, and North America.

One pressing question is why the systematic study of gender-coded symbols and women's participation in rituals has been so late in coming. This is especially puzzling when one considers that the subject of women in Islam has been a highly studied topic since the 1990s. There are numerous contributing factors. Since all the prophets and imams were male, and the narratives of the battle of Karbala have usually focused on the martyrs at Karbala, including ʿAlī ibn Abī Ṭālib (Ḥusayn) and his male followers on the battlefield, the focus of scholarship has similarly been on males and male symbols. However, beliefs and doctrines associated with prophecy, religious leadership, and sectarianism should not be limited exclusively to the prophets and imams. Likewise, the "event" of Karbala should not be defined as simply the battle itself; rather, it is best understood as including the events leading up to the battle, surrounding the battle (i.e., on the sidelines), and following the battle. Furthermore, these should all be placed within a universalist narrative beginning with the first prophet of Islam, Adam (or according to some theological views, even prior to Adam), and ending with the return of the Mahdi at the end of the temporal world, all of which has historically been included by most Shīʿī scholars within the discussion of the imamate and the tragedy of Karbala. For example, Fāṭimah's role as supporter of Muḥammad, and as mother and educator of Ḥasan and Ḥusayn, as well as her role as one of the purified fourteen who suffered persecution for the cause of true Islam (i.e., Shīʿī Islam) cannot be separated from the functions of imams or the Karbala event, even though she was not a prophet or imam herself, and was not present at the battle of Karbala itself (although in many narratives she is brought into the narrative symbolically).

While female characters have always served an important function in Shīʿī pious literatures, such as the "Karbala narratives," in texts from the premodern and early-modern periods, the female characters have most often been used as plot devices or as reflections of male characters, rather than taking on the aspects of fully independent characters in their own right. As a discourse on gender developed in various Shīʿī communities in the mid-twentieth century, Islamic ideals of womanhood were more explicitly articulated and placed in opposition to Western ideals, and, in some ways, in opposition to perceived traditional roles for women. In more recent narratives, female characters have been presented as more self-aware than in earlier representations, as Shīʿī writers have used these symbols to place gender issues at the center of political discourse. In the case of female characters, the modern era marks the first period in which female-gendered symbols were used as part of an anti-Western discourse focusing specifically upon gender roles. Thus, the transformation of the symbolic narrative form reflected a heightened consciousness of issues of gender, thus serving as both activist models and traditionalist models of behavior for Shīʿī women.

The shift in the focus of gender discourse that occurred in the second half of the twentieth century defined gender roles within a context in which it was perceived that westernization from outside combined with moral decay from within the Muslim community were detrimental to Islam and Muslim society. Thus, promoting more active roles for women in a society that nevertheless aimed to promote an Islamist vision of social morality, as conceptualized within gender categories, was increasingly viewed as a primary goal of religious scholars and intellectuals, as well as social and political movements.

There have been countless books published with such titles as "The Garden of Martyrs," "The Fourteen Purified Ones" or "Fāṭimah Fāṭimah ast," which present the biographies of the Imams, the Prophets, and Fāṭimah. These sacred personages are portrayed as suffering for the cause of Shīʿī Islam. The importance of Fāṭimah is demonstrated by the large number of poems and Muḥarram chants devoted to her memory. For example, Fāṭimah is given a great deal more coverage than most of the male characters in some narratives, like Va'iz Kashifi's canonical work, *Rawḍāt al-shuhadāʾ*. Similarly, Murtiza Mutahhari has portrayed Zaynab's role as spokesperson for the cause after the massacre as the second half of Ḥusayn's movement (i.e., not in merely a marginal role). Zaynab's public criticism of Yazid and his followers is a point that has been stressed in most Shīʿī narratives.

Syed Akbar Hyder has similarly shown the diverse ways in which Zaynab is represented in modern Urdu poems and pious elegies, in particular the elegies of the prominent South Asian Zaker Rashid Torabi, and other poets like Eftekhar Aref, Vahid Akhtar, and the female poet Parvin Shaker. He explores the central role of Zaynab as the "conqueror of Damascus" in the symbolic narratives of Karbala. Hyder's literary analysis explores the symbolic rhetoric and stylistic devices used in representing Zaynab within the South Asian tradition, and shows how Shīʿī symbols and ideals have been articulated within the modern discourses on gender in South Asia.

Lara Deeb also explores recent changes in Lebanese Shīʿī rituals that have been brought on by many factors, including urbanization, modernization, and the political ascendancy of Shīʿī parties, such as Amal and Hezbollah, over the past decade or so, and the mobilization of the Shīʿīs as a communal group in the 1970s by such leaders as Mūsā al-Ṣadr. In recent years, a new method of ritual performance has emerged alongside the more traditional rituals. These shifts in ritual practice were influenced by trends in Iran. Proponents of these new ritual practices argue that the newer practices are more "authentic" because they are closer to the original intent of the Karbala paradigm. Divergent interpretations of the role of Zaynab in the battle of Karbala are indicative of this discourse. The shift has been toward using Zaynab as a role model for women becoming more directly involved in social and political activism. Women's rituals have slowly transformed in tandem with the broader trends in ritual observance.

Ḥusayn's followers, both men and women, were prominent players in the events themselves, and therefore have been important sources of symbolism for Shiism, and have very often been role models to be emulated by both men and women. What has not been sufficiently developed in the scholarship on Shīʿī Islam are the ways in which certain qualities that important personages like Ḥusayn, Fāṭimah, and Zaynab represent have been gender-coded as "male," "female," or "gender-neutral." Using this approach, rather than thinking simplistically about "women role models for women," also shows how women have at times been talked about in these sources as role models not only for women, but also for men.

Loyalty to the prophets and imams, and courage in defending true Islam, are always central themes that are not gendered in any significant way. A similar case is righteousness and piety, which are universally praised for both men and women. There are countless stories of pious behavior by exemplary males and females. However, fighting and martyrdom are gendered themes. Men are depicted as the ideal fighters and martyrs, while the ideal woman is portrayed as sacrificing her loved ones, rather than becoming a martyr herself. In fact, it is clear from the narratives that women did not belong on the battlefield at all, although they were supposed to lend support nearby. It is generally argued in most sources that it was critically important for women to have accompanied Ḥusayn to Iraq. All of the adult male followers, (except for Zayn al-ʿĀbidīn, who refrained from participating in the combat due to illness) were killed, and their martyrdom is recounted in great detail. The story is different concerning females. While a few women, and in some cases girls, were martyred, they were small in number, and these stories are not recounted in the same degree of detail as those of the male martyrs. One example is the account of the newlyweds Wahb and his wife Haniya. She lost control out of love for her husband and ran out onto the battlefield to help him, but was called back to the tents by Imam Ḥusayn, thus reinforcing the idea that she should not be on the battlefield at all. It happened again and she was eventually martyred. However, in the narratives, the story is typically passed over in merely a few lines. The story of her husband, on the other hand, is given much more elaborate treatment. A similar event took place when Zaynab ran out onto the battlefield, which again resulted in Husayn calling her back to the tent area, with instructions to care for the women, the children, and the wounded. Therefore, it is clear that the ideal of the male fighter and martyr is well developed, whereas the model of the female fighter or martyr is not only underdeveloped, but is, in fact, discouraged in these narratives. Of course, this has obvious implications regarding spiritual equity, according to this conception of Islam, because women are denied access to the ranks of those Muslims who have made the greatest of sacrifice by becoming a martyr, and who will be rewarded accordingly on the Day of Judgment.

While men were the primary speakers before and during the battle, women participants served a critical function of becoming the spokespeople for the cause once they were taken into captivity and taken to Syria. Zaynab, in particular, was central to the preservation and spreading of the message at this point. This is significant in that it clearly develops this role as a responsibility for women and assures the centrality of Zaynab to the story. The role of spokesperson is closely related to the role played in relation to educating men or boys. Again, Zaynab is depicted as the ideal example, as she constantly coached the believers, and, in particular, her own sons, as did Fāṭimah. Another related theme that is also gender-coded as female in Shīʿī symbolism is humiliation through captivity. While Zayn al-ʿĀbidīn was taken captive in the story, the accounts of women being mistreated and humiliated are much more dominant. These stories are recounted in great detail, stressing disrespect of their status, their humiliation, and the general tragic nature of their being taken into captivity. Thus, women play the role of victims.

The depiction of women as mourners of the dead is also a prevalent theme. Although throughout history, men have definitely been presented as mourning the event of death, women have always played a very important (and somewhat different) role in this activity. For example, in teahouse/coffee shop paintings or other graphic representations of the tragedy, women have been used as graphic representations of the tragic loss. Men in such representations have usually been the actual warriors and martyrs, while the women were represented as mourning their loss. Hence, women have become the embodiment of the tragedy by becoming mourners.

A useful way to conceptualize this gendered dichotomy is to think of men as martyrs and women as mourners. It is also worth noting that there were several examples from the 1960s and 1970s of political leaders, such as Ali Sharīʿatī, Murtaza Mutahhari, and Salihi Najafabadi, who used the symbolism of Karbala to motivate the Iranian masses to participate in political rebellions against the shah. Parallel examples can be found in other Shīʿī communities, especially in Lebanon and Iraq. One of the main points of this discourse was that the act of merely mourning the tragedy was to be abandoned in favor of active rebellion. They often referred to the "wrong" practice as being what women commonly do, which is said to be pointless crying, rather than what men should be doing, which is active or armed rebellion. Although this did not necessarily preclude men from also being mourners, women as mourners are typically treated differently and have often been given precedence.

Shīʿī women have always been actively involved in religious rituals, both in women-only rituals and in gender-mixed public rituals. For example, during the Qājār period, wealthy women reinforced their social standing by being generous supporters of rituals themselves, including women's majalis and sufras (ritual dinners), as well as public *rowzeh khanis* and *taʿzīyahs*. One of the best-known female patrons of such performances was Nasir al-Din Shah's sister, Izzat al-Dowlah, who regularly sponsored very elaborate *taʿzīyahs* in her home in Sarchishmah. Women-only rituals are still extremely prevalent today in Shīʿī communities.

Elizabeth Warnock Fernea and Basima Q. Bezirgan have called into question the overly simplistic or rigid variants of the dichotomization of "public vs. private space" in Muslim societies. Instead, they propose using a far more nuanced conception that allows for relative fluidity between what would traditionally have been labeled "women's world" and "men's world," observing that men and women are both involved in public rituals. Furthermore, men play a supporting, or "instrumental" role in women-only rituals, while women play a supporting or "instrumental" role in male-dominated rituals. Fernea and Bezirgan further argue that the gender dynamics observed in the rituals are similar to the patterns one would see in other spheres of Middle Eastern society.

Just as Lara Deeb has explored recent changes in Lebanese Shīʿī rituals, Ingvild Flaskerud has explored the gender dynamics of ritual participation, visual representations of sacred themes, and the experiences of women participants in rituals. She analyzes women's religious rituals in modern Shiraz, especially ritual space, objects, and visual imagery, showing how Shīʿī women participate in rituals in order to achieve salvation and divine intercession in this world and the next. In addition to explaining the origins and dynamics of a distinctively Shīʿī aesthetic tradition, she discusses the iconography of images, space and objects in women's rituals in Shiraz. In addition, Mary Elaine Hegland has authored several important articles in which she explores the participation of women in South Asia, as well as North America, in terms of gender dynamics, ethnicity, class, and power relationships. For example, in the case of North America, she compares the two major Shīʿī immigrant communities in the United States—Iranians and South Asians. Her comparative analysis demonstrates that the religious practices of these two communities are quite distinct from one another. She argues that South Asian women are far more active in Shīʿī rituals than their Iranian counterparts because of the differing socio-economic backgrounds and demographics of these two communities, along with distinct religious and political experiences.

While Shīʿī symbols and rituals have been used at times to restrict women's activities and social roles, they have also served as a means for empowering women and have helped to promote a sense of gender-specific identities for women. Although there are various universalistic components to Shīʿī beliefs and practices, the religious experiences of Shīʿī women have generally been extremely diverse and varied, as practices vary based on personal preferences, religious interpretations, popular cultural practices, ideals or norms of gender interaction/segregation, regional customs, education levels, or socio-economic background.

While the state and various social groups (like the ulama and the guilds) have tried to enforce specific ideals of gender interaction, they usually have not been able to completely control the process of ritual performance. Usually, various participants have acted in accordance with their own priorities and ideals. Women in particular have often been very active and innovative in participating in rituals in ways that are consistent with their own interests and ideals, although assuming the role of the "martyr" is normally exclusive to males. One might be tempted to attribute this exclusion of women simply to concepts of female modesty and private vs. public space. However, these women (with the exception of some Arab women from southern Iran and Iraq) also do not typically perform these rituals in private. Furthermore, they are present in large numbers at these events, but serve in different capacities than men. Thus, apart from concern for public modesty, they are deterred by a series of interpretations concerning Shīʿī symbolism, and male-female participation in the rituals.

Although women do not generally participate as symbolic martyrs they do participate in large numbers along with men as "witnesses" and "mourners." The mourners follow the central procession and have usually been discussed by academics as being observers, rather than participants. However, women are not outside the ritual at all; rather, they are participating in the ritual in a very different capacity from the "martyrs" in the central procession. This practice dates back at least to the Qājār and Ṣafavid periods. Jean Chardin commented that women outdid the men, describing how mourners were "wailing and howling, especially the women, tearing themselves and crying in floods of tears." Ibn Kathir's much older account from the Būyid period, *al-Bidaya wa al-Nihaya,* also seems to allude to a similar practice in tenth century Baghdad.

This role of the "mourner" is different from that of the "martyr," in that it is not as highly structured, and it is not symbolic of martyrdom itself, but is rather the commemoration of the tragedy in the form of mourning, lending moral support, or bearing witness. Thus, rather than participating directly in the moving procession, or the structured self-flagellation, either by beating their chests or backs, the main activity of the mourners is to witness and mourn the tragedy being reenacted in front of them. As mourners, they generally cry in order to symbolize the tragedy of the event. Finally, they often take part in symbolic self-flagellation, which involves random chest beating, or, in some cases, striking of the hands against the head. These acts are usually performed with no real force at all, and are therefore only symbolic acts of self-mortification. Their main purpose is to ritually mourn and bear witness.

Space is gendered along similar lines, with a parallel being drawn between the battlefield in the original Battle of Karbala, and the space occupied by the central procession of "martyrs" or "penitents" in the Muharram procession. In the original narrative, the imam himself is portrayed as enforcing the gendered space by reprimanding the few women, such as Zaynab and Haniya, who violated the male space of the battlefield. Similarly, men and, in some cases, women, enforce the gendered spatial divisions during the rituals. The enforcement is most rigid in indoor rituals because this space is structured and is therefore more easily controlled. However, in public rituals, as well as indoor rituals performed in large public spaces, women often cross those barriers and claim entrance to the central space whenever possible.

Regardless of whether it is the state, the ulama, or the community organizers who try to promote patterns of behavior, other individuals and groups, and women in particular, have often been efficacious and innovative when participating in the rituals, in accordance with their preferences or ideals. These women have rarely rejected the fundamental symbolic understandings of gender roles as portrayed in the Karbala narrative. Instead, they have worked within the established parameters of the rituals, stretching and modifying the boundaries in subtle ways. The diversity of practices within these rituals demonstrates the inherent flexibility of the symbols and rituals themselves.

[*See also* Fāṭimah; *and* Zaynab bint ʿAlī.]

Bibliography

Aghaie, Kamran Scot. *The Martyrs of Karbala: Shiʿi Symbols and Rituals in Modern Iran.* Seattle: University of Washington Press, 2004.

Aghaie, Kamran Scot. *The Women of Karbala: The Gender Dynamics of Ritual Performances and Symbolic Discourses of Modern Shiʿi Islam.* Austin: University of Texas Press, 2005.

Beck, Lois, and Guity Nashat, eds. *Women in Iran: From 1800 to the Islamic Republic.* Urbana and Chicago: University of Illinois Press, 2004.

Bucar, Elizabeth M. *Creative Conformity: The Feminist Politics of U.S. Catholic and Iranian Shiʿi Women.* Washington, D.C.: Georgetown University Press, 2011.

Deeb, Lara. *An Enchanted Modern: Gender and Public Piety in Shiʿi Lebanon.* Princeton, N.J.: Princeton University Press, 2006.

Flakerud, Ingvild. *Visualizing Belief and Piety in Iranian Shiʿism.* London: Continuum, 2010.

Hegland, Mary Elaine. "Women of Karbala Moving to America: A Comparison of Iranian and South Asian Shiʿi Rituals in the United States of America." In *The Women of Karbala*, ed. Kamran Scot Aghaie. Austin: University of Texas Press, 2005.

Additional Reading

Brink, Judy, and Joan Mencher, eds. "A Mixed Blessing—Majales: Shiʿa Women's Rituals in NW Pakistan and the Politics of Religion, Ethnicity, and Gender." In *Mixed Blessings: Religious Fundamentalisms and Gender Cross-Culturally.* New York: Routledge, 1996.

Hegland, Mary Elaine "Shiʿa Women of NW Pakistan and Agency Through Practice: Ritual, Resistance, Resilience," *PoLAR: Political and Legal Anthropology Review* 18, no. 2 (1995): 1–14.

Hegland, Mary Elaine "The Power Paradox in Muslim Women's *Majales*: North-West Pakistani Mourning Rituals as Sites of Contestation over Religious Politics, Ethnicity, and Gender." *SIGNS* 23, no. 2 (Winter 1998): 391–428.)

Thurlkill, Mary F. *Chosen Among Women: Mary and Fatima in Medieval Christianity and Shiʿite Islam.* Notre Dame: University of Notre Dame Press, 2008.

Torab, Azam. *Performing Islam: Gender and Ritual in Iran.* Leiden: Brill, 2006.

Varzi, Roxanne. *Warring Souls: Youth, Media, and Martyrdom and Post-Revolutionary Iran.* Durham, N.C.: Duke University Press, 2006.

Kamran Scot Aghaie

SHRINE. The Arabic term *qubbah* (a tomb surmounted by a dome) refers throughout the Muslim world to saints' shrines and mausoleums and places of special spiritual significance. These shrines are often associated with natural phenomena—in Indonesia, for example, they are frequently located in elevated spots and have their own water sources. In North Africa, the shrines of marabouts, or *al-ṣāliḥūn* (sing. *ṣāliḥ* "pious ones") dot the landscape so pervasively that they are rarely out of sight. Some are squat, whitewashed buildings. Others are considerably more elaborate and linked to mosques and hostels. A visit to a shrine is thought to offer spiritual blessings. Every rural settlement has such a shrine, sometimes just a semi-derelict, sporadically maintained structure in a cemetery. In western Morocco, there is roughly one shrine for every 6 square kilometers and 150 people. These tombs constitute a framework that concretely symbolizes social groups and their relations. As alliances change, derelict shrines can be restored or new ones constructed to reflect new identities.

In addition to these modest local shrines, there are elaborate complexes linked to major religious figures. Major shrines have annual *mawsims* (festivals) that draw tens of thousands of pilgrims annually and have full-time caretakers, often descendants of the saint (*walī* or *ṣāliḥ*). The term *ṣāliḥ* is strongly preferred in North Africa because of its multiple meanings. It can imply someone living or dead outstanding in piety, and therefore acceptable even to neo-orthodox Muslims. For some, it can also imply the ability to work miracles or a special relationship with God. Jews in North Africa also have shrines, most of which have been maintained despite the diminution of the Jewish population since the 1950s. Indeed, some Jewish shrines have been relocated in Israel as their North African supporters have emigrated there. In Morocco, some shrines attract both Jewish and Muslim pilgrims. Morocco's kings regularly visit the major shrines, showing their continued significance in national and regional identity. In the Palestinian territories, Jews, Christians, and Muslims share some shrines, such as the Tomb of the Patriarchs near Hebron (Ar., al-Khalīl). In Morocco, as in the Palestinian territories and elsewhere, women participate equally with men in shrine visits and acts of piety.

In urban Cairo and towns elsewhere, there is a "politics of festivity" associated with major shrines that continues to play a wide range of social roles. In Java, as in Egypt, even if modernist Muslims discourage visits to shrines, the texts and oral traditions associated with them continue to offer many faithful a spatial representation of their history and identity. In India and Pakistan, where shrines are sometimes known by the Persian term *dargah*, shrines are often a place where women play leading ritual roles, activities that they are unable to perform in mosques. Major shrines often have subsidiary ones associated with them that are primarily dedicated to women or, as in North Africa, that are dedicated to the daughters, sisters, or mothers of leading male "pious ones," or saints. Women are fully integrated into the ritual life of shrines and the Ṣūfī rituals often related to them.

Shīʿī Muslims also have elaborate shrine complexes associated with the principal imams and religious centers, and many of these, such as Qom in Iran and Karbala in southern Iraq, have religious schools associated with them along with bureaucracies to accept donations, support humanitarian works, and administer the endowed properties (*awqāf*; sing. *waqf*) that produce revenue for their upkeep. Some of these shrines are big business, such as the shrine of Imam Reza, a revered ninth-century martyr, in Mashhad, northeastern Iran. Over 12 million Iranians, Iraqis, and other Shīʿī pilgrims visit the shrine annually. It is larger than the Vatican, and the business empire associated with it extends to pharmaceuticals, mines, agriculture, engineering, a textile factory, and construction projects elsewhere in the Muslim world.

Shrines and Sacred Space. The most important shrine complex in the Muslim world is that of the Kaʿbah and the Great Mosque in Mecca. Some Muslims believe that the Kaʿbah (literally, "cube") was brought to Abraham by the angel Gabriel. At first it was white, but it turned black through contact with the impurities of the pre-Islamic period. Others say that Adam built the Kaʿbah and that he is buried there. The Kaʿbah is the most sacred space in the Muslim world, the point to which all Muslims turn to pray, and the direction to which the head is pointed in burial. It is the most important place of *ḥajj* (pilgrimage) and is distinguished from visits to local or regional shrines, known as *ziyārahs*. As the spiritual center of the earth, actions at the Kaʿbah, such as its circumambulation, are duplicated in the heavens and at the throne of God. Unlike the weekly Friday mosque prayers, where women are generally separated from men or cannot participate, women are the full equals of men in all *ḥajj*-related rituals.

Shrines define sacred space, both for the Great Mosque in Mecca and for the local shrines throughout the Muslim world. These shrines are devoted to mythical figures, great scholars believed to have mystical powers, and persons of exceptional piety. Shrines in Indonesia are associated with the coming of Islam and also relate to sacred time. To obtain the most benefit, pilgrims often visit several shrines, calculating their arrival on the day most favorably associated with each shrine in complex, interlocking cycles of five- and seven-day weeks. Major shrines can have ten thousand to fifty thousand visitors on their most auspicious days. Some modernist Muslims have sought to ban visits to shrines, but such visits retain their popularity except in Saudi Arabia, where their cessation has almost been forced, except to those in Mecca and Medina.

Shrines also separate sacred and secular space. People seek sanctuary in them and await the intervention of religious intermediaries to negotiate a truce or settlement. Oaths sworn at shrines are especially binding, because their violation incurs the wrath of the shrine's *ṣāliḥ* or *walī*. Some are known as centers for healing. Visits to the shrine of Bū Yā ʿUmār, located near Marrakesh, Morocco, are reputed to cure the mentally ill.

Gendered Space and History. Gender divisions are often associated with shrines. The shrine for Lalla Ḥnīya, a daughter of Sīdī Muḥammad al-Sharqī, in Boujad, Morocco, is visited almost exclusively by women seeking a remedy for infertility. Visitors tear strips of cloth from their clothing and affix it to the door of the shrine as a *waʿd* (promise) to offer a gift or sacrifice if they bear a child. Such offerings are not made at Lalla Ḥnīya's tomb, but at the nearby shrine complex of her father. Until the 1950s, women in rural Turkey were largely confined to their homes or those of relatives, except for visits to local shrines on religious and secular festivals. Visits to shrines secure blessings for the household and can be used to signal changes in personal status—marriage, the birth of a child, or mourning. Women say prayers at these shrines and are more conscious than men of local sacred geography. Men occasionally visit shrines with women, but rarely do so on their own.

From the early centuries of Islam, women have played a consistently strong role in Muslim ritual and spiritual life, and in recent years this role has become more explicit and acknowledged. One of the earliest Muslim female saints was Umm Ḥarām bint Milḥām. By some accounts, she was the wet nurse of the Prophet Muḥammad and, like her husband, was a companion of the Prophet. She received the Prophet's permission to take part in the early Islamic conquests, which she finally did only in 648 CE, sixteen years after his death. By then elderly, she accompanied her husband on an expedition to Cyprus, where she fell off her mule during the siege of Larnaca, died, and was buried where she fell, rendering her a martyr. Under Ottoman rule, a mosque and shrine complex, called the Hala Sultan Tekke, were built around her tomb. As is the case with other sanctified figures, miracles are attributed to her.

One of the earliest and still influential female Muslim mystics was Rābiʿah al-ʿAdawīyah (714–801 CE) of Basra, in present-day Iraq. An ascetic, mystic, and author of devotional poetry in praise of the Prophet, she taught both women and men and continues to have prominence in the Ṣūfī tradition. In India and Pakistan, women and men can achieve strong reputations for *qawwālī* composition and recital, in which recitals are accompanied by musical instruments, and *Sufiānā ḥākim*, recitals using only the human voice. Complementary to the male-dominated ritual of mosques, these recitals are closely related to Sufism, invested with strong emotional significance, and open to intensely local and personal occasions, including birth and marriage.

The sacred geography of shrines is not confined to supposed vestiges of the past, although shrines, such as that at Mecca, had pre-Islamic significance, and other shrines, as in Java, are not associated exclusively with Muslim figures. Instead, they constitute a physical representation of the sacred, defining not only relations of particular social groups and categories with the divine but also the relations among social groups and between genders. Thus, they offer a rich means of ordering the religious and social universes, and for many, they serve as a means of aligning one with the other.

[*See also* Ḥajj, Women's Patronage of; Sainthood; Sufism and Women; *and* Ziyārah.]

BIBLIOGRAPHY

Abbas, Shemeem Burney. *The Female Voice in Sufi Ritual: Devotional Practices of Pakistan and India.* Austin: University of Texas Press, 2002. Offers an excellent historical and ethnographic context of women's role in devotional rituals in South Asia, including at shrines.

Eickelman, Dale F. *Moroccan Islam: Tradition and Society in a Pilgrimage Center.* Austin: University of Texas Press, 1976. Describes a major shrine complex in Morocco and the practices associated with it.

Esin, Emil. *Mecca the Blessed: Madinah the Radiant.* London: Elek, 1963. Beautifully written and illustrated account of Mecca and Medina as shrine complexes.

Fischer, Michael M. J. *Iran: From Religious Dispute to Revolution.* Cambridge, Mass.: Harvard University Press, 1980. Chapter 4, "Qum: Arena of Conflict," describes religious and political action in a major Shīʿī shrine center.

Fox, James J. "Ziarah Visits to the Tombs of the Wali, the Founders of Islam on Java." In *Islam in the Indonesian Social Context,* edited by Merle C. Ricklefs, pp. 19–38. Clayton, Australia: Centre of Southeast Asian Studies, Monash University, 1991.

McChesney, Robert. *Waqf in Central Asia: Four Hundred Years in the History of a Muslim Shrine.* Princeton, N.J.: Princeton University Press, 1991. Remains the best account for the historical continuity and changing significance of a major shrine in Central Asia.

Meri, Josef. *The Cult of Saints among Muslims and Jews in Medieval Syria.* Oxford and New York: Oxford University Press, 2003. Critically investigates the cult of saints among Muslims and Jews in medieval Syria and the Near East through case studies of saints and their devotees and analysis of ideas of "holiness" common to Muslims and Jews.

Pemberton, Kelly. *Women Mystics and Sufi Shrines in India.* Columbia: University of South Carolina Press, 2010. Superb sociohistorical account of the role of women in shrines and Ṣūfī ritual.

Schielke, Samuli. "Mawlids and Modernity: Danger of Fun." *ISIM Review* 17 (Spring 2006): 6–7. Brief but excellent overview of the struggle for sacred space in Egypt.

Smith, Margaret. *Rābiʿa the Mystic and Her Fellow-Saints in Islam.* Cambridge, U.K., and New York: Cambridge University Press, 1984. Originally published in 1928, a text-based early account of female mystics that remains essential reading.

Torab, Azam. *Performing Islam: Gender and Ritual in Islam.* Leiden, Netherlands: Brill, 2007. An excellent ethnography of women's ritual space and practice in contemporary Iran.

Weingrod, Alex. "Saints and Shrines, Politics and Culture: A Morocco-Israel Comparison." In *Muslim Travellers: Pilgrimage, Migration, and the Religious Imagination*, edited by Dale F. Eickelman and James Piscatori, pp. 217–235. Berkeley and Los Angeles: University of California Press, 1990.

DALE F. EICKELMAN

SISTERS IN ISLAM. Sisters in Islam (SIS) is a small but vocal and contentious Malaysian nongovernmental organization (NGO). Founded in 1988, SIS is premised on an understanding of Islam as supporting rights of equality and human dignity for men and women. Those practices and values that subordinate or demean women, SIS argues, stem from men's control of interpretation of the Qurʿān, and inaccurately represent both the best interests of the *ummah* (Muslim community) and the position of women in public life at the time of the Prophet.

SIS describes its mission as a committment "to promote an awareness of the true principles of Islam, principles that enshrine the concept of equality between women and men, and to strive towards creating a society that upholds the Islamic principles of equality, justice, freedom and dignity within a democratic state." (SIS, 2007) Its three core objectives are:

> To promote and develop a framework of women's rights in Islam, which takes into consideration women's experiences and realities; To eliminate injustice and discrimination against women by changing practices and values that regard women as inferior to men; To create public awareness, and reform laws and policies, on issues of equality, justice, freedom, dignity and democracy in Islam.

Based in a suburb of the Malaysian capital, Kuala Lumpur, SIS was founded by a group of eight Muslim female professionals. Initially an informal social and discussion group, it evolved into a more formal structure, with an emphasis on study, research, and public outreach. Most members still are professionals with largely secular education, including academics, journalists, artists, and lawyers. The group has never been a mass organization, though it aims to reach and influence the general public as well as religious and political officials.

Its primary approach is detailed textual analysis of the Qurʿān and secondary texts, presented in a series of booklets and other publications. SIS also runs a legal clinic, publishes a newsletter and regular columns on Islamic family law in local media, issues periodic letters to the editor and press releases, gives interviews to local and international media, and has organized study sessions, public lectures, and conferences on issues ranging from *aurat* (parts of the body required to be covered) and Islamic dress to HIV/AIDS. SIS also runs training workshops on women's rights in Islam for grassroots women's leaders, journalists, lawyers, and others. It has also addressed issues such as the implications of implementing *ḥudūd* (Islamic criminal law) or an Islamic state in Malaysia, women as *syariah* (Ar. *sharīʿah*, Islamic law) court judges, polygamy and divorce, reproductive health and rights, domestic violence, moral policing, and women's status and roles in Islam in general.

SIS also collaborates with other Malaysian NGOs, particularly women's groups. Most notably, SIS joined other local women's organizations in pressing for passage of a Domestic Violence Act in the early 1990s. SIS's contribution was especially important in ensuring that the act would cover both Muslims and non-Muslims; Malaysia has separate jurisdictions in family law under civil and *syariah* courts for non-Muslims and Muslims, respectively. The group also maintains ties with international Muslim women's organizations and activists.

Though tolerated by the government, SIS has come under repeated challenge in Malaysia from public officials, fellow activists, and the Islamist political opposition. Its positions and approaches remain controversial.

[*See also* Malaysia; *and* Women and Social Reform, *subentry on* Overview.]

BIBLIOGRAPHY

Saliha Hassan. "Islamic Non-Governmental Organisations." In *Social Movements in Malaysia: From Moral Communities to NGOs*, edited by Meredith L. Weiss and Saliha Hassan, pp. 97–114. London and New York: Routledge Curzon, 2003.

Sisters in Islam. http://www.sistersinislam.org.my (accessed Sept. 5, 2008) Official website of the organization.

Wadud-Muhsin, Amina. "Sisters in Islam: Effective Against All Odds." In *Silent Voices*, edited by Doug A. Newson and Bob J. Carrell, pp. 117–38. Lanham, Md., and London, 1995.

MEREDITH L. WEISS

SLAVERY. Slavery (*ubūdīyah, riqq*) was pervasive in many Muslim societies historically. Women participated in slave systems as both owners and owned. Enslaved women labored as servants and sexual partners. Early Islamic dogma affirmed that human beings were in essence free (*al-aṣl huwa al-ḥurrīyah*), yet it tacitly accepted slavery. Various rules protected freedom, promoted manumission (*ʿitq*), and softened the conditions of bondage. Although Islamic law forbade enslavement of foundlings, orphans, and free members of Islamic society, including non-Muslims residing in Islamic lands (*dhimmīs*), it nevertheless allowed for both the capture and purchase of slaves, as well as transmission of enslaved status from mother to child in some cases.

Slaves were both chattels and persons. They had certain rights and protections, which—as with free people—varied by gender. Owners were not to mutilate or kill their slaves. Muslim slaves had to fulfill ritual obligations and owners had to let them. Yet owners controlled the slaves' labor and, to a greater or lesser extent, property they accumulated. Male masters could exercise sexual rights over their unmarried female slaves (*ama, jāriyah*, or *fatāh*), with no need for the slave's consent, or could also marry them off to other men. (Though some masters did use male slaves sexually, jurists never condoned such use; female owners were prohibited from sexual use of slaves of either gender.)

Unlike in Roman or American slave systems, Muslim slaves of both sexes could, with their owners' permission, be validly married, though never to their owners. Anecdotes suggest that some slaves initiated marriages; more often, owners made matches based on their own interests. Marrying off female slaves brought both dower (paid to a free wife or to a slave's owner) and additional slaves to the master, since offspring born to a married slave woman were her master's property, regardless of whether her husband—whose paternity was recognized—was free or enslaved. The owner maintained control over a married slave woman's mobility and labor (Ali, 2010).

Muslim rules governing slave concubinage (*milk al-yamīn*) developed during the seventh and eighth centuries. A slave who bore her master's child (*umm walad* or *mustawlida*) would be automatically freed at the master's death. Any such child was free (opinion differed as to whether the master's formal acknowledgment of paternity was required, or merely the absence of denial) and of equal status to children born in marriage. An *umm walad* could not be sold, although jurists disagreed as to whether she could be married off without her consent as other female slaves could be. *Umm walads* figured heavily in certain courtly contexts, especially where families wanted to reproduce royal lines without being beholden to other powerful parties. Many Ottoman sultans were born to concubines.

In addition, both manumitted Mamluk women and women of the Ottoman harems themselves had numerous female slave servants. Manumitted slaves remained linked to their former owners by formal ties of clientage. They could be instrumental in political networking, including by arranged marriages. Thus, scholarship has emphasized the micropolitics of power in the slaver-enslaved relationship (Toledano, 2007, Zilfi, 2010), suggesting that the simple dichotomy of enslaved and free fails to capture not only the significance of personal ties, but also gradations of power and influence.

Most slaves were domestic menials, not only in royal but also in upper and middle class households. In the city and countryside, slaves worked in industry and agriculture, though little is known about women's participation. Military slavery, which involved conscripted soldiers and an elite class of freed military slaves, developed into a major institution in some regions and periods, including the Mamlūk sultanate (1254–1517), the Mughal state in India, and the Ṣafavid and Ottoman Empires. These slaves were divided and hierarchically organized by ethnic-racial origin and type of work, though personal relationships could bend rules. Indeed, research into legal manuals, fatwā collections, chronicles, medical records and, especially, court archives indicates that slavery in practice often deviated from the theory laid down by jurists.

An active slave trade existed in many Muslim societies through much of the nineteenth century, and large slave populations continued to exist in Arab lands, in the Indian subcontinent, and in Africa into the twentieth century. Muslim-majority societies have since formally abolished slavery, although slavery and slavery-like practices persist in some African nations, as well as in the brutal treatment of domestic immigrant labor in some Gulf nations. Women have been enslaved and used for sex in civil wars in Sudan and Somalia, and the Taliban are said to have captured and used Hazāra Shīʿī women as concubines.

BIBLIOGRAPHY

Ali, Kecia. *Marriage and Slavery in Early Islam*. Cambridge, Mass.: Harvard University Press, 2010.

Johansen, Baber. "The Valorization of the Body in Muslim Sunni Law." In *Law and Society in Islam*, ed. Devin J. Stewart, Baber Johansen, and Amy Singer. Princeton, N.J.: Markus Wiener, 1996.

Marmon, Shaun E. "Domestic Slavery in the Mamluk Empire: A Preliminary Sketch." In *Slavery in the Islamic Middle East*, ed. Shaun E. Marmon. Princeton, N.J.: Markus Wiener Publishers, 1999. Solid brief overview.

Toledano, Ehud R. As If Silent and Absent: Bonds of Enslavement in the Islamic Middle East. New Haven, Conn.: Yale University Press, 2007.

Zilfi, Madeline. *Women and Slavery in the Late Ottoman Empire: The Design of Difference*. Cambridge: Cambridge University Press, 2010.

DROR ZE'EVI
Updated by KECIA ALI

SOGHAGHTANI BEKI. (1198–1252), influential aristocrat of the Mongol Empire. Soghaghtani Beki, the youngest daughter of the tribal ruler Toghril-Ong Khan's brother, Ja-Gambu, was born into the aristocracy of the Kereit tribe, whose distinction was the number of women it had provided as wives for the Turco-Mongol nobility. Reared among the ruling elite, Soghaghtani Beki maintained her position at the heart of Chinggisid imperial power throughout her life and she made it her life's ambition to ensure that her sons earned for themselves prestige, wealth, and influence. Her marriage to Chinggis Khan's youngest son, Tolui, provided her ambitions with a tangible and very solid base on which to build. After her husband's early death, she resisted strongly all attempts to assign her through marriage to the "protection" of another royal prince. Such a move would have interfered with, and probably undermined, the plans she had for her four sons, Möngke, Kublai, Hülegü, and Arigböge, three of whom ruled as emperors, while her youngest, supported by a substantial part of the Turco-Mongol world, aspired to be Great Khan of the Eurasian steppelands.

Rashīd al-Dīn described her husband, Tolui, as "a great winner of battles" who had conquered more countries than any other prince, an enviable accolade for a Mongol man, though hardly suggestive of an ideal husband or attentive father. In 1231, at the age of forty, Tolui Khan died an enviable death brought on by excessive drinking and Soghaghtani continued single-handedly and single-mindedly to bring up her sons in her own inimitable way while pursuing her own ambitious career. She successfully resisted formidable pressure to marry the great khan, Ögödei's son and successor, Güyük Khan, and concentrated instead on her appanage Chen-ting in Hebei province, educating her sons through example in the arts of statecraft and administration. She taught her sons to respect and nurture the land and their subjects and ensured that the boys received a comprehensive education. ʿAṭā Malik Juwayni, the future governor of Baghdad and a chronicler of the Chinggisids, quoting a contemporary poet al-Mutanabbī, expressed his admiration for Soghaghtani Beki thus: "And if all women were like unto her, then would women be superior to men" (Juwayni, 1997, p. 552), words echoed by the Syriac cleric and chronicler Bar Hebraeus,

> This queen trained her sons so well that all the princes marvelled at her power of administration.... And it was in respect of her that a certain poet said, "If I were to see among the race of women another woman like this, I should say that the race of women was far superior to that of men." (1976, p. 398)

While ensuring that the traditional Mongol skills of riding, hunting, archery, and combat, were mastered, she saw to it that her sons were also schooled in literature, the arts, and sciences—for which task, she employed a Persian tutor from the northern Iranian city of Qazvin and an Uighur named Tolochu to teach them Mongolian literary skills:

> Thanks to her ability, when her sons were left by their father, some of them still children, she went to great pains in their education, teaching them various accomplishments and good manners and never allowing the slightest sign of strife to appear amongst them. She caused their wives also to have love in their hearts for one another, and by her prudence and counsel [she] cherished and protected her sons, their children and grandchildren, and the great emirs and troops that had been left by Chingiz-Khan and Tolui Khan and were now attached to them. And perceiving her to be extremely intelligent and able, they never swerved a hair's breadth from her command. (Rashīd al-Dīn Ṭabīb, 1971, p., 199)

Kublai's appanage of Hsing-chou that supported ten thousand households was close by her own appanage of Chen-ting and she used the closeness to demonstrate the differences in their approach to administering the land. Initially, the young Kublai, born 23 September 1215, adopted a laissez-faire attitude to the practices of his Mongol officers charged with administering the lands on his behalf, and he ignored the widespread abuses of power, excessive taxes, and exploitative labor demands imposed on his Chinese subjects. The resulting mass exodus from the land and the fall in taxation revenue, a pattern repeated over much of occupied northern China, contrasted sharply with the situation in the lands administered by his mother, where farms flourished and agriculture yielded rich rewards in taxation and trade. She encouraged the native agrarian economy with no attempt at imposing the pastoral practices more suited to Mongol nomadic practices and the resulting high return in taxes and supportive subjects was very clear. The lessons were not lost on her sons and the success of both the Ilkhanate (1258–1335) and Yuan China (1270–1369) can be attributed, in part, to the legacy of Soghaghtani Beki and her early recognition that the brutal and exploitative practices of the first generation of Mongol landowners were short-sighted, self-defeating, and disastrous for the economy of the region.

Kublai consequently replaced many of his Mongol overlords with Chinese officials and appointed administrators with experience rather than the retainers whom he had known from his youth. He drew up a committee of predominantly Chinese officials, named the *an-ch'a shih*, or Pacification Commission, which was tasked with enticing back the farmers and peasants who had joined the exodus so they might once more farm the province's estates and lands. By the early 1240s, with the implementation of a regularized system of taxation and an end to the imposition of extraordinary levies, Kublai's reforms began to show results and the province's agrarian economy again flourished.

But it was not only at the local level of administration that Soghaghtani Beki was adept. She was also a master of the machinations, intrigue, and manipulation needed to survive and had the ruthlessness and determination necessary to succeed in the courts of the Mongol elite.

Through a network of spies and her own contacts with the women of the elite whose friendships often crossed barriers inaccessible to men, she had learned of the perfidy of Güyük and his murderous designs against his cousins, all of which she had relayed to the kingmaker, Batu Khan of the Golden Horde. Heavily in her debt, Batu Khan was instrumental in ensuring the election of her eldest son Möngke Khan rather than Ögödei's grandson Shiremun as the next great khan and thus was Soghaghtani Beki's greatest ambition realized.

Soghaghtani Beki fell ill and died a few months after Möngke Khan's enthronement as great khan and she was buried in a Christian church in Gansu province. However in Maragha, the capital of her son Hülegü Khan (d. 1265), the first Ilkhan of Iran, there is a tomb tower named in her honor, even though no evidence exists that she ever visited Iran. This solitary tomb tower stands today in the courtyard of a girls' primary school in the small provincial market town of Maragha and bears silent witness to the memory of a remarkable woman and her extraordinary legacy.

BIBLIOGRAPHY

Bar Hebraeus, Gregory John. *The Laughable Stories*. Translated by E. A. Wallis Budge. New York: AMS Press, 1976. Originally published in 1897 (London: Luzac).

Juwayni, 'Alā' al-Dīn 'Aṭā Malik. Translated by John A. Boyle. *Genghis Khan: History of the World Conqueror*. Manchester, U.K.: Manchester University Press, 1997.

Lambton, Ann. *Continuity and Change in Medieval Persia: Aspects of Administrative, Economic, Social History in 11th–14th Century Persia*. London: I. B. Tauris, 1988.

Lane, George. *Daily Life in the Mongol Empire*. Westport, Conn.: Greenwood Press, 2006.

Morgan, David. *The Mongols*. 2d ed. Malden, Mass.: Wiley-Blackwell, 2007.

Rashīd al-Dīn Ṭabīb. Translated by Wheeler Thackston. *Rashiduddin Fazlullah's Jami'u't-Tawarikh: Compendium of Chronicles*. Parts 1–3. Sources of Oriental Languages and Literature 45. Cambridge, Mass: Harvard University, 1998–1999.

Rashīd al-Dīn Ṭabīb. Translated by John Andrew Boyle. *Successors of Genghis Khan*. New York: Columbia University Press, 1971.

GEORGE LANE

Sokoto Caliphate. The Sokoto Caliphate was established in the region now known as northwestern Nigeria in the aftermath of the Sokoto Jihad (1803–1830), which was launched to reform Islam in the area. Like the jihad, the Caliphate was led by Shehu (Hausa; Ar., *shaykh*) Usuman Dan Fodio, a Fulani preacher and teacher, and the patriarch of the Fodio (Fulfulde, "learned") clan. The effects of the Sokoto Caliphate continue to resonate in political and spiritual leadership in the region, and in the continuing model of women's extension education that was established early in the Caliphate by the Shehu's daughter, Nana Asma'u.

The Shehu was born into a Fulani clerical family in 1754 in Maratta, in what is now the Niger Republic, and then moved his family south to the village of Degel. The Shehu gathered a following as he preached against non-Islamic Hausa practices such as spirit possession. As his following grew, he was increasingly restricted by nominally Muslim Hausa rulers, who considered him a political threat. In 1793 the birth of his twins coincided with the beginning of the Shehu's Ṣūfī spiritual experiences and dreams, like the one in which he was given the "sword of Truth" for the defense of his community. He named his twin son Hassan but his twin daughter Asma'u instead of the traditional twin counterpart, Husseina. It is said that he anticipated her role would parallel that of the historical Asma, daughter of the Prophet Muḥammad's close companion, Abū Bakr. Asma'u did, in fact, prove to be as active in the Sokoto jihad as Asma had been in the conflicts of seventh-century Islam.

The Shehu was able to continue preaching until 1803, when a new local leader attacked him and his followers. In response, they retreated, declared the Shehu to be the commander of the Faithful, and then, at his command, launched a formal jihad of religious reform in 1804. Although some conflicts continued until 1830 in the eastern and southern regions, the Shehu and his followers had defeated most of the rulers of the Hausa states by 1808. In 1809 the new capital of Sokoto was established. Initially, the Shehu stayed in the village of Gwandu, where he resumed his teaching and writing. He moved to Sifawa and finally to Sokoto. The Shehu died in 1817, and his son Muhammad Bello succeeded him as the Sarkin Musulmi (king of the Muslims, H.; Ar., *Amir al-Mu'minin*). The Shehu's brother, Abdullahi, moved to Gwandu and administered the western part of the Caliphate, including Nupe and Ilorin, while Bello continued to rule the major portion of the Caliphate and write extensively until his own death in 1837.

Scholarship was of central importance to the Fodio clan: The Shehu had been educated at a young age by his mother and grandmother, according to the clan's customary model of education. He believed adamantly in the Qur'ānic mandate that all individuals should pursue knowledge and stated plainly that any man who did not facilitate women's education was not abiding by Islamic ethics. The jihad itself was a campaign based on intellectual considerations from those in his close circle of family-member advisors: Abdullahi; Muhammad Bello; Bello's friend Gidado; and Nana Asma'u. Each of these individuals was an active, productive scholar, and they relied on one another for strategic planning and spiritual sustenance during long years of battle and itinerancy in escaping the enemy. The principal supporters in the itinerancy of the jihad years included the Shehu's entire community: men remained on the battlefield, while the women maintained family life, prepared food, oversaw births and deaths, and attended to the details of daily needs, such as food preparation and textile production. During this time, the Fodio clan continued to write in Arabic, Fulfulde, and Hausa, and engage in intellectual debate. The Shehu himself composed over three hundred books and treatises. Caliph Bello, Asma'u, and Gidado also wrote works that continue to be studied in contemporary times.

The aftermath of the jihad resulted in long-lasting social change for the region. At one level, the effects of the jihad were clear in the installation of its key commanders in positions of leadership. They replaced Hausa traditional kings as Muslim Fulani emirs in city-states such as Kano, Kebbi, Ilorin, Nupe, Bauchi, Gombe, Adamawa, Hadejia, Kazaure, Katsina, Daura, Zaria, Misau, Zamfara, Jamaʿare, and Baghirmi. At the judicial level, these emirs appointed new judges to establish courts of Islamic law.

Meanwhile, the vast majority of the Hausa refugee population was in need of social welfare. Many widows and orphans had to be housed securely and educated in the ethical bases of Islamic society. Nana Asmaʾu was instrumental in the reparation of the social fabric by assisting rural women. While she continued her work teaching mixed-gender classes and writing poetic works in Fulfulde and Arabic that were known to Arabist scholars throughout the Maghreb, she also began to instruct a cadre of women teachers whose task it was to travel to rural areas to educate women there. This endeavor was significant in terms of social reform in the region and may indeed have had a far deeper effect on the transformation of local Islamic practices than even the new judicial system. Asmaʾu's realization that rural refugee Hausa women needed to learn Islamic principles led her to systematize her educational plan, calling it the the ʾYan Taru, the Associates. Each group of ʾYan Taru women had a designated leader, a Jaji. ʾYan Taru students studied with Asmaʾu to memorize her poems, written in Hausa for the masses, which functioned as lesson plans when they traveled to rural areas to teach other women.

In 1903 the British conquest of northern Nigeria was resisted unsuccessfully by Sultan Attahiru I at Giginya (Sokoto) and Burmi (Gombe). After the battles, the British established a system of indirect rule within the existing political and legal infrastructures, and worked through the new sultan and emirs until independence almost sixty years later. Through the entire colonial period, Asmaʾu's ʾYan Taru system of educating women was neither acknowledged nor supported beyond its grassroots level. Nevertheless, women perpetuated the program following Asmaʾu's death in 1864; it was especially important to a community in which colonial rulers focused attention and resources on boys' education. The ʾYan Taru system of educating women continued post-jihad, throughout the years of British colonial presence (1903–1960), and in the years following Nigerian independence in 1960.

After independence, the first and only premier of northern Nigeria was Ahmadu Bello, a direct descendant of Sultan Bello, who had been a contender for the sultanship with Abubakar III in 1937–1938. Ahmadu Bello's assassination by military officers in 1966 helped spark a civil war, from 1967 to 1970. Abubakar III remained the sultan until his death in 1988, and the sultanship then passed to Ibrahim Dasuki, from the Buhari branch of the Dan Fodio family. Dasuki was removed by the head of state, General Sani Abacha, for political reasons in 1996 and replaced by Muhammadu Maccido (r. 1996–2006), the son of Abubakar III. Maccido remained in office until his untimely death, along with his son, in a plane crash in October 2006.

Maccido's younger brother, Muhammadu Saʾadu Abubakar III, was installed as the twentieth Sultan of Sokoto on 3 March 2007. Unlike many of the previous sultans, Saʾad Abubakar was a "modern man." He was born on 24 August 1956; attended Barewa College, Zaria; and proceeded to the Nigerian Defense Academy, Kaduna, in 1975. He was commissioned in December 1977 as a second lieutenant and posted to the Nigerian Army Armored Corps, where he spent thirty-one years, including his work with

ECOWAS in Sierra Leone and serving as Nigeria's defense adviser in Pakistan, with concurrent accreditation in Iran, Iraq, Afghanistan, and Saudi Arabia, from February 2003 to February 2006. He returned to Nigeria in 2006 to attend the Senior Executive Course at the National Institute for Policy and Strategic Studies, in Kuru, where he wrote a paper "Religious Extremism as a National Security Problem: Strategies for Sustainable Solutions."

In October 2011 Alhaji Muhammad Sa'ad Abubakar III, sultan of Sokoto, was invited to deliver the Samuel L. and Elizabeth Jodidi Lecture on peacekeeping at Harvard Divinity School. As a direct descendant of Nana Asma'u, he also was interested in holding a forum on the tradition of women's education in northern Nigeria. To this end, he presided over a panel of scholars speaking on women's education, titled "Women's Religious Literacy: The Legacy of Nana Asma'u in the Twenty-first Century and Beyond" on 2 October 2011. That the sultan of Sokoto insisted on including a discussion of Nana Asma'u in his first visit to Harvard University as a distinguished speaker indicates clearly the esteem in which he holds his ancestor and her accomplishments. Men's roles in the Sokoto Caliphate have been studied extensively, but only recently has it been acknowledged widely that Nana Asma'u's model of women's education, the 'Yan Taru, is an enduring, productive legacy of the Sokoto Caliphate. It is active in the region in the twenty-first century and has become a model for Muslim women of Qādirīyah communities well beyond Nigeria, including many in the United States and elsewhere in the world.

BIBLIOGRAPHY

Boyd, Jean. *The Caliph's Sister*. London: Frank Cass, 1989. The definitive biography of Nana Asma'u.

Boyd, Jean, and Beverly Mack. *Asma'u's Legacy: An Enduring Model of Muslim Women's Scholarship*. London: Interface Press, 2012. A close study of jihad and caliphate life, the continued tradition of the 'Yan Taru, and its spread beyond Nigeria.

Boyd, Jean, and Beverly Mack. *The Collected Works of Nana Asma'u, Daughter of Usman dan Fodio, 1793–1864*. East Lansing: Michigan State University Press, 1997. Text and translation of Nana Asma'u's known works, historical footnotes.

Boyd, Jean, with Hamzat Maishanu. *Sir Siddiq Abubakar III, Sarkin Musulmi*. Ibadan, Nigeria: Spectrum Books, 1991. Thoughtful biography of Sultan Abubakar III, who ruled from 1937 to 1988, by an Englishwoman who worked in Sokoto for twenty-five years and had access to archival and local literatures.

Last, Murray. *The Sokoto Caliphate*. New York: Humanities Press, 1967. Major scholarly work on the subject.

Mack, Beverly, and Jean Boyd. *Nana Asma'u: Scholar and Scribe*. Bloomington: Indiana University Press, 2000. Descriptive feminist analysis of historical, literary, and anthropological views of the Sokoto Caliphate.

Sulaiman, Ibraheem. *The Islamic State and the Challenge of History: Ideals, Policies, and Operation of the Sokoto Caliphate*. London: Mansell, 1987. Sympathetic detailed interpretation of the jihad.

BEVERLY MACK

SOUTH AFRICA. Islam is a minority religion in South Africa, where Muslims, numbering an estimated 1.2 million, made up approximately 2.5 percent of the population in 2012. Women comprise roughly half of the Muslim population. Around 80 percent of Muslims are either descendents of slaves and political prisoners from Southeast Asia (mostly from Indonesia, but also from Madagascar, India, and Africa) who were brought to the Cape Colony by the Dutch East India Company during the seventeenth and eighteenth centuries, or indentured and non-indentured migrants from South Asia who settled originally in the province of Natal from 1860 onward and subsequently migrated to other parts of the country. The former, who are referred to by the generalized term "Malays," live mostly in the Western Cape, while Indian Muslims settled mainly in KwaZulu-Natal and Gauteng. The post-apartheid period has seen Muslims spread to most parts of the country, including the Orange Free State, whose racist policies had barred them entry from the 1880s until the end of apartheid in 1994. Indigenous Africans make up less than 10 percent of the Muslim population. There has been a sizable migration of Muslims from the Asian sub continent (India, Pakistan, Bangladesh), as well as from African countries such as Malawi and Somalia, in the post-apartheid period. They number in the tens of thousands, though there is no exact figure, as most keep a low profile either because they entered the country fraudulently or because of high levels of xenophobia. Most of these new migrants have opted to settle in townships and rural areas across the country in pursuit of business opportunities. Some of the male migrants have married indigenous women who have embraced Islam. Being in the townships has brought these migrants into proximity with indigenous Africans, but has also made them more susceptible to xenophobic attacks, as they are seen to take away scarce jobs and to monopolize business opportunities.

Historically, Cape Muslims have embraced a more egalitarian view of gender relations with less austere gender segregation. In contrast to Natal, women played an important role in early Islam in the Cape and in society generally, with some acquiring wealth and prominence. One example is Saartjie van de Kaap, a freed slave woman who, in 1809, purchased two properties in Cape Town. One of these properties was already used as a mosque and, in her will, Saartjie declared that it must continue to be used as a mosque. Although the institutionalization of Islam gradually marginalized women in the Cape, it was not to the same extent as in Natal. Overall, though, it would be fair to say that women have largely been excluded from participation in religious structures, even though decisions made in these bodies directly affects them. In addition, most Muslim women, being black, were also racially oppressed under successive white minority governments.

Despite the difficulties of indenture, Muslim immigrants in Natal set about re-establishing their culture and religion by building mosques, instituting prayer, and establishing festivals. Mosques were built in Natal and the Transvaal from at least the 1880s, but women were prohibited from entering this public space until at least the 1970s, when a group of women, led by Zuleikha Mayat of the Women's Cultural Group, secured the right to pray at the West Street Mosque, one of the premier mosques in Durban. Most other mosques resisted even this concession. Class differences usually determined whether or not women participated in religious festivals. Most working-class women were heavily involved in the very public Muharram festival while the less boisterous and more private Eid festivals were observed by middle-class women. It should be noted that, while Muharram is a predominantly Shīʿī festival, it has been celebrated by diasporic Indians everywhere who were almost entirely Sunnīs.

Historically, women have always participated in the public sphere. Many of the indentured were women and, during the formative decades of settlement, there was an economic need for poorer migrants to work. While educational opportunities were limited for Indians in general, women were doubly prejudiced because of the reluctance of parents to educate them. It was only from the 1950s that small numbers of Muslim women were able to access high school education. Early exceptions include Moseda Ismail, who qualified as a medical doctor at Edinburgh University in 1930; Hawa Patel, the first woman to complete a medical degree at the University of Cape Town; Khatija

Nagdee, the first woman to graduate at the University of Witwatersrand; and Fatima Mayer, the first Muslim woman to finish her medical studies at the University of Natal, where she subsequently became a professor of medicine. The numbers of Muslim women who completed high school and attended university increased considerably between the 1960s and the 1980s, and many women have made their mark in all professional fields. However, strong reformist impulses since the 1980s have also seen many parents opting to send their daughters to schools where they receive an exclusively Islamic education.

Muslims women began entering the political sphere in the 1930s and later participated fully in the public and secular spheres during the struggle against apartheid and the pursuit of human rights. They clearly did not heed the advice of Sir Kuma Reddi, the Indian Agent General in South Africa, who stated in 1930 that Indian women should stay out of politics as their menfolk were accomplished enough to do that. Women, instead, were told to tend to their homes and children. The editor of *Indian Opinion*, the newspaper founded by Mohandas K. Gandhi during his stay in South Africa, commented in an editorial on 26 December 1930 that he "respectfully disagree[d] with this view expressed by Sir Kurma." "Why," Gandhi asked, "should not our women take part in politics?" Cissie Gool and Halima Gool of Cape Town were iconic figures in the 1930s and 1940s through their participation in the Non-European Unity Front and the South African Communist Party. Halima Gool wrote an article in the newspaper *Indian Views* under the pseudonym "Muslim Girl." Males refused to believe that a woman could write such probing political analyses. Finally, on 19 August 1938, *Indian Views* published a supplement carrying her photograph to convince the public of her existence.

Women like Zainab Asvat, Cissie Gool, Ghadija Christopher, and Rookeya Docrat were imprisoned for participating in the passive resistance campaign from 1946 to 1948 in protest against land segregation in Natal. The likes of Rahima Moosa, Fatima Seedat, Amina Cachalia, and Fatima Meer, the first women to be banned in South Africa, participated in the 8 August 1956 National Women's anti-apartheid march. This day is now observed as an annual holiday in South Africa. Meer (1928–2010) achieved international fame as an anti-apartheid activist and sociologist. For this, she and her husband, I. C. Meer, were repeatedly banned from the country from the 1960s to the 1980s. Amina Desai was arrested in 1971 with schoolteacher Ahmed Timol, an anti-apartheid activist who was a friend of her son. Timol died in detention within a few weeks of his arrest, while Desai was imprisoned for the next six and half years, making her one of the longest serving female political prisoners in South Africa. In the post-apartheid period several Muslim women have served in government, with Naledi Pandor and Fathima Chohan being ministers in the ANC government.

Many Muslims found the assumption of power by the African National Congress in 1994 challenging, as the new secular democracy, unlike the apartheid government, did not patrol individual moral behavior, while the country's secular and liberal 1996 Constitution legalized same-sex relationships, abortion, and pornography. At the same time, globalization and the opening of borders, and the freer movement of people had economic and cultural repercussions. The communications revolution also made it difficult to control the information flow. These changes ushered or coincided with Muslims, including women, undergoing important transformations, such as a greater emphasis on personal piety, emphasis on simplifying such celebrations weddings and eradicating others such as birthdays, giving up watching television and films, the growth of Islamic and Muslim schools, many more Muslims going on pilgrimage to Saudi Arabia, and so on. There seemed to be a greater affinity with the global and transnational community of believers, the *ummah*. This is at the level of a political imaginary introduced by such events as the unresolved Palestinian question, the U.S. invasions of Iraq and Afghanistan, the drone attacks in Pakistan, and so on. At a practical level, this transnational flow has seen the arrival of Sufi *turuq*, visits of international scholars, establishment of a network of Turkish schools and madrasahs, and opening of the Nizamiye Turkish Mosque in Johannesburg in October 2012, which is the largest mosque in the Southern Hemisphere and a major tourist attraction with many local and overseas Muslims visiting to see the Ottoman Empire-style architecture. The mosque was funded by Turkish businessman Ali Katircioglu, who first visited South Africa in 2007. Katircioglu has also sought permission to open the first Islamic university in South Africa. This return to the roots on the part of many women does not mark a turn to the kind of "fundamentalism" that conservatives and policymakers in the Western world imagine. The process of re-Islamization is largely an attempt to create privatized Islamic spaces; few Muslims harbor any realistic ambitions of Islamizing the state.

There are intense internal and external debates over issues of correct Islamic rituals and practices. A conspicuous feature of this period has been the move to segregate the sexes. In response to the call from Ulama for the complete separation (*purdah*) of men and women, large numbers of women are fully veiled, even though there is disputation in Islam as to whether or not women need to cover their faces. This is part of the renewed endeavor by the Muslim Ulama to prevent what they perceive to be transgressions of gender norms. When local Ulama refer to veiling, they mean total seclusion from public life. Ironically, while Muslim women are covering their faces, they are far more visible in "new" public spaces, such as upmarket shopping malls, flea markets, coffee shops, the beachfront, and restaurants, than their predecessors of a generation ago. The kinds of spaces that women are able to access is influenced by class. Women have simultaneously become visible and invisible in the public sphere. While there is opposition to the veil from politicians and the general public in many Western countries, there is little overt opposition to it in South Africa.

Among the issues that women confront are the lack of secular education as part of this reformist drive and training to prepare them for any meaningful vocation. Like other women in South Africa, working-class Muslim women also have to confront high levels of domestic violence and must try to manage single-headed households. One of the most contentious issues among Muslims is Sharīʿah-based Muslim Personal Law (MPL). The South African Law Commission (SALC) released a draft bill on Muslim marriages in December 2001. While many women activists welcomed the bill, Muslim judicial bodies rejected aspects of it, such as the requirement that a man wanting to marry for a second time would have to obtain the permission of a civil court. Judicial bodies argue that enacting the legislation will make it subject to constitutional supremacy, which they find unacceptable as they regard the Qurʾān as the supreme law in Islam. As a result of these differences, the bill has sat with the Department of Justice and Constitutional Development for more than ten years. The result is that many Muslim women remain vulnerable because of the failure of the state to recognize religious marriages. They consequently do not enjoy the protection offered by civil marriages when it comes to such things as non-payment of maintenance, men's easy access to divorce, and being deprived of inheritance.

Although South African Muslim society generally deploys a conservative and, some may say, patriarchal approach to the Qur'ān, given that Muslims are a fractured entity, it is not surprising that there are discrepancies between the normative Islamic models of the mainly middle-class mainstream Ulama and the actual practices of Muslims in the townships and informal settlements and among the working classes. Even some middle-class Muslims have challenged traditional Ulama as they seek space for women's aspirations. Such women are inspired by the likes of Amina Wadud and Leila Ahmed, who argue that the Qur'ān upholds the equality of men and women but that this message has been subverted by Ulama to relegate women to a second-class status. Amina Wadud, for example, was invited to render a pre-khutbah (sermon) talk at a Friday congregational prayer at Claremont Main Road Mosque in Cape Town in August 1994, raising the ire of many Ulama. Shamima Shaikh (1960–1998) was a leading gender activist in her position as national co-ordinator of the Muslim Youth Movement's Gender Desk and editor of the progressive Muslim monthly *al-Qalam*. From 1993, she headed the "Equal Access to Mosques" campaign. Since the early 2000s, under the banner of "Taking Islam to the People," a "Family Eidgah" has been organized on the beachfront annually during the Eid festival.

While many Muslims believe that limiting the participation of women in the public sphere is a waste of human potential, traditional Ulama, by contrast, see those pushing for women's rights as misguided secularists spreading disinformation by misinterpreting religious texts for their own purposes. Muslim women have formed their own associations and are involved in a myriad of organizations, such as the Islamic Co-ordinating Council—Ladies Council, Cape Town; Islamic Da'wah Movement, Women's Wing, Durban; Islamic Women's Association, Durban; Jamaat-un-Nissa, Kimberley; Muslim Women's Federation, Cape Town; and Senior Citizens Comfort Group and Women's Cultural Group, Durban—all of which are engaged in the public sphere in various ways.

The growth of Islamic media has made it possible for many more voices to be heard in the public domain. Media, in the form of the radio, magazines, websites, books, audiocassettes, videocassettes, television, pod casting, and newspapers, have mushroomed over the past decade. This has blurred the boundaries between public and private and made it easier for counter-voices to articulate their agendas and thus reduce the regulatory capacities of Ulama. Like print before it, new forms of electronic communication involve new actors and sites of production and consumption. The impact of these new media forms is contradictory, as they tend to address groups defined by specific concerns and identities and reach narrow audiences and shape localized identities.

There are deep divisions of class, race, ethnicity, and language among South Africa's Muslim women, even if there is a tendency in the literature to view them as a monolith. Diversity has been deepened by the new waves of migration and the commodification of Islam through the consumption of designer cloaks, halaal certification, private schools, and so on, which is changing Muslim religious, as well as social, cultural, and economic, life. Given the vast differences of belief and behavior, the term "Muslim, for analytical purposes, is at best only a minimal common denominator for those who are described as such. For now, most Muslims, women included, feel very comfortable in South Africa, which they see as a land relatively free of Islamophobia, the fear of Islam and Muslims that became so prevalent in many parts of the Western world following the September 2001 attacks on the World Trade Center in New York, but one which has a much longer history rooted in Orientalism, colonialism, immigration, and racism. In South Africa, unlike in some European countries, Islam is not perceived as a threat to national identity, and the country's constitution allows for the expression of various beliefs. Muslims have not been marginalized in the post-apartheid period because of their religion, but are included in political and societal debates. This has engendered a sense of attachment to the post-apartheid nation among most Muslims, even if they oppose policy changes around sexuality and morality and feel aggrieved by policies such as affirmative action and the high levels of corruption in some sectors. The presence of post-1994 migrants from Africa and the Asian sub continent is an important new dimension to the Islamic experience in South Africa, and it remains to be seen how this will shape the Islamic experience in the country.

[*See also* Ahmed, Leila; *and* Wadud, Amina.]

BIBLIOGRAPHY

Bangstad, Sindre. "Facets of Secularisation and Islamization among contemporary Cape Muslims." Ph dissertation, Radboud University, Nijmegen, 2007.

Bradlow, F., and M. Cairns. *The Early Cape Muslims: A Study of Their Mosques, Genealogy, and Origins.* Cape Town: A.A. Balkema, 1978.

Da Costa, Y., and A. Davids, eds. *Pages from Cape Muslim History*. Pietermaritzburg, South Africa: Shuter 7 Shooter, 1994.

Esack, Farid. *On Being a Muslim. Finding a Religious Path in the World Today*. Oxford One World, 1999.

Jeppie, S. "Reclassifications: Coloured, Malay, Muslim." In *Coloured by History, Shaped by Place: New Perspectives on Coloured Identities in Cape Town*, by Z. Erasmus, pp. 80–96. Cape Town: Kwela and SA History Online, 2001.

Mahida, E. M. *History of Muslims in South Africa: A Chronology*. Durban: Arabic Study Circle, 1993.

Tayob, A. *Islam in South Africa. Mosques, Imams, and Sermons*. Gainesville, Fla.: University Press of Florida, 1999.

Vahed, G., and T. Waetjen. *Gender, Modernity, and Indian Delights: The Women's Cultural Group of Durban, 1954–2010*. Cape Town: HSRC Press, 2010.

Goolam Vahed

Southeast Asia and the Pacific.

Muslim women occupy a pivotal position in Southeast Asian countries, where their history and political participation intersect with nation-building programs, as well as complex multi-ethnic and plural religious realities. Aiming to follow the model of global Islamic revivalism, regional and national Islamic movements and political parties (especially in majority Muslim countries) have struggled to construct a modern society that is oriented toward universal Islamic revivalist values and downplays local traditions and customs. In some cases, this project has coincided with political action to introduce Islamic criminal law (for example, in northwestern Malaysian states, and in the now autonomous Aceh region of Indonesia). Although, historically, Islamic revival movements have proved essential in the establishment of postcolonial independent nations, nowadays these same forces put national cohesion to the test. Such movements fielded discourses focusing on women's roles as mothers, daughters, and wives in the creation of the nation, yet fully engaged in political participation. The tendency to limit women's participation in civil society and attempts to enforce a narrow Islamic view on their roles and conduct are constantly challenged by women's groups. The nature and the extent of these processes differ between majority Muslim countries (Indonesia, Malaysia, and Brunei) and countries where Muslims constitute a minority (Philippines, Thailand, Myanmar, Singapore, and Cambodia), especially in relation to family-law legislation.

History, Experience, and Activities. Revivalist movements in Indonesia provided women with access to education, greater rights, and the possibility to pursue a career. Religious and national consciousness was promoted at the same time as new political subjectivities arose, so that religiosity and political actions became inextricably linked. In Indonesia, women's activism targeted the opposition between public and private spheres, marking a meaningful relation between individual piety and national morality. Women's branches of political parties were established in the first half of the twentieth century. In 1917, Ahmad Dahlan established Aisyiyah, the women's branch of the Muhammadiyah movement, whose foremost women leaders were Siti Bariyah and Siti Badilah. It is presently chaired (2010–2015) by Hj. Siti Noordjannah. In 1940, Muslimat sprang from the more traditionalist organization, Nahdatul Ulama (NU), which follows the Shāfiʿī school of Islamic law and acts in opposition to the Muhammadiyah. In 1936, Persatuan Islam Istri became an autonomous branch of the modernist Islamic movement Persis. Other relevant organizations were Syarekat Perempuan Islam Indonesia (Federation of the Muslim Women of Indonesian Syarekat Islam) and the Women's Section of the Jong Islamieten Bond. Indonesian women's groups gathered for a general meeting in Yogyakarta on December 22–26, 1928, steering clear of certain issues that would have incurred the opposition of the parent organizations, such as gender equality in law and education. These groups joined under an umbrella organization that, in 1946, was renamed Kongres Wanita Indonesia (KOWANI, Indonesian Women's Congress). With Indonesian independence in 1945 new women's organizations flourished and maintained a specific focus on defending national sovereignty: Persatuan Wanita Indonesia (Perwani, Union of Indonesian Women); Wanita Republik Indonesia (PERWARI, Union of the Women of the Indonesian Republic); Laskar Wanita (Women's Army); and Gerakan Pemuda Islam Indonesia (Girls' Section of Islamic Youth Movement). Women also gained access to parliamentary representation and the Constituent Assembly.

The Gerakan Wanita Indonesia (GERWANI, Indonesian Women's Movement) was formed from the Partai Komunis Indonesia (PKI, Indonesian Communist Party). After the end of constitutional democracy in 1957, GERWANI and KOWANI became more antagonistic. GERWANI supported the attempted coup of 1965 and, with the beginning of Suharto's New Order in 1966, the movement was suppressed. Women belonging to the organization suffered defamatory propaganda and were jailed or sentenced to death as part of the government's anticommunist campaign. During the 1980s, new women's movements were created, specifically An Nisa Swasti Foundation, Srikandi Foundation, and Pusat Pengembangan Sumber Daya Wanita (Center for Women's Development), which emphasized the autonomy and agency of "directed" women's movements and applied a shared model of authority among their members, "even though they [risked] being interpreted as critics of the male patriarchal system" (Anwar, 2004, p. 91). Movements addressing gender issues more specifically in Indonesia are the young women's sections of NU (Fatayat) and Muhammadiyah (Nasyiatul Aisyiyah).

Although several NGOs engage with women's-rights issues and feminism (such as the group Rahima), some political parties (for example, the Partai Keadilan Sejahtera [PKS, Prosperous Justice Party], associated with the *dakwah* movement and founded in 2002) consider feminism un-Islamic. The Pembinaan Kesejahteraan Keluarga (PKK, Family Welfare Movement) was founded in 1975 and operates in rural and urban areas of Indonesia, focusing on issues of women's health, education, and training. The increasing engagement of women in political life in Indonesia reached a zenith with the election of Megawati Sukarnoputri to the presidency of Indonesia (2001–2004) after leading the Indonesian Democratic Party of Struggle.

Women's participation in Indonesia and Malaysia and, specifically, in NGOs gained momentum in 1998 following two separate events, namely protests against Suharto's regime in Indonesia and the arrest in Malaysia of the deputy prime minister, Anwar Ibrahim. Protesters crossing ethnic and religious boundaries joined forces to denounce corruption and state abuse in both countries. A number of associations encompassing increased participation by women originated in the student movements of the 1970s. One of the main channels for women's participation in political movements in Malaysia was ABIM (Malaysian Muslim Youth Organization), founded in 1971, mainly by students from the University of Malaya. One of its main aims was to address the ethnic issues in Malaysia by taking an Islamic approach to the construction of a multiethnic nation and an Islamically-oriented social order based on equality. In 1988, the Malaysian NGO Sisters in Islam (SIS) was founded by a group of women lawyers, academics, and activists. Its mission is "to promote the principles of gender equality, justice, freedom, and dignity in Islam and empower women to be advocates for change" (Sisters in Islam, "Mission Statement").

Women's activism is part of a wider program of democratization involving intellectuals, other faith communities, and groups working on citizenship rights. SIS organizes training programs, workshops, and public lectures, participates in policy-making by engaging the government through the issuing of memoranda (for example, on extending the Domestic Violence Act to Muslims and reforming Islamic family law and laws on polygamy) and addressing wider issues of democracy and civil liberties. A Malaysian woman who has reached the pinnacle of political leadership is Wan Azizah Wan Ismail, president of the main opposition party in Malaysia, Parti Keadilan Rakyat (People's Justice Party). She is the spouse of the former deputy prime minister, Anwar Ibrahim. Belonging to the same political organization, Fuziah Sallehis is also among the founders of the NGO Wanita Pertubuhan Jamaah Islah Malaysia (Wanita JIM) and a major figure within it. Among the prominent founding members of SIS are Zainah Anwar (SIS's executive director), Norani Othman, and Amina Wadud. Amina Wadud made global headlines when, on March 18, 2005, she was the first woman to lead the Friday prayers and sermon in New York before a mixed congregation. The event sparked a heated debate in Southeast Asia and the issuing of several legal pronouncements. Wanita JIM condemned the action, which demonstrates that, whereas women's political leadership and participation are increasingly accepted, religious leadership triggers a variety of opinions, including from women's organizations.

Gender Relations, Issues, and Challenges. Adherence to religious practice, modesty, piety, and engagement with conservative Islam constitute the foundation for the construction of new gendered selves, and, at the same time, challenge Muslim women on issues of gender relations. Gender equality and justice are high on the agenda of the Indonesian women's-rights organization Rahima (informally linked to NU), as well as the Malaysian Sisters in Islam (SIS). The two groups also campaign to break the monopoly on interpretation of Islamic tenets in the contemporary context. The concept of gender justice is favored over the more westernized concept of gender equality, but needs to accommodate existing situated ethics in order to attain social legitimacy. Women are still discriminated against in terms of access to specific careers, representation, and normatively prescribed roles. There remains a strong perception of women as mainly relegated to the domestic sphere, as carers and nurturers.

In Malaysia, the representation of the Malay mother during colonial times as "highly altruistic, long-suffering, and self-denying" was pervasive (Stivens, 2010, "Religion, Nation, and Mother-love," p. 394). An emblematic figure of a mother fighting against colonial administrative power and legislation is Aminah (Amina) Binte Mohamed, a Malaysian woman living in Java and later in Terengganu, who fought over the custody of the Dutch girl she had raised, Maria Hertogh, who was finally repatriated to the Netherlands. Maria's death in 2009 made headlines in both Malaysian and Singaporean newspapers. The story is relevant because it stages the opposition between Dutch and Islamic law, cast as paternal versus maternal rights. Focus on motherhood has not disappeared from contemporary political discourse and is still considered the basis for fostering a better Indonesia by women belonging to the PKS party. Rhetoric linked to family life is expressed in the concepts of *keluarga sakinah* ("happy family" or "harmonious family"), proposed in 1985 by the Indonesian group Aisiyah, and *keluarga maslahah* ("family welfare"), introduced by NU in 1969. Both attempt to reconcile the goal of creating a family founded on Islamic values with the government's family-planning programs.

Gender equality was addressed by women's movements in the post-independence era, attempting to attain an egalitarianism that, despite being declared in the Republic of Indonesia's law, was rarely translated into everyday practice and conditions. Although Indonesian women's movements were apparently unable to challenge patriarchal social and cultural values and norms, more recently the field of gender relations has been the battleground for activists against those who pursue an Islamization of the country.

Polygamy. Beginning in the first half of the twentieth century, family legislation in Indonesia and Malaysia was significantly modified, contributing to a decline in the previously high divorce rates. One of the major targets of the women's organizations in Indonesia was to emancipate women from some practices related to local customs (*adat*), such as "abuse of polygamy, forced marriage, child marriage, and one-sided right of repudiation" (Anwar, 2004, p. 97). On some issues, different Indonesian women's organizations held opposing views that were difficult to reconcile, especially on marriage law. Two organizations, Aisyiyah and Persatuan Islam, even contended that polygamy prevented prostitution. Following pressure from women's organizations, in 1950 the Indonesian government appointed a committee to study a reform of the marriage law; it was passed in 1974 and advocated monogamous marriage. Regulation was unified and jurisdiction over marriage and divorce passed to state courts. However, the envisioned roles for women still relegated them to the domestic sphere. Also, in Malaysia during the 1970s, several women's movements raised their voices against "easy divorce" initiated by the man (*talak* divorce) and general marital instability, with divorce rates reaching a staggering 71 percent in Kelantan state between 1948 and 1957. The new Islamic Family Law Act was passed in 1984, imposing some conditions on men who wanted to marry more than one woman, although states retained margins of discretion to amend specific aspects of the enactment, thus giving leeway to men, who could search for favorable pronouncements. Another viable subterfuge is for the man to enter polygamous marriage across national borders. Some Malaysian states accept marriage certificates issued by authorities in southern Thailand's four Muslim provinces, whereas others refuse any document issued by the Islamic Council of Thailand. In Malaysian law, the first wife needs to consent to a second marriage, a statement demonstrating sufficient financial means must be produced, and a Sharya court must grant permission. When polygamous marriages are contracted without registration in the court, the rights of the second wife are particularly weak should the man die or divorce. Women's groups exerted pressure when, in 2003, Perlis state reduced the conditions for the court to grant permission to polygamous marriages by making the written consent of the first wife unnecessary. Sisters in Islam proposed a special *taklik* recitation (accepted by the Ḥanbalī *madhhab*) by the husband that would give the existing wife space to apply for divorce for breaking those conditions, but the proposal was not accepted. This NGO is at the forefront of targeting gender bias and discrimination against women within a perspective of constructing a new *ummah* and challenging radical *ʿulamāʾ*.

Divorce. The 1984 Malaysia law also limited the man's right to pronounce the *talak*, as he is required to submit a formal request stating specific reasons for wanting a divorce and only after a reconciliatory process has been pursued without success. A *talak* without court approval is void and the man can be fined for acting outside legal boundaries. A woman can initiate a divorce procedure by accusing her husband of violating the marriage conditions (*taklik*), by asking to nullify the marriage (*faskh*), or by asking for a *khuluk* divorce when her husband refuses to pronounce a *talak*. The minimum age for marriage was set at sixteen for women and eighteen for men. All laws concerning family matters (except inheritance) were collected in one volume.

Inheritance. In matters of inheritance Malaysia witnesses an antagonism between different systems. The local customary law (*adat perpatih*) in Negeri Sembilan and a district of Malacca privileges matrilineal transmission of property and the collective ancestral ownership of land (*harta pusaka*); both of these principles clash with the complex Islamic law on inheritance privileging patrilineal descent (called *hukum faraid* in Malay) and now generally accepted. The other Malay states follow a bilateral descent system and a different customary law (*adat temenggong*) less at odds with the *hukum faraid* because it is inclined to privileging the patriliny. However, in Indonesia, the opposition *adat* (Islamic law) was formalized and reinforced by the Dutch colonial administration, whereas the relation between the two sets of legal rules was more fluid. When the Indonesian minister of religion Munawir Sjadzali (1983–1993) proposed that the Islamic law on inheritance needed to be modified and that sons and daughters should receive equal shares, his proposal was met with rejection by the Association of Muslim Intellectuals (ICMI).

Modern Courtship and Sexual Relations. Changes in gender relations, patterns of courtship, and premarital sexual relations are often attributed to the influence of Western models, which conflict with the widespread images of "Asian family" and "Asian values." In Malaysia in the 1990s, as the revivalist Islamic movement Al Arqam was banned from the country, a panic over young Muslim women's "loafing," hanging out in shopping centers, and engaging in dating was picked up by state agents and religious authorities. Reactions included the enforcement of dress codes in the northwestern Malaysian states of Terengganu and Kelantan, both of which are dominated by the PAS (Partai Islam se Malaysia). A comparable anxiety about the perceived spreading of a westernized youth culture is found in urban Indonesia, especially the capital Jakarta. Migration to Bangkok to pursue higher education and careers creates a new possibility for young Thai Muslims from the southern region to engage in romantic relations away from parental control and village lifestyles. Partaking in new models of gender relations, while at the same time maintaining religious identity, is a challenge for a growing number of Muslim women in the urban spheres of Southeast Asia. Although still stigmatized, occurrences of premarital sex are not accompanied by an appropriate knowledge of either contraception or STDs. General condemnation tends to face young women engaging in more liberated sexual behavior.

Dress Code and Veiling. Maintenance of Islamic identity has been upheld through the embodiment of specific interpretations of the Islamic values of modesty and femininity, expressed through dress codes. Far from being limited to individual representations of piety, changes in dress codes and veiling were associated with wider political and social transformations as a visible sign of the revivalist wave. Islamic dress codes were adopted by women in the workplace in Brunei on the wave of *dakwah* movements. In Malaysia, the emphasis and enforcement of specific dress codes for women in public places in Kelantan after the electoral victory of PAS in 1990 went hand in hand with the prohibition of women party members standing for political office. PAS receded on this point in 2004. Women's dress code is intended to protect women from sexual assault and at the same time to tame their "natural" sexual allure that leads men into temptation. Veiling is at times advocated by certain women as feminist and liberating. In the state of Selangor, indecent dressing is a criminal offense.

In countries with minority Muslim populations, veiling is linked to securing a sense of Islamic identity. In the Philippines and Singapore, very young schoolgirls are required to wear the *tudong* (headscarf) or mini-*telekung* (a longer veil covering the shoulders and bust); in southern Thailand, Muslim female students attending *madrasahs* wear veils of different lengths, some covering their whole upper body. In the late 1980s, a protest advocating the right for Thai Muslim female students attending the Yala Teacher Training College to wear the hijab triggered a nationwide movement. In 1997, a rule allowed Muslim students to wear the hijab in all schools, thus breaking the uniformity in attire required in educational establishments as well as government offices. The movement brought to the fore the pluralistic nature of Thai society against the government's ideal of homogenization of all peoples living in Thailand. Similar to Thailand, the spreading of veiling in Indonesia in the 1990s, culminating in permission being granted to wear the *jilbāb* in schools, can be considered as a form of opposition to the authoritarian government. During the last decade of his rule, Suharto encouraged organized Islam. In Singapore, the government and general public strongly oppose wearing of the *tudong* in schools, as it is seen as a threat to integration and harmonious multiculturalism.

[*See also* Family Law; Gender Equality; Hijab; Minorities, *subentry on* Muslim Minorities in Non-Muslim Societies; Political Activism, Women's, *subentry on* Contemporary Discourse; Sisters in Islam; *and* Women and Social Reform, *subentry on* Southeast Asia; *and* Women's Movements.]

BIBLIOGRAPHY

Amporn Marddent. *Sexual Culture among Young Migrant Muslims in Bangkok*. Chiang Mai, Thailand: Silkworm Books, 2007.

Anwar, Etin. "'Directed' Women's Movements in Indonesia: Social and Political Agency from Within." *Hawwa: Journal of Women of the Middle East and the Islamic World* 2, no. 1 (March 2004): 89–112.

Bennett, Linda Rae. "Modernity, Desire, and Courtship: The Evolution of Premarital Relationships in Mataram, Eastern Indonesia." In *Coming of Age in South and Southeast Asia: Youth, Courtship, and Sexuality*, edited by Lenore Manderson and Pranee Liamputtong, pp. 96–112. Richmond, U.K.: Curzon, 2002.

Brooks, Ann. "The Politics of Location in Southeast Asia: Intersecting Tensions around Gender, Ethnicity, Class, and Religion." *Asian Journal of Social Sciences* 31, no. 1 (March 2003): 86–106.

Fealy, Greg, and Virginia Hooker, eds. *Voices of Islam in Southeast Asia: A Contemporary Sourcebook*. Singapore: Institute of Southeast Asian Studies, 2006.

Hefner, Robert W. *Civil Islam: Muslims and Democratization in Indonesia*. Princeton, N.J.: Princeton University Press, 2000.

Iwu Dwisetyani Utomo. "Sexual Values and Early Experiences among Young People in Jakarta." In *Coming of Age in South and Southeast Asia: Youth, Courtship and Sexuality*, edited by Lenore Manderson and Pranee Liamputtong, pp. 207–227. Richmond, U.K.: Curzon, 2002.

Jones, Gavin W. *Marriage and Divorce in Islamic South-East Asia*. Oxford: Oxford University Press, 1997.

Ong, Aihwa. "Translating Gender Justice in Southeast Asia: Situated Ethics, NGOs, and Bio-Welfare." *Hawwa: Journal of Women of the Middle East and the Islamic World* 9, no. 1 (January 2011): 26–48.

Othman, Norani. "Muslim Women and the Challenge of Islamic Fundamentalism/Extremism: An Overview of Southeast Asian Muslim Women's Struggle for Human Rights and Gender Equality." *Women's Studies International Forum* 29, no. 4 (July 2006): 339–353.

Preeda Prapertchob. "Islam and Civil Society in Thailand: The Role of NGOs." In *Islam and Civil Society in Southeast Asia*, edited by Nakamura Mitsuo, Sharon Siddique, and Omar Farouk Bajunid, pp. 104–116. Singapore: Institute of Southeast Asian Studies, 2001.

Rinaldo, Rachel. "The Islamic Revival and Women's Political Subjectivity in Indonesia." *Women's Studies International Forum* 33, no. 4 (July–August 2010): 422–431.

Sharifah Zaleha Syed Hassan and Sven Cederroth. *Managing Marital Disputes in Malaysia: Islamic Mediators and Conflict Resolution in the Syariah Courts.* Richmond, U.K.: Curzon, 1997.

Sisters in Islam. "Mission Statement and Objectives." http:// www.sistersinislam.org.my.

Stivens, Maila. "The Hope of the Nation: Moral Panics and the Construction of Teenagerhood in Contemporary Malaysia." In *Coming of Age in South and Southeast Asia: Youth, Courtship, and Sexuality*, edited by Lenore Manderson and Pranee Liamputtong, pp. 188–206. Richmond, U.K.: Curzon, 2002.

Stivens, Maila. "Religion, Nation, and Mother-love: The Malay Peninsula Past and Present." *Women's Studies International Forum* 33, no. 4 (July–August 2010): 390–401.

Zaleha Kamaruddin and Raihanah Abdullah. "Protecting Muslim Women against Abuse of Polygamy in Malaysia: Legal Perspectives." *Hawwa: Journal of Women of the Middle East and the Islamic World* 6, no. 2 (2008): 176–201.

CLAUDIA MERLI

SOVEREIGNTY. As Islamic gender constructs continually evolve in the twenty-first century, the issue of sovereignty as it relates to women remains an essential subject within Islam and Islamic history.

Qurʾānic discourse states that God is the omnipotent and definitive owner of both heaven and earth. There is no other God, nor any equal, and, therefore, God is the ruler or "sovereign" of heaven and earth. Hence, sovereign can be defined as ruler. The theological belief in God as the sovereign of heaven and earth, however, has led to the practical question of who serves as God's physical representative in a sovereignesque capacity on earth, keeping in mind that a human sovereign is subordinate to God as divine sovereign. This is an issue that has been debated throughout Islamic history. It has manifested itself in a very real sense as problematic to the *ummah* via various exegetical interpretations of who constitutes a sovereign and what characteristics a person should display to qualify as a sovereign.

This brings into focus the issue of humans as vicegerents of God on earth. Khaled Abou El Fadl notes that, in Qurʾānic discourse, while God is the ultimate sovereign, God has also allowed for the delegation of God's sovereignty on earth in the form of human agency. Citing Qurʾān 2:30, he argues that the primary divine charge is to implement the principles of mercy and justice. God's sovereignty lies in God's authority to delegate the responsibility of achieving justice on earth by fulfilling these virtues as an approximation of divinity, provided that humans do not actually aspire to become divine themselves (Abou El Fadl, 2004). The terms "sovereign," "ruler," and "head vice-gerent" are, therefore, synonymous.

Within this construct of human agency and humans as vicegerents of God, representation of God on earth by humans is Qurʾānically mandated. The Qurʾān, though, as Ali Mohammad

Syed notes, provides no answer as to the gender of who should constitute God's ultimate human earthly representative, or sovereign (Syed, 2004). This silence leaves open the possibility of whether women might act as sovereigns, that is, as heads of state or government. Syed argues that there are multiple Qur'ānic verses in which men and women are equal in the eyes of God. Toshihiku Izutsu furthers Syed's thought, arguing that the characteristics which constitute a true or ideal Muslim believer, regardless of gender, are those characteristics that constitute a true or ideal Muslim sovereign. Such characteristics include continual devotional practices, avoidance of Jahili acts that God has forbidden, and respect for the importance of the Qur'ān as God's revealed word (Izutsu, 2002).

Quintan Wiktorowicz has proposed a political opportunity construct, observing that women have filled this space throughout Islamic history (Wiktorowicz, 2004). One must be extremely careful, however, to determine what title in a certain country's system of governance and the time period of that governance denotes a head of state or government, and, therefore, a sovereign. Historically, women served as sovereigns in a variety of locations and times, such as, for example, Sitt al-Mulk in Fāṭimid Egypt, Shajar al-Durr in Ayyubid Egypt, Radiyya bint Iltutmish in the Mughal Empire, and several women in the Sulayhid dynasty in Yemen. In a modern context, prominent examples include Benazir Bhutto, who served as the prime minister of Pakistan (head of state or government in the Pakistani system) twice, from 1988 to 1990 and 1993 to 1996, and Sheikha Hasina Wazed and Khaleda Zia, who have both served as the prime minister of Bangladesh.

Post-Arab Spring, this debate has regained momentum throughout the Middle East and North Africa. As new constitutions are drawn up in Tunisia and Egypt, among other nations, women's rights in general and women holding positions of political power have become important issues. In Tunisia, forty-nine women were elected to the 2011 Constituent Assembly. In Egypt, women now represent 2 percent of the Parliament. In Iran, though forty-two women registered as 2009 presidential candidates, all were disqualified by the Guardian Council but women represent 3 percent of the 2012 Iranian Parliament or Majlis. A woman has yet to be elected as head of state, and therefore sovereign, of any of these countries.

The idea of women as sovereigns remains fluid and ultimately depends on the views of the various political parties and individuals in governmental power. Debates about a woman's capacity to serve as a sovereign nevertheless are expected to gain momentum as women's role in the economy and achievements as educated professionals continue to grow.

BIBLIOGRAPHY

Abou El Fadl, Khaled. *Islam and the Challenge of Democracy*. Princeton, N.J.: Princeton University Press, 2004.

Esfandiari, Haleh. "The Women's Movement." In *Iran Primer*. United States Institute of Peace. http://www.iranprimer.usip.org/resource/womens-movement.

Izutsu, Toshihiko. *Ethico-Religious Concepts in the Quran*. Montreal: McGill-Queens University Press, 2002.

Pickard, Duncan. "How Well Did Women Really Fare in Tunisia's Elections?" Belfer Center for Science and International Affairs, Harvard Kennedy School. December 6, 2011. http://www.powerandpolicy.com/2011/12/06/how-well-did-women-really-fare-in-tunisia's-electi.

Sweis, Rana. "Women's Rights at a Standstill in Jordan." *New York Times*, November 7, 2012. http://www.nytimes.com/2012/11/08/world/middleeast/womens-rights-at-a-standstill-in-jordan.html?pagewanted=all.

Syed, Ali Mohammad. *The Position of Women in Islam: A Progressive View*. Albany: State University of New York Press, 2004.

United Kingdom House of Commons. Note SN/SG 1250.

United Nations Development Programme. "Women Play Major Role in Tunisia's Historic Election." http://www.undp.org/content/undp/en/home/ourwork/democraticgovernance.

Wiktorowicz, Quintan. *Islamic Activism: A Social Movement Theory Approach*. Bloomington: Indiana University Press, 2004.

CHRIS LAROSSA

STEREOTYPES IN MASS MEDIA. Most Americans come to know the world's approximately 280 million Arabs and more than one billion Muslims through the mainstream mass media—television programs and motion pictures in particular—which provide most of the images U.S. citizens have of the peoples of the world. An examination of more than a thousand pre-9/11 feature films and hundreds of television programs, comic books and strips, music recordings, video games, newspapers and magazines (including their advertisements, crossword puzzles, and editorial cartoons), as well as textbooks, novels and reference works, computer and video games, and scores of graphic images from other communication channels reveals stereotypical portraits of Arab Muslims long before nineteen Arab terrorists launched the 9/11 attacks, resulting in the deaths of nearly three thousand Americans.

Although more than 20 million Arab Christians reside in the Middle East—ranging from Eastern Orthodox to Roman Catholic to Protestant—they are invisible in the media. Thus, especially since the 9/11 tragedy and the March 2003 invasion of Iraq, the sweeping Arab-as-Muslim-terrorist stereotype has positioned itself firmly in peoples' minds around the world.

Seemingly mindlessly adopted and casually adapted, images present the Muslim as the bogeyman, the quintessential Other—how else to explain the message from a student at the University of Wisconsin to an Iranian student: "Death to all Arabs, die, Islamic scumbags" ("College Debate: Free Speech versus Freedom from Bigotry," p. 2)? Image makers often lump together Arab, Iranian, Turkish, or Pakistani Muslims as threateningly dark-complexioned, bearded men with thick accents.

Selective media framing makes it feasible to belittle Islam. Movies often reinforce audiences' misperceptions by portraying Muslim men as deceiving, suppressing, and abusing white Western females. In the film *Not Without My Daughter* (1991), for example, the Iranian protagonist treats his American wife like chattel; he slaps her face and keeps her prisoner in their home, boasting "I'm a Muslim." The film portrays Muslims as hypocrites: breaking his oath sworn on the Qurʾān, the husband says, "Islam is the greatest gift I can give my daughter." As his family leaves the mosque, we see posters of Ayatollah Ruhollah Khomeini, suggesting that all Muslims and a single controversial ayatollah are one and the same. In the book and documentary *Reel Bad Arabs: How Hollywood Vilifies a People* (2009), more than a thousand pre-9/11 motion pictures that include Arab characters or references, from *Fatima* (1896) to *The Mummy Returns* (2001) are examined, leading to the finding that Hollywood's Arabs were almost always portrayed as villains, and violent and uncivilized beings. The vast majority of reel villains were Palestinians, Egyptians, shaykhs, and Arab women. Also, about three hundred films that had nothing whatsoever to do with Arabs displayed gratuitous slurs and scenes. Only around a dozen films offered positive depictions, and fifty-four were neutral. All the others were negative, projecting Arabs and Muslims as subhumans, and as Public Enemy Number One. For example, in cinematic terms, America first went to war in Iraq in 1943; the action movie *Adventure in Iraq* features the U.S. Air Force staging a "shock and awe" bombing of Iraq's pro-Nazi "devil worshipers."

Fast-forward forty-nine years: in 1992, Disney's release of the children's film *Aladdin* began with an opening song that contained the lyric, "Where they cut off your ear / If they don't like your face," and referred to the setting of the film as "barbaric."

Regrettably, two years after Disney's *Aladdin* was released, the straight-to-video sequel, *The Return of Jafar* (1994), popped up on television screens, complete with offensive lyrics, such as "Pack your shield, pack your sword," and "You won't ever get bored,/Though beaten and gored."

A 1993 *New York Times* editorial ("It's Racist") complained that merely changing one line from the opening lyric was not enough: "To characterize an entire region with this sort of tongue-in-cheek bigotry, especially in a movie aimed at children, borders on the barbaric." On a positive note, these lines were deleted in the video/DVD version. Also, Disney executives said that the controversy over *Aladdin* prompted them to avoid the same kind of stereotyping with *Pocahontas* (1995). That film's director, Mike Gabriel, affirms that from the very beginning the image of Native Americans "was a clear concern since we had been blasted by Arab [American] groups for defamatory lyrics in 1992's *Aladdin*" (Rice).

Portrayals in the News. Rigid and repetitive news images of Osama Bin Laden and Saddam Hussein have been blended with scores of fictional motion pictures and television programs featuring Muslim terrorists shouting "Allah be praised," while murdering innocents. Deceptive portraits are common, and include skewed so-called documentaries funded and released by the Clarion Fund that encourage viewers to fear and hate all things Arab and Islam such as *Obsession: Radical Islam's War on the West* (2005) and *The Third Jihad* (2008). Books that encourage this fear have titles including *The Sword of Islam* (2002), *The Islamic Bomb* (1981), *The Assassins: Holy Killers of Islam* (1987), *Muslim Mafia: Inside the Secret Underworld that's Conspiring to Islamize America* (2009), *The Dagger of Islam* (1979), *The Fire of Islam, Holy Wars, Inflamed Islam, and Militant Islam*, while magazine essays are titled "The Roots of Muslim Rage" (*Atlantic Monthly*, 1990) and "The Muslims Are Coming, The Muslims Are Coming!" (*National Review*, 1990).

The Third Jihad and *Obsession* merit special attention because of their pervasiveness, anti-Islam messages, and political implications. Throughout *Obsession* viewers see scores of fanatical Muslims threatening to bring down Western civilization. Shockingly, the Clarion Fund managed to convince dozens of major newspapers throughout the country to distribute 28 million copies of the *Obsession* DVDs, free of charge. The DVDs were inserted in over 70 newspapers, predominantly in swing states before the 2008 presidential election; only five newspapers refused to distribute the DVD. The Clarion Fund is the same group that is behind the 72-minute propaganda film *The Third Jihad: Radical Islam's Vision for America* (2008), which was screened before 1,500 New York City police officers as a part of a terrorist training initiative. *Jihad's* narrator tells viewers that America's Muslims are a threat, and that most mainstream Muslim groups are not moderate. One of their primary tactics is deception. The film hammers home the myth that Muslims are deceptive, and implies that Islam and terrorism are synonymous. For example, viewers witness a black and white flag, denoted as the flag of Islam, flying over the White House. Though New York's Mayor Bloomberg has strongly condemned this film, he said that he doubted *Jihad* negatively affected any of the city's police officials.

Demonized and delegitimized, even America's Arab Muslims lack a human face. It began with TV movies such as *Under Siege* (1986) and *The President's Man: A Line in the Sand* (2002). Here, Arabs and Muslims from Dearborn, Michigan, and Dallas, Texas, are presented as anti-American "religious fanatics" willingly sacrificing their lives in "holy wars" for "the cause." In *President's Man*, they try to explode a nuclear bomb in Texas. In *Siege*, they topple the dome of the U.S. Capitol and kill scores of American civilians. The FBI director explains to his associate that "those people," meaing Arab and Iranian Muslims, are different than Americans. The writers and producers, unable to distinguish Arabs from Iranians, portray them as one ethnic group, even though each group has its own origin, ethnicity, language, and cultural heritage. Consequently, "Arab" is used throughout the film interchangeably with "Iranian." Referring to atrocities being committed by Muslims in the United States, the FBI director tells his associate: "It's a whole different ball game. I mean the East and the Middle East. They have their own notion of what's right and what's wrong, what's worth living for and dying for. But we insist on dealing with them as if they're the same as us. We'd better wake up!"

Beginning with the 2002–2003 television season, network producers introduced a threatening stereotype: the Arab-American and Muslim American neighbor as terrorist. TV shows regularly implied that America's own Arabs and Muslims (not to mention immigrants) were intent on waging a holy war against the U.S. As documented in the book, *GUILTY: Hollywood's Verdict on Arabs After 9/11*, since 2002, more than fifty programs have displayed stock villains and have repeated these negative images over and over. These televised images have suggested that America's Muslims are running shadowy terrorist sleeper cells inside mosques and shacks, from Los Angeles to Washington, D.C. These damaging programs helped generate a serious backlash against Arab Americans and Muslim Americans, punishing communities from Los Angeles to New York. Episodes from TV shows such as *The Practice, Judging Amy, The District, Sleeper Cell, The Agency, Treat Matrix, Sue Thomas F B Eye, The Unit,* and *Law and Order* projected Arab Americans and America's Muslims as backward religious radicals who merit profiling, imprisonment, torture, and death.

Continuously repeated, stereotypical images and statements transmitted by media have a telling effect on innocent people. In 1990, Iraq invaded Kuwait, leading to the Gulf War. During this time, two prominent Americans, Senator J. J. Exon of Nebraska and former U.S. Ambassador to Iraq Edward Peck, offered comparable commentary about Arabs and Muslims. In remarks for which he later apologized (according to Casey Kasem), Exon said, "In the Arab world, life is not as important as in the non-Arab world" (*Omaha World Herald*, August 30, 1990, p. 3). Edward Peck stated on television, "We in the West tend to think of our New Testament heritage, where you turn the other cheek and you let bygones be bygones and forgive and forget. [But] the people of the Middle East are the people of the Old Testament. With Muslims there's much more of an eye for an eye and a tooth for a tooth. You don't forget and you don't forgive; you carry on the vendetta and the struggle long after people in the West would be prepared to say it's all right, it's over, let's not worry about it any longer" (NBC Nightly News, January 16, 1991).

Otherness. To enhance the myth of the Muslim's otherness, image makers clothe him in foreign garb, such as strange "bedsheets." Made up with dark features, he is unattractive and in need of a shave. Speaking with a "foreign" accent, he poses an economic threat by using oil or terrorism as a weapon against "developed" societies. Most important, he is painted as worshiping a different deity and possessing an unprovoked hatred of "civilized" peoples, notably American Christians and Jews. "These bastards [Muslim hijackers] shot those people in cold blood. They think it's open season on Americans," explains a passenger in the television movie, *Hostage Flight*

(1985). Journalist Edward R. Murrow said that what we do not see is as important, if not more important, than what we do see: seldom do audiences see or read about a devout Muslim caring for his wife or children, writing poetry, or tending to the sick.

Children's cartoons, such as *Inspector Gadget* and *Heathcliff*, have shown Muslims not glorifying God, but idolizing Westerners, suggesting they are gullible and foolish. In an episode of *Heathcliff*, Egyptians, perceiving Heathcliff to be their ancient ruler, bow before the cat. When, in an *Inspector Gadget* episode, Gadget discovers an ancient relic, Arab hordes worship him. Falling to their knees, they mumble "the chosen one, the chosen one."

Consider how the media paint two holy cities, Mecca and Jerusalem. In 1991, on CBS's top-rated *60 Minutes* program, Teddy Kollek, the mayor of Jerusalem, neglected to mention Jerusalem's Muslim population when he said that Jerusalem is a city inhabited by "Christians, Jews, and Arabs." The city of Mecca is the birthplace of Muḥammad and the site of the Grand Mosque, the most sacred place in the Islamic world. Yet, media merchants transform Mecca into a corrupt town, where offensive antics reign. In 1966, producers of the successful television series *I Dream of Jeannie* (episode no. 16) represented Mecca not as a holy city with devout worshipers, but as a topsy-turvy bazaar filled with thieves robbing Western tourists. The plot focused on Jeannie, a two-thousand-year-old genie, who will soon die unless she visits Mecca's "thieves' market." In the episode "First National Bank of Mecca," Jeannie's friend performs ridiculous rituals. To save her life, he must "raise his right arm, face the minaret of the rising sun, and repeat the sacred words: 'bottle to genie, genie to master, master to Mecca. Ronda!' "

The dialogue and imagery in *I Dream of Jeannie* is designed to amuse, but instead it narrows our vision and blurs reality. In 1987, *Ishtar*, a $50-million comedy film starring Warren Beatty and Dustin Hoffman continued this trend. Riddled with anti-Arab sentiments, Arab culture is labeled "devious," and Hoffman is told, "Go act like an Arab." *Ishtar* also lampoons Mecca with "I Look to Mecca," a song concerning a romantic rendezvous under a tree. Islam's holiest city and the pilgrimage to Mecca, a sacred journey that Muslims look forward to making all their lives, are belittled with sexual innuendo. There is a dangerous and cumulative effect when image makers continually transmit repetitive stereotypical pictures of Muslims. Such imagery does not exist in a vacuum: teaching viewers and readers whom to fear and whom to hate, the Muslim stereotype affects perceptions and consequently U.S. public opinion and policy decisions.

Changing Attitudes. Some public figures are recognizing the differences between image and reality. On 8 March 8 1991, following the Gulf War, General Norman Schwarzkopf made these remarks to departing American troops in Dhahran, Saudi Arabia: "You are going to take back home the fact that 'Islam' is not a word to be feared, a religion to be feared. It's a religion to be respected, just as we respect all other religions. That's the American way." Although the general's comments appeared in the *Washington Post,* his statements about Islam were not widely circulated.

Even image makers are gradually addressing negative portraits of Muslims. Producers of documentaries and feature films, print journalists, and others are presenting more accurate and humane portraits. Anisa Mehdi's telling 2008 National Geographic documentary, *Inside Mecca*, about the annual pilgrimage to Mecca, is already considered to be a classic film on the Hajj. *Islam: A Civilization and Its Art* (1991) is an informative ninety-minute documentary focusing on Islamic civilization, culture, and art. *Legacy* (1992), a PBS television documentary series, points out that Islam is "the true basis" of our culture. Host Michael Wood shows that "the West's rediscovery of its ancient science and knowledge of the Italian Renaissance was indebted to the Muslims." Revealing scenes of mosques, mosaics, calligraphy, and devout Muslims at prayer underscore his commentary: "When Europe was still in the Dark Ages, the Fertile Crescent entered another glorious phase of its culture. Here, in the universities and libraries of Baghdad, Babylonian astronomy, Hindu mathematics, and Chinese science and technology were passed on by Arabs. It was one of the great multicultural epochs of all time. The triumph of the modern West was made possible by a flood of ancient learning and science from Islam."

Witness Hollywood's improved images of Arabs and Muslims in documentaries such as *Fordson: Faith, Fasting, and Football* (2011), about how high school students cope with prejudice and fasting while playing football. Equally impressive are feature films like *The Visitor* (2007), a beautifully told story about how the "war on terror" impacts and injures immigrants, *Rendition* (2009), about an Egyptian-American engineer who is wrongfully kidnapped and brutally tortured, and Roberto Benigni's *Tiger and the Snow* (2005). In this drama, set in Iraq during the 2003 US-led invasion, Benigni presents the Iraqi people as just that—people. And, two 2006 feature films, *Paradise Now* and *Babel*, project humane, three-dimensional images of Palestinians and Moroccans. In *Kingdom of Heaven* (2005), Islam is presented as a devout, compassionate faith, and *Robin Hood: Prince of Thieves* (1991), introduces Azeem, a Moorish Muslim who is devout, intelligent, innovative, and Robin's equal, both as a combatant and as a humanist. With Robin in the English countryside, Azeem takes his prayer rug, faces Mecca, and prays. He refuses to drink alcohol—"I must decline, Allah forbids it"—and he is tolerant of other faiths—"it is vanity to force other men to our religion." Also, Azeem embraces other races and colors: "Allah loves wondrous variety." Equipped with scimitar, Arab headdress, and robe, he manages not only to deliver a breech baby, but also to save Robin's life and the day by introducing the telescope and gunpowder to the British Isles. Robin acknowledges the Moor's humanity, saying, "You truly are a great one."

In *Chicago* magazine (April 1991, p. 26), journalist Gretchen Reynolds describes a service at a mosque, calling it "a revelation. Canonical and dignified, moving even if you don't know the language, it evokes deep visceral emotion in Muslims attending. Some of the women start to cry. The people attending stand and kneel, call back to the khatib leading them. Anyone looking to have western preconceptions of Arab religion confirmed would be disappointed: There is no fanaticism here, only faith."

Mindful that American Muslims are either dehumanized or neglected in the media, the U.S. Senate for the first time invited an imam, W. Deen Mohammed, to offer the opening prayer on 6 February 1992. Fifteen years later, Minnesota Democrat Keith Elllison, the first Muslim elected to the U.S, Congress, took the oath of office on the Holy Qur'ān.

The people of the "book"—Jews, Christians, and Muslims—are all children of Abraham. All three religions emphasize an ethic of humane behavior and belief in one God who reveals his will through the sacred scriptures. Central to all three faiths is peace, which is reflected in the similarities of their greetings: "Shalom aliechem" in Hebrew, "pax vobiscum" in Latin, and "salaam alaikum" in Arabic—all three can be roughly translated as "Peace be with you." Observed Mahatma Gandhi, "The Bible, Qur'ān, Torah and other holy books" remind us that "we are all children of one and the same creator. Every human... Muslim and non-Muslim, Christian and non-Christian, Jew and non-Jew, has exactly the same human worth."

As for the future, the ultimate, ideal result would be an image of the Arab and the Muslim as neither saint nor devil, but as a fellow human being, with all the potentials and frailties that condition implies.

BIBLIOGRAPHY

"College Debate: Free Speech versus Freedom from Bigotry." *Chicago Tribune*, March 8, 1991.

"It's Racist, but Hey, It's Disney." *New York Times*, July 14, 1993.

Lewis, Bernard. "The Roots of Muslim Rage," *Atlantic Monthly*, September 1990.

Pipes, Daniel. "The Muslims Are Coming, The Muslims Are Coming!" *National Review*, November 19, 1990.

Rice, Lynette. "Aladdin Sequel Draws Complaints," *Los Angeles Times*, May 19, 1994.

Shaheen, Jack. *GUILTY: Hollywood's Verdict on Arabs After 9/11*. Northampton, Mass.: Olive Branch Press, 2008.

Shaheen, Jack. *Reel Bad Arabs: How Hollywood Vilifies a People*. Rev. and updated ed. Northampton, Mass.: Olive Branch Press, 2009.

Jack G. Shaheen

Sub-Saharan Africa. Through earlier historical eras, as well as in contemporary times, the role of women in African societies has varied considerably because of regional political and cultural differences across the continent. Also, within specific modern countries, conditions in urban, compared with rural, areas are obviously distinct. Ecological conditions in Africa, as in every area of the world, are inextricably tied to economic questions, particularly the relative importance of agriculture, pastoralism, levels and nature of commercial activities, and urban and/or industrial development.

Where religious differences are apparent, in some cases resulting in communities of majority or minority Islamic populations, the status of Muslim women may also vary from region to region. In some cases, Islamic communities in Africa, and Muslim women within such communities, have been characteristically associated with certain patterns of economic activity. *Overall*, however, it is not possible to suggest that religious factors play a key role in the forms of economic activity in which African women may engage. Surrounding environment—rural or urban; desert, savannah, or forest; coastal or major river systems—tends to determine work patterns, no matter what ethnic or religious group is involved.

A number of different cultural patterns among African women do, however, stem from religious beliefs; some suggest an intertwining of religious and local ethnic traditions that have become almost inseparable. Strictly popular images of African women as seen from other places in the world over long stretches of time have tended to evolve from highly stereotyped and distorted conceptions of primitive simplicity or sensuality through more sophisticated characterizations that can be gleaned from a number of sources. Some perceptions of Muslim African women stem from visual impressions that are easily communicated to outsiders. Cultural differentiation among African women as a whole is often expressed by means of personal adornment, both in features of clothing and jewelry and, usually, among traditional ethnic or religious groups, display (or non-display) of hair, or intentional alteration of skin (tattooing, scarification) or other features of the body, such as lips and ears. In the case of Muslim women, such visual distinctions most often follow carefully defined rules, some of which are specifically mentioned in the Qur'ān, while others stem from the *ḥadīth* literature or local custom. A number of characteristic subjects (none strictly limited to African Islamic societies) appear repeatedly in the literature dealing with African countries that have majority-Islamic populations: Burkina Faso (estimated 58–60 percent), Gambia (est. 95 percent), Guinea (est. 84 percent), Niger (est. 98 percent), Senegal (est. 96 percent), and Sierra Leone (est. 70–72 percent); or countries with a significant minority-Islamic population: Benin (est. 25 percent); Guinea-Bissau (est. 42–50 percent), Ivory Coast (est. 36–40 percent), Nigeria (est. 48 percent), Tanzania (est. 30–35 percent), and Togo (est. 12–20 percent).

Polygyny, Fertility Rates, and the Controversial Issue of Female Genital Cutting. A very important issue affecting Muslim women in these countries (which, significantly, is not limited to Muslims, but can be found among Christians and several indigenous African religious groups) is the practice of polygyny. Probably the form of marriage with more than one wife most familiar to general observers is that sanctioned by Islam, which is recognized in the family law in many African countries. Islamic law stipulates that, if a man can assure appropriate and equal treatment for each spouse, he may marry up to four wives. In Islamic-majority but ethnically diverse regions (especially where Christianity has affected only portions of population), local communities may justify the practice of polygamy on sociocultural and economic grounds. Many societies (not only in Africa, and not only among Muslims) consider that having multiple wives assures recognition of a man's economic status and/or his position as a leader. Also, from the standpoint of shared physical labor so characteristic of rural African communities, multiple wives, particularly older wives, often consider "passing on" labor responsibilities to more recent or younger wives to be an advantage, as well as recognition of their familial hegemony.

An increasingly controversial and culturally sensitive issue affecting a considerable number of African women's physical as well as psychological health involves the practice of female genital cutting (FGC). In some African cultures (again, not necessarily Muslim communities), surgical removal of all or part of a woman's external genitalia has been practiced for centuries, often representing—like male circumcision—a religious rite. This is true among Muslim women from some countries, although it is not an obligatory Islamic practice per se. Opposition to FGC began to form in the second half of the twentieth century and has grown considerably. Opposition is based not only on medical and hygienic arguments, but also on principles that seek to defend individual human rights and dignity. A strong African international voice opposing FGC emerged under the aegis of the Inter-African Committee Against Harmful Traditional Practices (IAC), founded in the 1980s following a meeting of a number of African women's organizations in Dakar, Senegal. Broader international concern was voiced at the International Conference on Population and Development held in Cairo in 1994, and at the Fourth World Conference on Women in Beijing in 1995. Because such issues are extremely sensitive among different cultural and religious groupings, only very approximate statistical estimates exist suggesting the numbers of women affected by FGC in different regions of Africa. Notably low numbers of cases have been reported in some central African countries (Uganda, with a minority-Islamic population of about 12 percent, and the Democratic Republic of Congo, with even fewer Muslims), where about 5 percent among the total female population, regardless of religious affiliation, may be affected. Moreover, in some Islamic-majority countries with mixed ethnic and religious minority groups, even approximate statistics often show that non-Islamic subgroups are less likely to practice FGC. This is the case in Mali, where overall percentages are above 90 percent, but are very much lower among members of (for example) the Tamāshek non-Islamic minority communities.

Relative fertility rates and future population predictions in different areas of Africa have attracted the attention of demographers generally and—in areas where critical issues of family planning may be important for health or grassroots economic reasons—local social-service agencies. Although assumed distinctions between rural and town or city families may be gradually receding, African cultural traditions across the continent frequently consider large family size to be desirable. Statistics from international agencies, including the United Nations and the World Bank, list several African countries having fertility rates near the top of world averages. Niger occupies the number one position, averaging seven or more births per mother, and other African Islamic-majority countries (among these Mali, Burkina Faso, and Guinea-Bissau) generally appear in the next-to-highest category—between six and seven births per mother. It should be noted, however, that a number of countries that are not majority Islamic (e.g., Liberia, Democratic Republic of Congo, Burundi, Uganda, Sierra Leone, and Angola) are also in the second-highest category.

Several factors could affect long-term population growth rates. One is the difference between countries in public health measures and their effect on mortality rates. Other factors are linked to sociological patterns, such as the tendency of elite classes and even middle-class urban families to limit the number of births (in the latter case perhaps owing to limited economic opportunities and the high cost of educating children). Although such factors might be statistically visible at different socioeconomic levels in Islamic-majority countries, estimating the effect of socioeconomic differentiation on fecundity rates in Islamic-minority community zones would be considerably more problematic.

As in the case of family planning, the United Nations often acts as a monitoring agency concerned with a number of other issues relating to women's health in Africa, including the main Islamic-majority regions. With the emergence of the AIDS epidemic and the subsequent joint UN program on AIDS (founded in 1996, and since 2009 under executive director and UN under-secretary General Michel Sidibé of Mali), the challenge of establishing and supporting local African anti-AIDS organizations rapidly became the most widely publicized public health campaign in Africa. Working closer to the grassroots level are organizations like Ghana's Society for Women and AIDS in Africa, which hosted a multinational AIDS information and prevention conference in 2011 of different women's groups from (among many others) African countries with Islamic majority or minority populations. One of the most active spokespersons in the field of information on and prevention of AIDS, who speaks in the interest not only of the Islamic-minority community in his native South Africa but of the entire Islamic world, is the internationally recognized scholar Farid Esack, who co-edited with Sarah Chiddy the volume *Islam and AIDS: Between Scorn, Pity, and Justice* (2009). Esack has been closely involved with the work of the South African Muslim women's support group Positive Muslims, founded in 2000 and headed by Muslim South African women themselves. A principal goal of Positive Muslims is to help HIV-positive Muslim women overcome the moral stigma sometimes leveled against them by members of their own religious community.

Muslim Women in Positions of Leadership. Several international bodies have played indirect roles not only in monitoring the health status of African women but also in encouraging different forms of progress, particularly in the realm of women's access to basic and higher education and levels of political participation. With respect to the latter area, the Inter-Parliamentary Union, based in Geneva, helps gather statistics on African women's involvement in higher levels of executive, legislative, and judicial politics, as well as a variety of administrative functions. IPU's published reports reveal several general patterns since African countries with majority or minority Islamic populations gained independence in the second half of the twentieth century. In most, but certainly not all, regions there has been a substantial increase in the number of women elected to legislative assemblies or appointed to high executive positions. It remains difficult, however, to gauge the proportion of such gains accruing to Muslim women. Ellen Johnson Sirleaf, a Christian born in 1938, was the first woman to be elected to the presidency of an African country; she was elected in 2005 in Liberia, a predominantly Christian country with an Islamic minority of about 13 percent. In other African countries, a number of women, albeit most of them non-Muslims (Gambia being the exception), have served as prime ministers, speakers of national assemblies, or members of parliament in countries as far apart and different as Burundi, Mozambique, Zimbabwe, and the Republic of South Africa.

Closer examination shows, however, that the political experience of Muslim women in Africa has continued to rise over the last two decades. The African Inter-Parliamentary Union reported that the percentage of women serving in the legislature of the Central African Republic (with an Islamic minority community estimated to be between 9 and 15 percent) rose from three (3.53 percent) in 1995 to eleven (6.95 percent) in 2006. Comparable numbers were recorded for the Muslim-majority Republic of Mali, where (after electing its first woman to parliament in 1960), by 2004, 10.2 percent (fifteen legislators) were Muslim women and one-third of the cabinet posts were held by women ministers.

Examples of individual Muslim women in Africa who have achieved recognition as leaders in either the public or private sectors present a very diverse record. Historically distant landmarks known mainly to specialists (such as Amina Sarauniya, reputed to have ruled the Hausa city-state of Zazzau in the sixteenth century, or Setfon Njapdunkgkhe [d. 1913], who served in the late nineteenth century as regent and later "chief advisor" for her son, Ibrahim Njoya, who would rule as sultan of the Fumban region of modern Cameroon) take on a distinctly modern hue, beginning in the early postcolonial era and continuing into the contemporary period. Senegal's deputy president of the National Assembly between 1971 and 1984 (also serving between 1978 and 1981 as minister of social affairs, and from 1982 to 1983 as minister of state) was Caroline Faye Diop. At the same high level is Guinea's Haja Mahawa Bangoura Camara, who, in addition to serving as her country's minister of foreign affairs, was appointed in 1995 as ambassador to the United States and later served as Guinea's representative to the United Nations.

Other examples of Muslim women political leaders in Africa include: Aïssata Moumouni (vice premier of Niger from 1989 to 1999); Sy Kadiatou Sow (Malian minister of foreign affairs in the mid-1990s and governor of the district of Bamako from 1998 to 2000); Mame Madior Boye, Senegal's prime minister in 2001–2002 (later minister of defense); and Dr. Ngozi Okonjo-Iweala, who, after serving as vice president of the World Bank, became Nigeria's minister of finance (2003–2006) and minister of foreign affairs (2006).

Muslim Women's Associations. A growing number of women's associations, some political or professional, others more social and economic in orientation, are to be found in many different regions of Africa. Many are linked to international organizations, but a large number of very local groups have formed around community-specific issues. One of the most highly structured and active movements involves women jurists. The African Women Lawyers Association, for example, founded in Ghana in 1998, is a professional body that seeks to involve individual women jurists from different African countries, including those having an Islamic majority or important minority representation, in the pursuit of issues affecting both women and children and to bring such issues to the attention of government agencies in Africa, as well as international organizations from the United Nations downward. A nationally-based example of groups linking African women jurists especially devoted to issues relating to women and family law is the Association Camerounaise des Femmes Juristes, founded in 1989 in Cameroon, a country, like Ghana, with a substantial (18–20 percent) Islamic-minority population.

On a global level, there are a number of international associations dedicated to issues affecting African women. Many of these are tied to nongovernmental organizations with offices both in Africa and abroad. In most cases such groups do not make distinctions between confessional groupings. Locally founded women's associations, on the other hand, can be identified as representing the interests of women of particular religious groups. This is the case, for example, of Al Mu'minaat, based in Lagos, Nigeria, which devotes itself to "all-round development of women folks [and] claiming their rightful position in the community... thus building Muslim women to build the nation." Another Nigerian group in Abuja, An Nisâ, is made up mainly of businesswomen who make hospital visits and provide financial support to needy girl students. They also publish an Islamic magazine called *Sister to Sister*. Other associations, like the Federation of Muslim Women in Freetown, Sierra Leone, attempt to involve smaller local groups of Muslim women in a broad program emphasizing shared goals.

Actively feminist movements like Baobab, led by the Islamic scholar Dr. Ayesha Imam, an opponent of the implementation of Sharīʿah law in northern Nigeria, are generally less visible than more broadly based women's associations in most African countries. For example, participation in a leadership seminar organized by the (nearly century-old) International Federation of University Women in the mid-1990s led several Sierra Leone women to found the Sierra Leone Women's Forum to "promote... effective alliances among women by sharing information... on current and emerging issues of common concern." Such issues for Sierra Leone women—whatever their confessional background—eventually came to include legal and political reactions to abuses suffered by women during the country's extended experience of internal civil violence.

Muslim Women in the Public Workplace: Example of the Town Market. The growing presence of African women in increasingly diversified sectors of the workplace, including administration, as well as private economic activities, is largely a reflection of evolving opportunities for basic and advanced education. Traditionally, and still today, the most visible area of economic participation by marginally educated African women (beyond agriculture and pastoral tasks) has been in urban and village outdoor markets. Although this pattern is visible in all traditional African market settings, examples from Islamic-majority countries like Niger, Mali, or Senegal reflect typical experiences of Muslim women vendors. In markets in Dakar or Bamako or provincial towns in their hinterlands, Muslim women vendors offer not only traditional food commodities, but also household items and, particularly significant for Muslim buyers, many items of specific interest to Muslims.

Such activity may represent a key part of African women's accepted spheres of social contact with individuals of both sexes and—as in most traditional societies around the world—serves as a means for gathering and disseminating information of all sorts, ranging from daily gossip to politics. Not infrequently, African women in the marketplace are accompanied by their children, especially young babies, and may depend on youngsters to carry out diverse small services to further their business interests. Less established sellers typically engage in secondary or even tertiary markets, offering small miscellaneous items at streetside stalls or from makeshift displays on sidewalks or the bare ground. Women engaged in such trade are subject to very unpredictable conditions, not only in terms of extremely marginal chances for gaining a livelihood from their sales, but also because many such itinerant sales displays in urban areas are often subject to police controls and expulsion—events that can cause public furor if they reflect on religious perceptions of the Muslim woman's role in the public sphere.

Access to Public Education. Access by young African women to education, even at the primary level, is far from guaranteed, whether for Muslim women or members of other (majority or minority) communities. In some Muslim-majority areas of Africa the proportion of girls attending primary and secondary schools is well below the number of boys in school. Gambia's case, for example, reveals quite serious inequities in a country with a more than 95 percent majority-Muslim population. Although nearly 60 percent of boys attend primary school, the figure for girls is below 50 percent. At the secondary level, boys' attendance is slightly over 30 percent, while only about 18 percent of girls advance to the secondary level. On the other hand, if such statistics are truly reliable, some countries with Islamic-minority communities appear to have achieved parity. The Central African Republic, for example, with an Islamic-minority population between 9 and 15 percent, has about 88 percent attendance for both sexes at the primary level, and 45 percent for both boys and girls at the secondary level. Reasons for gender disparities and gaps between members of different religious communities may be connected to limitations in families' ability to pay for all their children's education, keeping girls at home to help in household tasks, or early-age marriage customs for girls in some cultures. In Muslim-majority countries like Mali, Senegal, or Nigeria, statistics gathered by UNICEF suggest that, although female participation in primary and secondary education has made considerable progress, some disparities are still visible. In Mali, estimates of net participation at the primary level between 2007 and 2010 suggest 70 percent among young boys against 62 percent among girls. Figures for secondary-school participation were much lower (38 percent for boys, 24 percent for girls). Senegal's record, although suggesting lower overall percentages at the primary level (without, however, distinguishing between rural and town or city environments), attest to near-parity between male and female pupils (close to 58 percent attendance for both boys and girls). A more detailed 2007 UNICEF country office study for Nigeria covering the decade 1991–2001 revealed a recurring gap separating male and female groups in school, but pointed to higher disparities in the northern majority-Islamic zones, where, for each girl in primary school, there were two, and sometimes three, boys enrolled.

Muslim Women in the Arts, Literature, and Journalism. In a totally different sphere, where statistics play a less obvious role but public perceptions are easier to trace, there has been a growing presence of African Muslim women recognized as writers, artists, and performers. Although examples of Muslim women writers and journalists can be found in many different African countries, contributions by the last decade of the twentieth century came largely from Senegal, Niger, and Nigeria in West Africa, and from

South Africa. The nature of publications by Muslim women authors runs the entire gamut from poetry and short stories to full-length novels. Often the subjects of fictional works are drawn from local folk traditions or reflect issues of social or cultural concern. The short novel *La grève des battus* (published in English in 1981 as *The Beggars' Strike*) by the Senegalese writer Aminata Sow Fall is an example of the latter genre. Fall also contributed to an edited monograph (with Rose Senghor) with a 1975 article titled "The Educational Role of African Women in Traditional Society." Another Senegalese writer, Annette D'Erneville M'baye, mainly known for her poetic writings, also tended in the 1960s and 1970s to concentrate on subjects relating to progressive measures affecting Senegalese women, mothers, and children. The writings of Mariama Bâ (also Senegalese), on the other hand, featured fiction set in traditional African town and village environments, notably in *Un chant écarlate* (*Scarlet Song*), published in the mid-1980s. While many (but not all) such Muslim authors produced works in Western languages established by their respective countries' colonial background and focused on literary or cultural genres that were not always tied to women's issues, the work of novelist Zaynab Alkali (b. 1950 in northern Nigeria, graduated from Bayero University in Kano in 1973) has garnered international attention for her realistic treatment of a number of feminist themes affecting African Muslim women. Her works published in the first decade of the new century included *The Descendants* (2005) and *The Initiates* (2007).

Increasing attention has been given in recent years to a variety of original creations by African women artists. Beyond the written word, on one hand (with what may often be restricted accessibility to more sophisticated works for many segments of the population), and in addition to demographically restricted access to the world of African women graphic artists, on the other, one finds a broad popular base of appreciation for African Muslim women performers, particularly in the domain of music and entertainment. African women's role as commercial entertainers is particularly notable in the domain of popular music. The number of local "stars" is very great, often crossing national borders within Africa. The Malian singer and actress Fatoumata Diwaraa, although clearly not unique, is a major example of an international success not only in Africa, but also in Europe. She has played key roles in French-language African films and plays in France and has expanded her popularity among French fans as well as Africans by adapting local Malian folk traditions to her own musical compositions.

In the totally different context prevailing in majority-Islamic regions like Hausaland in Nigeria, Muslim women poets and singers perform before mixed (but most frequently all-women) audiences. The subjects of their music and poetry often deal with social and cultural issues of interest to local women. Outstanding examples include the Hausa poet Hauwa Gwaram, the Hausa singers Hajiya Faji and Hauwa Mai Duala, and, in a different vein, Maizargadi, a very widely recognized (ceremonial) praise singer in the royal court of Kano.

Increasing Impact of Conservative Islamic Movements. Wherever the influence of what is commonly termed Salafist conservative Islam has been in Africa, one can expect increasing pressures for stricter observance of Sharīʿah rules affecting women. An example of conservative Islamic reactions affecting women's status has evolved over the years in the northern Muslim-majority provinces of the Federal Republic of Nigeria. In this case, long-standing pressures for political autonomy and (especially since the late 1990s) supremacy of Sharīʿah law in northern regions are from time to time reflected in highly publicized Sharīʿah rulings and/or general communal pressures involving Muslim women. The most common here, as in other Islamic communities around the world, has been the almost universal use of the hijab and even burqa attire. The practice of secluding women within their homes or other areas restricted to women only (termed *kulle* in Nigeria) is also reported to be on the rise.

Situations similar to those found in northern Nigeria may have long-term or evolutionary effects on the daily life of Muslim women—sometimes, but not always, overlapping with Salafist interpretations of the Sharīʿah. Another more recent and possibly more pressing example arose in northern Mali during 2012, when most of the country's vast northern region was occupied by Saharan forces under the influence of AQMI (al-Qaʿida in the Islamic Maghrib). In this case, several extremist actions involving physical punishment of individual women for purported contravention of Islamic law became the focus of international attention, specifically where charges of adultery were leveled and strict punishments applied. The longer-term significance of this sudden separatist movement and declaration of intent to apply even stricter Islamic sanctions against "errant" women remains to be seen, not only for Mali, but also for neighboring Muslim-majority states like Niger and Burkina Faso. Such issues raise serious questions for spokespersons representing the religious scholarly class of *ʿulamāʾ* in all areas of Africa.

In a totally different context, that of the Islamic-minority population of South Africa, there has been a somewhat controversial movement to facilitate integration—through a special marriage bill yet to be adopted—of certain procedural aspects of Sharīʿah law into the prevailing legal system, particularly where matters of marriage and divorce are concerned.

[*See also* Education and Women, *subentry on* Contemporary Discourse; Esack, Farid; Female Genital Cutting; International Laws and Treaties on Women's Status; Islamic Literature, *subentry on* Contemporary; Minorities; Nigeria; Political Activism, Women's, *subentry on* Contemporary Discourse; Polygyny; *and* South Africa.]

BIBLIOGRAPHY

Alidou, Ousseina. *Engaging Modernity: Muslim Women and the Politics of Agency in Postcolonial Niger.* Madison: University of Wisconsin Press, 2005.

Berrian, Brenda F. *Bibliography of African Women Writers and Journalists: Ancient Egypt–1984.* Washington, D.C.: Three Continents Press, 1985.

Edwin, Shirin. "We Belong Here, Too: Accommodating African Muslim Feminism in African Feminist Theory via Zaynab Alkali's *The Virtuous Woman* and *The Cobwebs and Other Stories.*" *Frontiers: A Journal of Women's Studies*, 2005.

James, Adeola, ed. *In Their Own Voices: African Women Writers Talk.* London: James Currey, 1990.

Mack, Beverly Blow. *Muslim Women Sing: Hausa Popular Song.* Bloomington: Indiana University Press, 2004.

Masquelier, Adeline. *Women and Islamic Revival in a West African Town.* Bloomington: Indiana University Press, 2009.

Sidikou, Aissata. *Recreating Words, Reshaping Worlds: The Verbal Art of Women from Niger, Mali, and Senegal.* Trenton, N.J.: Africa World Press, 2001.

Zakaria, Yakubu. "Entrepreneurs at Home: Secluded Muslim Women and Hidden Economic Activities in Northern Nigeria." *Nordic Journal of African Studies*, 2001.

BYRON CANNON

SUDAN. Islam was first introduced to Sudan in the mid-seventh century as Arab merchants, pilgrims, and armies traveled through the region; however, the number of local converts remained small.

Early Islam. For much of the Middle Ages, Christian Nubian kingdoms of northern Sudan maintained ties of trade and loose allegiance to Egypt's Faṭīmid and Mamlūk Empires. Islamization was slow and the widespread practice of Islam only began under the Funj sultanate (1504–1821), whose political stability encouraged Muslim scholars, notably of the Mālikī tradition, to permanently settle in Sudan. Under the sultanate, elite women established *khalwas*, local religious schools that taught the memorization of the Qurʾān to boys and girls. In 1821 armies of the Ottoman governor of Egypt, Muḥammad ʿAlī, conquered northern portions of the Sudan. Turco-Egyptian rule was harsh, but further centralized the administration and legal system of Sudan.

Revival under the Mahdī. In the last years of the nineteenth century, northern Sudan underwent a wave of Islamic reform and revival. In 1881 Muḥammad Aḥmad Ibn ʿAbd Allāh, a noted religious ascetic, declared himself the Mahdī, the rightly guided leader of Islam. ʿAbd Allāh's plan for religious renewal and a return to Islam's true origins within Sudan was comparable to that of other nineteenth-century Islamic reformers throughout Africa and the Middle East. His message of Islamic justice and the coming end-of-days was well timed during a period of weak government control and lost livelihoods due to the abolition of the slave trade. In January 1885 al-Mahdī's army defeated the last of the Turco-Egyptian troops, stationed in Khartoum under the command of British hero Major-General Charles Gordon, and effectively seized military and political control of much of northern Sudan. In the early twenty-first century, in light of his military victories and brief period of rule, the Sudanese remember al-Mahdī not just as a religious figure, but also as *Abu-al-istiqlāl* (the Father of independence).

Much of the earliest legislation of the Mahdīyah period (1881–1898) was aimed at regulating the behavior of women. In accordance with Mahdist interpretations of Islam, women were ordered to cover their heads and both men and women were instructed to avoid imported Western clothing styles. European observers recorded that unrelated men and women were not to meet in public and women were restricted from walking alone with their herds. These new social restrictions were critical as Mahdist troops and their accompanying families swelled the urban populations of Omdurman and Khartoum. Alarmed by the overwhelming number of Sudanese women in urban centers, al-Mahdī's successor, Khalīfah ʿAbdullāhi, ordered compulsory marriage for unmarried women and a lowering of bridewealth rates. Spaulding and Beswick (1995) note that serial polygamy became commonplace as elite officers quickly and inexpensively acquired new wives.

Education and Early Activism. In 1898, at the height of the European scramble for Africa, Great Britain and Egypt undertook a joint campaign to conquer and occupy Sudan. On 2 September 1898 Herbert Kitchener soundly defeated the Mahdist army at Omdurman and established the shared Anglo-Egyptian imperial administration of the Sudan. The new government immediately banned all Mahdist symbols and instead gave its support to traditional Islamic leaders who had opposed al-Mahdī. For the first three decades of imperial rule, the threat of a Mahdist resurgence, headed by al-Mahdī's posthumous son, Sayyid ʿAbd al-Raḥman al-Mahdī, was a constant fear for the British. Thus, they believed it prudent to leave matters of custom and personal status largely in the hands of local imams. As a result, northern Sudan did not experience British attempts at cultural civilizing campaigns that characterized other regions of the British Empire.

Formal education for Sudanese girls was one area in which British administrators did institute significant reform. In 1907 Sheikh Babikr Bedri, a Sudanese headmaster of a village boys' school, petitioned the government for permission to open a school for Sudanese girls. The first class was made up of just seventeen girls, nine of whom were from Bedri's own family. The school proved a success, and in 1911 the Anglo-Egyptian government officially took control of girls' education. Sudanese were divided over the appropriateness of girls' education. Many believed that Islam allowed for women to be educated in order to better instruct their children, but critics were concerned that a Sudanese woman who was too educated would not willingly carry out her domestic responsibilities or submit to the demands to her husband. Nevertheless, the popularity of girls' education grew. By the 1940s a Sudanese girl with some level of education was considered a better marriage prospect than her unschooled sisters.

In January 1952 a group of ten young, well-educated women met to discuss establishing a Sudanese Women's Union (Itiḥad al-nisā'ī al-sudānī, or SWU), a new kind of women's association that would actively address Sudanese women's social problems. Inspired by women's and nationalist movements in Egypt, Pakistan, and Iran and rising nationalism in Sudan, the Union advocated for increased social and political rights and heightened national consciousness. The earliest and biggest successes for the SWU were in the area of education. Union members ran popular and effective night schools for women of all ages. Long-serving president of the Union Fatima Ahmed Ibrahim founded a monthly women's magazine, *The Woman's Voice*, which offered news and advice and kept its readers informed about women's activism in Sudan and around the world. The Sudanese Women's Union would become Sudan's most popular and longest-lasting women's activist organization.

Though activists insisted that Islamic principles guided their plans for progress, they were divided over the question of Islam's permissiveness toward women's political participation. Two of the SWU's founding members believed that women's social progress did not need to extend to full political rights. They left the politically progressive Union and joined the newly established Women's Cultural Revival Society, led by women of Sayyid ʿAbd al-Raḥman al-Mahdī's family. The aims of the Revival Society were to improve the standard of women culturally, and only then politically, in accordance with Islam and its traditions.

Across political lines, women activists agreed on the need to speak out against the so-called harmful traditions of lip tattooing, facial scarring, and spirit possession that existed in Sudanese women's culture. The most persistent campaign was against female genital cutting (FGC), popularly known as "pharaonic circumcision," practiced on the large majority of young girls in northern Sudan. Historically, women in northern Sudan underwent the most extreme form of genital cutting, infibulation: the excision of all external genitalia (the clitoris, labia major, and labia minor) and then the stitching together of the vaginal skin, leaving only a small opening for menses and urine to pass. The operation carried a number of health risks. However, for the northern Sudanese, infibulation protected a girl's purity and fertility and marked her readiness for adulthood. In 1946 the British administration passed legislation outlawing FGC and criminalizing the midwives who continued to perform the procedure. Many Sudanese politicians and religious leaders supported the legislation and issued statements explaining that female genital cutting was not mandatory in Islam. However, the practice remains a defining characteristic of northern Sudanese womanhood and continues to the present in modified form.

Women in the New Nation. On 1 January 1956 the independent Republic of Sudan was declared. Bitter political rivalries and violence in the south of Sudan prompted Sudan's first military coup just two years later. In October 1964 a series of popular protests led by university students, the Muslim Brotherhood, women, and legal professionals overthrew the military regime and instituted a second civilian government.

Within this democratic period, Sudanese women significantly increased their political participation. After the October Revolution, literate women were granted the right to vote. In 1965 Fatima Ahmed Ibrahim became the first female member elected to Parliament. In 1970 Nagwa Kemal Farid became the first female justice appointed to Sudan's Sharīʿah courts and among the first female Sharīʿah jurists in the Middle East. More broadly, women's organizations progressed from addressing primarily educational and social concerns to directly petitioning the government for improved working conditions, equitable wages and pension rights, lengthier maternity leave, and increased financial support for divorced women with children.

Other women sought change through the Republican Brothers, an Islamic reform movement founded by Ustadh Maḥmūd Muḥammad Ṭāhā in the late 1940s. Ṭāhā had developed a radical new understanding of Qurʾān, which he termed the "second message of Islam." Ṭāhā believed that the verses revealed to the Prophet Muḥammad after his flight to Medina were critical teachings for establishing the structure of the first Muslim communities. In contrast, the earlier revelations that came to the Prophet Muḥammad in Mecca (those that guided his behavior and formed the *sunnah*) were universal and could be applied to life in the twentieth century. Crucial for Ṭāhā and his followers, the Qurʾānic teachings that describe women's subservient position to men may be found in the Medina verses. In 1967 female followers of Ustadh Ṭāhā established the Republican Sisters. The Sisters accompanied Ṭāhā on his speaking tours and sold social and religious pamphlets on the street. One of the most popular pamphlets, "Steps to Marriage in Islam," argued that true marriage in Islam was founded on monogamy, mutual consent of the bride and groom, and a dowry of no more than one Sudanese pound to emphasize the equality between men and women.

In 1969 a second military coup, supported by leftist parties and the Sudanese Women's Union, brought Colonel Jaʿfar Muḥammad Nimeiri to power. Nimeiri promoted a socialist platform and many hoped he would reform Sudan the way the Free Officers coup reorganized Egypt in 1952. However, after passing a number of laws favorable to working women, Nimeiri abruptly changed political tactics and turned from the support of the progressive left to the growing influence of the Muslim Brotherhood. The SWU was banned (though it continued to work underground) and all women's organizations brought under the control of the state.

Women who spoke publically and participated in politics risked public censure. Both the Sudanese Women's Union and the Republican Sisters required that their members be of good moral standing and modestly dressed. Despite these precautions, women from both groups reported being victims of verbal abuse and occasional physical violence. In the early 1980s Nimeiri imprisoned Fatima Ahmed Ibrahim; Communist Party member Niemat Malik; Republican Sister Asma Mahmoud Taha; and other women leaders for their opposition to the increasing Islamization of the country. Held for years without being charged, activists were placed in the same cells with prostitutes and poor women accused of illegally brewing beer. The women passed the time reading Islamic poetry, studying the Qurʾān, and teaching their cellmates to read.

Islamization of the State. In September 1983 President Nimeiri instituted Sharīʿah law as the governing principle of Sudan. These "September Laws" established an alms tax, interest-free banking, and Qurʾānic punishments of amputation and flogging for certain crimes. Many Sudanese who considered themselves faithful Muslims criticized Nimeiri's interpretation of Islam. Others argued that the imposition of Sharīʿah law effectively turned non-Muslims, notably the southern Sudanese, into second-class citizens. Many judges were deliberately slow to apply the new laws. In response, Nimeiri set up "quick decision" courts, headed by the Muslim Brothers, to administer his form of Islamic justice. In 1985 Ustadh Ṭāhā was arrested and hanged for apostasy. Months later popular demonstrations and strikes ousted Nimeiri from power.

But the National Islamic Front (NIF), an offshoot of the Muslim Brotherhood, continued to dominate Sudan's political systems. From 1985 to 1989 only two women served in the legislative People's Assembly, both of whom were members of the NIF. In 1989 the NIF orchestrated a coup that brought General ʿUmar al-Bashīr to power and dismissed thousands of unsympathetic government officials from their posts. In 1991 Bashīr's government introduced a sweeping set of legislation that established Sharīʿah law far beyond what had been proposed under Nimeiri.

The new Islamic state has paid particular attention to redefining women's rights and reforming women's behavior. Women are legal minorities who cannot travel, seek work, or visit relatives without the permission of their husband, father, or other male guardian. Women are prohibited from traveling alone at night or working in certain environments alongside men. Such restrictions have been particularly harmful for lower-class working women who make their living selling food and drink on the streets. Women convicted of breaking the law are fined, detained, and flogged.

Women's proper appearance is also legislated. In November 1991 Bashīr ruled that all female students and civil servants must wear a long dark dress to the ankles and a scarf covering the head and hair. A separate law concerning disorderly conduct requires all Sudanese to dress modestly. Yet in defiance of the dark robes mandated by the government, many women persisted in wearing the traditional Sudanese *tobe*—a large rectangle of fabric (often colorful) that is loosely wrapped around a woman's head and body. Despite harassment and physical abuse from neighborhood morality guards, women insisted that the *tobe* satisfied Islamic standards of modesty. Older generations of women continue to wear the *tobe* as part of their everyday dress and female civil servants are required to wear a white *tobe* to work. Students prefer to follow Islamic fashion trends and in recent years have donned the *ʿabāya* and ḥijab made popular in the Gulf states. In July 2009 Sudanese journalist Lubna Hussein and twelve other women were arrested for wearing trousers, an offense usually punished with flogging. Hussein insisted that the laws were unconstitutional and, after an internationally publicized trial, was found guilty and fined five hundred Sudanese pounds.

New Visions of Islam. Despite social and cultural restrictions, a number of Sudanese women have found professional and political opportunities within the Islamic state. Quotas of parliamentary seats are reserved for women and others have risen to serve as judges and government officials. In 2000, in an effort to better address women's issues, President Bashīr appointed Dr. Suad al-Fatih as a special advisor on women's affairs. This new Islamist community of female political leaders insists that men's discrimination toward women can only be redressed through the rightful application of Sharīʿah law. Thus, women's liberation has been recast in Islamic rhetoric. For these activists, it is not Islam but men who oppress women. Greater gender equity will be reached when men and women follow the laws and behaviors of Islam. However, secular and leftist activists have accused Bashīr and the Islamists of co-opting the energy of the women's movement and bringing all possibilities for change under the tight control of the state.

On a local level, greater access to Islamic teaching has provided Sudanese women with new avenues for questioning established gender roles. Communities have formed "mosque groups"—informal gatherings where women meet regularly to discuss Islam and its application to their everyday lives. Topics of discussion range from world events to the proper interpretation of men's charge over women. The mosque groups, unassociated with the state or NIF, provide women with direct access to the Qur'ān and opportunities for discussion in a safe space. Even women who do not claim to be political have used their new understandings of Islam to question familial relationship and cultural traditions. Thus, distinct from the state-mandated laws, it is through local community and daily practice that many Sudanese women are exercising a heightened personal relationship with Islam.

BIBLIOGRAPHY

Abdel Halim, Asma Mohamed. "Women's Organizations Seeking Gender Justice in the Sudan, 1964–1985." *Review of African Political Economy* no.121 (2009): 389–407. Insightful comparison of how the SWU and Republican Sisters have negotiated and challenged prevailing gender norms.

Badri, Haga Kashif. *Women's Movement in the Sudan*. 2d ed. Omdurman: MOB Center for Sudanese Studies, 2009. Highly detailed account of the origins of the women's movement, authored by a leading Sudanese activist.

Cuzzi, Guiseppe. *Fifteen Years Prisoner of the False Prophet*. Translated by Hildegund Sharma. Khartoum: Sudan Research Unit, University of Khartoum, 1968. A controversial account of Guiseppe Cuzzi's years in a Mahdist camp, where he was held captive.

Esposito, John L. "Sudan's Islamic Experiment." *The Muslim World* 76 (October 1986): 181–202.

Fluehr-Lobban, Carolyn. "Shari'a Law in the Sudan: History and Trends since Independence." *Africa Today* 28, no. 2 (1981): 69–77.

Hale, Sondra. *Gender Politics in Sudan: Islamism, Socialism, and the State*. Boulder, Colo.: Westview Press, 1996. An in-depth, feminist analysis of Sudanese women, politics, and political power in the twentieth century.

Hale, Sondra. "Mothers and Militias: Islamic State Construction of the Women Citizens of Northern Sudan." *Citizenship Studies* 3, no. 3 (1999): 373–386. An insightful look at the gendered activism of Islamist women.

Holt, P. M., and M. W. Daly. *A History of the Sudan, From the Coming of Islam to the Present Day*. 6th ed. Harlow, U.K.: Pearson, 2011. Concise and accessible history of Sudan.

Howard, W. Stephen. "Mahmoud Mohammad Taha and the Republican Sisters: A Movement for Women in Muslim Sudan." *Ahfad Journal* 23, no. 2 (2006): 31–49.

Nageeb, Salma Ahmed. *New Spaces and Old Frontiers: Women, Social Space, and Islamization in Sudan*. Lanham, Md.: Lexington Books, 2004. A compelling look at how women negotiate Islam and social space in their everyday lives.

Spaulding, Jay, and Stephanie Beswick. "Sex, Bondage, and the Market: The Emergence of Prostitution in Northern Sudan, 1750–1950." *Journal of the History of Sexuality* 5, no. 4 (1995): 512–534.

MARIE GRACE BROWN

SUFISM AND WOMEN.

[*This entry contains two subentries,*

Historical Overview *and*
Contemporary Thought and Practice.]

HISTORICAL OVERVIEW

Sufism (Ar. *taṣawwuf*) is a form of Islamic mysticism and a branch of Islamic knowledge and practice whose development historically parallels and intersects that of the other Islamic sciences, such as Qur'ān exegesis (*tafsīr*), jurisprudence (*fikh*), traditions of the Prophet Muḥammad (*ḥadīth*), theology (*kalām*), and philosophy (*falsafah*). From Sufism's roots in early Islamic asceticism (seventh to ninth centuries), to its transformation into a recognizable mystical tradition emphasizing love and intimate nearness to God (ninth to eleventh centuries), to the formation and continued popularity of institutionalized Ṣūfī orders (*tarekat*) (twelfth to sixteenth centuries), women have been active scholars (*faqiha*, *muhaddithat*), spiritual guides and teachers (*shaykha*, *ustādha*, *mu'addiba*), gnostics (*'arifat*), saints (*awlīyā*), disciples (*murida*), (*tāliba*), and lovers (*muhibba*) of the tradition. Extant Islamic biographical and hagiographical collections (*tabaqāt*, *tadhkirāt*) provide narrative accounts of some of these women, but owing to the relative absence of their primary writings, explicit details of their contributions to and participation in the tradition are less clear. Fewer women are highlighted in the hagiographical literature of later centuries, especially the seventeenth and eighteenth, while ethnographic, anthropological, and autobiographical accounts of Ṣūfī women of the nineteenth, twentieth, and twenty-first centuries have become new sources for their documentation.

As a spiritual path that emphasizes acute examination of personal desires, intentions, and awareness of God, Sufism is often described as an interiorization of Islamic faith and practice. Private disciplines of supererogatory prayer and fasting, repetition of God's names (*dhikr*), and seclusion (*khalwah*) may have offered women the opportunity to acquire a level of expertise not available in the other sciences, but that should not overshadow the fact that women have been active in vibrant communal aspects of Sufism: congregational *dhikr*, public sermons, shrine festivals, and community service. Many Ṣūfīs have been countercultural or social critics and activists—a fact demonstrating the ethical and social applications of insights derived from intensive spiritual disciplines. Ruth Roded points out that as Islam spread geographically in the early centuries, a number of ascetics arose as witnesses in critical opposition to an opulent Muslim ruling elite and a scholarly singular focus on legal issues. Yet this attitude exists in tension with some early ascetic and Ṣūfī women who demonstrated a more complex relationship between devotional practice and an emergent legal tradition, as their comments on seclusion, head covering (ḥijab), and *halal* food demonstrate. For example, when the Qura'ānic verse permitting her to unveil at her old age was read to Hafsa bint Sirin (early eighth century), the mystic legist asked, "'Is there anything else after that?'... We answered: 'But it is best for them to be modest.' Then she replied: 'This part of the verse is what confirms the use of the veil (ḥijab).'" These tensions and more are addressed by contemporary Ṣūfī women and scholars, who have transformed how one reads the hagiographical literature by casting a critical eye on the patriarchal interpretive tradition evident within it.

Early Ṣūfī Women. Ṣūfī hagiographers from the ninth to eleventh centuries root Sufism in the words and actions of the Prophet Muḥammad and his companions (*Ṣaḥābah*), among whom were a number of women noted for their piety and devotion, valued opinions, and miracles. Looking closely at these biographies, including *Ornaments of the Saints* (*Hilyat al-Awliya'*), by Abu Nu'aym al-Isfahani (d. 1038), and *Sifat al-safwa*, by Abu al-Faraj ibn al-Jawzi (d. 1201), among others, Ruth Roded (1994) shows that Ṣūfī biographies from this time contain a varying percentage of women (4 to 23 percent). A manuscript of the *Dhikr an-niswa al-Muta'abbidāt as-Sūffiyāt*, by Abu 'Abd al-Rahman al-Sulami (d. 1021), was found following Roded's publication and after being translated by Rkia Cornell (1999) has been critical to understanding these early Ṣūfī women.

By far the most well-known Ṣūfī woman, Rābi'a al-'Adawiyya (d. 801), also referred to as Rābi'a of Basra, is found not only in the above biographies, but also in works about the Ṣūfī path by al-Qushayri (d. 1072), al-Ghazali (d. 1111), and 'Attar (d. 1230), as illustrating Ṣūfī principles of repentance (*tawba*), patience (*sabr*), gratitude (*shukr*), hope (*raja'*) and fear (*khawf*), poverty (*faqr*), renunciation (*zuhd*), and love (*mahabba*). ʿAttar puts her "among the ranks of men" and defends his choice with the hadith "God does not regard your forms." Rābiʿa is often depicted in conversation with Hasan al-Basri and other well-known *shaykhs*, always appearing wiser through her vigilance against any form of egoism in devotion to God alone. She is considered the personality who transformed a growing Islamic asceticism into the vibrant tradition of love mysticism that became Sufism. Although Rābiʿa was the inheritor of a system of thought and practice rather than its founder, her poetry and the anecdotes about her have supplanted in popularity many of the women before and after her in the Ṣūfī collective memory.

Narratives of Ṣūfī women reveal a complex of demographics, behavior, ritual, and practice. Cornell outlines the historical trend of the first several centuries beginning in Basra sometime during the eighth century with a group of mostly non-Arab, recently converted women. They were characterized by highly ascetic practices of fasting and maintaining all-night vigils, often accompanied by profuse weeping, in addition to performing ritual prayer (*salat*), conversing with God through personal prayer (*duʾa*), and reflecting on the Qurʾān. Biographical transmissions of the ninth century, focusing on Syria, mention mostly free Arab women, highlighting their elevated intellect (*ʿaql*) and knowledge of religion (*din*). In the tenth century, Cornell (1999, p. 65) notes a distinctive paradigm shift from women being spiritual masters of other women to a marked decrease in their positions of leadership. The practice of *niswan*, service to one's companions or "institutionalized chivalry," also took hold among women Ṣūfīs at this time.

Among the early Ṣūfīs were women who were married and single, wealthy and poor, secluded and well traveled, and literate and illiterate. The often very short anecdotes and descriptions of these women reveal that they sought and were sought by male Ṣūfī *shaykhs*, were "masters of self-denial" (*mujahadat*), spoke words of ecstasy (*shath*), manifested signs (*āyat*) and miracles (*karamat*), and were preachers (*wa ʿiza*), reciters (*qarʾiat*), and interpreters (*mujtahida*) of the Qurʾān. Their "beautiful and melodious voice[s]," meditative states (*tafakkur*), and experiential knowledge of God (*mʾarifa*) attracted Ṣūfīs and non-Ṣūfīs alike, male and female. For example, Fatima of Nishapur (d. 849) traveled from Khurasan to Mecca a number of times and was noted for her knowledge of the Qurʾān. Dhu un-Nun (d. 859) called her a saint (*waliyat*) and his teacher (*ustadh*), and Bayezid Bistami (d. 874) called her a true woman.

Cornell (1999, p. 54) uses the phrase "theology of servitude" (*taʾabbud*) to highlight Sulami's own emphasis on the paradigm of service found among the women in his *dhikr*. Elaborating on this theme, Maria Dakake has examined the language of these seventh- to thirteenth-century Ṣūfī women and finds a gendered experience of God in terms of women's domestic social realities. Laury Silvers (2010), looking more closely at this "language of domesticity," refines Dakake's thesis by stating that these accounts must also be read as reflecting the development and polemics of the theological, political, and social concerns of their male transmitters. These kinds of critical analyses have been central to getting closer to the realities of early Ṣūfī women.

Middle and Late Period. Ṣūfī orders began to institutionalize in the twelfth and thirteenth centuries and were immensely popular throughout the fifteenth and sixteenth centuries. The growing centrality of the relationship between disciple (*murid*) and master (*shaykh*) and the closeness required for success on the path may be responsible for a growing discomfort with women's involvement. Women are noted to have attended congregational spiritual discourses (*sohbat*) given by Ṣūfī masters and to have joined in communal rituals of remembrance of God (*dhikr*), in which women and men are reported to have died in ecstasy. Wealthy women continued to be philanthropists of Ṣūfī activities (the Indian Mughal princess Jihān Ārā Begum, d. 1680), benefactresses of convents (Princess Tadhkaray, thirteenth century, Cairo), and because they were often educated, commentators on Ṣūfī treatises (Bibi Rasti, d. 1620, who was an expert on Fakhruddin Iraqi's *Lama'at*, and the *shaykha* Aisha al-Ba'uniyya d. Yusuf, d. 1516 CE. of Damascus, who authored several books on mysticism and taught and provided legal opinions in Cairo). During these centuries, the Ottomans entered Europe, and the Ṣūfī orders soon followed. Although scant, there are accounts of women dervishes throughout the Balkans and Greece who were connected to the Mevlevi, Halveti, and Naqshbandi orders, and the Bektashi order demonstrated a particularly high level of participation by women.

Along traveling routes and in cities, Ṣūfī lodges and retreat centers (Pers. *khaneqa*, Ar. *ribat* and *zawiya*, Turk. *tekke*) formed as gathering places for Ṣūfī *shaykh*s and *murid*s, including women. Leila Ahmed observes, "Women dwelling in ribats, and Sufi women in general, seem to have occupied a borderline status between the reputable and the disreputable" (1993, p. 115). With reference to their status as *wali* (saints), John Renard (2008, p. 152) calls Ṣūfī women "friends on the fringes," drawing attention to their marginalization during this period, despite often being in a demographic majority. These "friends" appear anecdotally in liminal places along the road, in the desert, and in the Holy City of Mecca. Ibn al-ʿArabī (d. 1240), in addition to mentioning women among his students, refers to a number of women Ṣūfī masters he had met in Andalusia (Shams, Mother of the Poor, and Nunah Fatima) and Mecca. However, as documented by Roded, overall the number of women mentioned in the biographical literature dropped significantly during this period.

As the centuries passed and the community of saints (*ʿawliya*) grew, so did ritual performance and attendance at their tombs (*mazar*, *dargah*, *turbe*, *keramat*). Shrines are places not only for devotion, but also for healing physical, psychological, and social ailments, and so have become popular pilgrimage sites for Muslim men and women. All over the Muslim world, there are tombs dedicated to women Ṣūfī saints, well known and obscure, the shrine of the Prophet's granddaughter, Sayyidnā Zaynab, in Cairo being one example. Shrine Sufism, as it has been called, has always garnered the participation of women and has drawn much attention in the last two centuries. It was first criticized by Muslim reformists (Deobandi, Tablighi Jamaat) as a general decline in Islamic practice, but scholars of the early twenty-first century have been attracted to it to understand Muslim women's embodied religiosity. At the tombs, women engaged in ritual remembrance of God (*dhikr*) and saint's day (*urs*, *mawlid*) festivities, including food preparation and listening to stories of the saint sung in poetic form (*na't*).

Women saints also hail from Senegal, Morocco, and Tunisia. Sayyida Manubiya of Tunisia, legendary student of Abu'l Hasan ash-Shadili (d. 1258), is still revered in weekly *dhikr* gatherings. Well-known male *shaykh*s often have related stories of their mothers, grandmothers, and great-grandmothers, extolling their saintly qualities and status as "friends of God," blessed with the ability to perform miracles and offer wise advice. For example, there are the stories of the mother and grandmother of Amadou Bamba (d. 1927), founder of the Senegalese Muridiyya Ṣūfī order, which has members currently far beyond Africa. These stories demonstrate how Ṣūfī women throughout the centuries are often related to their menfolk as disciples of their fathers or husbands. Although known to obtain some level of leadership within an order and to participate in male *dhikrs*, Ṣūfī women still struggled with criticism of its social propriety and with maintaining their levels of leadership. While there have been female *shaykhas* (*marabout*) in North and West Africa, any authority with decision-making power remained fleeting. Ṣūfī women thus experienced authority structures similar to those experienced by women in many other places in the world.

Ṣūfī women have also been artists. Poets master poetic forms from the metrical forms found in Central and South Asia and Turkey (*ghazal*, *rubiyat*) to the various indigenous forms found throughout Africa. Calligraphers master brushstrokes in calligraphy and other expressive media (*ebru*). Musicians, such as the internationally renowned *qawwali* singer Abida Parveen, sing Ṣūfī poetry. There are Ṣūfī Muslim women today who are active participants in grassroots Ṣūfī women's organizations addressing gender, educational, health, environmental, and political inequities by providing relief efforts and human and social services.

Contemporary and Current Trends. The growing presence of Ṣūfī orders in Europe and the Americas over the last two centuries is the consequence of a combination of factors. First, scholars and travelers have brought back Ṣūfī texts and practices from Muslim lands. Second, there has been increased immigration from colonial legacies reaching from South Asia to Africa. And last, travel and communication have become easier in a technological age. Women are not only active members in Ṣūfī orders in the West, but also have access to a transnational community of Ṣūfī women through the Internet and social media. In addition to a growing number of autobiographies, ethnographic, anthropological, and critical scholarship have provided more insights into the world of Ṣūfī women. Muslim feminist critique of the interpretive tradition in Islam, including Sufism, can be considered one contemporary manifestation of the Ṣūfī tradition. Zohara Simmons, a scholar of religion and Ṣūfī disciple of the Sri Lankan *shaykh* Bawa Muhaiyaddeen, and Leila Ahmed, a scholar of Muslim women, have found in Sufism theoretical bases and methods for challenging practices associated with Islam. For example, Ahmed, in addressing issues of gender construction, has noted that the Ṣūfī stress on the cultivation of the spiritual life should imply a de-emphasis of gender roles found in the legal and social obligations of women. She also points to a "pretextual or supratextual" hermeneutical process practiced by many Ṣūfī women, as opposed to a strictly linguistic one, when reading sacred literature. Simmons has concentrated on the impact of sharīʿah law on Muslim women, especially within the African-American Muslim communities of the United States.

Though Ṣūfī principles imply a contemporary transformation of gender relations in Islam, the Ṣūfī tradition as passed on by its male transmitters has displayed a patriarchal orientation toward gender and power not unlike other Islamic sciences. Addressing this concern, Rkia Cornell refers to the legacy of women in Sufism as a "veiled tradition," in which the perceived rarity of exemplary Ṣūfī women provides the false sense that it is nearly impossible for a woman to succeed on the Ṣūfī path. Kelly Pemberton, in her comparative and ethnographic study of women in three different branches of the Chishtī and Firdausi Ṣūfī orders in India, explores the disconnect between discourse and praxis, that is, how the description of women's (socially constructed and mediated) agency and autonomy does not match their broad participation and variety of roles in the Ṣūfī community. The scholarship on Ṣūfī women has come a long way since Margaret Smith's seminal work on Rābiʿa and other women mystics in Islam. Contemporary scholars are still working to balance the lives of saints with the realities of the many female Ṣūfīs and affiliates veiled by their ordinariness and surrender.

[*See also* Gender Themes, *subentry* Ṣūfī Devotional Literature.]

BIBLIOGRAPHY

Ahmed, Leila. *Women and Gender in Islam: Historical Roots of a Modern Debate.* New Haven, Conn.: Yale University Press, 1993.

Cornell, Rkia Elaroui. *Early Sufi Women: Dhikr an-Niswa al-Muta'abbidāt as-Sūffiyāt by Abū 'Abd Ar-Rahmān as-Sulamī.* Louisville, Ky.: Fons Vitae, 1999.

Dakake, M. "Guest of the Inmost Heart: Conceptions of the Divine Beloved Among Early Sufi Women." *Comparative Islamic Studies*, 3, (2007): 72–97.

Hoffman, V. J. *Sufism, Mystics, and Saints in Modern Egypt.* Columbia: University of South Carolina Press, 1995.

Pemberton, Kelly. *Women Mystics and Sufi Shrines in India.* Columbia: University of South Carolina Press, 2010. Focuses on women's participation in the Chishtī and Firdausi Ṣūfī orders in Rajasthan and Bihar.

Raudvere, Catharina. *The Book and the Roses: Sufi Women, Visibility, and Zikir in Contemporary Istanbul.* New York: I. B. Tauris, 2003.

Renard, John. *Friends of God: Islamic Images of Piety, Commitment, and Servanthood.* Berkeley: University of California Press, 2008.

Roded, Ruth. *Women in Islamic Biographical Collections: From Ibn Sa'd to Who's Who.* Boulder, Colo.: Lynne Rienner, 1994.

Schimmel, Annemarie. *My Soul Is a Woman: The Feminine in Islam.* New York: Continuum 1999. Contains a chapter, "Women in Sufism," that introduces a broad spectrum of early Ṣūfī women.

Silvers, Laury. "God Loves Me: Early Pious and Sufi Women and the Theological Debate over God's Love." *Journal for Islamic Studies* 30 (2010): 33–59. An excellent example of how critical scholarship can be applied to gendered texts to arrive at a better understanding of women's historical realities.

Smith, Margaret. *Rābi'a: The Life and Works of Rābi'a and Other Women Mystics in Islam.* Rockport, Mass.: Oneworld Publications, 1994.

Sultanova, Razia. *From Shamanism to Sufism: Women, Islam, and Culture in Central Asia.* New York: I. B. Tauris, 2010. Ethnography focusing on women's participation in Ṣūfī ritual, music, and healing in the Ferghana Valley, Uzbekistan.

MELINDA KROKUS

CONTEMPORARY THOUGHT AND PRACTICE

Women's contemporary engagement in Ṣūfī orders and in Ṣūfī-oriented rituals is obviously as diverse and complex as modern Muslim life at large. However, the conventional understanding of Sufism (*taṣawwūf*) as Islamic mysticism—with a focus on its orders (sing. *ṭarīqah*), specific theological discourses of spiritual progress, trust in the guidance of a master (*shaykh* or *murshid*), and participation in characteristic rituals (such as *wird*, *dhikr*, and *sama*) under his conduct—does not fully include women's participation in the wide range of devotional practices and civil engagement connected with Ṣūfī traditions. Women masters (sing. *shaykhah*) can be formally appointed within an order, and have been throughout history, or they can build their legitimacy to teach, preach, and lead rituals in local authority structures, or as deputies (sing. *khalīfah*) in relation to women's matters. Nevertheless, the search for women's Ṣūfī-related activities in the modern world must be based on a wider understanding of the concept of Sufism itself.

Affiliation with a Ṣūfī order has, by tradition, been a matter for the extended family, and even today fewer women than men take a formal vow of allegiance (*bay'ah*) with a *shaykh*, irrespective of whether their ritual life is practiced within the framework of an order or not. The ideal, and idealized, image of this master-disciple relationship, together with legendary history, provides narratives of the importance of women as saints and devotees. Yet in most Muslim societies, women's

Ṣūfī activities have developed in-parallel behind, and spatially separated from, men's activities. Women who practice Ṣūfī-influenced rituals are not necessarily members of an order and do not even identify themselves as Ṣūfī or dervishes. This ambiguous position has turned out to be as much a strategic advantage as an obstacle. On the one hand, a broad definition of Sufism based on ritual activities includes practices that have no direct connection to Ṣūfī theology, but rather with places invested with narratives of miracles and pious memory. On the other hand, a broad definition risks including too wide a cluster of devotional practices—and thereby confirming stereotypes of Sufism as primarily emotional and expressive. Hence, the term "Ṣūfī-oriented" is used to indicate the historical background of some devotional activities, as well as their location in less formalized social contexts.

Throughout history, Ṣūfī groups have been transnational and, through narratives and legendary history, have connected local communities with sites of pilgrimage and learning. In the age of globalization, transnational contacts have become even more emphasized, albeit in new directions. Processes like urbanization and international migration have not only moved people to new places, but also established new spaces for women to develop spiritually while being less dependent on traditional family ties and religious authorities (Deeb, 2006). Ṣūfī practices have been part of these fusions.

Devotional practices play a definitive role in women's Ṣūfī-oriented activities, and female lineages pass down authority as well as the local corpuses of repetitive prayers, narratives, and songs that constitute the core structure of many Ṣūfī rituals. Many women have learned the art of reciting the Qur'ān in these ritual contexts. The organized commemoration of the birth of the Prophet Muḥammad (*mawlid*) is an important genre in this framework and can include exegesis as well as sermons. Local mosques are rarely used for these activities. Rather, preference is for domestic spaces, with the hostess inviting women ritual specialist(s) to recite, sing, lead prayers, and preach to the crowd of guests at hand. The moral reputation of the hostess determines the social status of the meeting, but also important is the fact that in ritual events, learning is passed on to new generations over social boundaries. The repertoire and performing skills of the invited ritual leader(s) lend the rituals legitimacy and preaching authority. Modern Ṣūfī women express their religiosity in a web of ritual genres that consist of interrelated prayer genres, song traditions, and narratives performed at events which have both a religious and social character. Local pilgrim sites at tombs and mausoleums of saints (sing. *wali*), martyrs (sing. *shahid*), and other venerated persons are other important ritual arenas. Often repeated is the pattern of male objects of veneration and female visitors.

It is furthermore questionable whether it is correct to represent Ṣūfī terminology in Arabic, as most Ṣūfī women use their vernacular vocabulary to express their religiosity. Furthermore, some of the core regions with a rich Ṣūfī heritage are to be found in the formerly Ottoman lands, the Persian speaking world, South Asia, Indo-Pakistan, and Africa.

Modern living conditions and new lifestyles have affected the position of religious communities worldwide, including Sufism. The trend since the late nineteenth century has been a decreasing influence for formal religious institutions and for individuals a focus on personal choices as the modern mode of religiosity (Howell, 2007; Bruinessen, 2010).

In the wake of ideologically diverse grand-scale modernization projects of the twentieth century—with their mass-education programs, social mobility, and new authority hierarchies—not only have gender relations changed. There has also been a growing gap between the educated elite and the objects of reforms and disciplining efforts. Educated women early on became one of the icons of modernity, and religion was one of the presumed obstacles to emancipation. Hence, it was difficult for women to combine access to new arenas with traditional practices. Both ideological modernists and puritan reformers of Islam have expressed reluctance about local ritual practice, and this reticence has affected the image of Sufism and attitudes toward Ṣūfī practices (Sirriyeh, 1999).

The issue of controversial rituals is strongly connected to modern Islamic reform movements with both radical and liberal inclinations. These rituals need not be evident parts of Ṣūfī theology; rather, they are often embedded in the veneration of local saints and pilgrim routes and they are essential parts of healing rituals connected with tombs and shrines, vows, seeking protection from evil spirits, or foretelling the future by means of various divination rituals. The production and distribution of amulets also belong to this area of contested practices. The conceptual basis for these ceremonies is the blessing or spiritual power (*barakah*) that emanates from living persons or tombs of saints. An equally important part of this conceptual basis and its instrumentalization is the transmission of the blessing through tactile touching of the coffin of the venerated, water from a nearby fountain, and sweets and artifacts that are distributed far beyond the pilgrim site by visitors who thus bring the blessing back home as a gift and a memory.

Women's Engagement in Ṣūfī Activities. For portraying contemporary Ṣūfī activities of women in terms of expressive genres, ritual leadership, and theological authority, there are many cases to choose from. The following four have been selected to indicate regional variation, the complexity of modernity, and different aspects of the theme of women and Sufism in the modern era.

First, *Rebel and Saint* (1994), Julia Clancy-Smith's study of resistance in colonial Algeria, brings to attention an example of formal female leadership within a local branch of a Ṣūfī order. In the absence of sons, Zaynab succeeded her father as the local *shaykh* in 1897, but not without opposition from other male relatives. This recognition was an acceptance of the daughter as part of the legitimate chain of authority (*silsila*). This inherited spiritual blessing (*barakah*), combined with her personal qualifications as a well-versed woman of respectable conduct, made her the legitimate leader of the local lodge (*zawiya*). The unusual condition that she remain unmarried to devote her time to pious and charitable deeds added to her status as a revered woman. Due to her close relation to her father, Zaynab, without any formal education, had nevertheless acquired sufficient religious learning (*ilm*) and was able to successfully direct the *zawiya* as a hub of cultural resistance against the French. After her early death in 1904, both male and female followers continued to venerate her with an annual pilgrimage (*ziyārah*) to her mausoleum. Clancy-Smith's (1994) study of Zaynab's accomplishments points to women's religious engagement as an important tool in anticolonial activities as well as to the possibility of finding documents that illuminate Ṣūfī women's leadership in early modernity.

Second, Razia Sultanova (2011) presents Uzbek musical and narrative traditions in a long-term perspective with a special emphasis on how women teachers (sing. *otin*) integrate this highly Ṣūfī-flavored canon in an increasing conservative trend. The changes at all societal levels in post-Soviet Uzbekistan greatly affect contemporary practices, and the cases of individual *otin*s highlight the impact of politics on Ṣūfī activities, no matter how emotional they are. After a long period of repression of religion in general, the *otin*s are again more known to the general public, though they only perform in mono-gendered environments. The recitations that *otins* conduct at life cycle rituals, such as celebrations of holidays, commemoration of the dead, and praising martyrs, are part of a poetic web related to devotional gatherings. Classic Ṣūfī ceremonies like the repetitive *dhikr* prayer, also commonly performed outside the orders, are part of this larger context. The textual, musical, and rhythmical aspects of the repertoire are transmitted to apprentices, who meet with elder women for successive training, nowadays sometimes with formal Islamic training.

Third, in urban areas, new fellowships are developing as forums for maintaining Ṣūfī rituals, but not necessarily within the framework of the established orders. Catharina Raudvere (2002) shows, in an example from Istanbul, how Ṣūfī activities in semipublic spaces build on both local tradition and on younger women's ability to adapt to social and political changes. By establishing an endowment (*waqf*), the women in this case make use of a widely respected form for directing money to stipulated purposes. This framework makes for a more formalized organization that can go beyond domestic spaces and the conventional spheres of orders in the neighborhood. Women in leading positions combine traditional Islamic learning with secular education to navigate late modern local Ṣūfī life. By avoiding classic Ṣūfī terminology for ritual functions and leadership, the women of the endowment guard against being regarded as competitors with the local orders. The Ṣūfī inclinations of the group are manifested in practice rather than in theological discourse. They organize *dhikr* and *mawlid* events, as well as social-welfare commitments to those in need, along with basic Islamic education classes and preaching in local mosques. Their legitimacy to educate, preach, and lead rituals comes from a deceased male teacher (*hoca*). The group defines itself as keepers of the *hoca*'s instructions by editing and interpreting his recorded sermons, which emphasize a combination of spiritual knowledge (*marifet*) and welfare work (*hizmet*). This background male authority is transmitted into intense women's activities that serve as a platform for comments on contemporary issues.

Fourth, the colonial representation of Muslim women as secluded and passive has emphasized their absences from communal ritual events and has overshadowed the fact that women do assume authority as leaders within orders. Kelly Pemberton's (2010) study shows, with examples from women's activities at Ṣūfī shrines in India, how family bonds, social gifts to lead, and pious qualifications constitute the main paths to local authority, but within domains other than those of men. *Pir*, the Urdu honorary title for a Ṣūfī master, can also be applied to a woman, although not as a community leader but most often as a ritual specialist or healer for women.

Women's musical performances are an integral part of Ṣūfī activities activities in mixed-gender spaces in Pemberton's examples. Yet women are socialized into tacit knowledge about the precise limits for women's conduct and presence in the community. The commemoration of a saint or founder of an order (*urs*) at an anniversary day is a significant ritual for South Asian Islam. These are major public events that would not function without the contribution of women.

International Migration, Globalization and New Conditions for Ṣūfī Groups. Internal and international migration, caused by political conflicts or economic difficulties, has created environments where different lifestyles and moral standards come into contact. These are also the spaces where many contemporary Ṣūfī groups operate.

Most Muslim migration takes place within the Muslim world, but diaspora connotes shifts from Muslim majority societies to minority situations. Sometimes Ṣūfī groups can even find themselves to be a minority within the minority. Ṣūfī activities in diaspora are, in general, less visible than those organized by formal Muslim communities. In diaspora, Ṣūfī fellowships are more rarely in contact with local authorities and more in alliance with their transnational networks.

Most first-generation migrants nevertheless define their activities in ethnic or national frameworks, whereas their descendants see other opportunities (Werbner, 2003). Diasporic Ṣūfī life is thus a generational issue as much as a question of gender. Young people seem more open to fusing traditions and constructing ritual spaces relevant to new circumstances. Between generations, a shift can be noted from ethnic community practices to marked choices of theological and ritual preferences.

Ṣūfī traditions can play a double, if not contradictory, role in diaspora. On the one hand, they confirm ethnic/national belonging and give structure to diasporic ritual life. On the other, Ṣūfī traditions can offer more liberal modes of pious expression and links to Muslim identity without necessarily accepting the ethnically defined religious authorities. This latter tendency has been attractive to many converts. For several decades new branches of the established orders, especially among the Naqshbandi, appeared on the global Ṣūfī scene, sometimes discussed under the disputed label "neo-Ṣūfīs." With transnational communications conveying authority and charisma, their prolific leaders reach new crowds such as the Muslim urban middle class and converts. In local environments, the neo-Ṣūfī activities can be very open to new forms of spirituality and cultural expression such as rap, Internet communities, and martial arts. The fusion between diasporic groups can be creative as well as a source of conflict.

Sufism is sometimes a non-Muslim's first encounter with the practice of Islam and it has been an important vehicle for the spread of Islam throughout history. This remains true today. Sufism is already part of Western intellectual history and gives rise to artistic expressions that are easy to access—not the least via the Internet. The border zone between converts to Sufism and New Age spirituality, as well as the even broader scope of healing and mindfulness, are significant features in the kaleidoscope of contemporary Ṣūfī representation. This should not be read, however, to mean that contemporary Sufism in general represents a liberal theological agenda. Most Ṣūfī groups are conservative in social and moral matters. Such attitudes to a great extent define the spaces for and the limits of women's activities, and yet prove attractive to new followers.

Religion in the twenty-first century, with its emphasis on personal preferences and individual religiosity, has pushed for a transition from collective identities to more individualized choices. Ṣūfī milieus offer a variety of rituals and forms of piety to be performed privately or as a community. By tradition, women have been given leading and guiding roles embedded in local hierarchies and limited to mono-gendered spaces. Modernity has opened up educational and professional achievements as new sources of authority to meet a greater variety of religious counterparts, but many Ṣūfī orders are also part of the increasingly conservative Islamic trends worldwide.

BIBLIOGRAPHY

Bruinessen, Martin van. "Sufism, Popular Islam, and the Encounter with Modernity." In *Islam and Modernity: Key Issues and Debates*, edited by Khalid Masud, Armando Salvatore, and Martin van Bruinessen. Edinburgh: Edinburgh University Press, 2010.

Clancy-Smith, Julia A. *Rebel and Saint: Muslim Notables, Populist Protest, Colonial Encounters (Algeria and Tunisia, 1800–1904)*. Berkeley: University of California Press, 1994.

Deeb, Lara. *An Enchanted Modern: Gender and Public Piety in Shiʿi Lebanon*. Princeton: Princeton University Press, 2006.

Howell, Julia. "Modernity and Islamic Spirituality in Indonesia's New Sufi Networks." In *Sufism and the*

'Modern' in Islam, edited by Martin van Bruinessen and Julia Day Howell. London: I. B. Tauris, 2007.

Pemberton, Kelly. *Women Mystics and Sufi Shrines in India*. Columbia: University of South Carolina Press, 2010.

Pemberton, Kelly. "Women *Pirs*, Saintly Succession, and Spiritual Guidance in South Asian Sufism." *Muslim World* 96 (2006): 61–87.

Raudvere, Catharina. *The Book and the Roses: Sufi Women, Visibility, and Zikir in Contemporary Istanbul*. London: I. B. Tauris, 2002.

Sirriyeh, Elizabeth. *Sufis and Anti-Sufis: The Defense, Rethinking, and Rejection of Sufism in the Modern World*. London: RoutledgeCurzon, 1999.

Sultanova, Razia. *From Shamanism to Sufism: Women, Islam, and Culture in Central Asia*. London: I. B. Tauris, 2011.

Werbner, Pnina. *Pilgrims of Love: The Anthropology of a Global Sufi Cult*. London: Hurst, 2003.

CATHARINA RAUDVERE

SUFRA. Originally an Arabic term, *sufra* was used in Persian to mean a spread of food and drinks or tablecloth. In the context of contemporary Iranian, *sufra* refers to the female-led and religiously inspired custom of inviting female acquaintances (usually Shīʿī) to an oblational banquet themed around a holy Shīʿī figure who is supplicated for the fulfillment of a wish, or in gratitude of the latter's actualization. The *sufra* may be either an exceptional or annual event. While in urban areas, male attendance and sponsorship have been occasionally reported, rural *sufra*s explicitly prohibit male attendance.

The Shīʿī holy figure usually commemorated is Abu al-Fazl al-ʿAbbās (also referred to by the epithet "Qamar-i Bani Hāshim," the moon of the Hashemites), the son of ʿAlī, the first Shīʿī imam. Having been martyred alongside his half-brother Ḥusayn, the third imam, in the battle of Karbala in 680 CE, Sufrah-yi Ḥazrat-i ʿAbbās was established in his honor. Occasionally, one might decide to offer a *sufra* in the name of other hallowed Shīʿī figures, such as Imams Ḥasan or Ḥusayn; their mother and daughter of the Prophet, Fāṭimah; their sister Zaynab; the mother of Abu al-Fazl al-ʿAbbās, Umm al-Banin; and the young daughter of Imam Ḥusayn, Sayiddah Ruqayyah. In Iran's northeast province of Khorāsān, Sufrah-yi Bībī Sishanbah is offered on the last Tuesday of the lunar month of Shaʿbān, for Lady Tuesday, someone who is thought to have been born, married, and died on Tuesday. Associated with this figure are two women believed to be the daughters of the Prophet: Bībī Ḥūr and Bībī Nūr.

The diphasic structure of the *sufra*, especially in urban areas, involves an initial atmosphere of devotion and mourning, followed by serving of food that may, at times, take on the form of a joyful celebration. Although the content of the devotional phase varies, the usual recitation of the Qurʾān is accompanied by an emotionally charged recounting of the Karbala tragedy called *rawzah*—the abbreviated form for *Rawzah al-shuhadāʾ* (The garden of the martyrs), an early-sixteenth-century book on the martyrdom of the Imams. Upon listening to the *Rawzah*, the audiences weep. One study reports the existence, also, of a prayer specific to the vowed *sufra* (*duʿā-yi sufrah-ʾi nazrī*). In some rural *sufra* ceremonies, the liturgical use of folktales evokes their legendary origins. The items put on the *sufra* have symbolic meaning. Both the preparation and the serving of the ritual meal involve prescribed behaviors, including the verbal recital of texts. In these and other aspects, the Iranian Shīʿī ritual of *sufra* shares some features with similar practices among Iranian Zoroastrians.

Sufra gatherings have been criticized by some Shīʿī clergy as a "perversion of charity" and "a pseudoreligious excuse for a party" (Jamzadeh and Mills, 1986, pp. 35, 50). For the women involved, however, the *sufra* is not only a religious rite, but also a social event that provides psychological comfort and communal participation.

BIBIOGRAPHY

Jamzadeh, Laal, and Margaret Mills. "Iranian *Sofreh*: from Collective to Female Ritual." In *Gender and Religion: On the Complexity of Symbols*, edited by C. W. Bynum, et al., pp. 23–65. Boston: Beacon, 1986. This chapter compares the *sufra* as it is practiced among Zoroastrian and Shīʿī Muslim communities. Drawing on several scholarly and literary sources, the authors present a rather comprehensive examination of the social organization and symbolic interpretation of *sufra*. Though written in 1986, it is still one of the main sources on Shīʿī *sufra* in English.

Shirazi, Faegheh. "The *Sofreh*: Comfort and Community among Women in Iran." *Iranian Studies* 38, no. 2 (2005): 293–309. This article studies *sufra* offered in the name of different Shīʿī holy figures, and discusses the social and psychological functions of this rite for Iranian women.

MINA YAZDANI

SUICIDE. Suicide is defined as deliberately self-inflicted death. Suicidal ideation refers to thinking or communicating about killing oneself. A behavior is considered suicidal when it is intended as life-threatening. The outcome of a suicidal act is not a reliable measure of intent. Some suicidal acts intended as fatal do not result in death, and vice versa, depending on method, type and promptness of medical care, and other circumstances. Ambivalence about the outcome of a suicidal act is common among persons who engage in suicidal behavior.

In classical Islamic texts, the term used for suicide is *qatl al-nafs*, literally "self-murder." *Intiḥār*, meaning "cutting of the throat," is the common word for suicide in modern Arabic speech.

Religious and Legal Perspectives. Suicide is *ḥarām* (forbidden) within Islam as it is God who gives and takes life. To kill oneself is to assume God's prerogative. Islam's prohibition of suicide is linked with statements in the Qurʾān, such as the phrase: "O you who have believed! . . . [D]o not kill yourselves" (4:29). The connection of this phrase with suicide is, however, tenuous because *lā taqtulū anfusakum* may also be understood as meaning "do not kill each other." In any case, within the prophetic tradition (*ḥadīth*), there is clear condemnation of suicide. According to the *ḥadīths*, those who commit suicide shall reside in hell forever, with the punishment consisting of unending repetitions of the act by which the suicides delivered themselves to death.

In many Islamic-majority nations, suicide and nonfatal suicidal behavior are a criminal offense. As noted by Khan and colleagues, the prosecution of individuals who survive a suicidal act, however, is rare, the most common practice being harassment and extortion of survivors and their families. There are also serious negative social sanctions against the suicidal and their families. For these reasons, according to commentators, statistics on suicide in Muslim-majority communities are unreliable.

Rates and Patterns of Women's Suicide. According to World Health Organization (WHO) records, suicide rates in Muslim-majority countries are low (relative to rates in non-Muslim-majority countries), with suicide rates for women being lower than those of men. There is, however, significant variability in official suicide rates across Muslim-majority countries—from a low of 0.0 for women (and 0.1, 0.2, 0.2, 0.7, respectively, for men) in Egypt, Jordan, Syria, and the Maldives, to a high of 9.4 for women (43 for men) in Kazakhstan (these suicide rates are per 100,000 population, and for the most recent year for each country). Suicide rates are also typically reported as low among Muslims in non-Muslim-majority countries.

The low suicide rates recorded among Muslims likely represent, at least in part, a real phenomenon. One reason is that low suicide rates are more likely to be found in low-income societies, with which Muslim-majority societies still largely coincide. Another reason is that the negative legal, religious, and social consequences of suicide in Muslim societies likely discourage it.

At the same time, Islam's condemnation of suicide may also impact suicide records, with official suicide data likely being an underestimate. Indirect evidence of the underreporting of suicide in Muslim-majority countries comes from a study by Pritchard and Amanullah, who found that undetermined death rates in ten predominantly Muslim countries were considerably higher than the predominantly non-Muslim countries' average.

There are indications that Muslim suicide records may be unreliable by way of overestimate as well, with a portion of women's official suicides actually being murders. For example, in Iran, the murders of female rape victims may be reported as suicides. Similarly, some deaths by burning documented among women in Afghanistan, Egypt, Iran, Pakistan, Tajikistan, and Uzbekistan may have been suicides under pressure from family members because, for example, of the women's presumed infertility (see Campbell and Guiao, Groohi and colleagues, and Maghsoudi and colleagues, for a review of burns' morbidity and fatality patterns in Muslim-majority countries). In sum, in Muslim-majority countries, female suicide records may be unreliable as a result of both underreporting and misreporting.

Evidence from community studies conducted in Islamic-majority countries, including Bangladesh, Iran, Pakistan, and Turkey, suggests that suicide among Muslims is not as uncommon as generally assumed, based on official country records. Also, in some communities, women have significantly higher rates than men. For example, according to a study by Altindag, Ozkan, and Oto, women's suicide rate within a community in southeastern Turkey was 9.3 per 100,000 (compared to a male rate of 5.4 per 100,000).

Rates and Patterns of Women's Suicidal Ideation and Behavior. In Muslim-majority countries, women report higher rates of suicidal thoughts than men. Rates of suicidal ideation however vary significantly across predominantly Muslim countries. According to Karam, Hajjar, and Salamoun's review of community studies conducted in twelve Muslim-majority countries, lifetime suicidal ideation varied from 2.1 percent to 13.9 percent of the samples surveyed, with women as the typical ideator.

Women in predominantly Muslim countries also report higher rates of nonfatal suicidal behavior than men. Across studies, women represent half to nearly all cases of nonfatal suicidal behavior. Also, nonfatal suicidal behavior rates are not lower in Muslim-majority countries than in non-Muslim-majority countries. Rates of nonfatal suicidal behavior, however, vary significantly across predominantly Muslim countries. The review by Karam and colleagues found that nonfatal suicidal behavior rates ranged between 0.7 and 6.3 percent of the sample studied. According to a review by Lester, nonfatal suicidal behavior rates per 100,000 also vary significantly over time within Muslim-majority countries (for example, from 1.9 in 1993 to 12.8 in 1998, in Oman).

Explanations for Women's Fatal and Nonfatal Suicidal Behavior. There are no universal explanations for suicidal behavior. This is because suicidal behavior is culturally specific, with its meaning, forms, precipitants, typical scenario, method, and consequences (and consequently, its rates) varying across cultures, and at different historical times. In other words, different suicide scripts exist in different cultures, including cultures that share an important common feature, such as a religion. In some cultures, women's suicidality follows a distinct script, relative to men's, with regard to, for example, typical precipitant or method, whereas, in other cultures, women's and men's suicidality are more similar than different (see Canetto, and Canetto and Lester, for reviews).

There are also no simple general explanations for women's suicidality in Muslim-majority societies. This is because Islam is diverse, between and within Muslim-majority countries, in its beliefs and practices with regard to suicide, women, and women and suicide.

This said, a few themes have emerged from studies of Muslim women's suicidality. One is that Muslim women's suicidality (nonfatal as well as fatal) is highest during women's reproductive years. Another is that, among Muslim women, marriage is a risk factor for, not a protector against, suicidality—as is the case in non-Muslim-majority societies, particularly among men. A third is that suicidality is most common among poor rural women. Many reasons have been proposed to explain young, married, and poor rural women's high rates of suicidality. First, as noted by Rezaeian, in many Muslim societies, women are married young, often to much older men. For many poor rural women, marriage brings heavy domestic and caregiving burdens. Poor women in rural communities are also subject to major educational, social, and economic restrictions as a result of patriarchal traditions and customs. In support of this hypothesis, an Iranian study by Aliverdinia and Pridemore found that female suicide was highest in provinces with low levels of female education and labor force participation. The most important factor in the suicidality of Muslim married women, however, appears to be domestic violence. Across studies and countries, emotional and physical abuse by husbands has emerged as the most consistent precipitant of Muslim women's suicidality. Taken together, the findings of studies have been interpreted to suggest that Muslim women's suicidality is a way to protest against and/or escape from domestic violence, and from a life of extreme social restrictions. In Durkheim's language, Muslim women's suicidality can be described as fatalistic, that is, as the result of social hyper-regulation—in contrast to the social underregulation postulated as the cause of non-Muslim men's anomic suicide in high-income, non-Muslim-majority societies.

Prevention of Women's Fatal and Nonfatal Suicidal Behavior. With regard to the prevention of Muslim women's suicidality, social scientists and clinicians concur on the importance of social and economic factors. For example, Rezaeian argued that Muslim societies should prohibit child marriage; provide equal educational, economic, and social rights and opportunities for women and men; and promote "Islamic values rather than traditional customs" (2010, p. 40). The findings of the study by Aliverdinia and Pridemore also point to the role of employment and independent income as protectors against suicidal behavior among Muslim women.

The strong association, among Muslim women, of suicidality and being the victim of violence by family members, together with the evidence on the role of family violence in the suicidality of women in general (see, for example, the findings of Devries and collaborators' study of women's nonfatal suicidal behavior and domestic violence in Brazil, Ethiopia, Japan, Namibia, Peru, Samoa, Serbia, Thailand, and Tanzania) point to the necessity of prioritizing violence prevention in suicide prevention strategies for women.

BIBLIOGRAPHY

Aliverdinia, Akbar, and William Alex Pridemore. "Women's Fatalistic Suicide in Iran: A Partial Test of Durkheim in an Islamic Republic." *Violence Against Women* 15 (2009): 307–320.

Altindag, Abdurrhman, Mustafa Ozkan, and Remzi Oto. "Suicide in Batman, Southeastern Turkey." *Sui-*

cide and Life-Threatening Behavior 35 (2005): 478–482.

Campbell, Elizabeth A., and Isabelita Z. Guiao. "Muslim Culture and Female Self-Immolation: Implication for Global Women's Health Research and Practice." *Health Care for Women International* 25 (2004): 782–793.

Canetto, Silvia Sara. "Women and Suicidal Behavior: A Cultural Analysis." *American Journal of Orthopsychiatry* 78 (2008): 259–266.

Canetto, Silvia Sara, and David Lester. "Gender, Culture and Suicidal Behavior." *Transcultural Psychiatry* 35 (1998): 163–191.

Devries, Karen, Charlotte Watts, Mieko Yoshihama, et al. "Violence against Women Is Strongly Associated with Suicide Attempts: Evidence from the WHO Multi-Country Study on Women's Health and Domestic Violence against Women." *Social Science & Medicine* 73 (2011): 79–86.

Groohi, Bahram, Annette McKay Rossignol, Sergio Perez Barrero, and Reza Alaghehbandan. "Suicidal Behavior by Burns among Adolescents in Kurdistan, Iran: A Social Tragedy." *Crisis* 27, no. 1 (2006): 16–21.

Karam, Elie G., Ranya V. Hajjar, and Mariana M. Salamoun. "Suicidality in the Arab World Part 1: Community Studies." *Arab Journal of Psychiatry* 18, no. 2 (2007): 99–107.

Khan, Murad M., Naqvi Haider, Thave Durrane, and Martin Prince. "Epidemiology of Suicide in Pakistan: Determining Rates in Six Cities." *Archives of Suicide Research* 12 (2008): 155–160.

Lester, David. "Suicide and Islam." *Archives of Suicide Research* 10 (2006): 77–97.

Maghsoudi, Hemmat, Abasad Garadagi, Golam Ali Jafary, et al. "Women Victims of Self-Inflicted Burns in Tabriz, Iran." *Burns* 30 (2004): 217–220.

Okasha, Ahmed, and Tarek Okasha. "Suicide and Islam." In *Oxford Textbook of Suicidology and Suicide Prevention: A Global Perspective*, edited by Danuta Wasserman and Camilla Wasserman, pp. 49–56. Oxford: Oxford University Press, 2009.

Pritchard, Colin, and S. Amanullah. "An Analysis of Suicide and Undetermined Deaths in 17 Predominantly Islamic Countries Contrasted with the UK." *Psychological Medicine* 37 (2007): 421–430.

Rezaeian, Mohsen. "Suicide among Young Middle Eastern Muslim Females." *Crisis* 31, no. 1 (2010): 36–42.

The Qur'ān (English version) rev. ed. Saheeh International, eds. Jeddah, Saudi Arabia: Abul-Qasim Publishing House, 1997.

World Health Organization. *Suicide Rates per 1000,000 by Country, Year and Sex.* Geneva, Switzerland: World Health Organization, 2012. http://www.who.int/mental_health/prevention/suicide_rates/en/.

SILVIA SARA CANETTO

SUICIDE BOMBINGS. What is the role of women in jihadist ideology and action in the contemporary world? The answer has varied over time and place, according to circumstances and the prevailing current of religious thought.

The Geography of Suicide Bombings. In the 1980s, during the long war between Iran and Iraq (1980–1988), women's role as martyrs in the young Islamic Republic of Iran was only indirect: they could not take part in the war as soldiers and meet martyrdom in the same fashion as men. They could die as martyrs by nursing wounded soldiers and succumbing under the Iraqi bombings. They could be recognized as martyrs if they died, like many men, as a result of air strikes by Iraqi fighter jets. Yet women were denied direct participation as "martyr soldiers" in Basīj, the organization that mainly enrolled young volunteers in Iran, although there was a demand in that direction by many young revolutionary girls.

In other countries, women gained some foothold within jihadist organizations between 1985 and 2006. In Chechnya, their role was important (47 in Russia and Chechnya). In Palestine, 67 women became involved in suicide attacks during this time, whereas the number of women in the jihadist movement in Jordan (1), Egypt (none), Iraq (4), Lebanon (6), and Morocco (2) shows that their involvement was marginal. The highest number was in Sri Lanka (75). But in all these cases, the role of women was close to that of the foot soldier and not within the leadership of these movements.

The effective role of women in suicide operations increased in the late 1990s and the first years of the twenty-first century, mainly because they were not identified by the security services as dangerous and therefore could act more freely than men. In Chechnya, Iraq, Jordan, Egypt, Uzbekistan, and Palestine, women played a role in suicide bombings. What made them attractive for the plots was that they could hide their weapons, sometimes appearing pregnant, under their veils. The *mujahidāt* (feminine form of *mujāhidūn*, those who carry out jihad) were involved in many cases as sisters, mothers, or wives.

Between 1985 and 2006, there were more than 220 women suicide bombers, representing nearly 15 percent of the overall number of actual suicide bombers around the world and those intercepted in the final stages before the attack.

In the Palestinian suicide attacks, Wafa Idriss was the first to act, in January 2002. She killed one Israeli and injured more than 150 others in a Jerusalem shopping district. Four other Palestinian women committed suicide attacks in the four months following Wafa Idriss. Some women seem to have been involved as "mere women," contrary to the general rule in women's martyrdom operations, where they are involved as relatives of men. This was the case for Hanadi Jaradat, who detonated a bomb in an Arab-owned restaurant in Haifa, killing nineteen people. In a prerecorded video aired by Al Jazeera on August 24, 2005, she said, "By the power of God, I have decided to become the sixth female martyrdom seeker who will turn her body into shrapnel, which will reach the heart of every Zionist colonialist in my country" (Ali, 2006, p. 49).

In April 2003, two women in Iraq blew up their car at a checkpoint and killed three soldiers. The Jordanian Sajida Mubarak Arrous al-Rishawi and her husband detonated explosives in November 2005 in three hotels in Amman. Her husband died, but she survived because of the failure of the ignition system. In September 2005, an Iraqi woman took part in the assassination of job applicants, under the leadership of al-Qaʿida. Other incidents involved women as soldiers, like the April 2005 shootings by two veiled Egyptian women on a tourist bus in Cairo. In the latter case, the two women, both in their twenties, were related to a male activist, Ehab Yousri Yassin. One was his sister (Negat Yassin) and the other his fiancée (Iman Ibrahim Khamis). They acted out of revenge for Yassin's death at the hands of the Egyptian authorities. The two women then shot themselves.

Among converts, there are some women who engaged in suicide attacks against the Americans or their allies. The case of Muriel Degauque is rather exceptional, since there have not been many women converts directly involved in global jihad so far. She was a young convert from Charleroi, Belgium. On November 9, 2005, she triggered her explosive belt in Baʿqūbah, Iraq, killing five policemen and wounding civilians. A few days later, Americans killed her husband, a Belgian citizen of Moroccan origin. Another convert, Pascal Cruypenninck, wanted to commit a suicide bombing with his fiancée, a young African woman, but he was arrested.

A young Uzbek woman played a major role in a suicide attack in March 2003: nineteen-year-old Dilnoza Holmuradova detonated explosives at Tashkent's Chorsu Market, killing at least forty-seven people, including ten police officers. She came from a middle-class background, was well educated, spoke five languages, and, unlike the vast majority of Uzbek women, had a driver's license. In her case, intense modernization in a society without any social orientation after the collapse of the Soviet Union and the attraction of Islam in its radical version through the Islamic Jihad group seem to have played an important role in her radicalization.

The Ideology of Women's Jihad. There is a paradox in the jihadist movement vis-à-vis women. On the one hand, jihadists denounce the presence of women in the public sphere and fight for their return to the family. They reject the modern Western idea of the equality of men and women and propose a rigid view of the Sharīʿah and *fiqh* (Islamic law) that refuses to recognize a formal role for women in the political or even the economic and cultural sphere, other than that of mother, sister, or wife. But, on the other hand, the hard facts of the modern world push jihadists to accept with some reluctance the participation of women, at least within the family and the city, to spread jihadist ideology and promote radical action.

The major ideologue of women's jihad is Yūsuf al-Uyayri, who was killed by the Saudi police in 2003. He belongs to those young "soldier intellectuals" who attached a major importance to women. In his writings on women and their role in the jihad, he called out to Muslim women and asked for their assistance in a situation where there was, according to his view, a "new crusaders' war" against the world of Islam. Al-Uyayri summoned women to help because many Muslims, and women in particular, believed, from his perspective, that jihad should be avoided because it is the path to death for their family. According to al-Uyayri, the sad predicament of Muslims was due to their willingness to acquiesce to inferiority and humiliation and their lack of determination to undertake jihad because of their lethargy and love of life in this world. The only way to resolve the problem is through violent jihad.

For al-Uyayri, today's women as mothers, wives, daughters, or sisters are an obstacle to jihad, since they forbid their men to engage in the fight against the unbelievers. On the contrary, he argues, as true believers, women should educate their children for the sake of carrying out jihad; they should protect the sexual honor (*ʿird*) of their men, once they choose the path of jihad; and they should become more active in preparing men for holy war. Al-Uyayri asked women to end their role as "prostitutes" within the new sick culture spread by the West, where dancing or singing is given precedence over the genuinely Islamic role of taking part in jihad, as many women did during the time of the Prophet, when they helped men in battle. In so doing, al-Uyayri did not push women to become directly involved in jihad as fighting soldiers. Instead, he asked them to accept the sacrifice of their sons, husbands, or fathers and actively prepare them for this holy task, emulating the women of the Golden Age of Islam.

The martyrdom of women can not only incite men to take part in jihad, but also entice other women to become more involved in suicide operations. Women's martyrdom thus has a dual role: it calls into question men's sense of honor and pride (*ghira*, *ʿird*), and it provides a heroic example that other women can imitate. Their enrollment in jihadist operations can also be a quest for empowerment within Muslim societies that are deeply patriarchal, even though the primary aim of the women might not be to assert their equality with men.

The media play a role in the mobilization of women in the path of jihad. New technologies, particularly the Internet, enable women to act more freely than within traditional social networks, which are dominated by men. Jihadist media like *Ṣawt al-jihād* and *Minbar al-tawḥīd* urge women to take part in jihad. *Ṣawt al-jihād*, produced by al-Qaʿida in Saudi Arabia, devotes part of its editorials to women. The name adopted for the women's jihadist magazine online was *al-Khansaʾ*, the famous female Arab poet who embraced Islam at the time of the Prophet Muḥammad, and all four of whose sons were killed in the battle of Qādisīyah. *Al-Khansaʾ* exhorts women to fight against the enemies of Islam. What kind of role is assigned to women? "There are many ways a Muslim woman can participate in jihad. . . . The sisters' role on the battlefield is: 1.

Participation in the actual fighting; 2. Supporting the fighters in the battlefield; 3. Undertaking guard duty and protection" (*al-Khansaa*, 2004).

In general, even before the Arab Spring, jihadist action in the West had receded, and in the Muslim world it was mainly reduced to a few zones, namely Iraq, Afghanistan, and Pakistan. The Arab Spring showed the capacity of the Muslims to promote change without recourse to violence and ideologically pushed the radical Islamists onto the defensive.

[*See also* Arab Spring; Jihad; Martyrdom; Terrorism; *and* Warriors, *subentry on* Contemporary Women.]

BIBLIOGRAPHY

Ali, Farhana. "Ready to Detonate: The Diverse Profiles of Female Bombers." *The MIPT Terrorism Annual.* Tel Aviv: Jaffee Center for Strategic Studies, Tel Aviv University, 2006.

Al-Uyayri, Yusuf bin Saleh. "Dowr al nisā' fi jihād al a' da" (The Role of the Woman in the Jihad against the Enemies). *Minbar al-tawḥīd wal-jihād*, before 2003.

Cook, David. *Martyrdom in Islam.* New York: Cambridge University Press, 2007.

al-Khansaa. Online women's magazine launched by a Saudi branch of al-Qaʿida. 2004, closed down (the French server that hosted its inaugural issue removed it in August 2004 from its site).

Khosrokhavar, Farhad. *Inside Jihadism: Understanding Jihādī Movements Worldwide.* Boulder, Colo.: Paradigm Publishers, 2009.

Khosrokhavar, Farhad. *L'islamisme et la mort: Le martyre révolutionnaire en Iran.* Paris: Harmattan, 1995.

Schweitzer, Yoram, ed. *Female Suicide Bombers: Dying for Equality?* JCSS Memorandum 84. Tel Aviv: Jaffee Center for Strategic Studies, Tel Aviv University, 2006.

FARHAD KHOSROKHAVAR

ṢULAYḤIDS. The name of an Ismāʿīlī Shīʿī dynasty that ruled over various parts of Yemen from 1047 to around 1138 CE. Until 1132, the Ṣulayḥids recognized the sovereignty of the Fāṭimids. It was also through the Ṣulayḥids that Fāṭimid sovereignty was extended to other parts of Arabia, such as Oman and Bahrain.

After its initial rapid success in Yemen, in the second half of the ninth century, the Ismāʿīlī *daʿwah* or mission had subsequently remained active in that part of southern Arabia only in dormant form. In the course of the tenth century, the *daʿwah* received the secret allegiance of several Yemeni tribes, notably some clans of the influential Banū Hamdān. At the time Yemen was ruled by several independent dynasties, such as the Yuʿfirids and Najāḥids, while the Zaydī Shīʿī imams held Ṣaʿda in northern Yemen. By the beginning of the eleventh century, the chief Ismāʿīlī *dāʿī* in Yemen was Sulaymān b. ʿAbd Allāh al-Zawāḥī who operated from the mountainous region of Ḥarāz, southwest of Ṣanʿāʾ. Sulaymān chose as his successor ʿAlī b. Muḥammad who hailed from the Ṣulayḥī clan of the Yām branch of Banū Hamdān. In fact, the *dāʿī* Sulaymān himself had converted ʿAlī b. Muḥammad al-Ṣulayḥī, son of the Shāfiʿī *qāḍī* of Ḥarāz, to Ismailism; and subsequently, ʿAlī served as the *dāʿī*'s assistant.

An important Hamdānī chief who led pilgrim caravans to Mecca, ʿAlī b. Muḥammad rose in revolt in 1047 in the Jabal Masār, a locality in Ḥarāz and seized Ṣanʿāʾ from the Yuʿfirids, marking the beginning of Ṣulayḥid rule in Yemen. Receiving military support from various Hamdānī, Ḥimyarī, and other local tribes, ʿAlī now embarked on a campaign of conquest in Yemen, everywhere instituting the *khuṭbah* in the name of al-Mustanṣir, the reigning Fāṭimid caliph-imam. In 1060 ʿAlī seized Zabīd by killing its ruler, al-Najāḥ, founder of the Najāḥid dynasty who had earlier incited the Zaydīs of Ṣaʿda against the Ṣulayḥids. He subsequently expelled the Zaydīs from Ṣanʿāʾ, which now became the Ṣulayḥid capital. By 1063 ʿAlī had conquered all of Yemen, including Adan, though the Banū Maʿn were permitted to remain there for some time as rulers and tributaries of the Ṣulayḥids.

In 1062 ʿAlī al-Ṣulayḥī sent Lamak b. Mālik al-Ḥammādī, the chief *qāḍī* of Yemen, to Cairo to discuss his own future visit to the Fāṭimid capital, an event that did not occur. Lamak spent some five years at the Dār al-ʿIlm in Cairo with the chief Fāṭimid *dāʿī*, al-Muʾayyad fi'l-Dīn al-Shīrāzī (d. 1078), who furthered Lamak's Ismāʿīlī education. The Egyptian mission of Lamak, who upon returning to Yemen in 1067 became the head of the Ismāʿīlī *daʿwah* there, served to bring Ṣulayḥid Yemen closer to the Fāṭimid regime and the central headquarters of the *daʿwah* in Cairo.

In 1067 ʿAlī b. Muḥammad al-Ṣulayḥī set out on pilgrimage to Mecca, evidently on his way to Cairo, when he together with some relatives were murdered by the sons of al-Najāḥ, in revenge for their slain father. ʿAlī's wife Asmāʾ bint Shihāb was taken by the Najāḥids to Zabīd where she was held captive for a year. Educated, like many other Ṣulayḥid women, Asmāʾ enjoyed much influence at the Ṣulayḥid court, also acting as an advisor to her husband. ʿAlī al-Ṣulayḥī was succeeded by his son al-Mukarram Aḥmad (r. 1067–1084) who, in 1068, succeeded in rescuing his mother, Asmāʾ, in a battle that was to result in his paralysis. The same year al-Mukarram regained some of the territories seized earlier by the Najāḥids. Confusion in some sources notwithstanding, it was also in 1068 that the second Ṣulayḥid ruler conferred ʿAdan's governorship on two Hamdānī brothers, ʿAbbās and Mas ʿūd b. al-Karam, who founded the Ismāʿīlī dynasty of the Zurayʿids of southern Yemen.

In the earlier years of his reign, al-Mukarram's mother Asmāʾ continued to play an active role in the affairs of the Ṣulayḥid state until her death in 1074. The same year al-Mukarram retired to Dhū Jibla in central Yemen, relegating effective authority in the Ṣulayḥid state to his consort al-Sayyida Arwā bint Aḥmad al-Ṣulayḥī, who had been brought up by Asmāʾ. Known also as al-Malika al-Sayyida and al-Sayyida al-Ḥurra, she was a capable queen and a most remarkable personality. One of her first acts was to relocate the Ṣulayḥid capital from Ṣanʿāʾ to Dhū Jibla, where she built a new palace and transformed the old one into a mosque, at which Queen Arwā's tomb is still preserved.

After al-Mukarram Aḥmad's death in 1084, his and Arwā's son ʿAlī (known as al-Mukarram al-Aṣghar) and then other Ṣulayḥids ruled nominally, but Queen Arwā continued to exercise real authority in the Ṣulayḥid state. She was particularly concerned with the affairs of the Ismāʿīlī *daʿwah* and it was shortly after her husband's death that the Fāṭimid caliph-imam al-Mustanṣir appointed her the *ḥujja* of Yemen, the highest rank in the *daʿwah* hierarchy of any region. In that capacity, the Ṣulayḥid queen was also made responsible for extending *daʿwah* activities to Gujarat, in western India. The Ismāʿīlī community founded in India by Arab *dāʿīs* dispatched from Ṣulayḥid Yemen evolved into the modern-day Ṭayyibī Bohra community of South Asia.

In the Nizārī-Mustaʿlī succession dispute following the death of al-Mustanṣir in 1094, Queen Arwā upheld al-Mustaʿlī's succession rights and maintained the Ṣulayḥids' close relations with the Fāṭimid regime. Meanwhile, Lamak b. Mālik al-Ḥammādī had continued to operate as the head of the Yemeni *daʿwah*, under Arwā's supreme leadership; on Lamak's death around 1098, his son Yaḥyā assumed control of the Ismāʿīlī *daʿwah* in Yemen. However, subsequently during the reign of Fāṭimid al-Mustaʿlī's son and successor al-Āmir (r. 1101–1130), relations deteriorated between Queen Arwā and the Fāṭimid establishment. As a result, in the Ṭayyibī-Ḥāfiẓī schism, following al-Ḥāfiẓ's successful claim to the Fāṭimid caliphate and Mustaʿlian Ismāʿīlī imamate in 1132, Queen Arwā severed her relations completely with the Fāṭimids in Egypt.

The Yemeni *daʿwah*, in line with Arwā's position, refused to recognize al-Ḥāfiẓ and the later Fāṭimid caliphs as imams. Queen Arwā, in fact, recognized al-Āmir's infant son al-Ṭayyib as the next imam. By this decision, the Ṣulayḥid queen had, in fact, founded the Ṭayyibī Mustaʿlian *daʿwah* independently of the Fāṭimid regime. It is the belief of the Ṭayyibīs, the only surviving Mustaʿlian Ismāʿīlī community, that al-Ṭayyib and all the subsequent successors to the imamate have continued to remain in concealment. In the absence of a manifest imam, the Ṭayyibī *daʿwah* and community are led by a *dāʿī muṭlaq*, or supreme *dāʿī*, the first of whom (al-Dhuʾayb b. Mūsā) was appointed in 1132 by Queen Arwā.

Until her death in 1138 at age ninety-two, Queen Arwā made every effort to consolidate the Ṭayyibī *daʿwah* while the Ṣulayḥid state was gradually disintegrating under pressure from several local dynasties, including the Ḥāfiẓī Ismāʿīlī Zurayʿids of ʿAdan. In her will she also bequeathed her famous collection of jewelry to the Ṭayyibī *daʿwah*. Queen Arwā's death marked the effective end of the Ṣulayḥid dynasty. Subsequently, a few minor Ṣulayḥids held control of several isolated fortresses until the 1170s, when the Zurayʿids seized the remaining Ṣulayḥid outposts. Following the downfall of the Fāṭimid dynasty in 1171, the Sunnī Ayyūbids extended their hegemony from Egypt to Yemen in 1173, but Ṭayyibī Ismailism survived in Yemen, as it had been made independent of both the Fāṭimid and Ṣulayḥid regimes by the insightful Queen Arwā.

BIBLIOGRAPHY

Daftary, Farhad. *The Ismāʿīlīs: Their History and Doctrines*. 2d ed. Cambridge, U.K., and New York: Cambridge University Press, 2007.

Daftary, Farhad. "Sayyida Ḥurra: The Ismāʿīlī Ṣulayḥid Queen of Yemen." In *Women in the Medieval Islamic World*, edited by Gavin R. G. Hambly, pp. 117–130. New York: St. Martin's Press, 1998.

Hamdānī, Ḥusayn F. al-. *al-Ṣulayḥiyyūn waʾl-ḥaraka al-Fāṭimiyya fiʾl-Yaman*. Cairo, Egypt: Maktabat Miṣr, 1955.

Idrīs ʿImād al-Dīn b. al-Ḥasan. *The Fatimids and Their Successors in Yaman*. Vol. 7: *ʿUyūn al-akhbār*. Edited by Ayman F. Sayyid, with summary English translation by P. E. Walker and M. A. Pomerantz. London: I.B. Tauris, 2002.

Imad, Leila S. al-. "Women and Religion in the Fatimid Caliphate: The Case of al-Sayyidah al-Hurrah, Queen of Yemen." In *Intellectual Studies on Islam: Essays Written in Honor of Martin B. Dickson*, edited by Michel M. Mazzaoui and Vera B. Moreen, pp. 137–144. Salt Lake City: University of Utah Press, 1990.

Lowick, Nicholas M. "Some Unpublished Dinars of the Ṣulayḥids and Zurayʿids." *Numismatic Chronicle*, 7th ser., 4 (1964): 261–270. Reprinted in Lowick's *Coinage and History of the Islamic World*, edited by J. Cribb, article 3 Aldershot, U.K.: Variorum, 1990.

ʿUmāra b. ʿAlī al-Ḥakamī, Abū Ḥamza. *Taʾrīkh al-Yaman*. In *Yaman: Its Early Mediaeval History*, edited and translated by Henry C. Kay, text pp. 1–102, translation pp. 1–137. London: Edward Arnold, 1892.

FARHAD DAFTARY

SUNNĪ ISLAM AND WOMEN.

[*This entry contains two subentries,*

Historical Overview *and*

Contemporary Thought and Practice.]

HISTORICAL OVERVIEW

This entry on women in Sunnī Islam discusses the impact of Islam on women through history, their participation in Islam, and their role in the religion of Islam and society. In general, the roles of women, who have contributed significantly to their cultures as well as to their religion, remain ignored in history or are only minimally represented. One explanation is that the stories of women have disappeared because of the predominance of the male perspective, as mostly male historians were writing. *His*tory therefore, tells us in the first place the activities and achievements of men. Closer examination of various sources, however, reveals hidden layers of female contributions and influences through the ages. It is these contributions and influences that have become more and more visible during the latest decades. Regarding Islam specifically, there is also a growing interest in the contribution and role of women in the history of Islam. The complexity of the position of women and of their relation to Islam is determined by two elements: the Islamic texts and the history of Muslim societies and cultures. Before dealing concisely with the history of women in relation to Islam, a few critical comments about these two elements are necessary.

Critical Comments. The interest in the history of women in Islam accelerated in the second half of the twentieth century, as a result of the women's movements in the 1960s and 1970s, called the second wave of feminism, the growing interest in social history, and the publication of Edward Said's *Orientalism*. As a branch of history, social history was a major growth field in the 1960s and 1970s. It includes the history of ordinary people and their strategies for coping with life. This approach opened a space in history for formerly marginalized individuals and groups, such as peasants, workers, and women. The history of women quickly grew into a specific field. Said criticized the Orientalist approach, which was based on a dichotomous representation of the so-called inferior Eastern societies as opposed to the superior European societies. The Orientalist epistemology resulted from the inadequate methodology Orientalists use, which Said regarded as outdated. Through the study of key texts, especially written sources such as the Qurʾān, *aḥādīth*, commentaries on the sacred texts, treatises on religion, and jurisprudence, Orientalists imagined they knew Islamic societies, through time as well as space. The knowledge about the Orient that emerges from this approach resulted in the presentation of Islam, both as a religion and as a culture, as monolithic and unwilling to change. On the Muslim side, on the other hand, modernists like Muḥammad ʿAbduh, Jamāl al-Dīn al-Afghānī, and Muhammad Iqbal have been arguing since the nineteenth century in favor of a reinterpretation of Islam in response to the new challenges with which Muslim communities were confronted. They argued that Islam is a dynamic and progressive religion—a religion that is able to effect change. The gap that arose between the sacred text and its application in daily life made clear the dialectical nature of the relationship between scripture and the social context of the community. This is why attitudes concerning women in Islam, as in other religious traditions and societies, vary throughout time and continue to shift in modern times.

Studying women in Islam and Muslim societies reflects the multifarious realities of Muslim women and Muslim societies. This is why the position of women should always be studied in relation to the context. What is more, such a study cannot be performed from one single point of view. In her description of the diverse contexts in which Muslim women are living, Kandiyoti (1991) emphasizes that the positions of Muslim women can "neither be examined from a purely Islamic ideology or praxis, nor from a global process of Islamic or socio-economic transformation, and nor from a universalistic idea of feminist theories" (p. 2). A unilateral approach as a purely abstract analysis of women in Islam according to the ideals embodied in the Qurʾān and *aḥādīth* would ignore the interaction of the Islamic faith with different cultures, as well as the influence thereof. In addition, it should not be forgotten that the (local) interpretation of Islam was, and still is, the interpretation of the dominant group in society and that the first interpreters were men from these cultures. As a result, more important than the actual representation of women and the feminine symbolism in the sacred books are the interpretations of these performances within the respective traditions.

Historical Overview. Throughout Islamic history, the constructs, institutions, and modes of thought devised by early Muslim societies form the core discourses of Islam that have played a central role in defining women's place in Muslim societies. In her work *Women and Gender in Islam* (1992), Leila Ahmed involves the broader context of the Near East when she explains the impact of the context and its relevance to Islam. She refers to the impact of ethnic and religious groups other than the Muslims in the region (such as Mesopotamia, Greece, Egypt, and Iran) and their contributions to what is considered Islam or Islamic. Other scholars believe that the Islamic system of jurisprudence has evolved naturally without outside interference.

The question of whether and how Islam has affected the position and status of women in pre- and early Islamic Arabia and the Middle East is complicated, because of the very limited sources and other materials about women. The literary sources about the early history of Islam are poetry, the narratives of the *ayyām al-ʿarab*, Qurʾānic materials, and early Muslim literature (*sīrah*, *tafsīr*, *ḥadīth*, and biographical dictionaries). Many of these materials, however, contain clear evidence of later-added ideological, theological, and political content, which reduce their historical reliability. It complicates the use of these sources to explore the impact of Islam on women, on their participation in Islam, and on the tribal society of that time. It can be said that the sources concerning the position of women in the early history of Islam are used by scholars in different ways, with varying degrees of critical distance and sophistication in methodology. Common subjects in these studies are property and inheritance rights for women, marriage and divorce, polygyny, female honor, and female infanticide. Depending on the criticism and methodology, different results are noticeable: when one uses contrastive readings between time periods, scholars can argue that the coming of Islam had a positive impact on women's lives, while other scholars state that Islam negatively affected the position of women in Arabia and in the Islamic world in general. Questions about the method of contrastive readings of time periods to assess Islam's impact on the position of women in Arabia, and later the Islamic world, continue to occupy scholarly critical discourse.

Another distinctive approach among scholars exploring the impact of Islam on women during the transition from the pre-Islamic period to the period of early Islam is an analysis by means of fault lines. Several researchers address the position of women by tracing continuities or discontinuities. For example, Jane Smith (1985) indicates how the attempts to portray the condition of women in pre-Islamic Arabia as bad, in order to emphasize subsequent Islamic improvements, are overly naive. She explains how the Qurʾān helped to improve women's legal capability regarding family relations as compared to the situation immediately preceding Islam, but also stresses how Islam, as a religious and cultural system, limited women's opportunities to participate fully in society.

According to Karmi (1996), the stark disparity between pre-Islamic and Islamic realities as presented in some historical sources proves how a radical alteration of the social structures and gender roles by Islam does primarily have a theological function, and is not necessarily a historical claim. In this sense, several scholars assert that the Qurʾān outlines gender equality and argue that the first generations of Muslims watered down the Islamic revelation's commitment to women when coming into contact with already established civilizations. These transformations in the attitude of men toward women after the death of the Prophet Muḥammad make scholars less divided regarding the further development of women's position, as compared to the early period of Islam. More and more studies are showing how women had rights in the early period of Islam that were later taken from them. It became more or less a consensus among scholars that the status of women, as evidenced by post-Muḥammadan practices and jurisprudential injunctions, declined as a result of highly patriarchal sociosexual norms and practices already ingrained in Arabian social structures or in newly conquered territories.

However, traces of women in this period of history have been found, especially in biographical dictionaries, which are the richest sources for the history of women. Biographical dictionaries were used by the *ʿulamāʾ* to immortalize themselves. They contain a detailed picture of intellectual life and important material for social and economic history. Regarding the history of women, two groups of women about whom there is a critical mass of information can be discerned: the women of Mecca and Medina of the first Islamic century, on the one hand, and, on the other hand, the notable women of Egypt, Syria, and Arabia in the later Middle Ages (the fourteenth to fifteenth centuries). The first group of women entered literature because of their proximity to the Prophet, as witnesses who related *ḥadīth*. The meaning of the biographical dictionaries was twofold: not only the facts regarding the represented subject were important, but also the way these facts were represented. Such representation happens in a way that fits subjects, men and women, into certain "ideal types" of personality to which Islamic culture attributed value. Historical female figures who became ideal types are Khadījah, ʿĀʾisha, and Fāṭimah. Several authors indicate how ʿĀʾisha's life, in particular, became a role model for the lives of Sunnī Muslim women. Throughout the medieval period, Muslim scholars based the appearance of real women upon female archetypes found in the Qurʾān. The second group of women is accounted for in biographies of approximately 1,300 women of the fourteenth and fifteenth centuries. Their biographies are written by their contemporary Ibn Ḥajar (*al-Durar al-kāminah* [Hidden Pearls]) and his student al-Sakhāwī (*al-Ḍawʾ al-lāmiʿ* [Brilliant Light]). These dictionaries tell about the notables of the fourteenth and fifteenth centuries, mostly *ʿulamāʾ*, but also about the high-ranking officials of the Mamlūk establishment in cities such as Cairo, Damascus, Jerusalem, Mecca, and Medina. In his final volume (out of twelve), al-Sakhāwī addressed the women of the same families and classes, including concubines and women who were merchants, poets, midwives, and entertainers. Some women were famous for their transmission of Islamic learning or for their skill at calligraphy. These biographical dictionaries deliver the information required to understand the role late-medieval women played in Muslim learning. They contain evidence of women's involvement in economic life, property, and religious endowments. The analysis of the often detailed personal information in al-Sakhāwī's biographies gives information about, for example, the occurrence of marriage, divorce, remarriage, and polygamy.

Despite these traces of (religious) active women, history shows how the religious role and practice of women in society, and particularly regarding Islam, became more and more restricted. An increasing number of reasons were found by (male) religious scholars: "from moral degeneration in society to woman's tendency to be a source of temptation and social discord" (Esposito, 1998, p. xiii). The fact that the sources that lie at the basis of Islam have been interpreted mainly by men contributes legitimacy to this as well (p. ix). Religious orthodoxy in Islam fell into the hands of men. They are responsible for the religious context in which women move. Yet the image of seclusion of women given in medieval literature (such as *fiqh*) is more representative of how it was thought women should live than an actual representation of women's real lives. This becomes even more clear when comparing the observation of Shaykh Muḥammad al-Ghazālī in the mid-twentieth century that "ninety percent of the veiled women do not pray at all; nor do they know of the other duties of Islam more than their names" (Esposito, 1998, p. xiii) with Leila Ahmed's comment that women always have had "their understanding of Islam," which was "an understanding that was different from men's Islam, 'official' Islam" (Ahmed, 1999, p. 120).

Modern Trends. However, the normative view of Muslim women gained the upper hand, both for Muslims and for non-Muslims. The women issue became a central stumbling block in the debates about modernizing reforms in Islamic societies during the nineteenth and twentieth centuries. From that period onward, governments, intellectuals, and religious leaders have attempted to face the challenges set by European colonialism and the impact of the "modern" West. The lives of women throughout most of the nineteenth century remained the same as in the eighteenth. Depending on each particular country, women experienced only small changes brought about by the reforms by the nation-states. New state laws and reforms have undoubtedly given women greater access to public services (e.g., in education and health), political rights, and relative job equality. Yet although the intent might be equality, in practice, women mainly experienced worsening gender relations. After all, many of the assumptions of modern scholars—including *fuqahā'*—regarding the (historical) position of Muslim women were (and still are) not founded on reality. These assumptions hold their influence from the way the Qurʾān—like other scriptures—was used to build hegemonic patriarchal discourses. Beliefs about the seclusion of women, women's private work at home, veiling, men's responsibility as moral guides to their wives, men's right to divorce women at will while women's access to divorce is restricted, and polygyny, are all central subjects in these discourses. Since the 1960s and 1970s, scholars have more and more accepted that these discourses are constructed and have gained a life of their own, enforcing a reality that has little to do with the original message and laws they supposedly represent. Slowly, attention is shifting to the contention that women are not simply objects, but that they actually are subjects and active agents of both Islamic and secular modernizing schemes. Indeed, Muslim women frequently disrupt the Islamic/modern or religious/secular dichotomy, in order to act in their own interests.

Many Muslim women themselves have already gone beyond simply asking questions about their religion: they seek for themselves an Islam applicable to their life context. There is a growing number of studies about the role of women as derived from a rereading of the Qurʾānic text or a new consideration of the *ḥadīth* literature, and about the contribution of women in the interpretive legacy of Islamic exegesis of texts. They gradually make the traditionalists' views on what real Islam is evolve and change. These studies challenge the patriarchal order and the "orthodox" Sunnī readings of the Qurʾānic text and *ḥadīth* literature, by demonstrating how, not the texts themselves, but the interpretations thereof, have allowed patriarchal traditions to persist.

[*See also* Ahmed, Leila; Feminism; Ḥadīth; Islam and Women; Islamic Biographical Collections, Women in; Orientalism; Qurʾān; Shīʿī Islam and Women, *subentry on* Historical Overview; Sufism and Women, *subentry on* Historical Overview; Women and Islam; *and* Women's Rights.]

BIBLIOGRAPHY

Abbott, Nabia. *ʿĀʾishah, the Beloved of Mohammed.* Chicago: University of Chicago Press, 1946.

Abbott, Nabia. "Women and the State in Early Islam." *Journal of Near Eastern Studies* 1, no. 1 (1942): 106–126.

Ahmed, Leila. *A Border Passage: From Cairo to America—A Woman's Journey.* New York: Penguin Books, 1999.

Barazangi, Nimat H. *Woman's Identity and the Qurʾān: A New Reading.* Gainesville: University Press of Florida, 2004.

Barlas, Asma. *"Believing Women" in Islam: Unreading Patriarchal Interpretations of the Qurʾān.* Austin: University of Texas Press, 2002.

Esposito, John L. "Introduction: Women in Islam and Muslim Societies." In *Islam, Gender, and Social Change*, edited by Yvonne Y. Haddad and John L. Esposito, pp. ix–xxviii. New York: Oxford University Press, 1998.

Kandiyoti, Deniz, ed. *Women, Islam, and the State.* London: Macmillan, 1991.

Karmi, Ghada. "Women, Islam, and Patriarchalism." In *Feminism and Islam: Legal and Literary Perspectives*, edited by Mai Yamani, pp. 69–85. New York: New York University Press, 1996.

Said, Edward W. *Orientalism.* New York: Pantheon Books, 1978.

Smith, Jane. "Women, Religion, and Social Change in Early Islam." In *Women, Religion, and Social Change*, edited by Yvonne Y. Haddad and Ellison Findley, pp. 19–35. Albany: State University of New York Press, 1985.

Sonbol, Amira E. "Rethinking Women and Islam." In *Daughters of Abraham: Feminist Thought in Judaism, Christianity, and Islam*, edited by Yvonne Y. Haddad and John L. Esposito, pp. 108–146. Gainesville: University Press of Florida, 2001.

Spellberg, Denise A. "Political Action and Public Example: ʿĀʾishah and the Battle of the Camel." In *Women in Middle Eastern History: Shifting Boundaries in Sex and Gender*, edited by Nikkie R. Keddie and Beth Baron, pp. 45–57. New Haven, Conn.: Yale University Press, 1991.

Stowasser, Barbara F. "The Status of Women in Early Islam." In *Muslim Women*, edited by Freda Hussain, pp. 11–43. London: Croom Helm, 1984.

Stowasser, Barbara F. *Women in the Qurʾān, Traditions, and Interpretation.* New York: Oxford University Press, 1994.

Wadūd, Āmina. *Qurʾān and Woman: Rereading the Sacred Text from a Woman's Perspective.* Kuala Lumpur: Penerbit Fajar Bakati Sdn. Bhd., 1992.

Wiebke, Walther. *Women in Islam from Medieval to Modern Times.* Translated by C. S. V. Salt. Rev. ed. Princeton, N.J.: Markus Wiener, 2006.

ELS VANDERWAEREN

CONTEMPORARY THOUGHT AND PRACTICE

Sunnī Islam is the majority religious opinion across the Islamic world (at least 85 percent of Muslims) and is spread across diverse national, ethnic, and denominational groups, including indigenous communities in South and Central Asia, the Middle East, Southeast Asia, Africa, Europe, and diaspora and convert communities in the West. In each of these regions, distinct sociocultural, economic, and political contexts influence discourses about Muslim women, their lives, and their social roles. For women, this is further complicated by constantly changing sociopolitical fabrics in each of these communities. It is difficult to elucidate all contemporary thought and practice within Sunnī Islam that is relevant to women, but it is important to give an overview that can lead to further literary and research-based explorations.

According to *The Oxford Dictionary of Islam*, Sunnī life is guided by four schools of legal thought: Ḥanafī, Mālikī, Shāfiʿī, and Ḥanbalī. Although Sunnī Islam comprises a variety of theological and legal schools, attitudes, and outlooks conditioned by historical setting, locale, and culture, Sunnīs around the world share some common points, including acceptance of the legitimacy of the first four successors of Muḥammad (Abū Bakr, ʿUmar, ʿUthmān, and ʿAlī). Although the distinction between Sunnī and Shīʿī Islam is easily achieved in theology and religious-studies disciplines, it is not always possible within contemporary women's studies to distinguish between the two sides of the Sunnī–Shīʿī dichotomy, except perhaps where specific denominational or regional indicators are available.

The Category "Muslim Women." With regard to contemporary Muslim women's issues, the Sunnī–Shīʿī divide seems to be superseded by Muslim women's similar struggles: (1) for their social, religious, and civic rights, (2) against patriarchy, and (3) against stereotypical views of "invisible" Muslim women who are assumed to be absent from sociopolitical endeavors. In their struggles against patriarchy, Muslim women also share common ground with women from other religious and non-religious backgrounds who, in many contexts, have similar life experiences.

Discussions about gender issues in the Muslim world are further complicated by heterogeneity within the category "Muslim woman." The simultaneous fetishization and oversimplification of this category perpetuates stereotypical imagery of Muslim women, usually as meek and subjugated, epitomized in contemporary contexts by media images of Afghani women. More recently, some stereotypes associate Muslim women with political Islam and less commonly with violent extremism. This category of "Muslim woman" and associated stereotypes are often incapable of acknowledging the rich ethnic, cultural, and social diversities among Muslim women and the variations in their belief and faith practice, including, but not limited to, denominational differences and socioeconomic class.

Muslim women, like Muslim men, practice Islam in many diverse ways. Some are more devout than others. John Bowen tries to differentiate between *croyant* and *pratiquant*, or "believing Muslims" and "practicing Muslims." According to Bowen, a *croyant* may fast and eat only *ḥalāl* meat, but does not regularly pray. *Pratiquants* regularly pray and *pratiquant* women normally wear hijab. He also adds that "designating someone as a *pratiquant* can carry with it tones of fanaticism" (2007, pp. 195) because of Western media imagery inscribed upon Islamic belief and practices. Bowen's *croyant/pratiquant*-distinction is a useful illustration of different ways of being Muslim, but a caveat must be added that both categories are ambiguous and exceedingly problematic to define. There are also multiple stances that are possible between and beyond these categories.

Some of the complexities discussed above are clearly refuted by Muslim women's visible participation in the Arab Spring or uprisings in Middle Eastern and North African Muslim states (2011–2012). Some commentators describe women's visibility in these uprisings as "uncharacteristic." Nevertheless, women's contributions to this Arab Spring are both indicative and symptomatic of the complexities within contemporary thinking and practice relevant to women in Sunnī Islam, including women's access to wider social roles and participation. News coverage of protests in Tahrir Square (which became the focus of protests in Egypt, which is majority Sunnī) depict *ḥijābī* and non-*ḥijābī* Muslim women participating in protests, in a united show of women's strength and agency. Women and men shared the same space in protests—supporting and being supported by each other—which is characteristic of some forms of Islamic feminism. Finally, denominational and sectarian differences were not always visible.

Moving beyond the more optimistic imagery indicated in coverage of the Arab Spring, recent sociopolitical statistics provide a macro picture of the challenges Muslim women continue to face. The 2005 World Economic Forum report indicates that countries with majority Muslim populations rank lowest in women's empowerment, which implies that women in these countries have the lowest levels of economic participation and opportunity, political empowerment, and educational attainment. The Sachar Report

(2006) commissioned by the government of India is a high-profile investigation into the status of Muslims in India (Indian Muslims are mostly Sunnī). Its findings show that Muslim women have much lower literacy levels compared to women from other religious backgrounds. This disparity in the educational achievements of Indian Muslim women influences their careers, health, lives, and futures. If we compare that with Muslim women's situation in the United Kingdom, for example, the 2006 *Social Trends* report indicates that Muslim women have the highest level of economic inactivity, at 69 percent compared to between 25 percent and 36 percent for women belonging to other faith groups or for those who have no religion. (Muslims in the United Kingdom come from diverse ethnic and denominational backgrounds. Although exact statistics are not available, immigration patterns and research indicate a majority Sunnī population.)

Muslim women thus lag behind their counterparts from other communities in education, as well as in the workplace. Such statistics indicate the predominance of patriarchal interpretations of religious doctrine in some Muslim communities, which often discourage women from participating in wider society. Some thinkers attribute this continuing patriarchy to legacies of colonialism and Muslim political responses to colonial rulers, which, in their zeal to protect women, often restricted their movements and rights.

Islamic Scholarship "by and for" Women. Muslim women are, however, challenging patriarchy on many fronts, as is evident in the resurgence of activism and scholarship led by them. This genre of female Muslim scholarship, by interrogating patriarchal interpretations of Islam, establishes "women-friendly" arguments. Such scholarship extends to exegetical studies of Muslim religious scripture; pedagogies to empower Muslim women; explorations of religious and historical roles of Muslim women; sociological studies of Muslim women; Muslim women geographies; and the feminisms of Muslim women. This resurgence of scholarship by and for Muslim women includes male scholars and also scholars who are not Muslim. Such scholarship includes Sunnī and Shīʿī scholars and affects all Muslim women.

There is another brand of scholarship: Muslim women graduating from Muslim seminaries as *ʿālimah*s or female scholars, who are influencing faith practice in local communities and beyond. This genre of scholarship may seem more traditional and orthodox in outlook; nevertheless, by informing Muslim women of their rights, they give them agency. The work of the following three scholars is indicative of the diverse nature and potential of such female scholarship: Dr. Farhat Hashimi, a Pakistani Sunnī scholar who practices strict veiling, has used Internet resources and local knowledge to establish international networks of women who gather on a weekly basis to study Islam and the Qurʾān; Shaikha Halima Krausen, a convert to Islam and scholar who leads her mosque community in Hamburg, Germany, regularly runs courses on Islamic thought and interfaith dialogue; Houda al-Habash runs an Islamic school for girls in Syria that inspires them to progress into education and professions. These scholars and others are emerging as public figures in Muslim communities. A number of other traditionally trained female scholars work in their local communities without gaining wider recognition. These *ʿālimah*s undertake social work, interfaith activities, pastoral care, counseling, chaplaincy, and teaching in their local and religious communities.

There are, therefore, two aspects to scholarship that is "by and for" Muslim women. One genre is more academic and usually framed in Western epistemological thinking. The other is faith-based and is framed within classical Islamic sciences. In the past, these two strands developed independently of each other. Increasingly, the two genres are being bridged, usually by Muslim women who have an appreciation for and grasp of both types of thinking.

Activism by and for Muslim Women. Muslim women in many Sunnī contexts are challenging patriarchal interpretations of their faith and seek to garner rights and agency for themselves. Such activism is partly informed and inspired by Islamic religious scholarship and partly by their interactions with the wider pluralist world, made possible by increased educational and communication opportunities, including on the Internet. In Saudi Arabia, women's activism has been successful on some fronts: education, opening up of career pathways, and the first female Saudi athlete's participation in the 2012 London Olympics. On other fronts, their struggles continue—such as permission for women to drive. Pakistani and Indian women are articulating constructs of feminism that challenge Western secular constructs of women's liberation and also patriarchal constructs of Islam. These movements are distinctly Muslim, retain cultural characteristics of the women who articulate them, and involve both men and women.

In Malaysia, the work of the organization Sisters in Islam challenges discriminatory family laws and argues for greater social rights for women. Indonesian Muslim women activists draw inspiration from Islam for a variety of political reform projects. In Turkey, since the 1990s, religious Muslim women have begun to "reshape their identities and to demand participation instead of representation, and women who wore headscarves founded several organizations to participate in the political sphere and in the women's movements in Turkey" (Ozcetin, p. 111). In the West, women who promote "gender jihad" are creating an alternative discourse that subscribes neither to dogmatic traditionalist interpretations of Islam nor to secular liberal feminisms.

Islamic Feminisms. This leads to discussion about the feminisms of Muslim women and how they balance competing understandings of "femininity," "modesty," "modernity," "piety," and "agency," which are perceived differently by Muslim women, by their Muslim communities, and by wider pluralist settings (which some Muslim women inhabit and to which, in a globalized world, most Muslim women are connected). It is issues such as this difference between "being" and "perceiving" that influence Islamic feminist philosophies and their application to everyday situations. Islamic feminisms are usually grounded in the Islamic beliefs of these women and are underpinned by their sociocultural milieus. These feminisms are thus diverse and reflect global–local intersections of emancipatory feminist ideals; Islamic theological interpretations; national, ethnic, and cultural ontologies; and the individual Muslim woman.

According to Jeenah, "Islamic feminism is, first, an ideology that uses the Qurʾān and *sunnah* to provide the ideals for gender relationships, as well as weapons in the struggle to transform society so that gender equality is accepted as a principle around which society is structured. Secondly, it is the struggle of Muslim women and men for the emancipation of women based on this ideology" (2006, pp. 30). Islamic feminists insist that they are inspired by Islam and the women heroes of Islam who stood up for justice and human rights—that Islam is a force of empowerment, rather than of disempowerment.

This feminism seeks to challenge patriarchy and patriarchal understandings of faith, yet these "Islamic feminists" constantly achieve their goals and rights through partnerships with men. They also challenge stereotypical imagery of Muslim women and seek to replace this with images of Muslim women as contributing citizens in a pluralist world. Thus, this feminism is a dual struggle against vestiges of patriarchy in Muslim communities and against increasingly popular secular suspicions of visible religiosity.

However, Islamic feminism also remains a controversial and sensitive subject. Some Muslim women are suspicious of feminism. Others hold naïve views about feminist scholarship, associating it with practices that they consider incompatible with their faith or culture. A few embrace the label and the scholarship. In the end, what is common to many such women is that, although they avoid the label, many use feminist language and arguments. Instead of using the label "feminism," these women seem to prefer the tag "reclaiming faith." According to Al Farūqi, when it comes to feminism and Islam, there are no "pat answers" (1991, p. 23).

Hijab and Women in the Public Sphere. Muslim women's hijab is much debated in secular scholarship, in feminist literature, in Islamic theology, in Muslim communities, and within popular media. The nature of the debates varies from feminist arguments about the hijab's perceived "oppression" of women to the Muslim apologist's version that portrays the hijab as an emancipator of the women who wear it and as a hallmark of piety. Such over-signification of the hijab, evident both within Muslim communities and in multicultural society, distracts from other more important discussions that society needs to have about Muslim women. The media coverage and political discourse around the banning of burqas or face veils in France and Belgium is an example of this excessive focus on what Muslim women wear. By focusing on "hijab, the garment," such discourses usually fail to convey to readers the more nuanced meanings that "hijab, the concept" holds for the women who wear it, and who consider it to be a divinely ordained framework that defines guidelines for both male and female modesty. Also, existing literature surrounding the hijab often treats it as a homogeneous practice, failing to contextualize the multitude of cultural, regional, theological, linguistic, and individual understandings that influence the way it is practiced and worn.

Some scholars comment on the resurgence of the hijab and veiling practices, particularly among younger women in the West. This is sometimes associated with a rise in political Islam. Empirical work with Muslim women, however, indicates that their practice of hijab is part of their reclamation of religion from patriarchal interpretations of faith and their wearing of the hijab gives them religious authority and agency. Thus, particularly in Western pluralist contexts, the hijab becomes a feminist tool. It can also become a dialogical tool, signifying the wearer as an informed representative of her faith.

Summary. As discussed above, the hijab can potentially give its wearers a degree of authority within Muslim communities and in wider pluralist contexts. Further questions remain, however, about the extent and limits of Muslim women's authority in Sunnī Islam. This discussion has been politicized by sensationalism around the leading of mixed prayer congregations by the female American scholar Amina Wadud. These issues around authority constitute a serious discussion that many Muslim women and their communities are having. Women's leadership of mixed congregations remains a controversial area with which, according to empirical work, many Muslim women disagree. However, there are other areas of authority in scholarship, interpretation, and teaching, and in social, civil, political, and religious roles, that Muslim women are achieving for themselves. The significance, possibilities, and limitations of this emerging female leadership in Muslim communities needs to be recognized by the media and policy makers. There is also an urgent need to celebrate the contributions of such women leaders, to create role models for younger generations to emulate and be inspired by.

[*See also* Arab Spring; Education and Women, *subentry on* Contemporary Discourse; Feminism; Hijab; Islam and Women, *subentry on* Contemporary Debates; Political Activism, Women's; Religious Authority of Women; Shīʿī Islam and Women, *subentry on* Historical Overview; Sisters in Islam; Sufism and Women, *subentry on* Contemporary Thought and Practice; Veiling, *subentry on* Contemporary Discourse; Women and Islam; Women and Social Protest; Women and Social Reform; Women's Rights; *and* Workforce, Women in the, *subentry on* Contemporary Discourse.]

BIBLIOGRAPHY

Afshar, Haleh. "Muslim Women in West Yorkshire: Growing Up with Real and Imaginary Values amidst Conflicting Views of Self and Society." In *The Dynamics of "Race" and Gender: Some Feminist Interventions*, edited by Haleh Afshar and Mary Maynard, pp. 127–150. London: Taylor and Francis, 1994.

Afzal-Khan, F. "Betwixt and Between? Women, the Nation, and Islamization in Pakistan." *Social Identities* 13, no. 1 (January 2007): 19–29.

Ahmed, Leila. *Women and Gender in Islam: Historical Roots of a Modern Debate*. New Haven, Conn.: Yale University Press, 1992.

Al Farūqi, Lois Ibsen. *Women, Muslim Society, and Islam*. Indianapolis, Ind.: American Trust Publications, 1988.

Ali, Azra Ashgar. *The Emergence of Feminism among Indian Muslim Women, 1920–1947*. Oxford: Oxford University Press, 2000.

Alvi, Sajida, Homa Hoodfar, and Sheila McDonough, eds. *The Muslim Veil in North America: Issues and Debates*. Toronto: Women's Press, 2003.

Archer, B. "Family Law Reform and the Feminist Debate: Actually-Existing Islamic Feminism in the Maghreb and Malaysia." *Journal of International Women's Studies* 8, no. 4 (2007): 49–59.

Badran, M. "Between Muslim Women and the Muslimwoman." *Journal of Feminist Studies in Religion* 24, no. 1 (2008): 101–106.

Bakhtiar, Laleh, trans. *The Sublime Qurʾān*. Chicago: Kazi Publications, 2007.

Barazangi, Nimat Hafez. *Woman's Identity and the Qurʾān: A New Reading*. Gainesville: University Press of Florida, 2004.

Barlas, Asma. *"Believing Women" in Islam: Unreading Patriarchal Interpretations of the Qurʾān*. Austin: University of Texas Press, 2002.

Bewley, Aisha. *Islam: The Empowering of Women*. London: Ta-Ha, 1999.

Bewley, Aisha. *Muslim Women: A Biographical Dictionary*. London: Ta-Ha, 2004.

Bowen, John R. *Why the French Don't Like Headscarves: Islam, the State, and Public Space*. Princeton, N.J.: Princeton University Press, 2007.

Bullock, Katherine. *Rethinking Muslim Women and the Veil: Challenging Historical and Modern Stereotypes*. Herndon, Va.: International Institute of Islamic Thought, 2003.

Contractor, Sariya. "Marginalisation or an Opportunity for Dialogue: Exploring the Hijab as a Discursive Symbol of the Identity of Young Muslim Women." In *Islam and the Veil*, edited by Theodore Gabriel and Rabiha Hanan, pp. 129–141. New York and London: Continuum, 2011.

Contractor, Sariya. *Muslim Women in Britain: Demystifying the Muslimah*. London and New York: Routledge, 2012.

cooke, miriam. "Deploying the Muslimwoman." *Journal of Feminist Studies in Religion* 24, no. 1 (Spring 2008): 91–99.

cooke, miriam. *Women Claim Islam: Creating Islamic Feminism through Literature*. London: Routledge, 2001.

Engineer, Asghar Ali. *The Rights of Women in Islam*. London: C. Hurst, 1992.

Falah, Ghazi-Walid, and Caroline Nagel, eds. *Geographies of Muslim Women*. New York: Guilford Press, 2005.

Haddad, Yvonne Yazbeck, Jane I. Smith, and Kathleen M. Moore. *Muslim Women in America: The Challenge of Islamic Identity Today*. New York: Oxford University Press, 2006.

Hoodfar, Homa. "More than Clothing: Veiling as an Adaptive Strategy." In *The Muslim Veil in North America: Issues and Debates*, edited by Sajida Alvi, Homa Hoodfar, and Sheila McDonough, pp. 3–40. Toronto: Women's Press, 2003.

Jeenah, Na'eem. "The National Liberation Struggle and Islamic Feminisms in South Africa." *Women's Studies International Forum* 29 (2006), pp. 27–41.

Kahf, Mohja. *Western Representations of the Muslim Woman: From Termagant to Odalisque.* Austin: University of Texas Press, 1999.

Kalmbach, Hilary. "Introduction." In *Women, Leadership, and Mosques: Changes in Contemporary Islamic Authority,* edited by Masooda Bano and Hilary Kalmbach, pp. 1–30. Leiden: Brill, 2012.

Lopez-Claros, Augusto, and Saadia Zahidi. *Women's Empowerment: Measuring the Global Gender Gap.* Geneva: World Economic Forum, 2005.

Mahmood, Saba. *Politics of Piety: The Islamic Revival and the Feminist Object.*Princeton, N.J.: Princeton University Press, 2005.

Moghissi, Haideh. *Feminism and Islamic Fundamentalism: The Limits of Postmodern Analysis.* London: Zed, 1999.

Mukadam, Mohamed, Alison Scott-Baumann, Ashfaque Chowdhary, and Sariya Contractor. *The Training and Development of Muslim Faith Leaders: Current Practice and Future Possibilities.* London: Department for Communities and Local Government, 2010. http://www.communities.gov.uk/documents/communities/pdf/1734121.pdf.

Nadwi, Muhammad Akram. *Al-Muhaddithat: The Women Scholars in Islam.* Oxford: Interface Publications, 2007.

Ozcetin, H. "Breaking the Silence: The Religious Muslim Women's Movement in Turkey." *Journal of International Women's Studies* 11, no. 1 (2009): 106–119.

Rinaldo, Rachel. "Veiled Feminism: Islamic Religious Piety and the Women's Movement in Indonesia." Paper presented at the annual meeting of the American Sociological Association, Montreal Convention Center, Montreal, Quebec, Canada, August 11, 2006. http://www.allacademic.com/meta/p102538_index.html.

Sachar, R. *Social, Economic, and Educational Status of the Muslim Community of India: A Report.* New Delhi: Prime Minister's High Level Committee. 2006.

Scott-Baumann, Alison. "Unveiling Orientalism in Reverse." In *Islam and the Veil,* edited by Theodore Gabriel and Rabia Hanan, pp. 20–35. London: Continuum, 2011.

Shabanova. "Address to the Congress of the Peoples of the East, Baku, September 1920." Stenographic report. Translated by Brian Pierce; transcribed by Andy Blunden. New Park Publications, 1977. http://www.marxists.org/history/international/comintern/baku/index.htm.

Social Trends 36 (2006).
http://www.ons.gov.uk/ons/rel/social-trends-rd/social-trends/no--36--2006-edition/index.html.

Syed, A. "Why Here, Why Now? Young Muslim Women Wearing Hijab." *Muslim World* 95, no. 4 (October 2005): 515–530.

Tarlo, Emma. *Visibly Muslim: Fashion, Politics, and Faith.* Oxford: Berg, 2010.

Tohidi, N. "The Global-Local Intersection of Feminism in Muslim Societies: The Cases of Iran and Azerbaijan." *Social Research* 69, no. 3 (Fall 2002): 851–887.

Vyas, S. "Identity Experiences of Young Muslim American Women in the Post-9/11 Era." *Encounter: Education for Meaning and Social Justice* 21, no. 2 (2008): 15–19.

Wadūd, Āmina. *Qur'ān and Woman: Rereading the Sacred Text from a Woman's Perspective.* New York: Oxford University Press, 1999.

SARIYA CHERUVALLIL-CONTRACTOR

SURROGATE MOTHERHOOD. Surrogate motherhood is a voluntary process whereby a woman agrees to be impregnated by means of artificial insemination, carry the baby to term, and relinquish the baby to the couple or individual with whom she made the contractual agreement. The woman who agrees to undergo this type of pregnancy is thought of as a gestational surrogate. In the West, there are legal, ethical, and social complications surrounding surrogate pregnancy, which have so far been regulated by federal or state laws. For Muslim medical and religious authorities, surrogate motherhood presents a religious and legal quandary.

Surrogate pregnancy challenges the Qur'ānic and *sunnah* that see marriage and children as gifts from God. Marriage in Islam includes both monogamy and polygamy as the means to procreate. Qur'ān 16:72 states that "God has made for you mates (and companions) of your own nature, and made for you, out of them, sons and daughters and grandchildren, and provided for you sustenance of the best: will they then believe in vain things, and be ungrateful for God's favors." Similarly, 42:49–50 says, "To God belongs the dominion of the heavens and the earth. He creates what He wills [and plans]. He bestows [children] male or female according to His Will [and Plan]. Or He bestows both males and females and he leaves barren whom He will. For He is full of knowledge and power." Since marriage conveys the legitimacy of heredity, inheritance, and blood relation with the offspring, having a child should remain within the marriage. A *ḥadīth* narrated by Ibn Abī al-Dunyā forbids a husband to seed his sperm in a uterus other than his wife's.

Having children is of the utmost importance in Muslim cultures, especially for Muslim women. Their social status within the family and society is often defined by their ability to reproduce. Even though women are frequently blamed for their inability to reproduce, they are not encouraged to enter into surgery, or visit an obstetrician or gynecologist as often as men seek out medical assistance for their own health issues. Nevertheless, with medical advances and communication technologies, NGOs, and feminist associations in Muslim countries, more and more women are becoming aware of the possibility of treating infertility and their right to bear children, as science and medicine offer many ways to surpass the obstacles of nature, culture, and religion.

During the first decade of the twenty-first century, Muslim women's access to ARTs (Assisted Reproductive Technologies) increased. In the 1980s and 1990s, Muslim medical personnel confronted complex ethical questions surrounding the validity of courses of treatment—questions that Muslim jurists still struggle to address, sometimes offering creative solutions and sometimes postponing the debate. As early as 1980, authoritative *fatwā*s (religious decrees) issued by Egypt's famed al-Azhar University suggested that IVF (in vitro fertilization) and similar technologies are permissible as long as they do not involve any form of third-party donation (sperm, eggs, embryos, or uteruses). (Note that in 2000 the first uterus transplant from a live donor was attempted in Saudi Arabia, although the organ was removed three month later due to a blood clot.) In general, no third-party donation is allowed; surrogacy of any form falls under this legal opinion. In this regard, the al-Azhar Fatwā Committee of Egypt and Scholars Council of Indonesia issued a *fatwā* that permits the artificial insemination of a wife's ovum with her husband's sperm. Usually, the Muslim judicial logic behind the prohibition of a third-party donation derives from the fact that men do have the alternative of taking another wife (or additional wives) who might be fertile.

In Shiism, the situation is quite different. In the late 1990s, Ayatollah ʿAlī Khameneʾi issued a *fatwā* in which he stated that egg donation "is not in and itself legally forbidden," and that the egg donor and infertile mother must abide by religious codes regarding parenting. Thus, the child of the egg donor has the right to inherit from the gametes donor. As for the infertile woman who received the eggs, she is considered to be an adoptive mother. As for sperm donation, the child can only inherit from the sperm donor, since the infertile father is considered to be an adoptive father. In this vein, Shiism permits a polygamous or *mutʿah* wife as a surrogate (since she is considered to be a legal co-wife). Khameneʾi even went further and permitted surrogacy outside marriage. Again, the logic behind this fatwā is that *mutʿah* marriage (literally, "marriage of pleasure") permits a Shīʿī man to "marry" a Shīʿī women for a temporary period that varies from one hour to a lifetime, for an amount of money that the man must give to the woman who agrees to engage in *mutʿah* marriage. Thus, Shīʿī jurists have permitted egg donation because they have deduced that, if Shīʿī men and women can "marry" for a temporary period and "divorce" whenever they want, the same principle can be applied to third-party egg donation and to gestational surrogacy as well.

This begs the question of why Shīʿī jurists have permitted egg donation and surrogacy (even outside marriage) based on the principle of *mutʿah* marriage, whereas Sunnī jurists banned it under the pretext of polygamy, which in fact functions like, and is the structural equivalent of, *mutʿah* marriage in Shiism. Meanwhile, Khameneʾi's *fatwā* seems to have had some effect on not only Iranians, but also Shīʿī minorities in Lebanon. Since the 1990s, sperm and egg donation have become accepted practice in Lebanon, whereas, in Sunnī countries, the dominant trends have been the prohibition of surrogacy, the outlawing of any kind of surrogacy contract with a third party, and no adoption.

The al-Azhar Fatwā Committee of Egypt (Majlis al-Buhuth al-Islamiyyah) prohibits all forms of surrogacy, including gestational surrogacy, whereas the Islamic Fiqh Council initially permitted the possibility of "polygynous gestational surrogacy—that is, the transfer of the fertilized egg of a man and his wife to the uterus of the second wife of the same husband" (Inhorn, 2003). Later, the Council changed its *fatwā* to resemble that of al-Azhar. Any form of surrogacy is prohibited because of the unlawful means of assisted reproduction. If the sperm belongs to a donor, the child becomes illegitimate, which is tantamount to the child's being the product of adultery. In this case, the child should be given the mother's surname. A child born of a surrogate mother could not inherit from its genetic father and adoptive mother unless the father had legally married the surrogate mother. In states permitting polygamy, he could theoretically do so. During the 1990s, changes occurred in Sunnī countries when some of the most conservative jurists [Members of the Sharīʿah Council of the Muslim World Association; President of the Council, Grand Muftī of Saudi Arabia ʿAbd al-ʿAzīz ibn ʿAbd Allāh ibn Bāz (d. 1999)] recognized the technological achievement of artificial insemination and test-tube babies.

In 2001 the same Majlis al-Buhuth al-Islamiyyah at al-Azhar University gathered at a Cairo summit and the same religious and legal perspective was maintained, although the Majlis emphasized the prohibition of any intervention on the part of a third party, for example, egg donation, surrogacy, and so on, regardless if the gestational surrogate mother is a total stranger or if she is the second wife or one of the wives of the man to whom the sperm belongs. It is also worth mentioning that during this summit, many delegates of the Majlis were supportive of two possibilities: (1) that a third-party gestational surrogate could be permitted because it solves the fertility problem of many families and helps them avoid divorce, on the condition that the action results from pure altruism and does not include any payment, thus avoiding any commercialization of the body and its parts; (2) that a third-party gestational surrogate could be the second wife of the man to whom the sperm belongs since polygamy is permitted in Islam. It seems probable that, in the future, a gestational surrogate arrangement conducted without payment may one day be seriously considered within Sunnī Islam.

It is tempting to conclude that of all the possibilities given the new reproductive technology, the only one that would be legal under Sunnī Islamic law is artificial insemination by the husband, and possibly in vitro fertilization where the fertilized ovum comes from the married couple. It seems, however, that Muslim jurists will have to eventually deal with changing morality and the way women think about their bodies in the wake of new technologies like ARTs. Muslim jurists cannot continue to ignore the existence of "reproductive tourism," and the fact that many Muslim women, especially those from the wealthier classes, can travel abroad to places like Eastern Europe and gain access to all kinds of ARTs, not to mention that Muslim women who live in Europe and North America have open access to ARTs without any official religious or moral restrictions. Palestinian Muslim women who are citizens of the state of Israel are however excluded from surrogacy, despite the fact that surrogacy is allowed by Israeli law. The Israeli surrogacy law ensures that only Jewish families can be created by this practice, since Islam prohibits surrogacy.

At the end of the day, the *fatwās* of Muslim jurists are valid only for poor Muslim women who cannot afford to circumvent religious, moral, and political obstacles. This creates an urgency for Muslim jurists to consider all men and women's desire to have offspring and become parents, regardless of whether or not they will be called "genetic parents" or "social parents."

BIBLIOGRAPHY

Afary Janet. *Sexual Politics in Modern Iran*. Cambridge, U.K.: Cambridge University Press, 2009.

Birenbaum-Carmeli, Daphna, and Yoram S. Carmeli. *Kin, Gene, Community: Reproductive Technologies Among Jewish Israelis*. Oxford and New York: Berghahn Books, 2010. See pp. 121–122.

Clarke, Morgan. "Children of the Revolution: ʿAli Khamene'i's 'Liberal' Views on *in vitro* Fertilization." *British Journal of Middle Eastern Studies* 34, no. 3 (2007): 287–303.

Ebrahim, Abul Fadl Mohsin. *Abortion, Birth Control and Surrogate Parenting: An Islamic Perspective*. Indianapolis: American Trust Publications, 1989. See p. 139.

Ghuwaybah, Samīr. *al-Mutājarah bi-al-umūmah wa-bayʿ al-iʿḍāʾ al-basharīyah*. Cairo: Madbūlī Ṣaghīr, 1999. See p. 85.

Gindi, A. R. al-, ed. *Human Reproduction in Islam*. Translated by A. Asbahi. Kuwait: Islamic Organization for Medical Sciences, 1989.

Haeri, Shahla. *Law of Desire: Temporary Marriage in Shīʿī Iran*. Syracuse, N.Y.: Syracuse University Press, 1989.

Hathout, Hasan. "Islamic Concepts and Bioethics." In *Bioethics Yearbook*, Vol. 1: *Theological Developments in Bioethics: 1988–1990*, edited by Baruch A. Brody, et al., Dordrecht, the Netherlands, and Boston: Kluwer, 1991.

Inhorn, Marcia C. "Globalization and Gametes: Reproductive 'Tourism' Islamic Bioethics, and Middle Eastern Modernity." *Anthropology & Medicine* 18, no. 1 (2011): 87.

Inhorn, Marcia C. *Local Babies, Global Science: Gender, Religion, and In Vitro Fertilization in Egypt*. London: Routledge, 2003. See p. 97.

Inhorn, Marcia C. "Making Muslim Babies: IVF and Gamete Donation in Sunni Versus Shiʿa Islam." *Culture, Medicine, and Psychiatry* 30 (2006): 427–450.

Mahmoud, Farouk. "Controversies in Islamic Evaluation of Assisted Reproductive Technologies." In *Islam and Assisted Reproductive Technologies: Sunni and Shia Perspectives*, edited by Marcia C. Inhorn and Soraya Tremayne, p. 82. Oxford: Berghahn Books, 2012.

Rasyid, M. Hamdan, ed. *Fiqh Indonesia: Himpunan Fatwā- Fatwā Actual* (Fiqh of Indonesia: A Collection of Contemporary Fatwās). Jakarta, Indonesia: Al-Mawardi Prima, 2003. See p. 206.

Sanbahlī, Muḥammad Burhān al-Dīn. *Qaḍāyā fiqhiyya muʿāṣira* (Contemporary medical issues). Beirut: Dār al-qalam, 2009. See p. 72.

SHERIFA ZUHUR
Updated by ETIN ANWAR
Updated by SAMIR BEN-LAYASHI

SUWEIDAN, TARIQ AL-. (b. 1953), Kuwaiti religious leader. Dr. Tariq Muḥammad Ṣāliḥ al-Suweidan is a Muslim televangelist, author, Islamic reformer, and leading member of the Muslim Brotherhood in Kuwait. He received a traditional Islamic education during his youth. After obtaining a BS in petroleum engineering from the Pennsylvania State University in 1975, he went on to study the same subject at the University of Tulsa where he obtained an MSc in 1982 and PhD in 1990. Al-Suweidan has advised or served on the executive boards of numerous organizations in the Arab world, the United States, and Malaysia. His executive experience spans a diverse range of disciplines, including petroleum engineering, financial investment, personal development, management, education, journalism, and public relations.

Al-Suweidan is general manager of the Arabic satellite television station Al-Resala, which specializes in Islamic programming. He has produced and hosted dozens of television and audio programs principally focused on empowering Arab Muslim youth. These programs include *Eternal Women* (*nisāʾ khālidāt*), a show narrating the biographies of great women from Islamic history; *Leadership in the Twenty-First Century* (*al-qiyādah fī al-qarn al-ḥādī wa al-ʿishrīn*); *Innovation in Childhood Education* (*al-ibdāʿ fī tarbiyat al-banīn*); and *Stories of the Prophets* (*qiṣaṣ al-anbiyāʾ*). Al-Suweidan has also authored over two dozen books in Arabic on Islamic history, including a four-volume work called *Constructing Culture* (*ṣināʿat al-thaqāfah*).

Al-Suweidan is known for his progressive views on gender equality and women's rights in Arab and Muslim societies. He explains that, according to Islamic law (*Sharīʿah*), women are equal to men in all spheres of life, including wages (*ajar*), social responsibilities (*masʾūlīyah*), and accountability before the law (*taklīf*). Thus, Islam encourages women to freely and fully participate in society. He cites as examples in this vein, the Prophet Muḥammad's wives ʿĀʾishah bint Abī Bakr (d. 678 CE) and Umm Salamah (d. CE 680). Al-Suweidan believes that women's freedom in Western societies comes with sexual exploitation. By contrast, he contends that Islam honors and protects women with modesty, recognizing their intelligence, hard work, and dignity. He adds that the treatment of women in Islam cannot be judged by the repression of their rights in Muslim societies in the early twenty-first century, but rather through careful study of Islam's long history. In 2005 Al-Suweidan argued during the television program *Doha Debates* that "Arab women should have full equality with men," and called for the implementation of laws protecting their inheritance and their right to marry out of choice. In 2007 he debated the feminist Iqbāl Barakah concerning the importance of the Islamic headscarf (hijab), arguing that it is not a custom (*ʿādah*) but rather an act of worship (*ʿibā dah*).

Al-Suweidan is one of the most influential Islamic preachers in the world. Much of his popularity results from his modern approach to Islamic tradition, his fluency in addressing Arabic as well as English audiences, and his media experience. He is known for his advocacy on behalf of Islam and the Arab world, calling for dialogue between Western and Muslim societies in the wake of the Danish cartoon controversy in 2005 and the Swiss ban on minarets in 2009. Al-Suweidan has also been an outspoken critic of dictatorships in the Arab world and a supporter of the popular revolutions that spread throughout the region in 2011.

BIBLIOGRAPHY

Sakr, Naomi. *Arab Television Today*. London: I.B. Tauris, 2007, pp. 152–155.

al-Suweidan, Tariq. "Qalam al-suwaydān." http://www.suwaidan.com/index.jsp?inc=25&lang=ar.

Emran El-Badawi

Syncretism. Syncretism is the phenomenon by which the practices and beliefs of one religion fuse with those of another to create a new and distinctive tradition. By the terms of this definition, all religions, and most certainly all those that have come to be known as world religions, can be regarded as syncretic in their origins, because each was shaped in dialogue with other faiths. In modern scholarship, however, the concept of syncretism is usually restricted to those religious syntheses that take shape after the initial consolidation of a widely recognized "religion"; syncretisms thus diverge from the parent religion's core or ideal expression. Equally important, however, even as they diverge from normative ideals, syncretisms in believers' eyes maintain a residual identification with the parent faith. The actual degree of identification varies widely, however, with the result that it is often difficult to distinguish syncretism from simple religious innovation. These analytic problems suggest that the concept of syncretism is closely linked to that of "normative" religion and to the standards of belief and practice whereby believers determine what is and what is not allowable within the faith.

As with all other world religions, Muslim understandings of the normative core of their religion have varied over time and place. This means that any effort to delineate that which is Islamic from that which is syncretistic inevitably raises delicate problems of value and judgment. This controversy has been a recurring source of debate in nineteenth-through twenty-first-century Islam, as standards as to what is and what is not properly Islamic have changed and are contested.

Although the varieties of Islamic syncretism vary widely, a common focus of many has been the religious standing of women. For centuries, Muslim women have been disproportionately represented in the ranks of healers, curers, and mediums, roles regarded with suspicion by some Muslim scholars. These phenomena are by no means archaic. Since the first decades of the nineteenth century, spirit cults like the so-called *zār* have spread across large portions of Muslim Africa and the Middle East.

Whatever its precedence in pre-Islamic religion, the *zār* cult has developed contemporaneously with the rise of modern Islamic reform. Most commonly, *zār* possession afflicts married women. Diagnosis of the affliction requires the services of a female curer (the *shaykhah*). Once afflicted by a *zār*, a woman can never fully sever the spirit relationship. At best, she is obliged to sponsor intermittent ceremonies in which the spirit is invoked and, speaking through the mouth of its female host, its wishes are voiced and then satisfied.

The spread of *zār* cults contemporaneous with Islamic reform has led many observers to see in them an assertion of feminine dignity and authority in the face of social trends that have greatly restricted women's public activities and excluded them from prestigious religious roles. Whatever their complex social psychology, the cults testify to the ability of Muslims to develop new forms of religious expression in the face of changing needs and social circumstances. This same dynamic has motivated the development of syncretic movements throughout Islamic history.

Bibliography

Boddy, Janice. *Wombs and Alien Spirits: Women, Men, and the Zar Cult in Northern Sudan*. Madison: University of Wisconsin Press, 1989. Rich ethnographic study of the *zār* and its implications for men's and women's divergent understanding of spirits, Islam, and gender.

Laderman, Carol. *Taming the Wind of Desire: Psychology, Medicine, and Aesthetics in Malay Shamanistic Performance*. Berkeley and Los Angeles: University of California Press, 1991. Beautifully evocative ethnography of a syncretistic shamanistic tradition in modern Malaysia.

Picard, Michel, and Remy Madinier, eds. *The Politics of Religion in Indonesia: Syncretism, Orthodoxy and Religious Contention in Java and Bali*. London and New York: Routledge, 2011.

Robert W. Hefner

Syria. The history of women in Syria is rich and complex. During the nineteenth century, under Ottoman rule (1516–1918), a nascent women's activism started to flourish in Syrian urban centers. The greater Syrian cultural renaissance of the nineteenth century created a favorable climate that allowed the discussion of women's conditions. Individual women, such as Maryana Marrash (1848–1919), made an impact through their writings and call for women's education. Marrash was the first to enter the field of journalism and is credited with opening the first Arab intellectual salon in Aleppo.

In general, women's activism at this time concerned itself with charity work, providing education and training for women, and teaching mothers how to care for their children hygienically. Some prominent members of the movement were politically active in the struggle against Ottoman rule, such as Mary Ajami (1888–1965), who was credited with publishing the first Arab women's magazine in 1910.

After World War I, under the French Mandate (1920–1946), women's charities became more politicized. Some worked for independence and others built girls' schools where instruction was provided in Arabic to counter French schools. The first Women's Union of Syria and Lebanon, formed in 1924, advocated Arab nationalism. By the 1930s, women's groups campaigned for suffrage rights, without success.

In the two decades following World War I, women generally suffered from conservative reactions to the advance of modernity, nationalists' political strategies and some of the nationalists' fascination with Nazi male chauvinism, and women's willingness to subordinate their demands to the "national struggle." The general public was simply hostile. In addition to these factors, France did not grant female suffrage until 1944, so it could hardly be expected to support such rights for Syrian women.

Venturing into public space was risky, as women faced direct attacks (sometimes with acid) in the streets if they did not conform to established norms for dress and behavior. Campaigns prevented women from going to cinemas. The significant women's press of the 1920s declined steeply. Almost all women's magazines stopped publishing. Newspapers rarely mentioned women. If they did, it was to publish complaints about the dangers of allowing women to venture outside of the home.

In 1949, three years after independence, educated women were given the right to vote, and in 1953 all Syrian women gained suffrage. Between 1949 and 1958, eight legislative councils were elected, and no women candidates won. It was only by appointment in 1960, when Syria joined Egypt in the United Arab Republic (1958–1961), that two female parliamentarians joined the two hundred members of Syria's National Council. Free elections only highlighted a voting pattern that discouraged women's political participation.

Syrian-Egyptian unification left its authoritarian mark on the Syrian political system (shaken by repeated military coups since independence). The reign of the Baʿthist Party in 1963 and the assumption of power by Hafez Al Assad (1930–2000) in 1970 turned this into a Stalinist dictatorship. Nascent Syrian civil society with its independent women's organizations was crushed.

Between 1963 and 2000, two women's organizations were allowed to work in Syria. The Syrian Women's League (SWL), created in 1947, was a branch of the Syrian Communist Party. It was considered too progressive and had little political weight. The Syrian General Women's Union (GWU) was established in 1967 as the sole representative of all women's organizations in Syria. It was controlled by the government and followed the gender policy of the Baʿth Party.

The Syrian state engaged in "state feminism," establishing national machineries for the advancement of women. It mobilized women using the rhetoric of Arab nationalism and stressing the importance of women's contribution to public life. Baʿthist ideology endorses women's emancipation and adopted policies to that end, especially in education. Women were represented regularly in every new Syrian Parliament, and measures actively sought to incorporate them within all levels of the political sphere. But the actual improvements in women's lives (in areas of education, economic opportunities, and marriage) were often retarded by traditional and conservative attitudes in the region.

A word of caution should also be added here. The effects of Syrian state feminism were often weakened by the regime's politics of survival and its co-optation of societal Islamism, which preaches control of social behavior but refrains from engaging in politics. In addition, a high level of political representation is not synonymous with real ability to influence the decision-making process. Given the features of the Syrian political system, where a few strongmen of the same ʿAlawī sectarian background hold sway over politics, the army, and the economy, women's representation has remained ineffective. The appointment of Najah al-Attar as second vice president for cultural affairs in 2006 is an example.

The symbolic nature of women's political participation has not only been restricted to the ruling party but was also typical of other political parties, both those legally sanctioned by the regime and those that are not. Exclusion should be seen within its wider political and cultural context, as it has to do with an authoritarian pattern shaped by cultural perceptions.

Low levels of female engagement in politics is also explained by the dire consequences women can face as a result of political activity. In the 1980s, at the height of the confrontation between the Syrian regime and the Muslim Brothers, security forces committed grave human rights violations against female activists of the Muslim Brotherhood or female relatives of male members. They were often arrested, raped, and tortured either to force them to share information on the organization or to demoralize their male relatives.

Notwithstanding this, pioneer activists such as the lawyer Hanan Nijmeh continued to campaign for favorable changes in labor and family laws.

In 2000, when Bashar al-Assad assumed power, civil society organizations flourished during the brief Damascus Spring. Women's organizations, such as the Committee of Social Initiative (2001) and the Syrian Women Observatory (2005), publicly debated taboo issues, such as "honor" killing, the introduction of civil marriage, reforming the system of legal pluralism, and reform of Islamic family law.

When the Damascus Spring dissipated, security forces turned to intimidation, forcing female activists out of their jobs, holding them in custody, and even imprisoning them, as was the case with Dr. Fidaa al-Hourani, the chairwoman of the National Council of the Damascus Declaration for National Democratic Change.

Since March 2011, Syrian women have been active in the Syrian nonviolent protests that turned into civil war. They have advocated peaceful means of protest and documented atrocities committed. For example, the lawyer Razan Zaitouna has been particularly active in this regard. Women activists' lives and those of their male partners have been disrupted by the ongoing civil war. For example, writer and activist Samar Yazbik had to flee the country in July 2011 with her family after security forces threatened to arrest her daughter. Yet women continue to organize demonstrations, strikes, and all-women marches in solidarity with victims. Because security forces have been blocking access to hospitals, women and men treated injured protesters in makeshift clinics set up in mosques and private houses. There were reports that the security forces were using rape as a weapon of war. However, documenting these crimes is difficult because of fear of reprisals and stigmatization of victims.

BIBLIOGRAPHY

Fédération Internationale des Ligues des Droits de l'Homme (FIDH). "Women and the Arab Spring: The Rights of Women Are a Priority and Must Be at the Core of Political Reforms." 13 March 2012. Available online at http://www.fidh.org/Women-and-the-Arab-Spring-The. Accessed 31 October 2012.

Hill, Fiona. "The Gender of Tradition: The Syrian Woman and the Feminist Agenda." In *Remaking the Middle East*, edited by Paul J. White and William S. Logan, pp. 129–152. Oxford: Berg, 1997.

Keddie, Nikki R. *Women in the Middle East: Past and Present*. Princeton, N.J.: Princeton University Press, 2007.

Manea, Elham. *The Arab State and Women's Rights: The Trap of Authoritarian Governance*. London: Routledge, 2011.

Ṣāliḥ, Nabīl, ed. *Riwāyah ismuhā Sūrīyah: Mi'at shakhsīyah as'hamat fī tashkīl wa'y al-Sūrīyīn fī al-qarn al-'ishrīn*. Vol. 1. Damascus: Al Majmoua Al Moutaheda li'anasher wa al tasouiq [United Group for Publication and Advertisement and Marketing], 2007.

Tucker, Judith E. *In the House of the Law: Gender and Islamic Law in Ottoman Syria and Palestine*. Berkeley: University of California Press, 1998.

Van Dam, Nikolaos. *The Struggle for Power in Syrian: Politics and Society under Asad and the Ba'th Party*. Rev. ed. London: I. B. Tauris, 1996.

Elham Manea

T

ṬABAQĀT. The *Ṭabaqāt* (classes, layers, categories, strata, or generations) genre is a branch of historical writing unique to the Muslim community. These biographical dictionaries appeared around the beginning of the ninth century CE, with their defining feature being people. The earliest extant work is '*Kitāb al-ṭabaqāt al-kabīr*' by Ibn Saʿd (784–845), which deals with the generations of men and women from the time of the Prophet to his own time, using earlier written works and oral traditions. Entries included facts such as the surname, *kunya* (honorific), town, descent, *madhhab* (doctrine), knowledge, craft, position and his or her various teachers or students, dates of birth and death, and outstanding contributions.

Such works developed out of the need to identify transmitters of ḥadīth (the words and deeds of the Prophet Muḥammad). Some scholars attribute their origins to the Arabs' interest (pre- and early Islamic) in genealogy and biography. Afterward, kinship to the Prophet or *ṣābiqa* (date of conversion to Islam) decided or affected the share of distributed booty and state pensions. Other scholars believe they were constructed to transmit certain behavioral patterns, while still others argued that entries conveyed clichéd models of the authors' ideals, rather than genuine personality traits, pointing out that the same person's life was portrayed differently in diverse works.

Ṭabaqāt were used for religious and secular purposes and were devoted to various professions, such as Qurʾān reciters and exegists, jurists, ṣūfīs, grammarians, poets, scholars, judges, philosophers, and scientists, or to certain geographical areas or cities, such as Baghdad and Damascus. Although there are *ṭabaqāt* works of all sorts, from people with diseases or disabilities to chess players or singers, surprisingly, there are none for historians. Analyzing the author's preface reveals his motive, scope, method, selectivity and can also disclose his objectivity or subjectivity. They show that the history of the Islamic community was mainly viewed as the contribution of individual men and women to both building and transmitting its specific culture, and that their contributions were deemed worthy of being recorded for future generations. Hence, they were later supplemented with a *tahdhīb*, *zayl*, or *takmila*, to ensure their continuity and update. None was authored by women until the late nineteenth century. Some authors did not regard any woman as essential enough to merit a biographical entry, and none included women in proportion to their actual numbers in the population.

A study of forty bibliographical collections, dating from the ninth to the early twenty-first century, showed that up to the sixteenth century, compilers normally included a separate section on women at the end, while some scattered women's biographies among those of men, contradicting the view of Muslim women as marginal, secluded, and restricted. However, from the sixteenth century on, the number and proportion of women dropped significantly.

Thorough examination and comparison of the entries in biographical dictionaries from different periods reveal how changing social circumstances affected the portrayal of the lives of early Muslim women. Entries of female warriors who fought in the early raids were edited and manipulated to conform to the seclusion portrayed later by *fuqahā*ʾ (jurists), specifically in the Seljuk and Mamlūk periods, presenting a masculine "wish list" of desirable qualities in the modest and respectable Muslim lady of the late Middle Ages. Critical examination of *ṭabaqāt* works offers perspectives on social, political, and religious ideologies prevalent at the time they were authored.

BIBLIOGRAPHY

Afsaruddin, Asma. "Reconstituting Women's Lives: Gender and the Poetics of Narrative in Medieval Biographical Collections." *The Muslim World* 92, no. 3–4 (2002): 461–480.

Gibb, H. A. R. "Islamic Biographical Literature." In *Historians of the Middle East*, edited by B. Lewis, pp. 54–58. Oxford: Oxford University Press, 1962.

Hafsi, Ibrahim. "Recherches sur le genre des 'ṭabaqāt' dans la littérature arabe." Parts 1–3. *Arabica* 23, no. 3 (1976): 227–265; no. 1 (1977): 1–41; no. 2 (1977): 150–186.

Humphreys, R. Stephen. *Islamic History: A Framework for Inquiry*. London: I. B. Tauris, 1991.

Hurvitz, Nimrod. "Biographies and Mild Asceticism: A Study of Islamic Moral Imagination." *Studia Islamica* 85 (1997): 41–65.

Lutfi, Huda. "Al-Sakhawi's *Kitab al-Nisa* as a Source for the Social, and Economic History of Muslim Women during the Fifteenth Century A.D." *The Muslim World* 71 (1981): 104–124.

Khalidi, Tarif. "Islamic Biographical Dictionaries: A Preliminary Assessment." *The Muslim World* 63, no. 1 (January 1973): 53–65.

al-Qadi, W. "Biographical Dictionaries as the Scholar's Alternative History of the Muslim Community." In *Organizing Knowledge, Encyclopaedic Activities in the Pre-Eighteenth Century Islamic World*, edited by G. Endress, pp. 23–75. Leiden, Netherlands: Brill, 2006.

Roded, Ruth. *Women in Islamic Biographical Collections—From Ibn Sa'd to Who's Who*. Boulder, Colo.: Lynne Rienner, 1994.

Rosenthal, F. *A History of Muslim Historiography*. Leiden, Netherlands: Brill, 1968.

YASMIN AMIN

TAJ MAHAL. The Taj Mahal (Crown Palace) is associated unequivocally with the wife of the fifth Mughal emperor Shah Jahan (r. 1628–1658)—Mumtāz Maḥal (1593–1631)—not only because of its role as her burial place but also its multifaceted symbolic evocations, especially love and grief. Born as Arjumand Banu Begum, the future empress of the Mughal Empire was the niece of Nūr Jahān (1577–1645), the wife of the fourth Mughal emperor Jahāngīr (r. 1605–1627). Arjumand Banu Begum married Shah Jahan at the age of nineteen and assumed the title Mumtāz-i Maḥal (Excellence of the Palace). As an ideal consort, Mumtāz Maḥal was trusted by the emperor as a companion with whom he traveled all over the empire. When she accompanied the emperor on a military campaign in 1631, she died in Khandesh, while giving birth to her fourteenth child. Temporally buried at Burhanpur, her body was brought eventually to Agra in 1632, when the Taj Mahal was under construction.

The Taj Mahal belongs to the golden ages of Indo-Muslim architecture. Designed and built under the careful planning of Shah Jahan, who

desired to build the most beautiful mausoleum dedicated to his beloved wife, the erection of the Taj Mahal took some twenty years to complete (1631–1648) and employed some notable architects of the time as well as thousands of craftsmen. Tranquilly set on the south bank of the Yamuna River, the Taj Mahal is a large, oblong walled-in architectural complex (c. 1019 × 341 m) and is renowned for its masterful synthesis of architectural idioms and urban environments. Derived from the Persian architectural heritage, especially that developed under the Timūrid dynasty in Iran and Central Asia, as well as from indigenous Indian building conventions, the complex consists of the central tomb characterized by a tall, onion-shaped dome and is flanked by four minarets, together with a cross-axial, four fold garden (*char-bagh*) and a subsidiary courtyard structure.

The mausoleum has a square plan, and its lofty yet well-proportioned exterior bears feminine characters in appearance, evoking the renowned grace of Mumtāz Maḥal. Its architectural elegance is enhanced by an immaculate sense of whiteness, further accentuated by the abundant use of fine white marble quarried in Rajasthan. The intricacy of colorful inlay decoration, worked skillfully in precious and semiprecious stones, especially those found near the cenotaph of Mumtāz, which is placed next to that of Shah Jahan, also serves to demonstrate the delicacy of the building. Taken together, this funeral structure, whose estimated costs reached 32 million Indian rupees at that time, deserves its rank as the pinnacle of Mughal architectural craftsmanship.

Taj Mahal was listed as a UNESCO World Heritage Site in 1983 and continues to evoke an intangible feeling of immortality even today.

BIBLIOGRAPHY

"Agra: II. Buildings, 1. Taj Mahal." In the *Dictionary of Art*, edited by Jane Turner, Vol. 1, pp. 459–460. London: Grove, 1996.

Begley, W. "The Myth of the Taj Mahal and a New Theory of Its Symbolic Meaning." *Art Bulletin* 61, no. 1 (1979): 7–37.

Begley, W. E., and Z. A. Desai. *Taj Mahal: The Illumined Tomb: An Anthology of Seventeenth Century Mughal and European Documentary Sources*. Cambridge, Mass.: Aga Khan Program for Islamic Architecture, 1989.

Koch, E. "Tāj Maḥall." In the *Encyclopaedia of Islam*, 2d ed., Vol. 10, edited by H. A. R. Gibb, pp. 58–60. Leiden: Brill, 2000.

Koch, E. *The Complete Taj Mahal: And the Riverfront Gardens of Agra*. London: Thames & Hudson, 2006.

Koch, E. "The Taj Mahal: Architecture, Symbolism, and Urban Significance." *Muqarnas* 22 (2005): 128–149.

YUKA KADOI

TAJWĪD. Tajwīd is a comprehensive system of rules governing Qurʾānic recitation. Tajwīd also refers to the practice of recitation itself. The term derives from the Arabic three-letter root *jīm-wāw-dāl*, from which are formed words having to do with "good," "excellence," "making better," and "the bestowing of goodness." The science of *tajwīd* (*ʿilm al-tajwīd*) is the application of a collection of recitation practices that pertain to pronunciation, accent, phonetics, rhythm, and tempo. When applied to the performance of the verses and chapters of the Qurʾān, these practices preserve the original word of God as it was received by the Prophet Muḥammad in a series of revelations to him by the Angel Gabriel in seventh-century Arabia. The Qurʾān itself contains many references to the practice of recitation, beginning with Gabriel's command to Muḥammad, "Iqrāʾ bism Allāh" (Recite in the name of God). Muḥammad received and recited the entirety of the Qurʾān over a twenty-two- to twenty-three-year period, first in the Arabian city of Mecca and then in Medina, in a randomly ordered collection of verses that he taught progressively to his followers (*ṣaḥābah* s.; *ṣaḥābāt* pl.), in the oral tradition consisting of demonstration, repetition, correction, and practice that persists to this day.

Although the rules of *tajwīd* pertain to a written language, they are learned orally and aurally through the common experience for Muslims of learning to recite, and hearing the recited Qurʿān daily in any number of ritual, social, and pedagogical contexts, as well as through the mass media. Any Muslim man, woman, boy, or girl who practices recitation attempts to channel an archetypal recitation, a reproduction of the sounded text as it was heard in the original context of its revelation. Although reciters, both professional and amateur, strive for a standardized ideal, human talent and the individual quality of a voice are recognized, cultivated, and rewarded. Children who are heard to have potential are encouraged through group and individual training with expert reciters, and then nurtured as performers in ritual and social contexts as well as in organized competitions. Those who excel can achieve extraordinary fame, yet even those who do not achieve excellence in recitation or an extensive command of Qurʾānic verses are understood to receive God's blessing just from the practice. International competitions in Qurʾānic recitation bestow prizes on the best male and female reciters in the Muslim world. National and local competitions, for example, those in Indonesia, can be multi-day events that combine civic, religious, and commercial activities. In some cultures, excellent reciters maintain star status and a busy performance schedule, and can become teachers, civic leaders, and government officials.

The term *tajwīd* also refers to the practice of recitation in the more performance-oriented and melodic *mujawwad* style. This style demands sophisticated, virtuosic artistry involving the application of Arab melodic modes, a practice that is both related to and a model for the art of singing. *Mujawwad* recitation involves a selection of verses sounded in long, controlled phrases, each recited on a single breath, with a strong and voluminous vocal timbre produced from the chest (as distinct from a falsetto timbre produced from the head). Each melodic line within a recitation builds in intensity as the reciter expands the range of the melody and employs ornamentation, such as trills, or small melodic ideas, such as sequences. Several rules of pronunciation affect rhythmic and timbral aspects of recitation and particularly the melodic phrasing of the text, including the length of long and short vowels, *madd*; the prolongation of a long vowel sound, as in the *h-ī-ī-īm* of *rahīm*, a perfect place for melodic melisma and decoration; *ghunna*, the nasalized prolongation of closed consonants, for example, *mmmm* or *nnnn* or even *llll* and *rrrr*; and the rules *idgham*, *iqlab*, and *ikhfa*, which deal with the assimilation, alteration, or concealment of consonant sounds.

Qurʾānic recitation, a shared experience for Muslims, is considered to be the apex of language performance, and the *mujawwad* style, the perfect marriage of text and melody, influences significantly the performance of singing and instrumental music in the Arab and Islamic world.

[*See also* Music; *and* Qurʾānic Recitation Schools for Girls.]

BIBLIOGRAPHY

Nelson, Kristina. *The Art of Reciting the Qurʾan*. Reprint. Cairo: American University of Cairo Press, 2001.

Rasmussen, Anne K. *Women's Voices, the Recited Qurʾan, and Islamic Music in Indonesia*. Berkeley and Los Angeles: University of California Press, 2010.

Sells, Michael, trans. *Approaching the Qurʿān: The Early Revelations*. Ashland, Oreg.: White Cloud Press, 1999. With a compact disc recording of various reciters.

Surty, Muhammad Ibrahim H. I. *A Course in the Science of Reciting the Qurʿān*. Rev. ed. Leicestershire, U.K.: Islamic Foundation, 2000. With two cassette tapes of lessons and examples recited by al-Shaykh

Sayyid Karrar, introduced by Ibrahim Hewitt. http://www.islamic-foundation.org.uk.

ANNE K. RASMUSSEN

TALEGHANI, AZAM. (b. 1944), daughter of the renowned Ayatollah Mahmoud Taleghani, was born Azam Alaee Taleghani in Tehran, Iran.

She married in her teens and continued her education despite having four children. After receiving a bachelor's degree in Persian literature, Taleghani established a girl's high school in Iran. Azam Taleghani, akin to her father, fought against Mohammad Reza Pahlavi's repressive regime. She was arrested and tortured on numerous occasions by the shah's security forces for her anti-regime sentiments, sometimes in a cell adjoining her father's.

After the Iranian Revolution of 1979, Taleghani became a member of the Islamic Republic's first parliament. She founded the Society of Muslim Women to help train and empower women in different fields. She represented the Women's Society of Islamic Revolution and sent letters to Iran's leader, Ayatollah Khomeini, cautioning authorities against compulsory veiling. Similar to her father, Taleghani opposed the required wearing of the hijab in public, although she wore it herself. In 1980, she represented Iran at a United Nations Conference on "Women in Thailand," bringing to the fore gender issues in Iran.

After the war with Iraq ended in 1988, Taleghani became involved with a generation of female activists who struggled against all types of discrimination imposed on women. She founded a leading women's magazine called *Hagar's Message*, which focused on women's issues and human rights in Iran. It was closed down by the state first, for a period, in 1993, and permanently in the year 2000.

In 2003, she started a sit-in in front of Tehran's Evin prison to protest the treatment of political prisoners. She particularly criticized the solitary confinement of some prisoners, which she compared to a form of torture, resulting in their gradual death. She also protested against the death of Iranian-Canadian reporter Zahra Kazemi while in detention in Iran, warning authorities that the security and political system of the country was in danger and advising them to investigate the situation of all prisoners.

Despite suffering from a serious illness, Taleghani became the first woman in Iran's history to submit her candidacy for president, first in 2001, and then again in 2009. However, as in the case of all women's candidacies, Iran's Guardian Council rejected it. The Guardian Council argued that women cannot run for the presidency, citing a passage in Iran's Constitution that indicates the president should be elected from among religious and political *rijāl* (leading persons, meaning, men). Taleghani exploited the ambiguity of the writing in the constitution, arguing that the meaning of *rijāl* in the constitution means "mankind" and not "men" in the Persian language, and thus does not exclude women. By gaining the support of prominent ʿulamā, such as Ayatollah Yousef Sanei, and outlining the lack of consensus among ʿulamā on the notion of female authority in Islam, Taleghani successfully managed to reverse the eight-year-old ruling of the Guardian Council concerning women's access to the highest leadership positions.

Taleghani is pushing to alter Iran's Constitution to include gender equality. She is an active member of a coalition of women demanding that Iran ratify the UN Convention on the Elimination of All Forms of Discrimination against women (CEDAW). She continues her activism by speaking out against the house arrest of the leaders of Iran's Green Movement. She is an optimal example of a religious reformist who plays a significant role in the democratization of religious interpretation in the Islamic republic of Iran.

BIBLIOGRAPHY

Ahmadi, Fereshteh. "Islamic Feminism in Iran: Feminism in a New Islamic Context." *Journal of Feminist Studies in Religion* 22, no. 2 (2006): 33–53.

DeLong-Bas, Natana J. *Notable Muslims: Muslim Builders of World Civilization and Culture*. Oxford: Oneworld, 2006.

"Hasre Mousavi va Karroubi gheire ghanooni va naghze hoghooghe bashar hast," [The imprisonment of Mousavi and Karroubi is illegal and violates human rights], *Saham News*, accessed January 15, 2013, http://sahamnews.net/1390/04/64131/.

Keddie, Nikki. "Iranian Women's Status and Struggles Since 1979." *Journal of International Affairs* 60, no. 2. (2007): 17–33.

Moghadam, Valentine M. "Islamic Feminism and Its Discontents: Toward a Resolution of the Debate." *Journal of Women in Culture and Society* 27, no. 4 (2002): 1135–1171.

Taleghani, Azam. "Mikhaham taklife rejal ra roshan konam." [I want to make clear the issue of *rejal*]. *Zanan* 34 (1997): 6–7.

Vakil, Sanam. *Women and Politics in the Islamic Republic of Iran: Action and Reaction*. New York: Continuum, 2011.

SAMANEH OLADI GHADIKOLAEI

TALIBAN. The Taliban is an Afghan Islamic militia movement that coalesced amid the civil war (1992–1996) following Soviet withdrawal (1989) from Afghanistan. The Taliban, with its clerical leadership, came to control most of Afghanistan's major cities and provinces in the last years of the twentieth century. The English word "Taliban" is derived from the Arabic term *ṭālib* (student). Many of the early recruits into the movement were young Afghan refugees in Pakistan studying at Islamic religious schools. Da Afghinstan da Talibano Islami Tahrik (The Afghan Islamic Movement of Taliban), or "Taliban," was the name chosen by a splinter group of *mujāhidīn* who wanted "to distance themselves from the party politics of the *mujāhidīn* by promoting their own policy of cleansing Afghan society of war and un-Islamic behavior" (Rostami-Povey, 2007, *Afghan Women*, pp. 22–23).

The Taliban established relative peace and security in large parts of Afghanistan, although this was achieved in part through enforcement of a harsh version of Sunni Islamic law, which led to international notoriety. The Taliban's treatment of women was particularly egregious, as discrimination against women and girls was both systematic and institutionally sanctioned. This treatment stemmed not only from their austere interpretation of Islamic law but also from incorporating the norms and values of Pashtunwali, the Pashtun honor code, which they had absorbed in the Deobandī *madrasahs* when they were living in refugee camps in Pakistan. The Taliban's hostility toward women was shaped partially by early identity formation. Many of them grew up as orphans in segregated male refugee camps where they found meaning in life only through war and a puritanical interpretation of Islam (Rostami-Povey, 2007, *Afghan Women*, pp. 22–23). Once in power, the Taliban rigorously enforced a rule that women must wear a garment called a *chadari* (*chādor*) or burqa, which covered them from head to toe.

The image of the burqa-clad woman in the Western media, in particular, after the events of 11 September 2001, came to represent the oppressed Afghan woman in need of liberation. In an attempt to convey the complexity of the image of the burqa, Gillian Whitlock has described it as a complex symbol, a reminder of an oppressive regime, and an icon of brave and successful resistance. (Whitlock, 2005, p. 57) Indeed, Afghan women activists transported weapons, messages, and banned publications beneath their burqas. Yet the Taliban banned girls from going to school and issued decrees both forbidding women to work outside their homes and prohibiting them from traveling except when accompanied by a *maḥram* (male family member). Women's access to health care was dramatically limited. Women could only be examined by a male health worker in the presence of a male *maḥram* (Physicians for Human Rights, 1998, "Taliban's War on Women," p. 40). The ban on women working as teachers had adverse effects on the education of girls and boys. Women who did not comply with these policies faced threats, harassment, beatings, and death. Urban areas saw a rise in begging and prostitution owing to poverty and unemployment. Nevertheless, women in the rural areas continued to contribute to the functioning of the rural economy (Rostami-Povey, 2007, "Afghanistan," p. 183). Women also worked in aid agencies until a decree by the Taliban in July 2000 banned them from all aid agencies, except those in the health sector (ILO, 2001).

Afghan women resisted the rule of the Taliban through different means. Some wrote poetry against the Taliban, as well as eulogies for female martyrs (Jerome, 2007, p. 77). Secret schools were set up in homes where women taught classes. The Revolutionary Association of Afghan Women (RAWA), which was founded in Kabul in 1977, operated in secret during the Taliban rule (RAWA Web site).

The Taliban's human rights violations were not limited to discrimination and violence against women. In August 1998, they attacked the northern city of Mazār-i Sharīf and its largely Hazāra Shīʿa population, killing an estimated two thousand civilians. On 8 January 2001, in Yakaolang, approximately 170 Hazāra Shīʿa were massacred. The Taliban also sheltered Osama Bin Laden and his followers. In March 2001, they destroyed the Buddhist statues at Bāmiān, despite intense worldwide opposition. In May 2001, it was decreed that the few Hindus residing in Kabul should wear an identifying yellow patch.

In the aftermath of 11 September 2001, the United States launched Operation Enduring Freedom with a massive aerial bombardment of Taliban and al-Qaʿida infrastructure in Afghanistan. Under intense bombing by the United States and a ground assault by Northern Alliance fighters, the Taliban lost control of the country. After the fall of the Taliban, women made modest gains in their access to education, employment, health, and political office. However, more than a decade later, a reconstituted Taliban had restored aspects of its military and political power in significant ways. While they are not recognized as governing in any official capacity, the "new Taliban" and other insurgents continue to threaten and attack Afghan women (Semple, 2012, p. 58, and Human Rights Watch).

BIBLIOGRAPHY

"Afghanistan." ILO Web site, 2001, http://www.ilo.org/public/english/region/asro/bangkok/arm/afg.htm.

Euben, Roxanne L., and Muhammad Qasim Zaman, eds. *Princeton Readings in Islamist Thought: Texts and Contexts from al-Banna to Bin Laden*. Princeton, N.J.: Princeton University Press, 2009.

Human Rights in Afghanistan. Human Rights Watch, http://www.hrw.org/asia/afghanistan.

Jerome, Alexandra Scheherezada. "Arts: Poets and Poetry: Afghanistan." In *Encyclopedia of Women and Islamic Cultures*, edited by Suad Joseph. Vol. 5, *Practices, Interpretations and Representations*, p. 70. Leiden, Netherlands: Brill, 2007.

Revolutionary Association of the Women of Afghanistan (RAWA) Web site, http://www.rawa.org/index.php.

Rostami-Povey, Elaheh. *Afghan Women: Identity and Invasion*. London: Zed, 2007.

Rostami-Povey, Elaheh. "Afghanistan." In *Encyclopedia of Women and Islamic Cultures*, edited by Suad Joseph. Vol. 6, *Supplement and Index*, pp. 183–184. Leiden, Netherlands: Brill, 2007.

Semple, Michael. "The Revival of the Afghan Taliban, 2001–2011." *Orient* 2 (2012): 58–69.

Tarzi, Amin, and Kimberly McCloud. "Taliban." In *Encyclopedia of Islam and the Muslim World*, edited by Richard C. Martin, pp. 676–678. New York: Thomson Gale, 2004.

"The Taliban's War on Women: A Health and Human Rights Crisis in Afghanistan." Boston and Washington DC: Physicians for Human Rights, 1998.

Whitlock, Gillian. "The Skin of the Burqa: Recent Life Narratives from Afghanistan." *Biography* 28, no. 1 (Winter 2005): pp. 54–76.

ROJA FAZAELI

TAQWĀ. A crucial Islamic concept, *taqwā* signifies "God-consciousness" and the state of being "God-fearing," and, by extension, "piety," with which it seems to have a partially comparable semantic history. *Taqwā* and its derivatives occur more than 250 times in the Qurʾān. It has been rendered variously as: fear, God-fearing, godliness, piety, God-consciousness, right conduct, righteousness, virtue, warding-off-evil, and wariness. A survey of its usage in the Qurʾān indicates that *taqwā* is often paired with faith, goodness, justice, fairness, equity, guidance, truthfulness, perseverance, sincerity, purity, reliance on God, obedience to God, fulfillment of promises, and generosity. *Taqwā* is seen as a condition of God's rewards for good deeds. Women as well as men are enjoined to have *taqwā*; and good treatment of women by men in the context of marriage is seen as a sign of *taqwā*.

In Ṣūfī thought and practice, *taqwā* signifies God-consciousness and abstention from everything but God, and is considered as the mainstay of spiritual practice. It is also an important concept in Islamic moral, juristic, and theological discourse and in classical Arabic worldly literature. As a highly esteemed attribute, *taqwā* has an important function in Islamic social and political discourse, particularly in contemporary life.

In the Qurʾān, *taqwā* is enjoined as an attitude for both men and women, and several ḥadīths referring to *taqwā* are addressed to and transmitted on the authority of women, such as ʿĀʾishah. In both the Qurʾān and the ḥadīth, women, like men, are specifically enjoined to have *taqwā* within themselves and are considered ennobled by it. The Prophet, addressing ʿĀʾishah, is quoted as saying: "Piety is here [in the heart] (*al-taqwā hāhunā*)," while placing the palm of his hand on his chest.

The Qurʾān's declaration that "the noblest of you in the sight of God are those having the most *taqwā*" (49:13) is usually highlighted in the context of human equality generally, particularly the absence of racial or national distinction. This is often coupled with the ḥadīth: "No additional virtue attaches to an Arab over a non-Arab except by the criterion of *taqwā*." On the other hand, since the last decades of the twentieth century, Muslim feminists have used the same Qurʾānic verse, in its proper context in the Qurʾān, to emphasize gender equality. This has been particularly clearly articulated by Amina Wadud, who has often argued that distinctions between males and females are of little significance since it is *taqwā*, rather than gender, that is the real criterion of excellence and nobility of character in the eyes of God.

Wadud also uses another significant Qurʾānic expression—"the dress of *taqwā* (*libās al-taqwā*, 7:26)," in both its inherent metaphorical significance and its literal implications for Muslim women (and men) for modest dress—both to expound on the significance of *taqwā* in general, and to challenge the current polarizing debates about the "politics of the hijab."

Other Muslim feminist academics and activists, via various approaches and methodologies, including anthropological fieldwork, education-oriented workshops, participatory action research (PAR), and proactive lobbying for Muslim women's rights, have used *taqwā* as a motivating concept. They include Nimat Hafez Barazangi, Saba Mahmoud, and Meena Sharify-Funk, among several others, as well as activist groups, such as the Malaysia-based Sisters in Islam, and several Muslim women's study groups or projects in North America and elsewhere.

The notion of *taqwā* as a kind of Muslim "pietism," in the sense of personal or group religious discipline, seems to be self-consciously exhibited in some activities carried out during regular mosque attendance by women at prayers and induction lessons.

BIBLIOGRAPHY

Anwar, Zainah, ed. *Wanted: Equality and Justice in the Muslim Family*. Selangor, Malaysia: Musawah, 2009.

Barazangi, Nimat Hafez. "Understanding Muslim Women's Self-identity and Resistance to Feminism and Participatory Action Research." In *Travelling Companions: Feminism, Teaching, and Action Research*, edited by Mary Brydon-Miller, Patricia Maguire, and Alice McIntyre, pp. 21–39. Westport, Conn.: Praeger, 2004a.

Barazangi, Nimat Hafez. *Woman's Identity and the Qur'ān: A New Reading*. Gainesville: University Press of Florida, 2004b.

Jensen, Yolande. "Postsecularism, Piety and Fanaticism: Reflections on Jürgen Habermas' and Saba Mahmoud's Critiques of Secularism." *Philosophy and Social Criticism* 37 (2011): 977–998.

Kassis, Hanna E. *A Concordance of the Qur'ān*. Berkeley: University of California Press, 1983.

"Taḳwā." *Encyclopaedia of Islam, Second Edition*. Brill Online, 2013. Reference. 18 February 2013 http://referenceworks.brillonline.com/entries/encyclopaedia-of-islam-2/takwa-COM_1457.

Mahmood, Saba. *Politics of Piety: The Islamic Revival and the Feminist Subject*. Princeton, N.J.: Princeton University Press, 2005.

Ohlander, Erik S. "Fear of God (taqwā) in the Qur'ān: Some Notes on Semantic Shift and Thematic Context." *Journal of Semitic Studies* 50, no. 1 (2005): 137–152.

Shahrour, Muhammad. *Al-Qur'ān wal-Kitāb: Qirā'ah Mu'āsirah* [The Qur'ān and the Book: Contemporary Reading]. Damascus, Syria: al-Ahālī, 1990.

Sharify-Funk, Meena. *Encountering the Transnational: Women: Islam and the Politics of Interpretation*. Aldershot, U.K.: Ashgate, 2008.

Shboul, Ahmad. "Between Rhetoric and Reality: Islam and Politics in the Arab World." *Islam in World Politics*, edited by Nelly Lahoud and Anthony H. Johns, pp. 170–191. New York: Routledge, 2005.

Wadud, Amina. *Inside the Gender Jihad: Women's Reform in Islam*. Oxford: Oneworld, 2006.

Wadud, Amina. *Qur'ān and Woman: Rereading the Sacred Text from a Woman's Perspective*. Oxford: Oxford University Press, 1999.

AHMAD SHBOUL

TARZI, MAHMUD. (1865–1933), writer, poet, translator, and journalist who became one of Afghanistan's most well-known intellectuals and a pivotal influence in moving Afghanistan into the twentieth century. Tarzi was born August 23, 1865, in Ghazni in central-east Afghanistan, the son of Sardar Ghulam Muhammad Tarzi, a member of the Mohamedzai royal subtribe. In 1881, the *amīr* Abdur Rahman Khan exiled Ghulam Muhammad Tarzi, and the family went to live in Turkey. Mahmud Tarzi was educated in both Turkey and India, becoming fluent in Pashto, Persian, Turkish, French, Arabic, and Urdu. He was married to Asma Rasmiya, the daughter of Shaykh Saleh Al-Mossadiah, a *muezzin* at the Awamiyyah Umayyad mosque in Damascus, Syria.

Upon the *amīr's* death in 1901, the Tarzi family returned to Afghanistan. Tarzi translated a number of books by Jules Verne and other popular Western writers into Persian. He also began to write his own works, including his *Account of a Journey*, published in 1902. His novel *Travel across Three Continents in Twenty-Nine Days*, published in 1914, was the first true Afghan novel. He was also the founder and editor of the Kabul newspaper, *Seraj ul-akhbar afghaniya*, which was published from 1911 to 1918.

Tarzi was further known for his political reforms, particularly his opposition to religious extremism and his support for secularism and modernization, as influenced by the Young Turks. He served as Afghanistan's Minister of Foreign Affairs in 1919 during the Third Anglo-Afghan War, helping to negotiate the end to the conflict, which resulted in international acknowledgement of Afghanistan's independence. Tarzi then served as ambassador to France from 1922 to 1924, and Minister of Foreign Affairs from 1924 to 1927.

Tarzi's influence increased when his daughter, Soraya, married King Amanullah Khan. As the king's only wife, Soraya played a critical role in advocating for social justice and education, particularly for women. She was the first Muslim consort to appear in public with her husband. Tarzi himself played a pivotal role in promoting social reform as chief adviser to King Amanullah, including expanding girls' and women's access to public space and participation in society, including by attending schools and adopting Western modes of dress. In 1921, the government passed laws ending child marriage, compulsory dowries, and forced marriage. Queen Soraya herself removed her veil in public, and her husband spoke out against both the veil and polygamy. This led to rapid changes in the cities, especially Kabul, although changes in the countryside were much slower. The government also implemented a higher education program whereby young women between the ages of fifteen and eighteen were able to complete their education in Turkey, where education had been secularized.

When the King abdicated in 1929, the Tarzi family was again forced into exile. Tarzi died on 22 November 1933, in Istanbul. His influence in Afghanistan's history nevertheless remains, as shown by the establishment of the Mahmud Tarzi Cultural Foundation in Kabul in his memory in 2005, which focuses on education and advancing the status of children and women in Afghan society.

BIBLIOGRAPHY

Gregorian, Vartan. "Mahmud Tarzi and Saraj-ol-Akbar: Ideology of Nationalism and Modernization in Afghanistan." *Middle East Journal* 21, no. 3 (1967): 345–368.

Gregorian, Vartan. *The Emergence of Modern Afghanistan: Politics of Reform and Modernization, 1880–1946*. Stanford, Calif.: Stanford University Press, 1969.

Pullada, Leon B. *Reform and Rebellion in Afghanistan, 1919–1929: King Amanullah's Failure to Modernize a Tribal Society*. Ithaca, N.Y.: Cornell University Press, 1973.

JUSTIN J. CORFIELD AND NATANA J. DELONG-BAS

TELEVISION. The media in general, and television in particular, wield tremendous power in shaping how viewers see the world and form their attitudes toward themselves, their neighbors, and others in society and in the world. In the Arab world, television is the primary source of entertainment, news, and information for much of the population; the medium bypasses illiteracy barriers and appeals to cultures that look to find much of their entertainment at home, in family settings. For women in the Arab world, the importance of television is magnified, particularly in those cultures where freedom of movement and public association is proscribed by cultural and religious barriers.

The development of television in the Arab world began in the mid-1950s in Morocco, Kuwait, and Saudi Arabia. By the 1960s governments in the region, having realized television's potential to influence and mobilize the population, started operating television as monopolies. In almost all countries in the region, television services were brought under the control of ministries of information or other government authorities. Television broadcasting in the region functioned under an authoritarian system of broadcasting, with terrestrial networks owned and operated by government bodies that used the medium more as government propaganda machines than as independent sources of information. Programming in general was of poor quality with news broadcasts primarily addressing leadership speeches, official visits, and protocol activities. Access was strictly controlled and limited to government-approved topics and presenters. Most of these channels also provided viewers with very limited opportunities to watch Western or international programming. In 1992 Freedom House ranked five countries in the Middle East and North Africa as "partly free" in the media category, but by 1998 that number of countries ranked "partly free" had shrunk to three.

By the 1990s, following the launch of transnational satellite broadcasting, governments began a process of liberalization of television broadcasting. CNN's coverage of the first Gulf War was closely followed by Arab audiences and revealed their hunger for independent, high-quality news coverage. In 1991 the Middle East Broadcasting Corporation (MBC) launched a 24-hour news channel broadcast from London. The Egyptian Satellite Channel, owned and operated by the Egyptian government, was next. Other Arab satellite networks, both government-owned and private, quickly followed suit. The programming on these networks proved to be highly popular and opened Arab homes to a much wider range of programming in terms of both content and genre.

Al Jazeera, the most popular news channel in the region, was launched in 1996 and greatly changed the Arab media landscape. The highly popular network has broken many of the traditional taboos of news broadcasting in the Arab world, interviewing controversial figures, from Islamic radicals to Israeli politicians, attacking Arab governments, and discussing social and cultural issues such as female genital mutilation and forced marriages in formats that include call-in shows. The award-winning network has incensed many of the governments in the region, who have reacted to criticism or unfavorable coverage by banning journalists' access, cutting electricity during interviews, and disrupting satellite transmissions, among other actions. Al Jazeera changed audience expectations of news coverage and set the stage for the growth of high-quality television broadcasting throughout the region.

Research indicates that the total number of distinct free-to-air satellite channels has reached 642 and now exceeds the number of government-owned channels, with around three-quarters privately owned. Increased demand for programming combined with an increase in the number of channels has helped promote the growth of production centers in the region, particularly in Egypt, Lebanon, Syria, and Jordan. Although the amount of regional content is increasing, quality and availability remain problematic, and many broadcasters still rely on imported material. Mexican and Turkish soap operas have proven very popular throughout the region, especially among Arab women.

Satellite broadcasting plays a critical role in conveying news and information of general and specific interest, commenting on events, as well as offering opinion and perspectives, reinforcing social norms and cultural awareness through the dissemination of information about culture and society, providing specialized data for commercial promotion and services, and, finally, entertaining viewers. Satellite broadcasting continues to bring together Arab women, deepening the dialogue among Arab women regarding issues of concern, and strengthening their traditions and customs. It has also provided a forum for Arab women to discuss the challenges of the twenty-first century and the Arab Spring, and is empowering Arab women in the exercise of their right to seek and receive information and ideas.

Satellite broadcasting bypasses the two most important communication barriers in the region: illiteracy and government control of content. While in most Arab countries, the literacy rate is rising, illiteracy continues to be a problem, particularly for women. Since a relatively high percentage of Arab women are illiterate, the programming in Arabic on satellite broadcasters is of greater appeal to them than foreign programs, print media, and the Internet. As for government control of content, governments cannot censor satellite broadcasts originating outside their countries and cannot control what their people watch, except by prohibiting satellite viewing or by jamming satellite transmissions or otherwise impeding broadcasts. Such efforts have been made and have failed almost across the board. The access to uncensored programming that adheres in most cases to global production standards has made audiences more discerning, as well as less tolerant, of the protocol news and programming routinely broadcast on government-owned networks.

As a result, government-owned terrestrial networks, which still wield great influence within their own countries, have begun liberalizing to some extent the content they offer, introducing talk shows and other formats in an attempt to compete for audience share with the satellite networks. Terrestrial networks remain influential particularly among lower-middle class and lower-class audiences, who struggle against poverty, illiteracy, and isolation, all of which restrict the availability and accessibility of satellite viewing. The high cost of acquiring a satellite dish and the difficulty in affording pay television channels continue to restrict access, although audiences have found ways to work around these barriers by watching broadcasts in public areas such as coffee shops, purchasing illegal receivers, and pirating satellite signals. The relative freedom that satellite networks have used to their advantage does not apply to terrestrial networks, which continue to be primarily government-owned,-operated, and -controlled.

Islamic societies in general and Arab society in particular are notably defensive of their traditions and values, which are often envisioned as under attack from a post-modern Western society. Most countries in the Arab world have laws that prohibit content that would offend not only the adherents of Islam but also members of other religious faiths. In addition, most Arab countries have enacted laws that prohibit extreme violence and pornography and obscenity, nudity, sex—including kissing and premarital sex as well as homosexual acts, which are still illegal in most of these nations—and even divorce as a means to solve family problems or content that portrays criminals as heroes. Governments have also prohibited criticism of authority, either presidents or princes, along with anything that could harm their country's reputation—an ill-defined, catch-all category that has been used to suppress news reports as well as the discussion of controversial topics.

Arab society is still fearful of the cultural impact of unrestricted satellite viewing and any danger it might pose. The resulting laws have engendered a great deal of self-censorship and a reluctance to discuss controversial topics. Satellite television is exempt from such national laws, yet many satellite broadcasters, as well as terrestrial broadcasters, censor programming on their networks in recognition of the concerns of their audiences.

The fear that satellite broadcasts carry alien values to a vulnerable population is not confined to issues related to sex and violence. In recent years, Islamic fundamentalists have increasingly made use of technology to win converts and spread their brand of Islam. Digital *fatwās*, satellite sheiks, and the promotion of superstition bordering on black magic have stirred concern among Muslim scholars, policy makers, and secularists. Although in the West, the impact of this kind of programming might be limited, it is not difficult to imagine the effect of this sort of content on relatively unsophisticated Arab audiences who receive most of their

entertainment and information from television. The ability to reach millions of viewers can blur the distinction between popularity and the religious authority needed to issue *fatwās* and other opinions.

The growth of Islamic programming has been exponential. The Lebanese channel Al-Manar, operated by the Shiite Muslim group Ḥizbullāh, ranks among the ten most popular satellite channels in the region, according to the 2009 Annual Arab Public Opinion Survey. The region's first Islamic satellite channel, IQRAA, was launched in 1998 by the Saudi-based Arab Radio and Television (ART) network. One of the channel's most popular programs is hosted by influential Muslim television lay preacher Amr Khaled, named one of *TIME* magazine's most influential people in 2007. Khaled rejects extremism and promotes "faith-based development," encouraging individuals to improve themselves and their communities using faith as a motivator and a guide. Khaled has inspired thousands of young women to start wearing the hijab, the traditional Islamic head covering. Another channel, Huda (The right path), is an English-language, Saudi-funded Islamic station that targets non-Arabic-speaking audiences. MBC, Future TV, and Dubai TV have all added regular series about Islam in recent years, responding to the popularity of these programs.

Women are a visible part of this growing phenomenon. An Egyptian satellite television show *Women's Fatwa* is hosted by a female religious scholar and provides religious rulings on a wide range of subjects in a kind of virtual mosque for women. Sheikha Suad Saleh, the highest-ranking woman at Al-Azhar, the center of learning and authority in Sunnī Islam, along with her colleagues on similar shows, focuses primarily on women's issues. IQRAA broadcasts a call-in show called *Kadaya Al-Maraa* (Women's issues) as well as a show focused on the rights of women in Islam, *Magalet Al-Maraa* (Women's magazine). Egypt's Dream TV frequently invites popular female scholars to host religious shows because they attract many viewers, and Saudi billionaire prince Alwaleed Bin Talal's new Islamic channel, Al-Resalah (The message), airs four popular programs hosted by women that together attract more viewers than the rest of the station's programming combined. Al-Resalah portrays modern Islamic religious women as veiled but stylish who remember, if working outside the home, that their most important job is their family. Al-Resalah's founders are clear about the channel's intent to appeal to Arab audiences, particularly female viewers who represent the majority, by using celebrity and modern media formats.

In spite of fears, satellite broadcasting offers an important opportunity for Arab women to access information and bypass barriers of illiteracy and government control. These new forms of media are providing new avenues for diverse and critical views on life in the region and examples of women's leadership in government, politics, business, religion, culture, and society. As women access international channels for news and information, they are finding that women are publicly discussing topics that were previously considered taboo. Discussion of female genital mutilation as an international issue first took place when CNN International broadcast a comprehensive report about female circumcision during the UN Conference on Population and Development held in Cairo, Egypt, in 1994. The report, which included video of the circumcision and interviews with participants, shocked and horrified the local community for portraying something that was not publicly discussed. It attracted a great deal of international attention and put the issue on the Egyptian government agenda. Since the report's publication, both governmental and non governmental organizations have established projects, frequently headed by women, to eradicate the procedure.

While these new spaces provide enormous opportunities for Arab women, at the same time there remain substantial barriers. Women have advanced to leadership positions in television organizations, but they have experienced less success in altering the medium's portrayal of women. Changing economic and social conditions have led to increased sensitivity toward stereotypes of women as sex objects or submissive housewives, yet there are still few portrayals of women as professional, responsible, objective, and rational or of women in positions of responsibility over men. Queen Rania of Jordan, one of *Forbes* magazine's 100 most powerful women in 2011, called attention to the problem in 2004 by launching a media campaign to change stereotypes affecting Arab women and to boost their role in society, challenging broadcasters and asking Arab women to be more vocal on issues affecting them.

Satellite broadcasting has immense potential for Arab women—as a forum for the exchange of thoughts and ideas, as a means to gain a public platform for development and empowerment, as a medium for education that overcomes barriers of distance and time, and as a tool to advance communities, speed progress, and enhance development. Concerns exist about the impact of programming on values and culture, the rise of Islamic programming and its ability to influence opinion in the region, and the image of women in the media. The growing awareness on the part of broadcasters about the size and power of female audiences should result in programming that is more closely tied to the needs of its viewers and that more closely reflects the reality of Arab women.

BIBLIOGRAPHY

Amin, Hussein. "Arab Media Audiences: An Overview of Existing Research." In *Arab Media Power and Weakness*, edited by Kai Hafez. New York: Continuum, 2008.

Amin, Hussein. "Arab Women and Satellite Broadcasting." *Transnational Broadcasting Studies* 6 (Spring/Summer 2001). http://www.tbsjournal.com/Archives/Spring01/Amin.html.

Amin, Hussein. "Egypt, Status of Media." In *Encyclopedia of International Media and Communications*, edited by Donald H. Johnston. London: Academic Press, 2002.

Amin, Hussein, and James Napoli. "Press Freedom in Egypt." In *Press Freedom and Communication in Africa*, edited by William Jong-Ebot and Festus Eribo. Trenton, N.J.: Africa World Press, 1997.

"Arab FTA Sat TV Channels Grow by 19% in 2011." AMEinfo.com. 12 May 2012. http://boonplanet.com/?sbarticleid=1384&arab-fta-sat-tv-channels-grow-by-19-in-2011.

Ayish, Muhammed. "American-Style Journalism and Arab World Television: An Exploratory Study of News Selection at Six Arab World Satellite Television Channels." *Transnational Broadcasting Studies* 6 (Spring/Summer 2001). http://www.tbsjournal.com/Archives/Spring01/Ayish.html.

Gavlak, Dale. "Arab Women Stereotypes Tackled." *BBC News*. 3 March 2004. http://news.bbc.co.uk/2/hi/middle_east/3530223.stm.

Horan, Deborah. "Shifting Sands: The Impact of Satellite TV on Media in the Arab World." *International Center for Media Assistance*. 29 March 2010. http://cima.ned.org/sites/default/files/CIMA-Arab_Satellite_TV-Report.pdf.

Kraidy, Marwan. "Arab Satellite Television Between Regionalization and Globalization." *Global Media Journal* 1, no. 1 (2002). http://lass.calumet.purdue.edu/cca/gmj/fa02/gmj-fa02-kraidy.htm.

Nomani, A. "The Time 100: Amr Khaled." *TIME* magazine, 3 May 2007. http://www.time.com/time/specials/2007/time100/article/0,28804,1595326_1615754_1616173,00.html.

Obeidat, Reem. "Content and Representation of Women in the Arab Media." Paper presented at Meeting of United Nations Expert Group on the Participation and Access of Women to the Media and the Impact of Media on, and Its Use as an Instrument for the Advancement and Empowerment of Women, Beirut, Lebanon, 12–15 November 2002. http://www.un.org/womenwatch/daw/egm/media2002/reports/EP11Obeidat.

Otterman, Sharon. "Fatwas and Feminism: Women, Religious Authority, and Islamic TV." *Transnational Broadcasting Studies* 16 (2006). http://www.tbsjournal.com/Otterman.html.

Sakr, Naomi. "Satellite Television and Development in the Middle East." *Middle East Report: Reform or Reaction? Dilemmas of Economic Development in the Middle East* 29 (Spring 1999). http://www.merip.org/mer/mer210/satellite-television-development-middle-east.

Hussein Amin

Terrorism. Little research has been undertaken on the link between gender and terrorism. Female engagement in terrorist activities has occurred at a smaller scale than for men (Gonzalez-Perez, 2008). Despite the fact that women have long been involved in terrorism (in Zionist organizations, South America, Sri Lanka, India, Chechyna, Palestine, and Iraq), they have traditionally assumed secondary roles that reflect the gender hierarchy in their respective societies.

No overarching theory has been commonly agreed upon in relation to women and terrorism, perhaps because of the relative lack of attention to the topic and the diversity of disciplines involved (e.g., psychology, sociology, criminology, and cultural and media studies). Thus, there are competing hypotheses and a lack of comparative studies (Jacques and Taylor, 2009). For instance, Victor's study (2004) argues that women are motivated by private reasons; others claim that women have dualistic reasons for partaking in acts of terrorism, such as personal relationships with men involved in political violence (Yuval-Davis, 1997); Morgan (2001) asserts that terrorism is an inevitable by-product of patriarchy being played out through sexual politics; others argue that women involved in political violence are "deviant" and "unnatural" (Galvin, 1983); while still others believe that these women are "insane" or "bad" (Brumby, n.d.). Rarely do studies of male suicide bombers focus on psychological background and grievances with such detail (excluding studies in psychology itself). Some research raises questions about the multifaceted connection between gender and terrorism (Berko and Erez, 2007). Others (Hoogensen, 2004) argue that gender has been a motivating factor among resistance movements despite variations due to religious, secular, ethnic, or national factors.

In the early twenty-first century the threat of terrorism may seem more pronounced because of the accessibility of destructive tools of terror, the means of communication available to terrorists, and instantaneous global media coverage. However, terrorism is not a new phenomenon that just emerged. It has a long history that most contemporary analysis of terrorism and policy development overlooks. Silke (2007) found that a mere 3.9 percent of articles in the field examined noncontemporary terrorism and less than half of those examined a period prior to 1960. Nasser-Eddine et al. (2011) revealed a deficit of historical considerations in the research undertaken on terrorism since 2001. Duyvesteyn (2007) argues that the study of terrorism should include more historical analysis.

The rise of liberation ideologies based on democracy, nationalism, and Marxism was significant in the development of terrorism. The advance of the anticolonial movement and separatist tendencies is also critical to understanding "the evolution and development of modern, contemporary terrorism" (Duyvesteyn, 2007). Both women and men partook equally in these struggles (Cunningham, 2003). During the Cold War period, non-state armed groups seeking independence from (mostly European) colonizers could be labeled terrorists or freedom fighters, depending on one's political standpoint. The mid- to late 1980s to the very early years of the 1990s witnessed a reduction in acts of terrorism.

Since the 9/11 terrorist attacks of 2001, research has focused on "religiously inspired" terrorism (e.g., Zalman, 2008). Organizationally, this "new terrorism" is decentralized rather than hierarchical. It was rare to have individuals undertake sole acts of terror (as a lone wolf) in "old terrorism"; in the early twenty-first century, however, such is becoming more common.

Definition. Despite the decades of research undertaken in terrorism studies, no consensus has been reached on a definition of terrorism (Schmid and Jongman, 1988). Often definitions of terrorism used by governments and security agencies are defined broadly enough to include all forms of subversion. Everyone agrees that "terrorism" is a pejorative term. Because the label carries with it intrinsic condemnation, it is applied to one's enemies and generally not one's allies. Use of the term implies a moral judgment; if one party can successfully attach the label "terrorist" to its opponent, then it has indirectly persuaded others to adopt its moral viewpoint. Overall, the word and its usage are politically loaded and highly subjective (Corcoran-Nantes, 2011). It is, therefore, important to challenge underlying assumptions vested in the way political violence is named, paying close attention to who does the naming, what this naming actually means, and whose interests it serves.

Most definitions in academic literature generally require two elements: "actual or threatened violence against civilians or persons not actively taking part in hostilities" and "the implicit or explicit purpose of the act being to intimidate or compel a population, government or organization into some course of action" (Maogoto, 2003, p. 412; Schmid and Jongman, 1988; Knight, 2006; Winkates, 2006; Ganor, 2002). Scholars largely agree that terrorism is highly effective; each incident has peculiarities that make it incomparable; it is considered the weapon of the weak; and it is highly unpredictable (Schmid and Jongman, 1988).

Unresolved questions include the difference between a terrorist and guerrilla/freedom fighter; the difference between insurgent political violence/terrorism and state-sponsored terrorism; and why some individuals and groups seek to achieve their political goals through violent extremism or acts of terrorism, while others choose to attain them through peaceful means and political engagement.

Islam and Terrorism. In the post-9/11 environment, terrorism, violent extremism, and radicalization have been liberally used as concepts and simultaneously led to a reductive focus on Muslims and Islam. The focus on religiously inspired terrorism has caused tension as governments tighten national security, both internally and at the borders. However, government reactions to terrorism in a post-9/11 climate have left many concerned about the curtailment of civil liberties of Muslim citizens living as minorities. Government responses often fail to consider the historical impact of European colonialism and U.S. policy on many Muslim dominant countries. In some cases, these same foreign powers have played a role in supporting repressive regimes and denying democratic development, which can be root causes of terrorists' grievances.

Thus, although many acts of terror are linked to territorial, political, and economic grievances, in a post-9/11 climate, many initial Western approaches have responded through the lenses of defense and national security. Furthermore, little is done to ensure that women are involved in finding solutions to existing problems.

Instead, many researchers are examining the culture of the region, particularly Islamic religious beliefs and their treatment of women. This cultural framing redirects the focus away from political and historical explanations to religious and cultural factors. This metaphysically divides the world into Western civilization versus Islam

(Abu-Lughod, 2002). The justification given by many governments for invading Afghanistan and Iraq was the so-called liberation of these people from those who "oppose our way of life." These colonial resonances have stirred the emotions of people who were equally appalled by the terrorist attacks of 9/11. This was reinforced in a 2002 survey conducted by the Pew Institute, which found that respondents who believed that Islam was under threat were more likely to support terrorism than those who did not (Fair and Shephard, 2007).

Many terrorists have been motivated by issues of territory, politics, and economic and social rights. Islamic fundamentalism or religious ideology is not a common factor (Pape, 2003). Juergensmeyer (2003) argues that, although religion has played an important role (providing moral justifications and promising reward in the afterlife), such does not automatically equal the conclusion that religion causes violence.

Leaders of groups such as Hamas (on the Gaza Strip), Hezbollah (in Lebanon), and al-Qaʿida have invoked the Qurʾān and Islamic history as validation for their violence. Islam as a religion does not justify the killing of innocent civilians. Following the events of 11 September 2001, Grand Mufti and Muslim leaders around the world condemned the suicide bombings against civilians. However, within Islam (like other monotheistic religions), there are numerous sects and schools of jurisprudence. Thus, the Qurʾān, ḥadīth, and Islamic practices are interpreted differently. Some are concerned with what they perceive to be signs of unbelief (*Kufr*), particularly as demonstrated by the moral and political degradation of society. A segment of this *takfīrī* sect have used Islam to justify their violent means against fellow Muslims, foreigners, modernity, and societal practices that they deem to be "un-Islamic." This group does not represent mainstream Muslims.

Muslim Women and Terrorism. Gender-based terminology and imagery are often invoked to explain the values, beliefs, behavior, and motives of participants in terrorism (Berko and Erez, 2007). Although some national movements, such as the Palestinians, reaffirm the boundaries of culturally acceptable feminine conduct (Rubenberg, 2001), Muslim and Arab women have nevertheless functioned as collaborators, informers, recruiters, human shields, and sexual bait (Bloom, 2005). The relative ease in women's ability to go undetected was a primary motivator in involving more women in acts of political violence and terrorism (Zedalis, 2004). Other reasons include the ability of females to ensure an "element of surprise"; the advantage of cultural reluctance to physically search women and their ability to therefore evade detection; and their likely ability to evoke appreciation of the plight of the aggrieved (Dalton and Asal, 2011).

Female participation in acts of political violence in the Middle East is not a recent phenomenon. Leila Khaled became the symbol of Palestinian resistance in 1969 when she participated in the hijacking of an airliner. Such acts escalated during the early 2000s, especially when Palestinian and Iraqi women began to commit suicide bombings. This period clearly highlighted that the main motivators for these women were political history, particularly the Palestine question, Israeli or Western occupation; cultural and social pressures; religious justifications; and the role (and ambitions) of political and religious leaders in the Palestinian/Iraqi occupied territories (Victor, 2004). *Fatwās* (religious edicts) by Palestinian religious resistance organizations declaring that female suicide bombings were religiously acceptable became necessary when their secular political counterparts intentionally involved women in such practices. Despite these political developments, often the prospect of women having political agency is overlooked (Sjoberg, 2009;

Corcoran-Nantes, 2011). Instead, most commentary on Arab and Muslim women and terrorism is patriarchal in nature, that is, it reasserts the traditional conservative role of a mother, daughter, or sister.

Finally, one must beware the common assumption that Islam is a monolith and that all Muslims are the same. The historical, political, cultural, generational, regional, and subregional differences in belief, practices, and interpretations vary enormously from one country to the next and within sects themselves.

When trying to answer the question "What do Muslims think of terrorism?" one needs to acknowledge that a universal consensus is not possible. Thus, when sifting through research findings and open source material, one must differentiate between a third-generation Australian Muslim's response and that of a Muslim woman living in Saudi Arabia, Indonesia, Chechnya, or China. The topic is as problematic as it is diverse and complex. In any case, the key to understanding terrorism is not religion as much as long-standing historical, political, economic, and cultural grievances.

BIBLIOGRAPHY

Abu-Lughod, Lila. "Do Muslim Women Really Need Saving? Anthropological Reflections on Cultural Relativism and Its Others." *American Anthropologist* 104, no. 3 (2002): 783–790.

Berko, Anat, and Edna Erez. "Gender, Palestinian Women, and Terrorism: Women's Liberation or Oppression?" *Studies in Conflict & Terrorism* 30, no. 6 (2007): 493–519.

Bloom, Mia M. *Dying to Kill: The Allure of Suicide Terror*. New York: Columbia University Press, 2005.

Brumby, Roy. "Red Army Faction Brains 'Disappeared.'" http://news.bbc.co.uk/2/hi/europe/2484745.stm.

Corcoran-Nantes, Y. "Unnatural Beings: Gender and Terrorism." *Outskirts Online Journal*, 24 June 2011.

Cunningham, Karla. "Cross Regional Trends in Female Terrorism." *Studies in Conflict and Terrorism* 26 (2003): 171–195.

Dalton, Angela, and Victor Asal. "Is It Ideology or Desperation: Why Do Organizations Deploy Women in Violent Terrorists Attacks?" *Studies in Conflict & Terrorism* 34, no. 10 (2011): 802–819.

Duyvesteyn, I. "The Role of History and Continuity in Terrorism Research." In *Mapping Terrorism Research: State of the Art, Gaps and Future Direction*, edited by M. Ranstorp, pp. 51–75. Oxford: Routledge, 2007.

Fair, C. Christine, and Bryan Shephard. "Who Supports Terrorism? Evidence from Fourteen Muslim Countries." *Studies in Conflict & Terrorism* 29, no. 1 (2007): 51–74.

Galvin, D. M. "The Female Terrorists: A Socio-Psychological Perspective." *Behavioural Sciences and the Law* 1, no. 2, (1983): 19–32.

Ganor, B. "Defining Terrorism: Is One Man's Terrorist Another Man's Freedom Fighter?" *Police Practice and Research* 3, no. 4 (2002): 287–304.

Gonzalez-Perez, Margaret. *Women and Terrorism: Female Activity in Domestic and International Terror Groups*. Abingdon, U.K., and New York: Routledge, 2008.

Hoogensen, G. "Gender Identity and the Subject of Security." *Security Dialogue* 35, no. 2 (2004): 155–171.

Jacques, Karen, and Paul J. Taylor. "Female Terrorism: A Review." *Terrorism and Political Violence* 21, no. 3 (2009): 499–515.

Juergensmeyer, Mark. *Terror in the Mind of God: The Global Rise of Religious Violence*. 3d ed. Berkeley: University of California Press, 2003.

Knight, A. "Jihad and Cross-Cultural Media: Osama Bin Laden as Reported in the Asian Press." *Pacific Journalism Review* 13, no. 2 (2006): 155–174.

Loza, W. "The Psychology of Extremism and Terrorism: A Middle-Eastern Perspective." *Aggression and Violent Behavior* 12 (2007): 141–155.

Maogoto, J. N. "War on the Enemy: Self-Defence and State Sponsored Terrorism." *Melbourne Journal of International Law* 4 (2003): 406–438.

Morgan, Robin. *The Demon Lover*. London: Piatkus, 2001.

Nasser-Eddine, M., B. Garnham, K. Agostino, and G. Caluya. *Countering Violent Extremism (CVE) Literature Review*. Edinburgh, South Australia: Defence Science and Technology Organisation, 2011.

Pape, R. A. "The Strategic Logic of Suicide Terrorism." *American Political Science Review* 97, no. 3 (2003): 343–361.

Rubenberg, Cheryl. *Palestinian Women: Patriarchy and Resistance in the West Bank.* Boulder, Colo.: Lynne Rienner, 2001.

Schmid, A. P., and A. J. Jongman. *Political Terrorism: A New Guide to Actors, Authors, Concepts, Databases, Theories, and Literature.* Amsterdam: SWIDOC, 1988.

Silke, A. "The Impact of 9/11 on Research on Terrorism." In *Mapping Terrorism Research: State of the Art, Gaps and Future Direction*, edited by M. Ranstorp, pp. 76–93. Oxford: Routledge, 2007.

Sjoberg, L. "Feminist Interrogations of Terrorism/Terrorism Studies." *International Relations* 23, no. 69 (2009): 69–74.

Victor, Barbara. *Army of Roses: Inside the World of Palestinian Women Suicide Bombers.* London: Constable & Robinson, 2004.

Winkates, J. "Suicide Terrorism: Martyrdom for Organizational Objectives." *Journal of Third World Studies* 23, no. 1 (2006): 87–115.

Yuval-Davis, Nira. *Gender and Nation.* London: SAGE, 1997.

Zalman, A. *Countering Violent Extremism: Beyond Words.* New York: East West Institute, 2008.

Zedalis, Deborah. "Female Suicide Bombers." Carlisle Papers in Security Strategy. Carlisle, PA: U.S. Army War College, 2004.

AUGUSTUS RICHARD NORTON
Updated by JOSEPH A. KÉCHICHIAN
and MINERVA NASSER-EDDINE

THAILAND. Thai Muslim women's groups initially emerged in the 1980s on campuses and Islamic schools, under the influence of the domestic democratization movement and global Islamic revitalization. Many Thai Muslim women's groups have adapted strategies from movements that were influenced by Muslim modernist thinkers. The Thai Muslim Students Association (TMSA), established in 1965–1966, slowly started to depart from issues concerning the traditional practice of Islam to stressing adherence to faith, human rights, and rural community development. TMSA had played a central role in providing coordination and support for affiliated Muslim students' groups across the country. In the beginning, activities were not strictly segregated according to sex. Women-initiated programs gradually started to collaborate more effectively with reformist Muslim nongovernmental organizations, such as the Young Muslim Association of Thailand (YMAT). They set up women's wings, which were dominated by middle-class Muslim women trained by TMSA.

Elite Thai Muslim women from the traditional faction of YMAT supported Islamic-affairs activities at the national level by joining with the office of the Chularajmontri or Sheikhul Islam, the royally appointed representative of the Thai Muslim community. Thanpuying Samorn Bhuminarong, the president of the Chularajmontri Tuan Suwannasart Foundation, presented a Thai translation of the Qurʾān to Her Majesty Queen Sirikit of Thailand and also distributed copies to provincial Islamic committees around the country. Traditional Muslims were challenged, however, by what they regarded as inauthenticities proposed by the reformists associated with *salafi* puritanism.

Another active side of the Thai Muslim women's movement has gradually been exploring public space. This led to the foundation of the Muslim Women's Organization of Thailand (MWOT) in the late 1980s. Saowanee Jitmoud, one of the MWOT founders who had started out as an activist in the women's wing of TMSA, was the first leader of MWOT. The group coordinated with other women's groups with the aim of offering a more scriptural interpretation of the conventional roles of Muslim women. For instance, Muslim-women study circles, along with MWOT and the women's sections of YMAT and TMSA, offered training courses to strengthen the religious role of women. Wallapha Neelaphaijit, another important Thai Muslim woman from TMSA, became a leader of the women's wing of the Foundation of Islamic Center of Thailand

(FICT), which highlights social development activities.

The 1987–1988 Yala Teacher Training College incident led Thai Muslims to demand state permission to wear the hijab (veil) in secular educational institutions. The incident exploded in Yala, the southernmost province of Thailand. MWOT and TMSA became involved in this issue, uniting protesters, organizing demonstrations and forums on the issue of rights and responsibilities with regard to the hijab, and eventually persuading the Chularajmontri to take action. The protesters continued to demand the civil right of wearing the veil in official ceremonies, at the work place, and for identification documents. After Areepen Uttarasin, a Muslim member of parliament from Narathiwat and the deputy minister of education, introduced a bill in parliament allowing the hijab, wearing the hijab became popular among Thai Muslim women throughout the country.

In the south, the Three Tigers Malay Muslim women's group held gatherings in villages and Islamic boarding schools in the 1970s. The Three Tigers studied at Yayasan Pengajian Tinggi Islam Kelantan, a university in Malaysia. The group was led by three females who focused their activities on women's responsibilities to the *ummah*, the universal community of believers. The Three Tigers developed links between modernist Muslim women in southern Thailand and in the Indonesian and Malaysian women's movements.

In the 1990s and 2000s, young modernist women's groups, such as Banatul Huda, were much more interested in learning and practicing Islam as the literal and scriptural truth. Meanwhile, the first generation of Thai reformist Muslim women stressed interpersonal social relationships and activities. The groups' members interacted with each other to develop a Muslim model of society and promote orthodox gender perspectives.

The Pattani Muslim Women's Association, a Muslim women's group, has gradually grown since the early 2000s. Hamidah Adae from the Three Tigers group, a lecturer at the College of Islamic Studies, prince of Songkla University, continues to play a central role in this group. Social activists in the group are connected with local people and politicians. They have bridged the class and religious-orientation gaps between modern professional and traditional nonprofessional Muslim women.

The return of unrest in southern Thailand since 2004 has led to women's engagement in relief activities and healing of victim's families affected by the violence. In this new social context, the Thai Muslim Women's Friend is a noticeable group that has coordinated with Muslim and secular organizations, defending Muslim women's rights and providing support to victims of violence in the conflict area. They are famous for active participation in the struggle against unequal treatment for women.

A caucus of Thai Muslim women academics formed in 2005 under the name of Young Muslim Women of Thailand (YMWT). It was initiated as a network to provide analytical forums and research aimed at critical reflections on the constructive orthodox position on and idealized interpretation of Muslim women's role and gender equality. YMWT raised diverse voices and women's life experiences in discussion and reflections on notions of women in Islam.

NISA, a Muslim women's magazine, is a leading media outlet formed by former TMSA activists. They use the magazine as a forum to voice views about the role of women in Islam from Sunnī and Shīʿī perspectives. This is a challenging role for a Muslim women's magazine in Thai Muslim society with its Sunnī majority. *NISA* is also seen as a Muslim women's fashion magazine. The *NISA* editorial team has purveyed progressive ideas in the discourse on women's bodies and gender issues, questioning rigid views about Muslim women's role being adhered to.

Muslim women's groups in Thailand are increasingly broad. Thai Muslim women coming from various social classes and holding different gender and religious ideologies are coordinating with each other to work with male reformist and traditional religious leaders. The academic, media, and cultural activities of progressive women have created basic demands that in turn have given direction to religious activism.

[*See also* Southeast Asia and the Pacific.]

BIBLIOGRAPHY

Jitmoud, Saowanee. *Salamun*. Bangkok: Phisit Karnpim, 1994.

Liow, Joseph Chinyong. "Tradition and Reform in Islamic Education in Southern Thailand." In *Divided over Thaksin: Thailand's Coup and Problematic Transition*, edited by John Funston, pp. 135–149. Singapore: Institute of Southeast Asian Studies, 2009.

Marddent, Amporn. "Muslim Women's Movements in the Modern Thai State." In *Islam und Staat in den Ländern Südostasiens / Islam and State in Southeast Asia*, edited by Fritz Schulze and Holger Warnk, pp. 171–196. Wiesbaden, Germany: Harrassowitz, 2010.

Ministry of Information and Communication Technology. National Statistic Office of Thailand. "Saruppon Karn Samruad Karn Kaoruam Kidjakam Thang Wattanatham Por Sor Song Pan Haroi Si Sip Paed." [Summary of Participation in Cultural Activities, BE 2548]. http://service.nso.go.th/nso/nsopublish/service/survey/cult48.pdf.

Nation. "Korans for the South." http://www.nationmultimedia.com/2009/06/12/national/national_30104951.php.

Prapertchop, Preeda. "Islam and Civil Society in Thailand: The Role of NGOs." In *Dynamic Diversity in Southern Thailand*, edited by Wattana Sugunnasil, pp. 104–116. Chiang Mai, Thailand: Silkworm Books, 2005.

Satha-Anand, Chaiwat. "*Hijab* and Moments of Legitimation: Islamic Resurgence in Thai Society." In *Asian Visions of Authority: Religion and the Modern States of East and Southeast Asia*, edited by Charles F. Keyes, Laurel Kendall, and Helen Hardacre, pp. 279–300. Honolulu: University of Hawaii Press, 1994.

Scupin, Raymond. "The Politics of Islamic Reformism in Thailand." *Asian Survey* 20, no. 12 (December 1980): 1223–1235.

Yusuf, Imtiyaz, ed. *Understanding Conflict and Approaching Peace in Southern Thailand*. Bangkok: Konrad Adenauer Stiftung, 2006.

Imtiyaz Yusuf and Amporn Marddent

Third World Organization for Women in Science. The Third World Organization for Women in Science (TWOWS) is an independent, nonprofit, and non governmental organization based at the headquarters of the Third World Academy of Science in Trieste, Italy. The organization was officially launched during an international conference, Women's Vision of Science and Technology of Development, which was held in Egypt in January 1993.

The objectives of the organization are to: increase women's opportunities for better education in the sciences in third world countries (henceforth TWC); increase women's participation in science and technology leadership positions; advance women's roles in the decision-making process related to national and international development; increase the scientific productivity and efficiency of women scientists in the TWC; promote collaboration among women scientists and technologists in the TWC with the international scientific community as a whole; and, finally, encourage other international organizations to increase their activities concerned with promoting the role of women in science and technology in TWC.

Membership is open to all women scientists and scientific institutions located in third world countries. Membership was free until 2011. The organization recommends a voluntary contribution of $20 (U.S.) for full membership. There are more than three thousand members and thirty-nine institutions representing more than eighty-two developing countries. The organization has several chapters in various countries including Bangladesh, China, India, Malaysia, Yemen, Nigeria, and South Africa. Many of these countries have either a Muslim-majority population or a substantial Muslim population. A number of Muslim women assume leadership roles in organizing the local chapters, and some have achieved influential positions at the international level of the organization.

TWOWS is funded by multiple sources. Among them are the African Academy of Science, the International Council of Science, the Kuwait Foundation for the Advancement of Sciences, and the MacArthur Foundation. Recently, $5,000 awards were established to recognize the achievements of women scientists living in third world countries for their contributions to the development of scientific knowledge. Four awards are given each year, one for each of the geographic regions: Asia and the Pacific, Africa, the Arab world, and Latin America.

The flagship program for this organization is its postgraduate training fellowship, which enables women scientists from third world countries to finish their PhDs. The fellowship is for women younger than forty with master's degrees in science who hail from third world countries. The applicant must pursue her PhD at a host institution of a developing country, not the applicant's home country. The objective of this program is to create a new generation of women leaders in science and technology who will play appropriate roles in the development of their countries. One hundred and seven young women from various third world countries have earned their PhDs through this fellowship. Many of the awardees are Muslim women who reside in Asia, Africa, and the Arab world. Twenty-three have come from the least developed countries in Africa, fifty-two from other sub-Saharan countries, twenty-three from Asia and the Pacific, and nine from the Arab world.

The organization has held four general meetings in different parts of the world, including one in China in June 2010. The meeting focused on women scientists in a changing world. More than six hundred female scientists from thirty-five third world countries attended these meetings. During the meeting in China, a decision was made to change the official name of the organization to Organization for Women in Science for the Developing World (OWSDW).

BIBLIOGRAPHY

Chinese Committee for Third World Organization for Women in Science, Retrieved February 20, 2013, from http://owsdw.ictp.it/.

CTA Knowledge for Development, Retrieved February 20, 2013, from http://knowledge.cta.int/. http://knowledge.cta.int/en/layout/set/print/S-T-Organisation/International/.

Forestry Nepal, Retrieved February 20, 2013, from www.forestrynepal.org.

Girls In ICT Portal, Retrieved February 20, 2013, from http://girlsinict.org.

Organization for Women in Science for the Developing World, accessed June 19, 2012, Retrieved February 20, 2013, from http://owsdw.ictp.it/.

Third World Organization of Women in Science, Retrieved February 20, 2013, from http://www.unesco.org/education/educprog/ste/newsletter/eng_n1/twowssci.html.

UNICEF United States Fund, Retrieved February 20, 2013, from http://www.unicefusa.org/.

Ayad al- Qazzaz

Tīmūrid Dynasty. Territory in Iran, Afghanistan, Tajikistan, and Uzbekistan accumulated by Tīmūr Lang b. Taraghay Barlas (r. 1370–1405), more popularly known as Tīmūr or Tamerlane, was controlled by four generations of his descendants until 1506. Its remnants were incorporated into the dominions of the Ṣafavid, Uzbek, and Chaghatay Mongol dynasties. Tīmūr's obituary stated that he had eighteen wives and twenty-two concubines and that his direct descendants included seventeen women and thirty-three men. Chronicles of the period focus on the family's male members and rarely provide personal details about their female relations, although some trends can be distinguished by matching literary references with information about the buildings financed by Tīmūrid women.

As a dynasty and a family, the Tīmūrids combined traditions from the nomadic cultures of Central Asia with Islamic practices followed by the inhabitants of the region's cities. The position of women within this family and the roles they played in its history conform more closely to nomadic than Muslim customs. Many of the precedents established by Tīmūr endured until the dynasty's collapse following the death of Sultan Ḥusayn Baiqara in 1506. Tīmūr was generous to his female relations; he was particularly close to his elder sister, Turkan Aga (d. 1383), with whom he had sought refuge after reverses early in his career. The lavishly decorated tomb she constructed in the cemetery of Samarqand for her own use and to house the remains of her daughter Shad-i Mulk (d. 1371) is testimony of her importance to Tīmūr. Another tomb in the same cemetery built for his younger sister, Shirin Bika Aga (d. 1385/86), exemplifies the architectural features of Tīmūr's own constructions, such as the shrine for Aḥmad Yasavī erected 1397–1399, demonstrating that the same craftsmen worked on both structures.

Although Tīmūr made Samarqand his capital, when he was on campaign, he was often accompanied by his entire household, who set up camp in a secure location. That female family members continued to accompany the armies of Tīmūr's successors is confirmed by historical descriptions of a confrontation between the forces of Sultan Abū Saʿīd (r. 1451–1469) and those of Uzun Ḥasan Qara Qoyunlu. In a final attempt to prevent hostilities, the former sent his mother and a religious leader to negotiate a truce. Their mission failed and Abū Saʿīd was captured and executed, but the victor took precautions to protect the encampment containing the Tīmūrids' household. Tīmūr had supervised the marriages of his own daughters to important military figures or members of his retinue, but many of his granddaughters married their own relatives. When a female member of the dynasty was widowed, the male head of the family gave her to a new husband, a practice followed even in the case of Tīmūr's own wives and concubines. Women from outside the family appear to have been regarded as booty and those seized through conquest were distributed among Tīmūr's relatives and supporters in much the same way as other property, although the treatment afforded to any particular woman reflected her lineage as well as her personal qualities.

Structures financed by Tīmūrid women testify to their wealth and status, but the composition of their assets was rarely documented. Several constructed their own mausoleums that were often linked to other religious institutions, a pattern established by Tīmūr's wives, Saray Mulk Khanim and Tuman Aqa. Funds for the maintenance of such buildings would have derived from *waqf*s or endowments that the women had created from their personal wealth. Only the endowment deed of Afaq Begum, Sultan Ḥusayn's wife, survives. Her assets included revenue from agriculture with rents from commercial establishments. Most of the structures constructed by Tīmūrid women have vanished, probably because subsequent generations neglected their upkeep.

Although no Tīmūrid woman ruled independently, some participated in the affairs of state. The most important of Tīmūr's wives was Saray Mulk Khanim, whom he acquired in 1370 by defeating Amir Ḥusayn b. Amir Mūsā to whom she was previously married. Her importance at the Tīmūrid court derived in large part from her descent from Genghis Khan, which allowed Tīmūr to add the appellation "Küreken" (son-in-law) to his official titulature, a circumstance that enhanced his legitimacy. Some of Tīmūr's descendants were also married to Gengisizid women and thereby permitted to use this title, including his grandson, Ulugh Beg b. Shāh Rukh, and his great-grandson, Abū Saʿīd b. Muḥammad.

Hints of Saray Mulk Khanim's special status within the family are provided by the Spanish envoy, Ruy Gonzalez de Clavijo, who reveals that she participated in public events alongside men. Persian historians describe her success in protecting family members from Tīmūr's wrath. Clavijo, who was shown the jeweled tree and other treasures bestowed on her by Tīmūr from his booty, also describes her majestic appearance at court ceremonies. Dressed in flowing red silk robes with black hair falling to her shoulders, her face artificially whitened and rouged, she wore a towering headdress that required support from the back by attendants.

The woman who assumed the largest role in Tīmūrid political and military affairs was Gawhar Shad Begum, Shāh Rukh's principal wife, who was the dominant figure at his court. In his declining years, he even entrusted her with military tasks. In the chaos that followed his death in 1447, she tried to influence the choice of his successor. In response to these actions, she was executed in 1457 on the orders of the eventual victor, Abū Saʿīd, an action that was widely criticized, particularly because it took place during the month of Ramaḍān. Her obituary stressed her patronage of architecture, which included a mosque at the shrine of Imam Reza in Mashhad, which is still regarded as one of the masterpieces of Tīmūrid architecture, and a complex of buildings near Herat that included a mausoleum for Shāh Rukh and his family.

BIBLIOGRAPHY

Clavijo, Ruz Gonzalez de. *Embassy to Tamerlane: 1403–1406*. Translated by Guy Le Strange. London: RoutledgeCurzon, 2005.

Golombek, Lisa, and Donald Wilber. *The Timurid Architecture of Iran and Turan*. 2 vols. Princeton, N.J.: Princeton University Press, 1988.

Khwandamir, Giyas al-din. *Habib's-Siyar*. Vols. 3 and 4. Translated by Thackston Wheeler. Cambridge, Mass.: Harvard University, 1994. Chronicle of the Tīmūrid period.

Manz, Beatrice. "Women in Timurid Dynastic Politics." In *Women in Iran from the Rise of Islam to 1800*, edited by Guity Neshat and Lois Beck, pp. 121–139. Urbana: University of Illinois Press, 2003.

O'Kane, Bernard. *Timurid Architecture in Khurasan*. Undena, Calif.: Mazda, 1987.

Soucek, Priscilla. "Timurid Women: A Cultural Perspective." In *Women in the Medieval Islamic World*, edited by Gavin R. Hambly, pp. 199–226. New York: St. Martin's Press, 1998.

Subtelny, Maria, *Timurids in Transition*. Leiden, Netherlands: E.J. Brill, 2007. See for endowment deed of Afaq Begum.

PRISCILLA SOUCEK

TOPKAPI SARAY. The primary residence of the rulers of the Ottoman Empire from 1465 until 1856, Topkapi Saray consisted of ten domed buildings, including the Imperial Harem, which was the women's quarters for members of the ruling family and their staff. The palace was built in Istanbul by Mehmet II between 1459 and 1465 as a series of interlocking complexes with their own courtyards. Within the central part of the main complex, which is located in the west of the palace grounds, to the southwest of the Third Court, lived the many women who constituted the "harem," which at its peak numbered some one thousand women.

The word "harem" comes from the Arabic word *haram* "forbidden." The women living there included Muslims, Jews, Christians, slaves, and former slaves from elsewhere, as well as women who had been presented to the sultan by various foreign leaders and imperial governors. On their arrival, the girls and women were taught the rules and traditions of the harem. If they were not Turkish, they were taught the Turkish language, and learned about Turkish and Muslim culture, as well as modes of dress, styles of music, reading, writing, dancing, sewing, and embroidery. Although Western stereotypes have tended to portray the harem as having an exclusively sexual function, the harem was, more importantly, home to the sultan's mother (*valide sultan*), sisters, children, and their servants, as well as other princes and their female relatives. The Topkapi Saray harem thus was also the center of the public culture of sovereignty, directing royal ceremonies, monumental building projects, especially *awqāf*, and artistic production.

Although only a few women managed to achieve great power, many of those who lived in Topkapi Saray sought in vain to gain the attention of the sultans. Only four of them could become a legitimate wife (*kadim*) of the sultan, with others allowed to be concubines who earned the title *haseki sultan* if they had a son with the sultan, and *haseki kadin* if they had a daughter. Historical accounts often portray the wives and concubines as scheming to get their children into high positions, especially their sons, in the hopes that they might become the next sultan. Others were satisfied with the many titles that were awarded to them, such as Chief Mistress of the Robes, Keeper of the Baths, and Keeper of Jewels. Many funded public charity ventures and institutions.

The harem was closed down in 1909. The Palace is now open to the public as an enormous state museum honoring Ottoman history, including displays of Ottoman architecture, porcelain, robes, weapons, carriages, armor, Ottoman miniatures, Islamic calligraphic manuscripts, murals, jewelry, and costumes and embroideries from the harem. However, the area of the harem itself within the palace can only be visited with a guide.

BIBLIOGRAPHY

Durukan, Zeynep M. *The Harem of the Topkapi Palace*. Istanbul, Turkey: Hilal Koll, 1973.

Peirce, Leslie. *The Imperial Harem: Women and Sovereignty in the Ottoman Empire*. New York: Oxford University Press, 1993.

Penzer, N. M. *The Harem: An Account of the Institution as it Existed in the Palace of the Turkish Sultans, with a History of the Grand Seraglio from Its Foundation to Modern Times*. London: George G. Harrap, 1936.

Rogers, J. M. *The Topkapi Saray Museum: Costumes, Embroideries and Other Textiles*. New York: Little, Brown and Company, 1986.

JUSTIN J. CORFIELD *and* NATANA J. DELONG-BAS

TRADE. Western influence has had two lasting effects on the economic and trade policies of the Islamic countries, or members of the Organization of the Islamic Conference (OIC). (For a comprehensive historical background, see Tuma, 2009.) The available data are recent in origin, and the resulting trade policies have rarely been affected by Islamic thought or principles. The direction and composition of the trade baskets have been determined by economic specialization, technical advancement, and profitability. OIC country exports have been mostly primary and natural products, and their imports mostly manufactured goods that Islamic countries do not produce. Their trade has also mostly occurred with developed countries. Its pattern and composition are determined largely by underdevelopment, poverty, tradition, and the shortage of development capital. Technological advance is neither contradictory to Islam, nor has it been seriously attempted. The OIC has tried to promote trade between its members by encouraging the establishment of Islamic chambers of commerce. Those effects have been limited.

This lasting traditional pattern may also result from restrictions on women's role in economic development and business. Islam does not put any restrictions on women's economic and business activities. But, tradition does, often in the name of religion. Such restrictions start in childhood with the biased distribution of nutrition, educational and career opportunities, freedom of expression, inheritance, and decision making. In adulthood, these restrictions take the form of segregation from men and the obligation to follow male orders. Opportunities are limited, and male children get priority, according to tradition in tribal and clannish societies, and to a certain extent in more advanced countries. Even so, women in OIC countries have achieved some success in overcoming those obstacles and achieving positions of leadership in economic and business enterprises. Islam guides people in business to practice trust, justice and honesty, mutual respect, and refrainment from paying or accepting interest.

Muslim women have realized some important changes in their status. They have become more active outside the home, and in jobs other than child upbringing. Some have achieved positions of top management and leadership. According to *Forbes* magazine, ten Muslim women executives from the Middle East were among the "world's 100 most powerful women" in 2007. For example, Dr. Nahed Taher is chief executive of Saudi Arabia's Gulf One Investment Bank. Another Muslim woman is the first female president of the Arab Bankers Association in North America. Another is chairperson of Kuwait's Global Investment House. Lubna Olayan is CEO of Olayan Financing and, according to *Fortune* magazine, was one of the fifty most influential women outside the United States in 2004. Other Muslim women occupy positions of leadership in government, education, law, and medicine.

However, even these leaders feel discriminated against by their fellow professionals, especially when they participate wearing traditional dress, such as *ʿabāyahs* (cloaks), veils, or *niqābs* (hiding everything except the eyes). Muslim women don these garments in the name of religion, although Islam does not require such fashions, but husbands or other male relatives do. Interviews with fifteen women in positions of leadership in the United Arab Emirates indicate that women feel disadvantaged compared with their male colleagues. Interviewees believe that they are not included in decision-making meetings. They also believe that they have fewer chances for advancement in their careers, compared with male employees in the same enterprises. Top management explained that the *niqāb* does not fit in with modern images of their companies. Similar observations were expressed by a majority of the fifty American Muslim women interviewed in the first decade of this century by Donna Gehrke-White (2006).

Muslim women play an important role in local and national trade, especially in the informal sector, which comprises two-thirds of the national trade, in countries such as Egypt, Pakistan, Indonesia, and Nigeria. In the city of Kumasi, Ghana, about 80 percent of the female population make their living by trading. Women's involvement in domestic trade has been reinforced by the small business loan system, the Grameen system, which became operational in Bangladesh in 1983 and has spread worldwide since then. Mohammad Yunus, its founder, wanted to fight poverty, by emphasizing organization, unity, courage, and hard work. The Grameen Bank has extended small loans to about 85 million people, in 81,000 villages. Approximately 97 percent of the borrowers are women. For his efforts, Yunus was awarded the Nobel Peace Prize in 2006. Women's involvement in international trade and the corporate economy has been limited to banking, finance, and insurance, in addition to their achievements in law, medicine, and education, all of which relate to trade.

Changes in the status of Muslim women have accelerated, especially in 2011 with the so-called Arab Spring, which has left an impact worldwide. Muslim women have participated fearlessly in the demonstrations against dictatorship, discrimination, and economic and gender inequality. They continue to fight for freedom from the restrictions imposed on them in the name of religion. They debate with religious leaders who issue *fatāwā* (religious decrees) based on debatable interpretations of the Qurʾān. As a result, Islamic parties that have achieved a plurality in recent elections have promised to respect women's rights, including the "Personal Status Code, which makes women equal to men in divorce, and bars polygamy" (Associated Press, "Tunisian Women," 2011). The effects of the Arab Spring on Muslim and other women's role in the economy have yet to be determined, however.

Bibliography

Alserhan, Baker Ahmed. *Principles of Islamic Marketing*. Burlington, Vt.: Ashgate Publishing, 2011.

Associated Press. "Malaysia to Ban Obedient Wives Sex Book." November 3, 2011. Accessed 8/5/2015 at http://www.news24.com/World/News/Malaysia-to-ban-Muslim-womens-sex-book-20111103

Associated Press. "Tunisian Women Demonstrate to Protect Their Rights." 2 November 2011.

Associated Press. "Yemen Uprising Binds Women from Many Walks of Life." 6 November 2011.

Bumiller, Elisabeth. *May You Be the Mother of a Hundred Sons: A Journey Among the Women of India*. New York: Random House 1990.

Burn, Trudy. "Women Worry over Growing Strength of Islamist Parties." *The Sacramento Bee*, 1 November 2011.

Clark, Gracia. "Everyday Islam in Kumasi: Devout Lay Men and Women in Daily Life." http://westafricanism.matrix.msu.edu/kumasi/subject/traders/.

"France 'Liberated' Muslim Women by Confining Them to Their Homes." *The Olympian*, 6 May 2011.

Gehrke-White, Donna. *The Face Behind the Veil*. New York: Kensington, 2006.

Hubeiqa, Lewis. "Small Loans Effective Weapon Against Poverty." *Beirut Times*, no. 1316, 17 November 2011.

MacDonald, Elizabeth, and Megha Bahree. "Muslim Women in Charge." 30 August 2007. http://www.forbes.com/2007/08/30/muslim-wo.

Omair, Katlin. "Arab Women Managers and Identity Formation through Clothing." *Gender in Management: An International Journal* 24, no. 6 (2009): 412–431.

Phetdee, Wannapa. "Muslim Women Take Leading Role, Defying Stereotypes." *The Nation*, 3 September 2009.

Shaikh, Shazia. "The Critical Analysis of Fatwas Issued on Muslim Women in India." http://www.boell-India.org/web/52-771.html.

Sidani, Yusuf. "Women, Work, and Islam in Arab Societies." *Women in Management Review* 20, no. 7 (2005): 498–512.

Tuma, Elias. "Trade." In *The Oxford Encyclopedia of the Modern Islamic World*. edited by John L. Esposito, pp. 385–386. New York: Oxford University Press, 2009.

VerEecke, Catherine. "Muslim Women Traders of Northern Nigeria: Perspectives from the City of Yolla." *Ethnology* 32, no. 3 (Summer 1993): 217–236.

Elias H. Tuma

Tribal Societies and Women.

Tribes have long played important roles in the Islamic world by facilitating the rapid spread of Islam in the early Islamic period, contributing to the rise and fall of empires and states throughout the premodern era, and sustaining or weakening ruling regimes during modern times. As Islam spread across Central Eurasia in the premodern period, for example, local tribal groups accepted the new religion, while combining its beliefs and practices with their preexisting ones, such as pilgrimages to saints' tombs. Tribal groups have continued to exert power and influence in the modern period by stabilizing political processes within nation-states (such as Jordan and Kuwait), by opposing ruling regimes (such as Qadhdhāfī's in Libya in 2011), and by fighting against or allying with foreign occupying militaries (such as in Afghanistan and Iraq in the early 2000s).

Writers often use the English term "tribe" to describe, interchangeably, a group of people, a political entity, a form of social organization, or a structural type, and thus leave the definition vague. Although they often equate nomads and pastoralists with tribes, not all nomads or pastoralists have been tribally organized, and more tribal people have been settled than mobile. Often negatively, scholars and others associate the adjective "tribal" with certain cultural systems, ideologies, attitudes, and modes of behavior and imply that a "tribal mentality" is a narrow, partisan, or traditional outlook, as compared with a modern one. The expression "tribes with flags" conveys the notion that even nation-states in the modern era (such as Somalia and Yemen) may be little more than tribes disguised as more complex polities. Scholars usually neglect to consider tribal polities as part of a vibrant civil society in many countries throughout the Islamic world, but such entities have sometimes proven to be vital parts of postcolonial, modernizing, and democratizing societies, as witnessed by tribally based sectors of Kurdish society in urban Iraq, especially since 1991.

Tribal polities—broadly defined by anthropologists as named sociopolitical entities having hierarchical groups and leaders—in the Islamic world have taken different forms, but they all have served as alternative systems to those of premodern empires and states and modern nation-states, and have consistently provided their members with political, economic, and social benefits, such as personal and group protection, support, and identity, especially where empires and state institutions have not effectively reached tribal areas. Different kinds of tribal societies have emerged in various parts of the Islamic world. Some forms have been closely tied to nomadic pastoralism and were often territorially expansive (as in the Arabian Peninsula and North Africa), while others have been based in agricultural societies and more closely connected with markets, centralizing governments, and institutionalized religion (as in Kurdistan and northwestern Pakistan).

Throughout the Islamic world, the structure, organization, leadership, and identity of tribal societies have affected the statuses and roles of women. Real and fictive genealogies (an organizing principle of such entities) have been patrilineal, and women belonged to the lineages, clans, tribes, and confederacies of their fathers. Women have served as repositories of genealogical knowledge, especially women's kinship and marital interconnections, while men have tended to stress their more limited patrilineal and patrilateral ties. Some groups have practiced endogamy (marriage within a defined group), to retain kinswomen within their groups after marriage and to maintain control over property there. Islamic law provides inheritance rights to women, but not all Muslim societies have honored that tenet. Even in endogamous societies, some marriages have been exogamous in order to create alliances with other groups. As in most Islamic societies, polygyny among tribal peoples has been rare and was usually practiced only when a first wife did not bear children, and thus the husband needed heirs to perpetuate his lineage. Women in tribal societies have formed multigenerational and often mutually supportive ties, and their interrelationships were more personally affirming and less competitive than those of most men. In some areas, older women have served as tribal leaders at the local level or for their societies as a whole. In the few rare matrilineal tribal societies (in Saharan and sub-Saharan Africa) in the Islamic world, women have gained some further authority, but actual power has usually rested with their brothers, sons, and other male kin (as has usually been the case in matrilineal societies everywhere). Regardless of tracing descent through the father's or the mother's line, men often still controlled political and economic decision-making on behalf of their households and local communities.

Tribal women have retained the rich cultures of their societies, including oral traditions, rituals, and ceremonies, and they have perpetuated their often unique material cultures and technologies, especially those relating to their work as producers of textiles and other utilitarian objects. In charge of their households, women have provisioned the members with resources, food, and comfort. They have been responsible for raising and socializing children. At a certain age or level of physical ability, boys have left the domestic domain to join older boys and men's activities, while girls have remained with their mothers and other female kin to learn the lessons of their gender before they marry, join their husband's households, and produce and raise their own children.

Whether adhering to Sunnī, Shīʿī, Ṣūfī, or other divisions in Islam (and the diverse beliefs and practices within each one), tribal men have tended to emphasize the five basic pillars of the faith (including praying, fasting, and alms giving) and to engage in communal, often all-male rites, while women have focused more attention on domestic and family rituals, including local pilgrimages, vow-making, and rites of passage relating to birth, attainment of adulthood, marriage, and death. Older Ṣūfī women especially have played essential roles in community leadership in tribal societies, given the greater gender equality inherent in many Ṣūfī beliefs and practices. Men and women in all Islamic societies have arranged and celebrated marriages, each gender having its own specific rites, roles, and duties.

Women in tribal societies have often been less restricted in their dress, deportment, and mobility than the women in the nontribal societies located near them, partly because internal tribal structures and organizations provided them with adequate protection and security. They have not been as limited by the kinds of modest coverings ("veiling" in its many forms) and patterns of seclusion found among other women in nontribal urban and rural settings in the Islamic world. Modesty, chastity, and marital fidelity have been key values for all Muslim women, and to some extent for men as well, and the norms governing behavior prevalent in any Islamic society help to sustain these values. Notions of honor and shame are paired in most Islamic societies, especially tribal ones, with men responsible for upholding lineage and group honor, and women impeded from engaging in behaviors that would shame their kin and tribal groups.

Outsiders have often blamed tribal societies for values and customs that have subordinated women and female children and have subjected them to honor killings, child marriages, other forms of arranged unions, physical abuse, female genital cutting, and easy divorce for men. Such attitudes and practices, also found among Islamic societies that were not tribally organized (and among many non-Islamic societies as well), have stemmed instead from often universal notions of male supremacy, patriarchy, and patrilineality, which privileged men and boys over women and girls. Women in some tribal societies have been more protected against discrimination and abuse than women in some nontribal societies because of the constant protections offered by coresident, close-knit, kinship-related tribal groups. The covert, subversive power of women, expressed within families and local communities, has played a role in their relationships with men and hierarchical structures and has tempered the authority that these individuals and entities might have otherwise held over them. Aware that women could apply sanctions against them (by denying them food or comfort) or threaten their fragile sense of masculinity and individual honor (by spreading rumors about their impotence), men have learned to exercise caution in exerting abusive power over women.

Tribal men have generally been more involved than tribal women in the processes of Islamization (greater systemization of religious beliefs and practices and their dissemination), market expansion, modernization (including access to modern technology such as mobile telephones and computers), integration and assimilation in nation-states, and globalization. Women have continued to support the domestic domain and their local kinship, tribal, and work-related networks and to handle children's socialization. Formal education, including both Islamic and secular forms, has involved boys in greater numbers than girls, and the resulting occupational changes have affected more males than females. Even with women's higher education and increased participation in paid labor outside the home, society at large has continued to consider women responsible for performing most, if not all, domestic and child-related tasks. New or enhanced notions of national identity and a politicized Islam have impacted men more directly than women, who continued to uphold local-community, tribal, and ethnic identities and their social, ritual, and ceremonial expressions. Women's (and men's) affiliations with tribal polities have served to demarcate the space between their local communities and wider arenas such as nation-states and to offer them some protective mediation. In some places, young women have resisted against the societal and cultural norms that restricted their greater participation in the wider community and society, such as in Iran during the country-wide popular uprisings against oppressive monarchical and theocratic regimes in the late twentieth and early twenty-first centuries.

BIBLIOGRAPHY

Abu-Lughod, Lila. *Veiled Sentiments: Honor and Poetry in a Bedouin Society*. Berkeley: University of California Press, 1986.

Beck, Lois. *Nomad: A Year in the Life of a Qashqa'i Tribesman in Iran*. Berkeley: University of California Press, 1991.

Beck, Lois. "Qashqa'i Women in Postrevolutionary Iran." In *Women in Iran from 1800 to the Islamic Republic*, edited by Lois Beck and Guity Nashat, pp. 240–278. Urbana: University of Illinois Press, 2004.

Beck, Lois, and Julia Huang. "Tribes." In *The Oxford Encyclopedia of the Islamic World*, edited by John Esposito, vol. 5, pp. 390–398. New York: Oxford University Press, 2009. Historical and anthropological analyses of tribal polities in the Islamic world in premodern and modern times.

Beck, Lois, and Julia Huang. "Tribes." In *The Oxford Encyclopedia of Islam and Politics*, edited by Emad El-Din Shahin, forthcoming. Revised and updated "Tribes" entry from *The Oxford Encyclopedia of the Islamic World*.

Charrad, Mounira. *States and Women's Rights: The Making of Postcolonial Tunisia, Algeria, and Morocco*. Berkeley: University of California Press, 2001.

Hilal, Hissa (Rimiya). *Divorce and Kholu' Poetry: A Reading of the Status of Women in Tribal Society, Nabati Poetry as a Witness*. Abu Dhabi, United Arab Emirates: Abu Dhabi Authority for Culture and Heritage, 2010.

Huang, Julia. *Tribeswomen of Iran: Weaving Memories among Qashqa'i Nomads*. London: I. B. Tauris, 2009.

Lavie, Smadar. *The Poetics of Military Occupation: Mzeina Allegories of Bedouin Identity under Israeli and Egyptian Rule*. Berkeley: University of California Press, 1990.

Layne, Linda L. *Home and Homeland: The Dialogics of Tribal and National Identities in Jordan*. Princeton, N.J.: Princeton University Press, 1994.

Schatz, Edward. *Modern Clan Politics: The Power of "Blood" in Kazakhstan and Beyond*. Seattle: University of Washington Press, 2004.

Shahrani, M. Sharif. *The Kirghiz and Wakhi of Afghanistan: Adaptation to Closed Frontiers and War*. Seattle: University of Washington Press, 2002.

Tapper, Nancy. *Bartered Brides: Politics, Gender and Marriage in an Afghan Tribal Society*. Cambridge, U.K.: Cambridge University Press, 1991.

Weir, Shelagh. *A Tribal Order: Politics and Law in the Mountains of Yemen*. Austin: University of Texas Press, 2007.

LOIS BECK *and* JULIA HUANG

TUNISIA. The development of the Tunisian feminist movement is deeply rooted in the country's nationalist and reformist movements.

The Colonial Period: The Fathers of Tunisian Feminism. Influenced by the Nahdha movement in the Middle East, as early as 1867, Kheireddine Pacha (1822–1890) called for women's education. In 1897 Shaykh Muḥammad al-Sanusi (1851–1900) published *Tafatuh Al-Akmem aw dirassa hawla almar'a fil Islam* (The blooming of the flower or a study of woman in Islam), in which he defended Muslim women's education as a religious duty. Co-authored by César Ben Attar, El Hedi Sebai, and Abdelaziz Eth'aalbi, *The Liberal Spirit of the Quran* (1905) called for the education of Tunisian women and the abolition of the veil. These new ideas about women's emancipation were propagated not only through literary clubs like the Khaldūnīyah or Jamaâ Taht Essur, but also newspapers like *Ez-Zohra, Al-Hadhira, Es-Saweb, En-Nahdha, Murshid Al-Umma, Al-Badr, Lissan Ech-Chaâb, The Kheireddine Review, Tunis Socialiste*, and *L'Etendard Tunisien*.

In 1917 Hassan Hosni Abdelwahab (1884–1968) dedicated to his daughter the first biography of Tunisian women, titled *Shahirat al-Tunisiyat* (Most famous Tunisian women), hoping she could find "spiritual guidance" in the lives of Queen Kahina; Zanab Bint ʿUmar; Oum al-Banin or Fatima el-Fihriya (eighth century); Asma Bint Asad Bent al-Furat (daughter of the Ḥanafi Cadi who conquered Sicily in 827); the princess and poet Mahriyya al-Aghlabiya (Aghlabid dynasty); the folktale el-Jaziya el-Hilaliya (eleventh century); Saïda Manoubia (Ḥafṣid dynasty); Aziza Uthmana (Ottoman Tunisia); and Fatima Uthmana (Ḥusaynid dynasty).

In 1930 the nationalist and trade unionist al-Ṭāhir al-Ḥaddād (1899–1935) published his controversial book *Imra'atuna fi al Sharia wa al mujtama* (Our woman in the Sharīʿah law and society) in which he called for women's education, gender equity in inheritance and the abolition of the veil, polygamy, the triple divorce formula (whereby a wife is repudiated if the husband says three times: "You are divorced"), and the practice of marriage without consent. In al-Ḥaddād's nationalist and patriarchal feminism, women's emancipation fell within the larger project of liberating the nation from French colonialism. For him, the Tunisian woman existed only as the future mother and wife of male nationalist subjects, not as an individual.

In Search of the Mothers of Tunisian Feminism. It was not until the 1980s and 1990s that the stories of the mothers of Tunisian feminism came to light with the rise of a new generation of Tunisian women scholars. In her 1993 study, Elhem Marzouki unearthed several organizations led by women from the traditional bourgeoisie of Tunis in French colonial Tunisia, such as the Club of the Tunisian Young Woman presided over by Tawhida Farhat; the Muslim Union of the Women of Tunisia presided over by Bchira Ben Mrad, the daughter of Shaykh Muḥammad Salah Ben Mrad (1881–1979) who attacked al-Ḥaddād in *Al-hidad âla imra'at al-Haddad* (1931; Mourning over al-Haddad's woman); and the Women's Section in the Association of Young Tunisian Women headed by Suad Khattach, the wife of Shaykh Muḥammad Salah Ennaifer, one of the most prominent religious scholars at the Zaytūnah mosque. These associations were less interested in improving women's status than they were in supporting education, conducting social work, and defending Tunisia's Arab and Islamic identity against the threat of acculturation and assimilation into French culture. In 1937 the Union Musulmane des Femmes de Tunisie (UMFT) held a ceremony in honor of Tawhida Ben Sheikh, the first Tunisian woman to receive a medical degree. During the fight for independence, many women affiliated with these organizations were harassed and arrested for organizing secret meetings and participating in demonstrations against the French colonial authorities. The most famous of these occurred on 15 January 1952, the so-called Women's Demonstration of Beja, which sparked off several others throughout the country. Many Tunisian women were placed under house arrest, imprisoned, and even sent to labor camps in places like Ben Gardane and Remada. In 1952 the Red Cross reported the rape of women and the murder of children in the Tazerka, Maamoura, and Kelibia areas during the brutal Ratissage du Cap Bon operation launched on 28 January 1952 by the résident général Jean de Hauteclocque, who used terror to beat the nation into submission.

State Feminism in the Postcolonial Era. The postcolonial period was marked by two phases of institutional feminism: the state feminism of Habib Bourguiba (1903–2000) and that of President Zine el Abidine Ben Ali (b. 1936). Even though he defended the veil in 1928 as the symbol of Tunisia's Arabo-Islamic identity, once he assumed power in 1956, Bourguiba attacked the veil as a foreign custom and claimed for himself the paternity of both Tunisian feminism and nationalism. On 13 August 1956 Bourguiba promulgated the Personal Status Code (PSC), which as of 2013 remains unequaled in the Arab world in that it abolished polygamy and marriage without consent and replaced the practice of repudiation with divorce courts that grant both spouses the right to file for divorce. Through the National Union of Tunisian Women (UNFT), a feminist organization affiliated with the state, Bourguiba launched his family-planning campaign and urged women to remove the veil, which he often referred to as a "misérable chiffon" or "despicable rug" (Bessis, 1999). This emancipatory project came to a halt in the 1970s when, in an effort to undermine the left, Bourguiba started catering to the religious right. In 1973 the marriage of Muslim women to non-Muslim men was forbidden. As Sophie Bessis has pointed out, far from being entirely secular, the status of Tunisian women remains quite ambiguous. Treated as equal in public laws, such as those involving education and employment, Tunisian women are still denied equity in matters of family law, such as inheritance or custody of children in the event of divorce.

In a deliberate effort to undermine the myth of Bourguiba as the sole "Libérateur de la femme tunisienne," Ben Ali highlighted the feminist contributions of the other fathers of modern Tunisia, such as ʿAbd al-ʿAzīz al-Thaʿālibī, who was Bourguiba's political rival. Situating himself in opposition to Bourguiba's secularism, Ben Ali reopened the Zaytūnah mosque that was closed by his predecessor and renovated the mausoleum of the Ṣūfī saint Sidi Boulbaba in 1996 to emphasize Tunisia's Arabo-Islamic heritage. In 2009 Ben Ali's son-in-law Sakher El Materi opened the first Islamic bank in North Africa. After breaking with the Islamists in 1990, Ben Ali realigned himself with Bourguiba's legacy of state feminism to silence all criticism of his regime in the West. He created the Women's Center of Information and Documentation (1991) and the Ministry of the Affairs of Women, Children and Childhood (1992). Trying to surpass Bourguiba, he enacted laws recognizing the rights of single mothers and children born out of wedlock (1998), replaced the word "obedience" to a husband in clause 23 of the PSC with the word "kindness" (1993), and granted Tunisian women the right to pass on their citizenship to their children born of a foreign husband (1993).

This new law remains patriarchal because only the Tunisian woman needs the consent of her foreign husband to convey her citizenship to her children. The children of a Tunisian father are born citizens; the consent of a foreign wife is not needed. The prenuptial agreements law enacted on 5 April 1996 also gave a husband and wife the choice of dividing up any property acquired before and after marriage.

In opposition to this state brand of "feminism," an independent grassroots feminist movement emerged in Tunisia in the mid-1980s, one that demanded separation between state and religion, gender equity in inheritance, and full equality in citizenship. As Sana Ben Achour, head of the Association of Tunisian Women Democrats, points out (2001), state feminism, far from guaranteeing *muwatana*, or full citizenship, to Tunisian women has held them hostage of both the religious establishment and the political expediency of the state. The secular spirit of the Personal Status Code stands in contradiction to Article 1 of the Constitution, which holds Islam to be the country's official religion. All reforms pertaining to women's status (1956 and 1988) were framed within the Islamic paradigm of *ijtihād* not the 1984 Copenhagen Convention on the abolition of all forms of discrimination against women. The spirit of this movement is represented in the activities and contributions of the al-Taher al-Haddad Cultural Club, the Tabarka International Jazz Festival (1979), the periodical *Nissa* (1984), the Women's Committee in the Tunisian Syndicate, and the Commission on Women's Rights (1985) operating within the Tunisian Human Rights League.

Tunisian Feminism in the Post-Revolution. With the fall of the Ben Ali regime, a new feminism surfaced in Tunisia, inspired by both the Anglocentric discourse on Islamic democracy and the Islamic Gulf-style feminism that stresses gender complementarity rather than the language of human rights. The outburst of violence against university women after the 23 October 2011 elections is illustrative of the backlash against feminist activists in post-revolution Tunisia, with such women forced once again to defend the PSC rather than continue the fight for equal citizenship. The deliberate association of all feminist movements with the Ben Ali regime and the amalgamation between the state feminism of Ben Ali and the independent feminism of the Association of Tunisian Women Democrats by both the religious right and the liberal patriarchy on the left are meant to deny women full citizenship in post-revolutionary Tunisia. The recent vote of the Constitutional Assembly to make the PSC a basic law, rather than being a concession by the Islamists, is in fact a concession by the secularists who yet again find themselves in the defensive position of protecting rights already gained, rather than seeking new ones. The ambiguous discourse of ruling Ennahdha leaders regarding polygamy, *ʿurfi* marriage (marriage without official contract), the current adoption laws and the rights of single mothers and their children has propelled Tunisian feminist activists of both sexes toward street activism, as was manifested in the Bardo sit-ins in front of the Constitutent Assembly in November and December 2011.

Cyber activism is perhaps the latest development in the history of Tunisian feminism across the entire political spectrum. Even though on her Facebook page, Soumaya Ghannoushi, the London-educated and hijab-wearing daughter of Ennahdha Party leader Rāshid al-Ghannūshī, opposes true Islamic feminism (which centers on education, work, and health care) to the fake Parisian feminism of Bourguiba (which consists of wearing mini-skirts, smoking cigarettes, and drinking wine), the simplistic dichotomy she makes is ironically a reproduction of the very patriarchal state feminism of Bourguiba that she opposes. As noted by Elhem Marzouki (1993), Radhia Haddad (UNFT president under

Bourguiba) once warned that Tunisia has no place for those modern women who "wake up at midday" because they spend their evenings "in salons, joking, smoking cigarettes, and playing cards" (p. 173).

The Ennahdha Party's victory has thrust non-veiled feminist activists educated at Tunisian universities from the realm of academia into the battlefield of Tunisian politics. Olfa Youssef, Raja Ben Slama, and Amel Grami recently transformed into cyber political analysts, which has brought upon them the admiration of some and the scorn of others. Youssef and Ben Slama have received several death threats for their blasphemous readings of the veil and gay rights in the Qur'ān. In the cyber war over Tunisia's national identity, each side has developed its own mythologies. To the Islamic feminist ideal of the Mothers of the Believers, the secularists oppose the myth of Bourguibism and the Amazons of Carthage. If the current crisis of identity pitting the "secularists" against "Islamists" reveals anything, it is, ironically, the way both sides instrumentalize and exhibit the female body to gain political legitimacy, the first through unveiling and the second through hyper-veiling as illustrated in the controversy over the wearing of the *niqāb* in Tunisian academia.

BIBLIOGRAPHY

Abdelwahab, Hassan Hosni. *Shahirat al-Tunisiyat: Baḥth tarikhi adabi fī ḥayat al-nisa' al-nawaabigh bi-al-quṭr al-Tunisii min al fatḥ al-Islaami ilaa al-zaman al-ḥaḍir* (Most famous Tunisian women: A history and literary study of women prodigies in the country of Tunisia from the Muslim conquest to the present). Tunis: Maktabat al Manar, 1966.

Al Haddād, Tāhir. *Muslim Women in Law and Society: Annotated Translation of al-Ṭāhir al Haddād's Imra 'tuna fi 'l-sharia wa 'l-mujtama, with an Introduction.* Trans. Runak Hosni and Daniel L. Newman. London and New York: Routledge, 2007. Print. This is the English translation of a seminal text on the role of women in Muslim society by the early twentieth-century union activist, feminist, and social reformer al-Ṭāhir al Haddād whose ideas formed the basis of the Personal Status Code of 1956 that gave Tunisian women rights unequaled in the Arab world.

Ben Abdallah, Sami. «Le Drame tunisien: Les viols et massacres commis au Cap Bon avant l'indépendance de la Tunisie.» *Sami Ben Abdallah*, 11 Mars 2012. http://www.samibenabdallah.info/2012/03/11/le-drame-tunisien-les-viols-et-massacres-commis-au-cap-bon-avant-lindependance-de-la-tunisie/#more. In opposition to the Tunisian government's amnesia over French colonial war crimes, cyber activist Sami Ben Abdallah unearths on his blog the untold history of collective rapes and massacres in the Cap Bon area in the 1950s, using as his only sources French colonial archives such as *Le Livre blanc: Sur la détention politique en Tunisie* (1953) and *Le Drame tunisien* (1952) by Cahiers de témoignage Chrétien.

Ben Achour, Sana. "Féminisme d'État: Figure ou défiguration du féminisme?" In *Manifeste des libertés.* Tunis: Centre de Publication Universitaire, 2001. http://www.manifeste.org/article.php3?id_article=129.

Bessis, Sophie. "Le féminisme institutionnel en Tunisie: Ben Ali et la question féminine." *CLIO Histoire, femmes et sociétés* 9 (1999). http://clio.revues.org/index286.html.

Ḥaddād, al-Ṭāhir. *Imra'atuna fi al Sharia wa al mujtama'*. Tunis: Manshurat dar al Maârif li al tiba'a wa al nashr, 1997.

Marzouki, Elhem. *Le mouvement des femmes en Tunisie au XXème siècle.* Collection Enjeux. Paris: Maisonneuve et Larose, 1993.

LAMIA BEN YOUSSEF

TURĀBĪ, ḤASAN AL-. (b. 1932). Ḥasan 'Abd Allāh al-Turābī, commonly referred to as Ḥasan al-Turābī is a Sudanese political leader and Islamist intellectual. In 1955, he graduated with a BA in law from the University of Khartoum. Then he completed his postgraduate studies in London and Paris and returned to Sudan with a PhD in constitutional law from the

Sorbonne (Moussalli, 1994). In 1964, he emerged as the charismatic leader and principal ideologue of the Islamic movement in Sudan. Described as a soft-spoken revolutionary, Turābī has, since 1964, been a central actor in every key political development in Sudan (Esposito and Voll, 2001). In 1979, he became minister of justice under the military reign of Jaʿfar Muḥammad al-Nimeirī (president from 1969 to 1985). In 1988, Turābī was again appointed minister of justice, then minister of foreign affairs, and later deputy prime minister under the elected government of his brother-in-law, Ṣādiq al-Mahdī (prime minister from 1985 to 1989). A coup led by ʿUmar Ḥasan Aḥmad al-Bashīr on 30 June 1989 installed a military dictatorship heavily influenced by the Islamic movement spearheaded by Turābī (El-Affendi, 1991). In 1996, Turābī was appointed as the speaker of parliament. He was considered the mastermind behind the Islamic state's policies, until he fell out of favor with the president during Ramaḍān, 1999. Since then, he has been in and out of prison and house arrest (Gallab, 2008).

Turābī exerted tremendous influence on the development of the ideological tenets of the Islamic movement. For Turābī, the justification for an Islamic state in Sudan is based on *tawḥīd* (unity of God) as a comprehensive way of life, including political life (Morrison, 2001; Affendi, 1991). He conceptualizes *shūrā* (consultation) as the Islamic way of decision-making (Tønnessen, 2009; Moussalli, 2001). Turābī originates these ideas in the Islamic sources of the Qurʾān and the *sunnah*. However, by going back to the roots he simultaneously surpasses the traditional law schools and thereby attempts to develop a new way of Islamic thinking (Turabi, 1987). Whether in economics, foreign policy, or political philosophy, Turābī continuously advocates the need for change (*tajdīd*) in order to adapt Islamic texts to the challenges of modern society (ibid.).

Turābī is particularly renowned for his controversial Islamic standpoints on women (Lowrie, 1993). Already in 1973, Turābī published a pamphlet with the title "Women between the Teachings of Religion and the Customs of Society," arguing that male Islamic jurists interpreted Shariʿah granting authority to men liberally and expansively, while reading those imposing limitations on women literally and strictly. Differing sharply with the conservative views held by most Islamic movements at that time, Turābī came down decisively in favor of women's presence in the public realm, including the military. According to Turābī, women played a significant public role during the time of Prophet Muḥammad, contributing to the election of the third caliph. In contemporary Muslim societies, however, women are wrongfully denied their rightful place in political and public life (Turabi, 1983). The foremost task of Islamic movements is, therefore, to close the gap between the fallen historical reality and the desired model of ideal Islam (Turabi, in Hamidi, 1998). Turābī continues to spark debate, in 2006, by even stating that Islam does not prohibit female-led prayer; that a woman's testimony in court is equal to that of a man's; and that it is not obligatory for Muslim women to wear the headscarf. Historically and presently, he is considered controversial inside and outside of Sudan. On several occasions, he has been accused of apostasy by his detractors for his provocative interpretations of Islam (Ibrahim, 1999). He has also been heavily criticized for ultimately failing to implement his moderate ideas when he was in a position of power in Sudan (Al-Affendi, 2006).

[*See also* Sudan.]

BIBLIOGRAPHY

Al-Turabi, Hasan. *Women between the Teachings of Religion and the Customs of Society [Al- Marʾa bayna*

Ta'alim al-Din wa Taqlid al-Mujta'ma]. Jeddah: Al-Dar al-Su'udiya li al-Nashr wa al-Tawzi', 1973.
Al-Turabi, Hasan. "The Islamic State." In *Voices of Resurgent Islam*, edited by John Esposito, pp. 241–252. Oxford: Oxford University Press, 1983.
Al-Turabi, Hasan. *The Renewal of Islamic Thinking [Tajdid al-Fikr al-Islam]*. Jeddah: Al-Dar al-Su'udiya li al-Nashr wa al-Tawzi', 1987.
El-Affendi, Abdelwahab. "Hasan al-Turabi and the Limits of Modern Islamic Reformation." In *The Blackwell Companion on Contemporary Islamic Thought*, edited by Ibrahim M. Abu-Rabi. Oxford: Blackwell, 2006.
El-Affendi, Abdelwahab. *Turabi's Revolution: Islam and Power in Sudan*. London: Grey Seal, 1991.
Esposito, John, and John Voll. *Makers of Contemporary Islam*. Oxford: Oxford University Press, 2001.
Gallab, Abdullahi A. *The First Islamist Republic: Development and Disintegration of Islamism in the Sudan*. Aldershot, U.K.: Ashgate, 2008.
Hamidi, Mohamed. *The Making of an Islamic Political Leader: Conversations with Hasan al-Turabi*. Boulder, Colo.: Westview, 1998.
Ibrahim, Abdullahi Ali. "A Theology of Modernity: Hasan al-Turabi and Islamic Renewal in Sudan," *Africa Today*, 46, no. 3/4 (1999): 195–222.
Lowrie, Arthur L., ed. *Islam, Democracy, the State and the West: A Round Table with Dr. Hasan Turabi, May 10, 1992*. Tampa, Fla.: USA, 1993.
Morrison, Scott. "The Political Thought of Hasan al-Turabi of Sudan." *Islam and Christian-Muslim Relations*, 12, no. 2 (2001): 153–160.
Moussalli, Ahmad. "Hasan al-Turabi's Islamist Discourse on Democracy and Shura." *Middle Eastern Studies*, 30, no. 1 (1994): 52–63.
Moussalli, Ahmad. *The Islamic Quest for Democracy, Pluralism and Human Rights*, Gainesville: University of Florida Press, 2001.
Tønnessen, Liv. "Democratizing Islam and Islamizing Democracy: An Inquiry into Hasan al-Turabi's Conception of Shura in Light of Western Democratic Theory." *Nordic Journal of Human Rights*, 27, no. 3 (2009): 313–329.

LIV TØNNESSEN

TURKEY. Turkish women have remained in a "patriarchal paradox" (Arat, 1989) since the founding of modern Turkey in 1923. Although upper-class Ottoman women rallied for enfranchisement and succeeded in gaining entry to universities in the 1910s, enfranchisement was only procured when Mustafa Kemal Atatürk, the founder of modern Turkey, granted women most legal equalities in the 1920s and 1930s as part of the modernization process. However, despite some Turkish women being encouraged by men to participate in politics, men have also limited the amount of support they lend to women in the political sphere. Thus, women are present in the parliament, political parties, and nongovernmental organizations, but frequently are not powerful enough to affect change. Many women also continue to confront patriarchy in their professional and personal lives.

Atatürk's modernization reforms encouraged Turkish women to adopt European dress and discard the headscarf while instituting mandatory education for both sexes. Atatürk and his followers ensured that in the new civil code polygamy was banned and women were allowed the right to initiate divorce and inherit equally with men. In 1930, women became eligible to vote in local elections and, in 1934, in national elections. The first parliamentary elections in which women voted occurred in 1935, when eighteen women won election to parliament. After the 1935 elections, however, the state asked the primary women's political group to close, because the state proclaimed that women had already been emancipated and liberated. The organization complied. For many decades thereafter, gender-based questions were not a large part of politics.

On some occasions, individual women were held up by the state as role models. One such woman was Sabiha Gökçen, whom Atatürk adopted as a teenager. Gökçen later attended flying school and Turkey's Air Force Academy. In 1936 and 1937, she took part in combat missions, becoming the first female military pilot in Turkey and, according to many, in the world. Her accomplishments were praised in Turkish and international newspapers. However, Gökçen, like other prominent Turkish women, did not use her status to campaign for more rights for women.

From the 1930s to the 1970s, the state assured that citizens were treated equally regardless of gender. In the 1970s, communist and religious groups, both labeled "leftists" by the state, emerged. For most of these groups, gender issues again took a backseat to other concerns, although one group formed to lobby for women's rights in the workplace. But the political landscape changed dramatically after the military instigated a coup in 1980 in order to purge Turkey of the influence of communism.

Women's Concerns Emerge. After the 1980 coup, identity politics dominated political discourse, with Kurdish associations, Islamic groups, and women's nongovernmental organizations all becoming organized forces in formal politics. From 1983 to 1987, Western feminism became popular among urban elites, with women forming groups and reading societies dedicated to concerns such as second-wave feminism, violence against women, and state-mandated virginity tests for never-married women who were applying for government jobs. Feminist groups also worked to have the state recognize that there was a large gap between women's formal rights and their social conditions.

Şirin Tekeli was a key figure in the women's movement in the 1980s. Originally an academic, Tekeli left academia after the 1980 coup, stating that the military was trying to control academic life. Tekeli then became very involved in feminist politics. In fact, three notable components of Istanbul's twenty-first-century feminist community trace their beginnings to Tekeli: the Women's Library and Information Centre, which opened in 1990; the Purple Roof Women's Shelter, which remains one of few women's shelters in Turkey; and KA-DER, the Organization for the Support and training of Women Candidates.

The 1990s brought women with varying identities and ideologies to the forefront of Turkish politics. Leyla Zana, a Kurd from Diyarbakır Province, was elected to Parliament in 1994 at the age of thirty-three. Kurds, an ethnic group spread over Turkey, Iran, Syria, and Iraq, had long been a target of the states they inhabited. Within Turkey in the 1980s, Kurdish villages had been burned, many Kurds had been killed or "disappeared," and speaking Kurdish in public was illegal. The ongoing conflict between the Turkish state and the Kurds resulted in the formation of the Kurdistan Workers' Party (PKK), a terrorist organization, which allowed both men and women to become fighters. However, the vast majority of Turkish Kurds were not members of the PKK. Many Kurds fought for Kurdish rights through formal political channels, including Zana, who drew attention to the Kurdish cause by speaking part of her parliamentary oath in Kurdish. For this, Zana was charged with treason and sentenced to fifteen years in prison. After two Nobel Peace Prize nominations and several other awards, the European Union successfully lobbied for her release in 2004. The Turkish government's harassment of Zana did not stop, however: in 2008, 2009, and 2010, Zana was convicted of spreading terrorist propaganda and violating antiterrorism laws and sentenced to more prison time. Despite her pending incarceration, Zana was reelected to Parliament in 2011.

As a result of Zana's efforts and the efforts of many other Kurdish women, the Kurdish women's movement in Turkey blossomed in the 1990s and continues to expand through organizations such as KAMER, which supports women in gaining skills for employment and becoming financially independent, and provides counseling for women and their children. Another Kurdish women's organization, SELİS provides services for women dealing with issues of forced migration and internal displacement. Following the example of Argentina's Mothers of the Plaza de Mayo, the Saturday Mothers are a group of Kurdish women who protest on Saturday mornings in central Istanbul, seeking justice for relatives who have disappeared after showing opposition to the state. Many of the Kurdish women's organizations in Turkey have formal links to Kurdish women's organizations in Europe and elsewhere in the Middle East.

Another prominent woman in Turkish politics in the 1990s was Tansu Çiller, who served as prime minister from 1993 to 1996. Çiller's family was part of the Turkish urban elite, and Çiller had attended the most elite schools in Turkey, earned a PhD in economics in the United States, then returned to Turkey, promising to be a politician who would "protect secularism." She was a member of the Doğru Yol Partisi (True Path Party). Many thought a woman assuming the position of Turkish prime minister in the 1990s was unquestionably a sign of Turkey's developing modernity and gender equality. Çiller faced a difficult political climate, however. She became prime minister after the Cumhuriyet Halk Partisi (Republican People's Party, CHP) withdrew from a coalition government, leaving a fractured political arena for her to bring order to. During Çiller's tenure, Turkey faced high inflation, a violent Kurdish separatist movement, dissension within the CHP, and the rising influence of political Islam. These were compounded by Çiller's own political foibles, including failing to declare $4.5 million in real estate holdings in the United States. Her party lost influence in politics and was forced to enter into coalition governments. In order to garner more public support from the religious population, she started increasing the use of religious terminology in her speeches, sometimes donning the headscarf and praying in public, which caused many Turks to question her values and leadership. Çiller was consequently forced out as prime minister in 1996; she left politics altogether in 2002.

The man who took over for Çiller as prime minister, Necmettin Erbakan, became prime minister after being a long-standing figure in Turkish politics who advocated for the increased presence of Islam in the public sphere. His advocacy for Sharīʿah (Islamic) law during a 1997 rally led to an "e-coup," in which the military publicly threatened to stage a coup unless Erbakan retired from politics immediately. Not willing to risk damaging Turkey's economy, his own Refah Partisi (Welfare Party), or European Union accession talks, Erbakan stepped down and was banned from politics for life. The Welfare Party was later closed.

Women in the Era of Islamic Political Parties, from 1999. In 1999, the Fazilet Partisi (Virtue Party) was established to replace the Welfare Party. In the 1999 elections, Merve Kavakçı, a young mother who was educated in Turkey until the ban on students wearing headscarves at universities forced her to continue her schooling in the United States, was placed on the ballot as a candidate. Kavakçı began her career in politics by volunteering for the Welfare Party; many say she was handpicked by Erbakan to become a candidate for the Virtue Party. Kavakçı won the election despite declaring during her campaign that she would not take off her headscarf before entering Parliament to take her oath. There had never been a headscarved woman elected to parliament before, and since the 1980s headscarf-wearing women had been banned at times from attending universities or entering courtrooms and military bases. The situation became more severe after the 1997 e-coup, when the military standardized enforcement of the ban throughout the country. Headscarf issues had contributed to a growing secular-urban-elite/religious-migrant-lower-class divide in Turkish affairs. When Kavakçı entered the parliament's chambers to take her oath, she became the center of such a conflict: an educated, headscarf-wearing woman attempting to take a place in formal politics threatened the existing social order. She faced booing and screaming from other parliamentarians and, unable to take her oath, left the chamber. The media and other politicians alleged she was an "agent provocateur," signaling Islam's increasing power in Turkish society. Iranian women rallied in Tehran in support of Kavakçı, although Kavakçı openly criticized the Iranian regime and its lack of rights for women. Later, Kavakçı received death threats and briefly lost her Turkish citizenship; she returned to the United States.

The Fazilet Party was banned in 2001, and the Adalet ve Kalkınma Partisi (Justice and Development Party, AKP) formed in its place. As with the Welfare and Virtue Parties before it, the AKP has had remarkable success recruiting women to volunteer for its *kadın kolları* (women's branches, which help during elections to support the party's candidates and organize assistance projects for those in need. The AKP boasts that its women's arm, with over 2 million members, is the largest women's political organization in the world.

The AKP won nearly 35 percent of the vote in the general election of 2002 and over 40 percent of the vote in the 2007 and 2011 general elections. In 2007, the AKP's Abdullah Gül was nominated to become Turkey's president. Gül's wife, Hayrünnisa, wears a headscarf, which created controversy. Secularists noted that if Gül became president, Hayrünnisa would be banned from official functions within Turkey because of regulations banning the headscarf in some public places and questioned how a woman could claim to be loyal to the Republic while wearing a headscarf. Hayrünnisa Gül has publically stated that the decision to wear a headscarf should be a woman's choice.

Other religiously conservative women founded organizations and became involved in politics, especially in the 1990s and 2000s. Among these organizations are AK-DER (Ayrımcılığa Karşı Kadın Hakları Derneği, Women's Antidiscrimination Organization), which fights specifically for the rights of headscarf-wearing women, and the Başkent Kadın Platformu (Capital Women's Platform), which was founded by Hidayet Tuksal. Tuksal, who holds a PhD in Islamic theology, describes her views as those of a "religious feminist." She states that interpretations of Islam have become male-dominated over time and objects to the notion that Islam is inherently patriarchal. The organization tries to help women participate in social and political life by offering computer classes, language classes, book groups, and other projects.

Since the 1990s, this "Islamist-secularist" divide has affected the ability of women's organizations to work together, with organizations like Cumhuriyet Kadınları (Women of the Republic) and Çağdaş Yaşamı Destekleme Derneği (Association in Support of Contemporary Life) and groups with outwardly more observant women, such as AK-DER and the Capital Women's Platform, being defined as "Islamist" and "pro-headscarf." However, in 2004, a coalition of women's organizations, both religious and secular, bridged this divide and succeeded in lobbying for thirty amendments to the penal code to protect women's rights, including rewriting laws that let men who committed honor crimes receive lesser sentences than men who committed crimes unrelated to honor. Similarly, women's groups began working in 2011 to address the problem of domestic violence in Turkey; in a country of almost 80 million people, approximately seventy women's shelters were open nationwide in 2011. Owing to the estimate that 14 percent of marriages each year in Turkey begin when the wife is underage, women's groups have also prioritized preventing girls from becoming child brides and the elimination of honor crimes as important goals. Although domestic violence, child bride practices, and honor crimes are all banned by law, many women point to the gap between legislation and enforcement of legal codes securing women's rights as large obstacles for Turkish society.

The Position of Women in 2012. In addition to seeking the implementation of existing policies, some women are also targeting gender equality in political representation. The Kurdish Barış ve Demokrasi Partisi (Peace and Democracy Party, BDP) is the only party in Turkey that has adopted a quota system; it requires a minimum of 40 percent female representation. Until 1946, women typically constituted between 4 and 6 percent of Turkish members of Parliament (MPs). After 1950, however, the percentage of parliamentarians who were women dropped to around 0.5 percent. In the 1980s, the percentage increased slightly to 0.88–1.34 percent; in the 1990s, women's representation increased to 2–4 percent. In 2002, the number of female MPs was around 4 percent, then rose to around 8 percent in 2007, and almost doubled, to 14 percent, in 2011. In 2012, women constituted 30.5 percent of BDP MPs, 14 percent of CHP MPs, 13.8 percent of AKP MPs, and 5.6 percent of Milliyetçi Hareket Partisi (Nationalist Action Party) MPs. On the local level, in 2012, 1 out of 80 governors were women, 26 out of 2,924 mayors were women, and 65 out of 34,210 village heads were women. In the foreign ministry, 21 out of 185 representatives were women.

Despite gaining rights and an increasing number of women in parliament, Turkish women face difficult times ahead. Many women in Turkey have yet to forget Prime Minister Tayyip Erdoğan's words on International Women's Day in 2008, when he declared that every Turkish woman should have at least three children. After the 2011 elections, Erdoğan announced a cabinet reshuffling, and the cabinet position once dedicated to women's issues became the Minister for Women and Families, stirring outrage from women's groups. The decrease in the number of women in cabinet—down to one of twenty-six ministers—and the lone woman being the Minister for Family and Social Policy—leads many to question how committed the AKP is to advancing the place of women in society. In 2012, Erdoğan also began a campaign to reduce women's access to abortion in Turkey, proposing that the law, which allowed abortions during the first ten weeks of pregnancy, be changed to only allow abortions during the first four weeks of pregnancy. Erdoğan's proposal evoked outrage and protest from many women's groups and some men, resulting in it being withdrawn. But with a smaller percentage of Turkish women working in 2012 than in the 1980s and the government's emphasis on women's role as mothers, many feel that women are being pushed out of both political and professional life and being relegated to the home.

BIBLIOGRAPHY

Arat, Yeşim. *The Patriarchal Paradox: Women Politicians in Turkey*. Rutherford, N.J.: Fairleigh Dickinson University Press, 1989.

Arat, Yeşim. "Toward a Democratic Society: The Women's Movement in Turkey in the 1980s." *Women's Studies International Forum* 17, nos. 2–3 (1994): 241–248.

Diner, Çağla, and Şule Toktaş. "Waves of Feminism in Turkey: Kemalist, Islamist and Kurdish Women's Movements in an Era of Globalization." *Journal of Balkan and Near Eastern Studies* 12, no. 1 (March 2010): 41–57.

Esim, Simel, and Dilek Çindoğlu. "Women Organizations in 1990s Turkey: Predicaments and Prospects." *Middle Eastern Studies* 33, no. 1 (January 1999): 178–188.

Güneş-Ayata, Ayşe. "Women's Participation in Politics in Turkey." In *Women in Modern Turkish Society: A Reader*, edited by Şirin Tekeli, pp. 235–249. London: Zed, 1995.

"Kadın İstatisticikleri 2011–2012." http://www.ka-der.org.tr/tr/down/2012_KADIN_ISTATISTIKLERI.pdf.

Kandiyoti, Deniz. "Patterns of Patriarchy: Notes for an Analysis of Male Dominance in Turkish Society." In *Women in Modern Turkish Society: A Reader*, edited by Şirin Tekeli, 306–318. London: Zed, 1995.

Ozcetin, Hilal. "'Breaking the Silence': The Religious Muslim Women's Movement in Turkey." *Journal of International Women's Studies* 11, no. 1 (November 2009): 106–119.

Reinart, Ustun. "Ambition for All Seasons: Tansu Ciller." *Middle East Review of International Affairs* 3, no. 1 (March 1999): 80–83.

Tekeli, Şirin. "The Turkish Women's Movement: A Brief History of Success." *Quaderns de la Mediterrània* 14 (2010): 119–123.

Yavuz, M. Hakan. "Political Islam and the Welfare (*Refah*) Party in Turkey." *Comparative Politics* 30, no. 1 (October 1997): 63–82.

Sarah F. Fischer

TURKISH LITERATURE. This article examines Turkish women authors' attitudes toward and treatment of religion in a chronological way from the period of the Ottoman Empire to the present by situating their works in their historical, political, and social contexts.

The Ottoman Period. Ottoman literature is mainly built on a poetic tradition that has two variations: the highly erudite courtly *Dīvān* poetry of elite circles and the oral, generally, but not always, mystical, love poetry of itinerant poet singers (called *âşık*) roaming the countryside. Despite the differences in the way they are composed and the audiences they are meant for, both kinds of poetry share central characters, conceits, and a Ṣūfī worldview. The poet is the lover addressing a beautiful, unresponsive, and aloof beloved who is described in terms of clichéd similes such as a rose, a cypress, and so on. The beloved may be a reference to an actual woman, but more probably to an actual man, with whom union can only be achieved through death. The poet's hopeless love, described through metaphors of suffering and burning, is ultimately the coded expression of divine love for God. There are several female poets of this period, mainly writing courtly poetry, including Mihri Hatun (d. 1506), Zübeyde Fıtnat Hanım (d. 1780), Feride Hanım (1837–1903), and Nigâr Hanım (1826–1918). Because they wrote from within a highly stylized poetic tradition, they took on the voice of a male poet addressing a nominally female beloved, complaining of her cruelty.

These women came from elite families and had enlightened fathers who were personally invested in their daughters' education and encouraged their literary endeavors. Fatma Âliye Hanım (1862–1936) whose career spanned the transition to the Turkish Republic in 1923 is a case in point. She was the daughter of the grand-vizier and historian Ahmet Cevdet Paşa (1822–1895). She was taught Arabic and French and received science lessons from her brother's tutor in the chemistry lab built at home for her brother. In addition to poetry, she wrote prose in the form of articles and novels. Prose genres like the novel, short story, and drama were brand-new forms of writing, imported as cultural technologies of Westernization during the reform era of Tanzimat (1839–1876). Fatma Âliye wrote several novels, including the two-part *Hayal ve Hakikat* (Dream and reality, 1894) co-authored with the most prolific and popular male novelist of the time, Ahmet Mithat Efendi (1844–1912). She signed that novel simply as "a woman," but she published all her other novels and subsequent prose under her own name, becoming the first Turkish woman to do so.

Her novels *Muhazarat* (Useful information, 1892) and *Udi* (The lute player, 1899), among others, depict capable women who work outside the home, but only because their economic troubles require it. Fatma Âliye also penned articles on science and philosophy for newspapers, as well as pieces about women in the women's journal *Hanımlara Mahsus Gazete* (Women's gazette). Although she created bold, independent women in her novels, her essays were more conservative. She wrote books about Muslim women: *Namdaran-ı Zenan-ı Islamiyan* (Famous women of Islam, 1895) and *Nisvan-ı Islam* (Muslim women, 1896), which explained that polygamy and the veiling of women were social not religious customs, and refuted the contemporary claim that polygamy prevented prostitution. Her work was exhibited and attracted wide attention at the 1893 Chicago World's Fair.

In addition to her writing, Fatma Âliye devoted much time to charitable work. She was the first female member of the Red Crescent and the founder of a women's aid organization, Nisvan-ı Osmaniye Imdat Cemiyeti, in 1897. Women's organizations and journals were becoming widespread at that time. She did not see Islam as an impediment to women's education and campaigned for the acceptance of women to the university (which became co-ed in 1921), arguing that educated women were better mothers and wives. She herself bore four daughters.

Transition to the Period of the Turkish Republic. Motherhood was also an important concern for Halide Edib Adıvar (1884–1964), which she turned into a metaphor central to her fiction. She was the first female superstar of Turkish letters, whose work is still in print in Turkish and English. She both lived the transition to the Turkish republic and contributed to its creation. She was the daughter of a secretary of Sultan Abdülhamid II (1842–1918) and also the first Muslim girl to graduate from the American College for Girls in Istanbul in 1901. She started writing articles on women's issues in 1908 in the journal *Tanin* through the influence of her first husband, the astronomer and mathematician Salih Zeki, who was one of its writers. Her own writing evolved into novels about women's freedom and marriage. She divorced her husband when he took a second wife in 1910.

Halide Edib was an important contributor to the political discussions on Turkism and the future of the empire at her house and social clubs such as the Turkish Hearth (of which she was the first woman member in 1912). She worked as a school inspector in Istanbul, establishing modern curricula in the new centralized school system. She was sent to establish orphanages in Lebanon and Syria during the early days of World War I. She married her second husband, Adnan Adıvar, a doctor with the Red Crescent and a fellow nationalist, in 1917. With him, she joined Mustafa Kemal's resistance movement in Ankara, shortly after the invasion of Istanbul by Allied forces and after giving two famous public speeches that rallied the public in 1919. She worked with Mustafa Kemal (who received the surname Atatürk after the last name law of 1934) throughout the Independence War as a translator and intercommunications officer. She was one of the proponents of the new history thesis that valorizes Anatolia as the rediscovered homeland of Turks. Although the Ottoman Empire conceptualized itself as a Balkan Empire, this thesis came to terms with the new reality: Anatolia was the mainland left to the Turks after the war. Halide Edib went into exile in France and England with her husband in 1924 because of the latter's political falling out with Mustafa Kemal, and she did not return to Turkey until his death in 1939. Upon her return, she served in the National Assembly (1950–1954). She also established the faculty of English literature at Istanbul University, where she taught.

During her years in exile, she wrote her memoirs in English: *Memoirs of Halide Edib* (1926) and *The Turkish Ordeal* (1928), which, respectively, describe her early family life and the final days of the Ottoman Empire; and the period of the Independence War (1919–1922). She wrote other historical works that examine the creation of and problems facing the new nation: *Turkey Faces West* (1930) and *The Conflict of East and West in Turkey* (1935). She also wrote *Inside India* (1937) to recount her travels to India in 1935 in support of the new campus of the Muslim school Jamia Millia Islamia (which later became a university), as well as of an independent India.

Although Halide Edib wrote more than twenty novels, her most famous is *The Clown and His Daughter*, originally written in English in 1935 and translated into Turkish in 1936. In this novel about a neighborhood of upper- and lower-class characters during the reign of Abdülhamid II (1876–1909), as in her novels about the early struggles for independence, she is critical of a constrictively dogmatic religion embodied by an imam as a religious authority. She was an observant Muslim who grew up in the household of her religious maternal grandmother and Ṣūfī grandfather. She was taught her prayers quite young and learned to read from the Qurʾān. But this early grounding was offset by her exposure to Christianity at the American College for Girls, where English was taught through the Bible. In her memoirs, she recounts how many of her Bibles were intercepted at home, forcing her to ask for a new one at school. At one period during her schooling, she consciously thought about religion, comparing different religions and justifying her choice of Islam.

Although Halide Edib covered her head until the end of the independence war (when the new Hat Law of 1925 changed clothing guidelines), her understanding of religion was based on spirituality and humanism rather than dogma. This is reflected in the novel *The Clown and His Daughter*, with its wide range of spiritual choices as represented by a hard-line imam who only talks of hell, a former Catholic priest, a Ṣūfī dervish, and a fortune-teller reading omens. The central heroine is Rabia, the granddaughter of the imam. She carves out a career for herself, becoming a chanter of *Mevlud*, the birth story of the Prophet Muḥammad, emphasizing in her interpretation the maternal feelings of the Prophet's mother and turning his holy birth into the human triumph of every mother. Rabia marries the former priest Peregrini and moves back into the house of her dead grandfather, reanimating his empty house with a new humanism and forgiving compassion. Halide Edib conveys that religion is not only the scripture, but also has a spiritual component that makes us human and that enriches our relationships with other people by making us compassionate and forgiving.

Political and Social Changes in the Roles ofWomen and Religion (1923–2000s). The founding of the republic drastically changed the position of women and role of religion, reversing their realm of visibility. Although there was an endemic feminist movement, represented by establishment, in 1924, of the women's organization Türk Kadınlar Birliği (Turkish Women's Association, which originally wanted to become a political party) spearheaded by Nezihe Muhittin (1889–1958), the state co-opted its demands and dissolved the organization in 1935. With the republic, women were brought out of their homes into public lives, and religion was pushed into the home as a private concern.

The abolition of the caliphate in 1924 brought about the separation of state affairs and religion. Religious affairs were placed under the regulation of the Diyanet, the Directorate of Religious Affairs, in 1924. Laws affecting clothing took effect in 1925, banning the fez and discouraging headscarves. Religious lodges were closed the same year. This was accompanied by changes in time measurement and also the calendar in 1925, breaking up the relationship between time and religious observation. Family law was subsumed under civil law in 1926, granting women the right to divorce (with property and custody rights) and ending polygamy. Universal primary and secondary education, which was unified and standardized in 1924, became co-ed in 1927. Women were given the right to vote and run for office in 1934. State feminism, which shaped public and active lives for women, also used their uncovered public image as a sign of its modernity. No new religious schools or mosques were built during this first period of state secularism.

Religion's profile has risen in Turkish social life since the 1950s for three reasons. First, despite the ban on brotherhoods, loosely organized religious communities that gather for readings and lectures persist, particularly the Nūr (Light) movement, which follows Said Nursi (1873–1960), and the Fethullah Gülen movement, built around the teachings of Gülen (b. 1938). The Nūr movement critiques the materialism of science while arguing that science and modern life are compatible with Islam, idealizing the Ottoman past, and enforcing segregation of the sexes. The Fethullah Gülen movement is similarly built around the ideal of a conservative, both observant and active, Ottoman-Turkish identity.

A second reason for the rise of religion's visibility in public space is the emergence of political Islam, which led to the creation of the first Islamist party, Millî Nizam Partisi (National Order Party), in 1971 and various offshoots, including Millî Refah Partisi (National Welfare Party), in 1996 the first Islamist party to win any election, and Fazilet Partisi (Virtue Party), in 1998 founded as Refah's successor. Adalet ve Kalkınma Partisi (Justice and Development Party or AK Parti), established by the reformist members of Fazilet Partisi, has governed Turkey over ten years, winning elections by positioning itself as a conservative democratic party rather than a religious party. However, AK Parti governments have attempted to make Turkish society more conservative by trying, among other measures, to limit alcohol consumption, to change educational requirements and curricula, and to illegalize abortions.

The third factor in Islam's rise within the public sphere is the creation of affluent religious middle and upper classes whose taste and buying power support religious lifestyles and politics, following the privatization and neoliberal policies of the 1980s under prime minister Turgut Özal (1927–1993).

Women Writers and Religion (1950s to 2000s). ***Modern (westernized) and religious women (1950s to 1960s).*** All political and social changes in Turkey were accompanied—and, in a sense, the path for them was prepared and promulgated—by literary works, but hardly any works on religion by women authors appeared until the late 1960s, although the number of women writers greatly increased from the 1950s to the late 1980s. The only exceptions were the few female followers of the mystical shaykh Kenan Rifaî (1867–1950). The most influential of these was Samiha Ayverdi (1905–1993) who celebrated a Turkish-Ottoman identity that valorized the Ottoman Empire as a land of toleration and glory in her forty books, ranging from romances, to history books and memoirs. She founded the conservative Kubbealtı Cemiyeti (Under the Dome Society) in 1970, which evolved into a foundation, able to publish and support other works with the aim of furthering a Turkish-Islamic synthesis. Although she did not veil, she was an observant Muslim. She tried to reconcile a modern feminist sensibility with a religious worldview. In the Ṣūfī romances she wrote, such as *Aşk Bu Imiş* (Apparently this is love) in 1937 and *Yaşayan Ölü* (The living dead) in 1942, she followed the mystical plot of love found in courtly literature that unites the lover and beloved through death.

There were other women writers in the same circle who were not as observant, but still pursued spirituality while producing clearly feminist works.

One of these was the journalist and playwright Nezihe Araz (1920–2009). Araz published best-selling biographies of the Prophet Muḥammad, *Peygamberler Peygamberi Hazreti Muhammed* (The Prophet of prophets, Muḥammad) in 1960; of the Anatolian mystic Yunus Emre, *Dertli Dolap* (The mournful water wheel) in 1961; and of Rumi, *Aşk Peygamberi: Mevlana'nın Romanı* (The prophet of love: A novel about Rumi) in 1962. She also wrote feminist plays about women groundbreakers, such as her eponymous prize-winning play *Afife Jale* about the first Muslim female actress, Afife Jale (available in English).

Dominant discourse in women's writing: secularist and leftist (1970s–1990s). As was historically the case, Samiha Ayverdi and Nezihe Araz were the offspring of elite and politically prominent families. The 1950s began to reap the results of the seeds planted by state feminism in an explosion of female writers that lasted into the late 1980s, the most prominent of whom were Adalet Ağaoğlu (b. 1929), Sevim Burak (1931–1983), Leyla Erbil (b. 1931), Füruzan (b. 1935), Sevgi Soysal (1936–1976), Ayla Kutlu (b. 1938), Aysel Özakın (b. 1942), Pınar Kür (b. 1945), Nazlı Eray (b. 1945), Tezer Özlü (1943–1986), and Latife Tekin (b. 1957). Some of these came from working-class families and directly benefited from drives and scholarships to educate women. For example, Füruzan recounts winning a state scholarship in her short story "Parasız Yatılı" (The scholarship student) in 1971, even though she was not able to finish her formal education and became largely self-taught. Adalet Ağaoğlu describes her struggles to continue her education beyond elementary school through her alter ego Aysel's similar battles in *Ölmeye Yatmak* (Lying down to die, 1973), a multicharacter novel that depicts the lives of the republic's first generation of schoolchildren. Latife Tekin fictionalizes her similar struggles to attend school in *Sevgili Arsız Ölüm* (1983, available in English as *Dear Shameless Death*) that depicts her farming family's move from the eastern town of Kayseri to a squatter settlement in Istanbul. This squatter settlement bordered by many industrial factories is impressionistically portrayed in Tekin's *Berci-Kristin Çöp Masalları* (1984, translated as *Berci-Kristin Tales from the Garbage Hills*) that imbues it with magic-realist qualities.

None of these women wrote about religion. They were interested in social justice and involved in leftist politics, in most cases actively seeking to effect the change they imagined in their writing. They wrote about women, marriage, sex, body politics, family relationships, poverty, work, and social change. Their writing had a historical edge; they examined Turkey's three military coups and politics. They exposed the patriarchal nature of most social and state institutions, showing that even familial relationships and love were contaminated by it. Although they were also disillusioned with the masculinist stance of their leftist comrades, in most cases, they would not call themselves feminist. Adalet Ağaoğlu vehemently rejects this term, viewing it as a narrowing of her focus. She explains that she wants justice not only for women but also for all of humanity. The 1980 coup deflated this universalist claim because a great majority of leftist male activists were imprisoned, leaving women to finally start from their own particular circumstances and needs, as opposed to waiting for the realization of a leftist utopia that would eventually solve their problems, along with those of the rest of society. Grassroots feminism emerged during this period, based on the realities of women's lives and their bodies. The successful 1987 protest against domestic violence, which was named Dayağa Karşı Kadın Dayanışması (Women's Collaboration Against Domestic Violence), became a large rallying event and is memorialized every year. Journalist Duygu Asena's 1987 novel *Kadının Adı Yok* (Woman has no name), which tells the story of women through the biological experiences of their bodies like menstruation, loss of virginity, birth, and menopause, was the best seller of this era.

Rather than writing in a realist style, these women experimented with structural and temporal components of narrative, creating multiple timeframes and layers of contrasting points of view. Their fracturing representational strategies that shatter a coherent narrative formalistically repeat their questioning of absolutist and unified "truths" and expose reality as contextual. They show that what obliterates and hides this circumstantiality are the unevenness of power relations and unquestioning complicity of people. The story collection *Twenty Stories by Turkish Women Writers* offers a sample story from twenty of these women. In addition, Adalet Ağaoğlu's *Yazsonu* (1980) that focuses on the period between the 1971 and 1980 coups is available in English with the title *Summer's End*, as well as in Arabic. Her novel *Üç Beş Kişi* (1984), which examines the period before the 1980 coup, appeared in English translation as *Curfew*. Nazlı Eray's magic realist and intertextual style is represented in English by *Orpheus*, translated from the Turkish original titled *Orphee* (1983). Latife Tekin's work is available in English as *Swords of Ice* (*Buzdan Kılıçlar*, 1989) in addition to her two aforementioned novels about internal immigration and poverty. This novel creates a new secret language that hides as much as it reveals about the lives of a poor family's enterprising members.

The work of other Turkish feminist authors has been translated into English. Erendiz Atasü (b. 1947) retells Turkish history from the beginning of the republic in the 1920s to the political turmoil of the 1970s through the interlocking voices of three generations of women from the same family in *The Other Side of the Mountain* (*Dağın Öteki Yüzü*, 1996). Perihan Mağden's (b. 1960) gender-bending stories about mother–child relationships are represented by *Messenger Boy Murders* (*Haberci Çocuk Cinayetleri*, 1991). The word "boy" in the translated title is misleading because these messengers have no gender. Mağden depicts homosexual teenagers who do not yet know how to understand and express their sexuality in *Two Girls* (*Iki Genç Kızın Romanı*, 2002) and *Ali and Ramazan* (*Ali ile Ramazan*, 2010). Aslı Erdoğan (b. 1967) traces the dissolution of a female character's identity and subjectivity in the story of a graduate student who moves to a maze-like Brazil to study physics and gets lost in multiple ways in *The City in Crimson Cloak* (*Kırmızı Pelerinli Şehir*, 1998).

Alternative discourse of modernity: Islamist women of the political right (1970s–1990s). Although the dominant and canonical narrative of women's writing often only includes leftist and feminist writers, highly conservative and Islamist women writers also made their voices heard starting in the late 1960s. Their numbers grew with the development and spread of the Nūr and Gülen movements and political Islam. Their novels counter the values and claims of secular novelists, arguing that modernization made Turkish society godless and immoral. They nostalgically hearken back to a glorious Ottoman past when religion was part of identity. The markers of this worldview are the segregation of the sexes and the covering of women. Gender relationships in these novels reflect the complementary understanding of gender roles in Islam. Women are presented as ideal mothers and wives, taking care of the house, and men as good providers who serve as their bridge to external life. The main plot revolves around the conversion of a leftist materialist protagonist through the influence of inspirational Muslim characters. The unhappy Westernized character is most generally a woman who takes up wearing the headscarf as a declaration of her new faith. These novels follow a formula without care for aesthetic considerations and are deliberately written to be read quickly.

The writers are generally teachers who come from rural backgrounds, who are of the 1945–1955 generation, and who address their message to high school or university students. Because their ultimate aim is to convert readers, these books are called *hidayet* (salvation) novels.

The earliest and the most famous of these works is *Huzur Sokağı* (1970, Inner Peace street) by Şule Yüksel Şenler (b. 1938), which established the formula. In this novel, the university student, Westernized Feyza, discovers the peace afforded by traditional values when she falls in love with the Muslim hero Bilal upon her family's move to a house on his street. Şenler, a popular lecturer, started wearing the headscarf in 1965, tying it in the special way that has since become the sign of contemporary Islamism. Şerife Katırcı Turhal's *Müslüman Kadının Adı Var* (1988, Muslim woman has a name) follows this same formula and counters Duygu Asena's feminist anthem *Woman Has No Name*. In the Islamist narrative, Dilara is a medical student who falls in love with the religious widower Ibrahim after witnessing his recovery from a car accident that kills his wife. She starts to cover her head just before graduation, alienating her whole school. She finds happiness when she becomes a *ḥajj* doctor, accompanying believers on their pilgrimage to Mecca, and marries Ibrahim.

The 1980s Islamic narrative is communitarian and does not focus on individual desires or conflicts within the Muslim community. The everyday practice and lives of Islamists had changed by the 1990s with their business successes and the creation of spaces like gender-segregated beaches, hotels, and movie theaters catering to them. There were also many religious women who had advanced degrees, composing fiction while also writing newspaper columns and non-fiction books, such as Fatma K. Barbarosoğlu (b. 1962). The novels of this period critique the narrowness of women's choices despite their university educations. They were still mainly expected to stay at home; they could not easily find work. Emine Şenlikoğlu (b. 1953) began to critique men's domination over women in her novels of the 1990s, especially focusing on the issue of legally non-binding religious marriages and polygamy. Cihan Aktaş (b. 1968) has written short stories on the nature of ideological marriages. Halime Toros (b. 1960) in *Halkaların Ezgisi* (1997, Music of the spheres) depicts a believer-heroine Nisa who first dons the headscarf because her husband wants it and then removes her scarf, deciding that the meaning of the headscarf is so overdetermined by both secularists and Islamists that it cannot signify a personal choice.

Beyond identity politics: The commercial success of the middle in the 2000s. The salvation novels of the 1980s and the more critical and complicated Islamic novels of the 1990s are read mainly by an Islamist readership. Elif Shafak (b. 1971) was able to address both religious and secular audiences with her best seller *The Forty Rules of Love*, originally written in English. The novel was translated into Turkish and first published in Turkish under the title *Aşk* (Love) in 2009, and then released in English in 2010. This novel juxtaposes the medieval story of the mystic Rūmī's encounter and relationship with his shaykh Shams-i Tabrīzī in Konya with a contemporary narrative of the relationship between a bored Jewish Boston housewife Ella Rubenstein and her Dutch ex-hippie Ṣūfī lover Aziz Zahara, who suffers from AIDS. At the story's end, the couple arrives in Konya where he dies, and Ella's metaphorical discipleship ends in the place where Rūmī's real one started. Shafak's first novel *Pinhan* (1997, the Ṣūfī) also focuses on a mystical character. She has explored the issue of Armenian Turkish conflict in *The Bastard of Istanbul*, as a result of which a court case was brought against her in 2006 on the basis of a fictional character insulting Turkishness. Her latest novel *Honour* (2012), whose Turkish version

Iskender was published in 2011, investigates the issue of honor killings, which have increased exponentially in recent years, by focusing on a Turkish immigrant family in London. Raising these controversial issues to argue for tolerance has made Shafak a great commercial success.

BIBLIOGRAPHY

Aksoy, Nazan. *Kurgulanmış Benlikler: Otobiyografi, Kadın, Cumhuriyet* (Constructed identities: Autobiography, woman, the republic). Istanbul: Iletişim, 2009. Discusses the autobiographies of Halide Edib and Samiha Ayverdi, among other women, tracing how they constructed their identities along their public achievements.

Araz, Nezihe. *Afife Jale*. Translated by Nilüfer Mizanoğlu Reddy. In *Anatolia and Other Plays*, Vol. 2, edited by Talat Halman and Jayne Warner, pp. 245–301. Syracuse, N.Y.: Syracuse University Press, 2008. A feminist play about the first Turkish Muslim stage actress, depicting her success and downfall.

Çayır, Kenan. *Islamic Literature in Turkey: From Epic to Novel*. New York: Palgrave Macmillan, 2007. Analyzes Islamist fiction of the 1980s and 1990s and distinguishes their political messages and artistic merits as products of two distinct periods.

Çınar, Alev. *Modernity, Islam, Secularism in Turkey: Bodies, Places and Time*. Minneapolis: University of Minnesota Press, 2005. Traces use of the female body as a marker of various ideologies, focusing on beauty pageants, the headscarf, and the like.

Erol, Sibel. "Discourses on the Intellectual: The Universal, the Particular and Their Mediation in Nazlı Eray's Works." *New Perspectives on Turkey*, no. 11 (Fall 1994): 1–17.

Erol, Sibel. "A Review of Turkish Feminism." *New Perspectives on Turkey*, no. 8 (Spring 1992): 109–121.

Erol, Sibel. "Sexual Discourse in Turkish Fiction: Return of the Repressed Female Identity." *Edebiyat* 6, no. 2 (October 1995): 187–202. Discusses the symbolic role of the body in identity politics, referring to Duygu Asena and Adalet Ağaoğlu.

Findley, Carter Vaughn. *Turkey, Islam, Nationalism and Modernity: A History, 1789–2007*. New Haven, Conn., and London: Yale University Press, 2010. The author gives summaries of Fatma Âliye's, Halide Edib's, and Adalet Ağaoğlu's novels, among other fictional works, as one means of contextualizing his historical analysis.

Göle, Nilüfer. *The Forbidden Modern: Civilization and Veiling*. Ann Arbor: University of Michigan Press, 1997. One of the earliest arguments that contemporary piety is part of modernity. Göle examines the symbolic import of women's visibility and clothing in Turkish political discourse.

Ilkkaracan, Pınar. "How Adultery Almost Derailed Turkey's Aspirations to Join the European Union." In *Deconstructing Sexuality in the Middle East*, edited by Pınar Ilkkaracan, pp. 41–64. Farnham, Surrey, UK: Ashgate, 2008. Shows how the patriarchal state controls the female body in Turkey through concepts of virginity and honor.

Kızıltan, Mübeccel. "Divan Edebiyati Özelliklerine Uyarak Şiir Yazan Kadın Şairler" (Women poets who write within the tradition of courtly poetry). *Sonbahar* 21/22 1994: 104–169. Gives a comprehensive overview of female poets from the fifteenth to the early twentieth century, using archival materials.

Kulu, Şule. Interview with Elif Shafak about *Forty Rules of Love*. September 13, 2009. http://www.todayszaman.com/news-186937-safak-looks-forward-to-reaching-the-world-with-the-forty-rules-of-love.html.

Kuru, Ahmet. *Secularism and State Policies Toward Religion: The United States, France and Turkey*. Cambridge, UK, and New York: Cambridge University Press, 2009. Distinguishing between assertive secularism, as in Turkey and France, and passive secularism, as in the United States, Kuru argues that the opposite reactions to public veiling in these countries are the results of these approaches.

Navaro-Yashin, Yael. *Faces of the State: Secularism and Public Life in Turkey*. Princeton, NJ: Princeton University Press, 2002. Discusses the way in which political and cultural wars are waged through symbols like the headscarf or Atatürk photographs, which are turned into commodities. This book traces the process of ideological commodification with its markets and consumers.

Ongün, Selin. *Başörtülü Kadınlar Anlattı: Türbanlı Erkekler* (Veiled women talk: Men with headscarves). Istanbul: Destek Yayınevi, 2010. Prominent Islamist professional women describe their double marginalization by both secularists and Islamist men.

Pemberton, Kelly. "Reclaiming Muslim Space in the 21th Century in Turkey: The New Narratives on Women, Islam and Secularism." *Near East Quarterly*

(2011). http://www.neareastquarterly.com/index.php/2011/09/07/reclaiming-muslim-space-in-21st-century-turkey-the-new-narratives-on-women-islam-and-secularism/. Addresses the most recent examples of Islamist women's writing.

Reddy, Nilüfer Mizanoğlu. *Twenty Stories by Turkish Women Writers*. Bloomington: Indiana University, 1988. Examples of the themes and styles of Turkish women writers from the 1960s to the late 1980s.

Sılay, Kemal. "Singing His Words: Ottoman Poets and the Power of Patriarchy." In *Women in the Ottoman Empire*, edited by Madeline Zilfi, pp. 197–214. Leiden, Netherlands: Brill, 1997. Shows that Ottoman women poets had no recourse but to write in the masculine posture of the poetic tradition, but argues that this in itself turns into a critique.

Tezcan, Demet. *Bir Çığır Öyküsü: Şule Yüksel Şenler* (The story of an era). Istanbul: Timaş Yayınları, 2007. A biography of the author Şule Yüksel Şenler that draws heavily from Şenler's own writings and newspaper columns. Şenler created much controversy when she argued that Islam permits husbands to beat their wives.

Turam, Berna. *Between Islam and the State: The Politics of Engagement*. Stanford, Calif.: Stanford University Press, 2007. Examines Fethullah Gülen's schools and their co-optation of the state in promoting a Turkish identity. Turam focuses on the gender dynamics of the movement, which excludes women from public visibility.

SIBEL EROL

U

Uddin, Baroness Pola Manzila. (b. 1959) is a Bengali-British Muslim community activist and advocate for social reforms and equal rights. She was born in a village in Bangladesh and raised in London's East End after moving with her parents to the United Kingdom in 1973. Her education consisted of Plashet Grammar School and later the University of North London where she graduated with a social work qualification in 1988; she also has an honorary doctorate from Exeter University.

Her community work began in the 1970s while she lived in the East End, pioneering several forward-thinking services and organizations that were well received. Her professional political career began in 1988 when she began to work with Newham Social Services. She was also a Youth and Community worker at the Young Women's Christian Association (YWCA), Liaison Officer for Tower Hamlets Social Services, and Manager of Tower Hamlets Women's Health Project.

Her career has been marked by significant achievements and a substantial amount of social work and activism that propelled Islam into British society. She was elected as a Tower Hamlets councilor in 1990 (becoming Deputy Leader in 1994), a position that would result in even greater achievements and social championing.

Throughout her working life, Baroness Uddin has been a pioneer in social service and activism in Britain. She has an impressive list of achievements in the social realm of her career, which has influenced and led to her political success. Her accomplishments in social work include the development and initiation of several projects such as a women's health and advocacy project; counseling services for families (she leads the Breaking the Cycle Project, an organization assisting families affected by substance misuse); the construction of the Jagonari Women's Education Resource Centre, the first training and education center of its kind in the country. In 2009 she became the Chair of the Black, Asian and Minority Ethnic (BAME) Women Councilors Taskforce. (Founded in May 2008 by the Minister for Women and Equality, Harriet Harman, the taskforce's aim is to encourage ethnic women to join electoral politics.) She is also a board member of Autism Speak U.K; pioneering initiatives against domestic violence; working as a child protection officer; and is a patron of Bethnal Green and Victoria Park Housing Association, Women's Housing Forum, and Women's Aid.

When elected as a Tower Hamlets councilor, she was the first Bengali woman to hold local authority in Britain; she rose to peerage in 1998 as one of Tony Blair's working peers. Rt. Hon. Baroness Uddin of Bethnal Green was the youngest woman among the government benches, the first Bengali and the first Muslim woman to hold a seat in the House of Lords, and the only Muslim woman in Parliament at the time. She also ranked as Britain's sixth most powerful woman on the 2009 Muslim Women Power List. "A formidable champion for women" and "a campaigner on women's and ethnic minority issues" are just two of Baroness Uddin's unofficial titles due to her focus on minority, women, and disability rights throughout her career.

BIBLIOGRAPHY

"Baroness Pola Manzila Uddin." *www.Bbwhoswho.co.uk* British Bangladeshi Who's Who. 2008.

"Baroness Pola Manzila Uddin," in *Notable Muslims: Muslim Builders of World Civilization and Culture*, Natana DeLong-Bas. Oxford: Oneworld, 2006.

"Compass: Tomorrow's Islam Screening on ABC TV, Sunday 26 October 2003 at 9:50 p.m." *www.ABC.net.au*. Australian Broadcasting Corporation.

"Muslim Women Power List." *www. Guardian.co.uk* 25 March 2009.

Eren Tatari

ʿUdhrī Poetry. As for any given epoch, literature and, specifically, poetry may be viewed as the media outlet as well as the historical record of that designated time period. Fifteen centuries ago, in the heart of Arabia, the ability to recite poetry was considered an innate talent with which many males and females were born. Love poetry was a particularly important form of expression and is heavily present in both pre-Islamic and Islamic historical literature.

The structures of Arabian social norms and codes of conduct in male/female relations led to the birth of ʿUdhrī poetry, which reflects a love that is generally destined to remain in the virginal stage between the lover and the beloved.

From the pre-Islamic era, arranged marriages were customary among the population of Arabia. In the case of mutual love shared by a young couple, the girl's father might prevent his daughter from marrying her beloved in order to deny rumors that the couple entered into a premarital sexual relationship. A father might also preclude his daughter's marriage due to racial and/or social class differences, such as what occurred in the case of ʿAntarah ibn Shaddād al-ʿAbsi (d. 608) almost a hundred years before the advent of Islam.

The tribal inhabitants in the north of Hijaz were named the people of ʿUdhra (literally, "virginity") because they were famous for their love poetry that stemmed from strong sentimental passions, namely, chastity, purity, and virtue. Shawqī Ḍayf (1999) reports that a man from the ʿUdhra tribe was asked, "Is it possible that you are from among a community who, if they fall in love, they die?" He replied: "Yes, I swear I left thirty dying young men, their only disease is extreme fervent love" (Dayf, p. 21). In another example, Buthayna, Jamil's beloved, was told that her lover was suffering as a result of her love, and was asked if she could offer Jamil any assistance. She replied that she was only able to cry for Jamil's love until they could meet in the Hereafter. (Dayf, p. 21)

Despite the undeniably famous ʿUdhrī poetry of pre-Islamic poets such as ʿAntarah ibn Shaddād al-ʿAbsi and Imruʾ al-Qais (d. 561–65), a number of twentieth-century Arabic literary critics and observers have related ʿUdhrī poetry to Islamic teachings. For example, Aḥmad ʿAbd al-Sattār al-Jawārī asserts in his book *al-Ḥubb al-ʿudhrī* (2006) that this category of love initially appeared in

Arabic literature during the first fifty years of Islam. He ties such a view to Islamic injunctions forbidding all premarital sexual relations. Such critics find support for this argument in the largely immodest lifestyle for which pre-Islamic Arabia was famous, because of the absence of any religious prohibition of such relations. However, al-Jawārī's claim denies the existence of pre-Islamic era ʿUdhrī poetry. This may be argued against as follows: first, although fornication is a prohibited act, celibacy, the main element of ʿUdhrī love, is not celebrated by Islamic law. Second, the ʿUdhrī poetry genre pre-dates the advent of Islam, as is made clear by the fact that ʿAntarah and al-Qais composed their poetry beforehand and insisted on marrying their beloved women lawfully, even though prevalent pre-Islamic customs did not allow them to.

Female Poets. Although the history of Arabic literature offers an abundance of love poetry, there are only a few examples of ʿUdhrī poetry composed and recited by women, Layla al-Akhyaliyya (d. 704) and Rābiʿah al-ʿAdawīyah (d. 801) being the most widely known of such poets. Layla was born fifteen years after the advent of Islam, and was known for her beauty, bravery, chastity, and exceptional poetry. When she fell in love with a young man from a neighboring tribe named Tawba, she was forced to marry someone else. The news of Layla's popular love story and poetry reached the ears of the Umayyad caliph ʿAbd al-Malik ibn Marwān in Damascus as well as his governor in Baghdad, Ḥajjāj āj ibn Yūsuf al-Thaqafi (d. 714). Layla not only used her poetical talent to express her love to Tawba, she also made the most of this gift, earning a living and feeding her children through years of drought. She traveled east and west in order to offer praise poems to these political figures, breaking the social norms of her time, first by declaring her unlawful feelings for a man other than her husband, and second by entering the political courts and praising the caliph as well as the governor. By infiltrating the male poets' territory, Layla broke the social patriarchal chain, using her willpower and determination to create a career for herself. As for her passionate affection for Tawba, Layla made clear her indifference to suggestions that her love poetry confirmed the illicit suspicions surrounding this frowned-upon relationship. Because she was confident of her own chastity, she did not concern herself with what others thought of her.

Rābiʿah al-ʿAdawīyah is the other major female ʿUdhrī female poet. Her beloved is not a handsome heroic poet who wrote her love poems, but rather the Exceptional One, namely, God. Rābiʿah renounced worldly desires for the love to which many other male and female Ṣūfī poets and ascetics dedicated their passionate sentiments. Through the removal and elimination of the sexual component usually attached to the meaning of love, ʿUdhrī love remains pure, an element shared by Ṣūfī love. This eternal love of the Sublime that is central to Sufism finds its origin in the Qurʾān (5.59).

ʿUdhrī poetry emerged and evolved with the expansion of Islam both east and west. Ṣūfī poetry may be found in Persia, Southeast Asia, and Islamic Southern Spain (Andalusia), where ʿUdhrī poetry was discovered between the tenth and twelfth centuries. Among the last poets who were also Islamic scholars are the Iraqi Ibn Dawud (d. 909) and the Andalusian Ibn Ḥazm (d. 1063). Both showed the importance of elevating the lover's passion beyond any sexual aspiration.

A number of twentieth-century Islamic medieval literary critics such as Aḥmad ʿAbd al-Sattār al-Jawārī, Shawqī Ḍayf, and Taha Hussain claim that this genre, free from human carnal desire, has its origins in the peasantry of the semi-Bedouin Hijazi land of Arabia during the first fifty years of Islamic civilization in the 680s CE As the Muslims of Medina and Mecca became involved in the establishment of the new state, the Bedouin

Hijazis found solace and refuge from poverty and despair through love poetry and devotion.

BIBLIOGRAPHY

Ḍayf, Shawqī. *al-Ḥubb al-ʿudhrī ʿinda al-ʿArab*. Cairo: al-Dār al-Miṣrīyah al-Lubnānīyah, 1999.

Jawārī, Aḥmad ʿAbd al-Sattār al-. *al-Ḥubb al-ʿudhrī: nashʾatuhu wa- taṭawwuruh*. Beirut: al-Muʾassasah al-ʿArabīyah lil-Dirāsāt wa-al-Nashr, 2006.

Sajdi, Dana al-. "Trespassing the Male Domain: The Qasidah of Layla al-Akhyaliyah." *Journal of Arabic Literature* 31, no. 2 (2000): 121–146.

Sulafa Abousamra

Ulfah, Hajjah Maria. (b. 1955), Indonesian Qurʾān reciter and teacher. Internationally renowned, Hajjah Maria Ulfah has been a driving force promoting the art of women's Qurʾān recitation in not only Indonesia, but all of Southeast Asia. She is a celebrity comparable to a pop star. She and her husband Dr. Mukhtar Ikhsan, a pulmonologist, have three children.

Born on 21 December 1955 in Lamongan, East Java, Indonesia, to Hajji Mudhoffar and Hajjah Ruminah, she was the ninth of twelve children. Although her parents provided for the family by weaving fabrics and were not religious experts, they discerned at an early age their daughter's unique talent and arranged for private Qurʾān lessons with a teacher. Her older sister Siti Maimunah taught her the short chapters of the Qurʾān. As Ulfah's skills improved, her parents pushed her to recite the Qurʾān during public celebrations such as the *mawlid al-nabī*.

While Ulfah was attending high school, her father sent her to study in the prestigious *pesantren* of Kiai Wahab Chasbullah, one of the founders of the Nahdlatul Ulama (NU) organization. *Pesantren* students devote all of their time to the various disciplines connected to the study of the Qurʾān. Ulfah continued her undergraduate studies at the State Institute for Islamic Studies (IAIN) Sunan Ampel in Surabaya. During that time, her parents died and she started to teach the Qurʾān in order to fund her studies. In 1977 she became the first graduate student at the Institut Ilmu al-Qurʾan (IIQ) for women that Ibrahim Hosen (1917–2001) had just opened.

Ulfah's career emerged at the crossroads of several developments within Indonesian society: traditional Qurʾān schools such as the *pesantren* started to admit female students, who soon gained access to venues of upward mobility via the IIQ network. During the 1980s, study of the Qurʾān intensified, as evidenced by the brisk sales of cassettes and DVDs that teach it, and the enormous popularity of Qurʾān recitation competitions and festivals that cater to participants as young as five years old.

Ulfah's public career was launched in 1980 when she won the women's title in the international recitation contest in Kuala Lumpur, Malaysia. Since then she has performed public recitation sessions in many nations, including Kuwait, Saudi Arabia, Egypt, Hong Kong, Japan, Australia, the United States, Canada, and several European countries. She has mastered seven of the ten styles of Qurʾān recitation and is a specialist in *tajwīd*, the rules of recitation.

Ulfah earned her MA at the IIQ in Jakarta, Indonesia, where she has taught and served in a variety of roles since 1981. She is also the school's vice-rector and director of administrative affairs and finance. From 1997 to 2005 she was a lecturer at the Islamic State University in Jakarta.

Ulfah regularly serves as a judge during national and international Qurʾān reciting competitions. To prepare themselves for the contests, students from all over the Archipelago attend the school she opened opposite her house, the Pesantren al-Qurʾan, Baitul Qurraʾ. Here, she grooms women students from countries as far away as Malaysia, South Africa, and Japan to follow in her footsteps.

Ulfah's international recognition includes a 1984 Gold Plate Record Award from Musica Studio's, appearances on European television and at American universities, and a recording with Phonogrammarchiv at the Austrian Academy of Sciences.

BIBLIOGRAPHY

DeLong-Bas, Natana. *Notable Muslims: Muslim Builders of World Civilization and Culture*. Oxford: Oneworld, 2006.

Durkee, Noura. "Recited from the Heart." *Saudi Aramco World* 51, no. 3 (May–June 2000). http://www.saudiaramcoworld.com/issue/200003/recited.from.the.heart.htm.

Rasmussen, Anne K. *Women, the Recited Qur'an, and Islamic Music in Indonesia*. Berkeley: University of California Press, 2010.

Nelly van Doorn-Harder

Umm Kulthūm. (c. 1904–1975), Egyptian singer. Born Umm Kulthūm Ibrāhīm al-Sayyid al-Baltājī, the most famous Egyptian and, arguably, Arab singer of the twentieth century grew up in a poor family in the Egyptian delta. She learned to sing by imitating her father, who was the imam (leader) of the local mosque and religious singer, and her brother. She attended the local religious school with her brother and joined her father's and brother's singing troupe, traveling across the Egyptian delta performing religious songs for weddings and holidays. In the 1920s, she traveled to Cairo, where she transformed herself from an unknown rural singer into a well-established, respected one. In the 1920s and 1930s, she used key media, including recordings, radio, and film, to strengthen and broaden her career. She created a more conservative persona than the female singers with whom she was competing, and she established a place for the female singer of serious songs. Through her use of media, her strong social connections, and her musical talent and determination, she crafted a career on a par with that of her leading contemporary, the Egyptian composer and singer Muḥammad ʿAbd al-Waḥḥāb.

By adapting her repertoire and image, she extended her career through the 1940s and beyond. She performed songs in several genres that suited changing public tastes and targeted members of various Egyptian social strata. She also adapted to changing political conditions. Following the 1952 Revolution, she recorded numerous political anthems. After Egypt's defeat in the Six-Day War of 1967, she gave concerts across the Arab world and donated proceeds to the Egyptian postwar reconstruction effort, not only strengthening her relationships with listeners abroad, but also positioning herself as a still-relevant singer and activist as she entered the sixth decade of her career. Through her long career, strong connection to the Egyptian public, and construction of a patriotic and pious persona, she established herself as a national icon by the time of her death in 1975.

Umm Kulthūm's accomplishments can be assessed in both quantitative and qualitative terms. She recorded nearly three hundred songs spanning romantic, religious, and patriotic genres, starred in six films, led a nationally renowned instrumental ensemble, gave lengthy live performances broadcast on radio, and received numerous state awards from Egypt and other Arab nations. Her singing was rooted in principles of Qurʾānic recitation, and she was often praised for her clear enunciation, outstanding improvisatory skills, and ability to elevate the public's literary taste through her engaging renditions of poetry in both classical and Egyptian colloquial Arabic. Her popularity is even reflected in Egyptian folklore, with stories containing references about political and military figures delaying activities "because Umm Kulthūm was singing." She was a shrewd businesswoman and carefully crafted a lengthy career despite numerous obstacles. Through her repertoire, musical talent, and iconic status, she also influenced musicians of later generations. Many later musicians—both singers and instrumentalists, men and women, Egyptians and non-Egyptians—covered her songs in a variety of genres, ranging from near duplication of her originals to innovative jazz and house renditions. Through her own achievements and influence, she attained an iconic status perhaps only rivaled by the Lebanese star Fairouz.

BIBLIOGRAPHY

Danielson, Virginia. *The Voice of Egypt: Umm Kulthūm, Arabic Song, and Egyptian Society in the Twentieth Century*. Chicago: University of Chicago Press, 1997. Particularly thorough in its documentation of Umm Kulthūm's career up to 1964.

Goldman, Michal. *Umm Kulthūm: A Voice like Egypt*. DVD. Seattle: Arab Film Distribution, 2006.

Lohman, Laura. *Umm Kulthūm: Artistic Agency and the Shaping of a Legend, 1967–2007*. Middletown, Conn.: Wesleyan University Press, 2010.

LAURA LOHMAN

UMM WARAQA. A female companion of the Prophet Muḥammad whose role as a prayer leader (*imāmah*) has impacted modern debates on women prayer leaders for mixed congregations.

Umm Waraqa bint ʿAbdullah b. al-Ḥārith is a woman of significance in the history of Islam. Knowledge of her life can be gathered from *aḥadith* of Abū Dāʾūd (d. 889) and Aḥmad ibn Ḥanbal (d. 855) as well as a biography in the *Ṭabaqāt al-Kubrā* of Ibn Saʿd (d. 845 CE). She was a companion (*anṣār*) of Muḥammad and a resident of Medina or "Helper." Muḥammad referred to her as "the Martyr" (*al-shahīdah*), for she had asked permission to participate in the Battle of Badr as a caretaker for the wounded. As a devout Muslim, she knew the Qurʾān by heart. She was killed by a female and male servant during the time of ʿUmar's successorship.

Muḥammad's directive for her to lead prayers has been of central interest to scholars for centuries. What, or who, Umm Waraqa led in prayer has been the crux of the debate on whether women are permitted to lead mixed congregations or only female groups. For most, the interpretation hinges on the definition of *dār*, for she led her *dār* (literally *ahl dārihā*) in prayer. *Dār* has an array of meanings, from a house to an area, neighborhood, region, or country. Some scholars have argued that Umm Waraqa's congregation could have been as large as a neighborhood as it had a muezzin (*muʾadhdhin*) to call the party to prayer. Proponents of the opinion that Umm Waraqa guided a mixed congregation suggest that a household or area of this magnitude, having a muezzin, must have included males. A second line of argumentation in support of a woman heading mixed congregations is based on a lack of prohibition. None of the *aḥadith* granting Umm Waraqa the position of *imāmah* (female prayer leader) proscribe her from conducting prayer for a mixture of males and females.

Opponents have found numerous grounds upon which to question the veracity of such an interpretation. Narrators of the *aḥadith* providing the details of Umm Waraqa have been judged by some scholars to be questionable in authority. A sufficient number of disreputable and unknown transmitters in the chains of these reports has led some scholars to discount the reliability of these traditions. However, many scholars of Islam have long recognized the legitimacy of these *aḥadith*, as they comprise the framework for allowing a woman to lead congregations of women in prayer. Those who do accept the *aḥadith* may still argue for a restrictive interpretation of the term *dār*, suggesting that Umm Waraqa may have only been granted permission to lead the females of her house in prayer.

Details of Umm Waraqa's story have undergone alterations and interpolations in what some have claimed are attempts to mitigate her role and image. In the earlier texts, for example, she was commanded or ordered (*amarahā*) by Muḥammad to conduct prayer. Later texts state that she was given permission (*udhina lahā*). Furthermore, later texts not only stripped her of the honorific title "the Martyr" (*al-shahīdah*), but when she inquired about participating in the battle, she was told to remain in her home. Early texts never clearly indicate whether she participated, but later works completely dismiss such notions. Despite efforts to downplay her image and function in the community, Umm Waraqa remains a significant figure in the modern context on the debate of mixed-gender prayer groups being led by women.

BIBLIOGRAPHY

Abū Dā'ūd Sulaymān ibn al-Ashʿath al-Sijistānī. *Sunan Abī Dāwūd*. Beirut: Dār Ibn Ḥazm, 1997–1998.

Afsaruddin, Asma. "Early Women Exemplars and the Construction of Gendered Space: (Re-)Defining Feminine Moral Excellence." In *Harem Histories: Envisioning Places and Living Spaces*, edited by Marilyn Booth, pp. 23–48. Durham, N.C.: Duke University Press, 2010.

Calderini, Simonetta. "Contextualizing Arguments about Female Ritual Leadership (Women Imāms) in Classical Islamic Sources." *Comparative Islamic Studies* 5, no. 1 (2011): 5–32.

Ibn Ḥanbal, Aḥmad ibn Muhammad. *al-Musnad*. Edited by Aḥmad Muhammad Shākir. Cairo: Dār al-Ḥadīth, 1416/1995.

Ibn Saʿd, Muhammad. *al-Tabaqāt al-Kubrā'*. Beirut: Dār al-Kutub al-ʿIlmīyah, 1418/1997.

MATTHEW LONG

ʿUMRAH. *ʿUmrah* is minor pilgrimage to Mecca as mentioned in the Qur'ān (2:158, 196). This pilgrimage, like the *ḥajj*, is performed by both males and females and there is no space discrimination. Its entire duration is shorter than that of the *ḥajj*; it is performed within a few hours at any time of day or night. The *ʿumrah* contains all the features of a religious pilgrimage, such as travel and religious experiences along the lines of what Rudolf Otto described as *mysterium tremendum et fascinans*—mystery, awe, and fascination of the numinous or sacred—and *communitas*—fellowship and personal transformation at the end. The *ʿumrah* pilgrimage is based on the Qur'ānic narrative about Ibrāhīm, Ismāʿīl, and Hajar; it is a process of withdrawal from profanities, entrance into the world of the sacred, and return to the dual worlds of the sacred and profane.

There are two types of *ʿumrah* pilgrimage: the first can be performed anytime during the year except the eighth, ninth, and tenth of Dhū al-Ḥijjah, the days of the *ḥajj*, and is called *al-ʿUmrat al-mufradah*. The second type, *al-ʿUmrat al-tamattuʿ*, is performed from the first of the month of Shawwāl to the eighth of Dhū al-Ḥijjah and in conjunction with the *ḥajj*. For this type of pilgrimage, *ʿumrah* rituals are performed before those of the *ḥajj*.

In 632 CE the prophet Muḥammad performed the *ʿumrah* before the *ḥajj* and distinguished the two rituals by discontinuing the *iḥrām* in between, thereby showing the independence of each pilgrimage.

The *ʿumrah* pilgrimage begins with the donning of the *iḥrām* at one of the *mīqāt* marking approaches to Mecca. It consists of performing the following rituals conducted within the vicinity of the Grand Mosque of Mecca. The pilgrim enters the Grand Mosque from the northeast side or the Bāb al-Salaam, turns right, and begins with the *ṭawāf*—circumambulation around the Kaʿbah seven times, the first three rounds being of rapid pace and the last four at normal pace. During the *ṭawāf*, the pilgrim praises Allāh and makes supplication for him- or herself, relatives, and the

Muslim community. This is then followed by two *rakʿāt* prayers with the pilgrim facing the Kaʿbah at *al-Multazam*—the space between the Black Stone and the door of the Kaʿbah but behind the *Maqām Ibrāhīm*, the footprint of Abraham. After the prayer, the pilgrim touches and kisses the Black Stone. This is followed by the ritual of drinking the *Zamzam* water and performing the *al-saʿy*—running between the two hillocks of Safa and Marwah uttering prayer at each end. The final ritual is the clipping of hair or shaving of the head that marks the end of the *ʿumrah*. The *ʿumrah* pilgrimage is more an act of personal devotion and of intimate religious experience of the Divine at the center of one's being. *ʿUmrah* is an experience that integrates being with sacred space and time.

BIBLIOGRAPHY

Bianchi, Robert. *Guests of God: Pilgrimage and Politics in the Islamic World*. New York: Oxford University Press, 2008.

Eliade, Mircea. *Patterns in Comparative Religion*. Translated by Rosemary Sheed. Lincoln, Neb.: Bison Books, 1996. Originally published in 1958.

Otto, R. *The Idea of the Holy*. 2d ed. Translated by John W. Harvey. New York: Oxford University Press, 1958.

Peters, F. E. *The Hajj: The Muslim Pilgrimage to Mecca and the Holy Places*. Princeton, N.J.: Princeton University Press, 1995.

Wolfe, Michael, ed. *One Thousand Roads to Mecca: Ten Centuries of Travelers Writing about the Muslim Pilgrimage*. New York: Grove, 1998.

IMTIYAZ YUSUF

UNITED ARAB EMIRATES. Years of development and urbanization have not only transformed the landscape of the United Arab Emirates (UAE) since independence in 1971, they have also created an almost insurmountable rupture that separates the present from the past. Older Emiratis are often loath to talk about the past and the poverty they endured, while the younger generation seems incapable of imagining what life was like before the discovery of oil. This has created considerable angst on the part of the leaders who are concerned that Emiratis have lost their cultural identity in the midst of so much change, much of it brought about by the presence of millions of foreign workers. One aspect of cultural identity that is little discussed and apparently cause for no worry is religion. The vast majority of Emiratis follow Sunnī Islam, and the UAE is officially an Islamic country. However, as in many Islamic countries, the origins of traditions such as dress, as well as customs, norms, and mores, are clouded in time, and, consequently, many old and new traditions are ascribed to Islam. In the UAE, oil wealth and an imported working class have allowed for the entrenchment of new customs and norms that were decidedly not a part of Emirati culture previously. This is especially true when it comes to the segregation of the sexes and the social role of women.

The pre-oil economy of what was then called the Trucial States had four significant sectors: dates, pearls, fish, and trade. The date harvest in the oasis areas corresponded with the pearling season, and so a substantial portion of the men were on pearling ships when the dates were ready. Women were in charge of the harvest and the drying, preserving, and trade of dates that would sustain the families and tribes for the coming year. Bedouin men, often kin of one sort or another, stayed in the oasis with their families during the harvest to help with the hard labor and also traded livestock for preserved dates. So too with fish that was preserved by drying or salting on the coast and then transported to inland areas: the men did the fishing but the women did the processing and exchange. The cash economy was negligible in those days, as most currency was in the hands of pearl merchants and traders, but the little money that circulated outside of trade was firmly in the hands of the women (Bristol-Rhys, 2010). The social history of the country is somewhat obscured for two reasons. First, though it was a literate Islamic society, historical narratives were transmitted orally, often through poetry, and those have been mostly lost to time. Second, the written—or documented—history of the Trucial States has been the product of Britain's hegemonic position in the Gulf, so that the historical record focuses primarily on treaties, British agents dealings with rulers, and, later, oil concessions and the hunt for oil. Precious few remarks are made about the people and their lives except to note the lack of water, poverty, and isolation.

The visible and rigidly maintained gender segregation in the UAE is often explained as "being from Islam," but that is correct only if qualified with "the post-oil, Saudi- (Wahhābī) influenced Islam," which has had an impact on most of the Gulf countries and, indeed, many of the Muslim regions elsewhere whose members have spent time in the Gulf as migrant workers. The same might be argued about the adoption of the black *ʿabāyah* worn by all but a tiny minority of Emirati women. Photographs taken in the 1940s, 1950s, and 1960s illustrate clearly that Emirati women of all ages covered their hair and married women wore the face burqa, but they did not cover their clothes with another garment of any color.

Gender segregation is sometimes interpreted to mean that women have little or no social role and so do not participate in the economic and political life of the country. This is not the case in the UAE. Women in the UAE are active in all sectors of the society including the police, military, science, research, medicine, education, humanitarian aid, foreign affairs, and diplomacy. While many of these new roles are opportunities that have emerged within the post-oil development of the federated nation, we know from stories and poems that women played important social and economic roles historically as well. Sadly, there is little historical documentation of women's role in the premodern period; in fact, there is precious little documented about the social life of Emiratis; the record we have is primarily from the British, and they dealt with rulers exclusively.

In the modern period, there were several publicly prominent women whose wisdom, behavior, and influence are still referred to today. Most notable of these is Shaykhah Salāmah bint Būṭī, who was the mother of Shaykh Shakhbut bin Sulṭān and Shaykh Zāyid bin Sulṭān, both of whom ruled Abu Dhabi. Shaykh Zāyid forged the federation of the seven individually ruled Emirates and was the architect of the UAE's development trajectory. Shaykhah Salāmah, whose husband was assassinated in a power struggle in 1926, is credited not only with rearing her family in adversity, especially the two sons who would rule, but with ending the cycle of violence that had ripped the ruling family apart (Maitra, 2007, p. 4). Shaykhah Ḥiṣṣah bint Muḥammad bin Khalīfah al-Nahayān, the mother of the president, Shaykh Khalīfah, is seen by many as the driving force behind the development of schools in Abu Dhabi. Characteristically modest, Shaykhah Ḥiṣṣah claims that she selfishly did not want her son to have to leave the country to be educated and so insisted that schools be opened. Shaykhah Fāṭimah bint Mubārak al-Kitbi is the most influential woman in the UAE by virtue of her work to promote women's rights and equal opportunities, her sponsorship of associations and the Women's Union, and the fact that her four sons, often referred to as the *Banī Fāṭimah*, rule Abu Dhabi and control many of the federal institutions. Other notable women in the public sphere are Shaykhah Lubnah al-Qāsimī, the minister for foreign trade, whose appointing as the minister of the economy in

2005 marked the first time an Emirati woman led a federal ministry. Women now serve as UAE ambassadors and judges, and are both elected and appointed to the Federal National Council, the country's bicameral advisory and consultative parliamentary body. The UAE is very proud of its record with regard to empowering women, and the official website, UAE Interact (www.uaeinteract.com), cites the United Nations Development Programme's Gender-related Development Index for 2011 showing the UAE ranking thirty-eighth among 187 reporting countries. However, many challenges to full empowerment remain, including the current family law, which requires a child of an Emirati woman, born in the UAE, to apply for citizenship at age eighteen, whereas all children of Emirati men are recognized as citizens at birth.

BIBLIOGRAPHY

Bristol-Rhys, Jane. *Emirati Women: Generations of Change*. London: Hurst, 2010.

Maitra, Jayanti. *Zayed: From Challenges to Union*. Abu Dhabi: Center for Documentation and Research, 2007.

Soffan, Linda Usra. *The Women of the United Arab Emirates*. London: Croom Helm, 1980.

United Nations Development Programme. *Arab Development Challenges Report 2011: Towards the Developmental State in the Arab Region*. Cairo: United Nations Development Programme, Regional Centre for Arab States.

United Nations Development Programme, Center of Arab Women for Training and Research, and Arab Gulf Programme for United Nations Development Organizations. *Globalization and Gender: Economic Participation of Arab Women*. Tunis: Center of Arab Women for Training and Research, 2001.

JANE E. BRISTOL-RHYS

UN DEVELOPMENT FUND FOR WOMEN (UNIFEM). United Nations Resolution 3520 of 15 December 1975 proclaimed the period from 1976 to 1985 the UN Decade for Women: Equality, Development and Peace. Its Voluntary Fund became the blueprint for the UN Development Fund for Women (UNIFEM).

The Voluntary Fund was established to support the poorest women in the poorest countries following the 1975 World Conference of the International Women's Year in Mexico City. Among the pledges to the newly formed Voluntary Fund was $1 million donated by Princess Ashraf Pahlavi of Iran. Iran also made another pledge, of the same amount, toward an International Research and Training Institute for the Advancement of Women (INSTRAW), which was to be established in Tehran. However, as a consequence of the fall of the Pahlavi dynasty (1925–1979) and the establishment of the Islamic Republic of Iran in 1979, INSTRAW was ultimately located in the Dominican Republic.

The mandate of the Voluntary Fund was extended in 1985 at the end of the UN Decade for Women, at which point it became UNIFEM, an autonomous organization associated with the UN Development Programme (UNDP). UNIFEM headquarters were set up in New York City under the direction of Margaret Snyder. The organization's goals are to provide financial and technical assistance for innovative approaches aimed at fostering women's empowerment in order to ensure women's participation in mainstream development planning and decision making. UNIFEM aims to eliminate gender discrimination and to promote women's rights and gender equality worldwide.

UNIFEM activities extend over one hundred nations, with fifteen regional offices, ten country-specific programs, and forty-four project offices. In 1994 UNIFEM established a regional West Asia office in Amman, Jordan, with the goal of strengthening institutions for the development of women-owned enterprises in Jordan, Syria, and

Lebanon. In 1996 Jordanian Princess Basma bint Talal was named UNIFEM goodwill ambassador.

UNIFEM's work in Muslim-majority countries has been extensive. In Morocco, UNIFEM has supported programs in education, HIV/AIDS, and legal reform alongside that nation's Ministries of Education and Health. Through its Arab Women Parliamentarians program, to advance the training of women parliamentarians and their knowledge of, and leadership in, governance structures and reforms, UNIFEM has worked with Jordan, Kuwait, Egypt, Syria, Lebanon, Bahrain, and the United Arab Emirates. In Afghanistan, the organization has supported that nation's Ministries of the Interior and Women's Affairs in providing refuge and 24-hour legal advice for women struggling with the issues of elopement, divorce, domestic violence, and land rights. In 2010, as part of a broader UN reform program, UNIFEM merged with three other UN organizations: the Division for the Advancement of Women (DAW), the International Research and Training Institute for the Advancement of Women (INSTRAW), and the Office of the Special Adviser on Gender Issues and Advancement of Women (OSAGI), to collectively form the United Nations Entity for Gender Equality and the Empowerment of Women (UN Women).

BIBLIOGRAPHY

"Agencies of the UN: UNIFEM." http://www.un.cv/agency-unifem.php.

Husseini, Randa. "Promoting Women Entrepreneurs in Lebanon: The Experience of UNIFEM." *Gender and Development* 5, no. 1 (February 1997): 49–53.

Pietilä, Hilka. *The Unfinished Story of Women and the United Nations*. New York and Geneva, Switzerland: United Nations, 2007.

Snyder, Margaret. "The Politics of Women and Development." In *Women, Politics, and the United Nations*, edited by Anne Winslow, pp. 95–116. Washington, D.C.: George Washington University, 1995.

Snyder, Margaret. "Walking My Own Road: How a Sabbatical Year Led to a United Nations Career." In *Developing Power, How Women Transformed International Development*, edited by Arvonne S. Fraser and Irene Tinker, pp. 38–49. New York: Feminist Press, City University of New York, 2004.

"UNIFEM Worldwide: Arab States." http://www.unifem.org/worldwide/arab_states/.

"UNIFEM Worldwide: Asia & the Pacific." http://unifem.org/worldwide/asia_pacific/.

"UN Women: Projects List." http://www.unifem.org.jo/pages/projectslist.aspx?gn=17.

"UN Women: World Conference of the International Women's Year." http://www.un.org/womenwatch/daw/beijing/mexico.html.

ROJA FAZAELI

UNITED NATIONS POPULATION FUND.

Formerly known as the United Nations Fund for Population Activities, the United Nations Population Fund (UNFPA) is an international development agency founded in 1969 under the aegis of the United Nations that promotes health and equal opportunities for all women, men, and children. UNFPA supports countries' use of population data to reduce poverty, unwanted pregnancies, and the spread of HIV/AIDS, while encouraging safe mothering and assuring the human rights and dignity of women and girls. It particularly focuses on gender equality, women's empowerment, and assisting governments in delivering universal access to sexual and reproductive health services, including family planning. UNFPA also works to address violence against women that results from war, particularly the concomitant rise of the use of rape and forced pregnancies as war tools and rising incidences of domestic violence, particularly among refugees. UNFPA has long-standing partnerships with governments, NGOs, foundations, communities, other UN agencies, and the private sector in order to address these issues at both the national and grassroots levels.

A key UNFPA priority has been improving maternal health and assuring safe motherhood, particularly by seeking to eliminate obstetric fistula (a medical complication that occurs when a woman has been in obstructed labor for too long and which typically results in the baby's death and, if not death, at least extensive and permanent damage to the birth canal that results in incontinence for the mother). Because this condition is treatable by Cesarean section, guaranteeing women access to this medical service is critical to its elimination, which means not only assuring that appropriate medical facilities exist, but also that women have viable transportation options to access them. Also critical to the success of UNFPA initiatives is involving men, so that they understand the importance of women's access to health and reproductive services and support their right to make use of them.

UNFPA's gender framework considers girls' education, women's economic and political empowerment, and women's self-capacity to control their own fertility as critical to the advancement of gender equality globally. Nevertheless, UNFPA also recognizes the need for cultural awareness and sensitivity in approaching human, women's, and reproductive rights in various settings. This has particularly proven to be the case in Muslim-majority countries, where public conversations about sex, sexuality, reproduction, and family planning are considered taboo because these are considered to be private family matters, rather than appropriate for public discussion. Also controversial has been UNFPA's stated goal of eliminating practices deemed to be harmful according to international standards of human rights, including female genital cutting (FGC), honor killings, and early marriage for girls and adolescents. Because these are sensitive cultural issues in some countries, opposition to UNFPA programs in general has resulted, with opponents voicing concerns about imposition of Western cultural standards on non-Western societies.

Particular awareness of cultural sensitivities, and constructive methods of encouraging communities to address them, were hallmark concerns of the former executive director Thoraya Obaid (2000–2010), the first Saudi Arabian national to head a UN agency. The executive director, Dr. Babatunde Osotimehin (2011–present), is a Nigerian physician and public health expert.

BIBLIOGRAPHY

"About UNFPA," *United Nations Population Fund*, accessed January 16, 2013, http://www.unfpa.org/public/home/about.

DeLong-Bas, Natana J. *Notable Muslims: Muslim Builders of World Civilization and Culture*. Oxford: Oneworld, 2006.

NATANA J. DELONG-BAS

UNITED STATES OF AMERICA. Muslims in America currently number around 3 to 6 million and constitute one of the most diverse populations of Muslims around the globe in terms of their ethnic and geographic backgrounds, as well as their ways of understanding and practicing Islam. In keeping with general global trends, American Muslims are majority Sunnī, with Shīʿī Muslims constituting about a fifth of the population. A small but noteworthy minority identifies with heterodox groups. While prior to 11 September 2001 Muslim Americans were less visible on the national stage, with subsequent increased public attention, at times including or verging on religious and racial persecution, Muslim Americans have become increasingly vocal, strengthening their community organizations and outreach activities to meet the exigent demands. Overall, American Muslims are highly integrated into the American sociocultural fabric;

abundant survey data suggests that their attitudes and views, income levels, and educational attainment closely follow general trends within the population at large.

Community Growth and Constitution. The origins of Islam in America stretch at least as far as the trans-Atlantic slave trade, although the extent of the Muslim presence in this period is difficult to determine. In the case of African Muslims brought to the Americas as slaves, the vast majority were assimilated into Christianity and given Anglicized names. However, the ancestral connection to African Muslims has constituted an impetus for African American conversion to Islam. In the early decades of the twentieth century, the outreach of the Aḥmadīyah Muslim mission, a distinct group originating in the Punjab region of South Asia, was very successful in spreading Islamic literacy particularly among African Americans in Chicago and other American metropolises. Many more African Americans embraced Islamic teachings in conjunction with black nationalist rhetoric and the struggle for civil rights during the mid-twentieth century. Early twentieth-century estimates place the proportion of African American Muslims at slightly over one-third of American Muslims, and growing at a rapid pace, with as many as twenty thousand conversions per year. This pattern of growth combined with immigration from Muslim-majority countries, is pacing the Muslim community to become the second-largest religious denomination in the United States.

Immigrant Muslims and their children, grandchildren, and even great-grandchildren are estimated at about one-third to one-half of the American Muslim population. Incredibly heterogeneous in their countries of origin and their religious backgrounds, these individuals were drawn to America for job opportunities and quality of living, as well as to reunite with family members who had immigrated in previous waves. The numbers of Muslims immigrating to the United States increased dramatically as a result of the Immigration and Naturalization Act of 1965, which attracted in particular Asian families from skilled and educated backgrounds. Despite this dramatic increase, Muslim immigrants had been arriving in the United States since the late nineteenth and early twentieth centuries, drawn predominantly from regions of the Levant. These early waves of immigrants often performed assembly-line manufacturing jobs in connection with the automobile industry. Today, many third, fourth, and even fifth generation Arab Muslims make up large percentages of the population in several locales, the most famous of which is the city of Dearborn, Michigan. Since the late twentieth century, Muslim immigrants have also come from many parts of Africa, Asia, and the Middle East. Some come to the United States as refugees of political conflicts, such as in Somalia, Sudan, Palestine, Iran, Iraq, Afghanistan, and other locales. Alongside political asylum, both job opportunities and high standards of living remain a compelling incentives for immigration to the United States.

Finally, adding to this unique population of American Muslims are converts from European, Native American, Latin American, and Caribbean backgrounds, many of whom were exposed to Islam either through Muslim community outreach efforts or through academic studies of Islamicate cultures and histories at institutions of learning in the United States. Including the population of African American converts, approximately two-thirds of converts come from Protestant Christian backgrounds. Transnational Ṣūfī communities with American branches are also contributing to the spread of Islamic teachings to an ethnically and religiously diverse cross-section of the population.

Women's Engagements. Muslim American women constitute the most heterodox grouping of Muslims in the world, and, as such, generalizing about their religious affiliations, pious practices, gender-related views, or community roles is difficult. Some are religiously observant, and others are Muslim by cultural identity or familial custom. Many are highly active in community life and have professional careers; some are more exclusively focused on domestic roles. Some women choose forms of dress that resemble traditional or neotraditional styles in majority-Muslim societies; others follow mainstream American fashion trends more closely. Generational and socioeconomic differences compound differences in ethnicity, religiosity, and custom.

Despite this great diversity, it is possible to observe that, in the post-9/11 atmosphere, increased public attention to the perceived mistreatment of women in Islam has prompted many women to articulate their unique personal narratives and understandings of religious, ethnic, and national identity. In the early 21st century, titles emphasizing Muslim women's voice and agency have populated the shelves of mainstream booksellers and are being consumed by a general American readership curious to know more about the Islamic faith and the personal lives of Muslim women. Such publicity, coupled with targeted educational efforts, is gradually serving to break down stereotypes of Muslims that have circulated within larger American public discourses. At the same time, stereotypes of Muslim men as being violent, domineering, or otherwise inclined toward excess have also begun to be dismantled as legacies of a missionary and imperialist age. In this broad effort to represent Islam and American Muslims positively, traditional and social media have been instrumental. Women-led NGOs, magazines, and online forums have a wide reach, both within the Muslim community and beyond.

Nonetheless, anti-Muslim bigotry continues to be an issue affecting American Muslims. For instance, organizations such as the Council on American-Islamic Relations (CAIR), America's most influential Muslim civil liberties organization, regularly handle complaints on behalf of female Muslims who wear headscarves and allege discriminatory practices on the part of employers. Other organizations, such as the Islamic Networks Group, specialize in providing professional associations and companies with information that can better help them serve, work alongside, or employ Muslims.

In addition to advancing a more nuanced public discourse on Islam, many Muslim women have long been involved in strengthening their local religious communities through enhancing educational programming, strengthening social service initiatives, or forging interfaith partnerships. In such ways, women have been at the forefront of making American mosques hospitable and effective institutions for multiple decades. While in a majority of American mosques women's representation in mosque governance is still lacking, focused campaigns to address this issue are underway by a number of large Muslim American organizations, as well as by concerned individuals. Ensuring that adequate prayer space is available to women in North American mosques is also on the agenda of Muslim advocacy groups. On a much smaller scale, lesbian and gay Muslims have been advocating for better reception in their religious and ethnic communities.

The education and religious enculturation of Muslim children in America remains an area of mobilization on the part of American Muslim women in particular. While some Muslim schools have long waiting lists, keeping up enrollment can present a significant challenge for some religious schools, particularly those located in more remote areas of the country. For some schools, qualified staffing is an issue; others have found a solution by opening employment opportunities to non-Muslims who are respectful of Islamic cultures and beliefs. One established model has been the Sister Clara Muhammad Schools, named after Clara Muhammad (1899–1972), wife of Elijah Muhammad (1897–1975) and mother of Warith Deen Muhammad (1933–2008). Beyond schools, also influential are youth organizations such as the Muslim Youth of North America (MYNA), a division of the Islamic Society of North America (ISNA), which holds camps and activities where youth can interact and study religion in structured, chaperoned environments.

On the level of the family, Muslim American households follow broader national trends with respect to income levels and numbers of children. Even divorce rates among Muslim couples are approaching the national average. Some Muslim households uphold various levels of gender segregation with extended family and guests; others socialize in more typically American mixed-gender environments. Some Muslim women follow the traditional dictates of their religion and marry only Muslim men; others are marrying outside the faith. While Muslim men have traditionally been given religious sanction to marry Christian and Jewish women, often women of such marriages adopt Islamic faith and Muslim customs. Also consistent with the larger U.S. population, Muslims in America are also remaining single longer, with many choosing to pursue career options rather than beginning families.

American Muslim Contributions to Public Discourse and Religious Scholarship. In many respects, American institutions have provided some of the most influential forums for advancing Muslim women's contributions to religious scholarship. Analyses on the part of female Muslim scholars, as well as their male counterparts, have become a central medium for advancing critiques of militant Islam, rigidly juridical Islam, ethnocentric Islam, patriarchal Islam, and other ideological orientations that are not conducive to Muslim integration into a cosmopolitan, religiously plural, Western society. Inspired by visions for a more equitable and just society, leading Muslim thinkers are engaging in communal self-reflection and at the same time are chiming in on discourses about the meaning and makeup of American values. In this context, a considerable number of American Muslim women scholars are increasingly vocal in seeking to analyze, and mitigate where possible, vestiges of patriarchy, prejudice, and parochialism, whether within religious discourses or as a result of structural dynamics in their own contemporary contexts.

Muslim scholars and activists face a number of potentially contentious issues: the demand for a progressive reconciliation of monotheistic claims with religiously plural societies, demands for racial and gender equity, many variant readings of foundational texts, many claims of interpretive authority, extremists of various types, including hardliner assailants and bigoted critics, and, for recent immigrants, current or looming political instability in countries of origin, as well as a marked need to preserve continuity with religious and cultural heritages as religious minorities. For converts, challenges include explaining their new religious affiliation to friends and family who may have hostile views of Islam. With all of these dynamics at play, the body of high-quality literature on Islam in America continues to expand, spurred on by a wider public interest in East-West relations, Jewish-Christian-Muslim relations, interfaith relations more generally and, of course, the habits, status, roles, and opinions of Muslim women in the United States and their connections to Muslims abroad.

[*See also* Islamic Society of North America; KARAMAH (Muslim Women Lawyers for Human Rights); Muslim Women's League; *and* Sisters in Islam.]

BIBLIOGRAPHY

Abdul-Ghafur, Saleemah, ed. *Living Islam Out Loud: American Muslim Women Speak.* Boston: Beacon, 2005.

Ahmed, Leila. *A Quiet Revolution: The Veil's Resurgence, from the Middle East to America*. New Haven, Conn.: Yale University Press, 2011.

Ali, Wajahat, and Zahra Suratwala, eds. *All-American: 45 American Men on Being Muslim*. Ashland, Oreg.: White Cloud, 2012.

Bullock, Katherine, ed. *Muslim Women Activists in North America: Speaking for Ourselves*. Austin: University of Texas Press, 2005.

Ebrahimji, Maria M., and Zahra T. Suratwala, eds. *I Speak for Myself: American Women on Being Muslim*. Ashland, Oreg.: White Cloud, 2011.

Esposito, John L., and Ibrahim Kalin, eds. *Islamophobia: The Challenge of Pluralism in the 21st Century*. New York: Oxford University Press, 2011.

GhaneaBassiri, Kambiz. *A History of Islam in America: From the New World to the New World Order*. New York: Cambridge University Press, 2012.

Haddad, Yvonne Yazbeck, Jane I. Smith, and Kathleen M. Moore. *Muslim Women in America: The Challenge of Islamic Identity Today*. New York: Oxford University Press, 2006.

Hibri, Azizah al-. "Islamic Law and Muslim Women in America." In *One Nation under God? Religion and American Culture*, edited by Marjorie Garber and Rebecca L. Walkowitz, pp. 128–144. London: Routledge, 1999.

Karim, Jamillah. *American Muslim Women: Negotiating Race, Class, and Gender within the Ummah*. New York: New York University Press, 2009.

Manji, Irshad. *The Trouble with Islam: A Muslim's Call for Reform in Her Faith*. New York: St. Martin's, 2004.

Mattu, Ayesha, and Nura Maznavi, eds. *Love, InshAllah: The Secret Love Lives of American Muslim Women*. Berkeley, Calif.: Soft Skull, 2012.

Safari, Elli, dir. *The Noble Struggle of Amina Wadud*. DVD. New York: Distributed by Women Make Movies, 2007.

Smith, Jane I. *Islam in America*. 2d ed. New York: Columbia University Press, 2010.

Webb, Gisela, ed. *Windows of Faith: Muslim Women Scholar-Activists in North America*. Syracuse, N.Y.: Syracuse University Press, 2000.

Celene Ayat Lizzio

Universities. Women have been establishing themselves in higher education across the Middle East and North Africa (MENA) since 1929, when Suhair el-Qalamwi (1911–1997) became the first woman to attend a university in an Arab country. However, MENA governments did not make women's participation in higher education a priority until the 1990s. Since then, women have made significant advances in accessing education. From 1999 to 2009, shifts brought new gender parity in enrollment at institutions of upper secondary education in Arab states, reflecting larger global trends. Female enrollment in tertiary education in 2009 ranged from regional lows of 28 percent in Mauritania and 29 percent in Yemen, to regional highs of 64 percent in Qatar and 60 percent in both Tunisia and the United Arab Emirates. As of 2012, statistics released by the United Nations suggested that the gender gap in education at the university level has closed for many women in the Middle East. In two-thirds of Middle Eastern countries, the total number of female students is equal to or higher than the number of male students.

Although women's participation has greatly expanded at the university, it has been restricted to particular fields. A popular belief is that only certain fields, such as the humanities, education, and medicine are appropriate for women, since the resulting jobs are in sex-segregated industries. These restrictions are generally self-imposed, although, in 2012, Iran formally restricted which fields women are allowed to study.

Egypt. In 1909, Egyptian University hosted a series of lectures by women and for women. Nevertheless, women did not gain access to most institutions of higher education until much later. Suhair el-Qalamwi graduated from Cairo University in 1933, but it was not until 1962 that women gained admittance to al-Azhar University, when it added a women's faculty as part of a larger reorganization.

Enrollment has reached gender parity in many Egyptian institutions. For example, women make up 52 percent of the student body at Cairo

University. In other institutions, such as Ain-Shams University, separate women-only colleges have been established. Enrollment numbers for women in postsecondary education are lowest in governorates in Upper Egypt, generally considered to be the most conservative region in the country. Similar to the regional trend, women in Egypt tend to specialize in the fields of education, the humanities, and the arts, although women's enrollment in basic sciences and medicine exceeds that of men. These disparities are reflected at the level of faculty. As of 2012, women constituted a third of the teaching staff at Egyptian universities. While small in number, these women are responsible for calls for significant reform. Su'ad Salih, professor of Islamic jurisprudence at al-Azhar Unviersity and Dean of the Girl's College, is currently leading the fight for women to be appointed *muftis*. At the administrative level, although the educational bureaucracy continues to be dominated by men, women do hold some significant positions. Salwa al-Ghareb, for example, is the Secretary-General of the Higher Council for Universities.

Gulf States. Women's involvement in higher education in the Gulf states began in 1961 when King Sa'ud University opened admission to women through correspondence courses in the colleges of arts and administrative sciences. They were permitted to begin on-campus instruction during the 1975–1976 school year. Since that time, female enrollment has skyrocketed. These numbers are unusually high in the Gulf states because large numbers of men leave the region for education or are able to find employment without pursuing postsecondary studies. As a result, institutions that enroll both men and women tend to be dominated by the latter. At the National University in Qatar, for example, 76 percent of students were female during the 2008–2009 school year. At the University of Sharjah, 79 percent of graduates in 2007 were female. At the same time, the region houses a number of women's-only colleges, including the Dubai Women's College, Zayed University with campuses in Dubai and Abu Dhabi, Dar al-Hekma University in Jeddah, and Princess Nora Bint Abdul Rahman University in Riyadh, the largest women-only university in the world. A notable woman in higher education administration is Sheikha Abdulla al-Misnad, who became the president of the University of Qatar in 2003 and the Minister of Education in 2010.

Palestine. Bir Zeit University houses the unique Institute of Women's Studies (IWS). Founded in 1994 by a group of female academics as the Women's Studies Program, the institute added a full-time staff and a graduate program in 1997. Its master's degree in Gender and Development was the first of its kind in the region. The institute aims to facilitate scholarship on women, contribute to women's studies more generally, and to promote and inform advocacy work on behalf of Palestinian women.

Lebanon. American Presbyterian missionaries founded the American School for Girls in Beirut in 1860. The institution was reformed into the American Junior Women's College in 1924 and renamed the Beirut College for Women in 1955, when it received a charter as a four-year college. Emily Nasrallah, the noted Lebanese writer and activist, was one of the first women in Lebanon to attend. She obtained her bachelor's degree in education in 1958. In 1973, the institution changed its name to Beirut University College and began admitting men. In that same year, the Institute for Women's Studies in the Arab World (IWSAW), dedicated to the study of women in the Arab world, was founded. In 1994, the university's name was changed to Lebanese American University.

Turkey. Unlike the other countries in the region, Turkey struggles to attain female parity in enrollment at universities. As of 2002, females made up 42 percent of the student body at Ankara

University and only 37 percent at the Middle East Technical University, also located in Ankara. This is likely due to both formal and informal restrictions on the participation of women who veil at public universities. In addition to reducing female enrollment, the ban also severely limits job opportunities for female academics, who must teach in smaller private institutes with fewer resources than the large public universities if they want to wear the veil. Some students have taken to wearing wigs in order to be able to attend or work at the public universities.

BIBLIOGRAPHY

Abu-Lughod, Lila, ed. *Remaking Women: Feminism and Modernity in the Middle East.* Princeton, N.J.: Princeton University Press, 1998.

Badran, Adnan. *At the Crossroads: Education in the Middle East.* New York: Paragon House, 1989.

Christina, Rachel, Golnar Mehran, and Shabana Mir. "Education in the Middle East: Challenges and Opportunities." In *Comparative Education: The Dialectic of the Global and the Local,* 3d ed., edited by Robert F. Arnove and Carlos Alberto Torres, pp. 311–332. Plymouth, U.K.: Rowman and Littlefield, 2007.

"Higher Education and the Middle East: Empowering Underserved and Vulnerable Populations." Special issue, *Viewpoints* (October 2010): http://www.mei.edu/sites/default/files/publications/EducationVPVol.II_.pdf.

Kejanlioğlu, D. Beybin, and Oğuzhan Taş. 2009. "Regimes of Un/veiling and Body Control: Turkish Students Wearing Wigs." *Social Anthropology: Journal of the European Association of Social Anthropologists* 17 (November 2009): 424–438.

Lack, Stephen, and Nagwa Megahed. "Colonial Legacy, Women's Rights and Gender-Educational Inequality in the Arab World with Particular Reference to Egypt and Tunisia." *International Review of Education* 57 (August 2011): 397–418.

Lindsey, Ursula. "Arab Women Make Inroads in Higher Education but Often Find Dead Ends." *The Chronicle of Higher Education* 58 (January 29, 2012).

Malik, L. P. "Social and Cultural Determinants of the Gender Gap in Higher Education in the Islamic World." *Journal of Asian and African Studies* 30 (1995): 181–193.

Massialas, Byron, and Samir Ahmad Jarrar. *Arab Education in Transition: A Source Book.* New York: Garland Publishing, 1991.

Mattar, Philip, ed. *Encyclopedia of the Modern Middle East and North Africa.* Detroit, Mich.: Macmillan Reference USA, 2004.

Moghadam, Valentine. *Modernizing Women: Gender and Social Change in the Middle East.* 2d ed. Boulder, Colo.: Lynne Rienner, 2003.

Obst, Daniel, and Daniel N. Kirk. *Innovation Through Education: Building the Knowledge Economy in the Middle East.* New York: Institute of International Education, 2010.

UNESCO Institute for Statistics. "Global Education Digest 2011: Comparing Education Statistics Across the World." http://www.uis.unesco.org/Education/Documents/ged-2011-en.pdf.

ANN WAINSCOTT

V

VEILING.

[*This entry has two subentries:* Historical Discourse *and* Contemporary Discourse.]

HISTORICAL DISCOURSE

The historical production of what we now refer to as the "Islamic veil" has been the work not only of Muslim scholars, but also ordinary Muslim believers, as well as non-Muslims. This entry will look at three particularly influential realms of debate: (1) theological interpretations about Qurʾānic directives to veil, (2) medieval legal debates surrounding obligations of women to cover, and (3) modern political rhetoric about the significance of the Islamic veil in the context of various colonial experiences.

Veiling Directives in the Qurʾān. There are three verses commonly cited as Qurʾānic evidence of the Islamic veil: 33:53, 33:59–60, and 24:30–31. There is an enormous diversity among these verses, even with the terms that are translated as "veil" (*hijab*, *jilbāb*, *khimār*). In addition, who is asked to veil, for what reasons, and in front of whom differs in these verses, which complicates what norms are implied by the Qurʾānic directives to cover.

Verse 33:53: Privacy in the home. Verse 33:53, sometimes referred to as "the verse of the *hijab*," is chronologically the first revelation related to Islamic veiling. Drawing on reports recorded in the ḥadīth, there is scholarly consensus that this revelation occurred within five years of the Muslim community's emigration from Mecca to Medina when the Prophet's leadership had expanded from spiritual leader of a Muslim minority to the political leader of the majority. With this new political authority came enormous demands on the Prophet's time. The ḥadīth describe, for instance, the common occurrence of Muslims seeking advice and favors while visiting the Prophet, often in the private quarters of one of his wives.

Ḥadīth reports claim the revelation recorded in verse 33:53 occurred after the marriage of the Prophet to Zaynab. A number of wedding guests lingered in Zaynab's house after the wedding celebration, causing the Prophet to become annoyed. 33:53 asks all Muslims to abide by various rules when visiting the Prophet, such as waiting for permission to enter his private quarters and not lingering after their business is completed.

In the second part of the verse, the way privacy is maintained is specified: Muslim men are told to address the Prophet's wives with a *hijab* between them. Although *hijab* today is used to refer to the Islamic veil, or even more generally to any form of women's Islamic dress, it has a more generic meaning in the Qurʾān. In the other places it is used, *hijab* separates things, such as gods from mortals (42:51), wrong-doers from the righteous (7:46), believers from unbelievers (41:5, 17:45), and light from darkness (38:32). In fact, other than verse 33:53, *hijab* refers to women in only one other place in the Qurʾān, 19:17, where it mentions Mary, the mother of Jesus. This means the Qurʾānic *hijab* is not necessarily an article of clothing, nor is it tied necessarily to women. At its most basic level, *hijab* in the Qurʾān is a term used merely to connote borders and establish thresholds.

Verse 33:59: Protection outside the home. Verse 33:59 is sometimes called the "mantle verse." In this revelation, all Muslim women are encouraged to draw close their *jilbāb*, to avoid being harassed on the street. Some context for this revelation is helpful: Ḥadīth reports describe the public harassment of women in Medina as so common that any woman who went out at night to relieve herself risked attack. In that specific cultural context, slave women were understood to be available to free men for sex. *Jilbāb* was, therefore, a way to visually mark someone as a free woman and, therefore, not sexually available in the same way as a slave.

The understanding of this specific context (harassment of women on the streets of Medina) and purpose (to prevent harassment of free Muslim women) remained mostly consistent in Qurʾānic commentary on this verse from the ninth to fifteenth centuries, even as the definition of what *jilbāb* was, and what parts of a woman's body it covered, changed. The challenge for contemporary application is that there is no way to know for sure what seventh-century *jilbāb* looked like.

Verse 24: 30–31: Sexual modesty. The third piece of Qurʾānic evidence often quoted in support of veiling is verse 24:30–31, in which Muslim women are directed not to reveal some sort of hidden *zināh* and to cover their *ʿawrāh* in front of men, except close male relatives or male servants.

Verse 24:30–31 is difficult to interpret, which is not helped by the absence of any solid ḥadīth concerning the occasion of its revelation, because the meanings of both *zināh* and *awrāt* are unclear in this text. *Zināh* has the specific meaning of illicit sex in Islamic law; however, it has a much more general meaning the forty-three times it occurs in the Qurʾān. At times, it refers to people (10:24 and 13:33), but it also describes the beauty of the stars (37:6), heaven (41:12), and sky (50:6). This means, in general terms, that the Qurʾānic meaning of *zināh* is morally neutral: it is merely a state of attractiveness.

There is no scholarly consensus about the definition of a woman's *awrāt*. One isolated but influential ḥadīth recorded by Tirmidhi states, "Women is *ʿawra*. If she goes out, Satan attempts to control her." This is referenced in legal opinions that indicate women should cover from head to toe, sometimes including their faces. For other scholars, a woman's *awrāt* does not include her face and hands; for others, only her bosom, neck, and head; for still others, only her genitals.

The text directs both men and women to adopt modesty; however, it devotes substantially more time to discussing women's modesty. Specific actions are required for women (such as covering bosoms—*juyub*—and *awrāt*) and others are forbidden (such as drawing attention to themselves). Verse 24:30–31 also explicitly references an article of clothing (*khimār*) that is sometimes used to cover a head (even if no reference to the head or hair is made).

Summary. The three relevant Qurʾānic verses contain tremendous diversity, especially in regard to what the veil is, who has a duty to veil, and for what reason. Three different Arabic words are used in the Qurʾān that might be translated as the

Islamic "veil": *hijab, jilbāb, khimār. Jilbāb* and *khimār* refer to articles of clothing, but not the same ones. The common Qur'ānic meaning of *hijab* is not clothing at all, but rather a separation. All three terms can be interpreted as gender barriers, but they separate men and women in different ways (hiding, making recognizable, covering) for different norms (privacy, bodily integrity, modesty).

The three verses address different groups of women for whom the veil is recommended. To complicate the matter further, men are also discussed in the sacred texts, both as the reason why the *hijab* is drawn, as well as having their own duty to be modest. In fact, the ḥadīth as a whole is more concerned with the modest dress of men than women, especially with regard to prayer, and during the *ḥajj*, when special ritualized clothing is prescribed.

Another difference between the three verses is why a separation of men and women is required in the first place and thus the moral norm the separation supports. In verse 33:53, the veil safeguards the *privacy* of the Prophet's home life. Here, seclusion ensures that the Prophet's wives are not bothered in their own home through creating a separation of public and private spaces. By contrast, in 33:59, the concern is the protection of the *bodily integrity* of Muslim women. The veil here protects women from unjust sexual harassment and assault when they are outside their homes. Finally, verse 24:31 establishes guidelines for interactions between men and women in order to encourage *modesty* and prevent inappropriate sexual relations.

Fundamental to understanding these sacred texts on the issue of the veil is the presumption that these verses are intimately related. In fact, a Qur'ānic "Islamic veil" is only possible through a holistic reading of the Qur'ān that links these verses and semantically expands the meaning of each. In other words, only by interpolating the revelation recorded in 33:59 about harassment of women and cloaks, the revelation in verse 24:31 about sexual modesty and kerchiefs, and verse 33:53 about the Prophet's privacy and a curtain is the concept of *an* "Islamic veil" sensible. Only by linking the key terms (*hijab, jilbāb, khimār*) and norms (privacy, bodily integrity, modesty) can the scriptural basis for an Islamic veil that applies to all women be seen.

Concern with Women's Bodies in Medieval *Fiqh*. Legal reasoning has had enormous influence on the development of Muslim meanings for the veil. Islamic scholars work to elaborate, apply, and explain the meaning of the veil as described in sacred texts, and Islamic legal thought referenced in contemporary efforts to establish national legislation requiring the veil. Early *fiqh* discussed veiling in the context of prayer, and in general saw veiling as an issue of social status and physical safety. This changed in medieval *fiqh*. Although women's dress was not a central concern of medieval legal scholars, themes and concepts that emerged in legal reasoning during this time period remain relevant in modern discussions of the veil.

One interesting trend in medieval legal reasoning was an increase in discussions about the interpretation of *awrāt* and whether or not a woman should cover her face. However, in medieval legal reasoning, face-veiling gained some prominence. There was by no means a legal consensus, but a majority legal opinion (women should cover everything except their face and hands) and a minority opinion (women should cover everything except their eyes) emerged. It was Ibn Taymīyah's (d. 1328) opinion, for example, that women should cover their faces in public, and this became the standard Ḥanbalī and Shāfiʿī position. In contrast, the Ḥanafī scholar Burhan al-Din al-Marghinani (d. 1197) wrote about the importance of women's faces and hands remaining uncovered, especially during everyday business transactions with men. For the most part, Mālikī and Ḥanafī legal experts did not consider a woman's face or hands *awrāt*. Nonetheless, even these standard legal positions within specific schools were not universal.

Another common pattern of legal reasoning in medieval *fiqh* is the linkage of *awrāt* (vulnerability) and *fitnah*. Specifically, it was during this time that jurists began to rely on a doctrine of *fitnah*, or worldly disorder, to justify rulings on a wide range of issues. The word *fitnah* appears in a number of places in the Qur'ān where it refers to nonsexual temptations, such as money, that lead to discord or worldly disorder. It is not, however, used in the sacred text as a reason for veiling, or to refer to actions and things that produce sexual arousal and lead to sexual sin. However, the majority of medieval legal scholars utilized a doctrine of *fitnah* to explain why the covering of women was required. The disorder at stake was the chaos that sexual desire outside of marriage can cause (such as distraction from completing other duties). Centuries later, this same concern motivates the arguments of some emerging Islamic governments, who claim that their stability depends on the public veiling of all women.

When medieval legal experts discussed *awrāt* or *fitnah*, their main focus was not on veiling per se, but the prevention and punishment of illicit sexual encounters. Nevertheless, they linked *fitnah* to the veil, thereby marking women's bodies as dangerous and disorderly. At the same time, their reliance on local veiling practices to determine what constitutes *awrāt* continued the legal precedent for multiple and varied interpretations of what the veil should cover and what it physically looked like.

Colonialism and the Symbolic Power of the Islamic Veil. During the colonization and decolonization of Muslim-majority regions, particular interactions between occupying powers and local populations made Islam more important to emerging forms of nationalism. During this process, the veil, in particular, took on new significance through discourse about religion, gender, and modernity.

Three important themes emerge. First, colonial empires were concerned with veiling, which they interpreted as a sign of underdevelopment. The occupiers' discourse on the veil also affected local understanding of veiling. Resistance narratives reproduced the idea of the Islamic veil as a symbol of the status of women and the status of Islam in politics in general. Even those who rejected the idea that women had to be unveiled to be modern adopted the premise that veiling epitomized Islamic culture. This reappropriation marked a significant shift in Islamic discourse about the veil in many regions, and the veil gained new powerful cultural and political symbolic meanings in this historical period.

Second, although women were active in the nationalist debates and independence movements—even taking on combatant roles—when it came to veiling debates, women were for the most part pawns in the political battles of men. Women in general were either indifferent to veiling or considered it an issue of gender equality, not a litmus test for patriotism or modernity.

Third, during colonization, the veil became an important political symbol, but the content of that symbol differed across contexts. In Egypt, the colonialists identified the veil as antimodern, and some nationalists also began to see the face-veil as a sign of Egypt's underdevelopment. Under colonial rule in Algeria, the French saw the veil as a symbol of resistance to their assimilation policies; for Algerians, the veil became a potential antidote to imperial domination. During the Intifada, the veil became a sign of allegiance to Palestinian liberation and unveiling a sign of collaboration with Israeli occupation. Islamic veiling functioned simultaneously as a practice that was regulatory and emancipatory, controlling and liberating, even within the same national context. If, as Leila Ahmed has famously stated, the veil became "pregnant with meanings" because of colonial encounters, these meanings vary between different people in different places in different historical contexts.

BIBLIOGRAPHY

Ahmed, Leila. *Women and Gender in Islam*. New Haven, CT: Yale University Press, 1992.

Badran, Margot. *Feminists, Islam, and Nation: Gender and the Making of Modern Egypt*. Princeton, NJ: Princeton University Press, 1995.

Bucar, Elizabeth. *The Islamic Veil: A Beginner's Guide*. Oxford: Oneworld, 2012. See especially 28–66.

El Fadl, Khaled Abou. *Speaking in God's Name: Islamic Law, Authority, and Women*. Oxford: Oneworld, 2001.

Fanon, Frantz. *A Dying Colonialism*. Translated by H. Chevalier. New York: Grove, 1965. With an introduction by A. Gilly.

Hajjaji-Jarrah, Soraya. "Women's Modesty in Qur'anic Commentaries: The Founding Discourse." In *The Muslim Veil in North America*, edited by S. S. Alvi, H. Hoodfar, and S. McDonough, pp. 118–213. Toronto: Women's Press, 2003.

Hoffman, Valerie. "Quranic Interpretation and Modesty Norms for Women." In *The Shaping of an American Islamic Discourse*, edited by E. Waugh and F. Denny, pp. 89–112. Atlanta: Scholars Press, 1998.

Mernissi, Fatima. *The Veil and the Male Elite*. Translated by M. J. Lakeland. Reading, MA: Perseus, 1991.

Stowasser, Barbara. *Women in the Qur'an, Traditions, and Interpretation*. New York: Oxford University Press, 1994.

Tucker, Judith. *In the House of the Law: Gender and Islamic Law in Ottoman Syria and Palestine*. Berkeley: University of California Press, 1998.

ELIZABETH M. BUCAR

CONTEMPORARY DISCOURSE

In the 1970s in Egypt, often to the consternation of family and friends at that time, young urban college women in the most competitive majors, some of whom had previously dressed in miniskirts and sleeveless tops, voluntarily and almost suddenly changed appearance and donned the "veil" (headscarf, *hijab*, or *niqāb*). An empirical ethnographic study classified the phenomenon as a particular form of religiousness expressed outwardly in new forms of appearance and dress contextualized in the wider society and culture. The change in appearance attracted the attention of many observers and scholars, although most observers focused on it as a women's phenomenon and on the new *hijab* as a "return to veiling."

The word *hijab*, prominently associated with this new form of appearance, developed historically in the Arab region. It has cultural and linguistic roots that are integral to Islamic (and Arab) culture and derives from the Arabic etymological root *h-j-b*; its verbal form *hajaba* translates as "to veil, to seclude, to screen, to conceal, to form a separation, to mask." Therefore, *hijab* translates as "cover, wrap, curtain, veil, screen, partition." The same word is used to refer to amulets carried on one's person (particularly for children or persons in a vulnerable state) to protect against harm. Another derivative, *ḥājib*, means "eyebrow" (protector of the eye) and was also the word used during the *khilāfah* (caliphate) historical periods for the official who screened the caliph from an unwanted audience and applicants seeking to meet him.

It is not clear how far back in history the term *hijab* was employed, but possibly it had a well-defined meaning by the ninth century CE when it was integral to the Arabian Arabic vocabulary in early Islam. While other terms were simultaneously used, the phrase *ḍarb* (adopting) *al-hijab* was employed in Arabia in discourse about the seclusion of the wives of the Prophet. By the nineteenth century upper-class urban Muslim and Christian women in Egypt and elsewhere in the Arab region wore the *ḥabarah*, which consisted of a long skirt, a head cover, and a *burquʿ*, a long rectangular cloth of white transparent muslin placed below the eyes, covering the lower nose and the mouth and falling to the chest. However, when veiling entered feminist nationalist discourse during the British colonial occupation of Egypt, *hijab* was the term used by feminists, nationalists, and secularists alike. The phrase used for the removal of urban women's face or head cover was *raf'*(lifting) *al-hijab* (not *al-ḥabarah*: the term used for "cloak" or "veil" among upper-class Egyptian women up to the early 1900s). *Niqāb* is one of several terms referring to a face cover, some concealing, some revealing the eyes.

Interestingly, in the contemporary Arabian Gulf, women insist that their traditional dress of *'abāyah* and *shayla* (often worn by young women over tight designer jeans; provocatively bold-colored, spike high-heels; and heavy makeup for the eyes and face) is, in fact, a *hijab*. However, using the term *hijab* for traditional forms of dress simply because they cover the body stresses only material aspects and misses the more fundamental meaning of *hijab*, its cultural base. As Islamic dress, *hijab* represents a conceptual complex, including the notions of *hurma*, *ḥishmah*, *satr*, *haya'*, etc., summed up in English as "sanctity, reserve, and respect," that is fundamental to notions of womanhood and society in Islamic imagery. It is not simply a material object to cover certain body parts.

In the 1970s in Egypt, the "veil" expressed this conceptual complex and gradually became a movement, containing an element of assertive resistance, expanding throughout urban Egypt, and spreading beyond Egypt to the rest of the Arab world, particularly among college students. It had no precedence in modern times, or in the original Islamic community, as a model to support the new appearance of *muḥajjabah* and *munaqqabah*. At first, families opposed this change in appearance but only secularists, including Muslim women and men, continue to do so to this day. The large majority of Muslim women in today's world choose to at least cover their hair and wear long clothes.

By the 1990s this change in appearance had evolved (changing in form and color) and gradually became routinized. In the early twenty-first century it is a normal part of the social landscape wherever Muslims live. Extreme reactions developed in Europe and the United States against veiling (first against the headscarf, then against the *hijab*, then against the *niqāb*), frequently becoming controversial and confrontational. The West argues in defense of secularist public life and Muslims see racist discrimination and hypocrisy.

In popular perception, the veil is associated most strongly with Arab Eastern women and Islam regardless of its real origins. This persists despite the lack of a single Arabic word that can be accurately used as equivalent to the English term "veil" commonly used to refer to Middle Eastern and South Asian women's traditional head, face (eyes, nose, or mouth), or body cover, although the South Asian institution of *purdah* is not exactly equivalent to "veiling."

Hijab is not the Arabic equivalent of veil. Related to *hijab* is the concept *of satr*, the Arabic derivative of the root (*s-t-r*), which also means "veil, curtain, and sanctity." The verb (*satara* or *yastur*) means "to shield, guard, cover, protect, or veil." In the Arabic-English dictionary, synonyms for *satr* include *hijab* and *niqāb*, terms of dress denoting a head or face cover. The European term "veil" fails to capture these differences, and oversimplifies a complex, nuanced, and multilayered phenomenon.

The absence of a single, monolithic term in the language(s) of the people who today most pervasively practice "veiling" suggests a conceptual complexity and diversity of form and function that cannot be captured in one expression. And herein lies the problem; the English-language referent is used indiscriminately, monolithically, and ambiguously to mean any of the multiplicity of forms and a complex of nuanced behaviors appearing in different eras in different cultures.

The veil is not a monolithic phenomenon. There were various forms, various contexts of use and meanings that differed across eras and cultural regions. The association of the veil with Arab and Muslim women persists despite the fact that the term "veil" has no single equivalent referent in Arabic—the spoken and written language of about 300 million people and the religious language of 1 billion people in the early twenty-first century. Instead, numerous Arabic terms are used to refer to diverse articles of women's clothing that vary in body part coverage, region, local dialect, and historical era. Some of these numerous Arabic terms are: *burquʿ*, *ʿabāyah*, *ṭarḥah*, *burnus*, *jilbāb*, *jellāba*, *haik*, *milāyah*, *gargush*, *ginaʿ*, *mungub*, *lithām*, *yashmik*, *ḥabarah*, and *shayla*, among others (for a discussion of dress in the Arabian Gulf, refer to El Guindi and al-Othman, 2010).

In Arabic, certain terms refer to covers similar in form for both sexes. Outer garments, such as cloaks and face covers, are worn by both women and men. As an example, *lithma* is a dual-gendered term for a face cover used in Yemen by women (and elsewhere) and associated with femaleness, and elsewhere by some Bedouin and Berber men and associated with virility and maleness. Other examples include the neutral-gendered terms *ʿabāyah* or *ʿabā* of Arabia and *burnus* of the Maghrib—overgarments for both sexes. While similar, even identical in form, they are "worn" differently by women and men. Femininity and masculinity are maintained through gait and body language as culturally scripted. Neutral-gendered headgear or overgarments in Arab society should not evoke the idea of a unisex style, in apparel or behavior, as is the case in Western culture. In Arab society, the gender line is drawn clearly, shifting the marker from the material to the behavioral in body and movement.

Also, a gender-neutral term in one society can be used as single-gender term in another. For example, the term *ʿabāyah* when used in the Arabian Gulf refers specifically to a woman's black outer garment. A man's outer cloak is known as a *bisht*, which is different from a woman's overgarment not only in its name but also in its form, use, shape, fabric, and color.

The veil has been the subject of discussion in the scholarly literature almost entirely from the perspective of religious studies, area studies, or women's studies, which situated the veil in texts, geographical region, or as a women's phenomenon. These were not adequate contexts for understanding the complexity embedded in the subject of the veil and led to false assumptions and inaccuracies of fact. A reframing was needed. El Guindi's classic and authoritative, comprehensive analysis of the veil and the practice of veiling (1999a) did exactly that, after which the entire discourse on the veil shifted. The study cast doubt on a number of assumptions: first, Middle Eastern veiling was assumed to be associated necessarily with *seclusion*. While originally veiling, as it developed over millennia and across civilizations within the Persian-Mesopotamian-Hellenic-Byzantine regional complex, was associated in some regions (prominently in Christian and Judaic thought and society) with practices of seclusion, evidence in Islamic society challenges such an association. Veiling among Muslims is instead about privacy and not seclusion (El Guindi 1999a also suggests how veiling can be about resistance and is embedded in notions of space).

Second, there is a false assumption that this form of dress and appearance is a direct reflection or cause of women's oppression through the ages, grounding the discourse on the patriarchal nature of Arab society in particular. Veiling in this discourse becomes the expression of female oppression by men. The strongest argument against this position derives from the important observation that Muslim women veil by choice. Conceptually, veiling has been shown to be grounded in the notion of privacy, not the primary or secondary status of women in society. The privacy of home, family, and women is fundamental to Arabo-Islamic society and is reflected in many domains other than the behavioral, such as architecture, cross-sex interaction, space, modern institutions, etc. Ethnographic evidence shows veiling in different cultural and subcultural contexts to be a marker of group identity, individual maturity, kinship relationship, marital status, etc. Another ethnographic point against such a claim is that men in Arab society historically and currently veil, too. If men also veil, the argument of patriarchy becomes irrelevant. Men's veiling has other implications as next discussed.

Third is the false assumption that only women veil, such that all studies on veiling prior to 1999 (an exception to this is Murphy, 1964, an early study that concentrated on Tuareg men veiling and social distance) focused on this aspect without an awareness of the ethnographic and historical evidence on veiling by men, not only the North African group known as the Tuareg (North African, traditionally nomadic, Muslim Arabized groups), but also Arabian men prior to Islam and including the Prophet Muḥammad himself with the advent of Islam. "Veiled masculinity" is a term that has been coined to argue that "[a] crucial, neglected and overlooked fact about veiling is the clear evidence that men in Arab society veil" (El Guindi, 2003, p. 117). Historical evidence shows that, for at least several centuries prior to the advent of Islam, Arab men veiled. Less known are the reported incidents during which Muḥammad himself, the Prophet and Messenger of Islam, face-veiled on specific occasions. The entire focus of observers and scholars was the fact that young college women had turned to a conservative form of dress which included veiling. Is veiling then to be considered the same for both sexes? This question emerged during an ethnographic field project on the Islamic movement in Egypt in the 1970s when research uncovered that the focus must shift from material appearance to an underlying code since college men had by then also begun to "veil." Men started to wear long *gallabiyahs* (long white cotton shirt-dresses) and don *kaffiyehs* (headcovers) to cover their heads.

Male veiling is also known to occur among the Tuareg, where it serves as a vehicle of communicating degrees of proximity between people, as well as relative levels of power and prestige.

A holistic understanding of the phenomenon of the "veil" is needed: a focus and paradigm shift from material appearance to the intangible sphere of an underlying code, and on both sexes rather than on women only. Analysis that includes the material, social, and conceptual sheds deeper light on the phenomenon of the veil and the practice of veiling, body and space, and codes of conduct in social and public spaces.

Bibliography

Ahmed, Leila. *Women and Gender in Islam: Historical Roots of a Modern Debate*. New Haven, CT: Yale University Press, 1992.

El Guindi, Fadwa. *By Noon Praryer: The Rhythm of Islam*. Oxford and New York: Berg, 2008.

El Guindi, Fadwa. "Hijab." In *Encyclopedia of Clothing and Fashion*, edited by S. Valerie. Farmington Hills, MI: Charles Scribner's Sons, 2005, pp. 209–213.

El Guindi, Fadwa. "Is There an Islamic Alternative? The Case of Egypt's Contemporary Islamic Movement." *Middle East Insight* 1, no. 4 (1981a): 19–24.

El Guindi, Fadwa. "Religious Revival and Islamic Survival in Egypt." *International Insight* 1, no. 2 (1980): 6–10.

El Guindi, Fadwa. "The Killing of Sadat and After: A Current Assessment of Egypt's Islamic Movement." *Middle East Insight* 2, no. 5 (1982): 20–27.

El Guindi, Fadwa. *Veil: Modesty, Privacy and Resistance*. Oxford and New York: Berg, 1999a. Reprinted in 2003.

El Guindi, Fadwa. "Veiled Activism: Egyptian Women in the Contemporary Islamic Movement." *Peuples Mediterraneans (Femmes de la Mediterranee)* 22–23 (1983): 79–89.

El Guindi, Fadwa. "Veiled Men, Private Women in Arabo-Islamic Culture." *ISIM Newsletter* 4 (1999b).

El Guindi, Fadwa. "Veiling Infitah with Muslim Ethic: Egypt's Contemporary Islamic Movement." *Social Problems* 28, no. 4 (1981b): 465–485.

El Guindi, Fadwa, and Wesam al-Othman. "Dress from the Gulf States, Bahrain, Kuwait, Qatar, UAE." In *Berg Encyclopedia of World Dress and Fashion: Central and Southwest Asia*, Vol. 5, edited by J. B. Eicher, pp. 245–251. Oxford and New York: Berg, 2010.

Keenan, Jeremy. *The Tuareg: People of Ahaggar*. New York: St. Martin's, 1971.

Lhote, Henri. *Les Touaregs du Hoggar*. Paris: Payot, 1955.

Murphy, Robert. "Social Distance and the Veil." *American Anthropologist* 66, no. 6 (1964): 1257–1274.

Nicolaisen, Johannes. "Essai sur la religion et la magie touaregues." *Folk* 3 (1961): 113–162.

Papanek, H. "Purdah: Separate Worlds and Symbolic Shelter." *Comparative Studies in Society and History* 15, no. 3 (1973): 289–325.

Sharma, U. "Women and Their Affines: The Veil as a Symbol of Separation." *Man* 13 (1978): 218–233.

Williams, John Alden. "A Return to the Veil in Egypt." *Middle East Review* 11, no. 3 (1979): 49–54.

Williams, John Alden. "Veiling in Egypt as a Political and Social Phenomenon." *In Islam and Development: Religion and Sociopolitical Change*, edited by John L. Esposito, pp. 71–86. Syracuse, NY: Syracuse University Press, 1980.

FADWA EL GUINDI

W

WADUD, AMINA. Amina Wadud (b. 1952) is an American-Muslim female academic, theologian, and activist of African descent. Trained in Islamic studies and Arabic at the University of Michigan, her scholarship and international activism center on "gender jihad," an expression she adopted to denote a struggle for Islamic gender equality. In her pioneering book *Qur'an and Woman*, which has been translated into Arabic, Dutch, Spanish, Malay, Persian, Turkish, and Indonesian, Wadud creates a female-inclusive hermeneutical approach to reading the Qur'ān. She eschews both the traditional and the reactive interpretive approaches that have yielded patriarchal Qur'ānic interpretations of women, relying instead on a holistic model based on *tawḥīd* (absolute monotheism). By using a "tawhidic paradigm" to reinterpret gender, she rethinks the legal, ethical, and spiritual relations between women and men on the basis of their singular appointment as God's moral agent (*khalīfah*) on earth. *Qur'an and Woman* simultaneously recovers the requisite female voice in rereading scriptural sources.

Furthering her *tawḥīdic* paradigm in *Inside the Gender Jihad*, Wadud continues to advocate for gender justice in the wider pursuit of an "Islamic justice tradition." Her objective is to demonstrate how Islam can be reinformed by its own egalitarian principles as a dynamic system whose practices fulfill the goal of justice at the same time that its concepts of justice are adaptable to actual historical and cultural situations. By using a flexible interpretive approach, she hopes to illustrate that the legal system can be responsive to the myriad forms of oppression—gender and otherwise—that pervade the Muslim world. Wadud's scholarship powerfully critiques the male reformist practice of silencing women's voices or marginalizing their roles and experiences; this, she argues, has ultimately left the Muslim historical record, and therefore Islamic law, asymmetrical and patriarchal.

Wadud led a mixed congregational prayer in New York that spawned a global controversy in March 2005; this act works in tandem with her ongoing gender jihad. Friday prayer has traditionally been led by men; however, following the historical precedent of the Prophet Muḥammad's appointment of Umm Waraqah, a respected early follower, to lead prayer in her domain, Wadud's role as the *imāmah* (Friday prayer leader) was intended to break the gridlock of gender disparity in Islamic public ritual by reconstructing Islamic leadership as female inclusive. To include women's experiences as a *khalīfah* in a collective ritual is to integrate their reality into the normative Muslim identity, and therefore public space. Wadud's aim is to question and transform the hegemonic nature of leadership as normatively male, given that primary Islamic sources permit legitimate alternative meanings premised on women's full moral agency. She argues that without women's contributions to general public discourse, they are left without their God-given agency and full humanity.

Wadud's recent research project involves reinterpreting traditional Islamic ethics and ethical theory in pursuit of a more gender-inclusive, faith-oriented formulation. A global activist and lecturer, the recipient of prestigious grants and awards, and the mother of five, Wadud contributes a theological intervention that permits the development of interpretive possibilities that redress Islamic androcentrism.

[*See also* Qur'ān: Women's Exegesis; *and* Women and Social Reform, *subentry* An Overview.]

BIBLIOGRAPHY

Wadud, Amina. *Inside the Gender Jihad: Women's Reform in Islam*. Oxford: Oneworld, 2006.

Wadud, Amina. *Qur'an and Woman: Rereading the Sacred Text from a Woman's Perspective*. 2d ed. New York: Oxford University Press, 1999.

Wadud, Amina. "Towards a Qur'anic Hermeneutics of Social Justice: Race, Class and Gender." *Journal of Law and Religion* 12, no. 1 (1995–1996): 37–50.

HIBBA ABUGIDEIRI

WAHHĀBĪYAH. An eighteenth-century religious revival (*tajdīd*) and reform (*iṣlāḥ*) movement founded in Najd in Arabia by the scholar and jurist Muḥammad Ibn ʿAbd al-Wahhāb (1702/3–1791/2 CE). Although originally founded as a religious movement designed to purify society of un-Islamic practices, it took on a political dimension in 1744 when an alliance was formed between Ibn ʿAbd al-Wahhāb and Muḥammad Ibn Saʿūd (d. 1767) that placed religious scholars in an advisory and legitimating role to political authority. This symbiotic relationship between the Al Saʿūd and the Āl al-Shaykh (descendants of Ibn ʿAbd al-Wahhāb) has remained intact and continues through the present Saudi state. Also known popularly and pejoratively as "Wahhabism," this movement has been accused in the contemporary era of inspiring militant extremism and being especially oppressive toward women.

The hallmark of Wahhābīyah has been its dedication to absolute monotheism (*tawḥīd*) and rejection of association of anyone or anything with God (*shirk*). Ibn ʿAbd al-Wahhāb's most famous treatise, *Kitāb al-tawḥīd*, detailed the implications of belief in *tawḥīd*, outlining behaviors to be followed and avoided, making no distinction between men and women. Despite the extreme degrees to which his followers sometimes literally sought to destroy *shirk*, Ibn Abd al-Wahhāb himself taught that the appropriate method of addressing *shirk* was to provide education and engage in discussion with the offending party in order to explain why the practice was incorrect. The result of this approach was that education for both men and women became central to the movement, as reflected in biographies of women from central Arabia who were known for their social and educational work, charitable contributions, oral poetry, and status within the community based on their learning, including female descendants of Ibn ʿAbd al-Wahhāb who served as community leaders and educators.

Throughout his writings, Ibn ʿAbd al-Wahhāb spoke of the responsibility of both men and women to carry out matters related to worship, presenting a view of both men and women as divinely created people who are expected to play an active role in establishing an Islamic society on earth, both privately within the family and publicly as part of the community (*ummah*), as an obligation of their faith. He further taught that any mature man or woman, even a menstruating woman, was permitted to recite the Qur'ān and pray.

With respect to women, Ibn ʿAbd al-Wahhāb himself is most notoriously associated with the stoning of a confessed adulteress, which is often taken to be the defining characteristic of the Wahhābīyah approach to women. However, Ibn ʿAbd al-Wahhāb also made it clear that the male partner in such an illicit sexual relationship was also deserving of the death penalty, thus highlighting a more balanced approach to the topic than is often followed in contemporary courts.

Ibn ʿAbd al-Wahhāb's writings on marriage and divorce, as contained in *Kitāb al-nikāḥ*, outline and underscore women's rights with respect to family law, typically in line with the Ḥanbalī *madhhab*, although reflecting familiarity with all the major Sunnī law schools, in addition to the Shīʿī Jaʿfarī school. In cases where he significantly departed from the teachings of other jurists, such as his opposition to concubinage, his prohibition of a father or grandfather compelling a virgin minor daughter or granddaughter into marriage, his requirement of the mature woman's consent for a marriage to be valid, regardless of her status as a virgin or deflowered, and the woman's right to stipulate conditions in the marriage contract, his interpretation tended to place greater decision-making power in the hands of the woman. He also insisted on the importance of a couple having the opportunity to meet and see each other in order to determine whether they are compatible before marriage (*Kitāb al-nikāḥ*, 638–639).

Once they were married, Ibn ʿAbd al-Wahhāb applied the standard obligations to husband and wife, including the wife's entitlement to *mahr* (dower) and *nafaqah* (maintenance) as a legal requirement for the marriage to be valid, although he held that the wife is not obligated to cook or bake bread for her husband (*Kitāb al-nikāḥ*, 682). He also emphasized the Qur'ānic injunction for men to live in kindness and equity with women (4:19 and 2:228) and not to abuse their wives, either physically or emotionally, by demonstrating dislike of them. Instead, he taught that husbands and wives should smile, be cheerful with, and protect each other as evidence of the kindness commanded by God (*Kitāb al-nikāḥ*, 680). Finally, with respect to the problem of domestic violence and whether a husband with a *nushuz* (disobedient) wife is permitted to beat her, he limited the definition of *nushuz* to sexual matters, thus restricting the circumstances under which a wife could be declared *nushuz*. With respect to Qur'ān 4:34, which is often used to justify a man's right to physically strike a disobedient wife, Ibn ʿAbd al-Wahhāb noted the verse's emphasis on other means, particularly verbal admonishment and parting of company, with the strike being a method of last resort and then only to be undertaken "other than violently" and "other than forcefully," thus denying the husband any right to demonstrate physical power or dominance over his wife (*Kitāb al-nikāḥ*, 681–682).

The focus of *Kitāb al-nikāḥ* is to enforce the rights of women as recorded in the Qur'ān and *ḥadīth*, even in cases where this did not coincide with local practice or custom. He demonstrated consistent concern for women's vulnerability in sexual matters, stating preference for a man refraining from sexual relations with slave women on the basis that this rendered slave women as prostitutes, a status prohibited by the Qur'ān and *ḥadīth*, and insisting on Muslim men's responsibility to control their sexual urges and keep them within the confines of marriage. He similarly denounced rape, regardless of the woman's status as slave or free, declaring that there is no loss of honor or shame for a woman who has been raped.

In matters of divorce, Ibn ʿAbd al-Wahhāb taught a balance of rights, so that both men and women had the right to initiate divorce. He forbade the practice of the triple *ṭalāq* pronounced by the man all at once (*Kitāb al-nikāḥ*, 688) and insisted that men inform their wives of a divorce (*Kitāb al-nikāḥ*, 690)—a practice not followed in many places through the present. He further empowered women with the right to initiate a *khul*ʿ divorce as a matter of her prerogative based on her recognition of her own inability to continue in the marriage, setting return of the *mahr* as the compensation owed to the husband (*Kitāb al-nikāḥ*, 683–685). This was intended to preclude the possibility of a husband preventing his wife from seeking a divorce or setting the cost of the divorce beyond what she could afford—practices that have occurred elsewhere through the present day.

Finally, Ibn ʿAbd al-Wahhāb asserted the right of women to meet with non-*maḥram* (nonrelated) men in certain circumstances, such as to conduct business transactions or if a woman needed assistance, sanctuary, or medical treatment provided by a male physician. In these cases, he taught that the overarching principle of the preservation of human life had a higher priority than preservation of female modesty (*Kitāb al-nikāḥ*, 639).

In contemporary Saudi Arabia, debate has revived over the legacy of Ibn ʿAbd al-Wahhāb and the teachings of Wahhābīyah as it developed historically. Although Ibn ʿAbd al-Wahhāb's teachings have not necessarily been consistently followed since his lifetime, they nevertheless address issues that continue to be important, suggesting that a return to the origins of Wahhābīyah might bolster reforms that could continue to expand women's rights in contemporary Saudi Arabia.

BIBLIOGRAPHY

DeLong-Bas, Natana J. *Wahhabi Islam: From Revival and Reform to Global Jihad*. New York: Oxford University Press, 2004.

Esposito, John L. with Natana J. DeLong-Bas. *Women in Muslim Family Law*. 2d ed. Syracuse, NY: Syracuse University Press, 2000.

al-Harbi, Dalal Mukhlid. *Prominent Women from Central Arabia*. Reading, UK: Ithaca Press, 2008.

Kitāb al-nikāḥ. In *Muʾallafāt al-Shaykh al-Imām Muḥammad Ibn ʿAbd al-Wahhāb*. Vol. 2. Riyadh: Jāmiʿat al-Imām Muḥammad Ibn Saʿūd al-Islāmīyah, 1981.

Kitāb al-tawḥīd. In *Muʾallafāt al-Shaykh al-Imām Muḥammad Ibn ʿAbd al-Wahhāb*. Vol. 1. Riyadh: Jāmiʿat al-Imām Muḥammad Ibn Saʿūd al-Islāmīyah, 1981.

Lippman, Thomas W. *Saudi Arabia on the Edge: The Uncertain Future of an American Ally*. Washington, DC: Potomac Books, 2012.

Muʿamalāt al-Shaykh al-Imām Muḥammad Ibn ʿAbd al-Wahhāb: Mulhaq al-musnifat. Riyadh: Jāmiʿat al-Imām Muḥammad Ibn Saʿūd al-Islāmīyah, 1981.

Muʿamalāt al-Shaykh al-Imām Muḥammad Ibn ʿAbd al-Wahhāb: Qism al-ḥadīth. 4 vols. Riyadh: Jāmiʿat al-Imām Muḥammad Ibn Saʿūd al-Islāmīyah, 1981.

Yamani, Maha A. Z. *Polygamy and Law in Contemporary Saudi Arabia*. Reading, UK: Ithaca Press, 2008.

NATANA J. DELONG-BAS

WALLĀDAH BINT AL-MUSTAKFĪ. (c. 1011–1091), poet and person of letters from the Umayyad ruling family in al-Andalus (modern-day Spain). Wallādah was born during the turbulent final years of the Umayyad dynasty in Córdoba, the daughter of al-Mustakfī and a slave woman of European origin. She received an excellent early education in the palace. Her father became caliph when she was entering her teenage years, but he seems to have been weak and dissolute, and he was deposed and killed after only seventeen months of rule. Thereafter the Umayyad dynasty collapsed, giving way to the divided Party Kings. When she was in her twenties,

Wallādah set herself up in an elegant Córdoban residence and began to host a literary salon that soon was the talk of Córdoba's elites. A witty blonde princess of extraordinary beauty, Wallādah captured hearts, and her courtyard became "an arena for the stallions of poetry and prose" that competed to impress her (Ibn Bassām, 1975, p. 429). She also encouraged female literary talent, taking under her wing Muhja bint al-Tiyyānī, the daughter of a local fig seller, and furthering her education until she developed into a poet, although the latter eventually turned on Wallādah and composed about her sexually explicit satire.

Wallādah is best known, however, for her troubled liaison with Ibn Zaydūn (1003–1071), considered the finest poet from the period of Arab-Islamic civilization in al-Andalus. Upon making his acquaintance, Wallādah took the initiative, bold for a lady of her day, and invited Ibn Zaydūn to visit her privately. There developed an intimacy between them, and Wallādah composed affecting lines about her passion for him and the impatience that she felt during his absence. Yet he committed errors in his courtship that cost him dearly. Once he suggested edits to a love poem that she had composed for him. On another occasion, following a singing girl's performance at one of her soirees, he forgot himself and enthusiastically called for an encore without first considering Wallādah. She rebuked him at preferring the girl and subsequently began to take an interest in Ibn ʿAbdūs, vizier to the new ruler of Córdoba, Ibn Jahwar. This change in her attitude prompted an extreme reaction from Ibn Zaydūn, including attempts to arouse her jealousy, warnings and threats aimed at his rival, and recourse to a satiric letter ("Al-Risālah al-hazliyyah") addressed to the vizier that he signed in Wallādah's name. Wallādah responded to his initiatives scornfully, dubbing him "the Sixer" in a line of invective, for his alleged sexual perversions and thievery. Ibn ʿAbdūs, meanwhile, arranged for Ibn Zaydūn to be put in prison. Over a year later, following his escape and flight to Seville, Ibn Zaydūn composed and sent to Wallādah his "Nūniyyah," the most famous love poem in Arabic literature. In fifty lines of great eloquence and emotion, he reminds her of their former happy times, extols her unique qualities, and attempts to rekindle her passion. But no doubt remembering his recent actions too well, Wallādah did not respond, and though he continued to pine for her in verse, she maintained her silence.

Wallādah remained in Córdoba until her death. Though she chose never to marry and had no children, she continued her relationship with Ibn ʿAbdūs until his death ten years before hers.

In Arabic literature, Wallādah has gained fame as a marvelous beloved whose affection was cherished never so much as when it was lost. In addition, she has come to symbolize, to an extent, the free woman of al-Andalus. However, being palace-born and palace-raised, able to bear on her own the expenses of hosting a prominent literary salon, and willing to take the lead in her romances with men, she was certainly more exceptional than typical.

BIBLIOGRAPHY

Farrin, Raymond. *Abundance from the Desert: Classical Arabic Poetry*. pp. 190–213. Syracuse, N.Y.: Syracuse University Press, 2011.

Ibn Bassām. *Al-Dhakhīra fī maḥāsin ahl al-Jazīrah* (The Rich Repository of the Merits of the People of the Iberian Peninsula). Edited by Iḥsān ʿAbbās. Pt. 1, vol. 1, pp. 429–437. Beirut, Lebanon: Dār al-Thaqāfah, 1975.

Ibn Khāqān. *Qalāʾid al-ʿiqyān* (The Necklaces of Gold). Edited by Muḥummad al-Ṭāhir ibn ʿĀshūr. pp. 175–199. Tunis, Tunisia: Al-Dār al-Tūnisiyyah lil-Nashr, 1990.

Ibn Saʿīd. *Al-Mughrib fī ḥulā al-Maghrib* (The Extraordinary Account of the Ornaments of the West). Edited by Shawqī Ḍayf. Vol. 1, pp. 63–69, 143. Cairo: Dār al-Maʿārif, 1964.

Al-Maqqarī. *Nafḥ al-ṭīb min ghuṣn al-Andalus al-sraṭīb* (The Diffusion of Fragrance from the Tender Branch of al-Andalus). Edited by Maryam Qāsim Ṭawīl and Yūsuf ʿAlī Ṭawīl. Vol. 5, pp. 340–346. Beirut, Lebanon: Dār al-Kutub al-ʿIlmiyyah, 1995.

RAYMOND FARRIN

WAN AZIZAH WAN ISMAIL. Yang Berbahagia Datuk Seri Wan Azizah Wan Ismail (b. 1952) is a Malaysian politician and the wife of the country's former deputy prime minister, Datuk Seri Anwar Ibrahim. She was born on 3 December 1952, in the state of Kedah in northwestern Malaysia. Although from a Malay Muslim family, she has a Straits Chinese grandfather. She was educated at St. Nicholas Convent School in Alor Setar in Kedah and Tunku Kurshiah College in Seremban, in central Malaysia, before studying medicine at the Royal College of Surgeons in Ireland, in Dublin, where she received a gold medal for obstetrics and gynecology and graduated as an ophthalmologist. She practiced medicine for fourteen years before shifting to volunteer work in support of her politician husband.

Ibrahim began his political career as a cabinet minister in 1983. In 1993, he was appointed deputy prime minister of Malaysia. As his wife, Wan Azizah became patron of the Majlis Kanser Nasional (National Cancer Council). The arrest of her husband on September 20, 1998, on apparently trumped up charges owing to the perception that he posed a political threat to then prime minister, Mahathir bin Mohamad, led to a large number of demonstrations throughout the country and the emergence of the Reformasi (Reform) movement, which campaigned against Mohamad's continued political dominance.

With her husband in jail, Wan Azizah became the leader of the Social Justice Movement and, on April 4, 1999, established the political party Parti Keadilan Nasional. This party became the spearhead of the Reformasi movement, calling for social justice and opposing corruption. In November 1999, Wan Azizah won her husband's former seat in parliament. She was reelected in 2004 and again in 2008.

Wan Azizah's party merged with the Parti Rakyat Malaysia (Malaysian People's Party) in 2003 to form the People's Justice Party. She was elected president of the new party, holding the seat of Permataung Pauh, and was the leader of the opposition in the Malaysian Parliament from March 9, 2008 until she resigned from parliament on July 31, 2008 to allow her husband to stand for the seat, which he won in a by-election on August 26, 2008, after the end of the five-year ban on him standing for elected office.

During her time as a politician, Wan Azizah gained respect for the humble and graceful manner of her public addresses and interviews. Soft-spoken and underspoken in her criticism of others, she has, in her words, chosen the politics of inspiration over the politics of slander and hatred, seeing herself in a supporting role to her husband. In addition to her important role in Malaysian politics, she has campaigned for political change in Myanmar through her vice-chairmanship of the Malaysian Parliamentary Caucus for Democracy in Myanmar and membership in the ASEAN Inter-Parliamentary Myanmar Caucus.

For her contributions to politics, Wan Azizah was awarded the Darjah Panglima Pangkuan Negeri (Order of the Defender of the Realm) in 2008.

BIBLIOGRAPHY

Halim Shah. *Sumpah & air mata Azizah*. Shah Alam, Malaysia: Piramid Perdana, 1999.

Hatta al-Mukmin. *Dr. Mahathir vs Dr. Wan Azizah*. Kuala Lumpur: Mukminin, 2002.

Mohd, Sayuti Omar. *Cinta dan perjuangan: Nonaku Azizah*. Kuala Lumpur: Tinta Merah, 1999.

Morais, J. Victor. *Anwar Ibrahim: Resolute in Leadership*. Kuala Lumpur: Arenabuku, 1984.
Who's Who in the World, 2002. New Providence, N.J.: Marquis Who's Who, 2001.

JUSTIN J. CORFIELD *and* NATANA J. DELONG-BAS

WAQF, WOMEN'S CONSTRUCTIONS OF.

The Islamic institution of the *waqf* has a long history, going back to the time of the Prophet Muḥammad and one of his closest companions, the future caliph ʿUmar ibn al-Khaṭṭāb, in the seventh century. According to a *ḥadīth* recorded in al-Bukhārī, ʿUmar asked the Prophet what he could do for Muslims. The Prophet replied that ʿUmar could set aside property in perpetuity whose revenues would be pledged to poor Muslims. The specific property, part of ʿUmar's land at Khaybar, could not be sold, bequeathed, or given as a gift. These essential attributes—the endowment of property in perpetuity with revenues to support charity among the Muslims—became the guiding principles of the practice of charitable religious endowments known as *waqfs*.

There is nothing in the Qurʾān about *waqfs*, but there is a great deal about *ṣadaqah*, or charitable giving. In Islamic history, the principles governing the establishment of the earliest *waqfs* were transformed into legal principles directing how, by whom, and for what purposes a religious endowment could be established. Originally, the only type of religious endowment created by donors was the *waqf khayri*, which pledged the income of the donor's property to charitable purposes only. Eventually, however, the *waqf* evolved into another form, called the family *waqf* (*waqf ahli*), also known as the *waqf dhurri*, in which endowed property benefitted the donor for life and designated heirs until the family line was extinguished. Only then were *waqf* revenues used to support the charities designated by the donor. A third type of *waqf* evolved, the *mushtarik*, or mixed *waqf*, in which the donor designated half as a family *waqf* and half as a charitable *waqf*. The family *waqf* had clear benefits for women, allowing them to put their income-producing property in a trust overseen by the courts and thus to protect it from predatory male relatives, to benefit monetarily from the *waqf* during their lifetimes, and to benefit other women by naming them as heirs or administrators of the *waqf*. One of the advantages to men and women who made family *waqfs* was that it prevented the fragmentation of property that results from the division of the deceased's estate according to the Islamic rules of inheritance mandated by the Qurʾān. Both men and women could evade the division of property stipulated in the Qurʾān by making a will, which allowed the testator to choose the heirs to the estate and the share that each would receive. However, only a third of the testator's estate could be willed, while the remaining two-thirds was subject to Islamic inheritance law. The advantage to the donor of a family *waqf* was that all of her property could be included in the endowment, which remained intact for the benefit only of the heirs named in the endowment deed. Another benefit was that it allowed a donor to allocate the income of the *waqf* to her daughters and sons equally, while Islamic inheritance law required that females inherit roughly one-half of a male's share.

From the beginning, Muslim women were associated with *waqfs*, first as examples of charitable giving and then as donors. For example, among the wives of the Prophet, Zaynab bint Khuzayma was known as the mother of the poor for her charity and was extolled by the Prophet himself as a model for his other wives. Another women, Zaynab (d. 831), the wife of the caliph Hārūn al-Rashīd, endowed many public works, such as hospices for Muslim travelers and pilgrims, as well as additions to the water supply along the pilgrimage route from Iraq to Mecca.

There was a tradition of *waqf* endowment among the women of the Ayyūbids, the Seljuk-Turks, the Seljuks of Rum (the predecessors of the Ottoman Turks in Anatolia), and among royal and elite Ottoman women.

Adult women could make *waqfs* because they had rights under Islamic law that allowed them to buy, sell, bequeath, inherit, and endow their private wealth and property. Property rights were contingent on the right to make a contract, a necessity for the purchase, sale, or rental of property, as well as for making a will or creating an endowment. Because property rights and the ability to make a contract established women as legal persons able to act on their own and without a male guardian, women under Islamic law could achieve a high degree of personal and economic autonomy and use the courts to defend their rights.

Historical research into the archives of the Islamic courts before and during the Ottoman period in the Middle East show that women of all classes were active users of the courts for various reasons, including to make religious endowments. In Egypt there is evidence from the Fatimid period through the Mamlūk Sultunate to the Ottoman conquest in 1516 that women were involved in both endowing and administering *waqfs*. Using the roughly 1,000 *waqfs* catalogued and analyzed by Muhammad Amin in his monumental work *Catalogue des documents d'archives du Caire de 239/853 à 922/1516*, Carl Petry (1991) isolated the 283 listed under a woman's name. He found that the majority were estates managed by a woman as the designated administrator of a husband's or father's *waqf*, while the minority were estates endowed by women themselves composed of property they owned independently of men. Acting as the administrator (*nazira*) of a *waqf* gave a woman not only an income but also real authority over property and enhanced her influence with her family or household.

In Egypt during the eighteenth century, women donors were 24 percent of the total number of donors whose religious endowment deeds (*waqfiyyat*) can be found in the archives (*daftarkhana*) of the Ministry of Awqaf (religious endowments). This is consistent with results obtained by other researchers for both the Arab provinces and Anatolia during the Ottoman period—results showing women donors comprised from 20 to almost 37 percent of total donors. For example, Haim Gerber's (1983) analysis of *waqf* records from fifteenth- and sixteenth-century Edirne shows that women made 20 percent of the new *waqfs*. Gabriel Baer's (1983) analysis of the Istanbul register (*tahrir*) of 1546 shows that women made 36.8 percent of the new *waqfs*. Baer also cites evidence from eighteenth-century Aleppo showing that women made 36.3 percent of the *waqfs*, that in Jerusalem between 1805 and 1820 women accounted for 24 percent, and that in Jaffa during the entire Ottoman period, they accounted for 23.4 percent. Beshara Doumani's (1998) study of *waqf* donors in Nablus and Tripoli between 1800 and 1860 revealed that 11.6 percent of the *waqfs* in Nablus, and 47 percent in Tripoli, were made by women. The majority of *waqfs* endowed by men and women were family *waqfs*: 79 percent of 211 *waqfs* in Tripoli and 96 percent of 138 *waqfs* in Nablus.

In Nablus most women endowed residential property, while in Tripoli most endowed revenue-producing agricultural property. Doumani observed a significant difference related to inheritance stipulations between donors in Nablus and Tripoli. Endowers in Nablus generally excluded the female line of descent, preferring to transmit property and its revenues within the male line. In Tripoli, in contrast, transmission strategies were more pluralistic, more egalitarian, and less competitive. In fact, in the Tripoli *waqfs*, a significant proportion of donors designated women as primary beneficiaries, and one-third even required equal shares among males and females. The transmission strategies in Tripoli were comparable to those of eighteenth-century women donors in Egypt, who stipulated equal shares to their female and male relatives, as well as to female and male slaves. Randi Deguilhem (2003) studied the *waqfs* of two Damascus women who made *waqfs* two centuries apart: Nafiza Hanum in 1776 and Hafiza Hanum in 1880. Like the Egyptian women, they named themselves the administrators of their *waqfs* during their lifetimes. Hafiza Hanum had extensive investments in commercial properties in Damascus, including a bread oven and fifteen shops in the heart of the city's commercial quarter. Her endowed properties were a mix of those that she bought herself and other properties that she inherited from her husband. Both she and her husband came from notable families, called *aʿyān*, that had influence and wealth from commercial and agricultural holdings in Damascus and the countryside.

One of the most famous Ottoman-era women and *waqf* donors was Hürrem Sultan, the wife of the Ottoman sultan Süleyman I and the mother of his son Selim II and his favorite daughter, Mihrima. In the 1550s construction began on the Hasseki Sultan ʿImaret in Jerusalem. An *ʿimaret* in Ottoman Turkish usage, also known as a *takiyya*, is traditionally a hostelry for Ṣūfīs offering lodging and food to students and a small stipend. The Hasseki Sultan complex included a mosque, 55 rooms for Muslim pilgrims who wanted to be near the Muslim Holy Places, an inn for travelers, and at the center of the complex, a soup kitchen providing food for the poor. The properties endowed to fund it were 25 villages in Palestine, 16 of which were in the province (*sanjak*) of Gaza/Ramle, 8 of which were in the province of Jerusalem, and 1 of which was in Tripoli in north Lebanon. Hürrem also built mosques in Istanbul and Edirne and a soup kitchen in Mecca. Her mother-in-law, Hafsa Sultan, also endowed a mosque, a primary school, and a Ṣūfī hospice in Manisa.

In Egypt during the eighteenth century, the elite women from Mamlūk households tended to make family or mixed *waqfs* rather than to build religious or charitable institutions. Shawikar Qadin, the concubine of one of the most powerful Mamlūks and the wife of another, made a family *waqf* in which she endowed considerable agricultural, commercial, and residential property; named herself as the overseer of the *waqf* during her lifetime; and named as her heirs her children and her slaves, males and females equally. One of her former female slaves, Mahbuba, became the administrator of her *waqf* after her death. One notable exception was Nafisa al-Bayda, whose waqf included property to support a sabil-kuttab, a public drinking fountain with a school for boys above it, which still stands today near the Bab Zuwayla gate in Cairo. Nafisa was the wife of ʿAli Bey al-Kabīr and, after his death, Murad Bey, two of the most powerful and famous Mamlūk emirs. Women of all classes made *waqfs*, as the documents from Cairo demonstrate. For example, Ruqya Khatun, the freed slave of an artisan identified as al-Haj Muhammad al-Nahhas, a coppersmith, endowed a property inside a tenement above a market that was the center of the copper trade. This could be a substantial investment, since the property could be used as either a coppersmithy or a shop or even a residence. The thriving commercial economies of cities like Cairo and Aleppo provided women of all classes with opportunities for investment.

Muslim women who endowed *waqfs* left across Islamic lands a legacy in stone that included schools, mosques, inns for Muslim pilgrims and travelers, public water fountains, soup kitchens, and other public benefits. These constructions also benefitted the public in other ways, notably in providing employment to the architects and builders of various structures and to those who carried out the various activities associated with them. The endowment of the Hürrem Sultan, for example, employed hundreds of persons as cooks, clerks, bakers, millers, food inspectors, dishwashers, cleaners, repairmen, doorkeepers, and an imam for the mosque.

In the nineteenth century, the legal environment that fostered and administered *waqfs* began to change with the arrival across the Middle East, Africa, and Asia of European colonizers who sought to control the administration and funds of the *waqfs*. After independence, some new nation-states established government agencies to oversee the management of *waqfs* directly and instituted laws allowing the government to control the funds generated by *waqfs*. States like Libya, Syria, and Turkey abolished family *waqfs*, seized the assets of all *waqfs*, and took charge of preserving historic buildings or charities that were funded through *waqfs*. For example, the *waqf* established by Hafiza Hanum in 1880 was liquidated in 1950 following passage in 1949 in newly independent Syria of a law that ordered the dismemberment of the former system of *waqfs*. In Egypt, India, and Pakistan, however, local resistance has made it difficult for governments to dominate the system of *waqfs* totally.

[*See also* Inheritance *and* Property.]

Bibliography

Amin, Muhammad Muhammad. *Catalogue des documents d'archives du Caire de 239/853 à 922/1516*. Cairo: Institut Français d'Archéologie Orientale du Caire, 1981.

Baer, Gabriel "Women and Waqf: An Analysis of the Istanbul Tahrir of 1546." *Asian and African Studies* 17 (1983): 9–27.

Deguilhem, Randi. "Gender Blindness and Societal Influence in Late Ottoman Damascus: Women as Creators and Managers of Endowments." *Hawwa: Journal of Women in the Middle East and the Islamic World* 1, no. 3 (2003): 329–350.

Deguilhem, Randi. "History of Waqf and Case Studies from Damascus in Late Ottoman and French Mandatory Times." PhD dissertation, New York University, 1986.

Deguilhem, Randi. "Naissance et Mort du Waqf Damascene de Hafiza Hanum al- Murahli 1880–1950." In *Le waqf dans l'espace islamique: Outil de pouvoir socio-politique*, edited by Randi Deguilhem, pp. 203–225. Damascus, Syria: Institut Français de Damas, 1995.

Doumani, Beshara. "Endowing Family: Waqf, Property Devolution, and Gender in Greater Syria, 1800–1860." *Comparative Studies in Society and History* 40 (1998): 3–41.

Fay, Mary Ann. "From Concubines to Capitalists: Women, Property, and Power in Eighteenth-Century Egypt." *Journal of Women's History*, Autumn 1998: 118–140. Anthologized in *Bodies in Contact: Rethinking Colonial Encounters in World History*, edited by Tony Ballantyne and Antoinette Burton, pp. 125–142. Durham, N.C.: Duke University Press, 2005.

Fay, Mary Ann. "Women and Waqf: Property, Power, and the Domain of Gender in Eighteenth-Century Egypt." In *Women in the Ottoman Empire: Middle Eastern Women in the Early Modern Period*, edited by Madeline Zilfi, pp. 28–47. Leiden, Netherlands: Brill, 1997.

Gerber, Haim. "The *Waqf* Institution in Early Ottoman Edirne." *Asian and African Studies* 17 (1983): 29–45.

Kozlowski, Gregory. "The Changing Political and Social Contexts of Muslim Endowments: The Case of Contemporary India." In *Le waqf dans l'espace islamique: Outil de pouvoir socio-politique*, edited by Randi Deguilhem, pp. 277–291. Damascus, Syria: Institut Français de Damas, 1995.

Meriwether, Margaret L. "Women and Waqf Revisited: The Case of Aleppo, 1770–1840." In *Women in the Ottoman Empire: Middle Eastern Women in the Early Modern Period*, edited by Madeline Zilfi, pp. 128–152. Leiden, Netherlands: Brill, 1997.

Peri, Oded. "Waqf and Ottoman Welfare Policy: The Poor Kitchen of Hasseki Sultan in Eighteenth-Century Jerusalem." *Journal of the Economic and Social History of the Orient* 35, no. 2 (1992): 167–186.

Petry, Carl F. "Class Solidarity versus Gender Gain: Women as Custodians of Property in Later Medieval Egypt." In *Women in Middle East History: Shifting Boundaries in Sex and Gender*, edited by Nikki R.

Keddie and Beth Baron, pp. 122–142. New Haven, Conn.: Yale University Press, 1991.
Salati, Marco. "Urban Notables, Private Waqf, and Capital Investment: The Case of the Seventeenth-Century Zuhrawi Family of Aleppo." In *Le waqf dans l'espace islamique: Outil de pouvoir socio-politique*, edited by Randi Deguilhem, pp. 187–201. Damascus, Syria: Institut Français de Damas, 1995.
Singer, Amy. *Constructing Ottoman Beneficence: An Imperial Soup Kitchen in Jerusalem*. Albany: State University of New York Press, 2002.

MARY ANN FAY

WARRIORS. [*This entry contains two sub-entries,*

Women *and*
Contemporary Women.]

WOMEN

Women engaging in armed combat are not a phenomenon usually associated with Islamic culture. Yet it has often been stated, both by Arab historians of the past and by modern scholars, that Arab women played an active role in the tribal conflicts of pre-Islamic days (*ayyām al-ʿarab*) and in the raids and wars of conquest of early Islam (*maghāzī* and *futūḥ*). There is little evidence, however, that women actually fought in combat. Their role was restricted mostly to encouraging the men and occasionally killing wounded enemies, at men's request (Lichtenstädter, 1935, and literature given there; see also Rosenthal, 1979).

Semilegendary warrior queens have played a role as opponents in the Islamic tradition. Such warrior queens include Georgian queens (Canard, 1969) and the Berber queen known as al-Kāhina, who led Berber resistance against the Arab invasion and continues to play a part in Algerian popular imagination (Déjeux, 1983). Islamic history has also known female rulers, though not in great numbers. Few of these women actually wielded power, however. They usually were just figureheads for a man behind the throne, and none of them is reported to have led armies or participated in combat, not even the few who actually exercised power, such as Arwa (lived 1048, less probably 1052–1138), also known as Sayyida ḥurra, of the Yemeni Sulayhids (Daftary, 1998), and Ḍayfa Khātūn, sultan of Aleppo on behalf of her young grandson from 1236–1242 (el-Azhari, 2000).

References to women actually going to war are not completely absent from Arabic sources, but they are rare and usually very brief. A remarkable case is that of Sajāḥ of the Bānū Tamīm, a prophetess who set herself against Islam and is reported to have married the prophet Musaylima. Sajāḥ came to the fore in 632/3, managed to unite the tribe of ḥanzala under her command and lead them against Medina (Vacca, 2000).

To give another example, a certain Abū Umāma reports that women took part in the fighting during the battle of Yarmūk (636), among them Juwayrīya, the daughter of Abū Sufyān, who found herself together with her husband after some heavy fighting (al-Tabarī, vol. 1, pp. 2100–2101). In another case, the two sisters of Sāliḥ bin ʿAlī, Umm ʿīsā and Lubāba, joined him in the campaign to Byzantine territory in the year 756 because they had vowed to go on holy war if the reign of the Umayyads came to an end. Nothing is said about their carrying armor of any kind (Ibn al-Athīr, vol. 5, p. 372). A report about an expedition under Yazīd ibn Mazyad sent by the Caliph Hārūn al-Rashīd against the Kharijite leader al-Walīd ibn ṭarīf mentions that the latter was accompanied by his sister Laylā bint ṭarīf, carrying arms and wearing a breast plate (or coat of mail) and a helmet. She started to attack and was recognized. Yazīd went up to her and struck the backside of her horse with his spear, telling her in strong terms to go away because she had brought shame on her father's clan. She felt deeply ashamed, and Yazīd received much praise for his action (al-Iṣbahānī, 1927–1974, vol. 12, p. 96). The report is noteworthy because it demonstrates the negative attitude toward martial women at the time.

Arab historians of the Crusades note with amazement the presence of armed women in the Frankish army, such as Queen Alienor, wife of Louis XII (Ciggaar, 1995), without giving any indication that the phenomenon was familiar to them. It is indeed unlikely that these historians knew this from actual reality, but they could have gathered this notion from literature, for warrior women were a prominent feature in the popular literature of that time, notably *sīra shaʿbīya*, the long epic tales that formed the stock in trade of popular storytellers and that also circulated in written form.

The genre is closely connected to the legendary stories about the wars of early Islamic times (*maghāzī* and *futūḥ*) and has a number of motifs in common with this literature, such as the warrior woman. In some of these epic tales, the wars against unbelievers, notably Byzantines and Crusaders, play an important part. The Arabic genre of popular epic consists of a number of often very long adventure tales, written in poetry, rhymed prose, and prose, or a combination of these. Their composition can be traced back to the twelfth to fifteenth centuries.

There are obvious connections between Arabic-popular-epic and Persian-epic literature, such as Firdawsī's *Shāhnāmah* and literature of the *dastān* genre. This genre also has offshoots in other Islamic literatures (Turkish, Urdu, Malay). The Greek Alexander novel (which includes Alexander's meeting with an Amazon queen), which has many offshoots in the Middle Eastern tradition, also has left its traces. In this whole corpus of epic literature, the warrior woman is a standard figure (Gaillard, 2005). Sometimes a warrior princess even gets her own epic, or epic cycle, such as Rustam's daughter Bānu Goshasb (Khaleghi-Motlagh, 1982– ; the text of the epic was published in Tehran in 2003) and ʿAntar's daughter ʿUnaytira in the last part of the Arabic *Sīrat ʿAntara*, while Princess Fāṭima Dhāt al-Himma is the major eponymous hero of the long (more than 6,000 pages in print) Arabic *Sīrat al-amīra Dhāt al-Himma*.

The warrior woman appears in various forms in Arabic popular epic (Kruk, 1993, 1994; Lyons, 1995, vol. 1, pp. 109–118). She may be a foreign princess later converted to Islam, but also an intrepid Bedouin girl. Typical characteristics are her beauty (if young), physical strength, prowess in combat, eagerness to demonstrate her superiority to men, unwillingness to submit to marriage, unless a suitor manages to defeat her in single combat, and dealing with motherhood. Many warrior women continue to take part in battle after marriage, often in the company of sons, sometimes even daughters. She may live to a considerable age without losing her authority and martial prowess, such as Princess Fāṭima Dhāt al-Himma. In the case of the hero, male or female, age simply is not a factor. Old women who are cast as enemies, however, are treated differently: even though they may be shrewd and excellent fighters, emphasis is laid on their disgusting physical aspects and lewdness, aspects that reflect social attitudes regarding old women.

The traveler Ibn Baṭūta (or his ghost writer Ibn Juzayy) uses familiar motifs of the warrior women tradition in his description of the foreign warrior queen Urdūja, whom he reportedly visited on his travels (*Riḥla*, 1964, pp. 625–627), the most obvious being the queen's entourage of female officials and her insistence that she would only marry a man who defeated her in single combat.

While the warrior woman is present in most Arabic popular epics, attitudes toward her vary from epic to epic. She is fully accepted in some of them (*Sīrat Dhāt al-Himma*, *Sīrat ʿAntara ibn Shaddād*, and *Sīrat al-malik Sayf ibn Dhī Yazan*), yet her martial role is less appreciated in others. Hamza in *Qiṣṣat Hamza al-Bahlawān* and Baybars in *Sīrat al-Zāhir Baybars* disapprove of her activities and insist that she stay home, especially after marriage.

Only in the way in which these views are expressed do these tales possibly reflect actual social attitudes to women, and then only to a very limited extent. Since the popular epic is, broadly speaking, literature composed by men for a male audience, to the extent that this literature reflects male attitudes toward strong and independent women, the intriguing question is why the warrior woman is such a frequently encountered figure in popular epics. In some respects the obvious answer is that male audiences enjoyed the exciting description of her beauty and of the close contact with her body during combat, gradually leading up to the discovery that the brave opponent is not male but female. But what about the many cases in which she gets the better of a man, defeating him, tying him up, and humiliating him? One possible explanation is cross-gender identification, along the lines suggested by Carol Glover (1992) for the role of women in modern horror films.

In modern times, women engaging in armed combat, or women soldiers in general, are still not a familiar feature in the modern Islamic world, apart from such marginal phenomena as the female body guard of the Libyan leader Colonel Muʿammar al-Qadhdhāfī. Since the end of the twentieth century, however, the picture has been changing: women occasionally started to participate in Islamic militant activism, especially as suicide bombers, for instance, in the group known as al-Aqsa Martyr Brigades and in Iraq. Whether this indicates that women take an increasingly important role in these movements is a matter of discussion. It has been argued that female suicide bombers are mere tools, easily disposable, useful only because they raise less suspicion than men.

Yet there seems to be a shift in the attitude toward martial Muslim women, not only in actual life (martial arts, for instance, especially kickboxing, are popular nowadays among Moroccan girls in the Netherlands), but also in popular fiction (several Muslim female heroes figure in the comic *The 99*, by the Kuwaiti author Naif al-Mutawa, fighting terrorism and narrow-minded attitudes).

[*See also* Suicide Bombings.]

BIBLIOGRAPHY

Azhari, Taef Kamal el-. "Ḍayfa Khātūn, Ayyubid queen of Aleppo 634–640 A.H./1236–1242 A.D." *Annals of Japan Association for Middle East Studies* 15 (2000): 27–55.

Bānu Goshasp-nāma. Tehran, Iran: Institute for Humanities and Cultural Studies, 2003.

Canard, M. "Les reines de Géorgie dans l'histoire et la légende musulmanes." *Revue des études islamiques* 1 (1969): 3–20.

Ciggaar, K. "La dame combattante: Thème épique et thème courtois au temps des croisades." In *Aspects de l'épopée romane: Mentalités, idéologies, intertextualités*, edited by Hans van Dijk and Willem Noomen, pp. 121–130. Groningen, Netherlands: E. Forsten, 1995.

Daftary, Farhad. "Sayyida ḥurra: The Ismaʿīlī Sulayḥid Queen of Yemen." In *Women in the Medieval Islamic World*, edited by Gavin R. G. Hambly, pp. 117–130. New York: St. Martin's Press, 1998.

Déjeux, J. "La Kahina: De l'histoire à la fiction littéraire: Mythe et épopée." *Studi Maghrebini* 15 (1983): 1–42.

Gaillard, Marina. "Héroïnes d'exception: Les femmes ʿAyyār dans la prose romanesque de l'Iran médiéval." *Studia iranica* 34, no. 2 (2005): 163–198.

Glover, Carol J. *Men, Women, and Chainsaws: Gender in the Modern Horror Film*. Princeton: Princeton University Press, 1992.

Ibn al-Athīr. *Al-Kāmil fī al-taʾrīkh*. Leiden, Netherlands: Brill, 1867–1876.

Ibn Baṭṭūta, *Riḥla*. Beirut, Lebanon: Dâr Sâdir, 1964. First published in 1384.

Iṣbahānī, Abū l-Faraj ʿAlī al-Husayn al-. *Kitāb al-aghānī*. Cairo, Egypt: Dâr al-Kutub, 1927–1974.

Khaleghi-Motlagh, Jalal. "Gushasb, Bānu." In *Encyclopaedia Iranica*, edited by Ehsan Yarshater, vol. 11, pp. 170–171. London: Routledge and Kegan Paul, 1982.

Kruk, Remke. "Clipped Wings: Medieval Arabic Adaptations of the Amazon Myth." *Harvard Middle Eastern and Islamic Review* 1, no. 2 (November 1994): 132–151.

Kruk, Remke. "Warrior Women in Arabic Popular Romance: Qannāsa bint Muzāḥim and Other Valiant Ladies, Part I." *Journal of Arabic Literature* 24 (1993): 213–230.

Lichtenstädter, Ilse. *Women in the Aiyām al-ʿArab: A Study of Female Life during Warfare in Preislamic Arabia*. London: Royal Asiatic Society, 1935.

Lyons, M. C. *The Arabian Epic: Heroic and Oral Storytelling*. Vol. 1: *Introduction*. Vol. 2: *Analysis*. Vol. 3: *Texts*. Cambridge, U.K.: Cambridge University Press, 1995.

Rosenthal, Franz. "Fiction and Reality: Sources for the Role of Sex in Medieval Muslim Society." In *Society and the Sexes in Medieval Islam*, edited by Afaf Lutfi al-Sayyid-Marsot, pp. 3–22. Malibu, Calif.: Undena Publications, 1979.

Tabarī, al-. *Taʾrīkh al-rusul wa-l-muluk*. Leiden, Netherlands: Brill, 1879–1901.

Vacca, V. "Sajāh." In *Encyclopaedia of Islam*, new edition, vol. 8, pp. 738–739. Leiden, Netherlands: Brill, 2000.

Remke Kruk

Contemporary Women

Ancient characterization of the just warrior/beautiful soul dichotomy continues to resonate both in contemporary discourse and popular understanding. While the just warrior is a man who shed blood for the common good, beautiful soul is a woman who needs male protection. This is paralled with the stereotype that men are rational and women are passionate. The tradition of women warriors is a familiar phenomenon in many parts of the world; however, it is viewed as disconcerting, transgressing, and unsettling to patriarchal order. An investigation of hidden women warriors' histories is found critical, particularly by feminist scholars, not only to discuss women's subjectivity and agency, but also to reform the cultural understanding of heroism and male-centered war narratives.

Many disciplines ranging from sociology to anthropology, literature, cultural studies, media studies, and women's studies are interested in women warriors. The concept is used broadly to depict powerful women in unconventional roles, particularly women in state armies and combat units, as well as women in difficult situations facing poverty or defending rights. Films and television episodes have cast women as warriors or "girl-power heroes" whose capacity to fight for just causes matches or exceeds that of their male colleauges. Women warriors are widely examined through books and scholarly articles specifically addressing American combat women in Vietnam and Iraq. These studies aim to reveal the determination of women as similar to male heroes, as well as to delineate gender restrictions on women. Moreover, the concept is utilized in some books to discuss women's historical role/new defining role in the Judeo-Christian tradition.

In modern times, Muslim female suicide bombers are referred to as women warriors. The most famous of them is Leila Khaled, who was a member of the Popular Front for the Liberation of Palestine (PFLP) involved in the 1969 hijacking of TWA flight 840. Another example is the first female Palestinian suicide bomber, Wafa Idris, who detonated a bomb in Jerusalem on January 27, 2002. Chechen and Kurdish militant women were also involved in several suicide bombings against state security forces. The issue here is not to condone or condemn but to study what social conditions allow women to play such roles. Narratives on Muslim female suicide bombers suggest that they are often inspired by their grievances; they see their roles as a defense against aggression, preserving their nations/societies and saving life through taking lives of enemies and sacrificing their bodies, which seem the only available resources, and which, in some conflicts, might be subject to rape and mutilation by the army of the enemy.

Since 9/11, the media has paid attention to Muslim women involved in terrorist networks in the West. Women connected with Islamist terrorism are referred to as Muslim women warriors as well. The most prominent of them are Muriel Dugauque, a Belgian woman who blew herself up in Iraq on November 9, 2005, and Sajida Mubaraka al-Rishawi, the failed Iraqi bomber who took part in the 2005 Amman bombings in Jordan. In their scholarly work, Groen, Kranenberg, and Naborn (2006) examine women of an informal network called Hofstad that was related to al-Qaeda in the Netherlands by calling them "Women warriors for Allah." Drawing on their field research, they argue that women warriors are in control of their lives and have chosen freely to share those lives with members of terrorist networks. In some cases, they became the ideologues of the networks. They are therefore not passive victims or brainwashed women, in contrast to stereotypes about Muslim women.

It is clear that the limited focus on the issue stems from lack of interest in women warriors because it defies the orientalist portrayal of Eastern and Muslim women as passive and oppressed. Worth mentioning here is that women are not accepted as conscripts in the army in the majority of Muslim countries, with the exception of Libya, Malaysia, and Tunisia.

Bibliography

Groen Janny, Annieke Kranenberg, and Robert Naborn. *Women Warriors for Allah: An Islamist Network in the Netherlands.* Philadelphia: University of Pennsylvania Press, 2006.

Holmstedt, Kirsten. *Band of Sisters: American Women at War in Iraq*. Mechanicsburg, Pa.: Stackpoe Books, 2008.

Holmstedt, Kirsten. *The Girls Come Marching Home: Stories of Women Warriors Returning from the War in Iraq*.Mechanicsburg: Pa.: Stackpoe Books, 2009.

Inness, Sherrie. *Tough Girls: Women Warriors and Wonder Women in Popular Culture*, Philadelphia: University of Pennsylvania Press, 1998.

Standish, Katerina. *Human Security and Gender: Female Suicide Bombers in Palestine and Chechnya.* Ciudad Colón, Costa Rica: University of Peace, 2006.

Stur, Marie Heather. *Beyond Combat: Women and Gender in the Vietnam War Era.* New York: Cambridge University Press, 2011.

Wise, James E., and Scott Baron. *Women at War: Iraq, Afghanistan, and Other Conflicts.* Annapolis, Md.: Naval Institute Press, 2006.

Zeynep Şahin-Mencütek

Wazed, Sheikh Hasina. (b. 1947), Sheikh Hasina Wazed is the current prime minister of Bangladesh and leader of the Bengali Awami League party. She served her first term in office from 1996 to 2001 and was re-elected in 2009. Wazed's terms in office have alternated with Bangladesh's first female prime minister, Khaleda Zia, making Bangladesh the only modern Muslim country to have been led by women for two decades continuously.

Wazed was born on 28 September 1947 in East Pakistan [now Bangladesh] to Wazed Sheikh Mujibur Rahman, leader of the Awami League (then the prime minister) and a key figure in the secession of Bangladesh from Pakistan. Wazed was active in Bangladeshi politics from the 1960s, including in the struggle for Bangladeshi independence. After her father and most of her family were assassinated in 1975 by elements of the military, Wazed became the leader of the Awami League and went into exile until the early 1980s due to fears for her safety. Since her return to Bangladesh,

Wazed has been a strong supporter of democracy and human rights. One of her most significant achievements has been her collaboration with Khaleda Zia during the 1980s to bring an end to military rule under General Ershad. Wazed was instrumental in this, forging an alliance of over ten political parties against military rule and issuing the ultimatum that would lead to the end of autocratic rule in Bangladesh in 1990.

In some estimations, Wazed, like Zia, secured a strong position in Bangladeshi politics as a result of her dynastic background. However, regardless of whether Wazed did or did not initially obtain her position in the Awami League because of her father's legacy, her position has been confirmed through democratic elections (as has Zia's). Wazed, like most prominent Bangladeshi politicians, has publically shown a commitment to aspects of Islamic traditions and norms as practiced in Bangladesh, despite leading a relatively secular party. For example, she has been keen to impart that her party is not opposed to "the will of God" and chose to dress in what might be considered a typically Islamic manner for women in the region (with a headscarf and long sleeves), both in the lead-up to and after the 1996 national elections in Bangladesh. Various commentators have seen this as incompatible with feminism, as a ploy to win votes in a state in which much of the population are observant Muslims, while others have pointed out that this can be read as a personal choice influenced by a variety of factors not necessarily linked to political maneuvering. Wazed's feminist credentials are better assessed through her engagement with women's policy issues. Wazed and the Awami League have strong links to prominent feminist groups, and, under Wazed's leadership, Bangladesh has seen the enacting of legislation aimed at eliminating institutionalized discrimination against women, and changes to the law around marriages and divorces that, while respecting Islamic tradition, give women more rights than previously conferred.

[*See also* Zia, Khaleda.]

BIBLIOGRAPHY

Basu, Amrita. "Women, Political Parties, and Social Movements in South Asia." In *Governing Women: Women's Political Effectiveness in Contexts of Democratization and Governance Reform*, ed. Anne Marie Goetz, 87–111. New York and Abingdon, Oxon: Routledge, 2009.

Cuno, Kenneth M. *Family, Gender, and Law in a Globalizing Middle East and South Asia.* Syracuse, New York: Syracuse University Press, 2009.

Hossain, Kamrul. "In Search of Equality: Marriage-related Laws for Muslim Women in Bangladesh." *Journal of International Women's Studies* 5, no. 1 (2003): 96–113.

Richter, Linda K. "Exploring Theories of Female Leadership in South and Southeast Asia." *Pacific Affairs* 63, no. 4 (1991): 524–540.

Shehabuddin, Elora. *Reshaping the Holy: Democracy, Development, and Muslim Women in Bangladesh.* New York and Chichester, West Sussex: Columbia University Press, 2008.

MARYAM KHALID

WEALTH, WELFARE, AND LABOR (THEORETICAL OVERVIEW). The articles contained within Wealth, Welfare and Labor would normally be divided among topics such as Art and Architecture; Economics; and Institutions, Organizations, and Movements. We created this theme with the purpose of looking not at the external function of the object, organization, or trend, but rather at the outcome it produces in terms of its impact on people's lives, whether by the creation and distribution of wealth, the provision of welfare or well-being, or the relative empowerment resulting from paid employment. In other words, we wanted to go beyond theory into practice as a means of analyzing women's relative agency in a variety of fields.

Analysis of art and architecture, for example, goes beyond discussion of the objects themselves into questions of women's agency, such as expressed through patronage of the construction of mosques, caravanserai, and palaces, or through the patronage, production, and consumption of other art forms, such as painting, textiles, and ceramics. By doing this, we address the reality of women as agents and consumers of artistic production, rather than simply as subjects of art or objects for artistic representation.

We also sought to restore women's voices and agency to the history of labor and the workforce by presenting women's agency as employers and employees, consumers and business owners, borrowers and creditors, landowners, and entrepreneurs throughout the Muslim world. Restoring women to the historical marketplace, bazaar, and labor force offers important precedents for contemporary women and provides some context for analyzing contemporary developments and their likely impact. For example, special attention is given to the contemporary realities of increased educational levels among Muslim women. Not only have these provided a change in women's welfare from the perspective of increased literacy, but they are also expected to, if they have not already, lead to increased representation of women in the labor force. This leads to questions about what the future implications of this might be, whether in terms of increased negotiating capacity within the changing family unit or in terms of legal reforms that reflect the new reality of the wife as a contributor to the family's income, rather than merely as the recipient of maintenance paid by the husband.

Because women's economic activity has been legitimated since the time of Muḥammad, as shown through the example of his first wife, Khadījah, who was involved in the caravan trade, contemporary Muslim women consider the business world a legitimate public space for them to occupy and are working for higher levels of inclusion, such as by being elected to the boards of various Chambers of Commerce and Industry. Particularly in Saudi Arabia, where gender segregation is generally strictly observed, reference to Muḥammad's time and example has proven empowering. In addition, satisfactory job performance at the level of the workplace has led to suggestions that women might also serve at higher levels of authority and participate more fully in decision-making processes, based on their merit, such as by voting and serving on the Saudi Shūrā (Consultative) Council, first as advisors, and, in 2013, as full members.

Also highlighted in this theme is the important role women have played in charitable and philanthropic work, both historically and in the contemporary era, to show that women are not simply the objects of charitable activity, but often are those leading charitable efforts. We have included articles on the *ḥajj* and women's travel in this section to shed light on women's agency in charitable giving and attention to provision of hospitality for pilgrims, rather than focusing exclusively on *ḥajj* as a religious event. By doing this, we hope to offer insight onto the importance of community (*ummah*) that is expressed at multiple levels in the practice of Islam, showing the interconnection between themes.

In addition, welfare is examined from the broader perspective of society. Although environmental issues have begun to be discussed among Muslim scholars only since the 1960s, women have already taken on a leading role in redressing abuse of the environment and the need for a healthier relationship with God's creation. As feminist theologians in other faith traditions have noted, the relationship of subjugation and authority over the earth by human beings has often served as a metaphor for the subjugation of and authority over women that men hold, both within the family and within the state. Thus, placing articles on domestic violence and child abuse, as well as environmental activism, within this theme was designed to draw attention to the complexity of the question of welfare as both a private and public, as well as global, concern.

Finally, although the Arab Spring is typically represented and discussed as a political development, we have elected to place it in the category of Wealth, Welfare, and Labor to draw attention to the common underlying causes of the revolutions in different countries—namely, perceptions of corruption, lack of justice, authoritarianism, and economic failure as evidenced by high rates of unemployment and underemployment and the skyrocketing cost of living. All of these issues are inherently tied to the welfare of the people—and the state's failure to provide for it effectively. What this suggests is that solutions that focus on the construction of a new or alternative political system without taking into account the deeper underlying cause of welfare are not likely to create future stability. Replacing an authoritarian regime with some sort of democracy will not necessarily redress the deeper failures of the prior state to provide for the well-being of its citizens. The insight provided by consideration of the issue from the perspective of the impact regimes have on people's lives may help to understand, and hopefully effectively address, the longer term challenges faced by the new regimes, regardless of what political form they take.

Natana J. DeLong-Bas

West Bank and Gaza. The West Bank and Gaza Strip (WBGS) refer to the two disconnected areas that, together with East Jerusalem, are commonly referred to as "the occupied Palestinian territories." They constitute what remains of the Arab Palestinian state outlined by the United Nations' General Assembly Resolution 181 (the Partition Plan) of 1947. This plan proposed to separate the former British Mandate territory into one Jewish and one Arab state on 56 and 43 percent of the territory respectively. Jerusalem was designated as a *corpus separatum* under international administration. The plan was rejected by the Arab neighbor states, and, when Israel declared its "independence" on May 14, 1948, war broke out. Victorious in the war, Israel conquered 21 percent of the territory intended for the Arab state, as well as the western part of Jerusalem. One part of the remaining territory—the Gaza Strip—was governed by Egypt, and one part—the West Bank, along with East Jerusalem—was governed by Jordan. An estimated 750,000 Palestinians were made refugees as a result of the war, which is referred to as *al-Nakba*, the catastrophe. The majority of the 3.7 million Palestinians presently living in the WBGS and East Jerusalem are Sunnī Muslim: 99.3 percent on the Gaza Strip and 92 percent in the West Bank. The rest belong to various Christian denominations.

1948–1967. The West Bank (Arabic: Al-Ḍaffa al-Gharbiyya) is a landlocked area of 5640 km^2 (including East Jerusalem). Jordan formally annexed the West Bank and East Jerusalem in 1950 and made the inhabitants Jordanian citizens with Jordanian passports. This move more than tripled Jordan's prewar population to 1,250,000, and it is estimated that 400,000 of those citizens were refugees. The Gaza Strip (Arabic: Qitā' Ghazza) is coastal area of 360 km^2. After *al-Nakba*, 250,000 refugees were added to the original population of about 80,000. Egypt retained control over the Gaza Strip after the 1949 armistice agreement with Israel. Nominally, the All-Palestine Government ruled until 1959, but the area was for all practical purposes under Egyptian military administration. Given that a large majority of the population were refugees, the United Nations

Relief and Works Agency (UNRWA) shared administrative responsibility with Egypt from 1950.

During this period, economic and infrastructural development was lacking and both areas remained mainly agricultural with high unemployment rates. The Jordanian rulers practiced discriminatory economic policies discouraging investment on the West Bank in favor of Transjordan. Egyptian rule changed after Nasser became president in 1956, and his social, educational, and security reform program was carried over to the Gaza Strip. The socioeconomic upheaval of *al-Nakba* meant that many peasant families lost their means of subsistence, forcing an unprecedented number of women to seek employment outside of the home. Women's organizations providing social services were established in major WBGS towns from the 1950s onward. The best known organization is In'ash al-Usra (the Family Rejuvenation Society), established in al-Bireh on the West Bank in 1965 and headed by Samiha Khalil. Such societies expanded their activities from charity to education and vocational training for women, enabling them to find jobs outside the home. Khalil ran against Yasser Arafat in the presidential election in 1996, garnering 11.5 percent of the vote.

Following the annexation, the West Bank and East Jerusalem became subject to Jordanian law. In 1951, the Jordanian and Palestinian *Sharīʿah* courts were unified and a Jordanian Law of Family Rights was promulgated. The Egyptian governor issued a Law of Family Rights in 1954, pertaining to the Gaza Strip only. The Jordanian Law of Family Rights was amended in 1976, and both laws remain in force today. The laws govern personal status issues, including marriage, divorce, child custody, and inheritance for Muslims, and both are derived from the Ḥanafī law school. For Christians of the WBGS, ecclesiastic courts govern personal status issues according to the person's denomination.

Under Jordanian and Egyptian rule, political activities in the WBGS were severely restricted; after Nasser's coup in 1952, all political parties were banned in Egypt. Jordan invoked a state of emergency in 1956 and banned all political parties the year after, except for the Muslim Brotherhood. Given that it was allowed to operate openly, the West Bank-Jordanian branch of the Muslim Brotherhood developed in a more moderate, less militaristic direction than the suppressed Gaza Strip-Egyptian one. Although Pan-Arabism was the dominant ideology, Palestinian nationalist movements developed in exile. The policy of Yasser Arafat's Fatah (Harakat al-Tahrir al-Watani al-Falastini; the Palestinian National Liberation Movement) was to develop a Palestinian revolutionary authority on the WBGS. When the Palestinian Liberation Organisation (PLO) was established in 1964, Nasser gave it nominal authority over the Gaza Strip. In 1965, Palestinian women's activism was unified and included in the PLO under the umbrella organization General Union of Palestinian Women (GUPW). The GUPW worked toward the participation of women in all aspects of the struggle to liberate Palestine, and, according to its charter, for women's equality with men "in all rights and privileges for the purpose of liberating the homeland."

1967–1993. Following the Six-Day War of June, 1967, Israel occupied the WBGS, gaining control of the remaining 23 percent of the British Mandate area. With reference to international law, the WBGS are recognized as occupied territories by the international community and designated as such by the United Nations. Israel challenges this, and refers to the WBGS as "disputed territories," arguing that they were never internationally recognized as sovereign prior to 1967. The territories were governed by an Israeli military administration, while East Jerusalem was formally annexed to the Israeli state. This annexation is not recognized as legal by the international community.

Among the consequence of the occupation was that 1 million Palestinians were brought under Israeli rule, and Palestinians of the WBGS could now resume contact with each other, as well as with Palestinians who are Israeli citizens. Importantly, the Israeli labor market was opened to Palestinians, and, from the 1970s, around half of the Palestinian workforce was employed in Israel, predominantly as unskilled laborers (Tamari). Israel has argued that this contributed to increasing Palestinian income levels and living standards, that health and education services improved, and that electricity and piped water were made available to more Palestinians as a result of the occupation. This claim is challenged by those who argue that the economic integration with Israel contributed to a "de-development" that severely limited progress in WBGS agriculture and industry, keeping internal economic growth at a low structural level and impeding independent development in the WBGS.

The process of settling Israeli Jewish citizens in the WBGS and East Jerusalem was initiated in the late 1960s and accelerated from 1977 onwards. The purpose has been to create a territorial continuity between the Israeli state and the occupied territories, as well as to serve security and strategic purposes. Israel has utilized various strategies to acquire land in WBGS for settlement construction. All settlements are considered illegal under international law, but Israel disputes this and distinguishes between state-sanctioned settlements and so-called outposts. The present settler population is estimated at 300,000 on the West Bank and 200,000 in East Jerusalem, living in around 150 settlements and 100 outposts. The settlements on the Gaza Strip were evacuated in 2005.

Israel outlawed most kinds of political activism, and leading activists, both male and female, operated in exile after 1967. A number of women were involved in militant activities; Souhaila Andrawes and Leila Khaled of the Popular Front for the Liberation of Palestine (PFLP)—one of the Marxist PLO factions—carried out several air plane hijackings. On the WBGS, grassroots activism grew in the late 1970s through the so-called popular committees, which were sponsored by the various PLO factions. Among these were women's popular committees, which were well organized and highly decentralized and drew support and commitment from camp and village women. Although their main activities were directed toward national liberation, the organizations also included the emancipation and formal equality of Palestinian women in employment and education as part of their mandate.

When the first popular uprising against the occupation—known as the Intifada—erupted in December 1987, these grassroots groups played an active role in initiating and sustaining many forms of civil disobedience and mostly nonviolent protests. These activities were coordinated by an underground group known as the United National Leadership of the Uprising (UNLU) with ties to PLO in exile. The Intifada created international attention and sympathy for the Palestinians' plight. In 1988, PLO's National Council adopted the Palestinian Declaration of Independence, declaring the State of Palestine as WBGS, with East Jerusalem as its capital. These territories continue to form the basis for the claim to sovereign statehood put forward in negotiations between Israel and the Palestinians.

Islamic groups—most notably Hamas (Ḥarakat al-Muqāwamah al-Islāmīyah, the Islamic Resistance Movement), an offshoot of the Muslim Brotherhood in the Gaza Strip—emerged during the Intifada, promoting a clearly religious agenda, in contrast to and in competition with the nationalist and largely secular discourses of the PLO. One example of this was the hijab campaign on the Gaza Strip, in which women and girls were admonished, even threatened, to adhere to a modest dress code associated with the modern

Islamic dress promoted by groups associated with the Muslim Brotherhood (Hammami). By 1990, most of the leaders of UNLU had been arrested, and, even if the Intifada continued for a few more years, it was more sporadic in character.

Although initially barred from the negotiations, the PLO leadership became involved in peace talks with Israel beginning with the Madrid conference in 1991 and the largely secret Oslo talks thereafter. During these talks, Hanan Ashrawi, an academic and prominent Intifada leader, served as official spokesperson for the Palestinian delegation. These talks culminated in the 1993 Declaration of Principles (DOP) based on mutual recognition between Israel and the PLO. Pursuant to the DOP, the Palestinian National Authority (PNA) was established as an interim self-government authority. The PNA was to gradually assume control over the WBGS in concurrence with withdrawal of Israeli forces and transfer of authority from the Israeli army's civil administration from 1994 onward. The agreement stipulated further Israeli withdrawals from the West Bank in a five-year interim period, during which key issues—borders, settlements, refugees, water rights, and the status of Jerusalem—were to be discussed and resolved. A two-state solution was envisioned as the end goal of this process, but this has yet to be realized. The PNA has, since its inception, exercised only limited control over parts of the WBGS.

1993–Present. Following the DOP, the PLO leadership in exile, headed by Yasser Arafat, returned to the WBGS and, to a large extent, took control over the PNA. Although largely male dominated, Arafat's government included long-time Fatah member and GUPW leader Intissar al-Wazir as Social Affairs Minister, Ashrawi as Minister of Education, and Zahira Kamal as Minister of Women's Affairs. The women's movement quickly began lobbying to develop the legal framework for the future Palestinian state in a gender-sensitive direction. In 1994, the Women's Charter was launched, demanding that the Palestinian Basic Law adhere to international human rights principles, including the Convention on the Elimination of All Forms of Discrimination (CEDAW). The law, signed into effect by President Arafat in 2002, incorporates the affirmation that "(a)ll Palestinians are equal under the law and judiciary, without discrimination because of race, sex, color, religion, political views, or disability" (The Amended Basic Law, title 2, article 9). However, the Basic Law also affirmed that personal status issues were to be governed by Sharīʿah and religious courts, and efforts to amend existing Family Law regimes have so far failed.

Women activists have also attempted to amend Palestinian citizenship rules, which are currently governed by the 1964 Palestinian National Charter and which state that Palestinian citizenship is passed on from the father. Notable victories include the fact that married women do not need their husband's consent to apply for a Palestinian passport, and unmarried women older than age eighteen do not need a guardian's consent. Also, changes in the election law include a women's quota. In the 1996 election, only five of eighty-eight seats in the legislative assembly were won by women. Although women lobbied for a 30 percent quota before the 2004 municipal elections, the current election law states that all the election lists must have a minimum of one woman among the three first candidates, two women among the eight first, and three women among the first fifteen to be approved. All municipal and village councils must include at least two women.

Further reform processes have stalled as the state-building progress itself was suspended. Failure to meet their obligations and mutual distrust impeded further peace negotiations from succeeding. The second Intifada that erupted in September 2000 was far more violent than the previous one, and, on the Palestinian side, dominated largely by armed groups from both Islamist and nationalist factions. Following a spate of attacks, Israeli forces reentered the previously evacuated areas in 2002. Over the following years, a system of roadblocks, checkpoints, and a separation barrier partially built on West Bank land limited freedom of movement in WBGS and contributed to dramatic increases in poverty levels, as well as physical and social isolation. This, together with a lack of security, has arguably contributed to increased conservatism and a return to traditional law enforcement mechanisms.

In November 2004, Yasser Arafat passed away after having spent eighteen months in his Ramallah compound surrounded by Israeli forces. Fatah strongman Mahmud Abbas was elected president. When the long overdue legislative elections were held in January 2006, the Change and Reform List, consisting mainly of Hamas members, scored an unexpected victory, capitalizing on popular frustration with the failed peace process and distrust of the PNA. Women gained 17 out of 132 seats. Six of these were Hamas representatives. Among them was Maryam Saleh, who was appointed Minister of Women's Affairs; Muna Mansour, widow of a Hamas leader assassinated by Israel in Nablus; and Maryam Farhat from Gaza, mother of three suicide attackers. Economic and political sanctions were enacted to pressure the Hamas government, led by Ismail Haniya, to recognize Israel, comply with agreements between Israel and the PLO, and renounce violence. Attempts were made to form a national unity government consisting of both Hamas and Fatah, but these were cut short when Hamas wrested control over the Gaza Strip in June 2007. While sanctions against the West Bank were eased, Israel proceeded to impose a complete blockade on the Gaza Strip. Tensions between Israel and the Gaza Strip erupted in December 2008 when Israel launched an airstrike and subsequent ground invasion. On the West Bank, further peace talks between Israel and the Palestinians have stalled as Abbas insists Israel must cease settlement expansion as a precondition for negotiations. Abbas' latest move—to have the UN Security Council recognize Palestine as a UN member state in September 2011 failed to get the required number of votes. One hundred and thirty UN member states presently recognize a Palestinian state on the West Bank and Gaza Strip.

Bibliography

Cohen, Amnon. *Political Parties in the West Bank under the Jordanian Regime, 1949–1967*. Ithaca, N.Y.: Cornell University Press, 1982.

Feldman, Ilana. *Governing Gaza: Bureaucracy, Authority, and the Work of Rule, 1917–1967*. Durham, N.C.: Duke University Press, 2008.

Gerner, Deborah J. *Mobilizing Women for Nationalist Agendas: Palestinian Women, Civil Society, and the State-Building Process*. Paper presented the Fulbright Conference "Women in the Global Community," Istanbul, Turkey, September, 2002.

Haddad, Yvonne. "Palestinian Women: Patterns of Legitimation and Domination." In *The Sociology of the Palestinians*, edited by Khalil Nakhleh and Elia Zureik. London: Croom Helm.

Hammami, Rema. "Women, the Hijab and the Intifada." *Middle East Report*. No. 164/165 (1990): 24–28, 71, 78.

Jamal, Amal. *The Palestinian National Movement. Politics of Contention, 1967–2005*. Bloomington and Indianapolis: Indiana University Press, 2005.

Roy, Sara. "The Gaza Strip. A Case of Economic De-Development." *Journal of Palestine Studies* 17, no. 1 (1987): 56–88.

Tamari, Salim. "The Palestinians in the West Bank and Gaza: The Sociology of Dependency." In. *The Sociology of the Palestinians*, edited by Khalil Nakhleh and Elia Zureik. London: Croom Helm.

United Nations Office for the Coordination of Humanitarian Affairs. "The Humanitarian Impact of Israeli Settlement Policies." http://www.ochaopt.org/documents/ocha_opt_settlements_FactSheet_January_2012_english.pdf.

Weighill, Marie-Louise. "Palestinians in Exile: Legal, Geographical and Statistical Aspects." In *The Palestinian Exodus 1948–1998*, edited by Ghada Karmi and Eugene Cotran. Reading, U.K.: Garnet Publishing.

Welchman, Lynn. *Islamic Family Law: Text and Practice in Palestine*. Jerusalem: Women's Centre for Legal Aid and Counselling (WCLAC), 1999.

HILDE GRANÅS KJØSTVEDT

WET NURSES. A wet nurse is a woman who breast feeds another's infant if the mother dies or is unable or unwilling to feed her baby. To feed the nursling, the wet nurse may leave her own baby in the care of others. In Muslim societies, the mother is expected to breastfeed her child for two years, unless, by mutual consent, the parents decide to wean the infant or to seek out a wet nurse to live in the same house as the baby's mother. Should the mother decline to feed her child, as in the case of divorce, the father is obliged seek out and compensate a wet nurse. Wet-nursing appears to have been common in pre-Islamic societies, but within Islam it received religious endorsement and regulation, not just as a short-lived physiological relationship between infant and wet nurse, but more importantly as a vehicle of physical and spiritual qualities that created milk kinship between the nursling, the wet nurse, and her kin, even across religious boundaries (Giladi, 1999, p. 142). The Prophet himself was fostered in infancy by Ḥalīma, a wet nurse from a desert tribe (Giladi, 1999, pp. 34–35). Milk kinship, though not universal, is not confined to Muslim or Middle Eastern societies, and may be found even today in the Balkans and in Africa. Milk kin cannot marry, are obliged to help one another, and may be a source of support to women in patriarchal societies. Among Muslims, children nursed by different wives of the same man become milk kin, hence the concept of sire's milk and the saying "The man is owner of the milk" (Altorki, 1980, p. 234). Giladi suggests that the Prophet endorsed milk sharing to discourage marriage among patrilateral kin and to promote links within the wider Muslim community. In the nineteenth-century Hindu Kush (Pakistan), wet nursing was used to create networks of allegiance over the generations, overriding rival and stratified patrilineal formations (Parkes, 2006). Although commercial wet nursing is mentioned in medieval texts, most nonmaternal breast feeding in Muslim societies is viewed positively as a gift from a social equal, whereas in stratified European societies, where it was widespread throughout known history, it was generally mercenary. The services of the wet nurse, a social subordinate, were transacted between the father of the nursling and the nurse's male affines. Any bonds of affection that she established with the nursling's family were without legal implications. Often the child was transferred to her household until it was weaned. Wet nurses were hired by hospitals and orphanages from at least the fifteenth century onward to feed premature and orphaned babies, and from the late eighteenth century onward they were supervised by male medical personnel, who managed wet nursing as a form of "technology." Its decline in industrialized countries led to the development of milk banks in the 1920s and the artificial milk formula. With the recent promotion of breast feeding, milk banks have returned as a resource for ill and premature infants. Although banked milk enjoys a sort of medical guarantee, some Muslims fear that its use may cause them to contract involuntary milk kinship or even forbidden marriages with anonymous strangers. The gift of banked milk is not only anonymous; it also appears to be ungendered and conveys no long-term social advantages to women. Yet many parents gratefully acknowledge its contribution to their children's survival.

[*See also* Motherhood *and* Pregnancy and Childbirth.]

BIBLIOGRAPHY

Altorki, Soraya. "Milk Kinship in Arab Society: An Unexplored Problem in the Ethnography of Marriage." *Ethnology* 19 (1980): 223–244.

Gila'di, Avner. *Infants, Parents, and Wet Nurses: Medieval Islamic Views on Breastfeeding and Their Social Implications.* Leiden, Netherlands: Brill, 1999.

Maher, Vanessa, ed. *The Anthropology of Breast-feeding: Natural Law or Social Construct.* Oxford: Berg, 1992.

Parkes, Peter. "Alternative Social Structures and Foster Relations in the Hindu Kush: Milk Kinship Allegiance in the Former Mountain Kingdoms of Northern Pakistan." *Comparative Studies in Society and History* 43, no. 1 (2001): 1–36.

Vanessa Maher

Wives of the Prophet. Just as the men of the community took Muḥammad as their role model, the women also looked to his wives as examples of the right manner of living. The honorific title "Mothers of the Believers" in Verse 33:6 raised their status and 33:53 prevented their remarriage. Verse 33:34 enjoined them to report the revelations received in their houses, informing the community about the minute details of the Prophet's life, how he lived and worshipped; to facilitate and clear up matters in general and matters of worship in particular, his mannerisms and behavior patterns, which were to be emulated; and later to provide a base for rulings in *fiqh* (jurisprudence). The women of the community sometimes shied away from discussing private or delicate issues with the Prophet and, hence, his wives spoke on their behalf. They also were the original authority for a great deal of material relating to their gender and served as the medium through which a vast number of traditions, referring to the *sunnah* of the Prophet—a standard of behavior for the whole community—were transmitted.

Mothers of the Believers. The number of Muḥammad's wives in the sources varies, as some authors include women he proposed to or who offered themselves to him and marriages that were not consummated. Some sources claim that a marriage took place, while others regard these women as *sara'ir* (slaves/concubines). Consensus has it that the Prophet had thirteen wives, of whom nine survived him:

1. **Khadījah bint Khuwaylid**, a wealthy merchant woman, proposed marriage to him when he was twenty-five and she was forty years old. They had four daughters: Zaynab, Ruqayyah, Umm Kulthūm, and Fāṭimah, but all their sons died in infancy. She was the first person to accept Islam and is portrayed in all sources, Sunnī and Shī'ah, as being the Prophet's most respected and beloved wife.
2. **Sawdah bint Zam'a**, an elderly widow and immigrant to Abyssinia, married the Prophet two years after Khadījah's death to help raise his daughter Fāṭimah. Some sources report that the Prophet divorced her, but repudiated the divorce after the revelation of Verse 4:128.
3. **'Ā'ishah bint Abī Bakr**, the youngest of the Prophet's wives, married him in Mecca. Her age at the time of their marriage is disputed in the sources and ranges between nine years at consummation of the marriage to twenty-one. She was said to have been one of only two virgin wives, the other being Māriyah al-Qibtiyya. 'Ā'ishah is frequently described in Sunnī sources as the Prophet's favorite wife; however, this standing seems to have been exaggerated after the Prophet's death. The Shī'ah view of 'Ā'ishah is negative. She is portrayed as a key player in the rebellion against 'Uthmān ibn 'Affān. Her participation in the battle of the Camel was considered contempt for *ahl-al-bayt* (the Prophet's family) and animosity toward 'Alī ibn Abī Ṭālib.

4. **Ḥafṣa bint ʿUmar ibn al-Khaṭṭāb**, a widow who could read and write, played an important role in compiling the Qurʾān, as she kept a private copy based on a version written directly from the Prophet's recitations and is said to have given it to ʿUthmān for the preparation of the ʿUthmānic codex. Sources report that the Prophet divorced her once, yet repudiated the divorce after a visit by Jibrīl, who told him she was *sawwama qawwama* (righteous and pious, observing her fasts and worshipping during the night). The Shīʿah view of Ḥafṣa is generally negative. She is criticized and portrayed in unflattering ways, probably related to the fact that she was ʿUmar's daughter rather than any particular personal characteristic.
5. **Zaynab bint Khuzayma [Umm Al Masakīn**ʾ (Mother of the Poor)] was a divorcee and widow, the maternal sister of Maymūna Bint al-Hārith; she died a few months after her marriage.
6. **Umm Salamah (Hind) bint Abī Umayyah ibn al-Mughīra**, a widow, was revered for her beauty and wisdom and advised the Prophet during the treaty of Ḥudaybīyah. The Shīʿah view of her is very positive. Imām Jaʿfar al-Ṣādiq is quoted as saying that she kept ʿAlī's books and then gave them to Ḥasan, from him to Ḥusayn, and finally to ʿAlī ibn Ḥusayn, designating her as keeper of the *naṣṣ* (text), an essential legitimization for a Shīʿah imam.
7. **Zaynab bint Jaḥsh**, the Prophet's first maternal cousin, married him after her divorce from his adoptive son Zayd ibn Ḥāritha. She was the first of his wives to die and her burial necessitated a change in practice. It had been customary until then to carry the body on an open litter, exposed to public view, but because the strict seclusion of Muḥammad's wives from all men, necessitated the use of a *naʿsh* (coffin) for the first time to hide the body.
8. **Juwayriyya bint al-Ḥārith** of the Khuzāʿa tribe was captured in an attack on her tribe, and upon her marriage, all prisoners of war were set free. For the Muslims, it was considered shameful to own relatives of a wife of the Prophet.
9. **Ṣafiyya bint Ḥuyayy**'s status is disputed and sources do not agree if she was first a concubine or a later wife. Shīʿī sources present a favorable picture of her because of her alleged humiliation by Hafsa and ʿĀʾishah due to her Jewish descent. Shīʿī sources report that the Prophet left instructions that, in the event of his death, Ṣafiyya should be given in care to ʿAlī as his most trusted family member.
10. **Umm Ḥabība (Ramla) bint Abī Sufyān**, a widow, who on the occasion of her marriage, after her return from Abyssinia, is said to have inspired the revelation of Verse 60:7. Shīʿī sources are critical of Umm Ḥabība, accusing her of playing a role in instigating the First Civil War, by sending ʿUthmān's bloody shirt to her brother Muʿāwiyah in Syria, which he then publicly displayed to rally people's support for the cause of avenging ʿUthmān.
11. **Maymūna bint al-Ḥārith**, twice widowed, was Muḥammad's last wife and was married right after *ʿumrah* (lesser pilgrimage). She is portrayed positively in Shiite sources because of her descent from the Banū Hāshim clan and favorable disposition toward ʿAlī.
12. **Māriyah bint Shamʿūn [Māriyah al-Qibtiyya]** was sent to the Prophet as a gift by Egypt's ruler, al-Muqawqis. Her status as a wife or concubine is disputed. She bore Muḥammad a son, Ibrāhīm, who died before he was two.
13. **Rayḥāna bint Zayd** was captured in an attack on the Jewish Banū Qurayẓa tribe. Sources disagree about her status and whether or not she converted to Islam or remained a Jewess.

In addition, there were other wives: Fāṭimah bint Shurayḥ, who was explicitly mentioned in the sources after offering herself to Muḥammad, hence the reason for the revelation of Verse 22:50;

Hind bint Yazīd al-Kilābīyya, who was divorced the next day due to a skin disease (or leprosy); Asmāʾ bint al-Nuʿmān, a Yemenite from Kinda, who was also divorced the next day, because she invoked Allāh's protection when Muḥammad wanted to consummate the marriage; and Umm Sharīk of Banū al-Naggar or Umm Sharīk Sanaʾ bint Asmāʾ bint al-Ṣalt of Banū Sālīm.

Concubines. The sources are in disagreement about the status of both Māriyah and Rayḥāna. They are regarded along with Rubayḥa or Zulaykha al-Qaraziya as concubines, said to have been spoils of war. Some sources claim that Rubayḥa, Zulaykha, and Rayḥāna are one and the same. Ibn Kathīr mentions another concubine, gifted to Muḥammad by Zaynab bint Jaḥsh to appease him after he had deserted her for three months. Two others are also mentioned in the same context: Jamīla and Nafīsa.

Reasons for Multiple Marriages. Before Islam, the practice of unlimited polygyny was common. Verse 4:3 restricted the number to four wives, provided the husband was able to treat them equally. However, Verse 4:129 disputes the ability to satisfy this condition; hence, some exegetes argued that monogamy was preferable, leaving polygyny as a solution to gender imbalance following wars. Verse 33:50 defined the women whom the Prophet was allowed to marry, yet his multiple marriages gave rise to many attacks on his character. Some exegetes used Verse 33:50 to argue that all wives, though more than the four allowed in Verse 4:3, were divinely approved. Muḥammad ʿAbdū, among many, wrote in the Prophet's defense, stating that there was a divine reason for each marriage. His marriage to Khadījah had established an important precedent in that a woman could initiate a marriage. Khadījah and Sawdah were older than him, indicating that a difference in age between a wife and husband did not matter. Marriages to Hafs-a and ʿĀʾishah occurred for political reasons: to honor their fathers, his most loyal companions. His marriage to Zaynab bint Jaḥsh abolished adoption, while his marriage to Juwayriyya freed her people. He married Umm Salamah for her wisdom, showing that good qualities in a wife are desirable, and married Umm Ḥabība for her lineage and to honor her. Although her father was one of Muḥammad's ardent enemies, she was a believer in spite of him. The marriages to Ṣafiyya, Rayḥāna, and Māriya showed that marrying Jewish and Christian women was lawful. Marriage to Maymūna set another precedent: that marriage immediately after *ʿumrah* was permitted.

Modern Feminism and the Prophet's Wives. In addition to historical works, two important sources of representation of the Prophet's wives are the Qurʾān—with its *asbāb al-nuzūl* (reasons for revelation)—and the *ḥadīth*. The Qurʾān does not mention the wives by name. *Ḥadīth* literature, however, mentions them frequently as part of events depicted in the *matn* (content/text), as transmitters and first narrators, reporting the Prophet's words with intimate details of his life, preferences, dislikes, responses to particular political or social situations, serving later on as precedents for legal rulings. In their acknowledged role as "Mothers of the Believers," they guided the community after his death as role models. Although Qurʾān 33:32 says that they "are unlike any other women," *ḥadīth* did not always present them in a flattering light. They were prototypes of what women should be, but also of what they couldn't help but be and should strive to overcome, as offered by Sells and Walker (1999).

From the mid-nineteenth century onward, Muslim writers portrayed the Prophet's wives in different ways to project their own agendas (Roded, 2006). Feminist writers portrayed them as perhaps the first feminists, despite the word and underlying concepts originating in modern times, arguing that, historically, women in different parts of the world had developed a concept of feminism long before there was a specific name for it (Badran, 1988). Although feminists mainly use ʿĀʾishah's example, Mernissi (1991) considers Umm Salamah a real feminist, a champion of the cause of women.

Each period had its own interpretations about the lives of the "Mothers of the Believers," affected by popular cultural and moral values and social norms. Hence, the emphasis on the Prophet's wives did not originate from their historical personalities, but rather from the continuous modifications, alterations, interpretations, and modernizations of their portrayed personalities. They were used to justify a great variety of attitudes. "They were portrayed as ideal, obedient, gentle, affectionate, content, pious, inside their houses, veiled, but also as jealous, angry, quarrelling, having great *kayd* (cunning), sowing *fitna* and sometimes with an imperfect mind, yet also as erudite teachers, daring, strong personalities, intelligent, political activists, even leaders in wars and of course, feminists" (Ascha, 1995, p. 107). The main feminist argument, outlined in Badran (1988), was that Islam granted rights to women, which the male-imposed customs and traditions denied them; this was a view also adopted by reformists, such as Muḥammad ʿAbdūh advocating a return to the early Islamic sources for fresh interpretations.

Unlike Khadījah and ʿĀʾishah, who have been thoroughly studied, other wives have not yet been given their due in scholarly research. Shiite literature, with ʿĀʾishah, Umm Salamah, and Umm Ḥabība being the exceptions, diminishes the roles played by the Prophet's wives and enhances those assumed by the members of ʿAlī ibn Abī Ṭālib's bloodline.

BIBLIOGRAPHY

ʿAbdu, Muḥammad. *Ḥikmat taʿaddud Zawjāt al-Nabī*. Cairo: Dār al-Ḥaramayn, 1999.

Ali, Kecia. *Sexual Ethics and Islam—Feminist Reflections of Qurʾan, Hadith and Jurisprudence*. Oxford: Oneworld, 2006.

ʿAmily, Zainab bt. Ali b. Husayn b. Fawaz al-. *Al-Durr al-manthūr fīṭabaqāt rabbat al-Khudūr*. Cairo, Egypt: Al-matbaʾa al-Kubra al-Amiriya fi-Bulaq, 1894, p. 314.

Ascha, Ghassan. "The 'Mothers of the Believers': Stereotypes of the Prophet Muhammad's Wives." In *Female Stereotypes in Religious Traditions*, edited by Ria Kloppenborg and Wouter J. Hanegraaf, pp. 89–107. Leiden, Netherlands: E.J. Brill, 1995.

Badran, Margot. "Dual Liberation: Feminism and Nationalism in Egypt 1870s–1925." *Feminist Issues* 8, no. 1 (1988): 15–34.

Balādhurī, Aḥmad Ibn Yaḥyá al- (d. ca. 892 CE). *Ansāb al-ashrāf*. Cairo, Egypt: Dār al-Maʿārīf, 1987.

Dakake, Maria Massi. *The Charismatic Community: Shiʿite Identity in Early Islam*. Albany: State University of New York Press, 2007.

Ḥalabī, ʿAlī Ibn Burhān al-Dīn al- (d. 1549 CE). *ʾInsān al-ʿuyūn fī sīrat al-amīn al-maʾmūn*. Beirut, Lebanon: al-Maktab al-Islāmī, 1902. Also known as *Al-sīrā al-Ḥalabīyya*.

Ibn ʿAsākir, ʿAlī ibn al-Ḥasan (d. 1125 CE). *Tārīkh madīnat Dimashq*. Beirut, Lebanon: Dār al-Fikr, 1995.

Ibn Ḥajjar, Shihāb al-Dīn Abī al-Faḍl Aḥmad ibn ʿAlī ibn Muḥammad ibn Muḥammad ibn ʿAlī al-Kinānī al-ʿAsqalānī thumma al-Miṣrī al-Shāfiʿī (d. 1449 CE). *al-Iṣābah fī tamyīz al-Ṣaḥābah*. Cairo, Egypt: Maṭbaʿat al-Saʿādah, 1907.

Ibn Kathīr al-Dimashqī, ʿImād al-Dīn Ismāʿīl Ibn ʿUmar (d. 1373 CE). *al-Bidāyah wa-al-nihāyah*. Beirut, Lebanon: Maktabat al-Maʿārif, 1966.

Ibn al-Muthannā (Abū ʿUbayda), Maʿmar b. al-Muthannā al-Tamīmī bi-al-Walāʾ al-Baṣrī. *Azwāj al-Nabi wa Awladuhu*. Cairo, Egypt: Dār al-Ḥaramayn, 1999.

Ibn Qutaybah, Abī Muḥammad ʿAbd Allāh ibn Muslim (d. 889 CE). *Al-imāmah wa-al-siyāsah*. Beirut, Lebanon: Dār Al-Kutub al-ʿIlmiyah, 2006.

Ibn Saʿd, Muḥammad (d. 845 CE). *Kitāb al-ṭabaqāt al-kabīr*. Leiden, Netherlands: E.J. Brill, 1920.

Mernissi, Fatima. *Women and Islam—An Historical and Theological Enquiry*. Oxford: Blackwell, 1991.

Roded, R. "Lessons by a Syrian Islamist from the Life of the Prophet Muhammad." *Middle Eastern Studies* 42, no. 6 (2006): 855–872.

Sells, M. A., and A. M. Walker. "The Wiles of Women and Performative Intertextuality: Aisha, the Hadith of the Slander, and the Sura of Yusuf." *Journal of Arabic Literature* 30, no. 1 (1999): 55–77.
Sha'rāwī, M. M. al-. *Zawjāt al-Nabī wa-Āl al-Bayt.* Beirut, Lebanon: Al-Maktabat al-'Aṣrīyah, 2003.
Spellberg, Denise. *Politics, Gender, and the Islamic Past: The Legacy of 'A'isha bint Abi Bakr.* New York: Columbia University Press, 1994.
Stern, Gertrude H. *Marriage in Early Islam.* London: Royal Asiatic Society, 1939.
Stowasser, Barbara Freyer. *Women in the Qur'an, Traditions, and Interpretation.* New York: Oxford University Press, 1994.
Watt, W. Montgomery. *Muhammad at Medina.* Oxford: Oxford University Press, 1956.

Yasmin Amin

Women and Islam.

[*This entry contains two subentries:*

Role and Status of Women *and*
Women's Religious Observances]

Role and Status of Women

The Qur'ān, Islam's holy book, changed women's status considerably from that of the pre-Islamic (*jāhilīyah*) period. Before Islam, both polyandrous and polygamous marriages were practiced, and matrilineal, uxorilocal marriages in which the woman remained with her tribe and the man either visited or resided with her were also quite common. Many women selected and divorced their own husbands, and women were neither veiled nor secluded; some were poets and others even fought in wars alongside men. As Leila Ahmed observes, although these "practices do not necessarily indicate the greater power of women or the absence of misogyny, they do correlate with women's enjoying greater sexual autonomy than they were allowed under Islam" (Ahmed, 1992, p. 42). At the same time that Islam eliminated polyandrous marriages, it also limited the number of female spouses to a maximum of four (Qur'ān 4:1) as early Arabian Muslims gradually moved from a matrilineal to a patrilineal society. Women's status was raised in other dimensions, such as by outlawing the pre-Islamic practice of female infanticide (81:8–9) and making the dower (*mahr*), which in pre-Islamic times was paid directly to a woman's male guardian (*walī*), payable directly to the woman (4:3), who was also given the right to inherit property (4:7).

Women's Status in the Qur'ān. The creation of the female is attributed, along with that of the male, to a single soul (4:1) from which the other is created as its mate (4:1). Another verse declares: "God created you from dust, then from a little fluid, then He made you pairs" (35:11). Thus, the Qur'ān grants both sexes equality from the perspective of origin and spiritual status. Men and women are equally accountable to God for their faith, actions, and moral behavior (33:35). However, from a contemporary perspective, such equality is not reflected in the social sphere, even though, in its own time, the Qur'ān greatly advanced women's status. For instance, the Qur'ān entitled women to inherit (4:7), but only half the portions received by men (4:11); women were considered legal persons (long before they were in the Western hemisphere), but two women's testimonies counted in weight to that of one man's (2:282); and women were given the right to economic security, but men were considered to "have preference over women" because they were made responsible for women's upkeep (4:34). In Islamic law, women are restricted to monogamy, which, although not specified in the Qur'ān, is implied in the injunction that "all married women" are forbidden to men (4:24). Men are allowed up to four wives on the condition that they are treated equally, followed by the comment that if men fear that they cannot do justice to that number, they should marry only one, or possess as many concubines as they can afford ("their right hand may possess") (4:3). Men may marry any of the women of the *ahl al-kitāb* (peoples of the Book) (5:5), whereas women may marry only Muslim men (again, not a Qurʾānic injunction, but a traditional stipulation). Conjugal relations are forbidden with menstruating women (2:222); otherwise, conjugal relations are permitted at will (2:223). Disobedient wives are subject to a graduated set of measures interpreted as ranging from admonishment to beating, depending on how the term *daraba* is interpreted (4:34). Should a conflict arise between the couple, then an arbiter from each one's kinsfolk should be appointed to attempt a reconciliation (4:35). According to the Qurʾān, men who forswear their wives must wait four months (2:226) during which they may change their minds; however, if divorce is determined as a course of action, then women must wait a term of three menses to ensure that they are not impregnated, in which case the husband is recommended to take them back (2:227). Should divorce nonetheless proceed, the wife is entitled to support until she gives birth (65:4), and, if mutually agreeable, while she nurses (65:6).

Women in Muslim Culture. Contemporary Muslim scholars such as Amina Wadud and Asma Barlas suggest that one should distinguish between Islam as a religion and the differing cultural contexts in which Islam was revealed, institutionalized, and practiced. Islam as a religion refers to regulations pertaining to piety, ethics, and belief. These spiritual aspects of Islam are considered duties of worship (*ʿibādāt*) and hence called "roots" or "foundations" (*uṣūl*) of the faith. They include cardinal beliefs in the singularity of God; the final prophecy of Muḥammad; and obligatory practices such as prayer, almsgiving, fasting, and the pilgrimage to Mecca. On this religious level, men and women are moral equals in the sight of God. Evidence for this is found in numerous Qurʾānic verses (2:187, 3:195, 4:1, 4:32, 9:71–72, 24:12, 30:21, 33:35–36, 40:40, 48:5, 57:12), which render the only distinction between women and men to be their piety (*taqwā*), not their sex. Islam as a culture refers to the ideas and practices of Muslims in the context of changing social, economic, and political circumstances. People not only worship God but also interact in social relationships, *muʿāmalāt* (transactions). They make contracts, trade, fight, arbitrate disputes, collect taxes, and so on. Collectively, these constitute the *furūʿ* (the branches or "superstructure").

On this cultural level, women have not been treated as men's equals. Such inequality has evolved largely as an artifact of the preferences and actions of patriarchal authorities after the Prophet's death, including a number of rulers and administrators, most jurists, and some intellectuals. In many instances, their patriarchal "readings" of the Qurʾānic text were driven by the cultural contexts supplied by the expansion of Muslim rule over former Byzantine and Sassanid territories, where patriarchy was already a well-established form of social organization. For instance, one of the earliest Qurʾānic commentators, al-Ṭabarī (d. 923 CE) imported the biblical account found in Gen 2:20–22 according to which the woman was created from Adam's rib, hence making the creation of the female secondary and in service to the male. In contrast, the Qurʾān asserts that male and female are created from a single soul, thereby retaining ontological equality between the two sexes, similar to that found in Genesis 1:26–27, in which both male and female are made in God's image. Al-Ṭabarī also draws on traditions that blame the woman for Adam's downfall, despite the fact that the Qurʾān names Adam as disobedient to God (20:121), or blames the couple (7:20–22), but not the woman alone. Al-Ṭabarī thereby conceptualized women as less rational and more morally reprehensible than men. Such essentialized sexual differentiation then became the basis for subsequent commentaries on the Qur'ān and became imbricated in laws pertaining to women developed by the legal schools. However, a number of nineteenth- and twentieth-century scholars, leaders of women's movements, and a minority of *'ulamā* (religious scholars) agree that the Qur'ān itself does not support later categorical claims that justify women's inequality in Islam based on essentialist characteristics attributed to her by al-Ṭabarī and other Qur'ānic commentators for her disobedience to God.

Qur'ānic verses do assign women's testimony half the value of men's in matters relating to transactions, so that, if one woman makes a mistake, the other might remind her (2:282); permit men to divorce their wives unilaterally (2:236); permit polygyny (4:3); and favor men over women respecting inheritance (4:11). However, stipulations in the Qur'ān itself and existing legal principles adduced by jurists may be invoked to maintain that, because the social, cultural, and economic context of those verses has changed, the sanction for gender inequality is no longer legitimate. For instance, scholars such as Amina Wadud argue that "each new Islamic society must understand the principles intended by the particulars... which were manifestations particular to that [that is, seventh-century Arabian] context" (Wadud, 1994, 9–10).

Contemporary woman-friendly scholars support their arguments by reference to the holy text itself. For instance, God says in the Qur'ān that a people's condition will not be changed until they change what is in themselves (13:11). According to contemporary scholars, this verse, as well as a sound tradition ascribed to the Prophet stating, "As for matters of your world, you know better," calls on Muslims to use their intrinsic endowment of reason to maximize their welfare. Thus, it would be irrational to accept gender inequality when God enjoins the spiritual equality of all Muslims; moreover, Asma Barlas argues that God cannot be accused of misogyny or maltreatment of women, which can never be justified on the basis of God's self-revelation in the Qur'ān. Jurists have over the centuries employed a number of legal devices that vindicate the use of reason in pursuing the welfare of Muslims, including (1) public interest (*al-maslahah al-mursalah*); (2) the common expression, "necessities make permissible what are forbidden" (*al-darūrāt tubīhu al-mahzūrāt*); and (3) the application of discretion (*istihsān*) in reaching a ruling.

Careful attention to lexical meanings of a term also suggest that a Qur'ānic verse such as 4:34, which says that men are preferred over (*qawwamūna 'ala*) women, could also be read as saying that men are a support to women, and the term *daraba*, which has commonly been understood as "beating," may also be understood as "setting an example." In addition, such scholars argue, it must be determined whether a Qur'ānic verse has placed a limitation on itself; for instance, 4:3 makes polygyny applicable only to the (female) orphans under one's care, not to all Muslim women. Moreover, not only does the Qur'ān make polygyny conditional on equitable treatment for all wives (4:3), but also explicitly asserts such treatment to be impossible (4:129).

Many Muslims claim that the Qur'ān and *sunnah* (practice of the Prophet) mandate veiling and seclusion. However, some scholars believe such arguments are tendentious. Of the seven Qur'ānic verses using the word "veil" (hijab), six were revealed at Mecca (7:46, 17:45, 19:17, 38:32, 41:5, 42:51), and none of them refer to veiling Muslim women. The seventh verse (33:53), revealed at Medina, requests male guests to address the Prophet's wives "from behind a hijab" when they ask something of them. Although the verse does not pertain to Muslim women in general, some Muslims argue that what applies to the Prophet's wives, exemplars of chastity, inheres all the more for Muslim women, on the assumption that they are less chaste. The hijab in the verse is clearly intended to be a curtain rather than a head-covering, and may have signaled the seclusion of the Prophet's wives. However, medieval Islamic commentators coupled this verse with verses specifying general Muslim women's clothing (24:30–31), in which women are asked to draw their scarves (*khumūr*) over their bosoms (*juyūb*), to enable Muslim women in ʿAbbāṣid times to emulate the cultural tradition of veiling and seclusion observed by Byzantine and Persian upper-class women. Qurʾānic scholars such as al-Wāḥidī, in his *Asbāb al-nuzūl,* and others maintain that the reference in 24:31 to *khumūr (s. khimār),* a garment that should cover both the head and the bosom, was based on the need to differentiate among free women and slaves. The story is told of the caliph ʿUmar who slapped a female slave for wearing a *khimār.* Thus, some Muslims argue that if *khumūr* were used to distinguish free women from slaves, then the abolition of slavery in the contemporary times has eliminated this reason for covering oneself.

In contemporary times, the veil has made a comeback as Muslim women are exhorted to take it on as a sign of their piety and to express through their clothing their proud identity as Muslims in a postcolonial era. Such calls for the pious display of faith may be understood in part as a struggle for cultural nativism in the face of an ever-globalizing American culture, preceded by Western colonization. The colonial British identification of Muslim backwardness with the seclusion and veiling of women has, in a reverse move, made veiling (and not necessarily seclusion) the signifier of all that is authentic in Islamic culture, where the woman is valued for her mind and her morals rather than for the amount of skin she shows. Veiling has allowed women to enter the public sphere without fear of retribution for entering previously male-dominated spaces, whether they are in the street or in the boardroom. With steady increases in women's education and employment, and as more women enter the legal and public professions, legal and cultural impediments barring women from assuming equality have been challenged. This is nowhere more apparent than in countries such as Iran, where public debates in print and in parliament question attitudes and laws that keep women out of public office, and in Pakistan, where challenges to laws such as the Ḥudud Ordinances are being vigorously voiced and are now being struck down or are under revision.

The Qurʾān does not support or assert notions of inherent female inferiority, nor can women be judged less rational, more emotional, or less competent than men on the basis of the Qurʾān. Certain *aḥādīth* are sometimes cited to the effect that the Prophet regarded women as incapable of leadership. However, some scholars doubt the veracity of a number of these traditions and believe that they were invented by later generations to justify restrictions on the activities of women. Indeed, many *aḥādīth* offer evidence that the Prophet consulted women and weighed their opinions seriously. Ibn Ḥanbal, founder of one of the four Sunnī schools of law, notes that at least one woman, Umm Waraqah, was appointed as the imām or leader of prayers for her household by the Prophet. Historical and canonical records demonstrate women's important and respected role in Muslim life, as reflected in the story of an older woman who corrected the authoritative ruling (*fatwā*) of the second caliph ʿUmar ibn al-Khaṭṭāb on the dower (*mahr*). Scholars cite the fact that women prayed in mosques unsegregated from men, and were involved in the transmittal of *aḥādīth* (Ibn Saʿd, the famous early biographer, records seven hundred cases of women who performed this important function) to show that women participated alongside men in religious and cultural life. Biographies of distinguished women, especially in the Prophet's household, show that women behaved autonomously in early Islam. The women about whom the most data are available are Khadījah, the Prophet's first wife; ʿĀʾishah, his favorite wife; Fāṭimah, his youngest daughter; Zaynab, his granddaughter; Sukaynah, his great-granddaughter; and ʿĀʾishah bint Ṭalḥah, the niece of her namesake. Women were known to give sanctuary (*jiwār*) to men. Women owned and disposed of property and engaged in commercial transactions, and wealthy women in the Islamic medieval period patronized large-scale architectural projects. Like men, women were encouraged to seek knowledge, which, indeed, they pursued in the Prophet's own home, and women have been identified both as instructors and pupils throughout Islamic history. The Prophet's favorite wife, ʿĀʾishah, was a well-known authority in medicine, history, and rhetoric and is noted for the number of *aḥādīth* that cite her as a source.

As to politics, the Qurʾān refers to women who, independently of their male kin, pledged the oath of allegiance (*bayʿah*) to the Prophet (60:12). Additional examples of women choosing to make such pledges to the Prophet, often before their men did, occurred at al-ʿAqabah, al-Riḍwān, and al-Shajarah. Caliph ʿUmar appointed women to serve as officials (*muḥtasibs*) in the market of Medina, and Ḥanbalī jurisprudence upholds the qualifications of women to serve as judges. Examples of women's involvement in politics as well as governance are found in almost every century, among the most notable being Sitt al-Mulk (tenth century), the Ṣulayḥīd queen Sayyidah al-Ḥurrah (eleventh century), Shajarat al-Durr and Rādīyah Sultānah Sulṭāna (Radiyya bint Iltutmish) (both thirteenth century), the Indonesian queens of Aceh (seventeenth century), and various female Muslim heads of state in the contemporary period in Pakistan, Bangladesh, and Indonesia.

Role and Status in Various Muslim Lands. The seclusion and confinement of women in urban settings prevailed without significant change until the early twentieth century, but numerous attempts to modify personal status law have been made since then. Before the early twentieth century, the colonial state in Muslim-majority regions left control over women and the family in the hands of patriarchal kinship groups and to Islamic Sharīʿah courts, both of which conceptualized the law based on sexual differences. In contrast to its highly interventionist behavior in Islamic civil, commercial, and penal law, the colonial state declined the very risky enterprise of tampering with personal status regulations, the very core of Muslim (masculine) identity. The patriarchal control of women's behavior and the family unit were central to the construction of this identity. Ultimately, however, the postcolonial state's reluctance began to give way, not least because of the pressure brought to bear by women's groups under the leadership of prominent women in countries such as Egypt and throughout the Ottoman Empire, and also as a result of pressures to modernize the labor market in an increasingly globalized economy.

In the past, inquiries into the role of women and the family often overemphasized the content of sacred texts, assuming these texts were the driving force behind people's behavior. In reaction to this "religious" approach, some scholars have stressed the relevance of conditions in "civil society" (e.g., legal protections offered by the state, economic realities, literacy and employment rates, and access) for understanding women's subordinate status. More recently, it has been suggested that neither the "sacred texts" nor the "civil society" approach are in themselves sufficient to explain the content of personal status legislation at any given time because they ignore the state's autonomy in pursuing its own economic and political agenda in this area.

For instance, the state has broadened its base of support by enfranchising women, in the process weaning them away from the kinship groups that traditionally have controlled them and redirecting their terminal loyalties to itself. Iran and Turkey at various times in recent history exemplify this pattern. However, in so doing, the state risks the growing disenchantment of more traditional Muslim scholars, who generally view such developments to be "anti-Islamic." Thus, the state may attempt to conciliate such groups by enforcing modesty codes or curtailing women's public presence. Post-1979 Pakistan, Afghanistan, and Iran, along with Sudan and Egypt after 1985, provide relevant examples of such conduct.

In balancing the conflicting demands of women and traditionalists, the state has generally followed a cautious policy of reform. Such reforms have made polygynous marriages more difficult or abolished them outright (notably in Turkey, Tunisia, and Syria); permitted wives to sue for divorce by having recourse to religious courts, especially in cases of cruelty, desertion, or dangerous contagious disease; provided women with the right to contract themselves in marriage; required husbands to find housing for a divorced wife during her custody over children; increased the minimum marital age of spouses; limited the ability of guardians to contract women in marriage against their wishes; provided opportunities for minor girls wed against their wishes to abrogate their marriage on reaching majority; enhanced the rights of women in regard to child custody; and allowed women to write clauses into marriage contracts limiting their husbands' authority over them, for example, by his ex ante grant to his wife of the right to divorce him.

Assessment. The Qurʾān improved women's status relative to the pre-Islamic period by emphasizing the ontological and spiritual equality of women and men. Although certain social and economic regulations in the scripture seemingly favor men, the social conditions prevailing at the time of the revelation, which seemed to justify such inequality, have lapsed. The Qurʾān itself provides mechanisms for a fresh interpretation of women's roles and status. Reforms begun in the twentieth century in personal status law, achieved through recourse to such instruments and arguments, have gradually moved in the direction of gender equality, but a certain degree of backsliding has occurred as a consequence of the rise of ideologies reinscribing patriarchal control over women's dress, comportment, and desired equity before the law in a platform that includes a sometimes unyielding, even violent, confrontation with the state (itself at times co-opted) and reformist groups.

[*See* HIJAB.]

BIBLIOGRAPHY

ʿAbduh, Muḥammad. "Ḥijāb al-nisāʿ min al-jihah al-dīnīyah." In *Fī qaḍḍāyā al-marʾah*. Beirut, Lebanon, 1988.

Ahmed, Leila. *Women and Gender in Islam: Historical Roots of a Modern Debate*. New Haven, Conn.: Yale University Press, 1992.

Amin, Husayn Ahmad. "ʿAwdah al-nisāʿ ilā al-ḥijāb." In *Ḥawla al-Daʿwah ilā taṭbīq al-sharīʿah al-Islamīyah*. 2d ed., pp. 227–251. Cairo, Egypt: Dar al-Nahdah al-Arabiyyah, 1987.

Barlas, Asma. "Believing Women" in *Islam: Unreading Patriarchal Interpretations of the Qurʾan*. Austin, Tex.: University of Texas Press, 2002.

Beck, Lois, and Nikki R. Keddie, eds. *Women in the Muslim World*. Cambridge, Mass.: Harvard University Press, 1978.

Esposito, John L. with Natana J. DeLong-Bas. *Women in Muslim Family Law*, 2d ed. Syracuse, N.Y.: Syracuse University Press, 2001.

Haddad, Yvonne Yazbeck. "Islam, Women, and Revolution in Twentieth-Century Arab Thought." *Muslim World* 74 (1984): 137–160.

Hambly, Gavin R. G., ed. *Women in the Medieval Islamic World*. New York: Palgrave Macmillan, 1999.

Hoffman-Ladd, Valerie J. "Polemics on the Modesty and Segregation of Women in Contemporary Egypt." *International Journal of Middle East Studies* 19, no. 1 (February 1987): 23–50.

Kandiyoti, Deniz, ed. *Women, Islam, and the State*. Philadelphia: Temple University Press, 1991.

Mernissi, Fatima. *The Forgotten Queens of Islam*. Minneapolis: University of Minnesota Press, 1993.

Moghadam, Valentine M. *Modernizing Women: Gender and Social Change in the Middle East*. Boulder, Colo.: Lynne Rienner, 2003.

Sharīʿatī, ʿAlī. *Fatima Is Fatima*. Translated by Laleh Bakhtiar. Tehran, Iran, 1981.

Sonbol, Amira El Azhary, ed. *Women, the Family, and Divorce Laws in Islamic History*. Syracuse, N.Y.: Syracuse University Press, 1996.

Stern, Gertrude. "The First Women Converts in Early Islam." *Islamic Culture* 13, no. 3 (1939): 290–305.

Stowasser, Barbara. "The Status of Women in Early Islam." In *Muslim Women*, edited by Freda Hussain, pp. 11–43. London: St. Martin's Press, 1984.

Stowasser, Barbara. "Religious Ideology, Women, and the Family: The Islamic Paradigm." In *The Islamic Impulse*, edited by Barbara Freyer Stowasser, pp. 262–296. London: Center for Contemporary Arab, 1987.

Stowasser, Barbara Freyer. *Women in the Qur'an, Traditions, and Interpretation*. New York: Oxford University Press, 1994.

Wadud, Amina. *Qur'an and Woman*. Kuala Lumpur, Malaysia: Penerbit Fajar Bakti Sdn. Bh.d., 1992.

Al-Wāḥidī, ʿAlī ibn Ahmad. *Asbāb al-nuzūl*. Cairo, Egypt: Dar al-Yamamah, 1968.

Zuhur, Sherifa. *Revealing Reveiling: Islamist Gender Ideology in Contemporary Egypt*. Albany, N.Y.: SUNY Press, 1992.

Soraya Altorki
Updated by Zayn Kassam

Women's Religious Observances

Although women and men are assigned the same religious duties and promised the same spiritual rewards in the Qurʾān, social conventions, illiteracy, and Islamic requirements of ritual purity have all tended to restrict women's access to many aspects of Islamic religious life. These restrictions are not uniform across the Muslim world, and neither are women's responses to them. Regional variations in women's religious lives have not been sufficiently documented to make possible a truly balanced description of women's religious observances. Furthermore, social changes in this century have radically altered the situation of women in society, opening new opportunities for women in the religious domain as well.

Women and Basic Islamic Obligations. Women are expected to perform the five daily prayers and the Ramaḍān fast, though they may not pray, fast, or touch (or even, according to some interpretations, recite) the Qurʾān during menstruation or postpartum bleeding. According to *ḥadīth*, the exemption during menstruation denotes women's religious deficiency, just as the devaluation of their legal testimony, worth only half that of a man, denotes their purported mental deficiency. Women are rendered much more susceptible to ritual impurity than men, not only by menstruation and childbirth, but also through their contact with young children, who may soil them. Although not required to fast while pregnant or nursing a baby, many women do observe the fast during these times, either totally or partially. Days of fasting that are missed because of these exemptions must be made up for later.

Although later Muslims would disallow women from serving as prayer leader (*imām*) for men, there is one instance of the Prophet commanding a woman to serve as *imām* for her household. Congregational prayer is said to be twenty-seven times more meritorious than prayer performed alone, and *aḥādīth* from the Prophet enjoin men not to forbid women from praying in the mosque. Still, other *aḥādīth* encourage women to pray in their homes. In the Prophet's day, women performed the dawn prayer in rows behind the men, and, according to *ḥadīth*, left the mosque before the men. Thus, theoretically, all contact between the sexes was avoided. During the caliphate of

ʿUmar ibn al-Khaṭṭāb (r. 634–644), women prayed in a separate room of the mosque with their own *imām*.

Previously women had gathered for social purposes in the mosque as well, but ʿUmar forbade this activity and, according to al-Ghazālī (d. 1111), women were banned from the mosque altogether in the generation after the Prophet. Al-Ghazālī justified this reversal of the Prophet's edict by claiming that widespread moral deterioration made public spaces unsafe for any but elderly women, encouraging women not to leave their homes for any reason.

Ethnographic studies from a number of different Islamic countries indicate that women are commonly regarded a source of temptation in public spaces. The exclusion of women is thus considered necessary to preserve the holiness and dignity of religious ceremonies. For instance, the Friday noon prayer in the mosque is mandatory for men but not for women, and according to Edward Lane, no women or young boys were allowed to be present in the mosque at any time of prayer in different Muslim societies. Although many mosques have segregated spaces for women, whether curtained areas, separate rooms, or balconies, mosques have until recently been considered male spaces to which a proper woman would not go. However, the Islamic resurgence that has swept the Muslim world since the 1970s, enlisting the active involvement of women, has helped change such attitudes. Most recently constructed mosques provide considerably more space for women than earlier ones. However, the actual spatial arrangement of the architecture reinforces women's marginality to life in the mosque, often isolating them in areas where they cannot see or hear the *imām*, or preacher.

Sexual segregation does not necessarily imply that Muslim women have no religious life. In the Ḥaḍramawt region of southeast Yemen, women rarely work outside the home or run errands and must cover their faces in public. Nonetheless, women have religious meetings—Qurʾān lessons, lessons in Islamic law, or Ṣūfī *dhikr*—several evenings per week, and the teachers and leaders at these meetings are always women. In China, there are special women's mosques, and, in Oman, it is customary to build small mosques for women on well-traveled routes.

On the pilgrimage to Mecca, the sexes are not segregated, and Islamic law stipulates that women should not cover their faces during the pilgrimage. This integration of the sexes also occurs during festivities at saints' shrines, indicating that, at the loci of most intense holiness and access to God, one is in a liminal state where gender barriers collapse.

Religious Education for Women. Women have always played a role in the transmission of religious knowledge. The role of ʿĀʾishah, Muḥammad's youngest wife, as a transmitter of *ḥadīth* was so important that Muḥammad is said to have told the Muslims they would receive half their religion from a woman. Muḥammad himself provided religious lessons for women, although later Muslims often complained that education would be used by women for unholy ends. Literacy was a rare achievement for women in later medieval Muslim society. Throughout Islamic history, some daughters of wealthy families have been favored with private education in the home. More often, women were excluded from formal education, although they might serve as patrons or even supervisors of educational institutions. The Ḥanbalī jurist ibn Taymīyah of Syria (d. 1328) listed two women among his teachers, and some female descendants of the Prophet, such as his granddaughter Zaynab and his great-great-great-great-granddaughter Nafīsah, are recognized as women of learning and wisdom as well as piety.

Although girls' schools in subjects such as midwifery, crafts, and housekeeping skills opened in the nineteenth century in many countries, and, since independence, secular education has been made available to girls as well as to boys throughout most of the Islamic world, religious education has lagged behind. Occasionally, women have become recognized as distinguished religious scholars through their writings and academic achievements alone, without attending institutions of higher Islamic education. ʿĀʾishah ʿAbd al-Raḥmān, the Egyptian Qurʾān exegete, and Khānum-i Amīn, the Iranian *mujtahid*, are examples. As part of Egyptian president Nasser's revamping of the Islamic University of al-Azhar, a College for Girls was opened in 1962, and graduates in the field of religion have been employed as teachers in religion classes in public schools. Al-Azhar began a limited program to train women as preachers in 1988. Women are not generally deemed fit to teach men, so it is assumed that these women are being trained only to serve women's religious needs. Nevertheless, two Egyptian women, Suʿad Saleh and Abla al-Kahlawy, have achieved such high levels of learning that al-Azhar has approved them as *muftiyah*s, or scholars authorized to issue *fatāwā* (independent legal opinions). In Iran, religious schools in the holy city of Qom were opened to girls in 1976. However, private education and apprenticeship has produced innumerable women who serve as Qurʾān reciters in both Sunnī and Shīʿī communities, and as leaders of women's gatherings to commemorate the martyrdom of the imams among the Shīʿī. In addition, in the twentieth century, two Iranian women, Noṣrat Amīn and Zohreh Ṣefātī, became recognized as ayatollahs for their scholarly achievements.

Ṣūfī Orders. Mysticism is by definition a sphere that depends more on individual reputation for holiness and receptivity to spiritual impulses than on literacy and institutional certification. It is therefore not surprising that Sufism has been more open to women than have the more legalistic and scholastic dimensions of Islamic religious life. The most famous Ṣūfī woman is Rābiʿa al-ʿAdawīyah (d. 801), credited with introducing the concept of selfless love into Sufism. Her poems of love for God have inspired mystics to the present day, and Ṣūfī tradition depicts her outwitting her male colleagues. She is listed alongside the men in Farīd al-Dīn ʿAṭṭār's (d. 1220) Ṣūfī biographical dictionary, because "when a woman becomes a 'man' in the path of God, she is a man and one cannot any more call her a woman" (ʿAṭṭār, 40). Rābiʿa is not unique in Ṣūfī tradition. Javād Nūrbakhsh has translated into English the brief biographies of some 124 Ṣūfī women, including Fāṭimah of Nishapur (d. 838), who was described by Dhū al-Nūn al-Miṣrī as the highest among the Ṣūfīs of his age. The great mystic Ibn al-ʿArabī (d. 1240) listed two women among his teachers and claimed that the most perfect contemplation of God for a man is in woman.

In spite of its greater hospitality to female participants, Ṣūfī tradition is not uniform in its praise of women. Al-Ghazālī (d. 1111) scarcely spoke of women in the mystical path except as assets or obstacles to the spiritual life of men. Although Muslim tradition recommends marriage, in imitation of the example of the Prophet, the Ṣūfī ʿAlī al-Hujwīrī (d. 1073) held celibacy to be the ideal, declaring that all the evils in the world had been caused by women.

Celibacy and rigorous fasting were practiced by many early Ṣūfīs. In addition to aiding in the training of the soul and spiritual concentration, these may have been tools for women to avoid ritual impurity—refusing marriage and childbirth through celibacy and preventing menstruation by fasting—and thereby aspiring to uninterrupted access to and worship of God.

Ṣūfī *shuyūkh* were the most effective religious teachers in Muslim society and often served as popular counselors and healers, so it is not surprising that they touched the feminine world more than the mosque-centered sphere of religious scholars. Some Ṣūfī *shuyūk* in the Mamlūk and Ottoman periods admitted women into their orders, although their participation in the orders and in *dhikr*, the distinctive Ṣūfī ritual of chanting the names of God with special breath control and movement, was controversial. Women sometimes founded Ṣūfī retreat houses for men as a pious act. Annemarie Schimmel documents an Anatolian woman of the late fourteenth century who was head of a Ṣūfī retreat center with male disciples. A Ṣūfī retreat house for women was established in Cairo in Mamlūk times in honor of a prominent woman Ṣūfī, Zaynab Fāṭimah bint ʿAbbās (late thirteenth–early fourteenth century), and according to Ibn Ḥajar al-ʿAsqalānī, there were women *shuyūk* and scholars of the law, most of them divorcees, who lived in extreme abstinence and worship in Ṣūfī hospices. In contrast to early Sufism, it seems that, in the later medieval period, only women who had already completed their duty of marriage were free to devote themselves to the mystical life.

Ṣūfī men argued about whether women should be allowed to give their oaths to a Ṣūfī master and be included in a line of spiritual transmission. Although some writers argued that it is legitimate, others raised fears regarding the potential for immoral behavior if a woman were allowed to enter into a master–disciple relationship with a male *shaykh*. Accusations of immorality leveled against the Bektashiyya, a popular order in Anatolia, are connected precisely with this concern over the dangers of the mixing of men and women. The founder of the Bektashiyya was the disciple of a woman, and two twentieth-century Moroccan women appear in the spiritual genealogy of the powerful West African order, the Tijaniyya. One of them is known as *al-shaykha 'l-qari'a*, "the Shatterer," for having transcended previous bounds of sainthood.

Moroccan and Algerian orders frequently have women's auxiliaries with female leadership, and, in many countries, women's organizations with female leadership complement those of men. In contemporary Egypt, however, concerns with propriety in the face of reformist criticisms of Sufism have led to the official banning of female membership by the Supreme Council of Ṣūfī Orders, a government-sponsored body. Women nonetheless continue to participate in all aspects of life in many Egyptian Ṣūfī orders. Some women become recognized as "spiritual mothers" to both men and women, or as heirs of the "spiritual secrets" of their fathers who were *shuyūk*. In this latter case, the official position of *shaykh* is inherited by the deceased's eldest son, although actual spiritual leadership may be exercised by the daughter. In some Egyptian orders, women participate in *dhikr* on a par with men, but, in many orders, and in society at large, it is considered improper for a woman to expose herself by rising to join a *dhikr*. Women who do so often shroud their faces, but, more often, women participate silently, sitting among the observers. When women do participate in *dhikr*, they are rarely as vocal as men, and use smaller, more contained movements. This is in marked contrast to Shīʿī commemorative assemblies in Iran, in which the women are said to be more emotionally expressive than the men. Women seem to be caught between competing social norms that say, on the one hand, that they are more emotional than men and, on the other hand, dictate that they suppress all public displays of emotion.

In Egypt, and probably in other places as well, some Ṣūfīs believe that once they have entered into the spirit, they may transcend the barriers of the flesh; "male" and "female" become meaningless categories. Ṣūfīs in such a state may exercise freedom in interpersonal relations between the sexes, a sanction considered shocking to society at large. Ṣūfīs are sometimes criticized as immoral for the way in which men and women mingle at their ceremonies, and women sometimes avoid saints'-day celebrations because of the dangers presented to their modesty by the dense crowds.

Saints and Spirits. Whereas ordinary mosques are usually regarded as male spaces, saints' shrines are traditionally open to women. Saints are men and women who are popularly recognized as *walī*s (friends of God). They are believed to be able to intercede with God on behalf of the faithful, and miracles occur at their hands. After their deaths, their tombs or reputed tombs become shrines and places of refuge for their devotees and other troubled individuals. Because they are, in some sense, champions of the downtrodden, and because the rituals surrounding their cult require no education, women are frequent visitors to their shrines, where they feel themselves able to plead with the saints on a par with men. Fatima Mernissi wrote that saints' shrines in Morocco are more like a social space for women than a religious space where prayers are made, and that male visitors may feel like intruders. This is not the case in Egypt, where shrines are definitely sacred spaces in which it is considered appropriate to pray, and where women are seldom in the majority. Women are indeed very much in evidence—even in the small towns of Upper (southern) Egypt, where women are kept veiled and secluded, they might feel free to sit in the vicinity of the tomb, nursing their babies—but, in some shrines, special rooms are designated for women to prevent them from sitting by the tomb. The country's most important shrine of all, that of the Prophet's grandson Ḥusayn, does not allow women to enter after sunset.

Some shrines cater specifically to women's needs, such as fertility. In India, some Muslim saints' shrines are designated as women's shrines, while others are for men. In Iran and Iraq, Shīʿī women visiting the tombs of the martyred imams acquire a prestige similar to that of those performing the pilgrimage. The great saints'-day festivals (*mawlid*s) that commemorate particular saints, usually on the anniversary of their death, form the major focus of Ṣūfī devotion in Egypt, as Ṣūfīs travel from one such festival to another, setting up hospitality stations and performing *dhikr*. During the *mawlids* of Sayyida Zainab in Cairo or Sayyid Aḥmad al-Badawī in Tanta in the Egyptian Delta or Abu Al Hassan al-Shazli in upper Egypt, the entire floor of the vast mosque associated with the shrine is transformed into a campground inhabited by a crowd of men, women, and children, without any segregation of the sexes. The activities at saints' shrines are a popular target of reformist criticism, and, frequently, the presence of women is deemed inappropriate, both for considerations of modesty and because the Prophet allegedly prohibited women from visiting tombs. The practice of saint-shrine veneration has its defenders, however, who rely on the same type of scriptural sources used by its critics. Regardless of this criticism, the visitation of saints' shrines has formed an essential component of the religious lives of women all over the Muslim world.

Women in many countries participate in spirit possession cults such as the *zār* of North and East Africa and the *bori* of West Africa. These cults are based on the assumption that both physical and emotional illness may be caused by spirits, whose anger must be appeased through the hosting of a feast and the performance of dances peculiar to the spirit in question. They often have both male and female functionaries, and the power and wealth of the "priestesses" may be considerable. Although the cults are non-Islamic in origin, the scripturally endorsed belief in spirits and their effects on humans make Islam a hospitable environment for the introduction and spread of such cults. Public *zār*s in Egypt utilize male musical troupes singing praises to the Prophet in Ṣūfī style, and some of the spirits are those of great

Muslim saints. Women *zār* musicians use a more African beat. Public criticism of the *zār* cult in Egypt has been vociferous enough that even illiterate women are aware of it.

Twentieth-Century Developments. Religious reformers of all types have criticized the saint cult as idolatrous and the spirit cults as un-Islamic. The hue of illegitimacy has been cast over the very aspects of Islamic religious life that have traditionally been most open to women. In *The Emancipation of Women* (1899), the Egyptian judge Qāsim Amīn (d. 1908) urged that women be educated in order to dispel the myths and superstitions they supposedly perpetuate among the young, and the Syrian-born writer Rashīd Riḍā (d. 1935) urged in his journal, *Al-Manār*, that women be integrated into orthodox religious life, as they were in the days of the Prophet. Throughout the twentieth century, independently founded Islamic voluntary associations have assumed the task of providing religious education for women, in addition to offering courses in literacy and crafts. The Muslim Brotherhood, founded in 1928 by Ḥasan al-Bannā in Egypt, had a women's auxiliary, the Muslim Sisters, that never succeeded on the level of its male counterpart. Zaynab al-Ghazālī founded the Muslim Women's Association in 1936 as an Islamic response to the Egyptian Feminist Union. Today there are approximately fourteen thousand Islamic voluntary associations in Egypt, and many of them offer religious classes for women. In addition, many government-operated mosques offer religious lessons to women. In many cases, the teachers are themselves women, although male instructors continue to predominate.

The Islamist movement began among universities in the 1970s and has since swept the entire Muslim world, garnering the support of many women as participants and propagandists. Women in the movement wear Islamic dress, a loose-fitting garment that covers the entire body except the face and hands. Although Islamic dress was an anomaly when it appeared in the early 1970s, by 1980, it became the uniform of the aggressively religious woman. The women who wear this dress are usually well educated, often in the most prestigious university faculties of medicine, engineering, and the sciences, and their dress signifies that, although they pursue an education and career in the public sphere, they are religious, moral women. Whereas other women are frequently harassed in public places, such women are honored and even feared. By the late 1980s, Islamic dress had become the norm for middle-class women who do not want to compromise their reputation by their public activities. Boutiques offer Parisian-style fashions adapted to Islamic modesty standards, thereby subverting somewhat the original intent of the movement.

Despite the high visibility of female participation in the Islamist movement throughout the Muslim world, it espouses a conservative ideology regarding women's social roles, idealizing their importance as mothers and stressing allegedly innate gender differences that make work outside the home unsuitable for women. This rhetoric, both inclusive and exclusionary, may appeal to women who are doubly burdened when they take on jobs outside the home, perhaps out of economic necessity, and feel degraded by their "public" conditions. The Islamic movement also encourages women to struggle on behalf of Islam, as their counterparts did in early Islam. The contradictory rhetoric of the Islamic movement has been particularly effective in Iran, where women have been incorporated into a nationalist movement through symbolic appeals to female purity, while, at the same time, employment and educational opportunities for women have been curtailed since the Revolution and modesty norms have been strictly enforced. Although the rank-and-file of the Islamic movement includes many women, its leadership remains largely male.

Zaynab al-Ghazālī of Egypt and Nadia Yassine of Morocco are among the few women to attain prominence as Islamic activists.

[*See also* Dress; Education and Women, *subentry on* Women's Religious Education; Ghazālī, Zaynab al-; Menstruation; Friday Prayer; Rābiʿah al-ʿAdawīyah; Sainthood; Shrine; *and* Sufism and Women.]

BIBLIOGRAPHY

Abbas, Shemeem Burney. *The Female Voice in Sufi Ritual: Devotional Practices of Pakistan and India.* Austin: University of Texas Press, 2002.

Abbott, Nabia. "Women and the State in Early Islam." *The Journal of Near Eastern Studies* 1 (1942): 106–126.

Antoun, Richard T. "On the Modesty of Women in Arab Muslim Villages: A Study in the Accommodation of Tradition." *American Anthropologist* new series, 70, no. 4 (1968): 671–697.

ʿAṭṭār, Farīḍ al-Dīn. *Muslim Saints and Mystics.* Translated from the Persian by A. J. Arberry. Oxford: Penguin, 1966.

Bellhassen, Souhayr. "Femmes tunisiennes islamistes." *Annuaire de l'Afrique du Nord*, 1979, pp. 77–94. Paris: Centre National de la Recherche Scientifique, 1980.

Berkey, Jonathan P. "Women and Islamic Education in the Mamlūk Period." In *Women in Middle Eastern History: Shifting Boundaries in Sex and Gender*, edited by Nikki R. Keddie and Beth Baron, pp. 143–157. New Haven, Conn., and London: Yale University Press 1991.

Bop, Codou. "Roles and the Position of Women in Sufi Brotherhoods in Senegal." *Journal of the American Academy of Religion* 73, no. 4 (December 2005): 1099–1119.

Clancy-Smith, Julia. "The House of Zainab: Female Authority and Saintly Succession." In *Women in Middle Eastern History: Shifting Boundaries in Sex and Gender*, edited by Nikki R. Keddie and Beth Baron, pp. 254–274. New Haven, Conn., and London: Yale University Press, 1991.

Dwyer, Daisy Hilse. "Women, Sufism, and Decision-Making in Moroccan Islam." In *Women in the Muslim World*, edited by Lois Beck and Nikki R. Keddie, pp. 585–598. Cambridge, Mass.: Harvard University Press, 1978.

Elias, Jamal. "Female and Feminine in Islamic Mysticism." *Muslim World* 78 (1988): 210–211.

Farah, Madelain. *Marriage and Sexuality in Islam: A Translation of al-Ghazālī's Book on the Etiquette of Marriage from the Iḥyāʿ*. Salt Lake City: University of Utah Press, 1984.

Friedl, Erika. "Islam and Tribal Women in a Village in Iran." In *Unspoken Worlds: Women's Religious Lives in Non-Western Cultures*, edited by Nancy E. Auer Falk and Rita M. Gross, pp. 159–173. San Francisco; Harper and Row, 1980.

Gemmeke, Amber B. "Marabout Women in Dakar: Creating Authority in Islamic Knowledge." *Africa: Journal of the International African Institute* 79, no. 1 (2009): 128–147.

Haddad, Yvonne Yazbeck, Jane I. Smith, and Kathleen M. Moore, eds. *Muslim Women in America: The Challenge of Islamic Identity Today.* New York: Oxford University Press, 2006.

Haeri, Shahla. "Obedience vs. Autonomy: Women and Fundamentalism in Iran and Pakistan." In *Fundamentalisms and Society: Reclaiming the Sciences, the Family, and Education*, edited by Martin E. Marty and R. Scott Appleby, pp. 181–213. Chicago: University of Chicago Press, 1993.

Helminski, Camille Adams. *Women of Sufism, A Hidden Treasure: Writings and Stories of Mystic Poets, Scholars and Saints.* Boston and London: Shambhala, 2003.

Hoffman, Valerie J. "Oral Traditions as a Source for the Study of Muslim Women: Women in the Sufi Orders." In *Beyond the Exotic: Women's Histories in Islamic Societies*, edited by Amira El-Azhary Sonbol, pp. 365–380. Syracuse, N.Y.: Syracuse University Press, 2005.

Hoffman-Ladd, Valerie J. "Polemics on the Modesty and Segregation of Women in Contemporary Egypt." *International Journal of Middle East Studies* 19.1 (February 1987): 23–50.

Hoffman, Valerie J. *Sufism, Mystics, and Saints in Modern Egypt.* Columbia: University of South Carolina Press, 1995.

Hujwīrī, ʿAlīibnʿUthmān. *The Kashf al-Maḥjūb: The Oldest Persian Treatise on Sūfiism.* Translated by R. A. Nicholson. 2d ed. London: HardPress Publishing, 1976.

Hutson, Alaine S. "The Development of Women's Authority in the Kano Tijaniyya, 1894–1963." *Africa Today* 46, no. 3–4 (1999): 43–63.

Hutson, Alaine. "We Are Many: Women Sufis and Islamic Scholars in Twentieth Century Kano, Nigeria." Unpublished Ph.D. dissertation, Indiana University, 1997.

Ibn al-ʿArabī. *The Sufis of Andalusia: The "Rūhal-quds" and "al-Durrat al-fākhirah."* Translated by R. W. J. Austin. London: Beshara Publications, 1971.

Jaschok, Maria, and Jingjun Shui. *The History of Women's Mosques in Chinese Islam: A Mosque of Their Own.* Richmond, U.K.: Routledge, 2000.

Lane, Edward. *An Account of the Manners and Customs of the Modern Egyptians.* London: Charles Knight & Co., 1836.

Lewis, I. M. "The Past and Present in Islam: The Case of African 'Survivals.'" *Temenos* 19 (1983): 55–67.

Macleod, Arlene Elowe. *Accommodating Protest: Working Women, the New Veiling, and Change in Cairo.* New York: Columbia University Press, 1991.

Mahmood, Saba. *Politics of Piety: The Islamic Revival and the Feminist Subject.* Princeton, N.J.: Princeton University Press, 2005.

Mernissi, Fatima. "Women, Saints, and Sanctuaries." *Signs: Journal of Women in Society and Culture* 3 (1977): 101–112.

Nelson, Cynthia. "Self, Spirit Possession, and World View: An Illustration from Egypt." *International Journal of Social Psychiatry* 17 (1971): 194–209.

Nūrbakhsh, Javād. *Sufi Women.* New York: Khaniqahi Nimatullahi Publications, 1983.

Raudvere, Catharina. *The Book and the Roses. Sufi Women, Visibility and Zikir in Contemporary Istanbul.* Istanbul: I.B. Tauris, 2003.

Rausch, Margaret. *Bodies, Boundaries and Spirit Possession: Moroccan Women and the Revision of Tradition.* Somerset, N.J.: Transaction Books, 2002.

Rosen, Lawrence. "The Negotiation of Reality: Male-Female Relations in Sefrou, Morocco." In *Women in the Muslim World,* edited by Lois Beck and Nikki R. Keddie, pp. 561–584. Cambridge, Mass.: Harvard University Press, 1978.

Saunders, Lucie Wood. "Variants in Zār Experience in an Egyptian Village." In *Case Studies in Spirit Possession,* edited by Vincent Crapanzano and Vivian Garrison, pp. 177–193. New York: John Wiley & Sons, 1977.

Schimmel, Annemarie. "Women in Mystical Islam." *Women's Studies International Forum* 5 (1982): 148.

Sengers, Gerda. *Women and Demons: Cult Healing in Islamic Egypt.* International Studies in Sociology and Social Anthropology. Leiden, The Netherlands: Brill, 2003.

Sharīʿatī, ʿAlī.*Fatima Is Fatima.* Translated by Laleh-Bakhtiar. Tehran: The Shariah Foundation, 1981.

Smith, Jane I, and Yvonne Yazbeck Haddad. "Women in the Afterlife: The Islamic View as Seen from Qurʿan and Tradition." *Journal of the American Academy of Religion* 43 (1975): 39–50.

Smith, Margaret. *Muslim Women Mystics: The Life and Work of Rabia and Other Women Mystics in Islam.* Oxford: Oneworld, 2001.

Veinstein, Gilles and Nathalie Clayer. "L'Empire ottoman." In *Les Voies d'Allah: Les ordres mystiques dans le monde musulman des origines a aujourd'hui,* edited by Alexandre Popovic and Gilles Veinstein. Paris: Fayard, 1996.

von Schlegell, Barbara. "Sufism and Social Innovation under Women Masters in Damascus." Unpublished paper presented at the Berkshire Conference, Chapel Hill, North Carolina, June 6, 1996.

Winter, Michael. *Society and Religion in Early Ottoman Egypt: Studies in the Writings of ʿAbd al-Wahhāb al-Shaʿrānī.* New Brunswick, N.J.: Transaction Books, 1982.

Zuhur, Sherifa. *Revealing Reveiling: Islamist Gender Ideology in Contemporary Egypt.* Albany, N.Y.: State University of New York Press, 1992.

VALERIE J. HOFFMAN

WOMEN AND SOCIAL PROTEST.

[*This entry includes two subentries:*

Contemporary *and*
Historical]

CONTEMPORARY

Decisions and policies are made every day, whether by individuals or groups, the private sector, or the government. Although these policies are often made jointly and representatively, this doesn't guarantee their automatic acceptance by the public. Policy decisions trigger reactions from the public, either pro or con, and responses can occur in various ways and forms. One of those forms is protest, defined as a statement or action, such as a demonstration, that expresses strong disagreement with or opposition to something. In many Muslim-majority countries today, from Africa to the Middle East to Southeast Asia, as well as non-Muslim majority countries in which Muslims have a significant presence, such as throughout Europe and the United States, women are using protests as a means of challenging patriarchal culture and discrimination on the basis of gender, ethnicity, tribe, and religion, and are fighting for their rights—as Muslims, citizens, and women. Some protests are individual efforts; others are led by organizations or politicians. In every case, the perception of a quest for justice of some sort lies at the heart of activism. These efforts have been either rewarded or punished by the state, society, and even families. In some cases, women have been arrested, jailed, beaten, tortured, sexually abused, shot, and even killed in the act of protesting. In others, they have received both national and international awards, including the Nobel Peace Prize. In many cases, outsiders have also protested either in favor of or against women activists, showing that women and social protest is a multidimensional phenomenon requiring analysis not just of the protesters themselves or the causes they espouse but also of the reactions they provoke and the tangible outcomes of all of these types of protest.

Perhaps some of the most prominent 21st-century social protests led and participated in by women were those of the Arab Spring. In Yemen, for example, the journalist and human rights activist Tawakul Karman earned the nickname "mother of the Arab revolution" for her nonviolent protests against the corruption and authoritarianism of President ʿAlī ʿAbd Allāh Ṣāliḥ's regime, including failure to respect freedom of the press and human rights. Karman's protests ranged from removing her veil, declaring it to be a matter of tradition rather than religion and a barrier to communication with other people, to founding schools geared toward redressing high rates of female illiteracy, to leading weekly protests against a variety of issues, ranging from the political (regime reform or replacement) to the social (opposing child marriage). In some cases, such as by removing her veil, Karman engaged in individual protest to make her point. In other cases, she successfully mobilized increasingly large cross sections of the population to bring pressure on the government. In both instances, she made it clear that she undertook her protests actively identifying as a Muslim woman and asserting through her own example that Muslim women should be active in the process of social change because of their religion, not despite it. Karman illustrates the capacity of the individual to engage in both personal and collective nonviolent protest. Her work has been rewarded both nationally, with the abdication of President Ṣāliḥ, and internationally, through the International Courageous Women Award in 2010 and the Nobel Peace Prize in 2011.

In Germany, Egyptian-born Marwa El-Sherbini became a tragic symbol of religious hatred in July 2009 when she was murdered by her neighbor. Called the "headscarf martyr," El-Sherbini was a pharmacist who proudly wore a hijab as a symbol of her faith, despite name-calling and harassment by her neighbor. When she called the police to intervene and in the midst of the court processing her case, her neighbor stabbed her to death, decrying the presence of Muslim immigrants in Germany. He also shot her husband. El-Sherbini's story received little coverage by the European media, despite clearly having been a documented hate crime. Massive protests against the injustice to El-Sherbini, both by her killing—and the killing of her unborn child (she was three months pregnant)—and by the media, erupted in Egypt and Iran. El-Sherbini represents an individual protesting in favor of something—her right to freedom of religious expression and her right to control her own body and how it is presented to the public—despite harassment. Responses to her death represent collective protest of injustice at the state's failure to protect her freedom of religious expression, as well as her life.

In the case of Saudi Arabia, much media and government attention has been given to the ban on women driving, with outsiders protesting the ban as discrimination against women and failure to respect their human rights and insiders protesting that the ban is based on culture and tradition rather than religion. Yet Saudi women themselves do not necessarily consider driving as the only or even the most important issue at stake. For many Saudi women activists, the bigger picture issue is acquiring access to public space in all of its dimensions. Because political parties and formal organizations are banned in the kingdom, Saudi women, perhaps more than women elsewhere, have had to rely on creative methods of making their point and demanding their rights without upsetting the political equation.

A flashpoint in Saudi women's quest for equal access to public space occurred in 2006, when a team from the King Fahd Institute for Hajj Research, under the approval of Mecca governor Prince Abdul Majeed, unveiled a plan to segregate men and women worshipping at the Grand Mosque, the holiest site in Islam. This move had no historical precedent, as women have always had equal access to the mosque. Nor were women included in the planning committee or even as part of the conversation. Ostensibly, the plan to move women elsewhere was due to purported overcrowding at the Mataf (place where the ritual of *ṭawāf*, or circumambulation of the Kaʿbah, occurs). Such segregation had already been implemented at the Prophet's Mosque in Medina, where visitation by women is limited to a few hours per day, while visitation by men is permitted at any time. Nevertheless, the plan evoked major, vocal protests from Saudi women, in particular, questioning whether men had any greater claim on the Kaʿbah than women and why such an innovation would be introduced, given that there was no historical precedent for such segregation at the Grand Mosque. Led by Hatoon al-Fassi, many Saudi women, as well as international figures, both male and female, quickly and publicly raised their voices in protest, declaring the plan to be discriminatory against women and taking the unusual step of criticizing the move in newspaper articles published in the Saudi press. Although the planning committee continued to insist that the plan would be "better" for women and invited women to allow the committee to explain the plan to them, women nevertheless remained adamant that the plan was discriminatory. This protest, undertaken simply by the raising of voices and public criticism, resulted in the plan being canceled. Addressing the issue by questioning the religious legitimacy of such a move struck a deep chord in Saudi Arabia as it tangentially raised questions about the monarchy's legitimacy, which is supposed to be rooted in its defense of Islam and its holy sites.

Another sphere of protest for Saudi women has to do with the sale of lingerie and makeup. Although the Saudi government passed a law in 2009 requiring that only female salespersons be permitted to sell such items, the government was not able to enforce the law because shopkeepers protested that the measures were impossible to implement, either because there weren't enough trained female salespersons, because women employees weren't reliable, or because no women applied for the jobs because of ongoing social concerns about women in the public sphere. What tipped the balance with respect to enforcement of the legislation was a series of social media and public awareness campaigns by women—some for it and some against it—bringing the matter to public consciousness. In the end, more people believed that having Saudi women purchase undergarments from unrelated male salespersons was a greater violation of Saudi women's dignity and modesty than working in a lingerie store. This case highlights the reality that religion can be used effectively as an argument both for and against women's presence in the public sphere and that women are capable of creative campaigns of protest while remaining within certain socially prescribed roles. It also shows women's capacity to harness new technologies in the service of projecting their message to a broad audience.

Attention to women's rights and access to public space in Saudi Arabia has been one of the hallmarks of the reign of King ʿAbd Allāh. Not only has women's access to educational and professional life been expanded, such as by the scholarship program for study abroad and the opening of certain previously prohibited disciplines such as engineering to women, but the king has also granted women the right to vote, run for office, serve as full members of the Shoura Council, and practice as licensed lawyers. Nevertheless, despite these important achievements, the right to drive remains elusive.

Because Saudi women cannot drive, they remain dependent on a man—whether father, husband, brother, or hired driver—to transport them to school, work, or wherever else they need to go. Having a hired driver who is a non–family member creates a conundrum for Saudi culture—Saudi women are not supposed to be in the presence of a non-*maḥram* man (non-unmarriageable) without a chaperone, yet the ban on women driving leaves women with no choice but to depend on someone else, in many cases a non-*maḥram* hired driver, of whom there are over 800,000 in the kingdom. Because hiring a male driver is expensive and because public transportation remains widely unavailable for the time being (metro projects are being undertaken in most major cities), many women who wish to work outside of the home cannot do so unless they have a male family member able and willing to regularly drive them there. Because of the constraints that inability to drive places on women, women's demand for the right to drive has continuously resurfaced since the initial infamous 1991 event in which Saudi women activists publicly drove in Riyadh, leading to a *fatwā* by then-Grand Mufti ʿAbd al-ʿAzīz bin Bāz, forcefully declaring a ban on women driving. Since then, Saudi women have engaged in a variety of means of protest against the ban, including, most recently, the Women2Drive campaign initiated by Manal al-Sharif, when she posted a video of herself driving in Khobar on YouTube. Al-Sharif said she was inspired to post the video after hearing the story of Bahia al-Mansour, a university student who often failed exams because of the constraints and difficulties of not having a reliable driver and not being able to drive herself. Al-Sharif was initially detained by local police for violating the ban, but was released and has continued to work to bring public attention to the matter, including through campaigns on Facebook and Twitter to raise awareness of the fact that the ban has no basis in the Sharīʿah and that there is no written law forbidding women from driving. Protests against her arrest were held by other women, who participated in collective driving in varying Saudi cities. In many cases, confrontations occurred with local police and the women were escorted home. One woman, Shaima Jastaina, was sentenced to ten lashes for driving, although King ʿAbd Allāh pardoned her.

Another method of protesting the ban on women driving has been for Saudi women to go to departments issuing driver's licenses to apply for them. There is no law prohibiting women from applying for a driver's license, yet the explanation given for al-Sharif's arrest, as well as others', is that they were not driving on a valid Saudi driver's license. Bringing attention to the bureaucratic gap was not only another method of highlighting the lack of an appropriate office but also a challenge to the driving ban. Al-Sharif, like many other Saudi women who have lived and studied abroad, possesses a valid driver's license from another country.

That these methods of protesting the ban have been successful is evidenced by the number of male Saudi citizens raising their voices in support of women's right to drive and the willingness of some Saudi men to ride in a car with a woman driver, even at the risk of being arrested themselves. Perhaps also indicative of the success of the Women2Drive campaign, in particular, was the report by a male Saudi academic to the Shoura Council warning that, if women were given the right to drive, there would be no virgins left in the kingdom within ten years, suggesting that public opinion has swayed in favor of women driving to the point where religious conservatives feel threatened.

In Indonesia, protests have focused on defending the rights of Indonesia's numerous migrant workers who go abroad, often to Gulf countries, to work as domestic help. Saudi Arabia has been particularly notorious for cases of abuse against domestic workers, with a number of cases that have been publicized internationally. In one of the most shocking, in June 2012, Ruyati binti Satubi was beheaded for murdering her employer. No information was provided to the Indonesian embassy, and there remained questions as to whether the killing was a matter of self-defense. This case was particularly shocking as the Indonesian president, Susilo Bambang Yudhoyono, had just given a speech describing six government programs to protect Indonesian migrant workers.

In response to the execution, mass demonstrations broke out in Indonesia, with participants ranging from activists to artists and businesspeople, led by the Ruyati's three daughters. The protests began at the labor department and spread to the state court, with protesters demanding the commitment of the president to guarantee the safety of overseas workers. The public also demanded a thorough investigation into the case. A civil society coalition of nongovernmental organizations and interfaith leaders called for the repatriation of Ruyati's body and raised funds to pay for the cost. Although the funds were raised and one daughter, along with supporters from the coalition, traveled to Saudi Arabia to recover Ruyati's body and property, they were unable to recover either. The Indonesian government responded by establishing a team called Satuan Tugas Tenaga Kerja Indonesia (Task Force for Protection of Indonesian Migrant Workers; Satgas TKI), which aims to protect Indonesian migrant workers from the death penalty abroad by seeking either life imprisonment as an alternative or release. There are currently 212 people under the sentence of death in various countries. In 2011, thirty-seven people were released. Many Indonesians also called for a moratorium on workers going to Saudi Arabia, which has been implemented periodically as ongoing negotiations between the Saudi and Indonesian governments have taken place, securing the rights of migrant workers along the lines of similar arrangements that have been made between the governments of Saudi Arabia and the Philippines.

All of these cases illustrate the capacity of women to spark, lead, and participate in protests, whether individual or communal, making the personal political. The variety of methods and responses highlights women's creative capacity to challenge unjust systems in new and meaningful ways, sometimes achieving change and sometimes raising public consciousness about issues of concern in order to build national consensus. Although such protests necessarily often occur outside of official channels, in many cases they have succeeded in bringing about change through official channels. It is clear that, having harnessed the power of protest, women are likely to continue to seek their rights and press for change at multiple levels of society. Yet the cost of protesting can still remain very high, as the case of Malala Yousafzai starkly reminds us. While traveling home from school in October 2012, she was shot in the head by an extremist claiming affiliation with the Taliban, who oppose girls' education. The Taliban continues to vow to kill her for her outspokenness against their occupation of her hometown and her protesting of their attempts to limit women's movements, particularly by preventing girls from seeking education. Yet Yousafzai has vowed to continue her struggle, exemplifying a quote by Margaret Mead: "Never doubt that a small group of thoughtful, committed citizens can change the world. Indeed, it is the only thing that ever has."

Bibliography

Arivia, Gadis. *Feminisme: Sebuah Kata Hati*. Jakarta, Indonesia: Kompas, 2006.

DeLong-Bas, Natana J. "The Freedoms Saudi Women Really Want." Middle East Institute, October 2009, http://www.mei.edu/content/freedoms-saudi-women-really-want.

International Labour Office. *Domestic Workers in Southeast Asia: A Decent Work Priority*. Jakarta, Indonesia: International Labour Office, 2006. Available online at http://www.ilo.org/wcmsp5/groups/public/---asia/---ro-bangkok/---ilo-jakarta/documents/publication/wcms_122290.pdf.

Rofiah, Nur, and Ala'i Nadjib. *Mari Kenali Hak-Hak Buruh Migran Indonesia: Perspektif Islam dan Perempuan*. Jakarta, Indonesia: PP Fatayat NU, 2010.

Tong, Rosemarie. *Feminist Thought: A More Comprehensive Introduction*. 3d ed. Boulder, Colo.:Westview, 2009.

Yuval-Davis, Nira. *Gender and Nation*. London: SAGE, 1997.

Online Resources

Hauslohner, Abigail. "Tragic Symbol: Egypt's Headscarf Martyr." *Time*, July 12, 2009, http://www.time.com/time/world/article/0,8599,1910030,00.html.

"Indonesia Group Raps Saudi Beheading." PressTV, 29 June 2011, http://www.presstv.ir/detail/186737.html.

MR. "Saudi Salafi Scholars: Women Not Allowed Near the Kaaba." *Mujahideen Ryder* (blog), September 2, 2006, http://www.mujahideenryder.net/2006/09/02/saudi-salafi-scholars-women-not-allowed-near-the-kaaba/.

"Presiden SBY Mempesona di Sidang ILO-Swiss, Sampaikan 6 Program untuk Buruh." *Berita-Terbaru.com* (blog), June 14, 2011, http://www.berita-terbaru.com/uncategorized/presiden-sby-mempesona-di-sidang-ilo-swiss-sampaikan-6-program-untuk-buruh.htm.

"Saudi King Abdullah Talks to Barbara Walters." *20/20*, October 14, 2005. Transcript online at http://abcnews.go.com/2020/International/story?id=1214706.

Vinograd, Cassandra. "Shot Pakistani Girl Malala Recovering as Father Arrives in UK." *Christian Science Monitor*, October 26, 2012, http://www.csmonitor.com/World/Latest-News-Wires/2012/1026/Shot-Pakistani-girl-Malala-recovering-as-father-arrives-in-UK.

VIVAnews. "New Findings in Ruyati Case: Ms. Ruyati Had Not Had Legal Aid from the Government during the Trials in Saudi Arabia." HRWG, October 12, 2011, http://www.hrwg.org/en/hrwg/news/national/item/3303-new-findings-in-ruyati-case-ms-ruyati-had-not-had-legal-aid-from-the-government-during-the-trials-in-saudi-arabia.

Watson, Katy. "Saudi Women Turn to Social Media for the Right to Drive." BBC News, June 27, 2011, http://www.bbc.co.uk/news/business-13928215.

Ala'i Nadjib and Natana J. DeLong-Bas

Historical

In traditional societies, such as that of early Islam, women have little opportunity to protest as individuals. Rather, they resort to their naturally perceived roles as wives, mothers, daughters, or sisters. Despite such limitations, however, women's protests can resound, and powerfully so. There are three women from the family of the Prophet Muḥammad who not only serve as role models in a general sense but also spoke out vigorously and effectively against wrongdoing and injustice during their respective times. They are ʿĀʾishah bint Abū Bakr, who was the Prophet's youngest and favorite wife; Fāṭimah, his daughter and single surviving child, the wife of ʿAlī ibn Abī Ṭālib; and, finally, Zaynab bint ʿAlī, his granddaughter and daughter of Fāṭimah and ʿAlī. In what follows, the narrative traditions about the lives of these three women are examined for the purpose of investigating how their words and actions reveal in general the mentalities of women's social protest in Islamic civilization.

What these narrative traditions actually say will be treated here as historical evidence. But this evidence reveals not necessarily what really happened but rather how people throughout the history of Islamic civilization were thinking about what happened. This thinking was not restricted to the historical context of the three women whose lives were being narrated. Rather, it extended diachronically through the entire history of Islamic thought, all the way to modern times. These three women, as we will see, were "good to think with" throughout the historical vicissitudes of the Islamic world. Their expressions of protest, in both word and action, have become collective prototypes for the full range of women's protest in Islamic civilization (Ruffle, 2010, p. 96; Hann-Kassam, 2002, passim).

ʿĀʾishah. ʿĀʾishah publically challenged two caliphs, ʿUthmān and ʿAlī. Although she was mostly confined to her home, out of the public eye, a confinement she took upon herself willingly in order to remain the Prophet's wife or else be released without blame (see *sūrah* 33:30–35), she managed to have sizable public influence. In her case, the interior life of a woman who is simply living at home was used paradoxically to exteriorize the message of her interiority. This way, conversely, the exterior life of this woman's famous men could in turn be appropriated into the interior space of her home. A case in point is the historical fact that the home of ʿĀʾishah eventually housed not only the body of the Prophet Muḥammad but those of the first two caliphs, Abū Bakr, her father, and ʿUmar, as well.

When the third caliph, ʿUthmān, overreached in his position by practicing egregious nepotism and dabbling in embezzlement of public funds, one of the Prophet's in-laws, ʿAmmār ibn Yāsir, spoke out against ʿUthmān and was consequently flogged within an inch of his life. Outraged by such injustice, ʿĀʾishah brought out from her home some relics of the Prophet—some hair, a shirt, and a sandal, in full view for all to see—exclaiming that the practice (*sunnah*) has been forgotten before these items had ever had a chance to disintegrate. ʿUthmān had no response to this gesture, which clearly incited public outrage, and was forced to take refuge in a mosque. Needless to say, ʿĀʾishah earned a great deal of public respect for her speech act and clever use of relics to shame ʿUthmān publically. She subsequently became a leading figure in the growing opposition movement. Once again we see here the exteriorization of the interior life of women, who are trusted as guardians and even controllers of their men's interior existence.

ʿĀʾishah defended the honest treasurer of Kufa, ʿAbd Allāh ibn Masʿūd, a man who had refused to allow ʿUthmān's cronies to embezzle from the treasury of Kufa. ʿUthmān removed him from power, using the excuse that ʿAbd Allāh ibn Masʿūd was really ʿUthmān's personal treasurer and should do his bidding. But ʿAbd Allāh ibn Masʿūd refused to comply, saying he was treasurer for the Muslim community only. Tensions between the two came to a head when ʿUthmān, while compiling the definitive copy of the Qurʾān, demanded that ʿAbd Allāh ibn Masʿūd relinquish for destruction whatever text he had in his possession, but ʿAbd Allāh ibn Masʿūd refused. Heated words were exchanged in the mosque, and ʿĀʾishah sided with ʿAbd Allāh ibn Masʿūd. ʿUthmān had ʿAbd Allāh ibn Masʿūd thrown out of the mosque with such force that he broke two ribs. ʿĀʾishah was so horrified at the way a companion of the Prophet was treated that she, as the historian Yaʿqūbī wryly states, responded most effectively: "And then ʿĀʾishah spoke and she said plenty" (Yaʿqūbī, in Abbott). When ʿAbd Allāh ibn Masʿūd died, he left orders that in no way should ʿUthmān pray over his body. The authority behind the public rebuke here comes again from the control of the woman over household affairs, which can be metaphorically compared in the public world to the treasurer's control over the affairs of the Muslim community.

ʿĀʾishah later had another chance to rebuke ʿUthmān publically—this time for refusing to admonish his brother, Walīd ibn ʿUqbah, for attempted embezzlement and public drunkenness. In response to the rebuke, ʿUthmān called attention to the status of ʿĀʾishah as Muḥammad's widow, trying to use it against her by saying to her that her place was in her house, far away from the public domain. That gambit opened up a heated, if not violent, debate as to whether ʿĀʾishah in particular and women in general have the right to object publically to wrongdoing. The debate may not have been resolved then—or even now—but Walīd ibn ʿUqbah was deposed and flogged for public drunkenness. Here again the metaphor of the home comes into play, since the act of embezzlement can be seen as a violation of the interior integrity of a household. And such interior integrity can also apply as a metaphorical counterweight to the loss of exterior integrity by way of public drunkenness.

ʿUthmān's ongoing leadership led to more nepotism, more attempts to have his rivals murdered, and a host of other wanton acts. What resulted was a general outcry for his abdication, a cry driven by ʿĀʾishah's remarks about his corruption. Her epigrammatic remarks became epigrams in and of themselves. Still, ʿUthmān refused to abdicate and angered the population so much that they laid siege to his house. Finally cowed, he promised to mend his ways and even to make no further appointments unless he cleared it with the wives of the Prophet and with an agreed-upon counsel. Whether ʿĀʾishah had any influence in this decision of his is unknown, but it is remarkable that the wives of the Prophet could wield such influence on the public from the confines of their houses. Once again, the same metaphor applies: the interiority of good housekeeping becomes the model for the exteriority of sound management for the government in power. Eventually, ʿUthmān's food and water supply was cut off, and he appealed to the wives of the Prophet and to the Prophet's extended family, as well as to his own kinsmen in Mecca and Syria and to his extended family, for aid and supplies. The principle applies: just as charity begins at home, good economics must begin at home, and home is where women manage the housekeeping.

ʿĀʾishah did not respond to the distress call of ʿUthmān, using the excuse that she did not want to be molested and dishonored by the crowds, as some had been, and she subsequently distanced herself completely from the uprising by leaving Medina and going to Mecca for *ḥajj*. The rebels, led by ʿĀʾishah's brother, Muḥammad ibn Abī Bakr, broke into ʿUthmān's house and attacked him while he was reading the Qurʾān. The wife of ʿUthmān, Naʾilah, attempted to protect him with her own hands and lost her fingers in the process. ʿUthmān was killed by a mob, offering no resistance, and the event had its consequences: Muslims shedding Muslim blood. ʿUthmān was buried secretly, and ʿAlī succeeded him as caliph. He did nothing about addressing the regicide or punishing the perpetrators.

ʿAlī's succession was accepted, but with reservations, especially among ʿUthmān's kinsmen, who wanted some sort of redress for his murder. ʿUthmān's blood-soaked shirt with Naʾilah's missing fingers stitched to it became a gruesome banner for rallying an opposition—and calling for revenge.

ʿĀʾishah, upon hearing about ʿUthmān's murder, set out to return to Medina, but once she heard that ʿAlī was accepted as the new caliph, she turned around and went back to Mecca. She claimed that she was outraged that the rabble had murdered the caliph and taken command. She felt that in order to restore order and strengthen Islam, ʿUthmān needed to be avenged. She then went to the Kaʿbah, ceremoniously veiled herself (thus creating an interior space and even a "home" for herself in within a public space), and addressed a crowd of ʿUthmān's kin, among others, giving a public speech in the mode of a lament. She excused all of ʿUthmān's transgressions on the grounds that these were merely things that go along with being a leader. Then she made a case that ʿUthmān had promised to reform. But. she said, "They shed sacred blood, desecrated the sacred city, seized sacred funds, and profaned the sacred month. By 'God, ʿUthmān's fingers are far better than a whole world filled with the likes of them." After telling the crowd to distance themselves from these perpetrators, she said: "By 'God, even if that which they imputed to him [ʿUthmān] were indeed a fault, he has been purged of it as gold is purged of its dross or a garment of its dirt; for they rinsed him in his own blood as a garment is rinsed in water" (Yaʿqūbī, in Abbott). One cannot help but recall the gruesome banner made of ʿUthmān's bloodied shirt with Naʾilah's severed fingers stitched to it. ʿĀʾishah roused the crowd at Mecca, who rallied around her, calling for revenge for ʿUthmān's murder. Her speech exonerated her from any suggestion that she was an opportunist who had spoken out against ʿUthmān on several occasions, because she had cloaked her speech as a lament, calling out genuinely for revenge. And that cloaking was formalized by her wearing a veil.

ʿĀʾishah managed to gain about three thousand followers in her quest to avenge ʿUthmān and set off to Basra to garner more support for her cause. ʿAlī, upon hearing that ʿĀʾishah was advancing with an army in her quest to avenge ʿUthmān, looked to Kufa for support. At the Battle of the Camel, ʿĀʾishah asked her general to lead her camel into the middle of the battle. Her general was killed in the action, and then, from the middle of the battle, in her *howdah* on her camel, she commanded her troops, stirring them up by calling for the avenging of ʿUthmān's death. She acted in true pre-Islamic form, since women would be placed in the middle of battle to encourage their men to protect them and preserve their honor. Many died protecting ʿĀʾishah. ʿAlī commanded that her camel be hamstrung and, as she fell, so did her cause.

Fāṭimah. Fāṭimah, the only surviving child of the Prophet Muḥammad and the wife of ʿAlī, is the paradigm in the Shīʿah tradition of forbearance, humility, and patience. When her father died, she was to inherit the Garden of Fadak, a piece of property given solely to Muḥammad for his personal use. However, Abū Bakr denied her the rights of inheritance, claiming that prophets neither inherit nor pass on inheritance. Anything they owned becomes alms for the poor. Fāṭimah objected, but to no avail. So she went to the mosque and addressed all the women there, first praising everything Islamic, then praising her father in particular and all that he had done for the nascent Muslim community. As the story proceeded, Fāṭimah continued by praising the Qurʾān and the wisdom and justice it contains, in particular its guidance for property inheritance, and then she stated outright that anyone going against the teachings of the Qurʾān is among either the ignorant or the hypocrites. She then got right to the point and stated unequivocally that she was indeed the daughter of the Prophet Muḥammad and had the right to inherit his personal property;

she cited cases within the text of the Qurʾān where prophets inherit and pass on their inheritance to their descendants; and she pointed out that God made no exception for Muḥammad. She finally reminded the gathering crowd that it was their duty to speak out against injustice and act accordingly. In this case, the woman's words of protest were spoken in the mode of a man, not a woman, since legal cases of inheritance cannot be argued by women. (On Fadak, see Ruffle, "May You Learn from Their Model," 2011, pp. 25–27, and Soufi, 1997, pp. 104ff. Soufi also provides full bibliography of all primary sources. See also the extensive article by Veccia Vaglieri, 1965.) Unlike ʿĀʾishah, then, Fāṭimah in this narrative took action that was masculinized by her circumstances.

According to the Shīʿah tradition, Fāṭimah ultimately succeeded in persuading Abū Bakr. However, when he was on his way to give Fāṭimah the deeds to the property, ʿUmar intercepted him and tore up the deeds. At this point, Fāṭimah switched her rhetoric from male to female discourse. She now extended her protest, after being forced out of the public arena, by grieving loudly day and night near the tombs of the fallen, calling to her father and bewailing the injustice that she had to bear. Some men complained to ʿAlī about her wailing in the open, and so ʿAlī built her a house where she could go every day, with her two sons, and complain loudly to her father as she mourned his death. Here we see the male world in the act of confining a protesting woman by putting her in her place, so to speak, back into an interior space that will be her supposedly permanent home.

Zaynab. Zaynab, the daughter of ʿAlī and granddaughter of the Prophet Muḥammad, joined her brother, Ḥusayn, in his cause against the forced acceptance of Muʿāwiyah's son, Yazīd, as the legitimate caliph. She was fifty-five at the time. Ḥusayn's retinue was on its way to Kufa to gather more supporters when they were intercepted and besieged by Yazīd's men. They were outnumbered, being only seventy-three to Yazīd's three thousand men. All the men, with the exception of a young and sickly nephew, ʿAlī Zayn al-ʿĀbidīn, Ḥusayn's son, were killed, and the women were stripped of their veils, humiliated, and abused. When they were paraded as captives in Kufa, Zaynab publically berated the crowd, in a very eloquent speech, for abandoning Husay's cause (full text of the speech in Sipihr, 1978, pp. 281–283). Here, the woman's deprivation of her veil forced her to go public in ways that would have been impossible in normal circumstances. Now that she was forcibly deprived of her veil, which would have been her home away from home, she was able to go public and speak freely like a man, venting her anger and hatred upon her enemies in her protestations.

Weeks later, Zaynab and the remainder of her kin were marched to Damascus and was humiliated for the six-hundred-mile journey as she was paraded, unveiled, from village to village. Once in Damascus, Yazīd insulted her and her nephew, ʿAlī Zayn al-ʿĀbidīn, but both stood up to him. When Yazīd reacted by calling for the execution of ʿAlī Zayn al-ʿĀbidīn, Zaynab protested that he had to kill her first. She then publically berated Yazīd for his ungodly behavior toward the Prophet's family and for his perverse leadership. (Full text of her *khuṭbah* in Yazīd's presence in Sipihr, 1978, pp. 386–389.)

At this point, Yazīd was ready to kill them both, but was prevented by dissent among his courtiers, since they felt great discomfort about his treatment of the prophet's grandchildren. Zaynab and ʿAlī Zayn al-ʿĀbidīn were eventually released and given permission to return to Medina. Before she left Damascus, however, Zaynab led a public mourning, lamenting Ḥusayn's death and those of Ḥasan and ʿAlī, blaming them all on Yazīd, as she painstakingly described the cruelty she and her kinsfolk had to endure (ibid. Sipihr, 1978, pp. 470–471). When leaving Damascus for Medina, she refused to be transported in an elegant litter, preferring one draped in the black flags of mourning. At every stop, she mourned in front of the gathering people and lamented her mistreatment. Once in Medina, she went to where Muḥammad was buried and very publicly mourned and bewailed her mistreatment and the mistreatment of all of Muḥammad's descendants. Her story reached the ears of many. Just as the humiliation of being deprived of her veil was permanent, the new freedom that Zaynab won for herself in the face of this humiliation could now make it possible for her to go public again in ways that would have been impossible in normal circumstances. Her opportunity to protest was made permanent.

Conclusion. In looking briefly at current women's protests in the Islamic world that occur within distinctly Islamic contexts, we can see broad brushstrokes of the historical forces outlined here at work. Most forms of women's protest in Islamic contexts employ the rhetoric of invoking traditional Islamic values in questioning a wide range of wrongs committed by those in power. The protestations tend to target such age-old forms of injustice as violence, sexual degradation, racism, sexism, and hypocrisy. The modes of protest range from traditional gestures of mourning at funerals to impassioned reasoning disseminated in print or electronic media. If the protest is met with attempts at repression, then the moral force of the suffering righteous can be activated, leading to further protest.

One ideal stands out in women's expressions of protest: the need for bravery, which most often takes the form of refusing to skulk away in shame when an injustice is committed against women in particular and humanity in general.

BIBLIOGRAPHY

ʿĀʾISHA BINT ABĪ BAKR

Abbott. Nabia. *Aishah, the Beloved of Mohammed.* Chicago: University of Chicago Press, 1942.

Elias, Jamal J. "The *Ḥadīth* Traditions of ʿĀʾisha as Prototypes of Self-Narrative." *Edebiyât*, n.s., 7 (1997): 215–233.

Geissinger, Aisha. "The Exegetical Traditions of ʿĀʾisha: Notes on Their Impact and Significance." *Journal of Qurʾanic Studies* 6, no. 1 (2004): 1–20.

Spellberg, D. A. *Politics, Gender, and the Islamic Past: The Legacy of ʿAʾisha bint Abi Bakr.* New York: Columbia University Press, 1994.

FĀṬIMĀh

Amīnī, ʿAbd al-ḤusaynAhmad. *Fāṭimah al-zahrā: Umm abīhā*, Tehran: Muʾassasah-e Intishārāt-e Amīr Kabīr, 1984.

Amīnī, Ibrāhīm. *Bānu-ye namūneh-ye islām: Fāṭimah zahrā alayhā al-salām.* Qom, Iran: Intishārāt-e Shafaq, 1970.

Calmard, Jean. "Fāṭema, Daughter of the Prophet Moḥammad." *Encyclopædia Iranica Online*, http://www.iranicaonline.org/articles/fatema.

Clohessy, Christopher Paul. *Fatima, Daughter of Muhammad.* Piscataway, N.J.: Gorgias, 2009. Also available as an e-book. Extensive bibliography of primary and secondary sources.

Gorgi, Monir, and Massoumeh Ebtekar. "The Life and Status of Fatima Zahra: A Woman's Image of Excellence." *Farzaneh* 8 (1997): 1–10. Available online at http://en.farzanehjournal.com/index.php/articles/no-8/44-no-8-2-the-life-and-status-of-fatima-zahra-a-womans-image-of-excellence.

Hann-Kassam, Zaya. "Transcendence and the Body: Fatimah as a Paradigmatic Model." *Feminist Theology* 10 (2002): 77–93.

Ibn al-Shahrāshūb, Muḥammad ibnʿAlī. *Manāqib āl abī ṭālib.* 4 vols. Qom, Iran: al-Matbaʿ al-ʿIlmiyya, 1980.

Kashani-Sabet, Firoozeh. "Who Is Fatima? Gender, Culture, and Representation in Islam." *Journal of Middle East Women's Studies* 1, no. 2 (Spring 2005): 1–24.

Kashefi, Husain Vaʿez. *Rowżat al-shohadāʾ.* Tehran: Kitab Forushi-yeIslamiyya, 1979.

Klemm, Verena. "Image Formation of an Islamic Legend: Fāṭima, the Daughter of the Prophet

Muḥammad." In *Ideas, Images, and Methods of Portrayal: Insights into Classical Arabic Literature and Islam*, edited by Sebastian Günther, pp. 181–208. Leiden, Netherlands: Brill, 2005.

Massignon, Louis. "La mubahala de Médine et l'hyperdulie de Fatima." In *Opera minora*, edited by Y. Moubarac, pp. 550–572. Beirut: Dar al-Maaref, 1963.

Massignon, Louis. "La notion de voeu et la devotion musulmane à Fatima." In *Opera minora*, edited by Y. Moubarac, pp. 573–591. Beirut: Dar al-Maaref, 1963.

Pinault, David. *Horse of Karbala: Muslim Devotional Life in India*. New York: Palgrave, 2001.

Rowe, Ruth E. "Lady of the Women of the Worlds: Exploring Shi'i Piety and Identity through a Consideration of Fatima al-Zahra." M.A. thesis, University of Arizona, 2008.

Ruffle, Karen G. "May Fatimah Gather Our Tears: The Mystical and Intercessory Powers of Fatimah al-Zahra in Indo-Persian Shi'i Literature and Performance." *Comparative Studies of South Asia, Africa and the Middle East* 30, no. 3 (2010): 386–397.

Ruffle, Karen G. "May You Learn from Their Model: The Exemplary Father-Daughter Relationship of Mohammad and Fatima in South Asian Shiism." *Journal of Persianate Studies* 4 (2011): 12–29.

Sered, Susan. "Rachel, Mary, and Fatima." *Cultural Anthropology* 6, no. 2 (May 1991): 131–146.

Shariati, Ali. *Fatima is Fatima*. Tehran: Shariati Foundation, 1981. Available online at: http://www.al-islam.org/fatimaisfatima/. Also translations into French and German.

Soufi, Denise. "The Image of Fatima in Classical Muslim Thought." PhD dissertation, Princeton University, 1997.

Tabarsi, Abu'Ali al-Fadl ibn al-Hasan ibn al-Fadl al-. *Beacons of Light: Muḥammad the prophet and Fāṭimah the radiant; A partial translation of I'lāmu 'l-warā bi a'lāmi 'l-hudā of Abū 'Alī al-Faḍl ibn al-Ḥasan ibn al-Faḍl aṭ-Ṭabrisī (c. 468/1076–548/1154)*. Translated by Mahmoud Ayoub and Lynda G. Clarke. Tehran: World Islamic Services, 1986.

Thurlkill, Mary F. *Chosen among Women: Mary and Fatima in Medieval Christianity and Shi'ite Islam*. Notre Dame, Ind.: University of Notre Dame Press, 2007.

Veccia Vaglieri, L. "Fātima," *Encyclopedia of Islam*, 2d ed., vol. 2. Edited by H. A. R. Gibb, pp. 841–850. Leiden, Netherlands: E. J. Brill, 1965.

ZAYNAB

Chelkowski, Peter, J., ed. *Ta'ziyeh: Ritual and Drama in Iran*. New York: New York University Press, 1979.

Pelly, Lewis, comp. *The Miracle Play of Hasan and Husain*. Revised by Arthur N. Wollaston. London: W. H. Allen, 1879.

Pinault, David. "Zaynab bint 'Ali and the Place of the Women of the Household of the First Imams in Shi'ite Devotional Literature." In *Women in the Medieval Islamic World: Power, Patronage, and Piety*. Edited by Gavin R. G. Hambly, pp. 69–98. New York: St. Martin's, 1998.

Sipihr, 'Abbās Qulī. *Al-Ṭaraz al-madhhab fi aḥwāl sidatnā Ziynab ālihā al-sal'am*. Vol. 9 of *Nāsikh al-tawārīkh*. Edited by Muḥammad-Bāqir Bihbūdī. Tehran: Kitābfurūshī-e Islāmīyah, 1978. Very long and detailed. Crucial.

MEDIEVAL PERIOD

Ahmed, Leila. "Early Islam and the Position of Women: The Problem of Interpretation." In *Women in Middle Eastern History: Shifting Boundaries in Sex and Gender*, edited by Nikki R. Keddie and Beth Baron, pp. 58–73. New Haven, Conn.: Yale University Press, 1991.

Ahmed, Leila. *Women and Gender Islam: Historical Roots of a Modern Debate*. New Haven, Conn.: Yale University Press, 1992.

Keddie, Nikki R. "Problems in the Study of Middle Eastern Women." *International Journal of Middle East Studies* 10 (1979): 225–240.

Malti-Douglas, Fedwa. *Woman's Body, Woman's Word: Gender and Discourse in Arabo-Islamic Writing*. Princeton, N.J.: Princeton University Press, 1991.

Meisami, Julie Scott. "Writing Medieval Women: Representations and Misrepresentations." In *Writing and Representation in Medieval Islam: Muslim Horizons*, edited by Julia Bray, pp. 47–87. Abingdon, U.K.: Routledge, 2006.

Ruffle, Karen G. *Gender, Sainthood, and Everyday Practice in South Asian Shi'ism*. Chapel Hill: University of North Carolina Press, 2011.

Stuard, Susan Mosher, ed. *Women in Medieval History and Historiography*. Philadelphia: University of Pennsylvania Press, 1987.

Waines, David. "Through a Veil Darkly: The Study of Women in Muslim Societies." *Comparative Studies in Society and History* 24 (1982): 642–659.

OLGA DAVIDSON

WOMEN AND SOCIAL REFORM. [*This entry includes five subentries*:

An Overview
Middle East
North Africa
South Asia *and*
Southeast Asia.]

AN OVERVIEW

Social reform in Muslim countries has been a long struggle that has entailed different political, economic, and cultural factors and has witnessed progress and regression since the early twentieth century. The years since 1980 have witnessed the intensification of economic and political crises in the Middle East region. The change from state-led development to privatization has contributed to severe economic crises manifested in the spread of poverty and large-scale unemployment, especially among the young men and women of the working and middle classes. The Islamist opposition movements, for one, hold a traditional vision on the division of labor between men and women and a family-centered imagination; yet their rising influence was a result of their strategy to use these economic situations to underline the failures of the nation-state and to represent themselves as reformers offering solutions. When these Islamist political movements achieved electoral gains, their successes provoked violent political reactions from many states, leading to the weakening of both forces. The political outcomes of the struggles between the state and its Islamist opponents since 1990 have increasingly underlined the authoritarian character of nation-states, which continue to monopolize political power, eroding their national basis of legitimacy as they govern societies characterized by glaring inequalities between classes, genders, and ethnic groups.

Economic and Political Crises and the Reform of Gender Inequalities. During the 1990s, as economic crises in the Middle East intensified, privatization decreased the state's role in the provision of vital social services including education, health, and, most importantly, employment. According to the 2002 Arab Human Development Report, one of the significant results of this structural adjustment process was the regional feminization of poverty and unemployment, exacerbating gender inequality. In Egypt and Bahrain, for example, female unemployment was three times as high as that of men, and in Morocco, Syria, Jordan, and Oman, it was twice as high (Moghadam, 2004). In response, Islamist oppositional groups and many of the nation-states in the region encouraged women to return home. This strategy was not feasible for female-headed households, whose large numbers were documented in Egypt, Lebanon, Yemen, and the West Bank and Gaza, and for working-class families whose women had increased their participation in the informal sector of the economy.

In a region where women's literacy more than doubled between 1970 and 1985, women still represented two-thirds of the illiterate population. Since 1985, total state expenditures on education in Arab states progressively declined, with serious consequences for the rate of working-class girls who had to drop out of school to assist with housework as their mothers entered the work force.

In the face of these acute crises, the Islamists have attempted to respond to the grievances of groups who have been excluded in the new privatized economies. They were rewarded by electoral and political gains in Tunisia and Egypt (in the late 1980s) and Algeria (in the early 1990s), leading these states to move against them—representing them as "terrorists" who posed a security threat to the political stability of these societies and continued modernization. Both sides targeted women, used the traditional roles of women to score political points against each other, and provoked different responses from women.

Egypt. In Egypt, the state and the national/secular political elites accused the Islamists of undermining the long history of Egyptian nationalist modernization/enlightenment by emphasizing a return to traditionalism, represented by the emphasis they placed on women's adherence to the Islamic mode of dress. Nawāl al-Saʿdāwī, the well-known feminist, offered a one-sided position with regard to hijab, describing the Muslim women's head cover adopted by many women as a sign of lack of full use of their reasoning abilities. Others represented women's embrace of Islamism typified by the Islamic mode of dress as undermining the nationalist discourse on the liberation of women, developed by early male reformers like Qāsim Amīn, with its emphasis on education and participation in public life. They argued that the discussion of women's roles in society was a civil matter, not a religious one. Finally, they offered the familiar argument that the liberation of Arab women is inseparable from the liberation of Arab men and the liberation of society itself. This assertion pointed out the nationalization of the concerns of women by putting them in the service of the broader social and political project of the modern state.

In response, the Islamists accused the state and its elites of sacrificing the Islamic character of society in the name of modernization, without being able to meet the developmental needs of the unemployed younger generations of men and women and the underdeveloped southern region of the country. Some Islamist women concurred with this analysis; they described their decision to embrace the Islamist project as a means of grounding the construction of daily life in Islamic principles and developing an Islamic sensibility that is more concrete and less abstract. Prominent Islamist women, theorizing on the importance of contemporary Islamism as an alternative to Western feminism, offered revisionist views of Egyptian women's history. Zaynab al-Ghazālī charged early Egyptian feminists with contributing to the alienation of Muslim women from the religion that provided them with a dignified status and important role models. Nationalists turned their backs on Islamic tradition, while Islamist women sought to extract more balanced interpretations of Islam's support of women's rights. Similarly, Heba Raouf Ezzat rejected feminism as a Western import that showed limited appreciation for the important roles that Muslim women played in the family. Her critique focused on how feminism promised women individual liberty in exchange for a weakened family unit, thus depriving women of an important source of social protection and support.

Tunisia. In Tunisia, the Islamists used the economic crisis to attract the support of young men and women with limited social mobility. In addition to their economic critique of state policies, the Islamists represented the free mixing of men and women in universities, Western modes of dress, and the violation of religious rules as the "manifestations of moral delinquency." The government of Zayn al-ʿĀbidīn bin ʿAlī and its Islamist opponents quickly focused on the Personal Status Law, the centerpiece of the national modernizing project, in their attempts to subvert each other's political discourses. The Islamists saw it as a deviation from Islamic tradition, and the state saw it as part of the National Pact by which political parties needed to abide.

In response, the Islamists' called their new political party al-Nahḍah, (the Renaissance), appropriating the key concept of Arab modernity to describe their political project. Bin ʿAlī responded by posing a national challenge to the Islamists in the form of a new National Pact: "Nothing justifies the creation of a group as long as it has not defined the type of society that it commends, clarified its position towards a certain number of civilizational issues and committed itself to respect the equality of rights and duties of citizens, men and women as well as the principles of tolerance and of the liberty of conscience." Also in the pact, the state emphasized Tunisia's "Arabo-Islamic identity," protecting itself against Islamist critics and appropriating a key source of their appeal.

Tunisian women were split in their support of these different political forces and their gender agendas. The official Union of Tunisian Women and relatively independent women's groups supported the state as the defender of the rights of women. In contrast, Islamist women used the Islamic mode of dress to fight sexism in the public arena, criticize their families' practice of religion, and develop support networks. With the elimination of the Islamist threat, the state tightened its control of the gender agenda and emerging feminist groups, but it also began an undeclared campaign of discrimination against Islamist women. They were warned to give up their mode of dress if they wanted to keep their jobs, and those who worked for the state and resisted faced termination of their employment.

Algeria. The confrontation between the state and its Islamist opponents was the most bloody in Algeria—it resulted in a prolonged civil war that claimed the lives of many men and women. Consequently, the pitch of the polemical exchanges between Islamists and nationalists was unparalleled in the region. Because some of the nationalists and feminists had internalized the French cultural frame of reference, they addressed themselves largely to French and Western audiences. For example, Khalida Messaoudi wrote, "The hijab is like a yellow star for women, the first step towards their physical elimination." Similarly, Rachid Mimouni suggested, "A women to an Islamist is like a Jew to a Nazi." This minority view clearly addressed a Western audience that privileged the Holocaust as an example of genocidal oppression that had great currency in the West. It said nothing about what Algerian women who took on the Islamic mode of dress thought and what the Islamic system of representation meant to them.

The views of Algerian Islamist women were not very different from those expressed by Tunisians and Egyptians. Some saw the hijab as providing them with equality before God, greater public freedom, a basis for bodily integrity in crowded social facilities, and greater individuality. Algerian women researchers also pointed out that there were few differences between the aspirations of Islamist and non-Islamist women for education, work, and public participation.

Iran and Turkey. The non-Arab cases of Iran's Islamic republic and Turkey's secular republic offer contrasting perspectives on the possibilities of reform under Islamist governments. Since 1990, women and young people in Iran were able to use the republican principles of their religious government to back the election of President Moḥammad Khātamī as the representative of a reformist segment of the clerical establishment. As part of this reformist trend, many women were elected to parliament, and, upon his election, Khātamī expressed his gratitude to women as a constituency by appointing a woman vice president. The new opening encouraged the emergence of a new alliance between feminist and Islamist women that pushed for gender agendas that supported more rights for women within and outside the family. Equally important, in women's publications and within some segments of the clerical establishment, debates began about how the creation of the Islamic republic pressured the clerics of the religion to develop interpretations that were friendly to women, to rebut Western claims that Islam was unfair to women and/or inhospitable to their rights.

The conservative clerical establishment in Iran was successful in blocking the efforts of the reformists in parliament and disqualifying their candidates in the elections of 2004; this led to the election of the conservative Mahmoud Ahmadinejad. His government reinstated the restrictive social environment and the strict surveillance of women in an effort to distract from the economic and political failures of the new regime.

The history of the secular republic in Turkey, whose commitment to nationalist modernization and attempt to join the European Union, which entails conforming to specific human rights requirements, made it a regional role model for women-friendly policies, revealing a new kind of openness. It has responded to the rise of Islamism and its spread among women in surprisingly repressive ways. Using the commitment to secularism as a stick, the republican state passed administrative laws in the late 1980s that discriminated against religious women who wore headscarves, by denying them the right to education, work, and political participation. The result was the familiar split observed in many Arab states, between women who supported the nationalist discourses on modernization and those who embraced Islamism. Interestingly, despite the important role that women played in the election of Islamist political parties, once they were elected, the steps they took to reverse the discriminatory laws that prevented their women supporters from exercising their rights of citizenship were minimal. This showed the extent to which Islamist governments were similar to secularist governments in subordinating women's interests to general political interests, especially in their relations with their nationalist and Kemalist counterparts. The priority was given to demonstrating to the secularist political establishment and its public their willingness to operate within the set secular rules.

September 11 and Gender Discourses. The events of 11 September 2001 have injected international issues into the debate about the future of Muslim women and their societies. It imported the "clash of civilization" thesis to characterize the struggle between the West (and its secular state allies in the region) and Islam/Islamism as a new source of global conflict. The neoconservative theorists of the war on terrorism borrowed, without the benefit of critical analysis, the perspectives of the Middle Eastern states on Islamism to characterize al-Qaʿida as a security threat that could be eliminated through the use of force to overthrow the Taliban regime in Afghanistan and that of Saddam Hussein in Iraq in order to improve the prospects of democratization of Islamic societies and to improve women's rights. United States intervention in Afghanistan and Iraq has not improved the conditions of women. The war exacerbated the sectarian and ethnic divisions among the Shīʿī, the Sunnīs, and the Kurds and created a new space for conservative religious discourse on the rights of women. The war has also increased the burdens of women in taking care of their families. In addition, it gave al-Qaʿida a regional stage from which it could attempt to strengthen the Islamists as defenders of Islamic lands against the new crusaders.

The Arab Spring and the Role of Women. Nevertheless, despite all of these attempts to marginalize women in the public sphere and to manipulate the images of women to promote various agendas, women were key players in the protests of the Arab Spring that led to the fall of many regimes since 2010. In Tunisia, Egypt, and Yemen, women's presence cannot be overlooked, and women's hopes were high that a new political context would empower women. Women in Tunisia are present in the ruling Nahda Party and the deputy of the constitutional assembly is a woman. Yet the unexpected rise of Salafism is a source of concern, and the gap between women in different political parties has not yet been bridged. In Egypt, the marginalization of women's issues in parties' political agendas as well as the new draft of the constitution, violation of female activists' bodies by the military through virginity tests and the "blue bra" case of stripping a female demonstrator, and rising sexual harassment on the streets keep the horizons unclear for women's equal citizenship. In Yemen, women still face poverty and the shadows of war, and the Libyan scene with its rising tribalism is still unclear regarding future social reform. Severe economic instability carries more challenges for poor women, as well as working women, and the fact that Islamists are now in power might prove to be an obstacle to further development of a social agenda of legal reform that supports women's empowerment.

[*See also* Algeria; Egypt; Feminism; Iran; Tunisia; Turkey; *and* Women and Social Reform, *subentries on* North Africa *and* Middle East.]

BIBLIOGRAPHY

Asfour, Gaber. "Kalimāt amin ʿam al-majlis al-ʿala lil thaqafa," in *Maʾat ʿam ʿala taḥrir al-marʿat*, pp. 13–14. Cairo, 2001.

Beck, Lois, and Guity Nashat, eds. *Women in Iran from 1800 to the Islamic Republic*. Urbana: University of Illinois Press, 2004.

Brand, Laurie. *Women, the State, and Political Liberalization: Middle Eastern and North African Experiences*. New York: Columbia University Press, 1998.

Burgat, François. *Face to Face with Political Islam*. London: I. B. Tauris, 2003.

Ezzat, Heba Raouf. "Secularism, the State, and the Social Bond: The Withering Away of the Family." In *Islam and Secularism in the Middle East*, edited by Azzam Tamimi and John Esposito, pp. 124–138. New York: New York University Press, 2000.

Fernea, Elizabeth Warnock, ed. *Women and the Family in the Middle East: New Voices of Change*. Austin: University of Texas Press, 1985.

Hatem, Mervat F. "Discourses on the 'War on Terrorism' in the U.S. and its Views of the Arab, Muslim, and Gendered 'Other.'" *Arab Studies Journal* 11/12 (2003–2004): 77–103.

Hatem, Mervat F. "Egyptian Discourses on Gender and Political Liberalization: Do the Secularist and the Islamist Views Really Differ?" *Middle East Journal* 48 (Autumn 1994): 661–676.

Hatem, Mervat F. "Liberalization, Gender, and the State." In *Political Liberalization and Democratization in the Arab World*, vol. 1, *Theoretical Perspectives*, edited by Rex Brynen, Bahgat Korany, and Paul Nobel, pp. 187–208. Boulder, Colo.: Lynne Rienner, 1995.

Ismail, Salwa. *Rethinking Islamist Politics: Culture, the State, and Islamism*. London: I. B. Tauris, 2003.

Kassem, Maye. *Egyptian Politics: The Dynamics of Authoritarian Rule*. Boulder, Colo.: Lynne Rienner, 2004.

Kavakçı, Merve. "Questioning Turkey's Role Model Status: A Critical Examination of the Social and Political Implications of the Headscarf Ban in Turkey." PhD dissertation, Howard University, 2007.

Kian-Thiébaut, Azadeh. "Political and Social Transformations in Post-Islamist Iran." *Middle East Report* 212 (Fall 1999): 12–16.

Korany, Bahgat, and Rabab El-Mahdi. *Arab Spring in Egypt: Revolution and Beyond*. Cairo: American University in Cairo Press, 2012.

Mahmood, Saba. *The Politics of Piety: The Islamic Revival and the Feminist Subject*. Princeton, N.J.: Princeton University Press, 2005.

Mir-Hosseini, Ziba. "Fatemeh Haqiqatjoo and the Sixth Majles: A Woman in Her Own Right." *Middle East Report* 233 (Winter 2004): 38–39.

Moghadam, Valentine. "Population Growth, Urbanization, and the Challenges of Unemployment." In *Understanding the Contemporary Middle East*, edited by Deborah J. Gerner and Jillian Schwedler, pp. 273–298. 2d ed. Boulder, Colo.: Lynne Rienner, 2004.

Saadawi, Nawal El. *The Hidden Face of Eve: Women in the Arab World*. Translated by Sherif Hetata. London: Zed, 1980.

Shukrallah, Salma. "10,000 Egyptian Women March Against Military Violence and Rule." *Jadaliyya*, December 20, 2011. http://www.jadaliyya.com/pages/index/3671/10000-egyptian-women-march-against-military-violen.

Solh, Camillia el-. *Women and Poverty in the ESCWA Region: Issues and Concerns*. New York: United Nations, 1995.

Soueif, Ahdaf. Cairo: *My City, Our Revolution*. London: Bloomsbury, 2012.

United Nations Development Programme and Arab Fund for Economic and Social Development. *Arab Human Development Report 2002: Creating Opportunities for Future Generations*. New York: United Nations Publications, 2002.

United Nations Economic and Social Commission for Western Asia. *Maseh lil tatwurat al-iqtisadiyah wa al-ijtimaʿa fi manṭiqat al-ISKWA*. New York: United Nations, 1996.

United Nations Office at Vienna, Centre for Social Development and Humanitarian Affairs. *World Survey on the Role of Women in Development, 1989*. New York: United Nations, 1990.

MERVAT HATEM
Updated by HEBA RAOUF EZZAT

MIDDLE EAST

The general inability of the modern Middle Eastern nation-state to fulfill promises of political and economic development, alongside a widespread perception of deteriorating public morality, have rekindled the historical conflict between the political and religious orders—between a Muslim state (presumably modeled after the original Islamic order) and a modern secular state, or between nationalism and utopian Islamic universalism (based on the concept of the *ummah*). The historical disputes over the legitimacy of the political order and the identity of an Islamic state became an apparently irreconcilable political and ideological conflict, exemplified by the Iranian Islamic Revolution of 1979, the spread of Islamist movements in the 1980s, and the Algerian civil conflict of the 1990s. The dual crises of legitimacy and identity underscore the fiercely competing religious and secular political discourses ("reformists," "modernists," "traditionalists," and "Islamists") vying for power, political constituencies, and, ultimately, the ethical direction of society. Since the 1980s, the continuing friction between the state and religious institutions has rendered social reform all the more contentious, especially in the domain of women and the family. The 2011 political revolutions in Tunisia and Egypt renewed questions about the capacity of Islamist parties, which won elections there and in Morocco, to bring about social reforms that are inclusive of the rights of women and of religious and ethnic minorities. This essay briefly sketches some patterns of family-law reform and the status of Middle Eastern women in that context.

Contours of Family Law: Marriage, Divorce, Child Custody, and Guardianship. In Islam, marriage (*nikāḥ*) is an exchange contract (*ʿaqd*) between unequal partners, involving a complex set of marital rights and reciprocal obligations. On the basis of the controversial Qurʾānic verse 4:3, traditional Islamic law gives Muslim men the right to marry up to four wives simultaneously. Shīʿī men may further contract an unlimited number of temporary marriages (*mutʿah*, or *sīgheh* in Farsi), legitimated in their view by the Qurʾān (4:24; following the second caliph's ban on temporary marriage in the seventh century, Sunnīs reject this practice). The legal possibility of polygyny and *mutʿah* is an element of insecurity for women in Islamic marriage. As a result, some legislatures in the Middle East and North Africa adopted reforms to regularize Islamic marriage and divorce and provide for women's security. In other cases, governments strengthened conservative provisions that benefit male kin.

For example, conditions not contrary to the essence of Muslim marriage (e.g., that the husband divorce a former wife) may be added to the marriage contract to safeguard the rights of the wife. Child marriage, a problem endemic to many Muslim societies, has been discouraged by raising the minimum age for marriage for both boys and girls. Generally it stands at eighteen for boys, but for girls it varies from fifteen to eighteen. In contrast, the Islamic Republic of Iran abolished the Iranian Family Protection Law of 1975, reverting to the Shīʿī minimum marriage age of fifteen for boys and nine for girls (New Civil Law, clause 1041). In all cases, the age restrictions may be waived at the discretion of a judge.

"Of all things permissible, divorce [*ṭalāq*] is the most reprehensible," states a saying popularly attributed to the Prophet Muhammad (Ḥadīth 2173). Nonetheless, Islamic law grants the unilateral right of divorce to the husband (Qurʾān 2:226–237; 65:1). In attempting legal reforms, many Middle Eastern states preserved unchallenged the right of the man to repudiate his wife, while allowing greater latitude for women seeking divorce in cases of cruelty, failure of the man to provide for his wife, and abandonment.

A divorce may take several forms; the most common is the revocable divorce. A revocable (*rajʿī*; literally "returnable") divorce is semifinal: the bonds of marriage are not completely severed. Although the husband and wife may separate physically, he has the unilateral right to return to his wife during the three months of her waiting period and to resume his marital rights and duties. The wife's consent is not sought or required, and she cannot remarry within the same period. Parallel to his right of return, she has the right to financial support. Islamic law grants a repentant husband the right to return to his wife and revoke the divorce twice, but, after the third divorce, he can no longer do so, for this last divorce becomes irrevocable (Qurʾān 2:229). Traditionally, Sunnī *Sharīʿah* permitted the single pronouncement of a triple "I divorce you," but in states such as Egypt, Syria, and Kuwait, such triple divorce became null and was counted as only one (Nasir, 1990, p. 76). Shīʿī law prohibits the triple pronouncement of repudiation altogether (Anderson, 1971).

An irrevocable (*bāʾin*) divorce occurs when the dissolution of marriage is final from the moment of pronouncement. In this form of divorce, the husband's right to return and the wife's right to maintenance are both curtailed, but only the woman has to maintain three months' sexual abstinence.

On specific grounds (e.g., absence of maintenance), Muslim women can apply for divorce, recognized as divorce of *khulʿ* (Qurʾān 2:229). A fundamental difference, however, exists between *khulʿ* and *ṭalāq* (divorce). Divorce is a unilateral (*īqā*) act in which the wife's consent is not necessary, whereas *khulʿ* is a contract to which the husband must agree. Under this provision, however, women are obliged to forgo their bride-price (*mahr*) and the three months' alimony.

Potentially, the most threatening issues facing a married Muslim woman are a unilateral and capricious divorce and an absence of alimony beyond the three months' waiting period (*ʿiddah*) following divorce. Islamic law and norms consider that women are sufficiently compensated by the *mahr*, although the deferred bride-price can be forfeited if the wife is deemed to have been at fault in the divorce. In some countries, some efforts to compensate divorced women were made. For example, under the heading of "compensation for repudiation," Kuwaiti law states that, in the case of a wife's arbitrary divorce, she is entitled to an amount "not in excess of a year's maintenance" above her three months' *ʿiddah* period. However, she is not entitled to any provision if the divorce is on the basis of the husband's insolvency or the wife's injurious behavior or her consent, or if the divorce is initiated by the wife.

Under the principle of guardianship, men have the responsibility of protecting their female kin and maintaining their wives and children. This guardianship also gives men rights to child custody after divorce. In the case of small children, the mothers are allowed to keep them until the ages of seven, nine, or eleven (depending on the country and legal interpretation in place), when they are returned to their father. In the latter half of the twentieth century, Middle Eastern reformers made minimal and conditional provisions for women's maintenance after divorce, while leaving the wrenching issue of custody of children—religiously and legally a father's prerogative—generally unchanged.

Family Law Reform in Historical Perspective. The codification of personal status matters and family law reform is associated with larger processes of state building, modernization, or political reforms. In general, the pace of legal and political reforms accelerated in the 1950s, 1960s, and 1970s, when most states in the Middle East and North Africa were at their reformist peak. The changes were aimed at loosening the political, economic, and moral hold that the religious establishment had for centuries enjoyed over the domestic domain. The success of the legal reforms and of their implementation was not uniform. Depending on their sociopolitical strength, economic resources, and relationship with the clergy or kin structures, states pursued different strategies (Charrad, 2001; Nasir, 1990, pp. 119–136).

The Ottoman Law of Family Rights of 1917 set in motion the earliest legal reform in a Muslim society, restricting the male privileges of plural marriage and divorce by permitting women to seek justice. The law, however, did not limit the husband's right to repudiate his wives without cause (Kandiyoti, 1991, p. 11; White, 1978, p. 56). In 1926, as part of the Kemalist revolution, the state adopted the Turkish Civil Code, severing all links with the *Sharīʿah*. It banned polygyny and gave marriage partners equal rights to divorce and child custody. At about the same time, Egypt enacted a series of personal laws (1920–1929) that raised the marriage age for both girls and boys, prohibited marriage without the couple's consent, and restricted divorce by giving women the right to divorce on specified grounds (Coulson and Hinchcliffe, 1978, p. 49). Social reforms under President Gamal Abdel Nasser did not, however, eliminate polygamy or men's privileges in divorce.

In 1951, Jordan reformed the Law of Family Rights (amended in 1976), restricting polygamy and divorce and giving women the right to divorce on certain grounds. A "fair" alimony was provided for the wife if a judge determined that she had been divorced arbitrarily. Syria enacted the Law of Personal Status in 1953 (amended in 1975), adding a right to financial support for a divorced wife of up to three years after arbitrary divorce. The law restricted, but did not ban, polygyny and unilateral divorce.

In late 1967, Iran introduced the Family Protection Law, revised in 1975. It restricted polygyny and divorce and was the only case of reform to accord the wife an equal right to the custody of children. It also made provision for alimony for either partner, to be determined on the basis of income. The Family Protection Law was abolished after the 1979 Islamic Revolution, and Islamic precepts were reinstated, with no restriction on polygyny or temporary marriage and minimal conditional limitation on arbitrary and unilateral divorce.

In Iraq, the Baʿth party amended the Personal Status Law in 1978 (adopted in 1959, and amended in 1963), an emendation that, though limited in its objectives, aimed at reducing the control of the husband in plural marriages and unilateral divorce. A husband's desire for a second marriage had to be approved by a judge.

Lebanese ethnic heterogeneity prompted the state to delegate family matters, divorce, and marriage to the control of each specific religious establishment. Consequently, the Lebanese state did not legislate a national family code, but issued some sixteen separate codes for eighteen religious sects.

Between the 1950s and 1970s, the most progressive family laws or personal status codes were to be found in Tunisia (adopted in 1956) and in the People's Democratic Republic of Yemen (adopted in 1967). While the former was based on a liberal interpretation of the Sharīʿah, while also drawing on Western (especially French) norms of the time, the latter drew heavily on the laws and norms of the socialist world.

During this period, Saudi Arabia, North Yemen, and the Gulf states—Bahrain, Kuwait, the United Arab Emirates, Oman, and Qatar—were a case apart, as they held deeply conservative views on women's status in the family and their social participation. Saudi Arabia particularly resisted change and strictly enforces its version of Islamic law. Morocco, too, instituted a very conservative family law—the Moudawana of 1957—after independence, in contrast to developments in neighboring Tunisia and Algeria.

The overall objective of codification or reforms in traditional Islamic family law was to accommodate Muslim women within a religiously and culturally relevant context. As such, Middle Eastern states (apart from Turkey) incorporated aspects of the different jurisprudential schools of Islamic law in all the changes made in family law. For example, they tended to restrict the husband's right to plural marriages by making it conditional on the wife's consent or the court's permission. This confronted Muslim women with an unenviable choice: either give their consent or sue for divorce.

For the most part, states initiated family law reforms in the 1950s and 1960s timidly, only to come under strong criticism from Islamists beginning in the late 1970s and throughout the 1980s. Taking a literal approach to the Sharīʿah, Islamists believe its laws to be divine, unchanging, and fundamental to maintaining a distinctly Islamic way of life. They view family legal reform as deviating from Islamic law and as inspired by the West.

The conflict over the proper Islamic approach to the role and status of women in the family and in the public domain became especially intense in the 1980s and 1990s, with Islamist movements largely succeeding in forcing states to retreat from earlier social reforms. This occurred most dramatically in Iran, but also in Egypt and in Yemen after the 1990 unification. At the same time, Middle Eastern women—particularly those who had gained access to education and employment and desired more participation and rights—began to mobilize in opposition to state concessions to Islamist pressures. Thus, in contrast with the earlier period of social reform in the Middle East, the impetus for the most recent wave of reform has come largely from women's organizations, which began to proliferate in the 1990s.

Women's Movements and Family Law Reforms in the Twenty-First Century. In the 1980s and 1990s, heavy pressure from increasingly vocal Islamists forced many states to reconsider family reforms, to Islamize their rhetoric, or to reformulate them within an Islamic framework. The Islamists, unlike the "traditionalists," are not exclusively against women's social participation, provided that their public roles are legitimated within an Islamic framework and that women uphold Islamic identity by observing Islamic conduct and veiling. Still, they have opposed liberalization of family laws, and this has galvanized women's rights activism on two fronts. On one, women with religious convictions are questioning historical patriarchal assumptions and practices; they are returning to the Qurʾān and giving it their own emancipatory and egalitarian interpretation (see writings by Leila Ahmed, Aziza al-Hibri, Margot Badran, Asma Barlas, Fatima Mernissi, Amina Wadud) in what some have called Islamic feminism. On the other front, women's rights organizations, comprising politically aware secular feminists, draw on international standards and norms and on culturally appropriate discourses to demand improvements in the legal status and social positions of women. The global women's rights agenda, crafted and promoted by the United Nations, has been especially important in legitimizing Middle Eastern women's struggles for equal rights in the family and in public domains.

Egypt's personal status laws were amended by presidential decree in June 1979 and came to be known as "Jihan's Law" for the wife of then-president Anwar el-Sadat. Because of pressure from Islamists, the decree was declared unconstitutional in May 1985, but was legally adopted by the People's Assembly in July of the same year, albeit with some changes. It left unchanged the right of the husband to divorce and to marry more than one wife, and removed a wife's automatic right to a divorce if her husband took another wife, but divorce now had to be mediated by the court, registered, and witnessed, and the wife promptly and officially informed. The 1985 law provided for maintenance for as long as the divorced mother nursed or cared for the small children, but removed her right to dwell in the unrented home (An-Naim, 2002, p. 170). The age range for which the mother has automatic custody of children was raised to ten and twelve (from seven and nine) for boys and girls, respectively. In the years following enactment of this law, Egyptian feminists worked to introduce a marriage contract that would stipulate the rights of the wife, including the right to a *khul'* divorce. They succeeded in doing so in 2000.

In December 2001, the Jordanian Cabinet approved several amendments to the Civil Status Law. The legal age for marriage was raised from fifteen for women and sixteen for men to eighteen for both, and Jordanian women were given legal recourse to divorce. New restrictions on polygyny required a man to inform his first wife of plans to marry again and to submit evidence of his financial ability to support more than one wife. Interpretation of guardianship to justify the so-called honor killing of a female family member deemed sexually transgressive was challenged, and women's rights activists successfully pushed for reform of the penal code to criminalize this extreme form of family violence.

In North Africa, women's rights and feminist organizations formed the Collectif 95 Maghreb Egalité, which was the major organizer behind the Muslim Women's Parliament at the NGO Forum that preceded the UN's Fourth World Conference on Women in Beijing in September 1995. The Collectif formulated an alternative "egalitarian family code" and promoted women's political participation. Moroccan women's groups launched a campaign to obtain one million signatures for family law reform, and in 1998 they received the support of the new government. The plan to reform the Mudawana came under attack by conservative Islamic forces, but victory came in October 2003, after a royal commission recommended reform and the new king issued a decree supporting reform. In January 2004, the parliament adopted Morocco's new family law, which is far more egalitarian in spirit and letter. While it does not ban polygyny, it makes it extremely difficult for a man to take an additional wife and establishes the principle of divorce by mutual consent. Moreover, the law gives the wife self-guardianship and confers on the wife, as well as the husband, responsibility for the family. Newly formed family courts will adjudicate issues of matrimonial property division and child custody following divorce.

In the Islamic Republic of Iran, an opposition trend in social reform may be observed. The abrogation of the 1975 Family Protection Act was followed by conservative legislation on women, men, and the family, along with compulsory veiling. But the patriarchal agenda of the Islamic Republic was resisted by segments of the society, while changes in the characteristics of the female population—notably higher education levels, delayed marriage, fewer children, and various forms of social participation—resulted in women's activism for change in the family laws. The

One Million Signatures Campaign, modeled after the successful campaign in Morocco in the 1990s, was launched in 2006; it entailed both a petition drive and social-awareness raising. The authorities responded by accusing the women's rights activists of undermining national security, harassing and arresting activists, confiscating computers, and forcing others into exile. In 2008, the Ahmadinejad government introduced a controversial Family Protection Bill that imposed taxation of the *mahr*, removed the requirement to register temporary marriages, and eliminated the need for a husband to prove financial solvency or ask his wife's permission before marrying another woman. This was too outrageous even for Ahmadinejad's supporters in parliament and their female constituencies, and it was rescinded. But, in 2012, two other measures were introduced: a quota placing a cap on female enrollments in universities in a number of fields of study; and a reversal of the family planning policy in favor of higher fertility (Roudi, 2012).

Calls for family law reform in some countries seek to eliminate gender injustices such as child marriages, male privileges in divorce, and the absence of a concept of matrimonial property. In other cases, reform is needed to close the gap between outdated laws subordinating women to husbands or male kin and the new social realities of educated, active, and empowered women. But social reform that challenges religious precepts and moves closer to gender equality continues to be contested by conservative forces, as seen in the Middle East and North Africa in 2011–2012. In post-Qadhdhāfī Libya, the new interim leader declared that polygamy would be restored. In Turkey, the president created a firestorm when he declared his intention to ban abortion. And, in the new Tunisia, controversy arose when members of the Islamist-dominated constituent assembly announced their intent to replace the word "equality," referring to men and women, with "complimentarity" or "partnership." The years ahead will reveal the extent to which the Arab Spring has contributed to social reform that is inclusive of women and women's rights.

[*See also* Family Law, Marriage, Divorce, Muʿtah, *and* Polygyny.]

BIBLIOGRAPHY

Ahmed, Leila. *Women and Gender in Islam: Historical Roots of a Modern Debate*. New Haven, Conn.: Yale University Press, 1992.

Anderson, J. N. D. "The Role of Personal Statutes in Social Development in Islamic Countries." *Comparative Studies in Society and History* 13, no. 1 (1971): 16–31.

An-Na'im, Abdullahi A., ed. *Islamic Family Law in a Changing World: A Global Resource Book*. London: Zed, 2002.

Charrad, Mounira M. *States and Women's Rights: The Making of Postcolonial Tunisia, Algeria, and Morocco*. Berkeley: University of California Press, 2001.

Collectif 95 Maghreb Egalité. *Guide to Equality in the Family in the Maghreb*. Bethesda, Md.: Women's Learning Partnership Translation Series, 2005.

Coulson, Noel J., and Doreen Hinchcliffe. "Women and Law Reform in Contemporary Islam." In *Women in the Muslim World*, edited by Lois Beck and Nikki Keddie, pp. 37–51. Cambridge, Mass.: Harvard University Press, 1978.

Haeri, Shahla. *Law of Desire: Temporary Marriage in Shi'i Iran*. Syracuse, N.Y.: Syracuse University Press, 1989.

Hinchcliffe, Doreen. "The Iranian Family Protection Act." *International and Comparative Law Quarterly* 17, no. 2 (1968): 516–521.

Hussein, Aziza. "Recent Amendments to Egypt's Personal Status Law." In *Women and the Family in the Middle East: New Voices of Change*, edited by Elizabeth Warnock Fernea, pp. 229–232. Austin: University of Texas Press, 1985.

Joseph, Suad, ed. *Gender and Citizenship in the Middle East*. Syracuse, N.Y.: Syracuse University Press, 2000.

Kandiyoti, Deniz, ed. *Women, Islam, and the State*. Philadelphia: Temple University Press, 1991.

Mernissi, Fatima. *The Veil and the Male Elite: A Feminist Interpretation of Women's Rights in Islam.* Translated by Mary Jo Lakeland. Reading, Mass.: Addison-Wesley, 1991.

Moghadam, Valentine M. *Modernizing Women: Gender and Social Change in the Middle East.* 2d ed. Boulder, Colo.: Lynne Rienner, 2003.

Moghadam, Valentine M., and Elham Gheytanchi. "Political Opportunities and Strategic Choices: Comparing Feminist Campaigns in Morocco and Iran." *Mobilization* 15, no. 3 (September 2010): 267–288.

Nasir, Jamal J. *The Status of Women under Islamic Law and Under Modern Islamic Legislation.* London: Graham & Trotman, 1990.

Roudi, Farzaneh. *Iran Is Reversing Its Population Policy.* Viewpoints 7. Washington, D.C.: Woodrow Wilson Center, Middle East Program, 2012.

Shehadeh, Lamia. "The Legal Status of Married Women in Lebanon." *International Journal of Middle East Studies* 30, no. 4 (1998): 501–519.

Wadud, Amina. *Qur'an and Woman: Rereading the Sacred Text from a Woman's Perspective.* 2d ed. New York: Oxford University Press, 1999.

White, E. H. "Legal Reforms as an Indicator of Women's Status in Muslim Nations." In *Women in the Muslim World,* edited by Lois Beck and Nikki Keddie, pp. 52–68. Cambridge, Mass.: Harvard University Press, 1978.

SHAHLA HAERI
Updated by VALENTINE M. MOGHADAM

NORTH AFRICA

North African women have participated in social change efforts for decades. They were involved in anticolonial movements and postindependence reforms. Mobilization efforts have increased considerably since the 1990s and during the Arab Spring, as women-led organizations strive to uphold women's human rights.

Colonial Period. While the French controlled Algeria (1830–1962), Tunisia (1881–1956), and Morocco (1912–1956), few reforms were directed at the status of women. Instead, traditional female roles were often stressed as symbols of cultural authenticity. Early nationalist groups in all three countries favored reform, although education for women had limited support. Just as significant for postindependence reform was the participation of women in all three anticolonial struggles. Their activities in Algeria's 1954–1962 war of independence have been best documented. Nearly eleven thousand women participated, and 20 percent were jailed or killed. Although revolutionaries deferred the process of changing female roles until after independence (or later), women's wartime heroism remains an important symbol of their potential.

Postindependence Period. After independence (Morocco, 1956; Tunisia, 1956; and Algeria, 1962), each country laid out its own path to social reform, including the establishment of a constitution, legal codes, and government agencies to promote change. In order to build viable national political constituencies and to reconcile the competing interests of Islam and nationalism, however, reforms concerning women were limited. Nonetheless, Tunisian women received the vote in 1957, Algerian women in 1962, and Moroccan women in 1963.

Maghribī Women in the Twenty-First Century. Advocates of social reform for Maghribī women include conservatives and liberals, secularists and scripturalists. Their reform agendas may be quite different, however.

Social and economic changes. Significant changes have occurred since independence, with important consequences for women's status and rights. The average age at first marriage has risen, and more women are staying single or not marrying at all. The percentage of never-married women ages thirty-five to thirty-nine stands at 17 percent, 12 percent, and 15 percent for Algeria, Morocco, and Tunisia, respectively, a drastic change since independence, and an indicator of the reality of different family forms.

Fertility rates have declined substantively, and all three countries are below 2.5 births per woman.

The shift from larger to smaller families has been the most drastic in Morocco, decreasing from 7.2 in 1968 to 2.5 in 2008. However, youth under the age of fifteen represent close to 30 percent of the population in Algeria and Morocco and 24 percent in Tunisia.

School enrollment rates for women are another area with considerable change. While few attended school before independence, in 2010–2011 the primary school completion rate for girls was 82 percent in Morocco, 96 percent in Algeria, and 92 percent in Tunisia (World Bank, 2012). Yet in all countries, the quality of education, school dropout rates, and the gender gap remain problems. The increased number of individuals receiving formal education does not translate directly into higher rates of employment and pay. Having paid employment often can increase women's leverage within the family and in society at large, although there remain many instances of husbands commandeering the wife's salary, women being pressured to register property in their husband's name, harassment of working women by their families, and husbands being pressured to divorce working wives. In 2011, the percentage of women over fifteen in the labor force was 26.2 in Morocco, 15.0 in Algeria, and 25.5 in Algeria (World Bank, 2012).

Legal Status of Women. Morocco, Algeria, and Tunisia are parties to the major United Nations human rights conventions, including the Convention on the Elimination of all Forms of Discrimination against Women (Morocco, 1993; Algeria, 1996; and Tunisia, 1985). In response to advocacy by local women's rights groups and United Nations recommendations, Algeria (2009) and Morocco (2011) withdrew their reservations on the compatibility of the convention's definition of gender equality with Islamic Sharīʿah.

Despite adhesion to UN conventions and Constitutional guarantees of equality, North African women still suffer from de jure and de facto discrimination. While formal equality for all citizens is explicitly proclaimed in all three constitutions, declaring Islam as the official religion provides decision makers with an opt-out concerning women's rights.

In all three countries, marriage, divorce, child custody and guardianship, and property matters are governed by family, or "personal status" laws. While other legislation is based on secular, European-style civil codes (contracts, torts, criminal matters, and commerce), family laws are based on the Mālikī school of Sunnī Islam. This religious exceptionalism created by national laws—the Moroccan Family Code as reformed in 2004, the Algerian Family Code as amended in 2005, and the 1956 Tunisian Personal Status Code—impacts women's status.

A royal commission initiated Moroccan Family Law reforms, building on decades of advocacy by women's groups. The new law raised women's age of marriageability from fifteen to eighteen; eliminated the husband's status as "head of household"; placed polygamy, repudiation, and underage marriage under judicial control; made the *walī*—a bride's male marital tutor—optional; and introduced divorce by mutual consent or for irreconcilable differences. Algerian Family Code amendments issued by presidential decree in 2005 were far less extensive—a *walī* is still mandatory for brides, and verbal marriages without a written contract are still legal. Both Moroccan and Algerian reforms allowed spouses to include a property contract agreeing on management, ownership, and division of assets acquired during the marriage.

Despite these reforms, Moroccan and Algerian women still have limited access to divorce; polygamy remains legal; and women have fewer rights than their husbands when it comes to child custody and guardianship.

The 1956 Tunisian Personal Status Law prohibits polygamy, eliminates the *walī*, only recognizes judicial divorce (granted equally to men and women), and outlaws repudiation. It allows adoption, grants legal guardianship of children to the mother upon the father's death, establishes the legal age of marriage as eighteen for girls and boys, and establishes paternity testing for abandoned children. A 1998 law instituted an optional community property regime for spouses.

In all three countries, women are not guaranteed access to adequate housing during marriage or upon divorce; alimony is not generally awarded upon divorce; and women's unpaid household work is rarely taken into account when dividing marital property. Further, social norms can limit or deny women's freedoms to study or work or to control their own sexual and reproductive health, as well as their freedom from violence. None of the countries have legislation governing violence against women. Reforms of women's rights in the three countries have frequently been imposed from the top down and used for political expediency, rather than accompanied by awareness-raising campaigns to inform the population and mobilize support, which is necessary to ensure the reforms' acceptance and application.

In addition, reforms have not been accompanied by government measures to monitor and control their implementation. Monitoring reports by women's rights nongovernmental organizations (NGOs) in all three countries describe how even laws that are positive on the face of it are not enforced by officials charged with applying them. Authorities themselves are often unaware of the laws, hostile to women's rights, or influenced by corruption. These circumstances help explain the fragility of these legislative gains.

Reform Processes and the Role of local NGOs. Several obstacles have limited widespread women's participation in reform processes—illiteracy, top-down state hierarchies, traditional attitudes towards women, and beliefs that family laws are sacred and untouchable. Despite this, beginning in the mid-1980s and increasing significantly since the late 1990s, hundreds of local associations promoting women's rights have proliferated, notably in Morocco and Algeria. These groups provide a variety of services including popular legal rights education, legal advice, and representation. Increased support by the international community for women's rights as a strategy for economic development, democratization, and the fight against terrorism has also contributed to the development of women's advocacy organizations.

However, women are often faced with a triple struggle: against sexist traditions, extremist religious groups, and state repression. To combat these, activists and academics use varied arguments to promote women's rights, including those based on international human rights, examples of progressive family laws from other Muslim countries, national constitutional equality guarantees, interpretations of Islam by women that are positive for women's rights, sociological imperatives based on family harmony, and arguments based on economic development and modernization. One example is through scholarship like *The Veil and the Male Elite* (Mernissi, *Veil and the Male Elite*, 1991), in which Fatima Mernissi identifies the misogyny behind certain *ḥadīths* traditionally used to support male privilege and finds evidence for early Islam's egalitarianism.

In Tunisia, the Ben Ali regime had severely repressed independent local NGOs, especially those working on human rights issues. Since the Tunisian Revolution of January 14, 2011, which ended the twenty-four-year regime, autonomous local associations working on women's rights have been created across the country.

The Rise of Islamism and the Arab Spring. The economic, social, and political power of Islamist groups, of which there are several varieties, has grown considerably since 1990 and more recently as a result of the 2011 elections in Tunisia and

Morocco. Women join Islamist groups for various reasons: they provide basic social services to communities and individuals; they promote a roadmap of religiously based values and a sense of identity and legitimacy; they offer women an opportunity to mobilize as part of a social and political movement; and they link national efforts with Islamists in other countries, thus contributing to a sense of a larger global movement.

In all three countries, an increasing number of Maghribī women, including educated professionals, are electing to wear the hijab. This modern-day version of the Muslim veil leaves the face uncovered and is worn with an ample gown or a loose tunic and slacks. Women adopt the hijab for many complex reasons, not necessarily to acquiesce to male power. Although it is perceived by most Westerners as a symbol of female oppression, for many Maghribī women wearing the hijab represents a commitment to Islamic authenticity and has also taken on contemporary functions. The hijab meets the need for an overt expression of Islamic religious and cultural identity, while accommodating women's expanded public presence within an Islamic framework. The veil ensures its wearer her private space (including freedom from male harassment), whatever the context.

For women wearing the hijab, the societal rewards are twofold. First, through their overt statement of virtue and commitment to Islam, they gain the respect and consideration of traditional men. Second, the initiative taken by these women, deliberately choosing to wear the veil, is empowering for many, creating a strong self-image and providing unimpeded physical mobility in public space. While for some the veil represents a retrograde mechanism of female oppression, for others it is psychologically liberating and facilitates access to a professional life. Paradoxically, then, the hijab, advocated by the Islamists, has the potential for being a liberating device while strengthening constraints traditionally imposed on Maghribī women.

The three countries have had to address the issue of what political space to allow for political parties based on religion. The Arab Spring has brought this issue to the forefront, with demands for democratization manifested in the ousting of Tunisian president Ben Ali, and in ongoing protests in Algeria and in Morocco since early 2011. Active in protests and lobbying as in past movements, women activists have also expanded their reach through the widespread use of social media such as Facebook and Twitter.

The status of women and family relations is central to the larger power struggle for authority and legitimacy between extremists and the state, due to the religious basis of the family and personal status codes. The major point of contention is who has the power to interpret and promote their vision of Islam as concerns women's rights.

The new Moroccan constitution, approved by referendum in July 2011, guarantees equal civil, political, economic, social, cultural, and environmental rights for men and women (article 19), providing fresh opportunities for advocating for women's rights, although the reaffirmation of Islam as the official religion still provides an opt-out.

Elections in Morocco and Tunisia in the fall of 2011 brought a large group of Islamists into the governments. In the Tunisian Constituent Assembly, 37 percent of seats went to the previously outlawed Islamist Ennahdha Party, and in Moroccan national elections 27 percent of seats in the House of Representatives went to the Justice and Development Party (PJD), the only legal Islamist party. While a 50 percent quota for women was set for candidates for the Tunisian elections, women only won 49 out of 217 seats on the Constituent Assembly, 42 from Ennahdha. The forty-one-member cabinet includes only three women. While a Moroccan national list reserved sixty seats in the House of Representatives for women, only seven others were elected to the Parliament through the local lists. The PJD-led coalition government has eleven PJD cabinet members, including the only woman minister—of Solidarity, Women, Family, and Social Development. Thus in 2010–2011, women held 16.9 percent of parliamentary seats in Morocco, 7.7 percent in Algeria, and 22.6 percent in Tunisia. By comparison, women then held 16.8 percent of the 435 seats in the U.S. House of Representatives.

In Algeria, a proposed bill to establish a quota for women in the 2012 legislative elections generated controversy. The version eventually adopted rejected the original one-third quota for women proposed by the president, and instead created a variable rate of women candidates by electoral district.

Conclusion. Women's advocacy related to their rights represents a historic moment for gender reform in the early twenty-first century. Women's full participation in society is necessary in order for there to be truly democratic processes in the Maghrib. While women's activism has increased greatly, international observers as well as local activists also express concern about the future of women's rights in the post–Arab Spring context with the visible presence of Salafi movements in the public and political sphere.

BIBLIOGRAPHY

Family Codes

Algerian Family Code French version: http://www.joradp.dz/TRV/FFam.pdf, accessed January 22, 2012. Arabic version: http://www.joradp.dz/TRV/AFam.pdf.

Moroccan Family Code (Mudawana)

Complete Arabic version: http://www.justice.gov.ma/ar/droits/droits.aspx?_iddt=1, accessed January 22, 2012.

Complete French version: http://www.sgg.gov.ma/textes_codes_pdf/code_fam_fr.pdf, accessed March 11, 2013.

English translation: http://www.hrea.org/moudawana.html, accessed 22 January 2012.

Tunisian Personal Status Code

French version: http://www.jurisitetunisie.com/tunisie/codes/csp/Csp1040.htm, accessed 22 January 2012. French version is also available at http://www.e-justice.tn/fileadmin/fichiers_site_francais/codes_juridiques/Statut_personel_Fr.pdf.

Arabic version: http://www.e-justice.tn/fileadmin/fichiers_site_arabe/codes_juridiques/code_statut_personel_ar_01_12_2009.pdf.

Secondary Sources

Abderrazak, Moulay R'chid. *La femme et la loi au Maroc*. Casablanca, Morocco: Editions le Fennec, 1991. Focuses on legislation in Morocco as it pertains to men's and women's roles, status, rights, and duties.

Abouzeid, Leila. *Year of the Elephant: A Moroccan Woman's Journey Toward Independence, and Other Stories*. Translated by Barbara Parmenter. Austin: University of Texas Press, 1989. Semibiographical account of women's roles in the Moroccan independence struggle.

An-Na'im, Abdullahi A., ed. *Islamic Family Law in a Changing World: A Global Resource Book*. London: Zed, 2002.

Assaad, Ragui, and Farzaneh Roudi-Fahimi. *Youth in the Middle East and North Africa: Demographic Opportunity or Challenge?* Washington, D.C.: Population Reference Bureau, 2005. Available online at http://www.prb.org/Publications/PolicyBriefs/YouthinMENA.aspx.

Badran, Margot. "Between Secular and Islamic Feminism/s: Reflections on the Middle East and Beyond." *Journal of Middle East Women's Studies* 1, no. 1 (2005): 6–28. Discusses how Islamic and secular feminisms differ and how they intersect, with extensive bibliography.

Belarbi, Aïcha, ed. *Femmes et Islam*. Casablanca, Morocco: Editions Fennec, 1998. A volume of the Fennec Approches series on women, this focuses mainly on Morocco with discussions of women, legal reform, and fundamentalism in French and Arabic.

Bodman, Herbert L., and Nayereh Tohidi, eds. *Women in Muslim Societies: Diversity within Unity*. Boulder, Colo.: Lynne Rienner, 1998.

Bordat, Stephanie Willman, and Saida Kouzzi. "The Challenge of Implementing Morocco's New Personal Status Law." *Arab Reform Bulletin* 2, no. 8. (2004): 8–9. An initial assessment of the challenges to local NGOs and the government in applying the Moroccan Family Code just after its promulgation.

Bordat, Stephanie Willman, and Saida Kouzzi. "The Maghreb: Algeria, Morocco, and Tunisia." In *Africa: A Practical Guide for Global Health Workers*, edited by Laurel A. Spielberg and Lisa V. Adams, pp. 91–121. Hanover, N.H.: Dartmouth College Press, 2011. Description of women's rights, legal status, and NGO activism in the three countries of the Maghrib.

Bordat, Stephanie Willman, Susan Schaefer Davis, and Saida Kouzzi. "Women as Agents of Grassroots Change: Illustrating Micro-Empowerment in Morocco." *Journal of Middle Eastern Women's Studies* 7, no. 1 (2011): 90–119. Women and reform at the grassroots, case-study level.

Bourqia, R., M. Charrad, and N. Gallagher, eds. *Femmes, culture, et société au Maghreb*. 2 vols. Casablanca, Morocco: Afrique Orient, 1996.

Brand, Laurie A. *Women, the State, and Political Liberalization: Middle Eastern and North African Experiences*. New York: Columbia University Press, 1998.

Chamari, Alya Chérif. *La femme et la loi en Tunisie*. Casablanca, Morocco: Éditions le Fennec 1991. Focuses on legislation in Tunisia as it pertains to men's and women's roles, status, rights, and duties.

Charrad, Mounira M. "State and Gender in the Maghreb." *Middle East Report* 163 (1990): 19–24. Summarizes women's conditions and analyzes the reasons each Maghribī state has dealt differently with changes related to gender.

Charrad, Mounira M. *States and Women's Rights: The Making of Postcolonial Tunisia, Algeria, and Morocco*. Berkeley: University of California Press, 2001.

Cuno, Kenneth M., and Manisha Desai, eds. *Family, Gender, and Law in a Globalizing Middle East and South Asia*. Syracuse, N.Y.: Syracuse University Press, 2009. Only one article on North Africa, good on changing the *mudawwana*, but the collection provides a useful geographic overview from colonial times to the twenty-first century of the complex interaction of women's agency, political mobilization, and collective action to claim rights.

Daoud, Zakya. *Féminisme et politique au Maghreb: Soixante ans de lutte*. Paris: Maisonneuve & Larose, 1993. Exhaustive examination of three stages of feminism in all three countries, by a respected local journalist and author.

Eisenberg, Ann M. "Law on the Books vs. Law in Action: Under-Enforcement of Morocco's Reformed 2004 Family Law, the *Moudawana*." *Cornell International Law Journal* 44, no. 3 (2011): 693–728. Available online at http://scholarship.law.cornell.edu/cllsrp/1. Provides hard-to-find data on the underenforcement of the 2004 Moroccan Mudawana.

Esposito, John L., with Natana J. DeLong-Bas. *Women in Muslim Family Law*. 2d ed. Syracuse, N.Y.: Syracuse University Press, 2001.

Fanon, Frantz. *A Dying Colonialism*. New York: Grove, 1965. Contains lucid descriptions of the psychological importance of female veiling and traditional behavior in the maintenance of cultural authenticity.

Gaunt, Marilyn, dir. *A Veiled Revolution*. London: Royal Anthropological Institute, 1982. Videocassette (VHS), 25 minutes. While not new, this film beautifully illustrates multiple attitudes about wearing the veil in interviews with Egyptian women, replacing stereotypes with insight.

Haddad, Yvonne Yazbeck, and Ellison Banks Findly, eds. *Women, Religion, and Social Change*. Albany: State University of New York Press, 1985. See especially the introduction, "Islam, Women, and Twentieth-Century Arab Thought," and Haddad's discussion of how women are influenced by, and can influence, religion to accomplish social change.

Ilkkaracan, Pınar, ed. *Women and Sexuality in Muslim Societies*. Istanbul, Turkey: Women for Women's Human Rights (WWHR), 2000.

Kandiyoti, Deniz, ed. *Women, Islam, and the State*. Philadelphia: Temple University Press, 1991. Explores interrelationships between religion, family, politics, culture, and the state.

Keddie, Nikki R. *Women in the Middle East: Past and Present*. Princeton, N.J.: Princeton University Press, 2007.

Knaus, Peter R. *The Persistence of Patriarchy: Class, Gender, and Ideology in Twentieth Century Algeria*. New York: Praeger, 1987. Stresses male domination, but thoroughly examines women's roles from precolonial times to the mid-1980s and includes an extensive bibliography.

Labidi, Lilia. "The Nature of Transnational Alliances in Women's Associations in the Maghreb: The Case of AFTURD and ATFD in Tunisia." *Journal of Middle East Women's Studies* 3, no. 1 (2007): 6–34. Focused on Tunisia, this article includes information on female activists in the three Maghrib states working together, initially through the network Collectif 95 Maghreb Egalité, with bibliographic citations of their work.

Lazreg, Marnia. "Gender and Politics in Algeria: Unraveling the Religious Paradigm." *Signs* 15, no. 4 (1990): 755–780. Well-documented discussion of Algerian women and their changing roles, from Algeria's independence to the present.

Mernissi, Fatima. *Beyond the Veil: Male-Female Dynamics in Modern Muslim Society*. Rev. ed. Bloomington: Indiana University Press, 1987. See p. xii. The introduction vividly portrays changes for women, as well as Mernissi's view of the bases and goals of Moroccan Islamist groups.

Mernissi, Fatima. *The Veil and the Male Elite: A Feminist Interpretation of Women's Rights in Islam*. Translated by Mary Jo Lakeland. Reading, Mass.: Addison-Wesley, 1991. A Moroccan feminist examines religious texts from her perspective.

Micaud, Charles A., Leon Carl Brown, and Clement Henry Moore. *Tunisia: The Politics of Modernization*. New York: Praeger, 1964. Covers social change involving women during the protectorate and in the early years of independence.

Mir-Hosseini, Ziba. *Marriage on Trial: A Study of Islamic Family Law: Iran and Morocco Compared*. London: I. B. Tauris, 1993.

Moghadam, Valentine M., and Fatima Sadiqi, eds. "Women's Activism and the Public Sphere." Special issue, *Journal of Middle East Women's Studies* 2, no. 2 (2006).

Pittman, Alexandra. *Cultural Adaptations: The Moroccan Women's Campaign to Change the Moudawana*. Brighton, U.K.: Institute for Development Studies, 2007. Available online at http://www.ids.ac.uk/download.cfm?downloadfile=84C59482-5056-8171-7BADD324D280F913&typename=dmFile&fieldname=filename, accessed March 11, 2013. Provides a detailed view of the processes Moroccan women's groups used to influence reform in the Mudawana, or Personal Status Code.

Sadiqi, Fatima, and Moha Ennaji. "The Feminization of Public Space: Women's Activism, the Family Law, and Social Change in Morocco." *Journal of Middle East Women's Studies* 2, no. 2 (2006): 86–114. Available online at http://eyas.free.fr/AMEWS%20Article.pdf, accessed January 20, 2012. Discusses the contribution of women's activism to more general democracy in Morocco.

Saadi, Nouredine. *La femme et la loi en Algérie*. Casablanca, Morocco: Éditions le Fennec, 1991. Focuses on legislation in Algeria as it pertains to men's and women's roles, status, rights, and duties.

World Bank. "Labor Participation Rate, Female (% of Female Population Ages 15+)." http://data.worldbank.org/indicator/SL.TLF.CACT.FE.ZS/countries/MA?display=graph, accessed January 22, 2012. Provides data by gender on many topics for most countries.

SUSAN SCHAEFER DAVIS, LEILA HESSINI, AND STEPHANIE WILLMAN BORDAT

SOUTH ASIA

Various attempts at social and legal reform have provoked integral changes in Muslim women's lives in the South Asian subcontinent throughout the past century. Attention to Muslim women's status and efforts to improve it began as an offshoot of two separate kinds of movements: the larger social reform movement in British India and the growing Muslim nationalist movement. In the postpartition era, the issue of social reform and Muslim women largely has been associated with the discourse regarding the role Islam can and/or should play in a modern state. Importantly, it addresses the extent to which the civil rights common in most Western democracies are appropriate in the South Asian Muslim context and whether they should override Islamic injunctions in the realm of family law, or vice versa. While this discourse is exemplified by events in Pakistan, it has also been important in Bangladesh and India.

Although Muslims in the nineteenth century did not have to contend with such social issues as abolishing sati (a Hindu custom in which a widow was burnt to ashes with her dead husband) or promoting widow remarriage, as Hindu reformers did, they had an uphill struggle in introducing female education, easing some of the extreme restrictions on women's activities associated with purdah, restricting polygyny, and ensuring women's legal rights under Islamic law. Sir Sayyid Ahmad Khān's Mohammedan Educational Conference, which began promoting modern education for Muslims in the 1870s, included many of the earliest proponents of female education and of raising women's social status in wider society. The intent was to advance girls' technical knowledge (evidenced in sewing and cooking classes) within a religious framework, thereby reinforcing Islamic values. A women's section of the Mohammedan Educational Conference was formed in 1896, followed three years later by the opening of the first teacher training school for girls. Progress was slow in opening more Muslim girls' schools; by 1921, only four out of every thousand Muslim females had enjoyed the benefits of education.

The promotion of female education was a first step in removing the bonds stipulated by traditional views of purdah. It contributed to transforming the very idea of purdah, the symbolic curtain that separates the world of men from the world of women. Many writers and social groups emerged, ostensibly promoting female literacy but in effect advocating women's rights.

The nationalist struggle also tore at the threads in that curtain. Two important groups were soon established: the politically oriented All-India Muslim Ladies Conference, predominantly wives of leaders active in the Muslim League, and the social-reform-oriented Anjuman-i Khavātīn-i Islām, the precursor to other social-welfare-oriented women's groups. Although these groups remained within the bounds of tradition, the precedent was set to challenge purdah itself. In the gradual building up of support for a Muslim homeland, women's roles were being questioned and their empowerment linked to the larger issues of nationalism and independence. The demand for Muslim women to inherit property as well as other rights Muslims had lost with the Anglicization of certain civil laws was rectified somewhat in 1937 with the enactment of the Muslim Personal Law.

After independence, elite Muslim women in Pakistan continued to advocate women's political empowerment through legal reforms. They mobilized support that eventually resulted in the passage of the Muslim Personal Law of Sharia (1948), which recognized a woman's right to inherit all forms of property, and were behind the futile attempt to include a Charter of Women's Rights in the 1956 constitution. The most important socio-legal reform was the 1961 Family Laws Ordinance, regulating marriage and divorce, which is still widely regarded in Pakistan and Bangladesh as empowering to women.

Two issues—promoting women's political representation and finding some accommodation between Muslim family law and civil democratic rights—came to define the discourse regarding women and socio-legal reform in Pakistan in the years following the 1971 war that resulted in East Pakistan seceding from the federal union and becoming Bangladesh. The latter issue became particularly prominent during the era of the government of President Muhammad Zia ul-Haq (1977–1988) as women's groups emerged in urban areas in response to the promulgation of an Islamization program that many feared would discriminate against women.

Discourse about the position of women in Islam and women's roles in a modern Islamic state was sparked by the Pakistan government's attempts to formalize a specific interpretation of Islamic law and exposed the controversy surrounding its various interpretations and role in a modern state. It was in the highly visible arena of law that women were able to articulate their objections to the Islamization program initiated by the government in 1979. Protests against the 1979 Enforcement of Hudood (Ar., *ḥudūd*) Ordinance focused on its failure to distinguish between adultery (*zinah*) and rape (*zināh bi al-jabr*), and that its enforcement was discriminatory to women. Further protests in 1983–1984 questioned the promulgation of the Qānūn-i Shahādah (Law of Evidence), which many felt did not give equal weight to men's and women's legal testimony. Importantly, the controversy surrounding the Qānūn-i Shahādah raised the issue of whether or not women and men are equal economic actors and the extent to which Western parliamentary and civil rights are applicable in a modern Muslim context.

The Shariat Bill and the Ninth Amendment (that all laws in Pakistan should be in conformity with Sharīʿah), proposed in 1986, were opposed by a range of women's groups on the grounds that it would give rise to sectarianism and divide the nation. They were concerned that Sharīʿah would now come to be identified solely with the relatively conservative interpretation of Islam supported by Zia's government. They also felt the Shariat Bill and the Ninth Amendment could potentially reverse many of the rights women in Pakistan had already won. In April 1991, a compromise version of the Shariat Bill was promulgated, but the debate over the issue of which kind of law—civil or Islamic—should prevail remains controversial.

No pivotal legislation was passed to further affect the rights of women during the democratic interregnum (1988–1999), which found Benazir Bhutto's Pakistan People's Party (PPP) and Nawaz Sharif's Pakistan Muslim League (PML) jockeying for power. Despite both parties' rhetoric of working for the empowerment of women, neither ever attempted to reverse the Hudood Ordinances, reinstate reserved seats for women in the provincial and national assemblies, or develop other substantive measures to transform Pakistani society in ways that could ensure women's rights in popular practices.

The government of Pervez Musharraf, which came to power in Pakistan following a coup in October 1999, incorporated women's empowerment as a substantive component of its policies to promote Pakistan's progress and alleviate poverty; it reinstated reserved seats for women in the 2001 elections, encouraged a variety of educational initiatives targeting improving female literacy, and introduced various microcredit and other financial schemes to facilitate increasing women's earning power. Importantly, and despite protests from Islamist parties now organized into a coalition, the Muttahida Majlis-e-Amal (MMA), which had risen to become leader of the opposition in the National Assembly, Musharraf's government reformed the Hudood Ordinances in November 2006 by removing the *zinah* clauses and placing the crime of rape back into Pakistan's Penal Code with the promulgation of the Protection of Women Act.

Since the coming to power of the Pakistan People's Party in February 2008, further social reform legislation affecting women has been implemented. Unanimously passed in the National Assembly in January 2010, the Protection against Harassment for Women at the Workplace Act 2009 makes provisions for the protection against sexual harassment of women in public spaces. Two additional bills, both modifying the Pakistan Penal Code and the Code of Criminal Procedure, have pushed the legal empowerment of women in Pakistan further. Passed in December 2011, the Anti-Women Practices Bill lists specific punishable offenses including compelling women to marry, especially "in consideration of settling a civil dispute or criminal liability," prohibiting *wanni* and *swara* (exchange marriages and marriage as a form of compensation), as well as barring women from inheriting property or facilitating a woman marrying the Qur'ān or other "anti-women practices." The second bill, commonly referred to as the "acid-throwing legislation," specifically imposes penalties for causing harm or disfigurement by using a "corrosive substance," punishable by long imprisonment and fines up to a million rupees.

A final act of legislation promises to make perhaps the greatest difference of all affecting women's rights and empowering them in the future—the elevation of the National Commission on the Status of Women (NCSW) in early February 2012 and the subsequent appointment of long-time women's rights activist Khawar Mumtaz as its chairperson. Importantly, the NCSW has been granted greater administrative autonomy to review laws, make recommendations, confer with the provincial governments, and, overall, gain greater scope, funding, and impact on redressing violations of women's rights.

While the federal government of Pakistan has articulated its development priorities within a global framework (skills training, poverty alleviation strategies, improvement of the educational infrastructure, and promoting the empowerment of women), it cannot leave behind the language of Islam, as this would provide its Islamist opposition with the opportunity to claim they are the only viable Islamic alternative on the political landscape. The government of Bangladesh has found itself in the grip of a similar debate since the 1980s: the extent to which Islamic law should be instituted as the supreme law in the country. While the rights granted women under the 1961 Family Laws Ordinance are still in force, they are being threatened by efforts to assert mandatory dress codes and conduct for women, and may be affected if legal changes are instituted.

Similar issues have been raised regarding Muslim women and social reform in postindependence India. As members of a minority community, Indian Muslims are caught in the dilemma of maintaining a communal identity and needing to adapt to the larger Indian society. A watershed event concerning socio-legal reform for Muslim women in India was the 1986 passage of the Muslim Women's Protection of the Right of Divorce Bill, which revoked Muslim women's rights to maintenance granted to Indian women under the state's civil laws. This question remains pertinent in the 21st century, as Indian Muslims continue to question the relationship between civil and religious laws.

[*See also* Ḥudūd *and* Seclusion.]

BIBLIOGRAPHY

Ahmad, Sadaf, ed. *Pakistani Women: Multiple Locations and Competing Narratives.* Oxford: Oxford University Press, 2010.

Ahmad, Sadaf. *Transforming Faith: the Story of al-Huda and Islamic Revivalism among Urban Pakistani Women.* Syracuse, N.Y.: Syracuse University Press, 2009.

Committee on the Status of Women in India. *Towards Equality: Committee on the Status of Women in India.* New Delhi: Government of India, Ministry of Education and Social Welfare, Department of Social Welfare, 1974. Groundbreaking recommendations by a government-appointed commission to promote the empowerment of women in India.

Jayawardena, Kumari. *Feminism and Nationalism in the Third World.* London: Zed, 1986.

Lateef, Shahida. *Muslim Women in India: Political and Private Realities, 1890s–1980s.* London: Zed, 1990.

Minault, Gail. "Political Change: Muslim Women in Conflict with Parda; Their Role in the Indian Nationalist Movement." In *Asian Women in Transition*, edited by Sylvia A. Chipp and Justin J. Green, pp. 194–203. University Park: Pennsylvania State University Press, 1980.

Minault, Gail. "Shaikh Abdullah, Begum Abdullah, and Sharif Education for Girls at Aligarh." In *Modernization and Social Change among Muslims in India*, edited by Imtiaz Ahmad, pp. 207–236. New Delhi: Manohar, 1983.

Mirza, Sarfaraz Hussain. *Muslim Women's Role in the Pakistan Movement.* Lahore: Research Society of Pakistan, University of the Punjab, 1969. Thorough account of the history of the Muslim women's reform movement in South Asia.

Mumtaz, Khawar, and Farida Shaheed. *Women of Pakistan: Two Steps Forward, One Step Back?* London: Zed, 1987.

Pakistan Commission on the Status of Women. *Report of the Pakistan Commission on the Status of Women.* Islamabad: Pakistan Commission on the Status of Women, 1986. Controversial document produced by a commission appointed by President Zia ul-Haq, which condemns the conditions under which women in Pakistan live and the lack of government action to rectify them.

Shahid, Ayesha. *Silent Voices: Untold Stories: Women Domestic Workers in Pakistan and their Struggle for Empowerment.* Karachi: Oxford University Press, 2010.

Thanawi, Ashraf ʿAli. *Perfecting Women: Maulana Ashraf ʿAli Thanawi's* Bihishti Zewar: *A Partial Translation with Commentary.* Translated by Barbara D. Metcalf. Berkeley: University of California Press, 1990.

Weiss, Anita M. "Crisis and Reconciliation in Swat through the Eyes of Women." In *Beyond Swat: History, Society and Economy along the Afghanistan-Pakistan Frontier*, edited by Benjamin Hopkins and Magnus Marsden, pp. 179–192. New York: Columbia University Press, 2012.

Weiss, Anita M. Moving Forward with the Legal Empowerment of Women in Pakistan. USIP Special Report 305. Washington, D.C.: United States Institute of Peace, 2012. Available online at http://www.usip.org/files/resources/SR305.pdf.

Weiss, Anita M. "Straddling CEDAW and the MMA: Conflicting Visions of Women's Rights in Contemporary Pakistan." In *Family, Gender, and Law in a Globalizing Middle East and South Asia*, edited by Kenneth M. Cuno and Manisha Desai, pp. 256–284. Syracuse, N.Y.: Syracuse University Press, 2009.

Weiss, Anita M., and S. Zulfiqar Gilani, eds. *Power and Civil Society in Pakistan.* Karachi: Oxford University Press, 2001.

ANITA M. WEISS

SOUTHEAST ASIA

Women's roles in Muslim societies in Southeast Asia have been defined largely by two interrelated factors. First, traditional Southeast Asian societies have been based on bilateral kinship systems, in contrast to pre-Islamic Middle Eastern societies, which were largely patrilineal. Second, Southeast Asian societies at the time Islam was introduced had already been profoundly influenced by other world religious traditions, most notably Hinduism and Buddhism. Although women enjoyed a relatively emancipated status in these two religious traditions, they also heavily influenced and shaped the contemporary social gender attitude in Southeast Asian Muslim societies, which generally involves acceptance of male authority. Many prejudicial customs that prevailed in Muslim social gender perceptions in Southeast Asia can be traced back to earlier religious traditions. In peasant societies, women were laborers and petty traders, and in court societies there are examples of women rulers. However, women's royal authority had little influence on average Muslim women's everyday lives. In Southeast Asian Muslim societies, the primary role of women always was, and still is, as mothers and wives. Nevertheless, the demand for a larger labor force since the industrialization in this region in the 1990s has led to mass participations by Muslim women in the workforce. This industrialization ultimately shaped the contemporary concept of Southeast Asian womanhood, which considers a woman's primary role to be a mother and a wife, with a secondary role as a worker (Ariffin, 1994).

Adherence to traditional customary law, or *adat*, was a vital part of the societal orientation of Southeast Asian Muslims. Many scholars, for example, have been fascinated by how the Minangkabau, a matrilineal society reputed to be the most pious Muslim community in Indonesia, have managed to retain many elements of their matrilineal system, when it would appear to contradict the patrilineal nature of Islamic law and custom. Nikki Keddie argues that the answer may be found in the fact that the Minangkabau appear to stress matters of worship and individual ethics (*ʿibādāt*) while paying relatively little attention to the worldly questions of Islamic law (Sharīʿah) and jurisprudence.

Traditionally, Southeast Asian Muslim societies have emphasized *ʿibādāt* and the acquisition of an early familiarity with the five pillars of Islam. The transmitters in this socialization process are women, in their roles as mothers and as religious teachers (*asātidhah*, sg. *ustādh*). However, Muslim women's religious teachings were, and still are, generally limited to children and women students. The formulation and implementation of Sharīʿah, in contrast, was a male purview, and is generally restricted to family law.

In the modern Islamic revival, the preoccupation with *ʿibādāt* has translated into a desire to take on a more overt Islamic identity; this extends to learning to read Arabic, studying the Qurʾān, and strictly performing the five daily prayers. All these are manifestations of a quest for Muslim religious piety. Thus women activists draw inspiration from Islam for a variety of political, social, and economic reform projects. For advocates of gender equality, Islam is a crucial resource for mobilization.

What is new at the beginning of the twenty-first century is the gathering shift to implementing Sharīʿah in Muslim communities. What type of Sharīʿah, how it should be accommodated within existing legal codes, and who should be empowered to determine its contents and formulate its judgments are all subjects of intense debate among Southeast Asian Muslims. In Malaysia and Indonesia, this means reconciling three legal systems: *adat* (customary) law; adaptations of Western law (British in Malaysia and Dutch in Indonesia); and Islamic law. Hitherto, Islamic law had been largely restricted to family law; the situation is similar for Muslims in Singapore, Thailand, and the Philippines. This appears to be changing, as the scope of Sharīʿah is broadened, especially with the introduction of alternative educational and economic models and structures that match similar changes in other places in the Muslim world.

Colonial Period. Southeast Asian Muslims have long recognized that it was as important for women to acquire a religious education as it was for men, as women are expected to raise and teach their children. Religious education thus helped to pave the way for some acceptance of secular education for women, particularly for upper-class women in the Dutch East Indies. Raden Kartini (1879–1904) was the Dutch-educated daughter of a Javanese regent (*bupati*) whose correspondence with a young Dutch woman has inspired generations of Indonesian women. Kartini argued that while there was much value in acquiring a progressive Western education, this must not supersede the religious education that provides a firm anchor in one's own traditional culture and value system.

Kartini inspired a small circle of aristocratic Indonesian women to dedicate themselves to establishing educational opportunities for women. The first organization set up for this purpose was the Putri Mardika (Liberated Women), founded in Jakarta in 1912 as a women's wing of the Budi Utomo (Pure Endeavor, the first native political society in the Dutch East Indies). Aisyiyah was formed as the women's section of the Muhammadiyah, a reformist organization founded in 1912 in Yogyakarta and led by the wife of the founder. Other groups in the Dutch East Indies included the women's wing of the Nahdlatul Ulama, the Nahdlatul Fatayat, and the Wanodya Utomo of the Sarekat Islam.

A pattern emerged for the foundation of women's organizations, whether secular or religious, generally as counterparts to exclusively male organizations, and particularly with the women directly involved in their formation generally being the wives of the founders of the male organizations. These women's organizations focused on the education of women as their primary mission. Toward this end, they established magazines and newsletters and published widely.

The emphasis on the education of women took on another dimension in the 1930s when Muslim women became actively involved in the nationalist movements in the Dutch East Indies and British Malaya. Given the prevailing belief that women and men had an equal right to education (particularly Qurʾānic education), it followed that Islam served as a legitimating base for women's entry into political activity. Even so, there is ongoing debate on the degree to which Muslim women should be allowed to participate in politics and whether or not Islam permits them to do so. In the context of Malaysia, it is argued that women can take part in politics as long as they conform to a certain role: they must be conciliatory and able to establish harmony, while relying on male patronage. In an interview in December 1998, Rashila Ramli, the head of the Department of Political Science at Universiti Kebangsaan Malaysia, argued that Southeast Asian politics is a man's game and that, in the context of Malaysia, women who take part in this always have to demonstrate that they can balance their family life and work. They must show that they are good wives and mothers, and play a supporting role in politics. As this is difficult to do, many women who are in high political office in Malaysia are mostly past childbearing age.

Two Malay women who later went on to become prominent Malaysian politicians, Aishah Ghani and Sakinah Junid, were both associated with one of the first women's movements in British Malaya, the Angkatan Wanita Sedar (AWAS, or Progressive Women's Corps). AWAS was the women's section of the Malay Nationalist Party (MNP), a radical party dedicated to establishing an Indonesian republic that included Malaya.

Postindependence Period. The contributions of Muslim women in the independence movements of the 1930s helped to ensure their smooth entrance into the postindependence political arena. In British Malaya, both leading Malay political parties established women's wings. The women's wing of the United Malays National Organization (UMNO) was called Kaum Ibu (later Kaum Wanita), and that of the opposition Partai Islam Se-Malaysia (PAS) was called Dewan Muslimat (Women's Section).

In Malaysia, the rights of women as citizens to participate in the political and administrative functions of the nation have been recognized and safeguarded in the federal constitution. Similarly, in Indonesia, the 1945 constitution ensures rights and equal responsibilities for men and women.

The women's wings of religious reform movements have played active roles in advocating and implementing social and educational reforms. In Indonesia, Aisyiyah organizes religious courses, Qurʾān-reading groups, and kindergartens. It also runs orphanages, maternity clinics, hospitals, day-care centers, family planning units, and girls' dormitories. Its role as a catalyst for change is exemplified by its dissemination of family planning information and methods. When planning was first introduced in Indonesia, the Muslim response was generally negative. After the Muhammadiyah issued a *fatwā* in support of family planning in 1971, Aisyiyah began to recommend it in the context of total environmental welfare for families. Although Muslim women have continued to play an active role in politics, they are underrepresented in elected political offices. For example, in Indonesia in 2007, fewer than 12 percent of the members of the national parliament were women, and more than half of the country's 440 district legislatures had no women members at all.

Late Twentieth-Century Developments. Since the early 1970s, Islamic reformist movements have gained prominence in Southeast

Asia. In Malaysia, the leading *dakwah* (from the Arabic *daʿwah*, response to a call) organization has been the Malaysian Muslim Youth Movement (ABIM), which followed the pattern of other Malay organizations by establishing a women's branch, HELWA (women's affairs unit).

The reformist wave that began in the late twentieth century has clearly had an impact on the status and role of women in Southeast Asia. In contrast to earlier twentieth-century reform movements, there appears to be a greater preoccupation with elaborating a model for Islamic women that is distinct from the Western model.

In the early twenty-first century, many Southeast Asian women do not see a contradiction between wearing a headscarf (*jilbāb*, *tudong*, hijab), and being a feminist, even though most Muslim women do not directly accept a "Western" feminist identification. However, they do accept that women have not been given equal opportunities and that this needs to be acknowledged and changed. For some Southeast Asian Muslim women, Islam offers an alternative modernity, in that the institutionalization of Islam provides a path to middle-class education and jobs.

Muslim women in Southeast Asia have also increasingly focused their attention on the process of, and preoccupation with, the implementation of Sharīʿah in Muslim communities and nation-states. The expanded implementation of Islamic law is affecting the legal status of Muslim women, as well as the social and political perception of their roles in society. In Malaysia, the most controversial element of this effort has been the call to introduce ḥudūd laws. Some Muslim scholars in Indonesia have also advocated the expansion of the domain of Islamic law. Much of this concerns morality codes, as exemplified by the rejected attempt to introduce a pornography law in 2011.

Muslim women in contemporary Southeast Asia have been a significant part of these socio-political reform endeavors. Their constant efforts can be observed in the increase in veiling—albeit stylish and fashionable—among Muslim female students throughout Southeast Asian universities, reflecting a struggle to meld their individual autonomy and modern education with a commitment to Islamic discourse and lifestyle. It also can be observed in the rising awareness among female Muslim activists and intellectuals in Southeast Asian societies of women's rights and gender equality in Islam.

Besides a range of activities in research, advocacy, public education, publications, and networking in the social and political arena, Muslim women are also taking steps to reform the legal status and conditions of women. In Indonesia, the 1974 Marriage Law and the Compilation of Islamic Law (Kompilasi Hukum Islam, or KHI) have been widely criticized by Muslim feminists, and since 2004 there have been calls to reform it as it no longer meets the spirit of gender equality in Islam and violates human rights (Mulia, 2007). In Malaysia, Muslim female intellectuals are pursuing reform to Islamic laws, Islamic administration, and Islamic interpretation (Foley, 2001). An increasing number of conferences, seminars, and workshops on women and Islam, which are mostly organized by various women's groups, reveals an avid interest in the "woman question" among female audiences seeking to understand their position within Islam and subsequently engaging in a discourse on reforming interpretations of women and Islam. Women in countries where Muslims are minorities, such as the Philippines and Singapore, are also striving for change, despite a growing sense of Islamic identity that is leading many Muslims to advocate a greater emphasis on authentic Islamic education (especially for female children) to be administered in the *madrasahs* rather than the national secular schools.

However, women's access to justice under the law, particularly Muslim family laws and the state's administrative policies and procedures relating to religion, poses substantial challenges in any reform efforts undertaken. In order for Muslim women in Southeast Asian societies to advocate for necessary sociopolitical and legal reforms and to reclaim their justice in Islam and under its laws, Muslim women themselves need to actively engage with the interpretation of religious texts, along with forming broader local and global alliances and support networks (Othman, 2006). All of this requires strong education and access to public space, while Muslim women remain faithful to Islamic lifestyle, albeit on their own terms.

True to their heritage, Southeast Asian Muslim women are playing an active role in debates on the redefinition of women's social, cultural, legal, and economic roles in their modernizing societies. Groups of professional Muslim women are spearheading a reexamination of traditional Islamic sources for answers to these complex questions. Among these groups are the Malaysian organizations Sisters in Islam and Musawah and the Indonesian Fahmina Institute, all of which have been active in publishing books and pamphlets, organizing seminars and training sessions, and reinforcing the relevancy of Kartini's observation of more than a century ago—that education is the key to progress for women.

[*See also* Family Law; Family Planning; *and* Women's Movements.]

BIBLIOGRAPHY

Anwar, Zainah. *Islamic Revivalism in Malaysia: Dakwah among the Students.* Petaling Jaya, Malaysia: Pelanduk, 1987.

Ariffin, Rohana. "Assessing Patriarchy in Labour Organizations." *Kajian Malaysia* 12, no. 2 (1994): 47–72.

Badran, Margot. "Understanding Islam, Islamism, and Islamic Feminism." *Journal of Women's History* 13, no. 1 (Spring 2001): 47–52.

Foley, Rebecca C ,2001. "The Challenge of Contemporary Muslim Women Activists in Malaysia." PhD dissertation, Monash University.

Karim, Wazir Jahan. *Women and Culture: Between Malay Adat and Islam.* Boulder, Colo.: Westview, 1992.

Keddie, Nikki R. "Islam and Society in Minangkabau and in the Middle East: Comparative Reflections." *Sojourn* 2, no. 1 (February 1987): 1–30.

Muhammad, Husein, Faqihuddin Abdul Kodir, Lies Marcoes Natsir, and Marzuki Wahid, eds. *Dawrah Fiqh Concerning Women: Manual for a Course on Islam and Gender.* Translated by Marlene Indro Nugroho-Heins. Cirebon, Indonesia: Fahmina Institute, 2006.

Mulia, Siti Musdah. *Islam dan Inspirasi Kesetaraan Gender.* Yogyakarta, Indonesia: Kibar, 2007. See esp. pp. 131–149.

Othman, Norani. "Muslim Women and The Challenge of Islamic Fundamentalism/Extremism: An Overview of Southeast Asian Muslim Women's Struggle for Human Rights and Gender Equality." *Women's Studies International Forum* 29 (2006): 339–353.

Robinson, Kathryn, and Sharon Bessell, eds. *Women in Indonesia: Gender, Equity, and Development.* Singapore: Institute of Southeast Asian Studies, 2002.

van Doorn-Harder, Pieternella. *Women Shaping Islam: Indonesian Women Reading the Qur'an.* Urbana: University of Illinois Press, 2006.

SHARON SIDDIQUE
Updated by FARJANA MAHBUBA

WOMEN LIVING UNDER MUSLIM LAWS. Women Living under Muslim Laws (WLUML) is an international support and solidarity network of Muslim and secular feminists who link with other women's networks to advance the human rights of women in the Muslim world. Although several such transnational feminist networks exist today, WLUML was the first to emerge, in 1984, in response to concerns about changes in family laws and growing Islamist movements in the countries from which the founding members came.

The group came together on the initiative of Marieme Helie Lucas, an Algerian citizen and lecturer at the University of Algiers who left for Europe in 1982. This was a time of transition in Algeria, from the era of Arab socialism under Houari Boumediénne (who had died in December 1979) to a period of economic restructuring under Chedli Benjedid. The new government also was drafting a patriarchal family law that alarmed many women and led to the formation of an Algerian feminist movement.

In July 1984, nine women—from Algeria, Sudan, Morocco, Pakistan, Bangladesh, Iran, Mauritius, and Tanzania—set up an Action Committee of Women Living under Muslim Laws to critique patriarchal family laws and growing fundamentalism. By early 1985, the committee had evolved into an international network of information, solidarity, and support, and Helie Lucas became the guiding light behind the WLUML network. Individuals and groups associated with the network have included Farida Shaheed and Khawar Mumtaz of Pakistan's Shirkat Gah, Ayesha Imam of Nigeria's Baobob, Malaysia's Sisters in Islam, and Salma Sobhan of Bangladesh.

Since the first planning meeting in July 1986, WLUML has linked women across the world who are active in their local and national movements but who meet periodically to reach consensus on a Plan of Action that guides the network's activities for the next five to seven years. Key strategies are information dissemination on discriminatory laws and violations of women's human rights; campaigns on specific cases that include petition drives and action alerts; and a variety of publications.

WLUML typically engages in grassroots networking but occasionally attends international conferences. The UN's World Conference on Human Rights, held in Vienna, Austria, in 1993, was the first UN conference that WLUML officially attended, and it did so largely to raise awareness at the women's tribunal about Islamist violence against Algerian women. WLUML also participated in the 1994 UN conference on population and development, held in Cairo, Egypt, where it joined other feminist networks in criticizing efforts by the Vatican, conservative states, and Christian and Muslim fundamentalists to remove references to women's reproductive rights in the conference declaration.

The Koranic Interpretation by Women project was launched in Lahore in 1990 and entailed an independent reading and interpretation of the Qur'ān, *ḥadīth*, and existing Islamic laws. The multi-year project, in which Sisters in Islam were especially active, culminated in a 1997 book—*For Ourselves: Women Reading the Qur'ān*—written to increase awareness of the misapplication of Islamic law in the Muslim world. Sections deal with interpretation and jurisprudence; "the foundational myths" and the controversial "Sūrat al-Nisā'" (Qur'ānic chapter 4 on women); women in the family; women in society; and recommendations for action and strategies. A subsequent related project produced *Knowing Our Rights: Women, Family, Laws, and Customs in the Muslim World*. In November 2002, WLUML expanded its work through a Web site called *Fundamentalisms: A Web Resource for Women's Human Rights*, a joint initiative with the Association for Women's Rights in Development (AWID). WLUML also continues to reach its vast network through periodic electronic dispatches, which summarize news, information, appeals, and alerts—in English and French—pertaining to women in the Muslim world and beyond.

BIBLIOGRAPHY

Helie Lucas, Marie-Aimee. "Women Living Under Muslim Laws." In *Ours By Right: Women's Rights as Human Rights*, ed. Joanna Kerr. London: Zed Books, 1993.

Kazi, Seema. "Muslim Laws and Women Living Under Muslim Laws." In *Muslim Women and the Politics of Participation*, ed. Mahnaz Afkhami and Erika Friedl. Syracuse, NY: Syracuse University Press, 1997.

Moghadam, Valentine M. *Globalizing Women: Transnational Feminist Networks*. Baltimore, MD: Johns Hopkins University Press, 2005.

Shaheed, Farida. "Controlled or Autonomous: Identity and the Experience of the Network Women Living Under Muslim Laws." WLUML Occasional Paper No. 5. July 1994.

Valentine M. Moghadam

Women of the Prophet's Household: Interpretation. The women of the Prophet's household include women in three "categories" that are discussed below. These women to varying extents played roles in the Prophet's household and contributed to the development of Islamic thought and practice. These women continue to have enduring influence on Muslim women's and men's thoughts, lives, and activism and are described as role models for men and for women.

Prophet's Wives. The Prophet's wives were Khadīja bint Khuwaylid, Sawdah bint Zamʾa, ʿĀʾishah bint Abu Bakr, Hafsah bint Umar, Zaynab bint Khuzaymah, Umm Salamah (Hind bint Abi Umayya), Zaynab bint Jahsh, Umm Habiba (Ramla bint Abi Sufyan), Juwayriyyah bint al-Harith, Safiyyah bint Huyayy, and Maymunah bint al-Harith. The Prophets wives are respected as *Ummahāt al-Muʾminīn*, or mothers of the believers, and, according to the Qurʾān, they were not allowed to remarry after the Prophet's death. Within this category, two women—Khadīja and ʿĀʾishah—are perhaps more significant and occupy a more visible place within both Islamic history and Muslim collective memory. Khadīja is recognized as the Prophet's first wife with whom he shared a monogamous relationship for fifteen years. Khadīja was a powerful and rich woman who is recognized as the first benefactor and patron of Islam. According to a ḥadīth narrated by Abdullah ibn Abbas, Khadīja,along with Assiya (the wife of Pharaoh and foster mother of Moses), Mary (the mother of Jesus), and Fāṭimah (the Prophet's daughter), are the best of women or, alternatively, the leaders of women in Paradise. ʿĀʾishah is significant for her scholarship and contributions to the recording and transmission of *ḥadīth* and Islamic history. ʿĀʾishah is criticized in some Shīʿī sources for her role in the Battle of the Camel (or the Battle of *Jamal*) in 656 AH during which she led forces against Ali (the Prophet's cousin and son-in-law and the then-reigning Caliph).

Prophet's Daughters. The Prophet's daughters were Zaynab, Ruqayyah, Umm Kulthum and Fāṭimah. Most Sunni sources and many Shīʿī sources agree that Muḥammad had four daughters all borne by his first wife Khadīja. Some Shīʿī dispute this and say that he only had one daughter, Fāṭimah, and that the other three were Khadīja's nieces. Fāṭimah is an extremely important figure both in Sunnī and Shīʿī Islam and is widely recognised as the person who will be holding the reins of Prophet's camel while leading it into Heaven. It is believed that, in practice, she will be the first woman to enter Heaven. As mentioned in the section about Khadīja, Fāṭimah is recognized as among the best of women.

Rayhana and Māriyah. Rayhana bint Zayd and Māriyah bint Shaʿmun also know as al-Qibtiyya, or the Copt, are included in this listing of women in the Prophet's household. The relationship to the Prophet of these two women is debated, with most sources indicating that they were slaves (Rayhana was enslaved after her tribe the Banū Qurayẓah was defeated, and Māriyah was given to Muḥammad by the patriarch of Alexandria). According to some sources, Muḥammad married these two women after they converted to Islam. Both these women were accorded much respect in early Muslim communities and are recognised as *Ummahāt ul-Mu'minīn*. Māriyah is a particularly important figure as she was the mother of the Prophet's son Ibrahim who died in infancy. Depending on whether or not these two women are included, Prophet Muḥammad is said to have married either 11 or 13 wives altogether, although not simultaneously.

Some Popular Interpretations. There is a plethora of literature from religious and academic perspectives that investigate the lives of these women. Depending on the standpoint that the author takes, the lives of these women are handled in extremely different ways and the imagery created about them ranges from cutting-edge scholarship to quiet submissiveness. Some literature sources present the reader with commentaries on these women's lives which clarify the emancipatory effect of Islam on the lives of women through history, during the lifetime of the Prophet and beyond. These women often had public roles and were businesswomen, scholars, teachers, and warriors. Mohammad Akram Nadwi's (2007) work about the women scholars of Islam (also Bewley 1999, 2004) provides evidence of the position of public authority that these women, and, particularly Khadīja, ʿĀ'ishah, and Fāṭimah, enjoyed in the Islamic societies that they lived in and also in contemporary Islamic society.

There are other literature sources which present more patriarchal renditions of the life stories of these same women. While such narratives have the same starting point, their interpretations of these women's lives portray different images. Their narratives are underpinned by notional suggestions about the sheltered nature of these women's lives. Such literature tends to "focus on the spiritual status of women" rather than their religious, literary, social, and moral achievements (Ansari et al. 2003; Bewley 1999). In such literature, it may be, for example, that the strict veiling practices of the Prophet's wives and daughters are presented as exemplars for Muslim women to emulate rather than Khadīja's business acumen, ʿĀ'ishah's scholarly prowess, or Sawdah's expertise in manufacture and trade (she treated, tanned, and sold animal skins and is reputed to have made considerable profits out of these activities).

Feminist Interpretations. It is such patriarchal stereotypes that Aisha Bewley (1999: 6) alludes to when she says that "it is time to re-examine the sources and re-assess how Muslim women in the past acted so that we can escape the limiting perspectives which have come to be the norm" for Muslim women. From a feminist perspective, an interrogation of patriarchal interpretations of these women's lives can lead to a reclamation of knowledge and scholarship that is by and for Muslim women. Khadīja, the first wife of Prophet Muḥammad (pbuh), is often described as a wife and as a mother, which are important attributes. However, the Muslim feminist's point of dissent with such narratives of Khadīja's life is that very little is mentioned of her independence, her career as a businesswoman, her role as a benefactor for early Muslim communities and also as a counselor to Prophet Muḥammad (*pbuh*) during the early days of prophethood when he lacked self-confidence and was unsure about himself (Contractor and Scott-Baumann 2011). Feminist scholars assert the importance of such holistic interpretations and their value in motivating young Muslim women.

Some 'feminist' interpretations about these women's lives may also be problematic. For example, it is sometimes claimed that because Khadīja achieved her successes (in business) before the advent of Islam in Arabia, she had more independence and autonomy, as compared to ʿĀ'ishah who was born in the Islamic era (Ahmed 1992). Such arguments are weakened by their failure to recognize ʿĀ'ishah's religious authority in early Islamic history (Bewley 1999, Ansari et al. 2003; Abdul Qadir 2006) as a narrator of ḥadīths and as one of the greatest living scholars of her time who autonomously issued *fatwas* or religious verdicts (Ansari et al. 2003). By failing to acknowledge ʿĀʾishah's reputation as an Islamic scholar, such views can be disempowering for all Muslim women (Contractor 2012).

[*See also* Khadīja bint Khuwaylid, ʿĀʾishah, *and* Fāṭimah.]

BIBLIOGRAPHY

Abdul Qadir, M. *Leading Ladies: Who made a Difference in the Lives of Others*. New Delhi: Adam Publishers & Distributors, 2006.

Ansari, S., A. Nadvi, and S. Nadvi. *Women Companions of the Holy Prophet and Their Sacred Lives*. New Delhi: Islamic Book Service, 2003.

Bewley, A. *Islam: The Empowering of Women*. London: Ta-Ha Publishers, 1999.

Bewley, A. *Muslim Women—a Biographical Dictionary*. London: Taha, 2004.

Contractor, S. *Muslim Women in Britain: Demystifying the Muslimah*. London: Routledge, 2012.

Contractor, S. and A. Scott-Baumann. "Encouraging Muslim women into higher education through partnerships and collaborative pathways." York, Yorks HEA Islamic Studies Network, 2011. http://www.islamicstudiesnetwork.ac.uk/assets/documents/islamicstudies/Final_report_August_2011_ASB_SC.doc.

Nadwi, M. *Al-Muhaddithat: the Women Scholars in Islam*. Oxford: Interface Publications, 2007.

Stowasser, Barbara Freyer. *Women in the Qurʾān, Traditions and Interpretation*. New York: Oxford University Press, 1994.

Sariya Cheruvallil-Contractor

Women's Action Forum. Formed in 1981 in response to the Pakistani government's implementation of an Islamic penal code, the Women's Action Forum (WAF; Khavātāin Ma ā-i ʿAmal) seeks to strengthen women's position in society by raising public consciousness and awareness of both women's rights and adverse propaganda against women. Members feared that many of the proposed laws put forward by the martial law government of General Zia ul-Haq might be discriminatory against women and compromise their civil status, as had occurred with the Ḥudūd Ordinances of 1979, when women were indicted after having been raped. Women, mostly from elite families, banded together under the principle of collective leadership in the three major cities of Karachi, Lahore, and Islamabad to formulate policy statements and engage in political action to safeguard women's legal position.

The WAF has played a central role in initiating public discussion of controversies surrounding various interpretations of Islamic law, its role in a modern state, and ways in which women can play a more active political role. The WAF's first major political action was in early 1983, when members in Lahore and Karachi openly marched in protest against the Majlis-i Shūrā's (Consultative Assembly) recommendation to President Zia that he promulgate the Qānūn-i Shahādat (Law of Evidence). As initially proposed, the law would require oral testimony and attestation of either two male witnesses or that of one male and two females; the witness of two or more females without corroboration by a male would not be sufficient, and no testimony by a woman would be admissible in the most severe Ḥudūd cases (cases that require mandatory punishments for crimes against God) as stipulated in the Sunnah. A revised evidence law was eventually promulgated in October 1984 following nearly two years of protests.

WAF members used Islamic precepts as the basis of their protest. They argued that the proposed Qānūn-i Shahādat was not the only acceptable evidence law in Islam, and that there is only one instance in the Qurʾān (2.282) in which two women are called to testify in the place of one man. They contended that the latter was in regard to a specific financial matter and the role of the second woman was to remind the first about points that she may have forgotten. They argued for interpretation that considered the intent (*nīyah*) of the law—namely, helping women and not discriminating against them. The protesters claimed that criteria for witnesses as stated in the Qur'ān are possession of sight, memory, and the ability to communicate; as long as witnesses have these, testimony should be weighed equally, regardless of gender. They also argued that the rigid interpretation of the Qur'ān that would support the Qānūn-i Shahādat (reading "male" for the generic word "man") would virtually exclude women from being members of the religious community. Opponents of the evidence law also feared that women might be restricted from testifying in certain kinds of Ḥudūd cases, such as when a woman is the sole witness to her father's or husband's murder. The final adopted version restricts to financial cases the testimony of two women being equal to that of one man; in other instances, acceptance of a single woman's testimony has been left to the discretion of the judge.

In the autumn of 1983, the WAF and other women's groups organized demonstrations throughout the country to protest both the Qānūn-i Shahādat and the public flogging of women. In 1984, the now separate WAF groups mounted a campaign against the promulgation of the proposed Qiṣāṣ and Dīyat (Retaliation and Blood Money) Ordinance, which stated that the compensation to the family of a female victim be only half that given to the family of a male victim.

After martial law was lifted in December 1985, the WAF became instrumental in organizing protests (which included nearly thirty other groups) in the wake of the debate over the Shariat Bill and the Ninth Amendment. The remaining years of the Zia regime (until 1988) found WAF members focused on protesting against the Ninth Amendment, instituting legal aid cells for indigent women, opposing the gendered segregation of universities, and playing an active role in condemning the growing incidents of violence against women and bringing them to the attention of the public.

During Benazir Bhutto's Pakistan People's Party's first tenure heading the government (December 1988–August 1990), the WAF was faced with the difficult task of transforming itself from protesting based on a collective moral conscience to advocacy. With the displacement of that government, it then focused its activities on three goals: securing women's political representation in the parliament; working to raise women's consciousness, particularly in the realm of family planning; and countering suppression and raising public awareness by taking stands and issuing statements on events as they occurred.

The government of Pervez Musharraf (1999–2008) was more responsive to WAF's recommendations. Although most WAF members criticized the government because it was a military regime, Musharraf's government nevertheless reinstated reserved seats for women in 2001 in provincial and national elections (a key demand of WAF), moved forward with a variety of microcredit schemes for women and, finally, in November 2006, reformed the Ḥudūd laws, which had been a key target of WAF's objections. Under the Pakistan People's Party that came to power following the February 2008 election, WAF has remained an activist voice supporting domestic violence legislation, among other legal reforms advancing the empowerment of women.

[*See also* Women and Social Reform, *subentry on* South Asia.]

BIBLIOGRAPHY

Government of Pakistan. The Protection of Women (Criminal Laws Amendment) Act, November 2006.

This act formally reformed the Ḥudūd laws by putting the crime of *zinah* (adultery) back into the Pakistan penal code.

Mumtaz, Khawar, and Farida Shaheed. *Women of Pakistan: Two Steps Forward, One Step Back?* London: Zed Books, 1987. Thorough review of the history of the Pakistan women's movement, with a strong focus on the Women's Action Forum.

National Commission on the Status of Women. "Recommendations of the NCSW on Hudood Ordinances 1979: Why It is Essential to Repeal it?", n.d.

Pakistan Commission on the Status of Women. "Report of the Commission on the Status of Women in Pakistan," 1986. Controversial report by a commission appointed by President Zia ul-Haq that condemned the conditions under which women in Pakistan live and the lack of government action to rectify them.

Weiss, Anita M. "Benazir Bhutto and the Future of Women in Pakistan." *Asian Survey* 30, no. 5 (May 1990): 433–445.

Weiss, Anita M. "Implications of the Islamization Program for Women." In *Islamic Reassertion in Pakistan: The Application of Islamic Laws in a Modern State*, edited by Anita M. Weiss, pp. 97–110. Syracuse, N.Y.: Syracuse University Press, 1986.

Weiss, Anita M. "Interpreting Women's Rights: The Dilemma Over Eliminating Discrimination Against Women in Pakistan." *International Sociology* 18, no. 3 (September 2003): 581–601.

Women's Action Forum. "Law of Evidence: WAF (National) Position Paper," 1983.

Women's Action Forum. "Law of Qiṣāṣ and Dīyat as Proposed by the Council of Islamic Ideology: Position Paper of WAF (National)," February 1984.

ANITA M. WEISS

WOMEN'S ENTREPRENEURSHIP.

[*This entry contains two subentries,*

Contemporary Practice *and*
Historical Practice.]

CONTEMPORARY PRACTICE

An entrepreneur is commonly defined as one who owns, launches, manages, and assumes the risks of an economic venture. Thus, entrepreneurship is distinct from a corporate effort. The complexity of the topic necessitates a nuanced definition. Given the perils of trying to evaluate the Muslim world as a whole, this article begins with a general discussion and then emphasizes the Middle East and North Africa (MENA) region.

There has been a recent increase in participation of women in the economy as entrepreneurs, and growing attention to the issue. The Global Entrepreneurship Monitor (GEM) project documents that, in many countries, women entrepreneurs constitute around 30 percent of total entrepreneurs. More interestingly, at the global level, women are starting businesses at a rate twice as fast as that of men. The percentage of women entrepreneurs seems to be growing in some parts of the world faster than others. This is true of countries such as Canada, Denmark, Finland, and New Zealand, where the rates exceed 30 percent, although there are exceptions, such as Norway.

The topic of gender and entrepreneurship of large ownership and the formal sector has been highly under-published in academia: in eight academic journals related to the issue, only 6 to 7 percent of the publications were on women and entrepreneurship. Moreover, the scarcity of gender and entrepreneurship literature is not limited to the subject matter itself; it extends to area- or country-specific studies and surveys. This has recently changed, however, and the topic now receives a great deal of media, academic, and policy attention.

The literature on women entrepreneurs as large-firm owners examines why women are discriminated against and underrepresented and what factors explains their lower presence. Some of these factors also apply to women in small and medium enterprises (SMEs). Some of the issues that create barriers to women's entrepreneurship are: lack of access to credit and collateral because of lower ownership of assets; the attitude of banks toward women, which in turn is related to negative social stereotypes against women; and the fact that women tend to have less human and social capital. There are still gaps in education and skills (human capital), even in rich countries, as well as social capital, especially in the form of social networks. Some researchers believe that lack of access to capital, at least in the case of large businesses, results from lower access to informal financial networks.

The issue of social network is an interesting facet of entrepreneurship and gender. Shaw et al. have articulated the topic using Pierre Bourdieu's work. They argue that social networks can reproduce and reinforce social inequalities at the same time that they can and do enhance social capital, but often to the benefit of those already in power, that is, men with high income. There seems to be a tendency for women, especially women of low-income background, to be outside of economically empowering circles.

Gender Inequality, Cross-National Data, and International Development Efforts. Muravyev et al., using a household data survey of thirty-four countries and the Business Environment and Enterprise Performance survey, found that women who own or manage a firm have a 5 percent lower probability of receiving a loan than their male counterparts. Moreover, the interest rate for women is about 0.5 percent higher. The result, controlled for other variables and focused on gender, shows that this occurs despite the fact that there is a tendency for lower rejection rates and lower collateral requirements for female entrepreneurs in more economically developed countries. Muravyev et al. argue (in line with Gary Becker's theory of human capital and the "U-shaped" theory outlined in Goldin) that rising economic development, once it reaches a certain stage, will reduce gender barriers to entering into entrepreneurship: as countries reach high income levels, women benefit.

Generally, women are more likely to be owners of SMEs than of large enterprises, throughout the world. This is partly because of the persistence of cultural factors, namely negative social stereotypes. As Bourdieu argues, individuals' positions are affected by the social structure as well as their own perception. Bourdieu identifies four categories of stereotype: economic, social, cultural, and symbolic. The last two—cultural and symbolic—refer to social stereotypes by which women tend to be viewed by the society as less capable in a male-dominated world. It appears that some women internalize those stereotypes; their perception of their own abilities puts them at a disadvantage. There is evidence that both factors can be at work in the underrepresentation of women in the entrepreneurial world.

Women are underrepresented not only in large enterprises, but also in SMEs (especially at the higher end). This is further reflected in their low profile of self-employment as compared to men. There is plenty of evidence indicating that women are underrepresented at the high end of self-employed jobs. Self-employed women have a tendency to be at the low end of the category and have lower capital and lower debt–equity ratio.

Although some of what has been discussed is universal, it should be noted that, in certain countries, gender discrimination has declined. In many cases, women of high-income background, especially in rich countries, have benefited significantly, narrowing the gender gap. Yet there seem to be overgeneralization and underlying assumptions in many research projects and publications, which: a) put all women into a single category, overlooking differences of class, race, and other factors, and b) presume that all economies can and will prosper, so that countries of low and middle income will unfailingly become high-income countries (an assumed necessary condition for the gender gap to narrow). Here it is worth mentioning that, even in rich countries, massive inequalities plague millions of women and there is ample evidence that, although a large number of women are in SMEs, their position as entrepreneurs of micro enterprises are precarious and far from ideal. This is particularly true of low-income women, women of color, immigrants, and, in some countries such as Canada, women from the native communities.

Nonetheless, it must be emphasized that the issue of women and entrepreneurship has gathered a great deal of attention and there have been efforts to enhance their role. For example, the Organisation for Economic Co-operation and Development portal on the topic "Promoting Entrepreneurship amongst Women," supported by the European Commission, aims to create a network and disseminate information. There are other initiatives supported by national and international agencies, such as Les Femmes Chefs d'Entreprises Mondiales, a France-based association uniting women business owners from around the world. The Diana Project International received early funding from the Entrepreneurship and Small Business Research Institute (Sweden), the Kauffman Center for Entrepreneurial Leadership, and the U.S. Small Business Administration and National Women's Business Council, and is now an international organization. The link to their 2010 conference provides a large list of organizations related to the topic. In addition, Goldman Sachs' 10,000 Women Initiative provides scholarships for women entrepreneurs, constituting a vast resource throughout the world, nationally as well as internationally (mainly in the Western countries), and is designed to promote women's entrepreneurship. It is perhaps not surprising that GEM reports that, in 2010, 108 million women in 59 countries (all the countries that are members of GEM) have become entrepreneurs.

Some of these efforts have been the result of pressures brought by professional women who have become successful and wish to promote female entrepreneurship. In general, though, it seems that the main purpose of such efforts, at least in the terms in which they are framed by some international development organizations, is to enable women to compete in what is considered an ideal situation (free market) in order to bring prosperity to the economy. Increasingly, mainstream policy makers, such as the World Bank, and national agencies support such initiatives and are in tune with international efforts, such as the International Association of Women Entrepreneurs Online. These efforts seek to empower women to engage in the free market and to compete with men in a neoclassical economic structure. These efforts in some cases target women who live in low-income countries and do not have access to resources.

Other Sides of the Story. Although there are some generalities to be made about women across the board, it is highly problematic to consider women as a single category. In fact, the reason that women's entrepreneurship is under-researched academically is that the definition of female entrepreneurs is biased towards large-firm owners in the formal sector; women as micro entrepreneurs, especially in the informal sector, have thus not been viewed as entrepreneurs.

Nevertheless, there is a rich literature on poverty and the role of women as micro entrepreneurs in the informal economy. It generally argues that the most dominant form of informal entrepreneurship venture involves low-paying jobs. This literature claims that not only has neoclassical economics not been beneficial to this type of employment, but, on the contrary, the growth of low-paying jobs in the informal sector and for women as self-employed, home-worker, or micro-enterprise owners has been the result of market drivers and deregulation of the world economy. Throughout the South, millions of the poor, a growing number of whom are women, are working as vendors, hawkers, small-store saleswomen, peddlers, and domestic home-care givers and help. They work without labor-law protection, have no or minimal access to credit or means of production, and remain without social protection.

The literature on women in the informal sector is growing as this sector is expanding. The "informal sector" refers to the sector of the economy that is outside of government taxation and legal protection. It employs some 1.8 billon worldwide, many of them women. This has raised concerns and led to the formation of some international organizations such as WIEGO (Women in Informal Employment: Globalizing and Organizing) and SEWA (Self-Employed Women's Association of India). Some of the mainstream international organizations, such as the International Labour Organization and the International Development Research Centre of Canada, have been preoccupied with these issues for some time. These types of organizations are mainly concerned with addressing poverty, social justice, and gender justice as part of a greater social inequality.

Recently, there has been a new take on the topic of women in the informal sector. The ILO has shown that women are increasingly entering this sector as self-employed and entrepreneurs. As the world is witnessing an expansion of the sector, contrary to an earlier assumption by mainstream economists who believed the informal sector would disappear, the topic is becoming more important. The sector has especially become noticeable in the face of declining employment opportunities in the formal sector because of the global economic crisis. For this reason, debates over women's employment in this sector have shifted from their main focus on poverty and now include women as micro enterprise and SME owners.

Some of this shift is the result of micro-data (in this case from Iran) showing that some women enter this type of employment by choice and they may even find ways to transform their situation (Bahramitash 2013). Nonetheless, precarious and unprotected types of employment are not to be advocated, as world evidence shows close ties between poverty and informal low-paying jobs, especially for women. Instead one may argue that, in view of the expansion of this sector, there is an even greater sense of urgency for bringing such employment under social protection by national and international policy makers and advocates.

More importantly, the earlier, celebratory views of the informal sector as a way of alleviating poverty, originating from the work of de Soto in the late 1980s, need to be questioned. This type of approach argues that, if the economy could take women from low-income households and turn them into small entrepreneurs, the issue of poverty would disappear (the argument has gained some credibility in the case of Peru). Yet, for the most part, the celebration of new informal entrepreneurship seems to be more of a populist support for mobilizing market-driven reforms and fails to see that social inequalities continue to persist if the topic of women (and workers in general) in the informal economy is not approached in combination with concerns over pay, working conditions, terms of employment, and some type of plan for organizing and formalizing. This debate shows the complexity of defining who is an entrepreneur and what their working conditions should be.

Women in the Muslim World. In the Muslim world, there has been a long tradition of female ownership of financial resources, beginning with the first woman to become a Muslim—Khadījah, whom the Prophet married—who was an entrepreneur. The spread of Islam relied on her resources from the start. Throughout the history of the MENA region, there is evidence of female property ownership. In other Muslim countries, such as Indonesia, the largest Muslim country in the world, women's role as entrepreneurs is significant. In Bangladesh, the most important micro-credit initiative, the Grameen Bank, thrives. In Bosnia and Herzegovina, GEM Bosnia and Herzegovina has created the Women's Business Network project with the support of USAID. GEM Malaysia reports on the creation of the Federation of Women Entrepreneur Associations Malaysia (FEM), which brings together nine different organizations. One of these organizations is the National Association of Women Entrepreneurs of Malaysia (NAWEM), launched in 1992 in an attempt to encourage, support, and inspire women in business.

Nevertheless, Muslim countries of the MENA region have a low profile in entrepreneurship and it has been argued that barriers to female entrepreneurship remain. These take the form of gender segregation and rising conservative interpretations of Islam in countries like Saudi Arabia, where women are not allowed to drive cars and many public places are already segregated. However, the 2006 Arab Development Report indicates that throughout the MENA region, women have made unequivocal gains in areas such as education, maternal mortality rate, life expectancy, and other important indicators, including a lower birth rate. Moreover, the employment figures show that women in this region have a higher rate of entry into the labor market than any other region of the world. This is in spite of the fact that women in MENA have the lowest participation in formal and paid work compared to all other regions of the world. The fact that a huge number of educated women are entering the labor market will undoubtedly have a major impact on their role as entrepreneurs. As the World Bank has documented, women entrepreneurs in MENA play a major role in the economy.

Furthermore, the GEM recent report shows that in some Muslim countries of MENA and Sub-Saharan Africa as well as Bosnia and Herzegovina and Malaysia women's perception of opportunities and confidence in their capabilities for entrepreneurship are high. Even more intriguing is that women in MENA not only have more positive attitudes about their abilities and higher aspirations, but there is also less fear of failure than in countries with more advanced economies. The same report, however, points out that women's access to business networks is much weaker than that of men.

A recent data analysis using the World Enterprise Survey indicated that in MENA countries (Algeria, Egypt, Jordan, Iran, Syria, the West Bank and Gaza, Turkey, Lebanon, Morocco, and Saudi Arabia), women entrepreneurs are overrepresented at the top—a pattern in contrast with other regions of the world. Among all female-owned and -managed enterprises, there are more women at the high end of the scale in MENA countries than in the rest of the world. The Enterprise Survey data show that, in 81.8 percent of MENA countries, women's ownership increases as the size of the enterprise increases. The corresponding percentages in other regions are 36.4 percent for Asia and the Pacific, 32.3 percent for Africa, 15.8 percent for Latin America and the Caribbean, 15 percent for Eastern and Central Europe, and 14.3 percent for the Caucasus and Central Asia.

Such a striking difference between MENA and the rest of the world calls for policies that will enhance the role of women in areas other than large firms, namely SMEs, but not in the pattern seen in the rest of the world, where such enterprises typically provide low pay and precarious employment terms and remain outside of government protection. Advocacy along these lines should take into account several factors. Strengthening women in the economy must be done in a way that translates into political and social empowerment. This can be achieved through promotion of SMEs within a framework of protected and decent work parameters geared to bringing equality. Since previous research indicates that women tend to hire women in their enterprises at a higher level than men do, supporting women-owned SMEs will boost female employment. Last but not least, energizing women's role in SMEs can become a catalyst for gender equity, as Naila Kabeer has shown.

[*See also* Borrowing and Credit, Women's: Contemporary and Historical Practice; Business Ownership and Women: Historical and Contemporary Practice; Economics and Finance; Gender Equality; Investment and Commerce, Women's: Historical Practices; *and* Workforce, Women in the.]

BIBLIOGRAPHY

Arenius, P., N. Langowitz, and M. Minniti. *2004 Report on Women and Entrepreneurship*. Babson Park, Mass. and London: Center for Women's Leadership, Babson College, London Business School, 2005.

Bahramitash, R. *Gender, Micro Entrepreneurship and the Informal Sector in Iran*, New York: Palgrave Macmillan, 2013.

Bahramitash, R., and H. Salehi-Esfahani. "A Quantitative Analysis of Women's Entrepreneurship in MENA: Similarities and Differences with Other Regions." Paper presented at the International Conference of The Middle East Economic Association (MEEA), Speyer, Germany, March 2013.

Brass, D. J. "Men's and Women's Networks: A Study of Interaction Patterns and Influence in an Organization." *Academy of Management Journal* 28 (1985): 327–343.

Brush, C. G., E. J. Gatewood, P. G. Greene, and M. M. Hart. *Growth-Oriented Women Entrepreneurs and Their Businesses: A Global Research Perspective*. Cheltenham, U.K.: Edward Elgar, 2006.

Carter, S., and E. Shaw. *Women's Business Ownership: Recent Research and Policy Developments. Report to the Small Business Service*. Stirling and Glasgow: Small Business Service, 2006.

Castells, Manuel, and Alejandro Portes. "World Underneath: The Origins, Dynamics, and Effects of the Informal Economy." In *The Informal Economy: Studies in Advanced and Less Developed Countries*, edited by Alejandro Portes, Manual Castells, and Lauren A. Benton, pp. 11–40. Baltimore: Johns Hopkins University Press, 1989.

Chamlou, Nadereh. *The Environment for Women's Entrepreneurship in the Middle East and North Africa*. Orientations in Development Series. Washington, D.C.: World Bank, 2008.

Cinar, E. Mine. *The Economics of Women and Work in the Middle East and North Africa*. London: Elsevier Science, 2001.

de Bruin, A., C. G. Brush, and F. Welter. "Introduction to the Special Issue: Towards Building Cumulative Knowledge on Women's Entrepreneurship." *Entrepreneurship Theory and Practice* 30, no. 5 (2006): 585–593.

de Soto, F. *The Other Path: The Economic Answer to Terrorism*. New York: Harper and Row, 1989.

Diana Project International. "Diana Conference for Women Entrepreneurs." http://womenentrepreneursgrowglobal.org/tag/diana-project/.

Global Entrepreneurship Monitor (GEM). "GEM 2010 Report: Women Entrepreneurs Worldwide." In *Global Entrepreneurship Monitor*, edited by D. J. Kelley, C. G. Brush, P. Greene, and Y. Litovsky. Babson Park, Mass.: Babson College and the Global Entrepreneurship Research Association, 2011. http://www.gemconsortium.org/docs/download/768.

Goldin, C. *The U-Shaped Female Labour Force Function in Economic Development and Economic History*. Working Paper 4707. National Bureau of Economic Research, 1994.

Greene, P. G, C. Brush, M. Hart, and P. Saparito. "An Exploration of the Venture Capital Industry: Is Gender an Issue?" In *Frontiers of Entrepreneurship Research*, edited by P. D. Reynolds, W. Bygrave, S. Manigart, C. Mason, G. D. Meyer, H. Sapienzia, and K. G. Shaver, pp. 63–83. Wellesley, Mass.: Babson College, 1999.

Greve, A., and J. W. Salaff. "Social Networks and Entrepreneurship." *Entrepreneurship: Theory and Practice* 28, no. 1 (2003): 1–22.

Hughes, K. D., J. E. Jennings, C. Brush, S. Carter, and F. Welter. "Extending Women's Entrepreneurship Research in New Directions." *Entrepreneurship: Theory and Practice* 36, no. 3 (2012): 449–442.

Ibarra, H. "Personal Networks of Women and Minorities in Management: A Conceptual Framework." *The Academy of Management Review* 18, no. 1: 56–87.

International Association of Women Entrepreneurs Online. http://www.iaweo.com.

International Labour Conference. *Decent Work and the Informal Economy*. Geneva: International Labour Organization, 2002.

International Labour Conference. *Women and Men in the Informal Economy: A Statistical Picture*. Geneva: International Labour Office, 2002.

Jütting, Johannes P., and Juan R. de Laiglesia. "Employment, Poverty Reduction, and Development: What's New?" In *Is Informal Normal? Towards More and Better Jobs in Developing Countries*, edited by Johannes P. Jütting and Juan R. de Laiglesia, Paris: OECD, 2009.

Kabeer, N. *Women's Economic Empowerment and Inclusive Growth: Labour Markets and Enterprise Development*. London: Department of International Development and International Development Research Center, School of Oriental Studies, 2012.

Kapoor, A. "The SEWA Way: Shaping Another Future for Informal Labour." *Futures* 39 (2007): 554–568.

Lerner, M., C. G. Brush, and R. Hisirch. "Israeli Women Entrepreneurs: An Examination of Factors Affecting Performance." *Journal of Business Venture* 12, no. 4 (1997): 315–339.

Meyer, G. D., H. Sapienzia, and K. G. Shaver, eds. *Frontiers of Entrepreneurship Research*. Wellesley, Mass.: Babson College.

Olm, K., A. L. Carsrud, and L. Alvey. "The Role of Networks in New Venture Funding for the Female Entrepreneur: A Continuing Analysis." Paper presented at the Frontiers of Entrepreneurship Research conference, Babson College, Wellesley, Mass., 1988.

Reynolds, P. D., W. D. Bygrave, and E. Autio. *GEM 2003 Global Report*. Babson Park, Mass.: Global Entrepreneurship Monitor, 2004.

Saffu, K., and T. Manu. *Strategic Capabilities of Ghanaian Female Business Owners and the Performance of the Ventures*. Paper presented at the 49th Annual Meeting of the International Council for Small Business (ICSB), Johannesburg, South Africa, 20th–23rd June 2004.

Sassen, S. *Informalisation in Advanced Market Economies*. Issues in Development Discussion Paper. Geneva: International Labour Organization, 1997.

Shaw, E., W. Lam, S. Carter, and F. Wilson. *Theory, Practice, and Policy: An Integrated View on Gender, Networks, and Social Capital*. International Council for Small Business, 2006.

United Nations Development Programme. *The Arab Human Development Report 2005: Towards the Rise of Women in the Arab World*. New York: UNDP, Regional Bureau for Arab States, 2006.

Roksana Bahramitash

Historical Practice

Topics related to women's economic role in Muslim countries seems to be under-researched despite the fact that female employment in the Middle East and North Africa (MENA) region has increased at a rate faster than any other region in the world. Although it is true that women in the region have the lowest participation rate compared to the rest of the world, it seems that they may be catching up, provided that political upheaval does not translate into major setbacks for them. However, given the massive increase in educational attainment, and especially the rising number of women seeking higher education, including in the business schools, it is likely that the trend will continue. One of the areas in which women from the region have proven to be making advances is in the area of female entrepreneurship.

In the proceedings of a 2007 CAWTAR (Center of Arab Women for Training and Research) conference, in which the focus was women's growing economic participation in the MENA and the growing awareness of women's economic contributions, an estimate, based on various surveys and statistical sources, was given that between one-quarter and one-third of all firms in the formal sector are owned or managed by women throughout the world. The share is even greater in the informal sector. The issue was at the center of attention even before the political and economic instability of the Middle East and North Africa that began in December 2010. The World Bank and other international organizations have endorsed empowering women entrepreneurs as a way of enhancing economic growth, especially in the context of the MENA region and with a view to increasing female employment. This endorsement is at the core of a World Bank publication on the topic in 2007.

There has been a visible trend since the early 2000s toward a rise in women-owned businesses. The role of entrepreneurship can be empowering to women in the context of development and has gained international attention.

Islam and Female Entrepreneurship. It is often assumed that women's role in Muslim countries is curtailed because of Islam. Traditionally and in Islamic law, the Shariʿah, there are no differences between men and women regarding commercial interactions and rights. Yet there are indirect potential barriers to women's economic activities because of the structure of the family. Of those with a direct impact, the most notable is the need for a husband's permission to leave the house in countries where this provision is included in the legal code. Inheritance law is another aspect of Shariʿah law that may limit women's economic activity. A son inherits twice as much as a daughter (Qurʾān 4:7–12), and widows have less entitlement to their husband's assets than it is the case with male's entitlement to their wife's possessions'. On the other hand, some of these traditional barriers work to the advantage of women, such as the husband's obligation to provide for his family (which is based on the traditional male-breadwinner model). What is interesting is that, under Islamic law, women are not obligated to share their income, assets, or any kind of possession with their husbands. The traditions that allow women to exercise control over their assets date to the time of the Prophet, as the first woman who became a Muslim, the Prophet's wife Khadījah, was an entrepreneur and had her husband as her employee. Interestingly, the superintendents at the market at Medina were all women. Later, this tradition was followed by Muslims during the Ottoman Empire, and historical records show that women were managers of property of the *waqf* (family trust or endowment). This is highly significant, as the records show that in sixteenth-century Istanbul, one-third of all founders of *awqāf* were women.

Historical Record of Women's Role in the Economy. In the case of Egypt, Judith Tucker argues that the historical evidence shows that women were engaged in a range of urban occupations and that court records illustrate that women owned many properties (at a time when British women had no ownership rights). As in the Ottoman case, women played a major role in *waqf* in Upper Egypt. Similar evidence from Syria in Margaret Meriwether's research of Aleppo women during the nineteenth century indicates that women were highly involved in the textile industry, although this industry suffered under colonial rule and European competition, resulting in losses of jobs for women. Aleppo women played a key role in the real-estate market and were in charge of most *waqf* administration.

As in the case of Aleppo women's roles in the textile industry, the colonial process seems to have undermined women's traditional access to property and production and minimized their role as entrepreneurs more generally throughout the region, as was seen in the heavy decline of the cotton and silk industry in Egypt. Moreover, modernization has led to a decline of the subsistence economy and an increase in cash crops, undermining women's access to means of production.

In Judith Tucker's *Arab Women: Old Boundaries, New Frontiers*, Evelyn's work, on the contemporary *baladi* (traditional) women of Egypt demonstrates that *baladi* women are entrenched in economic and bureaucratic networks, which are both national and international in scope. These networks provide women with opportunities to become involved in their communities and can help secure employment for their male relatives, such as taxi driving and construction work in Saudi Arabia. A *baladi* woman may also be a producer of goods herself, and may contract a family member to travel to the Persian Gulf to sell her goods on her behalf and act as middle merchants returning from a buying trip abroad. This very much complicates attempts to distinguish strictly between traditional and modern, in both the historical and the contemporary settings.

Characteristics of Female Entrepreneurs in MENA. On average about 13 percent of businesses are female-owned in MENA, although this number varies considerably across countries, with the highest rates being found in Lebanon (30 percent) and the lowest in Syria and Morocco (10 percent). Two of the most interesting findings of a 2008 World Bank study are that female-owned firms are more likely to hire women workers and also more likely to export, although this also varies by country. Issues that entrepreneurs identify as constraints include taxation, macroeconomic instability, access to and the cost of financing, and availability of skilled workers. While in some cases, female entrepreneurs report that these are more of a problem than male workers do, in other cases no gender difference is in evidence. One of the most surprising findings is that, in Yemen and Lebanon, constraints seem the most gendered, although these are two countries that in other ways look very different.

One of the more interesting characteristics of female-owned businesses is that they tend to hire women for jobs at managerial levels. In Egypt, for example, women make up 19 percent of the workers in female-owned firms, but only 16 percent in male-owned firms (Elgeziri, 2010).

It is particularly important to note that in the MENA region, the rate of female unemployment in some cases remains disproportionately higher than men's. In Yemen, for example, 40.9 percent of women are unemployed compared to 11.5 percent of men; in the West Bank, 38.85 percent of women are unemployed compared to 13.9 percent of men; in Egypt, the percentages for women and men are 19.2 and 5.9 respectively. In Saudi Arabia, there is a remarkable difference between unemployment among women, at 15.9 percent, and men, at 3.5 percent. Jordan shows major differences between the sexes: 24.1 percent of Jordanian women are unemployed compared to 10.3 percent of their male counterparts. Iranian female unemployment shows similar discrepancies: 16.8 percent for women compared to 9.1 percent for men. In a few other countries, female unemployment is marginally higher than male, such as in Turkey, where female unemployment is 14.9 percent compared to 13 percent for men. In Algeria, female unemployment is slightly less than men's, at 10.1 percent for women compared to 11 percent for men (Chamlou, 2008).

Informal Sector and Micro Enterprises. Although men constitute the majority of large-firm owners in the formal sector, women throughout the world are represented in the low end of the informal sector and/or home workers. As micro entrepreneurs, many women in the Muslim world continue to provide essential income for their family's survival. This is particularly noteworthy as the number of female-headed households in the region is increasing (UNDP, 2006). Irene Tinker argues that the role of women in micro enterprises is significant to many households in some Muslim countries, as documented by the Self-Employed Women's Association of India: 59 percent of households in Senegal rely on the income generated by women street vendors, and in Dakar 67 percent of households "were de facto headed by women" who work in the informal sector and as micro entrepreneurs (Tinker, 2008). Muslim women have proven to be highly industrious, and perhaps it is no surprise that the Grameen Bank, which has become a world success, has flourished in a Muslim country, Bangladesh.

In the face of rising micro enterprises, especially in the informal sector where there is a tendency for low pay and precarious working conditions because of the nature of the sector (M. A. Chen, 2001; M.A. Chen, Vanek, and Heintz, 2006), efforts to unionize informal micro entrepreneurs are important for their own economic protection. Many of them are confined to the house as home workers. The issue has been taken up by organizations such as SEWA (Self-Employed Women's Association), WIEGO (Women in Informal Employment: Globalizing and Organizing), and StreetNet, all of which seek to call attention to women's informal employment in order to lobby for protective legislation and unionization.

It is important to point out that one of the major obstacles for the female entrepreneur, whether in large, medium, or small enterprises, is access to credit. Generally, since women have much lower property ownership than men do, this has translated into a much bigger challenge for women in obtaining loans and credit for their companies than men face. It is for these reasons that development initiatives place such great emphasis on female entrepreneurship. There have been efforts to provide documentation on the importance of female-owned companies as the engine of economic growth in many parts of the Muslim world in general and in MENA in particular. Obviously large, medium, and small firms in the formal sector face fewer challenges in accessing credit than those in the informal sector. Therefore, solving the problem for women in the informal sector, in small and micro enterprises especially, means that increased access to credit must be a priority.

The concept of interest-free loans in Islamic culture is especially noteworthy. Such access will undoubtedly work to the benefit of women entrepreneurs, especially in micro enterprises. In some parts of the Muslim world, rotating saving and credit associations (small groups of women who bring their savings together and take turns borrowing the total sum for a fixed duration) have created a source of credit and are potentially a major resource for cash vital to starting a micro enterprise.

[*See also* Borrowing and Credit, Women's; Business Ownership and Women; Economics and Finance; Investment and Commerce, Women's; Khadīja bint Khuwaylid; Ottoman Empire, Women's Socioeconomic Role; Waqf, Women's Constructions of; *and* Workforce, Women in the.]

BIBLIOGRAPHY

Afshar, Haleh. *Women, Development, and Survival in the Third World.* London and New York: Longman, 1991.

Benería, Lourdes. *Gender, Development, and Globalization: Economics As If All People Mattered.* New York: Routledge, 2003.

Benería, Lourdes, and G. Sen. "Accumulation, Reproduction, and Women's Role in Economic Development: Boserup Revisited." *Sign: Journal of Women in Culture and Society* 7 (1981): 279–296.

Boserup, Ester. *Woman's Role in Economic Development.* New ed. London and Sterling, Va.: Earthscan, 1989.

Center of Arab Women for Training and Research (CAWTAR). *Globalization and Gender: Economic Participation and Arab Women.* Arab Women's Development Report. Tunis: CAWTAR, 2001.

Center of Arab Women for Training and Research (CAWTAR) and International Finance Corporation (IFC). *Women Entrepreneurs in the Middle East and North Africa: Characteristics, Contributions, and*

Challenges. Washington, D.C. and Tunis: CAWTAR and IFC, 2007.

Chamlou, Nadereh. *The Environment for Women's Entrepreneurship in the Middle East and North Africa*. Orientations in Development Series. Washington, D.C.: World Bank, 2008.

Chant, Sylvia, and Cathy McIlwaine. *Geographies of Development in the 21st Century: An Introduction to the Global South*. Cheltenham, U.K.: Edward Elgar, 2009.

Chen, M. A. "Women in the Informal Sector: A Global Picture, the Global Movement." *SAIS Review* 21 (2001): 71–82.

Chen, M. A., J. Vanek, and J. Heintz. "Informality, Gender, and Poverty: A Global Picture." *Economic and Political Weekly* 41, no. 21: 2131–2139, May 26, 2004.

Cinar, M. *The Economics of Women and Work in the Middle East and North Africa*. London: Elsevier Science, 2001.

Cuno, K. M. "A Tale of Two Villages: Family, Property, and Economic Activity in Rural Egypt in the 1840s." In *Agriculture in Egypt: From Pharaonic to Modern Times*, edited by Alan K. Bowman and Eugene Rogan, pp. 301–329. Oxford: Oxford University Press, 1999.

Elgeziri, M. "Wading through Treacle: Female Commercial School Graduates (CGSS) in Egypt's Informal Economy." *Feminist Formations* 22, no. 3 (2010): 10–50.

Elson, D. "Gender-Aware Analysis and Development Economics." *Journal of International Development* 5, no. 2 (1993): 176–190.

Harcourt, Wendy, ed. *Feminist Perspectives on Sustainable Development*. London: Zed Books, 1994.

Karshenas, M. "Economic Liberalization, Competitiveness, and Women's Employment in the Middle East and North Africa." In *Labor and Human Capital in the Middle East*, edited by Djavad Salehi-Isfahani, pp. 92–147. Reading, U.K.: Ithaca Press, 2001.

Karshenas, M., and V. Moghadam. "Female Labor Force Participation and Economic Adjustment in the MENA Region." In *The Economics of Women and Work in the Middle East and North Africa*, edited by M. Cinar, pp. 51–74. New York: JAI Press, 2001.

Meriwether, Margaret L. "Women and Economic Change in Nineteenth-Century Syria: The Case of Aleppo." In *Arab Women: Old Boundaries, New Frontiers*, edited by Judith E. Tucker, pp. 65–83. Bloomington: Indiana University Press, 1999.

Moghadam, Fatemeh Etemad. "Commoditization of Sexuality and Female Labor Participation in Islam: Implications for Iran, 1960–90." In *In the Eye of the Storm*, edited by Mahnaz Afkhami and Erika Friedl, 80–97. Syracuse, N.Y.: Syracuse University Press, 1994.

Mundy, M. "The Family, Inheritance, and Islam: A Re-examination of the Sociology of Faraid Law." In *Islamic Law: Social and Historical Contexts*, edited by Aziz al-Azmeh. New York: Routledge, 1988.

Nahvandi, M., and S. Ajavarlo. "Motaleh vaziateh zanan sarparast khanevar ba takid bar zanan-e dast forosh-e metro" [Research on Metro Vendor Female Heads of Households]. Paper presented at the Empowerment and Capacity Building of Female Heads of Households conference, Tehran, 2009. Conference Proceeding translated to English from Persian.

Nashat, Guity, and Judith E. Tucker. *Women in the Middle East and North Africa: Restoring Women to History*. Bloomington: Indiana University Press, 1999.

Peterson, Janice, and Margaret Lewis, eds. *The Elgar Companion to Feminist Economics*. Northampton, Mass.: Edward Elgar, 1999.

Rezai-Rashti, G. M. "Exploring Women's Experience of Higher Education and the Changing Nature of Gender Relations in Iran." In *Gender in Contemporary Iran: Pushing the Boundaries*, edited by Roksana Bahramitash and Eric Hooglund, pp. 45–61. New York: Routledge, 2011.

Tinker, I. "Sub-Saharan Africa." In *Encyclopedia of Women and Islamic Cultures*, edited by Suad Joseph and Afsaneh Najmabadi, Leiden, Netherlands: Brill, 2008.

Tucker, Judith E. *Egyptian Women in the Work Force: An Historical Survey*. Middle East Research and Information Project, 1976.

Tucker, Judith E., ed. *Arab Women: Old Boundaries, New Frontiers*. Bloomington: Indiana University Press, 1993.

Tucker, Judith E. *Egyptian Women in the Work Force: An Historical Survey*. MERIP Reports No. 50 (Aug., 1976) 3–9+26.

United Nations Development Programme (UNDP). *The Arab Human Development Report 2005: Towards the Rise of Women in the Arab World*. Amman, Jordan: Regional Bureau of Arab States, 2006.

ROKSANA BAHRAMITASH

WOMEN'S ISLAMIC INITIATIVE IN SPIRITUALITY AND EQUALITY (WISE).

Women's Islamic Initiative in Spirituality and Equality (WISE) is a social network and grassroots social justice movement composed of thousands of Muslim women from over 100 countries who are representing women's rights within an Islamic framework in order to tackle the central cause of women's disempowerment and grievances. It aims at building a cohesive, international movement of Muslim women who are reclaiming gender justice in Islam, enabling them to have greater agency in decision-making and to partake in constructing equal opportunities in their societies. By instituting an international network of in-country collaborative projects and support, WISE attempts to realize its goals at a local level. Such projects include the eradication of female genital cutting in Egypt; the imam-training program on women's rights in Afghanistan; and a domestic violence awareness campaign in Pakistan.

Launched in 2006 by Daisy Khan, WISE is a program of the American Society for Muslim Advancement (ASMA), a non-profit organization committed to strengthening the expression of Islam through interfaith dialogues, women's empowerment, and support for Muslim women's movements. By creating a space for diverse groups of female activists to connect and unite, WISE leads joint efforts to increase women's social and economic sovereignty and reinforce women's voices at all junctures of socio-political and religious discourse. In October 2011, WISE held a conference in Istanbul, Turkey titled "Muslim Women Leaders: At the Frontlines of Change." Over 175 Muslim women leaders of diverse backgrounds and religious ideologies from 45 countries partook in this event in an effort to disseminate women's voices.

Unlike secular organizations, WISE offers religion as an alternative frame of reference. It addresses the need for a Muslim women's movement with religious credentials and legitimacy. By stressing that substantial change should be produced through the interpretation of religious texts, WISE has instigated a global Muslim women's Shūrā Council of Muslim women scholars and activists, designed to promote gender justice within an Islamic framework through education and advocacy, affirming gender equality as an inherent part of religion. The Council also educates women on the principles of women's rights and socio-political and economic justice in the Islamic faith, and challenges discriminatory analysis of Islamic law and its primary texts by offering analyses that are in conformity with Islamic jurisprudence and a vision of gender justice.

Drawing upon its members' expertise in Islamic law, humanities, and social sciences, the Shūrā Council issues informed and religiously authentic opinions on contentious issues of relevance to Muslim women in their public and private lives. Although WISE faces criticism from some religious leaders who believe this organization is westernized and lacks the appropriate legal training to instigate a Shūrā Council, the members of this organization continue engage in reinterpretations of religious texts. By applying the Islamic legal traditions to the most urgent issues facing Muslim women at present, WISE attempts to develop strategies for creating social change.

[*See also* Khan, Daisy.]

BIBLIOGRAPHY

Abou El Fadl, Khaled. *Speaking in God's name: Islamic Law, Authority and Women.* Oxford: Oneworld, 2001.

Ahmed, Leila. *A Quiet Revolution: The Veil's Resurgence, from the Middle East to America.* New Haven, Conn.: Yale University Press, 2011.

Ali, Kecia. *Marriage and Slavery in Early Islam.* Cambridge, Mass.: Harvard University Press, 2010.

Khan, Daisy. "Islamophobia Is America's Real Enem." *The Guardian*, 9 Feb. 2012. http://www.guardian.co.uk/commentisfree/2012/feb/09/islamophobes-us-muslims-enemy.

Khan, Daisy, and Siddiqui Fazeela. "Training Afghani Imams to End Violence Against Women." *Huffington Post*, Feb 21, 2012. http://www.huffingtonpost.com/daisy-khan/afghanistan-imams-end-violence-against-muslim-women_b_1287885.html.

Wadud, Amina. *Inside the Gender Jihad: Women's Reform in Islam*. Oxford: Oneworld, 2006.

"Women's Islamic Initiative in Spirituality and Equality." Last modified August 2012. http://www.wise-muslimwomen.org/.

Samaneh Oladi Ghadikolei

Women's Magazines. Women's magazines are popular media products tied to the context within which they are produced and read. In Muslim majority countries, this is no exception. From Morocco to Afghanistan and from Iran to Indonesia, women's magazines have been shaped by histories of colonialism, nationalism, and the complicated trajectories of postcolonial modernity in these societies. Since their emergence, women's magazines have been entangled in debates about change and authenticity, the affirmation of cultural identities, and the management of postcolonial anxieties. The "women question" has been central in these debates. Magazines have been both reflective of and participants in reconfiguring women's status, conditions, and responsibilities in modern Muslim states. Magazines' roles have evolved over time to adapt to women's multilayered lives. As such, they provide a valuable record of societal (re)definitions of gender roles and norms and the ideals of womanhood, motherhood, and femininity. Magazines have also served as a vibrant space for women's self-expression, self-representation, and identity formation. Given the many ideological forces shaping the magazines' form and content, the publications have over the years taken on different ideological positions about women's rights and made different commitments to their emancipation and empowerment. Their vacillation between "trend-setting" and "trend-following" speaks to larger tensions and contradictions characterizing Muslim societies in the early twenty-first century.

This article sheds light on some of the major characteristics and trends defining women's magazines in the Muslim world. It first provides a brief overview of the conditions under which women's publications emerged and then focuses on the broad ideological currents that have shaped women's magazines since the second half of the twentieth century: feminism, consumerism, and Islamism. The argument made here is that, although these ideologies are at odds with each other, they invariably compete, collide, and even converge on the pages of women's magazines. This explains the "ideological messiness" of the publications as they adjust to changing local realities and negotiate global influences. The article concludes with a reflection on women's magazines in the age of cyber-publishing and interconnectivity.

Foundations and Legacies. Magazines for Muslim women emerged within contexts of colonialism, nationalist movements, and the rise of the developmental state. Their appearance under colonial administrations gave them a distinctive character: of militantism and reformism. Their founders were neither property owners nor business entrepreneurs—as was the case for early Euro-American publications. They were individuals and small groups invested in the sociopolitical change of their countries as activists, writers, and founders of associations.

In the Middle East and North Africa (MENA), this tradition was established by Lebanese, Syrian, and Egyptian middle-class women from multiethnic and multireligious backgrounds. Early pioneers underplayed their differences to privilege their shared language, cultural heritage, and Eastern identity. When the first women's monthly *Al-Fatah* (The Young Woman) appeared in Alexandria, Egypt, in November 1892, its editor Hind Nawal called it "the first of its kind under the Eastern sky" and promised to "adorn its pages with pearls from the pens of women." Egyptian publications were the source of inspiration for North African magazines, although these did not emerge for several more decades.

In Turkey, women's magazines started appearing when the Young Turks instituted Ottoman reforms. At least forty women's journals began publication prior to the pre-Republican period (1919–1923), but a few of these were owned by women or counted only women writers. Nonetheless, titles such as *Terakki-i Muhaddarat* (Progress of Women, 1869–1870), *Şűkûfezar* (Flower Garden, 1883–1884), and *Demet* (*Bouquet*, 1908–1909) debated women's rights and demanded their education and inclusion in the workforce.

Muslim women in India could choose among early magazines printed in Urdu, with *Tahzib un-Niswan* being a long-lasting publication (1898–1950s). Founded by the reformist Sayyid Mumtaz Ali and his wife Muhammadi Begam, the magazine was conceived as a "practical guide" to educate Muslim women about their rights as granted them by religion but denied by society. This and subsequent publications (*Khatun d'Aligarh*, 1904–1914; *Ismat*, 1908) called for social reforms to broaden women's roles in society.

Early women's magazines in Indonesia targeted middle-class women, starting in 1912 with *Poetri Mardika* (The Independent Lady) that raised questions about education, early marriage, and polygamy. At least seven other Indonesian publications appeared in the first half of the twentieth century. Most were published by religious groups, including *Soeara Aisyiyah* (The Voice of Aisyiyah)—a women's movement affiliated with the Islamic organization Muhammadiyah. After Independence in 1945, magazines were published by women's groups such as the Indonesian Female Workers Organization, which produced *Karya* (The Achievement), and the Indonesian Women's Consciousness Movement, the leftist women's organization at the University of Indonesia. Only one publication survived by the time the New Order (the military regime of General Suharto, 1965 till 1998) came to power.

There are a few significant commonalities among the first generation of women's publications across the Muslim world. First, given the colonial context under which magazines emerged, women entered the print culture as a politicized and problematized subject. Their roles and responsibilities, whether debated on or off the magazines' pages, were framed by nationalistic ambitions and ethos. The education of Muslim women unified voices beyond ideological or cultural differences. Justifications for their education, however, created divisions among those who linked it to state modernization, those who tied it to cultural/identity preservation, and those who demanded it for women's emancipation. Calls for women's emancipation by magazine editors were usually controversial and ran the risk of being labeled either "anti-nationalist" or "anti-religious," or both. The entanglement of women's issues with broader religious, cultural, and political considerations is one of the powerful legacies still impacting how women and their magazines are discussed.

Second, a contemporary reading of early magazines can easily cast doubts on the meaning of emancipation they advocated. Placed in their historical contexts, however, many early pioneers had unmistakable feminist aspirations. Echoes of the women's suffrage movement in Europe reached Muslim women as topics for discussion and inspiration. Those who participated in the magazines were brave and daring enough to approach controversial issues of divorce, veiling, or polygamy at a time when their societies were unprepared for their voices. As historical documents, early magazines recorded how calls for women's rights initiated heated debates and ideological confrontations that reverberated across religious and political circles.

Third, early magazines are also records of the emergence of women as writing and reading subjects active in the dissemination of knowledge in their societies. Magazines were the space for self-expression and celebration of one's own literary talents. Although this was the case for an urban-based minority, many had to brave social and psychological barriers to develop a voice and presence in the public space. Finally, a common concern of early pioneers was the production of an indigenous model of women's magazines despite the Western origin of the genre. This search for indigeneity reflected then, as it does now, a larger preoccupation with finding a "local" vocabulary and model for advancing women's emancipation.

Feminism and the Passion for Fashion. In Western societies, the "commercialization of gender" and "gendering of commerce" were twin processes shaping women's magazines beginning in the eighteenth century. Feminists and media critics have since approached such publications as purveyors of oppressive patriarchal and capitalist ideologies. Similar concerns did not apply to women's magazines in Muslim countries until the market started to refashion their form and content after the Second World War.

However, reducing all magazines to mere commercial/patriarchal vehicles simplifies the complex relations they have with the changing realities of Muslim women and undermines the diversity of ideologies that claim and are claimed by them. A more apt characterization would describe the magazines as products that sit rather uncomfortably between feminist drives, commercial vibes, and Islamist considerations, especially since the 1990s. Magazines for Muslim women tend to fall within three broad categories: feminist, commercial, and Islamist magazines. However, the boundaries between these categories are strikingly porous: Different ideologies often collide and compete in the magazines despite the claims of coherence by their editors. Virtually all deploy discourses of women's rights and empowerment to attract readers with the promise of meeting their specific needs. Virtually all adopt a glossy outlook and most advertise consumer products for which they provide ideological justifications, as discussed below.

Few magazines self-identify as feminist in the early twenty-first century and fewer still have survived censorship in Muslim countries. The Iranian *Zanan* (Women) folded in 2008 after the regime declared it a threat to the "psychological security of the society." *Zanan*, like feminist magazines in other contexts, was produced by women's rights activists with a passion for and commitment to justice. This was also the case of the Arab-language *Thamania Mars* (March 8, 1983–1995), the Arab-language *Nissa' al Marghreb* (Moroccan Women, 1986), and the French-language *Kalima* (Word, 1986–1989). The first two magazines were founded by the leaders of the Moroccan secular women's movement, while the third pioneered the art of taboo-breaking.

Censorship looms large not just for feminist magazines. The trajectory of the Egyptian weekly *Hawa'*, for instance, tells us that censorship is often unpredictable and arbitrary.

Hawa' was banned in Muʿammar al-Qadhdhāfī's Libya and in Saudi Arabia because its editor was declared a "heretic" supporting women's liberation. Yet, the magazine is neither radically feminist nor is it free from consumerist ideologies. This author's review of one issue of the magazine reveals that out of its seventy pages, twenty-nine are devoted to fashion and beauty products (Skalli, 2006). Its feminism is "diluted" by a strong dose of consumerism.

Breaking taboos, however, still energizes the younger generation of activists who deploy their artistic talents in creative ways. When the Lebanese *JASAD* (Body) appeared in 2009, it shocked the Muslim public by mixing articles on women's sexuality and sexual orientation with graphic images. Contributors to the magazine from various MENA nations embraced the magazine's refusal to be intimidated by critics or threatening hate mail. In defense of her self-financed project, Joumana Haddad has invited her critics to "go back to our own literary heritage which includes 'The Perfumed Garden' and 'Thousand and One Nights," (Zablit, 2009). A similar use of artistic expression distinguishes the Turkish *Bayan Yani*, a satirical women's magazine that mixes social criticism and acid humor to break gender-related taboos. Its founders take the controversies ignited by the magazine as a sign of its success, which is also confirmed by the large circulation numbers (over fifty thousand) in a country with low readership.

In general, however, it is the mix of "soft" feminism and glossy commercialism that seems to dominate magazines for Muslim women. Women's increasing education and mobility have encouraged magazines to offer them advice on how to make sense of themselves and their changing world, and with commercial products that "assist" them in this process. The Moroccan glossies *Femmes du Maroc* and *Citadine* best exemplify this trend. When their first issues appeared in the mid-1990s, the magazines introduced high-end fashion products along with calls for reform in women's legal status. The editor of *Femmes du Maroc* defined this as "modern feminism" with which most readers can identify. The presentation of feminism with a glossy look started as early as the 1970s in MENA, India, and Indonesia. Many magazines embraced the "Cosmo phenomenon" for inspiration: The American *Cosmopolitan* (first published in 1965) revolutionized magazine production by paying "tribute" to the capitalist system while "popularizing" basic feminist ideas in ways no other publications succeeded.

Many magazines, however, made an overt commercial and conservative commitment. Lebanese periodicals played a leading role. After the Lebanese Civil War, big media industries moved to Europe and the journalistic expertise of emigrants was traded for the petrodollars of Saudi investors. This resulted in a new breed of women's magazines that created a local market for an Arabized version of major European magazines such as the French editions of *Elle*, *Vogue*, and *Burda*. The unapologetic consumerism of these magazines meshed well with the conservatism of their founders who believed in women's limited roles and capabilities. The weekly *Sayidaty* (My Lady) is a classic example in this category. Published since the 1970s by Saudi money in London, *Sayidaty* is distributed across MENA, Europe, and America. Its selection of safe topics (fashion, beauty, entertainment and family life) has attracted numerous readers and advertisers. *Zahrat Al Khaleej* (The Gulf Flower) in making the same safe choices has enjoyed a similarly long life.

Faith and Fashion: The Rise of Islamist Magazines. In 2011 al-Qa'ida launched a 31-page women's magazine *Al-Shamikha* (Majestic Woman) that glorifies beauty and fashion with martyrdom and sacrifice. The glossy's first editorial recognized women's contribution to fighting Islam's enemies: It gives voice to martyrs' wives and provides singletons tips for marrying a martyr. Although *Al-Shamikha* is a rare example of radical Islamist magazines, it reflects important changes in the sociopolitical landscapes of Muslim societies. Not so extremist are women's magazines, such as *Zahoor* (Flowers), which are produced by Saudi-funded Islamist groups targeting women as valuable voters and mothers of the next Islamist generations.

Islamist ideologies of piety and modesty have also started to shape the growing market of Islamic fashion for women and the magazines that supports it. The large popularity of the Islamic magazine *Noor* in post-Suharto Indonesia resides in its combination of faith and fashion, and translation of "virtue into value via the image of the feminine" (Jones, 2010, p. 92). Although the magazine's editors refuse to view their glossy as capitalism in religious garb, their magazine serves the thriving Islamic consumer culture as much as it caters to the modern Muslim woman. Like *Femmes du Maroc* that helped popularize women's traditional dress in Morocco, *Noor* supports the Islamic fashion industry in Indonesia. Both magazines sponsor designer shows, organize media coverage of those events, and provide in-depth treatment in special issues. Other magazines, such as the Egyptian Hijab, promote Islamic fashion without the pretense of any other missions.

The emergence and popularity of these magazines point to the complex ways in which a woman's body, visibility, and piety are represented in the Muslim world, and the extent to which the latter is traversed by larger market forces. By inhabiting spaces of contradictions and controversy, Islamist magazines often stimulate social dialogue over unaddressed issues. This is the case of the Turkish *Âlâ* (Beautiful Lifestyle) that gained instant public attention when its first issue (published in the summer of 2011) featured the Islamic headscarf on its cover. The cover ignited a debate among Turkish secularists and traditional Muslims about the congruence of fashion and Islam. Critics on and off social media spaces dubbed the glossy an "Islamic *Vogue*" that violates Islamic ideals of modesty. What the debate confirms is that women's fashion and publications remain entangled with broader issues of nationalism, religion, modernity, and capitalism.

Net Generation Magazines. Magazines on the Net include those with an existing print edition (*Sayidaty* or *Femmes du Maroc)* and those with both a print and cyber-copy (*Muslim Girl*, *Azizah*, or *Emel*). Although e-magazines have yet to receive the scholarly attention they deserve, their emergence signals yet another stage in the visibility of Muslim women and articulation of their needs. The high number of e-magazines suggests new possibilities of knowledge production and circulation, women's freedom of selection, and increased opportunities for interconnectivity among Muslim women including those in the Diaspora. These promises are not without limitations.

Magazines in cyberspace are the initiative of what this author elsewhere has referred to as "cultural brokers": a generation of young cosmopolitans who are mediators between local realities and global cultural trends (Skalli, 2006). Some are educated in European languages and institutions, most are widely traveled, and all are tech-savvy. While these brokers understand the appeal of Western-style consumerism, they also respond to the realities of their local "niche" markets. In addition, they recognize the rewards of addressing Muslim women as modern citizens with transformative powers and consumer preferences. Not surprisingly, magazines draw extensively on the feminist vocabulary of empowerment and/or Islamic piety when necessary.

The challenge for the researcher in the early twenty-first century is not simply to provide answers to "who reads what, where and for what purposes." Rather, the challenge is to understand how these magazines complicate issues surrounding the accessibility, visibility, and identity of Muslim women while acknowledging their agency as well as the power of competing ideologies.

With rare exceptions, research on women's magazines has remained strongly biased toward content analysis and is rather weak when it comes to including the voices of the readers and producers of the magazines. A balanced approach would provide a more cogent analysis of how Muslim women make sense of the magazines that target them in today's media- and consumer-saturated environment.

BIBLIOGRAPHY

Azeharie, Suzie. "Representations of Women in *Femina*, an Indonesian Women's Magazine." Masters by Research thesis, Murdoch University, Perth, Australia,1997. http://www.researchrepository.murdoch.edu.au/193/.

Damon-Moore, Helen. *Magazines for the Millions: Gender and Commerce in the Ladies' Home Journal and Saturday Evening Post*. New York: New York University Press, 1994.

Human Rights First. "What's at Stake? Protest Closure of Iranian Women's Magazine." February 12, 2008. http://action.humanrightsfirst.org/campaign/Zanan/explanation.

Jones, Carla. "Images of Desire: Creating Virtue and Value in an Indonesian Islamic Lifestyle Magazine." *Journal of Middle East Women's Studies* 6, no. 3 (Fall 2010): 91–117.

Letsch, C. "Turkey: Islamic Women's Magazine Sparks Debate over Role of Fashion in Islam." 2011. http://www.eurasianet.org/node/64542.

Lewis, Reina. "Marketing Muslim Lifestyle: A New Media Genre." *Journal of Middle East Women's Studies* 6, no. 3 (Fall 2010): 58–90.

Minault, Gail. "Les revues féminines en langue urdu au début du XX e siècle." *Women Living Under Muslim Laws*, 9–10 (1991). http://www.wluml.org/sites/wluml.org/files/import/french/pubs/rtf/dossiers/dossier9-10/D9-10-07-revues.rtf.

Skalli, Loubna H. *Through a Local Prism: Gender, Globalization and Identity in Moroccan Women's Magazines*. Lanham, MD: Lexington Books, 2006.

Toksabay, Ece. "Feature with Satire: Woman's Magazine Tackles Taboos in Turkey." 2011. http://www.reuters.com/article/2011/07/20/turkey-women-magazine-idUSLDE76H0LI20110720.

Zablit, Jocelyne. "*Jasad* Magazine Casts an Unprecedented Spotlight on Sexuality in the Arab World." March 31, 2009. http://doctorbulldog.wordpress.com/2009/03/30/jasad-magazine-casts-an-unprecedented-spotlight-on-sexuality-in-the-arab-world/.

LOUBNA H. SKALLI

WOMEN'S MOVEMENTS. Muslim women's participation in social movements and the emergence of women's associations, leagues, and organizations involved in nationalist, charitable, gender-centered, political, economic, or religious activities began in the nineteenth century and continued into the twenty-first. Important debates over women's status first emerged in the nineteenth century. These debates concerning the education, segregation, and full veiling of certain women expanded to other aspects of women's roles in public life, affording them greater opportunities in a gradual fashion, especially for upper-class women and in combination with state-led reforms. With the rise of Islamism, a response to the earlier modernist view of sex-role expansion and reform arose, as well as a new activism by some Islamist women. Also, women continued organized efforts to reform family, criminal, and commercial laws, as well as cultural practices affecting women. With the burgeoning number of nongovernmental organizations (NGOs) in the 1990s, more emphasis on activities and agendas for women was included.

The Nineteenth Century. From the early nineteenth century onward, different Muslim societies began to discuss the need for social, educational, and political reform. Muslim women's oppression was an area requiring reform; hence, debate about women and gender relations among Muslims also rang with overtones concerning the role of the West in the Muslim world. Certain women and men questioned the legal and social restrictions on women, especially with regard to education, female seclusion (known as purdah in the Indian subcontinent), strict veiling of the face, polygamy, the marriage of very young women to much older men by family arrangement, women's slavery, and, in some cases, concubinage. Egyptian male reformers wrote on women's behalf, among them Aḥmad Fāris al-Shidyāq, author of *One Leg Crossed Over the Other* (1855); Rifāʿah Rāfiʿ al-Ṭahṭāwī (1801–1871); Muḥammad ʿAbduh (1849–1905), a founder of the Islamic reform movement; Qāsim Amīn, whose book *Women's Emancipation* (1899) unleashed furious discussion; and Aḥmad Luṭfī al-Sayyid, publisher of *al-Jarīdah*. Turkish counterparts included Namık Kemal and Ahmet Mithat.

Educated women, such as Wardah al-Yāzijī and Wardah al-Turk in Syria and ʿĀʾishah al-Taymūrīyah in Egypt, began writing to each other in the 1860s and 1870s regarding reform for women, as women later did for women's publications. As part of a growing women's press, Hind Nawfal (1860–1920), a Syrian immigrant to Alexandria, published and edited *al-Fatāh*, a women's Arabic monthly; Zaynab Fawwāz (1860–1914), who immigrated from Tibnin to the same city, founded the newspaper *al-Nīl* in 1891. Persian women also began writing and publishing women's journals, the earliest being *Danesh* (1907).

In Turkey, early feminists included the well-known Halide Edib Adıvar (1883–1964) and Fatma Âliye Hanım (b. 1862), who published *Nisvani İslam* and *A Newspaper for Ladies*. During this period, women in various Muslim countries began to establish schools for girls. Somewhat earlier, some Iranian women had participated in the Bābī movement, an offshoot of Shiism; its leaders included Rustamah and the martyr Qurrat al-ʿAyn (1815–1851), who appeared unveiled and preached against polygamy and the veil. In Indonesia, a famous advocate of women's education and emancipation was Raden Adjeng Kartini (1879–1904). She wrote and founded a school for daughters of Javanese officials, becoming most influential after her death.

The Effect of Nationalist Movements. Women also engaged in philanthropy and in nationalist movements. Both impulses instructed women in social mobilization and gave rise to associations run for and by women. In Iran, women took part in the Tobacco Rebellion and subsequently in the Constitutional Revolution (1908) and its aftermath, when mainly upper-class women organized separate *anjumans* (political societies), seeking education and the right to vote.

However, leaders and reformers such as Muṣṭafā Kāmil (1874–1908) and Talʿat Ḥarb in Egypt opposed the end of veiling, and, in 1882, Sayyid Aḥmad Khān of India asserted that purdah should be maintained and female education postponed. As women gained the right to professional educations and entered the workforce, some twentieth-century discourse characterized working women as a social drain or, in those instances where women worked with men, as a source of potential immorality. Often the primacy of the national struggle forced feminist issues onto the back burner. Examples were the later arrival of female suffrage in various countries and the primacy of national over gender issues in the Palestinian and Algerian national struggles. However, Palestinian women's activism provided important links to popular needs. It was paralleled by the organizing of Islamist women, especially after the Oslo peace process.

Women's participation in nationalist movements eroded the preexisting custom of female seclusion, allowing women into various public forums. Upper-class women in the early twentieth century ventured to meetings in elite salons—Eugénie Le Brun's in Egypt, and later to the literary salon of May Ziyada. Women's gatherings included lecture sessions, study groups, demonstrations, and formal associations. Individuals became well known; Hudā Shaʿrāwī (1879–1947), for example, became a symbol of feminist activism.

Philanthropic activities of elite and middle-class women actually formed the basis for the Egyptian state's social services and demonstrated women's managerial expertise. In Palestine, after the dispersal of the Palestinian people in 1948, middle-class women conducted relief efforts until the establishment of UNRWA refugee camps and facilities. In exile and at home, charitable associations formed the major focus for Palestinian women's organized activities until the 1967 war. Women's interest in social services later translated into participation in developmental programs, such as the Bangladesh Jatiyo Mahila Sangshtha (National Women's Organization), which coordinated programs under official sponsorship.

Postwar State Feminism. Nationalist movements and the new states that emerged in the post–World War I period perceived women and gender issues as crucial to social development. Atatürk of Turkey, Reza Shah of Iran, and later Habib Bourguiba of Tunisia, leaders with unassailable nationalist credentials, initiated new policies to reform women's status and weaken the power base of the *ʿulamāʾ*. These actions were controversial, as were, in Afghanistan, Amānullāh Khan's reforms of the family code in 1921, the banning of polygamy for state employees, and the public appearance of his wife, Queen Suraya, unveiled. Turkish and Iranian reforms from above also attacked the veil (or headscarf). Later amendments in Iran, Tunisia, and Egypt addressed various areas of personal status, including divorce, child custody, women's rights to the family home, and alimony, as did the Family Law ordinance (1961) in West and East Pakistan. State-controlled education and laws provided women with at least a basic education. State policies enabled groups of women to enter the male-dominated political sphere and professions previously closed to women, although the same policies may have caused a popular and religious aversion to state intervention in gender matters.

Women in political life might promote women's issues, but they and some activists were often isolated from lower-class women, who did not necessarily favor changes to current practices, such as the suggested reduction of *mahr* (bride price), or the listing of the bride's property, or the insertion of stipulations in marriage contracts, or, in Egypt, the custom of female circumcision.

Egypt. Egyptian women were accorded voting rights in 1956, in part as a consequence of long-term advocacy, but also through unprecedented public activism under Durrīyah Shafīq (1908–1975), who was later ill-regarded by the Nasser regime. Early activist women's groups included the Wafdist Women's Committee, the Egyptian Feminist Union, and the Bint al-Nīl association. Women also organized through a wing of Ḥasan al-Bannā's Muslim Brotherhood (founded in 1928) in the Association of Muslim Women established by Zaynab al-Ghazālī. These Islamist women wore the veil and eventually adopted a white *khimār* (head cover). They held that women must preserve their modesty, morals, and loyalty to their role in the home. The Muslim Brotherhood spread in the Arab world, opposing the female vote and coeducation in the 1950s, but later proposing reform of women's status in an Islamic manner.

Algeria. Women were involved in the resistance movements of North Africa. In Algeria, the National Liberation Front (FLN) incorporated women in its rebellion against French authority. The Front's conception of Algerian identity linked religion and nationalism. Its leadership was male, but so many men were imprisoned or in hiding that women served as fighters, intelligence operatives, and liaison agents, as well as in nursing and supply operations. Initially, the veil provided cover, as the French were reluctant to search women, who became increasingly involved in carrying bombs and arms. Later, women were imprisoned and tortured, and in the process some became national heroines. However, the post-revolutionary government required the registration of their activities, and many lost benefits and recognition because they were illiterate or because, as women, they were designated "civilian" rather than "military" participants. With time, Islamist parties gained large followings, including women who proposed a more conservative view of gender. At times, women in public spaces who were not abiding by these more conservative views, such as veiling, were subject to harassment and physical violence.

Oman and Yemen. In the Omani resistance movement, women were also empowered by the military nature of their engagement. In the former People's Democratic Republic of Yemen, after the revolution, various official agencies and associations were created for women, but their goal was the economic well-being of the state rather than a reform of gender inequities. Nonetheless, reforms were enacted that fostered women's education and increased their participation in the workforce. Women started holding official posts and became members in different cabinets. Yemeni women surprised the world with their active participation in the revolution, and the Yemeni activist Tawakul Karman won the Nobel Peace Prize in 2011.

Iraq. In Iraq, prior to World War I, Jamil Sidqi al-Zahawi wrote an attack on veiling and women's treatment under Sharīʿah that caused controversy. A small elite group of feminists were active in King Faysal's era, and the Iraqi Communist Party promoted an agenda for women. Later, in both Iraq and Syria, the Baaʿth Party featured women's associations. These movements were not able to translate their goals successfully or equally to all classes of society.

In post-Saddam Iraq, many international projects that aimed to provide income or other aid to women were interrupted by violence. Kidnappings and attacks on women forced many into exile, or to cease attending school, and many adopted the hijab out of fear of attacks, when unveiled women, those driving, and some with businesses were targeted. Iraqi women successfully prevented a law that would require them to attend family courts of their own sect. A small women's movement is offset by politicians who argue for Islamist interpretations of the law.

Syria. In Syria, uniformed high-school girls serve as clean-up crews in villages and participate in youth leagues, but are still encouraged to marry early and enter "female" professions, such as teaching. Women have been important in religious opposition groups within Syria, including the outlawed Muslim Brotherhood. When urban Sunnī women adopted the hijab, some were met by officially organized demonstrations of ʿAlawī Baʿthī women, who unsuccessfully protested the wearing of hijab in school and work settings.

Women as part of the ruling party and state feminism in an authoritarian regime meant that women figures in the party and ruling elites did not represent a grassroots struggle. After the situation in Syria deteriorated during 2012, women became far more vulnerable, living with their families under threats and displaced due to military clashes.

Malaysia. Women's participation in student movements has been a feature of Islamic revival in Malaysia, known generally as *dakwah* (Ar., *daʿwah*). Dissension arose over the increase in veiling, particularly when universities required it. Similarly, debate continues over the appropriate level of female participation in the public sphere, ranging from sermons emphasizing a strong Muslim family life, to the complete segregation of female *dakwah* communal members, to the activism of other women such as those in Sisters in

Islam. In Malaysia, the gender discussion combines with concerns of national identity, as the Malay majority coexists with other communities (Chinese, Indian, and aboriginal) who are legally free to observe their own faiths. The religious revival was propagated by several organizations, including the Islamic Youth League of Malaysia, Dar ul Arqam, and the more traditional Jemaat Tabligh. Clusters of adherents to revivalist groups had formed same-sex "family" groups (*usrah*). Islamization, including that of the laws in some areas, has continued.

Indonesia. In Indonesia, the Muhammadiyah organization, begun in 1912, typifies apolitical educational and service activities. The Aisyiyah was the women's branch of this party, allowing for mobilization beyond the traditional teacher-peasant dynamic existing in Indonesia, as well as Malaysia. After the Sukarno era, religious political parties were banned under Suharto, and the four existing Islamic parties combined into the Partai Persatuan Pembangunan (PPP). Nonetheless, religiosity has been on the rise in Indonesia, along with contemporary Islamic dress. Groups such as the Association of Islamic Students eschew militancy, but view gender issues as integrally tied to Muslim identity. At the same time, the women's wings of Nahdlatul Ulama, Fatayat, and Muhammadiyah, Nasyiatul Aisyiyah, are challenging traditional Islamic teachings about gender in favor of contextualized reinterpretations that expand women's rights.

Pakistan. The most important locus of Islamist activity in Pakistan, prior to the emergence of al-Qaʿida and the Taliban, was the Jamāʿat-i Islāmī and the Tablīghī Jamāʿat. Both proposed countering secularization and Western gender identity with a Muslim notion of modesty and piety. With the growth of Islamist parties and persons in politics, disputes over gender issues increased, including legal debates over whether rape victims can be prosecuted as adulteresses. Veiling and separation of the sexes have continued, though nuanced by the changing fortunes of the various political actors and parties, with al-Qaʿida supporters calling for much stricter regulations on women. The 2007 assassination of Benazir Bhutto, a turning of the political tide against the Musharraf regime, and post-9/11 concern over radicalism could portend more support for women's issues and groups supporting them.

Iran. The emergence of the Islamic Republic of Iran sparked new interest in women's role in the revolution and response to the Republic's legislation of gender. Many women, Islamist and non-Islamist, had been involved in opposition to Shah Muhammad Reza Pahlavi and had protested the Western commodification of women. However, when the government imposed Islamic dress and removed women from legal, judicial, and other offices, many Iranians fled. Nonetheless, women actively participated in the Mujāhidīn-i Khalq, an organization of Marxist-Islamic orientation not fully defeated in Iran until 1981–1982. A patrol and information division called the Zaynab Sisters and other women's associations began operating in Iran. A penal and family code revised along Islamic lines was imposed, but women, though now excluded from holding judgeships and other positions, kept alive a debate about fairer treatment of women under the law. Women parliamentarians in the Sixth Majlis challenged certain discriminatory laws, but these eleven women were banned from running for office in the Seventh Majlis, which included only conservative female figures and reversed some legal reforms. Between 2003 and 2007, an Iranian movement for women's rights reasserted itself in the One Million Signatures and Abolish Stoning Forever campaigns. Former judge and prominent human and women's rights activist Shirin Ebadi became the first Muslim woman and first Iranian to win the Nobel Peace Prize in 2003.

Sudan. The Islamization of Muslim society, both organized and informal, increased in the 1980s. Women were fully involved in the process, whether by personal choice, familial loyalties, or active recruitment. For example, in Sudan, where women had been active in one of the strongest Communist parties in the region, reversals in the public sphere have occurred. Women's issues became important to the National Islamic Front as well, and the liberal Islamist group of legal specialists, the Republican Brothers and Sisters, was suppressed. By the 1990s, Sudanese women had gained greater access to the Qurʾān and Islamic teachings through "mosque groups," enabling them to encounter Islam in an alternative venue to the legal system, as well as to question cultural traditions and family roles and relationships.

Lebanon. In some areas, nationalist and Islamist goals interact and mobilize women, as among the Shīʿī of southern and eastern Lebanon. Necessity impelled many women to make use of political networks in the absence of their imprisoned or fighting men. Women resisted Israeli occupiers when possible and were harassed, attacked, and arrested. Most adopted the hijab and a more actively anti-Western stance in reaction to the Israeli occupation and in order to assert communal identity. In postwar Lebanon, a small reformist women's movement has campaigned unsuccessfully for an optional civil law of personal status, and successfully against a law permitting reduced sentences for honor killings. That movement contrasts with the less-organized emphasis on public piety as "women's jihad" in the Shīʿī community in Beirut.

West Bank and Gaza. Women were crucial to the waging of the *intifāḍah* in the occupied West Bank and the Gaza Strip. They participated at the grassroots level and through the four women's committees of the PLO, founded in 1981, which have sponsored economic, health, and political projects. These committees and the General Union of Palestinian Women's Associations in diaspora include both Muslim and Christian women. Much tension has arisen between these activist women and supporters of Ḥamās and Islamic Jihad, when attempts were made to impose the hijab in Gaza and elsewhere. Although these attempts were reined in, Islamist women's associations and agendas have come to parallel the efforts made by non-Islamist women, though they have different aims.

International Trends. Tensions between transnational feminist goals and those of local groups, whether Islamic feminists or those who disavow a feminist agenda altogether, have continued for over a quarter-century. With global migration, large groups of Muslim women are now living outside historically Muslim lands. Some explicitly Muslim groups have begun to organize, such as the North American Association of Muslim Women (founded in 1992) or the Women's Islamic Initiative in Spirituality and Equality (launched in 2006), an endeavor of the American Muslim Society for Advancement. Western branches of the long-standing General Union of Palestinian Women did not deal with specifically Muslim issues but with national ones. A Muslim feminist group in France, Ni Putes Ni Soumises (Neither Whores nor Repressed), organized to battle violence against women, obligatory hijab-wearing, and forced marriage—thus, some say, enacting the French New Right's agenda.

Many women's organizations ranging from Islamic feminist to profession-oriented or human rights groups now exist in Muslim countries. Nawāl al-Saʿdāwī's Arab Women's Solidarity Association was dissolved in Egypt in 1992 in response to Islamist and regime pressure, although it continued to exist outside the country. Other issue-oriented groups, such as al-Marʿah al-Jadīdah (The New Woman), the Bint al-Ard (Daughter of the Earth), and the FGM Taskforce, continued to operate. Numerous conferences and events in the region display the activities of gender-oriented NGOs, among them the Turkish-based Women for Women's Human Rights working on the issue of sexual rights, which the group defines as the proper focus for women's rights. Some attention has also been given to women *mujahidāt* and *shahīdāt*, or suicide bombers, in various incidents from Iraq to Jordan to Palestine, as a social phenomenon.

[*See also* Family Law; Feminism; Shaʿrāwī, Hudā; Women and Islam; *and* Women and Social Reform.]

BIBLIOGRAPHY

Al-Ali, Nadje. *Secularism, Gender, and the State in the Middle East: The Egyptian Women's Movement*. Cambridge, U.K.: Cambridge University Press, 2000.

Araffin, Rohana. "Feminism in Malaysia." *Women's Studies International Forum* 22, no. 4 (1999): 417–423.

Arat, Yesim. *Rethinking Islam and Liberal Democracy: Islamist Women in Turkish Politics*. Albany: State University of New York Press, 2006.

Badran, Margot. *Feminism in Islam: Secular and Religious Convergences*. Oxford: Oneworld, 2009.

Bullock, Katherine, ed. *Muslim Women Activists in North America: Speaking for Ourselves*. Austin: University of Texas Press, 2005.

cooke, miriam. "Islamic Feminism Before and After September 11th." *Duke Journal of Gender Law and Policy* 227 (2002): 227–235. Also appears in Zuhur (2003) listed below.

Hijab, Nadia. *Womanpower: The Arab Debate on Women at Work*. Cambridge, U.K.: Cambridge University Press, 1988.

Joseph, Suad, ed. *Gender and Citizenship in the Middle East*. Syracuse, N.Y.: Syracuse University Press, 2000.

Keddie, Nikki. *Women in the Middle East: Past and Present*. Princeton: Princeton University Press, 2007.

Khan, Shahnaz. *Zina, Transnational Feminism, and the Moral Regulation of Pakistani Women*. Vancouver, B.C.: ABC Press, 2006.

Mahmood, Saba. *Politics of Piety: The Islamic Revival and the Feminist Subject*. Princeton: Princeton University Press, 2005.

Nouraei-Simone, Fereshteh, ed. *On Shifting Ground: Muslim Women in the Global Era*. New York: Feminist Press, 2005.

Schweitzer, Yoram, ed. *Female Suicide Bombers: Dying for Equality?* Tel Aviv: Tel Aviv University, 2006.

Zuhur, Sherifa. "Empowering Women or Dislodging Sectarianism? Civil Marriage in Lebanon." *Yale Journal of Law and Feminism* 14, no. 1 (2002): 177–208.

Zuhur, Sherifa. *Iraq, Women's Empowerment, and Public Policy*. Carlisle Barracks, Penn.: US Army War College, 2007.

Zuhur, Sherifa. "The Mixed Impact of Feminism in Egypt of the 1990s." *Middle East Review of International Affairs (MERIA)* 6, no. 1 (2001).

Zuhur, Sherifa, ed. *Women and Gender in the Islamic World Today*. Berkeley: University of California Press, 2003. New edition published in 2008 (Carlisle Barracks, Penn.: US Army War College).

SHERIFA ZUHUR

WOMEN'S RELIGIOUS CELEBRATIONS.

Throughout the year, Muslims gather to celebrate particularly important events and figures in their religio-spiritual history. Throughout the Islamic world, Muslims celebrate joyous events such as the birthday of the Prophet Muḥammad, the end of the month of fasting in Ramadan, weddings, births, and the death anniversaries (*ʿurs*) of Ṣūfī saints and Shīʿī imams. The ritual celebrations of these events and holy figures are distinctly gendered in their performance and significance. For women, many of these celebrations are simultaneously spiritual, therapeutic, and reinforcing of female-centered support networks. Focusing on rituals celebrating the birth of the Prophet Muḥammad, marriage, Shīʿī votive meals, and pilgrimage to the tombs of Ṣūfī saints highlights the importance of the complex interpersonal relationships that Muslim women establish with God, holy figures, and other women.

Birth of Prophet Muḥammad. The birth of the Prophet Muḥammad in 570 CE produced over time a genre of panegyric poetry (Turkish *mevlūd*, Arabic *mawlūd*, Persian and Urdu *durūd-e sharīf*) describing Muḥammad's life, personality, and exemplary spiritual accomplishments. The birth of the Prophet Muḥammad (Mawlid al-Nabī) on 17 Rabīʿ al-Awwal is, along with the feast of the sacrifice (ʿĪd al-Aḍḥā) and the feast ending the fasting month of Ramadan (ʿĪd al-Fiṭr), one of the most important Muslim celebrations. *Mawlūd* poetry is recited throughout the year in sex-segregated religious gatherings, although in Turkey, South Asia, and Iran, it has become a distinctively women's celebration.

Varying in length, *mawlūd* poetry is composed in a series of chapters describing Muḥammad's birth, the visitations of angels, the foretelling of his birth by past prophets, Muḥammad's journey into the heavens (*miʿrāj*), and a petition for the Prophet's intercession on the Day of Judgment. The recitation of *mawlūd* poetry in women's gatherings typically focuses on the accounts of Muḥammad's miraculous birth and his mother Āmīnah's exceptional qualities. Poems honoring Muḥammad's birth are recited by both Sunnī and Shīʿī women throughout the Islamic world. In Turkey, women recite *mevlūd* poetry on a number of occasions, including Friday prayer meetings and such life cycle events as birth and death. In Iran, *mawlūds* are recited for the Prophet Muḥammad, his daughter Fāṭimah al-Zahraʾ, and, since the 1979 Islamic Revolution, in celebration of the former Supreme Leader Ayatollah Ruhollah Khomeini's birthday. At various times throughout Islamic history, Muslim reformists have debated the permissibility of celebrating Muḥammad's birthday, and the recitation of *mawlūd* poetry and the performance of other rituals have been criticized as innovation (*bidʿah*) and women's folk religion.

Marriage Rituals. Marriage and the family are the fundamental social units of Muslim society. The importance of marriage in Islam is attested to in Muḥammad's declaration that "marriage is my *sunnah*. He who does not act upon it shall not be mine" (*Saḥīḥ al-Bukhārī*, vol. 7, book 62, number 1). Marriage is one of the most significant life cycle events for Muslims, for it establishes sexual relations between a man and woman as legally permissible, and sex is expected to be enjoyable although intended for the purpose of procreation. The legal requirements for marriage are simple, including the ritualized performance of the bride's acceptance (*qabūl*) and the signing of a marriage contract (*ʿaqd al-nikāḥ*) in the presence of two witnesses, but a rich and varied tradition of women's wedding rituals has developed throughout the Islamic world.

In preparation for her wedding, a bride from North Africa to South Asia undergoes a ceremonial bathing ritual in which her skin in scrubbed, rubbed with perfumed oils, and decorated with henna designs (Arabic *laylat al-ḥinnā*; Urdu *sāchaq* or *mehndī*). Often such henna designs on the bride's hands and feet are elaborate, integrating the bridegroom's name among intricate floral motifs and religious symbols. Henna not only beautifies the bride, it also symbolizes her vitality and health and protects her from the evil eye. Women gather to sing songs in honor of the upcoming wedding and to teach the bride about what to expect from married life. The henna ceremony serves a variety of purposes, most obviously making the bride beautiful for her wedding day, but more significantly, this ritual introduces her into a support network of married female relations and friends.

***Sofreh* (*Dastārkhwān*).** *Sofreh* refers to the cloth on which meals are eaten on the floor. From a religious perspective, the *sofreh* is a votive meal (*sofreh-ye naẕrī*) held by a group of women in honor of a member of the Prophet Muḥammad's family (*ahl al-bayt*), especially his daughter Fāṭimah al-Zahra' and Imam Husayn's half-brother 'Abbas Ibn 'Ali. Originally practiced in Iran by Zoroastrians and Jews, the *sofreh* is now commonly practiced by women in Shīʿī communities in Iran, Iraq, Syria, Lebanon, Afghanistan, Pakistan, and India (in South Asia, this same ritual is known as *dastārkhwān*). *Sofreh* gatherings are specifically women-only; even pregnant women are not able to participate in the ritual activities, lest the expectant mother is carrying a male fetus. *Sofrehs* are held for a variety of reasons: a *sofreh* may be held annually in honor of a particular member of the *ahl al-bayt*; in fulfillment of a vow made in seeking the assistance of a particular holy person; and as an opportunity for female guests to make their own offerings and prayers.

The *sofreh* is an important venue for women's fellowship, one that is mediated through the making and fulfillment of vows (*naẕr*) that reaffirm individual and collective relationships with various members of the *ahl al-bayt*. Food plays a central role in the *sofreh* and special dishes are served in honor of each member of the *ahl al-bayt*. The *du'a'-ye sofreh-ye naẕrī* (the prayer of the votive table) that is recited at the beginning of a votive meal describes the food offering and the reward that will be earned from a particular member of the *ahl al-bayt*. For example, those who make an offering of sweets will receive the intercession of Fāṭimah al-Zahra' and the offering of cucumbers will bring closeness to Imam Husayn. Regardless of the occasion and individual being honored and appeased, each *sofreh* follows a similar format: only women attend; prayers are conducted; the hostesses' intention is publicly declared; special food (*ḥalwā*, *khichṛī*, cut fruits) is prepared in honor of the holy figure and consumed by the guests. If the wish of the hostess is granted, she is obligated to fulfill her votive request (*naẕr*) at least once the following year.

Pilgrimage. While not necessarily a religious celebration, pilgrimage to the shrines of Ṣūfī saints (Arabic *mazār*; Persian and Urdu *dargāh* or *ziyāratgāh*; Turkish *ziyāret*) and tombs of the Shīʿī imams and members of the *ahl al-bayt* (*imāmzādah*, *rowzeh*) is an important part of the spiritual and ritual life of many Muslim women throughout the Islamic world. A number of scholars (Tapper 1990; Werbner 2010; Mernissi 1977; Fernea 1965) have argued that *ziyārat* (visitation) is a gendered practice in which women travel outside the home and establish interpersonal relationships with each other and with God through the intercessory powers of the saint. Pilgrimage in the forms of *ziyārat* to the shrine-tombs of Ṣūfī and Shīʿī saints and of *ḥajj* to Mecca allows women to enter into a liminal state in which the rules of sex segregation are relaxed and inversion of gender roles might even take place.

Many Muslim women and men perform pilgrimage in order to experience the Divine blessing (*barakah*) that emanates from the saint's shrine-tomb. Proof of being endowed with *barakah* is manifested in the miracles (*karāmāt*) that the saint performs from the grave. Women who are unable to conceive make a pilgrimage to the tombs of Ṣūfī saints such as Sidi Moussa Doukkali of Salé, Morocco, and Sayyid Baba Sharf al-Din Suhrawardī at Pahaṛ-e Sharif in Hyderabad, India. At the shrine, supplicants pay their respects to the saint through rituals of greetings and prayers, offerings of incense, tying strings or locks to the tomb's grillwork, and making vows in order to benefit from the saint's healing powers. Marital problems, illnesses, the evil eye and black magic, and mental illness are some of the reasons why women perform *ziyārat*. In her study of gendered practices in Ṣūfī healing traditions, Joyce Flueckiger (2006) notes that Ṣūfī healing traditions appeal to many women because they benefit from the emotional support of other women, and for quite a few, hospitals and doctors are too expensive and their intervention is perceived as less effective than that of the saint. Like the *mawlid* celebrations and the *sofreh*, pilgrimage provides women with an opportunity to obtain blessings, solve problems, and develop relationships and support networks with other women.

Assessment. Women's religious celebrations privilege interpersonal and spiritual relationships. Because women have often been excluded from the masculine space of the mosque and patriarchal religious educational institutions, pilgrimage to saints' shrines, the *sofreh* votive meal, and birthday celebrations for the Prophet Muḥammad, Fāṭimah al-Zahra', and other holy figures allow women to participate in and transform the public religious sphere into a spiritually and socially efficacious feminine space.

BIBLIOGRAPHY

Fernea, Elizabeth Warnock. *Guests of the Sheikh: An Ethnography of an Iraqi Village.* New York: Anchor Books, 1965. Based on fieldwork in an Iraqi village, this book includes chapters on wedding rituals and women's pilgrimage to Karbala.

Flueckiger, Joyce Burkhalter. *In Amma's Healing Room: Gender and Vernacular Islam in South India.* Bloomington: Indiana University Press, 2006.

Katz, Marion Holmes. *The Birth of the Prophet Muhammad: Devotional Piety in Sunni Islam.* New York: Routledge, 2007.

Mernissi, Fatima. "Women, Saints, and Sanctuaries." *Signs* 3, no. 1 (Autumn 1977): 101–112. Examines the role of Ṣūfī shrines in Morocco as therapeutic spaces for women.

Ruffle, Karen G. *Gender, Sainthood, and Everyday Practice in South Asian Shiʿism.* Chapel Hill: University of North Carolina Press, 2011. Chapter 4 examines the gendered aspects of Muslim marriage rituals.

Shirazi, Faegheh. "The *Sofreh*: Comfort and Community among Women in Iran." *Iranian Studies* 38, no. 2 (2005): 293–309.

Tapper, Nancy. "Ziyaret: Gender, Movement, and Exchange in a Turkish Community." In *Muslim Travellers: Pilgrimage, Migration, and the Religious Imagination*, edited by Dale F. Eickelman and James Piscatori, pp. 236–263. Berkeley: University of California Press, 1990.

KAREN G. RUFFLE

WOMEN'S RIGHTS.

"Women's rights" in Islam is a contentious topic. Although in some respects the role of women in the Qurʾān was a definite amelioration of women's status in pre-Islamic Arabia, the Islamic tradition did not break all links with its pre-Islamic past. Some gender discriminatory laws persisted. Shaheen Sardar Ali asserts, "Despite an entirely new ideological perspective, Islam's view of the feminine was influenced by the very culture it had come to change" (2000, p. 44). Azizah al-Hibri identifies the persistence of patriarchy in Qurʾānic interpretations that have left many Muslim women feeling conflicted. They want to be "good Muslims," al-Hibri writes, while also wanting equal rights (1997, p. 3).

The Qurʾān, as the primary source of Islamic law, is said to be egalitarian and nondiscriminatory. However, looking at the Qurʾān textually there are verses, although few (for example, 2:221; 2:228; 2.282; 24:30; 4:3; 4:34), which, according to different readings and interpretations, reinforce gender hierarchy and discrimination. Beyond the verses that grant women complete equality with men (for example, 39:6, 7:18-26, 33:35, 40:17, 6:164, 74:38, 24:2-4, 3:285, 4:7, 4:32), there are also verses that are meant to protect women in a male-dominated environment, verses whose literal translations are deemed to be discriminatory against women, and verses meant to correct discrimination against women.

One categorization of Qur'ānic verses made by Muhammad Abduh distinguishes between *'ibadat* (doctrines, beliefs, and rituals), which are seen as immutable and not open to interpretation, "and *muamalat* (human relations), the political, economic, cultural, social, and educational issues that should be reinterpreted for each age" (Sardar Ali, 2000, p. 48). John Esposito and Natana De-Long-Bas employ a framework similar to this contextualized interpretation, which they term the "hierarchization of Quranic values." (2001, p. 133) In it, they imply that Qur'ānic values were applied in the context of seventh-century Arabia by differentiating between socioeconomic and ethno-religious categories in Qur'ānic legislation. The intent of Abduh and Esposito in each instance is to justify Islamic legal reform. Their strong theoretical arguments on the nature of social relations, or *mu'āmalāt*, suggest, among other outcomes, that, where one finds inequality of genders, such inequality is subject to change.

Understanding the concept of equality in the Qur'ān underpins much of the women's rights debate. Although "the Qur'ān acknowledges the anatomical distinction" between the two genders, it does not prefer men over women or one race or tribe over the other (Amina Wadud, 1999). From the time of creation, men and women have been equal. "People, be midful of your Lord, who created you from a single *nafs* (soul), and from it created its *zawj* (mate), and from them spread countless men and women far and wide" (Qur'ānic 4:1, A new translation by M.A.S. Abdel Haleem).

While considered secondary texts to the Qur'ān, the *ḥadīth* literature has also had an undeniable impact on both the Shī'ah and the Sunnī understandings of gender and rights. A considerable number of prophetic *aḥadīth* were related by females, including 'Ā'ishah, one of Muḥammad's wives. Women's images in the *ḥadīth* literature vary greatly, spanning from saintly to sinful. Whether related by women or men, there are several examples of authoritative *aḥadīth* that are discriminatory against women. These *aḥadīth* are said to go against the egalitarian nature of the Qur'ān. Take, for example, the egalitarian act of creation in the Qur'ān cited above as compared to certain narrated *aḥadīth* that clearly contradict this principle of equality. One such *ḥadīth* as narrated by Abu Hurayra reads, "God's Apostle said, 'Treat women nicely, for a women is created from a rib, and the most curved portion of the rib is its upper portion, so, if you should try to straighten it, it will break, but if you leave it as it is, it will remain crooked. So treat women nicely'" (*Sahih Bukhari*, Vol. 4, Book 55, No. 548). This *ḥadīth* asserts both imperfection and inferiority in women.

Yet, for the majority of the discriminatory *aḥadīth*, one can nearly always find another that contradicts the spirit of the first. The above *ḥadīth*, for example, is contradicted by the spirit of equality embedded in the following: "All people are equal, as equal as the tooth of a comb. There is no claim of merit of an Arab over a non-Arab or a white over a black person, or a male over a female. Only God-fearing people merit a preference with God" (Eissa, 1999, p. 5).

The first *ḥadīth* not only contradicts the second but it also contradicts the Qur'ānic essence of equality. As observed by Eissa, the first *ḥadīth* is seldom referred to where men and women's equality is concerned. It is also widely believed that the idea of Eve having been created from Adam's left rib has penetrated Islam from Abrahamic religions, in particular Christianity. As such, Eissa observes "that what is commonly understood today about women's status in Islam is the product of biased interpretation and selective acknowledgment of textual sources from which rights have been derived" (1999, p. 5).

These kinds of contradictions are also visible in different Qur'ānic interpretations. This underscores the fact that Qur'ānic *tafsīr* historically has been a male domain and that Islam is interpreted and practiced differently the world over. Much of what one might think is Islamic or grounded in Islamic notions is "not based on Islam as a religion but, rather, depends on an array of social, political, and economic conditions pertinent to the specific Muslim context" (Ibrahim, 2005, p. 102). In this regard, cultural notions of the feminine and the masculine have had a definite effect on the subjective interpretation of the Qur'ān and *ḥadīth* literature. Deniz Kandiyoti correctly asserts that "using the Quran, the hadith and the lives of prominent women in the early period of Muslim history as sources, conservatives confirmed that existing gender asymmetries are divinely ordained, while feminists discerned possibilities for a more progressive politics of gender based on the egalitarian ideals of early Islam" (1991, p. 9). Clearly, it is not only the feminists' or the conservatives' interpretations of Islamic doctrine that determine women's rights in Islamic countries. Other factors, such as socioeconomics, class, identity (national identity), state, politics, foreign aid, and power, also bear on Muslim women's status.

Bibliography

Eissa, Dahlia. "Constructing the Notion of Male Superiority over Women in Islam: The Influence of Sex and Gender Stereotyping in the Interpretation of the Qur'an and the Implications for a Modernist Exegesis of Rights." Women Living Under Muslim Law Occasional Paper No. 11, November 1999, pp. 5–55. May be downloaded at WLUML's website, http://www.wluml.org/node/443.

Esposito, John L. with Natana J. DeLong-Bas. *Women in Muslim Family Law*. 2d ed. Syracuse, N.Y.: Syracuse University Press, 2001.

Hibri, Azizah al-. "Islam, Law and Custom: Redefining Muslim Women's Rights." *American University International Law Review* 12, no. 1 (1997): 1–44.

Ibrahim, Saad Eddin. "The Causes of Muslim Countries' Poor Record of Human Rights." In *Islam and Human Rights, Advancing a U.S.-Muslim Dialogue*, edited by Shirin Hunter and Huma Malik, pp 100–109. Washington, D.C.: Center for Strategic and International Studies, 2005.

Kandiyoti, Deniz. "Women, Islam and the State." *Middle East Report* 173 (Nov. -Dec. 1991): 9–14.

Sahih Bukhari. Vol. 4, Book 55, No. 548.

Sardar Ali, Shaheen. *Gender and Human Rights in Islam and International Law: Equal Before Allah, Unequal Before Man*. The Hague: Kluwer Law International, 2000.

Stowasser, Barbara F. "The Status of Women in Early Islam." In *Muslim Women*, edited by Freda Hussain, pp. 11–43, London, Sydney: Croom Helm, 1984.

The Qur'an, A new translation by M.A.S. Abdel Haleem, New York: Oxford University Press, 2004.

Wadud, Amina, *Qur'an and Woman, Rereading the Sacred Text from a Woman's Perspective*, New York: Oxford University Press, 1999.

Roja Fazaeli

Women's Travel, Historical. Historical study of travel in Muslim societies is still a developing field. Muslim women's travel has not received consistent attention, with research depending on male-authored records, whether in medieval or modern times. The majority of medieval sources are in Arabic, followed in frequency by the Ottoman records for later centuries. Since the women left no descriptions of their journeys, we learn of them from such Arabic books as the *Marvels (Wonders) of India* by Buzurg ibn Shāhriyār (953 CE), the *Rihla* (Journey) of Ibn Jubayr (d. 1217), and the *Travels* of Ibn Baṭṭūṭah (1304–1377?). These Arabic authors were pious Muslims from Persia, Spain, and Morocco, respectively. Even the Timurid Mughal princess Gulbadan (c. 1523–1603), who wrote an account (*Humāyūn Nāmā)* of life at court during the reign of her father, brother, and nephew—the emperors Bābur, Humāyūn, and Akbar, failed to describe her seven-year pilgrimage to the Hejaz (or Hijaz) in the 1570s. The earliest known pilgrimage records by a woman is a poem of 1,200 verses in Persian about her late-seventeenth-century *ḥajj* by the anonymous widow of Mīrzā Khalīl, the *raqamnavīs* (royal scribe) of the divan who served the last Ṣafavid ruler Shah Sultan Husayn (1694–1722). A member of the lettered Urdūbādī family, she modestly calls herself Bānū-yi Iṣfahānī, a lady of Isfahan. The first published record of a journey authored by a Muslim woman was an epistolary memoir of the 1863–1864 *ḥajj* by Nawāb Sikandar Bēgum of Bhopal, composed in Urdu, but first published in English in 1870.

The British colonial connection facilitated Muslim, especially Indian women's travel to England and elsewhere in Europe. Greater mobility, higher literacy, print culture, and Islamic reformist movements of the late nineteenth century boosted the Muslim women's emergent travel writing beyond pilgrimage accounts. Among the first such published records are books like *Six Years in Europe: Sequel to Thirty Years in the Harem* (1873) by Melek Hanum, wife of H. H. Kibrizli-Mehemet-Pasha, and Emilie Said-Ruete's *Memoirs of an Arabian Princess: Princess Salme bint Said ibn Sultan al-Bu Saidi of Oman and Zanzibar* (1888). In the early twentieth century, the *ḥajj* narratives of Hyderabad's ʿAmmat al-Ghānī Nūr al-Nisā (*Safarnāmāh-i-Hijāz, Shām ō Misr*, 1909) and Nawāb Sultan Jahan Bēgum of Bhopal's *The Story of a Pilgrimage to Hijaz* (Calcutta, 1909) appeared. The latter author was a granddaughter of Sikandar. European travelogues were represented by those of Atiya Fyzee, a Bohrā Muslim from Bombay, who studied in England in 1906–1907, and Nazli Rafia Sultan Nawāb Bēgum Sahiba who, traveling with Atiya only a little while later, produced *Sair-i-Yurōp* (Lahore, 1908). Sultan Jahan's daughter-in-law Shahbano Bēgum Maimoona Sultan documented her journey to Britain via mainland Europe, Turkey, and Egypt for the coronation of George V in 1911 in her *Siyāsat-i sultānī*, also published in English translation as *A Trip to Europe* (1914). Sughra Humayun Mirza of Hyderabad published a two-volume description of her trips to Europe and West Asia as *Safārnāmāh-i-Yurōp* (1926). During the same period, the first female Western converts to Islam began to publish their impressions of Mecca: Asian-Australian Winifred Stegar (1927) and British Evelyn Cobbold (1933), a great-niece of the intrepid Jane Digby (1807–1881). In addition to more recent memoirs, there are now numerous guidebooks and websites for the female pilgrim and for Muslim women traveling to non-Muslim countries.

Islam arose in Arabian society where nomadic migration, travel for commerce, and pilgrimage were common. Women participated in these activities alongside men, but the hazards and discomfort of travel made it undesirable. Concerns for safety, privacy, and prestige led women to avoid travel. Medieval Muslim women of various social classes traveled relatively infrequently, but sometimes they did traverse great distances. The prophetic *ḥadīth* encouraged Muslims to travel for education and gain, saying, "Seek knowledge even as far as China" and "Travel so that you many remain hale and hearty. Travel so that you may derive benefit and get a windfall." The travels of upper-class women are better documented, but middle-class scholarly and Ṣūfī women traveled as well. Women's travel away from home was socially acceptable, though certain laws and rules of propriety had to be observed. In general, Muslim women were not to travel beyond the realm of Islam and had to have a male escort subject to legal specifications. Free women had the right to refuse to accompany their husbands on their journeys. Slave women were normally not given the choice, but in principle, servants could not be compelled to travel with their masters against their will.

Islam spread as well among non-Arab nomadic societies where women's spatial mobility traditionally was less restricted. Despite the rise of veiling and seclusion, which especially affected free urban Muslim women, perceived need was sufficient cause for women to travel without men or under unusual circumstances. Brides traveled to join prospective husbands; wives accompanied husbands and journeyed to visit their natal families while married, or to return home if widowed or divorced. Ibn Baṭṭūṭah's first marriage was negotiated with her father in the woman's absence while passing through Tunis in a caravan; the bride was then sent to Tripoli where the caravan had moved in the meantime. This match was quickly abandoned, and Ibn Baṭṭūṭah found another candidate in the daughter of a fellow traveler from Fez; she, too, had to be sent for. Princesses often married abroad. Ibn Baṭṭūṭah traveled to Constantinople in the train of a Byzantine princess who was married to a Muslim Mongol ruler and returning home to give birth. In the thirteenth and fourteenth centuries, Mongol princes and their wives, including those who accepted Islam, were expected to travel long distances to the annual meeting of the extended ruling family in Inner Asia. Bābur's daughter Gulbadan lived in Kabul, Lahore, Delhi, Agra, and Fatehpour Sikri, moving from one royal residence to another.

Mamlūk women, many of them coming from a steppe background, enjoyed both travel and the outdoors, and were accomplished horsewomen. The Egyptian chronicler Taqī al-Dīn al-Maqrīzī records that when the Mamlūk sultan al-Ṣāliḥ ʿImād al-Dīn Ismāʿīl (r. 1342–1345) made his seasonal rides from the citadel to the village of Siriyāqūs or the Pyramids, his mother, with another two hundred women, would accompany him on horseback. They were escorted by eunuchs from the citadel to the promenading grounds, where they might play polo. When the Nile was in flood, pleasure boats appeared in the 5-km-long canal Khalīj al-Hākimī. Under the events of 1306, Maqrīzī describes women sitting in these boats next to men, with their faces uncovered, drinking wine. Also around 1300, the sultan of Delhi Alā al-Dīn Khiljī (r. 1296–1316) was described camping in a jungle together with his seraglio, on a hunting trip. A canvas wall (*kanāt*) was pitched round an extensive enclosure to form a curtain (*pardah*) to enable members of the harem to hunt the game freely. One of the queens, galloping in pursuit of a deer, jumped over the canvas, and the scene shows noblewomen on horseback roaming the countryside. Numerous Indian miniatures depict women playing polo, hunting, and even riding into battle. Ṣafavid women, too, show striking mobility even when only traveling between female spaces.

The pre-Islamic custom of women accompanying men to the battlefield continued among Arabs for a while under Islam, and the first Muslim sailors were encouraged to bring their wives on board. A lady of the Anṣār family, Umm Harām bint Milhān, is said to have joined the first Muslim naval expedition, led by the future caliph Muʿāwiyah against Cyprus in 649. She died from a fall from her horse upon disembarking there. In an expedition against Constantinople in 652–653, Muʿāwiyah's wife ʿĀtiqa traveled with him. Sometimes, travel was forced by danger. After a short reign over Egypt (1250), Queen Shajar al-Durr attempted to find sanctuary in Jerusalem. Princess Radiyya of Delhi (r. 1236–1240) was deposed, raised a rebellion, and was killed in flight. Royal exiles (women or men with their consorts) often ended up in Mecca and Medina. Some royal women accompanied early Ottoman sultans on campaigns, with the queens traveling at least a distance of a few days out of the capital. Legend has that Süleyman the Magnificent's daughter Mihr-i-māh (1522–1578) accompanied her father on his campaigns and even followed him into the battle of the Pyramids in Egypt (the battle, in fact, took place in 1517 before her birth). These "sultanas" also moved between royal cities; some were sent to reside at the Edirne palace harem, and others were allowed to stay at summer facilities. Boat rides on the Golden Horn were not uncommon, with the ladies shielded from the public view by curtains wrapped around the deck. The tradition of traveling with the harem continued to the twentieth century.

Finally, there was migration, in both directions, East and West. Thus, several *seyyid* families from Hadramaut in southern Arabia established themselves in India, with many Arabs settling in Calicut. These migrants were merchants who owned ships used in the spice trade and the transport of pilgrims. Iranian migrants achieved a highly influential position in the seventeenth-century sultanate of Golconda in southeast India. Scholars and merchants went also to southeast Asia. Even the Portuguese could not stop these movements, including Arab settlement in Malacca. There was less migration southward, but both Arab and Persian migrants came to the east coast of Africa; however, women's participation in these migrations was somewhat limited until modern times. The Muslim slave trade, which always included women, continued into the twentieth century.

Pilgrimage. Travel for religious reasons was especially meritorious. It could be for a range of purposes, such as emigration away from unbelievers (*hijrah*), pilgrimage to Mecca (*ḥajj*), visits to other holy places (*ziyārah*), and the search for education (*ʿilm*, true knowledge). These high goals made it possible for single ladies, married women without their husbands, and groups of women to travel without opprobrium. The first emigration of Muslim converts from Mecca to Ethiopia included several women, among them the Prophet Muḥammad's daughter Ruqayyah and her husband, the future caliph ʿUthmān. Among the emigrants from Mecca to Medina there were some wives who had converted and left their pagan husbands behind. After Islam's success over Mecca was ensured, a number of Meccan women traveled the distance of 200 miles to Muḥammad at Medina to bring him the "women's oath." Everywhere in the Islamic world, including the Hejaz, *ziyārahs* are dominated by women; it was probably so in the Middle Ages as well. Ṣūfī women traveled both on *ziyārahs*, their journeys then often timed to saints' holidays (*mawlids*) and for education. Ibn Baṭṭūṭah met two such women in the Hejaz. One of them was Shaykha Zaynab (1248–1339), nicknamed "the goal of the world's travel," a reference to the many people who journeyed great distances to study with her. Another was Sitt Zāhida (d. 1326), famous for her piety and served by a group of male mystic devotees. Women also performed *ʿumrah*, the "lesser pilgrimage" rites at Mecca not limited to the month of Dhū al-Ḥijjah. Jerusalem was visited by Muslim women as well, including royal ladies. Ottoman royal women favored picnic visits to tombs far from the palace—in Istanbul at the far end of the Golden Horn, or on the Asian side (in Üsküdar).

Islam legitimized travel for all Muslims on the occasion of pilgrimage to Mecca (*ḥajj*). Required once in a lifetime, this journey gave women considerable freedom. The wife did not need her husband's consent for it (although if she went against his will, she was not entitled to support for her travel). During *ḥajj* ceremonies, the woman is not subject to her husband's authority, the use of the veil is limited to covering the hair, and the face must remain open. The veil worn on the pilgrimage journey was often preserved by its owner throughout her life. Going to Mecca required settling the debts one owed and renouncing anything worldly except for necessities, but travel could be combined with trade to pay the expenses of the journey. In caravans destined for Mecca, the number of women was greater than usual; for protection, they usually stayed in the middle of the caravan. Classical scholars disapproved of women pilgrims traveling by sea, possibly because only the largest ships had cabins that could be used as accommodations for ladies or families of paying passengers. Mediterranean shipping increasingly involved Muslims sailing on Christian vessels, as done by both Ibn Jubayr and Ibn Baṭṭūṭah.

Pilgrimage allowed women extended absence and even prolonged stays away from home. Some used it to escape control. Abū Bakr's granddaughter ʿĀʾishah bint Ṭalḥah was said to have illicit activities in her tent during her *ḥajj* pilgrimage. On a visit to Mali, Ibn Baṭṭūṭah made an effort to dissuade the local ruler from traveling to Mecca with a woman to whom he was not married. The Ṣafavid widow on *ḥajj* may have decided on a pilgrimage after her husband's death, in part, to expiate her love for a female companion from the past. However, sexual relations within limits allowed by Islamic law are permitted up to and after the days reserved for pilgrimage rites. In fact, the sacred ground around the Kaʿbah was a popular meeting place where marriages were contracted. John Lewis Burckhardt (1784–1817), also known as Johann Ludwig, reported special marital arrangements between locals and pilgrims for the duration of the *ḥajj* season or more extended sojourn in the Hejaz. Western authors report nightly celebration at caravan rest stops. However, with the rise of Wahhābīs in central Arabia, tomb visitation, music and song, and even the wearing of jewelry by women pilgrims were increasingly limited.

From the earliest times, women of the Muslim elite became not only devout pilgrims, but also generous benefactors of the holy cities of Mecca and Medina, their permanent settlers and pilgrims. Among them was Muʿāwiyah's granddaughter Umm al-Banīn ʿĀtika bint Yazīd, wife of the Umayyad caliph ʿAbd al-Malik ibn Marwān (r. 685–705), who traveled from Damascus. The consort of the Abbasid caliph al-Mahdī Khayzurān made her first pilgrimage of 787 as a slave concubine; in 788 she came to Mecca from Baghdad as queen-mother of the caliph Hārūn al-Rashīd (r. 786–809). His wife Zubayda was a four-time pilgrim. Research suggests that a significant number of princesses and royal consorts went on pilgrimage through the ages. Since sultans and princes practically never appeared in the Hejaz, the occasional presence of royal women went beyond demonstrations of piety and charity and acquired a strong political connotation. Ibn Jubayr reported the large pilgrimage of Malika Khātun, the wife of the Zangid ruler of Aleppo, Nūr al-Dīn (r. 1174–1181). Sitt Hadaq, a highly placed woman at the court of a Mamlūk sultan of Egypt and a pilgrim to Mecca in 1328, commemorated her return from pilgrimage by erecting a mosque in Cairo. The mother of the Egyptian Mamlūk sultan al-Ashraf Shaʿbān II, Baraka Khānum, was honored by a magnificent pilgrimage procession in 1368, called the "Year of the Sultan's Mother." In 1507 the last Mamlūk sultan Qānsuh al-Ghawrī sent a particularly lavish caravan with several princesses. From Iran came the consort of Shah Tahmasp of Iran (r. 1524–1576), the mother of Prince Ismāʿīl, and his sister Pērikhān. In the Ottoman period, such royal ladies included the mother of Sultan Selim (r. 1512–1520), the conqueror of Arab countries; under his successor Süleyman the Magnificent (r. 1520–1566) came his consort Hürrem Sultan (the famous Roxelana), their daughter Mihr-i-Māh (d. 1578), and a sister. The brother of the Mughal emperor Humāyūn (r. 1530–1556), Kamran, settled in the holy cities with his wife Māh Chichek Begam. The emperor Akbar (r. 1556–1605) was represented by one of his wives, Salīma, and his aunt, the court historian Gulbadan Bēgum.

In the colonial period, royal female visitors from India who recorded and published their impressions included Nawāb Sikandar Bēgum of

Bhopal (1864) and Nawāb Bēgum of Bhopal, Nawāb Faizunnesā (1834–1903), who performed the *ḥajj* in 1894. In the early twentieth century, Western Muslim women came from Europe, Australia, and North America. Some of them traveled on their own, although those highly placed did not hesitate to use their local contacts to facilitate their travel. Contemporary Muslim women increasingly perform the *ḥajj* unaccompanied by male relatives, although conservative websites still instruct women not to go on the *ḥajj* without a male escort.

Transport and Logistics. The hardships and dangers of travel are consistently reflected in the narratives until the advent of modern transportation in the twentieth century. Women joined caravans because it was both customary and also more secure. In caravans destined for Mecca, the number of women was greater than usual; for protection, they usually stayed in the middle of the caravan. In case of attack, women, even those of high rank, could be robbed, raped, enslaved, or held for ransom. Paradoxically, *ḥajj* caravans could be both more and less secure. Because the *ḥajj* must be accomplished in the early days of Dhū al-Ḥijjah, the last month of the Islamic calendar, the Bedouin and the pirates knew in advance when and where caravans and passengers might be found. In March 1187 Saladin (Ar., Ṣalāḥ al-Dīn al-Ayyūbī) had to send troops to protect a pilgrim caravan threatened by Crusaders in which his sister was returning from Mecca. Male travelers like Ibn Baṭṭūṭah were sometimes extended protection by well-protected and supplied queens and princesses.

Most overland journeys to Mecca required months or even years. Ibn Jubayr, the most compact in space and time, describes a round-trip of about two years—the average span of the journey before steamships, trains, and airplanes. Festivities accompanied both the departure and return of major caravans. Families and friends of pilgrims prepared gifts and walked out of town in a procession to welcome the returning pilgrims en route. Because the timing of the *ḥajj* advanced about 10 days every year (due to the lunar calendar of 355 days), approximate dates of departures for caravans from the Maghrib, Cairo, Damascus, Baghdad, or Yemen (carrying pilgrims from India) required flexibility and included ample time for rest, travelers catching up, and waiting for provisioning, official escorts, and permits. Animals bought or hired from the Bedouin for pilgrims, cargo, food, and sacrifice, counted in the tens of thousands. In 1503 Varthema counted 64,000 camels in the Cairo caravan, escorted by a 100 Mamlūks on horseback. In 1575 an anonymous European source adds two caravans, from Damascus and Arabia, for a total of 200,000 to 300,000 animals. In 1807 Ali ben Abbasi counted 5,000 men only in the caravan from Cairo to Suez, before embarking on a ship. In 1814 at Arafat, Burckhardt counted 80,000 men; 2,000 women; 1,000 little children; and 60,000–70,000 camels, asses, and horses. It took 500 camels to transport the baggage of the wife of Muḥammad ʿAlī of Egypt, the mother of Tusun Pasha and Ibrāhīm Pasha, from Jiddah to Mecca. Her tent was, in fact, an encampment consisting of a dozen tents of different sizes, inhabited by her women, "the whole enclosed by a wall of linen cloth 800 paces in circuit, the single entrance to which was guarded by eunuchs in splendid dresses. Around this enclosure there were pitched the tents of the men who formed her numerous suite" (Wolfe, 1997, p. 183), In Mecca and Medina, there were hostels for arrivals of different ethnicities. In other major cities, some hotels (*funduq, wakālah*) had "family suites" on the upper floors. There were also women's hospices (*ribāṭ al-nisāʾ*), supported by charity.

Obviously, the level of comfort varied depending on status and wealth. Zubayda started the tradition of traveling in richly decorated litters.

When Ibn Jubayr witnessed the lavish pilgrimage of the wife of the ruler of Aleppo, Nūr al-Dīn (1174–1181), he described, "Palanquins fastened atop camels, draped, some of them with all sorts of silk fabric, others with fine linen stuff, according to the wealth and luxury of their owners; everyone put on a public display according to his means.... The most remarkable of the ones we saw was the palanquin of the Sharifa Jumāna, daughter of Fulayta [Sharif of Mecca, 1123–1132] and the paternal aunt of the Amir Mukthir, since the end of her curtains trailed in waves upon the ground...." (Wolfe, 1997, p. 40) The tradition continued, and a similar spectacle was described in 1432 by the Christian pilgrim to the East, Bertrandon de la Brocquière, who saw in Damascus a caravan returning from Mecca: "Behind this [*mahmal*] camel...came a Turkish lady, a relation of the Grand Seigneur, in a litter borne by two camels with rich housings. There were many of these animals covered with cloth of gold." (Peters, 1994, p. 80) The lady had been to Mecca at least three times. In the fourteenth century, a Moroccan caravan carrying the princess Maryam to Mecca stopped at Cairo, occasioning much talk and celebration. Mamlūk sultan al-Nāṣir Muḥammad (r. 1309–1341), who made three pilgrimages, traveled in comfort, sustained by access to his portable vegetable garden carried on frames atop the backs of his camels. In the mid-seventeenth century François Bernier watched with awe the procession of sixty-six elephants who departed from Delhi carrying the princess Raushanārā Begam, Awrangzīb ʿĀlamgīr's younger sister, and her entourage. He described a troop of female servants that surrounded her elephant: Tartars and Kachmerys, fantastically attired and riding handsome pad-horses.

Merchant and pilgrim caravans moved with different speed. A pre-Islamic journey from Yemen to Aqaba took seventy days. Richard Francis Burton specifies *rakb* and *tayyāra* return caravans to Damascus; *rakb* passengers traveled on dromedaries and were allowed only saddlebags for baggage. For comfort, travelers hired sedans and litters carried by animals. The litter was variously called *rafraf* (cushion) or *mihaffa* (palanquin). *Shuqduf* was a two-person sedan carried on the back of a camel. It was a litter divided into two square panniers, hanging over each side of the camel, with a cushioned wood framework supplemented with ropework and cover. Sometimes also called *shibriyya*, this was the litter available to commoners. In India, there were bullock-drawn carriages (*rath*); the *pālkī*, a medium-sized litter, requiring fewer bearers; and the *dolī*, the smallest-size litter. Dignitaries and elite women, when not on horseback, traveled in a variety of conveyances: rich palanquins called *takhtrūn* or, again, *shibriyya*, its shafts supported on two camels or mules, one behind the other. Before the nineteenth century, such litters were reserved for *ḥajj* dignitaries; they were mounted by ladder or pole. In Syria, this kind of litter was also called *khashab* (plank) and *mahāra* (shell or scoop). Curtained litters could be carried by camels, horses, or two to four donkeys; Islamized Mongols migrated with yurt tents placed on carts. Indian princesses used the closed elephant howdah (*ʿamārī*); the litter slung between two camels (*kajāba*); or *chandūl*, the largest Indian litter handled by human bearers (up to twenty). For short distances carrying female passengers, and especially for entering into or exiting from the women's quarter (*zenāna*), female slave bearers were used.

Ships of the Indian Ocean depended on monsoons and safe conduct. The ruler of the city of Cochin often sent ships to Jiddah protected by a Portuguese safe conduct. The most important shipowners were the Mughal rulers residing in Delhi and Agra. Their ships were explicitly defined as pilgrims' ships; they transported a large amount of trade goods for rulers and merchants as well as most pilgrims who financed their journeys by carrying wares they hoped to sell. In 1662 a ship owned by the queen of the southern state of Bijapur appeared in the port of Aden, carrying fifteen hundred passengers and four hundred bales of goods. At Surat in March 1735, Henry Lowther of the East India Company observed African Sidis, in theory the naval guardians of the port, arresting all the ships laden for the Red Sea, making the *ḥājjīs* afraid to be late for pilgrimage (and eventually plundering six vessels).

Modern transportation, while making *ḥajj* more accessible, also increased overcrowding and raised the danger of epidemics. The first cholera epidemic in Mecca was brought in 1831 by pilgrims from British India; another major epidemic in 1865 came on pilgrim ships from Dutch East India. Quarantine was introduced; Mohammad Farahani experienced it in 1885–1886 and described such in his book. This Persian bureaucrat traveled by novel routes, by boat and railway via Baku in the Russian Empire, next by a Black Sea steamship to Ottoman Turkey, and then to Hejaz. *Ḥajj* traffic declined, as most pilgrims now came from India and by ship to Jiddah. Some land traffic was lost because of a safer sea route from Jiddah to Janbo. By the turn of the twentieth century, the number of *ḥajj* caravans had shrunk from six to three. The Damascus *ḥajj* route (*darb al-ḥajj*), more difficult than the one from Cairo via Suez and Sinai, was eased by dynamiting some rocks to make for easier passage. The short-lived Hejaz Railway was designed mainly with pilgrims in mind, to make the journey faster and safer from the Bedouin. Winifred Stegar reported in 1927 that when the Turkish subsidy to nomads ceased, they started to attack the railway and trains; to prevent plunder, Ibn Saʿūd resumed the subsidy. In 1933 Lady Evelyn Cobbold traveled by car, including transportation to the Mina valley and Arafat. Saida Miller Khalifa's 1977 book describes the conditions of women's pilgrimage in the 1970s. In the early twenty-first century, pilgrimage air traffic is directed to the Jeddah Airport Hajj Terminal (among the world's largest) and to Medina.

BIBLIOGRAPHY

Dunn, Ross E. *The Adventures of Ibn Battuta: A Muslim Traveler of the Fourteenth Century.* Berkeley: University of California Press, 1986.

Eickelman, Dale F., and James Piscatori, eds. *Muslim Travellers: Pilgrimage, Migration, and the Religious Imagination.* Berkeley: University of California Press, 1990.

Faroqhi, Suraiya. *Pilgrims and Sultans: The Hajj under the Ottomans 1517–1683.* London and New York: I. B. Tauris, 1994.

Johnson, Kathryn. "Royal Pilgrims: Mamluk Accounts of the Pilgrimage to Mecca of the Khawand al-Kubra (Senior Wife of the Sultan)." *Studia Islamica* 91 (2000): 107–131.

Lambert-Hurley, Siobhan, ed. *A Princess's Pilgrimage: Nawab Sikandar Begum's* A Pilgrimage to Mecca. Bloomington: Indiana University Press, 2008.

Lambert-Hurley, Siobhan, and Sunil Sharma. *Atiya's Journeys: A Muslim Woman from Colonial Bombay to Edwardian Britain.* New Delhi: Oxford University Press, 2010.

Netton, Ian, ed.*Golden Roads: Migration, Travel and Pilgrimage in Mediaeval and Modern Islam.* Richmond, Surrey, U.K.: Curzon Press, 1993.

Peters, Francis E. *The Hajj: The Muslim Pilgrimage to Mecca and the Holy Places.* Princeton: Princeton University Press, 1994.

Tolmacheva, Marina. "Female Piety and Patronage in the Medieval Hajj." In *Women in the Medieval Islamic World: Power, Patronage, and Piety*, edited by Gavin R. G. Hambly, pp. 161–178. New York: St. Martin's Press, 1998.

Tolmacheva, Marina. "Ibn Battuta on Women's Travel in the Dar al-Islam." In *Women and the Journey: The Female Travel Experience*, edited by Bonnie Frederick and Susan H. McLeod, pp. 119–140. Pullman: Washington State University Press, 1993.

Touati, Houari. *Islam and Travel in the Middle Ages.* Translated by by Lydia G. Cochrane. Chicago: University of Chicago Press, 2010.

Wolfe, Michael, ed. *One Thousand Roads to Mecca: Ten Centuries of Travelers Writing about the Muslim Pilgrimage*. New York: Grove Press, 1997.

Online Resources

For *Oxford Bibliographies Online: Islamic Studies* (Andrew Rippin, gen. ed.) and *Pilgrimage and Religious Travel: Oxford Bibliographies Online Research Guide*, Kindle ed. (Yousef Meri, comp.), go to http://www.oup.com/online/. The latter is also available through Amazon Digital Services.

Marina Tolmacheva

Workforce, Women in the

[*This entry has two subentries:*

Historical Discourse *and*
Contemporary Discourse.]

Historical Discourse

Women have always been active in the workforce in the Muslim world, whether their contributions are formally recognized in the form of financial remuneration for their services or are informally present, such as through unpaid agricultural work on family property. Because women often worked as independent contractors, small business owners, and labor-for-hire, typically in the domestic arena or in service to other women, and because most working women were not members of the elite classes, records of their activities are scarce. Nevertheless, historical records, particularly court documents, tax records, and contemporary writings, provide hints at the variety of occupations women have fulfilled over the centuries.

During the lifetime of the Prophet Muḥammad, women were known to have worked in the caravan trade and in the marketplace. He met his first wife, Khadījah, when she hired him to accompany her caravan to Syria to sell her goods. Another of his wives, Sawdah, earned her own income through leather-working.

The Pre-Modern Period. In the pre-modern, pre-industrial period, women were actively involved in small-scale commerce, such as sewing, embroidery, and textile production, particularly the production of silk, which involved unraveling the silk thread, reeling it, weaving it into cloth, and then dying it. Lower-class women worked in a variety of paid professions, including as midwives, healers, greengrocers, sellers of foodstuffs, bakers, matchmakers, hairdressers, *dalallas* (peddlers of goods such as clothing, jewelry, and embroidery to harems, as well as carriers of gossip), singers, dancers, mourners, washers of the dead, bath attendants, orderlies in hospitals, and even prostitutes. Occasionally, lower-class women might embark on a more unusual, specialized occupation, such as raising carrier pigeons that could be sold or hired out.

Some elite and middle-class women were known to provide religious education to other women, although it is not clear whether there was formal remuneration for these services, as would have been the case for men. Upper-class women were also important employers of other women, typically as domestic slaves who would cook food and clean houses, but also as professional singers and dancers for weddings and births. Mamlūk women were particularly known as major employers of female domestic servants. One Mamlūk princess reportedly had a household staff of seven hundred women, including a treasurer (*khazindara*) and general supervisor (*ra's nawba*).

Frequent mention is made of women working as prostitutes in eighteenth-century Cairo and Aleppo. Although the profession was considered disreputable, the state nevertheless permitted its practice in order to tax it and thereby gain revenue. Aleppo required prostitutes to be licensed by a state officer to whom prostitutes additionally had to pay protection money. Arab sources from the time indicate that there were guilds of sorts for prostitutes, singers, and dancers, although it has been speculated that these guilds were simply organizational structures that facilitated state control and taxation. Prostitutes were also present in Isfahan, where fourteen thousand of them were registered as taxpayers in 1666. They lived together in special caravanserais under the control of female "superiors" who hired them out. Similarly, although the professions of poets, singers, dancers, Ṣūfi *dhikr* chanters, and professional mourners were looked down on socially, the government nevertheless required them to pay taxes and hired female officers (*daminat al-maghani*) to collect remittances.

In the pre-modern era, the most common trade for lower-class women was spinning, as often portrayed in miniatures showing women either at a spinning wheel or with a spindle under their arm. Some women became particularly renowned for their skill in working linen and other materials, as well as for embroidery in gold and silver thread. The market for cotton and linen cloth was particularly strong, providing many women, such as in nineteenth-century Cairo, with the opportunity to purchase raw cotton or linen at their own expense, process it in their own homes, and then resell it for a profit. Others received from traders their cotton or linen, which they took home, spun or carded. They returned the finished thread to the trader, who would then sell it to a weaving workshop. This kind of work was paid at a piece rate, typically very low wages. Similar patterns have been found in eighteenth-century Aleppo and seventeenth-century Bursa, in Turkey. Some women expanded beyond making cloth to sewing the cloth into clothing items, which they further enhanced with embroidery in order to produce luxury goods for the wealthy. Some hired young girls at low wages to serve as apprentices. Others were hired by the families of young girls to teach them their skills.

Impact of European Industrialization. Women's place in the cloth market—one of the few remunerative labor options available to them—was threatened in the late eighteenth-century by the importation of cheaper, factory-produced European goods. Although state factories were established in Egypt to try to compete with European factories, the state factories were plagued by a variety of problems that led to their ultimate failure. By the 1840s, this led to a major shift in the Egyptian economy, namely, an imbalance of trade in which raw materials were exported from Egypt and European finished goods were imported into Egypt. Women's independence as contractors had already been impinged upon when they were hired by state factories, placing them under state control at only two-thirds of the wages paid to men. As local merchants were pushed aside in favor of European companies and products, women not only lost placement of the goods they produced, but also suffered severe financial losses in cases where they had invested in local trade.

At the same time, new land tenure laws were introduced, concentrating land in the hands of a few large landowners and largely dispossessing peasants. As major agricultural projects, such as the construction and restoration of dikes and canals, were undertaken and small farmers were displaced, women and children often ended up working alongside men at the work sites, earning poor pay, engaging in hard labor, and working under difficult conditions. In other cases, families retained a nominal claim to the land, but the males were conscripted into the army, leaving the women to take on all of the agricultural labor, in addition to their other work, or risk loss of the land.

Public Education and the Workforce. Despite these developments and their negative impact on women's ability to participate in the workforce, other opportunities opened during the nineteenth century, largely due to the introduction of public education for women. For example, in Egypt in 1832, a school for *hakimas* (women doctors) was established in order to train medical practitioners who would provide services, both outpatient and inpatient, to other women at the Civil Hospital in Cairo. These *hakimas* were also responsible for vaccinating children, both in private homes and at the hospital. Expansion of education also led to openings in positions as teachers and governesses. Although these educational endeavors initially targeted upper-class women, progressive middle-class families also began to demand access to education for their daughters, including up to the university level, although they were still not willing to allow them to work outside the home. It took time for social perceptions about women's work outside the home to change, as this had previously been associated with lower-class women. Nevertheless, many educated women argued that their interest in work was not financial in nature, but for the sake of having a career.

By the early 1930s, Egyptian women began entering new professions—journalism, medicine, law, and university teaching. Upper- and middle-class women also engaged in volunteer work in medical and social services, such as by addressing public health concerns, disaster relief, and war relief with the onset of World War II. Although some women found employment in the cigarette, textile, and pharmaceutical industries, they constituted only about 3 percent of the workforce. The majority of women remained employed in either agriculture or domestic service.

Bibliography

Abd ar-Raziq, Ahmad. *La Femme au temps des Mamlouks en Egypte*. 2 vols. Cairo: Institut Français d'Archeologie Orientale du Caire, 1973.

Ahmed, Leila. *Women and Gender in Islam*. New Haven, Conn.: Yale University Press, 1992.

Gerber, Haim. "Social and Economic Position of Women in an Ottoman City: Bursa, 1600–1700." *International Journal of Middle East Studies* 12, no. 3 (1980): 231–244.

Lutfi, Huda. "Al-Sakhawi's Kitab al-Nisa' as a Source for the Social and Economic History of Muslim Women during the Fifteenth Century A.D." *Muslim World* 71, no. 2 (1981): 104–124.

Tucker, Judith. *Women in Nineteenth Century Egypt*. Cambridge, U.K.: Cambridge University Press, 1985.

Walther, Wiebke. *Women in Islam: From Medieval to Modern Times*. Princeton: Markus Wiener, 1995.

Natana J. DeLong-Bas

Contemporary Discourse

This article will discuss women in the workforce in the Middle Eastern and North African (MENA) countries with special reference to Iran. It will be argued that despite women's high level of education and low fertility rate in many MENA countries, their access to the formal economy is limited and they do not occupy decision-making positions. On the other hand women work in various forms in the informal economy. Patriarchal gender relations are a real obstacle in the path of women, leading to marginalization of women in the workforce. However, women throughout the region have been challenging gender inequalities. Their struggle for gender justice, including economic gender justice, has resulted in some changes in laws and regulations in favor of women, paving their way for further gender equality. In this context women's contribution to the economy as a whole, including their work in the informal economy, is important, as the whole economy is the site of gender contestation. This analysis suggests that change in material (education, health, employment) circumstances and women's struggle for gender equality greatly impact patriarchal gender relations.

Making Women's Participation in the MENA Workforce Visible. In the second decade of the twenty-first century, women's level of education is high in most countries around the world.

In the MENA countries, with the exception of East Asia, education has expanded faster than other regions, especially for women, who in recent years have overtaken men in this respect. In the Middle East the percentage of women in universities is high, and in some countries such as in Iran the majority of university students are women.

The age of marriage is high, ranging from mid- to late twenties both for women and men. The fertility rate has also declined substantially. Iran has the lowest fertility rate (1.7), followed by Lebanon (1.8) and Tunisia (1.8). Syria has the highest rate (2.9), followed by Oman (2.8) and Saudi Arabia (2.8). Micro- and macro-level studies have historically demonstrated that education and fertility rates are important indicators for women's participation in the workforce. Economic development, industrialization, and urbanization in this region have also contributed to women's rising participation in the economy. However, women's participation in the formal workforce in this region is 26 percent, which is lower than any other region (East Asia and the Pacific, 69 percent; Latin America and the Caribbean, 42 percent; South Asia, 43 percent; sub-Saharan Africa, 62 percent). Women's formal political participation in this region is also lower than other regions.

Access to employment, especially in the formal economy, is crucial for women's empowerment and their ability to struggle for gender equality. However, in order to make women's work and their struggle for gender equality visible, we need to look at the discourses of women in the workforce through the lens of the sexual division of labor and the economy as a whole (formal and informal). The analysis of women's agency, of changing gender identities, and of women's capacity to contest oppressive practices—at work and other institutions—are crucial to evaluate the majority of women's contribution to the economy and society as a whole through paid, unpaid, and voluntary work. In this context, a review of the literature reveals a number of interrelated issues:

1. Gendered division of labor is the source of women's marginalization in the workforce. However, the definition of "women's work" varies considerably in different societies according to change in economic circumstances and male-dominated gender ideologies.
2. Informal employment includes a wide range of economic activities, ranging from wage work, unpaid work, self-employment, and voluntary work. Women work in family businesses, in various forms of informal enterprises and microenterprises. They work as subcontract workers and outsource workers. Another aspect of the informal economy is home-based work of various sorts—globally 80 percent of women are home-based workers. The prevalence of women's multiple occupations clearly demonstrates why women's work is underreported. Thus the analysis of the economy as a whole (formal and informal) is more important than focusing solely on the labor market.
3. The persistence of the informal economy suggests that the informal labor is a structural feature of capitalist accumulation. Within the informal labor some activities can easily be defined as production. Others are not directly linked to the market but there is a recognition that these activities contribute to social reproduction and the maintenance of the economy, but women's contribution within the informal economy has been undercounted in labor statistics and national income accounts. However, the invisible contribution of women could yield billions of dollars annually.

These discussions suggest that the focus should be on recognizing the importance of the informal workers, mainly women, and their location within the larger economy. The emphasis should be on the level of earnings; the nature of contracts; the access to social services; the affiliation to labor organizations; the integration of the formal and the informal sectors and their dependence on each other; and the fact that the informal economy plays an important role in the functioning of the formal economy and thus the whole economy.

The case study of Iran. Women's mass participation in the 1979 revolution empowered many women and gave them confidence to explicitly challenge male domination. Originally the modern Islamic interpretation of women's issues removed some of the obstacles and encouraged women to participate in socioeconomic and sociopolitical spheres. The Islamisation of state and society, hijab, and sex segregation opened up opportunities for many religious middle-class and working-class women to enter the public sphere of economy and society. Female formal labor force participation in state enterprises increased from 29 percent in 1971 to 34 percent in 2008. And its participation in industries increased from 8 percent in 1972 to 11 percent in 2007.

However, the patriarchal gender relations based on conservative interpretations of Iranian and Islamic culture were soon reconstructed. Laws and regulations, a male-dominated society and culture, and a highly male-centered state policy have created a web of obstacles to women's progress. Since the mid-1990s, few women have occupied high government positions such as ministers, vice presidents, deputy ministers, regional governors, and regional deputy governors. Furthermore women's participation at the higher levels of employment—such as political leadership, managerial, and decision-making positions—have not increased more than 2 percent. The gendered division of labor is based on the idea that men are the sole breadwinners and women's access to work depends on men's permission. Thus the dominant state ideology advocates that men should have access to employment and reach high positions and women may take up whatever employment and positions are left over and not wanted by men. Many women have specialized in science, social science, art, and humanities, but they have not been absorbed into the formal workforce, especially in high positions. In cases where they are included, they are not promoted even if they have higher educational degrees and more years of work experience compared to their male colleagues.

Despite the deeply rooted patriarchal attitudes at the level of family, state, and society, women's struggle for gender equality has had a relatively positive impact on these institutions, and women's participation in socioeconomic and sociopolitical spheres has been made acceptable to society. Throughout the 1990s and into the twenty-first century, more than two thousand women have been elected in local council elections. This is significant as it demonstrates that despite patriarchal attitudes women are prepared to participate in elections as voters and as candidates, and in comparison with previous decades many women and some men are prepared to elect women to decision-making positions. Women's participation in elections as voters has been significantly high. In the 2009 presidential elections 65 percent of women and 62 percent of men participated in the election. Nevertheless, the percentage of women members of parliaments is 4 percent. In local urban and rural councils women constitute 1.5 percent and in high managerial positions, 2 percent. This is also because participation in electoral politics as candidates requires funding. Only through employment are women able to access the necessary funds to participate in elections as candidates and pay for their administrative costs. Many women, therefore, believe that if they have financial independence they can participate in electoral politics; they can be involved in policy-making decisions that could pave the way for women to have access to resources, including the formal workforce.

Despite all the barriers, many women systematically challenge patriarchal gender relations. Women's social knowledge and their role in economic activities are growing and changing the existing gendered division of labor and incorrect perceptions about women's place in the family, economy, and wider society. For many women economic independence is the prerequisite to achieve political power. It is through employment that women find the opportunity to gain experience, to be trained, and to be able to risk and ultimately gain power and challenge the subordination of women in society.

The female informal employment in Iran. The informal economy in Iran includes wageworkers in small private enterprises (carpet weaving and other handicrafts) and various types of unpaid family labor at home, including simple commodity production (production of dried herbs, pickles, purées, jams, blankets, sheets, cloths). Also a large number of women are voluntary workers. Their work is essential for the functioning of the economy and the well-being of their family and community. This large and growing workforce does not appear in the statistics and its contribution is not included in the national income. This pattern can be found in other MENA countries as well as all developing countries.

Since the 1990s, a large number of women work as self-employed and unpaid voluntary workers in nongovernmental organizations (NGOs). Many of these NGOs were born out of the women's movement and acted as civil society organizations. They created an autonomous space from the family, the state, and the market. Their struggle represented an unprecedented historical transformation, responding to profound changes in women's and men's consciousness. They provided opportunities for new sources of identity for individuals and groups of women. However, the creation of autonomous spheres of social activity for women has been undermined by a patriarchal social order and the multiple sites—the intertwining of civil society, state, religion, and family—through which social gender is constructed. Nevertheless, women in Iran have been challenging institutional power, especially gender-specific access and influence, and have achieved substantive goals. They are recognized as a social group that shares common interests and legitimate claims on society. The same pattern can be found in Egypt, Lebanon, and Palestine. Women's voluntary work in charity organizations and NGOs has played an important role in the provision of health, education, and social welfare where the states have failed to provide these resources for their citizens. As a recognized social group these women have also struggled for gender equality and challenged conservative gender ideologies.

Another aspect of women's informal employment in Iran is found in the increasing abundance of modern coffee shops where a large number of young women university graduates work. Many of them are not registered workers, as entry to and exit from these businesses are easy for women. Although there are disadvantages to this form of employment as there is no job security, for many women this line of work has the advantage of flexibility, allowing them to study or perform other forms of employment. Many women welcome the presence of female waitresses and argue that this phenomenon makes it easier for young women to sit in a coffee shop without being harassed by men. Also the character of coffee shops is changing from the traditional *ghahvekhaneh* (coffeehouse), which were and still are totally male institutions, serving men by men.

The culture of work within another male-dominated profession is also changing. A large number of female home-based workers are engaged in the property and money markets. The majority of those who are formally engaged in this profession are men. However, more and more young educated women as home-based workers are entering this profession. This is a profitable business for these women and demonstrates that the informal workers are not necessarily poor.

Women's Struggle for Gender Equality and Change in Patriarchal Gender Relations. These different categories of women's work amount to millions of invisible hours of labor; their monetary value is unknown as they are not counted in the statistics or the national incomes. However, these women are empowered by working and earning money in these informal economies and are confidently changing gender relations within the home and the wider society.

Women throughout the region—whether engaged in the formal economy or informal economy—as purposeful agents, devise work and other strategies to renegotiate aspects of gender relations within the patriarchal household, the state, the market, and other institutions. No doubt patriarchal gender relations and institutions are important obstacles for women's access to resources and women's employment in the formal economy. Moreover women's work is affected by family laws, education, and health issues, as well as employment laws and regulations. However, the dynamic of women's struggle for gender equality is changing gender relations. In many cases women have succeeded in reforms to family law, education, and employment law, which have had a relatively positive impact on women and work. These reforms have affected the work of women both in the formal and informal economy.

The concept of "patriarchal bargain" is useful. This discussion can be extended to women's struggle for change beyond the household and marriage and into the sphere of economy and society. In this context we see women who have access to the formal economy have greater degrees of bargaining power and are able to directly challenge gender relations by engaging in active agency at different levels of economic, social, political, and cultural life. However, the majority of women may not directly confront gender equality but their contribution to the economy and society as a whole end up being empowering for them. Thus different factors affect women's bargaining strength, including their participation in the informal economy.

Conclusion. Unequal power relations are derived from strict gendered divisions of labor. The barriers in the path of women are the way male-dominated structures are reproduced and reconstructed and patriarchal institutions are reluctant to include women in positions of power. However, gender relations are not static, and the dynamic nature of women's struggle is constantly changing male-dominated societies. A breakthrough in societal attitudes toward women is visible in the MENA societies and has positive implications for the future of these societies.

Women in the MENA region face many challenges. However, in the second decade of the twenty-first century, the ongoing political changes in this region are creating opportunities for women to gain greater economic and political power and secure a stronger voice in the socioeconomic and sociopolitical processes of their countries. Women's presence in these struggles is crucial. In Iran their presence is clearly visible; in other countries women's presence varies. Nevertheless their multiple struggles can lead to gender justice, economic justice, and democracy.

[*See also* Economics and Finance *and* Iran.]

BIBLIOGRAPHY

Agarwal, Bina. "'Bargaining' and Gender Relations: Within and Beyond the Household." *Feminist Economics* 3, no. 1 (Spring 1997): 1–51.

Aryan, Khadijeh. "The Boom in Women's Education." In *Women, Power and Politics in 21st Century Iran*, edited by Tara Povey and Elaheh Rostami-Povey. Burlington, Vt.: Ashgate, 2012.

Benería, Lourdes. *Gender, Development, and Globalization: Economics as if All People Mattered*. New York: Routledge, 2003.

Boserup, Ester. *Women's Role in Economic Development*. New York: St. Martin's, 1970.

Iran Statistical Yearbook. Statistical Centre of Iran. Tehran: Statistical Centre of Iran, 1977/8; 1986/7; 1996/7; 2002/3; 2008/9.

Kandiyoti, Deniz. "Gender, Power and Contestation: Rethinking 'Bargaining with Patriarchy.'" In *Feminist Visions of Development: Gender Analysis and Policy*, edited by Cecile Jackson and Ruth Pearson, pp. 135–151. London and New York: Routledge, 1998.

Koolaee, Elaheh. "Women in the Parliament." In *Women, Power and Politics in 21st Century Iran*, edited by Tara Povey and Elaheh Rostami-Povey. Burlington, Vt.: Ashgate, 2012.

Moghadam, Valentine M. *Modernizing Women: Gender and Social Change in the Middle East*. Boulder, Colo.: L. Rienner, 2003.

Nejadbahram, Zahra. "Women and Employment." In *Women, Power and Politics in 21st Century Iran*, edited by Tara Povey and Elaheh Rostami-Povey. Burlington, Vt.: Ashgate, 2012.

Pearson, Ruth. "Organising Home-Based Workers in the Global Economy: An Action-Research Approach." *Development in Practice* 14, no. 1/2 (February 2004): 136–148. (I am indebted to Professor Ruth Pearson for discussing this issue with me.)

Pearson, Ruth. "Plenary Presentation: Homeworkers Worldwide Mapping Project." Final Workshop, Uzice, Serbia, September 2004.

Rostami-Povey, Elaheh. *Iran's Influence: A Religious-Political State and Society in Its Region*. London and New York: Zed Books, 2010.

Rostami-Povey Elaheh. "Trade Unions and Women's NGOs: Diverse Civil Society Organisations in Iran." *Development in Practice* 14, nos. 1/2 (February 2004): 254–266.

Rostami-Povey, Elaheh [pseud. Maryam Poya]. *Women, Work and Islamism: Ideology and Resistance in Iran*. London and New York: Zed Books, 1999.

Salehi-Isfahani, Djavad. *Human Development Report in Middle East and North Africa 2010/26*. Human Development Research Paper Series. New York: United Nations Development Programme, 2010. Available at http://hdr.undp.org/en/reports/global/hdr2010/papers/HDRP_2010_26.pdf.

ELAHEH ROSTAMI-POVEY

X-Y

Xinjiang. Strategically located in northwest China, Xinjiang is not only China's largest province; it is also one of its most rich in natural resources, and the province most tightly controlled by the government. The region is known for its numerous mountain ranges, large deserts, oasis settlements, and multi-ethnic waves of migration dating back more than 2,000 years. In the past, the region that is now known as Xinjiang was referred to as Eastern Turkistan or Chinese Turkistan. The largest indigenous ethnic group in Xinjiang today are the Uighur, one of China's ten officially recognized minority ethnic groups who are predominantly Muslim. The Uighurs, like several of the other main groups in Xinjiang (the Kazakhs, Uzbeks, and Kirghiz) are a Turkic people who speak a Turkic language. Although, in the past, most of Xinjiang was controlled by the Uighur, it was never recognized as an independent state, and, given its strategic borders with Russia (and now Kazakhstan), Mongolia, Tibet, India, and other Central Asia states, it was frequently at the center of struggles for influence and control over trade routes dating back to the Silk Road. Over the centuries, China was able to exert varying degrees of control over Xinjiang.

Today, although Muslims living in all other regions of China enjoy a significant degree of freedom of religion, the situation for Muslims in Xinjiang, especially for the Uighur, is quite different. Children are not allowed to enter mosques, and government employees and, recently, even retired government employees, are forbidden to publicly practice Islam. During Ramadan, they are not allowed to fast, and teachers are expected to ensure that their students do not fast either. Men are forbidden to have mustaches or beards, and women are not allowed to wear any type of head covering. Although non-government employees are allowed to follow these religious and cultural practices, many, if not most, of the best jobs in the province have some link with the state.

In addition to the tight control of their religion, the Uighur communities of Xinjiang feel that their ethnic and cultural identity is very much under threat. Since 1949, the percentage of Han Chinese living in Xinjiang has risen from 6.7 percent to 40 percent. This huge influx of Han Chinese is the result of a massive government campaign to forcibly relocate Han Chinese to strategic minority regions, such as Xinjiang and Tibet, and, more recently, Han Chinese entrepreneurs and unemployed are seeking opportunities in a region targeted for economic development by the state.

Traditionally, Uighur women in Xinjiang were able to play a relatively active role in society. Women often produced a range of handiwork at home that they then sold in the markets. Divorce was not uncommon and often initiated by women. Not only was there no stigma attached to divorce, but divorced women usually had no problem remarrying. Ironically, it was during the forced socialist collectivization period in the early years of the People's Republic of China that women's lives became significantly more difficult. All forms of private business were no longer allowed, so women could not earn money through their handicrafts. They were forced to work in the fields while the care of their babies and pre-school children was handed over to the state who recruited older women and women who had just given birth to run the nurseries. One of the unintended consequences of combining Islamic traditions and state-run nurseries was that the young mothers taking care of others people's babies often had to breast feed these children as well. Given the prohibition against marriage between milk-siblings, the result was a major disruption of marriage practices within communities.

Over the past few decades, the disparity between the Uighur standard of living and that of the immigrant Han Chinese has grown even wider. While the government has instituted a variety of measures to ameliorate the situation, some see these efforts as undermining the religious and ethnic identity of the Uighurs.

The state started a program in 2000 that recruited the best minority middle school students in Xinjiang to continue their studies in boarding schools located in the more economically developed regions of China. This program has grown rapidly and now involves more than 50,000 students. A similar program had been set up for Tibetan students in 1990. In addition, relatively well-paying factory jobs have been allocated to minority Xinjiang young people in Shenzhen, located near Guangzhou along China's southeastern coast, literally on the other side of the country.

While both of these programs appear to be successful in terms of providing young students with an excellent education which will greatly increase their chance of being accepted into the nation's top universities, and the factory workers undoubtedly receive useful training as well, these opportunities come at the cost of being separated from family, friends, and culture at a crucial time in their lives.

Organizations, especially religious ones, are difficult to establish given the heavy surveillance by the state on such activities. As a result, it is difficult to document either the religious activities or concerns of the general population. There was one point in recent history during which Uighurs were allowed to form organizations. During that time, Rabiya Kadeer formed the group "A Thousand Mothers" to support job training and literacy among Uighur women. However, she was later imprisoned and sent into exile.

[*See also* Kadeer, Rabiya]

BIBLIOGRAPHY

Benson, Linda. "A Much-Married Woman: Marriage & Divorce in Xinjiang 1850–1950." *Muslim World* 83, nos. 3–4 (1993): 227–247.

Devastating Blows: Religious Repression of Uighurs in Xinjiang. Human Rights Watch report, vol. 17, no. 2(C), April 2005. Available at http://www.hrw.org/reports/2005/china0405/china0405.pdf.

Millward, James. *Eurasian Crossroads: A History of Xinjiang.* New York: Columbia University Press, 2007.

JACQUELINE ARMIJO

YAQOOB, SALMA. (b. 1971), is a British Muslim of Pakistani descent, antiwar campaigner, national commentator on race issues, and founder of the Respect Party. She was born in 1971 in

Bradford and raised in Alum Rock, Birmingham, with her six siblings. Her parents emigrated from Pakistan in the 1960s, and her father worked for some time in a mill before he joined the Royal Mail.

She studied biochemistry and psychology at Aston University and continued to do postgraduate work in psychotherapy, becoming a trained psychotherapist. While at Aston, she experimented with different religions (Christianity, Judaism, and Hinduism) before eventually returning to Islam. Her move into politics was triggered by one particular incident: two weeks after September 11, 2011, she was spat at while shopping with her three-year-old son in Birmingham city center. In the post-9/11 climate of Britain, after becoming pessimistic about all political parties as they followed "Blair philosophy" and voted for the Iraqi war, she spearheaded many antiwar movements. She temporarily suspended her doctorate to spend more time with her extended family and focus on her political career.

Yaqoob soon established herself as a powerful and outspoken political candidate on many social topics and was described as a "doughty fighter for Birmingham inner city communities." She first gained political renown in 2003 as chair of the Birmingham Stop the War Coalition, which formed in response to the invasion of Iraq. She would further cement her status as a noteworthy political adversary when she represented the Respect Party in Birmingham, Sparkbrook, and Small Heath during the 2005 general elections, in which she took second place (with one-third of the vote), beating both the Liberal Democratic and Conservative candidates. The next year she got nearly half the vote and was elected as city councilor for Sparkbrook Ward on Birmingham City Council. She was subsequently solicited by the Tories, Liberal Democrats, and Labour party, yet she decided to stay with the Respect Party, eventually becoming the party leader after its split. She would maintain her position as city councilor and party leader until July 7, 2011, when she announced her resignation as councilor for Sparkbrook for health reasons.

She was acknowledged for her work in 2006 when she received the Asian Jewel Award for Public Service Excellence for her achievements for social schemes for the prosperity of Britain's South Asian communities. She also ranked number 24 on Birmingham Post's 2009 Power 50 and number 18 on the 2009 Muslim Women Power List.

Her short political career is characterized by her views on local and national social issues. While she remains adamant in her views against the war, she also gained recognition for her outspoken opinions about many other topics, such as housing improvement, inner-city deprivation, current affairs (as discussed on her *Politics and Media* show, which aired on the Islam Channel), the role of Muslims and Muslim women as well as other race issues, overcoming traditional beliefs of proper behavior for Muslim women, Muslim and non-Muslim unity, and pro-Palestinian stance (as evidenced by the boycott of Israeli goods she called for in response to Israel's actions in Gaza). Throughout her political and social works, she has upheld the common principles of peace, social justice, and equality and continues to work toward creating a world that is free from "war, racism, and poverty." Her career pursuits, as well as those of the Respect Party, are documented on her web site, http://www.salmayaqoob.com.

BIBLIOGRAPHY

BBC. "Profile: Respect Party Leader Salma Yaqoob." *BBC*, April 8 2010. http://news.bbc.co.uk/2/hi/uk_news/politics/election_2010/8609297.stm.

Birmingham Post. "In the Frame—Andrew Mitchell, Paul Tilsley, Paul Bassi, Salma Yaqoob, Clive Dutton, and Jon Bounds." *Birmingham Post*, June 9, 2009. http://www.birminghampost.net/news/power-50/

2009/06/09/in-the-frame-andrew-mitchell-paul-tilsley-paul-bassi-salma-yaqoob-clive-dutton-and-jon-bounds-65233-23831663/.

Birmingham Post. "Power 50 Profiles: No. 24, Salma Yaqoob." *Birmingham Post*, 2009. http://www.birminghampost.net/news/power-50/power50-profiles09/2009/07/30/no-24-salma-yaqoob-65233-24276952/.

Bunting, Madeleine. "Respect Candidate Spearheads Quiet Revolution to Get Muslim Women Involved in Politics." *Guardian*, April 23, 2010. http://www.guardian.co.uk/politics/2010/apr/23/respect-candidate-muslim-women-politics.

Guardian. "Muslim Women Power List." *Guardian*, March 25, 2009. http://www.guardian.co.uk/society/gallery/2009/mar/25/muslim-women-power-list.

Lutz, Richard. "The Lutz Report: On Salma Yaqoob." *Stirrer*, March 9, 2010. http://thestirrer.thebirminghampress.com/March_10/the-lutz-report-on-salma-yaqoob-090310.html.

McFerran, Ann. "Relative Values: Salma Yaqoob and Her Father Mohammad." *Times of London*, July 22, 2007. http://women.timesonline.co.uk/tol/life_and_style/women/the_way_we_live/article2062769.ece.

Yaqoob, Salma. "Biography: Salma Yaqoob." *Salma Yaqoob.com*, January 1, 2010. http://www.salmayaqoob.com/2010/01/salma-yaqoob_31.html.

Yaqoob, Salma. "Time to Take a Step Back." *SalmaYaqoob.com*, July 7, 2011. http://www.salmayaqoob.com/2011/07/time-to-take-step-back.html.

EREN TATARI

YASSINE, NADIA. (b. 1958), a Moroccan activist and a high profile member of the Islamist political movement Al-ʿAdl wa l-Iḥsān (Justice and Spirituality), established in the early 1970s. As the daughter of the guide of the movement, ʿAbd al-Salām Yāsīn, her political role is closely linked to that of her father. Her interpretation of Islam is also in large part influenced by her father's mystical approach and by the Ṣūfī character of his movement.

Nadia Yassine was born in 1958 in Casablanca, Morocco. Although she received education in Arabic, she also attended the French system of primary and secondary education, graduating in 1977 from the Lycée Victor Hugo in Marrakesh. She obtained a bachelor's degree (*licence*) in political science from the faculty of law in Fes.

Al-ʿAdl wa l-Iḥsān has its origins in the Boutchihiyya ṭarīqa (Sūfī order), from which Yassine's father separated in 1972. Because it is a Ṣūfī society, her father is considered the *shaykh* (head) of the disciples who form its membership. The movement is not recognized by the monarchy, which labels it as part of the radical political opposition.

In 1973 Yassine's father sent a virulent letter to the king of Morocco, Hasan II, in the *naṣīḥa* (admonishment) style, exhorting him to surrender to God and establish a caliphate. As a result, he was sent to prison. Nadia was politically active while attending university, following in the footsteps of her father's movement, which denied the legitimacy of the Moroccan monarchy. She has since emerged as the movement's unofficial spokesperson, in particular for the Francophone media in Morocco and more largely in Europe.

Although she represents her father's political movement, she also benefits from a certain autonomy, owing perhaps to her status as the daughter of the guide. For instance, she heads the women's section, called *inṣāf* (equity), which operates as a space for mystical practices, community building, politics, and engagement with the media. Nadia also combines the mystical aspects of Al-ʿAdl wa l-Iḥsān with a larger project of social reform aimed at fighting poverty and social injustices, and critical of the political regime of Morocco for its lack of democracy and its corruption. She views the regime's processes of liberalization since the 1990s as superficial reforms that further consolidate the monarchy's authority in Morocco. She is one of the most outspoken high-profile members of Al-ʿAdl wa l-Iḥsān on such political and social questions. She allegedly coauthored the 2000 memorandum that her father sent to the young King Muḥammad VI of Morocco. This admonition was different from the more traditional admonition sent to his father King Hassan II in 1973: it was written in French, and it bears Nadia's style.

Nadia was deprived of her passport until 2003, after which she travelled to Europe and to the United States to give lectures. She often writes essays in the Moroccan press and has her own web site. She published *Full Sails Ahead* (2006), a book originally written in French under the title *Toutes voiles dehors* (2003). She acknowledges that her writings are not academic and are driven by her political critique of the monarchy and of Western imperialism. Though she rarely speaks about the political notions that her father developed, such as those of a caliphate and of the prophetic way (*al-minhāj al-nabawī*), she insists that a republic is the best regime for Morocco. One of her enduring themes is Sharīʿah (Islamic law) and women's rights. She argues that Sharīʿah law, if well understood, can be on the side only of women's rights.

BIBLIOGRAPHY

Yassine, Nadia. *Full Sails Ahead*. Iowa City, Iowa: Justice and Spirituality Publishing, 2006.

Zeghal, Malika. *Islamism in Morocco: Religion, Authoritarianism, and Electoral Politics*. Princeton, N.J.: Markus Wiener, 2008.

MALIKA ZEGHAL

YEMEN. Yemen was the home of two legendary women: the Queen of Sheba, or Bilqis as she is called in Arabic, and Queen Arwa. Both women ruled over important parts of present-day Yemen and continue to be important symbols for Yemeni women. However, little is known about the lives of ordinary Yemeni women before the twentieth century. Until 1970, the large majority of the population lived in the countryside, education was accessible only to the elite, there were hardly any health facilities, and infrastructure was poor. Yemeni society was highly stratified, affecting gender relations. Elite women often led secluded lives, but sometimes had access to religious education; women of tribal background were actively involved in agricultural and livestock activities; and women from the lower status groups performed manual and service labor, in addition to housekeeping and childcare. Literacy rates among both men and women were very low, life expectancy rates were around forty years of age, and infant- and child-mortality rates were very high. Many male Yemenis migrated to Africa, Asia, Europe, and the United States to escape the poor living conditions. They often left their wives and children behind.

Two Republics. The Republic of Yemen was formed after unification of North and South Yemen in 1990. North Yemen was for centuries a Zaydi Imamate ruled by religious leaders. In 1962, the Yemen Arab Republic (YAR) was established, followed by a seven-year-long civil war between republicans and royalists. Equality of all citizens, including gender equality, was a central element in the constitution. Women obtained, among other things, the right to education and employment, and to vote and run for parliament. Yet, women were discouraged from running in elections and continued to suffer from limited access to education and health care, early marriages, and high fertility rates. Conservative attitudes in families and society at large were the main reasons. South Yemen was colonized by Great Britain (1839–1967). Women participated actively in the independence struggle. The Yemeni Women's Association was established in the 1950s. In 1967, the People's Democratic Republic of Yemen (PDRY) was established by a Marxist liberation front. A progressive family law was introduced protecting women from early marriages, regulating polygyny, and giving women equal rights to divorce, for example. The situation of women in South Yemen was far better than in North Yemen. Radhiya Shamsir is one of the most important women activists in the South.

Migration. Labor migration became an important source of income after the oil-boom in Saudi Arabia and the Gulf States in the 1970s. This migration was highly gendered, with men migrating to take up work as unskilled workers in the infrastructure and service sector. Remittances led to increased access to foreign currencies, the growth of the import sector, new class differences and changing consumption patterns. Rural women's workload increased due to male migration, yet rarely led to more decision-making power. Urbanization increased as well, affecting women's lives in other ways. For some Yemeni women, migration to the city meant a decrease in workload as they no longer had agricultural tasks, but changing family structures could also mean more isolation and more work. Employing domestic workers became a common phenomenon among middle-and upper-middle class families in the main cities. The majority of these workers come from Ethiopia and Somalia.

Development Aid. Foreign development aid became another important source of income since the 1970s. Western, Arab, Asian, and former Communist nations have technically and financially supported projects in the fields of education and health care, infrastructure, water and sanitation, and the like. Gender issues received special attention in many development projects. National women's organizations, such as the Yemeni Women Union and the National Committee for Women, are supported by foreign donor organizations. The number of NGOs, particularly those focusing on women, increased considerably after unification in 1990, when a period of freedom of expression and democratization began. In addition, both Sana'a University and Aden University received foreign support to establish Women's Studies centers. Women also played an important role in the parliamentary elections, as voters and candidates. Yet, the number of female MPs and Ministers remains very small.

Political Instability. After unification, it soon became clear that women's rights deteriorated, particularly in South Yemen. The progressive family law was replaced by much more conservative laws. In 1994, a short war between the armies of former North and South Yemen was won by Northern troops. The Islamic Reform Party (Islah) obtained more political power. Islah attracted many women as it offers a way to combine charity work with being active in the public sphere. While women's education and employment have improved in urban areas in North Yemen, the situation in rural areas is lagging behind. In addition, widespread corruption, mismanagement, unemployment, and inflation have led to increasing frustration and despair. President Ali Abdullah Saleh, who had been in power since 1978, supported the U.S.-led "War on Terror," but did little to improve the living conditions of the population. Several violent clashes have taken place between government forces and an opposition movement in the far north of the country, resulting in hundreds of thousands of Internally Displaced People, among whom are many women and children. A popular movement in former South Yemen is fighting for independence. Countrywide nonviolent protests against the regime of Ali Abdullah Saleh, inspired by the developments in Tunisia and Egypt, started in February 2011. Women have played a large role in this movement. Tawakkul Karman, spokeswoman of the Youth of the Yemeni Revolution, received the Nobel Peace Prize that year for her nonviolent efforts to bring about change. In November 2011, Ali

Abdullah Saleh nominally stepped down in exchange for immunity. A transitional government under the leadership of President Abdel Mansour Hadi has the difficult task to bring back stability to the country. The promotion of human rights including gender equality, is a big challenge for the new government.

BIBLIOGRAPHY

Carapico, Sheila. "Gender and Status Inequalities in Yemen: Honour, Economics, and Politics." In *Patriarchy and Economic Development: Women's Positions at the End of the Twentieth Century*, edited by Valentine M. Moghadam, pp. 80–98. Oxford: Clarendon, 1996.

Dahlgren, Susanne. *Contesting Realities: The Public Sphere and Morality in Southern Yemen*. Syracuse, N.Y.: Syracuse University Press, 2010.

Paluch, Marta, ed. *Yemeni Voices: Women Tell Their Stories*. Sana'a: The British Council, 2001.

de Regt, Marina. *Pioneers or Pawns? Women Health Workers and the Politics of Development in Yemen*. Syracuse, N.Y.: Syracuse University Press, 2007.

MARINA DE REGT

YOUTH CULTURE. The Muslim youth culture that has begun burgeoning in the early twenty-first century is a reflection of the newly available social opportunities, as well as the frustrations, of a youth population whose numbers have exploded across the Muslim world since the postcolonial and independence era of the 1960s. The combination of basic infrastructural improvements and simple health measures put into place since that time has resulted in a sharp rise in young populations in Muslim-majority societies throughout sub-Saharan Africa, the Middle East, and South, Central, and Southeast Asia.

This so-called Muslim "youth bulge" is defined as occurring when people between the ages of fifteen and twenty-nine make up more than 40 percent of the population. The youth bulge in the Muslim world is distinctive not only with regard to its size (in some countries reaching well over 50 percent of the total population), but also due to its levels of education. A significant proportion of this postcolonial generation has experienced far higher rates of schooling than any previous generation. Not all countries conform to this pattern, however. Rates of educational achievement remain stubbornly low, for example, in Afghanistan and some parts of Muslim sub-Saharan African. Still, generally speaking, the current generation has greatly exceeded the levels of education achieved by their parents.

With education have come new social and economic aspirations. Many among the newly educated, especially in the urban middle classes (themselves greatly expanded as a result of urbanization and postcolonial population growth), come away from their educational experience with significantly changed self-perceptions and social ambitions. Many are reluctant to take low-paying and insecure menial employment, hoping instead to secure a white-collar or government position. The neoliberal structural reforms of the 1990s and 2000s, however, have diminished employment opportunities in the government sector and, even where jobs exist, educational systems often do not provide youth with the requisite skills and training. Anxiety revolving around securing employment remains a key feature of urban, middle class youth culture across large parts of the Muslim-majority world.

An equally important feature of this educational and aspirational shift has been its impact on young women. Although, at first, they were greatly underrepresented among postcolonial educational cohorts due to a widespread cultural emphasis on the education of boys, by the 1990s, women in most—although not all—Muslim countries were well represented in primary and secondary education. In a number of countries their representation in tertiary education has rivaled or—as in Egypt, Iran, Saudi Arabia, and Malaysia—exceeded that of males. To a much greater extent than was the case in Western societies after the 1960s, however, the impact of these educational and aspirational changes on women's employment outside of the household has varied. Some countries—among them, Morocco, Tunisia, Qatar, Malaysia, and Indonesia—have seen a noticeable upswing in numbers of women employed in the extra-familial workforce. In other countries, such as Saudi Arabia, Iran, and Afghanistan, patriarchal norms have continued to restrict women's participation in extra-household employment, even where young women have begun to participate more fully in higher education.

Whatever the precise impact of education on extra-familial employment, the combination of higher education and, where it occurs, a higher rate of female employment, has resulted in a social development of equally momentous importance for the development of youth culture: the deferral of marriage and the prolongation of the period of premarital youth. The pattern is additionally complicated by economic and class variables. Among the aspiring urban middle class, not least of all, the increasing costs associated with marriage and setting up an independent household have frustrated dreams of youthful marriage, raising the median age of marriage into the mid-twenties, and compounding social tensions. A distinctive feature of these tensions is that urbanization, education, and an expanding commercial environment present much greater possibilities for mixing between the sexes. These factors have led to new patterns of courtship and marriage, including, in countries like Iraq, Iran, Egypt, and Jordan, as well as the Arab Gulf states, a renewed interest in various forms of temporary marriage (*nikah al-mut'ah*). These same circumstances have also given rise to repeated moral panics with regard to sexual promiscuity and increased violence against women, including—in areas of the Middle East and Southwest Asia—honor killings for perceived moral transgressions on the part of girls.

Unlike the pattern seen in parts of the post-1960s West, these new practices of gender, sexuality, and marriage have for the most part coincided with an historically unprecedented Islamic awakening (*ṣaḥwah*), rather than a secularist surge in public life. This Islamic resurgence varies greatly across nations in its precise genealogy and public impact, but one of its trademark characteristics has been a heightened concern with sexual modesty, especially among young women. In some countries this has involved the imposition of regulations ostensibly based on sharīʿah law, as well as the policing of public forms of sexual expression. The new youth cultures so salient across large parts of the Muslim world have been sites of both dialogue and contestation over these issues of subjectivity, piety, sexuality, and sociability.

Adulthood Deferred. Youth represents a life stage positioned between the dependency of childhood and the mature responsibilities of adulthood, the latter phase typically defined in relation to marriage, employment, and parenthood. Across much of the Muslim-majority world, higher education has had the effect of significantly prolonging the former period of youthful exploration. Urbanization, expanded media, and new forms of consumption have served to further define the contours of this greatly expanded youth phase. Television series, radio talk shows, and inexpensive booklets and magazines disseminate discourses of self-improvement and offer models for the cultivation of new, more cosmopolitan, lifestyles for youth who have moved to cities and towns in unprecedented numbers in search of education and employment. Billboards and commercial advertisements, air-conditioned malls, and multistoried shopping centers all present enticing new images of consumption, sociability, and well-being.

For many youth, however, these new possibilities are frustratingly out of reach. Youth unemployment remains stubbornly high across most of the Middle East region. In the late 1990s and early 2000s, the figure among young people ages 15 to 24 had reached 25 percent. A similar pattern exists in sub-Saharan Africa, where the regional figure also exceeds 20 percent. In Muslim-majority countries like Nigeria and Senegal, over half of the youth population remains unemployed. Many more young people are economically inactive, waiting and hoping for their employment opportunities to improve. Without a job and a steady income, young people feel uncertain about the future—particularly with regard to marriage and the establishment of a family of their own. High levels of unemployment and underemployment among young people in many areas of the Muslim world remain a challenging issue and a major source of youth frustration. The situation has resulted in changing youth perceptions of life, family, and the government. It has expressed itself most recently in the "Arab Spring," a revolutionary wave of protests and demonstrations in opposition to the state that swept across the Middle East and Northern Africa beginning in December 2010.

New Patterns of Courtship and Marriage. Within this context of social and economic possibility and uncertainty, patterns of courtship and marriage have undergone great changes. Although young people are marrying considerably later, there is nonetheless still a strong marital imperative across much of the Muslim world. Shaped by a mix of scriptural directives and social expectations, most young people feel great pressures from their families, peers, and communities to marry. Not to marry consigns one to an incomplete adult status, and also excludes one from many of the most cherished public activities and traditions of adult social life. Significantly, since the 1960s, urban populations in much of the Muslim world have witnessed a relative shift away from arranged marriages and toward marriage determined by a greater measure of individual choice. However, the degree of choice and the degree to which parents and extended family members continue to play a role in some phase of spousal selection vary greatly.

In areas like South Asia, Muslim West Africa, and those portions of the Arab Muslim world where tribes and extended families play a central role in public and political life, parents still play an important role in marital arrangements. In these settings, family "honor" is a matter of passionate collective concern, and its force is nowhere felt more fully than in matters of sexuality and marriage. This is true even in modern urban societies, including Muslim immigrant societies. In those instances where extended family units remain socially important, arranged marriages are still common. In the United Kingdom, for example, where almost three-quarters of Muslims are of South Asian descent (the majority from a few districts in Pakistan and Bangladesh), nearly half of all marriages are parentally arranged (though typically with at least some degree of assent on the part of the couple). Among recent Yemeni immigrants in the United States as well, parents commonly arrange marriages for their children with individuals back in Yemen, both as a way to bring newcomers to the United States and in order to insure the continued cultural vitality of the Yemeni-American community.

Other areas of the Muslim world, however, have seen a marked increase in youth-initiated premarital relationships. In big cities like Tunis, Cairo, Jakarta, Kuala Lumpur, and Rabat, a Western- or East Asian-influenced "dating" culture has emerged, especially among the middle- and upper-middle classes. Computers and cell phones facilitate meetings in malls and coffee shops and, in some cases, nightclubs. Young couples fill the streets on Saturday nights, on their way to restaurants and movie theaters, or simply strolling and window-shopping. Nonetheless, men continue to play the more active role in courtship by initiating interaction, and "dating" is often only possible after a serious commitment has been made.

Moreover, although youth throughout the Muslim world are increasingly familiar with a globalized, rights-based discourse that emphasizes individual agency and a greater measure of gender equity, this awareness has not eradicated the double standard that exists for the evaluation of the sexual behavior of men and women. This is true particularly, but not only, with regard to premarital virginity. Urban, educated young women may become involved in modern-style relationships (which may or may not involve sex), only to discover that when it comes to marriage, they are rejected in favor of someone younger and purportedly less experienced. In countries like Egypt, Morocco, and Jordan, young women may resort to surgical procedures to physically reconstruct their virginity prior to their wedding night. In many areas of the Muslim world, educated women in their mid- to late twenties find it increasingly difficult to find an equally well-educated husband, as men continue to "marry down" in terms of age and education. In the context of a perceived dearth of available men, some women are willing to consider entering into temporary marriage or even a polygynous relationship.

Discipline and Defiance. In some Muslim-majority countries, the government has enacted more direct and systematic forms of state control and discipline in an attempt to contain the emerging cultures of youth and sexuality. In Iran, Saudi Arabia, and Afghanistan, state regulations severely limit sexual expression in the public sphere by requiring that women remain covered and by restricting interactions between unrelated men and women. Those who transgress and are caught may be harassed, jailed, or publicly flogged. In Iran, as in some other areas of the urban Middle East, an urban youth culture has developed that intentionally tests the limits of these policies. Even among urban populations, however, the pattern is marked by differences of class. Whereas the lower, and working classes in urban Iran have remained more faithful to state-sanctioned models of piety and propriety, levels of disaffection among the urban middle and upper classes have soared. Because the public sphere is so highly policed, many middle-class young people in cities like Tehran have shifted their socializing to private spaces within the household and family. In private house parties, Iranian youth from more affluent class backgrounds engage in heterosexual mixing, dancing, drinking, and, in some cases even drug use—which young people view not so much as political dissent, but rather as personal choice and individual expression. Other activities, however, pose a more direct challenge to state authority and involve youth from a variety of class backgrounds, as when young people orchestrate their own celebrations of Muharram (the Shīʿī month of mourning) by organizing "Hussein Parties," which draw thousands of youth into the streets and involve, not mourning and self-abasement, but self-assertion. These parties often lead to direct clashes with the morality police, the *Basiji*, sometimes resulting in large-scale arrests and beatings.

In Saudi Arabia, young people test the limits of government surveillance in equally risky, if typically nonpolitical, ways. In cities like Riyadh, disenfranchised rural youth, school drop-outs, Bedouins, and, in general, young men frustrated with their lack of prospects in the city—are drawn to the thrill and notoriety of "car skidding." Skidders (*mufahhatin*) report feeling excluded from Islamic youth groups that typically seek out the most securely middle-class students. Marginalized from these high-status activities, skidders seek alternative routes to fame and respect. They drive in caravans at top speeds, often destroying the cars in spectacular displays that sometimes result in their own or bystanders' death. Government officials' efforts to eradicate skidding, which they identify with glue sniffing, drinking, and homosexuality, have been largely ineffective. When one ringleader is arrested and jailed, another emerges to take his place. In an interesting parallel with gang culture in the United States, incarcerated skidders often repent and become street preachers, who attempt to use their own experience to reach out to and connect with other young *mufahhat*.

Awakened Youth. Improvements in education and increased contact with Muslims in other parts of the world, due to a globalized media, have also supported a resurgence of interest among young people in religious study and more normative forms of religious practice. A vibrant and self-consciously "Islamic" youth culture has developed in most countries with significant Muslim populations. This is clear from the growing numbers of young people who join Qur'ānic study groups, attend public sermons, and wear Islamic-style clothing. For young women, the new culture of piety almost always includes wearing a more encompassing headscarf, a loose tunic or top, and a long skirt or loose pants. Pious styles for men involve beards, collarless tunics, and ankle-length pants. These styles are especially common in urban areas and among high school and university students, a percentage of whom have been attracted to moderately conservative *daʿwah* (missionary or proselytizing) groups. From Egypt and Jordan to Malaysia and Indonesia, campus *daʿwah* organizations have exerted considerable influence on youth culture through their efforts to Islamize society "from the ground up." Their members have successfully organized campus study groups on the model of Egypt's Muslim Brotherhood, and have often secured leadership positions in student government. From these and other strategic perches, young reformists have sought to develop a youth culture both modern and pious, and often self-consciously opposed to patterns of dress, courtship, and media consumption seen as Western, individualistic, and irreligious.

The new Islamic groups have not, however, completely rejected popular youth culture. Instead, many have adapted select elements to their own ends. Since the 1990s, Indonesia, Malaysia, Egypt, Morocco, and Senegal have witnessed the emergence of a new generation of "hip" Muslim preachers (imam, *ustadz*, marabout) whose message is aimed specifically at young people. The preaching styles deployed by these young preachers incorporate elements of informal slang and use marketing techniques and pop psychology to address youthful concerns like proper social relations and sexuality. The new interest in Muslim styles of clothing has also fueled a booming Muslim fashion industry, which offers stylish creations in regional fabrics and eye-catching colors, some of which are far from demure. In the same way, a rapidly expanding industry of Islamic music, from Ṣūfī *qawwālī* and *nasheed* boy bands to religiously inflected hip hop and heavy metal, is now evident throughout the Muslim world.

Variety and Contestation. Across much of the Muslim world, then, a globalized media, higher levels of education (not least that of women and girls), and class-based consumption have all played a role in the emergence of new cultures of adolescence and youth. But this cultural globalization has not brought with it homogenization. Although urbanization and education have in some populations resulted in a greater measure of individual "choice" in courtship and marriage, the precise pattern has also been inflected by the relative strength of tribal- and extended-family groups. More generally, whereas in Western Europe the gender changes and individualizing currents of the post-1960s period took place against the backdrop of a growing secularization of public life, similar changes in Muslim majority countries have taken place against the backdrop of a general religious awakening. Muslim youth culture is situated at the intersection of these changes, and, as a result, it will continue to be highly varied and contested in its expression.

[*See also* Divorce, *subentry on* Modern Practice; Marriage *subentry on* Modern Practice; *and* Sexuality.]

BIBLIOGRAPHY

Dhillon, Navtej, and Tarik Yousef, eds. *Generation in Waiting: The Unfulfilled Promise of Young People in the Middle East*. Washington, D.C.: Brookings Institution Press, 2009. A collection of articles on Middle Eastern youth with a focus on issues of education, marriage, and employment.

Herrera, Linda, and Asep Bayat, eds. *Being Young and Muslim: New Cultural Politics in the Global South and North*. New York: Oxford University Press, 2010. Articles on Muslim youth from a variety of Muslim countries which take up issues of identity, gender, politics, and youth culture.

Heryanto, Ariel, ed. *Popular Culture in Indonesia: Fluid Identities in Post-Authoritarian Politics*. New York: Routledge, 2008.

Khosravi, Shahram. *Young and Defiant in Tehran*. Philadelphia: University of Pennsylvania Press, 2008. An ethnography of contemporary youth culture in Iran's capital.

Nilan, Pam, and Charles Feixa, eds. *Global Youth?: Hybrid Identities, Plural Worlds*. New York: Routlege, 2006. A collection of articles on youth culture and Identity.

Sarroub, Loukia K. *All American Yemeni Girls: Being Muslim in a Public School*. Philadelphia: University of Pennsylvania Press, 2005. An ethnography of Yemeni American girls in a southeastern Michigan community.

Schielke, Samuli. "Ambivalent Commitments: Troubles of Morality, Religiosity and Aspiration among Young Egyptians." *Journal of Religion in Africa* 39 (2009): 158–185.

Smith-Hefner, Nancy J. "The New Muslim Romance: Changing Patterns of Courtship and Marriage among Educated Javanese Youth." *Journal of Southeast Asian Studies* 36 (2005): 441–459, 2005.

NANCY J. SMITH-HEFNER

YUSUF HANSON, HAMZA. (b. 1958), American convert to Islam; Muslim scholar, teacher, and author.

Hamza Yusuf Hanson (formally Shaykh Hamza Yusuf) was born Mark Hanson in Walla Walla, Washington, and was raised in Santa Barbara, California, as a Greek Orthodox Christian by his parents, both American-born academics. He converted to Islam as a teenager in 1977 and promptly traveled to North Africa and the Middle East, including Algeria, Morocco, and the United Arab Emirates, studying philosophy, spiritual psychology, Arabic, and Islamic jurisprudence. He eventually traveled to a madrasah (school) in West Africa's Sahara Desert, where he studied under Shaykh Murabit al-Hajj. Upon returning to the United States, he obtained a BS in nursing at Imperial Valley College and an MA in religious studies at San José State University. Since then, he has continued to travel and lecture and co-founded Zaytuna College, an institution of higher education that combines the classical methodology of Islamic learning with a relatively liberal undergraduate education. He currently lives with his wife and five children in northern California.

Yusuf's primary focus appears to be reintroducing Islam while promoting an understanding that extends beyond the perceived misdoings of Islam. His newspaper and journal articles, in particular, stress the similarities between Islam and Western beliefs. He attributes his own interest in Islam to both its core values and what his own progressive mother taught him when he was younger. He has continuously advocated equality, peace, and social justice while pointing out the basic contradictions that exist in an "us versus them" ideology.

Yusuf is recognized at both the national and global levels. He is renowned for presenting Islam in a modern context, as well as showcasing classical Islam, leading to the resurgence of the traditional study of Islam and Islamic sciences and methods. He has published several books and newspaper and journal articles, and translated an equal amount of classical Arabic traditional texts into English. In the academic realm, he serves as advisor to Stanford University for its program on Islamic studies as well as Berkeley's Graduate Theological Union Centre for Islamic Studies. He was also the first American lecturer permitted to present and teach at the University of Al-Karaouine, Morocco's most prestigious and the world's oldest university located in Fez. He sits on the board of advisors for One Nation, a philanthropic organization that works to promote inclusion throughout America. He formed the Deen Intensive Foundation, which is dedicated to preserving and educating individuals on Islam's core sacred sciences as related from traditional sources.

One of Yusuf's most notable accomplishments is his co-founding of Zaytuna College, based in Hayward, California. Established in 1996, Zaytuna is currently undergoing the accreditation process, which would make it the first accredited Islamic college in the United States.

Outside of his prestige as a lecturer, translator, and scholar, Yusuf has also gained his fair share of notoriety for his previous anti-American and anti-Semitic sentiments and opinions. Since the September 11 attacks, Yusuf has modified his views, even advising U.S. president George W. Bush when he held office. He has expressed regret at his own frequent admonitions against America and Judaism, relating it back to the influence of having lived in the Arab world for over ten years. He also played a pivotal role in helping to calm the tensions that followed the Danish cartoon crisis in 2006.

In 2009 Yusuf was ranked as the Western world's most influential Islamic scholar on a list compiling the five hundred most influential Muslims. He continues to work and teach with the goal of increasing understanding and appreciation of the likenesses that bind the Muslim world and the West together.

BIBLIOGRAPHY

"Biography of Hamza Yusuf." http://sandala.org/about/hamzayusuf/.

Deen Intensive Foundation. "Teachers: Shaykh Hamza Yusuf." http://www.deen-intensive.com/teachers.htm#HYusuf.

Esposito, John, and Ibrahim Kalin, eds. *The 500 Most Influential Muslims in the World*. Amann, Jordan: Royal Islamic Strategies Studies Center, 2009.

O'Sullivan, Jack. "'If you hate the west, emigrate to a Muslim country.'" *The Guardian* 7, October 7, 2001. http://www.guardian.co.uk/world/2001/oct/08/.

Santella, Andrew. "Modern Lessons from an Ancient Faith." http://public.elmhurst.edu/home/news/ 84987267.html.

"Sheikh Hamza Yusuf." http://www.discoverthenetworks.org/individualProfile.asp?indid=1062.

Yusuf, Hamza. "Islam Has a Progressive Tradition Too: Most Western Views of Muslims Are Founded on Ignorance." *The Guardian*, June 18, 2002.

Eren Tatari

Z

ZĀWIYAH. Among Muslims the *zāwiyah* (corner, convent, or lodge) has evolved over centuries as an institution of learning and a Ṣūfī lodge where both women and men can engage in worship and social welfare activities. The *zāwiyah* continues to function in these ways in rural areas of the Muslim world, especially in the Maghreb. In cities, it continues to be a locus of spiritual study. The *zāwiyah* venue includes open space for worship and the recitation of religious litanies (*dhikr*), as well as sleeping spaces that can be used for solitary retreats through which one can seek advanced spiritual states with attention from the spiritual guide in residence. Often built in the vicinity of a venerated Ṣūfī saint's tomb, the *zāwiyah* is the site of many social activities that require religious blessing, such as funeral rituals, which proceed from the bathing of the dead to the last prayer after the shrouding, and celebrations of the annual anniversary of the birth of the Prophet Muḥammad, or of a local saint.

The move from prayer to education is a short step, for the Qurʾān advises that individuals seek knowledge at every step of their lives. Prior to colonial intervention, the *zāwiyah* was a significant center of learning for affiliates of Ṣūfī brotherhoods. Since the colonial establishment of public schools, which often favored boys' enrollment, the *zāwiyah* has continued to function as a venue for women's education in which they attend small, informal classes several times a week. The *zāwiyah* offers secure space for women to meet to discuss a wide range of topics from current politics to theological issues. They address their questions to the senior woman who is the designated leader, their teacher. In this way, the *zāwiyah* functions as a local educational center without the formalities of school fees, degree requirements, age limits, or even concern for literacy. The only aim is the acquisition of knowledge of all kinds. *Zāwiyah* classes allow women access to current news and continued learning even as they manage their domestic responsibilities to children and the home. For girls who are not able to pursue a regular program of public education and professional work, the *zāwiyah* provides a continued source of knowledge on a wide range of issues, in a context in which they feel free to talk among themselves without concern about mixed genders and the kinds of constraints that public education can entail.

The *zāwiyah* also is a place to which people take offerings for redistribution of social wealth, and where the handicapped and others incapable of meeting their needs are catered for and assured of food and lodging. In difficult times, the *zāwiyah* has constituted a unique welfare institution where the hungry have been fed, the homeless have secured refuge, and travelers, or any disenfranchised individual in need, has received sustenance and protection, even if that person is not a member of the local *ṭarīqah*. In the early centuries of Islam, it was customary for wealthy women to endow institutions of public benefit, such as universities and health clinics. An example of this is Turkey's network of *zāwiyah* enclosures, strategically placed a day's camel ride apart, in which travelers could find shelter, food, and security inside the walled structure by nightfall. The remains of these *zāwiyah* hostels are maintained in contemporary times as tourist sites throughout the countryside, with kiosks, and sometimes hotels nearby.

BIBLIOGRAPHY

Clancy-Smith, Julia A. *Rebel and Saint: Muslim Notables, Populist Protest, Colonial Encounters (Algeria and Tunisia 1800–1904)*. Los Angeles: University of California Press, 1994.

Raudvere, Catharina. *The Book and the Roses: Sufi Women, Visibility and Zikr in Contemporary Istanbul*. London: I. B. Tauris, 2002.

Sule, Balarabe B. M., and Priscilla Starratt. "Islamic Leadership Positions for Women in Contemporary Kano Society." In *Hausa Women in the Twentieth Century*, edited by Catherine Coles and Beverly Mack, pp. 29–49. Madison: University of Wisconsin, 1991.

Trimingham, J. S. *The Sufi Orders in Islam*. Oxford: Oxford University Press, 1971.

BEVERLY MACK

ZAYNAB BINT ʿALĪ. Zaynab was born in Medina c. 626/627 CE, the daughter of Fāṭimah al-Zahraʿ and ʿAlī ibn Abī Ṭālib. Much is uncertain concerning the details of her life. Pious legends from Shīʿī devotional sources describe her childhood: when the infant Zaynab was presented to her grandfather, the prophet Muhammad, the angel Gabriel wept and announced her predestined role as a mourner of the tragedy of Karbala. Another legend highlights the intensity of her childhood devotion to her older brother Husayn, so as to heighten the pathos of her presence at his martyrdom.

What is known of Zaynab with some certainty concerns the climactic events of her life: the battle of Karbala (680 CE) and its aftermath. According to the ʿAbbāsid historian al-Tabarī (d. 923 CE), Zaynab was among the women and children of Husayn's family captured at Karbala and led in captivity to Kufa. There she successfully interceded with the Kufan governor ʿUbaydallah ibn Ziyad on behalf of ʿAlī Zayn al-ʿĀbidīn, Husayn's surviving son. Tabarī also reports that when taken to the Damascus court of Husayn's rival Yazīd, she denounced Yazīd for his actions. The caliph subsequently released her, and she died shortly thereafter. Varying accounts of her death place Zaynab's burial site in Damascus and Cairo. Popular shrines in her honor exist in both cities.

Zaynab plays a prominent role in Shīʿī lamentation poetry on the martyrs of Karbala. Muhammad Bāqir al-Majlisī (d. 1698), in his *Bihār al-anwār* (The Oceans of Lights), presents an Arabic poem dramatizing an incident that is still recalled in Muharram sermons today—the moment when Zuljenah, Husayn's stallion, returns riderless from the combat at Karbala: And the horse came from the battlefield, deprived of its rider, Announcing the death of Husayn, shying with fright. Dyed with the blood of Husayn, it ran to the tents, Its saddle pulled awry. Zaynab said, "O Sakina, Husayn's horse has come. Look, behold its condition!"

A twentieth-century *nawhah* (lamentation poem) from Ladakh (in the Indian province of Jammu and Kashmir) has Zaynab address the riderless Zuljenah: "O horse, so spattered with blood, has martyrdom befallen my brother, king of Kauthar, who was thirsty and exhausted?"

Such poems feature prominently in the *majālis* (annual Muharram gatherings to commemorate Husayn's death). This genre of poetry, which is intended to induce sympathetic weeping in the audience, frequently evokes the shared suffering of Zaynab and her brother the martyr.

Muharram poems and sermons credit Zaynab with three achievements. She held the first *majlis* to mourn for Husayn, thereby establishing a precedent of lamentation rituals for later generations. She rescued Husayn's son from Yazīd's soldiers, thereby preserving the bloodline of the Shīʿī imams. And, while a prisoner in Yazīd's palace, she denounced the victorious caliph, thereby offering a model of defiance in defeat.

During the Iranian Revolution of the 1970s, Zaynab's image was employed for political purposes. Preachers and writers de-emphasized Fātimah al-Zahraʿ and Sakina bint Husayn, who are associated with silent suffering and passive endurance. Instead, the assertive and outspoken Zaynab was presented as an appropriate role model for mobilizing Shīʿī women in opposition to the reign of the Shah of Iran.

Bibliography

Majlisi, Muhammad Baqir al-. *Bihar al-anwar*. 110 vols. Teheran: al-Maktabah al-Islamiyah, 1966.

Pinault, David. *Horse of Karbala: Muslim Devotional Life in India*. New York: Palgrave, 2001.

David Pinault

Zia, Khaleda. Khaleda Zia (Khaleda Zia ur-Rahman) (b. 1945) is a former prime minister of Bangladesh (and the most-elected prime minister of Bangladesh) who served three terms in office: the first two from 1991 to 1996, and the third from 2001 to 2006. Her role in Bangladeshi politics has been particularly significant given her status as the first female prime minister of Bangladesh, and the second woman to serve as prime minister of a Muslim country.

Born Khaleda Mazumdar on August 15, 1945, in East Bengal, India [now Bangladesh], she married Ziaur Rahman in 1960, who, at the time, was a captain in the Pakistani army. In the early years of her marriage, she completed her college education and took on homemaker duties while her husband became a prominent figure in the East Pakistani independence movement and eventually became the first prime minister of Bangladesh six years after its establishment in 1977. During her husband's time in office and his leadership of the Islamic Bangladeshi Nationalist Party (BNP), Zia was not significantly involved in political affairs. After her husband's assassination in 1981, Zia entered Bangladeshi politics when she was elected unopposed as leader of the BNP in 1984. To some extent, Zia's entrance into politics came about because of the political maneuverings of the male leaders of the BNP who convinced Zia to become the successor to her husband's legacy, offering her the role of prime minister after the BNP's success in the 1991 national election.

However, Zia has played more than a simply symbolic role in Bangladeshi politics, and her position as prime minister is particularly significant given the previous lack of female participation in elite politics in the country. As the leader of a Muslim state, the role of Islam (and its particular expressions in Bangladeshi culture) in both bringing Zia to power and shaping her political stance, is significant and complex. While the image of the Muslim woman as wholly oppressed and lacking agency has currency in dominant Western discourses, Zia's role as a powerful political figure—re-elected three times to the highest office in her country—poses a challenge to this perception.

Zia has engaged with what can be described as a feminist position, within the framework of Islam and Bangladeshi culture. She has linked gender equality to national progress, speaking publicly of the need to educate girls and women, ensure they are given equal rights under the law, and increase women's participation in the workforce in order to alleviate poverty. She has introduced compulsory primary education for girls (and subsidized education for girls up to age ten), and also engaged with more controversial (in the mainstream Bangladeshi context) feminist concerns, such as the need to engage with family planning practices. She has also indicated her intent to end the dowry system. At the same time, Zia's feminist rhetoric and the powerful symbolism of a female head of a Muslim state is somewhat tempered by political maneuvers undertaken by the BNP. For example, during Zia's leadership, the BNP has aligned with the conservative Jaamat-e-Islami party; although Jaamat-e-Islami generally opposes women's political leadership, it was instrumental in securing Zia's re-election. This sits somewhat uncomfortably with Zia's rhetoric of women's rights, particularly as Jaamat-e-Islami has been vocal in calling for women to adhere to a socially conservative vision of what it considers appropriate Islamic conduct. Although there is no inherent contradiction between Islam and gender equality, the alliance points to the complexities of prospects for (Islamic) feminist activism in Bangladeshi politics.

BIBLIOGRAPHY

Basu, Amrita. "Women, Political Parties, and Social Movements in South Asia." In *Governing Women: Women's Political Effectiveness in Contexts of Democratization and Governance Reform*, ed. Anne Marie Goetz, pp. 87–111. New York and Abingdon, Oxon: Routledge, 2009.

Cuno, Kenneth M. *Family, Gender, and Law in a Globalizing Middle East and South Asia*. Syracuse: Syracuse University Press, 2009.

Hakim, S. Abdul. *Begum Khaleda Zia of Bangladesh: A Political Biography*. New Delhi: Vikas Publishing House Pvt Ltd, 1992.

Shehabuddin, Elora, *Reshaping the Holy: Democracy, Development, and Muslim Women in Bangladesh*. New York and Chichester, West Sussex: Columbia University Press, 2008.

Thompson, Mark R. "Female Leadership of Democratic Transitions in Asia." *Pacific Affairs* 75, no. 4 (2003): 535–555.

Maryam Khalid

Zinah. In Islamic law, the crime of unlawful sexual intercourse (*zinah*) is defined as the illicit penetration of the penis into the vagina. Muslim jurists sometimes included discussions of other illicit sex practices such as sodomy, prostitution, bestiality, and rape in chapters devoted to the subject. *Zinah* constitutes one of the *ḥudūd* crimes in Islamic law, offenses warranting a fixed—and often more severe—punishment. Crimes in this category also include *qadhf* (false accusation of *zinah*), apostasy, drinking alcohol, and highway robbery. According to verse 24:2, *zinah* committed by an unmarried male or female offender is to be punished with one hundred lashes each. Alternatively, jurists recommended that married offenders suffer the more severe punishment of death by stoning, a punishment that continues to be advocated for in many Muslim countries, despite its absence from the text of the Qurʾān. Due to the absence of a Qurʾānic reference, jurists cite ḥadīth traditions to support punishments such as stoning and from those traditions Muslim jurists have constructed detailed prescriptions for both flogging and executions by stoning. According to Qurʾān 24:4 as well as later juridical discussions, all cases of *zinah* must be proven by four male eyewitnesses to the actual act of penetration. Such strict evidentiary requirements make *zinah* cases virtually impossible to prove, in theory. Yet, recent work published on the application of *zinah* laws in Ottoman Aleppo found that stoning was not administered by its Sharīʿah courts. In the studies conducted thus far, there is little documentation of actual stoning outside of ḥadīth accounts and a few rare and isolated court cases from the Ottoman period, such as a high-profile stoning of an alleged Muslim adulteress and her Jewish lover in Istanbul's Hippodrome in 1680. Aside from these rare accounts, most documentation of actual stonings may be found in the twentieth century to the present. Some are in the form of video recordings. *Zinah* has become a more pressing issue in the modern period as nation-states and Islamic revivalists have engaged in campaigns against immorality and sexual licentiousness. Post-revolutionary Iran witnessed several highly publicized stonings, one of which was the subject of the book and subsequent film entitled *The Stoning of Soraya M.* (2008). Pending is the case of Sakineh Mohammadi Ashtiani who was convicted of adultery and sentenced to stoning in Iran in 2006. She faces execution; however, due to international outcry, the Iranian government has claimed it will not stone her and may commute the punishment to hanging. In other parts of the Islamic world, such as Algeria in the 1990s, women suspected of loose morals were targeted for assassination during its civil war by bands of Islamist militants. In addition, suspicion of *zinah* is cited as motivation for the murder of women, and to a lesser extent men suspected of homosexuality, by their families in Jordan, Yemen, Palestine, Iraq, and Turkey. Districts of northern Nigeria have worked to implement stoning in two high-profile cases against Safiya Husaini and Amina Lawal; both cases have been overturned by Nigeria's Supreme Court. Under Taliban rule in Afghanistan, suspected adulteresses were executed with machine guns publicly.

Regardless of legal prescriptions found in Islamic legal manuals, modern interpretations of *zinah* law have been much more lax in terms of evidence requirements and have applied double standards with regard to gender through disproportionate punishment applied to women. This is best demonstrated in Pakistan where rape victims are often imprisoned after admitting to illicit intercourse in the form of rape in accord with Zia al-Haq's 1979 Ḥudūd Ordinances. Victims bear an enormous burden of proof and are required to produce four male witnesses to the rape. On the contrary, gang rapes make it possible under modern codes for multiple male witnesses to testify against the victim; rarely if ever are the male offenders prosecuted. *Zinah* laws in Pakistan were only reformed in 2006 amid Islamist opposition but have not ameliorated the blurring of consensual sex and nonconsensual rape. Muslim reformer Tariq Ramadan has called attention to these inequities in the application of the law and requested a moratorium on stoning, arguing that the punishment is unjust because it is disproportionately applied to women and the poor, who are doubly victimized. Nonetheless, the subject of *zinah* remains a highly controversial issue, as it often masks deeper economic and political conflicts bubbling under the surface.

BIBLIOGRAPHY

Baer, Marc David. "Death in the Hippodrome: Sexual Politics and Legal Culture in the Reign of Mehmet IV." *Past and Present* 210, no. 1 (February 2011): 61–91.

Bennoune, Karima. "S.O.S. Algeria: Women's Human Rights Under Siege." In *Faith and Freedom: Women's Human Rights in the Muslim World*, edited by Mahnaz Afkhami, pp. 184–208. Syracuse: Syracuse University Press, 1995.

Imber, Colin. "Zina in Ottoman Law." In *Collection Turcica III: Contribution à l'histoire economique et sociale de l'empire ottoman*. Edited by Omer Lutfi Barkan et al., pp. 59–91. Leuven, Belgium: Peeters, 1983.

Peirce, Leslie. *Morality Tales: Law and Gender in the Ottoman Court of Aintab*. Berkeley: University of California Press, 2003.

Ramadan, Tariq. "An International Call for Moratorium on Corporal Punishment, Stoning and the Death Penalty in the Islamic World." March 30, 2005. http://www.tariqramadan.com.

el-Rouayheb, Khaled. *Before Homosexuality in the Arab-Islamic World, 1500–1800*. Chicago: University of Chicago Press, 2005.

Semerdjian, Elyse. *"Off the Straight Path": Illicit Sex, Law, and Community in Ottoman Aleppo* Syracuse: Syracuse University Press, 2008.

Ze'evi, Dror. *Producing Desire: Changing Sexual Discourse in the Ottoman Middle East, 1500–1900*. Berkeley: University of California Press, 2006.

ELYSE SEMERDJIAN

ZIYĀRAH. Literally, "visitation," *ziyārah* technically refers to visiting gravesites (*ziyārat al-qubūr*) for the purpose of praying for the dead and remembering death. Although it is often referred to as a pilgrimage, it is a supererogatory, rather than mandatory, practice and should not be confused with the ḥajj pilgrimage, which is required of all Muslims who are physically and financially able to make it at least once in a lifetime.

According to well-documented practices in all Sunni hadith compilations, at some point in the period between 610 and 622, the Prophet had apparently forbidden visitation to gravesites because of the exaggerated importance attached to the practice. However, when Islam came he made it lawful and recommended it, because "it will remind you of the hereafter" (al-Sayyid Sābiq, *Fiqh al-sunnah*, Beirut, 1977, vol. 1, p. 477). In another tradition, such visits are recommended in order to remind oneself of death. The overall religious significance of *ziyārah*, as it emerges in several narratives, is remembrance of death and reflection upon the hereafter. Therefore, some traditions even permit visitation of the graves of nonbelievers as reminders of the wrong that one commits against oneself by rejecting faith. It is also recommended to weep and to express one's need for God when passing through the graveyards of non-believers.

The rituals connected with *ziyārah* require that, when reaching the grave, one should turn one's face toward the dead, offer a greeting, and pray for that dead person. The Prophet used to visit the cemeteries and greet the dead, saying "Peace be upon you, O you the believers and the Muslims! We shall, God willing, join you. You have preceded us and we shall follow you. We pray to God for our and your well-being" (Sābiq, p. 477).

However, there was a problem with *ziyārah* by women. Again, the problem relates to pre-Islamic practices among the Arabs to which many narratives seem to be responding. The Mālikī and some Ḥanafī jurists deduced the permission of jurists on the basis of the narrative in which ʿĀʾishah, the Prophet's wife, one day was returning from having visited her brother's grave. When reminded of the Prophet's prohibition by ʿAbd Allāh ibn Ubayy, she replied: "Yes, he had forbidden the visitation of the graves [earlier], but had ordered [*amara bihi*] it afterwards" (Sābiq, p. 478). On the other hand, Ḥanbalīs, citing another tradition in which the Prophet cursed the women who visit graves, regard it as *makrūh* (reprehensible). They also argue that the reprehensibility is due to the belief that women are less patient and excessively overcome by grief.

The Wahhābīyah of Saudi Arabia, who also follow the Ḥanbalī school, extrapolate the same tradition to maintain an absolute interdiction for women to visit the gravesite (ʿAbd al-Raḥmān ibn Muḥammad ibn Qāsim al-ʿĀṣimī al-Najdī al-Ḥanbalī, *Ḥāshiyat al-Rawḍ al-murbiʿ sharḥ Zād al-mustaqniʿ*, Riyadh, 1982, vol. 3, pp. 144–146). It is for this reason that they prohibit women from entering the historic Baqīʿ cemetery in Medina where the Prophet's family, wives, and prominent Companions are buried. In 1925 the Wahhābīyah leveled all the structures that marked these graves.

Earlier, in 1801, they raided and destroyed the shrines at Karbala and Najaf. According to Wahhābī belief, shared by no one else in the Sunni community, the *ziyārah* in general amounts to "saint veneration," which potentially leads to the grave sin of *shirk*, associating divinity with these persons.

The Shafi'i and the Shī'ī jurists have no problem with visitation by women to gravesites. The Shī'ī jurists recommend that the visitor place his or her hand on the grave and read the *Fātiḥah*, the opening chapter of the Qur'ān ('Amilī, *Wasā'il al-Shī'ah*, vol. 2, p. 881ff.). Several traditions regarding the prohibition of women from performing the *ziyārah* and expressing grief during the visitation must be regarded as a later reaction to the pre-Islamic funeral practices, which included extravagant slapping of cheeks and tearing of clothes (Bukhārī, Janāiiz, ḥadīth 382). Otherwise there are traditions that explicitly establish that women did perform the *ziyārah*. In another tradition preserved by Bukhārī, the Prophet passed by a woman who was weeping beside a grave. He told her to fear God and be patient, without requiring her to leave the site or reminding her about any prohibition against her being there (Bukhārī, Janāiiz, ḥadīth 372).

The visitation to the tombs of the imams and their descendants (*imāmzādah*; formally extended only to male descendants, although female descendants are included as *sayyidah* or *bībī*) who were distinguished by special sanctity or by suffering martyrdom, and to the tombs of holy men and women, is treated as a supererogatory pilgrimage by both the Sunnis and the Shiah. Hence the universal practice of *ziyārah* of Medina among all Muslims. Visitation includes the shrines of famous women in Islam, including those of Sayyidah Zaynab, daughter of 'Alī ibn 'Abī Ṭālib, and Sayyidah Ruqayyah, daughter of Ḥusayn, in Damascus; Sayyidah Zaynab and Nafīsah in Cairo; Bībī Fāṭimah, daughter of Mūsā al-Kāẓim, the seventh imam, in Qom; Narjīs Khātūn, the twelfth imam's mother, and Ḥakīmah, the daughter of 'Alī al-Hādī, the tenth imam, in Sāmarrā'. It has always been common for both the Shia and Sunnis to perform visitations to these mostly Shii shrines. Unlike the *ḥajj*, which is performed at a set time, *ziyārah* to these shrines can be undertaken at any time, although some particular days are recommended. In the case of some shrines, pilgrimage is associated with a special lunar month or season of the year. Thus, the *ziyārah* of Sayyidah Zaynab in Cairo is performed in the month of Rajab, whereas the *ziyārah* of Imam Riḍā in Mashhad is recommended in the month of Dhū al-Qa'dah. The *ziyārah* of *imāmzādah* Sultān 'Alī near Kashan is held on the seventh day of autumn. Only the *ziyārah* of Ḥusayn in Karbala is recommended every Thursday evening, in addition to the major occasion of 'Āshūrā' (the day of his martyrdom). That evening, the *mashhad* of Karbala is filled with crowds of pilgrims from many lands. The performance of *ziyārah* is regarded by the pilgrims as an act of covenant renewal between the holy person and devotees. This is a covenant of love, sincere obedience, and devotion on the part of the believers. Through *ziyārah*, the person participates in the suffering and sorrows of the *ahl al-bayt* (the Prophet's family).

Someone who cannot undertake the arduous and expensive journey to the shrines of the imams can go into the wilderness, or onto a high roof of one's house, and then turn toward the *qiblah* (direction of Mecca) and pronounce the salutations. There are special *ziyāratnāmah* (salutations) for specific occasions. Although distinction is made between the *ziyārat* of the imams and other holy persons, Shī'ī scholars have regarded it permissible to show them all honor and respect by addressing them in a prescribed way. Thus in Tehran one can now do the ziyarat of Ayatollah Ruhullah Khomeini with official *ziyaratnamah* saluting the founder of the Islamic Republic of Iran. Some of these ancient salutations are taken from the words of the imams directly. However, the *ziyārah* of the imams is followed by two *rakʿah* (units of prayer) as a gift to the imam whose *ziyārah* is being performed. The *ziyārah* is concluded with a petition for the intercession of the Prophet and his family and praise to God.

[*See also* Shrine.]

BIBLIOGRAPHY

Ayoub, Mahmoud M. *Redemptive Suffering in Islam: A Study of the Devotional Aspects of ʿĀshūrāʾ in Twelver Shiʿism*. The Hague: Mouton, 1978. Discusses *ziyārah* and its prescribed rituals in Shīʿī piety.

Lambton, Ann K. S. "Imāmzāda." In *Encyclopaedia of Islam*. 3d ed., vol. 3, edited by Marc Gaborieau, Gudrun Kramer, John Nawas, and Everett Rowson, pp. 1169–1170. Leiden, Netherlands: Brill, 2007.

Taylor, C. S. *In the Vicinity of the Righteous: Ziyāra and the Veneration of Muslim Saints in Late Medieval Egypt*. Leiden: Brill, 1999.

ABDULAZIZ SACHEDINA

Topical Outline of Entries

Community and Society

Overview
Community and Society

Culture and Society
Child-Rearing Practices
Divorce: Historical Practice
Divorce: Modern Practice
Ethnicity
Family
Family Planning
Hospitality
Mahr
Marriage: Historical Practice
Marriage: Modern Practice
Suicide
Surrogate Motherhood
Tribal Societies and Women
Youth Culture

Religious Belief
Mourning

Religious Practice, Devotionalism, and Ritual
Names and Naming
Rites

Culture and Expression

Overview
Culture and Expression

Art and Architecture
Art, Women in Islamic
Ceramics, Women's Representation in
Palaces
Taj Mahal
Topkapi Saray

Arts and Literature
African Languages and Literature: East Africa
African Languages and Literature: West Africa
Arabic Literature: Gender in Arabic Literature
Arabic Literature: Overview
Calligraphy and Epigraphy
Central Asian Literatures
Dance
Devotional Poetry
Iconography
Islamic Literature: Contemporary
Islamic Literature: Historical
Literary Salons
Malay and Indonesian Literature
Medieval Court Poetry
Music
Painting: Overview
Painting: Women's Representation and Production
Persian Literature
Religious Biography and Hagiography
Turkish Literature
ʿUdhrī Poetry
Women's Magazines

Biographies
Adıvar, Halide Edip
Dorai, Fawzieh al-
Gorani, Hala
Nāṣif, Malak Ḥifnī
Saʿdāwī, Nawāl al-
Shaykh, Hanan al-
Ṭabaqāt
Ulfah, Hajjah Maria
Umm Kulthūm

Communications and Media
Cinema: Arab Women's Contributions
Cinema: Iranian Women's Contributions
Cinema: North African Women's Contributions
Cinema: Turkish Women's Contributions
Communications Media
Internet, Blogs, and Social Networking
Pamphlets and Tracts
Print Journalism
Television

Culture and Society
Jewelry and Gems

Women's Studies
Cultural Activities, Women's Historical

Immigration and Minorities

Overview
Immigration and Minorities

Biographies
Badawi, Jamal
Jameelah, Maryam
Joseph, Sarah
Khan, Daisy
Mattson, Ingrid
Mogahed, Dalia
Ramadan, Tariq
Rasul-Bernardo, Amina
Uddin, Baroness Pola Manzila
Wadud, Amina
Yakoob, Salma
Yusuf Hanson, Hamza

Institutions, Organizations, and Movements
Commission on International Religious Freedom
Islamic Society of North America
Muslim Council of Britain
Women's Islamic Initiative in Spirituality and Equality (WISE)

Islamic Law
Dhimmī
Women Living Under Muslim Laws

Religion and Politics
Minorities: Minorities in Muslim Societies
Minorities: Muslim Minorities in Non-Muslim Countries

Politics and Polity

Overview
Politics and Polity

Americas
Canada
Mexico
United States of America

Biographies
Baghdād Khātūn
Bhutto, Benazir
Bouhired, Djamila
Dashti, Rola
Roxelana, Hürrem
Kadeer, Rabiya
Khayr al-Nisa' Begam
Mubarak, Massouma al-
Nūr Jahān
Nana Asma'u
Pakzad, Surraya
Parī-Khān Khānum I
Qutlugh Terkān Khātūn
Radiyya bint Iltutmish
Ṣefātī, Zohreh
Shajarat al-Dur
Wan Azizah Ismail
Wazed, Sheikh Hasina
Yassine, Nadia
Zia, Khaleda

Central Asia and Caucasus
Afghanistan
Central Asia and the Caucasus
Chechnya
China
Xinjiang

Concepts and Terms
Black Widows

Dynastic States
Delhi Sultanate
Fāṭimid Dynasty
Mamlūk Dynasty
Mughal Empire
Ottoman Empire
Qājār Dynasty
Rasūlid Dynasty
Safavid Dynasty
Sokoto Caliphate

Sufra
ʿUmrah

Schools of Thought
Khawārij
Salafi Groups
Wahhābīyah

Scholarly Approaches and Theoretical Constructs

Overview
Scholarly Approaches and Theoretical Constructs

Biographies
Wives of the Prophet

Communications and Media
Stereotypes in Mass Media

Concepts and Terms
Gender Equality
Women and Social Protest: Contemporary
Women and Social Protest: Historical

Culture and Society
Veiling: Contemporary Discourse
Veiling: Historical Discourse

Institutions, Organizations, and Movements
Political Activism, Women's: Historical Discourse
Women's Movements

Islamic Law
Women's Rights

Islamic Studies
Orientalism

Overviews
Islam and Women: An Overview
Shīʿī Islam and Women: Historical Overview
Shīʿī Islam and Women: Contemporary Thought and Practice
Sufism and Women: Contemporary Thought and Practice
Sufism and Women: Historical Overview
Sunnī Islam and Women: Contemporary Thought and Practice
Sunnī Islam and Women: Historical Overview

Religion and Politics
Feminism: Concept and Debates
Feminism: Nature of Islamic Feminism
Feminism: Sources

Religious Practice, Devotionalism, and Ritual
Hagarism
Islam and Women: Eighteenth-Century to Early Twentieth-Century Debates
Islam and Women: Contemporary Discourses
Women and Islam: Women's Religious Observances

Women's Studies
Gender Construction: Historical
Gender Construction: Contemporary Practices
Gender Construction: Early Islam
Gender Studies and Women: History of the Field
Gender Studies and Women: Methodologies
Gender Themes: Ṣūfī Devotional Literature
Gender Themes: Shīʿī Devotional Literature
Gender Themes: Sunnī Devotional Literature
Islam and Patriarchy
Islamic Biographical Collections, Women in
Political Activism, Women's: Contemporary Discourse
Women and Islam: Role and Status of Women
Women and Social Reform: An Overview
Women and Social Reform: Social Reform in North Africa
Women and Social Reform: Social Reform in South Asia
Women and Social Reform: Social Reform in Southeast Asia
Women and Social Reform: Social Reform in the Middle East

Science, Medicine, and Education

Overview
Science, Medicine, and Education

Culture and Society
Abortion
Education and Women: Contemporary Discourse
Family Planning
Fertility and Infertility Treatments
Midwifery
Pregnancy and Childbirth
Sexual Education

Education
Astronomy and Astrology
Education and Women: Historical Discourse
Education and Women: Educational Reform
Education and Women: Women's Religious Education
Madrasah
Pesantren
Universities

Health and Medicine
Health Care
Health Issues
Medical Profession, Women in the: Historical and Contemporary Practice
Medicine: Contemporary Practice
Medicine: Traditional Practice

Institutions, Organizations, and Movements
Gender Advisory Board, United Nations Commission on Science and Technology for Development
Third World Organization for Women in Science

Self and Body

Overview
Self and Body

Concepts and Terms
Harem

Culture and Society
Abortion
Cemeteries
Chastity (*ʿIffa*)
Clitoridectomy
Concubinage
Cosmetics
Fertility and Infertility Treatments
Ḥammām
Midwifery
Pregnancy and Childbirth
Female Genital Cutting
Guardianship
Hijab
Honor
Honor Killings
Hygiene
ʿIddah
Menstruation
Modesty
Motherhood
Prostitution
Seclusion
Sexuality
Shame
Wet Nurses

Health and Medicine
Games and Sports

Religious Practice, Devotionalism, and Ritual
Dress: Contemporary
Dress: Historical

Sharīʾah, Fiqh, Philosophy, and Reason

Overview
Sharīʿah, Fiqh, Philosophy, and Reason

Biographies
Ahmed, Leila

Wealth, Welfare, and Labor

Property
Real Estate
Slavery
Trade
Workforce, Women in the: Contemporary Discourse
Workforce, Women in the: Historical Discourse

Institutions, Organizations, and Movements

Aga Khan Foundation
International League of Muslim Women
KARAMAH (Muslim Women Lawyers for Human Rights)
Muslim Women's League
NGOs and Women
One Million Signatures Campaign: Iran
One Million Signatures Campaign: Morocco
UN Development Fund for Women (UNIFEM)
United Nations Population Fund

Religion and Politics

Arab Spring
Refugees

Religious Practice, Devotionalism, and Ritual

Ḥajj, Women's Patronage of: Contemporary Practice
Ḥajj, Women's Patronage of: Historical Practice

Women's Studies

Ottoman Empire, Women's Socioeconomic Role
Women's Travel, Historical

Directory of Contributors

Tahir Abbas
Fatih University
Muslim Council of Britain

Deina Abdelkader
University of Massachusetts Lowell
Gender Studies and Women: History of the Field
Justice, Social

Najla Naeem Abdurrahman
Columbia University
Libya

Nisrine Abiad
Saint Joseph University
Child Abuse

Sulafa Abousamra
Clemson University
ʿUdhrī Poetry

Hibba Abugideiri
Villanova University
Science, Medicine, and Education (Theoretical Overview)
Community and Society (Theoretical Overview)
Wadud, Amina

Evelyne Accad
University of Illinois, Lebanese American University (Emeritus)
Rape as War Tool

Sabahat Adil
University of Chicago
Guilds

Asma Afsaruddin
Indiana University, Bloomington
Companions of the Prophet
Ezzat, Heba Raouf
Female Genital Cutting
Tajwīd
Rābiʿah al-ʿAdawīyah
Religion: Theory, Practice, and Interpretation of (Theoretical Overview)
Self and Body (Theoretical Overview)

Kamran Scot Aghaie
University of Texas at Austin
Shīʿī Islam and Women: Contemporary Thought and Practice

Anis Ahmad
Riphah International University
Friday Prayer
Khuṭbah
Muhājirūn

Sadaf Ahmad
Lahore University of Management Sciences
Hashmi, Farhat

Elif E. Akşit
Ankara University
Ottoman Empire, Overview

Asiya Alam
University of Texas at Austin
India

Sorarya Altorki
The American University in Cairo
Women and Islam: Role and Status of Women

Biancamaria Scarcia Amoretti
Università degli Studi di Roma "La Sapienza"
Safavid Dynasty

Khalid al-Azri
University of Oxford
Oman

Hatoon al-Fassi
King Saud University
Saudi Arabia

Souad T. Ali
Arizona State University
Barlas, Asma
Barazangi, Nimat Hafez
Gender Studies and Women: Methodologies

Samer Ali
University of Texas at Austin
Literary Salons
Medieval Court Poetry

Kecia Ali
Boston University
Slavery

Tariq al-Jamil
Swarthmore College
ʿIbādah

Nermin Allam
University of Alberta
Kahlawy, Abla al-

Pam Allen
University of Tasmania
Malay and Indonesian Literature

Zainab Alwani
Howard University School of Divinity
Domestic Violence

Yasmin Amin
Exeter University
Ṭabaqāt
Wives of the Prophet

Hussein Amin
The American University in Cairo
Television

Jon W. Anderson
The Catholic University of America
Honor
Shame

Vivienne SM. Angeles
La Salle University
Philippines

Ali Anooshahr
University of California, Davis
Delhi Sultanate

Etin Anwar
Hobert and William Smith Colleges
Female Genital Cutting

Ghazala Anwar
Starr King School for the Ministry
ʿĀʾishah
Asmāʾ al-Husna, al-
Fāṭimah
Mahr

Zainah Anwar
Musawah; Sisters in Islam
Musawah

Diane Apostolos-Cappadona
Georgetown University
Art, Women in Islamic
Painting: Women's Representation and Production

Jacqueline Armijo
Qatar University
China
Kadeer, Rabiya
Xinjiang

Iram Nisa Asif
University of Copenhagen
Pakistan

Yalda Asmatey
University of California Berkeley
Pakzad, Surraya

Eylem Atakav
University of East Anglia
Cinema: Turkish Women's Contributions

Abed Awad
Awad & Khoury, Attorneys at Law; Rutgers Law School; Pace Law School
Divorce: Legal Foundations
Marriage: Legal Foundations

Zahra M. S. Ayubi
University of North Carolina, Chapel Hill
Qur'ān: Women's Exegesis (Tafsir)
Revelation

Margot Badran
Georgetown University
Feminism: Concept and Debates
Feminism: Nature of Islamic Feminism
Shaʿrāwī, Hudā
Nāṣif, Malak Ḥifnī

Roksana Bahramitash
University of Montreal
Business Ownership and Women: Historical and Contemporary Practice
Women's Entrepreneurship: Historical Practice
Women's Entrepreneurship: Contemporary Practice
Iran

Laleh Bakhtiar
Institute of Traditional Psychology, Kazi Publications (USA)
Female Qurʾānic Figures
Khan, Daisy
Mattson, Ingrid

Lisa Balabanlilar
Rice University
Mughal Empire

Ellison Banks
Trinity College
Nūr Jahān

Daniel Bannoura
University of Chicago Divinity School
Astronomy and Astrology

Carolyn Baugh
University of Pennsylvania
Menstruation

Sara Bazoobandi
National University of Singapore
Investment and Commerce, Women's: Historical Practices

Zohra Ismail-Beben
College of William and Mary
Aga Khan Foundation

Lois Beck
Washington University in St. Louis
Tribal Societies and Women

Valérie Behiery
University of Montreal
Cultural Activities, Women's Historical

Samir Ben-Layashi
Tel Aviv University
Surrogate Motherhood
Abortion
Sexuality

Clinton Bennett
State University of New York at New Paltz
Microfinance

Kristina Benson
University of California, Los Angeles
Ḥadīth: Women and Gender in the

Robert R. Bianchi
National University of Singapore
Ḥajj, Women's Patronage of: Contemporary Practice

Sheila S. Blair
Boston College
Calligraphy and Epigraphy
Ceramics, Women's Representation in

Stephen P. Blake
University of Minnesota
Architecture and Women: India
Architecture and Women: Iran

Dominic T. Bocci
American Society for Muslim Advancement
Commission on International Religious Freedom
Gender Advisory Board, United Nations Commission on Science and Technology for Development
Modernization and Development

Stephanie Willman Bordat
Women's Rights Activist
Women and Social Reform: Social Reform in North Africa

Donna Lee Bowen
Brigham Young University
Family Planning

Jane E. Bristol-Rhys
Zayed University
United Arab Emirates

Dominic Parviz Brookshaw
Stanford University
Persian Literature

Nathan Brown
George Washington University
Gebaly, Tahany el

Marie Grace Brown
University of Kansas
Sudan

Silvia Bruzzi
Bologna University
African Languages and Literature: East Africa
African Languages and Literature: West Africa
Sainthood

Elizabeth M. Bucar
Northeastern University
Veiling: Historical Discourse

Katherine Bullock
University of Toronto Mississauga
Canada
Islamic Society of North America

Halim Calis
The University of Chicago, Divinity School
Five Pillars of Islam
Prophethood

Silvia Sara Canetto
Colorado State University
Suicide

Byron Cannon
University of Utah
Black Widows
Chechnya
Qadi
Qur'ān: Women's Status
Sub-Saharan Africa

Catherine Cartwright-Jones
Kent State University
Cosmetics
Ḥammām
Harem

Kenan Çayir
İstanbul Bilgi University
Islamic Literature: Contemporary

Manuela Ceballos
Emory University
Refugees

Sariya Cheruvallil-Contractor
University of Derby
Da'wah, Women's Activities in
Qur'ānic Schools for Girls
Sunnī Islam and Women: Contemporary Thought and Practice
Women of the Prophet's Household: Interpretation

Julia Clancy-Smith
University of Arizona
Barakah
Zaynab, Lalla

L. Clarke
Iddah

miriam cooke
Duke University
Arabic Literature: Gender in Arabic Literature

Yvonne Corcoran-Nantes
Flinders University of South Australia
Economics and Finance
Financial Institutions

Justin J. Corfield
Geelong Grammar School
Anwar, Zainah
Gorani, Hala
Joseph, Sarah
Rasul, Amina
Shaykh, Hanan al-
Tarzi, Mahmud
Topkapi Saray
Wan Azizah Ismail

Delia Cortese
Middlesex University
Concubinage

Jill Crystal
Auburn University
Qatar

Kenneth M. Cuno
Department of History, University of Illinois at Urbana-Champaign
Marriage: Historical Practice

Farhad Daftary
The Institute of Ismaili Studies
Sulayhids
Fāṭimid Dynasty

Ahmad S. Dallal
Yale University
Fatwā

Susan Muaddi Darraj
Harford Community College
Noor al-Hussein

Bahar Davary
University of San Diego
Islam and Patriarchy
Qur'ān: Portrayals of Women

Olga Davidson
Boston University
Women and Social Protest: Historical

Christopher Davidson
Durham University
Mouza bint Nasser Al-Misnad, Sheikha

Marina de Regt
Free University Amsterdam
Yemen

Natana J. DeLong-Bas
Boston College
Algeria
Barakah
Bouhired, Djamila
Culture and Expression (Theoretical Overview)
Dhimmī
Feminism: Concept and Debates
Feminism: Nature of Islamic Feminism
Gender Construction: Early Islam
Gorani, Hala
Honor
Hygiene
Immigration and Minorities (Theoretical Overview)
International League of Muslim Women
Islam and Women: Eighteenth-Century to Early Twentieth-Century Debates
Jameelah, Maryam
Joseph, Sarah
Khawārij
Mourning
Politics and Polity (Theoretical Overview)
Purification
Rasul-Bernardo, Amina
Scholarly Approaches and Theoretical Constructs (Theoretical Overview)
Sharī'ah, Fiqh, Philosophy, and Reason (Theoretical Overview)
Shaykh, Hanan al-
Women and Social Protest: Contemporary
Tarzi, Mahmud
Topkapi Saray
United Nations Population Fund
Wahhābīyah
Wealth, Welfare, and Labor (Theoretical Overview)

Benjamin B. DeVan
University of Durham; Candler School of Theology, Emory University
People of the Book
Popular Religion: Europe and the Americas

Zenepe Dibra
Intellectual Women of Shkodra
Albania

Nelly van Doorn-Harder
Wake Forest University
Ulfah, Hajjah Maria

Eleanor Abdella Doumato
Brown University
Shafiq, Durrīyah

Adis Duderija
University of Malaya
Gender Construction: Contemporary Practices

Abul Fadl Mohsin Ebrahim
University of Durban
Abortion

Dale F. Eickelman
Dartmouth College
Ethnicity
Popular Religion: Middle East and North Africa
Shrine

Fadwa El Guindi
Qatar National Research Fund, Qatar Foundation
Gender Construction: Historical
Hijab
Veiling: Contemporary Discourse

Nadine El Sayed
University of Westminster
Communications Media

Emran El-Badawi
University of Houston
Suweidan, Tariq al-

Zenepe Dibra
Intelektualet e rinj, Shprese (IRSH) [Young Intellectuals, Hope]
Albania

Sibel Erol
New York University
Turkish Literature

John L. Esposito
Georgetown University
Pluralism

Heba Raouf Ezzat
Cairo University
Gumaa, Ali
Women and Social Reform: An Overview

Elizabeth Faier
Eastern Michigan University
Hospitality Rituals

Raymond Farrin
American University of Kuwait
Wallādah bint al-Mustakfī

Mary Ann Fay
Morgan State University
Waqf, Women's Constructions of

Roja Fazaeli
Trinity College Dublin
Ayatollah
Convention on the Elimination of All Forms of Discrimination against Women (CEDAW)
Education and Women: Women's Religious Education
International Laws and Treaties on Women's Status
Kar, Mehrangiz
Martyrdom
Mujtahidah
Taliban
UN Development Fund for Women (UNIFEM)
Women's Rights

Elizabeth J. Fernea
University of Texas at Austin
Family

Michael M.J. Fischer
Massachusetts Institute of Technology
Bazaar

Sarah Fischer
American University
Political Activism, Women's: Historical Discourse
Turkey

Charles Fletcher
McGill University
Ahl al-Bayt
Miracles

Willem Floor
Independent Scholar
Mutʿah

Sylva Frisk
University of Göteborg
Malaysia

Alyssa Gabbay
University of Chicago
Bazaar

Nancy E. Gallagher
University of California, Santa Barbara
Medicine: Contemporary Practice

Aisha Geissinger
Carleton University
Aisha bint Saʿd bint ibn Abi Waqqas
Aʾisha bint Talha

Haim Gerber
The Hebrew University of Jerusalem
Ottoman Empire, Women's Socioeconomic Role

Avner Giladi
University of Haifa
Midwifery
Motherhood

Fatma Müge Göçek
University of Michigan
Gender Equality

Robert Gleave
University of Exeter
Medicine: Contemporary Practice

Mustafa Gokcek
Department of History, Niagara University
Central Asian Literatures

Rebecca Gould
Humanities, Yale-NUS College
Arabic Literature: Overview

Doris Gray
Department of Modern Languages, Florida State University
Murshida

Shahla Haeri
Department of Anthropology, Boston University
Mutʿah

Aaron Albert Haley
University of Washington
Orientalism

Fachrizal Halim
Institute of Islamic Studies, McGill University
Guardianship

Shehnaz Haqqani
The University of Texas, Austin
Muʿāmalāh

Nader Hashemi
University of Denver, Josef Korbel School of International Studies
Human Rights

Jane Hathaway
Department of History, Ohio State University
Households

Robert W. Hefner
Institute on Culture, Religion, and World Affairs; Boston University
Syncretism

Marcia K. Hermansen
Theology Department, Loyola University Chicago
Religious Biography and Hagiography

Leila Hessini
Global Fund for Women
Women and Social Reform: Social Reform in North Africa

Azizah Y. al-Hibri
C. Williams School of Law, University of Richmond
Modesty

Syarif Hidayatullah
State Islamic University, Jakarta
Women and Social Protest: Contemporary
Fatayat Nahdlatul ʿUlamā

Rebecca Hodges
Department of Anthropology, Washington University in St. Louis
Education and Women: Historical Discourse

Valerie J. Hoffman
Center for South Asian and Middle Eastern Studies, University of Illinois at Urbana-Champaign
Ghazālī, Zaynab al-
Raḥmān, ʿĀʾishah ʿAbd al-
Women and Islam: Women's Religious Observances

Nicholas S. Hopkins
Department of Anthropology, American University in Cairo (Emeritus)
Land Tenure

Julia Huang
The London School of Economics and Political Science
Tribal Societies and Women

Syed Rifaat Hussain
Department of Peace and Conflict Studies, National Defense University, Islamabad
Bhutto, Benazir

Rana Husseini
Senior Reporter, The Jordan Times
Honor Killings

Derya Iner
Centre for Islamic Studies and Civilization, Charles Sturt University, Sydney
Adivar, Halide Edip

Nazila Isgandarova
Emmanuel College of Victoria University of University of Toronto
Pregnancy and Childbirth
Gender Themes: Sunni Devotional Literature

Sarah Islam
Department of Near Eastern Studies, Princeton University
Family Law
Fertility and Infertility Treatments

Akel Ismail
Kahera School of Architecture, Prairie View A&M University
Mosque, Women's Space and Use of

Peter Jackson
School of Humanities, Keele University
Radiyya bint Iltutmish
Shajarat al-Dur

Abbas Jaffer
Harvard University
Ghamidi, Javed Ahmad
Popular Religion: South Asia

Maria Jaschok
International Gender Studies Centre (IGS) at Lady Margaret Hall, University of Oxford
Nü Ahong

Alexandra M. Jerome
Women's Studies, College of William & Mary
Iraq

Katrin Jomaa
Emory University
Chastity (ʿIffa)

Alan Jones
University of Oxford
Houris

Sabrina Joseph
Department of Humanities and Social Science, Zayed University
Real Estate

S. Ayse Kadayifci-Orellana
Program in Conflict Resolution, Georgetown University
Islam and Peacebuilding
Interfaith Dialogue

Yuka Kadoi
University of Edinburgh, UK
Iconography
Jewelry and Gems
Painting: Overview
Taj Mahal

Monzer Kahf
Islamic Development Bank, Jeddah, Saudi Arabia
Property

Ibrahim Kalin
Georgetown University
Akhlāq

Hilary Kalmbach
New College, University of Oxford
Religious Authority of Women

Marianne R. Kamp
Department of History, University of Wyoming
Central Asia and the Caucasus: Tajikistan, Turkmenistan, and Uzbekistan

Dženita Karić
Philological Department, Oriental Institute in Sarajevo
Afterlife
Bosnia and Herzegovina
Cerić, Mustapha
Devotional Poetry
Minorities: Muslim Minorities in Non-Muslim Countries

Lamia Karim
Department of Anthropology, University of Oregon
Bangladesh

Zayn Kassam
Religious Studies, Pomona College
Women and Islam: Role and Status of Women

Joseph A. Kéchichian
Kéchichian and Associates, LLC
Ramadan, Tariq

Mona Chemali Khalaf
Economist and Independent Gender Consultant
Lebanon

Maryam Khalid
University of New South Wales, School of Social Sciences and International Studies
Wazed, Sheikh Hasina
Zia, Khaleda

Nyla Ali Khan
Department of English, University of Oklahoma, Norman
Kashmir

SHENILA KHOJA-MOOLJI
Teachers College, Columbia University
Sexual Education

FARHAD KHOSROKHAVAR
Ecole des Hautes Etudes en Sciences Sociales, Paris
Arab Spring
Karman, Tawakul
Suicide Bombings

HILDE GRANÅS KJØSTVEDT
Chr Michelsen Institute, Bergem, Norway
Palestine
West Bank and Gaza

MARYAM KOUSHKIE JAHROMI
Physical Education and Sport Science Department, School of Education and Psychology, Shiraz University
Games and Sports

WANDA KRAUSE
Dept. of Social Sciences and Humanities, Hamad bin Khalifa University,
Qatar Foundation, QNRF
Rostamani, Amina al-
Fatima bint Mubarak, Sheikha

MELINDA KROKUS
Boston University
Environmental Activism
Sufism and Women: Historical Overview

REMKE KRUK
Leiden University Institute for Area Studies (LIAS), Leiden University
Warriors: Women

MIRJAM KÜNKLER
Department of Near Eastern Studies, Princeton University
Amīn, Nosrat
Muftiyah
Ṣefātī, Zohreh

GEORGE LANE
School of Oriental and African Studies, University of London
Qutlugh Terkān Khātūn
Baghdād Khātūn
Ābish Khātūn bint Sa'd II
Soghaghtani Beg

CHRIS LAROSSA
Alwaleed Bin Talal Center for Muslim-Christian Understanding, Georgetown University
Salafi Groups
Sovereignty

HILARY LIM
School of Law and Social Sciences, University of East London
Inheritance

CHRISTINA LINDHOLM
School of the Arts, Virginia Commonwealth University
Dress: Contemporary
Dress: Historical

MARK LINDLEY-HIGHFIELD OF BALLUMBIE CASTLE
Department of Religious Studies, The Open University; Faculty of Humanities, Cirencester College
Mexico

CELENE AYAT LIZZIO
Brandeis University
Fatwā
Obaid, Thoraya
United States of America

LAURA LOHMAN
Department of Music, California State University, Fullerton
Music
Qur'ān: Contemporary Female Reciters
Qur'ān: Historical Female Reciters
Qur'ānic Recitation Schools for Girls
Umm Kulthūm

MATTHEW LONG
Miami University
Fitnah
Hagarism
Umm Waraqa

SUSAN MACDOUGALL
School of Anthropology, Oxford University
Jordan

BEVERLY MACK
Department of African and African-American Studies, University of Kansas
Nana Asma'u
Sokoto Caliphate
Zāwiyah

Farjana Mahbuba
Religion and Society Research Center, University of Western Sydney
Women and Social Reform: Social Reform in Southeast Asia

Vanessa Maher
Department of Time, Space, Image, Society; University of Verona
Wet Nurses

Fedwa Malti-Douglas
Indiana University, Bloomington
Pamphlets and Tracts
Saʿdāwī, Nawāl al-

Elham Manea
Department of Political Science, University of Zurich
Syria

Amporn Marddent
Cultural Studies Program, Walialak University, Thailand
Thailand

Manuela Marín
CSIC, Madrid (Emeritus)
Andalus, Al-

Rudolph Matthee
Department of History, University of Delaware
Safavid Dynasty

Hany Mawla
Marriage: Legal Foundations

Zahraa McDonald
Department of Sociology, University of Johannesburg
Popular Religion: Sub-Saharan Africa

Claudia Merli
Department of Anthropology, Durham University
Southeast Asia and the Pacific

Valentine M. Moghadam
Sociology and International Affairs, Northeastern University
Family
Women Living Under Muslim Laws
Political Activism, Women's: Contemporary Discourse
Women and Social Reform: Social Reform in the Middle East

Moojan Momen
Independent Scholar
Qājār Dynasty
Shīʿī Islam and Women: Historical Overview

Hadia Mubarak
Department of Islamic Studies, Georgetown University
Khaled, Amr

Aisha Musa
Colgate University
Islam and Women: An Overview

Ala'i Nadjib
Fatayat NU, Lakpesdam (Institute of Human Resource Studies NU); State Islamic University Syarif Hidayatullah Jakarta
Women and Social Protest: Contemporary
Fatayat Nahdlatul ʿUlamā

Shuruq Naguib
Lancaster University
Saleh, Suʿad

Azim A. Nanji
University of Florida
Aga Khan Foundation

Fallou Ngom
Boston University
African Languages and Literature: West Africa

Seyyed Vali Reza Nasr
Naval Postgraduate School
Jameelah, Maryam

Minerva Nasser-Eddine
Flinders University
Terrorism

Ronald L. Nettler
University of Oxford and Mansfield College, (Emeritus)
Dhimmī

Emily Neumeier
University of Pennsylvania
Palaces

Mohd Anis Md Nor
University of Malaya
Dance

Augustus Richard Norton
Boston University
Terrorism

Samaneh Oladi Ghadikolaei
University of California Santa Barbara

Rahnavard, Zahra
Taleghani, Azam
Women's Islamic Initiative in Spirituality and Equality (WISE)

Soudeh Oladi
University of New Brunswick
Education and Women: Educational Reform

Zafer Öter
Izmir Katip Celebi University
Marriage: Modern Practice

Saba Ozyurt
Alliont International University
Muslim Women's League

Youshaa Patel
Duke University
Seclusion

David Stephen Pearl
University of East Anglia
Family Law

Kelly Pemberton
George Washington University
Relics
Gender Themes: Sufi Devotional Literature

Kenneth J. Perkins
University of South Carolina
Bouhired, Djamila

Rudolph Peters
Faculty of Humanities, University of Amsterdam
Ḥudūd
Jihad

Marie Juul Petersen
Danish Institute for International Studies
NGOs and Women

Anna Piela
University of Leicester
Internet, Blogs, and Social Networking

David Pinault
Santa Clara University
Zaynab bint Ali

Lisa Pollard
University of North Carolina, Wilmington
Egypt

Peter E. Pormann
University of Manchester
Medicine: Traditional Practice

Julie Pruzan-Jørgensen
Danish Institute for International Studies (DIIS)
Badran, Margot

Ayad al-Qazzaz
California State University, Sacramento
Third World Organization for Women in Science

Annika Rabo
Stockholm University
Bazaar

Naysan Rafati
University of Oxford
Israel

Yossef Rapoport
University of London
Mamlūk Dynasty

Anne K. Rasmussen
College of William and Mary
Tajwīd

Amal Rassam
City University of New York
Mernissi, Fatima

Catharina Raudvere
University of Copenhagen
Sufism and Women: Contemporary Thought and Practice

Maryanne Rhett
Washington State University
Aga Khan Foundation

D. S. Richards
University of Oxford
Fāṭimid Dynasty

Helen Mary Rizzo
The American University in Cairo
Dashti, Rola
Dorai, Fawzieh al-
Mubarak, Massouma al-

Ruth Roded
The Hebrew University of Jerusalem
Islamic Biographical Collections, Women in
Islamic Literature: Historical

Ruth Roded
Department of Islamic and Middle Eastern Studies, The Hebrew University of Jerusalem
Islamic Biographical Collections, Women in

ELAHEH ROSTAMI-POVEY
University of London
Borrowing and Credit, Women's: Contemporary and Historical Practice
Workforce, Women in the: Contemporary Discourse
Afghanistan

KAREN G. RUFFLE
University of Toronto
Gender Themes: Shīʿī Devotional Literature
Women's Religious Celebrations

SORAYA SAATCHI
Wayne State University
Law: Women's Legal Thought and Jurisprudence

ABDULAZIZ SACHEDINA
University of Virginia
Ziyārah

FATIMA SADIQI
University of Fez;
The International Institute for Languages and Cultures
Morocco

YASMIN SAFIAN
Medicine: Contemporary Practice

ZEYNEP ŞAHIN-MENCÜTEK
Gediz University
Philanthropy and Women, Contemporary and Historical
Warriors: Contemporary Women

MASHAL SAIF
Duke University
Rasūlid Dynasty

LENA SALAYMEH
Berkeley Law; University of California
Law: Courts

SARA SALJOUGHI
University of Minnesota
Cinema: Iranian Women's Contributions

PAULA SANDERS
Rice University
Clitoridectomy

ASMA SAYEED
University of California Los Angeles
Ḥadīth: Transmission
Mary

VERNON JAMES SCHUBEL
Kenyon College
Relics

MARK SEDGWICK
Aarhus University
Ablutions
Cemeteries

MAY SEIKALY
Wayne State University
Bahrain

ELYSE SEMERDJIAN
Whitman College
Prostitution
Zinah

ĐERMANA ŠETA
Center for Education and Research "Nahla"
Balkan States

CAROLINE SEYMOUR-JORN
University of Wisconsin – Milwaukee
Arabic Literature: Gender in Arabic Literature

JACK G. SHAHEEN
New York University
Stereotypes in Mass Media

DINA EL-SHARNOUBY
The American University in Cairo
Dorai, Fawzieh al-

AHMAD SHBOUL
University of Sydney
Taqwā

MIRI SHEFER-MOSSENSOHN
Tel Aviv University
Medical Profession, Women in the: Historical and Contemporary Practice
Medicine: Contemporary Practice

SHARON SIDDIQUE
Independent Scholar
Women and Social Reform: Social Reform in Southeast Asia

DINA SIJAMHODŽIĆ-NADAREVIĆ
University of Sarajevo
Education and Women: Contemporary Discourse

LOUBNA H. SKALLI
American University
Print Journalism
Women's Magazines

BIANCA J. SMITH
Universiti Brunei Darussalam
Madrasah
Popular Religion: Southeast Asia

NANCY J. SMITH-HEFNER
Boston University
Child-Rearing Practices
Indonesia Youth Culture

FARINA SO
Documentation Center of Cambodia (DC-Cam)
Cambodia

YUSHAU SODIQ
Texas Christian University
Nigeria

PRISCILLA SOUCEK
New York University
Timurid Dynasty

DENISE A. SPELLBERG
University of Texas at Austin
Khadīja bint Khuwaylid

RIEM SPIELHAUS
Erlangen Centre for Islam and Law in Europe (EZIRE), Friedrich-Alexander-University
Europe

CHARLES C. STEWART
University of Illinois, Urbana-Champaign
Popular Religion: Sub-Saharan Africa

DEVIN J. STEWART
Emory University
Arabic Literature: Overview

SITI SYAMSIYATUN
Sunan Kalijaga Islamic University
Aisyiyah, Nasyitaul

MARIA SZUPPE
Le Centre National de la Recherche Scientifique
Khayr al-Nisa' Begam
Parī-Khān Khānum I

ANARA TABYSHALIEVA
Marshall University
Central Asia and the Caucasus: Kazakhstan and Kyrgyzstan

LIYAKAT TAKIM
McMaster University
Judgment, Final

EREN TATARI
Rollins College
Badawi, Jamal
Bakhtiar, Laleh
Esack, Farid
Mogahed, Dalia
Uddin, Baroness Pola Manzila
Yakoob, Salma
Yusuf Hanson, Hamza

ABDULKADER I. TAYOB
Radboud University
Purification

GABRIELE TECCHIATO
Islamic Cultural Centre of Italy
Ablutions

MARY ANN TÉTREAULT
Trinity University
Kuwait

GUSTAV THAISS
York University (Emeritus)
Rawẓah Khvānī

LUCIENNE THYS-ŞENOCAK
Koç University
Architecture and Women: Turkey

MARIT TJOMSLAND
University of Bergen
Ahmed, Leila
Islam and Women: Contemporary Discourses
Hibri, Azizah al-

NAYEREH TOHIDI
California State University, Northridge
Ebadi, Shirin

MARINA TOLMACHEVA
Washington State University
Ḥajj, Women's Patronage of: Historical Practice
Women's Travel, Historical

LIV TØNNESSEN
Chr. Michelsen Institute (CMI)
Turābī, Ḥasan al-

Roberto Tottoli
Università di Napoli L'Orientale
Prophets

Elias H. Tuma
University of California, Davis (Emeritus)
Trade

Bryan S. Turner
City University of New York
Citizenship

Goolam Vahed
University of KwaZulu-Natal
South Africa

Ailya Vajid
MIIM Designs, LLC
KARAMAH (Muslim Women Lawyers for Human Rights)

Stefanie Van de Peer
University of St Andrews
Cinema: Arab Women's Contributions

Els Vanderwaeren
University of Antwerp
Sunnī Islam and Women: Historical Overview
Feminism: Sources

Maaike Voorhoeve
Harvard Law School
Divorce: Historical Practice
Divorce: Modern Practice
Iddah

Amina Wadud-Muḥsin
Virginia Commonwealth University
Revelation

Ann Wainscott
University of Florida
Universities

Christie S. Warren
William and Mary Law School
Polygyny

Heghnar Zeitlian Watenpaugh
University of California, Davis
Architecture and Women: Middle East and North Africa

Earle Waugh
Centre for Cross-Cultural Study of Health and Healing (CCCSHH); University of Alberta
Health Care
Health Issues
Minorities: Minorities in Muslim Societies
Names and Naming
Rites

Anita Weiss
University of Oregon
Women's Action Forum
Women and Social Reform: Social Reform in South Asia

Meredith L. Weiss
University of Oregon
Sisters in Islam

John Alden Williams
College of William and Mary
Fitnah
Khawārij

Rodney Wilson
University of Durham
Financial Institutions

Michael Wood
Dawson College
Pesantren

Lisa Worthington
University of Western Sydney
Mernissi, Fatima

Mina Yazdani
Eastern Kentucky University
Hay'at
Sufra

Özlem Öğüt Yazicioğlu
Boğaziçi University, Istanbul
Roxelana, Hürrem

Antonia Young
University of Bradford
Albania

Elizabeth L. Young
University of Michigan
Gender Equality

Imtiyaz Yusuf
Center for Buddhist-Muslim Understanding, Mahidol University, Thailand
Thailand
'Umrah

Lamia Ben Youssef
University of Alabama at Birmingham
Cinema: North African Women's Contributions
Tunisia

Dror Ze'evi
Bun Gurion University of the Negev
Slavery

Malika Zeghal
Harvard University
Yassine, Nadia

Farkhonda Zia Mansoor
International Islamic University
Islam and Women: Eighteenth-Century to Early Twentieth-Century Debates

Sherifa Zuhur
Institute of Middle Eastern, Islamic and Strategic Studies
Dress: Contemporary
Dress: Historical
Hijab
One Million Signatures Campaign: Iran
One Million Signatures Campaign: Morocco
Surrogate Motherhood
Women's Movements

INDEX

Page numbers in boldface refer to the main entry on a subject.

A

Abacha, Sani, **2:** 254
abandonment, divorce due to, **1:** 210, 215
Abaqa Khan, **2:** 149
'*abāya* (robe), **1:** 232, 233, 436; **2:** 399. *See also* dress; veiling
ethnicity and, **1:** 272
historical, **1:** 234
Abbas, Mahmoud, **2:** 424
'Abbās, al-
ceramics for, **1:** 132
in household of the Prophet, **1:** 20
rawẓah khvānī for, **2:** *164*
Sakīnah and, **1:** 385
'Abbās b. al-Karam, **2:** 303
Abbasi, Ali ben, **2:** 519
'Abbās I (Safavid shah), **1:** 53, 498; **2:** 116, 199–200
'Abbasi, Riza, **2:** 40
'Abbas Ibn 'Ali, **2:** 511
'Abbāsid Empire
astronomy and astrology, **1:** 69
concubinage, **1:** 180
courts, **1:** 581–582
dress, **1:** 235
education, **1:** 253
Fāṭimid conflict with, **1:** 300, 303
gender equality, **1:** 362
ḥajj, **1:** 410, 411
harems, **1:** 56
in household of the Prophet, **1:** 20
households, **1:** 446–447
Iran under, **1:** 53
Iraq, **1:** 503
love poetry, **1:** 387
medicine, **1:** 640
medieval court poetry, **1:** 652, 653
music, **1:** 704
palaces, **2:** 49, 50
patronage, **1:** 411
Qur'ānic schools for girls, **2:** 146
Qur'ān reciters, **2:** 128
women in the public sphere in, **1:** 585
'Abbās II (Safavid shah), **2:** 200
Abbey Sittidey (prayer ritual), **1:** 14
Abbott, Nabia, **1:** 536
'Abd Allāh (Saudi king), **2:** 446
'Abd Allāh, Muḥammad Aḥmad Ibn. *See* Mahdī, Muḥammad Aḥmad Ibn 'Abd Allāh al-
'Abd Allāh ibn Mas'ūd, **2:** 450–451
'Abd Allāh ibn Ubayy, **2:** 550
'Abd Allāh Khān Ostājalū, **2:** 56
'Abd al-Malik ibn Marwān, **1:** 652–653, 689; **2:** 377
Abdalova, Fatima, **1:** 131
'Abd al-Rahīm ibn Ilyās, **1:** 301–302
'Abd al-Raḥmān Jāmī, **1:** 202
Abdellatif, Dalia, **1:** 120
Abdellatif, Omayma, **2:** 204
Abdelwahab, Hassan Hosni, **2:** 355
Abderrahim, Souad, **1:** 523
'Abduh, Ibrāhim, **2:** 226
'Abduh, Muḥammad, **1:** 362, 575; **2:** 504
categorization of Qur'ān verses, **2:** 513
on education, **1:** 248, 254
on gender reform, **1:** 379
on *ḥadīth*, **1:** 407
legal thought, **1:** 586–587
modernism of, **1:** 99; **2:** 229
on modernization, **1:** 672
on people of the book, **2:** 57–58
on polygyny, **1:** 614
on reason and science, **1:** 585
reforms by, **1:** 525
Abdul-Ghafur, Saleemah, **2:** 90
Abdülhamid II (Ottoman sultan), **2:** 32, 366
Abdul Ḥasan Asaf Khan, **1:** 693
Abdullah (king of Saudi Arabia), **1:** 249
Abdullah, Sheikh Mohammad, **1:** 564
Abdullah, Sheikh Muhammed Nur, **1:** 540
'Abdullāh b. 'Umar, **1:** 337
Abdullahi, **2:** 253

E

F

G

H

I

J

K

L

O

P

Q

R

T

V

W

X

Y

Z